ILLUSTRATED

BIBLE DICTIONARY.

ILLUSTRATED
BIBLE
DICTIONARY

M. G. EASTON

BRACKEN BOOKS
LONDON

Originally published by
T. Nelson and Sons,
London, 1894

This edition published 1989 by Bracken Books
an imprint of Bestseller Publications ltd
Princess House, 50 Eastcastle Street
London W1N 7AP, England

ISBN 1 85170 364 0

Printed and bound in Finland

PREFACE.

HE ILLUSTRATED DICTIONARY OF THE BIBLE is the fruit of
many years of loving labour. No pains have been spared
to make it in all respects reliable and complete. The author
has sought to embody in the work, in as compact a form as
possible, the results of the most recent research in all departments of Biblical
literature—doctrinal, historical, biographical, archæological, and geographical.

The learned research and criticism which resulted in the Revised Version of the Scriptures have, probably for the first time, been here utilized in
a systematic way in a Bible Dictionary.

The abundant use of illustrations and sketch-maps, and the introduction
of chronological and other tables, will, it is believed, be found to add greatly
to the value of the book.

The author offers this work to the public in the hope that it may prove
to be worthy of a place on the table of all students of the Bible, and particularly of those who are engaged in the religious instruction of the young
in Sabbath schools, and be helpful as a convenient and trustworthy book of
reference on all Biblical subjects. He has taken cognizance of modern controversies bearing on the character and claims of the Word of God and on the
doctrines of the gospel, and, while avoiding everything of a sectarian character, has freely stated the conclusions he has reached, under the deep
impression that further study and research will only the more fully confirm
the truth of "those things which are most surely believed among us."

May the Lord, whose Word this book is intended to elucidate, graciously
vouchsafe His blessing with it, to His own glory !

M. G. E.

Darvel.

PREFACE TO THE SECOND EDITION.

I HAVE subjected this book to a thorough revision, improving and enlarging where that seemed necessary ; and I now send it forth again for the acceptance of Bible students, believing that they will find in it what it professes to give—full and reliable information on all questions of Bible history, literature, and doctrine.

M. G. E.

LIST OF BOOKS CONSULTED.

HE books the author has had occasion to consult in the preparation of this Dictionary have been very numerous. Besides those quoted or referred to in the work itself, the following may be mentioned :—

The Palestine Exploration Fund Quarterly Statements.
The Memoirs of the Survey of Western Palestine.
The Memoirs of the Egypt Exploration Fund.
The Negeb or South Country of Scripture, by Rev. E. WILTON, M.A.
The Desert of the Exodus, by E. H. PALMER, M.A.
Durch Gosen zum Sinai, von Dr. GEORG EBERS.
Ægypten und die Bücher Mose's, von Dr. GEORG EBERS.
Zeitschrift des Deutschen Palästina-Vereins.
Die Keilinschriften u. das Alte Testament, 2ᵗᵉ A., von EBERHARD SCHRADER.
Zeitschrift für Assyriologie u. Verwandte Gebiete.
Keilinschriften und Geschichtsforschung: Ein Beitrag zur Monumentalen Geographie der Assyrer, von EBERHARD SCHRADER.
Die bibl. Altertümer, von KINZLER.
Die bibl. Naturgeschichte u. die bibl. Geographie, Herausg. von dem Calwer Verlagsverein.
Bibel-Atlas u. bibl. Geographie, von Dr. R. v. RIESS.
Handwörterbuch des bibl. Alterthums, von E. C. H. RIEHM; 2ᵗᵉ Auflage, von Dr. F. BAETHGEN.
Einleitung in d. A. T., von F. BLEEK; Herausg. von J. BLEEK u. A. KEMPHAUSEN. 6ᵗᵉ Auflage, von J. WELLHAUSEN.
Realencyclopädie für Protest. Theol. u. Kirche, von HERZOG, PLITT, u. HAUCK. 2ᵗᵉ Auflage.
La Trouvaille de Deir-el-Behari, vingt Photographies, par M. E. BRUGSCH, Texte par G. MASPERO.
Hist. Ancienne de l'Orient, par M. LENORMANT.
The Hibbert Lectures. Lectures on the origin and growth of religion as illustrated by the religion of the ancient Babylonians. By Rev. A. H. SAYCE.
A Manual of Ancient History, by GEORGE RAWLINSON, M.A.
The Five Great Monarchies of the Ancient Eastern World, by GEORGE RAWLINSON, M.A.
History of Ancient Egypt, by GEORGE RAWLINSON, M.A.
A History of Art in Chaldea and Assyria, by GEORGES PERROT and CHARLES CLUPIEZ.
The Tell Amarna Tablets, translated by Major CONDER. 1893.
The Records of the Past.
An Introduction to the Literature of the O. T., by S. B. DRIVER, D.D.   [1894.
The "Higher Criticism" and the Verdict of the Monuments, by Rev. A. H. SAYCE.

The Bible and Modern Discovery (4th edition), by HARPER.
The Holy Land and the Bible, by GEIKIE.
The Bible by Modern Light, by GEIKIE. 1894.
The Student's Edition of the Speaker's Commentary, by M. FULLER, M.A., Professor
    of Ecclesiastical History, King's College, London.
Biblischer Commentar u. d. A. T., von KEIL u. DELITZSCH.
The By-Paths of Bible Knowledge.
Smith's Bible Dictionary.
Fausset's Critical and Expository Bible Cyclopædia.
Edersheim's Bible History.
*M'Clintock and Strong's Cyclopædia of Biblical, Theological, and Ecclesiastical
    Literature.*
Gesenius' Handwörterbuch u. d. A. T. Bearb. von Mühlau u. Volck. 11te Auflage.

ARABIC WORDS USED IN THE MODERN NAMES OF PLACES, ETC.

Ab, father. *Abu,* father of.

'*Ain* or *en,* a well; *lit.* the "eye" of the desert. '*Ayûn* (pl.), wells.

Amîr or *ameer,* prince.

Ard, earth.

Bahr, sea.

Beit, house.

Beni, sons of. *Ibn,* son.

Bîr or *beer,* fountain; an artificially sunk and enclosed well, as distinguished from '*ain.*

Birket, pool.

Dan, dwelling.

Deir, convent.

Derb, way.

Kalat, castle or fort.

Kefr, village.

Kasr, palace; pl. *kŭsûr.*

Khŭrbet, ruins.

Kŭrm, vineyard.

Malek, king.

Nahr, river.

Nebi, prophet.

Râs, headland; cape; summit.

Said, lord.

Tell, mound; hill.

Umm, mother.

Wâdy, rain stream, or the channel through which it flows.

ABBREVIATIONS.

A.V...........Authorized Version of the Bible.

R.V...........Revised Version of the Bible.

LXX.........Septuagint Version of the Bible.

Lat...........Latin.

Gr. ....Greek.

Heb. ....Hebrew.

Arab.........Arabic.

Aram.........Aramaic or Chaldee.

N.T. ....New Testament.

O.T...........Old Testament.

n.p............proper name.

cf..............compare.

i.e..............that is.

ibid..........the same.

q.v............which see.

l.c..............in the passage quoted.

e.g..............for example.

LIST OF ILLUSTRATIONS.

SCENES.

PLANTS AND ANIMALS.

ANTIQUARIAN.

MANNERS AND CUSTOMS.

LIST OF MAPS AND PLANS.

BIBLE DICTIONARY.

A, Alpha, the first letter of the Greek alphabet, as Omega is the last. These letters occur in the text of Rev. 1:8, 11; 21:6; 22:13, and are represented by "Alpha" and "Omega" respectively (omitted in R.V., 1:11). They mean "the first and the last." (Comp. Heb. 12:2; Isa. 41:4; 44:6; Rev. 1:11, 17; 2:8.) In the symbols of the early Christian Church these two letters are frequently combined with the cross or with Christ's monogram to denote his divinity.

A'aron, the eldest son of Amram and Jochebed, a daughter of Levi (Ex. 6:20). Some explain the name as meaning *mountaineer*, others *mountain of strength, illuminator*. He was born in Egypt three years before his brother Moses, and a number of years after his sister Miriam (2:1, 4; 7:7). He married Elisheba, the daughter of Amminadab of the house of Judah (6:23; 1 Chr. 2:10), by whom he had four sons—Nadab and Abihu, Eleazar and Ithamar. When the time for the deliverance of Israel out of Egypt drew nigh, he was sent by God (Ex. 4:14, 27-30) to meet his long-absent brother, that he might co-operate with him in all that they were required to do in bringing about the Exodus. He was to be the "mouth" or "prophet" of Moses—*i.e.*, was to speak for him, because he was a man of a ready utterance (7:1, 2, 9, 10, 19). He was faithful to his trust, and stood by Moses in all his interviews with Pharaoh.

When the ransomed tribes fought their first battle with Amalek in Rephidim, Moses stood on a hill overlooking the scene of the conflict with the rod of God in his outstretched hand. On this occasion he was attended by Aaron and Hur, his sister's husband, who held up his wearied hands till Joshua and the chosen warriors of Israel gained the victory (17:8-13).

Afterwards, when encamped before Sinai, and when Moses at the command of God ascended the mount to receive the tables of the law, Aaron and his two sons—Nadab and Abihu—along with seventy of the elders of Israel, were permitted to accompany him part of the way, and to behold afar off the manifestation of the glory of Israel's God (Ex. 19:24; 24:9-11). While Moses remained on the mountain with God, Aaron returned unto the people; and yielding through fear, or ignorance, or instability of character, to their clamour, made unto them a golden calf, and set it up as an object of worship (Ex. 32:4; Ps. 106:19). On the return of Moses to the camp, Aaron was sternly rebuked by him for the part he had acted in this matter; but he interceded for him before God, who forgave his sin (Deut. 9:20).

On the mount, Moses received instructions regarding the system of worship which was to be set up among the people; and in accordance therewith Aaron and his sons were consecrated to the priest's office (Lev. 8; 9). Aaron, as high priest, held henceforth the prominent place appertaining to that office.

When Israel had reached Hazeroth, in "the wilderness of Paran," Aaron joined with his sister Miriam in murmuring against Moses, "because of the Ethiopian woman whom he had married," probably after the death of Zipporah. But the Lord vindicated his servant Moses, and punished Miriam with leprosy (Num. 12). Aaron acknowledged his own and his sister's guilt, and at the intercession of Moses they were forgiven.

Twenty years after this, when the children of Israel were encamped in the wilderness of Paran, Korah, Dathan, and Abiram conspired against Aaron and his sons; but a fearful judgment from God fell upon them, and they were destroyed, and the next day thousands of the people also perished by a fierce pestilence, the ravages of which were only stayed by the interposition of Aaron (Num. 16). That there might be further evidence of the divine appointment of Aaron to the priestly office, the chiefs of the tribes were each required to bring to Moses a rod bearing on it the name of his tribe. And these, along with the rod of Aaron for the tribe of Levi, were laid up overnight in the tabernacle, and in the morning it was found that while the other rods remained unchanged, that of Aaron "for the house of Levi" budded, blossomed, and yielded almonds (Num. 17 : 1-10). This rod was afterwards preserved in the tabernacle (Heb. 9 : 4) as a memorial of the divine attestation of his appointment to the priesthood.

Aaron was implicated in the sin of his brother at Meribah (Num. 20 : 8-13), and on that account was not permitted to enter the Promised Land. When the tribes arrived at Mount Hor, "in the edge of the land of Edom," at the command of God Moses led Aaron and his son Eleazar to the top of that mountain, in the sight of all the people. There he stripped Aaron of his priestly vestments, and put them upon Eleazar; and there Aaron died on the top of the mount, being 123 years old (Num. 20 : 23-29. Comp. Deut. 10 : 6; 33 : 50), and was "gathered unto his people." The people, "even all the house of Israel," mourned for him thirty days. Of Aaron's sons two survived him—Eleazar, whose family held the high-priesthood till the time of Eli; and Ithamar, in whose family, beginning with Eli, the high-priesthood was held till the time of Solomon. Aaron's other two sons had been struck dead (Lev. 10 : 1, 2) for the daring impiety of offering "strange fire" on the altar of incense.

The Arabs still show with veneration the traditionary site of Aaron's grave on one of the two summits of Mount Hor, which is marked by a Mohammedan chapel. His name is mentioned in the Koran, and there are found in the writings of the rabbins many fabulous stories regarding him.

He was the first anointed priest. His descendants, "the house of Aaron," constituted the priesthood in general. In the time of David they were very numerous (1 Chr. 12 : 27). The other branches of the tribe of Levi held subordinate positions in connection with the sacred office.

Aaron was a type of Christ in his official character as the high priest. His priesthood was a "shadow of heavenly things," and was intended to lead the people of Israel to look forward to the time when "another priest" would arise "after the order of Melchizedek" (Heb. 6 : 20). (See MOSES.)

A'aronites, the descendants of Aaron, and therefore priests. Jehoiada, the father of Benaiah, led 3,700 Aaronites as "fighting men" to the support of David at Hebron (1 Chr. 12 : 27). Eleazar (Num. 4 : 16), and at a later period Zadok (1 Chr. 27 : 17), was their chief.

Abad'don — *destruction* — the Hebrew name (equivalent to the Greek Apollyon— *i.e.*, destroyer) of "the angel of the bottomless pit" (Rev. 9 : 11). It is rendered "destruction" in Job 26 : 6; 28 : 22; 31 : 12; Prov. 15 : 11; 27 : 20. In the last three of these passages the Revised Version retains the word "Abaddon." We may regard this word as a personification of the idea of destruction, or as sheol, the realm of the dead.

Abag'tha, one of the seven eunuchs in Ahasuerus's court (Esther 1 : 10; 2 : 21).

Ab'ana—*stony* (Heb. marg. "Amanah," *perennial*)—the chief river of Damascus (2 Kings 5 : 12). Its modern name is *Barada*, the Chrysorrhoas, or "golden stream," of the Greeks. It rises in a cleft of the Anti-Lebanon range, about 23 miles north-west of Damascus, and after flowing southward for a little way parts into three smaller streams—the central one flowing through Damascus, and the other two on each side of the city, diffusing beauty and fertility where otherwise there would be barrenness such as characterizes the con-

COURSE OF THE ABANA (BARADA).

tiguous plain. The river disappears in the marshy lakes on the east of the city. (See AMANA.)

Ab'arim—*regions beyond; i.e.*, on the east of Jordan—a mountain. or rather a mountain-chain, over against Jericho, to the east and south-east of the Dead Sea, in the land of Moab. From "the top of Pisgah" —*i.e.*, Mount Nebo (*q.v.*)—one of its summits, Moses surveyed the Promised Land (Deut. 3:27; 32:49), and there he died (34:1, 5). The Israelites had one of their encampments in the mountains of Abarim (Num. 33:47, 48) after crossing the Arnon.

Ab'ba. This Syriac or Chaldee word is found three times in the New Testament (Mark 14:36; Rom. 8:15; Gal. 4:6), and in each case is followed by its Greek equivalent, which is translated "father." It is a term expressing warm affection and filial confidence. It has no perfect equivalent in our language. It has passed into European languages as an ecclesiastical term, "abbot."

Ab'da—*servant.* (1.) The father of Adoniram, whom Solomon set over the tribute (1 Kings 4:6); *i.e.*, the forced labour (R.V., "levy").

(2.) A Levite of the family of Jeduthun (Neh. 11:17), also called Obadiah (1 Chr. 9:16).

Ab'deel—*servant of God*—(Jer. 36:26), the father of Shelemiah.

Ab'di—*my servant.* (1.) 1 Chr. 6:44. (2.) 2 Chr. 29:12. (3.) Ezra 10:26.

Ab'diel—*servant of God*—(1 Chr. 5:15), a Gadite chief.

Ab'don—*servile.* (1.) The son of Hillel, a Pirathonite, the tenth judge of Israel (Judg. 12:13-15). He is probably the Bedan of 1 Sam. 12:11.

(2.) The first-born of Gibeon of the tribe of Benjamin (1 Chr. 8:30; 9:36).

(3.) The son of Micah, one of those whom Josiah sent to the prophetess Huldah to ascertain from her the meaning of the recently discovered book of the law (2 Chr. 34:20). He is called Achbor in 2 Kings 22:12.

(4.) One of the "sons" of Shashak (1 Chr. 8:23).

This is the name also of a Levitical town of the Gershonites, in the tribe of Asher (Josh. 21:30; 1 Chr. 6:74). The ruins of *Abdeh*, some 8 miles north-east of Accho, probably mark its site.

Abed'nego—*servant of Nego=Nebo*—the Chaldee name given to Azariah, one of Daniel's three companions (Dan. 2:49). With Shadrach and Meshach, he was delivered from the burning fiery furnace (3:12-30).

A'bel (Heb. *Hebhel*)—*a breath*, or *vanity*— the second son of Adam and Eve. He was put to death by his brother Cain (Gen. 4:1-16). Guided by the instruction of their father, the two brothers were trained in the duty of worshipping God. "And in process of time" (marg. "at the end of days"—*i.e.*, on the Sabbath) each of them offered up to God of the first-fruits of his labours. Cain, as a husbandman, offered the fruits of the field; Abel, as a shepherd, of the firstlings of his flock. "The Lord had respect unto Abel and his offering; but unto Cain and his offering he had not respect" (Gen. 4:3-5). On this account Cain was angry with his brother, and formed the design of putting him to death; a design which he at length found an opportunity of carrying into effect (Gen. 4:8, 9. Comp. 1 John 3:12). There are several references to Abel in the New Testament. Our Saviour speaks of him as "righteous" (Matt. 23:35). "The blood of sprinkling" is said to speak "better things than that of Abel" (Heb. 12:24); *i.e.*, the blood of Jesus is the reality of which the blood of the offering made by Abel was only the type. The comparison here is between the sacrifice offered by Christ and that offered by Abel, and not between the blood of Christ calling for mercy and the blood of the murdered Abel calling for vengeance, as has sometimes been supposed. It is also said (Heb. 11:4) that "Abel offered unto God a more excellent sacrifice than Cain." This sacrifice was made "by faith;" this faith rested in God, not only as the Creator and the God of providence, but especially in God as the great Redeemer, whose sacrifice was typified by the sacrifices which, no doubt by the divine institution, were offered from the days of Adam downward. On account of that "faith" which looked forward to the great atoning sacrifice, Abel's offering was accepted of God. Cain's offering had no such reference, and therefore was rejected. Abel was the first martyr, as he was the first of our race to die.

A′bel (Heb. *'abhēl*)—*lamentation* (1 Sam. 6:18)—the name given to the great stone in Joshua's field whereon the ark was "set down." The Revised Version, however, following the Targum and the LXX., reads in the Hebrew text *'ebhen* (=a stone), and accordingly translates "unto the great stone, whereon they set down the ark." This reading is to be preferred.

A′bel (Heb. *'abhēl*), a grassy place, a meadow. This word enters into the composition of the following words :—

A′bel-beth-ma′achah—*meadow of the house of Maachah*—a city in the north of Palestine, in the neighbourhood of Dan and Ijon, in the tribe of Naphtali. It was a place of considerable strength and importance. It is called a "mother in Israel"—*i.e.*, a metropolis (2 Sam. 20:19). It was besieged by Joab (2 Sam. 20:14), by Benhadad (1 Kings 15:20), and by Tiglath-pileser (2 Kings 15:29) about B.C. 734. It is elsewhere called **A′bel-maim** —*meadow of the waters*—(2 Chr. 16:4). Its site is occupied by the modern *Abil* or *Abil-el-kamh*, on a rising ground to the east

of the brook Derdârah, which flows through the plain of Hûleh into the Jordan, about 6 miles to the west-north-west of Dan.

A′bel-chera′mim (Judg. 11:33, R.V.; A. V., "plain of the vineyards"), a village of the Ammonites, whither Jephthah pursued their forces.

A′bel-meho′lah — *meadow of dancing*, or *the dancing-meadow*—the birth-place and residence of the prophet Elisha, not far from Beth-shean (1 Kings 4:12), in the tribe of Issachar, near where the Wady el-Maleh emerges into the valley of the Jordan—" the rich meadow-land which extends about 4 miles south of Beth-shean; moist and luxuriant." Here Elisha was found at his plough by Elijah on his return up the Jordan valley from Horeb (1 Kings 19:16). It is now called *'Ain Helweh*.

A′bel-miz′raim—*meadow of Egypt*, or *mourning of Egypt*—a place "beyond," *i.e.*, on the west of Jordan, at the "threshing-floor of Atad." Here the Egyptians mourned seventy days for Jacob (Gen. 50:4–11). Its site is unknown.

A′bel-shit′tim — *meadow of the acacias*, frequently called simply "Shittim" (Num. 25:1; Josh. 2:1; Micah 6:5)—a place on the east of Jordan, in the plain of Moab, nearly opposite Jericho. It was the forty-second encampment of the Israelites, their last resting-place before they crossed the Jordan (Num. 33:49; 22:1; 26:3; 31:12; comp. 25:1; 31:16).

A′bez—*tin*, or *white*—a town in the tribe of Issachar (Josh. 19:20), at the north of the plain of Esdraelon. It is probably identified with the ruins of *el-Beida*.

Abi′a—*my father is the Lord*—the Greek form of Abijah, or Abijam (Matt. 1:7), instead of Abiah (1 Chr. 3:10). In Luke 1:5, the name refers to the head of the eighth of the twenty-four courses into which David divided the priests (1 Chr. 24:10).

A′bi-al′bon—*father of strength; i.e.*, "valiant"—one of David's body-guard of thirty mighty men (2 Sam. 23:31); called also Abiel (1 Chr. 11:32).

Abi′asaph—*father of gathering; the gatherer*—the youngest of the three sons of Korah the Levite, head of a family of

Korhites (Ex. 6 : 24) ; called Ebiasaph (1 Chr. 6 : 37).

Abi'athar—*father of abundance*, or *my father excels*—the son of Ahimelech the high priest. He was the tenth high priest, and the fourth in descent from Eli. When his father was slain with the priests of Nob, he escaped, and bearing with him the ephod, he joined David, who was then in the cave of Adullam (1 Sam. 22 : 20–23 ; 23 : 6). He remained with David, and became priest of the party of which he was the leader (1 Sam. 30 : 7). When David ascended the throne of Judah, Abiathar was appointed high priest (1 Chr. 15 : 11 ; 1 Kings 2 : 26) and the "king's companion" (1 Chr. 27 : 33). Meanwhile Zadok, of the house of Eleazar, had been made high priest. These appointments continued in force till the end of David's reign (1 Kings 4 : 4). Abiathar was deposed (the sole historical instance of the deposition of a high priest) and banished to his home at Anathoth by Solomon, because he took part in the attempt to raise Adonijah to the throne. The priesthood thus passed from the house of Ithamar (1 Sam. 2 : 30–36 ; 1 Kings 1 : 19 ; 2 : 26, 27). Zadok now became sole high priest. In Mark 2 : 26, reference is made to an occurrence in "the days of Abiathar the high priest." But from 1 Sam. 22, we learn explicitly that this event took place when Ahimelech, the father of Abiathar, was high priest. The apparent discrepancy is satisfactorily explained by interpreting the words in Mark as referring to the life-time of Abiathar, and not to the term of his holding the office of high priest. It is not implied in Mark that he was actual high priest at the time referred to. Others, however, think that the loaves belonged to Abiathar, who was at that time (Lev. 24 : 9) a priest, and that he either himself gave them to David, or persuaded his father to give them.

A'bib—*an ear of corn*—the month of newly-ripened grain (Ex. 13 : 4 ; 23 : 15) ; the first of the Jewish ecclesiastical year, and the seventh of the civil year. It began about the time of the vernal equinox, on 21st March. It was called Nisan, after the Captivity (Neh. 2 : 1). On the fifteenth day of the month, harvest was begun by gathering a sheaf of barley, which was offered unto the Lord on the sixteenth (Lev. 23 : 4–11).

Abi'da or **Abi'dah**—*father of knowledge; knowing*—one of the five sons of Midian, who was the son of Abraham by Keturah (1 Chr. 1 : 33), and apparently the chief of an Arab tribe.

Abi'dan—*father of judgment; judge*—head of the tribe of Benjamin at the Exodus (Num. 1 : 11 ; 2 : 22).

A'biel—*father (i.e., "possessor") of God* = "pious." (1.) The son of Zeror and father of Ner, who was the grandfather of Saul (1 Sam. 14 : 51 ; 1 Chr. 8 : 33 ; 9 : 39). In 1 Sam. 9 : 1, he is called the "father," probably meaning the grandfather, of Kish.

(2.) An Arbathite, one of David's warriors (1 Chr. 11 : 32) ; called also Abi-albon (2 Sam. 23 : 31).

Abie'zer—*father of help; i.e.,* "helpful." (1.) The second of the three sons of Hammoleketh, the sister of Gilead. He was the grandson of Manasseh (1 Chr. 7 : 18). From his family Gideon sprang (Josh. 17 : 2 ; comp. Judg. 6 : 34 ; 8 : 2). He was also called Jeezer (Num. 26 : 30).

(2.) One of David's thirty warriors (2 Sam. 23 : 27 ; comp. 1 Chr. 27 : 12).

(3.) The prince of the tribe of Dan at the Exodus (Num. 1 : 12).

Abi'ezrite—*father of help*—a descendant of Abiezer (Judg. 6 : 11, 24 ; 8 : 32).

Ab'igail—*father (i.e., "leader") of the dance*, or "of joy." (1.) The sister of David, and wife of Jether an Ishmaelite (1 Chr. 2 : 16, 17). She was the mother of Amasa (2 Sam. 17 : 25).

(2.) The wife of the churlish Nabal, who dwelt in the district of Carmel (1 Sam. 25 : 3). She showed great prudence and delicate management at a critical period of her husband's life. She was "a woman of good understanding, and of a beautiful countenance." After Nabal's death she became the wife of David (1 Sam. 25 : 14–42), and was his companion in all his future fortunes (1 Sam. 27 : 3 ; 30 : 5 ; 2 Sam. 2 : 2). By her David had a son called Chileab (2 Sam. 3 : 3), elsewhere called Daniel (1 Chr. 3 : 1).

Abiha'il—*father of might*. (1.) Num. 3:35. (2.) 1 Chr. 2:29. (3.) 1 Chr. 5:14.

(4.) The second wife of King Rehoboam (2 Chr. 11:18), a descendant of Eliab, David's eldest brother.

(5.) The father of Esther and uncle of Mordecai (Esther 2:15).

Abi'hu—*father of Him; i.e.,* "worshipper of God"—the second of the sons of Aaron (Ex. 6:23; Num. 3:2; 26:60; 1 Chr. 6:3). Along with his two brothers he was consecrated to the priest's office (Ex. 28:1). With his father and elder brother he accompanied the seventy elders part of the way up the mount with Moses (Ex. 24:1, 9). On one occasion he and Nadab his brother offered incense in their censers filled with "strange" (*i.e.,* common) fire—*i.e.,* not with fire taken from the great brazen altar (Lev. 6:9, etc.)—and for this offence they were struck dead, and were taken out and buried without the camp (Lev. 10:1-11; comp. Num. 3:4; 26:61; 1 Chr. 24:2). It is probable that when they committed this offence they were intoxicated, for immediately after is given the law prohibiting the use of wine or strong drink to the priests.

Abi'hud—*father* (*i.e.,* "possessor") *of renown.* (1.) One of the sons of Bela, the son of Benjamin (1 Chr. 8:3); called also Ahihud (ver. 7).

(2.) A descendant of Zerubbabel and father of Eliakim (Matt. 1:13, "Abiud"); called also Juda (Luke 3:26), and Obadiah (1 Chr. 3:21).

Abi'jah—*father* (*i.e.,* "possessor or worshipper") *of Jehovah.* (1.) 1 Chr. 7:8. (2.) 1 Chr. 2:24.

(3.) The second son of Samuel (1 Sam. 8:2; 1 Chr. 6:12). His conduct, along with that of his brother, as a judge in Beer-sheba, to which office his father had appointed him, led to popular discontent, and ultimately provoked the people to demand a royal form of government.

(4.) A descendant of Eleazar, the son of Aaron, a chief of one of the twenty-four orders into which the priesthood was divided by David (1 Chr. 24:10). The order of Abijah was one of those which did not return from the Captivity (Ezra 2:36-39; Neh. 7:39-42; 12:1).

(5.) The son of Rehoboam, whom he succeeded on the throne of Judah (1 Chr. 3:10). He is also called Abijam (1 Kings 14:31; 15:1-8). He began his three years' reign (2 Chr. 12:16; 13:1, 2) with a strenuous but unsuccessful effort to bring back the ten tribes to their allegiance. His address to "Jeroboam and all Israel," before encountering them in battle, is worthy of being specially noticed (2 Chr. 13:5-12). It was a very bloody battle, no fewer than 500,000 of the army of Israel having perished on the field. He is described as having walked "in all the sins of his father" (1 Kings 15:3; 2 Chr. 13:20-22). It is said in 1 Kings 15:2 that "his mother's name was Maachah, the daughter of Abishalom;" but in 2 Chr. 13:2 we read, "his mother's name was Michaiah, the daughter of Uriel of Gibeah." The explanation is that Maachah is just a variation of the name Michaiah, and that Abishalom is probably the same as Absalom, the son of David. It is probable that "Uriel of Gibeah" married Tamar, the daughter of Absalom (2 Sam. 14:27), and by her had Maachah. The word "daughter" in 1 Kings 15:2 will thus, as it frequently elsewhere does, mean grand-daughter.

(6.) A son of Jeroboam, the first king of Israel. On account of his severe illness when a youth, his father sent his wife to consult the prophet Ahijah regarding his recovery. The prophet, though blind with old age, knew the wife of Jeroboam as soon as she approached, and under a divine impulse he announced to her that inasmuch as in Abijah alone of all the house of Jeroboam there was found "some good thing toward the Lord," he only would come to his grave in peace. As his mother crossed the threshold of the door on her return, the youth died, and "all Israel mourned for him" (1 Kings 14:1-18).

(7.) The daughter of Zechariah (2 Chr. 29:1; comp. Isa. 8:2), and afterwards the wife of Ahaz. She is also called Abi (2 Kings 18:2).

(8.) One of the priests who "sealed the covenant" made by Nehemiah (Neh. 10:7; 12:4).

Abi'jam—*father of the sea; i.e.,* "seaman" —the name always used in Kings (except 1 Kings 14:1, which refers to another person) of the king of Judah elsewhere called Abijah (1 Kings 15:1, 7, 8).

Abile'ne—*a plain*—a district lying on the east slope of the Anti-Lebanon range; so called from its chief town, Abila (Luke 3:1), which stood in the Suk Wady Barada, between Heliopolis (Baalbec) and Damascus, 38 miles from the former and 18 from the latter. Lysanias was governor or tetrarch of this province.

Abima'el—*father of Mael*—one of the sons or descendants of Joktan, in Northern Arabia (Gen. 10:28; 1 Chr. 1:22).

Abim'elech—*my father a king,* or *father of a king*—a common name of the Philistine kings, as "Pharaoh" was of the Egyptian kings. (1.) The Philistine king of Gerar in the time of Abraham (Gen. 20:1–18). By an interposition of Providence, Sarah was delivered from his harem, and was restored to her husband Abraham. As a mark of respect he gave to Abraham valuable gifts, and offered him a settlement in any part of his country; while at the same time he delicately and yet severely rebuked him for having practised a deception upon him in pretending that Sarah was only his sister. Among the gifts presented by the king were a thousand pieces of silver as a "covering of the eyes" for Sarah; *i.e.,* either as an atoning gift and a testimony of her innocence in the sight of all, or rather for the purpose of procuring a veil for Sarah to conceal her beauty, and thus as a reproof to her for not having worn a veil which, as a married woman, she ought to have done. A few years after this Abimelech visited Abraham, who had removed southward beyond his territory, and there entered into a league of peace and friendship with him. This league was the first of which we have any record. It was confirmed by a mutual oath at Beer-sheba (Gen. 21:22–34).

(2.) A king of Gerar in the time of Isaac, probably the son of the preceding (Gen. 26:1–22). Isaac sought refuge in his territory during a famine, and there he acted a part with reference to his wife Rebekah similar to that of his father Abraham with reference to Sarah. Abimelech rebuked him for the deception, which he accidentally discovered. Isaac settled for a while here, and prospered. Abimelech desired him, however, to leave his territory, which Isaac did. Abimelech afterwards visited him when he was encamped at Beer-sheba, and expressed a desire to renew the covenant which had been entered into between their fathers (Gen. 26:26–31).

(3.) A son of Gideon (Judg. 9:1), who was proclaimed king after the death of his father (Judg. 8:33–9:6). One of his first acts was to murder his brothers, seventy in number, "on one stone," at Ophrah. Only one named Jotham escaped. He was an unprincipled, ambitious ruler, often engaged in war with his own subjects. When engaged in reducing the town of Thebez, which had revolted, he was struck mortally on his head by a mill-stone, thrown by the hand of a woman from the wall above. Perceiving that the wound was mortal, he desired his armour-bearer to thrust him through with his sword, that it might not be said he had perished by the hand of a woman (Judg. 9:54–57; comp. 2 Sam. 11:21).

(4.) The son of Abiathar, and high priest in the time of David (1 Chr. 18:16). In the parallel passage, 2 Sam. 8:17, we have the name Ahimelech.

(5.) The name given to Achish, king of Gath, in the title of Ps. 34. (Comp. 1 Sam. 21:10–15.)

Abin'adab—*father of nobleness; i.e.,* "noble." (1.) A Levite of Kirjath-jearim, in whose house the ark of the covenant was deposited after having been brought back from the land of the Philistines (1 Sam. 7:1). It remained there twenty years, till it was at length removed by David (1 Sam. 7:1, 2; 1 Chr. 13:7).

(2.) The second of the eight sons of Jesse (1 Sam. 16:8). He was with Saul in the campaign against the Philistines in which Goliath was slain (1 Sam. 17:13).

(3.) One of Saul's sons, who perished with his father in the battle of Gilboa (1 Sam. 31:2; 1 Chr. 10:2).

(4.) One of Solomon's officers, who "provided victuals for the king and his household." He presided, for this purpose, over the district of Dor (1 Kings 4:11).

Abin'oam—*father of kindness*—the father of Barak (Judg. 4:6; 5:1).

Abi'ram—*father of height; i.e.,* "proud." (1.) One of the sons of Eliab, who joined Korah in the conspiracy against Moses and Aaron. He and all the conspirators, with their families and possessions (except the children of Korah), were swallowed up by an earthquake (Num. 16:1-27; 26:9; Ps. 106:17).

(2.) The eldest son of Hiel the Bethelite, who perished prematurely in consequence of his father's undertaking to rebuild Jericho (1 Kings 16:34), according to the words of Joshua (6:26). (See JERICHO.)

Ab'ishag—*father of (i.e.,* "given to") *error*—a young woman of Shunem, distinguished for her beauty. She was chosen to minister to David in his old age. She became his wife (1 Kings 1:3, 4, 15). After David's death Adonijah persuaded Bathsheba, Solomon's mother, to entreat the king to permit him to marry Abishag. Solomon suspected in this request an aspiration to the throne, and therefore caused him to be put to death (1 Kings 2:17-25).

Abi'shai—*father of (i.e.,* "desirous of") *a gift*—the eldest son of Zeruiah, David's sister. He was the brother of Joab and Asahel (2 Sam. 2:18; 1 Chr. 2:16). The three brothers were devoted to their uncle David during his wanderings. Abishai was the only one who accompanied him when he went to the camp of Saul and took the spear and the cruse of water from Saul's bolster (1 Sam. 26:5-9). He had the command of one of the three divisions of David's army at the battle with Absalom (2 Sam. 18:2-12). He slew the Philistine giant Ishbi-benob, who threatened David's life (2 Sam. 21:15-17). He was the chief of the second rank of the three "mighties" (2 Sam. 23:18; 1 Chr. 11:20); and on one occasion withstood 300 men, and slew them with his own spear (2 Sam. 23:18).

Abish'ua—*father of welfare; i.e.,* "fortunate." (1.) The grandson of Benjamin (1 Chr. 8:4).

(2.) The son of Phinehas the high priest (1 Chr. 6:4, 5, 50; Ezra 7:5).

Ab'ishur—*father of the wall; i.e.,* "mason"—one of the two sons of Shammai of the tribe of Judah (1 Chr. 2:28, 29).

Ab'ital—*father of dew; i.e.,* "fresh"—David's fifth wife (2 Sam. 3:4).

Ab'itub—*father of goodness*—a Benjamite (1 Chr. 8:11).

Ab'jects (Ps. 35:15), the translation of a Hebrew word meaning *smiters;* probably, in allusion to the tongue, *slanderers.* (Comp. Jer. 18:18.)

Ablu'tion, or washing, was practised—(1.) When a person was initiated into a higher state: *e.g.,* when Aaron and his sons were set apart to the priest's office, they were washed with water previous to their investiture with the priestly robes (Lev. 8:6).

(2.) Before the priests approached the altar of God, they were required, on pain of death, to wash their hands and their feet to cleanse them from the soil of common life (Ex. 30:17-21). To this practice the Psalmist alludes, Ps. 26:6.

(3.) There were washings prescribed for the purpose of cleansing from positive defilement contracted by particular acts. Of such washings eleven different species are prescribed in the Levitical law (Lev. 12-15).

(4.) A fourth class of ablutions is mentioned, by which a person purified or absolved himself from the guilt of some particular act. For example, the elders of the nearest village where some murder was committed were required, when the murderer was unknown, to wash their hands over the expiatory heifer which was beheaded, and in doing so to say, "Our hands have not shed this blood, neither have our eyes seen it" (Deut. 21:1-9). So also Pilate declared himself innocent of the blood of Jesus by washing his hands (Matt. 27:24). This act of Pilate may not, however, have been borrowed from the custom of the Jews. The same practice was common among the Greeks and Romans.

The Pharisees carried the practice of ablution to great excess, thereby claiming extraordinary purity (Matt. 23:25). Mark (7:1-5) refers to the ceremonial ablutions.

The Pharisees washed their hands "oft," more correctly, "with the fist" (R.V., "diligently"), or as an old father, Theophylact, explains it, "up to the elbow." (Compare also Mark 7:4; Lev. 6:28; 11:32–36; 15:22.) (See WASHING.)

Ab'ner—*father of light; i.e.*, "enlightening"—the son of Ner and uncle of Saul. He was commander-in-chief of Saul's army (1 Sam. 14:50; 17:55; 20:25). He first introduced David to the court of Saul after the victory over Goliath (1 Sam. 17:57). After the death of Saul, David was made king over Judah, and reigned in Hebron. Among the other tribes there was a feeling of hostility to Judah; and Abner, at the head of Ephraim, fostered this hostility in the interest of the house of Saul, whose son Ish-bosheth he caused to be proclaimed king (2 Sam. 2:8). A state of war existed between these two kings. A battle fatal to Abner, who was the leader of Ish-bosheth's army, was fought with David's army under Joab at Gibeon (2 Sam. 2:12). Abner, escaping from the field, was overtaken by Asahel, who was "light of foot as a wild roe," the brother of Joab and Abishai, whom he thrust through with a back stroke of his spear (2 Sam. 2:18–32).

Being rebuked by Ish-bosheth for the impropriety of taking to wife Rizpah, who had been a concubine of King Saul, he found an excuse for going over to the side of David, whom he now professed to regard as anointed by the Lord to reign over all Israel. David received him favourably, and promised that he would have command of the armies. At this time Joab was absent from Hebron, but on his return he found what had happened. Abner had just left the city; but Joab by a stratagem recalled him, and meeting him at the gate of the city on his return, thrust him through with his sword (2 Sam. 3:27; 31–39; 4:12. Comp. 1 Kings 2:5, 32). David lamented in pathetic words the death of Abner— "Know ye not that there is a prince and a great man fallen this day in Israel?" (2 Sam. 3:33–38.)

Abomina'tion. This word is used— (1.) To express the idea that the Egyptians considered themselves as defiled when they ate with strangers (Gen. 43:32). The Jews subsequently followed the same practice, holding it unlawful to eat or drink with foreigners (John 18:28; Acts 10:28; 11:3).

(2.) Every shepherd was "an abomination" unto the Egyptians (Gen. 46:34). This aversion to shepherds, such as the Hebrews, arose probably from the fact that Lower and Middle Egypt had formerly been held in oppressive subjection by a tribe of nomad shepherds (the Hyksos), who had only recently been expelled, and partly also perhaps from this other fact that the Egyptians detested the lawless habits of these wandering shepherds.

(3.) Pharaoh was so moved by the fourth plague, that while he refused the demand of Moses, he offered a compromise, granting to the Israelites permission to hold their festival and offer their sacrifices in Egypt. This permission could not be accepted, because Moses said they would have to sacrifice "the abomination of the Egyptians" (Ex. 8:26); *i.e.*, the cow or ox, which all the Egyptians held as sacred, and which they regarded it as sacrilegious to kill.

(4.) Daniel (11:31), in that section of his prophecies which is generally interpreted as referring to the fearful calamities that were to fall on the Jews in the time of Antiochus Epiphanes, says, "And they shall place the abomination that maketh desolate." Antiochus Epiphanes caused an altar to be erected on the altar of burnt-offering, on which sacrifices were offered to Jupiter Olympus. (Comp. 1 Macc. 1:54). This was the abomination of the desolation of Jerusalem. The same language is employed in Dan. 9:27 (comp. Matt. 24:15), where the reference is probably to the image-crowned standards which the Romans set up at the east gate of the temple (A.D. 70), and to which they paid idolatrous honours. "Almost the entire religion of the Roman camp consisted in worshipping the ensign, swearing by the ensign, and in preferring the ensign before all other gods." These ensigns were an "abomination" to the Jews—the "abomination of desolation."

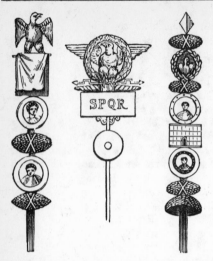

GROUP OF ROMAN STANDARDS.

This word is also used symbolically of sin in general (Isa. 66:3); an idol (44:19); the ceremonies of the apostate Church of Rome (Rev. 17:4); a detestable act (Ezek. 22:11).

A'bram—*exalted father;* **A'braham**—*father of a multitude*—son of Terah, named (Gen. 11:27) before his older brothers Nahor and Haran, because he was the heir of the promises. Till the age of seventy, Abram sojourned among his kindred in his native country of Chaldea. He then, with his father and his family and household, quitted the city of Ur, in which he had hitherto dwelt, and went some 300 miles north to Haran, where he abode fifteen years. The cause of his migration was a call from God (Acts 7:2-4). There is no mention of this first call in the Old Testament; it is implied, however, in Gen. 12. While they tarried at Haran, Terah died at the age of 205 years. Abram now received a second and more definite call, accompanied by a promise from God (Gen. 12:1, 2); whereupon he took his departure, taking his nephew Lot with him, "not knowing whither he went" (Heb. 11:8). He trusted implicitly to the guidance of Him who had called him.

Abram now, with a large household of probably a thousand souls, entered on a migratory life, and dwelt in tents. Pass-ing along the valley of the Jabbok, in the land of Canaan, he formed his first encampment at Sichem (Gen. 12:6), in the vale or oak-grove of Moreh, between Ebal on the north and Gerizim on the south. Here he received the great promise, "I will make of thee a great nation," etc. (Gen. 12:2, 3, 7). This promise comprehended not only temporal but also spiritual blessings. It implied that he was the chosen ancestor of the great Deliverer whose coming had been long ago predicted (Gen. 3:15). Soon after this, for some reason not mentioned, he removed his tent to the mountain district between Bethel, then called Luz, and Ai, towns about two miles apart, where he built an altar to "Jehovah." He again moved into the southern tract of Palestine, called by the Hebrews the *Negeb;* and was at length, on account of a famine, compelled to go down into Egypt. This took place in the time of the Hyksos, a Semitic race which now held the Egyptians in bondage. Here occurred that case of deception on the part of Abram which exposed him to the rebuke of Pharaoh (Gen. 12:18). Sarai was restored to him; and Pharaoh loaded him with presents, recommending him to withdraw from the country. He returned to Canaan richer than when he left it, "in cattle, in silver, and in gold" (Gen. 12:8; 13:2. Comp. Ps. 105:13, 14). The whole party then moved northward, and returned to their previous station near Bethel. Here disputes arose between Lot's shepherds and those of Abram about water and pasturage. Abram generously gave Lot his choice of the pasture-ground. (Comp. 1 Cor. 6:7.) He chose the well-watered plain in which Sodom was situated, and removed thither; and thus the uncle and nephew were separated. Immediately after this Abram was cheered by a repetition of the promises already made to him, and then removed to the plain or "oak-grove" of Mamre, which is in Hebron. He finally settled here, pitching his tent under a famous oak or terebinth tree, called "the oak of Mamre" (Gen. 13:18). This was his third resting-place in the land.

Some fourteen years before this, while

SEMITIC FAMILY BRINGING GIFTS INTO EGYPT, IN THE TIME OF ABRAHAM.
(From Egyptian Paintings.)

Abram was still in Chaldea, Palestine had been invaded by Chedorlaomer, king of Elam, who brought under tribute to him the five cities in the plain to which Lot had removed. This tribute was felt by the inhabitants of these cities to be a heavy burden, and after twelve years they revolted. This brought upon them the vengeance of Chedorlaomer, who had in league with him four other kings. He ravaged the whole country, plundering the towns, and carrying the inhabitants away as slaves. Among those thus treated was Lot. Hearing of the disaster that had fallen on his nephew, Abram immediately gathered from his own household a band of 318 armed men, and being joined by the Amoritish chiefs Mamre, Aner, and Eshcol, he pursued after Chedorlaomer, and overtook him near the springs of the Jordan. They attacked and routed his army, and pursued it over the range of Anti-Libanus as far as to Hobah, near Damascus, and then returned, bringing back all the spoils that had been carried away. Returning by way of Salem—i.e., Jerusalem—the king of that place, Melchizedek, came forth to meet them with refreshments. To him Abram presented a tenth of the spoils, in recognition of his character as a priest of the most high God (Gen. 14 : 18–20).

The history of this warlike exploit shows Abram as a great chief, having other chiefs in friendly alliance with him, and as a man of great power and social influence.

Having returned to his home at Mamre, the promises already made to him by God were repeated and enlarged (Gen. 14). "The word of the Lord" (an expression occurring here for the first time) "came to him" (15 : 1). He now understood better the future that lay before the nation that was to spring from him. Sarai, now seventy-five years old, in her impatience, persuaded Abram to take Hagar, her Egyptian maid, as a concubine, intending that whatever child might be born should be reckoned as her own. Ishmael was accordingly thus brought up, and was regarded as the heir of these promises (Gen. 16). When Ishmael was thirteen years old, God again revealed yet more explicitly and fully his gracious purpose; and in token of the sure fulfilment of that purpose the patriarch's name was now changed from Abram to Abraham (Gen. 17 : 4, 5), and the rite of circumcision was instituted as a sign of the covenant. It was then announced that the heir to these covenant promises would be the son of Sarai, though she was now ninety years old; and it was directed that his name should be Isaac. At the same time, in commemoration of the promises, Sarai's name was changed to Sarah. On that memorable day of God's thus revealing his design, Abraham and his son Ishmael and all the males of his house were circumcised (Gen. 17). Three months after this, as Abraham sat in his tent door, he saw three men approaching. They accepted his proffered hospitality, and, seated under an oak-tree, partook of the fare which Abraham and Sarah provided. One of the three visitants was none other than the Lord, and the other two were angels in the guise of men. The Lord renewed on this occasion his promise of a son by Sarah, who was rebuked for her unbelief. Abraham accompanied the three as they proceeded on their journey. The two angels went on toward Sodom; while the Lord tarried behind and talked with Abraham, making known to him the destruction that was about to fall on that guilty city. The patriarch interceded earnestly in behalf of the doomed city. But as not even ten righteous persons were found in it, for whose sake the city would have been spared, the threatened destruction fell upon it; and early next morning Abraham saw the smoke of the fire that consumed it as the "smoke of a furnace" (Gen. 19 : 1-28).

After fifteen years' residence at Mamre, Abraham moved southward, and pitched his tent among the Philistines, near to Gerar. Here occurred that sad instance of prevarication on his part in his relation to Abimelech the king (Gen. 20 ; 24). (See ABIMELECH.) Soon after this event, the patriarch left the vicinity of Gerar, and moved down the fertile valley about 25 miles to Beer-sheba. It was probably here that Isaac was born, Abraham being now an hundred years old. A feeling of jealousy now arose between Sarah and Hagar, whose son, Ishmael, was no longer to be regarded as Abraham's heir. Sarah insisted that both Hagar and her son should be sent away. This was done, although it was a hard trial to Abraham (Gen. 21:12). (See HAGAR; ISHMAEL.)

At this point there is a blank in the patriarch's history of perhaps twenty-five years. These years of peace and happiness were spent at Beer-sheba. The next time we see him his faith is put to a severe test by the command that suddenly came to him to go and offer up Isaac, the heir of all the promises, as a sacrifice on one of the mountains of Moriah. His faith stood the test (Heb. 11:17-19). He proceeded in a spirit of unhesitating obedience to carry out the command; and when about to slay his son, whom he had laid on the altar, his uplifted hand was arrested by the angel of Jehovah, and a ram, which was entangled in a thicket near at hand, was seized and offered in his stead. From this circumstance that place was called Jehovah-jireh—*i.e.*, "The Lord will provide." The promises made to Abraham were again confirmed (and this was the last recorded word of God to the patriarch); and he descended the mount with his son, and returned to his home at Beer-sheba (Gen. 22:19), where he resided for some years, and then moved northward to Hebron.

Some years after this Sarah died at Hebron, being 120 years old. Abraham acquired now the needful possession of a burying-place, the cave of Machpelah, by purchase from the owner of it, Ephron the Hittite (Gen. 23); and there he buried Sarah. His next care was to provide a wife for Isaac, and for this purpose he sent his steward, Eliezer, to Haran (or Charran, Acts 7:2), where his brother Nahor and his family resided (Gen. 11:31). The result was that Rebekah, the daughter of Nahor's son Bethuel, became the wife of Isaac (Gen. 24). Abraham then himself took to wife Keturah, who became the mother of

six sons, whose descendants were afterwards known as the "children of the east" (Judg. 6:3), and later as "Saracens." At length all his wanderings came to an end. At the age of 175 years, 100 years after he had first entered the land of Canaan, he died, and was buried in the old family burying-place at Machpelah (Gen. 25:1-10).

The history of Abraham made a wide and deep impression on the ancient world, and references to it are interwoven in the religious traditions of almost all Eastern nations. He is called "the friend of God" (James 2:23), "faithful Abraham" (Gal. 3:9), "the father of us all" (Rom. 4:16).

A'braham's bosom (Luke 16:22, 23) refers to the custom of reclining on couches at table, which was prevalent among the Jews—an arrangement which brought the head of one person almost into the bosom of the one who sat or reclined above him. To "be in Abraham's bosom" thus meant to enjoy happiness and rest (Matt. 8:11; Luke 16:23) at the banquet in Paradise. (See BANQUET; MEAL.)

Ab'ronah, one of Israel's halting-places in the desert (Num. 33:34, 35), just before Ezion-gaber.

Ab'salom—*father of peace; i.e.,* "peaceful"—David's son by Maacah (2 Sam. 3:3; comp. 1 Kings 1:6). He was noted

ABSALOM'S TOMB, JERUSALEM.

for his personal beauty and for the extraordinary profusion of the hair of his head (2 Sam. 14:25, 26). The first public act of his life was the blood-revenge he executed against Amnon, David's eldest son, who had basely wronged Absalom's sister Tamar. This revenge was executed at the time of the festivities connected with a great sheep-shearing at Baal-hazor. David's other sons fled from the place in horror, and brought the tidings of the death of Amnon to Jerusalem. Alarmed for the consequences of the act, Absalom fled to his grandfather at Geshur, and there abode for three years (2 Sam. 3:3; 13:23-38).

David mourned his absent son, now branded with the guilt of fratricide. As the result of a stratagem carried out by a woman of Tekoah, Joab received David's sanction to invite Absalom back to Jerusalem. He returned accordingly, but two years elapsed before his father admitted him into his presence (2 Sam. 14:28). Absalom was now probably the oldest surviving son of David, and as he was of royal descent by his mother as well as by his father, he began to aspire to the throne. His pretensions were favoured by the people. By many arts he gained their affection; and after his return from Geshur (2 Sam. 15:7; marg., R.V.) he went up to Hebron, the old capital of Judah, along with a great body of the people, and there proclaimed himself king. The revolt was so successful that David found it necessary to quit Jerusalem and flee to Mahanaim, beyond Jordan; where upon Absalom returned to Jerusalem and took possession of the throne without opposition. Ahithophel, who had been David's chief counsellor, deserted him and joined Absalom, whose chief counsellor he now became. Hushai also joined Absalom, but only for the purpose of trying to counteract the counsels of Ahithophel, and so to advantage David's cause. He was so far successful that by his advice, which was preferred to that of Ahithophel, Absalom delayed to march an army against his father, who thus gained time to prepare for the defence.

Absalom at length marched out against his father, whose army, under the command of Joab, he encountered on the borders of the forest of Ephraim. Twenty thousand of Absalom's army were slain in that fatal battle, and the rest fled. Absalom fled on a swift mule; but his long flowing hair, or more probably his head, was caught in the bough of an oak, and there he was left suspended till Joab came up and pierced him through with three darts. His body was then taken down and cast into a pit dug in the forest, and a heap of stones was raised over his grave. When the tidings of the result of that battle were brought to David, as he sat impatiently at the gate of Mahanaim, and he was told that Absalom had been slain, he gave way to the bitter lamentation: "O my son Absalom, my son, my son Absalom! would God I had died for thee, O Absalom, my son, my son!" (2 Sam. 18:33. Comp. Ex. 32:32; Rom. 9:3).

Absalom's three sons (2 Sam. 14:27; comp. 18:18) had all died before him, so that he left only a daughter, Tamar, who became the grandmother of Abijah.

Aca'cia (Heb. *shittim*)—Ex. 25:5, R.V.— probably the *Acacia seyal* (the gum-arabic

SHITTAH TREE (ACACIA SEYAL).

tree); called the "shittah" tree (Isa. 41:19). Its wood is called *shittim* wood (Ex. 26:15, 26; 25:10, 13, 23, 28, etc.). This species (*A. seyal*) is like the hawthorn, a gnarled and thorny tree. It yields the gum-arabic of commerce. It is found in abundance in the Sinaitic peninsula.

Ac'cad—*the high land* or *mountains*—a city in the land of Shinar. It has been identified with the mounds of *Akker Kuf*, some 50 miles to the north of Babylon; but this is doubtful. It was one of the cities of Nimrod's kingdom (Gen. 10:10). It stood close to the Euphrates, opposite Sippara. (See SEPHARVAIM.)

It is also the name of the country of which this city was the capital—namely, northern or upper Babylonia. The Accadians who came from the "mountains of the east," where the ark rested, attained to a high degree of civilization. In the Babylonian inscriptions they are called "the black heads" and "the black faces," in contrast to "the white race" of Semitic descent. They invented the form of writing in pictorial hieroglyphics, and also the cuneiform system, in which they wrote many books partly on papyrus and partly on clay. The Semitic Babylonians ("the white race"), or, as some scholars think, first the Cushites, and afterwards, as a second immigration, the Semites, invaded and conquered this country; and then the Accadian language ceased to be a spoken language, although for the sake of its literary treasures it continued to be studied by the educated classes of Babylonia. A large portion of the Ninevite tablets brought to light by Oriental research con-

PART OF TABLET SHOWING PRIMITIVE HIEROGLYPHICS AND CUNEIFORM CHARACTERS SIDE BY SIDE.

sists of interlinear or parallel translations from Accadian into Assyrian; and thus that long-forgotten language has been recovered by scholars. It belongs to the class of languages called *agglutinative*, common to the Tauranian race; *i.e.*, it consists of words "glued together," without declension or conjugation. These tablets in a remarkable manner illustrate ancient history. Among other notable records, they contain an account of the Creation which closely resembles that given in the book of Genesis, of the Sabbath as a day of rest, and of the Deluge and its cause. (See BABYLONIA, CHALDEA.)

Ac'cho—*sultry* or *sandy*—a town and harbour of Phœnicia, in the tribe of Asher, but never acquired by them (Judg. 1:31). It was known to the ancient Greeks and Romans by the name of Ptolemais, from Ptolemy the king of Egypt, who rebuilt it about B.C. 100. Here Paul landed on his last journey to Jerusalem (Acts 21:7). During the crusades of the Middle Ages it was called Acra; and subsequently, on account of its being occupied by the Knights Hospitallers of Jerusalem, it was called St. Jean d'Acre, or simply Acre.

Accus'er. Satan is styled the "accuser of the brethren" (Rev. 12:10. Comp.

Job 1:6; Zech. 3:1), as seeking to uphold his influence among men by bringing false charges against Christians, with the view of weakening their influence and injuring the cause with which they are identified. He was regarded by the Jews as the accuser of men before God, laying to their charge the violations of the law of which they were guilty, and demanding their punishment.

The same Greek word, rendered "accuser," is found in John 8:10 (but omitted in the Revised Version); Acts 23:30, 35; 24:8; 25:16, 18, in all of which places it is used of one who brings a charge against another.

Acel'dama, the name which the Jews gave in their proper tongue, i.e., in Aramaic, to the field which was purchased with the money which had been given to the betrayer of our Lord. The word means "field of blood." It was previously called "the potter's field" (Matt. 27:7, 8; Acts 1:19), and was appropriated as the burial-place for strangers. It lies on a narrow level terrace on the south face of the valley of Hinnom. Its modern name is *Hak ed-damm.*

ACELDAMA.

Achai'a, the name originally of a narrow strip of territory in Greece, on the northwest of the Peloponnesus. Subsequently it was applied by the Romans to the whole Peloponnesus, now called the Morea, and the south of Greece. It was then one of the two provinces (Macedonia being the other) into which they divided the country when it fell under their dominion. It is in this latter enlarged meaning that the name is always used in the New Testament (Acts 18:12, 16; 19:21; Rom. 15:26; 16:5, etc.). It was at the time when Luke wrote the Acts of the Apostles under the proconsular form of government; hence the appropriate title given to Gallio as the "deputy," i.e., proconsul, of Achaia (Acts 18:12).

Acha'ichus (1 Cor. 16:17), one of the members of the church of Corinth who, with Fortunatus and Stephanas, visited Paul while he was at Ephesus, for the purpose of consulting him on the affairs of the church. These two probably were the bearers of the letter from Corinth to the apostle to which he alludes in 1 Cor. 7:1.

A'chan, called also Achar—i.e., *one who troubles* (1 Chr. 2:7)—in commemoration of his crime, which brought upon him an awful destruction (Josh. 7:1). On the occasion of the fall of Jericho, he seized, contrary to the divine command, an ingot of gold, a quantity of silver, and a costly Babylonish garment, which he hid in his tent. Joshua was convinced that the defeat which the Israelites afterwards sustained before Ai was a proof of the divine displeasure on account of some crime, and he at once adopted means by the use of the lot for discovering the criminal. It was then found that Achan was guilty, and he was stoned to death in the valley of Achor. He and all that belonged to him were then consumed by fire, and a heap of stones was raised over the ashes.

Ach'bor—*gnawing=mouse.* (1.) An Edomitish king (Gen. 36 : 38 ; 1 Chr. 1 : 49).

(2.) One of Josiah's officers sent to the prophetess Huldah to inquire regarding the newly-discovered book of the law (2 Kings 22 : 12, 14). He is also called Abdon (2 Chr. 34 : 20).

A'chish—*angry*—perhaps only a general title of royalty applicable to the Philistine kings. (1.) The king with whom David sought refuge when he fled from Saul (1 Sam. 21 : 10–15). He is called Abimelech in the superscription of Ps. 34. It was probably this same king to whom David a second time repaired at the head of a band of 600 warriors, and who assigned him Ziklag, whence he carried on war against the surrounding tribes (1 Sam. 27 : 5–12). Achish had great confidence in the valour and fidelity of David (1 Sam. 28 : 1, 2), but at the instigation of his courtiers did not permit him to go up to battle along with the Philistine hosts (1 Sam. 29 : 2–11). David remained with Achish a year and four months.

(2.) Another king of Gath, probably grandson of the foregoing, to whom the two servants of Shimei fled. This led Shimei to go to Gath in pursuit of them, and the consequence was that Solomon put him to death (1 Kings 2 : 39–46).

Ach'metha (Ezra 6 : 2), called Ecbatana by classical writers, the capital of northern Media. Here was the palace which was the residence of the old Median monarchs, and of Cyrus and Cambyses. In the time of Ezra, the Persian kings resided usually at Susa or Babylon. But Cyrus held his court at Achmetha ; and Ezra, writing a century after, correctly mentions the place where the decree of Cyrus was found.

A'chor—*trouble*—a valley near Jericho,

so called in consequence of the trouble which the sin of Achan caused Israel (Josh. 7 : 24, 26). The expression "valley of Achor" probably became proverbial for that which caused trouble, and when Isaiah (65 : 10) refers to it he uses it in this sense : "The valley of Achor, a place for herds to lie down in ;" *i.e.*, that which had been a source of calamity would become a source of blessing. Hosea also (2 : 15) uses the expression in the same sense : "The valley of Achor, a door of hope ;" *i.e.*, trouble would be turned into joy, despair into hope. This valley has been identified with the *Wady Kelt.*

Ach'sah—*anklet*—Caleb's only daughter (1 Chr. 2 : 49). She was offered in marriage to the man who would lead an attack on the city of Debir, or Kirjath-sepher. This was done by Othniel (*q.v.*), who accordingly obtained her as his wife (Josh. 15 : 16–19 ; Judg. 1 : 9–15).

Ach'shaph—*fascination*—a royal city of the Canaanites, in the north of Palestine (Josh. 11 : 1 ; 12 : 20 ; 19 : 25). It was in the eastern boundary of the tribe of Asher, and is identified with the modern ruined village of *Kesaf* or *Yasif*, N.-E. of Accho.

Ach'zib—*falsehood.* (1.) A town in the Shephēlah, or plain country of Judah (Josh. 15 : 44) ; probably the same as Chezib of Gen. 38 : 5=*Ain Kezbeh.*

(2.) A Phœnician city (the Gr. *Ecdippa*), always retained in their possession though assigned to the tribe of Asher (Josh. 19 : 29 ; Judg. 1 : 31). It is identified with the modern *es-Zib*, on the Mediterranean, about 8 miles north of Accho.

A'cre is the translation of a word (*tse'med*), which properly means *a yoke,* and denotes a space of ground that may be ploughed by a yoke of oxen in a day. It is about an acre of our measure (Isa. 5 : 10 ; 1 Sam. 14 : 14).

Acts of the Apostles, the title now given to the fifth and last of the historical books of the New Testament. The author styles it a "treatise" (1 : 1). It was early called "The Acts," "The Gospel of the Holy Ghost," and "The Gospel of the Resurrection." It contains properly no account of any of the apostles except Peter and Paul. John is noticed only three times; and all that is recorded of James, the son of Zebedée, is his execution by Herod. It is properly therefore not the history of the "Acts of the Apostles," a title which was given to the book at a later date, but of "Acts of Apostles," or more correctly, of "Some Acts of Certain Apostles."

As regards its *authorship*, it was certainly the work of Luke, the "beloved physician" (comp. Luke 1:1-4; Acts 1:1). This is the uniform tradition of antiquity, although the writer nowhere makes mention of himself by name. The style and idiom of the Gospel of Luke and of the Acts, and the usage of words and phrases common to both, strengthen this opinion. The writer first appears in the narrative in 16:11, and then disappears till Paul's return to Philippi two years afterwards, when he and Paul left that place together (20:6), and the two seem henceforth to have been constant companions to the end. He was certainly with Paul at Rome (28; Col. 4:14). Thus he wrote a great portion of that history from personal observation. For what lay beyond his own experience he had the instruction of Paul. If, as is very probable, 2 Tim. was written during Paul's second imprisonment at Rome, Luke was with him then as his faithful companion to the last (2 Tim. 4:11). Of his subsequent history we have no certain information.

The design of Luke's Gospel was to give an exhibition of the character and work of Christ as seen in his history till he was taken up from his disciples into heaven; and of the Acts, as its sequel, to give an illustration of the power and working of the gospel when preached among all nations, "beginning at Jerusalem." The opening sentences of the Acts are just an expansion and an explanation of the closing words of the Gospel. In this book we have just a continuation of the history of the church after Christ's ascension. Luke here carries on the history in the same spirit in which he had commenced it. It is only a book of *beginnings*—a history of the *founding* of churches—the *initial* steps in the formation of the Christian society in the different places visited by the apostles. It records a cycle of "representative events."

All through the narrative we see the ever-present, all-controlling power of the ever-living Saviour. He worketh all and in all in spreading abroad his truth among men by his Spirit and through the instrumentality of his apostles.

The *time* of the writing of this history may be gathered from the fact that the narrative extends down to the close of the second year of Paul's first imprisonment at Rome. It could not therefore have been written earlier than A.D. 61 or 62, nor later than about the end of A.D. 63. Paul was probably put to death during his second imprisonment, about A.D. 64, or, as some think, 66.

The *place* where the book was written was probably Rome, to which Luke accompanied Paul.

The key to the *contents* of the book is in 1:8, "Ye shall be witnesses unto me in Jerusalem, and in all Judæa, and in Samaria, and unto the uttermost part of the earth." After referring to what had been recorded in a "former treatise" of the sayings and doings of Jesus Christ before his ascension, the author proceeds to give an account of the circumstances connected with that event, and then records the leading facts with reference to the spread and triumphs of Christianity over the world during a period of about thirty years. The record begins with Pentecost (A.D. 33) and ends with Paul's first imprisonment (A.D. 63 or 64). The whole contents of the book may be divided into these three parts:—

(1.) Chaps. 1-12, describing the first twelve years of the Christian church. This section has been entitled "From Jerusalem to Antioch." It contains the history of the planting and extension of the church among the Jews by the ministry of Peter.

(2.) Chaps. 13-19, Paul's missionary journeys, giving the history of the extension and planting of the church among the Gentiles.

(3.) Chaps. 20-28, Paul at Rome, and the events which led to this. Chaps. 13-28 have been entitled "From Antioch to Rome."

In tnis book it is worthy of note that no mention is made of the writing by Paul of any of his epistles. This may be accounted for by the fact that the writer confined himself to a history of the *planting* of the church, and not to that of its *training* or edification. The relation, however, between this history and the epistles of Paul is of such a kind—*i.e.*, brings to light so many undesigned coincidences—as to prove the genuineness and authenticity of both, as is so ably shown by Paley in his *Horæ Paulinæ.* "No ancient work affords so many tests of veracity; for no other has such numerous points of contact in all directions with contemporary history, politics, and topography, whether Jewish, or Greek, or Roman."—*Lightfoot.* (See PAUL.)

A'dah — *ornament.* (1.) The first of Lamech's two wives, and the mother of Jabal and Jubal (Gen. 4 : 19, 20, 23).

(2.) The first of Esau's three wives, the daughter of Elon the Hittite (Gen. 36 : 2, 4), called also Bashemath (26 : 34).

Ad'am—*red*—a Babylonian word, the generic name for man, having the same meaning in the Hebrew and the Assyrian languages. It was the name given to the first man, whose creation, fall, and subsequent history and that of his descendants are detailed in the first book of Moses (Gen. 1 : 27–ch. 5). "God created man [Heb., *Adam*] in his own image, in the image of God created he him; male and female created he them."

Adam was absolutely the first man whom God created. He was formed out of the dust of the earth (and hence his name), and God breathed into his nostrils the breath of life, and gave him dominion over all the lower creatures (Gen. 1 : 26 ; 2 : 7). He was placed after his creation in the Garden of Eden, to cultivate it, and to enjoy its fruits under this one prohibition : "Of the tree of the knowledge of good and evil thou shalt not eat ; for in the day thou eatest thereof thou shalt surely die."

The first recorded act of Adam was his giving names to the beasts of the field and the fowls of the air, which God brought to him for this end. Thereafter the Lord

caused a deep sleep to fall upon him, and while in an unconscious state took one of his ribs, and closed up his flesh again ; and of this rib he made a woman, whom he presented to him when he awoke. Adam received her as his wife, and said, "This is now bone of my bone, and flesh of my flesh : she shall be called Woman, because she was taken out of Man." He called her Eve, because she was the mother of all living.

Being induced by the tempter in the form of a serpent to eat the forbidden fruit, Eve persuaded Adam, and he also did eat. Thus man fell, and brought upon himself and his posterity all the sad consequences of his transgression. The narrative of the Fall comprehends in it the great promise of a Deliverer (Gen. 3 : 15), the "first gospel" message to man. They were expelled from Eden, and at the east of the garden God placed a flame, which turned every way, to prevent access to the tree of life (Gen. 3). How long they were in Paradise is matter of mere conjecture.

Shortly after their expulsion Eve brought forth her first-born, and called him Cain. Although we have the names of only three of Adam's sons—*viz.*, Cain, Abel, and Seth —yet it is obvious that he had several sons and daughters (Gen. 5 : 4). He died aged 930 years.

Adam and Eve were the progenitors of the whole human race. Evidences of varied kinds are abundant in proving the unity of the human race. The investigations of science, altogether independent of historical evidence, lead to the conclusion that God "hath made of one blood all nations of men for to dwell on all the face of the earth" (Acts 17 : 26. Comp. Rom. 5 : 12–21 ; 1 Cor. 15 : 22–47).

Ad'am, a type. The apostle Paul speaks of Adam as "the figure of him who was to come." On this account our Lord is sometimes called the second Adam. This typical relation is,described in Rom. 5 : 14–19.

Ad'am, the city of, is referred to in Josh. 3 : 16. It stood "beside Zarethan," on the west bank of Jordan (1 Kings 4 : 12). At this city the flow of the water was arrested and rose up "upon an heap" at the time of the Israelites' passing over (Josh. 3 : 16).

The site of this city is unknown. A trace of it has been supposed to be found near *Kurn Surtabeh*, at the Damieh ford of Jordan, south-east of Shechem.

Ad'amah—*red earth*—a fortified city of Naphtali, probably the modern *Damieh*, on the west of the sea of Tiberias (Josh. 19:33, 36).

Ad'amant (Heb. *shamir*)—Ezek. 3:9—a word meaning "unconquerable," used to denote hard stones, as the diamond, which is just a corruption of this word. It is an emblem of firmness in resisting adversaries of the truth (Zech. 7:12), and of hard-heartedness against the truth (Jer. 17:1).

A'dar—*large*—the sixth month of the civil and the twelfth of the ecclesiastical year of the Jews (Esther 3:7, 13; 8:12; 9:1, 15, 17, 19, 21). It included the days extending from the new moon of our March to the new moon of April. This name was first used after the Captivity. When the season was backward, and the lambs not yet of a paschal size, or the barley not forward enough for *Abib*, then a month called *Veadar, i.e.*, a second Adar, was intercalated.

Ad'beel—*miracle of God*—the third of the twelve sons of Ishmael, and head of an Arabian tribe (Gen. 25:13; 1 Chr. 1:29).

Ad'dar—*ample, splendid*—son of Bela (1 Chr. 8:3), called also Ard (Gen. 46:21).

Ad'der (Ps. 140:3; Rom. 3:13, "asp") is the rendering of—(1.) *Akshub* ("coiling" or "lying in wait"), properly an asp or viper, only found in this passage. (2.) *Pethen* ("twisting"), a viper or venomous serpent identified with the cobra (*Naja haje*) (Ps. 58:4; 91:13; elsewhere "asp"). (3.) *Tziphoni* ("hissing") (Prov. 23:32; elsewhere rendered "cockatrice," Isa. 11:8; 14:29; 59:5; Jer. 8:17), as it is here in the margin of the Authorized Version. The Revised Version has "basilisk." This may have been the yellow viper, the *Daboia xanthina*, the largest and most dangerous of the vipers of Palestine. (4.) *Shephiphon* ("creeping"), occurring only in Gen. 49:17, the small speckled venomous snake, the "horned snake," or cerastes. Dan is compared to this serpent, which springs from its hiding-place on the passers-by.

The terms adder and viper are nearly interchangeable, the latter being properly, however, the name of a genus of serpents

EGYPTIAN COBRA (NAJA HAJE).

which have their heads covered with scales. (See SERPENT.)

A "deaf adder that cannot be charmed" is a type of those whom no appeals to reason or conscience can restrain from evil (Ps. 58:4, 5; Jer. 8:17).

Ad'di—*ornament*—(Luke 3:28), the son of Cosam, and father of Melchi, one of the progenitors of Christ.

Ad'don—*low*—one of the persons named in Neh. 7:61 who could not "shew their father's house" on the return from captivity. This, with similar instances (ver. 63), indicates the importance the Jews attached to their genealogies.

A'diel—*ornament of God.* (1.) The father of Azmaveth, who was treasurer under David and Solomon (1 Chr. 27:25).

(2.) A family head of the tribe of Simeon (1 Chr. 4:36).

(3.) A priest (1 Chr. 9:12).

A'din—*effeminate.* (1.) Ezra 8:6. (2.) Neh. 10:16.

Ad'ina—*slender*—one of David's warriors (1 Chr. 11:42), a Reubenite.

Ad'ino, the Eznite, one of David's mighty men (2 Sam. 23:8). (See JASHOBEAM.)

Ad'juration, a solemn appeal whereby one person imposes on another the obligation of speaking or acting as if under an oath (1 Sam. 14:24; Josh. 6:26; 1 Kings 22:16).

CLAY TABLETS FROM TELL-EL-AMARNA, UPPER EGYPT.
(See Adoni-zedec, Ajalon, Egypt, Gibeon, Joshua, Melchizedek, Sepharvaim, etc.)
From *Helps to the Study of the Bible*. Oxford.

CLAY TABLET FROM TELL EL-HESY, SOUTHERN PALESTINE,
(See Lachish, page 413.)
By permission of the Committee of the Palestine Exploration Fund.

We have in the New Testament a striking example of this (Matt. 26 : 63; Mark 5 : 7), where the high priest calls upon Christ to avow his true character. It would seem that in such a case the person so adjured could not refuse to give an answer.

The word "adjure"—*i.e.*, cause to swear —is used with reference to the casting out of demons (Acts 19 : 13).

Ad'mah—*earth*—one of the five cities of the vale of Siddim (Gen. 10 : 19). It was destroyed along with Sodom and Gomorrah (19 : 24; Deut. 29 : 23). It is supposed by some to be the same as the Adam of Josh. 3 : 16, the name of which still lingers in *Damieh*, the ford of Jordan. (See ZEBOIM.)

Ad'nah — *delight*. (1.) A chief of the tribe of Manasseh who joined David at Ziklag (1 Chr. 12 : 20).

(2.) A general under Jehoshaphat, chief over 300,000 men (2 Chr. 17 : 14).

Adon'i-be'zek—*lord of Bezek*—a Canaanitish king who, having subdued seventy of the chiefs that were around him, made an attack against the armies of Judah and Simeon, but was defeated and brought as a captive to Jerusalem, where his thumbs and great toes were cut off. He confessed that God had requited him for his like cruelty to the seventy kings whom he had subdued (Judg: 1:4-7; comp. 1 Sam. 15:33).

Adoni'jah—*my Lord is Jehovah*. (1.) The fourth son of David (2 Sam. 3 : 4). After the death of his elder brothers, Amnon and Absalom, he became heir-apparent to the throne. But Solomon, a younger brother, was preferred to him. Adonijah, however, when his father was dying, caused himself to be proclaimed king. But Nathan and Bathsheba induced David to give orders that Solomon should at once be proclaimed and admitted to the throne. Adonijah fled and took refuge at the altar, and received pardon for his conduct from Solomon on the condition that he showed himself "a worthy man" (1 Kings 1 : 5-53). He afterwards made a second attempt to gain the throne, but was seized and put to death (1 Kings 2 : 13-25).

(2.) A Levite sent with the princes to teach the book of the law to the inhabitants of Judah (2 Chr. 17 : 8).

(3.) One of the "chiefs of the people" after the Captivity (Neh. 10 : 16).

Adoni'kam—*whom the Lord sets up*— one of those "which came with Zerubbabel" (Ezra 2 : 13). His "children," or retainers, to the number of 666, came up to Jerusalem (8 : 13).

Adoni'ram (**Ado'ram**, 1 Kings 12 : 18), the son of Abda, was "over the tribute," *i.e.*, the levy or forced labour. He was stoned to death by the people of Israel (1 Kings 4 : 6; 5 : 14).

Adon'i-ze'dec—*lord of justice or righteousness*—was king in Jerusalem at the time when the Israelites invaded Palestine (Josh. 10 : 1, 3). He formed a confederacy with the other Canaanitish kings against the Israelites, but was utterly routed by Joshua when he was engaged in besieging the Gibeonites. The history of this victory and of the treatment of the five confederated kings is recorded in Josh. 10 : 1-27. (Comp. Deut. 21 : 23). Among the Tell Amarna tablets (see p. 215) are some very interesting letters from Adoni-zedec to the King of Egypt. These illustrate in a very remarkable manner the history recorded in Josh. 10, and indeed throw light on the wars of conquest generally, so that they may be read as a kind of commentary on the book of Joshua. Here the conquering career of the *Abiri* (*i.e.*, Hebrews) is graphically described : "Behold, I say that the land of the king my lord is ruined"—"The wars are mighty against me"—"The Hebrew chiefs plunder all the king's lands"— "Behold, I the chief of the Amorites am breaking to pieces." Then he implores the king of Egypt to send soldiers to help him, directing that the army should come by sea to Ascalon or Gaza, and thence march to *Wru-sa-lim* (Jerusalem) by the valley of Elah.

Adop'tion, the giving to any one the name and place and privileges of a son who is not a son by birth.

(1.) *Natural.* Thus Pharaoh's daughter adopted Moses (Ex. 2 : 10), and Mordecai Esther (Esther 2: 7).

(2.) *National.* God adopted Israel (Ex. 4 : 22; Deut. 7 : 6; Hos. 11 : 1; Rom. 9 : 4).

(3.) *Spiritual.* An act of God's grace by

which he brings men into the number of his redeemed family, and makes them partakers of all the blessings he has provided for them. Adoption represents the new relations into which the believer is introduced by justification, and the privileges connected therewith—*viz.*, an interest in God's peculiar love (John 17 : 23 ; Rom. 5 : 5–8), a spiritual nature (2 Pet. 1 : 4 ; John 1 : 13), the possession of a spirit becoming children of God (1 Pet. 1 : 14 ; 2 John 6 ; Rom. 8 : 15–21 ; Gal. 5 : 1 ; Heb. 2 : 15), present protection, consolation, supplies (Luke 12 : 27–32 ; John 14 : 18 ; 1 Cor. 3 : 21–23 ; 2 Cor. 1 : 4), fatherly chastisements (Heb. 12 : 5–11), and a future glorious inheritance (Rom. 8 : 17, 23 ; James 2 : 5 ; Phil. 3 : 21).

Ado'ram. See ADONIRAM.

Adore', to worship; to express reverence and homage. The forms of adoration among the Jews were putting off the shoes (Ex. 3 : 5 ; Josh. 5 : 15), and prostration (Gen. 17 : 3 ; Ps. 95 : 6 ; Isa. 44 : 15, 17, 19 ; 46 : 6). To "kiss the Son" in Ps. 2 : 12 is to adore and worship him. (See Dan. 3 : 5, 6.) The word itself does not occur in Scripture.

Adram'melech—*Adar the king.* (1.) An idol; a form of the sun-god worshipped by the inhabitants of Sepharvaim (2 Kings 17 : 31), and brought by the Sepharvite colonists into Samaria.

(2.) A son of Sennacherib, king of Assyria (2 Kings 19 : 37 ; Isa. 37 : 38).

Adramyt'tium, a city of Asia Minor on the coast of Mysia, which in early times was called Æolis. The ship in which Paul embarked at Cæsarea belonged to this city (Acts 27 : 2). He was conveyed in it only to Myra, in Lycia, whence he sailed in an Alexandrian ship to Italy. It was a rare thing for a ship to sail from any port of Palestine direct for Italy. It still bears the name Adramyti, and is a place of some traffic.

A'dria (Acts 27 : 27 ; R.V., "the sea of Adria"), the Adriatic Sea, including in Paul's time the whole of the Mediterranean lying between Crete and Sicily. It is the modern Gulf of Venice, the *Mare Superum* of the Romans, as distinguished from the *Mare Inferum* or Tyrrhenian Sea.

A'driel—*flock of God*—the son of Barzillai, the Meholathite, to whom Saul gave in marriage his daughter Merab (1 Sam. 18 : 19). The five sons that sprang from this union were put to death by the Gibeonites (2 Sam. 21 : 8, 9. Here it is said that Michal "brought up" [R.V., "bare"] these five sons,—either that she treated them as if she had been their own mother, or that for "Michal" we should read "Merab," as in 1 Sam. 18 : 19).

Adul'lam, one of the royal cities of the Canaanites, now *'Aîd-el-mâ* (Josh. 12 : 15 ; 15 : 35). It stood on the old Roman road in the valley of Elah (*q.v.*), which was the scene of David's memorable victory over Goliath (1 Sam. 17 : 4), and not far from Gath. It was one of the towns which Rehoboam fortified against Egypt (2 Chr. 11 : 7). It was called "the glory of Israel" (Micah 1 : 15).

The *Cave of Adullam* has been discovered about 2 miles south of the scene of David's triumph, and about 13 miles west from Bethlehem. At this place is a hill some 500 feet high pierced with numerous caverns, in one of which David gathered together "every one that was in distress, and every one that was in debt, and every one that was discontented" (1 Sam. 22 : 2). Some of these caverns are large enough to hold 200 or 300 men. According to tradition this cave was at Wady Khureitûn, between Bethlehem and the Dead Sea, but this view cannot be well maintained.

Adul'lamite, an inhabitant of the city of Adullam (Gen. 38 : 1, 12, 20).

Adul'tery, conjugal infidelity. An adulterer was a man who had illicit intercourse with a married or a betrothed woman, and such a woman was an adulteress. Intercourse between a married man and an unmarried woman was fornication. Adultery was regarded as a great social wrong, as well as a great sin.

The Mosaic law (Num. 5 : 11–31) prescribed that the suspected wife should be tried by the ordeal of the "water of jealousy." There is, however, no recorded instance of the application of this law. In subsequent times the Rabbis made various regulations with the view of discovering the guilty party, and of bringing about a divorce. It has been inferred from John 8:1-8 that this sin became very common during the age preceding the destruction of Jerusalem.

Idolatry, covetousness, and apostasy are spoken of as adultery *spiritually* (Jer. 3:6, 8, 9; Ezek. 16:32; Hos. 1:2:3; Rev. 2:22). An apostate church is an adulteress (Isa. 1:21; Ezek. 23:4, 7, 37), and the Jews are styled "an adulterous generation" (Matt. 12:39). (Comp. Rev. 12.)

Adum'mim—*the red ones*—a place apparently on the road between Jericho and Jerusalem, "on the south side of the torrent" Wady Kelt, looking toward Gilgal, mentioned Josh. 15:7; 18:17. It was nearly half-way between Jerusalem and Jericho, and now bears the name of *Tal-at-ed-Dumm*. It is supposed to have been the place referred to in the parable of the Good Samaritan (Luke 10:33-37). The order of the "Knights Templars" sprang out of an association formed for the purpose of guarding this road, which was infested by robbers.

THE ROAD BETWEEN JERUSALEM AND JERICHO.

Ad'versary (Heb. *satan*), an opponent or foe (1 Kings 5:4; 11:14, 23, 25; Luke 13:17); one that speaks against another, a complainant (Matt. 5:25; Luke 12:58); an enemy (Luke 18:3), and specially the devil (1 Pet. 5:8).

Ad'vocate (Gr. *paraklētos*), one who pleads another's cause, who helps another by defending or comforting him. It is a name given by Christ three times to the Holy Ghost (John 14:16; 15:26; 16:7, where the Greek word is rendered "Comforter," *q.v.*). It is applied to Christ in 1 John 2:1, where the same Greek word is rendered "Advocate," the rendering which it should have in all the places where it occurs.

Tertullus "the orator" (Acts 24:1) was a Roman advocate whom the Jews employed to accuse Paul before Felix.

Æ'non—*springs*—a place near Salim where John baptized (John 3:23). It was probably near the upper source of the Wady Fâr'ah, an open valley extending from Mount Ebal to the Jordan. It is full of springs. A place has been found called *'Ainūn*, four miles north of the springs.

Affec'tion, feeling or emotion. Mention is made of "vile affections" (Rom. 1:26) and "inordinate affections" (Col. 3:5). Christians are exhorted to set their affections on things above (Col. 3:2). There is a distinction between natural and spiritual or gracious affections (Ezek. 33:32).

Affin'ity, relationship by alliance (2 Chr. 18:1) or by marriage (1 Kings 3:1). Marriages are prohibited within certain degrees of affinity, enumerated Lev. 18:6-17. Consanguinity is relationship by blood.

Afflic'tions—common to all (Job 5:7; 14:1; Ps. 34:19); are for the good of men (James 1:2, 3, 12; 2 Cor. 12:7) and the glory of God (2 Cor. 12:7-10; 1 Pet. 4:14), and are to be borne with patience by the Lord's people (Ps. 94:12; Prov. 3:12). They are all directed by God (Lam. 3:33), and will result in the everlasting good of his people (2 Cor. 4:16-18) in Christ Jesus (Rom. 8:35-39).

Ag'abus, a "prophet," probably one of the seventy disciples of Christ. He prophesied at Antioch of an approaching famine (Acts 11:27, 28). Many years afterwards he met Paul at Cæsarea, and warned him of the bonds and affliction that awaited him at Jerusalem should he persist in going thither (Acts 21:10-12).

A'gag—*flame*—the usual title of the Amalekite kings, as "Pharaoh" was of the Egyptian. (1.) A king of the Amalekites referred to by Balaam (Num. 24:7). He lived at the time of the Exodus.

(2.) Another king of the Amalekites whom Saul spared unlawfully, but whom Samuel on his arrival in the camp of Saul ordered, in *retributive* justice (Judg. 1), to be brought out and cut in pieces (1 Sam. 15:8-33. Comp. Ex. 17:11; Num. 14:45).

A'gagite, a name applied to Haman and also to his father (Esther 3:1, 10; 7:3, 5). Probably it was equivalent to Amalekite.

Ag'ate (Heb. *shebó*), a precious stone in the breast-plate of the high priest (Ex. 28:19; 39:12), the second in the third row. This may be the agate properly so called, a semi-transparent crystallized quartz, probably brought from Sheba, whence its name. In Isa. 54:12 and Ezek. 27:16, this word is the rendering of the Hebrew *cadcod*, which means "ruddy," and may probably denote the ruby or carbuncle, or, as others think, the chalcedony.

This word is from the Greek name given to a stone found in the river *Achates* in Sicily.

Age, used to denote the period of a man's life (Gen. 47:28), the maturity of life (John 9:21), the latter end of life (Job 11:17), a generation of the human race (Job 8:8), and an indefinite period (Eph. 2:7; 3:5, 21; Col. 1:26). Respect to be shown to the aged (Lev. 19:32). It is a blessing to communities when they have old men among them (Isa. 65:20; Zech. 8:4). The aged supposed to excel in understanding (Job 12:20; 15:10; 32:4, 9; 1 Kings 12:6, 8). A full age the reward of piety (Job 32:26; Gen. 15:15).

Ag'ee—*fugitive*—the father of Shammah, who was one of David's mighty men (2 Sam. 23:11).

Ag'ony, contest; wrestling; severe struggling with pain and suffering. Anguish is the reflection on evil that is already past, while agony is a struggle with evil at the time present. It is only used in the New Testament by Luke (22:44) to describe our Lord's fearful struggle in Gethsemane.

The verb from which the noun "agony" is derived is used to denote an earnest endeavour or striving, as "Strive [agonize] to enter" (Luke 13:24); "Then would my servants fight" [agonize] (John 18:36). Comp. 1 Cor. 9:25; Col. 1:29; 4:12; 1 Tim. 6:12; 2 Tim. 4:7—where the words "striveth," "labour," "conflict," "fight," are the renderings of the same Greek verb.

Ag'riculture. Tilling the ground (Gen. 2:15; 4:2, 3, 12) and rearing cattle were the chief employments in ancient times. The Egyptians excelled in agriculture. And after the Israelites entered into the possession of the Promised Land, their circumstances favoured in the highest degree a remarkable development of this art. Agriculture became indeed the basis of the Mosaic commonwealth.

The year in Palestine was divided into six agricultural periods :—

I. SOWING TIME.

MONTHS.

Tisri, latter half $\left\{\begin{array}{l}\text{beginning about}\\ \text{the autumnal}\\ \text{equinox.}\end{array}\right.$

Marchesvan.
Kisleu, former half. $\left.\begin{array}{l}\\ \\ \\ \\ \end{array}\right\}$ Early rain due=first showers of autumn.

II. UNRIPE TIME.

Kisleu, latter half.
Tebet.
Sebat, former half.

III. COLD SEASON.

Sebat, latter half.
Adar.
[Veadar.]
Nisan, former half. $\left.\begin{array}{l}\\ \\ \\ \\ \end{array}\right\}$ Latter rain due (Deut. 11: 14; Jer. 5: 24; Hos. 6: 3; Zech. 10: 1; James 5: 7; Job 29: 23).

IV. HARVEST TIME.

MONTHS.

Nisan, latter half. $\left\{\begin{array}{l}\text{Beginning about vernal}\\ \text{equinox. Barley green.}\\ \text{Passover.}\end{array}\right.$

Ijar.
Sivan, former half.—Wheat ripe. Pentecost.

V. SUMMER (total absence of rain).

Sivan, latter half.
Tammuz.
Ab, former half.

VI. SULTRY SEASON.

Ab, latter half.
Elul.
Tisri, former half.—Ingathering of fruits.

The six months from the middle of Tisri to the middle of Nisan were occu-

PLOUGHING.

pied with the work of cultivation, and the rest of the year mainly with the gathering in of the fruits. The extensive and easily-arranged system of irrigation from the rills and streams from the mountains made the soil in every part of Palestine richly productive (Ps. 1 : 3 ; 65 : 10 ; Prov. 21 : 1 ; Isa. 30 : 25 ; 32 : 2, 20 ; Hos. 12 : 11), and the appliances of careful cultivation and of manure increased its fertility to such an extent that in the days of Solomon, when there was an abundant population, "20,000 measures of wheat year by year" were sent to Hiram in exchange for timber (1 Kings 5 : 11), and in large quantities also wheat was sent to the Tyrians for the merchandise in which they traded (Ezek. 27 : 17). The wheat sometimes produced an hundredfold (Gen. 26 : 12; Matt. 13 : 23). Figs and pomegranates were very plentiful (Num. 13 : 23), and the vine and the olive grew luxuriantly and produced abundant fruit (Deut. 33 : 24).

Lest the productiveness of the soil should be exhausted, it was enjoined that the whole land should rest every seventh year, when all agricultural labour would entirely cease (Lev. 25 : 1-7 ; Deut. 15 : 1-10).

It was forbidden to sow a field with divers seeds (Deut. 22 : 9). A passer-by was at liberty to eat any quantity of corn or grapes, but he was not permitted to carry away any (Deut. 23 : 24, 25 ; Matt.

12:1). The poor were permitted to claim the corners of the fields and the gleanings. A forgotten sheaf in the field was to be left also for the poor. (See Lev. 19:9, 10; Deut. 24:19.)

Agricultural implements and operations. The sculptured monuments and painted tombs of Egypt and Assyria throw much light on this subject, and on the general operations of agriculture. Ploughs of a simple construction were known in the time of Moses (Deut. 22:10; comp. Job 1:14). They were very light, and required great attention to keep them in the ground (Luke 9:62). They were drawn by oxen (Job 1:14), cows (1 Sam. 6:7), and asses (Isa. 30:24); but an ox and an ass must not be yoked together in the same plough (Deut. 22:10). Men sometimes followed the plough with a hoe to break the clods (Isa. 28:24). The oxen were urged on by a "goad," or long staff pointed at the end, so that if occasion arose it could be used as a spear also (Judg. 3:31; 1 Sam. 13:21).

When the soil was prepared, the seed was *sown* broadcast over the field (Matt. 13:3-8). The "harrow" mentioned in Job 39:10 was not used to cover the seeds, but to break the clods, being little more than a thick block of wood. In highly irrigated spots the seed was trampled in by cattle (Isa. 32:20); but doubtless there was some kind of harrow also for covering in the seed scattered in the furrows of the field.

The *reaping* of the corn was performed either by pulling it up by the roots, or cutting it with a species of sickle, according to circumstances. The corn when cut was generally put up in sheaves (Gen. 37:7; Lev. 23:10-15; Ruth 2:7, 15; Job 24:10; Jer. 9:22; Micah 4:12), which were afterwards gathered to the threshing-floor or stored in barns (Matt. 6:26).

The process of *threshing* was performed generally by spreading the sheaves on the threshing-floor and causing oxen and cattle to tread repeatedly over them (Deut. 25:4; Isa. 28:28). On occasions flails or sticks were used for this purpose (Ruth 2:17; Isa. 28:27). There was also a "threshing instrument" (Isa. 41:15; Amos 1:3) which was drawn over the corn. It was called by the Hebrews a *moreg*—a threshing roller

THRESHING-FLOOR.

or sledge (2 Sam. 24:22; 1 Chr. 21:23; Isa. 4:15). It was something like the Roman *tribulum* or threshing instrument.

When the grain was threshed, it was *winnowed* by being thrown up against the wind (Jer. 4:11), and afterwards tossed with wooden scoops (Isa. 30:24). The

WINNOWING.
(From Egyptian monuments.)

shovel and the fan for winnowing are mentioned in Ps. 35:5; Job 21:18; Isa. 17:13. The refuse of straw and chaff was burned (Isa. 5:24). Freed from impurities, the grain was then laid up in granaries till used (Deut. 28:8; Prov. 3:10; Matt. 6:26; 13:30; Luke 12:18).

Agrip'pa I., the grandson of Herod the Great, and son of Aristobulus and Bernice. The Roman emperor Caligula made him governor first of the territories of Philip, then of the tetrarchy of Lysanias, with the title of king ("king Herod"), and finally of that of Antipas, who was banished, and of Samaria and Judea. Thus he became ruler over the whole of Palestine.

He was a persecutor of the early Christians. He slew James and imprisoned Peter (Acts 12 : 1–4). He died at Cæsarea in agony, being "eaten of worms" (Acts 12 : 23), A.D. 44. (Comp. Josephus, *Ant.* xix. 8, 2.)

Agrip'pa II., son of the foregoing, was born at Rome, A.D. 27. He was the brother of Bernice and Drusilla. The Emperor Claudius (A.D. 48) invested him with the office of superintendent of the Temple of Jerusalem, and with the right of nominating the high priest, and made him governor (A.D. 50) of Chalcis, which office his uncle Herod had held. He was afterwards raised to the rank of king, and made governor over the tetrarchy of Philip and Lysanias (Acts 25 : 13 ; 26 : 2, 7). It was before him that Paul delivered (A.D. 59) his speech recorded in Acts 26. He took part with the Romans against the Jews. His private life was very profligate. He died (the last of his race) at Rome, at the age of about seventy years, A.D. 100.

A'gue, the translation in Lev. 26 : 16 (R.V., "fever") of the Hebrew word *kaddah'ath,* meaning "kindling" — *i.e.,* an inflammatory or burning fever. In Deut. 28 : 22 the word is rendered "fever."

A'gur — *gatherer;* the *collector* — mentioned as author of the sayings in Prov. 30. Nothing is known of him beyond what is there recorded.

Ah! an exclamation of sorrow or regret (Ps. 35:25 ; Isa. 1:4, 24 ; Jer. 1:6 ; 22:18 ; Mark 15 : 29).

Aha! an exclamation of ridicule (Ps. 35 : 21 ; 40 : 15 ; 70 : 3). In Isa. 44 : 16 it signifies joyful surprise, so also in Job 39 : 25.

A'hab—*father's brother.* (1.) The son of Omri, whom he succeeded as the seventh king of Israel. His history is recorded in 1 Kings 16–22. His wife was Jezebel (*q.v.*), who exercised a very evil influence over him. To the calf-worship introduced by Jeroboam he added the worship of Baal. He was severely admonished by Elijah (*q.v.*) for his wickedness. His anger was on this account kindled against the prophet, and he sought to kill him. He undertook three campaigns against Benhadad II.,

king of Damascus. In the first two, which were defensive, he gained a complete victory over Benhadad, who fell into his hands, and was afterwards released on the condition of his restoring all the cities of Israel he then held, and granting certain other concessions to Ahab. After three years of peace, for some cause Ahab renewed war (1 Kings 22 : 3) with Benhadad by assaulting the city of Ramoth - gilead, although the prophet Micaiah warned him that he would not succeed, and that the 400 false prophets who encouraged him were only leading him to his ruin. Micaiah was imprisoned for thus venturing to dissuade Ahab from his purpose. Ahab went into the battle disguised, that he might if possible escape the notice of his enemies ; but an arrow from a bow "drawn at a venture" pierced him, and though stayed up in his chariot for a time he died towards evening, and Elijah's prophecy (1 Kings 21 : 19) was fulfilled. He reigned twenty-three years. Because of his idolatry, lust, and covetousness, Ahab is referred to as pre-eminently the type of a wicked king (2 Kings 8 : 18 ; 2 Chr. 22 : 3 ; Micah 6 : 16).

(2.) A false prophet referred to by Jeremiah (29 : 21), of whom nothing is known.

Ahasue'rus. There are three kings designated by this name in Scripture. (1.) The father of Darius the Mede, mentioned in Dan. 9 : 1. This was probably the Cyaxares I. known by this name in profane history, the king of Media and the conqueror of Nineveh.

(2.) The king mentioned in Ezra 4 : 6, probably the Cambyses of profane history, the son and successor of Cyrus (B.C. 529).

(3.) The son of Darius Hystaspes, the king named in the Book of Esther. He ruled over the kingdoms of Persia, Media, and Babylonia—"from India to Ethiopia." This was in all probability the Xerxes of profane history, who succeeded his father Darius (B.C. 485). In the LXX. version of the Book of Esther the name Artaxerxes occurs for Ahasuerus. He reigned for twenty-one years (B.C. 486–465). He invaded Greece with an army, it is said, of more than 2,000,000 soldiers, only 5,000 of whom returned with him. Leonidas, with his famous 300, arrested his progress at the Pass of Thermopylæ, and then he was defeated disastrously by Themistocles at Salamis. It was after his return from this invasion that Esther was chosen as his queen.

Aha′va—*water*—the river (Ezra 8 : 21) by the banks of which the Jewish exiles assembled under Ezra when about to return to Jerusalem from Babylon. In all probability this was one of the streams of Mesopotamia which flowed into the Euphrates somewhere in the north-west of Babylonia. It has, however, been supposed to be the name of a place (Ezra 8 : 15) now called *Hit*, on the Euphrates, east of Damascus.

A′haz—*possessor*. (1.) A grandson of Jonathan (1 Chr. 8 : 35 ; 9 : 42).

(2.) The son and successor of Jotham, king of Judah (2 Kings 16 ; Isa. 7-9 ; 2 Chr. 28). He gave himself up to a life of wickedness and idolatry. Notwithstanding the remonstrances and warnings of Isaiah, Hosea, and Micah, he appealed for help against Rezin, king of Damascus, and Pekah, king of Israel, who threatened Jerusalem, to Tiglath-pileser, the king of Assyria, to the great injury of his kingdom and his own humiliating subjection to the Assyrians (2 Kings 16 : 7, 9 ; 15 : 29). He also introduced among his people many heathen and idolatrous customs (Isa. 8 : 19 ; 38 : 8 ; 2 Kings 23 : 12). He died at the age of thirty-five years, after reigning sixteen years (B.C. 740-724), and was succeeded by his son Hezekiah. Because of his wickedness he was "not brought into the sepulchre of the kings."

Ahazi′ah—*held by Jehovah*. (1.) The son and successor of Ahab. He followed the counsels of his mother Jezebel, and imitated in wickedness the ways of his father. In his reign the Moabites revolted from under his authority (2 Kings 3 : 5-7). He united with Jehoshaphat in an attempt to revive maritime trade by the Red Sea, which proved a failure (2 Chr. 20 : 35-37). His messengers, sent to consult the god of Ekron regarding his recovery from the effects of a fall from the roof-gallery of his palace, were met on the way by Elijah, who sent them back to tell the king that

he would never rise from his bed (1 Kings 22 : 51).

(2.) The son of Joram, or Jehoram, and sixth king of Judah. Called Jehoahaz (2 Chr. 21 : 17 ; 25 : 23), and Azariah (2 Chr. 22 : 6). Guided by his idolatrous mother Athaliah, his reign was disastrous (2 Kings 8 : 24-29 ; 9 : 29). He joined his uncle Jehoram, king of Israel, in an expedition against Hazael, king of Damascus ; but was wounded at the pass of Gur when attempting to escape, and had strength only to reach Megiddo, where he died (2 Kings 9 : 22-28). He reigned only one year.

Ahi′am — *mother's brother* — one of David's thirty heroes (2 Sam. 23 : 33 ; 1 Chr. 11 : 35).

Ahie′zer—*brother of help ; i.e.*, "helpful." (1.) The chief of the tribe of Dan at the time of the Exodus (Num. 1 : 12 ; 2 : 25 ; 10 : 25).

(2.) The chief of the Benjamite slingers that repaired to David at Ziklag (1 Chr. 12 : 3).

Ahi′hud — *brother* (*i.e.*, "friend") *of union*. (1.) A son of Bela, the son of Benjamin (1 Chr. 8 : 7).

(2.) Name different in Hebrew—meaning *brother of Judah*. Chief of the tribe of Asher ; one of those appointed by Moses to superintend the division of Canaan among the tribes (Num. 34 : 27).

Ahi′jah—*brother* (*i.e.*, "friend") *of Jehovah*. (1.) One of the sons of Bela (1 Chr. 8 : 7).

(2.) One of the five sons of Jerahmeel, who was great-grandson of Judah (1 Chr. 2 : 25).

(3.) Son of Ahitub (1 Sam. 14 : 3, 18), Ichabod's brother ; the same probably as Ahimelech, who was high priest at Nob in the reign of Saul (1 Sam. 22 : 11). Some, however, suppose that Ahimelech was the brother of Ahijah, and that they both officiated as high priests—Ahijah at Gibeah or Kirjath-jearim, and Ahimelech at Nob.

(4.) A Pelonite, one of David's heroes (1 Chr. 11 : 36) ; called also Eliam (2 Sam. 23 : 34).

(5.) A Levite having charge of the sacred treasury in the temple (1 Chr. 26 : 20).

(6.) One of Solomon's secretaries (1 Kings 4 : 3).

(7.) A prophet of Shiloh (1 Kings 11 : 29 ; 14 : 2), called the "Shilonite," in the days of Rehoboam. We have on record two of his remarkable prophecies—1 Kings 11 : 31–39, announcing the rending of the ten tribes from Solomon ; and 1 Kings 14 : 6–16, delivered to Jeroboam's wife, fore-telling the death of Abijah the king's son, the destruction of Jeroboam's house, and the captivity of Israel "beyond the river." Jeroboam bears testimony to the high esteem in which he was held as a prophet of God (1 Kings 14 : 2, 3).

Ahi′kam—*brother of support = helper*—one of the five whom Josiah sent to consult the prophetess Huldah in connection with the discovery of the book of the law (2 Kings 22 : 12-14 ; 2 Chr. 34 : 20). He was the son of Shaphan, the royal secretary, and the father of Gedaliah, governor of Judea after the destruction of Jerusalem by the Babylonians (2 Kings 25 : 22 ; Jer. 40 : 5-16 ; 43 : 6). On one occasion he protected Jeremiah against the fury of Jehoiakim (Jer. 26 : 24). It was in the chamber of another son (Gemariah) of Shaphan that Baruch read in the ears of all the people Jeremiah's roll.

Ahim′aaz—*brother of anger = irascible.* (1.) The father of Ahinoam, the wife of Saul (1 Sam. 14 : 50).

(2.) The son and successor of Zadok in the office of high priest (1 Chr. 6 : 8, 53). On the occasion of the revolt of Absalom he remained faithful to David, and was of service to him in conveying to him tidings of the proceedings of Absalom in Jerusalem (2 Sam. 15 : 24-37 ; 17 : 15-21). He was swift of foot, and was the first to carry to David tidings of the defeat of Absalom, although he refrained, from delicacy of feeling, from telling him of his death (2 Sam. 18 : 19-33).

Ahi′man — *brother of a gift = liberal.* (1.) One of the three giant Anakim brothers whom Caleb and the spies saw in Mount Hebron (Num. 13 : 22) when they went in to explore the land. They were afterwards driven out and slain (Josh. 15 : 14 ; Judg. 1 : 10).

(2.) One of the guardians of the temple after the Exile (1 Chr. 9 : 17).

Ahim′elech—*brother of the king*—the son of Ahitub and father of Abiathar (1 Sam. 22 : 20-23). He descended from Eli in the line of Ithamar. In 1 Chr. 18 : 16 he is called Abimelech, and is probably the same as Ahiah (1 Sam. 14 : 3, 18). He was the twelfth high priest, and officiated at Nob, where he was visited by David (to whom and his companions he gave five loaves of the showbread) when he fled from Saul (1 Sam. 21 : 1-9). He was summoned into Saul's presence, and accused, on the information of Doeg the Edomite, of disloyalty because of his kindness to David ; whereupon the king commanded that he, with the other priests who stood beside him (86 in all), should be put to death. This sentence was carried into execution by Doeg in the most cruel manner (1 Sam. 22 : 9-23). Possibly Abiathar had a son also called Ahimelech, or the two names, as some think, may have been accidentally transposed in 2 Sam. 8 : 17 ; 1 Chr. 18:16, marg. ; 24 : 3, 6, 31.

Ahin′adab—*brother of liberality = liberal* —one of the twelve commissariat officers appointed by Solomon in so many districts of his kingdom to raise supplies by monthly rotation for his household. He was appointed to the district of Mahanaim (1 Kings 4 : 14), east of Jordan.

Ahi′noam — *brother of pleasantness = pleasant.* (1.) The daughter of Ahimaaz, and wife of Saul (1 Sam. 14 : 50).

(2.) A Jezreelitess, the first wife of David (1 Sam. 25 : 43 ; 27 : 3). She was the mother of Amnon (2 Sam. 3 : 2). (See 1 Sam. 30:5, 18 ; 2 Sam. 2 : 2.)

Ahi′o—*brotherly.* (1.) One of the sons of Beriah (1 Chr. 8 : 14).

(2.) One of the sons of Jehiel the Gibeonite (1 Chr. 8 : 31 ; 9 : 37).

(3.) One of the sons of Abinadab the Levite. While Uzzah went by the side of the ark, he walked before it guiding the oxen which drew the cart on which it was carried, after having brought it from his father's house in Gibeah (1 Chr. 13:7 ; 2 Sam. 6 : 3, 4).

Ahi′ra—*brother of evil = unlucky*, or *my*

brother is friend — chief of the tribe of Naphtali at the Exodus (Num. 1:15 ; 2:29).

Ahi'shar—*brother of song = singer*—the officer who was "over the household of Solomon" (1 Kings 4:6).

Ahith'ophel — *brother of insipidity* or *impiety*—a man greatly renowned for his sagacity among the Jews. At the time of Absalom's revolt he deserted David (Ps. 41:9 ; 55:12–14) and espoused the cause of Absalom (2 Sam. 15:12). David sent his old friend Hushai back to Absalom, in order that he might counteract the counsel of Ahithophel (2 Sam. 15:31–37). This end was so far gained that Ahithophel saw he had no longer any influence, and accordingly he at once left the camp of Absalom and returned to Giloh, his native place, where, after arranging his worldly affairs, he hanged himself, and was buried in the sepulchre of his fathers (2 Sam. 17:1–23). He was the type of Judas (Ps. 41:9).

Ahi'tub — *brother of goodness = good.* (1.) The son of Phinehas. On the death of his grandfather Eli he succeeded to the office of high priest, and was himself succeeded by his son Ahijah (1 Sam. 14:3 ; 22:9, 11, 12, 20).

(2.) The father of Zadok, who was made high priest by Saul after the extermination of the family of Ahimelech (1 Chr. 6:7, 8 ; 2 Sam. 8:17).

Ah'lab—*fatness*—a town of Asher lying within the unconquered Phœnician border (Judg. 1:31), north-west of the Sea of Galilee; commonly identified with Giscala, now *el-Jish.*

Aho'ah—*brotherly*—one of the sons of Bela, the son of Benjamin (1 Chr. 8:4). He is also called Ahiah (ver. 7) and Iri (1 Chr. 7:7). His descendants were called Ahohites (2 Sam. 23:9, 28).

Aho'hite, an epithet applied to Dodo, one of Solomon's captains (1 Chr. 27:4) ; to his son Eleazar, one of David's three mightiest heroes (2 Sam. 23:9 ; 1 Chr. 11:12) ; and to Zalmon, one of the thirty (2 Sam. 23:28 ; 1 Chr. 11:29)—from their descent from Ahoah.

Aho'lah—*she has her own tent*—a name used by Ezekiel (23:4, 5, 36, 44) as a symbol of the idolatry of the kingdom of Israel.

This kingdom is described as a lewd woman, an adulteress, given up to the abominations and idolatries of the Egyptians and Assyrians. Because of her crimes, she was carried away captive, and ceased to be a kingdom. (Comp. Ps. 78:67-69 ; 1 Kings 12:25–33 ; 1 Chr. 11:13–16.)

Aho'liab—*tent of the father*—an artist of the tribe of Dan, appointed to the work of preparing materials for the tabernacle (Ex. 31:6 ; 35:34 ; 36:1, 2 ; 38:23).

Aho'libah—*my tent is in her*—the name of an imaginary harlot, applied symbolically to Jerusalem, because she had abandoned the worship of the true God and given herself up to the idolatries of foreign nations. (Ezek. 23:4, 11, 22, 36, 44).

Aholiba'mah—*tent of the height*—the name given to Judith, the daughter of Beeri = Anah (Gen. 26:34 ; 36:2), when she became the wife of Esau. A district among the mountains of Edom, probably near Mount Hor, was called after her name, or it may be that she received her name from the district. From her descended three tribes of Edomites, founded by her three sons.

A'i—*ruins.* (1.) One of the royal cities of the Canaanites (Josh. 10:1 ; Gen. 12:8 ; 13:3). It was the scene of Joshua's defeat, and afterwards of his victory. It was the second Canaanite city taken by Israel (Josh. 7:2–5 ; 8:1–29). It was rebuilt and inhabited by the Benjamites (Ezra 2:28 ; Neh. 7:32 ; 11:31). It lay to the east of Bethel, "beside Beth-aven." The spot which is most probably the site of this ancient city is *Haiyan,* 2 miles east from Bethel. It lay up the Wady Suweinit, a steep, rugged valley, extending from the Jordan valley to Bethel.

(2.) A city in the Ammonite territory (Jer. 49:3). Some have thought that the proper reading of the word is Ar (Isa. 15:1).

Aij'eleth Sha'har—*hind of the dawn*—a name found in the title of Ps. 22. It is probably the name of some song or tune to the measure of which the psalm was to be chanted. Some, however, understand by the name some instrument of music, or an allegorical allusion to the subject of the psalm.

Air, the atmosphere, as opposed to the higher regions of the sky (1 Thess. 4 : 17; Rev. 9 : 2; 16 : 17). This word occurs once as the rendering of the Hebrew *ruah* (Job 41 : 16); elsewhere it is the rendering of *shamaiyim,* usually translated "heavens."

The expression "to speak into the air" (1 Cor. 14 : 9) is a proverb denoting to speak in vain, as to "beat the air" (1 Cor. 9 : 26) denotes to labour in vain.

Aj'alon and **Aij'alon**—*place of deer.* (1.) A town and valley originally assigned to the tribe of Dan, from which, however, they could not drive the Amorites (Judg. 1 : 35). It was one of the Levitical cities given to the Kohathites (1 Chr. 6 : 69). It was not far from Beth-shemesh (2 Chr. 28 : 18). It was the boundary between the kingdoms of Judah and Israel, and is frequently mentioned in Jewish history (2 Chr. 11 : 10; 1 Sam. 14 : 31; 1 Chr. 8 : 13). With reference to the valley named after the town, Joshua uttered the celebrated command, "Sun, stand thou still on Gibeon; and thou, Moon, in the valley of Ajalon" (Josh. 10 : 12). It has been identified as the modern *Yâlo,* at the foot of the Beth-horon pass (*q. v.*). In the Tell Amarna letters Adoni-zedek (*q. v.*) speaks of the destruction of the "city of Ascalon" by the invaders, and describes himself as "afflicted, greatly afflicted" by the calamities that had come on the land, urging the king of Egypt to hasten to his help.

(2.) A city in the tribe of Zebulun (Judg. 12 : 12), the modern *Jalun,* three miles north of Cabul.

Ak'kub (another form of **Jacob**). (1.) The head of one of the families of Nethinim (Ezra 2 : 45).

(2.) A Levite who kept the gate of the temple after the return from Babylon (1 Chr. 9 : 17; Ezra 2 : 42; Neh. 7 : 45).

(3.) A descendant of David (1 Chr. 3 : 24).

Akrab'bim — *scorpions* — probably the general name given to the ridge containing the pass between the south of the Dead Sea and Zin, *es-Sufah,* by which there is an ascent to the level of the land of Palestine. Scorpions are said to abound in this whole district, and hence the name (Num. 34 : 4). It is called "Maaleh-acrabbim" in Josh. 15 : 3, and "the ascent of Akrabbim" in Num. 34 : 4.

Al'abaster, occurs only in the New Testament in connection with the box of "ointment of spikenard very precious," with the contents of which a woman anointed the head of Jesus as he sat at supper in the house of Simon the leper (Matt. 26 : 7; Mark 14 : 3; Luke 7 : 37). These boxes were made from a stone found near Alabastron in Egypt, and from this circumstance the Greeks gave them the name of the city where they were made. The name was then given to the stone of which they were made; and finally to all perfume vessels, of whatever material they were formed. The woman "broke" the vessel; *i.e.,* she broke off, as was usually done, the long and narrow neck so as to reach the contents. This stone resembles marble, but is softer in its texture, and hence very easily wrought into boxes. Mark says (14 : 5) that this box of ointment was worth more than 300 pence—*i.e.,* denarii, each of the value of sevenpence halfpenny of our money, and therefore worth about £10. But if we take the denarius as the day's wage of a labourer (Matt. 20 : 2), say two shillings of our money, then the whole would be worth about £30, so costly was Mary's offering.

Ala'moth—*virgins*—a musical term (1 Chr. 15 : 20), denoting that the psalm which bears this inscription (Ps. 46) was to be sung by soprano or female voices.

Alarm, a particular quivering sound of the silver trumpets to give warning to the Hebrews on their journey through the wilderness (Num. 10 : 5, 6), a call to arms, or a war-note (Jer. 4 : 19; 49 : 2; Zeph. 1 : 16).

Al'emeth—*covering.* (1.) One of the nine sons of Becher, the son of Benjamin (1 Chr. 7 : 8).

(2.) One of the sons of Jehoadah, or Jarah, son of Ahaz (1 Chr. 8 : 36).

(3.) A sacerdotal city of Benjamin (1 Chr. 6 : 60), called also Almon (Josh. 21 : 18), now *Almit,* a mile north-east of the ancient Anathoth.

Alexan'der—*man-defender.* (1.) A relative of Annas the high priest, present when Peter and John were examined before the Sanhedrim (Acts 4 : 6).

(2.) A man whose father, Simon the Cyrenian, bore the cross of Christ (Mark 15 : 21).

(3.) A Jew of Ephesus who took a prominent part in the uproar raised there by the preaching of Paul (Acts 19 : 33). The Jews put him forward to plead their cause before the mob. It was probably intended that he should show that he and the other Jews had no sympathy with Paul any more than the Ephesians had. It is possible that this man was the same as the following.

(4.) A coppersmith who, with Hymenæus and others, promulgated certain heresies regarding the resurrection (1 Tim. 1 : 19 ; 2 Tim. 4 : 14), and made shipwreck of faith and of a good conscience. Paul excommunicated him (1 Tim. 1 : 20 ; comp. 1 Cor. 5 : 5).

Alexan'der the Great, the king of Macedonia, the great conqueror ; probably represented in Daniel by the "belly of brass" (Dan. 2 : 32), and the leopard and the he-goat (7 : 6 ; 11 : 3, 4). He succeeded his father Philip, and died at the age of thirty-two from the effects of intemperance, B.C. 323. His empire was divided among his four generals.

Alexan'dria, the ancient metropolis of Lower Egypt, so called from its founder,

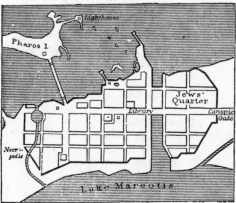

ANCIENT ALEXANDRIA.

Alexander the Great (about B.C. 333). It was for a long period the greatest of existing cities, for both Nineveh and Babylon had been destroyed, and Rome had not yet risen to greatness. It was the residence of the kings of Egypt for 200 years. It is not mentioned in the Old Testament, and only incidentally in the New. Apollos, eloquent and mighty in the Scriptures, was a native of this city (Acts 18 : 24). Many Jews from Alexandria were in Jerusalem, where they had a synagogue (Acts 6 : 9), at the time of Stephen's martyrdom. At one time it is said that as many as 10,000 Jews resided in this city. It possessed a famous library of 700,000 volumes, which was burned by the Saracens (A.D. 642). It was here that the Hebrew Bible was translated into Greek. This is called the *Septuagint* version, from the tradition that seventy learned men were engaged in executing it. It was, however, not all translated at one time. It was begun B.C. 280, and finished about B.C. 200 or 150. (See VERSION.)

Al'gum (2 Chr. 2 : 8 ; 9 : 10, 11), the same as **almug** (1 Kings 10 : 11).

A'lien, a foreigner, or person born in another country, and therefore not entitled to the rights and privileges of the country where he resides. Among the Hebrews there were two classes of aliens.

(1.) Those who were strangers generally, and who owned no landed property.

(2.) Strangers dwelling in another country without being naturalized (Lev. 22 : 10 ; Ps. 39 : 12).

Both of these classes were to enjoy, under certain conditions, the same rights as other citizens (Lev. 19 : 33, 34 ; Deut. 10 : 19). They might be naturalized and permitted to enter into the congregation of the Lord by submitting to circumcision and abandoning idolatry (Deut. 23 : 3-8).

This term is used (Eph. 2 : 12) to denote persons who have no interest in Christ.

Al'legory, used only in Gal. 4 : 24, where the apostle refers to the history of Isaac the free-born, and Ishmael the slave-born, and makes use of it allegorically.

Every parable is an allegory. Nathan (2 Sam. 12 : 1-14) addresses David in an allegorical narrative. In the eightieth Psalm there is a beautiful allegory: "Thou broughtest a vine out of Egypt," etc. In Eccl. 12 : 2-6, there is a striking allegorical description of old age.

Allelu'ia, the Greek form (Rev. 19:1, 3, 4, 6) of the Hebrew Hallelujah=*Praise ye Jehovah*, which begins and ends several of the psalms (106, 111, 112, 113, etc.).

Alli'ance, a treaty between nations, or between individuals, for their mutual advantage.

Abraham formed an alliance with some of the Canaanitish princes (Gen. 14:13), also with Abimelech (21:22–32). Joshua and the elders of Israel entered into an alliance with the Gibeonites (Josh. 9:3–27). When the Israelites entered Palestine they were forbidden to enter into alliances with the inhabitants of the country (Lev. 18:3, 4; 20:22, 23).

Solomon formed a league with Hiram (1 Kings 5:12). This "brotherly covenant" is referred to 250 years afterwards (Amos 1:9). He also appears to have entered into an alliance with Pharaoh (1 Kings 10:28, 29).

In the subsequent history of the kingdoms of Judah and Israel various alliances were formed between them and also with neighbouring nations at different times.

From patriarchal times a covenant of alliance was sealed by the blood of some sacrificial victim. The animal sacrificed was cut in two (except birds), and between these two parts the persons contracting the alliance passed (Gen. 15:10). There are frequent allusions to this practice (Jer. 34:18). Such alliances were called "covenants of salt" (Num. 18:19; 2 Chr. 13:5), salt being the symbol of perpetuity. A pillar was set up as a memorial of the alliance between Laban and Jacob (Gen. 31:52). The Jews throughout their whole history attached great importance to fidelity to their engagements. Divine wrath fell upon the violators of them (Josh. 9:18; 2 Sam. 21:1, 2; Ezek. 17:16).

Al'lon—*oak.* (1.) The expression in the Authorized Version of Josh. 19:33, "from Allon to Zaanannim," is more correctly rendered in the Revised Version, "from the oak in Zaanannim." The word denotes some remarkable tree which stood near Zaanannim, and which served as a landmark.

(2.) The son of Jedaiah, of the family of the Simeonites, who expelled the Hamites from the valley of Gedor (1 Chr. 4:37).

Al'lon-bach'uth—*oak of weeping*—a tree near Bethel, at the spot where Deborah, Rebekah's nurse, was buried (Gen. 35:8). Large trees, from their rarity in the plains of Palestine, were frequently designated as landmarks. This particular tree was probably the same as the "palm tree of Deborah" (Judg. 4:5).

Almo'dad — *immeasurable* — the first named of the sons of Joktan (Gen. 10:26), the founder of an Arabian tribe.

Al'mon—*hidden*—one of the sacerdotal cities of Benjamin (Josh. 21:18), called also Alemeth (1 Chr. 6:60).

Al'mond, a native of Syria and Palestine. In form, blossoms, and fruit it resembles the peach tree. Its blossoms are of a very

BRANCH OF ALMOND TREE.

pale pink colour, and appear before its leaves. Its Hebrew name, *shâked*, signifying "wakeful, hastening," is given to it on account of its putting forth its blossoms so early, generally in February, and sometimes even in January. In Eccl. 12:5, it is referred to as illustrative, probably, of the haste with which old age comes. There are others, however, who still contend for the old interpretation here. "The almond tree bears its blossoms in the midst of winter, on a naked, leafless stem, and these blossoms (reddish or flesh-coloured in the beginning) seem at the time of their fall exactly like white snow-flakes. In this way the almond blossom is a very fitting symbol of old age, with its silvery hair and its wintry, dry, barren, unfruitful condition." In Jer. 1:11—"I see a rod of an almond tree [*shâked*]......for I will hasten [*shâked*] my word to perform it "—the word is used as an emblem of promptitude. Jacob desired his sons (Gen. 43:11) to take with them into Egypt of the best fruits of the land, almonds, etc., as a present to Joseph, probably because this tree was not a native of Egypt. Aaron's rod yielded almonds (Num. 17:8; Heb. 9:4). Moses was directed to make certain parts of the candlestick for the ark of carved work "like unto almonds" (Ex. 25:33, 34). The Hebrew word *luz*, translated "hazel" in the Authorized Version (Gen. 30:37), is rendered in the Revised Version "almond." It is probable that *luz* denotes the wild almond, while *shâked* denotes the cultivated variety.

Alms. Not found in the Old Testament, but repeatedly in the New. The Mosaic legislation (Lev. 25:35; Deut. 15:7) tended to promote a spirit of charity, and to prevent the occurrence of destitution among the people. Such passages as these, Ps. 41:1; 112:9; Prov. 14:31; Isa. 10:2; Amos 2:7; Jer. 5:28; Ezek. 22:29, would also naturally foster the same benevolent spirit.

In the time of our Lord begging was common (Mark 10:46; Acts 3:2). The Pharisees were very ostentatious in their almsgivings (Matt. 6:2). The spirit by which the Christian ought to be actuated in this duty is set forth in 1 John 3:17. A regard to the state of the poor and needy is enjoined as a Christian duty (Luke 3:11; 6:30; Matt. 6:1; Acts 9:36; 10:2, 7), a duty which was not neglected by the early Christians (Luke 14:13; Acts 20:35; Gal. 2:10; Rom. 15:25-27; 1 Cor. 16:1-4). They cared not only for the poor among themselves, but contributed also to the necessities of those at a distance (Acts 11:29; 24:17; 2 Cor. 9:12). Our Lord and his attendants showed an example also in this (John 13:29).

In modern times the "poor-laws" have introduced an element which modifies considerably the form in which we may discharge this Christian duty.

Al′mug (1 Kings 10:11, 12) = **algum** (2 Chr. 2:8; 9:10, 11), in the Hebrew occurring only in the plural *almuggim* (indicating that the wood was brought in *planks*), the name of a wood brought from Ophir to be used in the building of the temple, and for other purposes. Some suppose it to have been the white sandal-wood of India, the *Santalum album* of botanists, a native of the mountainous parts of the Malabar coast. It is a fragrant wood, and is used in China for incense in idol-worship. Others, with some probability, think that it was the Indian red sandal-wood, the *Pterocarpus santalinus*, a heavy, fine-grained wood, the Sanscrit name of which is *valguka*. It is found on the Coromandel coast and in Ceylon.

A′loes (Heb. *'ahalîm*), a fragrant wood (Num. 24:6; Ps. 45:8; Prov. 7:17; Cant. 4:14), the *Aquilaria agallochum* of botanists, or, as some suppose, the costly gum or perfume extracted from the wood. It is found in China, Siam, and Northern India, and grows to the height sometimes of 120 feet. This species is of great rarity even in India. There is another and more common species, called by the Indians *aghil*, whence Europeans have given it the name of *Lignum aquilæ*, or eagle-wood. Aloewood was used by the Egyptians for embalming dead bodies. Nicodemus brought it (pounded aloe-wood) to embalm the body of Christ (John 19:39); but whether this was the same as that mentioned elsewhere is uncertain.

The bitter aloes of the apothecary is the produce of a totally different plant.

Alphae′us. (1.) The father of James the Less, the apostle and writer of the epistle (Matt. 10:3; Mark 3:18; Luke 6:15; Acts 1:13), and the husband of Mary (John 19:25). The Hebrew form of this name is Cleopas, or Clopas (*q.v.*).

(2.) The father of Levi, or Matthew (Mark 2:14).

Al′tar (Heb. *mizbe′âh*, from a word meaning "to slay"), any structure of earth

(Ex. 20:24) or unwrought stone (20:25) on which sacrifices were offered. Altars were generally erected in conspicuous places (Gen. 22:9; Ezek. 6:3; 2 Kings 23:12; 16:4; 23:8; Acts 14:13). The word is used in Heb. 13:10 for the *sacrifice* offered upon it—the sacrifice Christ offered.

Paul found among the many altars erected in Athens one bearing the inscription, "To the unknown God" (Acts 17:23), or rather "to an [*i.e.,* some] unknown God." The reason for this inscription cannot now be accurately determined. It afforded the apostle the occasion of proclaiming the gospel to the "men of Athens."

1. BRAZEN ALTAR.   2. GOLDEN ALTAR.

The first altar we read of is that erected by Noah (Gen. 8:20). Altars were erected by Abraham (Gen. 12:7; 13:4; 22:9), by Isaac (Gen. 26:25), by Jacob (33:20; 35:1, 3), and by Moses (Ex. 17:15, "Jehovah-nissi").

In the tabernacle, and afterwards in the temple, two altars were erected.

(1.) The *altar of burnt offering* (Ex. 30:28), called also the "brazen altar" (Ex. 39:39) and "the table of the Lord" (Mal. 1:7).

This altar, as erected in the tabernacle, is described in Ex. 27:1–8. It was a hollow square, 5 cubits in length and in breadth, and 3 cubits in height. It was made of shittim wood, and was overlaid with plates of brass. Its corners were ornamented with "horns" (Ex. 29:12; Lev. 4:18).

In Ex. 27:3 the various utensils appertaining to the altar are enumerated. They were made of brass. (Comp. 1 Sam. 2:13, 14; Lev. 16:12; Num. 16:6, 7.)

In Solomon's temple the altar was of larger dimensions (2 Chr. 4:1. Comp. 1 Kings 8:22, 64; 9:25), and was made wholly of brass, covering a structure of stone or earth. This altar was renewed by Asa (2 Chr. 15:8). It was removed by Ahaz (2 Kings 16:14), and "cleansed" by Hezekiah, in the latter part of whose reign it was rebuilt. It was finally broken up and carried away by the Babylonians (Jer. 52:17).

After the return from captivity it was re-erected (Ezra 3:3, 6) on the same place where it had formerly stood. (Comp. 1 Macc. 4:47.) When Antiochus Epiphanes pillaged Jerusalem the altar of burnt offering was taken away.

Again the altar was erected by Herod, and remained in its place till the destruction of Jerusalem by the Romans (70 A.D.).

The fire on the altar was not permitted to go out (Lev. 6:9).

In the Mosque of Omar, immediately underneath the great dome, which occupies the site of the old temple, there is a rough projection of the natural rock, of about 60 feet in its extreme length, and 50 in its greatest breadth, and in its highest part about 4 feet above the general pavement. This rock seems to have been left intact when Solomon's temple was built. It was in all probability the site of the altar of burnt offering. Underneath this rock is a cave, which may probably have been the granary of Araunah's threshing-floor (1 Chr. 21:22).

(2.) The *altar of incense* (Ex. 30:1–8), called also "the golden altar" (39:38; Num. 4:11), stood in the holy place "before the vail that is by the ark of the testimony." On this altar sweet spices were continually burned with fire taken from the brazen altar. The morning and the evening services were commenced by the high priest offering incense on this altar. The burning of the incense was a type of prayer (Ps. 141:2; Rev. 5:8; 8:3, 4).

This altar was a small movable table,

made of acacia wood overlaid with gold (Ex. 37:25, 26). It was 1 cubit in length and breadth, and 2 cubits in height.

In Solomon's temple the altar was similar in size, but was made of cedar-wood (1 Kings 6:20; 7:48) overlaid with gold. In Ezek. 41:22 it is called "the altar of wood." (Comp. Ex. 30:1-6.)

In the temple built after the Exile the altar was restored. Antiochus Epiphanes took it away, but it was afterwards restored by Judas Maccabæus (1 Macc. 1:23; 4:49). Among the trophies carried away by Titus on the destruction of Jerusalem the altar of incense is not found, nor is any mention made of it in Heb. 9. It was at this altar Zacharias ministered when an angel appeared to him (Luke 1:11). It is the only altar which appears in the heavenly temple (Isa. 6:6; Rev. 8:3, 4).

Altas'chith—*destroy not*—the title of Ps. 57, 58, 59, and 75. It was probably the name of some song to the melody of which these psalms were to be chanted.

A'lush, one of the places, the last before Rephidim, at which the Hebrews rested on their way to Sinai (Num. 33:13, 14). It was probably situated on the shore of the Red Sea.

Am'alek—*dweller in a valley*—the son of Eliphaz and grandson of Esau (Gen. 36:12; 1 Chr. 1:36); the chief of an Idumean tribe (Gen. 36:16). His mother was a Horite, a tribe whose territory the descendants of Esau had seized.

Am'alekite, a tribe that dwelt in Arabia Petræa, between the Dead Sea and the Red Sea. They were not the descendants of Amalek, the son of Eliphaz, for they existed in the days of Abraham (Gen. 14:7). They were probably a tribe that migrated from the shores of the Persian Gulf and settled in Arabia. "They dwelt in the land of the south......from Havilah until thou comest to Shur" (Num. 13:29; 1 Sam. 15:7). They were a pastoral, and hence a nomadic race. Their kings bore the hereditary name of Agag (Num. 24:7; 1 Sam. 15:8). They attempted to stop the Israelites when they marched through their territory (Deut. 25:18), attacking them at Rephidim (Ex.

17:8-13; comp. Deut. 25:17; 1 Sam. 15:2). They afterwards attacked the Israelites at Hormah (Num. 14:45). We read of them subsequently as in league with the Moabites (Judg. 3:13) and the Midianites (Judg. 6:3). Saul finally desolated their territory and destroyed their power (1 Sam. 14:48; 15:3), so that they were no longer formidable enemies to Israel, although on one occasion they invaded the land; but David pursued after them, and recovered all the booty they had carried away (1 Sam. 30:19, 20).

Ama'na or **Am'ana** — *perennial*. (1.) The Hebrew margin of 2 Kings 5:12 gives this as another reading of Abana (*q.v.*), a stream near Damascus.

(2.) A mountain (Cant. 4:8), probably the southern summit of Anti-Libanus, at the base of which are the sources of the Abana.

Amari'ah—*said by Jehovah*. (1.) One of the descendants of Aaron by Eleazar (1 Chr. 6:7, 52). He was probably the last of the high priests of Eleazar's line prior to the transfer of that office to Eli, of the line of Ithamar.

(2.) A Levite, son of Hebron, of the lineage of Moses (1 Chr. 23:19; 24:23).

(3.) A "chief priest" who took an active part in the reformation under Jehoshaphat (2 Chr. 19:11); probably the same as mentioned in 1 Chr. 6:9.

(4.) 1 Chr. 6:11; Ezra 7:3. (5.) One of the high priests in the time of Hezekiah (2 Chr. 31:15). (6.) Zeph. 1:1. (7.) Neh. 11:4. (8.) Neh. 10:3. (9.) Ezra 10:42.

Ama'sa—*burden*. (1.) The son of Abigail, a sister of king David (1 Chr. 2:17; 2 Sam. 17:25). He was appointed by David to command the army in room of his cousin Joab (2 Sam. 19:13), who afterwards treacherously put him to death as a dangerous rival (2 Sam. 20:4-12).

(2.) A son of Hadlai, and chief of Ephraim (2 Chr. 28:12) in the reign of Ahaz.

Amasa'i—*burdensome*. (1.) A Levite, son of Elkanah, of the ancestry of Samuel (1 Chr. 6:25, 35).

(2.) The leader of a body of men who joined David in the "stronghold," probably of Adullam (1 Chr. 12:18).

(3.) One of the priests appointed to precede the ark with blowing of trumpets on its removal from the house of Obed-edom (1 Chr. 15 : 24).

(4.) A Levite, one of the two Kohathites who took a prominent part at the instance of Hezekiah in the cleansing of the temple (2 Chr. 29 : 12).

Amash'ai, the son of Azareel, appointed by Nehemiah to reside at Jerusalem and do the work of the temple (Neh. 11 : 13).

Amasi'ah — *burden of* (*i.e.*, "sustained by") *Jehovah*—the "son of Zichri, who willingly offered himself unto the Lord," a captain over thousands under Jehoshaphat (2 Chr. 17 : 16; comp. Judg. 5 : 29).

Amazi'ah—*strengthened by Jehovah.* (1.) A Levite, son of Hilkiah, of the ancestry of Ethan the Merarite (1 Chr. 6 : 45).

(2.) The son and successor of Joash, and eighth king of the separate kingdom of Judah (2 Kings 14:1-4). He began his reign by punishing the murderers of his father (5–7; 2 Chr. 25 : 3–5). He was the first to employ a mercenary army of 100,000 Israelite soldiers, which he did in his attempt to bring the Edomites again under the yoke of Judah (2 Chr. 25 : 5, 6). He was commanded by a prophet of the Lord to send back the mercenaries, which he did (2 Chr. 25 : 7–10, 13), much to their annoyance. His obedience to this command was followed by a decisive victory over the Edomites (2 Chr. 25 : 14–16). Amaziah began to worship some of the idols he took from the Edomites, and this was his ruin, for he was vanquished by Joash, king of Israel, whom he challenged to battle. The disaster he thus brought upon Judah by his infatuation in proclaiming war against Israel probably occasioned the conspiracy by which he lost his life (2 Kings 14 : 8–14, 19). He was slain at Lachish, whither he had fled, and his body was brought upon horses to Jerusalem, where it was buried in the royal sepulchre (2 Kings 14 : 19, 20; 2 Chr. 25 : 27, 28).

(3.) A priest of the golden calves at Bethel (Amos 7 : 10–17).

(4.) The father of Joshah, one of the Simeonite chiefs in the time of Hezekiah (1 Chr. 4 : 34).

Ambas'sador. In the Old Testament the Hebrew word *tsîr*, meaning "one who goes on an errand," is rendered thus (Josh. 9 : 4; Prov. 13 : 17; Isa. 18 : 2; Jer. 49 : 14; Obad. 1). This is also the rendering of *melits*, meaning "an interpreter," in 2 Chr. 32 : 31; and of *malak*, a "messenger," in 2 Chr. 35 : 21; Isa. 30 : 4; 33 : 7; Ezek. 17 : 15. This is the name used by the apostle as designating those who are appointed by God to declare his will (2 Cor. 5 : 20; Eph. 6 : 20).

The Hebrews on various occasions and for various purposes had recourse to the services of ambassadors—*e.g.*, to contract alliances (Josh. 9 : 4), to solicit favours (Num. 20 : 14), to remonstrate when wrong was done (Judg. 11 : 12), to condole with a young king on the death of his father (2 Sam. 10 : 2), and to congratulate a king on his accession to the throne (1 Kings 5 : 1).

To do injury to an ambassador was to insult the king who sent him (2 Sam. 10 : 5).

Am'ber (Ezek. 1 : 4, 27; 8 : 2. Heb., *hashmal*, rendered by the LXX. *elektron*, and by the Vulgate *electrum*), a metal compounded of silver and gold. Some translate the word by "polished brass," others "fine brass," as in Rev. 1 : 15; 2 : 18. It is not certain what the original word really means. The word has no connection, however, with what is now called amber, which is a gummy substance, reckoned as belonging to the mineral kingdom though of vegetable origin—a fossil resin.

Am'bush. Joshua at the capture of Ai lay in ambush, and so deceived the inhabitants that he gained an easy victory (Josh. 8 : 4–26). Shechem was taken in this manner (Judg. 9 : 30–46. Comp. Jer. 51 : 12).

Amen'. This Hebrew word means *firm*, and hence also *faithful* (Rev. 3 : 14). In Isa. 65 : 16, the Authorized Version has "the God of truth," which in Hebrew is "the God of Amen." It is frequently used by our Saviour to give emphasis to his words, where it is translated "verily." Sometimes—only, however, in John's Gospel—it is repeated, "Verily, verily." It is used as an epithet of the Lord Jesus Christ (Rev. 3 : 14).

It is found singly and sometimes doubly at the end of prayers (Ps. 41:13; 72:19; 89:52), to confirm the words and invoke the fulfilment of them. It is used in token of being bound by an oath (Num. 5:22; Deut. 27:15, 17; Neh. 5:13; 8:6; 1 Chr. 16:36).

In the primitive churches it was common for the general audience to say "Amen" at the close of the prayer (1 Cor. 14:16).

The promises of God are Amen; *i.e.*, they are all true and sure (2 Cor. 1:20).

Am'ethyst, one of the precious stones in the breastplate of the high priest (Ex. 28:19; 39:12), and in the foundation of the New Jerusalem (Rev. 21:20). The ancients thought that this stone had the power of dispelling drunkenness in all who wore or touched it, and hence its Greek name formed from *a*, "privative," and *methuo*, "to get drunk." Its Jewish name, *ahlamah'*, was derived by the rabbins from the Hebrew word *halam*, "to dream," from its supposed power of causing the wearer to dream.

It is a pale-blue crystallized quartz, varying to a dark purple blue. It is found in Persia and India, also in different parts of Europe.

Amit'tai—*true*—the father of Jonah the prophet, a native of Gath-hepher (2 Kings 14:25; Jonah 1:1).

Am'mah—*a cubit*—the name of a hill which Joab and Abishai reached as the sun went down, when they were in pursuit of Abner (2 Sam. 2:24). It lay to the east of Gibeon.

Am'mi—*my people*—a name given by Jehovah to the people of Israel (Hos. 2:1, 23. Comp. 1:9; Ezek. 16:8; Rom. 9:25, 26; 1 Pet. 2:10).

Am'miel—*people of God.* (1.) One of the twelve spies sent by Moses to search the land of Canaan (Num. 13:12). He was one of the ten who perished by the plague for their unfavourable report (Num. 14:37).

(2.) The father of Machir of Lo-debar, in whose house Mephibosheth resided (2 Sam. 9:4, 5; 17:27).

(3.) The father of Bathsheba, the wife of Uriah, and afterwards of David (1 Chr. 3:5). He is called Eliam in 2 Sam. 11:3.

(4.) One of the sons of Obed-edom the Levite (1 Chr. 26:5).

Ammi'hud—*people of glory; i.e.*, "renowned." (1.) The father of the Ephraimite chief Elishama, at the time of the Exodus (Num. 1:10; 2:18; 7:48, 53).

(2.) Num. 34:20. (3.) Num. 34:28.

(4.) The father of Talmai, king of Geshur, to whom Absalom fled after the murder of Amnon (2 Sam. 13:37).

(5.) The son of Omri, and the father of Uthai (1 Chr. 9:4).

Ammin'adab—*kindred of the prince.* (1.) The father of Nahshon, who was chief of the tribe of Judah (Num. 1:7; 2:3; 7:12, 17; 10:14). His daughter Elisheba was married to Aaron (Ex. 6:23).

(2.) A son of Kohath, the second son of Levi (1 Chr. 6:22), called also Izhar (2, 18).

(3.) Chief of the 112 descendants of Uzziel the Levite (1 Chr. 15:10, 11).

Ammin'adib, a person mentioned in Cant. 6:12, whose chariots were famed for their swiftness. It is rendered in the margin "my willing people," and in the Revised Version "my princely people."

Ammishad'dai—*people of the Almighty*—the father of Ahiezer, who was chief of the Danites at the time of the Exodus (Num. 1:12; 2:25). This is one of the few names compounded with the name of God—*Shaddai*, "Almighty."

Ammiz'abad—*people of the giver*—the son of Benaiah, who was the third and chief captain of the host under David (1 Chr. 27:6).

Am'mon, another form of the name Ben-ammi, the son of Lot (Gen. 19:38). This name is also used for his posterity (Ps. 83:7).

Am'monite, the usual name of the descendants of Ammon, the son of Lot (Gen. 19:38). From the very beginning (Deut. 2:16–20) of their history till they are lost sight of (Judg. 5:2), this tribe is closely associated with the Moabites (Judg. 10:11; 2 Chr. 20:1; Zeph. 2:8). Both of these tribes hired Balaam to curse Israel (Deut. 23:4). The Ammonites were probably more of a predatory tribe, moving from place to place; while the Moabites were more settled. Their precise territory cannot be definitely ascertained. Originally they occupied a tract of country east of the Amorites, and separated by the river Arnon from the Moabites, and by the river Jabbok from Gilead or Bashan (Deut. 3:16; Josh. 12:2), which originally belonged to a gigantic race called Zamzummims (Deut. 2:19, 20). They showed no kindness to the Israelites when passing through their territory, and therefore they were prohibited from "entering the congregation of the Lord to the tenth generation" (Deut. 23:3). They afterwards became hostile to Israel (Judg. 3:13). Jephthah waged war against them, and "took twenty cities with a very great slaughter" (Judg. 11:33). They were again signally defeated by Saul (1 Sam. 11:11). David also defeated them and their allies the Syrians (2 Sam. 10:6–14), and took their chief city, Rabbah, with much spoil (2 Sam. 10:14; 12:26–31). The subsequent events of their history are noted in 2 Chr. 20:25; 26:8; Jer. 49:1; Ezek. 25:3, 6. One of Solomon's wives was Naamah, an Ammonite. She was the mother of Rehoboam (1 Kings 14: 31; 2 Chr. 12:13).

The prophets predicted fearful judgments against the Ammonites because of their hostility to Israel (Zeph. 2:8; Jer. 49:1–6; Ezek. 25:1–5, 10; Amos 1:13–15). The national idol worshipped by this people was Molech or Milcom, at whose altar they offered human sacrifices (1 Kings 11:5, 7). The high places built for this idol by Solomon, at the instigation of his Ammonitish wives, were not destroyed till the time of Josiah (2 Kings 23:13).

Am'non—*faithful*. (1.) One of the sons of Shemmai, of the children of Ezra (1 Chr. 4:20; comp. 17).

(2.) The eldest son of David, by Ahinoam of Jezreel (1 Chr. 3:1; 2 Sam. 3:2). Absalom caused him to be put to death for his great crime in the matter of Tamar (2 Sam. 13:28, 29).

A'mon—*builder*. (1.) The governor of Samaria in the time of Ahab. The prophet Micaiah was committed to his custody (1 Kings 22:26; 2 Chr. 18:25).

(2.) The son of Manasseh, and fourteenth king of Judah. He restored idolatry, and set up the images which his father had cast down. Zephaniah (1:4; 3:4, 11) refers to the moral depravity prevailing in this king's reign.

He was assassinated (2 Kings 21:18–26; 2 Chr. 33:20–25) by his own servants, who conspired against him.

(3.) An Egyptian god, usually depicted with a human body and the head of a ram, referred to in Jer. 46:25, where the word "multitudes" in the Authorized Version is more appropriately rendered "Amon" in the Revised Version. In Nah. 3:8 the expression "populous No" of the Authorized Version is rendered in the Revised Version "No-amon," where undoubtedly the reference is to the same idol, the Egyptian Jupiter.

(4.) Neh. 7:59.

Am'orites—*highlanders*, or *hillmen*—the name given to the descendants of one of the sons of Canaan (Gen. 14:7). They are mentioned as one of the nations whose country would be given to the posterity of Abraham (Gen. 15:21). The three confederates who took part with the patriarch were of this tribe (Gen. 14:13, 24). The southern slopes of the mountains of Judea are called the "mount of the Amorites" (Deut. 1:7, 19, 20). They seem to have originally occupied the land stretching from the height west of the Dead Sea (Gen. 14:7) to Hebron (13. Comp. 13:8; Deut. 3:8; 4:48), embracing "all Gilead and all Bashan" (Deut. 3:10), with the Jordan valley on the east of the river (4:49), the land of the "two kings of the Amorites," Sihon and Og (Deut. 31:4; Josh. 2:10; 9:10). The five kings of the Amorites were defeated with great slaughter by Joshua (10:10). They were again defeated at the waters of Merom by Joshua, who smote them till there were none remaining (Josh. 11:8). It is mentioned as a surprising circumstance that in the days of Samuel there was peace between them and the Israelites (1 Sam. 7:14). The discrepancy supposed to exist between Deut. 1:44 and Num. 14:45 is explained by the circumstance that the terms "Amorites" and "Amalekites" are used synonymously for the "Canaanites." In the same way we explain the fact that the "Hivites" of Gen. 34:2 are the "Amorites" of 48:22. Comp. Josh. 10:6; 11:19 with 2 Sam. 21:2; also Num. 14:45 with Deut. 1:44. It would appear that this was not the name of a distinct tribe, but rather the name denoting the inhabitants of a wide area in which separate and independent kings ruled, as Sihon and Og. The Amorites were warlike mountaineers. They are supposed to have been men of great stature; their king, Og, is described by Moses as the last "of the remnant of the giants" (Deut. 3:21). Only one word of the Amorite language survives—"Shenir," the name they gave to Mount Hermon (Deut. 3:9).

A'mos—*borne; a burden*—one of the twelve minor prophets. He was a native of Tekoa, the modern *Tekua*, a town about 12 miles south-east of Bethlehem. He was a man of humble birth, neither a "prophet nor a prophet's son," but "an herdman and dresser of sycomore trees," R.V. He prophesied in the days of Uzziah, king of Judah, and was contemporary with Isaiah and Hosea (Amos 1:1; 7:14, 15; Zech. 14:5), who survived him a few years. Under Jeroboam II. the kingdom of Israel rose to the zenith of its prosperity; but that was followed by the prevalence of luxury and vice and idolatry. At this period Amos was called from his obscurity to remind the people of the law of God's retributive justice, and to call them to repentance.

The BOOK of Amos consists of three parts:—

(1.) The nations around are summoned to judgment because of their sins (1:1-2:3). He quotes Joel 3:16.

(2.) The spiritual condition of Judah, and especially of Israel, is described (2:4-6:14).

(3.) In 7:1-9:10 are recorded five prophetic visions.

(*a*) The first two (7:1-6) refer to judgments against the guilty people.

(*b*) The next two (7:7-9; 8:1-3) point out the ripeness of the people for the threatened judgments. 7:10-17 consists of a conversation between the prophet and the priest of Bethel.

(*c*) The fifth describes the overthrow and ruin of Israel (9:1-10); to which is added the promise of the restoration of the kingdom and its final glory in the Messiah's kingdom.

The *style* is peculiar in the number of the allusions made to natural objects and to agricultural occupations. Other allusions show also that Amos was a student of the law as well as a "child of nature." These phrases are peculiar to him: "Cleanness of teeth" [*i.e.*, want of bread] (4:6); "The excellency of Jacob" (6:8; 8:7); "The high places of Isaac" (7:9); "The house of Isaac" (7:16); "He that createth the wind" (4:13). Quoted, Acts 7:42.

A'moz—*strong*—the father of the prophet Isaiah (2 Kings 19:2, 20; 20:1; Isa. 1:1; 2:1). As to his personal history little is positively known. He is supposed by some to have been the "man of God" spoken of in 2 Chr. 25:7, 8.

Amphip'olis—*city on both sides*—a Macedonian city, a great Roman military station, through which Paul and Silas passed on their way from Philippi to Thessalonica, a distance of 33 Roman miles from Philippi (Acts 17:1). It stood 3 miles from the sea, on the left bank of the navigable river Strymon, by which it was almost surrounded. It has long been in ruins. A village called Neophorio now occupies part of its site.

Am'plias, a Roman Christian saluted by Paul (Rom. 16:8).

Am'ram—*kindred of the High; i.e.*, "friend of Jehovah." (1.) The son of Kohath, the son of Levi. He married Jochebed, "his father's sister," and was the father of Aaron, Miriam, and Moses (Ex. 6:18; Num. 3:19). He died in Egypt at the age of 137 years (Ex. 6:20). His descendants were called Amramites (Num. 3:27; 1 Chr. 26:23).

(2.) Ezra 10:34.

Am'raphel—Bab. name, "Amarphal," *circle of life*—king of Shinar, southern Chaldea, one of the confederates of Chedorlaomer, king of Elam, in a war against Sodom and cities of the plain (Gen. 14:1, 4).

A'nab—*grape-town*—one of the cities in the mountains of Judah, from which Joshua expelled the Anakim (Josh. 11:21;

15 : 50). It still retains its ancient name. It lies among the hills, 10 miles south-south-west of Hebron.

A′nah—*speech.* (1.) One of the sons of Seir, and head of an Idumean tribe, called a Horite, as in course of time all the branches of this tribe were called from their dwelling in caves in Mount Seir (Gen. 36 : 20, 29 ; 1 Chr. 1 : 38).

(2.) One of the two sons of Zibeon the Horite, and father of Esau's wife Aholibamah (Gen. 36 : 18, 24).

A′nak—*long-necked*—the son of Arba, father of the Anakim (Josh. 15 : 13 ; 21 : 11, Heb. *Anok*).

Anakim′, the descendants of Anak (Josh. 11 : 21 ; Num. 13 : 33 ; Deut. 9 : 2). They dwelt in the south of Palestine, in the neighbourhood of Hebron (Gen. 23 : 2 ; Josh. 15 : 13). In the days of Abraham (Gen. 14 : 5, 6) they inhabited the region afterwards known as Edom and Moab, east of the Jordan. They were probably a remnant of the original inhabitants of Palestine before the Canaanites, a Cushite tribe from Babel, and of the same race as the Phœnicians and the Egyptian shepherd kings. Their formidable warlike appearance, as described by the spies sent to search the land, filled the Israelites with terror. They seem to have identified them with the *Nephilim*, the "giants" (Gen. 6 : 4 ; Num. 13 : 33) of the antediluvian age. There were various tribes of Anakim (Josh. 15 : 14). Joshua finally expelled them from the land, except a remnant that found a refuge in the cities of Gaza, Gath, and Ashdod (Josh. 11 : 22). The Philistine giants whom David encountered (2 Sam. 21 : 15–22) were descendants of the Anakim. (See GIANTS.)

A′namim, the name of an Egyptian tribe descended from Mizraim (Gen. 10 : 13 ; 1 Chr. 1 : 11).

Anam′me′lech, one of the gods worshipped by the people of Sepharvaim, who colonized Samaria (2 Kings 17 : 31). The name means "Anu is king." It was a female deity representing the moon, as Adrammelech (*q.v.*) was the male representing the sun.

A′nan—*cloud*—one of the Israelites who sealed the covenant after the return from Babylon (Neh. 10 : 26).

Anani′ah—*protected by Jehovah*—the name of a town in the tribe of Benjamin between Nob and Hazor (Neh. 11 : 32). It is probably the modern *Beit Hanina*, a small village 3 miles north of Jerusalem.

Anani′as, a common Jewish name, the same as Hananiah. (1.) One of the members of the church at Jerusalem, who conspired with his wife Sapphira to deceive the brethren, and who fell down and immediately expired after he had uttered the falsehood (Acts 5 : 5). By common agreement the members of the early Christian community devoted their property to the work of furthering the gospel and of assisting the poor and needy. The proceeds of the possessions they sold were placed at the disposal of the apostles (Acts 4 : 36, 37). Ananias might have kept his property had he so chosen ; but he professed agreement with the brethren in the common purpose, and had of his own accord devoted it all, as he said, to these sacred ends. Yet he retained a part of it for his own ends, and thus lied in declaring that he had given it all. "The offence of Ananias and Sapphira showed contempt of God, vanity and ambition in the offenders, and utter disregard of the corruption which they were bringing into the society. Such sin, committed in despite of the light which they possessed, called for a special mark of divine indignation."

(2.) A Christian at Damascus (Acts 9 : 10). He became Paul's instructor ; but when or by what means he himself became a Christian we have no information. He was "a devout man according to the law, having a good report of all the Jews which dwelt" at Damascus (22 : 12).

(3.) The high priest before whom Paul was brought in the procuratorship of Felix (Acts 23 : 2, 5, 24). He was so enraged at Paul's noble declaration, "I have lived in all good conscience before God until this day," that he commanded one of his attendants to smite him on the mouth. Smarting under this unprovoked insult, Paul quickly replied, "God shall smite thee, thou whited wall." Being reminded that Ananias was the high priest, to whose office all respect was to be paid, he answered, "I wist not, brethren, that he was the high priest" (Acts 23:5). This expression has occasioned some difficulty, as it is scarcely probable that Paul should have been ignorant of so public a fact. The expression may mean (a) that Paul had at the moment overlooked the honour due to the high priest; or (b), as others think, that Paul spoke ironically, as if he had said, "The high priest breaking the law! God's high priest a tyrant and a law-breaker! I see a man in white robes, and have heard his voice; but surely it cannot, it ought not to be, the voice of the high priest." (See Dr. Lindsay on Acts, in loco.) (c) Others think that from defect of sight Paul could not observe that the speaker was the high priest. In all this, however, it may be explained, Paul, with all his excellency, comes short of the example of his divine Master, who, when he was reviled, reviled not again.

A'nath—an answer; i.e., to "prayer"—the father of Shamgar, who was one of the judges of Israel (Judg. 3:31).

Anath'ema, anything laid up or suspended; hence anything laid up in a temple or set apart as sacred. In this sense the form of the word is anathĕma, once in plural used in the Greek New Testament, in Luke 21:5, where it is rendered "gifts." In the LXX. the form anathĕma is generally used as the rendering of the Hebrew word ḥĕrem, derived from a verb which means (1) to consecrate or devote; and (2) to exterminate. Any object so devoted to the Lord could not be redeemed (Num. 18:14; Lev. 27:28, 29); and hence the idea of exterminating connected with the word. The Hebrew verb (ḥaram) is frequently used of the extermination of idolatrous nations. It had a wide range of application. The anathĕma or ḥĕrem was a person or thing irrevocably devoted to God (Lev. 27:21, 28); and "none devoted shall be ransomed. He shall surely be put to death" (27:29). The word therefore carried the idea of devoted to destruction (Num. 21:2, 3; Josh. 6:17); and hence generally it meant a thing accursed. In Deut. 7:26

an idol is called a herem = anathĕma, a thing accursed.

In the New Testament this word always implies execration. In some cases an individual denounces an anathema on himself unless certain conditions are fulfilled (Acts 23:12, 14, 21). "To call Jesus accursed" [anathĕma] (1 Cor. 12:3) is to pronounce him execrated or accursed. If any one preached another gospel, the apostle says, "let him be accursed" (Gal. 1:8, 9); i.e., let his conduct in so doing be accounted accursed.

In Rom. 9:3, the expression "accursed" (anathema) from Christ — i.e., excluded from fellowship or alliance with Christ—has occasioned much difficulty. The apostle here does not speak of his wish as a possible thing. It is simply a vehement expression of feeling, showing how strong was his desire for the salvation of his people.

The anathema in 1 Cor. 16:22 denotes simply that they who love not the Lord are rightly objects of loathing and execration to all holy beings; they are guilty of a crime that merits the severest condemnation; they are exposed to the just sentence of "everlasting destruction from the presence of the Lord."

An'athoth—the name of one of the cities of refuge, in the tribe of Benjamin (Josh. 21:18). The Jews, as a rule, did not change the names of the towns they found in Palestine; hence this town may be regarded as deriving its name from the goddess Anat. It was the native place of Abiezer, one of David's "thirty" (2 Sam. 23:27), and of Jehu, another of his mighty men (1 Chr. 12:3). It is chiefly notable, however, as the birth-place and usual residence of Jeremiah (Jer. 1:1; 11:21-23; 29:27; 32:7-9). It suffered greatly from the army of Sennacherib, and only 128 men returned to it from the Exile (Neh. 7:27; Ezra 2:23). It lay about 3 miles north of Jerusalem. It has been identified with the small and poor village of 'Anâta, containing about 100 inhabitants.

Anch'or. From Acts 27:29, 30, 40, it would appear that the Roman vessels carried several anchors, which were attached to the stern as well as to the prow. The Roman anchor, like the modern one, had two teeth or flukes. In Heb. 6:19 the word is used metaphorically for that which supports or keeps one steadfast in the time of trial or of doubt. It is an emblem of hope.

> " If you fear,
> Put all your trust in God: that anchor holds."

An'cient of Days, an expression applied to Jehovah three times in the vision of Daniel (7 : 9, 13, 22) in the sense of eternal. In contrast with all earthly kings, his days are past reckoning.

An'drew—*manliness*—a Greek name; one of the apostles of our Lord. He was of Bethsaida in Galilee (John 1:45), and was the brother of Simon Peter (Matt. 4: 18; 10:2). On one occasion John the Baptist, whose disciple he then was, pointing to Jesus, said, "Behold the Lamb of God" (John 1:29); and Andrew, hearing him, immediately became a follower of Jesus, the first of his disciples. After he had been led to recognize Jesus as the Messiah, his first care was to bring also his brother Simon to Jesus. The two brothers seem to have after this pursued for a while their usual calling as fishermen, and did not become the stated attendants of the Lord till after John's imprisonment (Matt. 4:18, 19; Mark 1:16, 17). Very little is related of Andrew. He was one of the confidential disciples (John 6:8; 12:22), and with Peter, James, and John inquired of our Lord privately regarding his future coming (Mark 13:3). He was present at the feeding of the five thousand (John 6:9), and he introduced the Greeks who desired to see Jesus (John 12:22); but of his subsequent history little is known. It is noteworthy that Andrew thrice brings others to Christ—(1) Peter; (2) the lad with the loaves; and (3) certain Greeks. These incidents may be regarded as a key to his character.

Androni'cus—*man-conquering*—a Jewish Christian, the kinsman and fellow-prisoner of Paul (Rom. 16:7); "of note among the apostles."

A'nem—*two fountains*—a Levitical city

in the tribe of Issachar (1 Chr. 6:73). It is also called En-gannim (*q.v.*) in Josh. 19:21; the modern *Jenin*.

A'ner—*a boy*. (1.) A Canaanitish chief who joined his forces with those of Abraham in pursuit of Chedorlaomer (Gen. 14: 13, 24).

(2.) A city of Manasseh given to the Levites of Kohath's family (1 Chr. 6:70).

An'gel, a word signifying, both in the Hebrew and Greek, a "messenger," and hence employed to denote any agent God sends forth to execute his purposes. It is used of an ordinary messenger (Job 1:14; 1 Sam. 11:3; Luke 7:24; 9:52), of prophets (Isa. 42:19; Hag. 1:13), of priests (Mal. 2:7), and ministers of the New Testament (Rev. 1:20).

It is also applied to such impersonal agents as the pestilence (2 Sam. 24: 16, 17; 2 Kings 19:35), the wind (Ps. 104:4).

But its distinctive application is to certain heavenly intelligences whom God employs in carrying on his government of the world. The name does not denote their nature but their office as messengers. The appearances to Abraham at Mamre (Gen. 18:2, 22. Comp. 19:1), to Jacob at Peniel (Gen. 32:24, 30), to Joshua at Gilgal (Josh. 5:13, 15), of the *Angel of the Lord*, were doubtless manifestations of the Divine presence, "foreshadowings of the incarnation," revelations before the "fulness of the time" of the Son of God.

(1.) *The existence and orders* of angelic beings can only be discovered from the Scriptures. Although the Bible does not treat of this subject specially, yet there are numerous incidental details that furnish us with ample information. Their personal existence is plainly implied in such passages as Gen. 16: 7, 10, 11; John 13:1-21; Matt. 28:2-5; Heb. 1:4, etc.

These superior beings are very numerous. "Thousand thousands," etc. (Dan. 7:10; Matt. 26:53; Luke 2:13; Heb. 12:22, 23). They are also spoken of as of different ranks in dignity and power (Zech. 1:9, 11; Dan. 10:13; 12:1; 1 Thess. 4:16; Jude 9; Eph. 1:21; Col. 1:16).

(2.) As to their *nature*, they are spirits (Heb. 1:14), like the soul of man, but not incorporeal. Such expressions as "like the angels" (Luke 20:36), and the fact that whenever angels appeared to man it was always in a human form (Gen. 18:2; 19:1, 10; Luke 24:4; Acts 1:10), and the titles that are applied to them ("sons of God," Job 1:6; 38:7; Dan. 3:25; comp. 28) and to men (Luke 3:38), seem all to indicate some resemblance between them and the human race. Imperfection is ascribed to them as creatures (Job 4:18; Matt. 24:36; 1 Pet. 1:12). As finite creatures they may fall under temptation; and accordingly we read of "fallen angels." Of the cause and manner of their "fall" we are wholly ignorant. We know only that "they left their first estate" (Matt. 25:41; Rev. 12:7, 9), and that they are "reserved unto judgment" (2 Pet. 2:4). When the manna is called "angels' food," this is merely to denote its excellence (Ps. 78:25). Angels never die (Luke 20:36). They are possessed of superhuman intelligence and power (Mark 13:32; 2 Thess. 1:7; Ps. 103:20). They are called "holy" (Luke 9:26), "elect" (1 Tim. 5:21). The redeemed in glory are "like unto the angels" (Luke 20:36). They are not to be worshipped (Col. 2:18; Rev. 19:10).

(3.) Their *functions* are manifold. (*a*) In the widest sense they are agents of God's providence (Ex. 12:23; Ps. 104:4; Heb. 11:28; 1 Cor. 10:10; 2 Sam. 24:16; 1 Chr. 21:16; 2 Kings 19:35; Acts 12:23). (*b*) They are specially God's agents in carrying on his great work of redemption. There is no notice of angelic appearances to man till after the call of Abraham. From that time onward there are frequent references to their ministry on earth (Gen. 18; 19; 24:7, 40; 28:12; 32:1). They appear to rebuke idolatry (Judg. 2:1-4), to call Gideon (Judg. 6:11, 12), and to consecrate Samson (13:3). In the days of the prophets, from Samuel downward, the angels appear only in their behalf (1 Kings 19:5; 2 Kings 6:17;. Zech. 1-6; Dan. 4:13, 23; 10:10, 13, 20, 21).

The *Incarnation* introduces a new era in the ministrations of angels. They come with their Lord to earth to do him service while here. They predict his advent (Matt.

1:20; Luke 1:26-38), minister to him after his temptation and agony (Matt. 4:11; Luke 22:43), and declare his resurrection and ascension (Matt. 28:2-8; John 20:12, 13; Acts 1:10, 11). They are now ministering spirits to the people of God (Heb. 1:14; Ps. 34:7; 91:11; Matt. 18:10; Acts 5:19; 8:26; 10:3; 12:7; 27:23). They rejoice over a penitent sinner (Luke 15:10). They bear the souls of the redeemed to paradise (Luke 16:22); and they will be the ministers of judgment hereafter on the great day (Matt. 13:39, 41, 49; 16:27; 24:31). The passages (Ps. 34:7, Matt. 18:10) usually referred to in support of the idea that every individual has a particular guardian angel have no such meaning. They merely indicate that God employs the ministry of angels to deliver his people from affliction and danger, and that the angels do not think it below their dignity to minister even to children and to the least among Christ's disciples.

The "angel of his presence" (Isa. 63:9. Comp. Ex. 23:20, 21; 32:34; 33:2; Num. 20:16) is probably rightly interpreted of the Messiah as the guide of his people. Others have supposed the expression to refer to Gabriel (Luke 1:19).

An'ger, the emotion of instant displeasure on account of something evil that presents itself to our view. In itself it is an original susceptibility of our nature, just as love is, and is not necessarily sinful. It may, however, become sinful when causeless, or excessive, or protracted (Matt. 5:22; Eph. 4:26; Col. 3:8). As ascribed to God, it merely denotes his displeasure with sin and with sinners (Ps. 7:11).

A'nim—*fountains*—a city in the mountains of Judah (Josh. 15:50), now *el-Ghuwein*, near Eshtemoh, about 10 miles south-west of Hebron.

An'imal, an organized living creature endowed with sensation. The Levitical law divided animals into clean and unclean, although the distinction seems to have existed before the Flood (Gen. 7:2). The clean could be offered in sacrifice and eaten. All animals that had not cloven hoofs and did not chew the cud were unclean. The list of clean and unclean quadrupeds is set forth in the Levitical law (Deut. 14 : 3–20; Lev. 11).

An′ise. This word is found only in Matt. 23:23. It is the plant commonly known by the name of dill, the *Peucedanum graveolens* of the botanist. This name dill is derived from a Norse word which means to soothe, the plant having the carminative property of allaying pain. The common dill, the *Anethum graveolens*, is an annual growing wild in the cornfields of Spain and Portugal and the south of Europe generally. There is also a species of dill cultivated in Eastern countries known by the name of *shubit*. It was this species of garden plant of which the Pharisees

DILL (PEUCEDANUM GRAVEOLENS).

were in the habit of paying tithes. It is an umbelliferous plant, very like the caraway—its leaves, which are aromatic, being used in soups and pickles. The proper anise is the *Pimpinella anisum*, the seeds of which are used in the manufacture of cordials.

An′na—*grace*—an aged widow, the daughter of Phanuel. She was a "prophetess," like Miriam, Deborah, and Huldah (2 Chr. 34 : 22). After seven years of married life her husband died, and during her long widowhood she daily attended the temple services. When she was eighty-four years old, she entered the temple at the moment when the aged Simeon uttered his memorable words of praise and thanks to God that he had fulfilled his ancient

promise in sending his Son into the world (Luke 2 : 36, 37).

An′nas was high priest A.D. 7–14. In A.D. 25 Caiaphas, who had married the daughter of Annas (John 18 : 13), was raised to that office, and probably Annas was now made president of the Sanhedrim, or deputy or coadjutor of the high priest, and thus was also called high priest along with Caiaphas (Luke 3 : 2). By the Mosaic law the high-priesthood was held for life (Num. 3 : 10); and although Annas had been deposed by the Roman procurator, the Jews may still have regarded him as legally the high priest. Our Lord was first brought before Annas, and after a brief questioning of him (John 18 : 19–23) was sent to Caiaphas, when some members of the Sanhedrim had met, and the first trial of Jesus took place (Matt. 26 : 57–68). This examination of our Lord before Annas is recorded only by John. Annas was president of the Sanhedrim before which Peter and John were brought (Acts 4 : 6).

Anoint′. The practice of anointing with perfumed oil was common among the Hebrews. (1.) The act of anointing was significant of consecration to a holy or sacred use; hence the anointing of the high priest (Ex. 29 : 29; Lev. 4 : 3) and of the sacred vessels (Ex. 30 : 26). The high priest and the king are thus called "the anointed" (Lev. 4 : 3; 5 : 16; 6 : 15; Ps. 132 : 10). Anointing a king was equivalent to crowning him (1 Sam. 16 : 13; 2 Sam. 2 : 35, etc.). Prophets were also anointed (1 Kings 19 : 16; 1 Chr. 16 : 22; Ps. 105 : 15). The expression, "anoint the shield" (Isa. 21 : 5), refers to the custom of rubbing oil on the leather of the shield so as to make it supple and fit for use in war.

(2.) Anointing was also an act of hospitality (Luke 7 : 38, 46). It was the custom of the Jews in like manner to anoint themselves with oil, as a means of refreshing or invigorating their bodies (Deut. 28 : 40; Ruth 3 : 3; 2 Sam. 14 : 2; Ps. 104 : 15, etc.). This custom is continued among the Arabians to the present day.

(3.) Oil was used also for medicinal purposes. It was applied to the sick, and also to wounds (Ps. 109:18; Isa. 1:6; Mark 6:13; James 5:14).

(4.) The bodies of the dead were sometimes anointed (Mark 14:8; Luke 23:56).

(5.) The promised Deliverer is twice called the "Anointed" or Messiah (Ps. 2:2; Dan. 9:25, 26), because he was anointed with the Holy Ghost (Isa. 61:1), figuratively styled the "oil of gladness" (Ps. 45:7; Heb. 1:9). Jesus of Nazareth is this anointed One (John 1:41; Acts 9:22; 17:2, 3; 18:5, 28), the Messiah of the Old Testament.

Ant (Heb. *nemâlâh*, from a word meaning *to creep, cut off, destroy*), referred to in Prov. 6:6; 30:25, as distinguished for its prudent habits. It is "exceeding wise." The particular species thus spoken of has not been identified. It was evidently one or other of the species of "harvesting ants." "Two of the most common species of the Holy Land (*Atta barbara*, the black ant, and *Atta structor*, a brown ant) are strictly seed-feeders, and in summer lay up stores of grain for winter use.

An'tichrist—*against Christ*, or an *opposition Christ*, a *rival Christ*. The word is used only by the apostle John. Referring to false teachers, he says (1 John 2:18, 22; 4:3; 2 John 7), "Even now are there many antichrists."

(1.) This name has been applied to the "little horn" of the "king of fierce countenance" (Dan. 7:24, 25; 8:23-25).

(2.) It has been applied also to the "false Christs" spoken of by our Lord (Matt. 24:5, 23, 24).

(3.) To the "man of sin" described by Paul (2 Thess. 2:3, 4, 8-10).

(4.) And to the "beast from the sea" (Rev. 13:1; 17:1-18).

An'tioch. (1.) In Syria, on the river Orontes, about 16 miles from the Mediterranean, and some 300 miles north of Jerusalem. It was the metropolis of Syria, and afterwards became the capital of the Roman province in Asia. It ranked third, after Rome and Alexandria, in point of importance, of the cities of the Roman empire. It was called the "first city of the East." Christianity was early introduced into it (Acts 11:19, 21, 24), and the name "Christian" was first applied here to its professors (Acts 11:26). It is intimately connected with the early history of the gospel (Acts 6:5; 11:19, 27, 28, 30; 12:25; 15:22-25; Gal. 2:11, 12). It was the great central point whence missionaries to the Gentiles were sent forth. It was the birth-place of the famous Christian father Chrysostom, who died A.D. 407. It bears the modern name of *Antakia*, and is now a miserable, decaying Turkish town. Like Philippi, it was raised to the rank of a Roman colony. Such colonies were ruled by "prætors" (R.V. marg., Acts 16:20, 21).

MAP SHOWING POSITION OF SYRIAN ANTIOCH.

(2.) In the extreme north of Pisidia; was visited by Paul and Barnabas on the first missionary journey (Acts 13:14). Here they found a synagogue and many proselytes. They met with great success in preaching the gospel, but the Jews stirred up a violent opposition against them, and they were obliged to leave the place. On his return, Paul again visited Antioch for the purpose of confirming the disciples (Acts 14:21). It has been identified with the modern *Yalobatch*, lying to the east of Ephesus.

Anti'ochus, the name of several Syrian kings from B.C. 280 to B.C. 65. The most notable of these were—(1.) Antiochus the Great, who ascended the throne B.C. 223. He is regarded as the "king of the north" referred to in Dan. 11:13-19. He was succeeded (B.C. 187) by his son, Seleucus Philopater, spoken of by Daniel (11:20) as "a raiser of taxes"—in the Revised Version, "one that shall cause an exactor to pass through the glory of the kingdom."

ANTIOCHUS THE GREAT.

(2.) Antiochus IV., surnamed "Epiphanes"—i.e., the *Illustrious*—succeeded his brother Seleucus (B.C. 175). His career and character are prophetically described by Daniel (11:21-32). He was a "vile person." In a spirit of revenge he organized an expedition against Jerusalem, which he destroyed, putting vast multitudes of its inhabitants to death in the most cruel manner. From this time the Jews began the great war of independence under their heroic Maccabean leaders with marked

ANTIOCHUS EPIPHANES.

success, defeating the armies of Antiochus that were sent against them. Enraged at this, Antiochus marched against them in person, threatening utterly to exterminate the nation; but on the way he was suddenly arrested by the hand of death (B.C. 164).

An′tipas. (1.) Herod Antipas, a son of Herod the Great by his Samaritan wife Malthace. He was tetrarch of Galilee and

Peræa during the whole period of our Lord's life on earth (Luke 23:7). He was a frivolous and vain prince, and was chargeable with many infamous crimes (Mark 8:15; Luke 3:19; 13:31, 32). He beheaded John the Baptist (Matt. 14:1-12) at the instigation of Herodias, the wife of his half-brother Herod-Philip, whom he had married. Pilate sent Christ to him when he was at Jerusalem at the Passover (Luke 23:7). He asked some idle questions at him, and after causing him to be mocked, sent him back again to Pilate. The wife of Chuza, his house-steward, was one of our Lord's disciples (Luke 8:3).

He was at length deprived of his dominions, and banished to Lyons in Gaul.

(2.) A "faithful martyr" (Rev. 2:13), of whom nothing more is certainly known.

Antip′atris, a city built by Herod the Great, and called by this name in honour of his father, Antipater. It lay between Cæsarea and Lydda, two miles inland on the great Roman road from Cæsarea to Jerusalem. To this place Paul was brought by night (Acts 23:31) on his way to Cæsarea, from which it was distant 28 miles. It is identified with the modern *Râs-el-'Ain*, where rise the springs of Aujeh, the largest springs in Palestine.

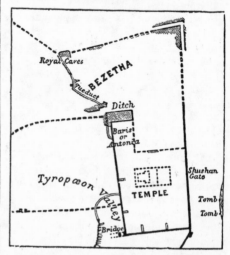

PLAN SHOWING POSITION OF ANTONIA.

Anto′nia, a fortress in Jerusalem, at the north-west corner of the temple area. It is called "the castle" (Acts 21:34, 37). From the stairs of this castle Paul delivered his famous speech to the multitude in the area below (Acts 22:1-21). It was originally a place in which were kept the vestments of the high priest. Herod fortified it, and called it Antonia in honour of his friend Mark Antony. It was of great size, and commanded the temple. It was built on a plateau of rock, separated on the north from the hill Bezetha by a ditch about 30 feet deep and 165 feet wide.

An'tothite, an inhabitant of Anathoth, found only in 1 Chr. 11:28; 12:3. In 2 Sam. 23:27 it is Anathothite; in 1 Chr. 27:12, Anetothite. (R.V. "Anthothite.")

An'vil, the rendering of the Hebrew word *pa'am,* "beaten," found only in Isa. 41:7.

Ape, an animal of the monkey tribe (1 Kings 10:22; 2 Chr. 9:21). It was brought from India by the fleets of Solomon and Hiram, and was called by the Hebrews *kōph,* and by the Greeks *kēpos,* both words being just the Indian Tamil name of the monkey, *kapi—i.e.,* swift, nimble, active. Apes are mentioned only in this connection in the Bible.

Apel'les, a Christian at Rome whom Paul salutes (Rom. 16:10), and styles "approved in Christ."

Aphar'sachites, a company of the colonists whom the Assyrian king planted in Samaria (Ezra 5:6; 6:6).

Aphar'sites, another of the tribes removed to Samaria (Ezra 4:9), or perhaps the same as the preceding.

A'phik (Judg. 1:31); **A'phek** (Josh. 13:4; 19:30)—*stronghold.* (1.) A city of the tribe of Asher. It was the scene of the licentious worship of the Syrian Aphrodite. The ruins of the temple—"magnificent ruins" in a "spot of strange wildness and beauty"—are still seen at *Afka,* on the north-west slopes of Lebanon, near the source of the river Adonis (now *Nahr Ibrahim*), 12 miles east of Gebal.

(2.) A city of the tribe of Issachar, near to Jezreel (1 Sam. 4:1; 29:1; comp. 28:4).

(3.) A town on the road from Damascus to Palestine, in the level plain east of Jordan, near which Benhadad was defeated by the Israelites (1 Kings 20:26, 30; 2

Kings 13:17). It has been identified with the modern *Fik,* 6 miles east of the Sea of Galilee, opposite Tiberias.

Apoc'alypse, the Greek name of the Book of Revelation (*q.v.*).

Apoc'rypha — *hidden, spurious* — the name given to certain ancient books which found a place in the LXX. and Latin Vulgate versions of the Old Testament, and were appended to all the great translations made from them in the sixteenth century, but which have no claim to be regarded as in any sense parts of the inspired Word.

(1.) They are not once quoted by the New Testament writers, who frequently quote from the LXX. Our Lord and his apostles confirmed by their authority the ordinary Jewish canon, which was the same in all respects as we now have it.

(2.) These books were written not in Hebrew but in Greek, and during the "period of silence," from the time of Malachi, after which oracles and direct revelations from God ceased till the Christian era.

(3.) The contents of the books themselves show that they were no part of Scripture.

The Old Testament Apocrypha consists of fourteen books, the chief of which are the Books of the Maccabees (*q.v.*), the Books of Esdras, the Book of Wisdom, the Book of Baruch, the Book of Esther, Ecclesiasticus, Tobit, Judith, etc.

The New Testament Apocrypha consists of a very extensive literature, which bears distinct evidences of its non-apostolic origin, and is utterly unworthy of regard.

Apollo'nia, a city of Macedonia between Amphipolis and Thessalonica, from which it was distant about 36 miles. Paul and Silas passed through it on their way to Thessalonica (Acts 17:1).

Apol'los, a Jew "born at Alexandria," a man well versed in the Scriptures and eloquent (Acts 18:24; R.V., "learned"). He came to Ephesus (about A.D. 49), where he spake "boldly" in the synagogue (18:25), although he did not know as yet that Jesus of Nazareth was the Messiah. Aquila and Priscilla instructed him more perfectly in "the way of God"—*i.e.,* in the knowledge of Christ. He then proceeded to Corinth, where he met Paul (Acts 18:27;

19:1). He was there very useful in watering the good seed Paul had sown (1 Cor. 2:9), and in gaining many to Christ. His disciples were much attached to him (1 Cor. 3:4-7, 22). He was with Paul at Ephesus when he wrote the First Epistle to the Corinthians; and Paul makes kindly reference to him in his letter to Titus (3:13). Some have supposed, although without sufficient ground, that he was the author of the Epistle to the Hebrews.

Apol'lyon—*destroyer*—the name given to the king of the hosts represented by the locusts (Rev. 9:11). It is the Greek translation of the Hebrew *Abaddon* (*q.v.*).

Apos'tle—*a person sent by another; a messenger; envoy.* This word is once used as a descriptive designation of Jesus Christ, the Sent of the Father (Heb. 3:1; John 20:21). It is, however, generally used as designating the body of disciples to whom he intrusted the organization of his church and the dissemination of his gospel—"the twelve," as they are called (Matt. 10:1-5; Mark 3:14; 6:7; Luke 6:13; 9:1). We have four lists of the apostles, one by each of the synoptic evangelists (Matt. 10:2-4; Mark 3:16; Luke 6:14), and one in the Acts (1:13). No two of these lists, however, perfectly coincide.

Our Lord gave them the "keys of the kingdom," and by the gift of his Spirit fitted them to be the founders and governors of his church (John 14:16, 17, 26; 15:26, 27; 16:7-15). To them, as representing his church, he gave the commission to "preach the gospel to every creature" (Matt. 28:18-20). After his ascension he communicated to them, according to his promise, supernatural gifts to qualify them for the discharge of their duties (Acts 2:4; 1 Cor. 2:16; 2:7, 10, 13; 2 Cor. 5:20; 1 Cor. 11:2). Judas Iscariot, one of "the twelve," fell by transgression, and Matthias was substituted in his place (Acts 1:21). Saul of Tarsus was afterwards added to their number (Acts 9:5-20; 20:4; 26:15-18; 1 Tim. 1:12; 2:7; 2 Tim. 1:11).

Luke has given some account of Peter, John, and the two Jameses (Acts 12:2, 17; 15:13; 21:18), but beyond this we know nothing from authentic history of the rest of the original twelve. After the martyrdom of James the Greater (Acts 12:2), James the Less usually resided at Jerusalem, while Paul, "the apostle of the uncircumcision," usually travelled as a missionary among the Gentiles (Gal. 2:8). It was characteristic of the apostles and necessary (1) that they should have seen the Lord, and been able to testify of him and of his resurrection from personal knowledge (John 15:27; Acts 1:21, 22; 1 Cor. 9:1; Acts 22:14, 15). (2.) They must have been immediately called to that office by Christ (Luke 6:13; Gal. 1:1). (3.) It was essential that they should be infallibly inspired, and thus secured against all error and mistake in their public teaching, whether by word or by writing (John 14:26; 16:13; 1 Thess. 2:13). (4.) Another qualification was the power of working miracles (Mark 16:20; Acts 2:43; 1 Cor. 12:8-11).

The apostles therefore could have had no successors. They are the only authoritative teachers of the Christian doctrines. The office of an apostle ceased with its first holders.

In 2 Cor. 8:23 and Phil. 2:25 the word "messenger" is the rendering of the same Greek word, elsewhere rendered "apostle."

Apoth'ecary, rendered in the margin and the Revised Version "perfumer," in Ex. 30:25; 37:29; Eccl. 10:1. The holy oils and ointments were prepared by priests properly qualified for this office. The feminine plural form of the Hebrew word is rendered "confectionaries" in 1 Sam. 8:13.

Appar'el. In Old Testament times the distinction between male and female attire was not very marked. The statute forbidding men to wear female apparel (Deut. 22:5) referred especially to ornaments and head-dresses. Both men and women wore (1) an under garment or tunic, which was bound by a girdle. One who had only this tunic on was spoken of as "naked" (1 Sam. 19:24; Job 24:10; Isa. 20:2). Those in high stations sometimes wore two tunics, the outer being called the "upper garment" (1 Sam. 15:27; 18:4; 24:5; Job 1:20). (2.) They wore in common an over-garment ("mantle," Isa. 3:22; 1 Kings 19:13; 2 Kings

2 : 13), a loose and flowing robe. The folds of this upper garment could be formed into a lap (Ruth 3 : 15; Ps. 79 : 12; Prov. 17 : 23; Luke 6 : 38). Generals of armies usually wore scarlet robes (Judg. 8 : 26; Nah. 2 : 3). A form of conspicuous raiment is mentioned in Luke 20 : 46; comp. Matt. 23 : 5.

Priests alone wore trousers. Both men and women wore turbans. Kings and nobles usually had a store of costly garments for festive occasions (Isa. 3 : 22; Zech. 3 : 4) and for presents (Gen. 45 : 22; Esther 4 : 4; 6 : 8, 11; 1 Sam. 18 : 4; 2 Kings 5 : 5; 10 : 22). Prophets and ascetics wore coarse garments (Isa. 20 : 2; Zech. 13 : 4; Matt. 3 : 4).

Appeal', a reference of any case from an inferior to a superior court. Moses established in the wilderness a series of judicatories such that appeals could be made from a lower to a higher (Ex. 18 : 13–26.)

Under the Roman law the most remarkable case of appeal is that of Paul from the tribunal of Festus at Cæsarea to that of the emperor at Rome (Acts 25 : 11, 12, 21, 25). Paul availed himself of the privilege of a Roman citizen in this matter.

Ap'phia—*increasing*—a female Christian at Colosse (Philemon 2), supposed by some to have been the wife of Philemon.

Ap'pii For'um—*i.e.*, "*the market of Appius*" (Acts 28 : 15, R.V.)—a town on the road, the "Appian Way," from Rome to Brundusium. It was 43 miles from Rome. Here Paul was met by some Roman Christians on his way to the capital. It was natural that they should halt here and wait for him, because from this place there were two ways by which travellers might journey to Rome.

Ap'ple (Heb. *tappûah*, meaning "fragrance"). Probably the apricot or quince is intended by the word, as Palestine was too hot for the growth of apples proper. It is enumerated among the most valuable trees of Palestine (Joel 1 : 12), and frequently referred to in Canticles, and noted for its beauty (2 : 3, 5; 8 : 5). There is nothing to show that it was the "tree of the knowledge of good and evil." The Bible does not mention "apples of Sodom," as some have apparently supposed, but it speaks of

the "vine of Sodom," only, however, metaphorically (Deut. 32 : 32). The "apple of the eye" is the rendering of the Hebrew *ishon*, meaning manikin—*i.e.*, the pupil of the eye (Prov. 7 : 2); so called from the image formed on the retina. (Comp. the promise, Zech. 2 : 8; the prayer, Ps. 17 : 8; and its fulfilment, Deut. 32 : 10.)

The so-called "apple of Sodom" some have supposed to be the *Solanum sanctum* (Heb. *hedek*), rendered "brier" (*q.v.*) in Micah 7 : 4, a thorny plant bearing fruit like the potato-apple. This shrub abounds in the Jordan valley. (See ENGEDI.)

A'pron, found in the Authorized Version in Gen. 3 : 7, of the bands of fig-leaves made by our first parents. In Acts 19 : 12, it denotes the belt or half-girdle worn by artisans and servants round the waist for the purpose of preserving the clothing from injury. In marg. of Authorized Version, Ruth 3 : 15, correctly rendered instead of "vail."

Aq'uila—*eagle*—a native of Pontus, by occupation a tent-maker, whom Paul met on his first visit to Corinth (Acts 18 : 2). Along with his wife Priscilla he had fled from Rome in consequence of a decree (A.D. 50) by Claudius commanding all Jews to leave the city. Paul sojourned with him at Corinth, and they wrought together at their common trade, making Cilician hair-cloth for tents. On Paul's departure from Corinth after eighteen months, Aquila and his wife accompanied him to Ephesus, where they remained, while he proceeded to Syria (Acts 18 : 25, 26). When they became Christians we are not informed, but in Ephesus they were (1 Cor. 16 : 19) Paul's "helpers in Christ Jesus." We find Aquila afterwards at Rome (Rom. 16 : 3) interesting himself still in the cause of Christ. They are referred to some years after this as being at Ephesus (2 Tim. 4 : 19). This is the last notice we have of them.

A'rab—*ambush*—a city in the mountains of Judah (Josh. 15 : 52), now *Er-Rabîyeh*.

Ara'bah—*plain*—in the Revised Version of 2 Kings 14 : 25; Josh. 3 : 16; 8 : 14; 2 Sam. 2 : 29; 4 : 7 (in all these passages the A.V. has "plain"); Amos 6 : 14 (A.V. "wilderness"). This word is found in the

Authorized Version only in Josh. 18:18. It denotes the hollow depression through which the Jordan flows from the Lake of Galilee to the Dead Sea. It is now called by the Arabs *el-Ghor*. But the Ghor is sometimes spoken of as extending 10 miles south of the Dead Sea, and thence to the Gulf of Akabah on the Red Sea is called the *Wady el-Arabah*.

Ara'bia—*arid*—an extensive region in the south-west of Asia. It is bounded on

Yemen. It lies between the Red Sea and the Persian Gulf. (2.) Arabia Deserta, the *el-Badieh* or "Great Wilderness" of the Arabs. From this name is derived that which is usually given to the nomadic tribes which wander over this region, the "Bedaween," or, more generally, "Bedouin." (3.) Arabia Petræa—*i.e.*, the Rocky Arabia, so called from its rocky mountains and stony plains. It comprehended all the north-west portion of the country, and is much better known to travellers than any other portion.

This country is, however, divided by modern geographers into (1) Arabia Proper, or the Arabian Peninsula; (2) Northern Arabia, or the Arabian Desert; and (3) Western Arabia, which includes the peninsula of Sinai and the Desert of Petra, originally inhabited by the Horites (Gen. 14:6, etc.), but in later times by the descendants of Esau, and known as the Land of Edom or Idumea, also as the Desert of Seir or Mount Seir.

The whole land appears (Gen. 10) to have been inhabited

MAP OF ARABIA.

the west by the Isthmus of Suez and the Red Sea, on the south by the Indian Ocean, and on the east by the Persian Gulf and the Euphrates. It extends far into the north in barren deserts, meeting those of Syria and Mesopotamia. It is one of the few countries of the world from which the original inhabitants have never been expelled.

It was anciently divided into three parts:—(1.) Arabia Felix (Happy Arabia), so called from its fertility. It embraced a large portion of the country now known by the name of Arabia. The Arabs call it

by a variety of tribes of different lineage—Ishmaelites, Arabians, Idumeans, Horites, and Edomites; but at length becoming amalgamated, they came to be known by the general designation of Arabs. The modern nation of Arabs is predominantly Ishmaelite. Their language is the most developed and the richest of all the Semitic languages, and is of great value to the student of Hebrew.

The Israelites wandered for forty years in Arabia. In the days of Solomon, and subsequently, commercial intercourse was to a considerable extent kept up with this country (1 Kings 10:15; 2 Chr. 9:14; 17:11). Arabians were present in Jerusalem at Pentecost (Acts 2:11). Paul retired for a season into Arabia after his conversion (Gal. 1:17). This country is frequently referred to by the prophets (Isa. 21:11; 42:11; Jer. 25:24, etc.).

A'rad. (1.) Now *Tell Arad*, a Canaanite city, about 20 miles south of Hebron. The king of Arad "fought against Israel and took of them prisoners" when they were retreating from the confines of Edom (Num. 21:1; 33:40; Judg. 1:16).

It was finally subdued by Joshua (12:14).

(2.) One of the sons of Beriah (1 Chr. 8:15).

A'ram, the son of Shem (Gen. 10:22); according to Gen. 22:21, a grandson of Nahor. In Matt. 1:3, 4, and Luke 3:33, this word is the Greek form of Ram, the father of Amminadab (1 Chr. 2:10).

The word means *high*, or *highlands*, and as the name of a *country* denotes that elevated region extending from the northeast of Palestine to the Euphrates. It corresponded generally with the Syria and

ARARAT.

Mesopotamia of the Greeks and Romans. In Gen. 25:20; 31:20, 24; Deut. 26:5, the word "Syrian" is properly "Aramean" (R.V., marg.). Damascus became at length the capital of the several smaller kingdoms comprehended under the designation "Aram" or "Syria."

A'ram-nahara'im—*Aram of the two rivers*—is Mesopotamia (as it is rendered in Gen. 24:10), the country enclosed between the Tigris on the east and the Euphrates on the west (Ps. 60, title); called also the "field of Aram" (Hos. 12:12, R.V.) —*i.e.*, the open country of Aram; in the Authorized Version, "country of Syria." Padan-aram (*q.v.*) was a portion of this country.

A'ram-zo'bah (Ps. 60, title), probably the region between the Euphrates and the Orontes.

Ar'an—*wild goat*—a descendant of Seir the Horite (Gen. 36:28).

Ar'arat—*sacred land* or *high land*—the name of a country on one of the mountains of which the ark rested after the Flood subsided (Gen. 8:4). The "mountains" mentioned were probably the Kurdish range of South Armenia. In 2 Kings 19:37, Isa. 37:38, the word is rendered "Armenia" in the Authorized Version, but in the Revised Version, "Land of Ararat." In Jer. 51:27, the name denotes the central or southern portion of Armenia. It is, however, generally applied to a high and almost inaccessible mountain which rises majestically on the plain of the Ar- axes. It has two conical peaks, about 7 miles apart, the one 14,300 feet, and the other 10,300 feet, above the level of the plain. Three thousand feet of the summit of the higher of these peaks is covered with perpetual snow. It is called *Kuh-i-nuh*— *i.e.,* "Noah's mountain"—by the Persians. This mountain stands midway between the Atlantic and the Pacific oceans. It is now the central boundary between Russia, Tur- key, and Persia.

"Nothing can be more beautiful than its shape, more awful than its height. All the surrounding mountains sink into insig- nificance when compared with it. It is perfect in all its parts; no rugged features, no unnatural prominences; everything is in harmony, and all combine to render it one of the sublimest objects in nature" (*Morier*). It was probably on one of the lower ledges of this enormous pyramid that the ark ultimately rested.

Arau'nah—*agile;* also called **Ornan** 1 Chr. 21:15—a Jebusite who dwelt in Jerusalem before it was taken by the Is- raelites. The destroying angel, sent to punish David for his vanity in taking a census of the people, was stayed in his work of destruction near a threshing-floor be- longing to Araunah which was situated on Mount Moriah. Araunah offered it to David as a free gift, together with the oxen and the threshing instruments; but the king insisted on purchasing it at its full price (2 Sam. 24:24; 1 Chr. 21:25), for, accord- ing to the law of sacrifices, he could not offer to God what cost him nothing. On the same place Solomon afterwards erected the temple (2 Sam. 24:16; 2 Chr. 3:1). (See ALTAR.)

Ar'ba—*four*—a giant, father of Anak. From him the city of Hebron derived its name of Kirjath-arba—*i.e.,* the city of Arba (Josh. 14:15; 15:13; 21:11; Gen. 13:18). (See HEBRON.)

Ar'bathite, a name given to Abi-albon, or, as elsewhere called, Abiel, one of David's warriors (2 Sam. 23:31; 1 Chr. 11:32), prob- ably as being an inhabitant of Arabah (Josh. 15:61), a town in the wilderness of Judah.

Archan'gel (1 Thess. 4:16; Jude 9), the prince of the angels; some highly-exalted being.

Arch, an architectural term found only in Ezek. 40:16, 22, 26, 29. The exact meaning of the word so rendered is in dis- pute. It probably denotes a portico with a colonnade or some moulding at the top of a column. There is no absolute proof that the Israelites employed arches in their buildings; but their non-existence cannot be inferred from the fact that there is no Hebrew word that can properly be so ren- dered. The arch was employed in the building of the pyramids of Egypt. The

REMAINS OF ARCH, TEMPLE WALL, JERUSALEM.

oldest existing arch is at Thebes, and bears the date B.C. 1350. There are also still found the remains of an arch of the bridge connecting Zion and Moriah. (See TYRO- PŒON VALLEY.) The spring of an arch has recently been discovered in "Solomon's stables," under the temple area.

Archela'us—*ruler of the people*—son of Herod the Great, by Malthace, a Samaritan woman. He was educated along with his brother Antipas at Rome. He inherited from his father a third part of his king- dom—*viz.,* Idumæa, Judæa, and Samaria, and hence is called "king" (Matt. 2:22). He was a cruel ruler, and in the tenth year of his reign was dethroned on account of his tyranny and banished to Vienne in Gaul, where he died. It was for fear of him that Joseph and Mary turned aside on their way back from Egypt. Till a few days before his death Herod had named Antipas as his successor, but in his last moments he named Archelaus.

Arch'er, a shooter with the bow (1 Chr. 10:3). This art was of high antiquity

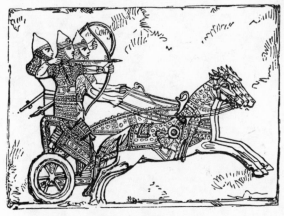

ARCHER.
(From Assyrian Sculptures.)

(Gen. 21:20; 27:3). Saul was wounded by the Philistine archers (1 Sam. 31:3). The phrase "breaking the bow" (Hos. 1:5; Jer. 49:35) is equivalent to taking away one's power, while "strengthening the bow" is a symbol of its increase (Gen. 49:24). The Persian archers were famous among the ancients (Isa. 13:18; Jer. 49:35; 50:1-42). (See Bow.)

Ar'chevite, one of the nations planted by the Assyrians in Samaria (Ezra 4:9); the men of Erech.

Ar'chi, a city on the boundary of Ephraim and Benjamin (Josh. 16:2), between Bethel and Beth-horon the nether.

Archip'pus—*master of the horse*—a "fellow-soldier" of Paul's (Philemon 2), whom he exhorts to renewed activity (Col. 4:17). He was a member of Philemon's family, probably his son.

Ar'chite, the usual designation of Hushai (2 Sam. 15:32; 17:5, 14; 1 Chr. 27:33), who was a native of Archi. He was "the king's friend"—*i.e.*, he held office under David similar to that of our modern privy councillor.

Arctu'rus—*bear-keeper*—the name given by the ancients to the brightest star in the constellation Boötes. In the Authorized Version (Job 9:9; 38:32) it is the rendering of the Hebrew word *'âsh*, which probably designates the constellation the Great Bear. This word (*'âsh*) is supposed to be derived from an Arabic word meaning *night-watcher*, because the Great Bear always revolves about the pole, and to our northern hemisphere never sets.

Ard—*descent*—a grandson of Benjamin (Num. 26:38-40). In 1 Chr. 8:3 he is called Addar. His descendants are mentioned in Num. 26:40.

Ar'don—*descendant*—the last of the three sons of Caleb by his first wife Azubah (1 Chr. 2:18).

Areop'agite, a member of the court of Areopagus (Acts 17:34).

Areop'agus, the Latin form of the Greek word rendered "Mars' hill." But it denotes also the council or court of justice which met in the open air on the hill. It was a rocky height to the west of the Acropolis at Athens, on the south-east summit of which the council was held which was constituted by Solon, and consisted of nine archons or chief magistrates who were then in office, and the ex-archons of blameless life.

On this hill of Mars (Gr. *Ares*) Paul delivered his memorable address to the "men of Athens" (Acts 17:22-31).

Ar'etas, the father-in-law of Herod Antipas, and king of Arabia Petræa. His daughter returned to him on the occasion of her husband's entering into an adulterous alliance with Herodias, the wife of Herod-Philip, his half-brother (Luke 3:19, 20; Mark 6:17; Matt. 14:3). This led to a war between Aretas and Herod Antipas. Herod's army was wholly destroyed (A.D. 36). Aretas, taking advantage of the complications of the times on account of the death of the Emperor Tiberius (A.D. 37), took possession of Damascus (2 Cor. 11:32; comp. Acts 9:24). At this time Paul returned to Damascus from Arabia.

Ar'gob—*stony heap*—an "island," as it has been called, of rock about 30 miles by

AREOPAGUS (MARS' HILL).

20, rising 20 or 30 feet above the table-land of Bashan; a region of crags and chasms wild and rugged in the extreme. On this "island" stood sixty walled cities, ruled over by Og. It is called Trachonitis ("the rugged region") in the New Testament (Luke 3:1). These cities were conquered by the Israelites (Deut. 3:4; 1 Kings 4:13). It is now called the *Lejah*. Here "sixty walled cities are still traceable in a space of 308 square miles. The architecture is ponderous and massive. Solid walls 4 feet thick, and stones on one another without cement; the roofs enormous slabs of basaltic rock, like iron; the doors and gates are of stone 18 inches thick, secured by ponderous bars. The land bears still the appearance of having been called the 'land of giants' under the giant Og." "I have more than once entered a deserted city in the evening, taken possession of a comfortable house, and spent the night in peace. Many of the houses in the ancient cities of Bashan are perfect, as if only finished yesterday. The walls are sound, the roofs unbroken,

and even the window-shutters in their places. These ancient cities of Bashan probably contain the very oldest specimens of domestic architecture in the world" (Porter's *Giant Cities*). (See BASHAN.)

Ari′eh—*the lion*—the name of one of the body-guard slain with Pekahiah at Samaria (2 Kings 15:25) by the conspirator Pekah.

A′riel—*the lion of God*. (1.) One of the chief men sent by Ezra to procure Levites for the sanctuary (Ezra 8:16).

(2.) A symbolic name for Jerusalem (Isa. 29:1, 2, 7) as "victorious under God," and in Ezek. 43:15, 16, for the altar (marg., Heb. *'ariel*) of burnt offerings, the secret of Israel's lion-like strength.

Arimathe′a, a "city of the Jews" (Luke 23:51), the birth-place of Joseph in whose sepulchre our Lord was laid (Matt. 27:57, 60; John 19:38). It is probably the same place as Ramathaim in Ephraim, and the birth-place of Samuel (1 Sam. 1:1, 19). Others identify it with Ramleh in Dan, or Rama (*q.v.*) in Benjamin (Matt. 2:18).

A′rioch—*lion-like, venerable*. (1.) A king of Ellasar who was confederate with Chedorlaomer against Sodom and Gomorrah (Gen. 14:1, 9).

(2.) The captain of the guard at Babylon to whose custody Daniel and his companions were intrusted (Dan. 2:14).

Aristar'chus—*best ruler*—a native of Thessalonica (Acts 20:4), a companion of Paul in his third missionary journey (Acts 19:29; 27:2). He was Paul's "fellow-prisoner" at Rome, and his "fellow-labourer" (Col. 4:10; Philemon 24).

Aristobu'lus, a Roman mentioned in Paul's Epistle to the Romans (16:10), whose "household" is saluted.

Ark. *Noah's ark*, a building of gopher-wood, and covered with pitch, 300 cubits long, 50 cubits broad, and 30 cubits high (Gen. 6:14-16); an oblong floating house of three stories, with a door in the side and a window in the roof. It was 120 years in building (Gen. 5:32; 7:6). It was intended to preserve certain persons and animals from the deluge which God was about to bring over the earth. It contained eight persons (Gen. 7:13; 2 Pet. 2:5), and of all "clean" animals seven pairs, and of "unclean" one pair, and of birds seven pairs of each sort (Gen. 7:2, 3). It was in the form of an oblong square, with flat bottom and sloping roof. Traditions of the Deluge, by which the race of man was swept from the earth, and of the ark of Noah have been found existing among all nations.

The ark of bulrushes in which the infant Moses was laid (Ex. 2:3) is called in the Hebrew *teebah*, a word derived from the Egyptian *teb*, meaning "a chest." It was daubed with slime and with pitch. The bulrushes of which it was made were the papyrus reed.

The sacred ark is designated by a different Hebrew word—*'aron'*, which is the common name for a chest or coffer used for any purpose (Gen. 50:26; 2 Kings 12:9, 10). It is distinguished from all others by such titles as the "ark of God" (1 Sam. 3:3), "ark of the covenant" (Josh. 3:6;

Heb. 9:4), "ark of the law" (Ex. 25:22). It was made of acacia or shittim wood, a cubit and a half broad and high and two cubits long, and covered all over with the purest gold. Its upper surface or lid—the mercy-seat—was surrounded with a rim of gold; and on each of the two sides were

ARK OF THE COVENANT.

two gold rings, in which were placed two gold-covered poles by which the ark could be carried (Num. 7:9; 10:21; 4:5, 19, 20; 1 Kings 8:3, 6). Over the ark, at the two extremities, were two cherubim, with their faces turned toward each other (Lev. 16:2; Num. 7:89). Their outspread wings over the top of the ark formed the throne of God, while the ark itself was his footstool (Ex. 25:10-22; 37:1-9). The ark was deposited in the "holy of holies," and was so placed that one end of the poles by which it was carried touched the veil which separated the two apartments of the tabernacle (1 Kings 8:8). The two tables of stone which constituted the "testimony" or evidence of God's covenant with the people (Deut. 31:26), the "pot of manna" (Ex. 16:33), and "Aaron's rod that budded" (Num. 17:10), were laid up in the ark (Heb. 9:4). (See TABERNACLE.) The ark and the sanctuary were "the beauty of Israel" (Lam. 2:1). During the journeys of the Israelites the ark was carried by the priests in advance of the host (Num. 4:5, 6; 10:33-36; Ps. 68:1; 132:8). It was borne by the priests into the bed of the Jordan, which separated, opening a pathway for the whole of the host to pass over (Josh. 3:15, 16; 4:7, 10, 11, 17, 18). It was borne in the procession round Jericho (Josh. 6:4, 6, 8, 11, 12). When carried it was always wrapped in the veil, the badgers' skins, and blue cloth, and carefully concealed even from the eyes of the Levites who carried it. After the settlement of Israel in Palestine the ark remained in the tabernacle at Gilgal for a season, and was then removed to Shiloh till the time of Eli—between 300 and 400 years (Jer. 7:12)—when it was carried into the field of battle so as to secure, as they supposed, victory to the Hebrews, and was taken by the Philistines (1 Sam. 4:3-11), who sent it back after retaining it seven months (1 Sam. 5:7, 8). It remained then at Kirjath-jearim (7:1, 2) till the time of David (twenty years), who wished to remove it to Jerusalem; but the proper mode of removing it having been neglected, Uzzah was smitten with death for putting "forth his hand to the ark of God," and in consequence of this it was left in the house of Obed-edom in Gath-rimmon for three months (2 Sam. 6:1-11), at the end of which time David removed it in a grand procession to Jerusalem, where it was kept till a place was prepared for it (12-19). It was afterwards deposited by Solomon in the temple (1 Kings 8:6-9). When the Babylonians destroyed Jerusalem and plundered the temple, the ark was probably taken away by Nebuchadnezzar and destroyed, as no trace of it is afterwards to be found. The absence of the ark from the second temple was one of the points in which it was inferior to the first temple.

Ar′kite (Gen. 10:17; 1 Chr. 1:15), a designation of certain descendants from the Phœnicians or Sidonians, the inhabitants of Arka, 12 miles north of Tripoli, opposite the northern extremity of Lebanon.

Arm, used to denote power (Ps. 10:15; Ezek. 30:21; Jer. 48:25). It is also used of the omnipotence of God (Ex. 15:16; Ps. 89:13; 98:1; 77:15; Isa. 53:1; John 12:38; Acts 13:17).

Armaged′don, occurs only in Rev. 16:16

(R.V., "Har-Magedon"), as symbolically designating the place where the "battle of the great day of God Almighty" (ver. 14) shall be fought. The word properly means the "mount of Megiddo." It is the scene of the final conflict between Christ and Antichrist. The idea of such a scene was suggested by the Old Testament great battle-field, the plain of Esdraelon (*q.v.*).

Arme′nia—*high land*—occurs only in Authorized Version, 2 Kings 19:37; in Revised Version, "Ararat," which is the Hebrew word. A country in western Asia lying between the Caspian and the Black Sea. Here the ark of Noah rested after the Deluge (Gen. 8:4). It is for the most part high table-land, and is watered by the Aras, the Kur, the Euphrates, and the Tigris. Ararat was properly the name of a part of ancient Armenia. Three provinces of Armenia are mentioned in Jer. 51:27—Ararat, Minni, and Ashchenaz. Some, however, think Minni a contraction for Armenia. (See ARARAT.)

Armo′ni—*inhabitant of a fortress*—the first-named of the two sons of Saul and Rizpah. He was delivered up to the Gibeonites by David, and hanged by them (2 Sam. 21:8, 9).

Ar′mour is employed in the English Bible to denote military equipment, both *offensive* and *defensive*.

(1.) The *offensive* weapons were different at different periods of history. The "rod of iron" (Ps. 2:9) is supposed to mean a mace or crowbar, an instrument of great power when used by a strong arm. The "maul" (Prov. 25:18; cognate Hebrew word rendered "battle-axe" in Jer. 51:20, and "slaughter weapon" in Ezek. 9:2) was a war-hammer or martel. The "sword" is the usual translation of *ḥereb*, which properly means "poniard." The real sword, as well as the dirk-sword (which was always double-edged), was also used (1 Sam. 17:39; 2 Sam. 20:8; 1 Kings 20:11). The spear was another offensive weapon (Josh. 8:18; 1 Sam. 17:7). The javelin was used by light troops (Num. 25:7, 8; 1 Sam. 13:22). Saul threw a javelin at David (1 Sam. 19:9, 10), and so virtually absolved him from his allegiance. The bow was, however, the chief weapon of offence. The arrows were carried in a quiver, the bow being always unbent till the moment of action (Gen. 27:3; 48:22; Ps. 18:34). The sling was a favourite weapon of the Benjamites (1 Sam. 17:40; 1 Chr. 12:2. Comp. 1 Sam. 25:29).

(2.) Of the *defensive* armour a chief place is assigned to the shield or buckler. There were the great shield or target (the *tzinnah*), for the protection of the whole person (Gen. 15:1; Ps. 47:9; 1 Sam. 17:6; Prov. 30:5), and the buckler (Heb. *mageen*) or small shield (1 Kings 10:17; Ezek. 26:8). In Ps. 91:4 "buckler" is properly a roundel appropriated to archers or slingers. The helmet (Ezek. 27:10; 1 Sam. 17:38), a covering for the head; the coat of mail or corselet (1 Sam. 17:5), or habergeon (Neh. 4:16), harness or breast-plate (Rev. 9:9), for the covering of the back and breast and both upper arms (Isa. 59:17; Eph. 6:14). The cuirass and corselet, composed of leather or quilted cloth, were also for the covering of the body. Greaves, for the covering of the legs, were worn in the time of David (1 Sam. 17:6). Reference is made by Paul (Eph. 6:14–17) to the panoply of a Roman soldier. The shield here is the *thureon*, a door-like oblong shield above all—*i.e.*, covering the whole person—not the small round shield. There is no armour for the back, but only for the front.

Ar′mour-bearer, an officer selected by kings and generals because of his bravery, not only to bear their armour, but also to stand by them in the time of danger. They were the adjutants of our modern armies (Judg. 9:54; 1 Sam. 14:7; 16:21; 31:6).

Armoury, the place in which armour was deposited when not used (Neh. 3:19; Jer. 50:25). At first each man of the Hebrews had his own arms, because all went to war. There were no arsenals or magazines for arms till the time of David, who had a large collection of arms, which he consecrated to the Lord in his tabernacle (1 Sam. 21:9; 2 Sam. 8:7–12; 1 Chr. 26:26, 27).

Army. The Israelites marched out of Egypt in military order (Ex. 13:18, "harnessed;" marg., "five in a rank"). Each tribe formed a battalion, with its own banner and leader (Num. 2:2; 10:14). In war the army was divided into thousands and hundreds under their several captains (Num. 31:14), and also into families (Num. 2:34; 2 Chr. 25:5; 26:12). From the time of their entering the land of Canaan to the time of the kings, the Israelites made little progress in military affairs, although often engaged in warfare. The kings introduced the custom of maintaining a body-guard (the *Gibborim; i.e.,* "heroes"), and thus the nucleus of a standing army was formed. Saul had an army of 3,000 select warriors (1 Sam. 13:2; 14:52; 24:2). David also had a band of soldiers around him (1 Sam. 23:13; 25:13). To this band he afterwards added the Cherethites and the Pelethites (2 Sam. 15:18; 20:7). At first the army consisted only of infantry (1 Sam. 4:10; 15:4), as the use of horses was prohibited (Deut. 17:16); but chariots and horses were afterwards added (2 Sam. 8:4; 1 Kings 10:26, 28, 29; 1 Kings 9:19). In 1 Kings 9:22 there is given a list of the various gradations of rank held by those who composed the army. The equipment and maintenance of the army were at the public expense (2 Sam. 17:28, 29; 1 Kings 4:27; 10:16, 17; Judg. 20:10). At the Exodus the number of males above twenty years capable of bearing arms was 600,000 (Ex. 12:37). In David's time it mounted to the number of 1,300,000 (2 Sam. 24:9).

Ar′non—*swift*—the southern boundary of the territory of Israel beyond Jordan, separating it from the land of Moab (Deut. 3:8, 16). This river (referred to twenty-four times in the Bible) rises in the mountains of Gilead, and after a circuitous course of about 80 miles through a deep ravine it falls into the Dead Sea nearly opposite Engedi. The stream is almost dry in summer. It is now called *el-Mujeb*. The territory of the Amorites extended from the Arnon to the Jabbok.

Ar′oer—*ruins*. (1.) A town on the north bank of the Arnon (Deut. 4:48; Judg. 11:26; 2 Kings 10:33), the southern boundary of the kingdom of Sihon (Josh. 12:2). It is now called *Aráir*, 13 miles west of the Dead Sea.

(2.) One of the towns built by the tribe of Gad (Num. 32:34) "before Rabbah" (Josh. 13:25), the Ammonite capital. It was famous in the history of Jephthah (Judg. 11:33) and of David (2 Sam. 24:5). (Comp. Isa. 17:2; 2 Kings 15:29.)

(3.) A city in the south of Judah, 12 miles south-east of Beersheba, to which David sent presents after recovering the spoil from the Amalekites at Ziklag (1 Sam. 30:26, 28). It was the native city of two of David's warriors (1 Chr. 11:44). It is now called *Ar'arah*.

Ar'pad (Isa. 10:9; 36:19; 37:13), also **Ar'phad**—*support*—a Syrian city near Hamath, along with which it is invariably mentioned (2 Kings 19:13; 18:34; Isa. 10:9), and Damascus (Jer. 49:23). After a siege of three years it fell (B.C. 742) before the Assyrian king Tiglath-pileser II. Now *Tell Erfûd.*

Arphax'ad, son of Shem, born the year after the Deluge. He died at the age of 438 years (Gen. 11:10–13; 1 Chr. 1:17, 18; Luke 3:36). He dwelt in Mesopotamia, and became, according to the Jewish historian Josephus, the progenitor of the Chaldeans.

Arrows. At first made of reeds, and then of wood tipped with iron. Arrows are sometimes figuratively put for lightning (Deut. 32:23, 42; Ps. 7:13; 18:14; 144:6; Zech. 9:14). They were used in war as well as in the chase (Gen. 27:3; 49:23). They were also used in divination (Ezek. 21:21).

The word is frequently employed as a symbol of calamity or disease inflicted by God (Job 6:4; 34:6; Ps. 38:2; Deut. 32:23. Comp. Ezek. 5:16), or of some sudden danger (Ps. 91:5), or bitter words (Ps. 64:3), or false testimony (Prov. 25:18). Children are compared to "arrows in the hands of a mighty man" (Ps. 127:4, 5). The arrow is also used to denote the irresistible energy of the word in the hands of the Messiah (Ps. 45:5).

Artaxer'xes, the Greek form of the name of several Persian kings. (1.) The king who obstructed the rebuilding of the temple (Ezra 4:7). He was probably the Smerdis of profane history.

(2.) The king mentioned in Ezra 7:1. in the seventh year (B.C. 458) of whose reign Ezra led a second colony of Jews back to Jerusalem, was probably Longimanus, who reigned for forty years (B.C. 464–425); the grandson of Darius, who, fourteen years later, permitted Nehemiah to return and rebuild Jerusalem.

Artif'icer, a person engaged in any kind of manual occupation (Gen. 4:22; Isa. 3:3).

Artil'lery—1 Sam. 20:40—(Heb. *keli*, meaning "apparatus;" here meaning collectively any missile weapons, as arrows and lances. In Revised Version, "weapons"). This word is derived from the Latin *artillaria* = equipment of war.

Ar'vad—*wandering*—(Ezek. 27:8), a small island and city on the coast of Syria, mentioned as furnishing mariners and soldiers for Tyre. The inhabitants were called Arvadites. They were descendants from one of the sons of Canaan (Gen. 10:18).

A'sa—*physician*—son of Abijah and grandson of Rehoboam, was the third king of Judah. He was zealous in maintaining the true worship of God, and in rooting all idolatry, with its accompanying immoralities, out of the land (1 Kings 15:8–14). The Lord gave him and his land rest and prosperity. It is recorded of him, however, that in his old age, when afflicted, he "sought not to the Lord, but to the physicians" (comp. Jer. 17:5). He died in the forty-first year of his reign, greatly honoured by his people (2 Chr. 16:1–13), and was succeeded by his son Jehoshaphat.

As'ahel—*made by God*—the youngest son of Zeruiah, David's sister. He was celebrated for his swiftness of foot. When fighting against Ish-bosheth at Gibeon, in the army of his brother Joab, he was put to death by Abner, whom he pursued from the field of battle (2 Sam. 2:18, 19). He is mentioned among David's thirty mighty men (2 Sam. 23:24; 1 Chr. 11:26).

Others of the same name are mentioned (2 Chr. 17:8; 31:13; Ezra 10:15).

A'saph—*convener*, or *collector*. (1.) A Levite; one of the leaders of David's choir (1 Chr. 6:39). Psalms 50 and 73–83 inclusive are attributed to him. He is mentioned along with David as skilled in music, and a "seer" (2 Chr. 29:30). The "sons of Asaph," mentioned in 1 Chr. 25:1, 2 Chr. 20:14, and Ezra 2:41, were his descendants, or more probably a class of poets or singers who recognized him as their master.

(2.) The "recorder" in the time of Hezekiah (2 Kings 18:18, 37).

(3.) The "keeper of the king's forests," to whom Nehemiah requested from Artaxerxes a "letter" that he might give him timber for the temple at Jerusalem (Neh. 2:8).

Ascension. See CHRIST.

As'enath—an Egyptian name, meaning "gift of the sun-god"—daughter of Potipherah, priest of On or Heliopolis, wife of Joseph (Gen. 41:45). She was the mother of Manasseh and Ephraim (50–52; 46:20).

Ash (Heb. *o'ren*, "tremulous"), mentioned only Isa. 44:14 (R.V., "fir tree"). It is rendered "pine tree" both in the LXX. and Vulgate versions. There is a tree called by the Arabs *aran*, found still in the valleys of Arabia Petræa, whose leaf resembles that of the mountain ash. This may be the tree meant. Our ash tree is not known in Syria.

Ash'dod—*stronghold*—a Philistine city (Josh. 15:47), about midway between Gaza and Joppa, and 3 miles from the Mediterranean. It was one of the chief seats of the worship of Dagon (1 Sam. 5:5). It belonged to the tribe of Judah (Josh. 15:47), but it never came into their actual possession. It was an important city, as it stood on the highroad from Egypt to Palestine, and hence was strongly fortified (2 Chr. 26:6; Isa. 20:1). Uzziah took it and held possession of it for a short time; but fifty years after his death it was taken by the Assyrians (B.C. 758), and its inhabitants were carried captive into Assyria.

The only reference to it in the New Testament, where it is called **Azotus,** is in the account of Philip's return from Gaza (Acts 8:40). It is now called *Eshdud.*

Ash'doth-pis'gah (Deut. 3:17; Josh. 12:3; 13:20) in Authorized Version, but in Revised Version translated "slopes of Pisgah." In Deut. 4:49 it is translated in the Authorized Version "springs of Pisgah." The name Ashdoth is translated "springs" in the Authorized Version, but "slopes" in the Revised Version, of Josh. 10:40 and 12:8. It has been identified with the springs under Mount Nebo, now called *'Ayûn Mûsa.*

Ash'er—*happy*—Jacob's eighth son; his mother was Zilpah, Leah's handmaid (Gen. 30:13). Of the tribe founded by him nothing is recorded beyond its holding a place in the list of the tribes (35:26; 46:17; Ex. 1:4, etc.). It increased in numbers twenty-nine per cent. during the thirty-eight years' wanderings. The place of this tribe during the march through the desert was between Dan and Naphtali (Num. 2:27). The boundaries of the inheritance given to it, which con-

MAP SHOWING THE TERRITORY OF ASHER.

tained some of the richest soil in Palestine, and the names of its towns, are recorded in Josh. 19:24–31; Judg. 1:31, 32. Asher and Simeon were the only tribes west of the Jordan which furnished no hero or judge for the nation. Anna the prophetess was of this tribe (Luke 2:36).

Ashe'rah, and pl. **Ashe'rim** in Revised Version, instead of "grove" and "groves" of the Authorized Version. This was the name of a sensual Canaanitish goddess Astarte, the feminine of the Assyrian Ishtar. Its symbol was the stem of a tree deprived of its boughs, and rudely shaped into an image, and planted in the ground. Such religious symbols ("groves") are frequently alluded to in Scripture (Ex. 34:13; Judg. 6:25; 2 Kings 23:6; 1 Kings 16:33, etc.). These images were also sometimes made of silver or of carved stone (2 Kings 21:7; "the graven image of Asherah," R.V.). (See GROVE [1]).

Ashes. The ashes of a red heifer burned entire (Num. 19:5) when sprinkled on the unclean made them ceremonially clean (Heb. 9:13).

To cover the head with ashes was a token of self-abhorrence and humiliation (2 Sam. 13:19; Esther 4:3; Jer. 6:26, etc.).

To feed on ashes (Isa. 44:20), means to seek that which will prove to be vain and unsatisfactory, and hence it denotes the unsatisfactory nature of idol-worship. (Comp. Hos. 12:1.)

Ash'kelon = Askelon = Ascalon, was one of the five cities of the Philistines (Josh. 13:3; 1 Sam. 6:17). It stood on the shore of the Mediterranean, 12 miles north of Gaza. It is mentioned on an inscription at Karnak in Egypt as having been taken by king Rameses II., the oppressor of the Hebrews. In the time of the judges (1:18) it fell into the possession of the tribe of Judah; but it was soon after retaken by the Philistines, who were not finally dispossessed till the time of Alexander the Great. Samson (2 Sam. 1:20) went down to this place from Timnath,

RUINS OF ASHKELON.

and slew thirty men and took their spoil. The prophets foretold its destruction (Jer. 25:20; 47:5, 7). It became a noted place in the Middle Ages, having been the scene of many a bloody battle between the Saracens and the Crusaders. It was besieged and taken by Richard the Lion-hearted, and "within its walls and towers now standing he held his court." Among the Tell Amarna tablets (see page 215) are found letters or official despatches from *Yadaya*, "captain of horse and dust of the king's feet," to the "great king" of Egypt, dated from Ascalon. It is now called *'Askalân.*

Ash'kenaz, one of the three sons of Gomer (Gen. 10:3), and founder of one of the tribes of the Japhetic race. They are mentioned in connection with Minni and Ararat, and hence their original seat must have been in Armenia (Jer. 51:27), probably near the Black Sea, which, from their founder, was first called Axenus, and afterwards the Euxine.

Ash'penaz, the master of the eunuchs of Nebuchadnezzar (Dan. 1:3), the "Rabsaris" of the court. His position was similar to that of the *Kislar-aga* of the modern Turkish sultans.

Ash'taroth, a city of Bashan, in the kingdom of Og (Deut. 1:4; Josh. 12:4; 13:12; 9:10). It was in the half-tribe of Manasseh (Josh. 13:12), and as a Levitical city was given to the Gershonites (1 Chr. 6:71). Uzziah, one of David's valiant men (1 Chr. 11:44), is named as of this city. It is identified with *Tell Ashterah*. Some identify it with the modern *Busrah*, capital of the Haurân, seeing it bears the name Beesh-terah (Josh. 21:27), a contraction for Beth-eshterah, *i.e.*, "the house of Ashtaroth."

Ash'teroth Karna'im—*Ashteroth of the two horns*—the abode of the Rephaim (Gen. 14:5). It may be identified with Ashtaroth preceding; called "Karnaim"—*i.e.*, the "two-horned" (the crescent moon). The Samaritan version renders the word by "Sunamein," the present *es-Sunamein*, 28 miles south of Damascus.

Ash'toreth, the moon goddess of the Phœnicians, representing the passive principle in nature, their principal female deity; frequently associated with the name of Baal, the sun-god, their chief male deity (Judg. 10: 6; 1 Sam. 7:4; 12:10). These names often occur in the plural (Ashtaroth, Baalim), probably as indicating either different statues or different modifications of the deities. This deity is spoken of as Ashtoreth of the Sidonians. She was the Ishtar of the Accadians and the Astarte of the Greeks (Jer. 44: 17; 1 Kings 11:5, 33; 2 Kings 23:13). There was a temple of this goddess among the Philistines in the time of Saul (1 Sam. 31:10). Under the name of Ishtar, she was one of the great deities of the Assyrians. The Phœnicians called her Astarte. Solomon

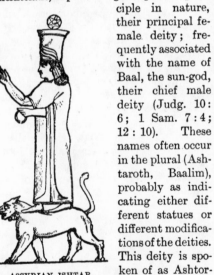

ASSYRIAN ISHTAR.

introduced the worship of this idol (1 Kings 11:33). Jezebel's 400 priests were probably employed in its service (1 Kings 18:19). It was called the "queen of heaven" (Jer. 44:25).

Ash'urites, mentioned among those over whom Ish-bosheth was made king (2 Sam. 2:9).

A'sia is used to denote Proconsular Asia, a Roman province which embraced the western parts of Asia Minor, and of which Ephesus was the capital, in Acts 2:9; 6:9; 16:6; 19:10, 22; 20:4, 16, 18, etc., and probably Asia Minor in Acts 19:26, 27; 21:27; 24:18, and 27:2. Proconsular Asia contained the seven churches of the Apocalypse (Rev. 1:11). The "chiefs of

PROCONSULAR ASIA AND THE SEVEN CHURCHES.

Asia" (Acts 19:31) were certain wealthy citizens who were annually elected to preside over the games and religious festivals of the several cities to which they belonged. Some of these "Asiarchs" were Paul's friends.

Asnap'per—probably the same as Assurbani-pal (Sardanapalos of the Greeks), styled the "great and noble" (Ezra 4:10) —was the son and successor (B.C. 670) of Esar-haddon (*q.v.*). He was "luxurious, ambitious, and cruel, but a magnificent patron of literature." He formed at Nineveh a library of clay tablets, numbering about 10,000. These are now mostly in the British Museum. They throw much light on the history and antiquities of Assyria. Asnapper had much difficulty in retaining possession of his vast empire. Before his death Egypt had successfully revolted from under his power, and Babylonia had regained much of its independence. He was succeeded by Esar-haddon II., the last of the Assyrian kings, and under his reign Nineveh was besieged and destroyed, and the second Assyrian empire perished hopelessly. (See NINEVEH.)

Asp (Heb. *pethen*)—Deut. 32:33; Job 20:14, 16; Isa. 11:8. It is the same as the adder mentioned in Ps. 58:4; 91:13. It was probably the Egyptian cobra (*Naja haje*), which was very poisonous (Rom. 3: 13; Gr. *aspis*). The peace and security of Messiah's reign are represented by the figure of a child playing on the hole of the asp. (See ADDER, COCKATRICE.)

Ass, frequently mentioned throughout Scripture. Of the domesticated species we read of—(1.) The she ass (Heb. *'athon*), so named from its slowness (Gen. 12:16; 45:23; Num. 22:23; 1 Sam. 9:3). (2.) The male ass (Heb. *ḥamor*), the common working ass of Western Asia, so called from its red colour. Issachar is compared to a strong ass (Gen. 49:14). It was forbidden to yoke together an ass and an ox in the plough (Deut. 22:10). (3.) The ass's colt (Heb. *'air*), mentioned Judg. 10:4; 12:14. It is rendered "foal" in Gen. 32: 15; 49:11. (Comp. Job 11:12; Isa. 30:6.) The ass is an unclean animal, because it does not chew the cud (Lev. 11:26. Comp. 2 Kings 6:25). Asses constituted a considerable portion of wealth in ancient times (Gen. 12:16; 30:43; 1 Chr. 27:30; Job 1:3; 42:12). They were noted for their spirit and their attachment to their master (Isa. 1:3). They are frequently spoken of as having been ridden upon—as by Abraham (Gen. 22:3), Balaam (Num. 22:21), the disobedient prophet (1 Kings 13:23), the family of Abdon the judge, seventy in number (Judg. 12:14), Zipporah (Ex. 4: 20), the Shunammite (1 Sam. 25:30), etc. Zechariah (9:9) predicted our Lord's triumphal entrance into Jerusalem, "riding upon an ass, and upon a colt," etc. (Matt. 21:5, R.V.).

Of wild asses two species are noticed— (1) that called in Hebrew *'arod*, mentioned

Job 39:5 and Dan. 5:21, noted for its swiftness; and (2) that called *pe're*, the wild ass of Asia (Job 39:6-8; 6:5; 11:12; Isa. 32:14; Jer. 2:24; 14:6, etc.). The wild ass was distinguished for its fleetness and its extreme shyness. In allusion to his mode of life, Ishmael is likened to a wild ass (Gen. 16:12. Here the word is simply rendered "wild" in the Authorized Version, but in the Revised Version, "wildass among men").

As'shur, second son of Shem (Gen. 10:22; 1 Chr. 1:17). He went from the land of Shinar and built Nineveh, etc. (Gen. 10:11, 12). He probably gave his name to Assyria, which is the usual translation of the word, although the form Asshur is sometimes retained (Num. 24:22, 24; Ezek. 27:23, etc.). In Gen. 2:14 "Assyria" ought rather to be "Asshur," which was the original capital of Assyria, a city represented by the mounds of *Kalah Sherghat*, on the west bank of the Tigris. This city was founded in the Accadian period, before the Semites migrated into Assyria. It is an Accadian word, meaning "water-bank." (See CALAH, NINEVEH.)

As'sos, a sea-port town of Proconsular Asia, in the district of Mysia, on the north shore of the Gulf of Adramyttium. Paul came hither on foot along the Roman road from Troas (Acts 20:13, 14), a distance of 20 miles. It was about 30 miles distant from Troas by sea. The island of Lesbos lay opposite it, about 7 miles distant.

Assur'ance. The resurrection of Jesus (Acts 17:31) is the "assurance" (Gr. *pistis*, generally rendered "faith") or pledge God has given that his revelation is true and worthy of acceptance. The "full assurance [Gr. *plērophoria*, 'full bearing'] of *faith*" (Heb. 10:22) is a fulness of faith in God which leaves no room for doubt. The "full assurance of *understanding*" (Col. 2:2) is an entire unwavering conviction of the truth of the declarations of Scripture—a joyful steadfastness on the part of any one of conviction that he has grasped the very truth. The "full assurance of *hope*" (Heb. 6:11) is a sure and well-grounded expectation of eternal glory (2 Tim. 4:7, 8). This assurance of hope is

ASSYRIAN HUNTING SCENE.

ASSUR-BANI-PAL AND HIS QUEEN FEASTING IN THEIR GARDEN.
(From Assyrian Sculptures.)

the assurance of a man's own particular salvation.

This infallible assurance, which believers may attain unto as to their *own personal salvation*, is founded on the truth of the promises (Heb. 6:18), on the inward evidence of Christian graces, and on the testimony of the Spirit of adoption (Rom. 8:16). That such a certainty may be attained appears from the testimony of Scripture (Rom. 8:16; 1 John 2:3; 3:14), from the command to seek after it (Heb. 6:11; 2 Pet. 1:10), and from the fact that it has been attained (2 Tim. 1:12; 4:7, 8; 1 John 2:3; 4:16).

This full assurance is not of the essence of saving faith. It is the *result* of faith, and posterior to it in the order of nature, and so frequently also in the order of time. True believers may be destitute of it. Trust itself is something different from the *evidence* that we do trust. Believers, moreover, are exhorted to go on to something beyond what they at present have when they are exhorted to seek the grace of full assurance (Heb. 10:22; 2 Pet. 1:5-10). The attainment of this grace is a duty, and is to be diligently sought.

"Genuine assurance naturally leads to a legitimate and abiding peace and joy, and to love and thankfulness to God; and these from the very laws of our being to greater buoyancy, strength, and cheerfulness in the practice of obedience in every department of duty."

This assurance may in various ways be shaken, diminished, and intermitted, but the principle out of which it springs can never be lost. (See FAITH.)

Assyr'ia, the name derived from the city Asshur on the Tigris, the original capital of the country, was originally a colony from Babylonia, and was ruled by viceroys from that kingdom. It was a mountainous region lying to the north of Babylonia, extending along the Tigris as far as to the high mountain range of Armenia, the Gordiæan or Carduchian mountains. It at length, in the seventeenth or sixteenth century B.C., became an independent and a conquering power, and shook off the yoke of its Babylonian masters. It subdued the whole of Northern Asia. The Assyrians were Semites (Gen. 10:22), but in process of time non-Semite tribes mingled with the inhabitants. They were a military people, the "Romans of the East."

Of the early history of the kingdom of Assyria little is positively known. In B.C. 1120 Tiglath-pileser I., the greatest of the Assyrian kings, "crossed the Euphrates, defeated the kings of the Hittites, captured the city of Carchemish, and advanced as far as the shores of the Mediterranean." He may be regarded as the founder of the first Assyrian empire. After this the Assyrians gradually extended their power, subjugating the states of Northern Syria. In the reign of Ahab, king of Israel, the Assyrian king marched an army against the Syrian states, whose allied army he encountered and vanquished at Karkar. This led to Ahab's casting off the yoke of Damascus and allying himself with Judah. Some years after this the Assyrian king marched an army against Hazael, king of Damascus. He besieged and took that city. He also brought under tribute Jehu, and the cities of Tyre and Sidon.

About a hundred years after this (B.C. 745) the crown was seized by a military adventurer called Pul, who assumed the name of Tiglath-pileser II. He directed his armies into Syria, which had by this time regained its independence, and took (B.C. 740) Arpad, near Aleppo, after a siege of three years, and reduced Hamath. Azariah (Uzziah) was an ally of the king of Hamath, and thus was compelled by Tiglath-pileser to do him homage and pay a yearly tribute.

In B.C. 738, in the reign of Menahem, king of Israel, Pul invaded Israel, and imposed on it a heavy tribute (2 Kings 15:8). Ahaz, the king of Judah, when engaged in a war against Israel and Syria, appealed for help to this Assyrian king by means of a present of gold and silver (2 Kings 16:8); who accordingly "marched against Damascus, defeated and put Rezin to death, and besieged the city itself." Leaving a portion of his army to continue the siege, "he advanced through the province east of Jordan, spreading fire and sword," and

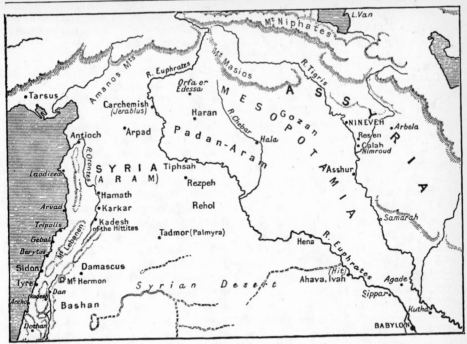

MAP OF ASSYRIA.

became master of Philistia, and took Samaria and Damascus. He died B.C. 727, and was succeeded by Shalmanezer IV., who ruled till B.C. 722. He also invaded Syria (2 Kings 17 : 5), but was deposed in favour of Sargon (*q.v.*) the Tartan, or commander-in-chief of the army, who took Samaria (*q.v.*) after a siege of three years, and so put an end to the kingdom of Israel, carrying the people away into captivity, B.C. 722 (2 Kings 17 : 1-6, 24 ; 18 : 7, 9). He also overran the land of Judah, and took the city of Jerusalem (Isa. 10 : 6, 12, 22, 24, 34). Mention is next made of Sennacherib (B.C. 705), the son and successor of Sargon (2 Kings 18 : 13 ; 19 : 37 ; Isa. 7 : 17, 18) ; and then of Esar-haddon, his son and successor, who took Manasseh, king of Judah, captive, and kept him for some time a prisoner at Babylon, which he alone of all the Assyrian kings made the seat of his government (2 Kings 19 : 37 ; Isa. 37 : 38).

After this there is no further mention made in Scripture of the kingdom of Assyria. From an early period of its history Assyria had entered on a conquering career, and having absorbed Babylon, the kingdoms of Hamath, Damascus, and Samaria, it conquered Phœnicia, and made Judea feudatory, and subjected Philistia and Idumea. At length, however, its power declined. In B.C. 727 the Babylonians threw off the rule of the Assyrians, under the leadership of the powerful Chaldean prince Merodachbaladan (2 Kings 20 : 12), who, after twelve years, was subdued by Sargon, who now reunited the kingdom, and ruled over a vast empire. But on his death the smouldering flames of rebellion again burst forth, and the Babylonians and Medes successfully asserted their independence (B.C. 625), and Assyria fell according to the prophecies of Isaiah (10 : 5-19), Nahum (3 : 19), and Zephaniah (3 : 13), and the many separate kingdoms of which it was composed ceased to recognize the "great king" (2 Kings 18 : 19 ; Isa. 36 : 4). Ezekiel (31) attests (about B.C. 586) how completely Assyria was overthrown. It ceased to be a nation. (See NINEVEH, BABYLON.)

Astrol'oger (Dan. 1 : 20 ; 2 : 2, 10, 27, etc.) —Heb. *'ashshaph'*, an *enchanter*—one who professes to divine future events by the appearance of the stars. This science flourished among the Chaldeans. It was positively forbidden to the Jews (Deut. 4:19; 18:10; Isa. 47:13).

Astronomy. The Hebrews were devout students of the wonders of the starry firmament (Amos 5:8; Ps. 19). In the Book of Job, which is the oldest book of the Bible in all probability, the constellations are distinguished and named. Mention is made of the "morning star" (Rev. 2:28; comp. Isa. 14:12), the "seven stars" and "Pleiades," "Orion," "Arcturus," the "Great Bear" (Amos 5:8; Job 9:9; 38:31), "the crooked serpent," *Draco* (Job 26:13), the *Dioscuri,* or *Gemini,* "Castor and Pollux" (Acts 28:11). The stars were called "the host of heaven" (Isa. 40:26; Jer. 33:22).

The oldest divisions of time were mainly based on the observation of the movements of the heavenly bodies, the "ordinances of heaven" (Gen. 1:14–18; Job 38:33; Jer. 31:35; 33:25). Such observations led to the division of the year into months, and the mapping out of the appearances of the stars into twelve portions, which received from the Greeks the name of the "zodiac." The word "Mazzaroth" (Job 38:32) means, as the margin notes, "the twelve signs" of the zodiac. Astronomical observations were also necessary among the Jews in order to the fixing of the proper time for sacred ceremonies—the "new moons," the "passover," etc. Many allusions are found to the display of God's wisdom and power as seen in the starry heavens (Ps. 8; 19:1–6; Isa. 51:6, etc.).

Asup'pim (1 Chr. 26:15, 17, Authorized Version; but in Revised Version, "storehouse"), properly the house of stores for the priests. In Neh. 12:25 the Authorized Version has "thresholds," marg. "treasuries" or "assemblies;" Revised Version, "storehouses."

A'tad—*buckthorn*—a place where Joseph and his brethren, when on their way from Egypt to Hebron with the remains of their father Jacob, made for seven days a "great and very sore mourning." On this account the Canaanites called it "Abel-mizraim"

(Gen. 50:10, 11). It was probably near Hebron. The word is rendered "bramble" in Judg. 9:14, 15, and "thorns" in Ps. 58:9.

At'aroth—*crowns.* (1.) A city east of Jordan, not far from Gilead (Num. 32:3).

(2.) A town on the border of Ephraim and Benjamin (Josh. 16:2, 7), called also Ataroth-adar (16:5). Now *ed-Dârieh.*

(3.) "Ataroth of the house of Joab" (1 Chr. 2:54), a town of Judah inhabited by the descendants of Caleb.

A'ter—*shut; lame.* (1.) Ezra 2:16. (2.) Neh. 10:17. (3.) Ezra 2:42.

Athali'ah—*whom God afflicts.* (1.) The daughter of Ahab and Jezebel, and the wife of Jehoram, king of Judah (2 Kings 8:18), who "walked in the ways of the house of Ahab" (2 Chr. 21:6), called "daughter" of Omri (2 Kings 8:26). On the death of her husband and of her son Ahaziah, she resolved to seat herself on the vacant throne. She slew all Ahaziah's children except Joash, the youngest (2 Kings 11:1, 2). After a reign of six years she was put to death in an insurrection (2 Kings 11:20; 2 Chr. 21:6; 22:10–12; 23:15), stirred up among the people in connection with Josiah's being crowned as king.

(2.) Ezra 8:7. (3.) 1 Chr. 8:26.

Ath'ens, the capital of Attica, the most celebrated city of the ancient world, the seat of Greek literature and art during the golden period of Grecian history. Its inhabitants were fond of novelty (Acts 17:21), and were remarkable for their zeal in the worship of the gods. It was a sarcastic saying of the Roman satirist that it was "easier to find a god at Athens than a man."

On his second missionary journey Paul visited this city (Acts 17:14; comp. 1 Thess. 3:1), and delivered in the Areopagus his famous speech (17:22–31). The altar of which Paul there speaks as dedicated "to the [properly *an*] unknown God" (23) was probably one of several which bore the same inscription. It is supposed that they originated in the practice of letting loose a flock of sheep and goats in the streets of Athens on the occasion of a plague, and of offering them up in sacrifice, at the spot

THE ACROPOLIS, ATHENS.
(From a Photograph.)

where they lay down, "to the god concerned."

Atone'ment. This word does not occur in the Authorized Version of the New Testament except in Rom. 5:11, where in the Revised Version the word "reconciliation" is used. In the Old Testament it is of frequent occurrence.

The meaning of the word is simply at-one-ment; i.e., the state of being at one or being reconciled, so that atonement is reconciliation. Thus it is used to denote the effect which flows from the death of Christ.

But the word is also used to denote that by which this reconciliation is brought about—viz., the death of Christ itself; and when so used it means satisfaction, and in this sense to make an atonement for one is to make satisfaction for his offences (Ex. 32:30; Lev. 4:26; 5:16; Num. 6:11), and, as regards the person, to reconcile, to propitiate God in his behalf.

By the atonement of Christ we generally mean his work by which he expiated our sins. But in Scripture usage the word denotes the reconciliation itself, and not the means by which it is effected. When speaking of Christ's saving work, the word "satisfaction," the word used by the theologians of the Reformation, is to be preferred to the word "atonement." Christ's satisfaction is all he did in the room and in behalf of sinners to satisfy the demands of the law and justice of God. Christ's work consisted of suffering and obedience, and these were vicarious; i.e., were not merely for our benefit, but were in our stead, as the suffering and obedience of our vicar, or substitute. Our guilt is expiated by the punishment which our vicar bore, and thus God is rendered propitious; i.e., it is now consistent with his justice to manifest his love to transgressors. Expiation has been made for sin; i.e., it is covered. The means by which it is covered is vicarious satisfaction, and the result of its being covered is atonement or reconciliation. To make atonement is to do that by virtue of which alienation ceases and reconciliation is brought about. Christ's mediatorial work and sufferings are the

ground or efficient cause of reconciliation with God. They rectify the disturbed relations between God and man, taking away the obstacles interposed by sin to their fellowship and concord. The reconciliation is mutual; i.e., it is not only that of sinners toward God, but also and pre-eminently that of God toward sinners, effected by the sin-offering he himself provided, so that consistently with the other attributes of his character his love might flow forth in all its fulness of blessing to men. The primary idea presented to us in different forms throughout the Scripture is that the death of Christ is a *satisfaction* of infinite worth rendered to the law and justice of God (*q.v.*), and accepted by him in room of the very penalty man had incurred. It must also be constantly kept in mind that the atonement is not the cause but *the consequence of God's love* to guilty men (John 3:16; Rom. 3:24, 25; Eph. 1:7; 1 John 1:9; 4:9). The atonement may also be regarded as *necessary*, not in an absolute but in a relative sense; i.e., if man is to be saved there is no other way than this, which God has devised and carried out (Ex. 34:7; Josh. 24:19; Ps. 5:4; 7:11; Nahum 1:2, 6; Rom. 3:5). This is God's plan, clearly revealed, and that is enough for us to know.

Atone'ment, Day of, the great day of national humiliation, "the fast" (Acts 27:9), and the only one commanded in the law of Moses. The mode of its observance is described in Lev. 16:3-10; 23:26-32; and Num. 29:7-11.

It was kept on the tenth day of the month Tisri—i.e., five days before the feast of Tabernacles—and lasted from sunset to sunset. (See AZAZEL.)

Attali'a, a town on the coast of Pamphylia, from which Paul and Barnabas sailed into Syria on their return to Antioch after the first missionary journey (Acts 14:25). It is now called *Antali.*

Augus'tus, the cognomen of the first Roman emperor, C. Julius Cæsar Octavianus, during whose reign Christ was born (Luke 2:1). His decree that "all the world should be taxed" was the divinely ordered occasion of Jesus' being born, according to prophecy (Micah 5:2), in Bethlehem. This name being simply a title meaning "majesty" or "venerable," first given to him by the senate (B.C. 27), was borne by succeeding emperors. Before his

death (A.D. 14) he associated Tiberius with him in the empire (Luke 3:1), by whom he was succeeded.

Augus'tus' band (Acts 27:1: literally, *of Sebaste*, the Greek form of *Augusta*, the name given to Cæsarea in honour of Augustus Cæsar). Probably this "band" or cohort consisted of Samaritan soldiers belonging to Cæsarea.

A'va, a place in Assyria from which colonies were brought to Samaria (2 Kings 17:24). It is probably the same with Ivah (18:34; 19:13; Isa. 37:13). It has been identified with *Hit* on the Euphrates.

A'ven—*nothingness; vanity.* (1.) Hosea speaks of the "high places of Aven" (10:8), by which he means Bethel. He also calls it Beth-aven—*i.e.*, "the house of vanity" (4:15)—on account of the golden calves Jeroboam had set up there (1 Kings 12:28).

(2.) Translated by the LXX. "On" in Ezek. 30:17. The Egyptian Heliopolis or city of On (*q.v.*).

(3.) In Amos 1:5 it denotes the Syrian Heliopolis, the modern *Baalbec.*

Aven'ger of blood (Heb. *goël*, from verb *gaäl*, " to be near of kin," " to redeem"), the nearest relative of a murdered person. It was his right and duty to slay the murderer (2 Sam. 14:7, 11) if he found him outside of a city of refuge. In order that this law might be guarded against abuse, Moses appointed six cities of refuge (Ex. 21:13; Num. 35:13; Deut. 19:1, 9). These were in different parts of the country, and every

facility was afforded the manslayer that he might flee to the city that lay nearest him for safety. Into the city of refuge the avenger durst not follow him. This arrangement applied only to cases where the death was not premeditated. The case had to be investigated by the authorities of the city, and the wilful murderer was on no account to be spared. He was regarded as an impure and polluted person, and was delivered up to the *goël* (Deut. 19:11–13). If the offence was merely manslaughter, then the fugitive must remain within the city till the death of the high priest (Num. 35:25).

A'vim, a people dwelling in Hazerim, or "the villages" or "encampments" on the south-west corner of the sea-coast (Deut. 2:23). They were subdued and driven northward by the Caphtorim. A trace of them is afterwards found in Josh. 18:23, where they are called Avites.

Awl, an instrument only referred to in connection with the custom of boring the ear of a slave (Ex. 21:6; Deut. 15:17), in token of his volunteering perpetual service when he might be free. (Comp. Ps. 40:6; Isa. 50:5.)

Axe, used in the Authorized Version of Deut. 19:5; 20:19; 1 Kings 6:7, as the translation of a Hebrew word which means "chopping." It was used for felling trees (Isa. 10:34) and hewing timber for building. It is the rendering of a different word in Judg. 9:48, 1 Sam. 13:20, 21, Ps. 74:5, which refers to its sharpness. In 2 Kings 6:5 it is the translation of a word used with reference to its being made of iron. In Isa. 44:12 the Revised Version renders by "axe" the Hebrew *maätsad*, which means a "hewing" instrument. In the Authorized Version it is rendered "tongs." It is also used in Jer. 10:3, and rendered "axe." The "battle-axe" (army of Medes and Persians) mentioned in Jer. 51:20 was probably, as noted in the margin of the Revised Version, a "maul" or heavy mace. In Ps. 74:6 the word so rendered means "feller." (See the figurative expression in Matt. 3:10; Luke 3:9.)

A'zal (Zech. 14:5) should perhaps be rendered "very near" = "the way cf escape shall be made easy." If a proper name, it may denote some place near the western extremity of the valley here spoken of near Jerusalem.

Azari'ah—*whom Jehovah helps.* (1.) Son of Ethan, of the tribe of Judah (1 Chr. 2:8).

(2.) Son of Ahimaaz, who succeeded his grandfather Zadok as high priest (1 Chr. 6:9; 1 Kings 4:2) in the days of Solomon. He officiated at the consecration of the temple (1 Chr. 6:10).

(3.) The son of Johanan, high priest in the reign of Abijah and Asa (2 Chr. 6:10, 11).

(4.) High priest in the reign of Uzziah, king of Judah (2 Kings 14:21; 2 Chr. 26:17-20). He was contemporary with the prophets Isaiah, Amos, and Joel.

(5.) High priest in the days of Hezekiah (2 Chr. 31:10-13). Of the house of Zadok.

(6.) Several other priests and Levites of this name are mentioned (1 Chr. 6:36; Ezra 7:1; 1 Chr. 9:11; Neh. 3:23, etc.).

(7.) The original name of Abed-nego (Dan. 1:6, 7, 11, 16). He was of the royal family of Judah, and with his other two companions remarkable for his personal beauty and his intelligence as well as piety.

(8.) The son of Oded, a remarkable prophet in the days of Asa (2 Chr. 15:1). He stirred up the king and the people to a great national reformation.

Aza'zel (Lev. 16:8, 10, 26, Revised Version only here; rendered "scape-goat" in the Authorized Version). This word has given rise to many different views. Some Jewish interpreters regard it as the name of a place some 12 miles east of Jerusalem, in the wilderness. Others take it to be the name of an evil spirit, or even of Satan. But when we remember that the two goats together form a type of Christ, on whom the Lord "laid the iniquity of us all," and examine into the root meaning of this word (*viz.*, "separation"), the interpretation of those who regard the one goat as representing the atonement made, and the other, that "for Azazel," as representing the effect of the great work of atonement (*viz.*, the *complete removal* of sin), is certainly to be preferred. The one goat which was "for Jehovah" was offered as a sin-offering, by which atonement was made. But the sins must also be visibly banished, and therefore they were symbolically laid by confession on the other goat, which was then "sent away for Azazel" into the wilderness. The form of this word indicates intensity, and therefore signifies the *total separation* of sin: it was wholly carried away. It was important that the result of the sacrifices offered by the high priest alone in the sanctuary should be embodied in a visible transaction, and hence the dismissal of the "scape-goat." It was of no consequence what became of it, as the whole import of the transaction lay in its being sent into the wilderness bearing away sin. As the goat "for Jehovah" was to witness to the demerit of sin and the need of the blood of atonement, so the goat "for Azazel" was to witness to the efficacy of the sacrifice and the result of the shedding of blood in the taking away of sin.

Azazi'ah—*whom Jehovah strengthened.* (1.) One of the Levitical harpers in the temple (1 Chr. 15:21).

(2.) The father of Hoshea, who was made ruler over the Ephraimites (1 Chr. 27:20).

(3.) One who had charge of the temple offerings (2 Chr. 31:13).

Aze'kah—*dug over*—a town in the Shephelah or low hills of Judah (Josh. 15:35), where the five confederated Amoritish kings were defeated by Joshua and their army destroyed by a hailstorm (10:10, 11). It was one of the places re-occupied by the Jews on their return from the Captivity (Neh. 11:30).

A'zel—*noble*—a descendant of king Saul (1 Chr. 8:37; 9:43, 44).

Azma'veth—*strong as death.* (1.) One of David's thirty warriors (2 Sam. 23:31).

(2.) An overseer over the royal treasury in the time of David and Solomon (1 Chr. 27:25).

(3.) A town in the tribe of Judah, near Jerusalem (Neh. 12:29; Ezra 2:24).

(4.) 1 Chr. 8:36.

Azo′tus, the Grecized form (Acts 8:40, etc.) of Ashdod (*q.v.*).

Azu′bah — *deserted.* (1.) The wife of Caleb (1 Chr. 2:18, 19).

(2.) The daughter of Shilhi, and mother of king Jehoshaphat (1 Kings 22:42).

Az′ur and **Az′zur** — *helper.* (1.) The father of Hananiah, a false prophet (Jer. 28:1).

(2.) The father of Jaazaniah (Ezek. 11:1).

(3.) One of those who sealed the covenant with Jehovah on the return from Babylon (Neh. 10:17).

B

Ba′al — *lord.* (1.) The name appropriated to the principal male god of the Phœnicians. It is found in several places in the plural BAALIM (Judg. 2:11; 10:10; 1 Kings 18:18; Jer. 2:23; Hos. 2:17). Baal is identified with Molech (Jer. 19:5). It was known to the Israelites as Baal-peor (Num. 25:3; Deut. 4:3), was worshipped

FIGURE OF BAAL CARRIED IN PROCESSION.

till the time of Samuel (1 Sam. 7:4), and was afterwards the religion of the ten tribes in the time of Ahab (1 Kings 16:31-33; 18:19, 22). It prevailed also for a time in the kingdom of Judah (2 Kings 8:27; comp. 11:18; 16:3; 2 Chr. 28:2), till finally put an end to by the severe discipline of the Captivity (Zeph. 1:4-6). The priests of Baal were in great numbers (1 Kings 18:19), and of various classes (2 Kings 10:19). Their mode of offering sacrifices is described in 1 Kings 18:25-29. Traces of the wide extent of this form of idolatry are found in the British Isles in the name Bel or Bal, which was the principal deity of the ancient inhabitants. Cairns found on the tops of many hills in Scotland are called "Bel's cairns," the tradition being that sacrifices were offered on them in ancient times.

(2.) A Benjamite, son of Jehiel, the progenitor of the Gibeonites (1 Chr. 8:30; 9:36).

(3.) The name of a place inhabited by the Simeonites, the same probably as Baalath-beer (1 Chr. 4:33; Josh. 19:8).

Ba′alah — *mistress; city.* (1.) A city in the south of Judah (Josh. 15:29), elsewhere called Balah (Josh. 19:3) and Bilhah (1 Chr. 4:29). Now *Khŭrbet Zebâlah.*

(2.) A city on the northern border of the tribe of Judah (Josh. 15:10), called also Kirjath-jearim, *q.v.* (15:9; 1 Chr. 13:6), now *Kŭriet-el-Enab,* or as some think, *'Erma.*

(3.) A mountain on the north-western boundary of Judah and Dan (Josh. 15:11).

Ba′alath, a town of the tribe of Dan (Josh. 19:44). It was fortified by Solomon (1 Kings 9:18; 2 Chr. 8:6). Some have identified it with *Bel′aîn,* in Wâdy Deir Balût.

Ba′alath-be′er — *Baalah of the well* — (Josh. 19:8), probably the same as Baal, mentioned in 1 Chr. 4:33, a city of Simeon.

Baal′bec, called by the Greeks *Heliopolis* — *i.e.,* "the city of the sun" — because of its famous Temple of the Sun, has by some been supposed to be Solomon's "house of the forest

RUINS OF BAALBEC.

of Lebanon" (1 Kings 7:2; 10:17; 2 Chr. 9:16); by others it is identified with *Baal-gad* (*q.v.*). It was a city of Cœle-Syria, on the lowest declivity of Anti-Libanus, about 42 miles north-west of Damascus. It was one of the most splendid of Syrian cities, existing from a remote antiquity. After sustaining several sieges under the Moslems and others, it was finally destroyed by an earthquake in 1759. Its ruins are of great extent.

Ba'al-be'rith—*covenant lord*—the name of the god worshipped in Shechem after the death of Gideon (Judg. 8:33; 9:4). In 9:46 he is called simply "the god Berith." The name denotes the god of the covenant into which the Israelites entered with the Canaanites, contrary to the command of Jehovah (Ex. 34:12), when they began to fall away to the worship of idols.

Ba'ale of Judah — *lords of Judah* — a city in the tribe of Judah from which David brought the ark into Jerusalem (2 Sam. 6:2). Elsewhere (1 Chr. 13:6) called Kirjath-jearim. (See BAALAH.)

Ba'al-gad—*lord of fortune*, or *troop of Baal*—a Canaanite city in the valley of Lebanon at the foot of Hermon, hence called Baal-hermon (Judg. 3:3; 1 Chr. 5:23), near the source of the Jordan (Josh. 13:5; 11:17; 12:7). It was the most northern point to which Joshua's conquests extended. It probably derived its name from the worship of Baal. Its modern representative is *Banias*. Some have supposed it to be the same as Baalbec.

Ba'al-ha'mon—*place of a multitude*—a place where Solomon had an extensive vineyard (Cant. 8:11). It has been supposed to be identical with Baal-gad, and also with Hamon in the tribe of Asher (Josh. 19:28). Others identify it with *Belamon*, in Central Palestine, near Dothaim.

Ba'al-ha'nan — *lord of grace.* (1.) A king of Edom, son of Achbor (Gen. 36:38, 39; 1 Chr. 1:49, 50).

(2.) An overseer of "the olive trees and sycamore trees in the low plains" (the Shephēlah) under David (1 Chr. 27:28).

Ba'al-ha'zor — *having a courtyard,* or *Baal's village*—the place on the borders of Ephraim and Benjamin where Absalom held the feast of sheep-shearing when Amnon was assassinated (2 Sam. 13:23). Probably it is the same with Hazor (Neh. 11:33), now *Tell 'Asûr*, 5 miles north-east of Bethel.

Ba'al-her'mon—*lord of Hermon.* (1.) A city near Mount Hermon inhabited by the Ephraimites (1 Chr. 5:23). Probably identical with Baal-gad (Josh. 11:17).

(2.) A mountain east of Lebanon (Judg. 3:3). Probably it may be the same as Mount Hermon, or one of its three peaks.

Ba'ali—*my lord*—a title the prophet (Hos. 2:16) reproaches the Jewish church for applying to Jehovah, instead of the more endearing title *Ishi*, meaning "my husband."

Ba'alim, plural of Baal; images of the god Baal (Judg. 2:11; 1 Sam. 7:4).

Ba'alis, king of the Ammonites at the time of the Babylonian captivity (Jer. 40:14). He hired Ishmael to slay Gedaliah, who had been appointed governor over the cities of Judah.

Ba'al-me'on—*lord of dwelling*—a town of Reuben (Num. 32:38), called also Beth-meon (Jer. 48:23) and Beth-baal-meon (Josh. 13:17). It is supposed to have been the birth-place of Elisha. It is identified with the modern *M'ain*, about 3 miles south-east of Heshbon.

Ba'al-pe'or—*lord of the opening*—a god of the Moabites (Num. 25:3; 31:16; Josh. 22:17), worshipped by obscene rites. So called from Mount Peor, where this worship was celebrated—the Baal of Peor. The Israelites fell into the worship of this idol (Num. 25:3, 5, 18; Deut. 4:3; Ps. 106:28; Hos. 9:10).

Ba'al-pera'zim — *Baal having rents, bursts,* or *destructions*—the scene of a victory gained by David over the Philistines (2 Sam. 5:20; 1 Chr. 14:11). Called Mount Perazim (Isa. 28:21). It was near the valley of Rephaim, west of Jerusalem. Identified with the modern *Jebel Aly.*

Ba'al-shali'sha — *lord of Shalisha* — a place from which a man came with provisions for Elisha, apparently not far from Gilgal (2 Kings 4:42). It has been identified with *Sirisia*, 13 miles north of Lydda.

Ba'al-ta'mar — *lord of palm trees* — a place in the tribe of Benjamin near Gibeah of Saul (Judg. 20:33). It was one of the sanctuaries or groves of Baal. Probably the palm tree of Deborah (Judg. 4:5) is alluded to in the name.

Ba'al-ze'bub—*fly-lord*—the god of the Philistines at Ekron (2 Kings 1:2, 3, 16). This name was given to the god because he was supposed to be able to avert the plague of flies which in that region was to be feared. He was consulted by Ahaziah as to his recovery.

Ba'al-ze'phon—*sanctuary to Typhon*—an Egyptian town on the shores of the Gulf of Suez (Ex. 14:1; Num. 33:7), over against which the children of Israel encamped before they crossed the Red Sea. It is probably to be identified with the modern *Jebel Deraj.* or *Kulalah*, on the western shore of the Gulf of Suez, a little below its head.

Ba'ana — *son of affliction.* (1.) One of Solomon's purveyors (1 Kings 4:12).

(2.) Son of Hushai, another of Solomon's purveyors (1 Kings 4:16).

(3.) Father of Zadok (Neh. 3:4).

Ba'anah—*son of affliction.* (1.) One of the two sons of Rimmon the Beerothite, a captain in Saul's army. He and his brother Rechab assassinated Ishbosheth (2 Sam. 4:2), and were on this account slain by David, and their mutilated bodies suspended over the pool at Hebron (5, 6, 12).

(2.) The father of Heled, who was one of David's thirty heroes (2 Sam. 23:29; 1 Chr. 11:30).

Ba'asha—*bravery*—the third king of the separate kingdom of Israel, and founder of its second dynasty (1 Kings 15, 16; 2 Chr. 16:1-6). He was the son of Ahijah of the tribe of Issachar. The city of Tirzah he made the capital of his kingdom, and there he was buried, after an eventful reign of twenty-four years (1 Kings 15:33). On account of his idolatries his family was exterminated, according to the word of the prophet Jehu (1 Kings 16:3, 4, 10-13).

Babe, used of children generally (Matt. 11:25; 21:16; Luke 10:21; Rom. 2:20). It is used also of those who are weak in Christian faith and knowledge (1 Cor. 3:1; Heb. 5:13; 1 Pet. 2:2). In Isa. 3:4 the word "babes" refers to a succession of weak and wicked princes who reigned over Judah from the death of Josiah downward to the destruction of Jerusalem.

Ba′bel, tower of, the name given to the tower which the primitive fathers of our race built in the land of Shinar after the Deluge (Gen. 11 : 1–9). Their object in building this tower was probably that it might be seen as a rallying-point in the extensive plain of Shinar, to which they had emigrated from the uplands of Armenia, and so prevent their being scattered abroad. But God interposed and defeated their design by confounding their language, and hence the name Babel, meaning "confusion." In the Babylonian tablets there is an account of this event, and also of the creation and the deluge. (See CHALDEA.)

The Temple of Belus, which is supposed to occupy its site, is described by the Greek historian Herodotus as a temple of great extent and magnificence, erected by the Babylonians for their god Belus. The treasures Nebuchadnezzar brought from Jerusalem were laid up in this temple (2 Chr. 36 : 7).

The *Birs Nimrûd*, at ancient Borsippa,

BIRS NIMRUD.

about 7 miles south-west of Hillah, the modern town which occupies a part of the site of ancient Babylon, and 6 miles from the Euphrates, is an immense mass of broken and fire-blasted fragments, of about 2,300 feet in circumference, rising suddenly to the height of 235 feet above the desert-plain, and is with probability regarded as the ruins of the tower of Babel. This is "one of the most imposing ruins in the country." Others think it to be the ruins of the Temple of Belus.

Bab′ylon—the Greek form of BABEL; Semitic form, *Babilu*, meaning "The Gate of God." In the Assyrian tablets it means "The city of the dispersion of the tribes." It stood on the Euphrates, about 200 miles above its junction with the Tigris, which flowed through its midst and divided it into two almost equal parts. The Elamites invaded Chaldea (*i.e.*, Lower Mesopotamia or Shinar, and Upper Mesopotamia or Accad, now combined into one) and held it in subjection. At length Hammurabi delivered it from the foreign yoke, and founded the new empire of Chaldea (*q.v.*), making Babylon the capital of the united kingdom. This city gradually grew in extent and grandeur, but in process of time it became subject to Assyria. On the fall of Nineveh (B.C. 606) it threw off the Assyrian yoke, and became the capital of the growing Babylonian empire. Under Nebuchadnezzar it became one of the most splendid cities of the ancient world.

After passing through various vicissitudes the city was occupied by Cyrus, "king of Elam," B.C. 538, who issued a decree permitting the Jews to return to their own land (Ezra 1). It then ceased to be the capital of an empire. It was again and again visited by hostile armies, till its inhabitants were all driven from their homes, and the city became a complete desolation, its very site being forgotten from among men.

On the west bank of the Euphrates, about 50 miles south of Bagdad, there is found a series of artificial mounds of vast extent. These are the ruins of this once famous proud city. These ruins are principally (1) the great mound called *Babil* by the Arabs. This was probably the noted Temple of Belus, which was a pyramid about 480 feet high. (2) The *Kasr* (*i.e.*, "the palace"). This was the great palace of Nebuchadnezzar. It is almost a square, each side of which is about 700 feet long. The little town of Hillah, near the site of Babylon, is built almost wholly of bricks taken from this single mound. (3) A lofty mound, on the summit of which stands a modern tomb called *Amran ibn-Ali*. This is probably the most ancient portion of the remains of the city, and represents the ruins of the famous hanging-gardens, or perhaps of some royal palace. The utter desolation of the

city once called "the glory of kingdoms" (Isa. 13:19) was foretold by the prophets (Isa. 13:4–22; Jer. 25:12; 50:2, 3; Dan. 2:31–38).

The Babylon mentioned in 1 Pet. 5:13 was not Rome, as some have thought, but the literal city of Babylon, which was inhabited by many Jews at the time Peter wrote.

In Rev. 14:8; 16:19; 17:5; and 18:2, "Babylon" is supposed to mean Rome, not considered as *pagan*, but as the prolongation of the ancient power in the *papal* form. Rome, pagan and papal, is regarded as one

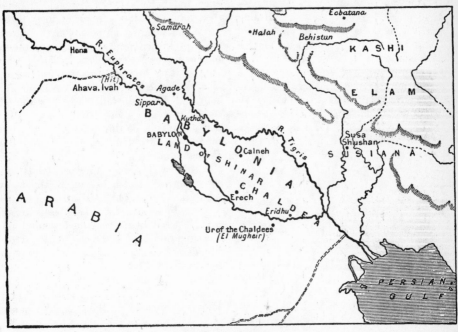

MAP OF BABYLONIA.

power. "The literal Babylon was the beginner and supporter of tyranny and idolatry ......This city and its whole empire were taken by the Persians under Cyrus; the Persians were subdued by the Macedonians, and the Macedonians by the Romans; so that Rome succeeded to the power of old Babylon. And it was her method to adopt the worship of the false deities she had conquered; so that by her own act she became *the heiress and successor* of all the Babylonian idolatry, and of all that was introduced into it by the immediate suc-

cessors of Babylon, and consequently of all the idolatry of the earth." Rome, or "mystical Babylon," is "that great city which reigneth over the kings of the earth" (17:18).

Bab′ylon, kingdom of, called "the land of the Chaldeans" (Jer. 24:5; Ezek. 12:13), was an extensive province in Central Asia along the valley of the Tigris from the Persian Gulf northward for some 300 miles. It was famed for its fertility and its riches. Its capital was the city of Babylon, a great commercial centre (Ezek.

17:4; Isa. 43:14). This kingdom consisted of Accad or Northern Babylonia, and Shinar or Southern Babylonia. It was always a land of mixed races. From the high table-land of Central Asia, the "womb of nations," wave after wave of migrating tribes went forth and settled in the plains of the Tigro-Euphrates valley (Gen. 11:2). These emigrants "from the east," their original home, a mountain-land, found in Shinar an aboriginal population akin to the inhabitants of the mountains of Elam. But they brought with them their language—the Accadian language—and their civilization, and establishing themselves in these Chaldean plains, laid the foundation of the Chaldean empire and civilization.

But another wave of emigrants from the west—Semitic nomads from the Syro-Arabian desert—invaded the valley of Shinar and settled in it, gradually becoming the predominant race. They adopted the cuneiform (wedge-shaped) mode of writing,

CUNEIFORM WRITING.

invented and used by the Accadians, but simplified it and invented the cursive style, which came to be in general use by the Babylonians and Assyrians. These Semites, "bred to a nomad life, wandering for hundreds of miles over their former desert homes, regarding war and plunder as their trade, came now under the influence of settled life and contact with a less hot-blooded people, and directed these characteristics into the channels of trade; and their caravans spread far and wide, bearing with them the elements of this new Semito-Accadian culture."

The two provinces, as they may be called—Shinar and Accad—became at length one, ruled by a king, who bore the title of "lord of the double crown" (i.e., ruler of the two provinces). This was the kingdom of Babylon or Chaldea.

Another result of the Semitic invasion was the founding of a colony on the banks of the Tigris, in the valley watered by the Upper and the Lower Zab. This became the "land of Assur," the kingdom of Assyria (q.v.). At first it was ruled by viceroys from Chaldea; but at length it threw off the Chaldean yoke, and became a conquering power and subdued Babylon (about B.C. 1350), and Nineveh, the capital of Assyria, became now the great centre of civilization.

Babylon once more gained her independence, and under Nebuchadnezzar (q.v.), who died B.C. 561, after a reign of forty-three years, attained great splendour. In the reign of Belshazzar the capital was taken by Darius the Median (Dan. 5:25–31), who entered it unexpectedly at the head of an army of Medes and Persians, as Isaiah (21:1–9) and Jeremiah (51:31) had predicted some 170 years before. Then began the decay and ruin of this proud city, and the kingdom of Babylon became a part of the Persian empire. In course of time the "great city" became "heaps," and "an astonishment, and a hissing, without an inhabitant" (Jer. 51:37–58).

Many of the Jews who had been carried captive to Babylon remained there, notwithstanding the decree of Cyrus. After the destruction of Jerusalem there was established at Babylon a school of Jewish learning of great repute. (See CYRUS.)

Babylo′nish garment, a robe of rich colours fabricated at Babylon, and hence of great value (Josh. 7:21).

Ba′ca, valley of (Ps. 84:6; R.V., "valley of weeping," marg., "or balsam trees"), probably a valley in some part of Palestine, or generally some one of the valleys through which pilgrims had to pass on their way to the sanctuary of Jehovah on Zion; or it may be figuratively "a valley of weeping."

Back′bite. In Ps. 15:3, the rendering of a word which means to run about tattling, calumniating; in Prov. 25:23, secret talebearing or slandering; in Rom. 1:30 and 2 Cor. 12:20, evil-speaking, maliciously defaming the absent.

Back′slide, to draw back or apostatize

in matters of religion (Acts 21 : 21 ; 2 Thess. 2 : 3 ; 1 Tim. 4 : 1). This may be either partial (Prov. 14 : 14) or complete (Heb. 6 : 4–6 ; 10 : 38, 39). The apostasy may be both doctrinal and moral.

Partial backsliding may take place when the heart is in reality right with God, so that it is not always to be taken as an evidence of hypocrisy, which is a studied profession of what has no reality. The causes of backsliding in the case of Christians are manifold, such as the cares of the world, self-indulgence, etc. ; and the cure is just giving a more earnest heed to the counsels and warnings of God's Word.

Badg'er. This word is found in Ex. 25 : 5 ; 26 : 14 ; 35 : 7, 23 ; 36 : 19 ; 39 : 34 ; Num. 4 : 6, etc. The tabernacle was covered with badgers' skins ; the shoes of women were also made of them (Ezek. 16 : 10). The true interpretation of the Hebrew word (*tahash*) has been a matter of some doubt. It has been by different interpreters regarded as denoting an animal like a weasel ; by others as a kind of wolf, or a seal, or a dugong (*Halicore Hemprichii*), a genus of marine pachydermata which are found in the Indian and Red Seas. "Seals' skins" is perhaps the best translation of the word, as in the Revised Version in the passages above referred to (but marg., "porpoise-skins").

Bag. (1.) A pocket of a cone-like shape in which Naaman bound two pieces of silver for Gehazi (2 Kings 5 : 23).

The same Hebrew word occurs elsewhere only in Isa. 3 : 22, where it is rendered "crisping-pins," but denotes the reticules (or as R. V., "satchels") carried by Hebrew women.

(2.) Another word (*kees*) so rendered means a bag for carrying weights (Deut. 25 : 13 ; Prov. 16 : 11 ; Micah 6 : 11). It also denotes a purse (Prov. 1 : 14) and a cup (23 : 31).

(3.) Another word rendered "bag" in 1 Sam. 17 : 40 is rendered "sack" in Gen. 42 : 25 ; and in 1 Sam. 9 : 7 and 21 : 5 "vessel," or wallet for carrying food.

(4.) The word rendered in the Authorized Version "bags," in which the priests bound up the money contributed for the restoration of the temple (2 Kings 12 : 10), is also rendered "bundle" (Gen. 42 : 35 ; 1 Sam. 25 : 29). It denotes bags used by travellers for carrying money during a journey (Prov. 7 : 20 ; Hag. 1 : 6).

(5.) The "bag" of Judas was a small box (John 12 : 6 ; 13 : 29).

Bahu'rim—*young men*—a place east of Jerusalem (2 Sam. 3 : 16 ; 19 : 16), on the road to the Jordan valley. Here Shimei resided, who poured forth vile abuse against David, and flung dust and stones at him and his party when they were making their way down the eastern slopes of Olivet toward Jordan (16 : 5) ; and here Jonathan and Ahimaaz hid themselves (17 : 18).

With the exception of Shimei, Azmaveth, one of David's heroes, is the only other native of the place who is mentioned (2 Sam. 23 : 31 ; 1 Chr. 11 : 33).

Ba'jith — *house* — probably a city of Moab, which had a celebrated idol-temple (Isa. 15 : 2). It has also been regarded as denoting simply the temple of the idol of Moab as opposed to the "high place."

Bake. The duty of preparing bread was usually, in ancient times, committed to the females or the slaves of the family (Gen. 18 : 6 ; Lev. 26 : 26 ; 1 Sam. 8 : 13) ; but at a later period we find a class of public bakers mentioned (Hos. 7 : 4, 6 ; Jer. 37 : 21).

The bread was generally in the form of long or round cakes (Ex. 29 : 23 ; 1 Sam. 2 : 36), of a thinness that rendered them easily broken (Isa. 58 : 7 ; Matt. 14 : 19 ; 26 : 26 ; Acts 20 : 11). Common ovens were generally used ; at other times a jar was half-filled with hot pebbles, and the dough was spread over them. Hence we read of "cakes baken on the coals" (1 Kings 19 : 6), and "baken in the oven" (Lev. 2 : 4). (See BREAD.)

Bake-meats, baked provisions (Gen. 40 : 17), literally "works of the baker," such as biscuits and cakes.

Ba'laam—*lord of the people ; foreigner* or *glutton*, as interpreted by others—the son of Beor, was a man of some rank among the Midianites (Num. 31 : 8 ; comp. 16). He resided at Pethor (Deut. 23 : 4), in Mesopotamia (Num. 23 : 7). It is evident that though dwelling among idolaters he had some knowledge of the true God; and was held in such reputation that it was supposed that he whom he blessed was blessed, and he whom he cursed was cursed. When the Israelites were encamped on the plains of Moab, on the east of Jordan, by Jericho, Balak sent for Balaam "from Aram, out of the mountains of the east," to curse them; but by the remarkable interposition of God he was utterly unable to fulfil Balak's wish, however desirous he was to do so. The apostle Peter refers (2 Pet. 2:15, 16) to this as an historical event. In Micah 6:5 reference also is made to the relations between Balaam and Balak. Though Balaam could not curse Israel, yet he suggested a mode by which the divine displeasure might be caused to descend upon them (Num. 25). In a battle between Israel and the Midianites (q.v.) Balaam was slain while fighting on the side of Balak (Num. 31:8).

The "doctrine of Balaam" is spoken of in Rev. 2:14, in allusion to the fact that it was through the teaching of Balaam that Balak learned the way by which the Israelites might be led into sin. (See NICOLAITANES.) Balaam was constrained to utter prophecies regarding the future of Israel of wonderful magnificence and beauty of expression (Num. 24:5-9, 17).

Bal'adan—*he has given a son*—the father of the Babylonian king (2 Kings 20:12; Isa. 39:1) Merodach-baladan (q.v.).

Ba'lah, a city in the tribe of Simeon (Josh. 19:3), elsewhere called Bilhah (1 Chr. 4:29) and Baalah (Josh. 15:29).

Ba'lak—*empty; spoiler*—a son of Zippor, and king of the Moabites (Num. 22:2, 4). From fear of the Israelites, who were encamped near the confines of his territory, he applied to Balaam (q.v.) to curse them; but in vain (Josh. 24:9).

Bal'ance occurs in Lev. 19:36 and Isa. 46:6, as the rendering of the Hebrew *kaneh'*, which properly means "a reed" or "a cane," then a rod or beam of a balance. This same word is translated "measuring reed" in Ezek. 40:3, 5; 42:16-18. There is another Hebrew word, *mozena'yim*—i.e.,

"two poisers"—also so rendered (Dan. 5:27). The balances as represented on the most ancient Egyptian monuments resemble those now in use.

BALANCE.

A "pair of balances" is a symbol of justice and fair dealing (Job 31:6; Ps. 62:9; Prov. 11:1). The expression denotes great want and scarcity in Rev. 6:5.

Bald'ness from natural causes was uncommon (2 Kings 2:23; Isa. 3:24). It was included apparently under "scab" and "scurf," which disqualified for the priesthood (Lev. 21:20). The Egyptians were rarely subject to it. This probably arose from their custom of constantly shaving the head, only allowing the hair to grow as a sign of mourning. With the Jews artificial baldness was a sign of mourning (Isa. 22:12; Jer. 7:29; 16:6); it also marked the conclusion of a Nazarite's vow (Acts 18:18; 21:24; Num. 6:9). It is often alluded to (Micah 1:16; Amos 8:10; Jer. 47:5). The Jews were forbidden to follow the customs of surrounding nations in making themselves bald (Deut. 14:1).

Balm, contracted from **Bal'sam**, a general name for many oily or resinous substances which flow or trickle from certain trees or plants when an incision is made through the bark.

(1.) This word occurs in the Authorized Version (Gen. 37:25; 43:11; Jer. 8:22; 46:11; 51:8; Ezek. 27:17) as the rendering of the Hebrew word *tsori* or *tseri*, which denotes the gum of a tree growing in Gilead (q.v.), which is very precious. It was celebrated for its medicinal qualities, and was circulated as an article of merchandise by Arab and Phœnician merchants. The shrub so named was highly valued, and was almost peculiar to Palestine. In the time of Josephus it was cultivated in the neighbourhood of Jericho and the Dead Sea. There is an Arab tradition that the tree yielding this balm was brought by the queen of Sheba as a present to Solomon, and that he planted it in his gardens at Jericho.

BALM OF GILEAD.

(2.) There is another Hebrew word, *basam* or *bosem*, from which our word "balsam," as well as the corresponding Greek *balsamon*, is derived. It is rendered "spice" (Cant. 5:1, 13; 6:2; margin of Revised Version, "balsam;" Ex. 35:28; 1 Kings 10:10), and denotes fragrance in general. *Basam* also denotes the true balsam-plant, a native of South Arabia (Cant. *l.c.*).

Ba'mah—*a height*—a name used simply to denote a high place where the Jews worshipped idols (Ezek. 20:29). The plural is translated "high places" in Num. 22:41 and Ezek. 36:2.

Ba'moth — *heights* — the forty-seventh station of the Israelites (Num. 21:19, 20) in the territory of the Moabites.

Ba'moth-Ba'al—*heights of Baal*—a place on the river Arnon, or in the plains through which it flows, east of Jordan (Josh. 13:17; comp. Num. 21:28). It has been supposed to be the same place as Bamoth.

Bands (1) of love (Hos. 11:4); (2) of Christ (Ps. 2:3); (3) uniting together Christ's body the church (Col. 2:19; 3:14; Eph. 4:3); (4) the emblem of the captivity of Israel (Ezek. 34:27; Isa. 28:22; 52:

2); (5) of brotherhood (Ezek. 37:15–28); (6) no bands to the wicked in their death (Ps. 73:4; Job 21:17; Ps. 10:6). Also denotes chains (Luke 8:29); companies of soldiers (Acts 21:31); a shepherd's staff, indicating the union between Judah and Israel (Zech. 11:7).

Ba'ni—*built*. (1.) 1 Chr. 6:46. (2.) One of David's thirty-seven warriors—a Gadite (2 Sam. 23:36). (3.) Ezra 2:10; 10:29, 34, 38. (4.) A Levite who was prominent in the reforms on the return from Babylon (Neh. 8:7; 9:4, 5). His son Rehum took part in rebuilding the wall of Jerusalem (Neh. 3:17).

Ban'ner. (1.) The flag or banner of the larger kind, serving for three tribes marching together. These standards, of which there were four, were worked with embroidery and beautifully ornamented (Num. 1:52; 2:2, 3, 10, 18, 25; Cant. 2:4; 6:4, 10).

(2.) The flag borne by each separate tribe, of a smaller form. Probably it bore on it the name of the tribe to which it belonged, or some distinguishing device (Num. 2:2, 34).

(3.) A lofty signal-flag, not carried about, but stationary. It was usually erected on a mountain or other lofty place. As soon as it was seen the war-trumpets were blown (Ps. 60:4; Isa. 5:26; 11:12; 13:2; 18:3; 30:17; Jer. 4:6. 21: Ezek. 27:7).

(4.) A "sign of fire" (Jer. 6:1) was sometimes used as a signal.

The banners and ensigns of the Roman army had idolatrous images upon them, and hence they are called the "abomination of desolation" (*q.v.*). The principal Roman standard, however, was an eagle. (See Matt. 24:28; Luke 17:37, where the Jewish nation is compared to a dead body, which the eagles gather together to devour.)

God's setting up or giving a banner (Ps. 20:5; 60:4; Cant. 2:4) imports his presence and protection and aid extended to his people.

Ban'quet, a feast provided for the entertainment of a company of guests (Esther 5, 7; 1 Pet. 4:3); such as was provided for our Lord by his friends in Bethany

(Matt. 26 : 6 ; Mark 14 : 3 ; comp. John 12 : 2). These meals were in the days of Christ usually called "suppers," after the custom of the Romans, and were partaken of toward the close of the day. It was usual to send a second invitation (Matt. 22 : 3 ; Luke 14 : 17) to those who had been already invited. When the whole company was assembled, the master of the house shut the door with his own hands (Luke 13 : 25 ; Matt. 25 : 10).

The guests were first refreshed with water and fragrant oil (Luke 7 : 38 ; Mark 7 : 4). A less frequent custom was that of supplying each guest with a robe to be worn during the feast (Eccles. 9 : 8 ; Rev.

3 : 4, 5 ; Matt. 22 : 11). At private banquets the master of the house presided ; but on public occasions a "governor of the feast " was chosen (John 2 : 8). The guests were placed in order according to seniority (Gen. 43 : 33), or according to the rank they held (Prov. 25 : 6, 7 ; Matt. 23 : 6 ; Luke 14 : 7).

As spoons and knives and forks are a modern invention, and were altogether unknown in the East, the hands alone were necessarily used, and were dipped in the dish, which was common to two of the guests (John 13 : 26). In the days of our Lord the guests reclined at table ; but the ancient Israelites sat around low tables,

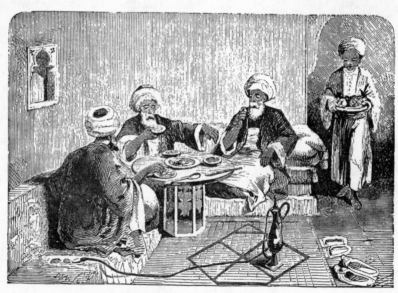

ORIENTALS SITTING AT MEAT.

cross-legged, like the modern Orientals. Guests were specially honoured when extra portions were set before them (Gen. 43 : 34), and when their cup was filled with wine till it ran over (Ps. 23 : 5). The hands of the guests were usually cleaned by being rubbed on bread, the crumbs of which fell to the ground, and were the portion for dogs (Matt. 15 : 27 ; Luke 16 : 21).

At the time of the three annual festivals at Jerusalem family banquets were common. To these the " widow, and the father-

less, and the stranger " were welcome (Deut. 16 : 11). Sacrifices also included a banquet (Ex. 34 : 15 ; Judg. 16 : 23). Birthday banquets are mentioned (Gen. 40 : 20 ; Matt. 14 : 6). They were sometimes protracted, and attended with revelry and excess (Gen. 21 : 8 ; 29 : 22 ; 1 Sam. 25 : 2, 36 ; 2 Sam. 13 : 23). Portions were sometimes sent from the table to poorer friends (Neh. 8 : 10 ; Esther 9 : 19, 22). (See MEALS.)

Bap′tism, Christian, an ordinance immediately instituted by Christ (Matt. 28 :

19, 20), and designed to be observed in the church, like that of the Supper, "till he come." The words "baptize" and "baptism" are simply Greek words transferred into English. This was necessarily done by the translators of the Scriptures, for no literal translation could properly express all that is implied in them.

The *mode* of baptism can in no way be determined from the Greek word rendered "baptize." Baptists say that it means "to dip," and nothing else. That is an incorrect view of the meaning of the word. It means both (1) to dip a thing into an element or liquid, and (2) to put an element or liquid over or on it. Nothing therefore as to the mode of baptism can be concluded from the mere word used. The word has a wide latitude of meaning, not only in the New Testament, but also in the LXX. Version of the Old Testament, where it is used of the ablutions and baptisms required by the Mosaic law. These were effected by immersion, and by affusion and sprinkling; and the same word, "washings" (Heb. 9:10, 13, 19, 21) or "baptisms," designates them all. In the New Testament there cannot be found a single well-authenticated instance of the occurrence of the word where it necessarily means immersion. Moreover, none of the instances of baptism recorded in the Acts of the Apostles (2:38-41; 8:26-39; 9:17, 18; 22:12-16; 10:44-48; 16:32-34) favours the idea that it was by dipping the person baptized, or by immersion, while in some of them such a mode was highly improbable.

The gospel and its ordinances are designed for the whole world, and it cannot be supposed that a form for the administration of baptism would have been prescribed which would in any place (as in a tropical country or in polar regions) or under any circumstances be inapplicable or injurious or impossible.

Baptism and the Lord's Supper are the two symbolical ordinances of the New Testament. The Supper represents the work of Christ, and Baptism the work of the Spirit. As in the Supper a small amount of bread and wine used in this ordinance exhibits in symbol the great work of Christ, so in Baptism the work of the Holy Spirit is fully seen in the water poured or sprinkled on the person in the name of the Father, Son, and Holy Ghost. That which is essential in baptism is only "washing with water," no mode being specified and none being necessary or essential to the symbolism of the ordinance.

The apostles of our Lord were baptized with the Holy Ghost (Matt. 3:11) by his *coming upon* them (Acts 1:8). The fire also with which they were baptized *sat upon* them. The extraordinary event of Pentecost was explained by Peter as a fulfilment of the ancient promise that the Spirit would be *poured out* in the last days (2:17). He uses also with the same reference the expression *shed forth* as descriptive of the baptism of the Spirit (33). In the Pentecostal baptism "the apostles were not dipped into the Spirit, nor plunged into the Spirit; but the Spirit was shed forth, poured out, fell on them (11:15), came upon them, sat on them." That was a real and true baptism. We are warranted from such language to conclude that in like manner when water is poured out, falls, comes upon or rests upon a person when this ordinance is administered, that person is baptized. Baptism is therefore, in view of all these arguments, "rightly administered by pouring or sprinkling water upon the person."

The *subjects* of baptism. This raises questions of greater importance than those relating to its mode.

1. The controversy here is not about "believers' baptism," for that is common to all parties. Believers were baptized in apostolic times, and they have been baptized in all time by all the branches of the church. It is altogether a misrepresentation to allege, as is sometimes done by Baptists, that their doctrine is "believers' baptism," and that the doctrine of the other branches of the church is "infant baptism." Every instance of adult baptism, or of "believers' baptism," recorded in the New Testament (Acts 2:41; 8:37; 9:17, 18; 10:47; 16:15; 19:5, etc.) is just

such as would be dealt with in precisely the same way by all branches of the Protestant Church—a profession of faith or of their being "believers" would be required from every one of them before baptism. The point in dispute is not the baptism of believers, but whether the infant children of believers—*i.e.*, of members of the church—ought to be baptized.

2. In support of the doctrine of infant baptism—*i.e.*, of the baptism of the infants, or rather the "children," of believing parents—the following considerations may be adduced :—

The Church of Christ exists as a divinely organized community. It is the "kingdom of God," one historic kingdom under all dispensations. The commonwealth of Israel was the "church" (Acts 7:38; Rom. 9:4) under the Mosaic dispensation. The New Testament church is not a new and different church, but one with that of the Old Testament. The terms of admission into the church have always been the same —*viz.*, a profession of faith and a promise of subjection to the laws of the kingdom. Now it is a fact beyond dispute that the children of God's people under the old dispensation were recognized as members of the church. Circumcision was the sign and seal of their membership. It was not because of carnal descent from Abraham, but as being the children of God's professing people, that this rite was administered (Rom. 4:11). If children were members of the church under the old dispensation, which they undoubtedly were, then they are members of the church now by the same right, unless it can be shown that they have been expressly excluded. Under the Old Testament parents acted for their children and represented them. (See Gen. 9:9; 17:10; Ex. 24:7, 8; Deut. 29:9-13.) When parents entered into covenant with God, they brought their children with them. This was a law in the Hebrew Church. When a proselyte was received into membership, he could not enter without bringing his children with him. The New Testament does not exclude the children of believers from the church. It does not deprive them of any privilege they enjoyed under the Old Testament. There is no command or statement of any kind, that can be interpreted as giving any countenance to such an idea, anywhere to be found in the New Testament. The church membership of infants has never been set aside. The ancient practice, originally appointed by God himself, must remain a law of his kingdom till repealed by the same divine authority. There are lambs in the fold of the Good Shepherd (John 21:15; comp. Luke 1:15; Matt. 19:14; 1 Cor. 7:14).

"In a company of converts applying for admission into Christ's house there are likely to be some heads of families. How is their case to be treated? How, for example, are Lydia and her neighbour the keeper of the city prison to be treated? Both have been converted. Both are heads of families. They desire to be received into the infant church of Philippi. What is Christ's direction to them? Shall we say that it is to this effect : 'Arise, and wash away your sins, and come into my house. But you must come in by yourselves. These babes in your arms—you must leave them outside. They cannot believe yet, and so they cannot come in. Those other little ones by your side—their hearts may perhaps have been touched with the love of God; still, they are not old enough to make a personal profession, so they too must be left outside......For the present you must leave them where they are and come in by yourselves.' One may reasonably demand very stringent proofs before accepting this as a fair representation of the sort of welcome Christ offers to parents who come to his door bringing their children with them. Surely it is more consonant with all we know about him to suppose that his welcome will be more ample in its scope, and will breathe a more gracious tone. Surely it would be more like the Good Shepherd to say, 'Come in, and bring your little ones along with you. The youngest needs my salvation; and the youngest is accessible to my salvation. *You* may be unable as yet to deal with them about either sin or salvation, but my gracious power can find its way into their hearts even now. I can impart to them pardon and a new life. From Adam they have inherited sin and death; and I can so unite them to myself that in me they shall be heirs of righteousness and life. You may without misgiving bring them to me. And the law of my house requires that the same day which witnesses your reception into it by baptism must witness their reception also'" (*The Church*, by Professor Binnie, D.D.).

Baptism of Christ. Christ had to be formally inaugurated into the public discharge of his offices. For this purpose he came to John, who was the representative of the law and the prophets, that by him he might be introduced into his offices, and thus be publicly recognized as the Messiah of whose coming the prophecies and types had for many ages borne witness.

John refused at first to confer his baptism on Christ, for he understood not what he had to do with the "baptism of repentance." But Christ said, "'Suffer it to be so *now*,'—NOW as suited to my state of humiliation, my state as a substitute in the room of sinners." His reception of baptism was not necessary on his own account. It was a voluntary act, the same as his act of becoming incarnate. Yet if the work he had engaged to accomplish was to be completed, then it became him to take on him the likeness of a sinner, and to fulfil all righteousness (Matt. 3 : 15).

The *official duty* of Christ and the *sinless person* of Christ are to be distinguished. It was in his official capacity that he submitted to baptism. In coming to John our Lord virtually said, "Though sinless, and without any personal taint, yet in my public or official capacity as the Sent of God, I stand in the room of many, and bring with me the sin of the world, for which I am the propitiation." Christ was not made under the law on his own account. It was as surety of his people—a position which he spontaneously assumed. The administration of the rite of baptism was also a symbol of the baptism of suffering before him in this official capacity (Luke 12 : 50). In thus presenting himself he in effect dedicated or consecrated himself to the work of fulfilling all righteousness.

Baptism, John's, was not Christian baptism, nor was that which was practised by the disciples previous to our Lord's crucifixion. Till then the New Testament economy did not exist. John's baptism bound its subjects to repentance, and not to the faith of Christ. It was not administered in the name of the Trinity, and those whom John baptized were rebaptized by Paul (Acts 18 : 24 ; 19 : 7).

Baptism for the dead, only mentioned in 1 Cor. 15 : 29. This expression as used by the apostle may be equivalent to saying, "He who goes through a baptism of blood in order to join a glorified church which has no existence [*i.e.*, if the dead rise not] is a fool." Some also regard the statement here as an allusion to the strange practice which began, it is said, to prevail at Corinth, in which a person was baptized in the stead of others who had died before being baptized, to whom it was hoped some of the benefits of that rite would be extended. This they think may have been one of the erroneous customs which Paul went to Corinth to "set in order."

Bar, used to denote the means by which a door is bolted (Neh. 3 : 3) ; a rock in the sea (Jonah 2 : 6) ; the shore of the sea (Job 38 : 10) ; strong fortifications and powerful impediments, etc. (Isa. 45 : 2 ; Amos 1 : 5) ; defences of a city (1 Kings 4 : 13). A bar for a door was of iron (Isa. 45 : 2), brass (Ps. 107 : 16), or wood (Nah. 3 : 13).

Barab'bas—*i.e., son of Abba* or *of a father*—a notorious robber whom Pilate proposed to condemn to death instead of Jesus, whom he wished to release, in accordance with the Roman custom (John 18 : 40 ; Mark 15 : 7 ; Luke 23 : 19). But the Jews were so bent on the death of Jesus that they demanded that Barabbas should be pardoned (Matt. 27 : 16–26 ; Acts 3 : 14). This Pilate did.

Bar'achel—*whom God has blessed*—a Buzite, the father of Elihu, one of Job's friends (Job 32 : 2, 6).

Barachi'ah—*whom Jehovah hath blessed*—the father of the prophet Zechariah (Zech. 1 : 1, 7 ; Matt. 23 : 35).

Ba'rak—*lightning*—the son of Abinoam (Judg. 4 : 6). At the summons of Deborah he made war against Jabin. She accompanied him into the battle, and gave the signal for the little army to make the attack, in which the host of Jabin was completely routed. The battle was fought (Judg. 4:16) in the plain of Jezreel (*q.v.*). This deliverance of Israel is commemorated in Judg. 5. Barak's faith is commended (Heb. 11:32). "The character of Barak, though pious, does not seem to have been heroic. Like Gideon, and in a sense Samson, he is an illustration of the words in Heb. 11:34, 'Out of weakness were made strong.'" (See DEBORAH.)

Barba'rian, a Greek word used in the New Testament (Rom. 1:14) to denote one of another nation. In Col. 3:11, the word more definitely designates those nations of the Roman empire that did not speak Greek. In 1 Cor. 14:11, it simply refers to one speaking a different language. The inhabitants of Malta are so called (Acts 28:1, 2, 4). They were originally a Carthaginian colony. This word nowhere in Scripture bears the meaning it does in modern times.

Bar'ber. Found only once, in Ezek. 5:1, where reference is made to the Jewish custom of shaving the head as a sign of mourning. The Nazarites were untouched by the razor from their birth (Num. 6:5). Comp. Judg. 16:19.

Barefoot. To go barefoot was a sign of great distress (Isa. 20:2, 3, 4), or of some great calamity having fallen on a person (2 Sam. 15:30).

Bari'ah—*fugitive*—one of Shemaiah's five sons. Their father is counted along with them in 1 Chr. 3:22.

Bar-je'sus—*son of Joshua*—the patronymic of Elymas the sorcerer (Acts 13:6), who met Paul and Barnabas at Paphos. Elymas is a word of Arabic origin meaning "wise."

Bar-jo'na—*son of Jonah*—the patronymic of Peter (Matt. 16:17; John 1:42), because his father's name was Jonas. (See PETER.)

Bar'kos—*painter*—(Ezra 2:53; Neh. 7:55). The father of some of the Nethinim.

Bar'ley, a grain much cultivated in Egypt (Ex. 9:31) and in Palestine (Lev. 27:16; Deut. 8:8). It was usually the food of horses (1 Kings 4:28). Barley bread was used by the poorer people (Judg. 7:13; 2 Kings 4:42). Barley of the first crop was ready for the harvest by the time of the Passover, in the middle of April (Ruth 1:22; 2 Sam. 21:9). Mention is made of barley-meal (Num. 5:15). Our Lord fed five thousand with "five barley loaves and two small fishes" (John 6:9).

Barn, a storehouse (Deut. 28:8; Job 39:12; Hag. 2:19) for grain, which was usually under ground, although also sometimes above ground (Luke 12:18).

Bar'nabas—*son of consolation*—the surname of Joses, a Levite (Acts 4:36). His name stands first on the list of prophets and teachers of the church at Antioch (13:1). Luke speaks of him as a "good man" (11:24). He was born of Jewish parents of the tribe of Levi. He was a native of Cyprus, where he had a possession of land (Acts 4:36, 37), which he sold. His personal appearance is supposed to have been dignified and commanding (Acts 14:8–12). When Paul returned to Jerusalem after his conversion, Barnabas took him by the hand and introduced him to the apostles (9:27). They had probably been companions as students in the school of Gamaliel.

The prosperity of the church at Antioch led the apostles and brethren at Jerusalem to send Barnabas thither to superintend the movement. He found the work so extensive and weighty that he went to Tarsus in search of Saul to assist him. Saul returned with him to Antioch and laboured with him for a whole year (Acts 11:25, 26). The two were at the end of this period sent up to Jerusalem with the contributions the church at Antioch had made for the poorer brethren there (11:28–30). Shortly after they returned, bringing John Mark with them, they were appointed as missionaries to the heathen world, and in this capacity visited Cyprus and some of the principal cities of Asia Minor (Acts 13:14). Returning from this first missionary journey to Antioch, they were again sent up to Jerusalem to consult with the church there regarding the relation of Gentiles to the church (Acts 15:2; Gal.

2:1). This matter having been settled, they returned again to Antioch, bringing the decree of the council as the rule by which Gentiles were to be admitted into the church.

When about to set forth on a second missionary journey, a dispute arose between Saul and Barnabas as to the propriety of taking John Mark with them again. The dispute ended by Saul and Barnabas taking separate routes. Saul took Silas as his companion, and journeyed through Syria and Cilicia; while Barnabas took his nephew John Mark, and visited Cyprus (15:36–41). Barnabas is not again mentioned by Luke in the Acts.

Bar′rel, a vessel used for keeping flour (1 Kings 17:12, 14, 16). The same word (*cad*) so rendered is also translated "pitcher," a vessel for carrying water (Gen. 24:14; Judg. 7:16).

Bar′ren. For a woman to be barren was accounted a severe punishment among the Jews (Gen. 16:2; 30:1–23; 1 Sam. 1:6, 27; Isa. 47:9; 49:21; Luke 1:25). Instances of barrenness are noticed (Gen. 11:30; 25:21; 29:31; Judg. 13:2, 3; Luke 1:7, 36).

Bar′sabas—*son of Saba*—the surname (1) of Joseph, also called Justus (Acts 1:23), —some identify him with Barnabas; (2) of Judas, who was a "prophet." Nothing more is known of him than what is mentioned in Acts 15:32.

Barthol′omew—*son of Tolmai*—one of the twelve apostles (Matt. 10:3; Acts 1:13); generally supposed to have been the same as Nathanael. In the synoptic gospels Philip and Bartholomew are always mentioned together, while Nathanael is never mentioned; in the fourth gospel, on the other hand, Philip and Nathanael are similarly mentioned together, but nothing is said of Bartholomew. He was one of the disciples to whom our Lord appeared at the Sea of Tiberias after his resurrection (John 21:2). He was also a witness of the Ascension (Acts 1:4, 12, 13). He was an "Israelite indeed" (John 1:47).

Bartimæ′us—*son of Timæus*—one of the two blind beggars of Jericho (Mark 10:46; Matt. 20:30). His blindness was miraculously cured on the ground of his faith.

Ba′ruch—*blessed*. (1.) The secretary of the prophet Jeremiah (32:12; 36:4). He was of the tribe of Judah (51:59). To him Jeremiah dictated his prophecies regarding the invasion of the Babylonians and the Captivity. These he read to the people from a window in the temple in the fourth year of the reign of Jehoiakim, king of Judah (Jer. 36). He afterwards read them before the counsellors of the king at a private interview; and then to the king himself, who, after hearing a part of the roll, cut it with a penknife, and threw it into the fire of his winter parlour, where he was sitting.

During the siege of Jerusalem by Nebuchadnezzar, he was the keeper of the deed of purchase Jeremiah had made of the territory of Hanameel (Jer. 32:12). Being accused by his enemies of favouring the Chaldeans, he was cast, with Jeremiah, into prison, where he remained till the capture of Jerusalem (B.C. 586). He probably died in Babylon.

(2.) Neh. 3:20; 10:6; 11:5.

Barzil′lai—*of iron*. (1.) A Meholathite, the father of Adriel (2 Sam. 21:8).

(2.) A Gileadite of Rogelim who was distinguished for his loyalty to David. He liberally provided for the king's followers (2 Sam. 17:27). David on his death-bed, remembering his kindness, commended Barzillai's children to the care of Solomon (1 Kings 2:7).

(3.) A priest who married a daughter of the preceding (Ezra 2:61).

Ba′shan—*light soil*—first mentioned in Gen. 14:5, where it is said that Chedorlaomer and his confederates "smote the Rephaim in Ashteroth," where Og the king of Bashan had his residence. At the time of Israel's entrance into the Promised Land, Og came out against them, but was utterly routed (Num. 21:33–35; Deut. 3:1–3). This country extended from Gilead in the south to Hermon in the north, and from the Jordan on the west to Salcah on the east. Along with the half of Gilead it was given to the half-tribe of Manasseh (Josh. 13:29–31). Golan, one of its cities, became a "city of refuge" (Josh. 21:27). Argob, in Bashan, was one of Solomon's commissariat districts (1 Kings 4:13). The cities of Bashan were taken by Hazael (2 Kings 10:33), but were soon after reconquered by Jehoash (2 Kings 13:25), who overcame the Syrians in three battles, according to the word of Elisha (19). From this time Bashan almost disappears from history, although we read of the wild cattle of its rich pastures (Ezek. 27:6; 39:18; Ps. 22:12), the oaks of its forests (Isa. 2:13; Zech. 11:2), and the beauty of its extensive plains (Amos 4:1; Ps. 68:15; Jer. 50:19). Soon after the Conquest, the name "Gilead" was given to the whole country beyond Jordan. After the Exile, Bashan was divided into four districts—(1.) Gaulonitis, or *Jaulân*, the most western; (2.) Auranitis, the *Haurân* (Ezek. 47:16); (3.) Argob or Trachonitis, now the *Lejah;* and (4.) Batanæa, now *Ard-el-Bathanyeh*, on the east of the Lejah, with many deserted towns almost as perfect as when they were inhabited. (See HAURAN.)

Ba'shan, Hill of (Ps. 68:15), probably another name for Hermon, which lies to the north of Bashan.

Ba'shan-hav'oth-ja'ir—*the Bashan of the villages of Jair*—the general name given to Argob by Jair, the son of Manasseh (Deut. 3:14), containing sixty cities with walls and brazen gates (Josh. 13:30; 1 Kings 4:13). (See ARGOB.)

Bash'emath—*sweet-smelling.* (1.) The daughter of Ishmael, the last of Esau's three wives (Gen. 36:3, 4, 13), from whose son Reuel four tribes of the Edomites sprung. She is also called Mahalath (Gen. 28:9). It is noticeable that Esau's three wives receive different names in the genealogical table of the Edomites (Gen. 36) from those given to them in the history (Gen. 26:34; 28:9).

(2.) A daughter of Solomon, and wife of Ahimaaz, one of his officers (1 Kings 4:15).

Bas'ilisk (in R.V., Isa. 11:8; 14:29; 59:5; Jer. 8:17), the "king serpent," as the name imports; a fabulous serpent said to be three spans long, with a spot on its head like a crown. Probably the yellow snake is intended. (See COCKATRICE.)

Ba'sin or **Ba'son.** (1.) A trough or laver (Heb. *aggan'*) for washing (Ex. 24:6); ren-

dered also "goblet" (Cant. 7:2) and "cups" (Isa. 22:24).

(2.) A covered dish or urn (Heb. *k'fōr*) among the vessels of the temple (1 Chr. 28:17; Ezra 1:10; 8:27).

(3.) A vase (Heb. *mizrâk*) from which to sprinkle anything. A metallic vessel; sometimes rendered "bowl" (Amos 6:6; Zech. 9:15). The vessels of the tabernacle were of brass (Ex. 27:3), while those of the temple were of gold (2 Chr. 4:8).

(4.) A utensil (Heb. *saph*) for holding the blood of the victims (Ex. 12:22); also a basin for domestic purposes (2 Sam. 17:28).

The various vessels spoken of by the names "basin, bowl, charger, cup, and dish," cannot now be accurately distinguished.

The basin in which our Lord washed the disciples' feet (John 13:5) must have been larger and deeper than the hand-basin.

Bas'ket. There are five different Hebrew words so rendered in the Authorized Version:—

(1.) A basket (Heb. *sal*, a twig or osier) for holding bread (Gen. 40:16; Ex. 29:3, 23; Lev. 8:2, 26, 31; Num. 6:15, 17, 19). Sometimes baskets were made of twigs peeled; their manufacture was a recognized trade among the Hebrews.

(2.) That used (Heb. *salsilloth'*) in gathering grapes (Jer. 6:9).

(3.) That in which the first fruits of the harvest were presented—Heb. *téne*—(Deut. 26:2, 4). It was also used for household purposes. In form it tapered downwards like that called *corbis* by the Romans.

(4.) A basket (Heb. *kelûb'*) having a lid, resembling a bird-cage. It was made of leaves or rushes. The name is also applied to fruit-baskets (Amos 8:1, 2).

(5.) A basket (Heb. *dûd*) for carrying figs (Jer. 24:2), also clay to the brick-yard (R.V., Ps. 81:6), and bulky articles (2 Kings 10:7). This word is also rendered in the Authorized Version "kettle" (1 Sam. 2:14), "caldron" (2 Chr. 35:13), "seething-pot" (Job 41:20).

In the New Testament mention is made of the basket (Gr. *kophĭnos*, small "wicker-basket") for the "fragments" in the miracle recorded Mark 6:43, and in that recorded Matt. 15:37 (Gr. *spuris*, large "rope-basket"); also of the basket in which Paul escaped (Acts 9 : 25, Gr. *spuris;* 2 Cor. 11 : 33, Gr. *sarganē,* "basket of plaited cords").

Bas′tard. In the Old Testament the rendering of the Hebrew word *mamzer′,* which means "polluted." In Deut. 23 : 2, it occurs in the ordinary sense of illegitimate offspring. In Zech. 9 : 6, the word is used in the sense of foreigner. From the history of Jephthah we learn that there were bastard offspring among the Jews (Judg. 11 : 1–7). In Heb. 12 : 8, the word (Gr. *nothoi*) is used in its ordinary sense, and denotes those who do not share the privileges of God's children.

Bastina′do—*beating*—a mode of punishment common in the East. It is referred to by "the rod of correction" (Prov. 22 : 15), "scourging" (Lev. 19 : 20), "chastening" (Deut. 22 : 18). The number of blows could not exceed forty (Deut. 25 : 2, 3).

Bat. The Hebrew word (*atalleph′*) so rendered (Lev. 11 : 19; Deut. 14 : 18) implies "flying in the dark." The bat is reckoned among the birds in the list of unclean animals. To cast idols to the "moles and to the bats" means to carry them into dark caverns or desolate places to which these animals resort (Isa. 2 : 20)—*i.e.,* to consign them to desolation or ruin.

Bath, a Hebrew liquid measure, the tenth part of an homer (1 Kings 7 : 26, 38; Ezek. 45 : 10, 14). It contained 8 gallons 3 quarts of our measure. "Ten acres of vineyard shall yield one bath" (Isa. 5 : 10) denotes great unproductiveness.

Baths. The use of the bath was very frequent among the Hebrews (Lev. 14 : 8; Num. 19 : 19, etc.). The high priest at his inauguration (Lev. 13 : 6), and on the day of atonement, was required to bathe himself (16 : 4, 24). The "pools" mentioned in Neh. 3 : 15, 16, 2 Kings 20 : 20, Isa. 22 : 11, John 9 : 7, were public bathing-places.

Bath′-rab′bim—*daughter of many*—the name of one of the gates of the city of Heshbon, near which were pools (Cant. 7 : 4).

Bath′-she′ba—*daughter of the oath,* or *of seven*—called also **Bath-shu′a** (1 Chr. 3 : 5), was the daughter of Eliam (2 Sam. 11 : 3) or Ammiel (1 Chr. 3 : 5), and wife of Uriah the Hittite. David committed adultery

with her (2 Sam. 11 : 4, 5; Ps. 51). The child born in adultery died (2 Sam. 12 : 15–19). After her husband was slain (11 : 15) she was married to David (11 : 27), and became the mother of Solomon (12 : 24; 1 Kings 1 : 11; 2 : 13). She took a prominent part in securing the succession of Solomon to the throne (1 Kings 1 : 11, 16–21).

Bat′tering-ram (Ezek. 4 : 2; 21 : 22), a military engine, consisting of a long beam of wood hung upon a frame, for making breaches in walls. The end of it which was brought against the wall was shaped like a ram's head.

Bat′tle-axe, a mallet or heavy war-club. Applied metaphorically (Jer. 51 : 20) to Cyrus, God's instrument in destroying Babylon.

Bat′tle-bow, the war-bow used in fighting (Zech. 9 : 10; 10 : 4). "Thy bow was made quite naked" (Hab. 3 : 9) means that it was made ready for use. By David's order (2 Sam. 1 : 18) the young men were taught the use, or rather the song of the bow. (See Armour, Bow.)

Bat′tlement, a parapet wall or balustrade surrounding the flat roofs of the houses, required to be built by a special

BATTLEMENT ON HOUSE-TOP.

law (Deut. 22 : 8). In Jer. 5 : 10, it denotes the parapet of a city wall.

Bay, denotes the estuary of the Dead Sea at the mouth of the Jordan (Josh. 15:5; 18:19), also the southern extremity of the same sea (15:2). The same Hebrew word is rendered "tongue" in Isa. 11:15, where it is used with reference to the forked mouths of the Nile.

Bay in Zech. 6:3, 7 denotes the colour of horses, but the original Hebrew means *strong*, and is here used rather to describe the horses as *fleet* or *spirited*.

Bay tree, named only in Ps. 37:35, Authorized Version. The Hebrew word so rendered is *ereḥ*, which simply means "native born"—*i.e.*, a tree not transplanted, but growing on its native soil, and therefore luxuriantly. If the psalmist intended by this word to denote any particular tree, it may have been the evergreen bay laurel (*Laurus nobilis*), which is a native of Palestine. Instead of "like a green bay tree" in the Authorized Version, the Revised Version has, "like a green tree in its native soil."

Bdell'ium, occurs only in Gen. 2:12, where it designates a product of the land of Havilah; and in Num. 11:7, where the manna is likened to it in colour. It was probably an aromatic gum like balsam which exuded from a particular tree (*Borassus flabelliformis*) still found in Arabia, Media, and India. It bears a resemblance in colour to myrrh. Others think the word denotes "pearls," or some precious stone.

Bea'con, a pole (Heb. *to'ren*) used as a standard or ensign set on the tops of mountains as a call to the people to assemble themselves for some great national purpose (Isa. 30:17). In Isa. 33:23 and Ezek. 27:5, the same word is rendered "mast." (See BANNER.)

Beali'ah—*whose Lord is Jehovah*—a Benjamite, one of David's thirty heroes of the sling and bow (1 Chr. 12:5).

Be'aloth—*citizens*—a town in the extreme south of Judah (Josh. 15:24); probably the same as Baalath-beer (19:8). In 1 Kings 4:16, the Authorized Version has "in Aloth," the Revised Version "Bealoth."

Beam occurs in the Authorized Version as the rendering of various Hebrew words. In 1 Sam. 17:7, it means a weaver's frame or principal beam; in Hab. 2:11, a crossbeam or girder; 2 Kings 6:2, 5, a crosspiece or rafter of a house; 1 Kings 7:6, an architectural ornament as a projecting step or moulding; Ezek. 41:25, a thick plank. In the New Testament the word occurs only in Matt. 7:3, 4, 5, and Luke 6:41, 42, where it means (Gr. *dokos*) a large piece of wood used for building purposes, as contrasted with "mote" (Gr. *karphos*), a small piece or mere splinter. "Mote" and "beam" became proverbial for little and great faults.

Beans, mentioned in 2 Sam. 17:28 as having been brought to David when flying from Absalom. They formed a constituent in the bread Ezekiel (4:9) was commanded to make, as they were in general much used as an article of diet. They are extensively cultivated in Egypt and Arabia and Syria.

Bear, a native of the mountain regions of Western Asia, frequently mentioned in Scripture. David defended his flocks against the attacks of a bear (1 Sam. 17:34–37). Bears came out of the wood and destroyed the children who mocked the prophet Elisha (2 Kings 2:24). Their habits are referred to in Isa. 59:11; Prov. 28:15; Lam. 3:10. The fury of the female bear when robbed of her young is spoken of (2 Sam. 17:8; Prov. 17:12; Hos. 13:8). In Daniel's vision of the four great monarchies, the Medo-Persian empire is represented by a bear (7:5).

Beard. The mode of wearing it was definitely prescribed to the Jews (Lev. 19:27; 21:5). Hence the import of Ezekiel's (5:1–5) description of the "razor"—*i.e.*, the agents of an angry providence being used against the guilty nation of the Jews. It was a part of a Jew's daily toilet to anoint his beard with oil and perfume (Ps. 133:2). Beards were trimmed with the most fastidious care (2 Sam. 19:24), and their neglect was an indication of deep sorrow (Isa. 15:2; Jer. 41:5). The custom was to shave or pluck off the hair as a sign of mourning (Isa. 50:6; Jer. 48:37; Ezra 9:3). The beards of David's ambassadors were cut off by Hanun (2 Sam. 10:4) as a mark of indignity.

EGYPTIAN MODES OF WEARING BEARD.

ASSYRIAN MODES OF WEARING BEARD.

On the other hand, the Egyptians carefully shaved the hair off their faces, and they compelled their slaves to do so also (Gen. 41:14).

Beast. This word is used of flocks or herds of grazing animals (Ex. 22:5; Num. 20:4, 8, 11; Ps. 78:48); of beasts of burden (Gen. 45:17); of eatable beasts (Prov. 9:2); and of swift beasts or dromedaries (Isa. 60:6). In the New Testament it is used of a domestic animal as property (Rev. 18:13); as used for food (1 Cor. 15:39), for service (Luke 10:34; Acts 23:24), and for sacrifice (Acts 7:42).

When used in contradistinction to man (Ps. 36:6), it denotes a brute creature generally, and when in contradistinction to creeping things (Lev. 11:2-7; 27:26), a four-footed animal.

The Mosaic law required that beasts of labour should have rest on the Sabbath (Ex. 20:10; 23:12), and in the Sabbatical year all cattle were allowed to roam about freely, and eat whatever grew in the fields (Ex. 23:11; Lev. 25:7). No animal could be castrated (Lev. 22:24). Animals of different kinds were to be always kept separate (Lev. 19:19; Deut. 22:10). Oxen when used in threshing were not to be prevented from eating what was within their reach (Deut. 25:4; 1 Cor. 9:9).

This word is used figuratively of an infuriated multitude (1 Cor. 15:32; Acts 19:29; comp. Ps. 22:12, 16; Eccl. 3:18; Isa. 11:6-8), and of wicked men (2 Pet. 2:12). The four beasts of Daniel 7:3, 17, 23 represent four kingdoms or kings.

Beat'en gold, in Num. 8:4, means "turned" or rounded work in gold. The Greek Version, however, renders the word "solid gold;" the Revised Version, "beaten work of gold." In 1 Kings 10:16, 17, it probably means "mixed" gold, as the word ought to be rendered—*i.e.*, not pure gold. Others render the word in these places "thin plates of gold."

Beat'en oil (Ex. 27:20; 29:40), obtained by pounding olives in a mortar, not by crushing them in a mill. It was reckoned the best. (See OLIVE.)

Beautiful gate, the name of one of the gates of the temple (Acts 3:2). It is supposed to have been the door which led from the court of the Gentiles to the court of the women. It was of massive structure, and covered with plates of Corinthian brass.

Be'cher—*first-born; a youth*—the second son of Benjamin (Gen. 46:21), who came down to Egypt with Jacob. It is probable that he married an Ephraimitish heiress, and that his descendants were consequently reckoned among the tribe of Ephraim (Num. 26:35; 1 Chr. 7:20, 21). They are not reckoned among the descendants of Benjamin (Num. 26:38).

Bed (Heb. *mittah*), for rest at night (Ex. 8:3; 1 Sam. 19:13, 15, 16, etc.); during sickness (Gen. 47:31; 48:2; 49:33, etc.); as a sofa for rest (1 Sam. 28:23; Amos 3:12). Another Hebrew word (*er'es*) so rendered denotes a canopied bed, or a bed with curtains (Deut. 3:11; Ps. 132:3), for sickness (Ps. 6:7; 41:4.)

In the New Testament it denotes sometimes a litter with a coverlet (Matt. 9:2, 6; Luke 5:18; Acts 5:15).

The Jewish bedstead was frequently merely the divan or platform along the sides of the house, sometimes a very slight portable frame, sometimes only a mat or one or more quilts. The only material for bed-clothes is mentioned in 1 Sam. 19:13. Sleeping in the open air was not uncommon, the sleeper wrapping himself in his outer garment (Ex. 22:26, 27; Deut. 24:12, 13).

EASTERN BEDS.

Be'dan, one of the judges of Israel (1 Sam. 12:11). It is uncertain who he was. Some suppose that Barak is meant, others Samson, but most probably this is a contracted form of Abdon (Judg. 12:13).

Bed-chamber, an apartment in Eastern houses, furnished with a slightly elevated platform at the upper end and sometimes along the sides, on which were laid mattresses. This was the general arrangement of the public sleeping-room for the males of the family and for guests, but there were usually besides distinct bed-chambers of a more private character (2 Kings 4:10; Ex. 8:3; 2 Kings 6:12). In 2 Kings 11:2 this word denotes, as in the margin of the Revised Version, a store-room in which mattresses were kept.

Bed'stead, used in Deut. 3:11, but elsewhere rendered "couch," "bed." In 2 Kings 1:4, 20:2, Ps. 132:3, Amos 3:12, the divan is meant by this word.

Bee. First mentioned in Deut. 1:44.

Swarms of bees, and the danger of their attacks, are mentioned in Ps. 118:12. Samson found a "swarm of bees" in the carcass of a lion he had slain (Judg. 14:8). Wild bees are described as laying up honey in woods and in clefts of rocks (Deut. 32:13; Ps. 81:16). In Isa. 7:18 the "fly" and the "bee" are personifications of the Egyptians and Assyrians, the inveterate enemies of Israel.

Beel'zebub (Gr. form **Beel'zebul**), the name given to Satan, and found only in the New Testament (Matt. 10:25; 12:24, 27; Mark 3:22). It is probably the same as Baalzebub (*q.v.*), the god of Ekron, meaning "the lord of flies," or, as others think, "the lord of dung," or "the dung-god."

Be'er—*well*. (1.) A place where a well was dug by the direction of Moses, at the forty-fourth station of the Hebrews in their wanderings (Num. 21:16-18) in the wilderness of Moab. (See WELL.)

(2.) A town in the tribe of Judah to which Jotham fled for fear of Abimelech (Judg. 9:21). Some have identified this place with Beeroth.

Be'er-e'lim—*well of heroes*—probably the name given to Beer, the place where the chiefs of Israel dug a well (Num. 21:16; Isa. 15:8).

Bee'ri—*illustrious*, or *the well-man*. (1.) The father of Judith, one of the wives of Esau (Gen. 26:34), the same as Anah (Gen. 36:2). (2.) The father of the prophet Hosea (1:1).

Be'er-lahai'-roi—*i.e.*, "the well of him that liveth and seeth me," or, as some render it, "the well of the vision of life"—the well where the Lord met with Hagar (Gen. 16:7-14). Isaac dwelt beside this well (24:62; 25:11). It has been identified with '*A in Muweileh*, or *Moilahhi*, south-west of Beersheba, and about 12 miles W. from Kadesh-barnea.

Bee'roth—*wells*—one of the four cities of the Hivites which entered by fraud into a league with Joshua. It belonged to Benjamin (Josh. 18:25). It has by some been identified with *el-Bireh* on the way to Nablûs, 10 miles north of Jerusalem.

Bee'roth of the children of Jaakan (Deut. 10:6). The same as Bene-jaakan (Num. 33:31).

Be′ershe′ba—*well of the oath*, or *well of seven*—a well dug by Abraham, and so named because he and Abimelech here entered into a compact (Gen. 21:31). On re-opening it, Isaac gave it the same name (Gen. 26:31-33). It was a favourite place of abode of both of these patriarchs (21: 33-22:1, 19; 26:33; 28:10). It is mentioned among the "cities" given to the tribe of Simeon (19:2; 1 Chr. 4:28). From Dan to Beersheba, a distance of about 144 miles (Judg. 20:1; 1 Chr. 21:2; 2 Sam. 24:2), became the usual way of designating the whole Promised Land, and passed into a proverb. After the return from the Captivity the phrase is narrowed into "from Beersheba unto the valley of Hinnom"

MOUTH OF ONE OF THE WELLS AT BEERSHEBA.

(Neh. 11:30). The kingdom of the ten tribes extended from Beersheba to Mount Ephraim (2 Chr. 19:4). The name is not found in the New Testament. It is still called by the Arabs *Bir es-Seba* — *i.e.*, "well of the seven"—where there are to the present day two principal wells and five smaller ones. It is nearly midway between the southern end of the Dead Sea and the Mediterranean.

Bee′tle (Heb. *hargol*, meaning "leaper"). Mention of it is made only in Lev. 11:22, where it is obvious the word cannot mean properly the beetle. It denotes some winged creeper with at least four feet, "which has legs above its feet, to leap withal." The description plainly points

to the locust (*q.v.*). This has been an article of food from the earliest times in the East to the present day. The word is rendered "cricket" in the Revised Version.

Beeves (an old English plural of the word *beef*), a name applicable to all ruminating animals except camels, and especially to the *Bovidæ*, or horned cattle (Lev. 22:19, 21; Num. 31:28, 30, 33, 38, 44).

Beg. That the poor existed among the Hebrews we have abundant evidence (Ex. 23:11; Deut. 15:11), but there is no mention of beggars properly so called in the Old Testament. The poor were provided for by the law of Moses (Lev. 19:10; Deut. 12:12; 14:29). It is predicted of the seed of the wicked that they shall be beggars (Ps. 37:25; 109:10).

In the New Testament we find not seldom mention made of beggars (Mark 10: 46; Luke 16:20, 21; Acts 3:2), yet there is no mention of such a class as vagrant beggars, so numerous in the East. "Beggarly," in Gal. 4:9, means worthless.

Behead′, a method of taking away life practised among the Egyptians (Gen. 40: 17-19). There are instances of this mode of punishment also among the Hebrews (2 Sam. 4:8; 20:21, 22; 2 Kings 10:6-8). It is also mentioned in the New Testament (Matt. 14:8-12; Acts 12:2).

Be′hemoth (Job 40:15-24). Some have supposed this to be an Egyptian word meaning a "water-ox." The Revised Version has here in the margin "hippopotamus," which is probably the correct rendering of the word. The word occurs frequently in Scripture, but, except here, always as a common name, and translated "beast" or "cattle."

Be′kah. Both the name and its explanation, "a half shekel," are given in Ex. 38:26. The word properly means a "division," a "part."

Bel, the Aramaic form of Baal, the national god of the Babylonians (Isa. 46: 1; Jer. 50:2; 51:44). It signifies "lord." (See BAAL.)

Be′la—*a thing swallowed*. (1.) A city on the shore of the Dead Sea, not far from Sodom, called also Zoar. It was the only one of the five cities that was spared at

Lot's intercession (Gen. 19:20, 36). It is first mentioned in Gen. 14:2, 8.

(2.) The eldest son of Benjamin (Gen. 46:21; Num. 26:38).

(3.) The son of Beor, and a king of Edom (Gen. 36:32, 33; 1 Chr. 1:43). He was a Chaldean by birth.

(4.) A son of Azaz, a Reubenite (1 Chr. 5:8).

Be'lial—*worthlessness*—frequently used in the Old Testament as a proper name. It is first used in Deut. 13:13. In the New Testament it is found only in 2 Cor. 6:15, where it is used as a name of Satan, the personification of all that is bad. It is translated "wicked" in Deut. 15:9; Ps. 41:8 (marg.); 101:3; Prov. 6:12, etc. The expression "son" or "man of Belial" means simply a worthless, lawless person (Judg. 19:22; 20:13; 1 Sam. 1:16; 2:12; 10:27, etc.).

Bell. The bells first mentioned in Scripture are the small golden bells attached to the hem of the high priest's ephod (Ex. 28:33, 34, 35). Their number is not given. Tradition mentions 66, also 72. The entrance into the holy place by the high priest was heralded by the sound of the bells which he wore. This sound also indicated to the people the time during which he was engaged in his sacred ministrations (Luke 1:9, 10).

The "bells of the horses" mentioned by Zechariah (14:20) were attached to the bridles or belts round the necks of horses trained for war, so as to accustom them to noise and tumult. But it is probable, as some have supposed, that the "bells" here spoken of were cymbals or flat pieces of brass attached to the horses as ornaments; and the circumstance that on these would be inscribed "Holiness to the Lord," denotes that in those happier days to come everything, from the highest to the lowest, the common events and things of life, would be sanctified to the Lord.

Bells of bronze with iron tongues have been found among the Assyrian ruins, but no notice of their existence has been found on the ancient monuments of Egypt.

Bel'lows occurs only in Jer. 6:29, in relation to the casting of metal. Probably they consisted of leather bags similar to those common in Egypt.

Belly, the seat of carnal affections (Titus 1:12; Phil. 3:19; Rom. 16:18). The word is used symbolically for the heart (Prov. 18:8; 20:27; 22:18, marg.). The "belly of hell" signifies the grave or under-world (Jonah 2:2).

Belshaz'zar—*Bel protect the king!*—the last of the kings of Babylon (Dan. 5:1). He was the son of Nabonadius by Nitocris, who was the daughter of Nebuchadnezzar and the widow of Nergal-sharezer. When still young he made a great feast to a thousand of his lords, and when heated by wine sent for the sacred vessels his "father".(Dan. 5:2)—or grandfather—Nebuchadnezzar had carried away from the temple in Jerusalem, and he and his princes drank out of them. In the midst of their mad revelry a hand was seen by the king tracing on the wall the announcement of God's judgment, which that night fell upon him. At the instance of the queen (*i.e.*, his mother) Daniel was brought in, and he interpreted the writing. That night the kingdom of the Chaldeans came to an end, and the king was slain (Dan. 5:30). (See NERGAL-SHAREZER.)

Belteshaz'zar—*Beltis protect the king!* —the Chaldee name given to Daniel by Nebuchadnezzar (Dan. 1:7).

Benai'ah—*built up by Jehovah.* (1.) The son of Jehoiada, the chief priest (1 Chr. 27:5). He was set by David over his body-guard of Cherethites and Pelethites (2 Sam. 8:18; 1 Kings 1:32; 1 Chr. 18:17). His exploits are enumerated in 2 Sam. 23:20, 21, 22; 1 Chr. 11:22. He remained faithful to Solomon (1 Kings 1:8, 10, 26), by whom he was ultimately raised to the rank of commander-in-chief of his whole army in room of Joab, whom he had put to death (1 Kings 2:25, 29, 30, 34, 35; 4:4).

(2.) A Pirathonite, one of David's thirty mighty men (2 Sam. 23:30; 1 Chr. 11:31).

(3.) A musical Levite in the time of David (1 Chr. 15:18, 20).

(4.) A priest appointed to blow the trumpet when the ark was brought into Jerusalem (1 Chr. 15:24; 16:6).

(5.) The son of Jeiel and father of Zechariah (2 Chr. 20:14).

Ben-am'mi—*son of my kindred; i.e.*, "born of incest"—the son of Lot by his youngest daughter (Gen. 19:38); called also Ammon.

Bench, the deck of a Tyrian ship, described by Ezekiel (27:6) as overlaid with box-wood.

Ben'e-ja'akan — *children of Jaakan* (Num. 33:31, 32)—the same as Beeroth (*q.v.*); the wells which the Jaakanites, the descendants of a grandson of Seir the Horite, had dug; the name of one of the encampments of Israel in the wilderness, identified with *el-Mayin*, 60 miles west of Mount Hor.

Ben-ha'dad, the standing title of the Syrian kings, meaning "the son of Hadad," the chief deity of the Syrians.

(1.) The king of Syria whom Asa, king of Judah, employed to invade Israel (1 Kings 15:18).

(2.) Son of the preceding, also king of Syria. He was long engaged in war against Israel. He was murdered probably by Hazael, by whom he was succeeded (2 Kings 8:7-15), after a reign of some thirty years.

(3.) King of Damascus, and successor of his father Hazael on the throne of Syria (2 Kings 13:3, 4). His misfortunes in war are noticed by Amos (1:4).

Ben'jamin—*son of my right hand.* (1.) The younger son of Jacob by Rachel (Gen. 35:18). His birth took place at Ephrath, on the road between Bethel and Bethlehem, at a short distance from the latter place. His mother died in giving him birth, and with her last breath named him Ben-oni—*son of my pain*—a name which was changed by his father into Benjamin. His posterity are called Benjamites (Gen. 49:27; Deut. 33:12; Josh. 18:21).

The *tribe of Benjamin* at the Exodus was the smallest but one (Num. 1:36, 37; Ps. 68:27). During the march its place was along with Manasseh and Ephraim on the west of the tabernacle. At the entrance into Canaan it counted 45,600 warriors. It has been inferred by some from the words of Jacob (Gen. 49:27) that the figure of a wolf was on the tribal standard. This tribe is mentioned in Rom. 11:1; Phil. 3:5.

The *inheritance* of this tribe lay immediately to the south of that of Ephraim, and was about 26 miles in length and 12 in breadth. Its eastern boundary was the Jordan. Dan intervened between it and the Philistines. Its chief towns are named in Josh. 18:21-28.

The *history* of the tribe contains a sad record of a desolating civil war in which they were engaged with the other eleven tribes. By it they were almost exterminated (Judg. 20:20, 21; 21:10). (See GIBEAH.)

The first king of the Jews was Saul, a Benjamite. A close alliance was formed between this tribe and that of Judah in the time of David (2 Sam. 19:16, 17), which continued after his death (1 Kings 11:13; 12:20). After the Exile these two tribes formed the great body of the Jewish nation (Ezra 11:1; 10:9).

The tribe of Benjamin was famous for its archers (1 Sam. 20:20; 36; 2 Sam. 1:22; 1 Chr. 8:40; 12:2) and slingers (Judg. 20:6).

The *gate of Benjamin* (Jer. 37:13; 38:7; Zech. 14:10) was so called because it led in the direction of the tribe of Benjamin, on the north side of Jerusalem. It is called by Jeremiah (20:2) "the high gate of Benjamin;" also "the gate of the children of the people" (17:19-27). Comp. 2 Kings 14:13.

Be'or—*a torch.* (1.) The father of Bela, one of the kings of Edom (Gen. 36:32).

(2.) The father of Balaam (Num. 22:5; 24:3, 15; 31:8). In 2 Pet. 2:15 he is called Bosor.

Be'ra—*gift*, or *son of evil*—king of Sodom at the time of the invasion of the four kings under Chedorlaomer (Gen. 14:2; 17:21).

Bera'chah—*blessing.* (1.) A valley not far from Engedi, where Jehoshaphat overthrew the Moabites and Ammonites (2 Chr. 20:26). It has been identified with the valley of *Bereikût*.

(2.) One of the Benjamite warriors, Saul's brethren, who joined David when at Ziklag (1 Chr. 12:3).

Bere'a, a city of Macedonia to which Paul with Silas and Timotheus went when persecuted at Thessalonica (Acts 17:10, 13), and from which also he was compelled to withdraw, when he fled to the sea-coast and thence sailed to Athens (14, 15). Sopater, one of Paul's companions, belonged to this city, and his conversion probably took place at this time (Acts 20:4). It is now called *Verria.*

Berechi'ah—*blessed by Jehovah.* (1.) Son of Shimea, and father of Asaph the musician (1 Chr. 6:39; 15:17).

(2.) One of the seven Ephraimite chieftains, son of Meshillemoth (2 Chr. 28:12).

(3.) The fourth of the five sons of Zerubbabel, of the royal family of Judah (1 Chr. 3:20).

(4.) The father of the prophet Zechariah (1:1, 7).

Be'red—*hail.* (1.) A town in the south of Palestine (Gen. 16:14), in the desert of Shur, near Lahai-roi.

(2.) A son of Shuthelah, and grandson of Ephraim (1 Chr. 7:20).

Beri'ah—*a gift,* or *in evil.* (1.) One of Asher's four sons, and father of Heber (Gen. 46:17).

(2.) A son of Ephraim (1 Chr. 7:20-23), born after the slaughter of his brother, and so called by his father "because it went evil with his house" at that time.

(3.) A Benjamite who with his brother Shema founded Ajalon and expelled the Gittites (1 Chr. 8:13).

Berni'ce—*bearer of victory*—the eldest daughter of Agrippa I., the Herod Agrippa of Acts 12:20. After the early death of her first husband she was married to her uncle Herod, king of Chalcis. After his death (A.D. 40) she lived in incestuous connection with her brother Agrippa II. (Acts 25:13, 23; 26:30). They joined the Romans at the outbreak of the final war between them and the Jews, and lived afterwards at Rome.

Bero'dach-bal'adan, the king of Babylon who sent a friendly deputation to Hezekiah (2 Kings 20:12). In Isa. 39:1 he is called Merodach-baladan (*q.v.*).

Ber'yl, the rendering in the Authorized Version of the Hebrew word *tarshish,* a precious stone; probably so called as being brought from Tarshish. It was one of the stones on the breastplate of the high priest (Ex. 28:20; R.V. marg., "chalcedony;" 39:13). The colour of the wheels in Ezekiel's vision was as the colour of a beryl-stone (1:16; 10:9; R.V., "stone of Tarshish"). It is mentioned in Cant. 5:14; Dan. 10:6; Rev. 21:20. In Ezek. 28:13 the LXX. render the word by "chrysolite," which the Jewish historian Josephus regards as its proper translation. This also is the rendering given in the Authorized Version in the margin. That was a gold-coloured gem, the topaz of ancient authors.

Be'som, the rendering of a Hebrew word meaning *sweeper,* occurs only in Isa. 14:23, of the sweeping away, the utter ruin, of Babylon.

Be'sor—*cold*—a ravine or brook in the extreme south-west of Judah, where 200 of David's men stayed behind because they were faint, while the other 400 pursued the Amalekites (1 Sam. 30:9, 10, 21). Probably the *Wâdy es Sheriah,* south of Gaza.

Bestead', the rendering in Isa. 8:21, where alone it occurs, of a Hebrew word meaning *to oppress,* or be in circumstances of hardship.

Be'tah—*confidence*—a city belonging to Hadadezer, king of Zobah, which yielded much spoil of brass to David (2 Sam. 8:8). In 1 Chr. 18:8 it is called Tibhath.

Beth occurs frequently as the appellation for a *house,* or *dwelling-place,* in such compounds as the words immediately following :—

Beth'ab'ara—*house of the ford*—a place on the east bank of the Jordan, where John was baptizing (John 1:28). It may be identical with Bethbara, the ancient ford of Jordan of which the men of Ephraim took possession (Judg. 7:24). The Revised Version reads "Bethany beyond Jordan." It was the great ford, and still bears the name of "the ford," *Makhadhet 'Abarah,* "the ford of crossing over," about 25 miles from Nazareth. (See BETHBARAH.)

Beth-a'nath—*house of response*—one of the fenced cities of Naphtali (Josh. 19:38). It is perhaps identical with the modern village *'Ainata,* 6 miles west of Kedesh.

Beth-a′noth—*house of answers*—a city in the mountainous district of Judah (Josh. 15 : 59). It has been identified with the modern *Beit-'Anûn*, about 3 miles north-east of Hebron.

Beth′any—*house of dates.* (1.) The Revised Version in John 1 : 28 has this word instead of Bethabara, on the authority of the oldest manuscripts. It appears to have been the name of a place on the east of Jordan.

(2.) A village on the south-eastern slope of the Mount of Olives (Mark 11 : 1), about 2 miles east of Jerusalem, on the road to Jericho. It derived its name from the number of palm-trees which grew there. It was the residence of Lazarus and his sisters. It is frequently mentioned in connection with memorable incidents in the life of our Lord (Matt. 21 : 17; 26 : 6; Mark 11 : 11, 12; 14 : 3; Luke 24 : 50; John 11 : 1; 12 : 1). It is now known by the name of *el-Azarîyeh—i.e.*, "place of Lazarus," or simply *Lazarîyeh.* Seen from a distance, the village has been described as "remarkably beautiful, the perfection of retirement and repose, of seclusion and lovely peace." Now a mean village, containing about twenty families.

BETHANY (EL-AZARÎYEH).

Beth-ar′abah—*house of the desert*—one of the six cities of Judah, situated in the sunk valley of the Jordan and Dead Sea (Josh. 18 : 22). In Josh. 15 : 61 it is said to have been "in the wilderness." It was afterwards included in the towns of Benjamin. It is called Arabah (Josh. 18 : 18).

Beth-a′ram—*house of the height; i.e.*, "mountain-house"—one of the towns of Gad, 3 miles east of Jordan, opposite Jericho (Josh. 13 : 27). Probably the same as Beth-haran in Num. 32 : 36. It was called by king Herod, Julias, or Livias, after Livia, the wife of Augustus. It is now called *Beit-haran.*

Beth-ar′bel—*house of God's court*—a place alluded to by Hosea (10 : 14) as the scene of some great military exploit, but not otherwise mentioned in Scripture. The Shalman here named was probably Shalmaneser, the king of Assyria (2 Kings 17 : 3).

Beth-a′ven—*house of nothingness; i.e.,* "of idols"—a place in the mountains of Benjamin, east of Bethel (Josh. 7:2; 18:12; 1 Sam. 13:5). In Hos. 4:15; 5:8; 10:5 it stands for "Bethel" (*q.v.*), and it is so called because it was no longer the "house of God," but "the house of idols," referring to the calves there worshipped.

Beth-ba′rah—*house of crossing*—a place south of the scene of Gideon's victory (Judg. 7:24). It was probably the chief ford of the Jordan in that district, and may have been that by which Jacob crossed when he returned from Mesopotamia, near the Jabbok (Gen. 32:22), and at which Jephthah slew the Ephraimites (Judg. 12:4). Nothing, however, is certainly known of it. (See BETHABARA.)

Beth′-car—*sheep-house*—a place to which the Israelites pursued the Philistines west from Mizpeh (1 Sam. 7:11).

Beth-da′gon—*house of Dagon.* (1.) A city in the low country or plain of Judah, near Philistia (Josh. 15:41); the modern *Beit Degan*, about 5 miles from Lydda.

(2.) A city near the south-east border of Asher (Josh. 19:27). It was a Philistine colony. It is identical with the modern ruined village of *Tell D'auk.*

Beth-dib′latha′im—*house of two cakes of figs*—a city of Moab, upon which Jeremiah (48:22) denounced destruction. It is called also Almon-diblathaim (Num. 33:46) and Diblath (Ezek. 6:14).

Beth′el—*house of God.* (1.) A place in Central Palestine, about 10 miles north of Jerusalem, at the head of the pass of Michmash and Ai. It was originally the royal Canaanite city of Luz (Gen. 28:19). The name Bethel was at first apparently given to the sanctuary in the neighbourhood of Luz, and was not given to the city itself till after its conquest by the tribe of Ephraim. When Abram entered Canaan he formed his second encampment between Bethel and Hai (Gen. 12:8); and on his return from Egypt he came back to it, and again "called upon the name of the Lord" (13:4). Here Jacob, on his way from Beersheba to Haran, had a vision of the angels of God ascending and descending on the ladder whose top reached unto heaven (28:10, 19);

and on his return he again visited this place, "where God talked with him" (35:1-15), and there he "built an altar, and called the place El-beth-el" (*q.v.*). To this second occasion of God's speaking with Jacob at Bethel, Hosea (12:4, 5) makes reference.

In troublous times the people went to Bethel to ask counsel of God (Judg. 20:18, 31; 21:2). Here the ark of the covenant was kept for a long time under the care of Phinehas, the grandson of Aaron (20:26-28). Here also Samuel held in rotation his court of justice (1 Sam. 7:16). It was included in Israel after the kingdom was divided, and it became one of the seats of the worship of the golden calf (1 Kings 12:28-33; 13:1). Hence the prophets (Amos 5:5; Hos. 4:15; 5:8; 10:5, 8) call it in contempt Beth-aven—*i.e.,* "house of idols." Bethel remained an abode of priests even after the kingdom of Israel was desolated by the king of Assyria (2 Kings 17:28, 29). At length all traces of the idolatries were extirpated by Josiah, king of Judah (2 Kings 23:15-18); and the place was still in existence after the Captivity (Ezra 2:28; Neh. 7:32). It has been identified with the ruins of *Beitin,* a small village amid extensive ruins some 9 miles south of Shiloh.

(2.) Mount Bethel was a hilly district near Bethel (Josh. 16:1; 1 Sam. 13:2).

(3.) A town in the south of Judah (Josh. 12:16; 15:30).

Beth′elite, a designation of Hiel (*q.v.*), who rebuilt Jericho and experienced the curse pronounced long before (1 Kings 16:34).

Be′ther—*dissection* or *separation*—certain mountains mentioned in Cant. 2:17; probably near Lebanon.

Bethes′da—*house of mercy*—a reservoir (Gr. *kolumbēthra,* "a swimming bath") with five porches, close to the sheep-gate or market (Neh. 3:1; John 5:2). Eusebius the historian (A.D. 330) calls it "the sheep-pool." It is also called "Bethsaida" and "Beth-zatha" (John 5:2, R.V. marg.). Under these "porches" or colonnades were usually a large number of infirm people waiting for the "troubling of the water." It is usually identified with the modern so-called *Fountain of the Virgin,* in the valley of the Kidron, and not far from the Pool of

Siloam (*q.v.*); and also with the *Birket Israel*, a pool near the mouth of the valley which runs into the Kidron south of "St. Stephen's Gate." Others again identify it with the twin pools called the "Souterrains," under the convent of the Sisters of Zion, situated in what must have been the rock-hewn ditch between Bezetha and the fortress of Antonia. But quite recently Schick has discovered a large tank, as sketched here, situated about 100 feet north-west of St. Anne's Church, which is, as he contends, very probably the Pool of Bethesda. No certainty as to its identification, however, has as yet been arrived at. (See FOUNTAIN.)

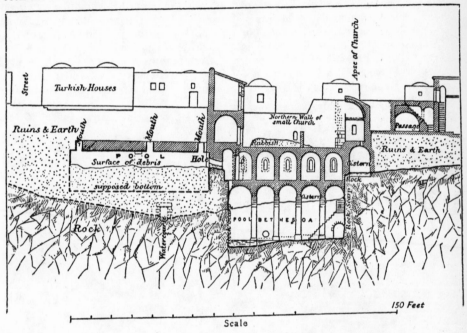

PROBABLE POOL OF BETHESDA. SECTION FROM EAST TO WEST.
(*By permission of the Committee of the Palestine Exploration Fund.*)

Beth-ga′mul—*camel-house*—a city in the "plain country" of Moab denounced by the prophet (Jer. 48 : 23); probably the modern *Um-el-Jemal*, near Bozrah, one of the deserted cities of the Hauran.

Beth-gil′gal—*house of Gilgal*—a place from which the inhabitants gathered for the purpose of celebrating the rebuilding of the walls on the return from exile (Neh. 12 : 29). (See GILGAL.)

Beth-hac′cerem—*house of a vineyard*—a place in the tribe of Judah (Neh. 3 : 14) where the Benjamites were to set up a beacon when they heard the trumpet against the invading army of the Babylonians (Jer. 6 : 1). It is probable that this place is the modern *'Ain Kârim*, or "well of the vineyards," near which there is a ridge on which are cairns which may have served as beacons of old, one of which is 40 feet high and 130 in diameter.

Beth-ho′ron—*house of the hollow*, or *of the cavern*—the name of two towns or villages (2 Chr. 8 : 5; 1 Chr. 7 : 24) in the territory of Ephraim, on the way from Jerusalem to Joppa. They are distinguished as Beth-horon "the upper" and Beth-horon "the nether." They are about 2 miles apart, the former being about 10 miles north-west of Jerusalem. Between the two places was the ascent and descent of Beth-horon, leading from Gibeon down to the western plain (Josh. 10 : 10, 11; 18 : 13, 14), down which the five kings of the Amorites were driven by

Joshua in that great battle, the most important in which the Hebrews had been as yet engaged, being their first conflict with their enemies in the open field. This was indeed one of the decisive battles of the world—"like the battle of the Milvian Bridge, which involved the fall of paganism; or the battle of Poitiers, which sealed the fate of Arianism; or like the battle of Lutzen, which determined the balance of power between Romanism and Protestantism in Germany." Jehovah interposed in behalf of Israel by a terrific hail-storm, which caused more deaths among the Canaanites than did the swords of the Israelites. (Comp. Ex. 9 : 19, 25; Job 38 : 22, 23; Ps. 18 : 12-14; Isa. 30 : 30.) The modern name of these places is *Beit-'ûr*, distinguished by *el-Fôka*, "the upper," and *el-Tahta*, "the nether." (See GIBEON.)

Beth-jesh'imoth—*house of wastes*, or *deserts*—a town near Abel-shittim, east of Jordan, in the desert of Moab, where the Israelites encamped not long before crossing the Jordan (Num. 33 : 49). It was within the territory of Sihon, king of the Amorites (Josh. 12 : 3).

Beth'lehem—*house of bread*. (1.) A city in the "hill country" of Judah. It was originally called Ephrath (Gen. 35 : 16, 19;

BETHLEHEM (BEIT-LAHM).

48 : 7; Ruth 4 : 11). It was also called Beth-lehem Ephratah (Micah 5 : 2), Beth-lehem-judah (1 Sam. 17 : 12), and "the city of David" (Luke 2 : 4). It is first noticed in Scripture as the place where Rachel died and was buried "by the wayside," directly to the north of the city (Gen. 48 : 7). The valley to the east was the scene of the story of Ruth the Moabitess. There are the fields in which she gleaned, and the path by which she and Naomi returned to the town. Here was David's birth-place, and here also, in after years, he was anointed as king by Samuel (1 Sam. 16 : 4-13); and it was from the well of Bethlehem that three of his heroes brought water for him at the risk of their lives when he was in the cave of Adullam (2 Sam. 23 : 13-17). But it was distinguished above every other city as the

birth-place of "Him whose goings forth were of old" (Matt. 2:6; comp. Micah 5:2). Afterwards Herod, "when he saw that he was mocked of the wise men," sent and slew "all the children that were in Bethlehem, and in all the coasts thereof, from two years old and under" (Matt. 2: 16, 18; Jer. 31:15).

Bethlehem bears the modern name of *Beit-Lahm—i.e.*, "house of flesh." It is about 5 miles south of Jerusalem, standing at an elevation of about 2,550 feet above the sea, thus 100 feet higher than Jerusalem.

There is a church still existing, built by Constantine the Great (A.D. 330), called the "Church of the Nativity," over a grotto or cave called the "holy crypt," and said to be the "stable" in which Jesus was born. All the facts and circumstances, however, are against this tradition. Close to it is another grotto, where Jerome the Latin father is said to have spent thirty years of his life in translating the Scriptures into Latin. (See VERSIONS.)

(2.) A city of Zebulun, mentioned only in Josh. 19:15. Now *Beit-Lahm*, a ruined village about 6 miles west-north-west of Nazareth.

Beth-le-Aph'rah (R.V. Micah 1:10)— *house of dust.* The Authorized Version reads "in the house of Aphrah." This is probably the name of a town in the Shephēlah, or "low country," between Joppa and Gaza.

Beth-pe'or—*house of Peor; i.e.*, "temple of Baal-peor"—a place in Moab, on the east of Jordan, opposite Jericho. It was in the tribe of Reuben (Josh. 13:20; Deut. 3:29; 4:46). In the "ravine" over against Beth-peor Moses was probably buried (Deut. 34:6).

Beth'-phage—*house of the unripe fig*—a village on the Mount of Olives, on the road from Jerusalem to Jericho (Matt. 21:1; Mark 11:1; Luke 19:29), and very close to Bethany. It was the limit of a Sabbath-day's journey from Jerusalem—*i.e.*, 2,000 cubits. It has been identified with the modern *Kefr-et-Tûr.*

Bethsai'da—*house of fish.* (1.) A town in Galilee, on the west side of the sea of Tiberias, in the "land of Gennesaret." It was the native place of Peter, Andrew, and Philip, and was frequently resorted to by Jesus (Mark 6:45; John 1:44; 12:21). It is supposed to have been at the modern *'Ain Tâbighah*, a bay to the north of Gennesaret.

(2.) A city near which Christ fed 5,000, and where the blind man had his sight restored (Luke 9:10), on the east side of the lake (Mark 8:22; John 6:17; Matt. 14:15–21), two miles up the Jordan. It stood within the region of Gaulonitis, and was enlarged by Philip the tetrarch, who called it "Julias," after the emperor's daughter. Or, as some have supposed, there may have been but one Bethsaida built on both sides of the lake, near where the Jordan enters it.

Beth-she'an—*house of security* or *rest*—a city which belonged to Manasseh (1 Chr. 7:29), on the west of Jordan. The bodies of Saul and his sons were fastened to its walls. In Solomon's time it gave its name to a district (1 Kings 4:12). The name is found in an abridged form, Beth-shan, in 1 Sam. 31:10, 12 and 2 Sam. 21:12. It is on the road from Jerusalem to Damascus, about 5 miles from the Jordan, and 14 from the south end of the Lake of Gennesaret. After the Captivity it was called *Scythopolis—i.e.*, "the city of the Scythians," who about B.C. 640 came down from the steppes of Southern Russia and settled in different places in Syria. It is now called *Beisân.*

Beth-she'mesh—*house of the sun.* (1.) A sacerdotal city in the tribe of Dan (Josh. 21:16; 1 Sam. 6:15), on the north border of Judah (Josh. 15:10). It was the scene of an encounter between Jehoash, king of Israel, and Amaziah, king of Judah, in which the latter was made prisoner (2 Kings 14: 11, 13). It was afterwards taken by the Philistines (2 Chr. 28:18). It is the modern ruined Arabic village *'Ain-shems*, on the north-west slopes of the mountains of Judah, 14 miles west of Jerusalem.

(2.) A city between Dothan and the Jordan, near the southern border of Issachar (Josh. 19:22), 7½ miles south of Beth-shean. It is the modern *Ain-esh-Shemsîyeh.*

(3.) One of the fenced cities of Naphtali

(Josh. 19:38), between Mount Tabor and the Jordan. Now *Khurbet Shema*, 3 miles west of Safed. But perhaps the same as No. 2.

(4.) An idol sanctuary in Egypt (Jer. 43:13); called by the Greeks Heliopolis, and by the Egyptians On (*q.v.*)—Gen. 41:45.

Beth-tap'puah—*house of apples*—a town of Judah, now *Tûffûh*, 5 miles west of Hebron (Josh. 15:53).

Bethu'el—*man of God*, or *virgin of God*, or *house of God*. (1.) The son of Nahor by Milcah; nephew of Abraham, and father of Rebekah (Gen. 22:22, 23; 24:15, 24, 47). He appears in person only once (24:50).

(2.) A southern city of Judah (1 Chr. 4:30); called also Bethul (Josh. 19:4) and Bethel (12:16; 1 Sam. 30:27).

Beth'zur—*house of rock*—a town in the mountains of Judah (Josh. 15:58), about 4 miles to the north of Hebron. It was built by Rehoboam for the defence of his kingdom (2 Chr. 11:7). It stood near the modern *ed-Dirweh*. Its ruins are still seen on a hill which bears the name of *Beit-Sûr*, and which commands the road from Beer-sheba and Hebron to Jerusalem from the south.

Betroth', to promise "by one's truth." Men and women were betrothed when they were engaged to be married. This usually took place a year or more before marriage. From the time of betrothal the woman was regarded as the lawful wife of the man to whom she was betrothed (Deut. 28:30; Judg. 14:2, 8; Matt. 1:18–21). The term is figuratively employed of the spiritual connection between God and his people (Hos. 2:19, 20).

Beu'lah—*married*—is used in Isa. 62:4 metaphorically as the name of Judea: "The land shall be married," *i.e.*, favoured and blessed of the Lord.

Bewray', to reveal or disclose; an old English word equivalent to "betray" (Prov. 27:16; 29:24, R.V., "uttereth;" Isa. 16:3; Matt. 26:73).

Beyond', when used with reference to Jordan, signifies in the writings of Moses the west side of the river, as he wrote on the east bank (Gen. 1:10, 11; Deut. 1:1, 5; 3:8, 20; 4:46); but in the writings of Joshua, after he had crossed the river, it means the east side (Josh. 5:1; 12:7; 22:7).

Bezal'eel—*in the shadow of God; i.e.*, "under his protection"—the artificer who executed the work of art in connection with the tabernacle in the wilderness (Ex. 31:2; 35:30). He was engaged principally in works of metal, wood, and stone; while Aholiab, who was associated with him and subordinate to him, had the charge of the textile fabrics (36:1, 2; 38:22). He was of the tribe of Judah, the son of Uri, and grandson of Hur (31:2). Mention is made in Ezra 10:30 of another of the same name.

Be'zek—*lightning*. (1.) The residence of Adoni-bezek, in the lot of Judah (Judg. 1:5). It was in the mountains, not far from Jerusalem. Probably the modern *Bezkah*, 6 miles south-east of Lydda.

(2.) The place where Saul numbered the forces of Israel and Judah (1 Sam. 11:8); somewhere in the centre of the country, near the Jordan valley. Probably the modern *Ibzik*, 13 miles north-east of Shechem.

Be'zer—*ore* of gold or silver. (1.) A city of the Reubenites; one of the three cities of refuge on the east of Jordan (Deut. 4:43; Josh. 20:8). It has been identified with the modern ruined village of *Burazin*, some 12 miles north of Heshbon; also with *Kasur-el-Besheir*, 2 miles south-west of Dibon.

(2.) A descendant of Asher (1 Chr. 7:37).

Bible, the English form of the Greek name *Biblia*, meaning "books," the name which in the fifth century began to be given to the entire collection of sacred books, the "Library of Divine Revelation." The name Bible was adopted by Wickliffe, and came gradually into use in our English language. The Bible consists of sixty-six different books, composed by many different writers, in three different languages, under different circumstances; writers of almost every social rank—statesmen and peasants, kings, herdsmen, fishermen, priests, tax-gatherers, tentmakers; educated and uneducated, Jews and Gentiles; most of them unknown to each other, and writing at various periods during the space of about 1600 years: and yet, after all, it is only *one* book dealing with only *one* subject in its numberless aspects and relations—the subject of man's redemption.

It is divided into the Old Testament, containing thirty-nine books, and the New Testament, containing twenty-seven books. The names given to the Old in the writings of the New are "the scriptures" (Matt. 21:42), "scripture" (2 Pet. 1:20), "the holy scriptures" (Rom. 1:2), "the law" (John 12:34), "the law, the prophets, and the psalms" (Luke 24:44), "the law and the prophets" (Matt. 5:17), "the old covenant" (2 Cor. 3:14, R.V.). There is a break of 400 years between the Old Testament and the New. (See APOCRYPHA.)

The Old Testament is divided into three parts:—1. The *Law* (*Tôrâh*), consisting of the Pentateuch, or five books of Moses. 2. The *Prophets*, consisting of (1) the former — namely, Joshua, Judges, the Books of Samuel, and the Books of Kings; (2) the latter—namely, the greater prophets, Isaiah, Jeremiah, and Ezekiel, and the twelve minor prophets. 3. The *Hagiographa*, or holy writings, including the rest of the books. These were ranked in three divisions:—(1) The Psalms, Proverbs, and Job, distinguished by the Hebrew name, a word formed of the initial letters of these books, *emeth*, meaning *truth*. (2) Canticles, Ruth, Lamentations, Ecclesiastes, and Esther, called the *five rolls*, as being written for the synagogue use on five separate rolls. (3) Daniel, Ezra, Nehemiah, and 1 and 2 Chronicles. Between the Old and the New Testament no addition was made to the revelation God had already given. The period of New Testament revelation, extending over a century, began with the appearance of John the Baptist.

The *New Testament* consists of (1) the historical books—*viz.*, the Gospels, and the Acts of the Apostles; (2) the Epistles; and (3) the book of prophecy, the Revelation.

The division of the Bible into chapters and verses is altogether of human invention, designed to facilitate reference to it.

The ancient Jews divided the Old Testament into certain sections for use in the synagogue service, and then at a later period, in the ninth century A.D., into verses. Our modern system of chapters for all the books of the Bible was introduced by Cardinal Hugo about the middle of the thirteenth century (he died 1263). The system of verses for the New Testament was introduced by Stephens in 1551 and generally adopted, although neither Tyndale's nor Coverdale's English translation of the Bible has verses. The division is not always wisely made, yet it is very useful. (See VERSIONS.)

Bier, the frame on which dead bodies were conveyed to the grave (Luke 7:14).

Big′tha—*garden,* or *gift of fortune*—one of the seven eunuchs or chamberlains who had charge of the harem of Ahasuerus (Esther 1:10).

Big′than, one of the eunuchs who "kept the door" in the court of Ahasuerus. With Teresh he conspired against the king's life. Mordecai detected the conspiracy, and the culprits were hanged (Esther 2:21-23; 6:1-3).

Bil′dad—*son of contention*—one of Job's friends. He is called "the Shuhite," probably as belonging to Shuah, a district in Arabia, in which Shuah, the sixth son of Abraham by Keturah, settled (Gen. 25:2). He took part in each of the three controversies into which Job's friends entered with him (Job 8:1; 18:1; 25:1), and delivered three speeches, very severe and stern in their tone, although less violent than those of Zophar, but more so than those of Eliphaz.

Bil′gah—*cheerful.* (1.) The head of the fifteenth sacerdotal course for the temple service (1 Chr. 24:14). (2.) A priest who returned from Babylon with Zerubbabel (Neh. 12:5, 18).

Bil′hah — *faltering; bashful* — Rachel's handmaid, whom she gave to Jacob (Gen. 29:29). She was the mother of Dan and Naphtali (Gen. 30:3-8). Reuben was cursed by his father for committing adultery with her (35:22; 49:4). He was deprived of the birth-right, which was given to the sons of Joseph.

Bil'shan—*son of the tongue; i.e.,* "eloquent "—a man of some note who returned from the Captivity with Zerubbabel (Ezra 2 : 2 ; Neh. 7 : 7).

Bird. Birds are divided in the Mosaic law into two classes—(1) the *clean* (Lev. 1 : 14-17 ; 5 : 7-10 ; 14 : 4-7), which were offered in sacrifice ; and (2) the *unclean* (Lev. 11 : 13-20). When offered in sacrifice, they were not divided as other victims were (Gen. 15 : 10). They are mentioned also as an article of food (Deut. 14 : 11). The art of snaring wild birds is referred to (Ps. 124 : 7 ; Prov. 1 : 17 ; 7 : 23 ; Jer. 5 : 27). Singing birds are mentioned in Ps. 104 : 12 ; Eccl. 12 : 4. Their timidity is alluded to (Hos. 11 : 11). The reference in Ps. 84 : 3 to the swallow and the sparrow may be only a comparison equivalent to, "What her house is to the sparrow, and her nest to the swallow, that thine altars are to my soul."

Bir'sha—*son of wickedness*—a king of Gomorrah whom Abraham succoured in the invasion of Chedorlaomer (Gen. 14 : 2).

Birth. As soon as a child was born it was washed, and rubbed with salt (Ezek. 16 : 4), and then swathed with bandages (Job 38 : 9 ; Luke 2 : 7, 11). A Hebrew mother remained forty days in seclusion after the birth of a son, and after the birth of a daughter double that number of days. At the close of that period she entered into the tabernacle or temple and offered up a sacrifice of purification (Lev. 12 : 1-8 ; Luke 2 : 22). A son was circumcised on the eighth day after his birth, being thereby consecrated to God (Gen. 17 : 10-12 ; comp. Rom. 4 : 11). Seasons of misfortune are likened to the pains of a woman in travail, and seasons of prosperity to the joy that succeeds child-birth (Isa. 13 : 8 ; Jer. 4 : 31 ; John 16 : 21, 22). The natural birth is referred to as the emblem of the new birth (John 3 : 3-8 ; Gal. 6 : 15 ; Titus 3 : 5, etc.).

Birth'-day. The observance of birthdays was common in early times (Job 1 : 4, 13, 18). They were specially celebrated in the land of Egypt (Gen. 40 : 20). There is no recorded instance in Scripture of the celebration of birth-days among the Jews.

On the occasion of Herod's birth-day John the Baptist was beheaded (Matt. 14 : 6).

Birth'right. (1.) This word denotes the special privileges and advantages belonging to the first-born son among the Jews. He became the priest of the family. Thus Reuben was the first-born of the patriarchs, and so the priesthood of the tribes belonged to him. That honour was, however, transferred by God from Reuben to Levi (Num. 3 : 12, 13 ; 8 : 18).

(2.) The first-born son had allotted to him also a double portion of the paternal inheritance (Deut. 21 : 15-17). Reuben was, because of his undutiful conduct, deprived of his birth-right (Gen. 49 : 4 ; 1 Chr. 5 : 1). Esau transferred his birth-right to Jacob (Gen. 25 : 33).

(3.) The first-born inherited the judicial authority of his father, whatever it might be (2 Chr. 21 : 3). By divine appointment, however, David excluded Adonijah in favour of Solomon.

(4.) The Jews attached a sacred importance to the rank of "first-born" and "first-begotten" as applied to the Messiah (Rom. 8 : 29 ; Col. 1 : 18 ; Heb. 1 : 4-6). As first-born he has an inheritance superior to his brethren, and is the alone true priest.

Bishop — *an overseer.* In apostolic times, it is quite manifest that there was no difference as to order between bishops and elders or presbyters (Acts 20 : 17-28 ; 1 Pet. 5 : 1, 2 ; Phil. 1 : 1 ; 1 Tim. 3). The term *bishop* is never once used to denote a different office from that of elder or presbyter. These different names are simply titles of the same office, "bishop" designating the *function*—namely, that of oversight—and "presbyter" the *dignity* appertaining to the office. Christ is figuratively called "the *bishop* [*episcopos*] of souls" (1 Pet. 2 : 25).

Bit, the curb put into the mouths of horses to restrain them. The Hebrew word (*metheg*) so rendered in Ps. 32 : 9 is elsewhere translated "bridle" (2 Kings 19 : 28 ; Prov. 26 : 3 ; Isa. 37 : 29). Bits were generally made of bronze or iron, but sometimes also of gold or silver. In James 3 : 3 the Authorized Version translates the Greek word by "bits," but the Revised Version by "bridles."

Bith'-ron—*the broken or divided place*—a district in the Arabah or Jordan valley, on the east of the river (2 Sam. 2:29). It was probably the designation of the region in general, which is broken and intersected by ravines.

Bithyn'ia, a province in Asia Minor, to the south of the Euxine and Propontis. Christian congregations were here formed at an early time (1 Pet. 1:1). Paul was prevented by the Spirit from entering this province (Acts 16:7). It is noted in church history as the province ruled over by Pliny as Roman proconsul, who was perplexed as to the course he should take with the numerous Christians brought before his tribunal on account of their profession of Christianity and their conduct, and wrote to Trajan, the emperor, for instructions (A.D. 107).

Bit'ter. Bitterness is symbolical of affliction, misery, and servitude (Ex. 1:14; Ruth 1:20; Jer. 9:15). The Chaldeans are called the "bitter and hasty nation" (Hab. 1:6). The "gall of bitterness" expresses a state of great wickedness (Acts 8:23). A "root of bitterness" is a wicked person or a dangerous sin (Heb. 12:15).

The Passover was to be eaten with "bitter herbs" (Ex. 12:8; Num. 9:11). The kind of herbs so designated is not known. Probably they were any bitter herbs obtainable at the place and time when the Passover was celebrated. They represented the severity of the servitude under which the people groaned; and have been regarded also as typical of the sufferings of Christ.

Bit'tern is found three times in connection with the desolations to come upon Babylon, Idumea, and Nineveh (Isa. 14:23; 34:11; Zeph. 2:14). This bird belongs to the class of cranes. Its scientific name is *Botaurus stellaris*. It is a solitary bird, frequenting marshy ground. The Hebrew word (*kippôd*) thus rendered in the Authorized Version is rendered "porcupine" in the Revised Version. But in the passages noted the *kippôd* is associated

with birds, with pools of water, and with solitude and desolation. This favours the idea that not the "porcupine" but the "bittern" is really intended by the word.

BITTERN.

Bit'umen (Gen. 11:3, R.V., margin, rendered in the A.V. "slime"), a mineral pitch. With this the ark was pitched (6:14. See also Ex. 2:3.) (See SLIME.)

Black, properly the absence of all colour. In Prov. 7:9 the Hebrew word means, as in the margin of the Revised Version, "the *pupil* of the eye." It is translated "apple" of the eye in Deut. 32:10; Ps. 17:8; Prov. 7:2. It is a different word which is rendered "black" in Lev. 13:31, 37; Cant. 1:5; 5:11; and Zech. 6:2, 6. It is uncertain what the "black marble" of Esther 1:6 was which formed a part of the mosaic pavement.

Blade, applied to the glittering point of a spear (Job 39:23) or sword (Nah. 3:3), the blade of a dagger (Judg. 3:22); the "shoulder blade" (Job 31:22); the "blade" of cereals (Matt. 13:26).

Blains occurs only in connection with the sixth plague of Egypt (Ex. 9:9, 10). In Deut. 28:27, 35, it is called "the botch of Egypt." It seems to have been the fearful disease of black leprosy, a kind of elephantiasis, producing burning ulcers.

Blas'phemy. In the sense of speaking evil of God this word is found in Ps. 74:18; Isa. 52:5; Rom. 2:24; Rev. 13:1, 6;

16:9, 11, 21. It denotes also any kind of calumny, or evil-speaking, or abuse (1 Kings 21:10; Acts 13:45; 18:6, etc.). Our Lord was accused of blasphemy when he claimed to be the Son of God (Matt. 26:65; comp. Matt. 9:3; Mark 2:7). They who deny his Messiahship blaspheme Jesus (Luke 22:65; John 10:36).

Blasphemy against the Holy Ghost (Matt. 12:31, 32; Mark 3:28, 29; Luke 12:10) is regarded by some as a continued and obstinate rejection of the gospel, and hence is an unpardonable sin, simply because as long as a sinner remains in unbelief he voluntarily excludes himself from pardon. Others regard the expression as designating the sin of attributing to the power of Satan those miracles which Christ performed, or generally those works which are the result of the Spirit's agency.

Blas'tus, chamberlain to king Herod Agrippa I. (Acts 12:20). Such persons generally had great influence with their masters.

Blem'ish, imperfection or bodily deformity excluding men from the priesthood, and rendering animals unfit to be offered in sacrifice (Lev. 21:17-23; 22:19-25). The Christian church, as justified in Christ, is "without blemish" (Eph. 5:27). Christ offered himself a sacrifice "without blemish," acceptable to God (1 Pet. 1:19).

Bless. (1.) God blesses his people when he bestows on them some gift temporal or spiritual (Gen. 1:22; 24:35; Job 42:12; Ps. 45:2; 104:24, 35).

(2.) We bless God when we thank him for his mercies (Ps. 103:1, 2; 145:1-3).

(3.) A man blesses himself when he invokes God's blessing (Isa. 65:16), or rejoices in God's goodness to him (Deut. 29:19; Ps. 49:18).

(4.) One blesses another when he expresses good wishes or offers prayer to God for his welfare (Gen. 24:60; 31:55; 1 Sam. 2:20). Sometimes blessings were uttered under divine inspiration, as in the case of Noah, Isaac, Jacob, and Moses (Gen. 9:26, 27; 27:28, 29, 40; 48:15-20; 49:1-28; Deut. 33). The priests were divinely authorized to bless the people

(Deut. 10:8; Num. 6:22-27). We have many examples of apostolic benediction (2 Cor. 13:14; Eph. 6:23, 24; 2 Thess. 3:16, 18; Heb. 13:20, 21; 1 Pet. 5:10, 11).

(5.) Among the Jews in their thank-offerings the master of the feast took a cup of wine in his hand, and after having blessed God for it and for other mercies then enjoyed, handed it to his guests, who all partook of it. Ps. 116:13 refers to this custom. It is also alluded to in 1 Cor. 10:16, where the apostle speaks of the "cup of blessing."

Blind. Blind beggars are frequently mentioned (Matt. 9:27; 12:22; 20:30; John 5:3). The blind are to be treated with compassion (Lev. 19:14; Deut. 27:18). Blindness was sometimes a punishment for disobedience (1 Sam. 11:2; Jer. 22:12), sometimes the effect of old age (Gen. 27:1; 1 Kings 14:4; 1 Sam. 4:15). Conquerors sometimes blinded their captives (2 Kings 25:7; 1 Sam. 11:2). Blindness denotes ignorance as to spiritual things (Isa. 6:10; 42:18, 19; Matt. 15:14; Eph. 4:18). The opening of the eyes of the blind is peculiar to the Messiah (Isa. 29:18). Elymas was smitten with blindness at Paul's word (Acts 13:11).

Blood. (1.) *As food*, prohibited in Gen. 9:4, where the use of animal food is first allowed. Comp. Deut. 12:23; Lev. 3:17; 7:26; 17:10-14. The injunction to abstain from blood is renewed in the decree of the council of Jerusalem (Acts 15:29). It has been held by some, and we think correctly, that this law of prohibition was only ceremonial and temporary; while others regard it as still binding on all. Blood was eaten by the Israelites after the battle of Gilboa (1 Sam. 14:32-34).

(2.) The *blood of sacrifices* was caught by the priest in a basin, and then sprinkled seven times on the altar; that of the passover on the doorposts and lintels of the houses (Ex. 12; Lev. 4:5-7; 16:14-19). At the giving of the law (Ex. 24:8) the blood of the sacrifices was sprinkled on the *people* as well as on the altar, and thus the people were consecrated to God, or entered into covenant with him, hence the *blood of the covenant* (Matt. 26:28; Heb. 9:19, 20; 10:29; 13:20).

(3.) *Human blood.* The murderer was to be punished (Gen. 9:5). The blood of the murdered "crieth for vengeance" (Gen. 4:10). The "avenger of blood" was the nearest relative of the murdered, and he was required to avenge his death (Num. 35:24, 27). No satisfaction could be made for the guilt of murder (Num. 35:31).

(4.) *Blood* used *metaphorically* to denote race (Acts 17:26), and as a symbol of slaughter (Isa. 34:3). To "wash the feet in blood" means to gain a great victory (Ps. 58:10). Wine, from its red colour, is called "the blood of the grape" (Gen. 49:11).

Blood and water issued from our Saviour's side when it was pierced by the Roman soldier (John 19:34). This has led pathologists to the conclusion that the proper cause of Christ's death was rupture of the heart. (Comp. Ps. 69:20.)

Bloody sweat, the sign and token of our Lord's great agony (Luke 22:44).

Blot, a stain or reproach (Job 31:7; Prov. 9:7). To blot out sin is to forgive it (Ps. 51:1, 9; Isa. 44:22; Acts 3:19). Christ's blotting out the handwriting of ordinances was his fulfilling the law in our behalf (Col. 2:14).

Blue, generally associated with purple (Ex. 25:4; 26:1, 31, 36, etc.). It is supposed to have been obtained from a shellfish of the Mediterranean, the *Helix ianthina* of Linnæus. The robe of the high priest's ephod was to be all of this colour (Ex. 28:31), also the loops of the curtains (26:4) and the ribbon of the breastplate (28:28). Blue cloths were also made for various sacred purposes (Num. 4:6, 7, 9, 11, 12). (See COLOURS.)

Boaner'ges—*sons of thunder*—a surname given by our Lord to James and John (Mark 3:17) on account of their fervid and impetuous temper (Luke 9:54).

Boar occurs only in Ps. 80:13. The same Hebrew word is elsewhere rendered "swine" (Lev. 11:7; Deut. 14:8; Prov. 11:22; Isa. 65:4; 66:3, 17). The Hebrews abhorred swine's flesh, and accordingly none of these animals were reared, except in the district beyond the Sea of Galilee.

In the psalm quoted above the powers that destroyed the Jewish nation are compared to wild boars and wild beasts of the field.

Bo'az — *alacrity.* (1.) The husband of Ruth, a wealthy Bethlehemite. By the "levirate law" the duty devolved on him of marrying Ruth the Moabitess (Ruth 4:1–13). He was a kinsman of Mahlon, her first husband.

(2.) The name given (for what reason is unknown) to one of the two (the other was called Jachin) brazen pillars which Solomon erected in the court of the temple (1 Kings 7:21; 2 Chr. 3:17). These pillars were broken up and carried to Babylon by Nebuchadnezzar.

Bo'chim—*weepers*—a place where the angel of the Lord reproved the Israelites for entering into a league with the people of the land. This caused them bitterly to weep, and hence the name of the place (Judg. 2:1, 5). It lay probably at the head of one of the valleys between Gilgal and Shiloh.

Boil (rendered "botch" in Deut. 28:27, 35), an aggravated ulcer, as in the case of Hezekiah (2 Kings 20:7; Isa. 38:21) or of the Egyptians (Ex. 9:9, 10, 11; Deut. 28:27, 35). It designates the disease of Job (2:7), which was probably the black leprosy.

Bol'led (Ex. 9:31), meaning "swollen or podded for seed," was adopted in the Authorized Version from the version of Coverdale (1535). The Revised Version has in the margin "was in blossom," which is the more probable rendering of the Hebrew word. It is the fact that in Egypt when barley is in ear (about February) flax is blossoming.

Bol'ster. The Hebrew word *kebir*, rendered "pillow" in 1 Sam. 19:13, 16, but in Revised Version marg. "quilt" or "network," probably means some counterpane or veil intended to protect the head of the sleeper. A different Hebrew word (*meraashoth'*) is used for "bolster" (1 Sam. 26:7, 11, 16). It is rightly rendered in Revised Version "at his head." In Gen. 28:11, 18 the Authorized Version renders it "for his pillows," and the Revised Version "under his head." In Ezek. 13:18, 21 another

Hebrew word (*kesathôth*) is used, properly denoting "cushions" or "pillows," as so rendered both in the Authorized and the Revised Version.

Bond, an obligation of any kind (Num. 30 : 2, 4, 12). The word means also oppression or affliction (Ps. 116 : 16; Phil. 1 : 7). Christian love is the "bond of perfectness" (Col. 3 : 14), and the influences of the Spirit are the "bond of peace" (Eph. 4 : 3).

Bond′age of Israel in Egypt (Ex. 2 : 23–25; 5), which is called the "house of bondage" (13 : 3; 20 : 2). This word is used also with reference to the captivity in Babylon (Isa. 14 : 3), and the oppression of the Persian king (Ezra 9 : 8, 9).

Bon′net (Heb. *pĕ̄er*)—Ex. 39 : 28 (R.V., "head-tires"); Ezek. 44 : 18 (R.V., "tires")

—denotes properly a turban worn by priests, and in Isa. 3 : 20 (R.V., "head-tires") a head-dress or tiara worn by females. The Hebrew word so rendered literally means an ornament, as in Isa. 61 : 10 (R.V., "garland"), and in Ezek. 24 : 17, 23 "tire" (R.V., "head-tire"). It consisted of a piece of cloth twisted about the head. In Ex. 28 : 40; 29 : 9 it is the translation of a different Hebrew word (*migbā'ah*), which denotes the turban (R.V., "head-tire") of the common priest as distinguished from the mitre of the high priest. (See Mitre.)

Book. This word has a comprehensive meaning in Scripture. In the Old Testament it is the rendering of the Hebrew word *sepher*, which properly means a "writing," and then a "volume" (Ex.

ANCIENT BOOKS.

17 : 14; Deut. 28 : 58; 29 : 20; Job 19 : 23) or "roll" (Jer. 36 : 2, 4).

Books were originally written on skins, on linen or cotton cloth, and on Egyptian papyrus, whence our word "paper." The leaves of the book were generally written in columns, designated by a Hebrew word properly meaning "doors" and "valves" (Jer. 36 : 23, R.V., marg. "columns").

Among the Hebrews books were generally rolled up like our maps, or if very long they were rolled from both ends, forming two rolls (Luke 4 : 17–20). Thus they were arranged when the writing was on flexible materials; but if the writing was on tablets of wood or brass or lead, then the several tablets were bound to-

gether by rings through which a rod was passed.

A *sealed book* is one whose contents are secret (Isa. 29 : 11; Rev. 5 : 1–3). To "eat" a book (Jer. 15 : 16; Ezek. 2 : 8–10; 3 : 1–3; Rev. 10 : 9) is to study its contents carefully.

The *book of judgment* (Dan. 7 : 10) refers to the method of human courts of justice as illustrating the proceedings which will take place at the day of God's final judgment.

The *book of the wars of the Lord* (Num. 21 : 14), the *book of Jasher* (Josh. 10 : 13), and the *book of the chronicles* of the kings of Judah and of Israel (1 Kings 14 : 19), were probably ancient documents known to the Hebrews, but not forming a part of the canon.

The *book of life* (Ps. 69:28) suggests the idea that as the redeemed form a community or citizenship (Phil. 3:20; 4:3), a catalogue of the citizens' names is preserved (Luke 10:20; Rev. 20:15). Their names are registered in heaven (Luke 10:20; Rev. 3:5).

The *book of the covenant* (Ex. 24:7), containing Ex. 20:22–23:33, is the first book actually mentioned as a part of the written word. It contains a series of laws, civil, social, and religious, given to Moses at Sinai immediately after the delivery of the decalogue. These were written in this "book."

Booth, a hut made of the branches of a tree. In such tabernacles Jacob sojourned for a season at a place named from this circumstance Succoth (Gen. 33:17). Booths were erected also at the feast of Tabernacles (*q.v.*)—Lev. 23:42, 43—which commemorated the abode of the Israelites in the wilderness.

Boot'y, captives or cattle or objects of value taken in war. In Canaan all that breathed were to be destroyed (Deut. 20:16). The "pictures and images" of the Canaanites were to be destroyed also (Num. 33:52). The law of booty as to its division is laid down in Num. 31:26–47. David afterwards introduced a regulation that the baggage-guard should share the booty equally with the soldiers engaged in battle. He also devoted of the spoils of war for the temple (1 Sam. 30:24–26; 2 Sam. 8:11; 1 Chr. 26:27).

Bor'row. The Israelites "borrowed" from the Egyptians (Ex. 12:35, R.V., "asked") in accordance with a divine command (3:22; 11:2). But the word (*sha'al*) so rendered here means simply and always to "request" or "demand." The Hebrew had another word which is properly translated "borrow" in Deut. 28:12; Ps. 37:21. It was well known that the parting was final. The Egyptians were so anxious to get the Israelites away out of their land that "they let them have what they asked" (Ex. 12:36, R.V.), or literally "made them to ask"—urged them to take whatever they desired and depart. (See LOAN.)

Bo'som. In the East objects are carried in the bosom which Europeans carry in the pocket. To have in one's bosom indicates kindness, secrecy, or intimacy (Gen. 16:5; 2 Sam. 12:8). Christ is said to have been in "the bosom of the Father"—*i.e.*, he had the most perfect knowledge of the Father, had the closest intimacy with him (John 1:18). John (21:20) was "leaning on Jesus' bosom" at the last supper. Our Lord carries his lambs in his bosom—*i.e.*, has a tender, watchful care over them (Isa. 40:11).

Bos'ses, the projecting parts of a shield (Job 15:26). The Hebrew word thus rendered means anything convex or arched, and hence the back, as of animals.

Bo'sor, the Chaldee or Aramaic form of the name Beor, the father of Balaam (2 Pet. 2:15).

Botch, the name given in Deut. 28:27, 35 to one of the Egyptian plagues (Ex. 9:9). The word so translated is usually rendered "boil" (*q.v.*).

Bot'tle, a vessel made of skins for holding wine (Josh. 9:4, 13; 1 Sam. 16:20:

BOTTLES.

Matt. 9:17; Mark 2:22; Luke 5:37, 38), or milk (Judg. 4:19), or water (Gen. 21:14, 15, 19), or strong drink (Hab. 2:15).

Earthenware vessels were also similarly used (Jer. 19:1–10; 1 Kings 14:3; Isa. 30:14). In Job 32:19 (comp. Matt. 9:17; Luke 5:37, 38; Mark 2:22) the reference is to a wine-skin ready to burst through the fermentation of the wine. "Bottles of wine" in the Authorized Version of Hos. 7:5 is properly rendered in the Revised Version by "the heat of wine"—*i.e.*, the fever of wine, its intoxicating strength.

The clouds are figuratively called the "bottles of heaven" (Job 38:37). A bottle blackened or shrivelled by smoke is referred to in Ps. 119:83 as an image to which the psalmist likens himself.

Bow. The bow was in use in early times both in war and in the chase (Gen. 21:20; 27:3; 48:22). The tribe of Benjamin were famous for the use of the bow (1 Chr. 8:40; 12:2; 2 Chr. 14:8; 17:17); so also were the Elamites (Isa. 22:6) and the Lydians (Jer. 46:9). The Hebrew word commonly used for bow means properly to *tread* (1 Chr. 5:18; 8:40), and hence it is concluded that the foot was employed in bending the bow. Bows of steel (correctly "copper") are mentioned (2 Sam. 22:35; Ps. 18:35).

The *arrows* were carried in a quiver (Gen. 27:3; Isa. 22:6; 49:2; Ps. 127:5). They were apparently sometimes shot with some burning material attached to them (Ps. 120:4).

The bow is a *symbol* of victory (Ps. 7:12). It denotes also falsehood, deceit (Ps. 64:34; Hos. 7:16; Jer. 9:3).

"The use of the bow" in 2 Sam. 1:18 (A.V.) ought to be "the song of the bow," as in the Revised Version.

Bowels (Phil. 1:8; 2:1; Col. 3:12), compassionate feelings; R.V., "tender mercies."

Bowing, a mode of showing respect. Abraham "bowed himself to the people of the land" (Gen. 23:7); so Jacob to Esau (Gen. 33:3); and the brethren of Joseph before him as the governor of the land (Gen. 43:28).

Bowing is also frequently mentioned as an act of adoration to idols (Josh. 23:7; 2 Kings 5:18; Judg. 2:19; Isa. 44:15), and to God (Josh. 5:14; Ps. 22:29; 72:9; Micah 6:6; Ps. 95:6; Eph. 3:14).

Bowl. The sockets of the lamps of the golden candlestick of the tabernacle are called bowls (Ex. 25:31, 33, 34; 37:17, 19, 20); the same word so rendered being elsewhere rendered "cup" (Gen. 44:2, 12, 16), and wine-"pot" (Jer. 35:5). The reservoir for oil, from which pipes led to each lamp in Zechariah's vision of the candlestick, is called also by this name (Zech. 4:2, 3); so also are the vessels used for libations (Ex. 25:29; 37:16).

Box, for holding oil or perfumery (Mark 14:3). It was of the form of a flask or bottle. The Hebrew word (*pak*) used for it is more appropriately rendered "vial" in 1 Sam. 10:1, and should also be so rendered in 2 Kings 9:1, where alone else it occurs.

Box-tree (Heb. *teashshûr*), mentioned in Isa. 60:13; 41:19, was, according to some, a species of cedar growing in Lebanon.

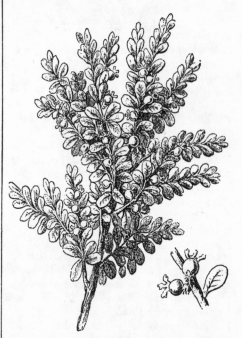

BRANCH OF BOX-TREE.

The words of Ezek. 27:6 literally translated are, "Thy benches they have made of ivory, the daughter of the *ashur* tree"——*i.e.*, inlaid with *ashur* wood. The *ashur* is the box-tree, and accordingly the Revised Version rightly reads "inlaid in box-wood." This is the *Buxus sempervirens* of botanists. It is remarkable for the beauty of its evergreen foliage and for the utility of its hard and durable wood.

Boz'rah—*enclosure; fortress.* (1.) The city of Jobab, one of the early Edomite kings (Gen. 36 : 33). This place is mentioned by the prophets in later times (Isa. 34 : 6 ; Jer. 49 : 13 ; Amos 1 : 12 ; Micah 2 : 12). Its modern representative is *el-Busseireh.* It lies in the mountain district of Petra, 20 miles to the south-east of the Dead Sea.

(2.) A Moabite city in the "plain coun-try" (Jer. 48 : 24)—*i.e.,* on the high level down on the east of the Dead Sea. It is probably the modern *Buzrah.*

Brace'let. (1.) Anklets (Num. 31 : 50 ; 2 Sam. 1 : 10), and with reference to men.

(2.) The rendering of a Hebrew word meaning *fasteners,* found in Gen. 24 : 22, 30, 47.

(3.) In Isa. 3 : 19, the rendering of a Hebrew word meaning *chains*—*i.e.,* twisted or chain-like bracelets.

(4.) In Ex. 35 : 22 it designates properly a *clasp* for fastening the dress of females. Some interpret it as a *nose-ring.*

(5.) In Gen. 38 : 18, 25, the rendering of a Hebrew word meaning "thread," and may denote the ornamental cord with which the signet was suspended from the neck of the wearer.

Bracelets were worn by men as well as by women (Cant. 5 : 14, R.V.). They were of many various forms. The weight of those presented by Eliezer to Rebekah was ten shekels (Gen. 24 : 22).

Bram'ble. (1.) Hebrew *atad,* Judg. 9 : 14 ; rendered "thorn," Ps. 58 : 9. The LXX. and Vulgate render by *rhamnus,* a thorny shrub common in Palestine, resembling the hawthorn.

(2.) Hebrew *hoah,* Isa. 34 : 13 (R.V. "thistles") ; "thickets" in 1 Sam. 13 : 6 ; "thistles" in 2 Kings 14 : 9, 2 Chr. 25 : 18, Job 31 : 40 ; "thorns" in 2 Chr. 33 : 11, Cant. 2 : 2, Hos. 9 : 6. The word may be regarded as denoting the common thistle, of which there are many species which encumber the corn-fields of Palestine. (See THORNS.)

Branch, a symbol of kings descended from royal ancestors (Ezek. 17 : 3, 10 ; Dan. 11 : 7) ; of prosperity (Job 8 : 16) ; of the Messiah—a branch out of the root of the stem of Jesse (Isa. 11 : 1), the "beautiful branch" (4 : 2), a "righteous branch" (Jer. 23 : 5), "the Branch" (Zech. 3 : 8 ; 6 : 12).

Disciples are branches of the true vine (John 15 : 5, 6). "The branch of the terrible ones" (Isa. 25 : 5) is rightly translated in the Revised Version "the song of the ter-rible ones"—*i.e.,* the song of victory shall be brought low by the destruction of Babylon and the return of the Jews from captivity.

The "abominable branch" is a tree on which a malefactor has been hanged (Isa. 14 : 19). The "highest branch" in Ezek. 17 : 3 represents Jehoiakim the king.

Brass, which is an alloy of copper and zinc, was not known till the thirteenth century. What is designated by this word in Scripture is properly copper (Deut. 8 : 9). It was used for fetters (Judg. 16 : 21 ; 2 Kings 25 : 7), for pieces of armour (1 Sam. 17 : 5, 6), for musical instruments (1 Chr. 15 : 19 ; 1 Cor. 13 : 1), and for money (Matt. 10 : 9).

It is a symbol of insensibility and ob-stinacy in sin (Isa. 48 : 4 ; Jer. 6 : 28 ; Ezek. 22 : 18), and of strength (Ps. 107 : 16 ; Micah 4 : 13).

The Macedonian empire is described as a kingdom of brass (Dan. 2 : 39). The "mountains of brass" Zechariah (6 : 1) speaks of have been supposed to represent the immutable decrees of God.

The *serpent of brass* was made by Moses at the command of God (Num. 21 : 4–9), and elevated on a pole, so that it might be seen by all the people when wounded by the bite of the serpents that were sent to them as a punishment for their murmurings against God and against Moses. It was af-terwards carried by the Jews into Canaan, and preserved by them till the time of Hezekiah, who caused it to be at length destroyed because it began to be viewed by the people with superstitious reverence (2 Kings 18 : 4). (See NEHUSHTAN.)

The brazen serpent is alluded to by our Lord in John 3 : 14, 15. (See SERPENT.)

Brav'ery (Isa. 3 : 18), an old English word meaning *comeliness* or *beauty.*

Breach, an opening in a wall (1 Kings 11:27; 2 Kings 12:5); the fracture of a limb (Lev. 24:20), and hence the expression, "Heal, etc." (Ps. 60:2). Judg. 5:17, a bay or harbour; R.V., "by his creeks."

Bread among the Jews was generally made of wheat (Ex. 29:2; Judg. 6:19), though also sometimes of other grains (Gen. 14:18; Judg. 7:13). Parched grain was sometimes used for food without any other preparation (Ruth 2:14).

Bread was prepared by kneading in wooden bowls or "kneading troughs" (Gen. 18:6; Ex. 12:34; Jer. 7:18). The dough was mixed with leaven and made into thin cakes, round or oval, and then baked. The bread eaten at the Passover was always unleavened (Ex. 12:15-20; Deut. 16:3). In the towns there were public ovens, which were much made use of for baking bread; there were also bakers by trade (Hos. 7:4; Jer. 37:21). Their ovens were not unlike those of modern times. But sometimes the bread was baked by being placed on the ground that had been heated by a fire, and by covering it with the embers (1 Kings 19:6). This was probably the mode in which Sarah prepared bread on the occasion referred to in Gen. 18:6.

In Lev. 2 there is an account of the different kinds of bread and cakes used by the Jews. (See BAKE.)

The *shew-bread* (*q.v.*) consisted of twelve loaves of unleavened bread prepared and presented hot on the golden table every Sabbath. They were square or oblong, and represented the twelve tribes of Israel. The old loaves were removed every Sabbath, and were to be eaten only by the priests in the court of the sanctuary (Ex. 25:30; Lev. 24:8; 1 Sam. 21:1-6; Matt. 12:4).

The word bread is used figuratively in such expressions as "bread of sorrows" (Ps. 127:2), "bread of tears" (80:5)—*i.e.*, sorrow and tears are like one's daily bread, they form so great a part in life. The bread of "wickedness" (Prov. 4:17) and "of deceit" (20:17) denote in like manner that wickedness and deceit are a part of the daily life.

Breast'plate. (1.) That piece of ancient armour that protected the breast. This word is used figuratively in Eph. 6:14 and Isa. 59:17. (See ARMOUR.)

(2.) An ornament covering the breast of the high priest, first mentioned in Ex. 25:7. It was made of embroidered cloth, set with four rows of precious stones, three in each row. On each stone was engraved the name of one of the twelve tribes (Ex. 28:15-29; 39:8-21). It was in size about ten inches square. The two upper corners were fastened to the ephod by blue ribbons. It was not to be "loosed from the ephod" (Ex. 28:28). The lower corners were fastened to the girdle of the priest. As it reminded the priest of his representative character, it was called the *memorial* (28:12, 29). It was also called the *breastplate of judgment* (28:15). (See PRIEST.)

Breech'es (Ex. 28:42), rather linen drawers, reaching from the waist to a little above the knee, worn by the priests (Ezek. 44:17, 18).

Bribe. None to be taken; "for the gift maketh open eyes blind, and perverteth the cause of the righteous" (Ex. 23:8, literally rendered).

Bricks, the making of, formed the chief labour of the Israelites in Egypt (Ex.

EGYPTIAN BRICK-MAKING.

1:13, 14). Those found among the ruins of Babylon and Nineveh are about a foot square and four inches thick. They were usually dried in the sun, though also sometimes in kilns (2 Sam. 12:31; Jer. 43:9; Nah. 3:14). (See NEBUCHADNEZZAR.)

The bricks used in the tower of Babel were burnt bricks, cemented in the building by bitumen (Gen. 11:3).

Bride, frequently used in the ordinary sense (Isa. 49:18; 61:10, etc.). The relation between Christ and his church is set forth under the figure of that between a bridegroom and bride (John 3:29). The church is called "the bride" (Rev. 21:9; 22:17). Compare parable of the Ten Virgins (Matt. 25:1–13).

Bri'dle. Three Hebrew words are thus rendered in the Authorized Version. (1.) Heb. *maḥsom'* signifies a muzzle or halter or bridle, by which the rider governs his horse (Ps. 39:2).

(2.) *Me'theg*, rendered also "bit" in Ps. 32:9, which is its proper meaning. Found in 2 Kings 19:28, where the restraints of God's providence are metaphorically styled his "bridle" and "hook." God's placing a "bridle in the jaws of the people" (Isa. 30:28; 37:29) signifies his preventing the Assyrians from carrying out their purpose against Jerusalem.

(3.) Another word, *re'sen*, was employed to represent a halter or bridle-rein, as used Ps. 32:9; Isa. 30:28. In Job 30:11 the restraints of law and humanity are called a bridle.

Bri'er. This word occurs frequently, and is the translation of several different terms. (1.) Micah 7:4, it denotes a species of thorn shrub used for hedges. In Prov. 15:19 the word is rendered "thorn" (Heb. *hedek*, "stinging"), supposed by some to be what is called the "apple of Sodom" (*q.v.*).

(2.) Ezek. 28:24, *sallon'*, properly a "prickle," such as is found on the shoots of the palm tree.

(3.) Isa. 55:13, probably simply a thorny bush. Some, following the Vulgate Version, regard it as the "nettle."

(4.) Isa. 5:6; 7:23–25, etc., frequently used to denote thorny shrubs in general. In 10:17; 27:4, it means troublesome men.

(5.) In Heb. 6:8 the Greek word (*tribŏlos*) so rendered means "three-pronged," and denotes the land *caltrop*, a low thorny shrub resembling in its spikes the military "crow-foot." Comp. Matt. 7:16, "thistle."

Brig'andine (Jer. 46:4; 51:3), an obsolete English word denoting a *scale* coat of armour, or habergeon, worn by light-armed "brigands." The Revised Version has "coat of mail."

Brim'stone, an inflammable mineral substance found in quantities on the shores of the Dead Sea. The cities of the plain were destroyed by a rain of fire and brimstone (Gen. 19:24, 25). In Isa. 34:9 allusion is made to the destruction of these cities. This word figuratively denotes destruction or punishment (Job 18:15; Isa. 30:33; 34:9; Ps. 11:6; Ezek. 38:22). It is used to express the idea of excruciating torment in Rev. 14:10; 19:20; 20:10.

Brook, a torrent. (1.) Applied to small streams, as the Arnon, Jabbok, etc. Isaiah (15:7) speaks of the "brook of the willows," probably the *Wady-el-Asha*.

(2.) It is also applied to winter torrents (Job 6:15; Num. 34:5; Josh. 15:4, 47), and to the torrent-bed or wady as well as to the torrent itself (Num. 13:23; 1 Kings 17:3).

(3.) In Isa. 19:7 the river Nile is meant, as rendered in the Revised Version.

Brother. (1.) In the natural and common sense (Matt. 1:2; Luke 3:1, 19).

(2.) A near relation, a cousin (Gen. 13:8; 14:16; Matt. 12:46; John 7:3; Acts 1:14; Gal. 1:19).

(3.) Simply a fellow-countryman (Matt. 5:47; Acts 3:22; Heb. 7:5).

(4.) A disciple or follower (Matt. 25:40; Heb. 2:11, 12).

(5.) One of the same faith (Amos 1:9; Acts 9:30; 11:29; 1 Cor. 5:11); whence the early disciples of our Lord were known to each other as brethren.

(6.) A colleague in office (Ezra 3:2; 1 Cor. 1:1; 2 Cor. 1:1).

(7.) A fellow-man (Gen. 9:5; 19:7; Matt. 5:22, 23, 24; 7:5; Heb. 2:17).

(8.) One beloved or closely united with another in affection (2 Sam. 1:26; Acts 6:3; 1 Thess. 5:1).

Brethren of Jesus (Matt. 1:25; 12:46, 50, 55; Mark 3:31; Gal. 1:19; 1 Cor. 9:5, etc.) were probably the younger children of Joseph and Mary. Some have supposed that they may have been the children of Joseph by a former marriage, and others that they were the children of Mary, the Virgin's sister, and wife of Cleophas. The first interpretation, however, is the most natural.

Bruit, a rumour or report (Jer. 10:22, R.V. "rumour;" Nah. 3:19).

Bucket, a vessel to draw water with (Isa. 40:15); used figuratively, probably, of a numerous issue (Num. 24:7).

Buckler. (1.) A portable shield (2 Sam. 22:31; 1 Chr. 5:18).

(2.) A shield surrounding the person; the targe or round form; used once figuratively (Ps. 91:4).

(3.) A large shield protecting the whole body (Ps. 35:2; Ezek. 23:24; 26:8).

(4.) A lance or spear; improperly rendered "buckler" in the Authorized Version (1 Chr. 12:8), but correctly in the Revised Version "spear."

The leather of shields required oiling (2 Sam. 1:21; Isa. 21:5), so as to prevent its being injured by moisture. Copper (="brass") shields were also in use (1 Sam. 17:6; 1 Kings 14:27). Those spoken of in 1 Kings 10:16, etc.; 14:26, were probably of massive metal.

The shields David had taken from his enemies were suspended in the temple as mementoes (2 Kings 11:10). (See ARMOUR, SHIELD.)

Building among the Jews was suited to the climate and conditions of the country. They probably adopted the kind of architecture for their dwellings which they found already existing when they entered Canaan (Deut. 6:10; Num. 13:19). Phœnician artists (2 Sam. 5:11; 1 Kings 5:6, 18) assisted at the erection of the royal palace and the temple at Jerusalem. Foreigners also assisted at the restoration of the temple after the Exile (Ezra 3:7).

In Gen. 11:3, 9, we have the first recorded instance of the erection of buildings. The cities of the plain of Shinar were founded by the descendants of Shem (10:11, 12, 22).

The Israelites were by occupation shepherds and dwellers in tents (Gen. 47:3); but from the time of their entering Canaan they became dwellers in towns, and in houses built of the native limestone of Palestine. Much building was carried on in Solomon's time. Besides the buildings he completed at Jerusalem, he also built Baalath and Tadmor (1 Kings 9:15, 24).

Many of the kings of Israel and Judah were engaged in erecting various buildings.

Herod and his sons and successors restored the temple, and built fortifications and other structures of great magnificence in Jerusalem (Luke 21:5).

The instruments used in building are mentioned as the plumb-line (Amos 7:7), the measuring-reed (Ezek. 40:3), and the saw (1 Kings 7:9).

Believers are "God's building" (1 Cor. 3:9); and heaven is called "a building of God" (2 Cor. 5:1). Christ is the only foundation of his church (1 Cor. 3:10–12), of which he also is the builder (Matt. 16:18).

Bul—*rainy*—the eighth ecclesiastical month of the year (1 Kings 6:38), and the second month of the civil year; later called *Marchesvan* (*q.v.*). (See MONTH.)

Bullock. (1.) The translation of a word which is a generic name for horned cattle (Isa. 65:25). It is also rendered "cow" (Ezek. 4:15), "ox" (Gen. 12:16).

(2.) The translation of a word always meaning an animal of the ox kind, without distinction of age or sex (Hos. 12:11). It is rendered "cow" (Num. 18:17) and "ox" (Lev. 17:3).

(3.) Another word is rendered in the same way (Jer. 31:18). It is also translated "calf" (Lev. 9:3; Micah 6:6). It is the same word used of the "molten calf" (Ex. 32:4, 8) and "the golden calf" (1 Kings 12:28).

(4.) In Judg. 6:25; Isa. 34:7, the Hebrew word is different. It is the customary word for bulls offered in sacrifice. In Hos. 14:2, the Authorized Version has "calves," the Revised Version "bullocks."

Bulrush. (1.) In Isa. 58:5 the rendering of a word which denotes "belonging to a marsh," from the nature of the soil in which it grows (Isa. 18:2). It was sometimes platted into ropes (Job 41:2; A.V., "hook," R.V., "rope," *lit.* "cord of rushes").

(2.) In Ex. 2:3, Isa. 18:2 (R.V., "papyrus") this word is the translation of the Hebrew *gomè*, which designates the plant as *absorbing* moisture. In Isa. 35:7 and Job 8:11 it is rendered "rush." This was the Egyptian papyrus (*papyrus Nilotica*). It was anciently very abundant in Egypt.

EGYPTIAN PAPYRUS.

The Egyptians made garments and shoes and various utensils of it. It was used for the construction of the ark of Moses (Ex. 2:3, 5). The root portions of the stem were used for food. The inside bark was cut into strips, which were sewed together and dried in the sun, forming the papyrus used for writing. It is no longer found in Egypt, but grows luxuriantly in Palestine, in the marshes of the Huleh, and in the swamps at the north end of the Lake of Gennesaret. (See CANE.)

Bulwarks, mural towers, bastions, were introduced by king Uzziah (2 Chr. 26:15; Zeph. 1:16; Ps. 48:13; Isa. 26:1). There are five Hebrew words so rendered in the Authorized Version, but the same word is also variously rendered.

Bunch. (1.) A bundle of twigs (Ex. 12:22). (2.) Bunch or cake of raisins (2 Sam. 16:1). (3.) The "bunch of a camel" (Isa. 30:6).

Burden. (1.) A load of any kind (Ex. 23:5). (2.) A severe task (Ex. 2:11). (3.) A difficult duty, requiring effort (Ex. 18:22). (4.) A prophecy of a calamitous or disastrous nature (Isa. 13:1; 17:1; Hab. 1:1, etc.).

Burial. The first burial we have an account of is that of Sarah (Gen. 23). The first commercial transaction recorded is that of the purchase of a burial-place, for which Abraham weighed to Ephron "four hundred shekels of silver current money with the merchants." Thus the patriarch became the owner of a part of the land of Canaan, the only part he ever possessed. When he himself died, "his sons Isaac and Ishmael buried him in the cave of Machpelah," beside Sarah his wife (Gen. 25:9).

Deborah, Rebekah's nurse, was buried under Allon-bachuth, "the oak of weeping" (Gen. 35:8), near to Bethel. Rachel died, and was buried near Ephrath; "and Jacob set a pillar upon her grave" (16–20). Isaac was buried at Hebron, where he had died (27, 29). Jacob, when charging his sons to bury him in the cave of Machpelah, said, "There they buried Abraham and Sarah his wife; there they buried Isaac and Rebekah; and there I buried Leah" (49:31). In compliance with the oath which he made him swear unto him (47:29–31), Joseph, assisted by his brethren, buried Jacob in the cave of Machpelah (50:2, 13). At the Exodus, Moses "took the bones of Joseph with him," and they were buried in the "parcel of ground" which Jacob had bought of the sons of Hamor (Josh. 24:32), which became Joseph's inheritance (Gen. 48:22; 1 Chr. 5:1; John 4:5). Two burials are mentioned as having taken place in the wilderness. That of Miriam (Num. 20:1), and that of Moses, "in the land of Moab" (Deut. 34:5, 6, 8). There is no account of the actual burial of Aaron, which probably, however, took place on the summit of Mount Hor (Num. 20:28, 29).

Joshua was buried "in the border of his inheritance in Timnath-serah" (Josh. 24:30, 33).

In Job we find a reference to burying-places, which were probably the Pyramids (3:14, 15). The Hebrew word for "waste places" here resembles in sound the Egyptian word for "pyramids."

Samuel, like Moses, was honoured with a national burial (1 Sam. 25:1). Joab (1 Kings 2:34) "was buried in his own house in the wilderness."

In connection with the burial of Saul and his three sons we meet for the first time with the practice of burning the dead (1 Sam. 31:11–13). The same practice is again referred to by Amos (6:7–10).

Absalom was buried "in the wood" where he was slain (2 Sam. 18:17, 18). The raising of the heap of stones over his grave was intended to mark abhorrence of the person buried (comp. Josh. 7:26 and 8:29). There was no fixed royal burying-place for the Hebrew kings. We find several royal burials taking place, however, "in the city of David" (1 Kings 2: 10; 11:43; 15:8; 2 Kings 14:19, 20; 15: 38; 1 Kings 14:31; 22:50; 2 Chr. 21:19, 20; 2 Chr. 24:25, etc.). Hezekiah was buried in the mount of the sepulchres of the sons of David; "and all Judah and the inhabitants of Jerusalem did him honour at his death" (2 Chr. 32:33).

Little is said regarding the burial of the kings of Israel. Some of them were buried in Samaria, the capital of their kingdom (2 Kings 10:35; 13:9; 14:16).

Our Lord was buried in a new tomb, hewn out of the rock, which Joseph of Arimathea had prepared for himself (Mark 15:46; John 19:41, 42).

The grave of Lazarus was "a cave, and a stone lay on it" (John 11:38). Graves were frequently either natural caverns or artificial excavations formed in the sides of rocks (Gen. 23:9; Matt. 27:60); and coffins were seldom used, unless when the body was brought from a distance.

Burnt offering—Hebrew 'ōlāh; i.e., "ascending," the whole being consumed by fire, and regarded as ascending to God while being consumed. Part of every offering was burnt in the sacred fire, but this was *wholly* burnt—a "whole burnt offering." It was the most frequent form of sacrifice, and apparently the only one mentioned in the book of Genesis. Such were the sacrifices offered by Abel (Gen. 4:3, 4, here called *minḥāh; i.e.,* "a gift"), Noah (8:20), Abraham (12:7; 22:2, 7, 8, 13), Jacob (33:20), and by the Hebrews in Egypt (Ex. 10:25).

The law of Moses afterwards prescribed the occasions and the manner in which burnt sacrifices were to be offered. There were "the continual burnt offering" (Ex. 29:38-42; Lev. 6:9-13), "the burnt offering of every sabbath," which was double the daily one (Num. 28:9, 10), "the burnt offering of every month" (28:11-15), the offerings at the Passover (19-23), at Pentecost (Lev. 23:16), the feast of Trumpets (23:23-25), and on the day of Atonement (Lev. 16).

On other occasions special sacrifices were offered, as at the consecration of Aaron

(Ex. 29) and the dedication of the temple (1 Kings 8:5, 62-64).

Free-will burnt offerings were also permitted (Lev. 1:13), and were offered at the accession of Solomon to the throne (1 Chr. 29:21), and at the reformation brought about by Hezekiah (2 Chr. 29: 31-35).

These offerings signified the complete dedication of the offerers unto God. This is referred to in Rom. 12:1. (See ALTAR, SACRIFICE.)

Bush, in which Jehovah appeared to Moses in the wilderness (Ex. 3:2; Acts 7:30). It is difficult to say what particular kind of plant or bush is here meant. Probably it was the *mimosa* or *acacia.* The words "in the bush" in Mark 12:26; Luke 20:37, mean "in the passage or paragraph on the bush;" i.e., in Ex. 3.

But'ler, properly *a servant in charge of the wine* (Gen. 40:1-13; 41:9). The Hebrew word, *mashkēh,* thus translated is rendered also (plural) "cup-bearers" (1 Kings 10:5; 2 Chr. 9:4). Nehemiah (1:11) was cup-bearer to king Artaxerxes. It was a position of great responsibility and honour in royal households.

Butter (Heb. *ḥemāh*), curdled milk (Gen. 18:8; Judg. 5:25; 2 Sam. 17: 29), or butter in the form of the skim of hot milk or cream, called by the Arabs *kaimak,* a semi-fluid (Job 20:17; 29:6; Deut. 32:14). The words of Prov. 30:33 have been rendered by some "the pressure [not churning] of milk bringeth forth cheese."

Buz—*contempt.* (1.) The second son of Nahor and Milcah, and brother of Huz (Gen. 22:21). Elihu was one of his descendants (Job 32:2).

(2.) One of the chiefs of the tribe of Gad (1 Chr. 5:14).

(3.) A district in Arabia Petrea (Jer. 25:23).

Bu'zi, the father of the prophet Ezekiel (1:3).

By, in the expression "by myself" (A.V., 1 Cor. 4:4), means, as rendered in the Revised Version, "against myself."

By and by, immediately (Matt. 13:21; R.V., "straightway;" Luke 21:9).

By-ways, only in Judg. 5:6 and Ps. 125:5; literally "winding or twisted roads." The margin has "crooked ways."

By-word—Hebrew *millah* (Job 30:9)—a word or speech, and hence object of talk;

Hebrew *mashal* (Ps. 44:14), a proverb or parable. When it denotes a sharp word of derision, as in Deut. 28:37, 1 Kings 9:7, 2 Chr. 7:20, the Hebrew *sheninah* is used. In Jer. 24:9 it is rendered "taunt."

C

Cab—*hollow* (R.V., "kab")—occurs only in 2 Kings 6:25; a dry measure, the sixth part of a seah, and the eighteenth part of an ephah, equal to about two English quarts.

Cabins — only in Jer. 37:16 (R.V., "cells")—arched vaults or recesses off a passage or room; cells for the closer confinement of prisoners.

Ca'bul—*how little! as nothing.* (1.) A town on the eastern border of Asher (Josh. 19:27), probably one of the towns given by Solomon to Hiram; the modern *Kabûl,* some 8 miles east of Accho, on the very borders of Galilee.

(2.) A district in the north-west of Galilee, near to Tyre, containing twenty cities given to Hiram by Solomon as a reward for various services rendered to him in building the temple (1 Kings 9:13), and as payment of the six score talents of gold he had borrowed from him. Hiram gave the cities this name because he was not pleased with the gift, the name signifying "good for nothing." Hiram seems afterwards to have restored these cities to Solomon (2 Chr. 8:2).

Cæsar, the title assumed by the Roman emperors after Julius Cæsar. In the New Testament this title is given to various emperors as sovereigns of Judæa without their accompanying distinctive proper names (John 19:15; Acts 17:7). The Jews paid tribute to Cæsar (Matt. 22:17), and all Roman citizens had the right of appeal to him (Acts 25:11). The Cæsars referred to in the New Testament are Augustus (Luke 2:1), Tiberius (3:1; 20:22), Claudius (Acts 11:28), and Nero (Acts 25:8; Phil. 4:22).

Cæsare'a (Palestinæ), a city on the shore of the Mediterranean, on the great road from Tyre to Egypt, about 70 miles north-west of Jerusalem, at the northern extremity of the plain of Sharon. It was built by Herod the Great (B.C. 10), who named it after Cæsar Augustus, hence called *Cæsarea Sebaste* (Gr. *Sebastos* = "Augustus"), on the site of an old town called "Strato's Tower." It was the capital of the Roman province of Judæa, the seat of the governors or procurators, and the headquarters of the Roman troops. It was the great Gentile city of Palestine, with a spacious artificial harbour. It was adorned with many buildings of great splendour, after the manner of the Roman cities of the West. Here Cornelius the centurion was converted through the instrumentality of Peter (Acts 10:1, 24), and thus for the first time the door of faith was opened to the Gentiles. Philip the evangelist resided here with his four daughters (21:8). From this place Saul sailed for his native Tarsus when forced to flee from Jerusalem (9:30), and here he landed when returning from his second missionary journey (18:22). He remained as a prisoner here for two years before his voyage to Rome (Acts 24:27; 25:1, 4, 6, 13). Here on a "set day," when games were celebrated in the theatre in honour of the emperor Claudius, Herod Agrippa I. appeared among the people in great pomp, and in the midst of the idolatrous homage paid to him was suddenly smitten by an angel, and carried out a dying man. He was "eaten of worms" (12:19-23), thus perishing by the same loathsome disease as his grandfather, Herod the Great. It still retains its ancient name *Kaiseriyeh,* but is now desolate. "The present inhabitants of the ruins are snakes, scorpions, lizards, wild

MOLE AND HARBOUR OF CÆSAREA (PALESTINÆ).

boars, and jackals." It is described as the most desolate city of all Palestine.

Cæsare'a Philip'pi, a city on the northeast of the marshy plain of *El-Hûleh*, 120 miles north of Jerusalem, and 20 miles north of the Sea of Galilee, at the "upper source" of the Jordan, and near the base of Mount Hermon. It is mentioned in Matt. 16:13 and Mark 8:27 as the northern limit of our Lord's public ministry. According to some its original name was *Baal-gad* (Josh. 11:17) or *Baal-hermon* (Judg. 3:3; 1 Chr. 5:23), when it was a Canaanite sanctuary of Baal. It was afterwards called *Panium* or *Paneas*, from a deep cavern full of water near the town. This name was given to the cavern by the Greeks of the Macedonian kingdom of Antioch because of its likeness to the grottoes of Greece, which were always associated with the worship of their god Pan. Its modern name is *Banias.* Here Herod built a temple which he dedicated to Augustus Cæsar. This town was afterwards enlarged and embellished by Herod

Philip, the tetrarch of Trachonitis, of whose territory it formed a part, and was called by him Cæsarea Philippi, partly after his own name and partly after that of the emperor Tiberias Cæsar. It is thus distinguished from the Cæsarea of Palestine. (See JORDAN.)

Cage (Heb. *kelub'*, Jer. 5:27, marg. "coop," rendered "basket" in Amos 8:1), a basket of wicker-work in which birds were placed after being caught. In Rev. 18:2 it is the rendering of the Greek *phulakē*, properly a prison or place of confinement.

Cai'aphas, the Jewish high priest (A.D. 27–36) at the beginning of our Lord's public ministry, in the reign of Tiberius (Luke 3:1), and also at the time of his condemnation and crucifixion (Matt. 26:3, 57; John 11:49; 18:13, 14). He held this office during the whole of Pilate's administration. His wife was the daughter of Annas, who had formerly been high priest, and was probably the vicar or deputy (Heb. *sagan*) of Caiaphas. He was of the sect of the Sadducees (Acts 5:17), and was a member of the council when he gave his opinion that Jesus should be put to death "for the people, and that the whole nation perish not" (John 11:50). In these words he unconsciously uttered a prophecy. "Like Saul, he was a prophet in spite of himself." Caiaphas had no power to inflict the punishment of death, and therefore Jesus was sent to Pilate, the Roman governor, that he might duly pronounce the sentence against him (Matt. 25:2; John 18:13, 28). At a later period his hostility to the gospel is still manifest (Acts 4:6). (See ANNAS.)

Cain — *a possession; a spear*. (1.) The first-born son of Adam and Eve (Gen. 4). He became a tiller of the ground, as his brother Abel followed the pursuits of pastoral life. He was "a sullen, self-willed, haughty, vindictive man; wanting the religious element in his character, and defiant even in his attitude towards God." It came to pass "in process of time" (marg. "at the end of days")—*i.e.*, probably on the Sabbath—that the two brothers presented their offerings to the Lord. Abel's offering was of the "firstlings of his flock and of the fat," while Cain's was "of the fruit of the ground." Abel's sacrifice was "more excellent" (Heb. 11:4) than Cain's, and was accepted by God. On this account Cain was "very wroth," and cherished feelings of murderous hatred against his brother, and was at length guilty of the desperate outrage of putting him to death (1 John 3:12). For this crime he was expelled from Eden, and henceforth led the life of an exile, bearing upon him some mark which God had set upon him in answer to his own cry for mercy, so that thereby he might be protected from the wrath of his fellow-men; or it may be that God only gave him some sign to assure him that he would not be slain (Gen. 4:15). Doomed to be a wanderer and a fugitive in the earth, he went forth into the "land of Nod"—*i.e.*, the land of "exile —which is said to have been in the "east of Eden," and there he builded a city, the first we read of, and called it after his son's name, Enoch. His descendants are enumerated to the sixth generation. They gradually

degenerated in their moral and spiritual condition till they became wholly corrupt before God. This corruption prevailed, and at length the Deluge was sent by God to prevent the final triumph of evil. (See ABEL.)

(2.) A town of the Kenites, a branch of the Midianites (Josh. 15:57), on the east edge of the mountain above Engedi; probably the "nest in a rock" mentioned by Balaam (Num. 24:21). It is identified with the modern *Yekin*, 3 miles south-east of Hebron.

Cai'nan — *possession; smith*. (1.) The fourth antediluvian patriarch, the eldest son of Enos. He was 70 years old at the birth of his eldest son Mahalaleel, after which he lived 840 years (Gen. 5:9-14), and was 910 years old when he died. He is also called Kenan (1 Chr. 1:2).

(2.) The son of Arphaxad (Luke 3:35, 36). He is nowhere named in the Old Testament. He is usually called the "second Cainan."

Cake. Cakes made of wheat or barley were offered in the temple. They were salted, but unleavened (Ex. 29:2; Lev. 2:4). In idolatrous worship thin cakes or wafers were offered "to the queen of heaven" (Jer. 7:18; 44:19).

Pancakes are described in 2 Sam. 13:8, 9. Cakes mingled with oil and baked in the oven are mentioned in Lev. 2:4, and "wafers unleavened anointed with oil," in Ex. 29:2; Lev. 8:26; 1 Chr. 23:29. "Cracknels," a kind of crisp cakes, were among the things Jeroboam directed his wife to take with her when she went to consult Ahijah the prophet at Shiloh (1 Kings 14:3). Such hard cakes were carried by the Gibeonites when they came to Joshua (9:5, 12). They described their bread as "mouldy;" but the Hebrew word *nikuddim*, here used, ought rather to be rendered "hard as biscuit." It is rendered "cracknels" in 1 Kings 14:3. The ordinary bread, when kept for a few days, became dry and excessively hard. The Gibeonites pointed to this hardness of their bread as an evidence that they had come a long journey.

We read also of honey-cakes (Ex. 16:31),

"cakes of figs" (1 Sam. 25:18), "cake" as denoting a whole piece of bread (1 Kings 17:12), and "a [round] cake of barley bread" (Judg. 7:13). In Lev. 2 is a list of the different kinds of bread and cakes which were fit for offerings.

Ca'lah, one of the most ancient cities of Assyria. "Out of that land he [*i.e.,* Nimrod] went forth into Assyria, and builded Nineveh, Rehoboth-Ir, and Calah, and Resen" (Gen. 10:11, R.V.). Its site is now marked probably by the *Nimrûd* ruins on the left bank of the Tigris. These cover an area of about 1,000 acres, and are second only in size and importance to the mass of ruins opposite Mosul. This city was at one time the capital of the empire, and was the residence of Sardanapalus and his successors down to the time of Sargon, who built a new capital, the modern *Khorsabad*. It has been conjectured that these four cities mentioned in Gen. 10:11 were afterwards all united into one and called Nineveh (*q.v.*).

Cal'amus—the Latin for *cane*, Hebrew *kâneh*—mentioned (Ex. 30:23) as one of the ingredients in the holy anointing oil, one of the sweet scents (Cant. 4:14), and among the articles sold in the markets of Tyre (Ezek. 27:19). The word designates an Oriental plant called the "sweet flag," the *Acorus calamus* of Linnæus. It is elsewhere called "sweet cane" (Isa. 43:24; Jer. 6:20). It has an aromatic smell, and when its knotted stalk is cut and dried and reduced to powder, it forms an ingredient in the most precious perfumes. It was not a native of Palestine, but was imported from Arabia Felix or from India. It was probably that which is now known in India by the name of "lemon grass" or "ginger grass," the *Andropogon schœnanthus*. (See CANE.)

Cal'col (1 Chr. 2:6)—*sustenance*—the same probably as Chalcol (1 Kings 4:31), one of the four sages whom Solomon excelled in wisdom; for "he was wiser than all men."

Ca'leb—*a dog.* (1.) One of the three sons of Hezron of the tribe of Judah. He is also called Chelubai (1 Chr. 2:9). His sons are enumerated (18, 19, 50).

(2.) A "son of Hur, the firstborn of Ephratah" (1 Chr. 2:50). Some would read the whole passage thus: "These [*i.e.,* the list in ver. 42–49] were the sons of Caleb. The sons of Hur, the firstborn of Ephratah, were Shobal, etc." Thus Hur would be the name of the son and not the father of Caleb (ver. 19).

(3.) The son of Jephunneh (Num. 13:6; 32:12; Josh. 14:6, 14). He was one of those whom Moses sent to search the land in the second year after the Exodus. He was one of the family chiefs of the tribe of Judah. He and Joshua the son of Nun were the only two of the whole number who encouraged the people to go up and possess the land, and they alone were spared when a plague broke out in which the other ten spies perished (Num. 13; 14). All the people that had been numbered, from twenty years old and upward, perished in the wilderness except these two. The last notice we have of Caleb is when (being then eighty-five years of age) he came to Joshua at the camp at Gilgal, after the people had gained possession of the land, and reminded him of the promise Moses had made to him, by virtue of which he claimed a certain portion of the land of Kirjath-arba as his inheritance (Josh. 14:6–15; 15:13–15; 21:10–12; 1 Sam. 25:2, 3; 30:14). He is called a "Kenezite" in Josh. 14:6, 14. This may simply mean "son of Kenez" (Num. 32:12). Some, however, read "Jephunneh, the son of Kenez," who was a descendant of Hezron, the son of Pharez, a grandson of Judah (1 Chr. 2:5). This Caleb may possibly be identical with (2).

(4.) Caleb gave his name apparently to a part of the south country (1 Sam. 30:14) of Judah, the district between Hebron and Carmel, which had been assigned to him. When he gave up the city of Hebron to the priests as a city of refuge, he retained possession of the surrounding country (Josh. 21:11, 12; comp. 1 Sam. 25:3).

Calf. Calves were commonly made use of in sacrifices, and are therefore frequently mentioned in Scripture. The "fatted calf" was regarded as the choicest of animal food; it was frequently also offered as a special sacrifice (1 Sam. 28:24; Amos 6:4; Luke 15:23). The words used in Jer. 34:18, 19, "cut the calf in twain," allude to the custom of dividing a sacrifice into two parts, between which the parties ratifying a covenant passed (Gen. 15:9, 10, 17, 18). The sacrifice of the lips —*i.e.*, praise—is called "the calves of our lips" (Hos. 14:2, R.V., "as bullocks the offering of our lips." Comp. Heb. 13:15; Ps. 116:7; Jer. 33:11).

The *golden calf* which Aaron made (Ex. 32:4) was probably a copy of the god Moloch rather than of the god Apis, the sacred ox or calf of Egypt. The Jews showed all through their history a tendency toward the Babylonian and Canaanitish idolatry rather than toward that of Egypt.

Ages after this, Jeroboam, king of Israel, set up two idol calves—one at Dan, and the other at Bethel—that he might thus prevent the ten tribes from resorting to Jerusalem for worship (1 Kings 12:28). These calves continued to be a snare to the people till the time of their captivity. The calf at Dan was carried away in the reign of Pekah by Tiglath-pileser, and that at Bethel ten years later, in the reign of Hoshea, by Shalmaneser (2 Kings 15:29; 17:33). This sin of Jeroboam is almost always mentioned along with his name (2 Kings 15:28, etc.).

Calk′ers, workmen skilled in stopping the seams of the deck or sides of vessels. The inhabitants of Gebel were employed in such work on Tyrian vessels (Ezek. 27:9, 27; marg., "strengtheners" or "stoppers of chinks").

Call. (1.) To cry for help, hence to pray (Gen. 4:26). Thus men are said to "call upon the name of the Lord" (Acts 2:21; 7:59; 9:14; Rom. 10:12; 1 Cor. 1:2).

(2.) God calls with respect to men when he designates them to some special office (Ex. 31:2; Isa. 22:20; Acts 13:2), and when he invites them to accept his offered grace (Matt. 9:13; 11:28; 22:4).

In the message of the gospel his call is addressed to all men—to Jews and Gentiles alike (Matt. 28:19; Mark 16:15; Rom. 9:24, 25). But this universal call is not inseparably connected with salvation, although it leaves all to whom it comes inexcusable if they reject it (John 3:14-19; Matt. 22:14).

An *effectual call* is something more than the outward message of the Word of God to men. It is internal, and is the result of the enlightening and sanctifying influence of the Holy Spirit (John 16:14; Acts 26:18; John 6:44), effectually drawing men to Christ, and disposing and enabling them to receive the truth (John 6:45; Acts 16:14; Eph. 1:17).

Calling, a profession, or as we usually say, a vocation (1 Cor. 7:20). The "hope of your calling" in Eph. 4:4 is the hope *resulting* from your being called into the kingdom of God.

Cal′neh — *fort* — one of the four cities founded by Nimrod (Gen. 10:10). It is the modern *Niffer*, a lofty mound of earth and rubbish situated in the marshes on the left—*i.e.*, the east—bank of the Euphrates, but 30 miles distant from its present course, and about 60 miles south-south-east from Babylon. It is mentioned as one of the towns with which Tyre carried on trade. It was finally taken and probably destroyed by one of the Assyrian kings (Amos 6:2). It is called *Calno* (Isa. 10:9) and *Canneh* (Ezek. 27:23).

Cal′vary, only in Luke 23:33, the Latin name *Calvaria*, which was used as a translation of the Greek word *Kranion*, by which the Hebrew word *Gulgoleth* was interpreted, "the place of a skull." It probably took this name from its shape, being a hillock or low, rounded, bare elevation somewhat in the form of a human skull. It is nowhere in Scripture called a "hill." The crucifixion of our Lord took place outside the city walls (Heb. 13:11-13) and near the public thoroughfare—"This thing was not done in a corner." (See GOLGOTHA.)

Cam′el, from the Hebrew *gâmal*, "to repay" or "requite," as the camel does the care of its master. There are two distinct species of camels, having, however, the common characteristics of being "ruminants without horns, without muzzle, with nostrils forming oblique slits, the upper lip divided and separately movable and extensile, the soles of the feet horny, with two toes covered by claws, the limbs long, the abdomen drawn up, while the neck, long and slender, is bent up and down— the reverse of that of a horse, which is arched."

(1.) The Bactrian camel is distinguished by two humps. It is a native of the high table-lands of Central Asia.

BACTRIAN CAMEL.

(2.) The Arabian camel or dromedary— from the Greek *dromos*, "a runner" (Isa. 60:6; Jer. 2:23)—has but one hump, and is a native of Western Asia or Africa.

ARABIAN CAMEL.

The camel was early used both for riding and as a beast of burden (Gen. 24:64; 37:25), and in war (1 Sam. 30:17; Isa. 21:7). Mention is made of the camel among the cattle given by Pharaoh to Abraham (Gen. 12:16). Its flesh was not to be eaten, as it was ranked among un-

clean animals (Lev. 11:4; Deut. 14:7). Abraham's servant rode on a camel when he went to fetch a wife for Isaac (Gen. 24 10, 11). Jacob had camels as a portion of his wealth (30:43), as Abraham also had (24:35). He sent a present of thirty milch camels to his brother Esau (32:15). It appears to have been little in use among the Jews after the conquest. It is, however, mentioned in the history of David (1 Chr. 27:30), and after the Exile (Ezra 2:67; Neh. 7:69). Camels were much in use among other nations in the East. The queen of Sheba came with a caravan of camels when she came to see the wisdom of Solomon (1 Kings 10:2; 2 Chr. 9:1). Benhadad of Damascus also sent a present to Elisha, "forty camels' burden" (2 Kings 8:9).

To show the difficulty in the way of a rich man's entering into the kingdom, our Lord uses the proverbial expression that it was easier for a camel to go through the eye of a needle (Matt. 19:24).

To strain at (rather, *out*) a gnat and swallow a camel was also a proverbial expression (Matt. 23:24), used with reference to those who were careful to avoid small faults, and yet did not hesitate to commit the greatest sins. The Jews carefully filtered their wine before drinking it, for fear of swallowing along with it some insect forbidden in the law as unclean, and yet they omitted openly the "weightier matters" of the law.

The raiment worn by John the Baptist was made of camel's hair (Matt. 3:4; Mark 1:6), by which he was distinguished from those who resided in royal palaces and wore soft raiment. This was also the case with Elijah (2 Kings 1:8), who is called "a hairy man," from his wearing such raiment. "This is one of the most admirable materials for clothing; it keeps out the heat, cold, and rain." The "sackcloth" so often alluded to (2 Kings 1:8; Isa. 15:3; Zech. 13:4, etc.) was probably made of camel's hair.

Ca'mon—*full of stalks*—a place (Judg. 10:5) where Jair was buried. It has usually been supposed to have been a city of Gilead, on the east of Jordan. It is probably, however, the modern *Tell-el-Kaimûn*, on the southern slopes of Carmel, the Jokneam of Carmel (Josh. 12 : 22 ; 1 Kings 4 : 12), since it is not at all unlikely that after he became judge, Jair might find it more convenient to live on the west side of Jordan ; and that he was buried where he had lived.

Camp. During their journeys across the wilderness, the twelve tribes formed encampments at the different places where they halted (Ex. 16 : 13 ; Num. 2 : 3). The diagram here given shows the position of the different tribes and the form of the encampment during the wanderings, according to Num. 1 : 53 ; 2 : 2–31 ; 3 : 29, 35, 38 ; 10 : 13–28.

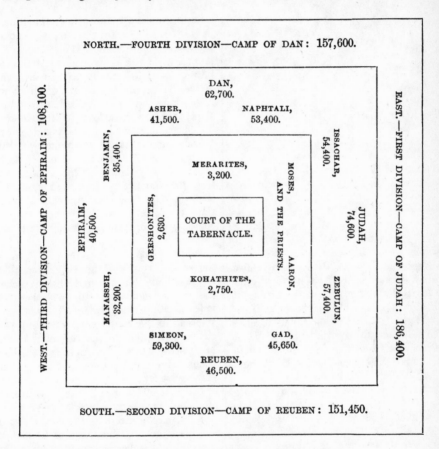

NORTH.—FOURTH DIVISION—CAMP OF DAN : 157,600.

The area of the camp would be in all about 3 square miles. After the Hebrews entered Palestine, the camps then spoken of were exclusively warlike (Josh. 11 : 5, 7 ; Judg. 5 : 19, 21 ; 7 : 1 ; 1 Sam. 29 : 1 ; 30 : 9, etc.).

Cam′phire (Heb. *côpher*)—mentioned in Cant. 1 : 14 (R.V., "henna-flowers"); 4 : 13 (R.V., "henna") — is the *al-henna* of the Arabs, a native of Egypt, producing clusters of small white and yellow odoriferous flowers, whence is made the *Oleum Cyprineum.* From its leaves is made the peculiar auburn dye with which Eastern women stain their nails and the palms of their hands. It is found only at Engedi, on the shore of the Dead Sea. It is known to botanists by the name *Lawsonia alba* or *inermis*, a kind of privet, which grows 6 or 8 feet high. The margin of the Authorized Version of the passages above referred to has "or cypress," not with reference to the conifer so called, but to the circumstance that one of the most highly appreciated species of this plant grew in the island of Cyprus.

CAMPHIRE.

Ca′na—*reedy*—a town of Galilee, near Capernaum. Here our Lord wrought his first miracle, the turning of water into wine (John 2:1–11; 4:46). It is also mentioned as the birth-place of Nathanael (21:2). It is not mentioned in the Old Testament. It has been identified with the modern *Kâna el-Jelîl*, also called *Khurbet Kâna*, a place 8 or 9 miles north of Nazareth. Others have identified it with *Kefr Kenna*, which lies on the direct road to the Sea of Galilee, about 5 miles north-east of Nazareth, and 12 in a direct course from Tiberias. It is called "Cana of Galilee," to distinguish it from Cana of Asher (Josh. 19:28).

Ca′naan. (1.) The fourth son of Ham (Gen. 10:6). His descendants were under a curse in consequence of the transgression of his father (9:22–27). His eldest son, Zidon, was the father of the Sidonians and Phœnicians. He had ten sons, who were the founders of as many tribes (10:15–18).

(2.) The country which derived its name from the preceding. The name as first used by the Phœnicians denoted only the maritime plain on which Sidon was built. But in the time of Moses and Joshua it denoted the whole country to the west of the Jordan and the Dead Sea (13:12; Deut. 11:30). In Josh. 5:12 the LXX. read, "land of the Phœnicians," instead of "land of Canaan."

The name signifies "the lowlands," as distinguished from the land of Gilead on the east of Jordan, which was a mountainous district. The extent and boundaries of Canaan are fully set forth in different parts of Scripture (Gen. 10:19; 17:8; Num. 13:29; 34:8). (See CANAANITES, PALESTINE.)

Ca′naan, the language of, mentioned in Isa. 19:18, denotes the language spoken by the Jews resident in Palestine. The language of the Canaanites and of the Hebrews was substantially the same. This is seen from the fragments of the Phœnician language which still survive, which show the closest analogy to the Hebrew. Yet the subject of the language of the "Canaanites" is very obscure. Being Hamites, their language could not be identical with that of the Jews, who were descendants of Shem. Yet, on the other hand, it is manifest that Abram, shortly after he entered into their country, could hold intercourse freely with the people.

Ca′naanites, the descendants of Canaan, the son of Ham. Migrating from their original home, they seem to have reached the Persian Gulf, and to have there sojourned for some time. They thence "spread to the west, across the mountain chain of Lebanon to the very edge of the Mediterranean Sea, occupying all the land which later became Palestine, also to the north-west as far as the mountain chain of Taurus. This group was very numerous, and broken up into a great many peoples, as we can judge from the list of nations (Gen. 10), the 'sons of Canaan.'" Six different tribes are mentioned in Ex. 3:8, 17; 23:23; 33:2; 34:11. In Ex. 13:5 the "Perizzites" are omitted. The "Girgashites" are mentioned in addition to the foregoing in Deut. 7:1; Josh. 3:10.

The "Canaanites," as distinguished from the Amalekites, the Anakim, and the Rephaim, were "dwellers in the lowlands" (Num. 13:29), the great plains and valleys, the richest and most important parts of Palestine. Tyre and Sidon, their famous cities, were the centres of great

TYPES OF THE ANCIENT RACES OF CANAAN.
From the Monuments. AFTER PETRIE.

commercial activity; and hence the name "Canaanite" came to signify a "trader" or "merchant" (Job 41:6; Prov. 31:24, *lit.* "Canaanites;" comp. Zeph. 1:11; Ezek. 17:4). The name "Canaanite" is also sometimes used to designate the non-Israelite inhabitants of the land in general (Gen. 12:6; Num. 21:3; Judg. 1:10).

The Israelites, when they were led to the Promised Land, were commanded utterly to destroy the descendants of Canaan then possessing it (Ex. 23:23; Num. 33:52, 53; Deut. 20:16, 17). This was to be done "by little and little," lest the beasts of the field should increase (Ex. 23:29; Deut. 7:22, 23). The history of these wars of conquest is given in the Book of Joshua. The extermination of these tribes, however, was never fully carried out. Jerusalem was not taken till the time of David (2 Sam. 5:6, 7). In the days of Solomon bond-service was exacted from the fragments of the tribes still remaining in the land (1 Kings 9:20, 21). Even after the return from captivity survivors of five of the Canaanitish tribes were still found in the land.

Under the name of *Kanana* they appear on Egyptian monuments, wearing a coat of mail and helmet, and distinguished by the use of spear and javelin and the battle-axe. Yet it would appear that, like the Phœnicians, they were much engaged in commerce.

The *war against the Canaanites* can be vindicated only on the ground that it was carried on at the express command of God. The Israelites were merely in this matter the instruments in executing God's purpose in exterminating these nations for their wickedness. They were clearly commissioned by God to carry out this work of judgment (Num. 33:52, 53; Deut. 7:1, 2).

Ca'naanite, a name given to the apostle Simon (Matt. 10:4; Mark 3:18). The word here does not, however, mean a descendant of Canaan, but is a translation, or rather almost a transliteration, of the Syriac word *Kanenyeh* (R.V. rendered "Canaanæan"), which designates the Jewish sect of the *Zealots*. Hence he is called elsewhere (Luke 6:15) "Simon Zelotes;" *i.e.,* Simon of the sect of the Zealots. (See SIMON.)

Can'dace, the queen of the Ethiopians whose "eunuch" or chamberlain was converted to Christianity by the instrumentality of Philip the evangelist (Acts 8:27). The country which she ruled was called by the Greeks *Meroë,* in Upper Nubia. It was long the centre of commercial intercourse between Africa and the south of Asia, and hence became famous for its wealth (Isa. 45:14).

It is somewhat singular that female sovereignty seems to have prevailed in Ethiopia, the name Candace (compare "Pharaoh," "Ptolemy," "Cæsar") being a title common to several successive queens. It is probable that Judaism had taken root in Ethiopia at this time, and hence the visit of the queen's treasurer to Jerusalem to keep the feast. There is a tradition that Candace was herself converted to Christianity by her treasurer on his return, and that he became the apostle of Christianity in that whole region, carrying it also into Abyssinia. It is said that he also preached the gospel in Arabia Felix and in Ceylon, where he suffered martyrdom. (See PHILIP.)

Candle—Heb. *ner*—Job 18:6; 29:3; Ps. 18:28; Prov. 24:20, in all which places the Revised Version and margin of Authorized Version have "lamp," by which the word is elsewhere frequently rendered. The Hebrew word denotes properly any kind of candle or lamp or torch. It is used as a figure of conscience (Prov. 20:27), of a Christian example (Matt. 5:14, 15), and of prosperity (Job 21:17; Prov. 13:9).

Candlestick, the lamp-stand, "candelabrum," which Moses was commanded to make for the tabernacle, according to the pattern shown him. Its form is described in Ex. 25:31-40; 37:17-24, and may be seen represented on the Arch of Titus at Rome. It was among the spoils taken by the Romans from the temple of Jerusalem (A.D. 70). It was made of fine gold, and with the utensils belonging to it was a talent in weight.

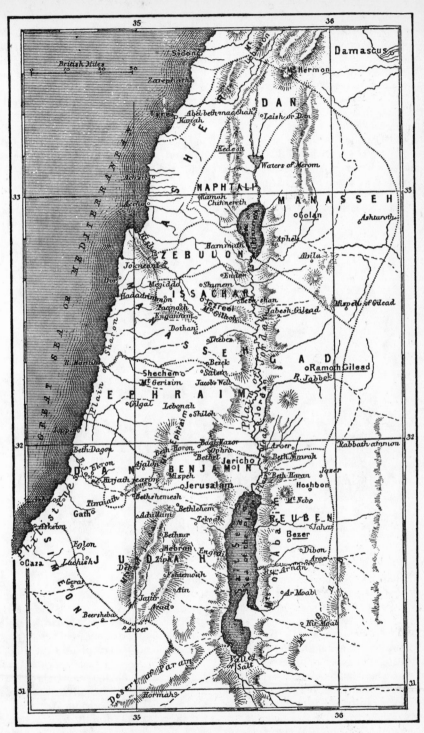

CANAAN AS DIVIDED AMONG THE TRIBES.
(The Six Cities of Refuge are underlined.)

The tabernacle was a tent without windows, and thus artificial light was needed. This was supplied by the candlestick, which, however, served also as a symbol of the church or people of God, who are "the light of the world." The light which "symbolizes the knowledge of God is not the sun or any natural light, but an artificial light supplied with a specially prepared oil; for the knowledge of God is in truth not natural nor common to all men, but furnished over and above nature."

This candlestick was placed on the south side of the Holy Place, opposite the table of showbread (Ex. 27:21; 30:7, 8; Lev. 24:3; 1 Sam. 3:3). It was lighted every evening, and was extinguished in the morning. In the morning the priests trimmed the seven lamps, borne by the seven branches, with golden snuffers, carrying away the ashes in golden dishes (Ex. 25: 38), and supplying the lamps at the same time with fresh oil. What ultimately became of the candlestick is unknown.

THE GOLDEN CANDLESTICK.
(*From the Arch of Titus.*)

In Solomon's temple there were ten separate candlesticks of pure gold, five on the right and five on the left of the Holy Place (1 Kings 7:49; 2 Chr. 4:7). Their structure is not mentioned. They were carried away to Babylon (Jer. 52:19).

In the temple erected after the Exile there was again but one candlestick, and like the first, with seven branches. It was this which was afterwards carried away by Titus to Rome, where it was deposited in the Temple of Peace. When Genseric

plundered Rome, he is said to have carried it to Carthage (A.D. 455). It was recaptured by Belisarius (A.D. 533), and carried to Constantinople and thence to Jerusalem, where it finally disappeared.

Cane, a tall sedgy plant with a hollow stem, growing in moist places. In Isa. 43:24; Jer. 6:20, the Hebrew word *kâneh* is thus rendered, giving its name to the plant. It is rendered "reed" in 1 Kings 14:15; Job 40:21; Isa. 19:6; 35:7. In Ps. 68:31 the expression "company of spearmen " is in the margin and the Revised Version " beasts of the reeds," referring probably to the crocodile or the hippopotamus as a symbol of Egypt. In 2 Kings 18:21; Isa. 36:6; Ezek. 29:6, 7, the reference is to the weak, fragile nature of the reed. (See CALAMUS.)

Cank′er, a *gangrene* or *mortification* which gradually spreads over the whole body (2 Tim. 2:17). In James 5:3 "cankered" means "rusted " (R.V.) or tarnished.

Cank′erworm (Heb. *yelek*), "the licking locust," which licks up the grass of the field ; probably the locust at a certain stage of its growth, just as it emerges from the caterpillar state (Joel 1:4; 2:25). The word is rendered "caterpillar " in Ps. 105:34; Jer. 51:14, 17 (but R.V. "canker-worm"). "It spoileth and fleeth away " (Nah. 3:16), or as some read the passage, "The cankerworm putteth off [*i.e.*, the envelope of its wings], and fleeth away."

Can′neh. Mentioned only in Ezek. 27:23. (See CALNEH.)

Can′on. This word is derived from a Hebrew and Greek word denoting a reed or cane. Hence it means something straight, or something to keep straight; and hence also a rule, or something ruled or measured. It came to be applied to the Scriptures, to denote that they contained the authoritative rule of faith and practice —the standard of doctrine and duty. A book is said to be of canonical authority when it has a right to take a place with the other books which contain a revelation of the Divine will. Such a right does not arise from any ecclesiastical authority, but from the evidence of the inspired authorship of the book. The canonical (*i.e.*, the inspired) books of the Old and New Testaments, are a *complete* rule, and the *only* rule, of faith and practice. They contain the whole supernatural revelation of God to men. The *New Testament Canon* was formed gradually under divine guidance. The different books as they were written came into the possession of the Christian associations which began to be formed soon after the day of Pentecost; and thus slowly the canon increased till all the books were gathered together into one collection containing the whole of the twenty-seven New Testament inspired books. Historical evidence shows that from about the middle of the second century this New Testament collection was substantially such as we now possess. Each book contained in it is proved to have, on its own ground, a right to its place; and thus the whole is of divine authority.

The *Old Testament Canon* is witnessed to by the New Testament writers. Their evidence is conclusive. The quotations in the New from the Old are very numerous, and the references are much more numerous. These quotations and references by our Lord and the apostles most clearly imply the existence at that time of a well-known and publicly acknowledged collection of Hebrew writings under the designation of "The Scriptures;" "The Law and the Prophets and the Psalms;" "Moses and the Prophets," etc. The appeals to these books, moreover, show that they were regarded as of divine authority, finally deciding all questions of which they treat; and that the whole collection so recognized consisted only of the thirty-nine books which we now possess. Thus they endorse as genuine and authentic the canon of the Jewish Scriptures. The Septuagint Version (*q.v.*) also contained every book we now have in the Old Testament Scriptures. As to the *time* at which the Old Testament canon was closed, there are many considerations which point to that of Ezra and Nehemiah, immediately after the return from Babylonian exile. (See BIBLE, EZRA, QUOTATIONS.)

Caper′naum—*Nahum's town*—a Galilean city frequently mentioned in the history of our Lord. It is not mentioned in the Old Testament. After our Lord's expulsion from Nazareth (Matt. 4:13-16; Luke 4:16-31), Capernaum became his "own city." It was the scene of many acts and incidents of his life (Matt. 8:5, 14, 15; 9:2-6, 10-17; 15:1-20; Mark 1:32-34, etc.). The impenitence and unbelief of its inhabitants after the many evidences our Lord gave among them of the truth of his mission, brought down upon them a heavy denunciation of judgment (Matt. 11:23).

It stood on the western shore of the Sea of Galilee. The "land of Gennesaret," near, if not in, which it was situated, was one of the most prosperous and crowded districts of Palestine. This city lay on the great highway from Damascus to Acco and Tyre. It has been identified with *Tell Hûm*, about two miles south-west of where the Jordan flows into the lake. Here are extensive ruins of walls and foundations, and also the remains of what must have been a beautiful synagogue, which it is conjectured may have been the one built by the centurion (Matt. 8:5), in which our Lord frequently taught (John 6:59; Mark 1:9; Luke 4:33). Others have conjectured that the ruins of the city are to be found at *Khân Minyêh*, some three miles further to the south on the shore of the lake. "If *Tell Hûm* be Capernaum, the remains spoken of are without doubt the ruins of the synagogue built by the Roman centurion, and one of the most sacred places on earth. It was in this building that our

TELL HÛM.

Lord gave the well-known discourse in John 6; and it was not without a certain strange feeling that on turning over a large block we found the pot of manna engraven on its face, and remembered the words: 'I am that bread of life: your fathers did eat manna in the wilderness, and are dead.'"— *The Recovery of Jerusalem*.

Caph′tor—*a chaplet*—the original seat of the Philistines (Deut. 2:23; Jer. 47:4; Amos 9:7). Some identify it with Crete, but most probably it was a part of Egypt, the *Caphtur* in the north Delta, since the Caphtorim were of the same race as the Mizraite people (Gen. 10:14; 1 Chr. 1:12).

Cappado′cia, the easternmost and the largest province of Asia Minor. Christianity very early penetrated into this country (1 Pet. 1:1). On the day of Pentecost there were Cappadocians at Jerusalem (Acts 2:9).

Cap′tain. (1.) Heb. *sar* (1 Sam. 22:2; 2 Sam. 23:19). Rendered "chief," Gen. 40:2; 41:9; rendered also "prince," Dan. 1:7; "ruler," Judg. 9:30; "governor," 1 Kings 22:26. This same Hebrew word denotes a military captain (Ex. 18:21; 2 Kings 1:9; Deut. 1:15; 1 Sam. 18:13, etc.), the "captain of the body-guard" (Gen. 37:36; 39:1; 41:10; Jer. 40:1), or, as the word may be rendered, "chief of the executioners" (marg.). The officers of the king's body-guard frequently acted as executioners. Nebuzar-adan (Jer. 39:13) and Arioch (Dan. 2:14) held this office in Babylon.

The "captain of the guard" mentioned in Acts 28:16 was the Prætorian prefect, the commander of the Prætorian troops.

(2.) Another word (Heb. *katsin*) so translated denotes sometimes a military (Josh. 10:24; Judg. 11:6, 11; Isa. 22:3 "rulers;" Dan. 11:18) and sometimes a civil command, a judge, magistrate—Arab. *kâdy*—(Isa. 1:10; 3:6; Micah 3:1, 9).

(3.) It is also the rendering of a Hebrew word (*shalish*) meaning "a third man," or "one of three." The LXX. render in plural by *tristatai; i.e.*, "soldiers fighting from chariots," so called because each warchariot contained three men, one of whom acted as charioteer while the other two fought (Ex. 14:7; 15:4; 1 Kings 9:22; comp. 2 Kings 9:25). This word is used also to denote the king's body-guard (2 Kings 10:25; 1 Chr. 11:11; 12:18) or aides-de-camp.

(4.) The "captain of the temple" mentioned in Acts 4:1 and 5:24 was not a military officer, but superintendent of the guard of priests and Levites who kept watch in the temple by night. (Comp. "the ruler of the house of God," 1 Chr. 9:11; 2 Chr. 31:13; Neh. 11:11.)

(5.) The *Captain of our salvation* is a name given to our Lord (Heb. 2:10), because he is the author and source of our salvation, the head of his people, whom he is conducting to glory. The "captain of the Lord's host" (Josh. 5:14, 15) is the name given to that mysterious person who manifested himself to Abraham (Gen. 12:7), and to Moses in the bush (Ex. 3:2, 6, etc.) —the Angel of the covenant. (See ANGEL.)

Cap'tive, one taken in war. Captives were often treated with great cruelty and indignity (1 Kings 20:32; Josh. 10:24; Judg. 1:7; 2 Sam. 4:12; Judg. 8:7; 2 Sam.

12:31; 1 Chr. 20:3). When a city was taken by assault, all the men were slain, and the women and children carried away captive and sold as slaves (Isa. 20; 47:3; 2 Chr. 28:9-15; Ps. 44:12; Joel 3:3), and exposed to the most cruel treatment (Nah. 3:10; Zech. 14:2; Esther 3:13; 2 Kings 8:12; Isa. 13:16, 18). Captives were sometimes carried away into foreign countries, as was the case with the Jews (Jer. 20:5; 39:9, 10; 40:7).

Captiv'ity. (1.) *Of Israel.* The kingdom of the ten tribes was successively invaded by several Assyrian kings. Pul (*q.v.*) imposed a tribute on Menahem of a thousand talents of silver (2 Kings 15:19, 20; 1 Chr. 5:26) (B.C. 762), and Tiglath-pileser, in the days of Pekah (B.C. 738), carried away the trans-Jordanic tribes and the inhabitants of Galilee into Assyria (1 Kings 15:29; Isa. 9:1). Subsequently Shalmaneser invaded Israel and laid siege to Samaria, the capital of the kingdom. During the siege he died, and was succeeded by Sargon, who took the city, and transported the great mass of the people into Assyria (B.C. 721), placing them in Halah and in Habor, and in the cities of the Medes (2 Kings 17:3, 5). Samaria was never again inhabited by the Israelites. The families thus removed were carried to distant cities, many of them not far from the Caspian Sea, and their place was supplied by colonists from Babylon and Cuthah, etc. (2 Kings 17:24). Thus terminated the kingdom of the ten tribes, after a separate duration of two hundred and fifty-five years (B.C. 975-721).

Many speculations have been indulged in with reference to these ten tribes. But we believe that all, except the number that probably allied themselves with Judah and shared in their restoration under Cyrus, are finally lost.

> "Like the dew on the mountain,
> Like the foam on the river,
> Like the bubble on the fountain,
> They are gone, and for ever."

(2.) *Of Judah.* In the third year of Jehoiachim, the eighteenth king of Judah (B.C. 605), Nebuchadnezzar having overcome the Egyptians at Carchemish, advanced to Jerusalem with a great army. After a brief siege he took that city, and carried away the vessels of the sanctuary to Babylon, and dedicated them in the Temple of Belus (2 Kings 24:1; 2 Chr. 36: 6, 7; Dan. 1:1, 2). He also carried away the treasures of the king, whom he made his vassal. At this time, from which is dated the "seventy years" of captivity (Jer. 25; Dan. 9:1, 2), Daniel and his companions were carried to Babylon, there to be brought up at the court and trained in all the learning of the Chaldeans. After this, in the fifth year of Jehoiachim, a great national fast was appointed (Jer. 36:9), during which the king, to show his defiance, cut up the leaves of the book of Jeremiah's prophecies as they were read to him in his winter palace, and threw them into the fire. In the same spirit he rebelled against Nebuchadnezzar (2 Kings 24:1), who again a second time (B.C. 598) marched against Jerusalem, and put Jehoiachim to death, placing his son Jehoiachin on the throne in his stead. But Jehoiachin's counsellors displeasing Nebuchadnezzar, he again a third time turned his army against Jerusalem, and carried away to Babylon a second detachment of Jews as captives, to the number of 10,000 (2 Kings 24:13; Jer. 24:1; 2 Chr. 36:10), among whom were the king, with his mother and all his princes and officers, also Ezekiel, who with many of his companions were settled on the banks of the river Chebar (q.v.). He also carried away all the remaining treasures of the temple and the palace, and the golden vessels of the sanctuary.

Mattaniah, the uncle of Jehoiachin, was now made king over what remained of the kingdom of Judah, under the name of Zedekiah (2 Kings 24:17; 2 Chr. 36:10). After a troubled reign of eleven years his kingdom came to an end (2 Chr. 36:11). Nebuchadnezzar, with a powerful army, besieged Jerusalem, and Zedekiah became a prisoner in Babylon. His eyes were put out, and he was kept in close confinement till his death (2 Kings 25:7). The city was spoiled of all that was of value, and then given up to the flames. The temple and palaces were consumed, and the walls of the city were levelled with the ground (B.C. 586), and all that remained of the people, except a number of the poorest class who were left to till the ground and dress the vineyards, were carried away captives to Babylon. This was the third and last deportation of Jewish captives. The land was now utterly desolate, and was abandoned to anarchy.

In the first year of his reign as king of Babylon (B.C. 536), Cyrus issued a decree liberating the Jewish captives, and permitting them to return to Jerusalem and rebuild the city and the temple (2 Chr. 36:22, 23; Ezra 1; 2). The number of the people forming the first caravan, under Zerubbabel, amounted in all to 42,360 (Ezra 2:64, 65), besides 7,367 men-servants and maid-servants. A considerable number, 12,000 probably, from the ten tribes who had been carried away into Assyria no doubt combined with this band of liberated captives.

At a later period other bands of the Jews returned (1) under Ezra (7:7) (B.C. 458), and (2) Nehemiah (7:66) (B.C. 445). But the great mass of the people remained still in the land to which they had been carried, and became a portion of the Jews of the "dispersion" (John 7:35; 1 Pet. 1:1). The whole number of the exiles that chose to remain was probably about six times the number of those who returned.

Car'buncle (Ex. 28:17; 39:10; Ezek. 28:13). Heb. *bārkath;* LXX. *smaragdos;* Vulgate, *smaragdus;* Revised Version, marg., "emerald." The Hebrew word is from a root meaning "to glitter," "lighten," "flash." When held up to the sun, this gem shines like a burning coal, a dark-red glowing coal, and hence is called "carbunculus" —i.e., a little coal. It was one of the jewels in the first row of the high priest's breastplate. It has been conjectured by some that the garnet is meant. In Isa. 54:12 the Hebrew word is *'ekdāh,* used in the prophetic description of the glory and beauty of the mansions above. Next to the diamond it is the hardest and most costly of all precious stones.

Car'case, contact with a, made an Israelite ceremonially unclean, and made whatever he touched also unclean, according to the Mosaic law (Hag. 2 : 14 ; comp. Num. 19 : 16, 22 ; Lev. 11 : 39).

Car'chemish—*fortress of Chemosh*—a city on the west bank of the Euphrates (Jer. 46 : 2 ; 2 Chr. 35 : 20), not, as was once supposed, the Circesium at the confluence of the Chebar and the Euphrates, but a city considerably higher up the river, and commanding the ordinary passage of the Euphrates ; probably identical with Hierapolis. It was the capital of the kingdom of the northern Hittites. The Babylonian army, under Nebuchadnezzar, the son of Nabopolassar, here met and conquered the army of Pharaoh-necho, king of Egypt (B.C. 607). By this victory the Babylonians became masters of the whole of Western Asia.

Car'mel—*a park;* generally with the article, "*the* park." (1.) A prominent headland of Central Palestine, consisting of several connected hills extending from the plain of Esdraelon to the sea, a distance of some 12 miles or more. At the east

MOUNT CARMEL FROM HAIFA.

end, in its highest part, it is 1,728 feet high, and at the west end it forms a promontory to the bay of Acre about 600 feet above the sea. It lay within the tribe of Asher. It was here, at the east end of the ridge, at a place called *el-Mūkhrakah* (*i.e.*, the place of burning), that Elijah brought back the people to their allegiance to God, and slew the prophets of Baal (1 Kings 18). Here were consumed the "fifties" of the royal guard ; and here also Elisha received the visit of the bereaved mother whose son was restored by him to life (2 Kings 4 : 25–37). "No mountain in or around Palestine retains its ancient beauty so much as Carmel. Two or three villages and some scattered cottages are found on it ; its groves are few but luxuriant ; it is no place for crags and precipices or rocks of wild goats ; but its surface is covered with a rich and constant verdure." "The whole mountain-side is dressed with blossom, and flowering shrubs, and fragrant herbs." The western extremity of the ridge is, however, more rocky and bleak than the eastern. The head of the bride in Cant. 7 : 5 is compared to Carmel. It is ranked with Bashan on account of its rich pastures (Isa. 33:9; Jer. 50:19; Amos 1:2). The whole ridge is deeply furrowed with rocky ravines filled with dense jungle. There are many caves in its sides, which at one time were inhabited by swarms of monks. These caves are referred to in Amos 9:3. To them Elijah and Elisha often resorted (1 Kings 18:19, 42; 2 Kings 2:25). On its north-west summit there is an ancient establishment of Carmelite monks. Vineyards have recently been planted on the mount by the German colonists of Haifa. The modern Arabic name of the mount is *Kŭrmul*, but more commonly *Jebel Mar Elyas*—i.e., Mount St. Elias, from the Convent of Elias.

(2.) A town in the hill country of Judah (Josh. 15:55), the residence of Nabal (1 Sam. 25:2, 5, 7, 40), and the native place of Abigail, who became David's wife (1 Sam. 27:3). Here king Uzziah had his vineyards (2 Chr. 26:10). The ruins of this town still remain under the name of *Kŭrmŭl*, about 10 miles south-south-east of Hebron, close to those of Maon.

Car'mi—*vine-dresser.* (1.) The last named of the four sons of Reuben (Gen. 46:9).

(2.) A descendant of Judah (1 Chr. 4:2). He is elsewhere (2:18) called Caleb (*q.v.*).

(3.) The son of Zimri, and the father of Achan (Josh. 7:1), "the troubler of Israel."

Car'nal. Unconverted men are so called (1 Cor. 3:3). They are represented as of a "carnal mind, which is enmity against God" (Rom. 8:6, 7). Enjoyments that minister to the wants and desires of man's animal nature are so called (Rom. 15:27; 1 Cor. 9:11). The ceremonial of the Mosaic law is spoken of as "carnal," because it related to things outward, the bodies of men and of animals, and the purification of the flesh (Heb. 7:16; 9:10). The weapons of Christian warfare are "not carnal"—that is, they are not of man's device, nor are wielded by human power (2 Cor. 10:4).

Car'penter, an artificer in stone, iron, and copper, as well as in wood (2 Sam. 5:11; 1 Chr. 14:1; Mark 6:3). The tools used by carpenters are mentioned in 1 Sam. 13:19, 20; Judg. 4:21; Isa. 10:15; 44:13. It was said of our Lord, "Is not this the carpenter's son?" (Matt. 13:55); also, "Is not this the carpenter?" (Mark 6:3). Every Jew, even the rabbis, learned some handicraft: Paul was a tent-maker. "In the cities the carpenters would be Greeks, and skilled workmen; the carpenter of a provincial village could only have held a very humble position, and secured a very moderate competence."

Car'riage. In the Authorized Version this word is found as the rendering of many different words. In Judg. 18:21 it means valuables, wealth, or booty. In Isa. 46:1 (R.V., "the things that ye carried about") the word means a load for a beast of burden. In 1 Sam. 17:22 and Isa. 10:28 it is the rendering of a word ("stuff" in 1 Sam. 10:22) meaning implements, equipments, baggage. The phrase in Acts 21:15, "We took up our carriages," means properly, "We packed up our baggage," as in the Revised Version.

Cart, a vehicle moving on wheels, and usually drawn by oxen (2 Sam. 6:3). The Hebrew word thus rendered, *'agâlâh* (1 Sam. 6:7, 8), is also rendered "waggon" (Gen. 45:19). It is used also to denote a war-chariot (Ps. 46:9). Carts were used for the removal of the ark and its sacred utensils (Num. 7:3, 6). After retaining the ark amongst them for seven months, the Philistines sent it back to the Israelites. On this occasion they set it in a new cart—probably a rude construction, with solid wooden wheels like that still used in Western Asia—which was drawn by two milch cows, which conveyed it straight to Beth-shemesh.

A "cart rope," for the purpose of fastening loads on carts, is used (Isa. 5:18) as a symbol of the power of sinful pleasures or habits over him who indulges them. (See CORD.) In Syria and Palestine wheel-carriages for any other purpose than the conveyance of agricultural produce are almost unknown.

Carve. The arts of engraving and carving were much practised among the Jews. They were practised in connection with the construction of the tabernacle and the

ORIENTAL OX-CART.

temple (Ex. 31:2, 5; 35:33; 1 Kings 6:18, 35; Ps. 74:6), as well as in the ornamentation of the priestly dresses (Ex. 28:9-36; Zech. 3:9; 2 Chr. 2:7, 14). Isaiah (44:13-17) gives a minute description of the process of carving idols of wood.

Case'ment, a barrier of open-work placed before windows (Prov. 7:6). In Judg. 5:28 the Hebrew word is rendered "lattice," in the LXX. "network," an opening through which cool air is admitted.

Casiph'ia—*silver*—a place between Babylon and Jerusalem, where Iddo resided (Ezra 8:17); otherwise unknown.

Cas'luhim—*fortified*—a people descended from Mizraim (Gen. 10:14; 1 Chr. 1:12). Their original seat was probably somewhere in Lower Egypt, along the sea-coast to the south border of Palestine.

Cas'sia. (1.) Hebrew *kiddah'*—*i.e.,* "split." One of the principal spices of the holy anointing oil (Ex. 30:24), and an article of commerce (Ezek. 27:19). It is the inner bark of a tree resembling the cinnamon (*q.v.*)—the *Cinnamomum cassia* of botanists—and was probably imported from India.

(2.) Hebrew pl. *ketzi'oth* (Ps. 45:8). Mentioned in connection with myrrh and aloes as being used to scent garments. It was probably prepared from the peeled bark, as the Hebrew word suggests, of some kind of cinnamon.

Cast'away—Gr. *adokimos*—(1 Cor. 9:27), one regarded as unworthy (R.V., "rejected"); elsewhere rendered "reprobate" (2 Tim. 3:8, etc.); "rejected" (Heb. 6:8, etc.).

Castle, a military fortress (1 Chr. 11:7), also probably a kind of tower used by the priests for making known anything discovered at a distance (1 Chr. 6:54). Castles are also mentioned (Gen. 25:16) as a kind of watch-tower, from which shepherds kept watch over their flocks by night. The "castle" into which the chief captain commanded Paul to be brought was the quarters of the Roman soldiers in the fortress of Antonia (so called by Herod after his patron Mark Antony), which was close to the north-west corner of the temple (Acts 21:34), which it commanded.

Cas'tor and Pol'lux—the "Dioscuri"—two heroes of Greek and Roman mythology. Their figures were probably painted or sculptured on the prow of the ship which Luke refers to (Acts 28:11). They were regarded as the tutelary divinities of sailors. They appeared in the heavens as the constellation Gemini.

Cat'erpillar—*the consumer.* Used in the Old Testament (1 Kings 8:37; 2 Chr. 6:28; Ps. 78:46; Isa. 33:4) as the translation of a word (*hasil*) the root of which means "to devour" or "consume," and which is used also with reference to the locust in Deut. 28:38. It may have been a species of locust, or the name of one of the transformations through which the locust passes—*locust-grub.*

It is also found (Ps. 105:34; Jer. 51:14, 27; R.V., "cankerworm") as the rendering of a different Hebrew word, *yelek*—a word elsewhere rendered "cankerworm" (*q.v.*)—Joel 1:4; 2:25. (See LOCUST.)

Ca'tholic epistles, the epistles of James, Peter, John, and Jude; so called because they are addressed to Christians in general, and not to any church or person in particular.

Cat'tle abounded in the Holy Land. To the rearing and management of them the inhabitants chiefly devoted themselves (Deut. 8:13; 12:21; 1 Sam. 11:5; 12:3; Ps. 144:14; Jer. 3:24). They may be classified as—

(1.) *Neat cattle.* Many hundreds of these were yearly consumed in sacrifices or used for food. The finest herds were found in Bashan, beyond Jordan (Num. 32:4). Large herds also pastured on the wide fertile plains of Sharon. They were yoked to the plough (1 Kings 19:19), and were employed for carrying burdens (1 Chr. 12:40). They were driven with a pointed rod (Judg. 3:31) or goad (*q.v.*).

According to the Mosaic law, the mouths of cattle employed for the threshing-floor were not to be muzzled, so as to prevent them from eating of the provender over which they trampled (Deut. 25:4). Whosoever stole and sold or slaughtered an ox must give five in satisfaction (Ex. 22:1); but if it was found alive in the possession of him who stole it, he was required to make double restitution only (22:4). If an ox went astray, whoever found it was required to bring it back to its owner (23:4; Deut. 22:1, 4). An ox and an ass could not be yoked together in the plough (Deut. 22:10).

(2.) *Small cattle.* Next to herds of neat cattle, sheep formed the most important of the possessions of the inhabitants of Palestine (Gen. 12:16; 13:5; 26:14; 21:27; 29:2, 3). They are frequently mentioned among the booty taken in war (Num. 31:32; Josh. 6:21; 1 Sam. 14:32; 15:3). There were many who were owners of large flocks (1 Sam. 25:2; 2 Sam. 12:2, comp. Job 1:3). Kings also had shepherds "over their flocks" (1 Chr. 27:31), from which they derived a large portion of their revenue (2 Sam. 17:29; 1 Chr. 12:40). The districts most famous for their flocks of sheep were the plain of Sharon (Isa. 65:10), Mount Carmel (Micah 7:14), Bashan and Gilead (Micah 7:14). In patriarchal times the flocks of sheep were sometimes tended by the daughters of the owners. Thus Rachel, the daughter of Laban, kept her father's sheep (Gen. 29:9); as also Zipporah and her six sisters had charge of their father Jethro's flocks (Ex. 2:16). Sometimes they were kept by hired shepherds (John 10:12), and sometimes by the sons of the family (1 Sam. 16:11; 17:15). The keepers so familiarized their sheep with their voices that they knew them, and followed them at their call. Sheep, but more especially rams and lambs, were frequently offered in sacrifice. The shearing of sheep was a great festive occasion (1 Sam. 25:4; 2 Sam. 13:23). They were folded at night, and guarded by their keepers against the attacks of the lion (Micah 5:8), the bear (1 Sam. 17:34), and the wolf (Matt. 10:16; John 10:12). They were liable to wander over the wide pastures and go astray (Ps. 119:176; Isa. 53:6; Hos. 4:16; Matt. 18:12).

Goats also formed a part of the pastoral wealth of Palestine (Gen. 15:9; 32:14; 37:31). They were used both for sacrifice and for food (Deut. 14:4), especially the young males (Gen. 27:9, 14, 17; Judg. 6:19; 13:15; 1 Sam. 16:20). Goat's hair was used for making tent cloth (Ex. 26:7; 36:14), and for mattresses and bedding (1 Sam. 19:13, 16). (See GOAT.)

Caul (Heb. *yothe'reth; i.e.,* "something redundant"), the membrane which covers the upper part of the liver (Ex. 29:13, 22; Lev. 3:4, 10, 15; 4:9; 7:4; marg., "midriff"). In Hos. 13:8 (Heb. *s*ĕ*ghōr; i.e.,* "an enclosure") the *pericardium*, or parts about the heart, is meant.

Cauls. In Isa. 3:18 this word (Heb. *shebîsîm*), in the marg. "networks," denotes network caps to contain the hair, worn by females. Others explain it as meaning "wreaths worn round the forehead, reaching from one ear to the other."

Cause'way, a raised way, an ascent by steps, or a raised slope between Zion and the temple (1 Chr. 26:16, 18). In 2 Chr. 9:11 the same word is translated "terrace."

Cave. There are numerous natural caves among the limestone rocks of Syria, many of which have been artificially enlarged for various purposes.

The first notice of a cave occurs in the history of Lot (Gen. 19:30).

The next we read of is the cave of Machpelah (*q.v.*), which Abraham purchased from the sons of Heth (Gen. 25:9, 10). It was the burying-place of Sarah and of Abraham himself, also of Isaac, Rebekah, Leah, and Jacob (Gen. 49:31; 50:13).

The cave of Makkedah, into which the five Amorite kings retired after their defeat by Joshua (10:16, 27).

The cave of Adullam (*q.v.*), an immense natural cavern, where David hid himself from Saul (1 Sam. 22:1, 2).

The cave of Engedi (*q.v.*), now called *Ain Jidy* — *i.e.*, the "Fountain of the Kid"—where David cut off the skirt of Saul's robe (24:4). Here he also found a shelter for himself and his followers to the number of 600 (23:29; 24:1). "On all sides the country is full of caverns which might serve as lurking-places for David and his men, as they do for outlaws at the present day."

CEDARS OF LEBANON.

The cave in which Obadiah hid the prophets (1 Kings 18:4) was probably in the north, but it cannot be identified.

The cave of Elijah (1 Kings 19:9), and the "cleft" of Moses on Horeb (Ex. 33:22), cannot be determined.

In the time of Gideon the Israelites took refuge from the Midianites in dens and caves, such as abounded in the mountain regions of Manasseh (Judg. 6:2).

Caves were frequently used as dwelling-places (Num. 24:21; Cant. 2:14; Jer. 49:16; Obad. 3). "The excavations at Deir Dubbân, on the south side of the wady leading to Santa Hanneh, are probably the dwellings of the Horites," the ancient inhabitants of Idumea Proper. The pits or cavities in rocks were also sometimes used as prisons (Isa. 24:22; 51:14; Zech. 9:11). Those which had niches in their sides were occupied as burying-places (Ezek. 32:23; John 11:38).

Ce'dar (Heb. *e'rez*, Gr. *kedros*, Lat. *cedrus*), a tree very frequently mentioned in Scripture. It was stately (Ezek. 31:3–5), long-branched (Ps. 80:10; 92:12; Ezek.

31 : 6–9), odoriferous (Cant. 4 : 15, 16 ; Hos. 14 : 6), durable, and therefore much used for boards, pillars, and ceilings (1 Kings 6 : 9, 10 ; 7 : 2 ; Jer. 22 : 14), for masts (Ezek. 27 : 5), and for carved images (Isa. 44 : 14).

It grew very abundantly in Palestine, and particularly on Lebanon, of which it was "the glory" (Isa. 35 : 2 ; 60 : 13). Hiram supplied Solomon with cedar trees from Lebanon for various purposes connected with the construction of the temple and the king's palace (2 Sam. 5 : 11 ; 7 : 2, 7 ; 1 Kings 5 : 6, 8, 10 ; 6 : 9, 10, 15, 16, 18, 20 ; 7 : 2, 3, 7, 11, 12 ; 9 : 11, etc.). Cedars were used also in the building of the second temple under Zerubbabel (Ezra 3 : 7).

Of the ancient cedars of Lebanon there remain now only some seven or eight. They are not standing together. But beside them there are found between three hundred . and four hundred of younger growth. They stand in an amphitheatre fronting the west, about 6,400 feet above the level of the sea.

The cedar is often figuratively alluded to in the sacred Scriptures. "The mighty conquerors of olden days, the despots of Assyria and the Pharaohs of Egypt, the proud and idolatrous monarchs of Judah, the Hebrew commonwealth itself, the warlike Ammonites of patriarchal times, and the moral majesty of the Messianic age, are all compared to the towering cedar, in its royal loftiness and supremacy (Isa. 2 : 13 ; Ezek. 17 : 3, 22, 23 ; 31 : 3–9 ; Amos 2 : 9 ; Zech. 11 : 1, 2 ; Job 40 : 17 ; Ps. 29 : 5 ; 80 : 10 ; 92 : 12, etc.)."—Groser's *Scrip. Nat. Hist.* (See Box-tree.)

Ce′dron—*the black torrent*—the brook flowing through the ravine below the eastern wall of Jerusalem (John 18 : 1). (See Kidron.)

Ceil′ing, the covering (1 Kings 7 : 3, 7) of the inside roof and walls of a house with planks of wood (2 Chr. 3 : 5 ; Jer. 22 : 14). Ceilings were sometimes adorned with various ornaments in stucco, gold, silver, gems, and ivory. The ceilings of the temple and of Solomon's palace are described 1 Kings 6 : 9, 15 ; 7 : 3 ; 2 Chr. 3 : 5, 9.

Cel′lar, a subterranean vault (1 Chr. 27 : 28), a storehouse. The word is also used to denote the treasury of the temple (1 Kings 7 : 51) and of the king (14 : 26). The Hebrew word is rendered "garner" in Joel 1 : 17, and "armoury" in Jer. 50 : 25.

Cen′chrea—*millet*—the eastern harbour of Corinth, from which it was distant about 9 miles east, and the outlet for its trade with the Asiatic shores of the Mediterranean. When Paul returned from his second missionary journey to Syria, he sailed from this port (Acts 18 : 18). In Rom. 16 : 1 he speaks as if there were at the time of his writing that epistle an organized church there. The western harbour of Corinth was Lechæum, about a mile and a half from the city. It was the channel of its trade with Italy and the west.

Cen′ser, the vessel in which incense was presented on "the golden altar" before the Lord in the temple (Ex. 30 : 1–9). The priest filled the censer with live coal from the sacred fire on the altar of burnt-offering, and having carried it into the sanctuary, there threw upon the burning coals the sweet incense (Lev. 16 : 12, 13), which sent up a cloud of smoke, filling the apartment with fragrance. The censers in daily use were of brass (Num. 16 : 39), and were designated by a different Hebrew name— *miktéreth* (2 Chr. 26 : 19 ; Ezek. 8 : 11); while those used on the day of Atonement were of gold, and were denoted by a word (*mahtâh*) meaning "something to take fire with ;" LXX. *pureion*=a fire-pan. Solomon prepared for the temple censers of pure gold (1 Kings 7 : 50 ; 2 Chr. 4 : 22). The angel in the Apocalypse is represented with a golden censer (Rev. 8 : 3, 5). Paul speaks of the golden censer as belonging to the tabernacle (Heb. 9 : 4). The Greek word *thumiaterion*, here rendered "censer," may more appropriately denote, as in the margin of Revised Version, "the altar of incense." Paul does not here say that the *thumiaterion* was *in* the holiest, for it was in the holy place, but that the holiest *had* it—*i.e.,* that it belonged to the holiest (1 Kings 6 : 22). It was intimately connected with the high priest's service in the holiest.

The manner in which the censer is to be used is described in Num. 4 : 14 ; Lev. 16 : 12.

Cen'sus. There are five instances of a census of the Jewish people having been taken. (1.) In the fourth month after the Exodus, when the people were encamped at Sinai. The number of men from twenty years old and upward was then 603,550 (Ex. 38 : 26). (2.) Another census was made just before the entrance into Canaan, when the number was found to be 601,730, showing thus a small decrease (Num. 26 : 51). (3.) The next census was in the time of David, when the number, exclusive of the tribes of Levi and Benjamin, was found to be 1,300,000 (2 Sam. 24 : 9 ; 1 Chr. 21 : 5). (4.) Solomon made a census of the foreigners in the land, and found 153,600 ablebodied workmen (2 Chr. 2 : 17, 18). (5.) After the return from Exile the whole congregation of Israel was numbered, and found to amount to 42,360 (Ezra 2 : 64). A census was made by the Roman government in the time of our Lord (Luke 2 : 1). (See TAXING.)

Centu'rion, a Roman officer in command of a hundred men (Mark 15 : 39, 44, 45). Cornelius, the first Gentile convert, was a centurion (Acts 10 : 1, 22). Other centurions are mentioned in Matt. 8 : 5, 8, 13 ; Luke 7 : 2, 6 ; Acts 21 : 32 ; 22 : 25, 26 ; 23 : 17, 23 ; 24 : 23 ; 27 : 1, 6, 11, 31, 43 ; 28 : 16. A centurion watched the crucifixion of our Lord (Matt. 27 : 54 ; Luke 23 : 47), and when he saw the wonders attending it, exclaimed, "Truly this man was the Son of God." "The centurions mentioned in the New Testament are uniformly spoken of in terms of praise, whether in the Gospels or in the Acts. It is interesting to compare this with the statement of Polybius (vi. 24), that the centurions were chosen by merit, and so were men remarkable not so much for their daring courage as for their *deliberation, constancy,* and *strength of mind.*"—Dr. Maclear's *N. T. Hist.*

Ce'phas, a Syriac surname given by Christ to Simon (John 1 : 42), meaning "rock." The Greeks translated it by *Petros,* and the Latins by *Petrus.*

Cesarea. See CÆSAREA.

Chaff, the refuse of winnowed corn. It was usually burned (Ps. 83 : 13 ; Isa. 5 : 24 ; Matt. 3 : 12). This word sometimes, however, means dried grass or hay (Isa. 5 : 24 ; 33 : 11). Chaff is used as a figure of abortive wickedness (Ps. 1 : 4 ; Matt. 3 : 12). False doctrines are also called chaff (Jer. 23 : 28), or more correctly rendered "chopped straw." The destruction of the wicked, and their powerlessness, are likened to the carrying away of chaff by the wind (Isa. 17 : 13 ; Hos. 13 : 3 ; Zeph. 2 : 2).

Chain. (1.) A part of the insignia of office. A chain of gold was placed about Joseph's neck (Gen. 41 : 42) ; and one was promised to Daniel (5 : 7). It is used as a symbol of sovereignty (Ezek. 16 : 11). The breast-plate of the high-priest was fastened to the ephod by golden chains (Ex. 39 : 17, 21).

(2.) It was used as an ornament (Prov. 1 : 9 ; Cant. 1 : 10). The Midianites adorned the necks of their camels with chains (Judg. 8 : 21, 26).

(3.) Chains were also used as fetters wherewith prisoners were bound (Judg. 16 : 21 ; 2 Sam. 3 : 34 ; 2 Kings 25 : 7 ; Jer. 39 : 7). Paul was in this manner bound to a Roman soldier (Acts 28 : 20 ; Eph. 6 : 20 ; 2 Tim. 1 : 16). Sometimes, for the sake of greater security, the prisoner was attached by two chains to two soldiers, as in the case of Peter (Acts 12 : 6).

Chalced'ony. Mentioned only in Rev. 21 : 19, as one of the precious stones in the foundation of the New Jerusalem. The name of this stone is derived from Chalcedon, where it is said to have been first discovered. In modern mineralogy this is the name of an agate-like quartz of a bluish colour. Pliny so names the Indian ruby. The mineral intended in Revelation is probably the Hebrew *nóphekh,* translated "emerald" (Ex. 28 : 18 ; 39 : 11 ; Ezek. 27 : 16 ; 28 : 13). It is rendered "anthrax" in the LXX., and "carbunculus" in the Vulgate. (See CARBUNCLE.)

Chalde'a. The southern portion of Babylonia — Lower Mesopotamia — lying chiefly on the right bank of the Euphrates, but commonly used of the whole of the Mesopotamian plain. The Hebrew name is *Kasdim,* which is usually rendered "Chaldeans" (Jer. 50 : 10 ; 51 : 24, 35 ;

Ezek. 16:29). It has been suggested that *Kasdim* may be derived from the Assyrian word *kasidi*, meaning "conquerors," a name applicable to the Semitic conquerors of Accad—*i.e.*, of Northern Babylonia—and Shumir or Shinar, the southern half of the pre-Semitic Babylonia. The name "Chaldeans" is of Greek origin, and is derived from *Kaldai*, the name of a tribe inhabiting the shores of the Persian Gulf. Under Merodach-baladan, the Kaldai conquered Babylonia, and gave their name to the country (2 Chr. 36:17; Dan. 9:1).

The country so named is a vast plain formed by the deposits of the Euphrates and the Tigris, extending to about 400 miles along the course of these rivers, and about 100 miles in average breadth. "In former days the vast plains of Babylon were nourished by a complicated system of canals and water-courses, which spread over the surface of the country like a network. The wants of a teeming population were supplied by a rich soil, not less bountiful than that on the banks of the Egyptian Nile. Like islands rising from a golden sea of waving corn stood frequent groves of palm-trees and pleasant gardens, affording to the idler or traveller their grateful and highly-valued shade. Crowds of passengers hurried along the dusty roads to and from the busy city. The land was rich in corn

CHALDEAN ACCOUNT OF BABEL.

and wine. How changed is the aspect of that region at the present day! Long lines of mounds, it is true, mark the courses of those main arteries which formerly diffused life and vegetation along their banks, but their channels are now bereft of moisture and choked with drifted sand; the smaller offshoots are wholly effaced. 'A drought is upon her waters,' says the prophet (Jer. 50:38); 'and they shall be dried up.' All that remains of that ancient civilization, that 'glory of kingdoms,' 'the praise of the whole earth,' is recognizable in the numerous mouldering heaps of bricks and rubbish which overspread the plain. Instead of the luxuriant fields,

the groves and gardens, nothing now meets the eye but an arid waste; the dense population of former times is vanished, and no man dwells there."—Loftus's *Chaldea*.

The first *towns* mentioned in Scripture—Babel, Erech, Accad, and Calneh, in the land of Shinar (Gen. 10:10)—are Chaldean cities. They were populous and prosperous cities, the centres of great activity. Ur was one of the principal ports, from which ships traded to many distant regions. Abraham grew up in the midst of all this busy life, surrounded by the idolatry and superstition which, through the gradual blending of the old Accadian religious system with that of the Cushite invaders, had grown up to a system of great and complicated power. "Strange to say, some of the very hymns which marked the growing development of Chaldean idolatry remain to our day; hymns which Abraham may often have heard rising in measured chant and antiphony from priestly choirs at Ur." Amid all this idolatry there still lingered indeed traditions of the creation, the fall of man, the deluge, the tower of Babel and the confusion of tongues, and of the Sabbath as "the day of rest for the heart;" but this was no place for Abraham, who remained true to the better faith he had brought from his native mountains, and God "called" him to leave Ur of the Chaldees. (See BABYLON; ABRAHAM.)

Chal'dee language, employed by the sacred writers in certain portions of the Old Testament — viz., Dan. 2:4-7, 28; Ezra 4:8-6:18; 7:12-26; Gen. 31:46; Jer. 10:11. It is the Aramaic dialect, as it is sometimes called, as distinguished from the Hebrew dialect. It was the language of commerce and of social intercourse in Western Asia, and after the Exile gradually came to be the popular language of Palestine. It is called "Syrian" in 2 Kings 18:26. Some isolated words in this language are preserved in the New Testament (Matt. 5:22; 6:24; 16:17; 27:46; Mark 3:17; 5:41; 7:34; 14:36; Acts 1:19; 1 Cor. 16:22). These are specimens of the vernacular language of Palestine at that period. The term "Hebrew" was also sometimes applied to the Chaldee because it had become the language of the Hebrews (John 5:2; 19:20).

Chal'dees, or **Chalde'ans,** the inhabitants of the country of which Babylon was the capital. They were so called till the time of the Captivity (2 Kings 25; Isa. 13:19; 23:13), when, particularly in the Book of Daniel (5:30; 9:1), the name began to be used with special reference to a class of learned men ranked with the magicians and astronomers. These men cultivated the ancient Cushite language of the original inhabitants of the land, for they had a "learning" and a "tongue" (1:4) of their own. The common language of the country at that time had become assimilated

to the Semitic dialect, especially through the influence of the Assyrians, and was the language that was used for all civil purposes. The Chaldeans were the learned class, interesting themselves in science and religion, which consisted, like that of the ancient Arabians and Syrians, in the worship of the heavenly bodies. There are representations of this priestly class, of magi and diviners, on the walls of the Assyrian palaces.

Cham'ber "on the wall," which the Shunammite prepared for the prophet Elisha (2 Kings 4:10), was an upper chamber over the porch through the hall toward the street. This was the "guest chamber" where entertainments were prepared (Mark 14:14). There were also "chambers within chambers" (1 Kings 22:25; 2 Kings 9:2). To enter into a chamber is used metaphorically of prayer and communion with God (Isa. 26:20). The "chambers of the south" (Job 9:9) are probably the constellations of the southern hemisphere. The "chambers of imagery" — i.e., chambers painted with images—as used by Ezekiel (8:12), is an expression denoting the vision the prophet had of the abominations practised by the Jews in Jerusalem.

Cham'bering (Rom. 13:13), wantonness, impurity.

Cham'berlain, a confidential servant of the king (Gen. 37:36; 39:1). In Rom. 16:23 mention is made of "Erastus the chamberlain." Here the word denotes the treasurer of the city, or the quæstor, as the Romans styled him. He is almost the only convert from the higher ranks of whom mention is made (comp. Acts 17:34). Blastus, Herod's "chamberlain" (Acts 12:20), was his personal attendant or valet-de-chambre. The Hebrew word saris, thus translated in Esther 1:10, 15; 2:3, 14, 21, etc., properly means an eunuch (as in the marg.), as it is rendered in Isa. 39:7; 56:3.

Chame'leon, a species of lizard which has the faculty of changing the colour of its skin. It is ranked among the unclean animals in Lev. 11:30, where the Hebrew word so translated is coah (R.V., "land crocodile"). In the same verse the Hebrew *tanshemeth,* rendered in Authorized Version "mole," is in Revised Version "chameleon," which is the correct rendering. This

CHAMELEON.

animal is very common in Egypt and in the Holy Land, especially in the Jordan valley.

Cham′ois—only in Deut. 14:5 (Heb. *zemer*)—an animal of the deer or gazelle species. It bears this Hebrew name from its leaping or springing. The animal intended is probably the wild sheep (*Ovis tragelephus*), which is still found in Sinai and in the broken ridges of Stony Arabia. The LXX. and Vulgate render the word by *camelopardus*—*i.e.*, the giraffe; but this is an animal of Central Africa, and is not at all known in Syria.

Cham′pion (1 Sam. 17:4, 23), properly "the man between the two," denoting the position of Goliath between the two camps. Single combats of this kind at the head of armies were common in ancient times. In ver. 51 this word is the rendering of a different Hebrew word, and properly denotes "a mighty man."

Chance (Luke 10:31). "It was not by chance that the priest came down by that road at that time, but by a specific arrangement and in exact fulfilment of a plan; not the plan of the priest, nor the plan of the wounded traveller, but the plan of God. By coincidence (Gr. *sungkuria*) the priest came down—that is, by the conjunction of two things, in fact, which were previously constituted a pair in the providence of God. In the result

they fell together according to the omniscient Designer's plan. This is the true theory of the divine government." Compare the meeting of Philip with the Ethiopian (Acts 8:26, 27). There is no "chance" in God's empire. "Chance" is only another word for our want of knowledge as to the way in which one event falls in with another (1 Sam. 6:9; Eccl. 9:11).

Chan′cellor, one who has judicial authority—literally, a "lord of judgment;" a title given to the Persian governor of Samaria (Ezra 4:8, 9, 17).

Chan′ges of rai′ment were reckoned among the treasures of rich men (Gen. 45:22; Judg. 14:12, 13; 2 Kings 5:22, 23).

Chan′nel. (1.) The bed of the sea or of a river (Ps. 18:15; Isa. 8:7).

(2.) The "chanelbone" (Job 31:22 marg.), properly "tube" or "shaft," an old term for the collar-bone.

Chap′el, a holy place or sanctuary, occurs only in Amos 7:13, where one of the idol priests calls Bethel "the king's chapel."

Chap′iter, the ornamental head or capital of a pillar. Three Hebrew words are so rendered. (1.) *Cothereth* (1 Kings 7:16; 2 Kings 25:17; 2 Chr. 4:12), meaning a "diadem" or "crown." (2.) *Tzepheth* (2 Chr. 3:15). (3.) *Rosh* (Ex. 36:38; 38:17, 19, 28), properly a "head" or "top."

Chap′ter. The several books of the Old and New Testaments were from an early time divided into chapters. The Pentateuch was divided by the ancient Hebrews into 54 *parshioth* or sections, one of which was read in the synagogue every Sabbath day (Acts 13:15). These sections were afterwards divided into 669 *sidrim* or orders of unequal length. The Prophets were divided in somewhat the same manner into *haphtaroth* or passages.

In the early Latin and Greek versions of the Bible, similar divisions of the several books were made. The New Testament books were also divided into portions of various lengths under different names, such as *titles* and *heads* or *chapters*.

In modern times this ancient example was imitated, and many attempts of the kind were made before the existing division into chapters was fixed. The Latin Bible published by Cardinal Hugo of St. Cher in A.D. 1240 is generally regarded as the first Bible that was divided into our present chapters, although it appears that some of the chapters were fixed as early as A.D. 1059. This division into chapters came gradually to be adopted in the published editions of the Hebrew, with some few variations, and of the Greek Scriptures, and hence of other versions.

Char′ashim—*craftsmen*—a valley named in 1 Chr. 4:14. In Neh. 11:35 the Hebrew word is rendered "valley of craftsmen" (R.V. marg., *Gehaharashim*). Nothing is known of it.

Char′ger, a bowl or deep dish. The silver vessels given by the heads of the tribes for the services of the tabernacle are so named (Num. 7:13, etc.). The "charger" in which the Baptist's head was presented was a platter or flat wooden trencher (Matt. 14:8, 11; Mark 6:25, 28). The chargers of gold and silver of Ezra 1:9 were probably basins for receiving the blood of sacrifices.

Char′iot, a vehicle generally used for warlike purposes. Sometimes, though but rarely, it is spoken of as used for peaceful purposes.

The first mention of the chariot is when Joseph, as a mark of distinction, was

WAR CHARIOTS.
(*From Assyrian Sculptures.*)

placed in Pharaoh's second state chariot (Gen. 41:43); and the next, when he went

out in his own chariot to meet his father Jacob (46:29). Chariots formed part of the funeral procession of Jacob (50:9). When Pharaoh pursued the Israelites he took 600 war-chariots with him (Ex. 14:7). The Canaanites in the valleys of Palestine had chariots of iron (Josh. 17:18; Judg. 1:19). Jabin, the king of Canaan, had 900 chariots (Judg. 4:3); and in Saul's time the Philistines had 30,000. In his wars with the king of Zobah and with the Syrians, David took many chariots among the spoils (2 Sam. 8:4; 10:18). Solomon maintained as part of his army 1,400 chariots (1 Kings 10:26), which were chiefly imported from Egypt (29). From this time forward they formed part of the armies of Israel (1 Kings 22:34; 2 Kings 9:16, 21; 13:7, 14; 18:24; 23:30).

In the New Testament we have only one historical reference to the use of chariots, in the case of the Ethiopian eunuch (Acts 8:28, 29, 38).

This word is sometimes used figuratively for hosts (Ps. 68:17; 2 Kings 6:17). Elijah, by his prayers and his counsel, was "the chariot of Israel, and the horsemen thereof." The rapid agency of God in the phenomena of nature is also spoken of under the similitude of a chariot (Ps. 104:3; Isa. 66:15; Hab. 3:8).

Chariot of the cherubim (1 Chr. 28:18), the chariot formed by the two cherubs on the mercy-seat on which the Lord rides.

Chariot cities were set apart for storing the war-chariots in time of peace (2 Chr. 1:14).

Chariot horses were such as were peculiarly fitted for service in chariots (2 Kings 7:14).

Chariots of war are described in Ex. 14:7; 1 Sam. 13:5; 2 Sam. 8:4; 1 Chr. 18:4; Josh. 11:4; Judg. 4:3, 13. They were not used by the Israelites till the time of David.

Elijah was translated in a "chariot of fire" (2 Kings 2:11). Comp. 2 Kings 6:17. This vision would be to Elisha a source of strength and encouragement, for now he could say, "They that be with us are more than they which be with them."

Char'ity (1 Cor. 13), the rendering in the Authorized Version of the word which properly denotes *love*, and is frequently so rendered (always so in the Revised Version). It is spoken of as the greatest of the three Christian graces (1 Cor. 12:31-13:13).

Charm'er, one who practises serpent-charming (Ps. 58:5; Jer. 8:17; Eccl. 10:11). It was an early and universal opinion that the most venomous reptiles could be made harmless by certain charms or by sweet sounds. It is well known that there are jugglers in India and in other Eastern lands who practise this art at the present day.

In Isa. 19:3 the word "charmers" is the rendering of the Hebrew *'ittim*, meaning, properly, necromancers (R.V. marg., "whisperers"). In Deut. 18:11 the word "charmer" means a dealer in spells, especially one who, by binding certain knots, was supposed thereby to bind a curse or a blessing on its object. In Isa. 3:3 the words "eloquent orator" should be, as in the Revised Version, "skilful enchanter."

Char'ran, another form (Acts 7:2, 4) of Haran (*q.v.*).

Che'bar—*length*—a river in the "land of the Chaldeans" (Ezek. 1:3), on the banks of which were located some of the Jews of the Captivity (Ezek. 1:1; 3:15, 23; 10:15, 20, 22). It has been supposed to be identical with the river Habor, the Chaboras, or modern Khabour, which falls into the Euphrates at Circesium. To the banks of this river some of the Israelites were removed by the Assyrians (2 Kings 17:6). An opinion that has much to support it is that the "Chebar" was the royal canal of Nebuchadnezzar, the *Nahr Malcha*, the greatest in Mesopotamia, which connected the Tigris with the Euphrates, in the excavation of which the Jewish captives were probably employed.

Chedorla'omer (=*Khudur-Lagamar* of the inscriptions), king of Elam. That ambitious and warlike monarch for some reason proclaimed war against the five great cities of the Jordan valley, Sodom and four others, which were governed by as many kings. In this warlike expedition he associated with him the kings of Shinar (= Shumir or Southern Chaldea), and Larsam (Ellassar), and the "king of nations," as in the Authorized Version; but the Hebrew word *goim*, rendered "nations," probably denotes certain nomadic tribes who roamed about Chaldea—the "Guti," part of whom afterwards became the Assyrian nation. With the combined army he marched 1,200 miles across the desert, and subdued these cities, which he held in subjection for twelve years. Abraham was probably still in Haran when this expedition took place. In the thirteenth year they rebelled; and the next year the king fell upon them with his allies, and encountered and routed them in the vale of Siddim. "They took all the goods of Sodom and Gomorrah, and all their victuals, and went their way."

Lot, the nephew of Abraham, was taken captive with his family, and was being taken back among the prisoners to Elam, when Abraham, summoning his armed men together, pursued after the retreating army and routed them. Lot and his family were rescued; and Abraham brought back the spoil Chedorlaomer had carried away (Gen. 14:17). We hear no more of this king. Probably he perished in the battle.

Cheek. Smiting on the cheek was accounted a grievous injury and insult (Job 16:10; Lam. 3:30; Micah 5:1). The admonition (Luke 6:29), "Unto him that smiteth thee on the one cheek offer also the other," means simply, "Resist not evil' (Matt. 5:39; 1 Pet. 2:19-23). Ps. 3:7= that God had deprived his enemies of the power of doing him injury.

Cheese (A.S. *cese*). This word occurs three times in the Authorized Version as the translation of three different Hebrew words:—(1.) 1 Sam. 17:18, "ten cheeses;" *i.e.*, ten sections of curd. (2.) 2 Sam. 17:29, "cheese of kine" = perhaps curdled milk of kine. The Vulgate version reads "fat calves." (3.) Job 10:10, curdled milk is meant by the word.

Chem'arim—*black*—(Zeph. 1:4; rendered "idolatrous priests" in 2 Kings 23:5, and "priests" in Hos. 10:5). Some derive this word from the Assyrian *kamarû*, meaning "to throw down," and interpret it as describing the idolatrous priests who prostrate themselves before the idols. Others regard it as meaning "those who go about in black," or "ascetics."

Che'mosh—the *destroyer, subduer*, or *fish-god*—the god of the Moabites (Num. 21:29; Jer. 48:7, 13, 46). The worship of this god, "the abomination of Moab," was introduced at Jerusalem by Solomon (1 Kings 11:7), but was abolished by Josiah (2 Kings 23:13). On the "Moabite Stone" (*q.v.*), Mesha (2 Kings 3:5) ascribes his victories over the king of Israel to this god—"And Chemosh drove him before my sight."

Chena'anah—*merchant.* (1.) A Benjamite (1 Chr. 7:10). (2.) The father of Zedekiah (1 Kings 22:11, 24).

Chenani'ah—*whom Jehovah hath made*—"chief of the Levites," probably a Kohathite (1 Chr. 15:22), and therefore not the same as mentioned in 26:29.

Chephi'rah—*village*—one of the four cities of the Gibeonitish Hivites with whom Joshua made a league (9:17). It belonged to Benjamin. It has been identified with the modern *Kefîreh*, on the west confines of Benjamin, about 2 miles west of Ajalon and 11 from Jerusalem.

Cher'ethim (Ezek. 25:16), more frequently **Cherethites**, the inhabitants of Southern Philistia, the Philistines (Zeph. 2:5). The Cherethites and the Pelethites were David's life-guards (1 Sam. 30:14; 2 Sam. 8:18; 20:7, 23; 23:23). This name is by some interpreted as meaning "Cretans," and by others "executioners," who were ready to execute the king's sentence of death (Gen. 37:36, marg.; 1 Kings 2:25).

Cher'ith—*a cutting; separation; a gorge*—a torrent-bed or winter-stream, a "brook," in whose banks the prophet Elijah hid himself during the early part of the three years' drought (1 Kings 17:3, 5). It has by some been identified as the *Wâdy el-Kelt* behind Jericho, which is formed by the junction of many streams flowing from the mountains west of Jericho. It is dry in summer. Travellers have described it as one of the wildest ravines of this wild region, and peculiarly fitted to afford a secure asylum to the persecuted. But if the prophet's interview with Ahab was in Samaria, and he thence journeyed toward the east, it is probable that he crossed Jordan and found refuge in some of the ravines of Gilead. The "brook" is said to have been "before Jordan," which probably means that it opened toward that river, into which it flowed. This description would apply to the east as well as to the west of Jordan. Thus Elijah's hiding-place may have been the *Jermûk*, in the territory of the half-tribe of Manasseh.

Cher'ub, plural **cherubim**, the name of certain symbolical figures frequently mentioned in Scripture. They are first mentioned in connection with the expulsion of our first parents from Eden (Gen. 3:24). There is no intimation given of their shape or form. They are next mentioned when Moses was commanded to provide furniture for the tabernacle (Ex. 25:17-20; 26:1, 31). God promised to commune with Moses "from between the cherubim" (25:22). This expression was afterwards used to denote the Divine abode and presence (Num. 7:89; 1 Sam. 4:4; Isa. 37:16; Ps. 80:1; 99:1). In Ezekiel's vision (10:1-20) they appear as living creatures supporting the throne of God. From Ezekiel's description of them (1; 10; 41:18,19), they appear to have been compound figures, unlike any real object in nature; artificial images possessing the features and properties of several animals. Two cherubim were placed on the mercy-seat of the ark; two of colossal size overshadowed it in Solomon's temple. Ezekiel (1:4-14) speaks of four; and this number of "living creatures" is mentioned in Rev. 4:6. Those on the ark are called the "cherubim of glory" (Heb. 9:5)—*i.e.*, of the Shechinah, or cloud of glory—for on them the visible glory of God rested.

They were placed one at each end of the mercy-seat, with wings stretched upward, and their faces "toward each other and toward the mercy-seat." They were anointed with holy oil, like the ark itself and the other sacred furniture.

The cherubim were *symbolical.* They were intended to represent spiritual existences in immediate contact with Jehovah. Some have regarded them as symbolical of the chief ruling power by which God carries on his operations in providence (Ps. 18:10; Deut. 33:26; Ps. 68:4). Others interpret them as having reference to the redemption of men, and as symbolizing the great rulers or ministers of the church. Many other opinions have been held regarding them which need not be referred to. On the whole, it seems to be most satisfactory to regard the interpretation of the symbol to be variable, as is the symbol itself.

Their office was—(1) on the expulsion of our first parents from Eden, to prevent all access to the tree of life; and (2) to form the throne and chariot of Jehovah in his manifestation of himself on earth. He dwelleth between and sitteth on the cherubim (1 Sam. 4:4; Ps. 80:1; Ezek. 1:26, 28).

Ches'alon—*strength; confidence*—a place on the border of Judah, on the side of Mount Jearim (Josh. 15:10); probably identified with the modern village of *Kesla*, on the western mountains of Judah.

Che'sed—*gain*—the son of Nahor (Gen. 22:22).

Che'sil—*ungodly*—a town in the south of Judah (Josh. 15:30); probably the same as Bethul (19:4) and Bethuel (1 Chr. 4:30); now *Khelasa*.

Chest (Heb. *'âron*, generally rendered "ark"), the coffer into which the contributions for the repair of the temple were put (2 Kings 12:9, 10; 2 Chr. 24:8, 10, 11). In Gen. 50:26 it is rendered "coffin." In Ezek. 27:24 a different Hebrew word, *gĕnazîm* (plur.), is used. It there means "treasure-chests."

Chest'nut tree (Heb. *'armôn; i.e.,* "naked"), mentioned in connection with Jacob's artifice regarding the cattle (Gen.

30:37). It is one of the trees to which, because of its strength and beauty, the Assyrian empire is likened (Ezek. 31:8; R.V., "plane trees"). It is probably the Oriental plane tree (*Platanus orientalis*)

BRANCH OF ORIENTAL PLANE TREE.

that is intended. It is a characteristic of this tree that it annually sheds its outer bark—becomes "naked." The chestnut tree proper is not a native of Palestine.

Chesul'loth—*fertile places; the loins*—a town of Issachar, on the slopes of some mountain between Jezreel and Shunem (Josh. 19:18). It has been identified with *Chisloth-tabor*, 2½ miles to the west of Mount Tabor, and north of Jezreel; now *Iksâl*.

Che'zib—*deceitful*—a town where Shelah, the son of Judah, was born (Gen. 38:5). Probably the same as Achzib (*q.v.*).

Chi'don—*dart*—the name of the threshing-floor at which the death of Uzzah took place (1 Chr. 13:9). In the parallel passage in Samuel (2 Sam. 6:6) it is called "Nachon's threshing-floor." It was a place not far north-west from Jerusalem.

Chiefs of A'sia, "Asiarchs," the title given to certain wealthy persons annually appointed to preside over the religious festivals and games in the various cities of proconsular Asia (Acts 19:31). Some of these officials appear to have been Paul's friends.

Chief of the three, a title given to Adino the Eznite, one of David's greatest heroes (2 Sam. 23:8); also called Jashobeam (1 Chr. 11:11).

Chief priest. See PRIEST.

Child. This word has considerable latitude of meaning in Scripture. Thus Joseph is called a child at the time when he was probably about sixteen years of age (Gen. 37:3); and Benjamin is so called when he was above thirty years (44:20). Solomon called himself a little child when he came to the kingdom (1 Kings 3:7).

The descendants of a man, however remote, are called his children; as, "the children of Edom," "the children of Moab," "the children of Israel."

In the earliest times mothers did not wean their children till they were from thirty months to three years old; and the day on which they were weaned was kept as a festival day (Gen. 21:8; Ex. 2:7, 9; 1 Sam. 1:22-24; Matt. 21:16). At the age of five, children began to learn the arts and duties of life under the care of their fathers (Deut. 6:20-25; 11:19).

To have a numerous family was regarded as a mark of divine favour (Gen. 11:30; 30:1; 1 Sam. 2:5; 2 Sam. 6:23; Ps. 127:3; 128:3).

Figuratively the name is used for those who are ignorant or narrow-minded (Matt. 11:16; Luke 7:32; 1 Cor. 13:11). "When I was a child, I spake as a child." "Brethren, be not children in understanding" (1 Cor. 14:20). "That we henceforth be no more children, tossed to and fro" (Eph. 4:14).

Children are also spoken of as representing simplicity and humility (Matt. 19:13-15; Mark 10:13-16; Luke 18:15-17). Believers are "children of light" (Luke 16:8; 1 Thess. 5:5) and "children of obedience" (1 Pet. 1:14).

Chil′eab—*protected by the father*—David's second son by Abigail (2 Sam. 3:3); called also Daniel (1 Chr. 3:1). He seems to have died when young.

Chil′ion—*the pining one*—the younger son of Elimelech and Naomi, and husband of Orpah, Ruth's sister (Ruth 1:2; 4:9).

Chil′mad, a place or country unknown which, along with Sheba and Asshur, traded with Tyre (Ezek. 27:23).

Chim′ham—*pining*—probably the youngest son of Barzillai the Gileadite (2 Sam. 19:37-40). The "habitation of Chimham" (Jer. 41:17) was probably an inn or khan—which is the proper meaning of the Hebrew *geruth*, rendered "habitation"—established in later times in his possession at Bethlehem, which David gave to him as a reward for his loyalty in accompanying him to Jerusalem after the defeat of Absalom (1 Kings 2:7). It has been supposed that, considering the stationary character of Eastern institutions, it was in the stable of this inn or caravanserai that our Saviour was born (Luke 2:7).

Chin′nereth—*lyre*—the singular form of the word (Deut. 3:17; Josh. 19:35), which is also used in the plural form, **Chinneroth,** the name of a fenced city which stood near the shore of the lake of Galilee, a little to the south of Tiberias. The town seems to have given its name to a district, as appears from 1 Kings 15:20, where the plural form of the word is used.

The *Sea of Chinnereth* (Num. 34:11; Josh. 13:27), or of *Chinneroth* (Josh. 12:3), was the "lake of Gennesaret" or "sea of Tiberias" (Deut. 3:17; Josh. 11:2). Chinnereth was probably an ancient Canaanitish name adopted by the Israelites into their language.

Chi′os—mentioned in Acts 20:15—an island in the Ægean Sea, about 5 miles distant from the mainland, having a roadstead, in the shelter of which Paul and his companions anchored for a night when on his third missionary return journey. It is now called *Scio*.

Chis′leu, the name adopted from the Babylonians by the Jews after the Captivity for the third civil, or ninth ecclesiastical, month (Neh. 1:1; Zech. 7:1). It corresponds nearly with the moon in November.

Chit′tim or **Kittim,** a plural form (Gen. 10:4), the name of a branch of the descendants of Javan, the "son" of Japheth.

Balaam foretold (Num. 24:24) "that ships should come from the coast of Chittim, and afflict Eber." Daniel prophesied (11:13) that the ships of Chittim would come against the king of the north. It probably denotes Cyprus, whose ancient capital was called *Kition* by the Greeks.

The references elsewhere made to Chittim (Isa. 23:1, 12; Jer. 2:10; Ezek. 27:6) are to be explained on the ground that while the name originally designated the Phœnicians only, it came latterly to be used of all the islands and various settlements on the sea-coasts which they had occupied, and then of the people who succeeded them when the Phœnician power decayed. Hence it designates generally the islands and coasts of the Mediterranean and the races that inhabit them.

Chi'un occurs only in Amos 5:26 (R.V. marg., "shrine"). The LXX. translated the word by *Rhephan*, which became corrupted into Remphan, as used by Stephen (Acts 7:43; but R.V., "Rephan"). Probably the planet Saturn is intended by the name. Astrologers represented this planet as baleful in its influences, and hence the Phœnicians offered to it human sacrifices, especially children.

Chlo'e—*verdure*—a female Christian (1 Cor. 1:11), some of whose household had informed Paul of the divided state of the Corinthian church. Nothing is known of her.

Chor-a'shan—*smoking furnace*—one of the places where "David and his men were wont to hunt" (1 Sam. 30:30). It is probably identical with Ashan (Josh. 15:42; 19:7), a Simeonite city in the Negeb —*i.e.*, the south—belonging to Judah. The word ought, according to another reading, to be "*Bor-ashan.*"

Chora'zin, named along with Bethsaida and Capernaum as one of the cities in which our Lord's "mighty works" were done, and which was doomed to woe because of signal privileges neglected (Matt. 11:21; Luke 10:13). It has been identified by general consent with the modern *Kerâzeh*, about 2½ miles up the Wâdy Kerâzeh from Capernaum; *i.e.*, *Tell Hûm.*

Chosen, spoken of warriors (Ex. 15:4;

Judg. 20:16), of the Hebrew nation (Ps. 105:43; Deut. 7:7), of Jerusalem as the seat of the temple (1 Kings 11:13). Christ is the "chosen" of God (Isa. 42:1); and the apostles are "chosen" for their work (Acts 10:41). It is said with regard to those who do not profit by their opportunities that "many are called, but few are chosen" (Matt. 20:16). (See ELECTION.)

Choze'ba (1 Chr. 4:22), the same as Chezib and Achzib, a place in the lowlands of Judah (Gen. 38:5; Josh. 15:44).

Christ—*anointed*—the Greek translation of the Hebrew word rendered "Messiah" (*q.v.*), the official title of our Lord, occurring five hundred and fourteen times in the New Testament. It denotes that he was anointed or consecrated to his great redemptive work as Prophet, Priest, and King of his people. He is Jesus *the* Christ (Acts 17:3; 18:5; Matt. 22:42), the Anointed One. He is thus spoken of by Isaiah (61:1), and by Daniel (9:24-26), who styles him "Messiah the Prince."

The Messiah is the same person as "the seed of the woman" (Gen. 3:15), "the seed of Abraham" (Gen. 22:18), the "Prophet like unto Moses" (Deut. 18:15), "the priest after the order of Melchizedek" (Ps. 110:4), "the root out of the stem of Jesse" (Isa. 11:1, 10), the "Immanuel," the virgin's son (Isa. 7:14), "the branch of Jehovah" (Isa. 4:2), and "the angel of the covenant" (Mal. 3:1). This is he "of whom Moses in the law and the prophets did write." The Old Testament Scripture is full of prophetic declarations regarding the Great Deliverer and the work he was to accomplish. Jesus *the* Christ is Jesus the Great Deliverer, the Anointed One, the Saviour of men.

This name denotes that Jesus was divinely appointed, commissioned, and accredited as the Saviour of men (Heb. 5:4; Isa. 11:2-4; 49:6; John 5:37; Acts 2:22).

To believe that "Jesus is the Christ" is to believe that he is the Anointed, the Messiah of the prophets, the Saviour sent of God—that he was, in a word, what he claimed to be. This is to believe the gospel, by the faith of which alone men can be brought unto God. That Jesus is the Christ is the testimony of God, and the faith of this constitutes a Christian (1 Cor. 12:3; 1 John 5:1).

Christs, False. Our Lord warned his disciples that they would arise (Matt. 24: 24). It is said that no fewer than twenty-four persons have at different times appeared (the last in 1682) pretending to be the Messiah of the prophets.

Christian, the name given by the Greeks or Romans, probably in reproach, to the followers of Jesus. It was first used at Antioch. The names by which the disciples were known among themselves were "brethren," "the faithful," "elect," "saints," "believers." But as distinguishing them from the multitude without, the name "Christian" came into use, and was universally accepted. This name occurs but three times in the New Testament (Acts 11:26; 26:28; 1 Pet. 4:16).

Chron'icles—*the words of the days*—(1 Kings 14:19; 1 Chr. 27:24), the daily or yearly records of the transactions of the kingdom; events recorded in the order of time.

Chron'icles, Books of. The two books were originally one. They bore the title in the Massoretic Hebrew *Dibre hayyamîm*—i.e., "Acts of the Days." This title was rendered by Jerome in his Latin version "Chronicon," and hence "Chronicles." In the Septuagint version the book is divided into two, and bears the title *Paraleipomena*—i.e., "things omitted," or "supplements"—because containing many things omitted in the Books of Kings.

The *contents* of these books are comprehended under four heads. (1.) The first nine chapters of Book I. contain little more than a list of genealogies in the line of Israel down to the time of David. (2.) The remainder of the first book contains a history of the reign of David. (3.) The first nine chapters of Book II. contain the history of the reign of Solomon. (4.) The remaining chapters of the second book contain the history of the separate kingdom of Judah to the time of the return from Babylonian Exile.

The *time* of the composition of the Chronicles was, there is every ground to conclude, subsequent to the Babylonian Exile, probably between 450 and 435 B.C. The contents of this twofold book, both as to matter and form, correspond closely with this idea. The close of the book records the proclamation of Cyrus permitting the Jews to return to their own land, and this forms the opening passage of the Book of Ezra, which must be viewed as a continuation of the Chronicles. The peculiar form of the language—being Aramæan in its general character—harmonizes also with that of the books which were written after the Exile. The author was certainly contemporary with Zerubbabel, details of whose family history are given (1 Chr. 3:19).

The time of the composition being determined, the question of the *authorship* may be more easily decided. According to Jewish tradition, which was universally received down to the middle of the seventeenth century, Ezra was regarded as the author of the Chronicles. There are many points of resemblance and of contact between the Chronicles and the Book of Ezra which seem to confirm this opinion. The conclusion of the one and the beginning of the other are almost identical in expression. In their spirit and characteristics they are the same, showing thus also an identity of authorship.

In their general *scope* and *design* these books are not so much *historical* as *didactic*. The principal aim of the writer appears to be to present moral and religious truth. He does not give prominence to *political* occurrences, as is done in Samuel and Kings, but to ecclesiastical institutions. "The genealogies, so uninteresting to most modern readers, were really an important part of the public records of the Hebrew state. They were the basis on which not only the land was distributed and held, but the public services of the temple were arranged and conducted, the Levites and their descendants alone, as is well known, being entitled to the necessary allowances of tithes and first fruits set apart for that purpose." The "Chronicles" are an epitome of the sacred history from the days of

Adam down to the return from Babylonian Exile—a period of about 3,500 years. The writer gathers up "the threads of the old national life broken by the Captivity."

The *sources* whence the chronicler compiled his work were public records, registers, and genealogical tables belonging to the Jews. These are referred to in the course of the book (1 Chr. 27 : 24; 29 : 29; 2 Chr. 9 : 29; 12 : 15; 13 : 22; 20 : 34; 24 : 27; 26 : 22; 32 : 32; 33 : 18, 19; 27 : 7; 35 : 25). There are in Chronicles, and the books of Samuel and Kings, forty parallels, often verbal, proving that the writer both knew and used these records (1 Chr. 17 : 18; comp. 2 Sam. 7 : 8; 1 Chr. 19; comp. 2 Sam. 10, etc.).

As compared with Samuel and Kings, the Book of Chronicles omits many particulars there recorded (2 Sam. 6 : 20-23; 9; 11; 14-19, etc.), and includes many things peculiar to itself (1 Chr. 12; 22; 23-26; 27; 28; 29, etc.). Twenty whole chapters, and twenty-four parts of chapters, are occupied with matter not found elsewhere. It also records many things in fuller detail, as (*e.g.*) the list of David's heroes (1 Chr. 12 : 1-37), the removal of the ark from Kirjath-jearim to Mount Zion (1 Chr. 13; 15 : 2-24; 16 : 4-43; comp. 2 Sam. 6), Uzziah's leprosy and its cause (2 Chr. 26 : 16-21; comp. 2 Kings 15 : 5), etc.

It has also been observed that *another peculiarity* of the book is that it substitutes modern and more common expressions for those that had then become unusual or obsolete. This is seen particularly in the substitution of modern names of places, such as were in use in the writer's day, for the old names; thus Gezer (1 Chr. 20 : 4) is used instead of Gob (2 Sam. 21 : 18), etc.

The Books of Chronicles are ranked among the *khethubim* or *hagiographa.* They are alluded to, though not directly quoted, in the New Testament (Heb. 5 : 4; Matt. 12 : 42; 23 : 35; Luke 1 : 5; 11 : 31, 51).

Chron'icles of king David (1 Chr. 27 : 24) were statistical state records; one of the public sources from which the compiler of the Books of Chronicles derived information on various public matters.

Chronol'ogy is the arrangement of facts and events in the order of time. The writers of the Bible themselves do not adopt any standard era according to which they date events. Sometimes the years are reckoned, *e.g.*, from the time of the Exodus (Num. 1 : 1; 33 : 38; 1 Kings 6 : 1), and sometimes from the accession of kings (1 Kings 15 : 1, 9, 25, 33, etc.), and sometimes again from the return from Exile (Ezra 3 : 8).

Hence in constructing a system of Biblical chronology, the plan has been adopted of reckoning the years from the ages of the patriarchs before the birth of their first-born sons for the period from the Creation to Abraham. After this period other data are to be taken into account in determining the relative sequence of events.

As to the patriarchal period, there are three principal systems of chronology : (1) that of the Hebrew text, (2) that of the Septuagint version, and (3) that of the Samaritan Pentateuch, as seen in the scheme on the opposite page.

The Samaritan and the Septuagint have considerably modified the Hebrew chronology. This modification some regard as having been wilfully made, and to be rejected. The same system of variations is observed in the chronology of the period between the Flood and Abraham. Thus :—

	He-brew.	Septu-agint.	Sama-ritan.
From the birth of Arphaxad, 2 years after the Flood, to the birth of Terah.	220	1000	870
From the birth of Terah to the birth of Abraham......	130	70	72

The Septuagint fixes on seventy years as the age of Terah at the birth of Abraham, from Gen. 11 : 26; but a comparison of Gen. 11 : 32 and Acts 7 : 4 with Gen. 12 : 4 shows that when Terah died, at the age of two hundred and five years, Abraham was seventy - five years, and hence Terah must have been one hundred and thirty years when Abraham was born.

Thus, including the two years from the Flood to the birth of Arphaxad, the period from the Flood to the birth of Abraham was three hundred and fifty-two years.

The next period is from the birth of Abraham to the Exodus. This, according to the Hebrew, extends to five hundred and five years. The difficulty here is as to the four hundred and thirty years mentioned Ex. 12:40, 41; Gal. 3:17. These years are regarded by some as dating from the covenant with Abraham (Gen. 15), which was entered into soon after his sojourn in Egypt; others, with more proba-

	HEBREW TEXT.			SEPTUAGINT VERSION.			SAMARITAN PENTATEUCH		
	Lived years before birth of first son.	Lived after birth of first son.	Total life.	Lived years before birth of first son.	Lived after birth of first son.	Total life.	Lived years before birth of first son.	Lived after birth of first son.	Total life.
Adam	130	800	930	230	700	930	130	800	930
Seth....................	105	807	912	205	707	912	105	807	912
Enos....................	90	815	905	190	715	905	90	815	905
Cainan..................	70	840	910	170	740	910	70	840	910
Mahalaleel	65	830	895	165	730	895	65	830	895
Jared	162	800	962	162	800	962	62	785	947
Enoch...................	65	300	365	165	200	365	65	300	365
Methuselah	187	782	969	187	782	969	67	653	720
Lamech..................	182	595	777	188	565	753	53	600	653
Thus from Adam to the birth of Noah........	1056			1662			707		
From birth of Noah to the Flood...........	600			600			600		
From Adam to the Flood..	1656			2262			1307		

bility, reckon these years from Jacob's going down into Egypt. (See Exodus.)

In modern times the systems of Biblical chronology that have been adopted are chiefly those of Ussher and Hales. The former follows the Hebrew, and the latter the Septuagint mainly. Archbishop Ussher's (died 1656) system is called the short chronology. It is that given on the margin of the Authorized Version, but is really of no authority, and is quite uncertain.

	Ussher. B.C.	Hales. B.C.
Creation	4004	5411
Flood	2348	3155
Abram leaves Haran..	1921	2078
Exodus................	1491	1648
Destruction of the Temple...........	588	586

(For Chronological Tables see APPENDIX.)

To show at a glance the different ideas of the date of the creation, it may be interesting to note the following:—

From Creation to 1894.

According to Ussher, 5,898; Hales, 7,305; Zunz (Hebrew reckoning), 5,882; Septuagint (*Perowne*), 7,305; Rabbinical, 5,654; Panodorus, 7,387; Anianus, 7,395; Constantinopolitan, 7,403; Eusebius, 7,093; Scaliger, 5,844; Dionysius (from whom we take our Christian era), 7,388; Maximus, 7,395; Syncellus and Theophanes, 7,395; Julius Africanus, 7,395; Jackson, 7,320.

Chrysop'rasus—*golden leek*—a precious stone of the colour of leek's juice, a greenish-golden colour.

Chub, the name of a people in alliance with Egypt in the time of Nebuchadnezzar. The word is found only in Ezek. 30:5.

They were probably a people of Northern Africa, or of the lands near Egypt in the south.

Chun, one of the cities of Hadarezer, king of Syria. David procured brass (*i.e.*, bronze or copper) from it for the temple (1 Chr. 18:8). It is called Berothai in 2 Sam. 8:8; probably the same as Berothah in Ezek. 47:16.

Church. Derived probably from the Greek *kuriakon* (*i.e.*, "the Lord's house"), which was used by ancient authors for the place of worship.

In the New-Testament it is the translation of the Greek word *ecclesia*, which is synonymous with the Hebrew *kâhal* of the Old Testament, both words meaning simply an assembly, the character of which can only be known from the connection in which the word is found. There is no clear instance of its being used for a place of meeting or of worship, although in post-apostolic times it early received this meaning. Nor is this word ever used to denote the inhabitants of a country united in the same profession, as when we say the "Church of England," the "Church of Scotland," etc.

We find the word *ecclesia* used in the following senses in the New Testament:—

(1.) It is translated "assembly" in the ordinary classical sense (Acts 19:32, 39, 41).

(2.) It denotes the whole body of the redeemed—all those whom the Father has given to Christ—the invisible catholic church (Eph. 5:23, 25, 27, 30; Heb. 12:23).

(3.) A few Christians associated together in observing the ordinances of the gospel are an *ecclesia* (Rom. 16:5; Col. 4:15).

(4.) All the Christians in a particular city, whether they assembled together in one place or in several places for religious worship, were an *ecclesia*. Thus all the disciples in Antioch, forming several congregations, were one church (Acts 13:1); so also we read of the "church of God at Corinth" (1 Cor. 1:2), "the church at Jerusalem" (Acts 8:1), "the church of Ephesus" (Rev. 2:1), etc.

(5.) The whole body of professing Christians throughout the world (1 Cor. 15:9; Gal. 1:13; Matt. 16:18) are the church of Christ.

The *church visible* "consists of all those throughout the world that profess the true religion, together with their children." It is called "visible" because its members are known and its assemblies are public. Here there is a mixture of "wheat and chaff," of saints and sinners. "God has commanded his people to organize themselves into distinct visible ecclesiastical communities, with constitutions, laws, and officers, badges, ordinances, and discipline, for the great purpose of giving visibility to his kingdom, of making known the gospel of that kingdom, and of gathering in all its elect subjects. Each one of these distinct organized communities which is faithful to the great King is an integral part of the visible church, and all together constitute the catholic or universal visible church." A credible profession of the true religion constitutes a person a member of this church. This is "the kingdom of heaven," whose character and progress are set forth in the parables recorded in Matt. 13.

The children of all who thus profess the true religion are members of the visible church along with their parents. Children are included in every covenant God ever made with man. They go along with their parents (Gen. 9:9-17; 12:1-3; 17:7; Ex. 20:5; Deut. 29:10-13). Peter, on the day of Pentecost, at the beginning of the New Testament dispensation, announces the same great principle. "The promise [just as to Abraham and his seed the promises were made] is unto you, and to your children" (Acts 2:38, 39). The children of believing parents are "holy"—*i.e.*, are "saints"—a title which designates the members of the Christian church (1 Cor. 7:14). (See BAPTISM.)

The *church invisible* "consists of the whole number of the elect that have been, are, or shall be gathered into one under Christ, the head thereof." This is a pure society, the church in which Christ dwells. It is the body of Christ. It is called "invisible" because the greater part of those who constitute it are already in heaven or are yet unborn, and also because its members still on earth cannot certainly be distinguished by us. The qualifications of membership in it are internal and are hidden. It is unseen except by Him who "searches the heart." "The Lord knoweth them that are his" (2 Tim. 2:19). No human eye can accurately draw the line which separates this church from the world.

The church to which the attributes, prerogatives, and promises appertaining to Christ's kingdom belong, is not a visible organized community, but a spiritual body consisting of all true believers—*i.e.*, the church invisible. Viewed thus, the properties of the church are :—

(1.) Its *unity.* God has ever had only one church on earth. We sometimes speak of the Old Testament church and of the New Testament church, but they are one and the same. The Old Testament church was not to be changed but enlarged (Isa. 49: 13–23; 60:1-14). When the Jews are at length restored, they do not enter a new church, but are grafted again into "their own olive tree" (Rom. 11:18–24; comp. Eph. 2:11–22). The church is the same under both dispensations—having the same foundation, the same conditions of membership; the sacraments in both symbolize and seal the same grace. The apostles did not set up a new organization. Under their ministry disciples were "added" to the "church" already existing (Acts 2:47).

(2.) Its *universality.* It is the "catholic" church; not confined to any particular country or outward organization, but comprehending all believers throughout the whole world.

(3.) Its *perpetuity.* It will continue through all ages to the end of the world. It can never be destroyed. It is an "everlasting kingdom."

Churl, in Isa. 32:5, means a *deceiver.* In 1 Sam. 25:3, the word *churlish* denotes a man that is coarse and ill-natured, or, as the word literally means, "hard." The same Greek word as used by the LXX. here is found in Matt. 25:24, and there is rendered "hard."

Chu'shan-rishatha'im—*Cush of double wickedness,* or *governor of two presidencies*—the king of Mesopotamia who oppressed Israel in the generation immediately following Joshua (Judg. 3:8). After eight years the yoke of his oppression was broken by Othniel, Caleb's nephew (3:10). Rawlinson (*Ancient Mon.*) has conjectured that this king is identical with the Asshurris-ilim of the Assyrian inscriptions. This conjecture, however, has not been established. (See CUSHAN.)

Chu'za—*a seer*—the steward of Herod Antipas, whose wife, Joanna, was one of those women who accompanied our Lord in his journeyings (Luke 8:3). She was probably also one of the women who came early to his sepulchre (24:10).

Cili'cia, a maritime province in the south-east of Asia Minor. Tarsus, the birth-place of Paul, was one of its chief towns, and the seat of a celebrated school of philosophy. Its luxurious climate attracted to it many Greek residents after its incorporation with the Macedonian empire. It was formed into a Roman province, B.C. 67. The Jews of Cilicia had a synagogue at Jerusalem (Acts 6:9). Paul visited it soon after his conversion (Gal. 1: 21; Acts 9:30), and again, on his second missionary journey (15:41), "he went through Syria and Cilicia, confirming the churches." It was famous for its goat's-hair cloth, called *cilicium.* Paul learned in his youth the trade of making tents of this cloth.

Cin'namon—Heb. *kinamón,* the *Cinnamomum zeylanicum* of botanists—a tree of

CINNAMON.

the Laurel family, which grows only in India on the Malabar coast, in Ceylon, and

China. There is no trace of it in Egypt, and it was unknown in Syria. The inner rind when dried and rolled into cylinders forms the cinnamon of commerce. The fruit and coarser pieces of bark when boiled yield a fragrant oil. It was one of the principal ingredients in the holy anointing oil (Ex. 30:23). It is mentioned elsewhere only in Prov. 7:17; Cant. 4:14; Rev. 18:13. The mention of it indicates a very early and extensive commerce carried on between Palestine and the East.

Cin'nereth—*a harp*—one of the "fenced cities" of Naphtali (Josh. 19:35; comp. Deut. 3:17). It also denotes, apparently, a *district* which may have taken its name from the adjacent city or lake of Gennesaret, anciently called "the sea of Chinnereth" (*q.v.*), and was probably that enclosed district north of Tiberias afterwards called "the plain of Gennesaret." Called Chinneroth (R.V., Chinnereth) Josh. 11:2. The phrase "all Cinneroth, with all the land of Naphtali" in 1 Kings 15:20 is parallel to "the store cities of Naphtali" in 2 Chr. 16:4.

Cir'cuit, the apparent diurnal revolution of the sun round the earth (Ps. 19:6), and the changes of the wind (Eccl. 1:6). In Job 22:14, "in the circuit of heaven" (R.V. marg., "on the vault of heaven") means the "arch of heaven," which seems to be bent over our heads.

Circumcis'ion—*cutting around.* This rite, practised before, as some think, by divers races, was appointed by God to be the special badge of his chosen people—an abiding sign of their consecration to him. It was established as a national ordinance (Gen. 17:10, 11). In compliance with the divine command, Abraham, though ninety-nine years of age, was circumcised on the same day with Ishmael, who was thirteen years old (17:24-27). Slaves, whether homeborn or purchased, were circumcised (17:12, 13); and all foreigners must have their males circumcised before they could enjoy the privileges of Jewish citizenship (Ex. 12:48). During the journey through the wilderness, the practice of circumcision fell into disuse, but was resumed by the command of Joshua before they entered

the Promised Land (Josh. 5:2-9). It was observed always afterwards among the tribes of Israel, although it is not expressly mentioned from the time of the settlement in Canaan till the time of Christ, about 1,450 years. The Jews prided themselves in the possession of this covenant distinction (Judg. 14:3; 15:18; 1 Sam. 14:6; 17:26; 2 Sam. 1:20; Ezek. 31:18).

As a rite of the church it ceased when the New Testament times began (Gal. 6:15; Col. 3:11). Some Jewish Christians sought to impose it, however, on the Gentile converts; but this the apostles resolutely resisted (Acts 15:1; Gal. 6:12). Our Lord was circumcised, for it "became him to fulfil all righteousness," as of the seed of Abraham, according to the flesh; and Paul "took and circumcised" Timothy (Acts 16:3), to avoid giving offence to the Jews. It would render Timothy's labours more acceptable to the Jews. But Paul would by no means consent to the demand that Titus should be circumcised (Gal. 2:3-5). The great point for which he contended was the free admission of uncircumcised Gentiles into the church. He contended successfully in behalf of Titus, even in Jerusalem.

In the Old Testament a spiritual idea is attached to circumcision. It was the symbol of purity (Isa. 52:1). We read of uncircumcised lips (Ex. 6:12, 30), ears (Jer. 6:10), hearts (Lev. 26:41). The fruit of a tree that is unclean is spoken of as uncircumcised (Lev. 19:23).

It was a *sign and seal* of the covenant of grace as well as of the national covenant between God and the Hebrews. (1.) It sealed the promises made to Abraham, which related to the commonwealth of Israel — national promises. (2.) But the promises made to Abraham included the promise of redemption (Gal. 3:14), a promise which has come upon us. The covenant with Abraham was a dispensation or a specific form of the covenant of grace, and circumcision was a sign and seal of that covenant. It had a spiritual meaning. It signified purification of the heart, inward circumcision effected by the Spirit (Deut. 10:16; 30:6; Ezek. 44:7; Acts

7:51; Rom. 2:28; Col. 2:11). Circumcision as a symbol shadowing forth sanctification by the Holy Spirit has now given way to the symbol of baptism (*q.v.*). But the truth embodied in both ordinances is ever the same—the removal of sin—the sanctifying effects of grace in the heart.

Under the Jewish dispensation, church and state were identical. No one could be a member of the one without also being a member of the other. Circumcision was a sign and seal of membership in both. Every circumcised person bore thereby evidence that he was one of the chosen people, a member of the church of God as it then existed, and consequently also a member of the Jewish commonwealth.

Cis′tern, the rendering of a Hebrew word *bôr*, which means a receptacle for water conveyed to it; distinguished from *beer*, which denotes a place where water rises on the spot (Jer. 2:13; Prov. 5:15; Isa. 36:16)—a fountain. Cisterns are frequently mentioned in Scripture. The scarcity of springs in Palestine made it necessary to collect rain-water in reservoirs and cisterns (Num. 21:22). (See WELL.)

Empty cisterns were sometimes used as prisons (Jer. 38:6; Lam. 3:53; Ps. 40:2; 69:15). The "pit" into which Joseph was cast (Gen. 37:24) was a *beer* or dry well. There are numerous remains of ancient cisterns in all parts of Palestine.

Cit′izenship, the rights and privileges of a citizen in distinction from a foreigner (Luke 15:15; 19:14; Acts 21:39). Under the Mosaic law non-Israelites, with the exception of the Moabites and the Ammonites and others mentioned in Deut. 23:1-3, were admitted to the general privileges of citizenship among the Jews (Ex. 12:19; Lev. 24:22; Num. 15:15; 35:15; Deut. 10:18; 14:29; 16:10, 14).

The right of citizenship under the *Roman* government was granted by the emperor to individuals, and sometimes to provinces, as a favour or as a recompense for services rendered to the state, or for a sum of money (Acts 22:28). This "freedom" secured privileges equal to those enjoyed by natives of Rome. Among the most notable of these was the provision that a man could not be bound or imprisoned without a formal trial (Acts 22:25, 26), or scourged (16:37). All Roman citizens had the right of appeal to Cæsar (25:11).

City. The earliest mention of city-building is that of Enoch, which was built by Cain (Gen. 4:17). After the confusion of tongues, the descendants of Nimrod founded several cities (10:10-12). Next, we have a record of the cities of the Canaanites—Sidon, Gaza, Sodom, etc. (10:12, 19; 11:3, 9; 36:31-39). The earliest description of a city is that of Sodom (19:1-22). Damascus is said to be the oldest existing city in the world. Before the time of Abraham there were cities in Egypt (Num. 13:22). The Israelites in Egypt were employed in building the "treasure cities" of Pithom and Raamses (Ex. 1:11); but it does not seem that they had any cities of their own in Goshen (Gen. 46:34; 47:1-11). In the kingdom of Og in Bashan there were sixty "great cities with walls," and twenty-three cities in Gilead partly rebuilt by the tribes on the east of Jordan (Num. 21:21, 32, 33, 35; 32:1-3, 34-42; Deut. 3:4, 5, 14; 1 Kings 4:13). On the west of Jordan were thirty-one "royal cities" (Josh. 12), besides many others spoken of in the history of Israel.

A *fenced city* was a city surrounded by fortifications and high walls, with watchtowers upon them (2 Chr. 11:11; Deut. 3:5). There was also within the city generally a tower to which the citizens might flee when danger threatened them (Judg. 9:46-52).

A *city with suburbs* was a city surrounded with open pasture-grounds, such as the forty-eight cities which were given to the Levites (Num. 35:2-7).

There were six *cities of refuge*, three on each side of Jordan—namely, Kadesh, Shechem, Hebron, on the west of Jordan; and on the east, Bezer, Ramoth-gilead, and Golan. The cities on each side of the river were nearly opposite each other. The regulations concerning these cities are given in Num. 35:9-34; Deut. 19:1-13; Ex. 21:12-14.

When David reduced the fortress of the Jebusites which stood on Mount Zion, he built on the site of it a palace and a city, which he called by his own name (1 Chr. 11:5), the *city of David*. Bethlehem is also so called as being David's native town (Luke 2:11).

Jerusalem is called the *Holy City*—the holiness of the temple being regarded as extending in some measure over the whole city (Neh. 11:1).

Pithom and Raamses, built by the Israelites as "treasure cities," were not places where royal treasures were kept, but were fortified towns where merchants might store their goods and transact their business in safety, or cities in which munitions of war were stored. (See PITHOM.)

Clau′da, a small island off the southwest coast of Crete, passed by Paul on his voyage to Rome (Acts 27:16). It is about 7 miles long and 3 broad. It is now called *Gozzo*.

Clau′dia, a female Christian mentioned in 2 Tim. 4:21. It is a conjecture having some probability that she was a British maiden, the daughter of king Cogidunus, who was an ally of Rome, and assumed the name of the emperor, his patron, Tiberius Claudius, and that she was the wife of Pudens.

Clau′dius—*lame*. (1.) The fourth Roman emperor. He succeeded Caligula (A.D. 41). Though in general he treated the Jews, especially those in Asia and Egypt, with great indulgence, yet about the middle of his reign (A.D. 49) he banished them all from Rome (Acts 18:2). In this edict the Christians were included, as being, as was supposed, a sect of Jews. The Jews, however, soon again returned to Rome.

During the reign of this emperor, several persecutions of the Christians by the Jews took place in the dominions of Herod Agrippa, in one of which the apostle James was "killed" (12:2). He died A.D. 54.

(2.) **Clau′dius Ly′sias,** a Greek who, having obtained by purchase the privilege of Roman citizenship, took the name of Claudius (Acts 21:31-40; 22:28; 23:26).

Clay. This word is used of sediment found in pits or in streets (Isa. 57:20;

Jer. 38:6), of dust mixed with spittle (John 9:6), and of potter's clay (Isa. 41:25; Nah. 3:14; Jer. 18:1-6; Rom. 9:21). Clay was used for sealing (Job 38:14; Jer. 32:14). Our Lord's tomb may have been thus sealed (Matt. 27:66). The practice of sealing doors with clay is still common in the East. Clay was also in primitive times used for mortar (Gen. 11:3). The "clay ground" in which the large vessels of the temple were cast (1 Kings 7:46; 2 Chr. 4:17) was a compact loam fitted for the purpose. The expression literally rendered is, "in the thickness of the ground,"—meaning, "in stiff ground" or in clay.

Clean. The various forms of uncleanness according to the Mosaic law are enumerated in Lev. 11-15; Num. 19. The division of animals into clean and unclean was probably founded on the practice of sacrifice. It existed before the Flood (Gen. 7:2). The regulations regarding such animals are recorded in Lev. 11 and Deut. 14.

The Hebrews were prohibited from using as food certain animal substances, such as (1) blood; (2) the fat covering the intestines, termed the caul; (3) the fat on the intestines, called the mesentery; (4) the fat of the kidneys; and (5) the fat tail of certain sheep (Ex. 29:13, 22; Lev. 3:4-9; 9:19; 17:10; 19:26).

The chief design of these regulations seems to have been to establish a system of regimen which would distinguish the Jews from all other nations. Regarding the design and the abolition of these regulations the reader will find all the details in Lev. 20:24-26; Acts 10:9-16; 11:1-10; Heb. 9:9-14.

Clem′ent—*mild*—a Christian of Philippi, Paul's "fellow-helper," whose name he mentions as "in the book of life" (Phil. 4:3). It was an opinion of ancient writers that he was the Clement of Rome whose name is well known in church history, and that he was the author of an Epistle to the Corinthians, the only known manuscript of which is appended to the Alexandrian Codex, now in the British Museum. It is of some historical interest, and has given rise to much discussion among critics. It makes distinct reference to Paul's First Epistle to the Corinthians.

Cle'opas (abbreviation of *Cleopatros*), one of the two disciples with whom Jesus conversed on the way to Emmaus on the day of the resurrection (Luke 24:18). We know nothing definitely regarding him. It is not certain that he was the Clopas of John 19:25, or the Alphæus of Matt. 10:3, although he *may* have been so.

Cle'ophas (in the spelling of this word *h* is inserted by mistake from Latin MSS.), rather *Cleopas*, which is the Greek form of the word, while *Clopas* is the Aramaic form. In John 19:25 the Authorized Version reads, "Mary, the *wife* of Clopas." The word "wife" is conjecturally inserted here. If "wife" is rightly inserted, then Mary was the mother of James the Less, and Clopas is the same as Alphæus (Matt. 10:3; 27:56).

Cloak, an upper garment, "an exterior tunic, wide and long, reaching to the ankles, but without sleeves" (Isa. 59:17). The word so rendered is elsewhere rendered "robe" or "mantle." It was worn by the high priest under the ephod (Ex. 28:31), by kings and others of rank (1 Sam. 15:27; Job 1:20; 2:12), and by women (2 Sam. 13:18).

The word translated "cloke"—*i.e.*, outer garment—in Matt. 5:40 is in its plural form used of garments in general (Matt. 17:2; 26:65). The cloak mentioned here and in Luke 6:29 was the Greek *himation*, Latin *pallium*, and consisted of a large square piece of woollen cloth fastened round the shoulders, like the *abba* of the Arabs. This could be taken by a creditor (Ex. 22:26, 27), but the coat or tunic (Gr. *chitón*) mentioned in Matt. 5:40 could not.

The cloak which Paul "left at Troas" (2 Tim. 4:13) was the Roman *pœnula*, a thick upper garment used chiefly in travelling as a protection from the weather. Some, however, have supposed that what Paul meant was a travelling-bag. In the Syriac version the word used means a book-case. (See DRESS.)

Clos'et, as used in the New Testament, signifies properly a storehouse (Luke 12:

24), and hence a place of privacy and retirement (Matt. 6:6; Luke 12:3).

Cloud. The Hebrew so rendered means "a covering," because clouds cover the sky. The word is used as a symbol of the Divine presence, as indicating the splendour of that glory which it conceals (Ex. 16:10; 33:9; Num. 11:25; 12:5; Job 22:14; Ps. 18:11). A "cloud without rain" is a proverbial saying, denoting a man who does not keep his promise (Prov. 16:15; Isa. 18:4; 25:5; Jude 12). A cloud is the figure of that which is transitory (Job 30:15; Hos. 6:4). A bright cloud is the symbolical seat of the Divine presence (Ex. 29:42, 43; 1 Kings 8:14; 2 Chr. 5:14; Ezek. 43:4), and was called the *Shechinah* (*q.v.*). Jehovah came down upon Sinai in a cloud (Ex. 19:9); and the cloud filled the court around the tabernacle in the wilderness so that Moses could not enter it (Ex. 40:34, 35). At the dedication of the temple also the cloud "filled the house of the Lord" (1 Kings 8:10). Thus in like manner when Christ comes the second time he is described as coming "in the clouds" (Matt. 17:5; 24:30; Acts 1:9, 11). False teachers are likened unto clouds carried about with a tempest (2 Pet. 2:17). The infirmities of old age, which come one after another, are compared by Solomon to "clouds returning after the rain" (Eccl. 12:2). The blotting out of sins is like the sudden disappearance of threatening clouds from the sky (Isa. 44:22).

Cloud, the pillar of, was the glory-cloud which indicated God's presence leading the ransomed people through the wilderness (Ex. 13:22; 33:9, 10). This pillar preceded the people as they marched, resting on the ark (Ex. 13:21; 40:36). By night it became a pillar of fire (Num. 9:17-23).

Cni'dus, a town and harbour on the extreme south-west of the peninsula of Doris in Asia Minor. Paul sailed past it on his voyage to Rome after leaving Myra (Acts 27:7).

Coal. It is by no means certain that the Hebrews were acquainted with mineral coal, although it is found in Syria. Their common fuel was dried dung of animals and wood charcoal. Two different words are found in Hebrew to denote coal, both occurring in Prov. 26 : 21—"As coal [Heb. *peham; i.e.*, "black coal"] is to burning coal [Heb. *gehalim*]." The latter of these words is used in Job 41 : 21 ; Prov. 6 : 28 ; Isa. 44 : 19. The words "live coal" in Isa. 6 : 6 are more correctly "glowing stone." In Lam. 4 : 8 the expression "blacker than coal" is literally rendered in the margin of the Revised Version "darker than blackness." "Coals of fire" (2 Sam. 22 : 9, 13 ; Ps. 18 : 8, 12, 13, etc.) is an expression used metaphorically for lightnings proceeding from God. A false tongue is compared to "coals of juniper" (Ps. 120 : 4 ; James 3 : 6). "Heaping coals of fire on the head" symbolizes overcoming evil with good. The words of Paul (Rom. 12 : 20) are equivalent to saying, "By charity and kindness thou shalt soften down his enmity as surely as heaping coals on the fire fuses the metal in the crucible."

Coat, the tunic worn like the shirt next the skin (Lev. 16 : 4 ; Cant. 5 : 3 ; 2 Sam. 15 : 32 ; Ex. 28 : 4 ; 29 : 5). The "coats of skin" prepared by God for Adam and Eve were probably nothing more than aprons (Gen. 3 : 21). This tunic was sometimes woven entire without a seam (John 19 : 23); it was also sometimes of "many colours" (Gen. 37 : 3 ; R.V. marg., "a long garment with sleeves"). The "fisher's coat" of John 21:7 was obviously an outer garment or cloak, as was also the "coat" made by Hannah for Samuel (1 Sam. 2 : 19). (See DRESS.)

Coat of mail, the rendering of a Hebrew word meaning "glittering" (1 Sam. 17 : 5, 38). The same word in the plural form is translated "habergeons" in 2 Chr. 26 : 14 and Neh. 4 : 16. The "harness" (1 Kings 22 : 34), "breastplate" (Isa. 59 : 17), and "brigandine" (Jer. 46 : 4), were probably also corselets or coats of mail. (See ARMOUR.)

Cock'-crowing. In our Lord's time the Jews had adopted the Greek and Roman division of the night into four watches, each consisting of three hours, the first beginning at six o'clock in the evening (Luke 12 : 38 ; Matt. 14 : 25 ; Mark 6 : 48). But the ancient division, known as the first and second cock-crowing, was still retained. The cock usually crows several times soon after midnight (this is the *first* crowing), and again at the dawn of day (and this is the *second* crowing). Mark mentions (14 : 30) the two cock-crowings. Matthew (26 : 34) alludes to that only which was emphatically *the* cock-crowing— *viz.*, the second.

Cock'atrice, the mediæval name (a corruption of "crocodile") of a fabulous serpent supposed to be produced from a cock's egg. It is generally supposed to denote the *cerastes*, or "horned viper," a very poisonous serpent about a foot long. Others think it to be the yellow viper (*Daboia xanthina*), one of the most dangerous vipers, from its size and its nocturnal habits (Isa. 11 : 8 ; 14 : 29 ; 59 : 5 ; Jer. 8 : 17 ; in all which the Revised Version renders the Hebrew *tziph'oni* by "basilisk"). In Prov. 23 : 32 the Hebrew *tzeph'a* is rendered both in the Authorized Version and the Revised Version by "adder ;" margin of Revised Version "basilisk," and of Authorized Version "cockatrice."

Cock'le, occurs only in Job 31 : 40 (marg., "noisome weeds"), where it is the rendering of a Hebrew word (*b'oshah*) which means "offensive," "having a bad smell," referring to some weed perhaps which has an unpleasant odour. Or it may be regarded as simply any noisome weed, such as the "tares" or darnel of Matt. 13 : 30. In Isa. 5 : 2, 4 the plural form is rendered "wild grapes."

Cœ'le-Syr'ia—*hollow Syria*—the name (not found in Scripture) given by the Greeks to the extensive valley, about 100 miles long, between the Lebanon and the Anti-Lebanon range of mountains.

Cof'fer, the receptacle or small box placed beside the ark by the Philistines, in which they deposited the golden mice and the emerods as their trespass-offering (1 Sam. 6 : 8, 11, 15).

Cof'fin, used in Gen. 50 : 26 with reference to the burial of Joseph. Here, it means a mummy - chest. The same Hebrew word is rendered "money-chest" in 2 Kings 12 : 10, 11.

Cogita'tion (or "thought," as the Chaldee word in Dan. 7 : 28 literally means), earnest meditation.

Coin. Before the Exile the Jews had no regularly stamped money. They made use of uncoined shekels or talents of silver, which they weighed out (Gen. 23 : 16 ; Ex. 38 : 24 ; 2 Sam. 18 : 12). Probably the silver ingots used in the time of Abraham may have been of a fixed weight, which was in some way indicated on them. The "pieces of silver" paid by Abimelech to Abraham (Gen. 20 : 16), and those also for which Joseph was sold (37 : 28), were probably in the form of rings. The shekel was the common standard of weight and value among the Hebrews down to the time of the Captivity. Only once is a shekel of gold mentioned (1 Chr. 21 : 25). The "six thousand of gold" mentioned in the transaction between Naaman and Gehazi (2 Kings 5 : 5) were probably so many shekels of gold. The "piece of money" mentioned in Job 42 : 11; Gen. 33 : 19 (marg., "lambs") was the Hebrew *kesitah*, probably an uncoined piece of silver of a certain weight in the form of a sheep or lamb, or perhaps having on it such an impression. The same Hebrew word is used in Josh. 24 : 32, which is rendered by Wickliffe "an hundred yonge scheep."

Col'lar (Heb. *peh*), means in Job 30 : 18 the mouth or opening of the garment that closes round the neck in the same way as a tunic (Ex. 39 : 23). The "collars" (Heb. *nĕtiphôth*) among the spoils of the Midianites (Judg. 8 : 26; R.V., "pendants") were ear-drops. The same Hebrew word is rendered "chains" in Isa. 3 : 19.

Collec'tion. The Christians in Palestine, from various causes, suffered from poverty. Paul awakened an interest in them among the Gentile churches, and made pecuniary collections in their behalf (Acts 24 : 17 ; Rom. 15 : 25, 26 ; 1 Cor. 16 : 1–3 ; 2 Cor. 8 ; 9 ; Gal. 2 : 10).

Col'lege—Heb. *mishneh* (2 Kings 22:14; 2 Chr. 34 : 22), rendered in Revised Version "second quarter"—the residence of the prophetess Huldah. The Authorized Version followed the Jewish commentators, who, following the Targum, gave the Hebrew word its post-Biblical sense, as if it meant a place of instruction. It properly means the "second," and may therefore

denote the lower city (Acra), which was built after the portion of the city on Mount Zion, and was enclosed by a second wall.

Col'ony. The city of Philippi was a Roman colony (Acts 16 : 12)—*i.e.*, a military settlement of Roman soldiers and citizens, planted there to keep in subjection a newly-conquered district. A colony was Rome in miniature, under Roman municipal law, but governed by military officers (prætors and lictors), not by proconsuls. It had an independent internal government— the *jus Italicum; i.e.*, the privileges of Italian citizens.

Col'our. The subject of colours holds an important place in the Scriptures.

White occurs as the translation of various Hebrew words. It is applied to milk (Gen. 49 : 12), manna (Ex. 16 : 31), snow (Isa. 1 : 18), horses (Zech. 1 : 8), raiment (Eccl. 9 : 8). Another Hebrew word so rendered is applied to marble (Esther 1 : 6), and a cognate word to the lily (Cant. 2 : 16). A different term, meaning "dazzling," is applied to the countenance (Cant. 5 : 10).

This colour was an emblem of purity and innocence (Mark 16 : 5 ; John 20 : 12 ; Rev. 19 : 8, 14), of joy (Eccl. 9 : 8), and also of victory (Zech. 6 : 3 ; Rev. 6 : 2). The hangings of the tabernacle court (Ex. 27 : 9 ; 38 : 9), the coats, mitres, bonnets, and breeches of the priests (Ex. 39 : 27, 28), and the dress of the high priest on the day of Atonement (Lev. 16 : 4, 32), were white.

Black, applied to the hair (Lev. 13 : 31 ; Cant. 5 : 11), the complexion (Cant. 1 : 5), and to horses (Zech. 6 : 2, 6). The word rendered "brown" in Gen. 30 : 32 (R.V., "black") means properly "scorched"—*i.e.*, the colour produced by the influence of the sun's rays. "Black" in Job 30 : 30 means dirty, blackened by sorrow and disease. The word is applied to a mourner's robes (Jer. 8 : 21 ; 14 : 2), to a clouded sky (1 Kings 18 : 45), to night (Micah 3 : 6 ; Jer. 4 : 28), and to a brook rendered turbid by melted snow (Job 6 : 16). It is used as symbolical of evil in Zech. 6 : 2, 6 and Rev. 6 : 5. It was the emblem of mourning, affliction, calamity (Jer. 14 : 2 ; Lam. 4 : 8 ; 5 : 10).

Red, applied to blood (2 Kings 3 : 22), a

heifer (Num. 19 : 2), pottage of lentils (Gen. 25 : 30), a horse (Zech. 1 : 8), wine (Prov. 23 : 31), the complexion (Gen. 25 : 25 ; Cant. 5 : 10).

This colour is symbolical of bloodshed (Zech. 6 : 2 ; Rev. 6 : 4 ; 12 : 3).

Purple, a colour obtained from the secretion of a species of shell-fish (the *Murex trunculus*) which was found in the Medi-

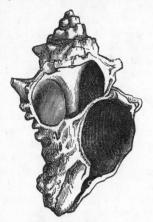

MUREX TRUNCULUS.

terranean, and particularly on the coasts of Phœnicia and Asia Minor. The colouring matter in each separate shell-fish amounted to only a single drop, and hence the great value of this dye. Robes of this colour were worn by kings (Judg. 8 : 26) and high officers (Esther 8 : 15). They were also worn by the wealthy and luxurious (Jer. 10 : 9 ; Ezek. 27 : 7 ; Luke 16 : 19 ; Rev. 17 : 4). With this colour was associated the idea of royalty and majesty (Judg. 8 : 26 ; Cant. 3 : 10 ; 7 : 5 ; Dan. 5 : 7, 16, 29).

Blue. This colour was also procured from a species of shell-fish—the *chelzon* of the Hebrews, and the *Helix ianthina* of modern naturalists. The tint was emblematic of the sky—the deep dark hue of the Eastern sky. This colour was used in the same way as purple. The ribbon and fringe of the Hebrew dress were of this colour (Num. 15 : 38). The loops of the curtains (Ex. 26 : 4), the lace of the high priest's breastplate, the robe of the ephod, and the lace on his mitre, were blue (Ex. 28 : 28, 31, 37).

Scarlet, or *Crimson*. In Isa. 1 : 18 a Hebrew word is used which denotes the worm or grub whence this dye was procured. In Gen. 38 : 28–30 the word so rendered means " to shine," and expresses the brilliancy of the colour. The small parasitic insects from which this dye was obtained somewhat resembled the cochineal which is found in Eastern countries. It is called by naturalists *Coccus ilicis.* The dye was procured from the female grub alone. The only natural object to which this colour is applied in Scripture is the lips, which are likened to a scarlet thread (Cant. 4 : 3). Scarlet robes were worn by the rich and luxurious (2 Sam. 1 : 24 ; Prov. 31 : 21 ; Jer. 4 : 30 · Rev. 17 : 4). It was also the hue of the warrior's dress (Nah. 2 : 3 ; Isa. 9 : 5). The Phœnicians excelled in the art of dyeing this colour (2 Chr. 2 : 7).

These four colours—white, purple, blue, and scarlet—were used in the textures of the tabernacle curtains (Ex. 26 : 1, 31, 36), and also in the high priest's ephod, girdle, and breastplate (Ex. 28 : 5, 6, 8, 15). Scarlet thread is mentioned in connection with the rites of cleansing the leper (Lev. 14 : 4, 6, 51) and of burning the red heifer (Num. 19 : 6). It was a crimson thread that Rahab was to bind on her window as a sign that she was to be saved alive (Josh. 2 : 18 ; 6 : 25) when the city of Jericho was taken.

Vermilion, the red sulphuret of mercury, or cinnabar ; a colour used for drawing the figures of idols on the walls of temples (Ezek. 23 : 14), or for decorating the walls and beams of houses (Jer. 22 : 14).

Colos′sæ, or **Colos′se**, a city of Phrygia, on the Lycus, which is a tributary of the Mæander. It was about 12 miles above Laodicea, and near the great road from Ephesus to the Euphrates, and was consequently of some mercantile importance. It does not appear that Paul had visited this city when he wrote his letter to the church there (Col. 1 : 2). He expresses in his letter to Philemon (ver. 22) his hope to visit it on being delivered from his imprisonment. From Col. 1 : 7 ; 4 : 12 it has been concluded that Epaphras was the founder of the Colossian church. This town afterwards fell into decay, and the modern town of *Chonas* or *Chonum* occupies a site near its ruins.

Colos'sians, Epistle to the, was written by Paul at Rome during his first imprisonment there (Acts 28:16, 30), probably in the spring of A.D. 57, or, as some think, 62, and soon after he had written his Epistle to the Ephesians. Like some of his other epistles (*e.g.*, those to Corinth), this seems to have been written in consequence of information which had somehow been conveyed to him of the internal state of the church there (Col. 1:6-8). Its object was to counteract false teaching. A large part of it is directed against certain speculatists who attempted to combine the doctrines of Oriental mysticism and asceticism with Christianity, thereby promising the disciples the enjoyment of a higher spiritual life and a deeper insight into the world of spirits. Paul argues against such teaching, showing that in Christ Jesus they had all things. He sets forth the majesty of Christ's person and the completeness of his redemption. The mention of the "new moon" and "sabbath days" (2:16) shows also that there were here Judaizing teachers who sought to draw away the disciples from the simplicity of the gospel.

Like most of Paul's epistles, this consists of two parts—a doctrinal and a practical.

(1.) The doctrinal part comprises the first two chapters. His main theme is developed in chapter 2. He warns them against being drawn away from Him in whom dwelt all the fulness of the Godhead, and who was the head of all spiritual powers. Christ was the head of the body of which they were members; and if they were truly united to him, what needed they more?

(2.) The practical part of the epistle (3-4) enforces various duties naturally flowing from the doctrines expounded. They are exhorted to mind things that are above (3:1-4), to mortify every evil principle of their nature, and to put on the new man (3:5-12). Many special duties of the Christian life are also insisted upon as the fitting evidence of the Christian character. Tychicus was the bearer of the letter, as he was also of that to the Ephesians and to Philemon, and he would tell them of the state of the apostle (4:7-9). After friendly greetings (10-14), he bids them interchange this letter with that he had sent to the neighbouring church of Laodicea. He then closes this brief but striking epistle with his usual autograph salutation. There is a remarkable resemblance between this epistle and that to the Ephesians (*q.v.*). The genuineness of this epistle has not been called in question.

Com'forter, the designation of the Holy Ghost (John 14:16, 26; 15:26; 16:7; R.V. marg., "or Advocate, or Helper; Gr. *paraclētos*"). The same Greek word thus rendered is translated "Advocate" in 1 John 2:1 as applicable to Christ. It means properly "one who is summoned to the side of another" to help him in a court of justice by defending him—"one who is summoned to plead a cause." "Advocate" is the proper rendering of the word in every case where it occurs.

It is worthy of notice that although Paul nowhere uses the word *paraclētos*, he yet presents the idea it embodies when he speaks of the "intercession" both of Christ and the Spirit (Rom. 8:27, 34).

Coming of Christ—(1) with reference to his first advent "in the fulness of the time" (1 John 5:20; 2 John 7), or (2) with reference to his coming again the second time at the last day (Acts 1:11; 3:20, 21; 1 Thess. 4:15; 2 Tim. 4:1; Heb. 9:28).

The expression is used *metaphorically* of the introduction of the gospel into any place (John 15:22; Eph. 2:17), the visible establishment of his kingdom in the world (Matt. 16:28), the conferring on his people of the peculiar tokens of his love (John 14:18, 23, 28), and his executing judgment on the wicked (2 Thess. 2:8).

Command'ments, the Ten (Ex. 34:28; Deut. 10:4, marg. "ten words")—*i.e.*, the Decalogue (*q.v.*)—is a summary of the immutable moral law. These commandments were first given in their written form to the people of Israel when they were encamped at Sinai, about fifty days after they came out of Egypt (Ex. 19:10-25). They were written by the finger of God on two tables of stone. The first tables were broken by Moses when he brought them down from the mount (32:19), being thrown by him on the ground. At the command of God he took up into the mount two other tables, and God wrote on them "the words that were on the first tables" (34:1). These tables were afterwards placed in the ark of the covenant (Deut. 10:5; 1 Kings 8:9). Their subsequent history is unknown. They are as a whole called "the covenant" (Deut. 4:13), and "the tables of the covenant" (9:9, 11; Heb. 9:4), and "the testimony."

They are obviously "ten" in number, but their division is not fixed, hence different methods of numbering them have been adopted. The Jews make the "Preface" one of the commandments, and then combine the first and second. The Roman Catholics and Lutherans combine the first and second and divide the tenth into two. The Greek and the Reformed Churches divide them according to the method now common amongst us. The Lutherans and Roman Catholics and Jews refer three commandments to the first table and seven to the second. The Reformed Church refers four to the first and six to the second table. (See LAW.)

Commu'nion, fellowship with God (Gen. 18:17-33; Ex. 33:9-11; Num. 12:7, 8), between Christ and his people (John 14:23), by the Spirit (2 Cor. 13:14; Phil. 2:1), of believers with one another (Eph. 4:1-6). The Lord's Supper is so called (1 Cor. 10:16, 17), because in it there is fellowship between Christ and his disciples, and of the disciples with one another.

Conani'ah—*whom Jehovah hath set*—a Levite placed over the tithes brought into the temple (2 Chr. 35:9).

Concis'ion (Gr. *katatomē; i.e.*, "mutilation"), a term used by Paul contemptuously of those who were zealots for circumcision (Phil. 3:2). Instead of the warning, "Beware of the circumcision" (*peritomē*)—*i.e.*, of the party who pressed on Gentile converts the necessity of still observing that ordinance—he says, "Beware of the concision;" as much as to say, "This circumcision which they vaunt of is in Christ only as the gashings and mutilations of idolatrous heathen."

Con'cubine in the Bible denotes a female conjugally united to a man, but in a relation inferior to that of a wife. Among the early Jews, from various causes, the difference between a wife and a concubine was less marked than it would be amongst us. The concubine was a wife of secondary rank. There are various laws recorded providing for their protection (Ex. 21:7; Deut. 21:10-14), and setting limits to the relation they sustained to the household to which they belonged (Gen. 21:14; 25:6). They had no authority in the family, nor could they share in the household government.

The immediate cause of concubinage might be gathered from the conjugal histories of Abraham and Jacob (Gen. 16; 30). But in process of time the custom of concubinage degenerated, and laws were made to restrain and regulate it (Ex. 21:7-9).

Christianity has restored the sacred institution of marriage to its original character, and concubinage is ranked with the sins of fornication and adultery (Matt. 19:5-9; 1 Cor. 7:2).

Concu'piscence—*desire*—Rom. 7:8 (R.V., "coveting"); Col. 3:5 (R.V., "desire"). The "lust of concupiscence" (1 Thess. 4:5; R.V., "passion of lust") denotes evil desire, indwelling sin.

Con'duit, a water-course or channel (Job 38:25). The "conduit of the upper pool" (Isa. 7:3) was formed by Hezekiah for the purpose of conveying the waters from the upper pool in the valley of Gihon to the west side of the city of David (2 Kings 18:17; 20:20; 2 Chr. 32:30). In carrying out this work he "stopped the waters of the fountain which were without the city"—*i.e.*, "the upper water-course of Gihon"—and conveyed it down from the west through a canal into the city, so that in case of a siege the inhabitants of the city might have a supply of water, which would thus be withdrawn from the enemy. (See SILOAM.)

There are also the remains of a conduit which conducted water from the so-called "Pools of Solomon," beyond Bethlehem, into the city. Water is still conveyed into the city from the fountains which supplied these pools by a channel which crosses the valley of Hinnom.

Co'ney (Heb. *shâphan; i.e.*, "the hider"), an animal which inhabits the mountain gorges and the rocky districts of Arabia Petræa and the Holy Land. "The conies are a feeble folk, yet make they their houses

CONIES.

in the rocks" (Prov. 30 : 26; Ps. 104 : 18). They are gregarious and "exceeding wise," and are described as chewing the cud (Lev. 11 : 5; Deut. 14 : 7).

The animal intended by this name is known among naturalists as the *Hyrax Syriacus*. It is neither a ruminant nor a rodent, but is regarded as akin to the rhinoceros. When it is said to "chew the cud," the Hebrew word so used does not necessarily imply the possession of a ruminant stomach. "The lawgiver speaks according to appearances; and no one can watch the constant motion of the little creature's jaws, as it sits continually working its teeth, without recognizing the naturalness of the expression" (Tristram, *Natural History of the Bible*). It is about the size and colour of a rabbit, though clumsier in structure, and without a tail. Its feet are not formed for digging, and therefore it has its home not in burrows but in the clefts of the rocks. "Coney" is an obsolete English word for "rabbit."

Confec'tion (Ex. 30 : 35, "ointment" in ver. 25; R.V., "perfume"). The Hebrew word so rendered is derived from a root meaning to compound oil and perfume.

Confec'tionaries, only in 1 Sam. 8 : 13, those who make confections—*i.e.*, perfumers, who compound spices and perfumes.

Confes'sion. (1.) An open profession of faith (Luke 12 : 8). (2.) An acknowledgment of sins to God (Lev. 16 : 21; Ezra 9 : 5-15; Dan. 9 : 3-12), and to a neighbour whom we have wronged (James 5 : 16; Matt. 18 : 15).

Congrega'tion (Heb. *kâhal*), the Hebrew people collectively as a holy community (Num. 15 : 15). Every circumcised Hebrew from twenty years old and upward was a member of the congregation. Strangers resident in the land, if circumcised, were, with certain exceptions (Ex. 12 : 19; Num. 9 : 14; Deut. 23 : 1-3), admitted to the privileges of citizenship, and spoken of as members of the congregation (Ex. 12 : 19; Num. 9 : 14; 15 : 15). The congregation were summoned together by the sound of two silver trumpets, and they met at the door of the tabernacle (Num. 10 : 3). These assemblies were convened for the purpose of engaging in solemn religious services (Ex. 12 : 47; Num. 25 : 6; Joel 2 : 15), or of receiving new commandments (Ex. 19 : 7, 8). The elders, who were summoned by the sound of one trumpet (Num. 10 : 4), represented on various occasions the whole congregation (Ex. 3 : 16; 12 : 21; 17 : 5; 24 : 1).

After the conquest of Canaan, the people were assembled only on occasions of the highest national importance (Judg. 20; 2 Chr. 30 : 5; 34 : 29; 1 Sam. 10 : 17; 2 Sam. 5 : 1-5; 1 Kings 12 : 20; 2 Kings 11 : 19; 21 : 24; 23 : 30). In subsequent times the congregation was represented by the Sanhedrim; and the name synagogue, applied in the Septuagint version exclusively to the congregation, came to be used to denote the places of worship established by the Jews. (See CHURCH.)

In Acts 13 : 43, where alone it occurs in the New Testament, it is the same word as that rendered "synagogue" (*q.v.*) in ver. 42.

Congrega'tion, mount of the (Isa. 14 : 13), has been supposed to refer to the place where God promised to meet with his people (Ex. 25 : 22; 29 : 42, 43)—*i.e.*, the mount of the Divine presence, Mount Zion. But here the king of Babylon must be taken as expressing himself according to his own heathen notions, and not according to those of the Jews. The "mount of the congregation" will therefore in this case mean the northern mountain, supposed by the Babylonians to be the meeting-place of their gods. In the Babylonian inscriptions mention is made of a mountain which is described as "the mighty mountain of Bel, whose head rivals heaven, whose root is the holy deep." This mountain was regarded in their mythology as the place where the gods had their seat.

Con'science, that faculty of the mind, or inborn sense of right and wrong, by which we judge of the moral character of human conduct. It is common to all men. Like all our other faculties, it has been perverted by the Fall (John 16:2; Acts 26:9; Rom. 2:15). It is spoken of as "defiled" (Titus 1:15), and "seared" (1 Tim. 4:2). A "conscience void of offence" is to be sought and cultivated (Acts 24:16; Rom. 9:1; 2 Cor. 1:12; 1 Tim. 1:5, 19; 1 Pet. 3:21).

Consecra'tion, the devoting or setting apart of anything to the worship or service of God. The race of Abraham and the tribe of Levi were thus consecrated (Ex. 13:2; 12:15; Num. 3:12). The Hebrews devoted their fields and cattle, and sometimes the spoils of war, to the Lord (Lev. 27:28, 29). According to the Mosaic law the first-born both of man and beast were consecrated to God.

In the New Testament, Christians are regarded as consecrated to the Lord (1 Pet. 2:9).

Consola'tion of Israel, a name for the Messiah in common use among the Jews, probably suggested by Isa. 11:1; 49:13. The Greek word thus rendered (Luke 2:25, *paraklēsis*) is kindred to that translated "Comforter" in John 14:16, etc.—*paraklētos.*

Constella'tion, a cluster of stars, or stars which appear to be near each other in the heavens, and which astronomers have reduced to certain figures (as the "Great Bear," the "Bull," etc.) for the sake of classification and of memory. In Isa. 13:10, where this word only occurs, it is the rendering of the Hebrew *kesil*—*i.e.,* "fool." This was the Hebrew name of the constel-

lation Orion (Job 9:9; 38:31), a constellation which represented Nimrod, the symbol of folly and impiety. The word some interpret by "the giant" in this place— "some heaven-daring rebel who was chained to the sky for his impiety."

Content'ment, a state of mind in which one's desires are confined to his lot whatever it may be (1 Tim. 6:6; 2 Cor. 9:8). It is opposed to envy (James 3:16), avarice (Heb. 13:5), ambition (Prov. 13:10), anxiety (Matt. 6:25, 34), and repining (1 Cor. 10:10). It arises from the inward disposition, and is the offspring of humility, and of an intelligent consideration of the rectitude and benignity of divine providence (Ps. 96:1, 2; 145), the greatness of the divine promises (2 Pet. 1:4), and our own unworthiness (Gen. 32:10); as well as from the view the gospel opens up to us of rest and peace hereafter (Rom. 5:2).

Conversa'tion, generally the goings out and in of social intercourse (Eph. 2:3; 4:22; R.V., "manner of life"); one's deportment or course of life. This word is never used in Scripture in the sense of verbal communication from one to another (Ps. 50:23; Heb. 13:5).

In Phil. 1:27 and 3:20, a different Greek word is used. It there means one's relations to a community as a citizen—*i.e.,* citizenship.

Conver'sion, the turning of a sinner to God (Acts 15:3).

In a general sense the heathen are said to be "converted" when they abandon heathenism and embrace the Christian faith; and in a more special sense men are converted when, by the influence of divine grace in their souls, their whole life is changed—old things pass away, and all things become new (Acts 26:18). Thus we speak of the conversions at Pentecost (Acts 2), the conversion of the Philippian jailer (16:19-34), of Paul (9:1-22), of the Ethiopian treasurer (8:26-40), of Cornelius (10), of Lydia (16:13-15), and others. (See REGENERATION.)

Convoca'tion, a meeting of a *religious* character as distinguished from congregation, which was more general, dealing with political and legal matters. Hence it is called an "holy convocation." Such convocations were the Sabbaths (Lev. 23:2, 3), the Passover (Ex. 12:16; Lev. 23:7, 8; Num. 28:25), Pentecost (Lev. 23:21), the feast of Trumpets (Lev. 23:24; Num. 29:1), the feast of Weeks (Num. 28:26), and the feast of Tabernacles (Lev. 23:35, 36). The great fast, the annual day of atonement, was "the holy convocation" (Lev. 23:27; Num. 29:7).

Cook, a person employed to perform culinary service. In early times among the Hebrews cooking was performed by the mistress of the household (Gen. 18:2–6; Judg. 6:19), and the process was very expeditiously performed (Gen. 27:3, 4, 9, 10). Professional cooks were afterwards employed (1 Sam. 8:13; 9:23). Few animals, as a rule, were slaughtered (other than sacrifices), except for purposes of hospitality (Gen. 18:7; Luke 15:23). The paschal lamb was roasted over a fire (Ex. 12:8, 9; 2 Chr. 35:13). Cooking by boiling was the usual method adopted (Lev. 8:31; Ex. 16:23). No cooking took place on the Sabbath day (Ex. 35:3).

Co'os (should be written **Cos**), a small island, one of the Sporades in the Ægean Sea, in the north-west of Rhodes, off the coast of Caria. Paul, on his return from his third missionary journey, passed the night here after sailing from Miletus (Acts 21:1). It is now called *Stanchio*.

Cop'per, derived from the Greek *kupros* (the island of Cyprus), called "Cyprian brass," occurs only in the Authorized Version in Ezra 8:27. Elsewhere the Hebrew word (*nehosheth*) is improperly rendered "brass," and sometimes "steel" (2 Sam. 22:35; Jer. 15:12). The "bow of steel" (Job 20:24; Ps. 18:34) should have been "bow of copper" (or "brass," as in the R.V.). The vessels of "fine copper" of Ezra 8:27 were probably similar to those of "bright brass" mentioned in 1 Kings 7:45; Dan. 10:6.

Tubal-cain was the first artificer in brass and iron (Gen. 4:22). Hiram was noted as a worker in brass (1 Kings 7:14). Copper abounded in Palestine (Deut. 8:9; Isa. 60:17; 1 Chr. 22:3–14). All sorts of vessels in the tabernacle and the temple were made of it (Lev. 6:28; Num. 16:39; 2 Chr. 4:16; Ezra 8:27); also weapons of war (1 Sam. 17:5, 6, 38; 2 Sam. 21:16). Iron is mentioned only four times (Gen. 4:22; Lev. 26:19; Num. 31:22; 35:16) in the first four books of Moses, while copper (rendered "brass") is mentioned forty times. (See BRASS.)

We find mention of Alexander (*q.v.*), a "coppersmith" of Ephesus (2 Tim. 4:14).

Cor. This Hebrew word, untranslated, denotes a *round* vessel used as a measure both for liquids and solids. It was equal to one homer, and contained ten ephahs in dry and ten baths in liquid measure (Ezek. 45:14). The Rabbins estimated the cor at forty-five gallons, while Josephus estimated it at about eighty-seven. In 1 Kings 4:22; 5:11; 2 Chr. 2:10; 27:5, the original word is rendered "measure."

Cor'al—Heb. *râmôth*, meaning "heights;" *i.e.*, "high-priced" or valuable things, or, as some suppose, "that which grows high," like a tree (Job 28:18; Ezek. 27:16)—according to the Rabbins, *red coral*, which was in use for ornaments.

The coral is a cretaceous marine product, the deposit by minute polypous animals of calcareous matter in cells in which the animal lives. It is of numberless shapes as it grows, but usually is branched like a tree. Great coral reefs and coral islands abound in the Red Sea, whence probably the Hebrews derived their knowledge of it. It is found of different colours—white, black, and red. The red, being esteemed the most precious, was used, as noticed above, for ornamental purposes.

Cor'ban, a Hebrew word adopted into the Greek of the New Testament and left untranslated. It occurs only once (Mark 7:11). It means a *gift* or *offering* consecrated to God. Anything over which this word was once pronounced was irrevocably dedicated to the temple. Land, however, so dedicated might be redeemed before the year of jubilee (Lev. 27:16–24). Our Lord condemns the Pharisees for their false doctrine, inasmuch as by their traditions they had destroyed the commandment which requires children to honour their father and mother, teaching them to find excuse from helping their parents by the device of pronouncing "Corban" over their goods, thus reserving them to their own selfish use.

Cord—frequently used in its proper sense—for fastening a tent (Ex. 35:18; 39:40), yoking animals to a cart (Isa. 5:18), binding prisoners (Judg. 15:13; Ps. 2:3; 129:4), and measuring ground (2 Sam. 8:2; Ps. 78:55). Figuratively, death is spoken of as the giving way of the tent-cord (Job 4:21. "Is not their tent-cord plucked up?" R.V.). To gird one's self with a cord was a token of sorrow and humiliation. To stretch a line over a city meant to level it with the ground (Lam. 2:8). The "cords of sin" are the consequences or fruits of sin (Prov. 5:22). A "threefold cord" is a symbol of union (Eccl. 4:12). The "cords of a man" (Hos. 11:4) means that men employ, in inducing each other, methods such as are suitable to men, and not "cords" such as oxen are led by. Isaiah (5:18) says, "Woe unto them that draw iniquity with cords of vanity, and sin as it were with a cart rope." This verse is thus given in the Chaldee paraphrase: "Woe to those who begin to sin by little and little, drawing sin by cords of vanity: these sins grow and increase till they are strong and are like a cart rope." This may be the true meaning. The wicked at first draw sin with a slender cord; but by-and-by their sins increase, and they are drawn after them by a cart rope. Henderson in his commentary says: "The meaning is that the persons described were not satisfied with ordinary modes of provoking the Deity, and the consequent ordinary approach of his vengeance, but, as it were, yoked themselves in the harness of iniquity, and, putting forth all their strength, drew down upon themselves, with accelerated speed, the load of punishment which their sins deserved."

Corian'der—Heb. *gad*—(Ex. 16:31; Num. 11:7), seed to which the manna is likened in its form and colour. It is the *Coriandrum sativum* of botanists, an umbelliferous annual plant with a round stalk, about two feet high. It is widely cultivated in Eastern countries and in the south of Europe for the sake of its seeds, which are in the form of a little ball of the size of a peppercorn. They are used medicinally and as a spice. The Greek name of this plant is *korion* or *koriannon*, whence the name "coriander."

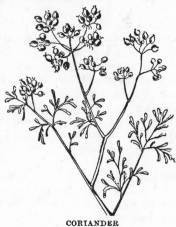

CORIANDER

Cor'inth, a Grecian city, on the isthmus which joins the Peloponnesus to the mainland of Greece. It is about 48 miles west of Athens. The ancient city was destroyed by the Romans (B.C. 146), and that mentioned in the New Testament was quite a new city, having been rebuilt about a century afterwards and peopled by a colony of freedmen from Rome. It became under the Romans the seat of government for Southern Greece or Achaia (Acts 18:12-16). It was noted for its wealth, and for the luxurious and immoral and vicious habits of the people. It had a large mixed population of Romans, Greeks, and Jews. When Paul first visited the city (A.D. 51 or 52), Gallio, the brother of Seneca, was proconsul. Here Paul resided for eighteen months (18:1-18). Here he first became acquainted with Aquila and Priscilla, and soon after his departure Apollos came to it from Ephesus. After an interval he visited it a second time, and remained for three months (20:3). During this second visit his Epistle to the Romans was written (probably A.D. 55). Although there were many Jewish converts at Corinth, yet the Gentile element prevailed in the church there.

Some have argued from 2 Cor. 12:14; 13:1, that Paul visited Corinth a *third* time (*i.e.*, that on some unrecorded occasion he visited the city between what are usually called the first and second visits). But the passages referred to only indicate Paul's *intention* to visit Corinth (comp. 1 Cor. 10:5, where the Greek present tense denotes an intention)—an intention which was in some way frustrated. We can hardly suppose that such a visit could have been made by the apostle without more distinct reference to it.

Corinth'ians, First Epistle to the, was written from Ephesus (1 Cor. 16:8) about the time of the Passover in the third year of the apostle's sojourn there (Acts 19:10; 20:31), and when he had formed the purpose to visit Macedonia, and then return to Corinth (probably A.D. 57).

The news which had reached him, however, from Corinth frustrated his plan. He had heard of the abuses and contentions that had arisen among them, first from Apollos (Acts 19:1), and then from a letter they had written him on the subject, and also from some of the "household of Chloe," and from Stephanas and his two friends who had visited him (1 Cor. 1:11; 16:17). Paul thereupon wrote this letter, for the purpose of checking the factious spirit and correcting the erroneous opinions that had sprung up among them, and remedying the many abuses and disorderly practices that prevailed. Titus and a brother whose name is not given were probably the bearers of the letter (2.Cor. 2:13; 8:6, 16–18).

The epistle may be divided into four parts :—

(1.) The apostle deals with the subject of the lamentable divisions and party strifes that had arisen among them (1 Cor. 1–4).

(2.) He next treats of certain cases of immorality that had become notorious among them. They had apparently set at nought the very first principles of morality (5; 6).

(3.) In the third part he discusses various questions of doctrine and of Christian ethics in reply to certain communications they had made to him. He especially rectifies certain flagrant abuses regarding the celebration of the Lord's supper (7–14).

(4.) The concluding part (15; 16) contains an elaborate defence of the doctrine of the resurrection of the dead, which had been called in question by some among them, followed by some general instructions, intimations, and greetings.

This epistle "shows the powerful self-control of the apostle in spite of his physical weakness, his distressed circumstances, his incessant troubles, and his emotional nature. It was written, he tells us, in bitter anguish, 'out of much affliction and pressure of heart......and with streaming eyes' (2 Cor. 2:4); yet he restrained the expression of his feelings, and wrote with a dignity and holy calm which he thought most calculated to win back his erring children. It gives a vivid picture of the early church......It entirely dissipates the dream that the apostolic church was in an exceptional condition of holiness of life or purity of doctrine." The apostle in this epistle unfolds and applies great principles fitted to guide the church of all ages in dealing with the same and kindred evils in whatever form they may appear.

This is one of the epistles the authenticity of which has never been called in question by critics of any school, so many and so conclusive are the evidences of its Pauline origin.

The subscription to this epistle states erroneously in the Authorized Version that it was written at Philippi. This error arose from a mistranslation of 1 Cor. 16:5, "For I do pass through Macedonia," which was interpreted as meaning, "I am passing through Macedonia." In 16:8 he declares his intention of remaining some time longer in Ephesus. *After that,* his purpose is to "pass through Macedonia."

Corinth'ians, Second Epistle to the. Shortly after writing his first letter to the Corinthians, Paul left Ephesus, where intense excitement had been aroused against him—the evidence of his great success—and proceeded to Macedonia. Pursuing the usual route, he reached Troas, the port of departure for Europe. Here he expected to meet with Titus, whom he had sent from Ephesus to Corinth, with tidings of the effects produced on the church there by the first epistle; but was disappointed

(2 Cor. 1:8; 2:12, 13; 4:10, 11). He then left Troas and proceeded to Macedonia; and at Philippi, where he tarried, he was soon joined by Titus (2 Cor. 7:6, 7), who brought him good news from Corinth, and also by Timothy. Under the influence of the feelings awakened in his mind by the favourable report which Titus brought back from Corinth, this second epistle was written. It was probably written at Philippi, or, as some think, Thessalonica, early in the year A.D. 58, and was sent to Corinth by Titus. This letter he addresses not only to the church in Corinth, but also to the saints in all Achaia—*i.e.*, in Athens, Cenchrea, and other cities in Greece.

The *contents* of this epistle may be thus arranged:—

(1.) Paul speaks of his spiritual labours and course of life, and expresses his warm affection toward the Corinthians (2 Cor. 1–7).

(2.) He gives specific directions regarding the collection that was to be made for their poor brethren in Judea (8; 9).

(3.) He defends his own apostolic claim (10–13), and justifies himself from the charges and insinuations of the false teacher and his adherents.

This epistle, it has been well said, shows the individuality of the apostle more than any other. "Human weakness, spiritual strength, the deepest tenderness of affection, wounded feeling, sternness, irony, rebuke, impassioned self-vindication, humility, a just self-respect, zeal for the welfare of the weak and suffering, as well as for the progress of the church of Christ and for the spiritual advancement of its members, are all displayed in turn in the course of his appeal."—Lias, *Second Corinthians.*

Of the effects produced on the Corinthian church by this epistle we have no definite information. We know that Paul visited Corinth after he had written it (Acts 20:2, 3), and that on that occasion he tarried there for three months. In his letter to Rome, written at this time, he sent salutations from some of the principal members of the church to the Romans.

Cor'morant (Lev. 11:17; Deut. 14:17) —Heb. *shâlak,* "plunging," or "darting down (the *Phalacrocorax carbo*)—ranked among the "unclean" birds; of the same family group as the pelican. It is a "plunging" bird, and is common on the coasts and the inland seas of Palestine.

CORMORANT.

Some think the Hebrew word should be rendered "gannet" (*Sula bassana,* "the solan goose"); others that it is the "tern" or "sea swallow," which also frequents the coasts of Palestine as well as the Sea of Galilee and the Jordan valley during several months of the year. But there is no reason to depart from the ordinary rendering.

In Isa. 34:11, Zeph. 2:14 (but in R.V., "pelican") the Hebrew word rendered by this name is *kâ'ath'.* It is translated "pelican" (*q.v.*) in Ps. 102:6. The word literally means the "vomiter," and the pelican is so called from its vomiting the shells and other things which it has voraciously swallowed. (See PELICAN.)

Corn. The word so rendered (*dâgan'*) in Gen. 27:28, 37, Num. 18:27, Deut. 28:51, Lam. 2:12, is a general term representing all the commodities we usually describe by the words corn, grain, seeds, peas, beans. With this corresponds the use of the word in John 12:24.

In Gen. 41:35, 49, Prov. 11:26, Joel 2:24 ("wheat"), the word thus translated (*bar; i.e.,* "winnowed") means corn purified from chaff. With this corresponds the use of the word in the New Testament (Matt. 3:12; Luke 3:17; Acts 7:12). In Ps. 65:13 it means "growing corn."

In Gen. 42:1, 2, 19, Ex. 8:5, Neh. 10: 31 ("victuals"), the word (*shéber; i.e.,* "broken," *i.e.,* grist) denotes generally victuals, provisions, and corn as a principal article of food.

From the time of Solomon, corn began to be exported from Palestine (Ezek. 27: 17; Amos 8:5). "Plenty of corn" was a part of Isaac's blessing conferred upon Jacob (Gen. 27:28; comp. Ps. 65:13).

Corne'lius, a centurion whose history is narrated in Acts 10. He was a "devout man," and like the centurion of Capernaum, believed in the God of Israel. His residence at Cæsarea probably brought him into contact with Jews who communicated to him their expectations regarding the Messiah; and thus he was prepared to welcome the message Peter brought him. He became the first fruit of the Gentile world to Christ. He and his family were baptized and admitted into the Christian church (Acts 10:1, 44–48). (See CENTURION.)

Cor'ner. The angle of a house (Job 1: 19) or a street (Prov. 7:8). "Corners" in Neh. 9:22 denotes the various districts of the promised land allotted to the Israelites. In Num. 24:17, the "corners of Moab" denotes the whole land of Moab. The "corner of a field" (Lev. 19:9; 23:22) is its extreme part, which was not to be reaped. The Jews were prohibited from cutting the "corners," *i.e.,* the extremities, of the hair and whiskers running round the ears (Lev. 19:27; 21:5). The "four corners of the earth" in Isa. 11:12 and Ezek. 7:2 denotes the whole land. The "corners of the streets" mentioned in Matt. 6:5 means the angles where streets meet so as to form a square or place of public resort.

The *corner gate* of Jerusalem (2 Kings 14:13; 2 Chr. 26:9) was on the north-west side of the city.

Corner-stone (Job 38:6; Isa. 28:16), a block of great importance in binding together the sides of a building. The "head of the corner" (Ps. 118:22, 23) denotes the coping, the "coign of vantage"—*i.e.,* the topstone of a building. But the word "corner stone" is sometimes used to denote some person of rank and importance (Isa. 28:16). It is applied to our Lord, who was set in highest honour (Matt. 21: 42). He is also styled "the chief corner stone" (Eph. 2:20; 1 Pet. 2:6, 8). When Zechariah (10:4), speaking of Judah, says, "Out of him came forth the corner," he is probably to be understood as ultimately referring to the Messiah as the "corner stone." (See TEMPLE, SOLOMON'S.)

Cor'net—Heb. *shôphâr,* "brightness," with reference to the clearness of its sound (1 Chr. 15:28; 2 Chr. 15:14; Ps. 98:6; Hos. 5:8). It is usually rendered in the Authorized Version "trumpet." It denotes the long and straight horn, about eighteen inches long. The words of Joel, "Blow the trumpet," literally, "Sound the cornet," refer to the festival which was the preparation for the day of Atonement. In Dan. 3:5, 7, 10, 15, the word (*kĕrĕn*) so rendered is a curved horn. The word "cornet" in 2 Sam. 6:5 (Heb. *menaʿanʿîm,* occurring only here) was some kind of instrument played by being shaken like the Egyptian *sistrum,* consisting of rings or bells hung loosely on iron rods.

Cotes, pens or enclosures for flocks (2 Chr. 32:28, "cotes for flocks;" R.V., "flocks in folds").

Cot'tage. (1.) A booth in a vineyard (Isa. 1:8); a temporary shed covered with leaves or straw to shelter the watchman that kept the garden. These were slight

LODGE IN A GARDEN.

fabrics, and were removed when no longer needed, or were left to be blown down in winter (Job 27:18).

(2.) A lodging-place (rendered "lodge" in Isa. 1:8); a slighter structure than the "booth," as the cucumber patch is more temporary than a vineyard (Isa. 24:20). It denotes a frail structure of boughs supported on a few poles, which is still in use in the East, or a hammock suspended between trees, in which the watchman was accustomed to sleep during summer.

(3.) In Zeph. 2:6 it is the rendering of the Hebrew *kĕroth*, which some suppose to denote rather "pits" (R.V. marg., "caves") or "wells of water," such as shepherds would sink.

Couch (Gen. 49:4; 1 Chr. 5:1; Job 7:13; Ps. 6:6, etc.), a seat for repose or rest. (See BED.)

Coulter (1 Sam. 13:20, 21), an agricultural instrument, elsewhere called "ploughshare" (Isa. 2:4; Micah 4:3; Joel 3:10). It was the facing-piece of a plough, analogous to the modern coulter.

Coun'cil, spoken of counsellors who sat in public trials with the governor of a province (Acts 25:12).

The Jewish councils were the Sanhedrim, or supreme council of the nation, which had subordinate to it smaller tribunals (the "judgment," perhaps, in Matt. 5:21, 22) in the cities of Palestine (Matt. 10:17; Mark 13:9). In the time of Christ the functions of the Sanhedrim were limited (John 16:2; 2 Cor. 11:24). In Ps. 68:27 the word "council" means simply a company of persons.

In ecclesiastical history the word is used to denote an assembly of pastors or bishops for the discussion and regulation of church affairs. The first of these councils was that of the apostles and elders at Jerusalem, of which we have a detailed account in Acts 15.

Coun'sellor, an adviser (Prov. 11:14; 15:22), a king's state counsellor (2 Sam. 15:12). Used once of the Messiah (Isa. 9:6). In Mark 15:43, Luke 23:50, the word probably means a member of the Jewish Sanhedrim.

Courses. When David was not permitted to build the temple, he proceeded, among the last acts of his life, with the assistance of Zadok and Ahimelech, to organize the priestly and musical services to be conducted in the house of God. (1.)

He divided the priests into twenty-four courses (1 Chr. 24:1–19), sixteen being of the house of Eleazar and eight of that of Ithamar. Each course was under a head or chief, and ministered for a week, the order being determined by lot. (2.) The rest of the 24,000 Levites (23:4) were divided also into twenty-four courses, each to render some allotted service in public worship: 4,000 in twenty-four courses were set apart as singers and musicians under separate leaders (25); 4,000 as porters or keepers of the doors and gates of the sanctuary (26:1–19); and 6,000 as officers and judges to see to the administration of the law in all civil and ecclesiastical matters (20–32).

This arrangement was re-established by Hezekiah (2 Chr. 31:2); and afterwards the four sacerdotal courses which are said to have returned from the Captivity were re-divided into the original number of twenty-four by Ezra (6:18).

Court, the enclosure of the tabernacle (Ex. 27:9–19; 40:8), of the temple (1 Kings 6:36), of a prison (Neh. 3:25), of a private house (2 Sam. 17:18), and of a king's palace (2 Kings 20:4).

Cov'enant, a contract or agreement between two parties. In the Old Testament the Hebrew word *berith* is always thus translated. *Berith* is derived from a root which means "to cut," and hence a covenant is a "cutting," with reference to the cutting or dividing of animals into two parts, and the contracting parties passing between them, in making a covenant (Gen. 15; Jer. 34:18, 19).

The corresponding word in the New Testament Greek is *diathéke*, which is, however, rendered "testament" generally in the Authorized Version. It ought to be rendered, just as the word *berith* of the Old Testament, "covenant."

This word is used (1) of a covenant or compact between man and man (Gen. 21:32), or between tribes or nations (1 Sam. 11:1; Josh. 9:6, 15). In entering into a covenant, Jehovah was solemnly called on to witness the transaction (Gen. 31:50), and hence it was called a "covenant of the Lord" (1 Sam. 20:8). The marriage compact is called "the covenant of God" (Prov. 2:17), because the marriage was made in God's name. Wicked men are spoken of as acting as if they had made a "covenant with death" not to destroy them, or with hell not to devour them (Isa. 28:15, 18).

(2.) The word is used with reference to God's revelation of himself in the way of promise or of favour to men. Thus God's promise to Noah after the Flood is called a covenant (Gen. 9; Jer. 33:20, "my covenant"). We have an account of God's covenant with Abraham (Gen. 17, comp. Lev. 26:42), of the covenant of the priesthood (Num. 25:12, 13; Deut. 33:9; Neh. 13:29), and of the covenant of Sinai (Ex. 34:27, 28; Lev. 26:15), which was afterwards renewed at different times in the history of Israel (Deut. 29; Josh. 24; 2 Chr. 15; 23; 29; 34; Ezra 10; Neh. 9). In conformity with human custom, God's covenant is said to be confirmed with an oath (Deut. 4:31; Ps. 89:3), and to be accompanied by a sign (Gen. 9; 17). Hence the covenant is called God's "counsel," "oath," "promise" (Ps. 89:3, 4; 105:8–11; Heb. 6:13–20; Luke 1:68–75). God's covenant consists wholly in the bestowal of blessing (Isa. 59:21; Jer. 31:33, 34).

The term covenant is also used to designate the regular succession of day and night (Jer. 33:20), the Sabbath (Ex. 31:16), circumcision (Gen. 17:9, 10), and in general any ordinance of God (Jer. 34:13, 14).

A "covenant of salt" signifies an everlasting covenant, in the sealing or ratifying of which salt, as an emblem of perpetuity, is used (Num. 18:19; Lev. 2:13; 2 Chr. 13:5).

COVENANT OF WORKS, the constitution under which Adam was placed at his creation. In this covenant—(1.) The contracting parties were (a) God the moral Governor, and (b) Adam, a free moral agent, and representative of all his natural posterity (Rom. 5:12–19). (2.) The promise was "life" (Matt. 19:16, 17; Gal. 3:12). (3.) The condition was perfect obedience to the law—the test in this case being abstaining from eating the fruit of the "tree of knowledge," etc. (4.) The penalty was death (Gen. 2:16, 17).

This covenant is also called a covenant of nature, as made with man in his natural or unfallen state; a covenant of life, because "life" was the promise attached to obedience; and a legal covenant, because it demanded perfect obedience to the law.

The "tree of life" was the outward sign and seal of that life which was promised in the covenant, and hence it is usually called the seal of that covenant.

This covenant is *abrogated* under the gospel, inasmuch as Christ has fulfilled all its conditions in behalf of his people, and now offers salvation on the condition of faith.

It is *still in force*, however, as it rests on the immutable justice of God, and is binding on all who have not fled to Christ and accepted his righteousness.

COVENANT OF GRACE, the eternal plan of redemption entered into by the three persons of the Godhead, and carried out by them in its several parts. In it the Father represented the Godhead in its indivisible sovereignty, and the Son his people as their surety (John 17:4, 6, 9; Isa. 42:6; Ps. 89:3).

The *conditions* of this covenant were—(1.) On the part of the Father (a) all needful preparation to the Son for the accomplishment of his work (Heb. 10:5; Isa. 42:1–7); (b) support in the work (Luke 22:43); and (c) a glorious reward in the exaltation of Christ when his work was done (Phil. 2:6–11), his investiture with universal dominion (John 5:22; Ps. 110:1), his having the administration of the covenant committed into his hands (Matt. 28:18; John 1:12; 17:2; Acts 2:33), and in the final salvation of all his people (Isa. 35:10; 53:10, 11; Jer. 31:33; Titus 1:2). (2.) On the part of the Son the conditions were (a) his becoming incarnate (Gal. 4:4, 5); and (b) as the second Adam his representing all his people, assuming their place and undertaking all their obligations under the violated covenant of works; (c) obeying the law (Ps. 40:8; Isa. 42:21; John 9:4, 5), and (d) suffering its penalty (Isa. 53; 2 Cor. 5:21; Gal. 3:13), in their stead.

Christ, the mediator of, fulfils all its conditions in behalf of his people, and dispenses to them all its blessings. In Heb. 8:6; 9:15; 12:24, this title is given to Christ. (See DISPENSATION.)

Cov'ering of the eyes, occurs only in Gen. 20:16. In the Revised Version the rendering is "it [*i.e.*, Abimelech's present of 1,000 pieces of silver to Abraham] is for thee a covering of the eyes." This has been regarded as an implied advice to Sarah to conform to the custom of married women, and wear a complete veil, covering the eyes as well as the rest of the face.

Cov'etousness, a strong desire after the possession of worldly things (Col. 3:5; Eph. 5:5; Heb. 13:5; 1 Tim. 6:9, 10;

Matt. 6:20). It assumes sometimes the more aggravated form of avarice, which is the mark of cold-hearted worldliness.

Cow. A cow and her calf were not to be killed on the same day (Lev. 22:28; Ex. 23:19; Deut. 22:6, 7). The reason for this enactment is not given. A state of great poverty is described in the words of Isa. 7:21-25, where, instead of possessing great resources, a man shall depend for the subsistence of himself and his family on what a single cow and two sheep could yield.

Crane (Isa. 38:14; Jer. 8:7). In both of these passages the Authorized Version has reversed the Hebrew order of the

FRAGMENT OF CLAY TABLET WITH ASSYRIAN ACCOUNT OF THE CREATION.
(From *Helps to the Study of the Bible.* Oxford.)

words. "Crane or swallow" should be "swallow or crane," as in the Revised Version. The rendering is there correct. The Hebrew for crane is *'âgûr*, the *Grus cinerea*, a bird well known in Palestine. It is migratory, and is distinguished by its loud voice, its cry being hoarse and melancholy.

Crea'tion. "In the beginning" God created—*i.e.*, called into being—all things out of nothing. This creative act on the part of God was absolutely free, and for infinitely wise reasons. The cause of all things exists only in the will of God. The work of creation is attributed (1) to the Godhead (Gen. 1:1, 26); (2) to the Father (1 Cor. 8:6); (3) to the Son (John 1:3;

Col. 1:16, 17); (4) to the Holy Spirit (Gen. 1:2; Job 26:13; Ps. 104:30). The fact that he is the Creator distinguishes Jehovah as the true God (Isa. 37:16; 40:12, 13; 54:5; Ps. 96:5; Jer. 10:11, 12). The one great end in the work of creation is the manifestation of the glory of the Creator (Col. 1:16; Rev. 4:11; Rom. 11:36). God's works, equally with God's word, are a revelation from him; and between the teachings of the one and those of the other, when rightly understood, there can be no contradiction.

Traditions of the creation, disfigured by corruptions, are found among the records of ancient Eastern nations. (See ACCAD.) A peculiar interest belongs to the traditions of the Accadians, the primitive inhabitants of the plains of Lower Mesopotamia. These within the last few years have been brought to light in the tablets and cylinders which have been rescued from the long-buried palaces and temples of Assyria. They bear a remarkable resemblance to the record of Genesis.

Crea'ture, denotes the whole creation in Rom. 8:39; Col. 1:15; Rev. 3:14; the whole human race in Mark 16:15; Rom. 8:19-22.

The *living creatures* in Ezek. 10:15, 17, are imaginary beings, symbols of the Divine attributes and operations.

Cres'cens—*increasing*—probably one of the seventy disciples of Christ. He was one of Paul's assistants (2 Tim. 4:10), probably a Christian of Rome.

Cre'te, now called Candia, one of the largest islands in the Mediterranean, about 140 miles long and 35 broad. It was at one time a very prosperous and populous island, having a "hundred cities." The character of the people is described in Paul's quotation from "one of their own poets" (Epimenides) in his epistle to Titus: "The Cretans are alway liars, evil beasts, slow bellies" (Titus 1:12). Jews from Crete were in Jerusalem on the day of Pentecost (Acts 2:11). The island was visited by Paul on his voyage to Rome (Acts 27). Here Paul subsequently left Titus (1:5) "to ordain elders." Some have supposed that it was the original home of the Caphtorim (*q.v.*) or Philistines.

Crim'son. See COLOUR.

Crisp'ing-pin (Isa. 3:22; R.V., "satchel"), some kind of female ornament, probably like the modern *reticule*. The Hebrew word *harît* properly signifies pouch or casket or purse. It is rendered "bag" in 2 Kings 5:23.

Cris'pus—*curled*—the chief of the synagogue at Corinth (Acts 18:8). He was converted and, with his family, baptized by Paul (1 Cor. 1:14).

Cross, in the New Testament the instrument of crucifixion, and hence used for the crucifixion of Christ itself (Eph. 2:16; Heb. 12:2; 1 Cor. 1:17, 18; Gal. 5:11; 6:12, 14; Phil. 3:18). The word

is also used to denote any severe affliction or trial (Matt. 10:38; 16:24; Mark 8:34; 10:21).

The *forms* in which the cross is represented are these:—

1. The *crux simplex* (I), a "single piece without transom."

2. The *crux decussata* (X), or St. Andrew's cross.

3. The *crux commissa* (T), or St. Anthony's cross.

4. The *crux immissa* (†), or Latin cross, which was the kind of cross on which our Saviour died. *Above* our Lord's head, on the projecting beam, was placed the "title." (See CRUCIFIXION.)

After the conversion, so-called, of Constantine the Great (B.C. 313), the cross first came into use as an emblem of Christianity. He pretended at a critical moment that he saw a flaming cross in the heavens bearing the inscription, "In hoc signo vinces"—*i.e.,* By this sign thou shalt conquer—and that on the following night Christ himself appeared and ordered him to take for his standard the sign of this cross. In this form a new standard, called the *Labarum,* was accordingly made, and

LABARUM.

borne by the Roman armies. It remained the standard of the Roman army till the downfall of the Western empire. It bore the embroidered monogram of Christ—*i.e.,* the first two Greek letters of his name, X and P (*chi* and *rho*), with the Alpha and Omega. (See ALPHA.)

Crown. (1.) Denotes the plate of gold

in the front of the high priest's mitre (Ex. 29:6; 39:30). The same Hebrew word so rendered (*ne'zer*) denotes the diadem worn by Saul in battle (2 Sam. 1:10), and also that which was used at the coronation of Joash (2 Kings 11:12).

(2.) The more general name in Hebrew for a crown is *'atârah*, meaning a "circlet." This is used of crowns and head ornaments of divers kinds, including royal crowns. Such was the crown taken from the king of Ammon by David (2 Sam. 12:30). The crown worn by the Assyrian kings was a high mitre, sometimes adorned with flowers. There are sculptures also representing the crowns worn by the early Egyptian and Persian kings. Sometimes a diadem surrounded the royal head-dress of two or three fillets. This probably signified that

MODERN ASIATIC CROWNS.

the wearer had dominion over two or three countries. In Rev. 12:3; 13:1, we read of "many crowns," a token of extended dominion.

(3.) The ancient Persian crown (Esther 1:11; 2:17; 6:8) was called *kéther; i.e.,* "a chaplet," a high cap or tiara. Crowns were worn sometimes to represent honour and power (Ezek. 23:42). They were worn at marriages (Cant. 3:11; Isa. 61:10, "ornaments;" R.V., "garlands"), and at feasts and public festivals.

The crown was among the Romans and Greeks a symbol of victory and reward. The crown or wreath worn by the victors in the Olympic games was made of leaves of the wild olive; in the Pythian games, of laurel; in the Nemean games, of parsley; and in the Isthmian games, of the pine. The Romans bestowed the "civic crown" on

him who saved the life of a citizen. It was made of the leaves of the oak. In opposition to all these fading crowns the apostles speak of the incorruptible crown, the crown of life (James 1:12; Rev. 2:10) "that fadeth not away" (1 Pet. 5:4—Gr. *amarantinos;* comp. 1:4). Probably the word "amaranth" was applied to flowers we call "everlasting," the "immortal amaranth."

Crown of thorns, our Lord was crowned with a, in mockery by the Romans (Matt. 27:29). The object of Pilate's guard in doing this was probably to insult, and not specially to inflict pain. There is nothing to show that the shrub thus used was, as has been supposed, the *spina Christi*, which could not have been easily woven into a wreath. It was probably the thorny *nâbk*, which grew abundantly round about Jerusalem, and whose flexible, pliant, and round branches could easily be platted into the form of a crown. (See THORN, 3.)

Crucifix′ion, a common mode of punishment among heathen nations in early times. It is not certain whether it was known among the ancient Jews; probably it was not. The modes of capital punishment according to the Mosaic law were, by the sword (Ex. 21), strangling, fire (Lev. 20), and stoning (Deut. 21).

This was regarded as the most horrible form of death, and to a Jew it would acquire greater horror from the curse in Deut. 21:23.

This punishment began by subjecting the sufferer to scourging. In the case of our Lord, however, his scourging was rather *before* the sentence was passed upon him, and was inflicted by Pilate for the purpose, probably, of exciting pity and procuring his escape from further punishment (Luke 23:22; John 19:1).

The condemned one carried his own cross to the place of execution, which was outside the city, in some conspicuous place set apart for the purpose. Before the nailing to the cross took place, a medicated cup of vinegar mixed with gall and myrrh (the *sopor*) was given, for the purpose of deadening the pangs of the sufferer. Our Lord refused this cup, that his senses might be clear (Matt. 27:34). The spongeful of vinegar—sour wine, *posca*—the common drink of the Roman soldiers, which was put on a hyssop stalk and offered to our Lord in contemptuous pity (Matt. 27:48; Luke 23:36), he tasted to allay the agonies of his thirst (John 19:29). The accounts given of the crucifixion of our Lord are in entire agreement with the customs and practices of the Romans in such cases. He was crucified between two "malefactors" (Isa. 53:12; Luke 23:32), and was watched by a party of four soldiers (John 19:23; Matt. 27:36, 54), with their centurion. The "breaking of the legs" of the malefactors was intended to hasten death, and put them out of misery (John 19:31); but the unusual rapidity of our Lord's death (19:33) was due to his previous sufferings and his great mental anguish. The omission of the breaking of his legs was the fulfilment of a type (Ex. 12:46). He literally died of a broken heart—a ruptured heart—and hence the flowing of blood and water from the wound made by the soldier's spear (John 19:34). Our Lord uttered seven memorable words from the cross—namely, (1) Luke 23:34; (2) 23:43; (3) John 19:26; (4) Matt. 27:46, Mark 15:34; (5) John 19:28; (6) 19:30; (7) Luke 23:46.

Cruse, a utensil; a flask or cup for holding water (1 Sam. 26:11, 12, 16; 1 Kings 19:6) or oil (1 Kings 17:12, 14, 16).

In 1 Kings 14:3 the word there so rendered means properly a bottle—as in Jer. 19:1, 10—or pitcher. In 2 Kings 2:20, a platter or flat metal saucer is intended. The Hebrew word here used is translated "dish" in 21:13; "pans," in 2 Chr. 35:13; and "bosom," in Prov. 19:24; 26:15 (R.V., "dish").

Crys'tal (Ezek. 1:22, with the epithet "terrible," as dazzling the spectators with its brightness). The word occurs in Rev. 4:6; 21:11; 22:1. It is a stone of the flint order, the most refined kind of quartz. The Greek word here used means also literally "ice." The ancients regarded the crystal as only pure water congealed into extreme hardness by great length of time.

Cu'bit—Heb. *'ammâh; i.e.,* "*mother* of

the arm," the *fore*-arm—is a word derived from the Latin *cubitus*, the lower arm. It is difficult to determine the exact length of this measure, from the uncertainty whether it included the entire length from the elbow to the tip of the longest finger, or only from the elbow to the root of the hand at the wrist. The probability is that the longer was the original cubit. The common computation as to the length of the cubit makes it 20.24 inches for the ordinary cubit, and 21.888 inches for the sacred one. This is the same as the Egyptian measurements.

A rod or staff the measure of a cubit is called in Judg. 3:16 *gómed*, which literally means a "cut," something "cut off." The LXX. and Vulgate render it "span."

Cuck'oo (Heb. *shahaph*), from a root meaning "to be lean; slender." This bird is mentioned only in Lev. 11:16 and Deut. 14:15 (R.V., "sea-mew"). Some have interpreted the Hebrew word by "petrel" or "shearwater" (*Puffinus cinereus*), which is found on the coast of Syria; others think it denotes the "sea-gull" or "sea-mew." The common cuckoo (*Cuculus canorus*) feeds on reptiles and large insects. It is found in Asia and Africa as well as in Europe. It only passes the winter in Palestine. The Arabs suppose it to utter the cry *Yakûb*, and hence they call it *tîr el-Yakûb; i.e.,* "Jacob's bird."

Cu'cumbers (Heb. plur. *kishshuîm; i.e.,* "hard," "difficult" of digestion, only in Num. 11:5). This vegetable is extensively cultivated in the East at the present day, as it appears to have been in earlier times among the Hebrews. It belongs to the gourd family of plants. In the East its cooling pulp and juice are most refreshing. "We need not altogether wonder that the Israelites, wearily marching through the arid solitudes of the Sinaitic peninsula, thought more of the cucumbers and watermelons of which they had had no lack in Egypt, rather than of the cruel bondage which was the price of these luxuries."— Groser's *Scripture Natural History.*

Isaiah speaks of a "lodge" (1:8; Heb. *sukkâh*)—*i.e.,* a shed or edifice more solid than a booth—for the protection throughout the season from spring to autumn of the watchers in a "garden of cucumbers."

Cum'min (Heb. *kammôn; i.e.*, a "condiment"), the fruit or seed of an umbelliferous plant, the *Cuminum sativum*, still

CUMMIN.

extensively cultivated in the East. Its fruit is mentioned in Isa. 28:25, 27. In the New Testament it is mentioned in Matt. 23:23, where our Lord pronounces a "woe" on the scribes and Pharisees, who were zealous in paying tithes of "mint and anise and cummin," while they "omitted the weightier matters of the law." "It is used as a spice, both bruised, to mix with bread, and also boiled, in the various messes and stews which compose an Oriental banquet."—Tristram, *Natural History.*

Cup, a wine-cup (Gen. 40:11, 21), various forms of which are found on Assyrian and Egyptian monuments. All Solomon's drinking vessels were of gold (1 Kings 10:21). The cups mentioned in the New Testament were made after Roman and Greek models, and were sometimes of gold (Rev. 17:4).

The art of divining by means of a cup was practised in Egypt (Gen. 44:2-17), and in the East generally.

The "cup of salvation" (Ps. 116:13) is the cup of thanksgiving for the great salvation. The "cup of consolation" (Jer. 16:7) refers to the custom of friends sending viands and wine to console relatives in mourning (Prov. 31:6). In 1 Cor. 10:16, the "cup of blessing" is contrasted with the "cup of devils" (1 Cor. 10:21). The sacramental cup is the "cup of blessing," because of blessing pronounced over it (Matt. 26:27; Luke 22:17). The "portion of the cup" (Ps. 11:6; 16:5) denotes one's condition of life, prosperous or adverse. A "cup" is also a type of sensual allurement (Jer. 51:7; Prov. 23:31; Rev. 17:4). We read also of the "cup of astonishment," the "cup of trembling," and the "cup of God's wrath" (Ps. 75:8; Isa. 51:17; Jer. 25:15; Lam. 4:21; Ezek. 23:32; Rev. 16:19; comp. Matt. 26:39, 42; John 18:11). The cup is also the symbol of death (Matt. 16:28; Mark 9:1; Heb. 2:9).

Cup'-bearer, an officer of high rank with Egyptian, Persian, Assyrian, and Jewish monarchs. The cup-bearer of the king of Egypt is mentioned in connection with Joseph's history (Gen. 40:1-21; 41:9). Rabshakeh (*q.v.*) was cup-bearer in the Assyrian court (2 Kings 18:17). Nehemiah filled this office to the king of Persia (Neh. 1:11). We read also of Solomon's cup-bearers (1 Kings 10:5; 2 Chr. 9:4).

Cu'rious arts (Acts 19:19), magical arts; jugglery practised by the Ephesian conjurers. Ephesus was noted for its wizards and the "Ephesian spells;" *i.c.*, charms or scraps of parchment written over with certain formulæ, which were worn as a safeguard against all manner of evils. The more important and powerful of these charms were written out in books which circulated among the exorcists, and were sold at a great price.

Curse, denounced by God against the serpent (Gen. 3:14), and against Cain (4:11). These divine maledictions carried their effect with them. Prophetical curses were sometimes pronounced by holy men (Gen. 9:25; 49:7; Deut. 27:15; Josh. 6:26). Such curses are not the consequence of passion or revenge, they are *predictions.*

No one on pain of death shall curse father or mother (Ex. 21:17), nor the prince of his people (22:28), nor the deaf (Lev. 19:14). Cursing God or blaspheming was punishable by death (Lev. 24:10-16). The words "curse God and die" (R.V., "renounce God and die"), used by Job's wife (Job 2:9), have been variously interpreted. Perhaps they simply mean that as nothing but death was expected, God would by this cursing at once interpose and destroy Job, and so put an end to his sufferings.

Cur'tain. (1.) Ten curtains, each twenty-eight cubits long and four wide, made of fine linen, also eleven made of goat's hair, covered the tabernacle (Ex. 26:1–13; 36: 8–17).

(2.) The sacred curtain, separating the holy of holies from the sanctuary, is designated by a different Hebrew word (*peró-keth*). It is described as a "veil of blue, and purple, and scarlet, and fine twined linen of cunning work" (Ex. 26:31; Lev. 16:2; Num. 18:7).

(3.) "Stretcheth out the heavens as a curtain" (Isa. 40:22), is an expression used with reference to the veil or awning which Orientals spread for a screen over their courts in summer. According to the prophet, the heavens are spread over our heads as such an awning. Similar expressions are found in Ps. 104:2; comp. Isa. 44:24; Job 9:8.

Cush—*black.* (1.) A son, probably the eldest, of Ham, and the father of Nimrod (Gen. 10:8; 1 Chr. 1:10). From him the *land of Cush* seems to have derived its name. The question of the precise locality of the land of Cush has given rise to not a little controversy. The second river of Paradise surrounded the whole land of Cush (Gen. 2:13, R.V.). The term Cush is in the Old Testament generally applied to the countries south of the Israelites. It was the southern limit of Egypt (Ezek. 29:10, A.V. "Ethiopia," Heb. *Cush*), with which it is generally associated (Ps. 68:31; Isa. 18:1; Jer. 46:9, etc.). It stands also associated with Elam (Isa. 11:11), with Persia (Ezek. 38:5), and with the Sabeans (Isa. 45:14). From these facts it has been inferred that Cush included Arabia and the country on the west coast of the Red Sea. Rawlinson takes it to be the country still known as *Khuzi-stan*, on the east side of the Lower Tigris. But there are intimations which warrant the conclusion that there was also a Cush in Africa—the Ethiopia (so called by the Greeks) of Africa. Ezekiel speaks (29:10; comp. 30:

4–6) of it as lying south of Egypt. It was the country now known to us as Nubia and Abyssinia (Isa. 18:1; Zeph. 3:10, Heb. *Cush*). In ancient Egyptian inscriptions Ethiopia is termed *Kesh*. The Cushites appear to have spread along extensive tracts, stretching from the Upper Nile to the Euphrates and Tigris. At an early period there was a stream of migration of Cushites "from Ethiopia, properly so called, through Arabia, Babylonia, and Persia, to Western India." The Hamite races, soon after their arrival in Africa, began to spread north, east, and west. Three branches of the Cushite or Ethiopian stock, moving from Western Asia, settled in the regions contiguous to the Persian Gulf. One branch, called the Cossæans, settled in the mountainous district on the east of the Tigris, known afterwards as Susiana; another occupied the lower regions of the Euphrates and the Tigris; while a third colonized the southern shores and islands of the gulf, whence they afterwards emigrated to the Mediterranean and settled on the coast of Palestine as the Phœnicians. Nimrod was a great Cushite chief. He conquered the Accadians, a Tauranian race, already settled in Mesopotamia, and founded his kingdom, the Cushites mingling with the Accads, and so forming the Chaldean nation.

(2.) A Benjamite of this name is mentioned in the title of Ps. 7. "Cush was probably a follower of Saul, the head of his tribe, and had sought the friendship of David for the purpose of 'rewarding evil to him that was at peace with him.'"

Cu'shan, probably a poetic or prolonged name of the land of Cush—the Arabian Cush (Hab. 3:7).

Some have, however, supposed this to be the same as **Chushan-rishathaim** (Judg. 3:8, 10)—*i.e.*, taking the latter part of the name as a title or local appellation, Chushan "of the two iniquities" (=oppressing Israel, and provoking them to idolatry)—a Mesopotamian king, identified by Rawlinson with Asshur-ris-ilim (the father of Tiglath-pileser I.); but incorrectly, for the empire of Assyria was not yet founded. He held Israel in bondage for eight years.

Cush'ite. (1.) The messenger sent by

Joab to David to announce his victory over Absalom (2 Sam. 18 : 32).

(2.) The father of Shelemiah (Jer. 36:14).

(3.) Son of Gedaliah, and father of the prophet Zephaniah (1 : 1).

(4.) Moses married a Cushite woman (Num. 12 : 1). From this circumstance some have supposed that Zipporah was meant, and hence that Midian was Cush.

Cus'tom, a tax imposed by the Romans. The tax-gatherers were termed publicans (*q.v.*), who had their stations at the gates of cities, and in the public highways, and at the place set apart for that purpose, called the "receipt of custom" (Matt. 9 : 9 ; Mark 2 : 14), where they collected the money that was to be paid on certain goods (Matt. 17:25). These publicans were tempted to exact more from the people than was lawful, and were, in consequence of their extortions, objects of great hatred. The Pharisees would have no intercourse with them (Matt. 5 : 46, 47 ; 9 : 10, 11).

A tax or tribute (*q.v.*) of *half a shekel* was annually paid by every adult Jew for the temple. It had to be paid in Jewish coin (Matt. 22 : 17–19 ; Mark 12 : 14, 15). Money-changers (*q.v.*) were necessary, to enable the Jews who came up to Jerusalem at the feasts to exchange their foreign coin for Jewish money ; but as it was forbidden by the law to carry on such a traffic for emolument (Deut. 23 : 20, 21), our Lord drove them from the temple (Matt. 21 : 12 ; Mark 11 : 15).

Cu'thah, one of the Babylonian cities or districts from which Shalmaneser transplanted certain colonists to Samaria (2 Kings 17 : 24). Some have conjectured that the "Cutheans" were identical with the "Cossæans" who inhabited the hill-country to the north of the river Choaspes. Cuthah is now identified with *Tell Ibrahim,* 15 miles north-east of Babylon.

Cut'ting the flesh in various ways was an idolatrous practice—a part of idol-worship (Deut. 14 : 1 ; 1 Kings 18 : 28). The Israelites were commanded not to imitate this practice (Lev. 19 : 28 ; 21 : 5 ; Deut. 14 : 1). The tearing of the flesh from grief and anguish of spirit in mourn-ing for the dead was regarded as a mark of affection (Jer. 16 : 6 ; 41 : 5 ; 48 : 37).

Allusions are made in Revelation (13 : 16 ; 17 : 5 ; 19 : 20) to the practice of printing marks on the body, to indicate allegiance to a deity. We find also references to it, though in a different direction, by Paul (Gal. 6 : 7) and by Ezekiel (9 : 4). (See HAIR.)

Cym'bals (Heb. *tzeltzelim,* from a root meaning to "tinkle"), musical instruments, consisting of two convex pieces of brass, one held in each hand, which were clashed together to produce a loud clanging sound ; castanets ; "loud cymbals." "High-sounding cymbals" consisted of two larger plates, one held also in each hand (2 Sam. 6:5 ; Ps. 150:5 ; 1 Chr. 13:8 ; 15 : 16, 19, 28 ; 1 Cor. 13 : 1).

Cy'press (Heb. *tirzâh,* "hardness"), mentioned only in Isa. 44:14 (R.V., "holm-oak"). The oldest Latin version translates this word by *ilex — i.e.,* the evergreen oak—which may possibly have been the tree intended ; but there is great probability that our Authorized Version is correct in rendering it "cypress." This

BRANCH OF CYPRESS-TREE.

tree grows abundantly on the mountains of Hermon. Its wood is hard and fragrant, and very durable. Its foliage is dark and gloomy. It is an evergreen (*Cupressus sempervirens*). "Throughout the East it is used as a funereal tree ; and its dark, tall, waving plumes render it peculiarly appropriate among the tombs."

Cy'prus, one of the largest islands of the Mediterranean—about 148 miles long and 40 broad. It is distant about 60 miles from the Syrian coast. It was the "Chittim" of the Old Testament (Num. 24:24). The Greek colonists gave it the name of *Kypros*, from the *cyprus—i.e.*, the henna (see CAMPHIRE)—which grew on this island. It was originally inhabited by Phœnicians. In B.C. 477 it fell under the dominion of the Greeks; and became a Roman province B.C. 58. In ancient times it was a centre of great commercial activity. Corn and wine and oil were produced here in the greatest perfection. It was rich also in timber and in mineral wealth.

It is first mentioned in the New Testament (Acts 4:36) as the native place of Barnabas. It was the scene of Paul's first missionary labours (13:4–13), when he and Barnabas and John Mark were sent forth by the church of Antioch. It was afterwards visited by Barnabas and Mark alone (15:39). Mnason, an "old disciple," probably one of the converts of the day of Pentecost belonging to this island, is mentioned 21:16. It is afterwards mentioned in connection with the voyages of Paul (Acts 21:3; 27:4). After being under the Turks for three hundred years, it was given up to the British Government in 1878.

Cyre'ne, a city (now *Tripoli*) in Upper Libya, North Africa, founded by a colony of Greeks (B.C. 630). It contained latterly a large number of Jews, who were introduced into the city by Ptolemy, the son of Lagus, because he thought they would contribute to the security of the place. They increased in number and influence; and we are thus prepared for the frequent references to them in connection with the early history of Christianity. Simon, who bore our Lord's cross, was a native of this place (Matt. 27:32; Mark 15:21). Jews from Cyrene were in Jerusalem at Pentecost (Acts 2:10); and Cyrenian Jews had a synagogue at Jerusalem (6:9). Converts belonging to Cyrene contributed to the formation of the first Gentile church at Antioch (11:20). Among "the prophets and teachers" who "ministered to the Lord at Antioch" was Lucius of Cyrene (13:1).

Cyre'nius, the Grecized form of Quirinus. His full name was Publius Sulpicius Quirinus. Recent historical investigation has proved that Quirinus was governor of Cilicia, which was annexed to Syria at the time of our Lord's birth. Cilicia, which he ruled, being a province of Syria, he is called the governor, which he was *de jure*, of Syria. Some ten years afterwards he was appointed governor of Syria for the second time. During his tenure of office, at the time of our Lord's birth (Luke 2:2), a "taxing" (R.V., "enrolment;" *i.e.*, a registration) of the people was "first made;" *i.e.*, was made for the first time under his government. (See TAXING.)

Cy'rus (Heb. *Ko'resh*), the celebrated "king of Persia" (Elam) who was conqueror of Babylon, and issued the decree of liberation to the Jews (Ezra 1:1, 2). He was the son of Cambyses, the prince of Persia, and was born about B.C. 599. In the year B.C. 559 he became king of Persia, the kingdom of Media being added to it partly by conquest. Cyrus was a great military leader, bent on universal conquest. Babylon fell before his army (B.C. 538) on the night of Belshazzar's feast (Dan. 5:30), and then the ancient dominion of Assyria was also added to his empire (*cf.*, "Go up, O Elam"—Isa. 21:2).

Hitherto the great kings of the earth had only oppressed the Jews. Cyrus was to them as a "shepherd" (Isa. 44:28; 45:1). God employed him in doing service to his ancient people. He may possibly have gained, through contact with the Jews, some knowledge of their religion.

The "first year of Cyrus" (Ezra 1:1) is not the year of his elevation to power over the Medes, nor over the Persians, nor the year of the fall of Babylon, but the year succeeding the two years during which "Darius the Mede" was viceroy in Babylon after its fall. At this time only (B.C. 536) Cyrus became actual king over Palestine, which became a part of his Babylonian empire. The edict of Cyrus for the rebuilding of Jerusalem marked a great epoch in the history of the Jewish people (2 Chr. 36 : 22, 23 ; Ezra 1 : 1-4 ; 4 : 3 ; 5 : 13, 17 ; 6 : 3).

This decree was discovered "at Achmetha [or Ecbatana], in the palace that is in the province of the Medes" (Ezra 6 : 2). When Ezra wrote, about a century after Cyrus, the Persian kings usually held their court at Susa or at Babylon, visiting only occasionally the city of Achmetha. But Cyrus is known from profane history to have held his court permanently at Achmetha ; and hence it was here, among the archives of his reign, that this decree was found.

"The character of Cyrus and his actions, as indicated by Ezra and Daniel, are in remarkable agreement with the notices which we possess of him in profane history. ......He was distinguished for his mildness and clemency ; he was a hater of idolatry, and would naturally sympathize with such a people as the Jews, a people whose religious views bore so great a resemblance to his own." The restoration of the Jews, and "the edicts which he issued on the occasion (Ezra 1 : 2-4 ; 6 : 3-5), are alike suitable to his religious belief and the generosity of his character. His acknowledgment of one 'Lord and God of heaven' (1 : 2), his identification of this God with the Jehovah of the Jews, and his pious confession that he has received all the kingdoms over which he rules from this source, breathe the spirit of the old Persian religion (Zoroastrianism), of which Cyrus was a sincere votary ; while the delivery of the golden vessels from out of the treasury (1 : 7-11 ; 6 : 5), the allowance of the whole

expense of rebuilding the temple out of the royal revenue (6 : 4), and the general directions given to all Persian subjects to 'help with silver, and with gold, and with goods, and with beasts' (1 : 4), accord well with the munificence which is said to have been one of his leading characteristics."— Rawlinson's *Hist. Illust.* The inscriptions, however, show that Cyrus was really or from policy a worshipper of the Babylonian gods.

TOMB OF CYRUS AT MOURGHAB.

The remarkable thing about this great Medo-Persian monarch is that he is mentioned by name in prophecy long before his birth (Isa. 41 : 2-6 ; 44 : 28 ; 45 : 1-13 ; 46 : 11) as the deliverer of the Jews from their seventy years' captivity, and also as the hand of God in the overthrow of Babylon, raised up "in righteousness" to do his work. A tomb said to be that of Cyrus is shown at Mourghab, the ancient Pasargidæ.

D

Dab'erath—*pasture*—a Levitical town of Issachar (Josh. 19 : 12 ; 21 : 28), near the border of Zebulun. It is the modern small village of *Debûrieh*, at the base of Mount Tabor. Tradition has incorrectly made it the scene of the miracle of the cure of the lunatic child (Matt. 17 : 14).

Dæ'mon, the Greek form, rendered

"devil" in the Authorized Version of the New Testament. Dæmons are spoken of as spiritual beings (Matt. 8 : 16 ; 10 : 1 ; 12 : 43-45) at enmity with God, and as having a certain power over man (James 2 : 19 ; Rev. 16 : 14). They recognize our Lord as the Son of God (Matt. 8 : 29 ; Luke 4 : 41). They belong to the number of those angels that "kept not their first estate," "unclean spirits," "fallen angels," the angels of the devil (Matt. 25 : 41 ; Rev. 12 : 7, 9). They are the "principalities and powers" against which we must "wrestle" (Eph. 6 : 12).

Dæmon'iac, one "possessed with a devil." In the days of our Lord and his apostles evil spirits, "dæmons," were mysteriously permitted by God to exercise an influence both over the souls and bodies of men, inflicting dumbness (Matt. 9 : 32), blindness (12 : 22), epilepsy (Mark 9 : 17–27), insanity (Matt. 8 : 28 ; Mark 5 : 1-5). Dæmoniacs are frequently distinguished from those who are afflicted with ordinary bodily maladies (Mark 1 : 32 ; 16 : 17, 18 ; Luke 6 : 17, 18). The dæmons speak in their own persons (Matt. 8 : 29 ; Mark 1 : 23, 24 ; 5 : 7). This influence is clearly distinguished from the ordinary power of corruption and of temptation over men. In the dæmoniac his personality seems to be destroyed, and his actions, words, and even thoughts to be overborne by the evil spirit (Mark, *l.c.* ; Acts 19 : 15). It is plain that it was not an ordinary assault of Satan with his temptations and allurements. It was a real, direct power of evil spirits among men in that age, and in that age only. During his sojourn on earth, Christ met and overcame this foe to man at all points. He waged war with Satan's emissaries "before the eyes of men, to enable them not to infer but to see the virulence of diabolical power and the gracious efficacy of that omnipotence which came to counterwork it."

Da'gon—*little fish;* diminutive from *dâg* = a fish — the fish-god; the national god of the Philistines. This idol had the body of a fish with the head and hands of a man. It was an Assyrio-Babylonian deity, the worship of which was introduced among the Philistines through Chaldea.

The most famous of the temples of Dagon were at Gaza (Judg. 16 : 21-30) and Ashdod (1 Sam. 5 : 5, 6).

Da'gon's house (1 Sam. 5 : 2), or *Beth-dagon*, as elsewhere rendered (Josh. 15 : 41 : 19 : 27), was the sanctuary or temple of Dagon.

The *Beth-dagon* of Josh. 15 : 41 was one of the cities of the tribe of Judah, in the lowland or plain which stretches westward. It has not been identified.

The *Beth-dagon* of Josh. 19 : 27 was one of the border cities of Asher.

That of 1 Chr. 10 : 10 was in the western half-tribe of Manasseh, where the Philistines, after their victory at Gilboa, placed Saul's head in the temple of their god. (Comp. 1 Sam. 31 : 8-13.)

Daily sacrifice (Dan. 8 : 12 ; 11 : 31 ; 12 : 11), a burnt offering of two lambs of a year old, which were daily sacrificed in the name of the whole Israelitish people upon the great altar—the first at dawn of day, and the second at evening (Dan. 9 : 21), or more correctly, "between the two evenings." (See SACRIFICE.)

Dale, the king's, the name of a valley, the alternative for "the valley of Shaveh" (*q.v.*), near the Dead Sea, where the king of Sodom met Abraham (Gen. 14 : 17). Some have identified it with the southern part of the valley of Jehoshaphat, where Absalom reared his family monument (2 Sam. 18 : 18).

Dalmanu'tha, a place on the west of the Sea of Galilee, mentioned only in Mark 8 : 10. In the parallel passage it is said that Christ came "into the borders of Magdala" (Matt. 15 : 39). It is plain, then, that Dalmanutha was near Magdala, which was probably the Greek name of one of the many Migdols (*i.e.*, watchtowers) on the western side of the lake of Gennesaret. It has been identified in the ruins of a village about a mile from Magdala, in the little open valley of 'Ain-el-Bârideh, "the cold fountain," called *el-Mejdel*, possibly the "Migdal-el" of Josh. 19 : 38.

Dalma'tia, a mountainous country on the eastern shore of the Adriatic, a part of the Roman province of Illyricum. It still bears its ancient name. During Paul's second imprisonment at Rome, Titus left him to visit Dalmatia (2 Tim. 4 : 10) for some unknown purpose. Paul had himself formerly preached in that region (Rom. 15 : 19).

The present Emperor of Austria hears,

among his other titles, that of "King of Dalmatia."

Dam'aris—*a heifer*—an Athenian woman converted to Christianity under the preaching of Paul (Acts 17:34). Some have supposed that she may have been the wife of Dionysius the Areopagite.

Damas'cus—*activity*—the most ancient of Oriental cities; the capital of Syria (Isa. 7:8; 17:3); situated about 133 miles to the north of Jerusalem. Its modern name is *Esh-Shâm; i.e.,* "the East."

The *situation* of this city is said to be the most beautiful of all Western Asia. The whole region around it is unsurpassed in richness and beauty, which to a large extent it owes to the rivers Abana and Pharpar (*q.v.*).

It is first mentioned in Scripture in connection with Abraham's victory over the confederate kings under Chedorlaomer (Gen. 14:15). It was the native place of Abraham's steward (15:2). It is not again noticed till the time of David, when

DAMASCUS.

"the Syrians of Damascus came to succour Hadadezer" (*q.v.*)—2 Sam. 8:5; 1 Chr. 18:5. In the reign of Solomon, Rezon became leader of a band who revolted from Hadadezer (1 Kings 11:23), and betaking themselves to Damascus, settled there and made their leader king. There was a long war, with varying success, between the Israelites and Syrians, who at a later period became allies of Israel against Judah (2 Kings 15:37).

The Syrians were at length subdued by the Assyrians, the city of Damascus was taken and destroyed, and the inhabitants carried captive into Assyria (2 Kings 16:7-9; comp. Isa. 7:8). In this, prophecy was fulfilled (Isa. 17:1; Amos 1:4; Jer. 49:24). The kingdom of Syria remained a province of Assyria till the capture of Nineveh by the Medes (B.C. 625), when it fell under the conquerors. After passing through various vicissitudes, Syria was invaded by the Romans (B.C. 64), and Damascus became the seat of the government of the province. In A.D. 37 Aretas, the king of Arabia, became master of Damascus, having driven back Herod Antipas.

This city is memorable as the scene of Saul's conversion (Acts 9:1–25). The street called "Straight," in which Judas lived, in whose house Saul was found by Ananias, is known by the name *Sultany*, or "Queen's Street." It is the principal street of the city. Paul visited Damascus again on his return from Arabia (Gal. 1:16, 17). Christianity was planted here as a centre (19; Acts 9:20), from which it spread to the surrounding regions.

In A.D. 634 Damascus was conquered by the growing Mohammedan power. In A.D. 1516 it fell under the dominion of the Turks, its present rulers. It is now the largest city in Asiatic Turkey. Christianity has again found a firm footing within its walls.

Damna'tion, in Rom. 13:2, means "condemnation," which comes on those who withstand God's ordinance of magistracy. This sentence of condemnation comes not from the magistrate, but from God, whose authority is thus resisted.

In 1 Cor. 11:29 (R.V., "judgment") this word means condemnation, in the sense of exposure to severe temporal judgments from God, as the following verse explains.

In Rom. 14:23 the word "damned" means "condemned" by one's own conscience, as well as by the Word of God. The apostle shows here that many things which are lawful are not expedient; and that in using our Christian liberty the question should not simply be, Is this course I follow lawful? but also, Can I follow it without doing injury to the spiritual interests of a brother in Christ? He that "doubteth"—*i.e.*, is not clear in his conscience as to "meats"—will violate his conscience "if he eat," and in eating is condemned; and thus one ought not so to use his liberty as to lead one who is "weak" to bring upon himself this condemnation.

Dan—*a judge.* (1.) The fifth son of Jacob. His mother was Bilhah, Rachel's maid (Gen. 30:6, "God hath *judged me*"—Heb. *dânanni*). The blessing pronounced on him by his father was, "Dan shall judge his

people" (49:16), probably in allusion to the judgeship of Samson, who was of the tribe of Dan.

The *tribe of Dan* had their place in the march through the wilderness on the north side of the tabernacle (Num. 2:25, 31; 10:25). It was the last of the tribes to receive a portion in the Land of Promise. Its position and extent are described in Josh. 19:40–48.

The *territory* of Dan extended from the west of that of Ephraim and Benjamin to the sea. It was a small territory, but was very fertile. It included in it, among others, the cities of Lydda, Ekron, and Joppa, which formed its northern bound-

MAP SHOWING THE TERRITORY OF DAN.
(See also Map of Asher, page 59.)

ary. But this district was too limited. "Squeezed into the narrow strip between the mountains and the sea, its energies were great beyond its numbers." Being pressed by the Amorites and the Philistines, whom they were unable to conquer, they longed for a wider space. They accordingly sent out five spies from two of their towns, who went north to the sources of the Jordan, and brought back a favourable report regarding that region. "Arise," they said, "be not slothful to go, and to possess the land," for it is "a place where there is no want of any thing that is in the earth" (Judg. 18:10). On receiving this report, 600 Danites girded on their weapons of war, and taking with them their wives and their children, marched to the foot of Hermon, and fought against Leshem, and took it from the Sidonians, and dwelt therein, and changed the name of the conquered town to Dan (Josh. 19:47). This new city of Dan became to them a new home, and was wont to be spoken of as the northern limit of Palestine, the length of which came to be denoted by the expression "from Dan to Beersheba"—i.e., about 144 miles.

"But like Lot under a similar temptation, they seem to have succumbed to the evil influences around them, and to have sunk down into a condition of semi-heathenism from which they never emerged. The mounds of ruins which mark the site of the city show that it covered a considerable extent of ground. But there remains no record of any noble deed wrought by the degenerate tribe. Their name disappears from the roll-book of the natural and the spiritual Israel."—Manning's *Those Holy Fields*.

This old border city was originally called Laish. Its modern name is *Tell el-Kâdy*, "Hill of the Judge." It stands about four miles below Cæsarea Philippi, in the midst of a region of surpassing richness and beauty.

(2.) This name occurs in Ezek 27:19, Authorized Version; but the words there, "Dan also," should be simply, as in the Revised Version, "Vedan," an Arabian city, from which various kinds of merchandise were brought to Tyre. Some suppose it to have been the city of Aden in Arabia. (See MAHNEH-DAN.)

Dance, found in Judg. 21:21, 23; Ps. 30:11; 149:3; 150:4; Jer. 31:4, 13, etc., as the translation of *hul*, which points to the *whirling* motion of Oriental sacred dances. It is the rendering of a word (*rakad'*) which means to skip or leap for joy, in Eccl. 3:4; Job 21:11; Isa. 13:21, etc.

In the New Testament it is in like manner the translation of different Greek words—circular motion (Luke 15:25); leaping up and down in concert (Matt. 11:17), and by a single person (Matt. 14:6).

It is spoken of as *symbolical* of rejoicing (Eccl. 3:4. Comp. Ps. 30:11; Matt. 11:17). The Hebrews had their sacred dances expressive of joy and thanksgiving, when the performers were usually females (Ex. 15:20; 1 Sam. 18:6).

The ancient dance was very different from that common among Western nations. It was usually the part of the women only (Ex. 15:20; Judg. 11:34; comp. 5:1). Hence the peculiarity of David's conduct in dancing before the ark of the Lord (2 Sam. 6:14). The women took part in it with their timbrels. Michal should, in accordance with the example of Miriam and others, have herself led the female choir, instead of keeping aloof on the occasion and "looking through the window." David led the choir "uncovered"—i.e., wearing only the ephod or linen tunic. He thought only of the honour of God, and forgot himself.

From being reserved for occasions of religious worship and festivity, it came gradually to be practised in common life on occasions of rejoicing (Jer. 31:4). The sexes among the Jews always danced separately. The daughter of Herodias danced alone (Matt. 14:6).

Dan'iel—*God is my judge*, or *judge of God*. (1.) David's second son, "born unto him in Hebron, of Abigail the Carmelitess" (1 Chr. 3:1). He is called also Chileab (2 Sam. 3:3).

(2.) One of the four great prophets, although he is not once spoken of in the Old Testament as a prophet. His life and prophecies are recorded in the Book of Daniel. He was descended from one of the noble families of Judah (Dan. 1:3), and was probably born in Jerusalem about B.C. 623, during the reign of Josiah. At the first deportation of the Jews by Nebuchadnezzar (the kingdom of Israel had come to an end nearly a century before), or immediately after his victory over the Egyptians at the second battle of Carchemish, in the fourth year of the reign of Jehoiakim (B.C. 606), Daniel and other three noble youths were carried off to Babylon, along with part of the vessels of the temple. There he was obliged to enter into the service of the king of Babylon, and in accordance with the custom of the age received the Chaldean name of Belteshazzar—i.e., "prince of Bel," or "Bel protect the king!" His residence in Babylon was very probably in the palace of Nebuchadnezzar, now identified with a mass of shapeless mounds called the *Kasr*, on the right bank of the river.

His training in the schools of the wise men in Babylon (Dan. 1:4) was to fit him for service to the empire. He was distinguished during this period for his piety and his strict observance of the Mosaic law (1:8–16), and gained the confidence and esteem of those who were over him. His habit of attention gained during his education in Jerusalem enabled him soon to master the wisdom and learning of the Chaldeans, and even to excel his compeers.

At the close of his three years of discipline and training in the royal schools, Daniel was distinguished for his proficiency in the "wisdom" of his day, and was brought out into public life. He soon became known for his skill in the interpretation of dreams (1:17; 2:14), and rose to the rank of governor of the province of Babylon, and became "chief of the governors"(Chald. *Rab-signin*) over all the wise men of Babylon. He made known and also interpreted Nebuchadnezzar's dream; and many years afterwards, when he was now an old man, amid the alarm and consternation of the terrible night of Belshazzar's impious feast, he was called in at the instance of the queen-mother (perhaps Nitocris, the daughter of Nebuchadnezzar) to interpret the mysterious handwriting on the wall. He was rewarded with a purple robe and elevation to the rank of "third ruler." The place of "second ruler" was held by Belshazzar as associated with his father—Nabonidus—on the throne (5:16). Daniel interpreted the handwriting, and "in that night was Belshazzar the king of the Chaldeans slain."

After the taking of Babylon, Cyrus, who was now master of all Asia from India to the Dardanelles, placed Darius (*q.v.*), a Median prince, on the throne, during the two years of whose reign Daniel held the office of first of the "three presidents" of the empire, and was thus practically at the head of affairs, no doubt interesting himself in the prospects of the captive Jews (Dan. 9), whom he had at last the happiness of seeing restored to their own land, although he did not return with them, but remained

still in Babylon. His fidelity to God exposed him to persecution, and he was cast into a den of lions, but was miraculously delivered; after which Darius issued a decree enjoining "reverence for the God of Daniel" (6:26). He "prospered in the reign of Darius, and in the reign of Cyrus the Persian," whom he probably greatly influenced in the matter of the decree which put an end to the Captivity (B.C. 536).

He had a series of prophetic visions vouchsafed to him which opened up the prospect of a glorious future for the people of God, and must have imparted peace and gladness to his spirit in his old age as he waited on at his post till the "end of the days." The time and circumstances of his death are not recorded. He probably died at Susa, about eighty-five years of age.

Ezekiel, with whom he was contemporary, mentions him as a pattern of righteousness (14:14, 20) and wisdom (28:3). (See NEBUCHADNEZZAR.)

Daniel, Book of, is ranked by the Jews in that division of their Bible called the *Hagiographa* (Heb. *Khethubim*). (See BIBLE.) It consists of two distinct parts. The first part, consisting of the first six chapters, is chiefly historical; and the second part, consisting of the remaining six chapters, is chiefly prophetical.

The historical part of the book treats of the period of the Captivity. Daniel is "the historian of the Captivity, the writer who alone furnishes any series of events for that dark and dismal period during which the harp of Israel hung on the trees that grew by the Euphrates. His narrative may be said in general to intervene between Kings and Chronicles on the one hand and Ezra on the other, or (more strictly) to fill out the sketch which the author of the Chronicles gives in a single verse in his last chapter: 'And them that had escaped from the sword carried he [*i.e.*, Nebuchadnezzar] away to Babylon; where they were servants to him and his sons until the reign of the kingdom of Persia'" (2 Chr. 36:20).

The prophetical part consists of three visions and one lengthened prophetical communication.

The genuineness of this book has been much disputed, but the arguments in its favour fully establish its claims. (1.) We have the testimony of Christ (Matt. 24:15; 25:31; 26:64) and his apostles (1 Cor. 6:2; 2 Thess. 2:3) for its authority; and (2) the important testimony of Ezekiel (14:14, 20; 28:3). (3.) The character and records of the book are also entirely in harmony with the times and circumstances in which the author lived. (4.) The linguistic character of the book is, moreover, just such as might be expected. Certain portions (Dan. 2:4; 7) are written in the Chaldee language; and the portions written in Hebrew are in a style and form having a close affinity with the later books of the Old Testament, especially with that of Ezra. The writer is familiar both with the Hebrew and the Chaldee, passing from the one to the other just as his subject required. This is in strict accordance with the position of the author and of the people for whom his book was written. That Daniel is the writer of this book is also testified to in the book itself (7:1, 28; 8:2; 9:2; 10:1, 2; 12:4, 5).

Dan-ja′an—*woodland Dan*—a place probably somewhere in the direction of Dan, near the sources of the Jordan (2 Sam. 24:6). The LXX. and the Vulgate read "Dan-ja'ar"—*i.e.*, "Dan in the forest."

Dan′nah—*murmuring*—a city (Josh. 15:49) in the mountains of Judah about 8 miles south-west of Hebron.

Dar′da—*pearl of wisdom*—one of the four who were noted for their wisdom, but whom Solomon excelled (1 Kings 4:31).

Dar′ic, in the Revised Version of 1 Chr. 29:7; Ezra 2:69; 8:27; Neh. 7:70–72, where the Authorized Version has "dram." It is the rendering of the Hebrew *darkĕmôn* and the Greek *dareikos*. It was a gold coin, bearing the figure of a Persian king with his crown and armed with bow and arrow. It was current among the Jews after their return from Babylon—*i.e.*, while under the Persian domination. It weighed about 128 grains troy, and was of the value of about one guinea or rather more of our money. It is the first coin mentioned in Scripture, and is the oldest that history makes known to us.

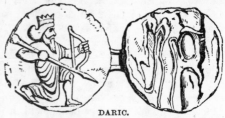

DARIC.

(Obverse: the King of Persia kneeling, bearing bow and javelin.)

Dari′us—*the holder* or *supporter*—the name of several Persian kings.

(1.) *Darius the Mede* (Dan. 11:1), "the son of Ahasuerus, of the seed of the Medes" (9:1). On the death of Belshazzar the Chaldean he "received the kingdom" of Babylon as viceroy from Cyrus. During his brief reign (B.C. 538–536) Daniel was promoted to the highest dignity (Dan. 6:1, 2); but on account of the malice of his enemies he was cast into the den of lions. After his miraculous escape, a decree was issued by Darius enjoining "reverence for the God of Daniel" (6:26). This king was probably the "Astyages" of the Greek historians. Nothing can, however, be with certainty affirmed regarding him. Some are of opinion that the name "Darius" is simply a name of office, equivalent to "governor," and that the "Gobryas" of the inscriptions was the person intended by the name.

(2.) *Darius, king of Persia,* was the son of Hystaspes, of the royal family of the Achæmenidæ. He did not immediately succeed Cyrus on the throne. There were two intermediate kings—*viz.*, Cambyses (the Ahasuerus of Ezra), the son of Cyrus, who reigned from B.C. 529–522, and was succeeded by a usurper named Smerdis, who occupied the throne only ten months, and was succeeded by this Darius (B.C. 521–486). Smerdis was a Magian, and therefore had no sympathy with Cyrus and Cambyses in the manner in which they had treated the Jews. He issued a decree prohibiting the restoration of the temple and of Jerusalem (Ezra 4:17–22). But soon after his death and the accession of Darius, the Jews resumed their work, thinking that the edict of Smerdis would be now null and void, as Darius was in known harmony with the religious policy of Cyrus. The enemies of the Jews lost no time in bringing the matter under the notice of Darius, who caused search to be made for the decree of Cyrus (*q.v.*). It was not found at Babylon, but at Achmetha (Ezra 6:2); and Darius forthwith issued a new decree, giving the Jews full liberty to prosecute their work, at the same time requiring the Syrian satrap and his subordinates to give them all needed help. It was with the army of this king that the Greeks fought the famous battle of Marathon (B.C. 490). During his reign the Jews enjoyed much peace and prosperity. He was succeeded by Ahasuerus, known to the Greeks as Xerxes, who reigned for twenty-one years.

(3.) *Darius the Persian* (Neh. 12:22) was probably the Darius II. (Ochus or Nothus) of profane history, the son of Artaxerxes Longimanus, who was the son and successor of Ahasuerus (Xerxes). There are some, however, who think that the king here meant was Darius III. (Codomannus), the antagonist of Alexander the Great (B.C. 336–331).

Dark′ness. The plague (the ninth) of darkness in Egypt (Ex. 10:21) is described as a darkness "which may be felt." It covered "all the land of Egypt," so that "they saw not one another." It did not extend to the land of Goshen (ver. 23).

When Jesus hung upon the cross (Matt. 27:45; Luke 23:44), from the "sixth hour there was darkness over all the land unto the ninth hour."

On Mount Sinai, Moses (Ex. 20:21) "drew near unto the thick darkness where God was." This was the "thick cloud upon the mount" in which Jehovah was when he spake unto Moses there. The Lord dwelt in the cloud upon the mercy-seat (1 Kings 8:12)—the cloud of glory. When the psalmist (Ps. 97:2) describes the inscrutable nature of God's workings among the sons of men, he says, "Clouds and darkness are round about him." God dwells in thick darkness.

Darkness (Isa. 13:9, 10; Matt. 24:29) also is a symbol of the judgments that attend on the coming of the Lord. It is a symbol of misery and adversity (Job 18:6; Ps. 107:10; Isa. 8:22; Ezek. 30:18). The "day of darkness" in Joel 2:2, caused by clouds of locusts, is a symbol of the obscurity which overhangs all divine proceedings. "Works of darkness" are impure actions (Eph. 5:11). "Outer darkness" refers to the darkness of the streets in the East, which are never lighted up by any public or private lamps after nightfall, in contrast with the blaze of cheerful light in the house. It is also a symbol of ignorance (Isa. 9:2; 60:2; Matt. 6:23) and of death (Job 10:21; 17:13).

Dart, an instrument of war; a light spear. "Fiery darts" (Eph. 6:16) are so called in allusion to the habit of discharging darts from the bow while they are on fire or armed with some combustible material. Arrows are compared to lightning (Deut. 32:23, 42; Ps. 7:13; 120:4).

Dar′ling (Ps. 22:20; 35:17) means an "only one."

DATE PALM.

Date, the fruit of a species of palm (*q.v.*), the *Phœnix dactilifera*. This was a common tree in Palestine (Joel 1:12; Neh. 8:15).

Palm branches were carried by the Jews on festive occasions, and especially at the feast of Tabernacles (Lev. 23:40; Neh. 8:15).

Da'than—*welled; belonging to a fountain*—a son of Eliab, a Reubenite, who joined Korah (*q.v.*) in his conspiracy, and with his accomplices was swallowed up by an earthquake (Num. 16:1; 26:9; Deut. 11:6; Ps. 106:17).

Daugh'ter. This word, besides its natural and proper sense, is used to designate—(1.) A niece or any *female* descendant (Gen. 20:12; 24:48; 28:6). (2.) Women as natives of a place, or as professing the religion of a place; as, "the daughters of Zion" (Isa. 3:16), "daughters of the Philistines" (2 Sam. 20). (3.) Small towns and villages lying around a city are its "daughters," as related to the metropolis or mother-city. Tyre is in this sense called the daughter of Sidon (Isa. 22:12). (4.) The people of Jerusalem are spoken of as "the daughters of Zion" (Isa. 37:22). (5.) The daughters of a tree are its boughs (Gen. 49:22). (6.) The "daughters of music" (Eccl. 12:4) are singing women.

Da'vid—*beloved*—the eighth and youngest son of Jesse, a citizen of Bethlehem. His father seems to have been a man in humble life. His mother's name is not recorded. Some think she was the Nahash of 2 Sam. 17:25. As to his personal appearance, we only know that he was "red-haired, with beautiful eyes and a fair face" (1 Sam. 16:12; 17:42).

His early occupation was that of tending his father's sheep on the uplands of Judah. From what we know of his after history, doubtless he frequently beguiled his time, when thus engaged, with his shepherd's flute, while he drank in the many lessons taught him by the varied scenes spread around him. His first recorded exploits were his encounters with the wild beasts of the field. He mentions that with his own unaided hand he slew a lion and also a bear, when they came out against his flock, beating them to death in open conflict with his club (1 Sam. 17:34, 35).

While David, in the freshness of ruddy youth, was thus engaged with his flocks, Samuel paid an unexpected visit to Bethlehem, having been guided thither by divine direction (1 Sam. 16:1-13). There he offered up sacrifice, and called the elders of Israel and Jesse's family to the sacrificial meal. Among all who appeared before him he failed to discover the one he sought. David was sent for, and the prophet immediately recognized him as the chosen of God—chosen to succeed Saul, who was now departing from the ways of God, on the throne of the kingdom. He accordingly, in anticipation, poured on his head the anointing oil. David went back again to his shepherd life, but from "that day forward the Spirit of the Lord came upon David," and "the Spirit of the Lord departed from Saul" (1 Sam. 16:13, 14).

Not long after this David was sent for to soothe with his harp the troubled spirit of Saul, who suffered from a strange melancholy dejection. He played before the king so skilfully that Saul was greatly cheered, and began to entertain great affection for the young shepherd. After this he went home to Bethlehem. But he soon again came into prominence. The armies of the Philistines and of Israel were in battle array in the valley of Elah, some 16 miles south-west of Bethlehem; and David was sent by his father with provisions for his three brothers, who were then fighting on the side of the king. On his arrival in the camp of Israel, David (now about twenty years of age) was made aware of the state of matters when the champion of the Philistines, Goliath of Gath, came forth to defy Israel. David took his sling, and with a well-trained aim threw a stone "out of the brook," which struck the giant's forehead, so that he fell senseless to the ground. David then ran and slew him, and cut off his head with his own sword (1 Sam. 17). The result was a great victory to the Israelites, who pursued the Philistines to the gates of Gath and Ekron.

David's popularity consequent on this heroic exploit awakened Saul's jealousy (1 Sam. 18:6-16), which he showed in various ways. He conceived a bitter hatred toward him, and by various stratagems sought his death (1 Sam. 17–ch. 30). The deep-laid plots of the enraged king, who could not fail to observe that David "prospered exceedingly," all proved futile, and only endeared the young hero the more to the people, and very specially to Jonathan, Saul's son, between whom and David a life-long warm friendship was formed.

A fugitive. To escape from the vengeance of Saul, David fled to Ramah (1 Sam. 19: 13–18) to Samuel, who received him, and he dwelt among the sons of the prophets, who were there under Samuel's training. It is supposed by some that the sixth, seventh, and eleventh Psalms were composed by him at this time. This place was only 3 miles from the residence of Saul, who soon discovered whither the fugitive had gone, and tried ineffectually to bring him back. Jonathan made a fruitless effort to bring his father to a better state of mind toward David (1 Sam. 20), who, being made aware of the fact, saw no hope of safety but in flight to a distance. We accordingly find him first at Nob (21: 1–9) and then at Gath, the chief city of the Philistines. The king of the Philistines would not admit him into his service, as he expected that he would, and David accordingly now betook himself to the stronghold of Adullam (22: 1–4; 1 Chr. 12: 8–18). Here in a short time 400 men gathered around him and acknowledged him as their leader. It was at this time that David, amid the harassment and perils of his position, cried, "Oh that one would give me drink of the water of the well of Bethlehem;" when three of his heroes broke through the lines of the Philistines and brought him the water for which he longed (2 Sam. 23: 13–17), but which he would not drink.

In his rage at the failure of all his efforts to seize David, Saul gave orders for the massacre of the entire priestly family at Nob—"persons who wore a linen ephod"— to the number of eighty-five persons, who were put to death by Doeg the Edomite. The sad tidings of the massacre were brought to David by Abiathar, a son of Ahimelech, the only one who escaped. Comp. Ps. 52.

Hearing that Keilah, a town on the western frontier, was harassed by the Philistines, David with his men relieved it (1 Sam. 23: 1–14); and then, for fear of Saul, he fled to the strongholds in the "hill country" of Judah. Comp. Ps. 31. While encamped there, in the forest in the district of Ziph, he was visited by Jonathan, who spoke to him words of encouragement (23: 16–18). The two now parted never to meet again. Saul continued his pursuit of David, who narrowly escaped from him at this time, and fled to the crags and ravines of Engedi, on the western shore of the Dead Sea (1 Sam. 24). Here Saul, who still pursued him with his army, narrowly escaped, through the generous forbearance of David, and was greatly affected by what David had done for him. He returned home from pursuing him, and David betook himself to Maon, where, with his 600 men, he maintained himself by contributions gathered from the district. Here occurred the incident connected with Nabal and his wife Abigail (1 Sam. 25: 2–44), whom David married after Nabal's death.

Saul again went forth (1 Sam. 26) in pursuit of David, who had hid himself "in the hill Hachilah, which is before Jeshimon," in the wilderness of Ziph, and was a second time spared through his forbearance. He returned home, professing shame and penitence for the way in which he had treated David, and predicting his elevation to the throne.

Fighting against Israel. Harassed by the necessity of moving from place to place through fear of Saul, David once more sought refuge among the Philistines (1 Sam. 27). He was welcomed by the king, who assigned him Ziklag as his residence. Here David lived among his followers for some time as an independent chief engaged in frequent war with the Amalekites and other tribes on the south of Judah.

Achish summoned David with his men to join his army against Saul; but the lords of the Philistines were suspicious of David's loyalty, and therefore he was sent back to Ziklag, which he found to his dismay had been pillaged and burnt during his brief absence. David pursued after the raiders, the Amalekites, and completely routed them. On his return to Ziklag tidings reached him of Saul's death (2 Sam. 1). An Amalekite brought Saul's crown and bracelet and laid them at his feet. David and his men rent their clothes and mourned for Saul, who had been defeated in battle near Mount Gilboa. David composed a beautiful elegy—the most beautiful of all extant Hebrew odes—a "lamentation over Saul and over Jonathan his son" (2 Sam. 1:18-27). It bore the title of "The Bow," and was to be taught to the children, that the memory of Saul and Jonathan might be preserved among them. "Behold, it is written in the book of Jasher" (*q.v.*).

David king over Judah. David and his men now set out for Hebron under divine direction (2 Sam. 2:1-4). There they were cordially welcomed, and he was at once anointed as king. He was now about thirty years of age.

But his title to the throne was not undisputed. Abner took Ish-bosheth, Saul's only remaining son, over the Jordan to Mahanaim, and there crowned him as king. Then began a civil war in Israel. The first encounter between the two opposing armies, led on the one side by Abner, and on the other by Joab, took place at the pool of Gibeon. It resulted in the defeat of Abner. Other encounters, however, between Israel and Judah followed (2 Sam. 3:1, 5), but still success was on the side of David. For the space of seven and a half years David reigned in Hebron. Abner now sided with David, and sought to promote his advancement; but was treacherously put to death by Joab in revenge for his having slain his brother Asahel at Gibeon (3:22-39). This was greatly to David's regret. He mourned for the death of Abner. Shortly after this Ish-bosheth was also treacherously put to death by two Canaanites of Beeroth; and there being now no rival, David was anointed king over all Israel (4:1-12).

David king over all Israel (2 Sam. 5:1-5; 1 Chr. 11:1-3). The elders of Israel now repaired to Hebron and offered allegiance to David in name of all the people, among whom the greatest enthusiasm prevailed. He was anointed king over all Israel, and sought out a new seat of government, more suitable than Hebron, as the capital of his empire. At this time there was a Jebusite fortress—"the stronghold"—on the hill of Zion, called also Jebus. This David took from the Jebusites, and made it Israel's capital, and established here his residence, and afterwards built for himself a palace by the aid of Tyrian tradesmen. The Philistines, who had for some time observed a kind of truce, now made war against David; but were defeated in battle at a place afterwards called, in remembrance of the victory, Baal-perazim. Again they invaded the land, and were a second time routed by him. He thus delivered Israel from their enemies.

David now resolved to bring up the ark of the covenant to his new capital (2 Sam. 6). It was in the house of Abinadab at Kirjath-jearim, about 7 miles from Jerusalem, where it had been for many years, from the time when the Philistines had sent it home (1 Sam. 6; 7). In consequence of the death of Uzzah (for it was a divine ordinance that only the Levites should handle the ark—Num. 4), who had put forth his hand to steady the ark when the cart in which it was being conveyed shook by reason of the roughness of the road, David stayed the procession, and conveyed the ark into the house of Obed-edom, a Philistine from Gath. After three months David brought the ark from the house of Obed-edom up to Jerusalem. Comp. Ps. 24. Here it was placed in a new tent or tabernacle which David erected for the purpose. About seventy years had passed since it had stood in the tabernacle at Shiloh. The old tabernacle was now at Gibeah, at which Zadok ministered. David now (1 Chr. 16) carefully set in order all the ritual of divine worship at Jerusalem, along with Abiathar the high priest. A new religious era began. The service of praise was for the first time introduced into public worship. Zion became henceforth "God's holy hill."

David's wars. David now entered on a series of conquests which "greatly extended and strengthened his kingdom" (2 Sam. 8). In a few years the whole territory from the Euphrates to the river of Egypt, and from Gaza on the west to Thapsacus on the east, was under his sway (2 Sam. 8 : 3–13 ; 10).

David's fall. He had now reached the height of his glory. He ruled over a vast empire, and his capital was enriched with the spoils of many lands. But in the midst of all this success he fell, and his character became stained with the sin of adultery (2 Sam. 11 : 2–27). It has been noted as characteristic of the Bible that while his military triumphs are recorded in a few verses, the sad story of his fall is given in detail—a story full of warning, and therefore recorded. This crime, in the attempt to conceal it, led to another. He was guilty of murder. Uriah, whom he had foully wronged—an officer of the Gibborim, the corps of heroes (23 : 39)—was, by his order, "set in the front of the hottest battle" at the siege of Rabbah, in order that he might be put to death. Nathan the prophet, whose name here appears for the first time, was sent by God to bring home his crimes to the conscience of the guilty monarch. He became a true penitent. He bitterly bewailed his sins before God. The thirty-second and fifty-first Psalms reveal the deep struggles of his soul, and his spiritual recovery.

Bathsheba became his wife after Uriah's death. Her first-born son died, according to the word of the prophet. She gave birth to a second son, whom David called Solomon, and who ultimately succeeded him on the throne (2 Sam. 12 : 24, 25).

Peace. After the successful termination of all his wars, David formed the idea of building a temple for the ark of God. This he was not permitted to carry into execution, because he had been a man of war. God, however, sent Nathan to him with a gracious message (2 Sam. 7 : 1–16). On receiving it he went into the sanctuary —the tent where the ark was—and sat before the Lord, and poured out his heart in words of devout thanksgiving (18–29). The building of the temple was reserved

for his son Solomon, who would be a man of peace (1 Chr. 22 : 9 ; 28 : 3).

A cloudy evening. Hitherto David's career had been one of great prosperity and success. Now cloudy and dark days came. His eldest son Amnon, whose mother was Ahinoam of Jezreel, was guilty of a great and shameful crime (2 Sam. 13). This was the beginning of the disasters of his later years. After two years Absalom terribly avenged the crime against Tamar, and put Amnon to death. This brought sore trouble to David's heart. Absalom, afraid of the consequences of his guilt, fled to Geshur beyond Jordan, where he remained for three years, when he was brought back through the intrigue of Joab (2 Sam. 14).

After this there fell upon the land the calamity of three years' famine (2 Sam. 21 : 1–14). This was soon after followed by a pestilence, brought upon the land as a punishment for David's sinful pride in numbering the people (2 Sam. 24), in which no fewer than 70,000 perished in the space of three days.

Rebellion of Absalom. The personal respect for David was sadly lowered by the incident of Bathsheba. There was a strong popular sentiment against the taking of the census, and the outburst of the plague in connection with it deepened the feeling of jealousy that had begun to manifest itself among some of the tribes against David. Absalom, taking full advantage of this state of things, gradually gained over the people, and at length openly rebelled against his father, and usurped the throne. Ahithophel was Absalom's chief counsellor. The revolt began in Hebron, the capital of Judah. Absalom was there proclaimed king. David was now in imminent danger, and he left Jerusalem (2 Sam. 15 : 13–20), and once more became a fugitive. It was a momentous day in Israel. The incidents of it are recorded with a fulness of detail greater than of any other day in Old Testament history. David fled with his followers to Mahanaim, on the east of Jordan. An unnatural civil war broke out. After a few weeks the rival armies were mustered and organized. They met in hostile array at the wood of Ephraim (2 Sam. 18:1-8). Absalom's army was defeated, and himself put to death by the hand of Joab (9-18). The tidings of the death of his rebellious son filled the heart of David with the most poignant grief. He "went up to the chamber over the gate, and wept" (33), giving utterance to the heart-broken cry, "Would God I had died for thee, O Absalom, my son, my son!" Peace was now restored, and David returned to Jerusalem and resumed the direction of affairs. An unhappy dispute arose between the men of Judah and the men of Israel (41-43). Sheba, a Benjamite, headed a revolt of the men of Israel. He was pursued to Abel-beth-maachah, and was there put to death, and so the revolt came to an end.

The end. After the suppression of the rebellion of Absalom and that of Sheba, ten comparatively peaceful years of David's life passed away. During those years he seems to have been principally engaged in accumulating treasures of every kind for the great temple at Jerusalem, which it was reserved to his successor to build (1 Chr. 22; 28; 29)—a house which was to be "exceeding magnifical, of fame and of glory throughout all countries" (22:5). The exciting and laborious life he had spent, and the dangers and trials through which he had passed, had left him an enfeebled man, prematurely old. It became apparent that his life was now drawing to its close. A new palace conspiracy broke out as to who should be his successor.

SUPPOSED TOMB OF DAVID, MOUNT ZION.

Joab favoured Adonijah. The chiefs of his party met at the "Fuller's spring," in the valley of Kidron, to proclaim him king; but Nathan hastened on a decision on the part of David in favour of Solomon, and so the aim of Adonijah's party failed. Solomon was brought to Jerusalem, and was anointed king and seated on his father's throne (1 Kings 1:11-53). David's last words are a grand utterance, revealing his unfailing faith in God, and his joyful confidence in his gracious covenant promises (2 Sam. 23:1-7).

After a reign of forty years and six months (2 Sam. 5:5; 1 Chr. 3:4) David died (B.C. 1015) at the age of seventy years, "and was buried in the city of David."

His tomb is still pointed out on Mount Zion.

Both in his prophetical and in his regal character David was a type of the Messiah (1 Sam. 16:13). The book of Psalms commonly bears the title of the "Psalms of David," from the circumstance that he was the largest contributor (about eighty psalms) to the collection. (See PSALMS.)

"The greatness of David was felt when he was gone. He had lived in harmony with both the priesthood and the prophets; a sure sign that the spirit of his government had been thoroughly loyal to the higher aims of the theocracy. The nation had not been oppressed by him, but had been left in the free enjoyment of its ancient liberties. As far as his power went he had striven to act justly to all (2 Sam. 8:15). His weak indulgence to his sons, and his own great sin besides, had been bitterly atoned, and were forgotten at his death in the remembrance of his long-tried worth. He had reigned thirty-three years in Jerusalem and seven and a half at Hebron (2 Sam. 5:5). Israel at his accession had reached the lowest point of national depression; its new-born unity rudely dissolved; its territory assailed by the Philistines. But he had left it an imperial power, with dominions like those of Egypt or Assyria. The sceptre of Solomon was already, before his father's death, owned from the Mediterranean to the Euphrates, and from the Orontes to the Red Sea."--Geikie's *Hours, etc.*, iii.

David, City of. (1.) David took from the Jebusites the fortress of Mount Zion. He "dwelt in the fort, and called it the city of David" (1 Chr. 11:7). This was the name afterwards given to the castle and royal palace on Mount Zion, as distinguished from Jerusalem generally (1 Kings 3:1; 8:1). It was on the south-west side of Jerusalem, opposite the temple mount, with which it was connected by a bridge over the Tyropœon valley.

(2.) Bethlehem is called the "city of David" (Luke 2:4, 11), because it was David's birth-place and early home (1 Sam. 17:12).

Day. The Jews reckoned the day from sunset to sunset (Lev. 23:32). It was originally divided into three parts (Ps. 55:17). "The heat of the day" (1 Sam. 11:11; Neh. 7:3) was at our nine o'clock, and "the cool of the day" just before sunset (Gen. 3:8). Before the Captivity the Jews divided the night into three watches —(1) from sunset to midnight (Lam. 2:19); (2) from midnight till the cock-crowing (Judg. 7:19); and (3) from the cock-crowing till sunrise (Ex. 14:24). In the New Testament the division of the Greeks and Romans into four watches was adopted (Mark 13:35). (See WATCHES.)

The division of the day by hours is first mentioned in Dan. 3:6, 15; 4:19; 5:5. This mode of reckoning was borrowed from the Chaldeans. The reckoning of twelve hours was from sunrise to sunset, and accordingly the hours were of variable length (John 11:9).

The word "day" sometimes signifies an indefinite time (Gen. 2:4; Isa. 2:12; 22:5; Heb. 3:8, etc.). In Job 3:1 it denotes a birth-day, and in Acts 17:31, and 2 Tim. 1:18, the great day of final judgment.

Day's journey. The usual length of a day's journey in the East, on camel or horseback, in six or eight hours, is about 25 or 30 miles. The "three days' journey" mentioned in Ex. 3:18 is simply a journey which would occupy three days in going and returning.

Days'man, an umpire or arbiter or judge (Job 9:33). This word is formed from the Latin *diem dicere*—*i.e.*, to fix a day for hearing a cause. Such an one is empowered by mutual consent to decide the cause, and to "lay his hand"—*i.e.*, to impose his authority—on both, and enforce his sentence.

Day'spring (Job 38:12; Luke 1:78), the dawn of the morning; daybreak. (Comp. Isa. 60:1, 2; Mal. 4:2; Rev. 22:16.)

Day'-star, which precedes and accompanies the sun-rising. It is found only in 2 Pet. 1:19, where it denotes the manifestation of Christ to the soul, imparting spiritual light and comfort. He is the "bright and morning star" of Rev. 2:28; 22:16.

Dea'con, Anglicized form of the Greek word *diaconos*, meaning a "runner," "messenger," "servant." For a long period a feeling of mutual jealousy had existed between the "Hebrews," or Jews proper, who spoke the sacred language of Palestine, and the "Hellenists," or Jews of the Grecian speech, who had adopted the Grecian language, and read the Septuagint version of the Bible instead of the Hebrew. This jealousy early appeared in the Christian community. It was alleged by the Hellenists that their widows were overlooked in the daily distribution of alms. This spirit must be checked. The apostles accordingly advised the disciples to look out for seven men of good report, full of the Holy Ghost, and men of practical wisdom, who should take entire charge of this distribution, leaving them free to devote themselves entirely to the spiritual functions of their office (Acts 6:1-6). This was accordingly done. Seven men were chosen, who appear from their names to have been Hellenists. The name "deacon" is nowhere applied to them in the New Testament; they are simply called "the seven" (21:8). Their office was at first secular, but it afterwards became also spiritual; for among other qualifications they must also be "apt to teach" (1 Tim. 3: 8-12). Both Philip and Stephen, who were of "the seven," preached; they did "the work of evangelists."

Dea′coness (Rom. 16:1, 3, 12; Phil. 4: 2, 3; 1 Tim. 3:11; 5:9, 10; Titus 2:3, 4). In these passages it is evident that females were then engaged in various Christian ministrations. Pliny makes mention of them also in his letter to Trajan (A.D. 110).

Dead Sea, the name given by Greek writers of the second century to that inland sea called in Scripture the "salt sea" (Gen. 14:3; Num. 34:12), the "sea of the plain" (Deut. 3:17), the "east sea" (Ezek. 47:18; Joel 2:20), and simply "the sea" (Ezek. 47:8). The Arabs call it *Bahr Lût—i.e.*, the Sea of Lot. It lies about 16 miles in a straight line to the east of

NORTH END OF THE DEAD SEA.

Jerusalem. Its surface is 1,292 feet below the surface of the Mediterranean Sea. It covers an area of about 300 square miles. Its depth varies from 1,310 to 11 feet. From various phenomena that have been observed, its bottom appears to be still subsiding. It is about 46 miles long, and of an average breadth of 10 miles. It has no outlet, the great heat of that region causing such rapid evaporation that its average depth, notwithstanding the rivers that run into it (see JORDAN), is maintained with little variation. The Jordan alone discharges into it no less than six million tons of water every twenty-four hours. It

is so much impregnated with salt, which flows into it as brine from the great salt mountain of Usdum at its south end, that three pounds of its water will yield one pound of solid salt. Bitumen, from which it anciently derived the name of the Lake Asphaltites, is still found on its shores, and sometimes floating in its waters. This was the "slime" spoken of in Gen. 14:10. Recent explorations have made it probable that this sea was at one time 1,400 feet above its present level, and that the whole Jordan valley, from Lebanon to the Red Sea, was once a branch of the Indian Ocean.

Nothing living can exist in this sea. "The fish carried down by the Jordan at once die, nor can even mussels or corals live in it; but it is a fable that no bird can fly over it, or that there are no living creatures on its banks. Dr. Tristram found on the shores three kinds of kingfishers, gulls, ducks, and grebes, which he says live on the fish which enter the sea in shoals, and presently die. He collected one hundred and eighteen species of birds, some new to science, on the shores, or swimming or flying over the waters. The cane-brakes which fringe it at some parts are the homes of about forty species of mammalia, several of them animals unknown in England; and innumerable tropical or semi-tropical plants perfume the atmosphere wherever fresh water can reach. The climate is perfect and most delicious, and indeed there is perhaps no place in the world where a sanatorium could be established with so much prospect of benefit as at Ain Jidi (Engedi)."—Geikie's *Hours, etc.*

Deal, Tenth. See OMER.

Dearth, a scarcity of provisions (1 Kings 17). There were frequent dearths in Palestine. In the days of Abram there was a "famine in the land" (Gen. 12:10), so also in the days of Jacob (47:4, 13). We read also of dearths in the time of the judges (Ruth 1:1), and of the kings (2 Sam. 21:1; 1 Kings 18:2; 2 Kings 4:38; 2 Sam. 21:2).

In New Testament times there was an extensive famine in Palestine (Acts 11:28) in the fourth year of the reign of the emperor Claudius (A.D. 44 and 45).

Death may be simply defined as the termination of life. It is represented under a variety of aspects in Scripture:—

(1.) "The dust shall return to the earth as it was" (Eccl. 12:7).

(2.) "Thou takest away their breath, they die" (Ps. 104:29).

(3.) It is the dissolution of "our earthly house of this tabernacle" (2 Cor. 5:1); the "putting off this tabernacle" (2 Pet. 1:13, 14).

(4.) Being "unclothed" (2 Cor. 5:3, 4).

(5.) "Falling on sleep" (Ps. 76:5; Jer. 51:39; John 11:13).

(6.) "I go whence I shall not return" (Job 10:21); "Make me to know mine end" (Ps. 39:4); "to depart" (Phil. 1:23).

The grave is represented as "the gates of death" (Job 38:17; Ps. 9:13; 107:18). The gloomy silence of the grave is spoken of under the figure of the "shadow of death" (Jer. 2:6).

Death is the *effect of sin* (Heb. 2:14), and not a "debt of nature." It is but once (9:27), universal (Gen. 3:19), necessary (Luke 2:28-30). Jesus has by his own death taken away its sting for all his followers (1 Cor. 15:55-57).

There is a spiritual death in trespasses and sins—*i.e.*, the death of the soul under the power of sin (Rom. 8:6; Eph. 2:1, 3; Col. 2:13).

The "second death" (Rev. 2:11) is the everlasting perdition of the wicked (Rev. 21:8), and "second" in respect to natural or temporal death.

THE DEATH OF CHRIST is the procuring cause incidentally of all the blessings men enjoy on earth. But specially it is the procuring cause of the actual salvation of all his people, together with all the means that lead thereto. It does not make their salvation merely possible, but certain (Matt. 18:11; Rom. 5:10; 2 Cor. 5:21; Gal. 1:4; 3:13; Eph. 1:7; 2:16; Rom. 8:32-35).

De'bir—*oracle town; sanctuary.* (1.) One of the eleven cities to the west of Hebron, in the highlands of Judah (Josh. 15:49; Judg. 1:11-15). It was originally one of the towns of the Anakim (Josh. 15:15), and was also called Kirjath-sepher (*q.v.*) and Kirjath-sannah (49). Caleb, who had conquered and taken possession of the town and district of Hebron (Josh. 14:6-15), offered the hand of his daughter to any one who would successfully lead a party against Debir. Othniel, his younger brother (Judg. 1:13; 3:9), achieved the conquest, and gained Achsah as his wife. She was not satisfied with the portion her father gave her, and as she was proceeding toward her new home, she "lighted off her ass" and said to him, "Give me a blessing" (*i.e.*, a dowry): "for thou hast given me a south land" (Josh. 15:19, A.V.); or, as in the Revised Version, "Thou hast set me in the land of the south"—*i.e.*, in the Negeb, outside the rich valley of Hebron, in the dry and barren land. "Give me also springs of water. And he gave her the upper springs, and the nether springs."

Debir has been identified with the modern *Edh-Dhâheriyeh—i.e.*, "the well on the ridge"—to the south of Hebron.

(2.) A place near the "valley of Achor" (Josh. 15:7), on the north boundary of Judah, between Jerusalem and Jericho.

(3.) The king of Eglon, one of the five Canaanitish kings who were hanged by Joshua (Josh. 10:3, 23) after the victory at Gibeon. These kings fled and took refuge in a cave at Makkedah. Here they were kept confined till Joshua returned from the pursuit of their discomfited armies, when he caused them to be brought forth, and "Joshua smote them, and slew them, and hanged them on five trees" (26).

Deb'orah—*a bee.* (1.) Rebekah's nurse. She accompanied her mistress when she left her father's house in Padan-aram to become the wife of Isaac (Gen. 24:59). Many years afterwards she died at Bethel, and was buried under the "oak of weeping"—Allon-bachuth (35:8).

(2.) A prophetess, "wife" (woman?) of Lapidoth. Jabin, the king of Hazor, had for twenty years held Israel in degrading subjection. The spirit of patriotism seemed crushed out of the nation. In this emergency Deborah roused the people from their lethargy. Her fame spread far and wide. She became a "mother in Israel" (Judg. 4:6, 14; 5:7), and "the children of Israel came to her for judgment" as she sat in her tent under the palm tree "between Ramah and Bethel." Preparations were everywhere made by her direction for the great effort to throw off the yoke of bondage. She summoned Barak from Kadesh to take the command of 10,000 men of Zebulun and Naphtali, and lead them to Mount Tabor on the plain of Esdraelon at its north-east end. With his aid she organized this army. She gave the signal for attack, and the Hebrew host rushed down impetuously upon the army of Jabin, which was commanded by Sisera, and gained a great and decisive victory. The Canaanitish army almost wholly perished. That was a great and ever-memorable day in Israel. In Judg. 5 is given the grand triumphal ode, the "song of Deborah," which she wrote in grateful commemoration of that great deliverance. (See LAPIDOTH, JABIN [2].)

Debt. The Mosaic law encouraged the practice of lending (Deut. 15:7; Ps. 37:26; Matt. 5:42); but it forbade the exaction of interest except from foreigners. Usury was strongly condemned (Prov. 28:8; Ezek. 18:8, 13, 17; 22:12; Ps. 15:5). On the Sabbatical year all pecuniary obligations were cancelled (Deut. 15:1-11). These regulations prevented the accumulation of debt.

Debt'or. Various regulations as to the relation between debtor and creditor are laid down in the Scriptures.

(1.) The debtor was to deliver up as a pledge to the creditor what he could most easily dispense with (Deut. 24:10, 11).

(2.) A mill, or millstone, or upper garment, when given as a pledge, could not be kept over night (Ex. 22:26, 27).

(3.) A debt could not be exacted during the Sabbatic year (Deut. 15:1-15).

For other laws bearing on this relation see Lev. 25:14, 32, 39; Matt. 18:25, 34.

(4.) A surety was liable in the same way as the original debtor (Prov. 11:15; 17:18).

Dec'alogue, the name given by the Greek fathers to the ten commandments; "the ten words," as the original is more literally rendered (Ex. 20:3-17). These commandments were at first written on two stone slabs (31:18), which were broken by Moses throwing them down on the ground (32:19). They were written by God a second time (34:1). The decalogue is alluded to in the New Testament five times (Matt. 5:17, 18, 19; Mark 10:19; Luke 18:20; Rom. 7:7, 8; 13:9; 1 Tim. 1:9, 10).

These commandments have been divided since the days of Origen the Greek father, as they stand in the Confession of all the Reformed Churches except the Lutheran.

The division adopted by Luther, and which has ever since been received in the Lutheran Church, makes the first two commandments one, and the third the second, and so on to the last, which is divided into two. "Thou shalt not covet thy neighbour's house" being ranked as ninth, and "Thou shalt not covet thy neighbour's wife," etc., the tenth. (See COMMANDMENTS.)

Decap'olis — *ten cities=deka*, ten, and *polis*, a city—a district on the east and south-east of the Sea of Galilee containing "ten cities," which were chiefly inhabited by Gentiles. It included a portion of Bashan and Gilead, and is mentioned three

MAP OF THE DISTRICT OF DECAPOLIS.

times in the New Testament (Matt. 4:25; Mark 5:20; 7:31). These cities were Scythopolis—*i.e.*, "city of the Scythians"—(ancient Bethshean, the only one of the ten cities on the west of Jordan), Hippos, Gadara, Pella (to which the Christians fled just before the destruction of Jerusalem), Philadelphia (ancient Rabbath - ammon), Gerasa, Dion, Canatha, Raphana, and Damascus. When the Romans conquered Syria (B.C. 65) they rebuilt, and endowed with certain privileges, these "ten cities," and the province connected with them they called "Decapolis."

Decision, Valley of, a name given to the valley of Jehoshaphat (*q.v.*) as *the vale of the sentence*. The ideal scene of Jehovah's signal inflictions on Zion's enemies (Joel 3:14).

Decrees of God. "The decrees of God are his eternal, unchangeable, holy, wise, and sovereign purpose, comprehending at once all things that ever were or will be in their causes, conditions, successions, and relations, and determining their certain futurition. The several contents of this one eternal purpose are, because of the limitation of our faculties, necessarily conceived of by us in partial aspects, and in logical relations, and are therefore styled *Decrees*." The decree being the act of an infinite, absolute, eternal, unchangeable, and sovereign Person, comprehending a plan including all his works of all kinds, great and small, from the beginning of creation to an unending eternity; ends as well as means, causes as well as effects, conditions and instrumentalities as well as the events which depend upon them, must be incomprehensible by the finite intellect of man. The decrees are eternal (Acts 15:18; Eph. 1:4; 2 Thess. 2:13), unchangeable (Ps. 33:11; Isa. 46:9), and comprehend all things that come to pass (Eph. 1:11; Matt. 10:29, 30; Eph. 2:10; Acts 2:23; 4:27, 28; Ps. 17:13, 14).

The decrees of God are (1) *efficacious*, as they respect those events he has determined to bring about by his own immediate agency; or (2) *permissive*, as they respect those events he has determined that free agents shall be permitted by him to effect.

This doctrine ought to produce in our minds "humility, in view of the infinite greatness and sovereignty of God, and of the dependence of man; confidence and implicit reliance upon the wisdom, righteousness, goodness, and immutability of God's purposes."

De'dan — *low ground.* (1.) A son of Raamah (Gen. 10:7). His descendants are mentioned in Isa. 21:13, and Ezek. 27:15. They probably settled among the sons of Cush, on the north-west coast of the Persian Gulf.

(2.) A son of Jokshan, Abraham's son by Keturah (1 Chr. 1:32). His descendants settled on the Syrian borders about the territory of Edom. They probably led a pastoral life.

Ded'anim, the descendants of Dedan, the son of Raamah. They are mentioned in Isa. 21:13 as sending out "travelling companies" which lodged "in the forest of Arabia." They are enumerated also by Ezekiel (27:20) among the merchants who supplied Tyre with precious things.

Dedica'tion, Feast of the (John 10:22, 42)—*i.e.*, the feast of *the renewing*. It was instituted B.C. 164 to commemorate the purging of the temple after its pollution by Antiochus Epiphanes (B.C. 167), and the rebuilding of the altar after the Syrian invaders had been driven out by Judas Maccabæus. It lasted for eight days, beginning on the 25th of the month Chisleu (December), which was often a period of heavy rains (Ezra 10:9, 13). It was an occasion of much rejoicing and festivity.

But there were other dedications of the temple. (1.) That of Solomon's temple (1 Kings 8:2; 2 Chr. 5:3); (2) the dedication in the days of Hezekiah (2 Chr. 29); and (3) the dedication of the temple after the Captivity (Ezra 6:16).

Deep, used to denote (1) the grave or the abyss (Rom. 10:7; Luke 8:31); (2) the deepest part of the sea (Ps. 69:15); (3) the chaos mentioned in Gen. 1:2; (4) the bottomless pit, hell (Rev. 9:1, 2; 11:7; 20:13).

Degrees, Song of—*song of steps*—a title given to each of these fifteen psalms, 120-134 inclusive. The probable origin of this name is the circumstance that these psalms came to be sung by the people on the ascents or goings up to Jerusalem to attend the three great festivals (Deut. 16:16). They were well fitted for being sung by the way from their peculiar form, and from the sentiments they express. "They are characterized by brevity, by a key-word, by epanaphora [*i.e.*, repetition], and by their epigrammatic style...More than half of them are cheerful, and all of them hopeful." They are sometimes called "Pilgrim Songs." Four of them were written by David, one (127) by Solomon, and the rest are anonymous.

Deha'vites—*villagers*—one of the Assyrian tribes which Asnapper sent to repopulate Samaria (Ezra 4:9). They were probably a nomad Persian tribe on the east of the Caspian Sea, and near the Sea of Azof.

Delai'ah—*freed by Jehovah*. (1.) The head of the twenty-third division of the priestly order (1 Chr. 24:18).

(2.) A son of Shemaiah, and one of the courtiers to whom Jeremiah's first roll of prophecy was read (Jer. 36:12).

(3.) The head of one of the bands of exiles that returned under Zerubbabel to Jerusalem (Ezra 2:60; Neh. 7:62).

Deli'lah—*languishing*—a Philistine woman who dwelt in the valley of Sorek (Judg. 16:4-20). She was bribed by the "lords of the Philistines" to obtain from Samson the secret of his strength and the means of overcoming it (Judg. 16:4-18). She tried on three occasions to obtain from him this secret in vain. On the fourth occasion she wrung it from him. She made him sleep upon her knees, and then called the man who was waiting to help her; who "cut off the seven locks of his head," and so his "strength went from him." (See SAMSON.)

Deluge, the name given to Noah's flood, the history of which is recorded in Gen. 7 and 8.

It began in the year 2516 B.C., and continued twelve lunar months and ten days, or exactly one solar year.

The cause of this judgment was the corruption and violence that filled the earth in the ninth generation from Adam. God in righteous indignation determined to purge the earth of the ungodly race. Amid a world of crime and guilt there was one household that continued faithful and true to God — the household of Noah. "Noah was a just man and perfect in his generation."

At the command of God, Noah made an ark 300 cubits long, 50 broad, and 30 high. He slowly proceeded with this work during a period of one hundred and twenty years (Gen. 6:3). At length the purpose of God began to be carried into effect.

The following table exhibits the order of events as they occurred :—

In the six hundredth year of his life Noah is commanded by God to enter the ark, taking with him his wife, and his three sons with their wives (Gen. 7 : 1-4).

The rain begins on the seventeenth day of the second month (Gen. 7 : 5-17).

The rain ceases—the waters prevail, fifteen cubits upward (Gen. 7 : 18-24).

The ark grounds on one of the mountains of Ararat on the seventeenth day of the seventh month, or one hundred and fifty days after the Deluge began (Gen. 8 : 1-4).

Tops of the mountains visible on the first day of the tenth month (Gen. 8 : 5).

Raven and dove sent out forty days after this (Gen. 8 : 6-9).

Dove again sent out seven days afterwards ; and in the evening she returns with an olive leaf in her mouth (Gen. 8 : 10, 11).

Dove sent out the third time after an interval of other seven days, and returns no more (Gen. 8 : 12).

The ground becomes dry on the first day of the first month of the new year (Gen. 8 : 13).

Noah leaves the ark on the twenty-seventh day of the second month (Gen. 8 : 14-19).

The historical truth of the narrative of the Flood is established by the references made to it by our Lord (Matt. 24 : 37 ; comp. Luke 17 : 26). Peter speaks of it also (1 Pet. 3 : 20 ; 2 Pet. 2 : 5). In Isa. 54 : 9 the Flood is referred to as "the waters of Noah." The Biblical narrative clearly shows that so far as the human race was concerned the Deluge was universal ; that it swept away all men living except Noah and his family, who were preserved in the ark ; and that the present human race is descended from those who were thus preserved.

Traditions of the Deluge are found among all the great divisions of the human family ; and these traditions, taken as a whole, wonderfully agree with the Biblical narrative, and agree with it in such a way as to lead to the conclusion that the Biblical is the authentic narrative, of which all these traditions are more or less corrupted versions. The most remarkable of these traditions is that recorded on tablets prepared by order of Assur-bani-pal, the king of Assyria. These were, however, copies of older records which belonged to some-

where about B.C. 2000, and which formed part of the priestly library at Erech (q.v.) —"the ineradicable remembrance of a real and terrible event." (See NOAH.)

De'mas, a companion and fellow-labourer of Paul during his first imprisonment at Rome (Philemon 24 ; Col. 4 : 14). It appears, however, that the love of the world afterwards mastered him, and he deserted the apostle (2 Tim. 4 : 10).

Deme'trius. (1.) A silversmith at Ephesus, whose chief occupation was to make "silver shrines for Diana" (q.v.)—Acts 19 : 24—i.e., models either of the temple of Diana or of the statue of the goddess. This trade brought to him and his fellow-craftsmen "great gain," for these shrines found a ready sale among the countless thousands who came to this temple from all parts of Asia Minor. This traffic was greatly endangered by the progress of the gospel, and hence Demetrius excited the tradesmen employed in the manufacture of these shrines, and caused so great a tumult that "the whole city was filled with confusion."

(2.) A Christian who is spoken of as having "a good report of all men, and of the truth itself " (3 John 12).

De'mon. See DÆMON.

Den, a lair of wild beasts (Ps. 10 : 9 ; 104 : 22 ; Job 37 : 8) ; the hole of a venomous reptile (Isa. 11 : 8) ; a recess for secrecy "in dens and caves of the earth" (Heb. 11 : 38) ; a resort of thieves (Matt. 21 : 13 ; Mark 11 : 17). Daniel was cast into "the den of lions" (Dan. 6 : 16, 17). Some recent discoveries among the ruins of Babylon have brought to light the fact that the practice of punishing offenders against the law by throwing them into a den of lions was common.

Dep'uty, in 1 Kings 22 : 47, means a prefect ; one set over others. The same Hebrew word is rendered "officer ;" i.e., chief of the commissariat appointed by Solomon (1 Kings 4 : 5, etc.).

In Esther 8 : 9 ; 9 : 3 (R.V., "governor ") it denotes a Persian prefect "on this side" —i.e., in the region west of—the Euphrates. It is the modern word *pasha*.

In Acts 13 : 7, 8, 12 ; 18 : 12, it denotes a

proconsul; *i.e.*, the governor of a Roman province holding his appointment from the senate. The Roman provinces were of two kinds—(1) senatorial and (2) imperial. The appointment of a governor to the former was in the hands of the senate, and he bore the title of *proconsul* (Gr. *anthupătos*). The appointment of a governor to the latter was in the hands of the emperor, and he bore the title of *propraetor* (Gr. *antistratēgos*).

Der'be, a small town on the eastern part of the upland plain of Lycaonia, about 20 miles from Lystra. Paul passed through Derbe on his route from Cilicia to Iconium, on his second missionary journey (Acts 16: 1), and probably also on his third journey (18:23; 19:1). On his first journey (14:20, 21) he came to Derbe from the other side; *i.e.*, from Iconium. It was the native place of Gaius, one of Paul's companions (20:4). He did not here suffer persecution (2 Tim. 3:11).

De'sert. (1.) Heb. *midbar*, "pasture-ground;" an open tract for pasturage; a common (Joel 2:22). The "backside of the desert" (Ex. 3:1) is the *west* of the desert, the region behind a man, as the east is the region in front. The same Hebrew word is rendered "wilderness," and is used of the country lying between Egypt and Palestine (Gen. 21:14, 21; Ex. 4:27; 19: 2; Josh. 1:4), the wilderness of the wanderings. It was a *grazing tract*, where the flocks and herds of the Israelites found pasturage during the whole of their journey to the Promised Land.

The same Hebrew word is used also to denote the wilderness of Arabia, which in winter and early spring supplies good pasturage to the flocks of the nomad tribes that roam over it (1 Kings 9:18).

The wilderness of Judah is the mountainous region along the western shore of the Dead Sea, where David fed his father's flocks (1 Sam. 17:28; 26:2). Thus in both of these instances the word denotes a country without settled inhabitants and without streams of water, but having good pasturage for cattle; a country of wandering tribes, as distinguished from that of a settled people (Isa.

35:1; 50:2; Jer. 4:11). Such, also, is the meaning of the word "wilderness" in Matt. 3:3; 15:33; Luke 15:4.

(2.) The translation of the Hebrew *Arâbah'*, "an arid tract" (Isa. 35:1, 6; 40: 3; 41:19; 51:3, etc.). The name *Arabah* is specially applied to the deep valley of the Jordan (the *Ghôr* of the Arabs), which extends from the lake of Tiberias to the Elanitic gulf. While *midbar* denotes properly a pastoral region, *arabah* denotes a wilderness. It is also translated "plains;" as "the plains of Jericho" (Josh. 5:10; 2 Kings 25:5), "the plains of Moab" (Num. 22:1; Deut. 34:1, 8), "the plains of the wilderness" (2 Sam. 17:16).

(3.) In the Revised Version of Num. 21: 20 the Hebrew word *jeshimôn'* is properly rendered "desert," meaning the waste tracts on both shores of the Dead Sea. This word is also rendered "desert" in Ps. 78:40; 106:14; Isa. 43:19, 20. It denotes a greater extent of uncultivated country than the other words so rendered. It is especially applied to the desert of the peninsula of Arabia (Num. 21:20; 23: 28), the most terrible of all the deserts with which the Israelites were acquainted. It is called "the desert" in Ex. 23:31; Deut. 11:24. (See JESHIMON.)

(4.) A dry place; hence a desolation (Ps. 9:6), desolate (Lev. 26:34); the rendering of the Hebrew word *ḥorbah'*. It is rendered "desert" only in Ps. 102:6, Isa. 48:21, and Ezek. 13:4, where it means the wilderness of Sinai.

(5.) This word is the symbol of the Jewish church when they had forsaken God (Isa. 40:3). Nations destitute of the knowledge of God are called a "wilderness" (32:15, *midbar*). It is a symbol of temptation, solitude, and persecution (Isa. 27:10, *midbar;* 33:9, *arabah*).

Desire of all nations (Hag. 2:7), usually interpreted as a title of the Messiah. The Revised Version, however, more correctly renders "the desirable things of all nations;" *i.e.*, the choicest treasures of the Gentiles shall be consecrated to the Lord.

Desola'tion, Abomination of (Matt. 24:15; Mark 13:14; comp. Luke 21:20), is interpreted of the eagles, the standards of the Roman army, which were an abomination to the Jews. These standards, rising over the site of the temple, were a sign that the holy place had fallen under the idolatrous Romans. The references are to Dan. 9 : 27. (See ABOMINATION.)

Destroy'er (Ex. 12 : 23), the agent employed in the killing of the first-born; the destroying angel or messenger of God. (Comp. 2 Kings 19 : 35; 2 Sam. 24 : 15, 16; Ps. 78 : 49; Acts 12 : 23.)

Destruc'tion in Job 26 : 6, 28 : 22 (Heb. *abaddon*) is sheol, the realm of the dead.

Destruc'tion, City of (Isa. 19 : 18; Heb. *Ir-ha-Heres*, "city of overthrow," because of the evidence it would present of the overthrow of heathenism), the ideal title of On or Heliopolis (*q.v.*).

Deuteron'omy. In all the Hebrew manuscripts the Pentateuch (*q.v.*) forms one roll or volume divided into larger and smaller sections called *parshioth* and *sedarim*. It is not easy to say when it was divided into five books. This was probably first done by the Greek translators of the book, whom the Vulgate follows.

The fifth of these books was called by the Greeks *Deuteronomion*—i.e., the second law—hence our name Deuteronomy, or a second statement of the laws already promulgated. The Jews designated the book by the two first Hebrew words that occur, *'Elle haddabhârim*—i.e., "These are the words." They divided it into eleven *parshioth*. In the English Bible it contains thirty-four chapters.

It consists chiefly of three discourses delivered by Moses a short time before his death. They were spoken to all Israel in the plains of Moab, in the eleventh month of the last year of their wanderings.

The *first discourse* (1–4 : 40) recapitulates the chief events of the last forty years in the wilderness, with earnest exhortations to obedience to the divine ordinances, and warnings against the danger of forsaking the God of their fathers.

The *second discourse* (5–26 : 19) is in effect the body of the whole book. The first address is introductory to it. It contains practically a recapitulation of the law already given by God at Mount Sinai, together with many admonitions and injunctions as to the course of conduct they were to follow when they were settled in Canaan.

The *concluding discourse* (ch. 27–30) relates almost wholly to the solemn sanctions of the law—the *blessings* to the obedient, and the *curse* that would fall on the rebellious. He solemnly adjures them to adhere faithfully to the covenant God had made with them, and so secure for themselves and their posterity the promised blessings.

These addresses to the people are followed by what may be called three *appendices*—namely (1), a song which God had commanded Moses to write (32 : 1–47); (2) the blessings he pronounced on the separate tribes (33 : 1–29); and (3) the story of his death (32 : 48–52) and burial (ch. 34), written by some other hand, probably that of Joshua.

These farewell addresses of Moses to the tribes of Israel he had so long led in the wilderness "glow in each line with the emotions of a great leader recounting to his contemporaries the marvellous story of their common experience. The enthusiasm they kindle, even to-day, though obscured by translation, reveals their matchless adaptation to the circumstances under which they were first spoken. Confidence for the future is evoked by remembrance of the past. The same God who had done mighty works for the tribes since the Exodus would cover their head in the day of battle with the nations of Palestine, soon to be invaded. Their great lawgiver stands before us, vigorous in his hoary age, stern in his abhorrence of evil, earnest in his zeal for God, but mellowed in all relations to earth by his nearness to heaven. The commanding wisdom of his enactments, the dignity of his position as the founder of the nation and the first of prophets, enforce his utterances. But he touches our deepest emotions by the human tenderness that breathes in all his words. Standing on the verge of life, he speaks as a father giving his parting counsels to those he loves; willing to depart and be with God he has served so well, but fondly lengthening out his last farewell to the dear ones of earth. No book can compare with Deuteronomy in its mingled sublimity and tenderness."—Geikie, *Hours*, etc.

The whole style and method of this book, its tone and its peculiarities of conception and expression, show that it must have come from one hand. That the author was none other than Moses is established by the following considerations :—(1.) The uniform tradition both of the Jewish and the Christian Church down to recent times. (2.) The book professes to have been written by Moses (1 : 1 ; 29 : 1 ; 31 : 1, 9–11, etc.), and was obviously intended to be accepted as his work. (3.) The incontrovertible testimony of our Lord and his apostles (Matt. 19 : 7, 8 ; Mark 10 : 3, 4 ; John 5 : 46, 47 ; Acts 3 : 22 ; 7 : 37 ; Rom. 10 : 19) establishes the same conclusion. (4.) The frequent references to it in the later books of the canon (Josh. 8 : 31 ; 1 Kings 2 : 9 ; 2 Kings 14 : 6 ; 2 Chr. 23 : 18 ; 25 : 4 ; 34 : 11 ; Ezra 3 : 2 ; 7 : 6 ; Neh. 8 : 1 ; Dan. 9 : 11, 13) prove its antiquity ; and (5) the archaisms found in it are in harmony with the age in which Moses lived. (6.) Its style and allusions are also strikingly consistent with the circumstances and position of Moses and of the people at that time.

This body of positive evidence cannot be set aside by the conjectures and reasonings of modern critics, who contend that the book was somewhat like a forgery, introduced among the Jews some seven or eight centuries after the Exodus.

Devil (Gr. *diabolos*)—*a slanderer*—the arch-enemy of man's spiritual interest (Job 1 : 6 ; Rev. 12 : 10 ; Zech. 3 : 1). He is called also "the accuser of the brethren" (1 Pet. 5 : 8).

In Lev. 17 : 7 the word "devil" is the translation of the Hebrew *saïr*, meaning a "goat" or "satyr" (Isa. 13 : 21 ; 34 : 14), alluding to the wood-dæmons, the objects of idolatrous worship among the heathen.

In Deut. 32 : 17 and Ps. 106 : 37 it is the translation of Hebrew *shed*, meaning *lord*, an *idol*, regarded by the Jews as a "demon," as the word is rendered in the Revised Version.

In the narratives of the Gospels regarding the "casting out of devils" a different Greek word (*daimon*) is used. In the time of our Lord there were frequent cases of demoniacal possession (Matt. 12 : 25–30 ; Mark 5 : 1–20 ; Luke 4 : 35 ; 10 : 18, etc.).

Dew. "There is no dew properly so called in Palestine, for there is no moisture in the hot summer air to be chilled into dew-drops by the coldness of the night. From May till October rain is unknown, the sun shining with unclouded brightness day after day. The heat becomes intense, the ground hard, and vegetation would perish but for the moist west winds that come each night from the sea. The bright skies cause the heat of the day to radiate very quickly into space, so that the nights are as cold as the day is the reverse—a peculiarity of climate from which poor Jacob suffered thousands of years ago (Gen. 31 : 40). To this coldness of the night air the indispensable watering of all plant-life is due. The winds, loaded with moisture, are robbed of it as they pass over the land, the cold air condensing it into drops of water, which fall in a gracious rain of mist on every thirsty blade. In the morning the fog thus created rests like a sea over the plains, and far up the sides of the hills, which raise their heads above it like so many islands. At sunrise, however, the scene speedily changes. By the kindling light the mist is transformed into vast snow-white clouds, which presently break into separate masses and rise up the mountain-sides, to disappear in the blue above, dissipated by the increasing heat. These are ' the morning clouds and the early dew that go away ' of which Hosea (6 : 4 ; 13 : 3) speaks so touchingly " (Geikie's *The Holy Land*, etc., i., p. 72). Dew is a source of great fertility (Gen. 27 : 28 ; Deut. 33 : 13 ; Zech. 8 : 12), and its withdrawal is regarded as a curse from God (2 Sam. 1 : 21 ; 1 Kings 17 : 1). It is the symbol of a multitude (2 Sam. 17 : 12 ; Ps. 110 : 3); and from its refreshing influence it is an emblem of brotherly love and harmony (Ps. 133 : 3), and of rich spiritual blessings (Hos. 14 : 5–7).

Di'adem, the tiara of a king (Ezek. 21 : 26 ; Isa. 28 : 5 ; 62 : 3); the turban (Job 29 : 14). In the New Testament a careful distinction is drawn between the diadem as a badge of royalty (Rev. 12:3; 13:1; 19:12) and the crown as a mark of distinction in private life. It is not known what the ancient Jewish "diadem" was. It was the mark of Oriental sovereigns. (See CROWN.)

Di'al, for the measurement of time, only once mentioned in the Bible, erected by Ahaz (2 Kings 20:11; Isa. 38:8). The Hebrew word (*ma'aloth*) is rendered "steps" in Ex. 20:26, 1 Kings 10:19, and "degrees" in 2 Kings 20:9, 10, 11. The *ma'aloth* was probably stairs on which the shadow of a column or obelisk placed on the top fell. The shadow would cover a greater or smaller number of steps, according as the sun was low or high.

Probably the sun-dial was a Babylonian invention. Daniel at Babylon (Dan. 3:6) is the first to make mention of the "hour."

Di'amond. (1.) A precious gem (Heb. *yahalom'*, in allusion to its hardness), otherwise unknown, the sixth—*i.e.*, the third in the second row—in the breastplate of the high priest, with the name of Naphtali engraven on it (Ex. 28:18; 39:11; R.V. marg., "sardonyx.")

(2.) A precious stone (Heb. *shamir'*, a sharp *point*) mentioned in Jer. 17:1. From its hardness it was used for cutting and perforating other minerals. It is rendered "adamant" (*q.v.*) in Ezek. 3:9, Zech. 7:12. It is the hardest and most valuable of precious stones.

Dia'na—so called by the Romans; called Artemis by the Greeks—the "great" goddess worshipped among heathen nations under various modifications. Her most noted temple was that at Ephesus. It was built outside the city walls, and was one of the seven wonders of the ancient world. "First and last it was the work of 220 years; built of shining marble; 342 feet long by 164 feet broad; supported by a forest of columns, each 56 feet high; a sacred museum of masterpieces of sculpture and painting. At the centre, hidden by curtains, within a gorgeous shrine, stood the very ancient image of the goddess, on wood or ebony reputed to have fallen from the sky. Behind the shrine was a

treasury, where, as in 'the safest bank in Asia,' nations and kings stored their most precious things. The temple as St. Paul saw it subsisted till A.D. 262, when it was ruined by the Goths" (Acts 19:23-35).— Moule on *Ephesians: Introd.*

Dib'laim—*doubled cakes* — the mother of Gomer, who was Hosea's wife (Hos. 1:3).

Diblatha'im--*two cakes* — a city of Moab, on the east of the Dead Sea (Num. 33:46; Jer. 48:22).

Di'bon —*pining; wasting.* (1.) A city in Moab (Num. 21:30); called also Dibon-gad (33:45), because it was built by Gad and Dimon (Isa. 15:9). It has been identified with the modern *Dibân*, about 3 miles north of the Arnon and 12 miles east of the Dead Sea. (See MOABITE STONE.)

(2.) A city of the tribe of Judah, inhabited after the Captivity (Neh. 11:25); called also Dimonah (Josh. 15:22). It is probably the modern *ed-Dheib.*

Did'ymus (Gr. *twin* = Heb. Thomas. *q.v.*)—John 11:16; 20:24; 21:2.

Dim'nah—*dunghill*—a city of Zebulun given to the Merarite Levites (Josh. 21:35). In 1 Chr. 6:77 the name "Rimmon" is substituted.

Di'nah—*judged; vindicated*—daughter of Jacob by Leah, and sister of Simeon and Levi (Gen. 30:21). She was seduced by Shechem, the son of Hamor, the Hivite chief, when Jacob's camp was in the neighbourhood of Shechem. This led to the terrible revenge of Simeon and Levi in putting the Shechemites to death (Gen.

STATUE OF DIANA.
(*From the Temple of Diana, Ephesus; now in the Museum at Naples.*)

34). Jacob makes frequent reference to this deed of blood with abhorrence and regret (Gen. 34 : 30 ; 49 : 5–7). She is mentioned among the rest of Jacob's family that went down into Egypt (Gen. 46 : 8, 15).

Dine (Gen. 43 : 16). It was the custom in Egypt to dine at noon. But it is probable that the Egyptians took their principal meal in the evening, as was the general custom in the East (Luke 14 : 12).

Din'habah—*robbers' den*—an Edomitish city, the capital of king Bela (Gen. 36 : 32). It is probably the modern *Dibdiba*, a little north-east of Petra.

Diony'sius, the Areopagite, one of Paul's converts at Athens (Acts 17 : 34).

Diot'rephes—*Jove-nourished*—rebuked by John for his pride (3 John 9). He was a Judaizer, prating against John and his fellow-labourers "with malicious words" (7).

Disci'ple—*a scholar*—sometimes applied to the followers of John the Baptist (Matt. 9 : 14), and of the Pharisees (22 : 16), but principally to the followers of Christ. A disciple of Christ is one who (1) believes his doctrine, (2) rests on his sacrifice, (3) imbibes his spirit, and (4) imitates his example (Matt. 10 : 24 ; Luke 14 : 26, 27, 33 ; John 6 : 69).

Dish, for eating from (2 Kings 21 : 13). Judas dipped his hand with a "sop" or piece of bread in the same dish with our Lord, thereby indicating friendly intimacy (Matt. 26 : 23). The "lordly dish" in Judg. 5 : 25 was probably the shallow drinking cup, usually of brass. In Judg. 6 : 38 the same Hebrew word is rendered "bowl."

The dishes of the tabernacle were made of pure gold (Ex. 25 : 29 ; 37 : 16).

Di'shan—*antelope*—the youngest son of Seir the Horite, head of one of the tribes of Idumæa (Gen. 36 : 21, 28, 30).

Dispensa'tion (Gr. *oikonomia*, "management," "economy"). (1.) The method or scheme according to which God carries out his purposes towards men is called a dispensation. There are usually reckoned three dispensations—the Patriarchal, the Mosaic or Jewish, and the Christian. (See COVENANT, *Administration of.*) These were so many stages in God's unfolding of his purpose of grace toward men. The word is not found with this meaning in Scripture.

(2.) A commission to preach the gospel (1 Cor. 9 : 17 ; Eph. 1 : 10 ; 3 : 2 ; Col. 1 : 25).

Dispensations of Providence are providential events which affect men either in the way of mercy or of judgment.

Disper'sion (Gr. *diaspŏra*, "scattered," James 1 : 1 ; 1 Pet. 1 : 1) of the Jews. At various times, and from the operation of divers causes, the Jews were separated and scattered into foreign countries "to the outmost parts of heaven" (Deut. 30 : 4).

(1.) Many were dispersed over Assyria, Media, Babylonia, and Persia, descendants of those who had been transported thither by the Exile. The ten tribes, after existing as a separate kingdom for two hundred and fifty-five years, were carried captive (B.C. 721) by Shalmaneser (or Sargon), king of Assyria. They never returned to their own land as a distinct people, although many individuals from among these tribes, there can be no doubt, joined with the bands that returned from Babylon on the proclamation of Cyrus.

(2.) Many Jews migrated to Egypt and took up their abode there. This migration began in the days of Solomon (2 Kings 18 : 21, 24 ; Isa. 39 : 7). Alexander the Great placed a large number of Jews in Alexandria, which he had founded, and conferred on them equal rights with the Egyptians. Ptolemy Philadelphus, it is said, caused the Jewish Scriptures to be translated into Greek (the work began B.C. 284), for the use of the Alexandrian Jews. The Jews in Egypt continued for many ages to exercise a powerful influence on the public interests of that country. From Egypt they spread along the coast of Africa to Cyrene (Acts 2 : 10) and to Ethiopia (7 : 27).

(3.) After the time of Seleucus Nicator (B.C. 280), one of the captains of Alexander the Great, large numbers of Jews migrated into Syria, where they enjoyed equal rights with the Macedonians. From Syria they found their way into Asia Minor. Antiochus the Great, king of Syria and Asia, removed 3,000 families of Jews from Mesopotamia and Babylonia, and planted them in Phrygia and Lydia.

(4.) From Asia Minor many Jews moved into Greece and Macedonia, chiefly for purposes of commerce. In the apostles' time they were found in considerable numbers in all the principal cities.

From the time of Pompey the Great (B.C. 63) numbers of Jews from Palestine and Greece went to Rome, where they had a separate quarter of the city assigned to them. Here they enjoyed considerable freedom.

Thus were the Jews everywhere *scattered abroad*. This, in the overruling providence of God, ultimately contributed in a great degree toward opening the way for the spread of the gospel into all lands.

Disper'sion *from the plain of Shinar.*

This was occasioned by the confusion of tongues at Babel (Gen. 11:9). They were scattered abroad "every one after his tongue, after their families, in their nations" (Gen. 10:5; 20:31).

The tenth chapter of Genesis gives us an account of the principal nations of the earth in their migrations from the plain of Shinar, which was their common residence after the Flood. In general, it may be said that the descendants of Japheth were scattered over the north, those of Shem over the central regions, and those of Ham over the extreme south.

The following table shows how the different families were dispersed:—

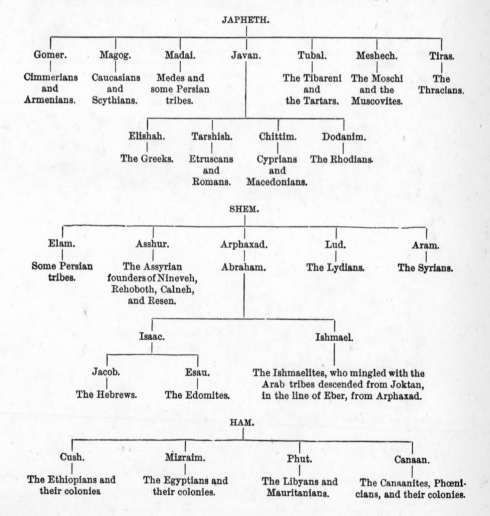

JAPHETH.

Gomer.	Magog.	Madai.	Javan.	Tubal.	Meshech.	Tiras.
Cimmerians and Armenians.	Caucasians and Scythians.	Medes and some Persian tribes.		The Tibareni and the Tartars.	The Moschi and the Muscovites.	The Thracians.

Elishah.	Tarshish.	Chittim.	Dodanim.
The Greeks.	Etruscans and Romans.	Cyprians and Macedonians.	The Rhodians.

SHEM.

Elam.	Asshur.	Arphaxad.	Lud.	Aram.
Some Persian tribes.	The Assyrian founders of Nineveh, Rehoboth, Calneh, and Resen.	Abraham.	The Lydians.	The Syrians.

Isaac.	Ishmael.

Jacob.	Esau.	
The Hebrews.	The Edomites.	The Ishmaelites, who mingled with the Arab tribes descended from Joktan, in the line of Eber, from Arphaxad.

HAM.

Cush.	Mizraim.	Phut.	Canaan.
The Ethiopians and their colonies.	The Egyptians and their colonies.	The Libyans and Mauritanians.	The Canaanites, Phoenicians, and their colonies.

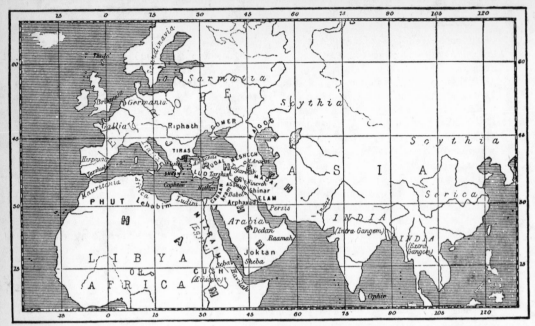

THE ANCIENT WORLD, SHOWING THE DISPERSION OF THE NATIONS AFTER THE FLOOD.
(*See page 199.*)

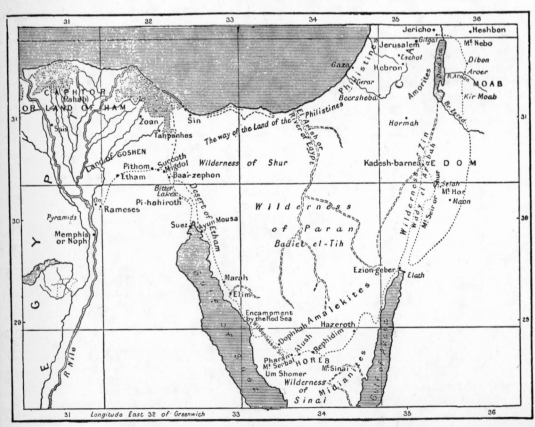

JOURNEYING OF THE ISRAELITES FROM EGYPT TO CANAAN.
(*See page 244.*)

Dis'taff (Heb. *pélek*, a "circle"), the instrument used for twisting threads by a whirl (Prov. 31:19).

Divina'tion of false prophets (Deut. 18: 10, 14; Micah 3:6, 7, 11), of necromancers (1 Sam. 28:8), of the Philistine priests and diviners (1 Sam. 6:2), of Balaam (Josh. 13:22). Three kinds of divination are mentioned in Ezek. 21:21—by arrows, consulting with images (the teraphim), and by examining the entrails of animals sacrificed. The practice of this art seems to have been encouraged in ancient Egypt. Diviners also abounded among the aborigines of Canaan and the Philistines (Isa. 2:6; 1 Sam. 28). At a later period multitudes of magicians poured from Chaldea and Arabia into the land of Israel, and pursued their occupations (Isa. 8:19; 2 Kings 21:6; 2 Chr. 33:6). This superstition widely spread, and in the time of the apostles there were "vagabond Jews, exorcists" (Acts 19:13), and men like Simon Magus (Acts 8:9), Bar-jesus (13:6, 8), and other jugglers and impostors (19:19; 2 Tim. 3:13). Every species and degree of this superstition was strictly forbidden by the law of Moses (Ex. 22:18; Lev. 19: 26, 31; 20:27; Deut. 18:10, 11).

But beyond these various forms of superstition, there are instances of divination on record in the Scriptures by which God was pleased to make known his will.

(1.) There was divination by lot, by which, when resorted to in matters of moment, and with solemnity, God intimated his will (Josh. 7:13). The land of Canaan was divided by lot (Num. 26:55, 56); Achan's guilt was detected (Josh. 7:16-19), Saul was elected king (1 Sam. 10:20, 21), and Matthias chosen to the apostleship, by the solemn lot (Acts 1:26). It was thus also that the scape-goat was determined (Lev. 16:8-10).

(2.) There was divination by dreams (Gen. 20:6; Deut. 13:2, 3; Judg. 7:13, 15; Matt. 1:20; 2:12, 13, 19, 22). This is illustrated in the history of Joseph (Gen. 41:25-32) and of Daniel (2:27; 4:19-28).

(3.) By divine appointment there was also divination by the Urim and Thummim (Num. 27:21), and by the ephod.

(4.) God was pleased sometimes to vouchsafe direct vocal communications to men (Deut. 34:10; Ex. 3:4; 4:3; Deut. 4:14,15; 1 Kings 19:12). He also communed with men from above the mercy-seat (Ex. 25: 22), and at the door of the tabernacle (Ex. 29:42, 43).

(5.) Through his prophets God revealed himself, and gave intimations of his will (2 Kings 13:17; Jer. 51:63, 64).

Divorce'. The dissolution of the marriage tie was regulated by the Mosaic law (Deut. 24:1-4). The Jews, after the Captivity, were required to dismiss the foreign women they had married contrary to the law (Ezra 10:11-19). Christ limited the permission of divorce to the single case of adultery. It seems that it was not uncommon for the Jews at that time to dissolve the union on very slight pretences (Matt. 5:31, 32; 19:1-9; Mark 10:2-12; Luke 16:18). These precepts given by Christ regulate the law of divorce in the Christian Church.

Diz'ahab—*region of gold*—a place in the desert of Sinai, on the western shore of the Elanitic gulf (Deut. 1:1). It is now called *Dehab*.

Doc'tor (Luke 2:46; 5:17; Acts 5:34), a teacher. The Jewish doctors taught and disputed in synagogues, or wherever they could find an audience. Their disciples were allowed to propose to them questions. They assumed the office without any appointment to it. The doctors of the law were principally of the sect of the Pharisees. Schools were established after the destruction of Jerusalem at Babylon and Tiberias, in which academical degrees were conferred on those who passed a certain examination. Those of the school of Tiberias were called by the title "rabbi," and those of Babylon by that of "master."

Dod'ai—*loving*—one of David's captains (1 Chr. 27:4). (See DODO [2].)

Dod'anim—*leaders*—a race descended from Javan (Gen. 10:4). They are known in profane history as the Dardani, originally inhabiting Illyricum. They were a semi-Pelasgic race, and in the ethnographical table (Gen. 10) they are grouped with the Chittim (*q.v.*). In 1 Chr. 1:7, they are called Rodanim. The LXX. and the Samaritan Version also read Rhodii, whence some have concluded that the Rhodians, the inhabitants of the island of Rhodes, are meant.

Do'do—*amatory; loving.* (1.) A descendant of Issachar (Judg. 10:1).

(2.) An Ahohite, father of Eleazar, who was one of David's three heroes (2 Sam. 23:9; 1 Chr. 11:12). He was the same with Dodai mentioned in 1 Chr. 27:4.

(3.) A Bethlehemite, and father of Elhanan, who was one of David's thirty heroes (2 Sam. 23:24).

Do'eg—*fearful*—an Edomite, the chief overseer of Saul's flocks (1 Sam. 21:7). At the command of Saul he slew the high priest Ahimelech (*q.v.*) at Nob, together with all the priests to the number of eighty-five persons. (Comp. Ps. 52.)

Dog, frequently mentioned both in the Old and New Testaments. Dogs were used by the Hebrews as a watch for their houses (Isa. 56:10), and for guarding their flocks (Job 30:1). There were also then as now troops of semi-wild dogs that wandered about devouring dead bodies and the offal of the streets (1 Kings 14:11; 16:4; 21:19, 23; 22:38; Ps. 59:6, 14).

As the dog was an unclean animal, the terms "dog," "dog's head," "dead dog," were used as terms of reproach or of humiliation (1 Sam. 24:14; 2 Sam. 3:8; 9:8; 16:9). Paul calls false apostles "dogs" (Phil. 3:2). Those who are shut out of the kingdom of heaven are also so designated (Rev. 22:15). Persecutors are called "dogs" (Ps. 22:16). Hazael's words, "Thy servant which is but a dog" (2 Kings 8:13), are spoken in mock humility=impossible that one so contemptible as he should attain to such power.

Doleful creatures (occurring only Isa. 13:21. Heb. *ochim*—*i.e.*, "shrieks;" hence "howling animals"), a general name for screech owls (*howlets*), which occupy the desolate palaces of Babylon. Some render the word "hyænas."

Doors moved on pivots of wood fastened in sockets above and below (Prov. 26:14). They were fastened by a lock (Judg. 3:23, 25; Cant. 5:5) or by a bar (Judg. 16:3; Job 38:10). In the interior of Oriental houses, curtains were frequently used instead of doors. The entrances of the tabernacle had curtains (Ex. 26:31-33, 36).

The "valley of Achor" is called a "door of hope," because immediately after the execution of Achan the Lord said to Joshua, "Fear not," and from that time Joshua went forward in a career of uninterrupted conquest. Paul speaks of a "door opened" for the spread of the gospel (1 Cor. 16:9; 2 Cor. 2:12; Col. 4:3). Our Lord says of himself, "I am the door" (John 10:9). John (Rev. 4:1) speaks of a "door opened in heaven."

Door-keeper. This word is used in Ps. 84:10 (R.V. marg., "stand at the threshold of," etc.), but there it signifies properly "sitting at the threshold in the house of God." The psalmist means that he would rather stand at the door of God's house and merely look in, than dwell in houses where iniquity prevailed.

Persons were appointed to keep the street door leading into the interior of the house (John 18:16, 17; Acts 12:13). Sometimes females held this post.

Door-posts. The Jews were commanded to write the divine name on the posts (*mezuzoth'*) of their doors (Deut. 6:9). The Jews, misunderstanding this injunction, adopted the custom of writing on a slip of parchment these verses (Deut. 6:4-9, and 11:13-21), which they enclosed in a reed or cylinder and fixed on the right-hand doorpost of every room in the house.

Doph'kah—*knocking*—an encampment of the Israelites in the wilderness (Num. 33:12). It was in the desert of Sin, on the eastern shore of the western arm of the Red Sea, somewhere in the Wâdy Feirân.

Dor—*dwelling*—the Dora of the Romans, an ancient royal city of the Canaanites (Josh. 11:1, 2; 12:23). It was the most southern settlement of the Phœnicians on the coast of Syria. The original inhabitants seem never to have been expelled, although they were made tributary by David. It was one of Solomon's commissariat districts (Judg. 1:27; 1 Kings 4:11). It has been identified with *Tantûra* (so named from the supposed resemblance

TANTÛRA (DOR).

of its tower to a *tantur*—*i.e.*, "a horn"—worn as an ornament on the head by the women of Lebanon and Hauran), about 8 miles north of Cæsarea, "a sad and sickly hamlet of wretched huts, on a naked sea-beach." Here are found the remains of an old Crusading fortress.

Dor'cas—*a female antelope*, or *gazelle*—a pious Christian widow at Joppa whom Peter restored to life (Acts 9 : 36–41). She was a Hellenistic Jewess, called Tabitha by the Jews and Dorcas by the Greeks.

Do'than—*two wells*—a famous pasture-ground where Joseph found his brethren watching their flocks. Here, at the sug-. gestion of Judah, they sold him to the Ishmaelite merchants (Gen. 37 : 17) who were on their way down to Egypt from the spice district of Gilead.

It was the residence of Elisha (2 Kings 6 : 13), and the scene of a remarkable vision of chariots and horses of fire surrounding the mountain on which the city stood. It is identified with the modern *Tell-Dothân*, on the south side of the plain of Jezreel, about 12 miles north of Samaria, among the hills of Gilboa. The "two wells" are still in existence, one of which bears the name of the "pit of Joseph" (*Jubb Yâsuf*).

Dough (*batsek*, meaning "swelling," *i.e.*, in fermentation). The dough the Israelites had prepared for baking was carried away by them out of Egypt in their kneading-troughs (Ex. 12 : 34, 39). In the process of baking, the dough had to be turned (Hos. 7 : 8).

Dove. In their wild state doves generally build their nests in the clefts of rocks, but when domesticated "dove-cots" are prepared for them (Cant. 2 : 14 ; Jer. 48 : 28 ; Isa. 60 : 8). The dove was placed on the standards of the Assyrians and Babylonians in honour, it is supposed, of Semiramis (Jer. 25 : 38 ; Vulg., "fierceness of the dove;" comp. Jer. 46 : 16 ; 50 : 16). Doves and turtle - doves were the only birds that could be offered in sacrifice, as they were clean according to the Mosaic law (Gen. 15 : 9 ; Lev. 5 : 7 ; 12 : 6 ; Luke 2 : 24). The dove was the harbinger of peace to Noah (Gen. 8 : 8, 10). It is often mentioned as the emblem of purity (Ps.

55 : 6–8). It is a symbol of the Holy Spirit (Gen. 1 : 2 ; Matt. 3 : 16 ; Mark 1 : 10 ; Luke 3 : 22 ; John 1 : 32) ; also of tender and devoted affection (Cant. 1 : 15 ; 2 : 14). David in his distress wished that he had the wings of a dove, that he might fly away and be at rest (Ps. 55 : 6–8). There is a species of dove found at Damascus "whose feathers, all except the wings, are literally as yellow as gold " (68 : 13).

Dove's dung (2 Kings 6 : 25) has been generally understood literally. There are instances in history of the dung of pigeons being actually used as food during a famine. Compare also the language of Rabshakeh to the Jews (2 Kings 18 : 27 ; Isa. 36 : 12). This name, however, is applied by the Arabs to different vegetable substances, and there is room for the opinion of those who think that some such substance is here referred to, as, *e.g.*, the seeds of a kind of millet, or a very inferior kind of pulse, or the root of the *ornithogalum*—*i.e.*, *bird-milk* —the star-of-Bethlehem.

STAR-OF-BETHLEHEM.

Dow'ry (*môhar; i.e., price* paid for a wife—Gen. 34 : 12 ; Ex. 22 : 17 ; 1 Sam. 18 : 25), a nuptial present ; some gift, as a sum of money, which the bridegroom offers to the father of his bride as a satisfaction before he can receive her. Jacob had no dowry to give for his wife, but he gave his services (Gen. 29 : 18 ; 30 : 20 ; 34 : 12).

Drag'on. (1.) Heb. *tannim*, plural of *tan*. The name of some unknown creature inhabiting desert places and ruins (Job 30 : 29 ; Ps. 44 : 19 ; Isa. 13 : 22 ; 34 : 13 ; 43 : 20 ; Jer. 10 : 22 ; Micah 1 : 8 ; Mal. 1 : 3) ; probably, as translated in the Revised Version, the jackal (*q.v.*).

(2.) Heb. *tannin*. Some great sea monster (Jer. 51:34). In Isa. 51:9 it may denote the crocodile. In Gen. 1:21 (Heb. plural *tanninim*) the Authorized Version renders "whales," and the Revised Version "sea monsters." It is rendered "serpent" in Ex. 7:9. It is used figuratively in Ps. 74:13; Ezek. 29:3.

In the New Testament the word "dragon" is found only in Rev. 12:3, 4, 7, 9, 16, 17, etc., and is there used metaphorically of "Satan." (See WHALE.)

Drag'on well (Neh. 2:13), supposed by some to be identical with the Pool of Gihon.

Dram. The Authorized Version understood the word *'adarkônim* (1 Chr. 29:7; Ezra 8:27), and the similar word *darkomnim* (Ezra 2:69; Neh. 7:70), as equivalent to the Greek silver coin the *drachma*. But the Revised Version rightly regards it as the Greek *dareikos*, a Persian gold coin (the daric) of the value of about £1, 2s., which was first struck by Darius, the son of Hystaspes, and was current in Western Asia long after the fall of the Persian empire. (See DARIC.)

Draught-house (2 Kings 10:27). Jehu ordered the temple of Baal to be destroyed, and the place to be converted to the vile use of receiving offal or ordure. (Comp. Matt. 15:17.)

Drawer of water (Deut. 29:11; Josh. 9:21, 23), a servile employment to which the Gibeonites were condemned.

Dream. God has frequently made use of dreams in communicating his will to men. The most remarkable instances of this are recorded in the history of Jacob (28:12; 31:10), Laban (31:24), Joseph (37:6–11), Gideon (Judg. 7), and Solomon (1 Kings 3:5). Other significant dreams are also recorded, such as those of Abimelech (Gen. 20:3–7), Pharaoh's chief butler and baker (40:5), Pharaoh (41:1–8), the Midianites (Judg. 7:13), Nebuchadnezzar (Dan. 2:1; 4:10, 18), the wise men from the east (Matt. 2:12), and Pilate's wife (27:19).

To Joseph "the Lord appeared in a dream," and gave him instructions regarding the infant Jesus (Matt. 1:20; 2:12, 13, 19). In a vision of the night a "man

of Macedonia" stood before Paul and said, "Come over into Macedonia and help us" (Acts 16:9; see also 18:9; 27:23).

Dredge (Job 24:6). See CORN.

Dregs (Ps. 75:8; Isa. 51:17, 22), the *lees* of wine which settle at the bottom of the vessel.

Dress. (1.) *Materials used.* The earliest and simplest an apron of fig-leaves sewed together (Gen. 3:7); then skins of animals (3:21). Elijah's dress was probably the skin of a sheep (2 Kings 1:8). The Hebrews were early acquainted with the art of weaving hair into cloth (Ex. 26:7; 35:6), which formed the sackcloth of mourners. This was the material of John the Baptist's robe (Matt. 3:4). Wool was also woven into garments (Lev. 13:47; Deut. 22:11; Ezek. 34:3; Job 31:20; Prov. 27:26). The Israelites probably learned the art of weaving linen when they were in Egypt (1 Chr. 4:21). Fine linen was used in the vestments of the high priest (Ex. 28:5), as well as by the rich (Gen. 41:42; Prov. 31:22; Luke 16:19). The use of mixed material, as wool and flax, was forbidden (Lev. 19:19; Deut. 22:11).

(2.) *Colour.* The prevailing colour was the natural white of the material used, which was sometimes rendered purer by the fuller's art (Ps. 104:1, 2; Isa. 63:3; Mark 9:3). The Hebrews were acquainted with the art of dyeing (Gen. 37:3, 23). Various modes of ornamentation were adopted in the process of weaving (Ex. 28:6; 26:1, 31; 35:25), and by needle-work (Judg. 5:30; Ps. 45:13). Dyed robes were imported from foreign countries, particularly from Phœnicia (Zeph. 1:8). Purple and scarlet robes were the marks of the wealthy (Luke 16:19; 2 Sam. 1:24).

(3.) *Form.* The robes of men and women were not very much different in form from each other.

(a) The "coat" (*kethôneth*), of wool, cotton, or linen, was worn by both sexes. It was a closely-fitting garment, resembling in use and form our shirt (John 19:23). It was kept close to the body by a girdle (John 21:7). A person wearing this "coat" alone was described as naked (1 Sam. 19:

24; Isa. 20:2; 2 Kings 6:30; John 21:7); deprived of it he would be absolutely naked.

(*b*) A linen cloth or wrapper (*sadin*) of fine linen, used somewhat as a night-shirt (Mark 14:51). It is mentioned in Judg. 14:12, 13, and rendered there "sheets."

(*c*) An upper tunic (*meïl*), longer than the "coat" (1 Sam. 2:19; 24:4; 28:14). In 1 Sam. 18:14 it is the mantle in which Samuel was enveloped; in 1 Sam. 24:4 it is the "robe" under which Saul slept.

The disciples were forbidden to wear two "coats" (Matt. 10:10; Luke 9:3).

(*d*) The usual outer garment consisted of a piece of woollen cloth like a Scotch plaid, either wrapped round the body or thrown over the shoulders like a shawl, with the ends hanging down in front, or it might be thrown over the head so as to conceal the face (2 Sam. 15:30; Esther 6:12). It was confined to the waist by a girdle, and the fold formed by the overlapping of the robe served as a pocket (2 Kings 4:39; Ps. 79:12; Hag. 2:12; Prov. 17:23; 21:14).

Female dress. The "coat" was common to both sexes (Cant. 5:3). But peculiar to females were (1) the "veil" or "wimple," a kind of shawl (Ruth 3:15; rendered "mantle," R. V., Isa. 3:22); (2) the "mantle," also a species of shawl (Isa. 3:22); (3) a "veil," probably a light summer dress (Gen. 24:65); (4) a "stomacher," a holiday dress (3:24). The outer garment terminated in an ample fringe or border, which concealed the feet (Isa. 47:2; Jer. 13:22).

The *dress of the Persians* is described in Dan. 3:21.

The *references to the art of sewing* are few, inasmuch as the garments generally came forth from the loom ready for being worn, and all that was required in the making of clothes devolved on the women of a family (Prov. 31:22; Acts 9:39).

Extravagance in dress is referred to in Jer. 4:30; Ezek. 16:10; Zeph. 1:8 (R.V., "foreign apparel"); 1 Tim. 2:9; 1 Pet. 3:3.

Rending the robes was expressive of grief (Gen. 37:29, 34), fear (1 Kings 21:27), indignation (2 Kings 5:7), or despair (Judg. 11:35; Esther 4:1).

Shaking the garments, or shaking the dust from off them, was a sign of renunciation (Acts 18:6); wrapping them round the head, of awe (1 Kings 19:13) or grief (2 Sam. 15:30); casting them off, of excitement (Acts 22:23); laying hold of them, of supplication (1 Sam. 15:27). In the case of travelling, the outer garments were girded up (1 Kings 18:46). They were thrown aside also when they would impede action (Mark 10:50; John 13:4; Acts 7:58).

Drink. The drinks of the Hebrews were water, wine, "strong drink," and vinegar. Their drinking vessels were the cup, goblet or "basin," the "cruse" or pitcher, and the saucer.

To drink water by measure (Ezek. 4:11), and to buy water to drink (Lam. 5:4), denote great scarcity. To drink blood means to be satiated with slaughter.

The Jews carefully strained their drinks through a sieve, through fear of violating the law of Lev. 11:20, 23, 41, 42. (See Matt. 23:24. "Strain at" should be "strain out.")

Drink, strong (Heb. *shekar'*), an intoxicating liquor (Judg. 13:4; Luke 1:15; Isa. 5:11; Micah 2:11) distilled from corn, honey, or dates. The effects of the use of strong drink are referred to in Ps. 107:27; Isa. 24:20; 49:26; 51:17–22. Its use prohibited, Prov. 20:1. (See WINE.)

Drink-offering consisted of wine (Num. 15:5; Hos. 9:4) poured around the altar (Ex. 30:9). Joined with meat-offerings (Num. 6:15, 17; 2 Kings 16:13; Joel 1:9, 13; 2:14), presented daily (Ex. 29:40), on the Sabbath (Num. 28:9), and on feast-days (28:14). One-fourth of an hin of wine was required for one lamb, one-third for a ram, and one-fourth for a bullock (Num. 15:5; 28:7, 14). "Drink offerings of blood" (Ps. 16:4) is used in allusion to the heathen practice of mingling the blood of animals sacrificed with wine or water, and pouring out the mixture in the worship of the gods, and the idea conveyed is that the psalmist would not partake of the abominations of the heathen.

Drom'edary (Isa. 60:6), an African or Arabian species of camel having only one hump, while the Bactrian camel has two.

It is distinguished from the camel only as a trained saddle-horse is distinguished from a cart-horse. It is remarkable for its speed (Jer. 2:23). Camels are frequently spoken of in patriarchal times (Gen. 12:16; 24:10; 30:43; 31:17, etc.). They were used for carrying burdens (Gen. 37:25; Judg. 6:5), and for riding (Gen. 24:64). The hair of the camel falls off of itself in spring, and is woven into coarse cloths and garments (Matt. 3:4). (See CAMEL.)

Drop′sy, mentioned only in Luke 14:2. The man afflicted with it was cured by Christ on the Sabbath.

Dross, the impurities of silver separated from the ore in the process of melting (Prov. 25:4; 26:23; Ps. 119:119). It is also used to denote the base metal itself, probably before it is smelted, in Isa. 1:22, 25.

Drought. From the middle of May to about the middle of August the land of Palestine is dry. It is then the "drought of summer" (Gen. 31:40; Ps. 32:4), and the land suffers (Deut. 28:23; Ps. 102:4), vegetation being preserved only by the dews (Hag. 1:11). (See DEW.)

Drown (Ex. 15:4; Amos 8:8; Heb. 11:29). Drowning was a mode of capital punishment in use among the Syrians, and was known to the Jews in the time of our Lord. To this he alludes in Matt. 18:6.

Drunk. The first case of intoxication on record is that of Noah (Gen. 9:21). The sin of drunkenness is frequently and strongly condemned (Rom. 13:13; 1 Cor. 6:9, 10; Eph. 5:18; 1 Thess. 5:7, 8). The sin of drinking to excess seems to have been not uncommon among the Israelites.

The word is used figuratively, when men are spoken of as being drunk with sorrow, and with the wine of God's wrath (Isa. 63:6; Jer. 51:57; Ezek. 23:33). To "add drunkenness to thirst" (Deut. 29:19, A.V.) is a proverbial expression, rendered in the Revised Version "to destroy the moist with the dry"—i.e., the well-watered equally with the dry land, meaning that the effect of such walking in the imagination of their own hearts would be to destroy one and all.

Drusil′la, third and youngest daughter of Herod Agrippa I. (Acts 12:1-4, 20-23). Felix, the Roman procurator of Judea, induced her to leave her husband, Azizus, the king of Emesa, and become his wife. She was present with Felix when Paul reasoned of "righteousness, temperance, and judgment to come" (Acts 24:24). She and her son perished in the eruption of Mount Vesuvius, A.D. 79.

Duke, derived from the Latin *dux*, meaning "a leader;" Arabic, "a sheik." This word is used to denote the phylarch or chief of a tribe (Gen. 36:15-43; Ex. 15:15; 1 Chr. 1:51-54).

Dul′cimer (Heb. *sumphoniah*), a musical instrument mentioned in Dan. 3:5, 15, along with other instruments there named, as sounded before the golden image. It was not a Jewish instrument. In the margin of the Revised Version it is styled the "bag-pipes." Luther translated it "lute," and Grotius the "crooked trumpet." It is probable that it was introduced into Babylon by some Greek or Western-Asiatic musician. Some Rabbinical commentators render it by "organ," the well-known instrument composed of a series of pipes, others by "lyre." The most probable interpretation is that it was a bag-pipe similar to the *zampagna* of Southern Europe.

Du′mah — *silence* — (comp. Ps. 94:17), the fourth son of Ishmael; also the tribe descended from him; and hence also the region in Arabia which they inhabited (Gen. 25:14; 1 Chr. 1:30).

There was also a town of this name in Judah (Josh. 15:52), which has been identified with *ed-Dômeh*, about 10 miles southwest of Hebron.

The place mentioned in the "burden" of the prophet Isaiah (21:11) is Edom or Idumea.

Dumb from natural infirmity (Ex. 4:11); not knowing what to say (Prov. 31:8); unwillingness to speak (Ps. 39:9; Lev. 10:3). Christ repeatedly restored the dumb (Matt. 9:32, 33; Luke 11:14; Matt. 12:22) to the use of speech.

Dung. (1.) Used as manure (Luke 13:8); collected outside the city walls (Neh. 2:13). Of sacrifices burnt outside the camp (Ex. 29:14; Lev. 4:11; 8:17;

Num. 19:5). To be "cast out as dung," a figurative expression (1 Kings 14:10; 2 Kings 9:37; Jer. 8:2; Ps. 18:42), meaning to be rejected as unprofitable.

(2.) Used as fuel, a substitute for fire-wood, which was with difficulty procured in Syria, Arabia, and Egypt (Ezek. 4:12–15), where cows' and camels' dung is used to the present day for this purpose.

Dung-gate (Neh. 2:13), a gate of ancient Jerusalem, on the south-west quarter. "The gate outside of which lay the piles of sweepings and offscourings of the streets," in the valley of Tophet.

Dung-hill, to sit on a, was a sign of the deepest dejection (1 Sam. 2:8; Ps. 113:7; Lam. 4:5).

Dun'geon, different from the ordinary prison in being more severe as a place of punishment. Like the Roman inner prison (Acts 16:24), it consisted of a deep cell or cistern (Jer. 38:6). To be shut up in, a punishment common in Egypt (Gen. 39:20; 40:3; 41:10; 42:19). It is not mentioned, however, in the law of Moses as a mode of punishment. Under the later kings imprisonment was frequently used as a punishment (2 Chron. 16:10; Jer. 20:2; 32:2; 33:1; 37:15), and it was customary after the Exile (Matt. 11:2; Luke 3:20; Acts 5:18, 21; Matt. 18:30).

Du'ra—*the circle*—the plain near Baby-lon in which Nebuchadnezzar set up a golden image, mentioned in Dan. 3:1. The place still retains its ancient name. On one of its many mounds the pedestal of what must have been a colossal statue has been found. It has been supposed to be that of the golden image.

Dust. Storms of sand and dust some-times overtake Eastern travellers. They are very dreadful, many perishing under them. Jehovah threatens to bring on the land of Israel, as a punishment for forsak-ing him, a rain of "powder and dust" (Deut. 28:24).

To cast dust on the head was a sign of mourning (Josh. 7:6); and to sit in dust, of extreme affliction (Isa. 47:1). "Dust" is used to denote the grave (Job 7:21). "To shake off the dust from one's feet" against another is to renounce all future

intercourse with him (Matt. 10:14; Acts 13:51). To "lick the dust" is a sign of abject submission (Ps. 72:9); and to throw dust at one is a sign of abhorrence (2 Sam. 16:13; comp. Acts 22:23).

Dwarf, a lean or emaciated person (Lev. 21:20).

Dwell. Tents were in primitive times the common dwellings of men. Houses were afterwards built, the walls of which were frequently of mud (Job 24:16; Matt. 6:19, 20) or of sun-dried bricks.

God "dwells in light" (1 Tim. 6:16; 1 John 1:7), in heaven (Ps. 123:1), in his church (Ps. 9:11; 1 John 4:12). Christ dwelt on earth in the days of his humilia-tion (John 1:14). He now dwells in the hearts of his people (Eph. 3:17-19). The Holy Spirit dwells in believers (1 Cor. 3:16; 2 Tim. 1:14). We are exhorted to "let the word of God dwell in us richly" (Col. 3:16; Ps. 119:11).

Dwell deep occurs only in Jer. 49:8, and refers to the custom of seeking refuge from impending danger, in retiring to the re-cesses of rocks and caverns, or to remote places in the desert.

Dwell'ings. The *materials* used in buildings were commonly bricks, sometimes also stones (Lev. 14:40, 42), which were held together by cement (Jer. 43:9) or bitumen (Gen. 11:3). The exterior was usually whitewashed (Lev. 14:41; Ezek. 13:10; Matt. 23:27). The beams were of sycamore (Isa. 9:10), or olive-wood, or cedar (1 Kings 7:2; Isa. 9:10).

The *form* of Eastern dwellings differed in many respects from that of dwellings in Western lands. The larger houses were built in a quadrangle enclosing a court-yard (Luke 5:19; 2 Sam. 17:18; Neh. 8:16) surrounded by galleries, which formed the guest-chamber or reception-room for visi-tors. The flat roof, surrounded by a low parapet, was used for many domestic and social purposes. It was reached by steps from the court. In connection with it (2 Kings 23:12) was an upper room, used as a private chamber (2 Sam. 18:33; Dan. 6:11), also as a bedroom (2 Kings 23:12), a sleeping apartment for guests (2 Kings 4:10), and as a sick-chamber (1 Kings 17:19).

The doors, sometimes of stone, swung on morticed pivots, and were generally fastened by wooden bolts. The houses of the more wealthy had a doorkeeper or a female porter (John 18:16; Acts 12:13). The windows generally opened into the court-yard, and were closed by a lattice (Judg. 5:28). The interior rooms were set apart for the female portion of the household.

The *furniture* of the room (2 Kings 4:10) consisted of a couch furnished with pillows (Amos 6:4; Ezek. 13:10), and besides this only chairs and lanterns or lamp-stands (2 Kings 4:10).

Dye. The art of dyeing is one of great antiquity, although no special mention is made of it in the Old Testament. The Hebrews probably learned it from the Egyptians (see Ex. 26:1; 28:5-8), who brought it to great perfection. In New Testament times Thyatira was famed for its dyers (Acts 16:14). (See COLOURS.)

E

Eagle (Heb. *nésher;* properly the griffon vulture or great vulture, so called from its *tearing* its prey with its beak),

GRIFFON VULTURE.

referred to for its swiftness of flight (Deut. 28:49; 2 Sam. 1:23), its mounting high in the air (Job 39:27), its strength (Ps. 103:5), its setting its nest in high places (Jer. 49:16), and its power of vision (Job 39:26-30).

This "ravenous bird" is a symbol of those nations whom God employs and sends forth to do a work of destruction, sweeping away whatever is decaying and putrescent (Matt. 24:28; Isa. 46:11; Ezek. 39:4; Deut. 28:49; Jer. 4:13;

48:40). It is said that the eagle sheds his feathers in the beginning of spring, and with fresh plumage assumes the appearance of youth. To this, allusion is made in Ps. 103:5 and Isa. 40:31. God's care over his people is likened to that of the eagle in training its young to fly (Ex. 19:4; Deut. 32:11, 12). An interesting illustration is thus recorded by Sir Humphry Davy:— "I once saw a very interesting sight above the crags of Ben Nevis. Two parent eagles were teaching their offspring, two young birds, the manœuvres of flight. They began by rising from the top of the mountain in the eye of the sun. It was about mid-day, and bright for the climate. They at first made small circles, and the young birds imitated them. They paused on their wings, waiting till they had made their flight, and then took a second and larger gyration, always rising toward the sun, and enlarging their circle of flight so as to make a gradually ascending spiral. The young ones still and slowly followed, apparently flying better as they mounted; and they continued this sublime exercise, always rising till they became mere points in the air, and the young ones were lost, and afterwards their parents, to our aching sight." (See Isa. 40:31.)

There have been observed in Palestine four distinct species of eagles—(1) the golden eagle (*Aquila chrysaëtos*); (2) the spotted eagle (*Aquila nævia*); (3) the common species, the imperial eagle (*Aquila heliaca*); and (4) the *Circaëtos gallicus,* which preys on reptiles.

The eagle was unclean by the Levitical law (Lev. 11 : 13 ; Deut. 14 : 12).

Ear, used frequently in a figurative sense (Ps. 34 : 15). To "uncover the ear" is to show respect to a person (1 Sam. 20 : 2 marg.). To have the "ear heavy," or to have "uncircumcised ears" (Isa. 6 : 10), is to be inattentive and disobedient. To have the ear "bored" through with an awl was a sign of perpetual servitude (Ex. 21 : 6).

Ear'ing, an Old English word (from the Latin *aro,* I plough), meaning "ploughing." It is used in the Authorized Version in Gen. 45 : 6 ; Ex. 34 : 21 ; 1 Sam. 8 : 12 ; Deut. 21 : 4 ; Isa. 30 : 24 ; but the Revised Version has rendered the original in these places by the ordinary word to plough or till.

Ear'nest. The Spirit is the earnest of the believer's destined inheritance (2 Cor. 1 : 22 ; 5 : 5 ; Eph. 1 : 14). The word thus rendered is the same as that rendered "pledge" in Gen. 38 : 17-20 ; "indeed, the Hebrew word has simply passed into the Greek and Latin languages, probably through commercial dealings with the Phœnicians, the great trading people of ancient days. Originally it meant no more than a pledge; but in common usage it came to denote that particular kind of pledge which is a part of the full price of an article paid in advance ; and as it is joined with the figure of a seal when applied to the Spirit, it seems to be used by Paul in this specific sense." The Spirit's gracious presence and working in believers is a foretaste to them of the blessedness of heaven. God is graciously pleased to give not only pledges but foretastes of future blessedness.

Ear'rings, rings properly for the ear (Gen. 35 : 4 ; Num. 31 : 51 ; Ezek. 16 : 12). In Gen. 24 : 47 the word means a nose-jewel, and is so rendered in the Revised Version. In Isa. 3 : 20 the Authorized Version has "ear-rings," and the Revised Version "amulets," which more correctly represents the original word (*leḥashim*), which means *incantations; charms* — thus remedies against enchantment, worn either

suspended from the neck or in the ears of females. Ear-rings were ornaments used by both sexes (Ex. 32 : 2).

Earth. (1.) In the sense of soil or ground, the translation of the word *adamah'*. In Gen. 9 : 20 "husbandman" is literally "man of the ground or earth." Altars were to be built of earth (Ex. 20 : 24). Naaman asked for two mules' burden of earth (2 Kings 5 : 17), under the superstitious notion that Jehovah, like the gods of the heathen, could be acceptably worshipped only on his own soil.

(2.) As the rendering of *érets,* it means the whole world (Gen. 1 : 2); the land as opposed to the sea (1 : 10). *Erets* also denotes a country (21 : 32); a plot of ground (23 : 15); the ground on which a man stands (33 : 3); the inhabitants of the earth (6 : 1 ; 11 : 1); all the world except Israel (2 Chr. 13 : 9). In the New Testament "the earth" denotes the land of Judea (Matt. 23 : 35); also things carnal in contrast with things heavenly (John 3 : 31 ; Col. 3 : 1, 2).

Earth'quake, mentioned among the extraordinary phenomena of Palestine (Ps. 18 : 7 ; comp. Hab. 3 : 6 ; Nah. 1 : 5 ; Isa. 5 : 25).

The first earthquake in Palestine of which we have any record happened in the reign of Ahab (1 Kings 19 : 11, 12). Another took place in the days of Uzziah, king of Judah (Zech. 14 : 5). The most memorable earthquake taking place in New Testament times happened at the crucifixion of our Lord (Matt. 27 : 54). An earthquake at Philippi shook the prison in which Paul and Silas were imprisoned (Acts 16 : 26).

It is used figuratively as a token of the presence of the Lord (Judg. 5 : 4 ; 2 Sam. 22 : 8 ; Ps. 77 : 18 ; 97 : 4 ; 104 : 32).

East. (1.) The orient (*mizrah*); the rising of the sun. Thus "the land of the east" is the country lying to the east of Syria, the Elymais (Zech. 8 : 7).

(2.) Properly what is in front of one, or a country that is before or in front of another ; the rendering of the word *kédem.* In pointing out the quarters, a Hebrew always looked with his face toward the east. The word *kédem* is used when the four quarters of the world are described (Gen. 13:14; 28:14); and *mizrah* when the east only is distinguished from the west (Josh. 11:3; Ps. 50:1; 103:12, etc.). In Gen. 25:6 "eastward" is literally "unto the land of *kédem;*" *i.e.*, the lands lying east of Palestine—namely, Arabia, Mesopotamia, etc.

East gate (Jer. 19:2), properly the Potter's gate, the gate which led to the potter's field, in the valley of Hinnom.

East, Children of the, the Arabs as a whole, known as the Nabateans or Kedarenes, nomad tribes (Judg. 6:3, 33; 7:12; 8:10).

East sea (Joel 2:20; Ezek. 47:18), the Dead Sea, which lay on the east side of the Holy Land. The Mediterranean, which lay on the west, was hence called the west sea (Num. 34:6).

East wind, the wind coming from the east (Job 27:21; Isa. 27:8, etc.). Blight caused by this wind, "thin ears" (Gen. 41:6); the withered "gourd" (Jonah 4:8). It was the cause and also the emblem of evil (Ezek. 17:10; 19:12; Hos. 13:15). In Palestine this wind blows from a burning desert, and hence is destitute of moisture necessary for vegetation.

East'er, originally a Saxon word (*Eostre*), denoting a goddess of the Saxons, in honour of whom sacrifices were offered about the time of the Passover. Hence the name came to be given to the festival of the Resurrection of Christ, which occurred at the time of the Passover. In the early English versions this word was frequently used as the translation of the Greek *pascha* (the Passover). When the Authorized Version (1611) was formed, the word "passover" was used in all passages in which this word *pascha* occurred, except in Acts 12:4. In the Revised Version the proper word, "passover," is always used.

Eating. The ancient Hebrews would not eat with the Egyptians (Gen. 43:32). In the time of our Lord they would not eat with Samaritans (John 4:9), and were astonished that he ate with publicans and sinners (Matt. 9:11). The Hebrews originally *sat* at table, but afterwards

adopted the Persian and Chaldean practice of *reclining* (Luke 7:36-50). Their principal meal was at noon (Gen. 43:16; 1 Kings 20:16; Ruth 2:14; Luke 14:12). The word "eat" is used metaphorically in Jer. 15:16; Ezek. 3:1; Rev. 10:9. In John 6:53-58, "eating and drinking" means believing in Christ. Women were never present as guests at meals (*q.v.*).

E'bal—*stony.* (1.) A mountain 3,076 feet above the level of the sea, and 1,200 feet above the level of the valley, on the north side of which stood the city of Shechem (*q.v.*). On this mountain six of the tribes (Deut. 27:12, 13) were appointed to take their stand and respond according to a prescribed form to the imprecations uttered in the valley, where the law was read by the Levites (11:29; 27:4, 13). This mountain was also the site of the first great altar erected to Jehovah (Deut. 27:5-8; Josh. 8:30-35). After this the name of Ebal does not again occur in Jewish history. (See GERIZIM.)

(2.) A descendant of Eber (1 Chr. 1:22), called also Obal (Gen. 10:28).

(3.) A descendant of Seir the Horite (Gen. 36:23).

E'bed—*slave*—the father of Gaal, in whom the men of Shechem "put·confidence" in their conspiracy against Abimelech (Judg. 9:26, 28, 30, 31).

E'bed-me'lech—*a servant of the king;* probably an official title—an Ethiopian, "one of the eunuchs which was in the king's house;" *i.e.*, in the palace of Zedekiah, king of Judah. He interceded with the king in Jeremiah's behalf, and was the means of saving him from death by famine (Jer. 38:7-13; comp. 39:15-18).

Eb'en-e'zer—*stone of help*—the memorial stone set up by Samuel to commemorate the divine assistance to Israel in their great battle against the Philistines, whom they totally routed (1 Sam. 7:7-12) at Aphek, in the neighbourhood of Mizpeh, in Benjamin, near the western entrance of the pass of Beth-horon. On this very battle-field, twenty years before, the Philistines routed the Israelites, "and slew of the army in the field about four thousand men" (4:1, 2; here, and at 5:1, called "Eben-ezer" by antici·

pation). In this extremity the Israelites fetched the ark out of Shiloh and carried it into their camp. The Philistines a second time immediately attacked them, and smote them with a very great slaughter, "for there fell of Israel thirty thousand footmen. And the ark of God was taken" (1 Sam. 4 : 10). And now in the same place the Philistines are vanquished, and the memorial stone is erected by Samuel (*q.v.*). The spot where the stone was erected was somewhere "between Mizpeh and Shen." Some have identified it with the modern *Beit Iksa*, a conspicuous and prominent position, apparently answering all the necessary conditions; others with *Deir Abân*, 3 miles east of 'Ain Shems.

E'ber— *beyond.* (1.) The third post-diluvian patriarch after Shem (Gen. 10 : 24; 11 : 14). He is regarded as the founder of the Hebrew race (10 : 21; Num. 24 : 24). In Luke 3 : 35 he is called Heber.

(2.) One of the seven heads of the families of the Gadites (1 Chr. 5 : 13).

(3.) The oldest of the three sons of Elpaal the Benjamite (8 : 12).

(4.) One of the heads of the families of Benjamites in Jerusalem (22).

(5.) The head of the priestly family of Amok in the time of Zerubbabel (Neh. 12 : 20).

Eb'ony, a black, hard wood, brought by the merchants from India to Tyre (Ezek. 27 : 15). It is the heart-wood of the *Diospyros ebenus*, which grows in Ceylon and Southern India.

Ebro'nah— *passage*—one of the stations of the Israelites in their wanderings (Num. 33 : 34, 35). It was near Ezion-geber.

Ecbat'ana (Ezra 6 : 2 marg.). (See ACHMETHA.)

Ecclesias'tes, the Greek rendering of the Hebrew *Koheleth*, which means "Preacher." The old and traditional view of the authorship of this book attributes it to Solomon. This view can be satisfactorily maintained, though others date it from the Captivity. The writer represents himself implicitly as Solomon (1 : 12). It has been appropriately styled The Confession of King Solomon. "The writer is a man who has sinned in giving way to selfishness and sensuality, who has paid the penalty of that sin

in satiety and weariness of life, but who has through all this been under the discipline of a divine education, and has learned from it the lesson which God meant to teach him." "The writer concludes by pointing out that the secret of a true life is that a man should consecrate the vigour of his youth to God." The key-note of the book is sounded in ch. 1 : 2—

" Vanity of vanities ! saith the Preacher,
  Vanity of vanities ! all is vanity !"

—*i.e.*, all man's efforts to find happiness apart from God are without result.

Eclipse of the sun alluded to in Amos 8 : 9; Micah 3 : 6; Zech. 14 : 6; Joel 2 : 10. Eclipses were regarded as tokens of God's anger (Joel 3 : 15; Job 9 : 7). The darkness at the crucifixion has been ascribed to an eclipse (Matt. 27 : 45); but on the other hand it is argued that the great intensity of darkness caused by an eclipse never lasts for more than six minutes, and this darkness lasted for three hours. Moreover, at the time of the Passover the moon was full, and therefore there could *not* be an eclipse of the sun, which is caused by an interposition of the moon between the sun and the earth.

Ed—*witness*—a word not found in the original Hebrew, nor in the LXX. and Vulgate, but added by the translators in the Authorized Version, also in the Revised Version, of Josh. 22 : 34. The words are literally rendered : " And the children of Reuben and the children of Gad named the altar. It is a witness between us that Jehovah is God." This great altar stood probably on the east side of the Jordan, in the land of Gilead, "over against the land of Canaan." After the division of the Promised Land, the tribes of Reuben and Gad and the half-tribe of Manasseh, on returning to their own settlements on the east of Jordan (Josh. 22 : 1–6), erected a great altar, which they affirmed, in answer to the challenge of the other tribes, was not for sacrifice, but only as a witness ('*Ed*) or testimony to future generations that they still retained the same interest in the nation as the other tribes.

E'dar—*tower of the flock*—a tower between Bethlehem and Hebron, near which Jacob first halted after leaving Bethlehem (Gen. 35:21). In Micah 4:8 the word is rendered "tower of the flock" (marg., "Edar"), and is used as a designation of Bethlehem, which figuratively represents the royal line of David as sprung from Bethlehem.

E'den—*delight.* (1.) The garden in which our first parents dwelt (Gen. 2: 8–17). No geographical question has been so much discussed as that bearing on its site. It has been placed in Armenia, in the region west of the Caspian Sea, in Media, near Damascus, in Palestine, in Southern Arabia, and in Babylonia. The site must undoubtedly be sought for somewhere along the course of the great streams the Tigris and the Euphrates of Western Asia, in "the land of Shinar" or Babylonia. The region from about lat. 33° 30′ to lat. 31°, which is a very rich and fertile tract, has been by the most competent authorities agreed on as the probable site of Eden. "It is a region where streams abound, where they divide and re-unite, where alone in the Mesopotamian tract can be found the phenomenon of a single river parting into four arms, each of which is or has been a river of consequence."

Among almost all nations there are traditions of the primitive innocence of our race in the garden of Eden. This was the "golden age" to which the Greeks looked back. Men then lived a "life free from care, and without labour and sorrow. Old age was unknown; the body never lost its vigour; existence was a perpetual feast without a taint of evil. The earth brought forth spontaneously all things that were good in profuse abundance."

(2.) One of the markets whence the merchants of Tyre obtained richly embroidered stuffs (Ezek. 27:23); the same, probably, as that mentioned in 2 Kings 19:12, and Isa. 37:12, as the name of a region conquered by the Assyrians.

(3.) Son of Joab, and one of the Levites who assisted in reforming the public worship of the sanctuary in the time of Hezekiah (2 Chr. 29:12).

E'der—*flock.* (1.) A city in the south of Judah, on the border of Idumea (Josh. 15:21).

(2.) The second of the three sons of Mushi, of the family of Merari, appointed to the Levitical office (1 Chr. 23:23; 24:30).

E'dom. (1.) The name of Esau (*q.v.*), Gen. 25:30—"Feed me, I pray thee, with that same red pottage [Heb. *haadom, haadom*—*i.e.,* 'the *red* pottage, the *red* pottage']......Therefore was his name called Edom"—*i.e., Red.*

(2.) Idumea (Isa. 34:5, 6; Ezek. 35:15). "The field of Edom" (Gen. 32:3), "the land of Edom" (Gen. 36:16), was mountainous (Obad. 8, 9, 19, 21). It was called the land, or "the mountain of Seir," the rough hills on the east side of the Arabah. It extended from the head of the Gulf of Akabah, the Elanitic gulf, to the foot of the Dead Sea (1 Kings 9:26), and contained, among other cities, the rock-hewn Sela (*q.v.*), generally known by the Greek name Petra (2 Kings 14:7). It is a wild and rugged region, traversed by fruitful valleys. Its old capital was Bozrah (Isa. 63:1). The early inhabitants of the land were Horites. They were destroyed by the Edomites (Deut. 2:12), between whom and the kings of Israel and Judah there was frequent war (2 Kings 8:20; 2 Chr. 28:17).

At the time of the Exodus they churlishly refused permission to the Israelites to pass through their land (Num. 20:14–21), and ever afterwards maintained an attitude of hostility toward them. They were conquered by David (2 Sam. 8:14; comp. 1 Kings 9:26), and afterwards by Amaziah (2 Chr. 25:11, 12). But they regained again their independence, and in later years, during the decline of the Jewish kingdom (2 Kings 16:6; R.V. marg., "Edomites"), made war against Israel. They took part with the Chaldeans when Nebuchadnezzar captured Jerusalem, and afterwards they invaded and held possession of the south of Palestine as far as Hebron. At length, however, Edom fell under the growing Chaldean power (Jer. 27:3, 6).

There are many prophecies concerning Edom (Isa. 34:5, 6; Jer. 49:7–18; Ezek. 25:13; 35:1–15; Joel 3:19; Amos 1:11; Obad.; Mal. 1:3, 4) which have been remarkably fulfilled. The present desolate condition of that land is a standing testimony to the inspiration of these prophecies. After an existence as a people for above seventeen hundred years, they have utterly disappeared, and their language even is forgotten for ever. In Petra, "where kings kept their court, and where nobles assembled; where manifest proofs of ancient opulence are concentrated; where princely mausoleums and temples retaining their external grandeur, but bereft of all their splendour, still look as if 'fresh from the chisel' —even there no man dwells: it is given by lot to birds and beasts and reptiles; it is a 'court for owls,' and scarcely are they frayed from their 'lonely habitations' by the tread of a solitary traveller from a far distant land, among deserted dwellings and desolated ruins."

Ed′rei—*mighty; strength.* (1.) One of the chief towns of the kingdom of Bashan (Josh. 12:4, 5). Here Og was defeated by the Israelites, and the strength of the Amorites broken (Num. 21:33-35). It subsequently belonged to Manasseh, for a short time apparently, and afterwards became the abode of banditti and outlaws (Josh. 13:31). It has been identified with the modern *Edr'a*, which stands on a rocky promontory on the south-west edge of the Lejah (the Argob of the Hebrews, and Trachonitis of the Greeks). The ruins of *Edr'a* are the most extensive in the Hauran. They are 3 miles in circumference. A number of the ancient houses still remain; the walls, roofs, and doors being all of stone. The wild region of which Edrei was the capital is thus described in its modern aspect: "Elevated about 20 feet above the plain, it is a labyrinth of clefts and crevasses in the rock, formed by volcanic action; and owing to its impenetrable condition, it has become a refuge for outlaws and turbulent characters, who make it a sort of Cave of Adullam...It is, in fact, an impregnable natural fortress, about 20 miles in length and 15 in breadth" (Porter's *Syria, etc.*). Beneath this wonderful city there is also a subterranean city, hollowed out probably as a refuge for the population of the upper city in times of danger. (See BASHAN.)

(2.) A town of Naphtali (Josh. 19:37).

Effectual call. See CALL.

Effectual prayer occurs in Authorized Version, James 5:16. The Revised Version renders appropriately: "The supplication of a righteous man availeth much in its working"—*i.e.*, "it moves the hand of Him who moves the world."

Egg (Heb. *beytsah*, "whiteness"). Eggs deserted (Isa. 10:14), of a bird (Deut. 22:6), an ostrich (Job 39:14), the cockatrice (Isa. 59:5). In Luke 11:12, an egg is contrasted with a scorpion, which is said to be very like an egg in its appearance, so much so as to be with difficulty at times distinguished from it. In Job 6:6 ("the white of an egg") the word for egg (*hallamuth'*) occurs nowhere else. It has been translated "purslain" (R.V. marg.), and the whole phrase "purslain-broth"—*i.e.*, broth made of that herb, proverbial for its insipidity; and hence an insipid discourse. Job applies this expression to the speech of Eliphaz as being insipid and dull. But the common rendering—"the white of an egg"—may be satisfactorily maintained.

Eg′lah—*a heifer*—one of David's wives, and mother of Ithream (2 Sam. 3:5; 1 Chr. 3:3). According to a Jewish tradition she was Michal.

Eg′laim—*two ponds*—(Isa. 15:8), probably En-eglaim of Ezek. 47:10.

Eg′lon—*the bullock; place of heifers.* (1.) Chieftain or king of one of the Moabite tribes (Judg. 3:12-14). Having entered into an alliance with Ammon and Amalek, he overran the trans-Jordanic region, and then crossing the Jordan, seized on Jericho, the "city of palm trees," which had been by this time rebuilt, but not as a fortress. He made this city his capital, and kept Israel in subjection for eighteen years. The people at length "cried unto the Lord" in their distress, and he "raised them up a deliverer" in Ehud (*q.v.*), the son of Gera, a Benjamite.

(2.) A city in Judah, near Lachish (Josh. 15:39). It was destroyed by Joshua (10: 5, 6). It has been identified with *Tell Nejileh*, 6 miles south of *Tell Hesy.* (See LACHISH.)

E′gypt, the land of the Nile and the pyramids, the oldest kingdom of which we have any record, holds a place of great significance in Scripture. Its Hebrew name is *Mizraim;* a dual form, pointing to the two divisions of the country, Upper and Lower Egypt, or, as some think, the two strips of fertile land on the two sides of the Nile. The common Coptic name of the country is *Keme* or *Kam* (*i.e.,* "the black land"), with reference to the colour of the soil. It is called also "the land of Ham" (Ps. 105:23, 27; comp. 78:51), and "Rahab" (87:4; 89:10, etc.). The origin of the name "Egypt," first met with in its Greek form in Homer, is unknown. It is supposed to mean "the land of the Copts."

Herodotus has called Egypt "the gift of the Nile." But for that river, it would have been a barren desert. From year to year, with wonderful regularity, the Nile begins to rise about the middle of July, attaining its greatest height in the end of September or beginning of October, when it begins, at first slowly, and afterwards more rapidly, to fall, till it reaches its lowest level in April or May. When at its height its waters spread over the whole valley, covering it with a black sediment which enriches the soil. This is soon covered with all manner of luxuriant crops.

Egypt is a great oasis, extending from where the Nile issues from the granite rocks of the First Cataract in a direct line to the Mediterranean, a distance of about 600 miles. This is divided into two parts. (1.) The Delta (so called from its resembling in form the Greek letter delta, Δ) is a large triangular plain, extending along the Mediterranean coast for about 200 miles, and up the Nile for 100 miles. (2.) From this point of the Nile to the First Cataract, a distance of about 500 miles, is the Nile valley, which ranges in breadth from 10 to 30 miles. The Delta and the Nile valley have together an area of about 9,600 square miles. Modern Egypt is, however, much more extensive. It is bounded on the north by the Mediterranean, on the south by Nubia, on the east by the Red Sea, and on the west by the Great Desert.

Egypt is of chief interest to us from its

THE NILE VALLEY.

place in Bible history. It was colonized at a very early period by the descendants of Mizraim, the second son of Ham, who probably came from the east along the Persian Gulf, then across Northern Arabia and the isthmus of Suez. It was an old, flourishing, and settled kingdom in the time of Abraham. "The first Egyptian monarchy had had its seat at Memphis ages before Jacob's day; and the kings of

SPHINX AND PYRAMIDS.

the Old Empire who flourished there had left monuments of their greatness which were old in the times of the patriarchs, and still astonish the world. Huge dikes like those of Holland were made by them to keep the Nile from flooding the cities, which themselves were built on artificial mounds raised high above the level of the annual inundations. The turquoise mines of the Sinai peninsula had been discovered, and were vigorously worked. The forced labour of tens of thousands had built the gigantic masses of the pyramids of lime-stone from the quarries of the neighbour-ing Arabian hills, cased with huge blocks of granite from Assouan at the First Cata-ract far up the river, wonderfully polished, and cut with an exactness which modern skill still envies."—Geikie's *Hours, etc.*, ii. 6.

The Old Empire founded by Menes at length came to an end, and was succeeded by the Middle Empire, the seat of govern-ment being shifted from Memphis to Thebes. After a short period the Hyksôs or shep-herd-kings successfully invaded the land,

and fixed their capital at Zoan (*q.v.*). The Hyksôs were ultimately expelled by Aah-mes, or, as he is sometimes called, Amosis, the first king of the eighteenth dynasty of purely Egyptian kings.

The nineteenth dynasty was founded by Seti I., the "king which knew not Joseph." He was succeeded by his son, the great Rameses II. (See PHARAOH.)

In the year B.C. 343 the Persians under Cambyses conquered the country, and after them the Greeks (B.C. 332) under Alexander ruled over it, and Egypt became a Greek kingdom. For the space of three hundred years the Ptolemies, the successors of Alex-ander, swayed the sceptre over the valley of the Nile, and the country flourished in all the arts of agriculture and commerce. After the battle of Actium in 30 A.D., Egypt be-came a Roman province, and on the division of the Roman empire (A.D. 337), it fell to the lot of Constantinople. In 638 A.D. it was subdued by the Moslems, and in 1517 by the Turks. It remains to this day nomin-ally a part of the Turkish empire.

When Abraham and Sarah went down into Egypt (B.C. 1920) it was ruled by Hyksós monarchs, who held their court at Zoan, and the king then on the throne bore the Egyptian title of Pharaoh. The inhabitants spoke the Semitic language, so that Abraham could converse with them. The history of Joseph (q.v.) begins a connection with Egypt full of momentous consequences for the descendants of the patriarch. Jacob and his family are at length brought down into Egypt, and have their dwellings in the land of Goshen (q.v.), where they "grew and multiplied exceedingly." The sacred narrative (Ex. 1:8, 14, etc.) reveals the oppression and cruel bondage to which the Hebrews were subjected, probably under Rameses II. (Sesostris of the Greeks), "Pharaoh of the oppression," and the wonderful interpositions of God in their behalf.

Egypt is the "monumental land of the earth," "the land of wonders." Its natural features and its history are alike extraordinary. Its ruined cities and palaces and

STONE WITH HIEROGLYPHICS

Found at the great temple of Karnak. The inscription is read from right to left. The first leaf (first line) represents *J*, the second *o*, the bird *u*. The hand (second line) represents *d*. The sign below the hand *h*. The next sign *m*, that above the lion *a*, the lion *l*, and the sign below the lion *k*. The sign at the bottom indicates that the name of a land is denoted. The whole inscription is read *Iudha Malek*. It is thought to denote the victory which Shishak, king of Egypt, gained over Rehoboam (1 Kings 14:25, 26).

temples, its pyramids and its obelisks, and its hieroglyphics, which scholars can now read and interpret, make it, of all countries

in the world, full of profound interest to the antiquary and to the student of the Bible, which receives numberless confirmations from the facts it now lays open to view.

A number of remarkable clay tablets were recently discovered at Tell-el-Amarna in Upper Egypt. The clay from different parts of Palestine differs, so that it has been found possible by the clay alone to decide where the tablets come from, when the name of the writer is lost. The inscriptions are cuneiform, and in the Aramaic language, resembling Assyrian. The writers are Phœnicians, Amorites, and Philistines, but in no instance Hittites, though Hittites are mentioned. The tablets consist of official despatches and letters, dating from B.C. 1480, addressed to the two Pharaohs, Amenôphis III. and IV., the last of this dynasty, from the kings and governors of Phœnicia and Palestine. There occur the names of three kings killed by Joshua—Adoni-zedec, king of Jerusalem, Japhia, king of Lachish (Josh. 10:3), and Jabin, king of Hazor (11:1); also the Hebrews (*Abiri*) are said to have come from the desert. "These letters are the most important historical records ever found in connection with the Bible. They most fully confirm the historical statements of the Book of Joshua, and prove the antiquity of civilization in Syria and Palestine."— Conder's *Tell Amarna Tablets*, page 6.

The principal prophecies of Scripture regarding Egypt are these, Isa. 19; Jer. 43: 8-13; 44:30; 46; Ezek. 29-32; and it might be easily shown that they have all been remarkably fulfilled. For example, the singular disappearance of Noph (*i.e.*, Memphis) is a fulfilment of Jer. 46:19; Ezek. 30:13.

E'hud—*union.* (1.) A descendant of Benjamin (1 Chr. 7:18)—his great grandson.

(2.) The son of Gera, of the tribe of Benjamin (Judg. 3:15). After the death of Othniel the people again fell into idolatry, and Eglon, the king of Moab, uniting his bands with those of the Ammonites and the Amalekites, crossed the Jordan and took the city of Jericho, and for eighteen years held that whole district in subjection, exacting from it an annual tribute. At length Ehud, by a stratagem, put Eglon to death with a two-edged dagger a cubit long, and routed the Moabites at the fords of the Jordan, putting 10,000 of them to death. Thenceforward the land, at least Benjamin, enjoyed rest "for fourscore years" (Judg. 3:12–30). (See QUARRIES [2].) But in the south-west the Philistines reduced the Israelites to great straits (Judg. 5:6). From this oppression Shamgar was raised up to be their deliverer.

Ek'ron—*firm-rooted*—the most northerly of the five towns belonging to the lords of the Philistines, about 11 miles north of Gath. It was assigned to Judah (Josh. 13: 3), and afterwards to Dan (19:43), but came again into the full possession of the Philistines (1 Sam. 5:10). It was the last place to which the Philistines carried the ark before they sent it back to Israel (1 Sam. 5:10; 6:1–8). There was here a noted sanctuary of Baal-zebub (2 Kings 1: 2, 3, 6, 16). With the other cities of the Philistines it is denounced by the prophets (Jer. 25:20; Amos 1:8; Zeph. 2: 4; Zech. 9:5, 7): "Ekron shall be rooted up."

E'lah—*terebinth* or *oak*. (1.) Valley of, where the Israelites were encamped when David killed Goliath (1 Sam. 17:2, 19). It was near Shochoh of Judah and Azekah (17: 1). It is the modern *Wâdy es-Sŭnt*—*i.e.*, "valley of the acacia." "The terebinths from which the valley of Elah takes its name still cling to their ancient soil. On the

VALLEY OF ELAH (WÂDY ES-SŬNT).

west side of the valley, near Shochoh, there is a very large and ancient tree of this kind known as the 'terebinth of Wady Sur,' 55 feet in height, its trunk 17 feet in circumference, and the breadth of its shade no less than 75 feet. It marks the upper end of the Elah valley, and forms a noted object, being one of the largest terebinths in Palestine."—Geikie's *The Holy Land, etc.*

(2.) One of the Edomite chiefs or "dukes" of Mount Seir (Gen. 36:41).

(3.) The second of the three sons of Caleb, the son of Jephunneh (1 Chr. 4:15).

(4.) The son and successor of Baasha, king of Israel (1 Kings 16:8–10). He was killed while drunk by Zimri, one of the captains of his chariots, and was the last king of the line of Baasha. Thus was fulfilled the prophecy of Jehu (6, 7, 11–14).

(5.) The father of Hoshea, the last king of Israel (2 Kings 15:30; 17:1).

E'lam—*highland*—the son of Shem (Gen. 10:22), and the name of the country inhabited by his descendants (14:1, 9; Isa.11:11; 21:2, etc.) lying to the east of Babylonia, and extending to the shore of the Mediterranean, a distance in a direct line of about 1,000 miles. The name *Elam* is an Assyrian word meaning "high." "*Elam* was itself a translation of the Accadian *Numma*, under which the Accadians included the whole of the highlands which bounded the plain of Babylonia on its eastern side. It was the seat of an ancient monarchy which rivalled in antiquity that of Chaldea itself, and was long a dangerous neighbour to the latter. It was finally overthrown, however, by Assur-bani-pal, the Assyrian king, about B.C. 645. The native title of the country was Anzan or Ansan; and the name of its capital, Susan or Shushan, seems to have signified 'the old town' in the language of its inhabitants" (A. H. Sayce). This country was called by the Greeks Cissia or Susiana. It was a strong kingdom in the days of Abraham (Gen. 14 : 1–12). It was a "province" of Babylonia in the time of Belshazzar, and afterwards formed a part of the Medo-Persian empire.

E'lamite (Ezra 4 : 9), an original inhabitant of the country of Elam, and a descendant of Shem (Gen. 10 : 22).

The Elamites who were in Jerusalem at the feast of Pentecost (Acts 2 : 9) were probably descendants of the captive tribes who had settled in Elam. (Comp. Isa. 11 : 11).

El'asah—*God made*. (1.) One of the descendants of Judah, of the family of Hezron (1 Chr. 2 : 39, "Eleasah").

(2.) A descendant of king Saul (1 Chr. 8 : 37; 9 : 43).

(3.) The son of Shaphan, one of the two who were sent by Zedekiah to Nebuchadnezzar, and also took charge of Jeremiah's letter to the captives in Babylon (Jer. 29 : 3).

E'lath—*grove; trees*—(Deut. 2 : 8), also in plural form **Eloth** (1 Kings 9 : 26, etc.); called by the Greeks and Romans Elana; a city of Idumea, on the east—*i.e.*, the Elanitic—gulf, or the Gulf of Akabah, of the Red Sea. It is first mentioned in Deut. 2 : 8. It is also mentioned along with Ezion-geber in 1 Kings 9 : 26. It was within the limits of Solomon's dominion, but afterwards revolted. It was, however, recovered and held for a time under king Uzziah (2 Kings 14 : 22).

El-Beth'el—*God of Bethel*—the name of the place where Jacob had the vision of the ladder, and where he erected an altar (Gen. 31 : 13; 35 : 7).

El'dad—*whom God has loved*—one of the seventy elders whom Moses appointed (Num. 11 : 26, 27) to administer justice among the people. He, with Medad, pro-

phesied in the camp instead of going with the rest to the tabernacle, as Moses had commanded. This incident was announced to Moses by Joshua, who thought their conduct in this respect irregular. Moses replied, "Enviest thou for my sake? would God that all the Lord's people were prophets" (Num. 11 : 24–30; comp. Mark 9 : 38; Luke 9 : 49).

Elder, a name frequently used in the Old Testament as denoting a person clothed with authority, and entitled to respect and reverence (Gen. 50 : 7). It also denoted a political office (Num. 22 : 7). The "elders of Israel" held a rank among the people indicative of authority. Moses opened his commission to them (Ex. 3 : 16). They attended Moses on all important occasions. Seventy of them attended on him at the giving of the law (Ex. 24 : 1). Seventy also were selected from the whole number to bear with Moses the burden of the people (Num. 11 : 16, 17). The "elder" is the keystone of the social and political fabric wherever the patriarchal system exists. At the present day this is the case among the Arabs, where the sheik (*i.e.*, "the old man") is the highest authority in the tribe. The body of the "elders" of Israel were the representatives of the people from the very first, and were recognized as such by Moses. All down through the history of the Jews we find mention made of the elders as exercising authority among the people. They appear as governors (Deut. 31 : 28), as local magistrates (16 : 18), administering justice (19 : 12). They were men of extensive influence (1 Sam. 30 : 26–31). In New Testament times they also appear taking an active part in public affairs (Matt. 16 : 21; 21 : 23; 26 : 59).

The Jewish eldership was transferred from the old dispensation to the *new*. "The creation of the office of elder is nowhere recorded in the New Testament, as in the case of deacons and apostles, because the latter offices were created to meet new and special emergencies, while the former was transmitted from the earliest times. In other words, the office of elder was the only permanent essential office of the church under either dispensation."

The "elders" of the New Testament church were the "pastors" (Eph. 4:11), "bishops or overseers" (Acts 20:28), "leaders" and "rulers" (Heb. 13:7; 1 Thess. 5:12) of the flock. Everywhere in the New Testament *bishop* and *presbyter* are titles given to one and the same officer of the Christian church. He who is called presbyter or elder on account of his age or gravity is also called bishop or overseer with reference to the duty that lay upon him (Titus 1:5-7; Acts 20:17-28; Phil. 1:1).

Elea′leh—*God has ascended*—a place in the pastoral country east of Jordan, in the tribe of Reuben (Num. 32:3, 37). It is not again mentioned till the time of Isaiah (15:4; 16:9) and Jeremiah (48:34). It is now an extensive ruin called *el-A'al*, about one mile north-east of Heshbon.

Elea′zar— *God has helped.* (1.) The third son of Aaron (Ex. 6:23). His wife, a daughter of Putiel, bore him Phinehas (Ex. 6:25). After the death of Nadab and Abihu (Lev. 10:12; Num. 3:4) he was appointed to the charge of the sanctuary (Num. 3:32). On Mount Hor he was clothed with the sacred vestments, which Moses took from off his brother Aaron and put upon him as successor to his father in the high priest's office, which he held for more than twenty years (Num. 20:25-29). He took part with Moses in numbering the people (26:3, 4), and assisted at the inauguration of Joshua. He assisted in the distribution of the land after the conquest (Josh. 14:1). The high-priesthood remained in his family till the time of Eli, into whose family it passed, till it was restored to the family of Eleazar in the person of Zadok (1 Sam. 2:25; comp. 1 Kings 2:27). "And Eleazar the son of Aaron died; and they buried him in a hill that pertained to Phinehas his son" (Josh. 24:33). The word here rendered "hill" is *Gibeah*, the name of several towns in Palestine which were generally on or near a hill. The words may be more suitably rendered, "They buried him in Gibeah of Phinehas"—*i.e.*, in the city of Phinehas, which has been identified, in accordance with Jewish and Samaritan traditions, with *Kefr Ghuweirah=′Awertah*, about 7

miles north of Shiloh, and a few miles south-east of Nablûs. "His tomb is still shown there, overshadowed by venerable terebinths." Others, however, have identified it with the village of Gaba or Gebena of Eusebius, the modern *Khŭrbet Jibia*, 5 miles north of Guphna towards Nablûs.

(2.) An inhabitant of Kirjath-jearim who was "sanctified" to take charge of the ark, although not allowed to touch it, while it remained in the house of his father Abinadab (1 Sam. 7:1, 2; comp. Num. 3:31; 4:15).

(3.) The son of Dodo the Ahohite, of the tribe of Benjamin, one of the three most eminent of David's thirty-seven heroes (1 Chr. 11:12) who broke through the Philistine host and brought him water from the well of Bethlehem (2 Sam. 23:9, 16).

(4.) A son of Phinehas associated with the priests in taking charge of the sacred vessels brought back to Jerusalem after the Exile (Ezra 8:33).

(5.) A Levite of the family of Merari (1 Chr. 23:21, 22).

Election of Grace. The Scripture speaks (1) of the election of individuals to office or to honour and privilege—*e.g.*, Abraham, Jacob, Saul, David, Solomon, were all chosen by God for the positions they held; so also were the apostles. (2) There is also an election of nations to special privileges—*e.g.*, the Hebrews (Deut. 7:6; Rom. 9:4). (3) But in addition there is an election of individuals to eternal life (2 Thess. 2:13; Eph. 1:4; 1 Pet. 1:2; John 13:18).

The ground of this election to salvation is the good pleasure of God (Eph. 1:5, 11; Matt. 11:25, 26; John 15:16, 19). God claims the right so to do (Rom. 9:16, 21).

It is not conditioned on faith or repentance, but is of sovereign grace (Rom. 11:4-6; Eph. 1:3-6). All that pertain to salvation, the means (Eph. 2:8; 2 Thess. 2:13) as well as the end, are of God (Acts 5:31; 2 Tim. 2:25; 1 Cor. 1:30; Eph. 2:5, 10). Faith and repentance and all other graces are the exercises of a regenerated soul; and regeneration is God's work, a "new creature."

Men are elected "to salvation," "to the adoption of sons," "to be holy and without blame before him in love" (2 Thess. 2:13; Gal. 4:4, 5; Eph. 1:4).

The ultimate end of election is the praise of God's grace (Eph. 1:6, 12). (See PRE-DESTINATION.)

Elect lady, to whom the Second Epistle of John is addressed (2 John 1). Some think that the word rendered "lady" is a proper name, and thus that the expression should be "elect Kyria."

El-elo′he-Is′rael—*mighty one; God of Israel*—the name which Jacob gave to the altar which he erected on the piece of land where he pitched his tent before Shechem, and which he afterwards purchased from the sons of Hamor (Gen. 33:20).

El′ements. In its primary sense, as denoting the first principles or constituents of things, it is used in 2 Pet. 3:10: "The elements shall be dissolved." In a secondary sense it denotes the first principles of any art or science. In this sense it is used in Gal. 4:3, 9; Col. 2:8, 20, where the expressions, "elements of the world," "weak and beggarly elements," denote that state of religious knowledge existing among the Jews before the coming of Christ—the rudiments of religious teaching. They are "of the world," because they are made up of types which appeal to the senses. They are "weak," because insufficient; and "beggarly," or "poor," because they are dry and barren, not being accompanied by an outpouring of spiritual gifts and graces, as the gospel is.

El′ephant, not found in Scripture except indirectly in the original Greek word (*elephantinos*) translated "of ivory" in Rev. 18:12, and in the Hebrew word (*shenhab-bim*, meaning "elephant's tooth") rendered "ivory" in 1 Kings 10:22 and 2 Chr. 9:21.

Elha′nan—*whom God has graciously bestowed*. (1.) A warrior of the time of David famed for his exploits. In the Authorized Version (2 Sam. 21:19) it is recorded that "Elhanan the son of Jaare-oregim, a Bethlehemite, slew *the brother of* Goliath." The Revised Version here rightly omits the words "the brother of." They were introduced in the Authorized Version to bring this passage into agreement with 1 Chr. 20:5, where it is said that he "slew Lahmi the brother of Goliath." Goliath the Gittite was killed by David (1 Sam. 17). The exploit of Elhanan took place late in David's reign.

(2.) The son of Dodo, and one of David's warriors (2 Sam. 23:24).

E′li—*ascent*—the high priest when the ark was at Shiloh (1 Sam. 1:3, 9). He was the first of the line of Ithamar, Aaron's fourth son (1 Chr. 24:3; comp. 2 Sam. 8:17), who held that office. The office remained in his family till the time of Abiathar (1 Kings 2:26, 27), whom Solomon deposed, and appointed Zadok, of the family of Eleazar, in his stead (35). He acted also as a civil judge in Israel after the death of Samson (1 Sam. 4:18), and judged Israel for forty years.

His sons Hophni and Phinehas grossly misconducted themselves, to the great disgust of the people (1 Sam. 2:27-36). They were licentious reprobates. He failed to reprove them so sternly as he ought to have done, and so brought upon his house the judgment of God (2:22-33; 3:18). The Israelites proclaimed war against the Philistines, whose army was encamped at Aphek. The battle, fought a short way beyond Mizpeh, ended in the total defeat of Israel. Four thousand of them fell in "battle array." They now sought safety in having the "ark of the covenant of the Lord" among them. They fetched it from Shiloh, and Hophni and Phinehas accompanied it. This was the first time since the settlement of Israel in Canaan that the ark had been removed from the sanctuary. The Philistines put themselves again in array against Israel, and in the battle which ensued "Israel was smitten, and there was a very great slaughter." The tidings of this great disaster were speedily conveyed to Shiloh, about 20 miles distant, by a messenger, a Benjamite from the army. There Eli sat outside the gate of the sanctuary by the wayside, anxiously waiting for tidings from the battle-field. The full extent of the national calamity was speedily made known to him: "Israel is fled before the Philistines, there has also been a great slaughter among the people, thy two sons Hophni and Phinehas are dead, and the ark of God is taken"(1 Sam. 4:12-18). When the old man, whose eyes were "stiffened" (*i.e.*, fixed, as of a blind eye unaffected by the light) with age, heard this sad story of woe, he fell backward from off his seat and died, being ninety and eight years old. (See ITHAMAR.)

Eli'—Heb. *ēli*, "my God"—(Matt. 27: 46), an exclamation used by Christ on the cross. Mark (15:34), as usual, gives the original Aramaic form of the word, *Eloi*.

Eli'ab—*to whom God is father*. (1.) A Reubenite, son of Pallu (Num. 16:1, 12; 26:8, 9; Deut. 11:6).

(2.) A son of Helon, and chief of the tribe of Zebulun at the time of the census in the wilderness (Num. 1:9; 2:7).

(3.) The son of Jesse, and brother of David (1 Sam. 16:6). It was he who spoke contemptuously to David when he proposed to fight Goliath (1 Sam. 17:28).

(4.) One of the Gadite heroes who joined David in his stronghold in the wilderness (1 Chr. 12:9).

Eli'ada—*whom God cares for*. (1.) One of David's sons born after his establishment in Jerusalem (2 Sam. 5:16).

(2.) A mighty man of war, a Benjamite (2 Chr. 17:17).

(3.) An Aramite of Zobah, captain of a marauding band that troubled Solomon (1 Kings 11:23).

Eli'akim—*whom God will raise up*. (1.) The son of Melea (Luke 3:30), and probably grandson of Nathan.

(2.) The son of Abiud, of the posterity of Zerubbabel (Matt. 1:13).

(3.) The son of Hilkiah, who was sent to receive the message of the invading Assyrians and report it to Isaiah (2 Kings 18: 18; 19:2; Isa. 36:3; 37:2). In his office as governor of the palace of Hezekiah he succeeded Shebna (Isa. 22:15-26). He was a good man (Isa. 22:20; 2 Kings 18:37), and had a splendid and honourable career.

(4.) The original name of Jehoiakim, king of Judah (2 Kings 23:34). He was the son of Josiah.

Eli'am—*God's people*. (1.) The father of Bathsheba, the wife of Uriah (2 Sam. 11:3). In 1 Chr. 3:5 his name is Ammiel.

(2.) This name also occurs as that of a Gilonite, the son of Ahithophel, and one of David's thirty warriors (2 Sam. 23:34). Perhaps these two were the same person.

Eli'as, the Greek form of Elijah (Matt. 11:14; 16:14, etc.), which the Revised Version has uniformly adopted in the New Testament. (See ELIJAH.)

Eli'ashib—*whom God will restore*. (1.) A priest, head of one of the courses of the priests of the time of David (1 Chr. 24:12).

(2.) A high priest in the time of Ezra and Nehemiah (Neh. 12:22, 23). He rebuilt the eastern city wall (3:1), his own mansion being in that quarter, on the ridge Ophel (3:20, 21). His indulgence of Tobiah the Ammonite provoked the indignation of Nehemiah (13:4, 7).

Eli'athah—*to whom God will come*—one of the fourteen sons of the Levite Heman, and musician of the temple in the time of David (1 Chr. 25:4).

Eli'dad—*whom God has loved*—son of Chislon, and chief of the tribe of Benjamin; one of those who were appointed to divide the Promised Land among the tribes (Num. 34:21).

Eli'el—*to whom God is might*. (1.) A chief of Manasseh, on the east of Jordan (1 Chr. 5:24).

(2.) A Gadite who joined David in the hold at Ziklag (1 Chr. 12:11).

(3.) One of the overseers of the offerings in the reign of Hezekiah (2 Chr. 31:13).

Eli'ezer—*God his help*. (1.) "Of Damascus," the "steward" (R.V., "possessor") of Abraham's house (Gen. 15:2, 3). It was probably he who headed the embassy sent by Abraham to the old home of his family in Padan-aram to seek a wife for his son Isaac. The account of this embassy is given at length in Gen. 24.

(2.) The son of Becher, and grandson of Benjamin (1 Chr. 7:8).

(3.) One of the two sons of Moses, born during his sojourn in Midian (Ex. 18:4; 1 Chr. 23:15, 17). He remained with his mother and brother Gershom with Jethro when Moses returned to Egypt (Ex. 18:4). They were restored to Moses when Jethro heard of his departure out of Egypt.

(4.) One of the priests who blew the trumpet before the ark when it was brought to Jerusalem (1 Chr. 15:24).

(5.) Son of Zichri, and chief of the Reubenites under David (1 Chr. 27:16).

(6.) A prophet in the time of Jehoshaphat (2 Chr. 20:37).

THE PLACE OF ELIJAH'S SACRIFICE, CARMEL.

Others of this name are mentioned Luke 3 : 29 ; Ezra 8 : 16 ; 10 : 18, 23, 31.

Eli'hu—*whose God is he.* (1.) "The son of Barachel, a Buzite" (Job 32 : 2), one of Job's friends. When the debate between Job and his friends is brought to a close, Elihu for the first time makes his appearance, and delivers his opinion on the points at issue (Job 32–37).

(2.) The son of Tohu, and grandfather of Elkanah (1 Sam. 1 : 1). He is called also Eliel (1 Chr. 6 ; 34) and Eliab (6 : 27).

(3.) One of the captains of thousands of Manasseh who joined David at Ziklag (1 Chr. 12 : 20).

(4.) One of the family of Obed-edom, who were appointed porters of the temple under David (1 Chr. 26 : 7).

Eli'jah—*whose God is Jehovah.* (1.) "The Tishbite," the "Elias" of the New Testament, is suddenly introduced to our notice in 1 Kings 17 : 1 as delivering a message from the Lord to Ahab. There is mention made of a town called Thisbe, south of Kadesh, but it is impossible to say whether this was the place referred to in the name given to the prophet.

Having delivered his message to Ahab, he retired at the command of God to a hiding-place by the brook Cherith, beyond Jordan, where he was fed by ravens. When the brook dried up God sent him to the widow of Zarephath, a city of Zidon, from whose scanty store he was supported for the space of two years. During this period the widow's son died, and was restored to life by Elijah (1 Kings 17: 2-24).

During all these two years a famine prevailed in the land. At the close of this period of retirement and of preparation for his work (comp. Gal. 1:17, 18) Elijah met Obadiah, one of Ahab's officers, whom he had sent out to seek for pasturage for the cattle, and bade him go and tell his master that Elijah was there. The king came and met Elijah, and reproached him as the troubler of Israel. It was then proposed that sacrifices should be publicly offered, for the purpose of determining whether Baal or Jehovah were the true God. This was done on Carmel, with the result that the people fell on their faces, crying, "The Lord, he is the God." Thus was accomplished the great work of Elijah's ministry. The prophets of Baal were then put to death by the order of Elijah. Not one of them escaped. Then immediately followed rain, according to the word of Elijah, and in answer to his prayer (James 5:18).

Jezebel, enraged at the fate that had befallen her priests of Baal, threatened to put Elijah to death (1 Kings 19:1-13). He therefore fled in alarm to Beersheba, and thence went alone a day's journey into the wilderness, and sat down in despondency under a juniper tree. As he slept an angel touched him, and said unto him, "Arise and eat; because the journey is too great for thee." He arose and found a cake and a cruse of water. Having partaken of the provision thus miraculously supplied, he went forward on his solitary way for forty days and forty nights to Horeb, the mount of God, where he took up his abode in a cave. Here the Lord appeared unto him and said, "What dost thou here, Elijah?" In answer to his despondent words God manifests to him his glory, and then directs him to return to Damascus and anoint Hazael king over Syria, and Jehu king over Israel, and Elisha to be prophet in his room (1 Kings 19:13-21; comp. 2 Kings 8:7-15; 9: 1-10).

Some six years after this he warned Ahab and Jezebel of the violent deaths

they would die (1 Kings 21:19-24; 22:38). He also, four years afterwards, warned Ahaziah (*q.v.*), who had succeeded his father Ahab, of his approaching death (2 Kings 1:1-16). (See NABOTH.) During these intervals he probably withdrew to some quiet retirement, no one knew where. His interview with Ahaziah's messengers on the way to Ekron, and the account of the destruction of his captains with their fifties, suggest the idea that he may have been in retirement at this time on Mount Carmel.

The time now drew near when he was to be taken up into heaven (2 Kings 2:1-12). He had a presentiment of what was awaiting him. He went down to Gilgal, where was a school of the prophets, and where his successor Elisha, whom he had anointed some years before, resided. Elisha was solemnized by the thought of his master's leaving him, and refused to be parted from him. "They two went on," and came to Bethel and Jericho, and crossed the Jordan, the waters of which were "divided hither and thither" when smitten with Elijah's mantle. Arrived at the borders of Gilead, which Elijah had left many years before, it "came to pass that while they went on and talked" they were suddenly separated by a chariot and horses of fire; and "Elijah went up by a whirlwind into heaven," Elisha receiving his mantle, which fell from him as he ascended.

No one of the old prophets is so frequently referred to in the New Testament. The priests and Levites said to the Baptist (John 1:25), "Why baptizest thou, if thou be not that Christ, nor Elias?" Paul (Rom. 11:2) refers to an incident in his history to illustrate his argument that God had not cast away his people. James (5:17) finds in him an illustration of the power of prayer. (See also Luke 4:25; 9:54.) He was a type of John the Baptist in the sternness and power of his reproofs (Luke 9:8). He was the Elijah that "must first come" (Matt. 11:11, 14), the forerunner of our Lord announced by Malachi. Even outwardly the Baptist corresponded so closely to the earlier prophet that he might be styled a second

Elijah. In him we see "the same connection with a wild and wilderness country; the same long retirement in the desert; the same sudden, startling entrance on his work (1 Kings 17:1; Luke 3:2); even the same dress—a hairy garment, and a leathern girdle about the loins (2 Kings 1:8; Matt. 3:4)."

How deep the impression was which Elijah made "on the mind of the nation may be judged from the fixed belief, which rested on the words of Malachi (4:5, 6), which many centuries after prevailed that he would again appear for the relief and restoration of the country. Each remarkable person as he arrives on the scene, be his habits and characteristics what they may—the stern John equally with his gentle Successor — is proclaimed to be Elijah (Matt. 11:13, 14; 16:14; 17:10; Mark 9:11; 15:35; Luke 9:7, 8; John 1:21). His appearance in glory on the mount of transfiguration does not seem to have startled the disciples. They were 'sore afraid,' but not apparently surprised."

(2.) The Elijah spoken of in 2 Chr. 21:12-15 is by some supposed to be a different person from the foregoing. He lived in the time of Jehoram, to whom he sent a letter of warning (comp. 1 Chr. 28:19; Jer. 36), and acted as a prophet in Judah; while the Tishbite was a prophet of the northern kingdom. But there does not seem any necessity for concluding that the writer of this letter was some other Elijah than the Tishbite. It may be supposed either that Elijah anticipated the character of Jehoram, and so wrote the warning message, which was preserved in the schools of the prophets till Jehoram ascended the throne after the Tishbite's translation, or that the translation did not actually take place till after the accession of Jehoram to the throne (2 Chr. 21:12; 2 Kings 8:16). The events of 2 Kings 2 may not be recorded in chronological order, and thus there may be room for the opinion that Elijah was still alive in the beginning of Jehoram's reign.

Eli'ka — *God is his rejecter* — one of David's thirty-seven distinguished heroes (2 Sam. 23:25).

E'lim—*trees*—(Ex. 15:27; Num. 33:9), the name of the second station where the Israelites encamped after crossing the Red Sea. It had "twelve wells of water and threescore and ten palm trees." It has been identified with the *Wâdy Ghurundel*, the most noted of the four wadies which descend from the range of *et-Tih* towards the sea. Here they probably remained some considerable time. The form of expression in Ex. 16:1 seems to imply that the people proceeded in detachments or companies from Elim, and only for the first time were assembled as a complete host when they reached the wilderness of Sin (*q.v.*).

Elim'elech—*God his king*—a man of the tribe of Judah, of the family of the Hezronites, and kinsman of Boaz, who dwelt in Bethlehem in the days of the judges. In consequence of a great dearth he, with his wife Naomi and his two sons, went to dwell in the land of Moab. There he and his sons died (Ruth 1:23; 2:1, 3; 4:3, 9). Naomi afterwards returned to Palestine with her daughter Ruth.

Elioe'nai—*toward Jehovah are my eyes* —the name of several men mentioned in the Old Testament (1 Chr. 7:8; 4:36; Ezra 10:22, 27). Among these was the eldest son of Neariah, son of Shemaiah, of the descendants of Zerubbabel. His family are the latest mentioned in the Old Testament (1 Chr. 3:23, 24).

Eliph'alet—*God his deliverance*—one of David's sons (2 Sam. 5:16); called also Eliphelet (1 Chr. 3:8).

Eli'phaz—*God his strength*. (1.) One of Job's "three friends" who visited him in his affliction (4:1). He was a "Temanite"—*i.e.*, a native of Teman, in Idumea. He first enters into debate with Job. His language is uniformly more delicate and gentle than that of the other two, although he imputes to Job special sins as the cause of his present sufferings. He states with remarkable force of language the infinite purity and majesty of God (4:12-21; 15:12-16).

(2.) The son of Esau by his wife Adah, and father of several Edomitish tribes (Gen. 36:4, 10, 11, 16).

Eli'pheleh—*God will distinguish him*—one of the porters appointed to play "on the Sheminith" on the occasion of the bringing up of the ark to the city of David (1 Chr. 15 : 18, 21).

Eli'phelet—*God his deliverance.* (1.) One of David's distinguished warriors (2 Sam. 23 : 34); called also Eliphal in 1 Chr. 11 : 35.

(2.) One of the sons of David born at Jerusalem (1 Chr. 3 : 6 ; 14 : 5); called Elipalet in 1 Chr. 14 : 5. Also another of David's sons (1 Chr. 3 : 8); called Eliphalet in 2 Sam. 5 : 16 ; 1 Chr. 14 : 7.

(3.) A descendant of king Saul through Jonathan (1 Chr. 8 : 39).

Elis'abeth—*God her oath*—the mother of John the Baptist (Luke 1 : 5). She was a descendant of Aaron. She and her husband Zacharias (*q.v.*) " were both righteous before God "(Luke 1 : 5, 13). Mary's visit to Elisabeth is described in 1 : 39–63.

Eli'sha—*God his salvation*—the son of Shaphat of Abel-meholah, who became the attendant and disciple of Elijah (1 Kings 19 : 16–19). His name first occurs in the command given to Elijah to anoint him as his successor (1 Kings 19 : 16). This was the only one of the three commands then given to Elijah which he accomplished. On his way from Sinai to Damascus he found Elisha at his native place engaged in the labours of the field, ploughing with twelve yoke of oxen. He went over to him, threw over his shoulders his rough mantle, and at once adopted him as a son, and invested him with the prophetical office (comp. Luke 9 : 61, 62). Elisha accepted the call thus given (about four years before the death of Ahab), and for some seven or eight years became the close attendant on Elijah till he was parted from him and taken up into heaven. During all these years we hear nothing of Elisha except in connection with the closing scenes of Elijah's life. After Elijah, Elisha was accepted as the leader of the sons of the prophets, and became noted in Israel. He possessed, according to his own request, " a double portion " of Elijah's spirit (2 Kings 2 : 9); and for the long period of about sixty years (B.C. 892–832)

held the office of " prophet in Israel " (2 Kings 5 : 8).

After Elijah's departure, Elisha returned to Jericho, and there healed the spring of water by casting salt into it (2 Kings 2 : 21). We next find him at Bethel (2 : 23), where, with the sternness of his master, he cursed the youths who came out and scoffed at him as a prophet of God: "Go up, thou bald head." The judgment at once took effect, and God terribly visited the dishonour done to his prophet as dishonour done to himself. We next read of his predicting a fall of rain when the army of Jehoram was faint from thirst (2 Kings 3 : 9–20); of the multiplying of the poor widow's cruse of oil (4 : 1–7); the miracle of restoring to life the son of the woman of Shunem (4 : 18–37); the multiplication of the twenty loaves of new barley into a sufficient supply for an hundred men (4 : 42–44); of the cure of Naaman the Syrian of his leprosy (5 : 1–27); of the punishment of Gehazi for his falsehood and his covetousness ; of the recovery of the axe lost in the waters of the Jordan (6 : 1–7); of the miracle at Dothan, half-way on the road between Samaria and Jezreel ; of the siege of Samaria by the king of Syria, and of the terrible sufferings of the people in connection with it, and Elisha's prophecy as to the relief that would come (2 Kings 6 : 24–7 : 2).

We then find Elisha at Damascus, to carry out the command given to his master to anoint Hazael king over Syria (2 Kings 8 : 7–15); thereafter he directs one of the sons of the prophets to anoint Jehu, the son of Jehoshaphat, king of Israel, instead of Ahab. Thus the three commands given to Elijah (9 : 1–10) were at length carried out.

We do not again read of him till we find him on his death-bed in his own house (2 Kings 13 : 14–19). Joash, the grandson of Jehu, comes to mourn over his approaching departure, and utters the same words as those of Elisha when Elijah was taken away : "My father, my father ! the chariot of Israel, and the horsemen thereof."

Afterwards when a dead body is laid in Elisha's grave a year after his burial, no sooner does it touch the hallowed remains than the man "revived, and stood up on his feet" (2 Kings 13 : 20–21).

Eli'shah, the oldest of the four sons of Javan (Gen. 10 : 4), whose descendants peopled Greece. It has been supposed that Elishah's descendants peopled the Peloponnesus, which was known by the name of *Elis.* This may be meant by "the isles of Elishah" (Ezek. 27 : 7).

Eli'shama—*whom God hears.* (1.) A prince of Benjamin, grandfather of Joshua (Num. 1 : 10 ; 1 Chr. 7 : 26). (2.) One of David's sons (2 Sam. 5 : 16). (3.) Another of David's sons (1 Chr. 3 : 6). (4.) A priest sent by Jehoshaphat to teach the people the law (2 Chr. 17 : 8).

Eli'shaphat—*whom God has judged*—one of the "captains of hundreds" associated with Jehoiada in the league to overthrow the usurpation of Athaliah (2 Chr. 23 : 1).

Eli'sheba—*God is her oath*—the daughter of Amminadab and the wife of Aaron (Ex. 6 : 23).

Eli'shua—*God his salvation*—a son of David, 2 Sam. 5 : 15 = Elishama, 1 Chr. 3 : 6.

Elka'nah— *God - created.* (1.) The second son of Korah (Ex. 6 : 24), or, according to 1 Chr. 6 : 22, 23, more correctly his grandson.

(2.) Another Levite of the line of Heman the singer, although he does not seem to have performed any of the usual Levitical offices. He was father of Samuel the prophet (1 Chr. 6 : 27, 34). He was "an Ephrathite" (1 Sam. 1 : 1, 4, 8), but lived at Ramah, a man of wealth and high position. He had two wives, Hannah, who was the mother of Samuel, and Peninnah.

El'kosh—*God my bow*—the birth - place of Nahum the prophet (Nah. 1 : 1). It was probably situated in Galilee, but nothing definite is known of it.

El'lasar—*the oak or heap of Assyria*—a territory in Asia of which Arioch was king (Gen. 14 : 1, 9). It is supposed that the old Chaldean town of *Larsa* was the metropolis of this kingdom, situated nearly half-way between Ur (now Mugheir) and Erech, on the left bank of the Euphrates. This town is represented by the mounds of *Senkereh*, a little to the east of Erech.

Elm—Hos. 4 : 13 ; rendered "terebinth" in the Revised Version. It is the *Pistacia terebinthus* of Linn., a tree common in Palestine, long-lived, and therefore often employed for landmarks and in designating places (Gen. 35 : 4 ; Judg. 6 : 11, 19. Rendered "oak" in both A.V. and R.V.). (See TEIL TREE.)

El'nathan—*whom God has given.* (1.) An inhabitant of Jerusalem, the father of Nehushta, who was the mother of king Jehoiachin (2 Kings 24 : 8). Probably the same who tried to prevent Jehoiakim from burning the roll of Jeremiah's prophecies (Jer. 26 : 22 ; 36 : 12). (2.) Ezra 6 : 16.

E'lon—*oak.* (1.) A city of Dan (Josh. 19 : 43). (2.) A Hittite, father of Bashemath, Esau's wife (Gen. 26 : 34). (3.) One of the sons of Zebulun (Gen. 46 : 14). (4.) The eleventh of the Hebrew judges. He held office for ten years (Judg. 12 : 11, 12). He is called the Zebulonite.

Elpa'ran—*oak of Paran*—a place on the edge of the wilderness bordering the territory of the Horites (Gen. 14 : 6). This was the farthest point to which Chedorlaomer's expedition extended. It is identified with the modern desert of *et-Tih.* (See PARAN.)

El'tekeh—*God is its fear*—a city in the tribe of Dan. It was a city of refuge and a Levitical city (Josh. 21 : 23). It has been identified with *Beit - Likia*, north-east of Latrum.

E'lul (Neh. 6 : 15), the name of the sixth month of the ecclesiastical year, and the twelfth of the civil year. It began with the new moon of our August and September, and consisted of twenty-nine days.

El'ymas — *magician* or *sorcerer* — the Arabic name of the Jew Bar-jesus, who withstood Paul and Barnabas in Cyprus. He was miraculously struck with blindness (Acts 13 : 11).

Embalm'ing, the process of preserving a body by means of aromatics (Gen. 50 : 2, 3, 26). This art was practised by the Egyptians from the earliest times, and there brought to great perfection. This custom probably originated in the belief in the future reunion of the soul with the body. The process became more and more complicated, and to such perfection was it carried that bodies embalmed thousands of years ago are preserved to the present day in the numberless mummies that have been discovered in Egypt.

The embalming of Jacob and Joseph was according to the Egyptian custom, which was partially followed by the Jews (2 Chr. 16:14), as in the case of king Asa, and of our Lord (John 19:39, 40; Luke 23:56; 24:1). (See PHARAOH.)

Embroi'der. The art of embroidery was known to the Jews (Ex. 26:36; 35:35; 38:23; Judg. 5:30; Ps. 45:14). The skill of the women in this art was seen in the preparation of the sacerdotal robes of the high priest (Ex. 28). It seems that the art became hereditary in certain families (1 Chr. 4:21). The Assyrians were also noted for their embroidered robes (Ezek. 27:24).

Em'erald—Heb. *nophek* (Ex. 28:18; 39:11); *i.e.*, the "glowing stone"— probably the carbuncle, a precious stone in the breastplate of the high priest. It is mentioned (Rev. 21:19) as one of the foundations of the New Jerusalem. The name given to this stone in the New Testament Greek is *smaragdos*, which means "live coal," a name given by the ancients to several glowing red stones resembling live coals, particularly rubies and garnets.

MUMMY CASE OF QUEEN NEFERT-ARI (*see page 543*).

The modern emerald is a species of beryl of a greenish colour.

Em'erod. See, HÆMORRHOIDS.

E'mims—*terrors*—a warlike tribe of giants who were defeated by Chedorlaomer and his allies in the plain of Kiriathaim. In the time of Abraham they occupied the country east of Jordan, afterwards the land of the Moabites (Gen. 14:5; Deut. 2:10). They were, like the Anakim, reckoned among the Rephaim, and were conquered by the Moabites, who gave them the name of Emims—*i.e.*, "terrible men" (Deut. 2:11). The Ammonites called them Zamzummims (2:20).

Emman'uel—*God with us*—(Matt. 1:23). (See IMMANUEL.)

Emma'us—*hot baths*—a village "threescore furlongs" from Jerusalem, where our Lord had an interview with two of his disciples on the day of his resurrection (Luke 24:13). This has been identified with the modern *el-Kubeibeh*, lying over 7 miles north-west of Jerusalem. This name, el-Kubeibeh, meaning "little dome," is derived from the remains of the Crusaders' church yet to be found there. Others have identified it with the modern *Khŭrbet Khamasa*—*i.e.*, "the ruins of Khamasa"—about 8 miles south-west of Jerusalem, where there are ruins also of a Crusaders' church. Its site, however, has been much disputed.

Em'mor — *an ass* — Acts 7:16. (See HAMOR.)

Encamp'. An encampment was the resting-place for a longer or shorter period of an army or company of travellers (Ex. 13:20; 14:19; Josh. 10:5; 11:5).

The manner in which the Israelites encamped during their march through the wilderness is described in Num. 2 and 3. The order of the encampment (see CAMP) was preserved in the march (Num. 2:17), the signal for which was the blast of two silver trumpets. Detailed regulations affecting the camp for sanitary purposes are given (Lev. 4:11, 12; 6:11; 8:17; 10:4, 5; 13:46; 14:3; Num. 12:14, 15; 31:19; Deut. 23:10, 12).

Criminals were executed without the camp (Lev. 4:12; comp. John 19:17, 20), and there also the young bullock for a sin-offering was burnt (Lev. 24:14; comp. Heb. 13:12).

In the subsequent history of Israel frequent mention is made of their encampments in the time of war (Judg. 7:18; 1 Sam. 13:2, 3, 16, 23; 17:3; 29:1; 30:9, 24). The temple was sometimes called "the camp of the LORD" (2 Chr. 31:2, R.V.; comp. Ps. 78:28). The multitudes who flocked to David are styled "a great host (*i.e.*, "camp;" Heb. *maḥaneh*), like the host of God" (1 Chr. 12:22).

Enchant'ments. (1.) The rendering of Hebrew *latim* or *lehatim*, which means "something covered," "muffled up;" secret arts, tricks (Ex. 7:11, 22; 8:7, 18), by which the Egyptian magicians imposed on the credulity of Pharaoh.

(2.) The rendering of the Hebrew *keshaphim*, "muttered spells" or "incantations," rendered "sorceries" in Isa. 47:9, 12—*i.e.*, the using of certain formulæ under the belief that men could thus be bound.

(3.) Hebrew *lehashim*, "charming," as of serpents (Jer. 8:17; comp. Ps. 58:5).

(4.) Hebrew *nehashim*, the enchantments or omens used by Balaam (Num. 24:1); his endeavouring to gain omens favourable to his design.

(5.) Hebrew *heber* (Isa. 47:9,10), "magical spells." All kinds of enchantments were condemned by the Mosaic law (Lev. 19: 26; Deut. 18:10-12). (See DIVINATION.)

End, in Heb. 13:7, is the rendering of the unusual Greek word *ekbasin*, meaning "outcome"—*i.e.*, death. It occurs only elsewhere in 1 Cor. 10:13, where it is rendered "escape."

En'dor—*fountain of Dor; i.e.*, "of the age"—a place in the territory of Issachar (Josh. 17:11) near the scene of the great victory which was gained by Deborah and Barak over Sisera and Jabin (comp. Ps. 83:9, 10). To Endor, Saul resorted to consult one reputed to be a witch on the eve of his last engagement with the Philistines (1 Sam. 28:7). It is identified with the modern village of *Endûr*, "a dirty hamlet of some twenty houses, or rather huts, most of them falling to ruin," on the northern slope of Little Hermon, about 7 miles from Jezreel.

En-eg'laim—*fountain of two calves*—a place mentioned only in Ezek. 47:10. Somewhere near the Dead Sea.

En-gan'nim—*fountain of gardens.* (1.) A town in the plains of Judah (Josh. 15: 34), north-west of Jerusalem, between Zanoah and Tappuah. It is the modern *Umm Jina.*

(2.) A city on the border of Machar (Josh. 19:21), allotted to the Gershonite Levites (21:29). It is identified with the modern *Jenîn*, a large and prosperous town

of about 4,000 inhabitants, situated 15 miles south of Mount Tabor, through which the road from Jezreel to Samaria and Jerusalem passes. When Ahaziah, king of Judah, attempted to escape from Jehu, he "fled by the way of the garden house"— *i.e.*, by way of En-gannim. Here he was overtaken by Jehu and wounded in his chariot, and turned aside and fled to Megiddo, a distance of about 20 miles, to die there.

Enge'di—*fountain of the kid*—a place in the wilderness of Judah (Josh. 15:62), on the western shore of the Dead Sea (Ezek. 47:10), and nearly equidistant from both extremities. To the wilderness near this town David fled for fear of Saul (Josh. 15:62; 1 Sam. 23:29). It was at first called Hazezon-tamar (Gen. 14:7), a city of the Amorites.

The vineyards of Engedi were celebrated in Solomon's time (Cant. 1:4). It is the modern *'Ain Jidy.* The "fountain" from which it derives its name rises on the mountain side about 600 feet above the sea, and in its rapid descent spreads luxuriance all around it. Along its banks the *osher* grows abundantly. That shrub is thus described by Porter:—"The stem is stout, measuring sometimes nearly a foot in diameter, and the plant grows to the height of 15 feet or more. It has a grayish bark and long oval leaves, which when broken off discharge a milky fluid. The fruit resembles an apple, and hangs in clusters of two or three. When ripe it is of a rich yellow colour, but on being pressed it explodes like a puff-ball. It is chiefly filled with air......This is the so-called 'apple of Sodom.'"—*Through Samaria, etc.* (See APPLE.)

En'gines. (1.) Heb. *hishshalon*—*i.e.*, "invention" (as in Eccl. 7:29)—contrivances indicating *ingenuity.* In 2 Chr. 26: 15 it refers to inventions for the purpose of propelling missiles from the walls of a town, such as stones (the Roman *balista*) and arrows (the *catapulta*).

(2.) Heb. *mechi kobolló*—*i.e.*, the *beating* of that which is in *front*—a battering-ram (Ezek. 26:9), the use of which was common among the Egyptians and the Assyrians.

Such an engine is mentioned in the reign of David (2 Sam. 20:15).

Engra'ver—Heb. *harash*—(Ex. 35:35; 38:23) means properly an *artificer* in wood, stone, or metal. The chief business of the engraver was cutting names or devices on rings and seals and signets (Ex. 28:11, 21, 36; Gen. 38:18).

En-hak'kore—*fountain of the crier*—the name of the spring in Lehi which burst forth in answer to Samson's prayer when he was exhausted with the slaughter of the Philistines (Judg. 15:19). It has been identified with the spring *'Ayûn Kara*, near Zoreah.

Enmity, deep-rooted hatred. "I will put enmity between thee and the woman, between thy seed and her seed" (Gen. 3:15). The friendship of the world is "enmity with God" (James 4:4; 1 John 2:15, 16). The "carnal mind" is "enmity against God" (Rom. 8:7). By the abrogation of the Mosaic institutes the "enmity" between Jew and Gentile is removed. They are reconciled, are "made one" (Eph. 2:15, 16).

E'noch—*initiated*. (1.) The eldest son of Cain (Gen. 4:17), who built a city east of Eden in the land of Nod, and called it "after the name of his son Enoch." This is the first "city" mentioned in Scripture.

(2.) The son of Jared, and father of Methuselah (Gen. 5:21; Luke 3:37). His

BIR EYÛB.

father was one hundred and sixty-two years old when he was born. After the birth of Methuselah, Enoch "walked with God three hundred years" (Gen. 5:22-24), when he was translated without tasting death. His whole life on earth was three hundred and sixty-five years. He was the "seventh from Adam" (Jude 14), as distinguished from the son of Cain, the third from Adam. He is spoken of in the catalogue of Old Testament worthies in the Epistle to the Hebrews (11:5). When he was translated, only Adam, so far as recorded, had as yet died a natural death, and Noah was not yet born. Mention is made of Enoch's prophesying only in Jude 14.

E'nos—*man*—the son of Seth, and grandson of Adam (Gen. 5:6-11; Luke 3:38). He lived nine hundred and five years. In his time "men began to call upon the name of the Lord" (Gen. 4:26), meaning either (1) then began men to call themselves by the name of the Lord (marg.) —*i.e.*, to distinguish themselves thereby from idolaters; or (2) then men in some public and earnest way began to call upon the Lord, indicating a time of spiritual revival.

En-ro'gel—*fountain of the treaders; i.e.,* "foot-fountain;" also called the "fullers' fountain," because fullers here trod the clothes in water. It has been identified with the "fountain of the virgin" (*q.v.*), the modern *'Ain Umm el-Daraj*. Others identify it, with perhaps some probability, with the *Bir Eyûb*, to the south of the Pool of

Siloam, and below the junction of the valleys of Kidron and Hinnom. (See FOUNTAIN.)

It was at this fountain that Jonathan and Ahimaaz lay hid after the flight of David (2 Sam. 17:17); and here also Adonijah held the feast when he aspired to the throne of his father (1 Kings 1:9).

The Bir Eyûb, or "Joab's well," "is a singular work of ancient enterprise. The shaft sunk through the solid rock in the bed of the Kidron is 125 feet deep......The water is pure and entirely sweet, quite different from that of Siloam ; which proves that there is no connection between them."—Thomson's *Land and the Book.*

En-she'mesh—*fountain of the sun*—a spring which formed one of the landmarks on the boundary between Judah and Benjamin (Josh. 15:7; 18:17). It was between the "ascent of Adummim" and the spring of En-rogel, and hence was on the east of Jerusalem and of the Mount of Olives. It is the modern *'Ain-Haud—i.e.*, the "well of the apostles"—about a mile east of Bethany, the only spring on the road to Jericho. The sun shines on it the whole day long.

En'sign. (1.) Heb. *'oth*, a military standard, especially of a single tribe (Num. 2:2). Each separate tribe had its own "sign" or "ensign."

(2.) Heb. *nês*, a lofty signal, as a column or high pole (Num. 21:8, 9); a standard or signal or flag placed on high mountains to point out to the people a place of rendezvous on the irruption of an enemy (Isa. 5:26; 11:12; 18:3; 62:10; Jer. 4:6, 21; Ps. 60:4). This was an occasional signal, and not a military standard. *Elevation* and *conspicuity* are implied in the word.

(3.) The Hebrew word *degel* denotes the standard given to each of the four divisions of the host of the Israelites at the Exodus (Num. 1:52; 2:2; 10:14). In Cant. 2:4 it is rendered "banner." We have no definite information as to the nature of these military standards. (See BANNER.)

Entertain. Entertainments, "feasts," were sometimes connected with a public festival (Deut. 16:11, 14), and accompanied by offerings (1 Sam. 9:13), in token of alliances (Gen. 26:30); sometimes in connection with

domestic or social events, as at the weaning of children (Gen. 21:8), at weddings (Gen. 29:22; John 2:1), on birth-days (Matt. 14:6), at the time of sheep-shearing (2 Sam. 13:23), and of vintage (Judg. 9:27), and at funerals (2 Sam. 3:35; Jer. 16:7).

The guests were invited by servants (Prov. 9:3; Matt. 22:3), who assigned them their respective places (1 Sam. 9:22; Luke 14:8; Mark 12:39). Like portions were sent by the master to each guest (1 Sam. 1:4; 2 Sam. 6:19), except when special honour was intended, when the portion was increased (Gen. 43:34).

The Israelites were forbidden to attend heathenish sacrificial entertainments (Ex. 34:15), because these were in honour of false gods, and because at such feasts they would be liable to partake of unclean flesh (1 Cor. 10:28).

In the entertainments common in apostolic times among the Gentiles were frequent "revellings," against which Christians were warned (Rom. 13:13; Gal. 5:21; 1 Pet. 4:3). (See BANQUET.)

Ep'aphras—*lovely*—spoken of by Paul (Col. 1:7; 4:12) as "his dear fellow-servant," and "a faithful minister of Christ." He was thus evidently with him at Rome when he wrote to the Colossians. He was a distinguished disciple, and probably the founder of the Colossian church. He is also mentioned in the Epistle to Philemon (23), where he is called by Paul his "fellow-prisoner."

Epaphrodi'tus—*fair, graceful;* belonging to *Aphrodite* or *Venus*—the messenger who came from Philippi to the apostle when he was a prisoner at Rome (Phil. 2:25-30; 4:10-18). Paul mentions him in words of esteem and affection. On his return to Philippi he was the bearer of Paul's letter to the church there.

Epæ'netus—*commendable*—a Christian at Rome to whom Paul sent his salutation (Rom. 16:5). He is spoken of as "the first fruits of Achaia" (R.V., "of Asia"—*i.e.*, of proconsular Asia, which is probably the correct reading). As being the first convert in that region, he was peculiarly dear to the apostle. He calls him his "well beloved."

E'phah—*gloom.* (1.) One of the five sons of Midian, and grandson of Abraham (Gen. 25 : 4). The city of Ephah, to which he gave his name, is mentioned Isa. 60 : 6, 7. This city, with its surrounding territory, formed part of Midian, on the east shore of the Dead Sea. It abounded in dromedaries and camels (Judg. 6 : 5).

(2.) 1 Chr. 2 : 46, a concubine of Caleb.

(3.) 1 Chr. 2 : 47, a descendant of Judah.

E'phah, a word of Egyptian origin, meaning *measure;* a grain measure containing "three seahs or ten omers," and equivalent to the *bath* for liquids (Ex. 16 : 36; 1 Sam. 17 : 17; Zech. 5 : 6). The double ephah in Prov. 20 : 10 (marg., "an ephah and an ephah"), Deut. 25 : 14, means two ephahs, the one false and the other just.

E'pher—*a calf.* (1.) One of the sons of Midian, who was Abraham's son by Keturah (Gen. 25 : 4).

(2.) The head of one of the families of trans-Jordanic Manasseh who were carried captive by Tiglath-pileser (1 Chr. 5 : 24).

E'phes-dam'mim—*boundary of blood*—a place in the tribe of Judah where the Philistines encamped when David fought with Goliath (1 Sam. 17 : 1). It was probably so called as having been the scene of frequent sanguinary conflicts between Israel and the Philistines. It is called Pas-dammim (1 Chr. 11 : 13). It has been identified with the modern *Beit Fased*—i.e., "house of bleeding"—near Shochoh (*q.v.*).

Ephe'sians, Epistle to, was written by Paul at Rome about the same time as that to the Colossians, which in many points it resembles.

Contents of. The Epistle to the Colossians is mainly polemical, designed to refute certain theosophic errors that had crept into the church there. That to the Ephesians does not seem to have originated in any special circumstances, but is simply a letter springing from Paul's love to the church there, and indicative of his earnest desire that they should be fully instructed in the profound doctrines of the gospel. It contains (1) the salutation (1 : 1, 2); (2) a general description of the blessings the gospel reveals—as to their source, means by which they are attained, purpose for which they are bestowed, and their final result, with a fervent prayer for the further spiritual enrichment of the Ephesians (1 : 3–2 : 11); (3) "a record of that marked change in spiritual position which the Gentile believers now possessed, ending with an account of the writer's selection to and qualification for the apostolate of heathendom—a fact so considered as to keep them from being dispirited, and to lead him to pray for enlarged spiritual benefactions on his absent sympathizers" (2 : 12–3 : 21); (4) a chapter on unity as undisturbed by diversity of gifts (4 : 1–17); (5) special injunctions bearing on ordinary life (4 : 17–6 : 10); (6) the imagery of a spiritual warfare, mission of Tychicus, and valedictory blessing (6 : 11-24).

Planting of the church at Ephesus. Paul's first and hurried visit for the space of three months to Ephesus is recorded in Acts 18 : 19–21. The work he began on this occasion was carried forward by Apollos (24–26) and Aquila and Priscilla. On his second visit, early in the following year, he remained at Ephesus "three years," for he found it was the key to the western provinces of Asia Minor. Here "a great door and effectual" was opened to him (1 Cor. 16 : 9), and the church was established and strengthened by his assiduous labours there (Acts 20 : 20, 31). From Ephesus as a centre the gospel spread abroad "almost throughout all Asia" (19 : 26). The word "mightily grew and prevailed" despite all the opposition and persecution he encountered.

On his last journey to Jerusalem the apostle landed at Miletus, and summoning together the elders of the church from Ephesus, delivered to them his remarkable farewell charge (Acts 20 : 18–35), expecting to see them no more.

The following parallels between this epistle and the Milesian charge may be traced :—

(1.) Acts 20 : 19 = Eph. 4 : 2. The phrase "lowliness of mind" occurs nowhere else.

(2.) Acts 20 : 27 = Eph. 1 : 11. The word "counsel," as denoting the divine plan, occurs only here and Heb. 6 : 17.

(3.) Acts 20 : 32 = Eph. 3 : 20. The divine ability.

(4.) Acts 20:32 = Eph. 2:20. The building upon the foundation.

(5.) Acts 20:32 = Eph. 1:14, 18. "The inheritance of the saints."

Place and date of the writing of the letter. It was evidently written from Rome during Paul's first imprisonment (3:1; 4:1; 6:20), and probably soon after his arrival there, about the year 62, four years after he had parted with the Ephesian elders at Miletus. The subscription of this epistle is correct.

There seems to have been no *special occasion* for the writing of this letter, as already noted. Paul's object was plainly not polemical. No errors had sprung up in the church which he sought to point out and refute. The object of the apostle is "to set forth the ground, the cause, and the aim and end of the church of the faithful in Christ. He speaks to the Ephesians as a type or sample of the church universal." The church's foundations, its course, and its end, are his theme. "Everywhere the foundation of the church is *the will of the Father;* the course of the church is by *the satisfaction of the Son;* the end of the church is *the life in the Holy Spirit.*" In the Epistle to the Romans, Paul writes from the point of view of justification by the imputed righteousness of Christ; here he writes from the point of view specially of union to the Redeemer, and hence of the oneness of the true church of Christ. "This is perhaps the profoundest book in existence." It is a book "which sounds the lowest depths of Christian doctrine, and scales the loftiest heights of Christian experience;" and the fact that the apostle evidently expected the Ephesians to understand it is an evidence of the "proficiency which Paul's converts had attained under his preaching at Ephesus."

Relation between this epistle and that to the Colossians (q.v.). "The letters of the apostle are the fervent outburst of pastoral zeal and attachment, written without reserve and in unaffected simplicity; sentiments come warm from the heart, without the shaping out, pruning, and punctilious arrangement of a formal discourse. There is such a fresh and familiar transcription of feeling, so frequent an introduction of colloquial idiom, and so much of conversational frankness and vivacity, that the reader associates the image of the writer with every paragraph, and the ear seems to catch and recognize the very tones of living address." "Is it then any matter of amazement that one letter should resemble another, or that two written about the same time should have so much in common and so much that is peculiar? The close relation as to style and subject between the epistles to Colosse and Ephesus must strike every reader. Their precise relation to each other has given rise to much discussion. The great probability is that the epistle to Colosse was first written; the parallel passages in Ephesians, which amount to about forty-two in number, having the appearance of being expansions from the epistle to Colosse.

Compare	with
Eph. 1:7	Col. 1:14.
,, 1:10	,, 1:20.
,, 3:2	,, 1:25.
,, 5:19	,, 3:16.
,, 6:22	,, 4:8.
,, 1:19–2:5	,, 2:12, 13.
,, 4:2–4	,, 3:12–15.
,, 4:16	,, 2:19.
,, 4:32	,, 3:13.
,, 4:22–24	,, 3:9, 10.
,, 5:6–8	,, 3:6–8.
,, 5:15, 16	,, 4:5.
,, 6:19, 20	,, 4:3, 4.
,, 5:22–6:9	,, 3:18–4:1.

"*The style* of this epistle is exceedingly animated, and corresponds with the state of the apostle's mind at the time of writing. Overjoyed with the account which their messenger had brought him of their faith and holiness (Eph. 1:15), and transported with the consideration of the unsearchable wisdom of God displayed in the work of man's redemption, and of his astonishing love towards the Gentiles in making them partakers through faith of all the benefits of Christ's death, he soars high in his sentiments on those grand subjects, and gives his thoughts utterance in sublime and copious expression."

Eph'esus, the capital of proconsular Asia, which was the western part of Asia Minor. It was colonized principally from

Athens. In the time of the Romans it bore the title of "the first and greatest metropolis of Asia." It was distinguished for the Temple of Diana (*q.v.*), who there had her chief shrine; and for its theatre, which was the largest in the world, capable of containing 50,000 spectators. It was, like all ancient theatres, open to the sky. Here were exhibited the fights of wild beasts and of men with beasts. (Comp. 1 Cor. 4: 9; 9:24, 25; 15:32.)

Many Jews took up their residence in this city, and here the seeds of the gospel were sown immediately after Pentecost (Acts 2:9; 6:9). At the close of his second missionary journey (about A.D. 51), when Paul was returning from Greece to Syria (18:18–21), he first visited this city. He remained, however, for only a short time, as he was hastening to keep the feast, probably of Pentecost, at Jerusalem; but he left Aquila and Priscilla behind him to carry on the work of spreading the gospel.

During his third missionary journey Paul reached Ephesus from the "upper coasts" (Acts 19:1)—*i.e.*, from the inland parts of Asia Minor—and tarried here for about three years; and so successful and abundant were his labours that "all they which dwelt in Asia heard the word of the Lord Jesus, both Jews and Greeks" (19: 10). Probably during this period the seven churches of the Apocalypse were founded, not by Paul's personal labours, but by

missionaries whom he may have sent out from Ephesus, and by the influence of converts returning to their homes.

On his return from his journey, Paul touched at Miletus, some 30 miles south of Ephesus (Acts 20:15), and sending for the presbyters of Ephesus to meet him there, he delivered to them that touching farewell charge which is recorded in Acts 20:18–35. Ephesus is not again mentioned till near the close of Paul's life, when he writes to Timothy exhorting him to "stay at Ephesus" (1 Tim. 1:3).

Two of Paul's companions, Trophimus and Tychicus, were probably natives of Ephesus (Acts 20:4; 21:29; 2 Tim. 4:12). In his second epistle to Timothy, Paul speaks of Onesiphorus as having "served him in many things" at Ephesus (2 Tim. 1:18). He also "sent Tychicus to Ephesus" (4:12), probably to attend to the interests of the church there. Ephesus is twice mentioned in the Apocalypse (1:11; 2:1).

The apostle John, according to tradition, spent many years in Ephesus, where he died and was buried.

A part of the site of this once famous city is now occupied by a small Turkish village, Ayasaluk, which is regarded as a corruption of the two Greek words, *hagios theologos; i.e.*, "the holy divine."

E'phod—something *girt*—a sacred vestment worn originally by the high priest (Ex. 28:4), afterwards by the ordinary priest (1 Sam. 22:18), and characteristic of his office (1 Sam. 2:18, 28; 14:3). It was worn by Samuel, and also by David (2 Sam. 6 : 14). It was made of fine linen, and consisted of two pieces, which hung from the neck, and covered both the back and front, above the tunic and outer garment (Ex. 28 : 31). That of the high priest was embroidered with divers colours. The two pieces were joined together over the shoulders (hence in Latin called *superhumerale*) by clasps or buckles of gold or precious stones, and fastened round the waist by a "curious girdle of gold, blue, purple, and fine twined linen" (28 : 6-12).

The breastplate, with the Urim and Thummim, was attached to the ephod.

Eph'phatha, the Greek form of a Syro-Chaldaic or Aramaic word, meaning "*Be opened,*" uttered by Christ when healing the man who was deaf and dumb (Mark 7 : 34). It is one of the characteristics of Mark that he uses the very Aramaic words which fell from our Lord's lips. (See 3 : 17; 5 : 41; 7 : 11; 14 : 36; 15 : 34.)

Eph'raim—*double fruitfulness* ("for God had made him fruitful in the land of his affliction"). The second son of Joseph, born in Egypt (Gen. 41 : 52; 46 : 20). The first incident recorded regarding him is his being placed, along with his brother Manasseh, before their grandfather, Jacob, that he might bless them (48 : 10; comp. 27 : 1). The intention of Joseph was that the right hand of the aged patriarch should be placed on the head of the elder of the two; but Jacob set Ephraim the younger before his brother, "guiding his hand wittingly." Before Joseph's death, Ephraim's family had reached the third generation (Gen. 50 : 23).

Eph'raim, The tribe of, took precedence over that of Manasseh by virtue of Jacob's blessing (Gen. 41 : 52; 48 : 1). The descendants of Joseph formed *two* of the tribes of Israel, whereas each of the other sons of Jacob was the founder of only one tribe. Thus there were in reality thirteen tribes; but the number twelve was preserved by excluding that of Levi when Ephraim and Manasseh are mentioned separately (Num. 1 : 32-34; Josh. 17 : 14, 17; 1 Chr. 7 : 20).

Territory of. At the time of the first census in the wilderness this tribe numbered 40,500 (Num. 1 : 32, 33); forty years later, when about to take possession of the Promised Land, it numbered only 32,500. During the march (see CAMP) Ephraim's place was on the west side of the tabernacle (Num. 2 : 18-24). When the spies were sent out to spy the land, "Oshea the son of Nun" of this tribe signalized himself.

The boundaries of the portion of the land assigned to Ephraim are given in Josh. 16 : 1-10. It included most of what was afterwards called Samaria as distinguished from Judea and Galilee. It thus lay in the centre of all traffic, from north to south, and from Jordan to the sea, and was about 55 miles long and 30 broad. The tabernacle and the ark were deposited within its limits at Shiloh, where it remained for four hundred years. During the time of the judges and the first stage of the monarchy this tribe manifested a domineering and haughty and discontented spirit. "For more than five hundred years—a period equal to that which elapsed between the Norman Conquest and the War of the Roses—Ephraim, with its two dependent tribes of Manasseh and Benjamin, exercised undisputed pre-eminence. Joshua the first conqueror, Gideon the greatest of the judges, and Saul the first king, belonged to one or other of the three tribes. It was not till the close of the first period of Jewish history that God 'refused the tabernacle of Joseph, and chose not the tribe of Ephraim but the tribe of Judah, even the Mount Zion which he loved' (Ps. 78 : 67, 68). When the ark was removed from Shiloh to Zion the power of Ephraim was humbled."

Among the causes which operated to bring about the disruption of Israel was Ephraim's jealousy of the growing power of Judah. From the settlement of Canaan till the time of David and Solomon, Ephraim had held the place of honour among the tribes. It occupied the central and fairest portions of the land, and had Shiloh and Shechem within its borders. But now when Jerusalem became the capital of the kingdom, and the centre of power and worship for the whole nation of Israel, Ephraim declined in influence. The discontent came to a crisis by Rehoboam's refusal to grant certain redresses that were demanded (1 Kings 12).

Eph'raim, Mount, the central mountainous district of Palestine occupied by the tribe of Ephraim (Josh. 17 : 15 ; 19 : 50 ; 50 : 7), extending from Bethel to the plain of Jezreel. In Joshua's time (Josh. 17 : 18) these hills were densely wooded. They were intersected by well-watered, fertile valleys, referred to in Jer. 50 : 19. Joshua was buried at Timnath-heres among the mountains of Ephraim, on the north side of the hill of Gaash (Judg. 2 : 9). This region is also called the "mountains of Israel" (Josh. 11 : 21) and the "mountains of Samaria" (Jer. 31 : 5, 6 ; Amos 3 : 9).

Eph'raim, Gate of, one of the gates of Jerusalem (2 Kings 14 : 13 ; 2 Chr. 25 : 23), on the side of the city looking toward Ephraim, the north side.

Eph'raim, Wood of, a forest in which a fatal battle was fought between the army of David and that of Absalom, who was killed there (2 Sam. 18 : 6, 8). It lay on the east of Jordan, not far from Mahanaim, and was some part of the great forest of Gilead.

Eph'raim in the wilderness (John 11 : 54), a town to which our Lord retired with his disciples after he had raised Lazarus, and when the priests were conspiring against him. It lay in the wild, uncultivated hill-country to the north-east of Jerusalem, between the central towns and the Jordan valley.

Eph'ratah—*fruitful.* (1.) The second wife of Caleb, the son of Hezron, mother of Hur, and grandmother of Caleb, who was one of those that were sent to spy the land (1 Chr. 2 : 19, 50).

(2.) The ancient name of Bethlehem in Judah (Gen. 35 : 16, 19 ; 48 : 7). In Ruth 1 : 2 it is called " Bethlehem-Judah," but the inhabitants are called "Ephrathites ;" in Micah 5 : 2, "Bethlehem - Ephratah ;" in Matt. 2 : 6, "Bethlehem in the land of Judah." In Ps. 132 : 6 it is mentioned as the place where David spent his youth, and where he heard much of the ark, although he never saw it till he found it long afterwards at Kirjath-jearim ; *i.e.,* the

"city of the wood," or the "forest-town" (1 Sam. 7 : 1 ; comp. 2 Sam. 6 : 3, 4).

Eph'rathite, a citizen of Ephratah, the old name of Bethlehem (Ruth 1 : 2 ; 1 Sam. 17 : 12), or Bethlehem-Judah.

Eph'ron—*fawn-like.* (1.) The son of Zohar a Hittite, the owner of the field and cave of Machpelah (*q.v.*), which Abraham bought for 400 shekels of silver (Gen. 23 : 8–17 ; 25 : 9 ; 49 : 29, 30).

(2.) A mountain range which formed one of the landmarks on the north boundary of the tribe of Judah (Josh. 15 : 9), probably the range on the west side of the *Wâdy Beit-Hanîna.*

Epicure'ans, followers of Epicurus (who died at Athens B.C. 270), or adherents of the Epicurean philosophy (Acts 17 : 18). This philosophy was a system of atheism, and taught men to seek as their highest aim a pleasant and smooth life. They have been called the "Sadducees" of Greek paganism. They, with the Stoics, ridiculed the teaching of Paul (Acts 17 : 18). They appear to have been greatly esteemed at Athens.

Epis'tles, the apostolic letters. The New Testament contains twenty-one in all. They are divided into two classes. (1.) *Paul's Epistles,* fourteen in number, including Hebrews. These are not arranged in the New Testament in the order of time as to their composition, but rather according to the rank of the cities or places to which they were sent. Who arranged them after this manner is unknown. Paul's letters were, as a rule, dictated to an amanuensis—a fact which accounts for some of their peculiarities. He authenticated them, however, by adding a few words in his own hand at the close. (See GALATIANS, EPISTLE TO.)

The epistles to Timothy and Titus are styled the Pastoral Epistles.

(2.) The *Catholic* or *General Epistles,* so called because they are not addressed to any particular church or city or individual, but to Christians in general, or to Christians in several countries. Of these, three are written by John, two by Peter, and one each by James and Jude.

It is an interesting and instructive fact

that a large portion of the New Testament is taken up with epistles. The doctrines of Christianity are thus not set forth in any formal treatise, but mainly in a collection of letters. "The causes of this peculiarity are not far to seek. Christianity was the first great missionary religion. It was the first to break the bounds of race and aim at embracing all mankind. But this necessarily involved a change in the mode in which it was presented. The prophet of the Old Testament, if he had anything to communicate, either appeared in person or sent messengers to speak for him by word of mouth. The one exception of any religious significance is the letter of Elijah to Jehoram in 2 Chr. 21. The narrow limits of Palestine made direct personal communication easy. But the case was different when the Christian Church came to consist of a number of scattered parts, stretching from Mesopotamia in the east to Rome or even Spain in the far west. It was only natural that the apostle by whom the greater number of these communities had been founded should seek to communicate with them by letter. He was enabled to do so by two things: first, the very general diffusion of the Greek language; and secondly, the remarkable facilities of intercourse afforded at this particular time. The whole world was at peace, and held together by the organized rule of imperial Rome."—Dr. Sanday's *Epistle to the Romans: Introduction.*

Eras'tus—*beloved.* (1.) The "chamberlain" of the city of Corinth (Rom. 16:23), and one of Paul's disciples. As treasurer of such a city he was a public officer of great dignity; and his conversion to the gospel was accordingly a proof of the wonderful success of the apostle's labours.

(2.) A companion of Paul at Ephesus, who was sent by him along with Timothy into Macedonia (Acts 19:22). Corinth was his usual place of abode (2 Tim. 4:20); but probably he may have been the same as the preceding.

E'rech (LXX., "Orech")—*length,* or *Moon-town*—one of the cities of Nimrod's kingdom in the plain of Shinar (Gen. 10:10); the Orchoë of the Greeks and Romans.

It was probably the city of the Archevites, who were transplanted to Samaria by Asnapper (Ezra 4:9). It lay on the left bank of the Euphrates, about 120 miles south-east of Babylon, and is now represented by the mounds and ruins of *Warka.* It appears to have been the necropolis of the Assyrian kings, as the whole region is strewed with bricks and the remains of coffins. "Standing on the summit of the principal edifice, called the Buwarizza, a tower 200 feet square in the centre of the ruins, the beholder is struck with astonishment at the enormous accumulation of mounds and ancient relics at his feet. An irregular circle, nearly 6 miles in circumference, is defined by the traces of an earthen rampart, in some places 40 feet high."

Esai'as, the Greek form for Isaiah, constantly used in the Authorized Version of the New Testament (Matt. 3:3; 4:14), but in the Revised Version always "Isaiah."

E'sarhad'don—*Assur has given a brother*—successor of Sennacherib (2 Kings 19:37;

ESARHADDON.
(From Assyrian Sculpture in British Museum.)

Isa. 37:38). He ascended the throne about B.C. 681. Nothing further is recorded of him in Scripture except that he settled certain colonists in Samaria (Ezra 4 : 2). But from the monuments it appears that he was the most powerful of all the Assyrian monarchs. He united Babylonia to his kingdom ; and was the only Assyrian king who actually reigned at Babylon, where he built a palace, the ruins of which remain to this day. The city had been almost destroyed by Sennacherib (B.C. 691), but he restored it to something of its former grandeur. During this period of his residence at Babylon, the last eleven years of his life, Manasseh, the king of Judah, was brought before him (2 Chr. 33 : 11), and detained as a prisoner, but was afterwards restored to his throne. From B.C. 725 to 672 the Ethiopian dynasty ruled in Egypt ; but he expelled Tirhakah, and reduced that country to the condition of an Assyrian dependency, which it continued to be till B.C. 660, when Psammetichus, a Lybian, became master of the country, and began the Greek epoch of its history.

He built many temples and palaces, the most magnificent of which was the south-west palace at Nimrûd, which is said to have been in its general design almost the same as Solomon's palace, only much larger (1 Kings 7 : 1–12).

Esarhaddon died at Babylon (B.C. 668), and was succeeded by his eldest son Assur-bani-pal, during whose reign of forty-three years Assyrian literature and art reached their highest perfection. After the death of Assur-bani-pal, Assyria declined, and Babylon (B.C. 625) gained independence ; and Nabopolassar, in alliance with the Medes under Cyaxares, laid Nineveh in ruins (B.C. 607). Babylon now rose to supremacy, which she retained till B.C. 530.

E'sau—*hairy*—Rebekah's first-born twin son (Gen. 25 : 25). The name of Edom—"red"—was also given to him from his conduct in connection with the red lentil "pottage" for which he sold his birthright (30, 31). The circumstances connected with his birth foreshadowed the enmity which afterwards subsisted between the twin brothers and the nations they founded (25 : 22, 23, 26). In process of time Jacob, following his natural bent, became a shep-

herd ; while Esau, a "son of the desert," devoted himself to the perilous and toilsome life of a huntsman. On a certain occasion, on returning from the chase, urged by the cravings of hunger, Esau sold his birthright to his brother Jacob, who thereby obtained the covenant blessing (Gen. 27 : 28, 29, 36 ; Heb. 12 : 16, 17). He afterwards tried to regain what he had so recklessly parted with, but was defeated in his attempts through the stealth of his brother (Gen. 27 : 4, 34, 38).

At the age of forty years, to the great grief of his parents, he married (Gen. 26 : 34, 35) two Canaanitish maidens—Judith, the daughter of Beeri, and Bashemath, the daughter of Elon. When Jacob was sent away to Padan-aram, Esau tried to conciliate his parents (28 : 8, 9) by marrying his cousin Mahalath, the daughter of Ishmael. This led him to cast in his lot with the Ishmaelite tribes ; and driving the Horites out of Mount Seir, he settled in that region. After some thirty years' sojourn in Padan-aram Jacob returned to Canaan, and was reconciled to Esau, who went forth to meet him (33 : 4). Twenty years after this, Isaac their father died, when the two brothers met, probably for the last time, beside his grave (35 : 29). Esau now permanently left Canaan, and established himself as a powerful and wealthy chief in the land of Edom (*q.v.*).

Long after this, when the descendants of Jacob came out of Egypt, the Edomites remembered the old quarrel between the brothers, and with fierce hatred they warred against Israel.

Eschew, from old French *eschever*, "to flee from" (Job 1 : 1, 8 ; 2 : 3 ; 1 Pet. 3 : 11).

Esdrae'lon, the Greek form of the Hebrew "Jezreel," the name of the great plain (called by the natives *Merj Ibn Amer ; i.e.,* "the meadow of the son of Amer") which stretches across Central Palestine from the Jordan to the Mediterranean, separating the mountain ranges of Carmel and Samaria from those of Galilee, extending about 14 miles from north to south, and 9 from east to west. It is drained by "that ancient river" Kishon, which flows westward to the Mediterranean. From the foot of Mount Tabor it branches out into three valleys,—that on the north passing between Tabor and Little Hermon (Judg. 4:14); that on the south between Mount Gilboa and En-gannim (2 Kings 9:27); while the central portion, the "valley of Jezreel" proper, runs into the Jordan valley (which is about 1,000 feet lower than Esdraelon) by Bethshean. Here Gideon gained his great victory over the Midianites (Judg. 7:1-25). Here also Barak defeated Sisera, and Saul's army was defeated by the Philistines, and king Josiah, while fighting in disguise against Necho, king of Egypt, was slain (2 Chr. 35:20-27; 2 Kings 23-29). This plain has been well called the "battle-field of Palestine." "It has been a chosen place for encampment in every contest carried on in this country, from the days of Nebuchadnezzar, king of the Assyrians, in the history of whose wars with Arphaxad it is mentioned as the Great Plain of Esdraelon, until the disastrous march of Napoleon Bonaparte from Egypt into Syria. Jews, Gentiles, Saracens, Crusaders, Frenchmen, Egyptians, Persians, Druses, Turks, and Arabs, warriors out of every nation which is under heaven, have pitched their tents

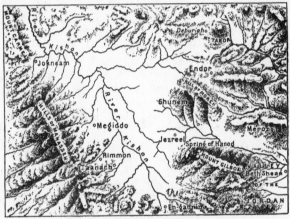

PLAIN OF ESDRAELON.

in the plain, and have beheld the various banners of their nations wet with the dews of Tabor and Hermon" (Dr. Clark).

E'sek—*quarrel*—a well which Isaac's herdsmen dug in the valley of Gerar, and so called because the herdsmen of Gerar quarrelled with them for its possession (Gen. 26:20).

Esh'ba'al—*man of Baal*—the fourth son of king Saul (1 Chr. 8:33; 9:39). He is also called Ish-bosheth (*q.v.*)—2 Sam. 2:8.

Esh'col—*bunch; brave*. (1.) A young Amoritish chief who joined Abraham in the recovery of Lot from the hands of Chedorlaomer (Gen. 14:13, 24).

(2.) A valley in which the spies obtained a fine cluster of grapes (Num. 13:23, 24; "the brook Eshcol," A.V.; "the valley of Eshcol," R.V.), which they took back with them to the camp of Israel as a speci-men of the fruits of the Promised Land. On their way back they explored the route which led into the south (the *Negeb*) by the western edge of the mountains at *Telilat el-'Anab*—i.e., "grape-mounds"—near Beersheba. "In one of these extensive valleys—perhaps in *Wâdy Hanein*, where miles of grape-mounds even now meet the eye—they cut the gigantic clusters of grapes, and gathered the pomegranates and figs, to show how goodly was the land which the Lord had promised for their inheritance."—Palmer's *Desert of the Exodus*.

Es'hean, a place in the mountains of Judah (Josh. 15:52), supposed to be the ruin *es-Simia*, near Dumah, south of Hebron.

Esh'taol—narrow *pass* or *recess*—a town (Josh. 15:33) in the low country, the *Shephêlah* of Judah. It was allotted to the tribe of Dan (Josh. 19:41), and was one of their strongholds. Here Samson spent his boyhood, and first began to show his mighty strength; and here he was buried in the burying-place of Manoah his father (Judg. 13:25; 16:31; 18:2, 8, 11, 12). It is identified with the modern *Yeshûa*, on a hill 2 miles east of Zorah. Others, however, identify it with *Kustûl*, east of Kirjath-jearim.

Eshtemo′a—*obedience*—a town in the mountains of Judah (Josh. 21:14; 1 Chr. 6:57), which was allotted, with the land round it, to the priests. It was frequented by David and his followers during their wanderings; and he sent presents of the spoil of the Amalekites to his friends there (1 Sam. 30:28). It is identified with *es-Semû′a*, a village about 3½ miles east of Socoh, and 7 or 8 miles south of Hebron, around which there are ancient remains of the ruined city. It is the centre of the "south country" or *Negeb*. It is also called "Eshtemoh" (Josh. 15:50).

Espouse′ (2 Sam. 3:14), to betroth. The espousal was a ceremony of betrothing, a formal agreement between the parties then coming under obligation for the purpose of marriage. Espousals are in the East frequently contracted years before the marriage is celebrated. It is referred to as figuratively illustrating the relations between God and his people (Jer. 2:2; Matt. 1:18; 2 Cor. 11:2). (See BETROTH.)

Esse′nes, a Jewish mystical sect somewhat resembling the Pharisees. They affected great purity. They originated about B.C. 100, and disappeared from history after the destruction of Jerusalem. They are not directly mentioned in Scripture, although they may be referred to in Matt. 19:11, 12, Col. 2:8, 18, 23.

Es′ther, the queen of Ahasuerus, and heroine of the book that bears her name. She was a Jewess named Hadas′sah (the *myrtle*), but when she entered the royal harem she received the name by which she henceforth became known (Esther 2:7). It is a Syro-Arabian modification of the Persian word *satârah*, which means a *star*. She was the daughter of Abihail, a Benjamite. Her family did not avail

themselves of the permission granted by Cyrus to the exiles to return to Jerusalem; and she resided with her cousin Mordecai, who held some office in the household of the Persian king at "Shushan in the palace." Ahasuerus having divorced Vashti, chose Esther to be his wife. Soon after this he gave Haman the Agagite, his prime minister, power and authority to kill and extirpate all the Jews throughout the Persian empire. By the interposition of Esther this terrible catastrophe was averted. Haman was hanged on the gallows he had intended for Mordecai (Esther 7); and the Jews established an annual feast—the feast of Purim (*q.v.*)—in memory of their wonderful deliverance. This took place about fifty-two years after the Return—the year of the great battles of Platæa and Mycale (B.C. 479).

Esther appears in the Bible as a "woman of deep piety, faith, courage, patriotism, and caution, combined with resolution; a dutiful daughter to her adopted father, docile and obedient to his counsels, and anxious to share the king's favour with him for the good of the Jewish people. There must have been a singular grace and charm in her aspect and manners, since 'she obtained favour in the sight of all that looked upon her' (Esther 2:15). That she was raised up as an instrument in the hand of God to avert the destruction of the Jewish people, and to afford them protection and forward their wealth and peace in their captivity, is also manifest from the Scripture account."

Es′ther, Book of. The *authorship* of this book is unknown. It must have been obviously written after the death of Ahasuerus (the Xerxes of the Greeks), which took place B.C. 465. The minute and particular account also given of many historical details makes it probable that the writer was contemporary with Mordecai and Esther. Hence we may conclude that the book was written probably about B.C. 444–434, and that the author was one of the Jews of the dispersion.

This book is more purely historical than any other book of Scripture; and it has this remarkable peculiarity that the name of God does not occur in it from first to last in any form. It has, however, been well observed that "though *the name* of God be not in it, his *finger* is." The book wonderfully exhibits the providential government of God.

E'tam—*eyrie.* (1.) A village of the tribe of Simeon (1 Chr. 4 : 32). Into some cleft ("top," A.V.; R.V., "cleft") of a rock here Samson retired after his slaughter of the Philistines (Judg. 15 : 8, 11). It was a natural stronghold. It has been identified with *Beit 'Atab,* west of Bethlehem, near Zorah and Eshtaol. On the crest of a rocky knoll, under the village, is a long tunnel, which may be the "cleft" in which Samson hid.

(2.) A city of Judah, fortified by Rehoboam (2 Chr. 11 : 6). It was near Bethlehem and Tekoah, and some distance apparently to the north of (1). It seems to have been in the district called Nephtoah (or Netophah), where were the sources of the water from which Solomon's gardens and pleasure-grounds and pools, as well as Bethlehem and the temple, were supplied. It is now '*Ain 'Atân,* at the head of the *Wâdy Urtâs,* a fountain sending forth a copious supply of pure water.

Eter'nal life. This expression occurs in the Old Testament only in Dan. 12 : 2 (R.V., "everlasting life").

It occurs frequently in the New Testament (Matt. 7 : 14; 18 : 8, 9; Luke 10 : 28; comp. 18 : 18). It comprises the whole future of the redeemed (Luke 16 : 9), and is opposed to "eternal punishment" (Matt. 19 : 29; 25 : 46). It is the final reward and glory into which the children of God enter (1 Tim. 6 : 12, 19; Rom. 6 : 22; Gal. 6 : 8; 1 Tim. 1 : 16; Rom. 5 : 21); their Sabbath of rest (Heb. 4 : 9; comp. 12 : 22).

The newness of life which the believer derives from Christ (Rom. 6 : 4) is the very essence of salvation, and hence the life of glory or the eternal life must also be theirs (Rom. 6 : 8; 2 Tim. 2 : 11, 12; Rom. 5 : 17, 21; 8 : 30; Eph. 2 : 5, 6). It is the "gift of God in Jesus Christ our Lord" (Rom. 6 : 23). The life the faithful have here on earth (John 3 : 36; 5 : 24; 6 : 47, 53-58) is inseparably connected with the

eternal life beyond—the endless life of the future, the happy future of the saints in heaven (Matt. 19 : 16, 29; 25 : 46).

Eter'nal death. The miserable fate of the wicked in hell (Matt. 25 : 46; Mark 3 : 29; Heb. 6 : 2; 2 Thess. 1 : 9; Matt. 18 : 8; 25 : 41; Jude 7). The Scripture as clearly teaches the unending duration of the penal sufferings of the lost as the "everlasting life," the "eternal life" of the righteous. The same Greek words in the New Testament (*aiōn, aiōnios, aidios*) are used to express (1) the eternal existence of God (1 Tim. 1 : 17; Rom. 1 : 20; 16 : 26); (2) of Christ (Rev. 1 : 18); (3) of the Holy Ghost (Heb. 9 : 14); and (4) the eternal duration of the sufferings of the lost (Matt. 25 : 46; Jude 6).

Their condition after casting off the mortal body is spoken of in these expressive words: "Fire that shall not be quenched" (Mark 9 : 45, 46), "fire unquenchable" (Luke 3 : 17), "the worm that never dies," the "bottomless pit" (Rev. 9 : 1), "the smoke of their torment ascending up for ever and ever" (Rev. 14 : 10, 11).

The idea that the "second death" (Rev. 20 : 14) is in the case of the wicked their absolute destruction, their annihilation, has not the slightest support from Scripture, which always represents their future as one of conscious suffering enduring for ever.

The supposition that God will ultimately secure the repentance and restoration of all sinners is equally unscriptural. There is not the slightest trace in all the Scriptures of any such restoration. Sufferings of themselves have no tendency to purify the soul from sin or impart spiritual life. The atoning death of Christ and the sanctifying power of the Holy Spirit are the only means of divine appointment for bringing men to repentance. Now in the case of them that perish these means have been rejected, and "there remaineth no more sacrifice for sins" (Heb. 10 : 26, 27).

E'tham, perhaps the Coptic word *atiom,* meaning "boundary of the sea," a place or rather district "in the edge of the wilderness"—*i.e.,* of the desert to the east of the present Suez Canal—where the Israelites made their third encampment

(Ex. 13:20; Num. 33:6). The camp was probably a little to the west of the modern town of Ismailia. Here the Israelites were commanded to change their route (Ex. 14:2), and "turn" towards the south, and encamp before Pi-hahiroth. (See EXODUS; PITHOM.)

E'than — *firm*. (1.) "The Ezrahite," distinguished for his wisdom (1 Kings 4:31). He is named as the author of the 89th Psalm. He was of the tribe of Levi.

(2.) A Levite of the family of Merari, one of the leaders of the temple music (1 Chr. 6:44; 15:17, 19). He was probably the same as Jeduthun. He is supposed by some to be the same also as (1).

Eth'anim, the *month of gifts*, *i.e.*, of vintage offerings; called Tisri after the Exile; corresponding to part of September and October. It was the first month of the civil year, and the seventh of the sacred year (1 Kings 8:2).

Eth-ba'al—*with Baal*—a king of Sidon (B.C. 940–908), father of Jezebel, who was the wife of Ahab (1 Kings 16:31). He is said to have been also a priest of Astarte, whose worship was closely allied to that of Baal, and this may account for his daughter's zeal in promoting idolatry in Israel. This marriage of Ahab was most fatal to both Israel and Judah. Dido, the founder of Carthage, was his granddaughter.

Ethio'pia--country of *burnt faces;* the Greek word by which the Hebrew *Cush* is rendered (Gen. 2:13; 2 Kings 19:9; Esther 1:1; Job 28:19; Ps. 68:31; 87:4)—a country which lay to the south of Egypt, beginning at Syene on the First Cataract (Ezek. 29:10; 30:6), and extending to beyond the confluence of the White and Blue Nile. It corresponds generally with what is now known as the Soudân (*i.e.*, the land of the blacks). This country was known to the Hebrews, and is described in Isa. 18:1; Zeph. 3:10. They carried on some commercial intercourse with it (Isa. 45:14).

Its inhabitants were descendants of Ham (Gen. 10:6; Jer. 13:23; Isa. 18:2, "scattered and peeled," A.V.; but in R.V., "tall and smooth"). Herodotus, the Greek historian, describes them as "the tallest and handsomest of men."

They are frequently represented on Egyptian monuments, and they are all of the type of the true negro. As might be expected, the history of this country is interwoven with that of Egypt.

Ethiopia is spoken of in prophecy (Ps. 68:31; 87:4; Isa. 45:14; Ezek. 30:4-9; Dan. 11:43; Nah. 3:8-10; Hab. 3:7; Zeph. 2:12).

Ethio'pian eunuch, the chief officer or prime minister of state of Candace (*q.v.*), queen of Ethiopia. He was converted to Christianity through the instrumentality of Philip (Acts 8:27). The northern portion of Ethiopia formed the kingdom of Meroë, which for a long period was ruled over by queens, and it was probably from this kingdom that the eunuch came.

Ethio'pian woman, the wife of Moses (Num. 12:1). It is supposed that Zipporah, Moses' first wife (Ex. 2:21), was now dead. His marriage of this "woman" descended from Ham gave offence to Aaron and Miriam.

Eu'nuch, literally *bed-keeper* or *chamberlain,* and not necessarily in all cases one who was mutilated, although the practice of employing such mutilated persons in Oriental courts was common (2 Kings 9:32; Esther 2:3). The law of Moses excluded them from the congregation (Deut. 23:1). They were common also among the Greeks and Romans. It is said that even to-day there are some in Rome who are employed in singing soprano in the Sistine Chapel.

Three classes of eunuchs are mentioned in Matt. 19:12.

Euni'ce—*happily conquering*—the mother of Timothy, a believing Jewess, but married to a Greek (Acts 16:1). She trained her son from his childhood in the knowledge of the Scriptures (2 Tim. 3:15). She was distinguished by her "unfeigned faith."

Euo'dias — *a good journey* — a female member of the church at Philippi. She was one who laboured much with Paul in the gospel. He exhorts her to be of one mind with Syntyche (Phil. 4:2). From this it seems they had been at variance with each other.

Euphra′tes. Hebrew, *Pĕrâth;* Assyrian, *Purât;* Persian cuneiform, *Ufratush,* whence Greek *Euphrates,* meaning "sweet water." The Assyrian name means "the stream," or "the great stream." It is generally called in the Bible simply "the river" (Ex. 23:31), or "the great river" (Deut. 1:7).

The Euphrates is first mentioned in Gen. 2:14 as one of the rivers of Paradise. It is next mentioned in connection with the covenant which God entered into with Abraham (15:18), when he promised to his descendants the land from the river of Egypt to the river Euphrates (comp. Deut. 11:24; Josh. 1:4), a covenant promise afterwards fulfilled in the extended conquests of David (2 Sam. 8:2-14; 1 Chr. 18:3; 1 Kings 4:24). It was then the boundary of the kingdom to the north-east. In the ancient history of Assyria, and Babylon, and Egypt many events are recorded in which mention is made of the "great river." Just as the Nile represented in prophecy the power of Egypt, so the Euphrates represented the Assyrian power (Isa. 8:7; Jer. 2:18).

It is by far the largest and most important of all the rivers of Western Asia. From its source in the Armenian mountains to the Persian Gulf, into which it empties itself, it has a course of about 1,700 miles. It has two sources—(1) the *Frat* or *Kara su* (*i.e.,* "the black river"), which rises 25 miles north-east of Erzeroum; and (2) the *Murad-chai* (*i.e.,* "the river of desire"), which rises near Ararat, on the northern slope of Ala tagh. At Kebban Maden, 400 miles from the source of the former, and 270 from that of the latter, they meet and form the majestic stream, which is at length joined by the Tigris at Koornah, after which it is called *Shat-el-Arab,* which runs in a deep and broad stream for above 140 miles to the sea. It is estimated that the alluvium brought down by these rivers encroaches on the sea at the rate of about one mile in thirty years.

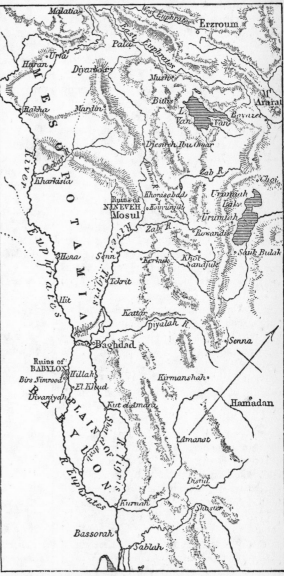

MAP SHOWING COURSE OF EUPHRATES.

Euroc′lydon — *south-east billow* — the name of the wind which blew in the Adriatic Gulf, and which struck the ship in which Paul was wrecked on the coast of Malta (Acts 27:14; R.V., "Euraquilo," *i.e.*, north-east wind). It is called a "tempestuous wind," *i.e.*, as literally rendered, a "typhonic wind," or a typhoon. It is the modern *Gregalia* or *Levanter*. (Comp. Jonah 1:4.)

Eu′tychus—*fortunate*—(Acts 20:9–12), a young man of Troas who fell through drowsiness from the open window of the third floor of the house where Paul was preaching, and was "taken up dead." The lattice-work of the window being open to admit the air, the lad fell out and down to the court below. Paul restored him to life again. (Comp. 1 Kings 17:21; 2 Kings 4:34.)

Evan′gelist, a "publisher of glad tidings;" a missionary preacher of the gospel (Eph. 4:11). This title is applied to Philip (Acts 21:8), who appears to have gone from city to city preaching the word (8:4, 40). Judging from the case of Philip, evangelists had neither the authority of an apostle, nor the gift of prophecy, nor the responsibility of pastoral supervision over a portion of the flock. They were itinerant preachers, having it as their special function to carry the gospel to places where it was previously unknown. The writers of the four Gospels are known as *the* Evangelists.

Eve—*life; living*—the name given by Adam to his wife (Gen. 3:20; 4:1). The account of her creation is given in Gen. 2:21, 22. The Creator, by declaring that it was not good for man to be alone, and by creating for him a suitable companion, gave sanction to monogamy. The commentator Matthew Henry says: "This companion was taken from his side to signify that she was to be dear unto him as his own flesh. Not from his head, lest she should rule over him; nor from his feet, lest he should tyrannize over her; but from his side, to denote that species of equality which is to subsist in the marriage state." And again, "That wife that is of God's making by special grace, and of God's bringing by special providence, is likely to prove a helpmeet to her husband." Through the subtle temptation of the serpent she violated the commandment of God by taking of the forbidden fruit, which she gave also unto her husband (1 Tim. 2:13–15; 2 Cor. 11:3). When she gave birth to her first son, she said, "I have gotten a man from the Lord" (R.V., "I have gotten a man with the help of the Lord," Gen. 4:1). Thus she welcomed Cain, as some think, as if he had been the Promised One, the "Seed of the woman."

E′vening, the period following sunset with which the Jewish day began (Gen. 1:5; Mark 13:35). The Hebrews reckoned two evenings of each day, as appears from Ex. 16:12; 30:8; 12:6 (marg.); Lev. 23:5 (marg. R.V., "between the two evenings"). The "first evening" was that period when the sun was verging towards setting, and the "second evening" the moment of actual sunset.

The word "evenings" in Jer. 5:6 should be "deserts" (marg. R.V.).

Everlast′ing=eternal, applied to God (Gen. 21:33; Deut. 33:27; Ps. 41:13; 90:2). We also read of the "everlasting hills" (Gen. 49:26); an "everlasting priesthood" (Ex. 40:15; Num. 25:13). (See ETERNAL.)

Evil eye (Prov. 23:6), figuratively, the envious or covetous. (Comp. Deut. 15:9; Matt. 20:15.)

E′vil-mer′odach—*Merodach's man*—the son and successor of Nebuchadnezzar, king of Babylon (2 Kings 25:27; Jer. 52:31, 34). He seems to have reigned but two years (B.C. 561–559). Influenced probably by Daniel, he showed kindness to Jehoiachin, who had been a prisoner in Babylon for thirty-seven years. He released him, and "spoke kindly to him." He was murdered by Nergal-sharezer=Neriglissar, his brother-in-law, who succeeded him (Jer. 39:3, 13).

Evil-speaking is expressly forbidden (Titus 3:2; James 4:11), and severe punishments are denounced against it (1 Cor. 5:11; 6:10). It is spoken of also with abhorrence (Ps. 15:3; Prov. 18:6, 7), and is foreign to the whole Christian character and the example of Christ.

Example, of Christ (1 Pet. 2:21; John 13:15); of pastors to their flocks (Phil. 3:17; 2 Thess. 3:9; 1 Tim. 4:12; 1 Pet. 5:3); of the Jews as a warning (Heb. 4:11); of the prophets as suffering affliction (James 5:10).

Execu'tioner (Mark 6:27). Instead of the Greek word, Mark here uses a Latin word, *speculator*, which literally means "a scout," "a spy," and at length came to denote one of the armed bodyguard of the emperor. Herod Antipas, in imitation of the emperor, had in attendance on him a company of *speculatores*. They were sometimes employed as executioners, but this was a mere accident of their office. (See MARK, GOSPEL OF.)

Exercise, bodily (1 Tim. 4:8). An ascetic mortification of the flesh and denial of personal gratification (comp. Col. 2:23) to which some sects of the Jews, especially the Essenes, attached importance.

Exile. (1.) Of the kingdom of Israel. In the time of Pekah, Tiglath-pileser II. carried away captive into Assyria (2 Kings 15:29; comp. Isa. 10:5, 6) a part of the inhabitants of Galilee and of Gilead (B.C. 741).

After the destruction of Samaria (B.C. 720) by Shalmaneser and Sargon (*q.v.*), there was a general deportation of the Israelites into Mesopotamia and Media (2 Kings 17:6; 18:9; 1 Chr. 5:26). (See ISRAEL, KINGDOM OF.)

(2.) Of the kingdom of the two tribes—the kingdom of Judah. Nebuchadnezzar, in the fourth year of Jehoiakim (Jer. 25:1), invaded Judah, and carried away some royal youths, including Daniel and his companions (B.C. 606), together with the sacred vessels of the temple (2 Chr. 36:7; Dan. 1:2). In B.C. 598 (Jer. 52:28; 2 Kings 24:12), in the beginning of Jehoiachin's reign (2 Kings 24:8), Nebuchadnezzar carried away captive 3,023 eminent Jews, including the king (2 Chr. 36:10), with his family and officers (2 Kings 24:12), and a large number of warriors (16), with very many persons of note (14), and artisans (16), leaving behind only those who were poor and helpless. This was the first *general* deportation to Babylon.

In B.C. 588, after the revolt of Zedekiah (*q.v.*), there was a second *general* deportation of Jews by Nebuchadnezzar (Jer. 52:29; 2 Kings 25:8), including 832 more of the principal men of the kingdom. He carried away also the rest of the sacred vessels (2 Chr. 36:18). From this period, when the temple was destroyed (2 Kings 25:9), to the complete restoration, B.C. 517 (Ezra 6:15), is the period of the "seventy years."

In B.C. 582 occurred the last and final deportation. The entire number Nebuchadnezzar carried captive was 14,600 heads of families with their wives and children and dependants (Jer. 52:30; 43:5-7; 2 Chr. 36:20, etc.). Thus the exiles formed a very considerable community in Babylon.

When Cyrus granted permission to the Jews to return to their own land (Ezra 1:5; 7:13), only a comparatively small number at first availed themselves of the privilege. It cannot be questioned that many belonging to the kingdom of Israel ultimately joined the Jews under Ezra, Zerubbabel, and Nehemiah, and returned along with them to Jerusalem (Jer. 50:4, 5, 17-20, 33-35).

Large numbers had, however, settled in the land of Babylon, and formed numerous colonies in different parts of the kingdom. Their descendants very probably have spread far into Eastern lands and become absorbed in the general population. (See JUDAH, KINGDOM OF; CAPTIVITY.)

Ex'odus, the great deliverance wrought for the children of Israel when they were brought out of the land of Egypt with "a mighty hand and a stretched out arm" (Ex. 12:51; Deut. 26:8; Ps. 114; 136), about B.C. 1490, and four hundred and eighty years (1 Kings 6:1) before the building of Solomon's temple.

The time of their sojourning in Egypt was, according to Ex. 12:40, the space of four hundred and thirty years. In the LXX., the words are, "The sojourning of the children of Israel which they sojourned in Egypt and *in the land of Canaan* was four hundred and thirty years;" and the Samaritan version reads, "The sojourning of the children of Israel *and of their fathers* which they sojourned *in the land of Canaan* and in the land of Egypt was four hundred and thirty years." In Gen. 15:13-16, the period is prophetically given (in round numbers) as four hundred years. This passage is quoted by Stephen in his defence before the council (Acts 7:6).

The chronology of the "sojourning" is variously estimated. Those who adopt the longer term reckon thus :—

Years.

From the descent of Jacob into Egypt to the death of Joseph.......................... 71
From the death of Joseph to the birth of Moses................................... 278
From the birth of Moses to his flight into Midian..................................... 40
From the flight of Moses to his return into Egypt................................ 40
From the return of Moses to the Exodus.... 1
                                    ——
                                    430

Others contend for the shorter period of two hundred and fifteen years, holding that the period of four hundred and thirty years comprehends the years from the entrance of Abraham into Canaan (see LXX. and Samaritan) to the descent of Jacob into Egypt. They reckon thus :—

Years.

From Abraham's arrival in Canaan to Isaac's birth..................................... 25
From Isaac's birth to that of his twin sons Esau and Jacob.......................... 60
From Jacob's birth to the going down into Egypt................................... 130
                                    ——
                                    215
From Jacob's going down into Egypt to the death of Joseph.......................... 71
From death of Joseph to the birth of Moses.. 64
From birth of Moses to the Exodus.......... 80
                                    ——
In all.... 430

During the forty years of Moses' sojourn in the land of Midian, the Hebrews in Egypt were being gradually prepared for the great national crisis which was approaching. The plagues that successively fell upon the land loosened the bonds by which Pharaoh held them in slavery, and at length he was eager that they should depart. But the Hebrews must now also be ready to go. They were poor ; for generations they had laboured for the Egyptians without wages. They asked gifts from their neighbours around them (Ex. 12 : 35), and these were readily bestowed. And then, as the first step towards their independent national organization, they observed the feast of the Passover, which was now instituted as a perpetual memorial.

The blood of the paschal lamb was duly sprinkled on the door-posts and lintels of all their houses, and they were all within, waiting the next movement in the working out of God's plan. At length the last stroke fell on the land of Egypt. "It came to pass, that at midnight Jehovah smote all the firstborn in the land of Egypt." Pharaoh rose up in the night, and called for Moses and Aaron by night, and said, "Rise up, get you forth from among my people, both ye and the children of Israel ; and go, serve Jehovah, as ye have said. And take your flocks and your herds, as ye have said, and be gone ; and bless me also." Thus was Pharaoh (*q.v.*) completely humbled and broken down. These words he spoke to Moses and Aaron "seem to gleam through the tears of the humbled king, as he lamented his son snatched from him by so sudden a death, and tremble with a sense of the helplessness which his proud soul at last felt when the avenging hand of God had visited even his palace."

The terror-stricken Egyptians now urged the instant departure of the Hebrews. In the midst of the Passover feast, before the dawn of the 15th day of the month Abib (our April nearly), which was to be to them henceforth the beginning of the year, as it was the commencement of a new epoch in their history, every family, with all that appertained to it, was ready for the march, which instantly began under the leadership of the heads of tribes with their various subdivisions. They moved onward, increasing as they went forward from all the districts of Goshen, over the whole of which they were scattered, to the common centre. Three or four days perhaps elapsed before the whole body of the people were assembled at Rameses, and ready to set out under their leader Moses (Ex. 12 : 37 ; Num. 33 : 3). This city was at that time the residence of the Egyptian court, and here the interviews between Moses and Pharaoh had taken place.

From Rameses they journeyed to Succoth (Ex. 12 : 37), identified with *Tel-el-Maskhuta*, about 12 miles west of Ismailia. (See PITHON.) Their third station was Etham (*q.v.*)—13 : 20—"in the edge of the wilderness," and was probably a little to the west of the modern town of Ismailia, on the Suez Canal. Here they were commanded "to turn and encamp before Pi-hahiroth, between Migdol and the sea"—*i.e.*, to change their route from east to due south. The Lord now assumed the direction of their march in the pillar of cloud by day and of fire by night. They were then led along the west shore of the Red Sea till they came to an extensive camping-ground "before Pi-hahiroth," about 40 miles from Etham. This distance from Etham may have taken three days to traverse, for the number of camping-places by no means indicates the number of days spent on the journey: *e.g.*, it took fully a month to travel from Rameses to the wilderness of Sin (Ex. 16:1), yet reference is made to only six camping-places during all that time. The exact spot of their encampment before they crossed the Red Sea cannot be determined. It was probably somewhere near the present site of Suez.

Under the direction of God the children of Israel went "forward" from the camp "before Pi-hahiroth," and the sea opened a pathway for them, so that they crossed to the farther shore in safety. The Egyptian host pursued after them, and, attempting to follow through the sea, were overwhelmed in its returning waters, and thus the whole military force of the Egyptians perished. They "sank like lead in the mighty waters" (Ex. 15:1–19; comp. Ps. 77:16-19).

Having reached the eastern shore of the sea, perhaps a little way to the north of 'Ayûn Musa ("the springs of Moses"), there they encamped and rested probably for a day. Here Miriam and the other women sang the triumphal song recorded in Ex. 15:1–21.

From 'Ayûn Musa they went on for three days through a part of the barren "wilderness of Shur" (22), called also the "wilderness of Etham" (Num. 33:8; comp. Ex. 13:20), without finding water. On the last of these days they came to Marah (*q.v.*), where the "bitter" water was by a miracle made drinkable.

Their next camping-place was Elim (*q.v.*),

where were twelve springs of water and a grove of "threescore and ten" palm trees (Ex. 15:27).

After a time the children of Israel "took their journey from Elim," and encamped by the Red Sea (Num. 33:10), and thence removed to the "wilderness of Sin" (to be distinguished from the wilderness of Zin, 20:1), where they again encamped. Here, probably the modern *el-Markha*, the supply of bread they had brought with them out of Egypt failed. They began to "murmur" for want of bread. God "heard their murmurings" and gave them quails and manna, "bread from heaven" (Ex. 16:4–36). Moses directed that an omer of manna should be put aside and preserved as a perpetual memorial of God's goodness. They now turned inland, and after three encampments came to the rich and fertile valley of Rephidim, in the Wâdy Feirân. Here they found no water, and again murmured against Moses. Directed by God, Moses procured a miraculous supply of water from the "rock in Horeb," one of the hills of the Sinai group (17:1–7); and shortly afterwards the children of Israel here fought their first battle with the Amalekites, whom they smote with the edge of the sword.

From the eastern extremity of the Wâdy Feirân the line of march now probably led through the Wâdy esh-Sheikh and the Wâdy Solaf, meeting in the Wâdy er-Rahah, "the enclosed plain in front of the magnificent cliffs of Ras Sufsâfeh." Here they encamped for more than a year (Num. 1:1; 10:11) before Sinai (*q.v.*).

The different encampments of the children of Israel, from the time of their leaving Egypt till they reached the Promised Land, are mentioned in Ex. 12:37-19; Num. 10–21; 33; Deut. 1, 2, 10.

It is worthy of notice that there are unmistakable evidences that the Egyptians had a tradition of a great exodus from their country, which could be none other than the exodus of the Hebrews. (See MAP, p. 198.)

Ex'odus, Book of. Exodus is the name given in the LXX. to the second book of the Pentateuch (*q.v.*). It means "departure" or "outgoing." This name was adopted in the Latin translation, and thence passed into other languages. The Hebrews called it by the first words, according to their custom, *Ve-êleh shemôth* (*i.e.*, "and these are the names").

It *contains*—(1.) An account of the increase and growth of the Israelites in Egypt (ch. 1). (2.) Preparations for their departure out of Egypt (2–12 : 36). (3.) Their journeyings from Egypt to Sinai (12 : 37–19 : 2). (4.) The giving of the law and the establishment of the institutions by which the organization of the people was completed—the theocracy, "a kingdom of priests and an holy nation" (19 : 3–ch. 40).

The *time* comprised in this book, from the death of Joseph to the erection of the tabernacle in the wilderness, is about one hundred and forty-five years, on the supposition that the four hundred and thirty years (12 : 40) are to be computed from the time of the promises made to Abraham (Gal. 3 : 17).

The *authorship* of this book, as well as of that of the other books of the Pentateuch, is to be ascribed to Moses. The unanimous voice of tradition and all internal evidences abundantly support this opinion.

Exor′cist (Acts 19 : 13). "In that sceptical and therefore superstitious age professional exorcists abounded. Many of these professional exorcists were disreputable Jews, like Simon in Samaria and Elymas in Cyprus (8 : 9 ; 13 : 6)." Other references to exorcism as practised by the Jews are found in Matt. 12 : 27 ; Mark 9 : 38 ; Luke 9 : 49, 50. It would seem that it was an opinion among the Jews that miracles might be wrought by invoking the divine name. Thus also these "vagabond Jews" pretended that they could expel dæmons.

The power of casting out devils was conferred by Christ on his apostles (Matt. 10 : 8), and on the seventy (Luke 10 : 17–19), and was exercised by believers after his ascension (Mark 16 : 17 ; Acts 16 : 18) ; but this power was never spoken of as exorcism.

Expia′tion. Guilt is said to be expiated when it is visited with punishment falling on a substitute. Expiation is made for our sins when they are punished not in ourselves but in another who consents to stand in our room. It is that by which reconciliation is effected. Sin is thus said to be "covered" by vicarious satisfaction.

The cover or lid of the ark is termed in the LXX. *hilasterion*, that which covered or shut out the claims and demands of the law against the sins of God's people, whereby he became "propitious" to them.

The idea of vicarious expiation runs through the whole Old Testament system of sacrifices. (See PROPITIATION.)

Eye (Heb. ʻ*ain*, meaning "flowing"), applied (1) to a fountain, frequently ; (2) to colour (Num. 11 : 7 ; R.V., "appearance," marg. "eye ") ; (3) the face (Ex. 10 : 5, 15 ; Num. 22 : 5, 11), in Num. 14 : 14, "face to face" (R.V. marg., "eye to eye "). "Between the eyes "—*i.e.*, the forehead (Ex. 13 : 9, 16).

The expression (Prov. 23 : 31), "when it giveth his colour in the cup," is literally, "when it giveth out [or showeth] its eye." The beads or bubbles of wine are thus spoken of. "To set the eyes " on any one is to view him with favour (Gen. 44 : 21 ; Job 24 : 23 ; Jer. 39 : 12). This word is used figuratively in the expressions an "evil eye" (Matt. 20 : 15), a "bountiful eye" (Prov. 22 : 9), "haughty eyes" (6 : 17 marg.), "wanton eyes " (Isa. 3 : 16), "eyes full of adultery" (2 Pet. 2 : 14), "the lust of the eyes " (1 John 2 : 16). Christians are warned against "eye-service" (Eph. 6 : 6 ; Col. 3 : 22). Men were sometimes punished by having their eyes put out (1 Sam. 11 : 2 ; Samson, Judg. 16 : 21 ; Zedekiah, 2 Kings 25 : 7).

The custom of *painting the eyes* is alluded to in 2 Kings 9 : 30, R.V.; Jer. 4 : 30 ; Ezek. 23 : 40, a custom which still prevails extensively among Eastern women.

Ezeki′as, Grecized form of Hezekiah (Matt. 1 : 9, 10).

Eze′kiel—*God will strengthen*. (1.) 1 Chr. 24 : 16, "Jehezekel."

(2.) One of the great prophets, the son of Buzi the priest (Ezek. 1 : 3). He was one of the Jewish exiles who settled at Tel-Abib, on the banks of the Chebar, "in the land of the Chaldeans." He was probably carried away captive with Jehoiachin (1:2; 2 Kings 24:14-16) about B.C. 597. His prophetic call came to him "in the fifth year of Jehoiachin's captivity" (B.C. 594). He had a house in the place of his exile, where he lost his wife, in the ninth year of his exile, by some sudden and unforeseen stroke (Ezek. 8:1; 24:18). He held a prominent place among the exiles, and was frequently consulted by the elders (8:1; 11:25; 14:1; 20:1). His ministry extended over twenty-three years (29:17), B.C. 595-573, during part of which he was contemporary with Daniel (14:14; 28:3) and Jeremiah, and probably also with Obadiah. The time and manner of his death are unknown. His reputed tomb is pointed out in the neighbourhood of Bagdad, at a place called Keffil.

Eze'kiel, Book of, consists mainly of three groups of prophecies. After an account of his call to the prophetical office (1-3:21), Ezekiel (1) utters words of denunciation against the Jews (3:22-24), warning them of the certain destruction of Jerusalem, in opposition to the words of the false prophets (4:1-3). The symbolical acts, by which the extremities to which Jerusalem would be reduced are described in ch. 4, 5, show his intimate acquaintance with the Levitical legislation. (See Ex. 22:30; Deut. 14:21; Lev. 5:2; 7:18, 24; 17:15; 19:7; 22:8, etc.)

(2.) Prophecies against various surrounding nations: against the Ammonites (Ezek. 25:1-7), the Moabites (8-11), the Edomites (12-14), the Philistines (15-17), Tyre and Sidon (26-28), and against Egypt (29-32).

(3.) Prophecies delivered after the destruction of Jerusalem by Nebuchadnezzar: the triumphs of Israel and of the kingdom of God on earth (Ezek. 33-39); Messianic times, and the establishment and prosperity of the kingdom of God (40; 48).

The closing visions of this book are referred to in the book of Revelation (Ezek. 38=Rev. 20:8; Ezek. 47:1-8=Rev. 22:1, 2). Other references to this book are also found in the New Testament. (Comp. Rom. 2:24 with Ezek. 36:2; Rom. 10:5, Gal. 3:12 with Ezek. 20:11; 2 Pet. 3:4 with Ezek. 12:22.)

It may be noted that Daniel, fourteen years after his deportation from Jerusalem, is mentioned by Ezekiel (14:14) along with Noah and Job as distinguished for his righteousness, and some five years later he is spoken of as pre-eminent for his wisdom (28:3).

Ezekiel's prophecies are *characterized by symbolical and allegorical representations,* "unfolding a rich series of majestic visions and of colossal symbols." There are a great many also of "symbolical *actions* embodying vivid conceptions on the part of the prophet" (4:1-4; 5:1-4; 12:3-6; 24:3-5; 37:16, etc.). "The mode of representation, in which symbols and allegories occupy a prominent place, gives a dark, mysterious character to the prophecies of Ezekiel. They are obscure and enigmatical. A cloudy mystery overhangs them which it is almost impossible to penetrate. Jerome calls the book 'a labyrinth of the mysteries of God.' It was because of this obscurity that the Jews forbade any one to read it till he had attained the age of thirty."

Ezekiel is singular in the frequency with which he refers to the Pentateuch (*e.g.,* Ezek. 27; 28:13; 31:8; 36:11, 34; 47:13, etc.). He shows also an acquaintance with the writings of Hosea (Ezek. 37:22), Isaiah (Ezek. 8:12; 29:6), and especially with those of Jeremiah, his older contemporary (Jer. 24:7, 9; 48:37).

Ez'el—*a separation*—(1 Sam. 20:19), a stone, or heap of stones, in the neighbourhood of Saul's residence, the scene of the parting of David and Jonathan (42). The margin of the Authorized Version reads, "The stone that sheweth the way," in this rendering following the Targum.

E'zer—*treasure.* (1.) One of the sons of Seir, the native princes, "dukes," of Mount Hor (Gen. 36:21, 27). (2.) 1 Chr. 7:21; (3.) 4:4. (4.) One of the Gadite champions who repaired to David at Ziklag (12:9). (5.) A Levite (Neh. 3:19). (6.) A priest (12:42).

E'zion-ge'ber—*the giant's backbone* (so called from the head of a mountain which runs out into the sea)—an ancient city and harbour at the north-east end of the Elanitic branch of the Red Sea, the Gulf of Akabah, near Elath or Eloth (Num. 33:35;

Deut. 2:8). Here Solomon built ships—"Tarshish ships," like those trading from Tyre to Tarshish and the west—which traded with Ophir (1 Kings 9:26; 2 Chr. 8:17); and here also Jehoshaphat's fleet was shipwrecked (1 Kings 22:48; 2 Chr. 20:36). It became a populous town, many of the Jews settling in it (2 Kings 16:6, "Elath"). It is supposed that anciently the north end of the gulf flowed further into the country than now, as far as 'Ain el-Ghudyân, which is 10 miles up the dry bed of the Arabah, and that Ezion-geber may have been there.

Ez'ra—*help.* (1.) A priest among those that returned to Jerusalem under Zerubbabel (Neh. 12:1).

(2.) The "scribe" who led the second body of exiles that returned from Babylon to Jerusalem B.C. 459, and author of the book of Scripture which bears his name. He was the son, or perhaps grandson, of Seraiah (2 Kings 25:18-21), and a lineal descendant of Phinehas, the son of Aaron (Ezra 7:1-5). All we know of his personal history is contained in the last four chapters of his book, and in Neh. 8 and 12:26.

In the seventh year of the reign of Artaxerxes Longimanus (see DARIUS), he obtained leave to go up to Jerusalem and to take with him a company of Israelites (Ezra 8). Artaxerxes manifested great interest in Ezra's undertaking, granting him "all his request," and loading him with gifts for the house of God. Ezra assembled the band of exiles, probably about 5,000 in all, who were prepared to go up with him to Jerusalem, on the banks of the Ahava, where they rested for three days, and were put into order for their march across the desert, which was completed in four months. His proceedings at Jerusalem on his arrival there are recorded in his book.

He was "a ready scribe in the law of Moses," who "had prepared his heart to seek the law of the Lord and to do it, and to teach in Israel statutes and judgments." "He is," says Professor Binnie, "the first well-defined example of an order of men who have never since ceased in the church; men of sacred erudition, who devote their lives to the study of the Holy Scriptures, in order that they may be in a condition to interpret them for the instruction and edification of the church. It is significant that the earliest mention of *the pulpit* occurs in the history of Ezra's ministry (Neh. 8:4). He was much more of a teacher than a priest. We learn from the account of his labours in the book of Nehemiah that he was careful to have the whole people instructed in the law of Moses; and there is no reason to reject the constant tradition of the Jews which connects his name with the collecting and editing of the Old Testament canon. The final completion of the canon may have been, and probably was, the work of a later generation; but Ezra seems to have put it much into the shape in which it is still found in the Hebrew Bible. When it is added that the complete organization of the synagogue dates from this period, it will be seen that the age was emphatically one of Biblical study" (*The Psalms: their History, etc.*).

For about fourteen years—*i.e.,* till B.C. 445—we have no record of what went on in Jerusalem after Ezra had set in order the ecclesiastical and civil affairs of the nation. In that year another distinguished personage—Nehemiah—appears on the scene. After the ruined wall of the city had been built by Nehemiah, there was a great gathering of the people at Jerusalem preparatory to the dedication of the wall. On the appointed day the whole population assembled, and the law was read aloud to them by Ezra and his assistants (Neh. 8:3). The remarkable scene is described in detail. There was a great religious awakening. For successive days they held solemn assemblies, confessing their sins and offering up solemn sacrifices. They kept also the feast of Tabernacles with great solemnity and joyous enthusiasm, and then renewed their national covenant to be the Lord's. Abuses were rectified, and arrangements for the temple service completed, and now nothing remained but the dedication of the walls of the city (Neh. 12).

Ez'ra, Book of. This book is the record of events occurring at the close of the Babylonian exile. It was at one time included in Nehemiah, the Jews regarding them as one volume. The two are still distinguished in the Vulgate version as I. and II. Esdras. It consists of two principal divisions :—

(1.) The history of the first return of exiles, in the first year of Cyrus (B.C. 536), till the completion and dedication of the new temple, in the sixth year of Darius Hystaspes (B.C. 515)—ch. 1-6. From the close of the sixth to the opening of the seventh chapter there is a blank in the history of about sixty years.

(2.) The history of the second return under Ezra, in the seventh year of Artaxerxes Longimanus, and of the events that took place at Jerusalem after Ezra's arrival there (7-10).

The book thus contains *memorabilia* connected with the Jews, from the decree of Cyrus (B.C. 536) to the reformation by Ezra (B.C. 456), extending over a period of about eighty years.

There is no quotation from this book in the New Testament, but there never has been any doubt about its being canonical.

Ezra was probably the *author* of this book, at least of the greater part of it (comp. 7 : 27, 28 ; 8 : 1, etc.), as he was also of the Books of Chronicles, the close of which forms the opening passage of Ezra.

Ez'rahite, a title given to Ethan (1 Kings 4 : 31 ; Ps. 89, title) and Heman (Ps. 88, title). They were both sons of Zerah (1 Chr. 2 : 6).

Ez'ri—*help of Jehovah*—the son of Chelub. He superintended, under David, those who "did the work of the field for tillage" (1 Chr. 27 : 26).

F

Fable, applied in the New Testament to the traditions and speculations—"cunningly devised fables"—of the Jews on religious questions (1 Tim. 1 : 4 ; 4 : 7 ; 2 Tim. 4 : 4 ; Titus 1 : 14 ; 2 Pet. 1 : 16). In such passages the word means anything false and unreal.

But the word is used as almost equivalent to parable. Thus we have (1) the fable of Jotham, in which the trees are spoken of as choosing a king (Judg. 9 : 8-15) ; and (2) that of the cedars of Lebanon and the thistle as Jehoash's answer to Amaziah (2 Kings 14 : 9).

Face means simply presence, as when it is recorded that Adam and Eve hid themselves from the "face [R.V., 'presence'] of the Lord God" (Gen. 3 : 8 ; comp. Ex. 33 : 14, 15, where the same Hebrew word is rendered " presence"). The "light of God's countenance" is his favour (Ps. 44 : 3 ; Dan. 9 : 17). "Face" signifies also anger, justice, severity (Gen. 16 : 6, 8 ; Ex. 2 : 15 ; Ps. 68 : 1 ; Rev. 6 : 16). To "provoke God to his face" (Isa. 65 : 3) is to sin against him openly.

The Jews prayed with their faces toward the temple and Jerusalem (1 Kings 8 : 38, 44, 48 ; Dan. 6 : 10). To "see God's face" is to have access to him and to enjoy his favour (Ps. 17 : 15 ; 27 : 8). This is the privilege of holy angels (Matt. 18 : 10 ; Luke 1 : 19). The "face of Jesus Christ" (2 Cor. 4 : 6) is the office and person of Christ, the revealer of the glory of God (John 1 : 14, 18).

Fair Havens, a harbour in the south of Crete, some 5 miles to the east of which was the town of Lasea (Acts 27 : 8). Here the ship of Alexandria in which Paul and his companions sailed was detained a considerable time waiting for a favourable wind. Contrary to Paul's advice, the master of the ship determined to prosecute the voyage, as the harbour was deemed incommodious for wintering in (9-12). The result was that, after a stormy voyage, the vessel was finally wrecked on the coast of Malta (27 : 40-44).

Fairs (Heb. *'izabhonîm*), found seven times in Ezek. 27, and nowhere else. The Authorized Version renders the word thus in all these instances, except in verse 33, where "wares" is used. The Revised

Version uniformly renders by "wares," which is the correct rendering of the Hebrew word. It never means "fairs" in the modern sense of the word.

Faith. Faith is in general the persuasion of the mind that a certain statement is true (Phil. 1 : 27 ; 2 Thess. 2 : 13). Its primary idea is trust. A thing is true, and therefore worthy of trust. It admits of many degrees up to full assurance of faith, in accordance with the evidence on which it rests.

Faith is the result of teaching (Rom. 10 : 14–17). Knowledge is an essential element in all faith, and is sometimes spoken of as an equivalent to faith (John 10 : 38 ; 1 John 2 : 3). Yet the two are distinguished in this respect, that faith includes in it assent, which is an act of the will in addition to the act of the understanding. Assent to the truth is of the essence of faith, and the ultimate ground on which our assent to any revealed truth rests is the veracity of God.

Historical faith is the apprehension of and assent to certain statements which are regarded as mere facts of history.

Temporary faith is that state of mind which is awakened in men (*e.g.*, Felix) by the exhibition of the truth and by the influence of religious sympathy, or by what is sometimes styled the common operation of the Holy Spirit.

Saving faith is so called because it has eternal life inseparably connected with it. It cannot be better defined than in the words of the Assembly's Shorter Catechism : "Faith in Jesus Christ is a saving grace, whereby we receive and rest upon him alone for salvation, as he is offered to us in the gospel."

The *object* of saving faith is the whole revealed Word of God. Faith accepts and believes it as the very truth most sure. But the special act of faith which unites to Christ has as its object the person and the work of the Lord Jesus Christ (John 7 : 38 ; Acts 16 : 31). This is the specific act of faith by which a sinner is justified before God (Rom. 3 : 22, 25 ; Gal. 2 : 16 ; Phil. 3 : 9 ; John 3 : 16–36 ; Acts 10 : 43 ; 16 : 31). In this act of faith the believer appro-

priates and rests on Christ alone as Mediator in all his offices.

This assent to or belief in the truth received upon the divine testimony has always associated with it a deep sense of sin, a distinct view of Christ, a consenting will, and a loving heart, together with a reliance on, a trusting in, or resting in Christ. It is that state of mind in which a poor sinner, conscious of his sin, flees from his guilty self to Christ his Saviour, and rolls over the burden of all his sins on him. It consists chiefly, not in the assent given to the testimony of God in his Word, but in embracing with fiducial reliance and trust the one only Saviour whom God reveals. This trust and reliance is of the essence of faith. By faith the believer directly and immediately appropriates Christ as his own. Faith in its direct act makes Christ ours. It is not a work which God graciously accepts instead of perfect obedience, but is only the hand by which we take hold of the person and work of our Redeemer as the only ground of our salvation.

Saving faith is a *moral* act, as it proceeds from a renewed will, and a renewed will is necessary to believing assent to the truth of God (1 Cor. 2 : 14 ; 2 Cor. 4 : 4). Faith, therefore, has its seat in the *moral* part of our nature fully as much as in the intellectual. The mind must first be enlightened by divine teaching (John 6 : 44 ; Acts 13 : 48 ; 2 Cor. 4 : 6 ; Eph. 1 : 17, 18) before it can discern the things of the Spirit.

Faith is *necessary* to our salvation (Mark 16 : 16), not because there is any merit in it, but simply because it is the sinner's taking the place assigned him by God—his falling in with what God is doing.

The *warrant* or ground of faith is the divine testimony—not the reasonableness of what God says, but the simple fact that he says it. Faith rests immediately on, "Thus saith the Lord." But in order to this faith the veracity, sincerity, and truth of God must be owned and appreciated, together with his unchangeableness. God's word encourages and emboldens the sinner personally to transact with Christ as God's gift, to close with him, embrace him, give himself to Christ, and take Christ as his. That word comes with power, for it is the word of God who has revealed himself in his works, and especially in the cross. God is to be believed for his word's sake, but also for his name's sake.

Faith in Christ secures for the believer freedom from condemnation, or justification before God; a participation in the life that is in Christ—the divine life (John 14:19; Rom. 6:4-10; Eph. 4:15,16, etc.); "peace with God" (Rom. 5:1); and sanctification (Acts 26:18; Gal. 5:6; Acts 15:9).

All who thus believe in Christ will certainly be saved (John 6:37, 40; 10:27, 28; Rom. 8:1).

The faith=the gospel (Acts 6:7; Rom. 1:5; Gal. 1:23; 1 Tim. 3:9; Jude 3).

Faithful, as a designation of Christians, means full of faith, trustful, and not simply trustworthy (Acts 10:45; 16:1; 2 Cor. 6:15; Col. 1:2; 1 Tim. 4:3, 12; 5:16; 6:2; Titus 1:6; Eph. 1:1; 1 Cor. 4:17, etc.).

It is used also of God's word or covenant as true and to be trusted (Ps. 119:86; 138; Isa. 25:1; 1 Tim. 1:15; Rev. 21:5; 22:6, etc.).

Fall of man, an expression probably borrowed from the Apocryphal Book of Wisdom, to express the fact of the revolt of our first parents from God, and the consequent sin and misery in which they and all their posterity were involved.

The *history* of the Fall is recorded in Gen. 2 and 3. That history is to be literally interpreted. It records facts which underlie the whole system of revealed truth. It is referred to by our Lord and his apostles not only as being true, but as furnishing the ground of all God's subsequent dispensations and dealings with the children of men. The record of Adam's temptation and fall must be taken as a true historical account, if we are to understand the Bible at all as a revelation of God's purpose of mercy.

The *effects* of this first sin *upon our first parents themselves* were (1) "shame, a sense of degradation and pollution; (2) dread of the displeasure of God, or a sense of guilt, and the consequent desire to hide

from his presence. These effects were unavoidable. They prove the loss not only of innocence but of original righteousness, and, with it, of the favour and fellowship of God. The state therefore to which Adam was reduced by his disobedience, so far as his subjective condition is concerned, was analogous to that of the fallen angels. He was entirely and absolutely ruined" (Hodge's *Theology*).

But the unbelief and disobedience of our first parents brought not only on themselves this misery and ruin, it entailed also the same sad consequences on all their descendants. (1.) The guilt—*i.e.*, liability to punishment—of that sin comes by imputation upon all men, because all were represented by Adam in the covenant of works (*q.v.*). (See IMPUTATION.)

(2.) Hence, also, all his descendants inherit a corrupt nature. In all by nature there is an inherent and prevailing tendency to sin. This universal depravity is taught by universal experience. All men sin as soon as they are capable of moral actions. The testimony of the Scriptures to the same effect is most abundant (Rom. 1; 2; 3:1-19, etc.).

(3.) This innate depravity is *total:* we are by nature "dead in trespasses and sins," and must be "born again" before we can enter into the kingdom (John 3:7, etc.).

(4.) Resulting from this "corruption of our whole nature" is our absolute moral inability to change our nature or to obey the law of God.

Commenting on John 9:3, Ryle well remarks: "A deep and instructive principle lies in these words. They surely throw some light on that great question— the origin of evil. God has thought fit to allow evil to exist in order that he may have a platform for showing his mercy, grace, and compassion. If man had never fallen there would have been no opportunity of showing divine mercy. But by permitting evil, mysterious as it seems, God's works of grace, mercy, and wisdom in saving sinners have been wonderfully manifested to all his creatures. The redeeming of the church of elect sinners is the means of 'showing to principalities and powers the manifold wisdom of God' (Eph. 3:10). Without the Fall we should have known nothing of the Cross and the Gospel."

On the monuments of Egypt are found representations of a deity in human form, piercing with a spear the head of a serpent. This is regarded as an illustration of the wide dissemination of the tradition of the Fall. The story of the "golden age," which gives place to the "iron age"—the age of purity and innocence, which is followed by a time when man becomes a prey to sin and misery, as represented in the mythology of Greece and Rome, has also been regarded as a tradition of the Fall.

Fallow-deer—Deut. 14:5 (R.V., "wild goat"); 1 Kings 4:23 (R.V., "roebucks"). This animal, called in Hebrew *yahmûr*, from a word meaning "to be red," is generally regarded as the common fallow-deer

FALLOW-DEER.

—the *Cervus dama*—which is said to be found very generally over Western and Southern Asia. It is called "fallow" from its pale-red or yellow colour. Some interpreters, however, regard the name as designating the bubale—*Antelope bubalus* (the "wild cow" of North Africa)—which is about the size of a stag, like the hartebeest of South Africa. A species of deer has been found at Mount Carmel which is called *yahmûr* by the Arabs. It is said to be very similar to the European roebuck.

Fallow-ground. The expression "Break

up your fallow ground" (Hos. 10:12; Jer. 4:3) means, "Do not sow your seed among thorns"—*i.e.*, break off all your evil habits; clear your hearts of weeds, in order that they may be prepared for the seed of righteousness. Land was allowed to lie fallow that it might become more fruitful; but when in this condition, it soon became overgrown with thorns and weeds. The cultivator of the soil was careful to "break up" his fallow ground—*i.e.*, to clear the field of weeds—before sowing seed in it. So says the prophet, "Break off your evil ways—repent of your sins—cease to do evil, and then the good seed of the word will have room to grow and bear fruit."

Familiar spirit. Sorcerers or necromancers, who professed to call up the dead to answer questions, were said to have a "familiar spirit" (Deut. 18:11; 2 Kings 21:6; 2 Chr. 33:6; Lev. 19:31; 20:6; Isa. 8:19; 29:4). Such a person was called by the Hebrews an *'ob*, which properly means a leathern bottle; for sorcerers were regarded as vessels containing the inspiring *dæmon*. This Hebrew word was equivalent to the *pytho* of the Greeks, and was used to denote both the person and the spirit which possessed him (Lev. 20:27; 1 Sam. 28:8; comp. Acts 16:16). The word "familiar" is from the Latin *familiaris*, meaning a "household servant," and was intended to express the idea that sorcerers had spirits as their servants ready to obey their commands.

Fam'ine. The first mentioned in Scripture was so grievous as to compel Abraham to go down to the land of Egypt (Gen. 26:1). Another is mentioned as having occurred in the days of Isaac, causing him to go to Gerar (Gen. 26:1, 17). But the most remarkable of all was that which arose in Egypt in the days of Joseph, which lasted for seven years (Gen. 41-45).

Famines were sent as an effect of God's anger against a guilty people (2 Kings 8:1, 2; Amos 8:11; Deut. 28:22-42; 2 Sam. 21:1; 2 Kings 6:25-28; 25:3; Jer. 14:15; 19:9; 42:17, etc.). A famine was predicted by Agabus (Acts 11:28). Josephus makes mention of the famine which occurred A.D. 45. Helena, queen of Adiabene, being at Jerusalem at that time, procured corn from Alexandria and figs from Cyprus for its poor inhabitants.

Fan, a winnowing shovel by which grain was thrown up against the wind that it might be cleansed from broken straw and chaff (Isa. 30:24; Jer. 15:7; Matt. 3:12). (See AGRICULTURE.)

Farm (Matt. 22:5). Every Hebrew had a certain portion of land assigned to him as a possession (Num. 26:33-56). In Egypt the lands all belonged to the king, and the husbandmen were obliged to give him a fifth part of the produce; so in Palestine Jehovah was the sole possessor of the soil, and the people held it by direct tenure from him. By the enactment of Moses, the Hebrews paid a tithe of the produce to Jehovah, which was assigned to the priesthood. Military service when required was also to be rendered by every Hebrew at his own expense. The occupation of a husbandman was held in high honour (1 Sam. 11:5-7; 1 Kings 19:19; 2 Chr. 26:10). (See LAND LAWS; TITHE.)

Farthing. (1.) Matt. 10:29; Luke 12:6. Greek *assarion*—*i.e.*, a small *as*, which was a Roman coin equal to a tenth

ASSARION.
(From a specimen in the British Museum.)

of a denarius or drachma, nearly equal to a halfpenny of our money.

(2.) Matt. 5:26; Mark 12:42 (Gr. *kodrantēs*), the *quadrant*, the fourth of an *as*,

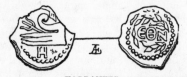

KODRANTES.
(From De Saulcy's "Numismatique Judaïque.")

equal to two *lepta*, mites. The *lepton* (mite) was the very smallest copper coin.

Fast. The sole fast required by the law of Moses was that of the great Day of Atonement (*q.v.*)—Lev. 23:26-32. It is called "the fast" (Acts 27:9).

The only other mention of a periodical fast in the Old Testament is in Zech. 7:1-7; 8:19, from which it appears that during their captivity the Jews observed four annual fasts.

(1.) The fast of the fourth month, kept on the seventeenth day of Tammuz, the anniversary of the capture of Jerusalem by the Chaldeans; to commemorate also the incident recorded Ex. 32:19. (Comp. Jer. 52:6, 7.)

(2.) The fast of the fifth month, kept on the ninth of Ab (comp. Num. 14:27), to commemorate the burning of the city and temple (Jer. 52:12, 13).

(3.) The fast of the seventh month, kept on the third of Tisri (comp. 2 Kings 25), the anniversary of the murder of Gedaliah (Jer. 41:1, 2).

(4.) The fast of the tenth month (comp. Jer. 52:4; Ezek. 33:21; 2 Kings 25:1), to commemorate the beginning of the siege of the holy city by Nebuchadnezzar.

There was in addition to these the fast appointed by Esther (4:16).

Public national fasts on account of sin or to supplicate divine favour were sometimes held. (1.) 1 Sam. 7:6; (2.) 2 Chr. 20:3; (3.) Jer. 36:6-10; (4.) Neh. 9:1.

There were also local fasts. (1.) Judg. 20:26; (2.) 2 Sam. 1:12; (3.) 1 Sam. 31:13; (4.) 1 Kings 21:9-12; (5.) Ezra 8:21-23; (6.) Jonah 3:5-9.

There are many instances of private occasional fasting (1 Sam. 1:7; 20:34; 2 Sam. 3:35; 12:16; 1 Kings 21:27; Ezra 10:6; Neh. 1:4; Dan. 10:2,3). Moses fasted forty days (Ex. 24:18; 34:28), and so also did Elijah (1 Kings 19:8). Our Lord fasted forty days in the wilderness (Matt. 4:2).

In the lapse of time the practice of fasting was lamentably abused (Isa. 58:4; Jer. 14:12; Zech. 7:5). Our Lord rebuked the Pharisees for their hypocritical pretences in fasting (Matt. 6:16). He himself appointed no fast. The early Christians, however, observed the ordinary fasts according to the law of their fathers (Acts 13:3; 14:23; 2 Cor. 6:5).

Fat (Heb. *heleb*) denotes the richest part of the animal, or the fattest of the flock, in the account of Abel's sacrifice (Gen. 4:4). It sometimes denotes the best of any production (Gen. 45:18; Num. 18:12; Ps. 81:16; 147:14). The fat of sacrifices was to be burned (Lev. 3:9–11; 4:8; 7:3; 8:25; Num. 18:17. Comp. Ex. 29:13–22; Lev. 3:3–5).

It is used figuratively for a dull, stupid state of mind (Ps. 17:10).

In Joel 2:24 the word is equivalent to "vat," a vessel. The Hebrew word here thus rendered is elsewhere rendered "winefat" and "press-fat" (Hag. 2:16; Isa. 63:2).

Father, a name applied (1) to any ancestor (Deut. 1:11; 1 Kings 15:11; Matt. 3:9; 23:30, etc.); and (2) as a title of respect to a chief, ruler, or elder, etc. (Judg. 17:10; 18:19; 1 Sam. 10:12; 2 Kings 2:12; Matt. 23:9, etc.). (3) The author or beginner of anything is also so called; *e.g.*, Jabal and Jubal (Gen. 4:20, 21; comp. Job 38:28).

Applied to God (Ex. 4:22; Deut. 32:6; 2 Sam. 7:14; Ps. 89:27, 28, etc.). (1.) As denoting his covenant relation to the Jews (Jer. 31:9; Isa. 63:16; 64:8; John 8:41, etc.).

(2.) Believers are called God's "sons" (John 1:12; Rom. 8:16; Matt. 6:4, 8, 15, 18; 10:20, 29). They also call him "Father" (Rom. 1:7; 1 Cor. 1:3; 2 Cor. 1:2; Gal. 1:4).

Fathom (Old A.S. *fæthm,* "bosom," or the outstretched arms), a span of six feet (Acts 27:28). Gr. *orguia* (from *oregō,* "I stretch"), the distance between the extremities of both arms fully stretched out.

Fatling. (1.) A fatted animal for slaughter (2 Sam. 6:13; Isa. 11:6; Ezek. 39:18. Comp. Matt. 22:4, where the word used in the original, *sitistos,* means literally "corn-fed;" *i.e.*, stalled, fat). (2.) Ps. 66:15 (Heb. *meah,* meaning "marrowy," "fat," a species of sheep). (3.) 1 Sam. 15:9 (Heb. *mishneh,* meaning "the second," and hence probably "cattle of a second quality," or lambs of the second birth—

i.e., autumnal lambs—and therefore of less value).

Fear of the Lord, the, is in the Old Testament used as a designation of true piety (Prov. 1:7; Job 28:28; Ps. 19:9). It is a fear conjoined with love and hope, and is therefore not a slavish dread, but rather filial reverence. (Comp. Deut. 32:6; Hos. 11:1; Isa. 1:2; 63:16; 64:8.) God is called "the Fear of Isaac" (Gen. 31:42, 53)—*i.e.*, the God whom Isaac feared.

A holy fear is enjoined also in the New Testament as a preventive of carelessness in religion, and as an incentive to penitence (Matt. 10:28; 2 Cor. 5:11; 7:1; Phil. 2:12; Eph. 5:21; Heb. 12:28, 29).

Feast, as a mark of hospitality (Gen. 19:3; 2 Sam. 3:20; 2 Kings 6:23); on occasions of domestic joy (Luke 15:23; Gen. 21:8); on birthdays (Gen. 40:20; Job 1:4; Matt. 14:6); and on the occasion of a marriage (Judg. 14:10; Gen. 29:22).

Feasting was a part of the observances connected with the offering up of sacrifices (Deut. 12:6, 7; 1 Sam. 9:19; 16:3, 5), and with the annual festivals (Deut. 16:11). "It was one of the designs of the greater solemnities, which required the attendance of the people at the sacred tent, that the oneness of the nation might be maintained and cemented together, by statedly congregating in one place, and with one soul taking part in the same religious services. But that oneness was primarily and chiefly a religious and not merely a political one; the people were not merely to meet as among themselves, but with Jehovah, and to present themselves before him as one body; the meeting was in its own nature a binding of themselves in fellowship with Jehovah; so that it was not politics and commerce that had here to do, but the soul of the Mosaic dispensation, the foundation of the religious and political existence of Israel, the covenant with Jehovah. To keep the people's consciousness alive to this, to revive, strengthen, and perpetuate it, nothing could be so well adapted as these annual feasts." (See FESTIVALS.)

Fe'lix—*happy*—the Roman procurator of Judea before whom Paul "reasoned" (Acts 24:25). He appears to have expected a bribe from Paul, and therefore had several interviews with him. The "worthy deeds" referred to in 24:2 was his clearing the country of banditti and impostors.

At the end of a two years' term, Porcius Festus was appointed in the room of Felix (A.D. 60), who proceeded to Rome, and was there accused of cruelty and malversation of office by the Jews of Cæsarea. The accusation was rendered nugatory by the influence of his brother Pallas with Nero. (See Josephus, *Ant.* xx. 8, 9.)

Drusilla, the daughter of Herod Agrippa, having been induced by Felix to desert her husband, the king of Emesa, became his adulterous companion. She was seated beside him when Paul "reasoned" before the judge. When Felix gave place to Festus, being "willing to do the Jews a pleasure," he left Paul bound.

Fel'lowship. (1.) With God—consisting in the knowledge of his will (Job 22:21; John 17:3); agreement with his designs (Amos 3:2); mutual affection (Rom. 8:38, 39); enjoyment of his presence (Ps. 4:6); conformity to his image (1 John 2:6; 1:6); and participation of his felicity (1 John 1:3, 4; Eph. 3:14-21).

(2.) Of saints with one another—in duties (Rom. 12:6; 1 Cor. 12:1; 1 Thess. 5:17, 18); in ordinances (Heb. 10:24; Acts 2:46); in grace, love, joy, etc. (Mal. 3:16; 2 Cor. 8:4); mutual interest, spiritual and temporal (Rom. 12:4, 13; Heb. 13:16); in sufferings (Rom. 15:1, 2; Gal. 6:1, 2; Rom. 12:15); and in glory (Rev. 7:9).

Fence (Heb. *gadēr*)— Num. 22:24 (R.V.). Fences were constructions of unmortared stones, to protect gardens, vineyards, sheepfolds, etc. From various causes they were apt to bulge out and fall (Ps. 62:3). In Ps. 80:12, R.V. (see Isa. 5:5), the psalmist says, "Why hast thou broken down her fences?" Serpents delight to lurk in the crevices of such fences (Eccl. 10:8; comp. Amos 5:19).

Fenced cities. There were in Palestine (1) cities, (2) unwalled villages, and (3) villages with castles or towers (1 Chr. 27:25). Cities, so called, had walls, and were thus fenced. The fortifications consisted of one or two walls, on which were towers or parapets at regular intervals (2 Chr. 32:5; Jer. 31:38). Around ancient Jerusalem were three walls, on one of which were ninety towers, on the second fourteen, and on the third sixty. The tower of Hananeel, near the north-east corner of the city wall, is frequently referred to (Neh. 3:1; 12:39; Zech. 14:10). The gateways of such cities were also fortified (Neh. 2:8; 3:3, 6; Judg. 16:2, 3; 1 Sam. 23:7).

The Hebrews found many fenced cities when they entered the Promised Land (Num. 13:28; 32:17, 34-42; Josh. 11:12, 13; Judg. 1:27-33), and we may estimate the strength of some of these cities from the fact that they were long held in possession by the Canaanites. The Jebusites, *e.g.*, were enabled to hold possession of Jerusalem till the time of David (2 Sam. 5:6, 7; 1 Chr. 11:5).

Several of the kings of Israel and Judah distinguished themselves as fortifiers or "builders" of cities.

Fer'ret—Lev. 11:30 (R.V., "gecko")—one of the unclean creeping things. It was perhaps the *Lacerta gecko* which was intended

A GECKO.

by the Hebrew word (*anâkah'*, a cry, "mourning," the creature which groans) here used—*i.e.*, the "fan-footed" lizard, the gecko which makes a mournful wail. The LXX. translate it by a word meaning "shrew-mouse," of which there are three species in Palestine. The Rabbinical writers regard it as the hedgehog. The translation of the Revised Version is to be preferred.

Fer′ry boat (2 Sam. 19:18), some kind of boat for crossing the river which the men of Judah placed at the service of the king. Floats or rafts for this purpose were in use from remote times (Isa. 18:2).

Fes′tivals, Religious. There were daily (Lev. 23), weekly, monthly, and yearly festivals, and great stress was laid on the regular observance of them in every particular (Num. 28:1-8; Ex. 29:38-42; Lev. 6:8-23; Ex. 30:7-9; 27:20).

(1.) The septenary festivals were—

(*a*) The weekly Sabbath (Lev. 23:1-3; Ex. 19:3-30; 20:8-11; 31:12, etc.).

(*b*) The seventh new moon, or the feast of Trumpets (Num. 28:11-15; 29:1-6).

(*c*) The Sabbatical year (Ex. 23:10, 11; Lev. 25:2-7).

(*d*) The year of jubilee (Lev. 23-35; 25:8-16; 27:16-25).

(2.) The great feasts were—

(*a*) The Passover. (*b*) The feast of Pentecost, or of weeks. (*c*) The feast of Tabernacles, or of ingathering.

On each of these occasions every male Israelite was commanded "to appear before the Lord" (Deut. 27:7; Neh. 8:9-12). The attendance of women was voluntary. (Comp. Luke 2:41; 1 Sam. 1:7; 2:19.) The promise that God would protect their homes (Ex. 34:23, 24) while all the males were absent in Jerusalem at these feasts was always fulfilled. "During the whole period between Moses and Christ we never read of an enemy invading the land at the time of the three festivals. The first instance on record is thirty-three years after they had withdrawn from themselves the divine protection by imbruing their hands in the Saviour's blood, when Cestius, the Roman general, slew fifty of the people of Lydda while all the rest had gone up to the feast of Tabernacles, A.D. 66."

These festivals, besides their religious purpose, had an important bearing on the maintenance among the people of the feeling of a national unity. The times fixed for their observance were arranged so as to interfere as little as possible with the industry of the people. The Passover was kept just before the harvest commenced, Pentecost at the conclusion of the corn

harvest and before the vintage, the feast of Tabernacles after all the fruits of the ground had been gathered in.

(3.) The Day of Atonement, the tenth day of the seventh month (Lev. 16:1, 34; 23:26-32; Num. 29:7-11). (See ATONEMENT, DAY OF.)

Of the *post-Exilian* festivals reference is made to the feast of Dedication (John 10:22). This feast was appointed by Judas Maccabæus in commemoration of the purification of the temple after it had been polluted by Antiochus Epiphanes. The "feast of Purim" (*q.v.*), Esther 9:24-32, was also instituted after the Exile. (Cf. John 5:1.)

Fes′tus, Por′cius, the successor of Felix (A.D. 60) as procurator of Judea (Acts 24:27). A few weeks after he had entered on his office the case of Paul, then a prisoner at Cæsarea, was reported to him. The "next day," after he had gone down to Cæsarea, he heard Paul defend himself in the presence of Herod Agrippa II. and his sister Bernice, and not finding in him anything worthy of death or of bonds, would have set him free had he not appealed unto Cæsar (Acts 25:11, 12). In consequence of this appeal Paul was sent to Rome. Festus, after being in office less than two years, died in Judæa. (See AGRIPPA.)

Fe′ver (Deut. 28:22; Matt. 8:14; Mark 1:30; John 4:52; Acts 28:8), a burning heat, as the word so rendered denotes, which attends all febrile attacks. In all Eastern countries such diseases are very common. Peter's wife's mother is said to have suffered from a "great fever" (Luke 4:38)—an instance of Luke's professional exactitude in describing disease. He adopts here the technical medical distinction, as in those times fevers were divided into the "great" and the "less."

Field (Heb. *sadêh*), a cultivated field, but unenclosed. It is applied to any cultivated ground or pasture (Gen. 29:2; 31:4; 34:7), or tillage (Gen. 37:7; 47:24). It is also applied to woodland (Ps. 132:6) or mountain top (Judg. 9:32, 36; 2 Sam. 1:21). It denotes sometimes a cultivated region as opposed to the wilderness (Gen. 33:19; 36:35). Unwalled villages or scattered houses are spoken of as "in the fields"

(Deut. 28 : 3, 16 ; Lev. 25 : 31 ; Mark 6 : 36, 56). The "open field" is a place remote from a house (Gen. 4 : 8 ; Lev. 14 : 7, 53 ; 17 : 5). Cultivated land of any extent was called a field (Gen. 23 : 13, 17 ; 41 : 8 ; Lev. 27 : 16 ; Ruth 4 : 5 ; Neh. 12 : 29).

Fig. First mentioned in Gen. 3 : 7. The fig-tree is mentioned (Deut. 8 : 8) as one of the valuable products of Palestine. It was a sign of peace and prosperity (1 Kings 4 : 25 ; Micah 4 : 4 ; Zech. 3 : 10). Figs were used medicinally (2 Kings 20 : 7), and

BRANCH OF FIG-TREE.

pressed together and formed into "cakes" as articles of diet (1 Sam. 30 : 12 ; Jer. 24 : 2).

Our Lord's cursing the fig-tree near Bethany (Mark 11 : 13) has occasioned much perplexity from the circumstance, as mentioned by the evangelist, that "the time of figs was not yet." The explanation of the words, however, lies in the simple fact that the fruit of the fig-tree appears before the leaves, and hence that if the tree produced leaves it ought also to have had fruit. It ought to have had fruit if it had been true to its

"pretensions," in showing its leaves at this particular season. "This tree, so to speak, vaunted itself to be in advance of all the other trees, challenged the passer-by that he should come and refresh himself with its fruit. Yet when the Lord accepted its challenge and drew near, it proved to be but *as* the others,—without fruit as they ; for indeed, as the evangelist observes, the time of figs had not yet arrived. Its fault, if one may use the word, lay in its pretensions, in its making a show to run before the rest when it did not so indeed " (Trench, *Miracles*).

The fig-tree of Palestine (*Ficus carica*) produces two and sometimes three crops of figs in a year—(1) the *bikkurâh,* or "early-ripe fig" (Micah 7 : 1 ; Isa. 28 : 4 ; Hos. 9 : 10, R.V.), which is ripe about the end of June, dropping off as soon as it is ripe (Nah. 3 : 12) ; (2) the *kermûs,* or "summer fig," then begins to be formed, and is ripe about August ; and (3) the *pag* (plural "green figs," Cant. 2 : 13 ; Gr. *olynthos,* Rev. 6 : 13, "the untimely fig "), or "winter fig," which ripens in sheltered spots in spring.

Fil′lets—Heb. *hashukîm,* plur., joinings (Ex. 27 : 17 ; 38 : 17, 28)—the rods by which the tops of the columns around the tabernacle court were joined together, and from which the curtains were suspended (Ex. 27 : 10, 11 ; 36 : 38).

In Jer. 52 : 21 the rendering of a different word, *hût,* meaning a "thread," and designating a measuring-line of 12 cubits in length for the circumference of the copper pillars of Solomon's temple.

Finer, a worker in silver and gold (Prov. 25 : 4). In Judg. 17 : 4 the word (*tsôreph*) is rendered "founder," and in Isa. 41 : 7 "goldsmith."

Fining pot, a crucible, melting - pot (Prov. 17 : 3 ; 27 : 21).

Fir, the uniform rendering in the Authorized Version (marg. R.V., "cypress ") of *berôsh* (2 Sam. 6 : 5 ; 1 Kings 5 : 8, 10 ; 6 : 15, 34 ; 9 : 11, etc.), a lofty tree (Isa. 55 : 13) growing on Lebanon (37 : 34). Its wood was used in making musical instruments and doors of houses, and for ceilings (2 Chr. 3 : 5), the decks of ships (Ezek. 27 : 5), floor-ings and spear-shafts (Nah. 2:3, R.V.). The true fir (*abies*) is not found in Palestine, but the pine tree, of which there are four species, is common.

The precise kind of tree meant by the "green fir tree" (Hos. 14:8) is uncertain. Some regard it as the sherbin tree, a cypress resembling the cedar; others, the Aleppo or maritime pine (*Pinus halepensis*), which resembles the Scotch fir; while others think that the "stone-pine" (*Pinus pinea*) is probably meant. (See PINE.)

Fire. (1.) *For sacred purposes.* The sacrifices were consumed by fire (Gen. 8:20). The ever-burning fire on the altar was first kindled from heaven (Lev. 6:9, 13; 9:24), and afterwards rekindled at the dedication of Solomon's temple (2 Chr. 7:1, 3). The expressions "fire from heaven" and "fire of the Lord" generally denote lightning, but sometimes also the fire of the altar was so called (Ex. 29:18; Lev. 1:9; 2:3; 3:5, 9).

Fire for a sacred purpose obtained otherwise than from the altar was called "strange fire" (Lev. 10:1, 2; Num. 3:4).

The victims slain for sin offerings were afterwards consumed by fire outside the camp (Lev. 4:12, 21; 6:30; 16:27; Heb. 13:11).

(2.) *For domestic purposes*, such as baking, cooking, warmth, etc. (Jer. 36:22; Mark 14:54; John 18:18). But on Sabbath no fire for any domestic purpose was to be kindled (Ex. 35:3; Num. 15:32–36).

(3.) *Punishment of death by fire* was inflicted on such as were guilty of certain forms of unchastity and incest (Lev. 20:14; 21:9). The burning of captives in war was not unknown among the Jews (2 Sam. 12:31; Jer. 29:22). The bodies of infamous persons who were executed were also sometimes burned (Josh. 7:25; 2 Kings 23:16).

(4.) *In war*, fire was used in the destruction of cities—as Jericho (Josh. 6:24), Ai (8:19), Hazor (11:11), Laish (Judg. 18:27), etc. The war-chariots of the Canaanites were burnt (Josh. 11:6, 9, 13). The Israelites burned the images (2 Kings 10:26; R.V., "pillars") of the house of Baal. These objects of worship seem to have

been of the nature of obelisks, and were sometimes evidently made of wood.

Torches were sometimes carried by the soldiers in battle (Judg. 7:16).

(5.) *Figuratively*, fire is a symbol of Jehovah's presence and the instrument of his power (Ex. 14:19; Num. 11:1, 3; Judg. 13:20; 1 Kings 18:38; 2 Kings 1:10, 12; 2:11; Isa. 6:4; Ezek. 1:4; Rev. 1:14, etc.).

God's word is also likened unto fire (Jer. 23:29). It is referred to as an emblem of severe trials or misfortunes (Zech. 12:6; Luke 12:49; 1 Cor. 3:13, 15; 1 Pet. 1:7), and of eternal punishment (Matt. 5:22; Mark 9:44; Rev. 14:10; 21:8).

The influence of the Holy Ghost is likened unto fire (Matt. 3:11). His descent was denoted by the appearance of tongues as of fire (Acts 2:3).

Fire′brand, Isa. 7:4, Amos 4:11, Zech. 3:2, denotes the burnt end of a stick (Heb. *'ûd*); in Judg. 15:4, a lamp or torch, a flambeau (Heb. *lappîd*); in Prov. 26:18 (comp. Eph. 6:16), burning darts or arrows (Heb. *zikkîm*).

Fire′pan (Ex. 27:3; 38:3), one of the vessels of the temple service (rendered "snuff-dish" Ex. 25:38; 37:23; and "censer" Lev. 10:1; 16:12). It was probably a metallic cinder-basin used for the purpose of carrying live coal for burning incense, and of carrying away the snuff in trimming the lamps.

Fir′kin. Used only in John 2:6; the Attic *amphora*, equivalent to the Hebrew

AMPHORA.
(From Pompeii.)

bath (*q.v.*), a measure for liquids containing about 8⅞ gallons.

Fir'mament, from the Vulgate *firmamentum*, which is used as the translation of the Hebrew *râkî'a*. This word means simply "expansion." It denotes the space or expanse like an arch appearing immediately above us. They who rendered *râkî'a* by *firmamentum* regarded it as a solid body. The language of Scripture is not scientific but popular, and hence we read of the sun rising and setting, and so also here the use of this particular word. It is plain that it was used to denote *solidity* as well as *expansion*. It formed a division between the waters above and the waters below (Gen. 1 : 7). The *râkî'a* supported the upper reservoir (Ps. 148 : 4). It was the support also of the heavenly bodies (Gen. 1 : 14), and is spoken of as having "windows" and "doors" (Gen. 7 : 11; Isa. 24 : 18; Mal. 3 : 10) through which the rain and snow might descend.

First-born sons enjoyed certain special privileges (Deut. 21 : 17; Gen. 25 : 23, 31, 34; 49 : 3; 1 Chr. 5 : 1; Heb. 12 : 16; Ps. 89 : 27). (See BIRTHRIGHT.)

The "first-born of the poor" signifies the most miserable of the poor (Isa. 14 : 30). The "church of the first-born" signifies the church of the redeemed.

The destruction of the first-born was the last of the ten plagues inflicted on the Egyptians (Ex. 11 : 1–8; 12 : 29, 30).

Menephtah is probably the Pharaoh whose first-born was slain. His son did not succeed or survive his father, but died early. The son's tomb has been found at Thebes unfinished, showing it was needed earlier than was expected. Some of the records on the tomb are as follows:—"The son whom Menephtah loves; who draws towards him his father's heart, the singer, the prince of archers, who governed Egypt on behalf of his father. Dead."

First-born, Sanctification of the. A peculiar sanctity was attached to the first-born both of man and of cattle. God claimed that the first-born males of man and of animals should be consecrated to him,—the one as a priest (Ex. 19 : 22, 24), representing the family to which he belonged, and the other to be offered up in sacrifice (Gen. 4 : 4).

First-born, Redemption of. From the beginning the office of the priesthood in each family belonged to the eldest son. But when the extensive plan of sacrificial worship was introduced, requiring a company of men to be exclusively devoted to this ministry, the primitive office of the first-born was superseded by that of the Levites (Num. 3 : 11–13), and it was ordained that the first-born of man and of unclean animals should henceforth be *redeemed* (18 : 15).

The laws concerning this redemption of the first-born of man are recorded in Ex. 13 : 12–15; 22 : 29; 34 : 20; Num. 3 : 45; 8 : 17; 18 : 16; Lev. 12 : 2, 4.

The first-born male of every clean animal was to be given up to the priest for sacrifice (Deut. 12 : 6; Ex. 13 : 12; 34 : 20; Num. 18 : 15–17).

But the first-born of unclean animals was either to be redeemed or sold and the price given to the priest (Lev. 27 : 11–13, 27). The first-born of an ass, if not redeemed, was to be put to death (Ex. 13 : 13; 34 : 20).

First - fruits. The first - fruits of the ground were offered unto God just as the first-born of man and animals.

The law required—(1.) That on the morrow after the Passover Sabbath a sheaf of new corn should be waved by the priest before the altar (Lev. 23 : 5, 6, 10, 12; 2 : 12).

(2.) That at the feast of Pentecost two loaves of leavened bread, made from the new flour, were to be waved in like manner (Lev. 23 : 15, 17; Num. 28 : 26).

(3.) The feast of Tabernacles was an acknowledgment that the fruits of the harvest were from the Lord (Ex. 23 : 16; 34 : 22).

(4.) Every individual, besides, was required to consecrate to God a portion of the first-fruits of the land (Ex. 22 : 29; 23 : 19; 34 : 26; Num. 15 : 20, 21).

(5.) The law enjoined that no fruit was to be gathered from newly-planted fruit-trees for the first three years, and that the first-fruits of the fourth year were to be consecrated to the Lord (Lev. 19 : 23–25). Jeremiah (2 : 3) alludes to the ordinance of "first-fruits," and hence he must have been acquainted with the books of Exodus, Leviticus, and Numbers, where the laws regarding it are recorded.

Fish, called *dâg* by the Hebrews, a word denoting great fecundity (Gen. 9:2; Num. 11:22; Jonah 2:1, 10). No fish is mentioned by name either in the Old or in the New Testament. Fish abounded in the Mediterranean and in the lakes of the Jordan, so that the Hebrews were no doubt acquainted with many species. Two of the villages on the shores of the Sea of Galilee derived their names from their fisheries— Bethsaida (the "house of fish") on the east and on the west. There was a regular fish-market apparently in Jerusalem (2

FISH FROM THE SEA OF GALILEE.

Chr. 33:14; Neh. 3:3; 12:39; Zeph. 1: 10), as there was a fish-gate which was probably contiguous to it.

Sidon is the oldest fishing establishment known in history.

Fisher. Besides its literal sense (Luke 5:2), this word is also applied by our Lord to his disciples in a figurative sense (Matt. 4:19; Mark 1:17).

Fish-hooks were used for catching fish (Amos 4:2; comp. Isa. 37:29; Jer. 16:16; Ezek. 29:4; Job 41:1, 2; Matt. 17:27).

Fish-pools (Cant. 7:4) should be simply "pools," as in the Revised Version. The reservoirs near Heshbon (*q.v.*) were probably stocked with fish (2 Sam. 2:13; 4:12; Isa. 7:3; 22:9, 11).

Fishing, the art of, was prosecuted with great industry in the waters of Palestine. It was from the fishing-nets that Jesus called his disciples (Mark 1:16–20), and it was in a fishing-boat he rebuked the winds and the waves (Matt. 8:26) and delivered that remarkable series of prophecies recorded in Matt. 13. He twice miraculously fed multitudes with fish and bread (Matt. 14:19; 15:36). It was in the mouth of a fish that the tribute-money was found (Matt. 17:27). And he "ate a piece of broiled fish" with his disciples after his resurrection (Luke 24:42, 43; comp. Acts 1:3). At the Sea of Tiberias (John 21:1–14), in obedience to his direction, the disciples cast their net "on the right side of the ship," and enclosed so many that "they were not able to draw it for the multitude of fishes."

Two kinds of fishing-nets are mentioned in the New Testament:—

(1.) The casting-net (Matt. 4:18; Mark 1:16).

(2.) The drag-net or *seine* (Matt. 13:48). Fish were also caught by the fishing-hook (Matt. 17:27). (See NET.)

Fitches (Isa. 28:25, 27), the rendering of the Hebrew *ketsah*, "without doubt the *Nigella sativa*, a small annual of the order *Ranunculaceæ*, which grows wild in the Mediterranean countries, and is cultivated in Egypt and Syria for its seed." It is rendered in margin of the Revised Version "black cummin." The seeds are used as a condiment.

In Ezek. 4:9 this word is the rendering of the Hebrew *kussemêth* (incorrectly rendered "rye" in the Authorized Version of Ex. 9:32 and Isa. 28:25, but "spelt" in the Revised Version). The reading "fitches" here is an error; it should be "spelt."

Flag (Heb., or rather Egyptian, *ahu*, Job 8:11), rendered "meadow" in Gen. 41:2, 18; probably the *Cyperus esculentus*, a species of rush eaten by cattle—the Nile reed. It also grows in Palestine.

In Ex. 2:3, 5, Isa. 19:6, it is the rendering of the Hebrew *sûph*, a word which occurs frequently in connection with *yam*; as *yam sûph*, to denote the "Red Sea" (*q.v.*) or the sea of weeds (as this word is rendered, Jonah 2:5). It denotes some kind of sedge or reed which grows in marshy places. (See PAPER, REED.)

Flag'on—Heb. *ashîshah*—(2 Sam. 6:19; 1 Chr. 16:3; Cant. 2:5; Hos. 3:1), meaning properly "a cake of pressed raisins." "Flagons of wine" of the Authorized Version should be, as in the Revised Version, "cakes of raisins" in all these passages.

In Isa. 22:24 it is the rendering of the Hebrew *nêbel*, which properly means a bottle or vessel of skin. (Comp. 1 Sam. 1:24; 10:3; 25:18; 2 Sam. 16:1, where the same Hebrew word is used.)

Flame of fire is the chosen symbol of the holiness of God (Ex. 3:2; Rev. 2:18), as indicating "the intense, all-consuming operation of his holiness in relation to sin."

Flax (Heb. *pishtâh—i.e.*, "peeled"—in allusion to the fact that the stalks of flax when dried were first split or peeled before being steeped in water for the purpose of destroying the pulp). This plant was cultivated from earliest times. The flax of Egypt was destroyed by the plague of hail when it "was bolled"—*i.e.*, was forming pods for seed (Ex. 9:31). It was extensively cultivated both in Egypt and Palestine. Reference is made in Josh. 2:6 to the custom of drying flax-stalks by exposing them to the sun on the flat roofs of houses. It was much used in forming articles of clothing such as girdles, also cords and bands (Lev. 13:48, 52, 59; Deut. 22:11). (See LINEN.)

Flea. David at the cave of Adullam thus addressed his persecutor Saul (1 Sam. 24:14): "After whom is the king of Israel come out? after whom dost thou pursue? after a dead dog, after a flea?" He thus speaks of himself as the poor, contemptible object of the monarch's pursuit—a "worthy object truly for an expedition of the king of Israel with his picked troops!" This insect is in Eastern language the popular emblem of insignificance. In 1 Sam. 26:20 the LXX. read "come out to seek my life" instead of "to seek a flea."

Fleece, the wool of a sheep, whether shorn off or still attached to the skin (Deut. 18:4; Job 31:20). The miracle of Gideon's fleece (Judg. 6:37–40) consisted in the dew having fallen at one time on the fleece without any on the floor, and at another time in the fleece remaining dry while the ground was wet with dew.

Flesh in the Old Testament denotes (1) a particular part of the body of man and animals (Gen. 2:21; 41:2; Ps. 102:5, marg.); (2) the whole body (Ps. 16:9); (3) all living things having flesh, and particularly humanity as a whole (Gen. 6 : 12, 13); (4) mutability and weakness (2 Chr. 32 : 8; comp. Isa. 31 : 3; Ps. 78 : 39). As suggesting the idea of softness it is used in the expression "heart of flesh" (Ezek. 11 : 19). The expression "my flesh and bone" (Judg. 9 : 2; Isa. 58 : 7) denotes relationship.

In the New Testament, besides these it is also used to denote the sinful element of human nature as opposed to the "Spirit" (Rom. 6 : 19; Matt. 16 : 17). Being "in the flesh" means being unrenewed (Rom. 7 : 5; 8 : 8, 9), and to live "according to the flesh" is to live and act sinfully (Rom. 8 : 4, 5, 7, 12).

This word also denotes the human nature of Christ (John 1 : 14, "The Word was made flesh." Comp. also 1 Tim. 3 : 16; Rom. 1 : 3).

Flesh-hook, a many-pronged fork used in the sacrificial services (1 Sam. 2 : 13, 14;

Ex. 27 : 3; 38 : 3) by the priest in drawing away the flesh. The fat of the sacrifice, together with the breast and shoulder (Lev. 7 : 29, 34), were presented by the worshipper to the priest. The fat was burned on the altar (3 : 3–5), and the breast and shoulder became the portion of the priests. But Hophni and Phinehas, not content with this, sent a servant to seize with a flesh-hook a further portion.

Flint abounds in all the plains and valleys of the wilderness of the forty years' wanderings. In Isa. 50 : 7 and Ezek. 3 : 9 the expressions, where the word is used, mean that the "Messiah would be firm and resolute amidst all contempt and scorn

which he would meet; that he had made up his mind to endure it, and would not shrink from any kind or degree of suffering which would be necessary to accomplish the great work in which he was engaged." (Comp. Ezek. 3 : 8, 9.) The words "like a flint" are used with reference to the hoofs of horses (Isa. 5 : 28).

Flood, an event recorded in Gen. 7 and 8. (See DELUGE.) In Josh. 24 : 2, 3, 14, 15, the word "flood" (R.V., "river") means the river Euphrates. In Ps. 66 : 6, this word refers to the river Jordan.

Flour. Grain reduced to the form of meal is spoken of in the time of Abraham (Gen. 18 : 6). As baking was a daily necessity, grain was also ground daily at the mills (Jer. 25 : 10). The flour mingled with water was kneaded in kneading-troughs, and sometimes leaven (Ex. 12 : 34) was added and sometimes omitted (Gen. 19 : 3). The dough was then formed into thin cakes nine or ten inches in diameter and baked in the oven.

Fine flour was offered by the poor as a sin-offering (Lev. 5 : 11–13), and also in connection with other sacrifices (Num. 15 : 3–12; 28 : 7–29).

Flowers. Very few species of flowers are mentioned in the Bible although they abounded in Palestine. It has been calculated that in Western Syria and Palestine from two thousand to two thousand five hundred plants are found, of which about five hundred probably are British wild-flowers. Their beauty is often alluded to (Cant. 2 : 12; Matt. 6 : 28). They are referred to as affording an emblem of the transitory nature of human life (Job 14 : 2; Ps. 103 : 15; Isa. 28 : 1; 40 : 6; James 1 : 10). Gardens containing flowers and fragrant herbs are spoken of (Cant. 4 : 16; 6 : 2).

Flute, a musical instrument, probably composed of a number of pipes, mentioned Dan. 3 : 5, 7, 10, 15.

In Matt. 9 : 23, 24, notice is taken of players on the flute, here called "minstrels" (but in R.V. "flute-players").

Flutes were in common use among the ancient Egyptians.

Fly—Heb. *zĕbûb*—(Eccl. 10 : 1; Isa. 7 : 18). This fly was so grievous a pest that the Phœnicians invoked against it the aid of their god Baal-zebub (*q.v.*).

Heb. *'arób*, the name given to the insects sent as a plague on the land of Egypt (Ex. 8:21–31; Ps. 78:45; 105:31). The LXX. render this by a word which means the "dog-fly," the *cynomuia*. The Jewish commentators regarded the Hebrew word here as connected with the word *'arab*, which means "mingled;" and they accordingly supposed the plague to consist of a mixed multitude of animals—beasts, reptiles, and insects. But there is no doubt that "the *'arób*" denotes a single definite species. Some interpreters regard it as the *Blatta orientalis*, the cockroach, a species of beetle. These insects "inflict very painful bites with their jaws; gnaw and destroy clothes, household furniture, leather, and articles of every kind, and either consume or render unavailable all eatables."

Foam (Hos. 10:7), the rendering of *ketseph*, which properly means twigs or splinters (as rendered in the LXX. and marg.

SHEEP-FOLD.

R.V.). The expression in Hosea may therefore be read, "as a chip on the face of the water," denoting the helplessness of the piece of wood as compared with the irresistible current.

Fodder—Heb. *belil*—(Job 6:5), meaning properly a mixture or *medley* (Lat. *farrago*), "made up of various kinds of grain, as wheat, barley, vetches, and the like, all mixed together, and then sown or given to cattle" (Job 24:6, A.V. "corn," R.V. "provender;" Isa. 30:24, "provender").

Fold, an enclosure for flocks to rest together (Isa. 13:20). Sheep-folds are mentioned Num. 32:16, 24, 36; 2 Sam. 7:8; Zeph. 2:6; John 10:1, etc. It was prophesied of the cities of Ammon (Ezek. 25:5), Aroer (Isa. 17:2), and Judæa, that they would be folds or couching-places for flocks. "Among the pots," of the Authorized Version (Ps. 68:13), is rightly in the Revised Version, "among the sheepfolds."

Food. Originally the Creator granted

the use of the vegetable world for food to man (Gen. 1:29), with the exception mentioned (2:17). The use of animal food was probably not unknown to the antediluvians. There is, however, a distinct law on the subject given to Noah after the Deluge (Gen. 9:2-5). Various articles of food used in the patriarchal age are mentioned in Gen. 18:6-8; 25:34; 27:3, 4; 43:11. Regarding the food of the Israelites in Egypt, see Ex. 16:3; Num. 11:5. In the wilderness their ordinary food was miraculously supplied in the manna. They had also quails (Ex. 16:11-13; Num. 11:31).

In the law of Moses there are special regulations as to the animals to be used for food (Lev. 11; Deut. 14:3-21). The Jews were also forbidden to use as food anything that had been consecrated to idols (Ex. 34:15), or animals that had died of disease or had been torn by wild beasts (Ex. 22:31; Lev. 22:8). (See also for other restrictions Ex. 23:19; 29:13-22; Lev. 3:4-9; 9:18, 19; 22:8; Deut. 14:21.) But beyond these restrictions they had a large grant from God (Deut. 14:26; 32:13, 14).

Food was prepared for use in various ways. The cereals were sometimes eaten without any preparation (Lev. 23:14; Deut. 23:25; 2 Kings 4:42). Vegetables were cooked by boiling (Gen. 25:30, 34; 2 Kings 4:38, 39), and thus also other articles of food were prepared for use (Gen. 27:4; Prov. 23:3; Ezek. 24:10; Luke 24:42; John 21:9). Food was also prepared by roasting (Ex. 12:8; Lev. 2:14). (See COOK.)

Foot'stool, connected with a throne (2 Chr. 9:18).

Jehovah symbolically dwelt in the holy place between the cherubim above the ark of the covenant. The ark was his footstool (1 Chr. 28:2; Ps. 99:5; 132:7). And as heaven is God's throne, so the earth is his footstool (Ps. 110:1; Isa. 66:1; Matt. 5:35).

Forces of the Gentiles (Isa. 60:5, 11; R.V., "the wealth of the nations") denotes the wealth of the heathen. The whole passage means that the wealth of the Gentile world should be consecrated to the service of the church.

Ford. Mention is frequently made of the fords of the Jordan (Josh. 2:7; Judg. 3:28; 12:5, 6), which must have been very numerous; about fifty perhaps. The most notable was that of Bethabara. Mention is also made of the ford of the Jabbok (Gen. 32:22), and of the fords of Arnon (Isa. 16:2) and of the Euphrates (Jer. 51:32).

Fore'head. The practice common among Oriental nations of colouring the forehead or impressing on it some distinctive mark as a sign of devotion to some deity is alluded to in Rev. 13:16, 17; 14:9; 17:5; 20:4.

The "jewel on thy forehead" mentioned in Ezek. 16:12 (R.V., "a ring upon thy nose") was in all probability the "nose-ring" (Isa. 3:21).

In Ezek. 3:7 the word "impudent" is rightly rendered in the Revised Version "hard of forehead." (See also ver. 8, 9.)

For'eigner, a Gentile. Such as resided among the Hebrews were required by the law to be treated with kindness (Ex. 22:21; 23:9; Lev. 19:33, 34; 23:22; Deut. 14:28; 16:10, 11; 24:19). They enjoyed in many things equal rights with the native-born residents (Ex. 12:49; Lev. 24:22; Num. 15:15; 35:15), but were not allowed to do anything which was an abomination according to the Jewish law (Ex. 26:10; Lev. 17:15,16; 18:26; 20:2; 24:16, etc.).

Foreknowl'edge of God (Acts 2:23; Rom. 8:29; 11:2; 1 Pet. 1:2), one of those high attributes essentially appertaining to him the full import of which we cannot comprehend. In the most absolute sense his knowledge is infinite (1 Sam. 23:9-13; Jer. 38:17-23; 42:9-22; Matt. 11:21, 23; Acts 15:18).

Forerun'ner. John the Baptist went before our Lord in this character (Mark 1:2, 3). Christ so called (Heb. 6:20) as entering before his people into the holy place as their head and guide.

For'est—Heb. *ya'ar*, meaning a dense wood, from its luxuriance. Thus all the great primeval forests of Syria (Eccl. 2:6; Isa. 44:14; Jer. 5:6; Micah 5:8). The most extensive was the trans-Jordanic forest of

Ephraim (2 Sam. 18:6, 8; Josh. 17:15, 18), which is probably the same as the wood of Ephratah (Ps. 132:6), some part of the great forest of Gilead. It was in this forest that Absalom was slain by Joab. David withdrew to the forest of Hareth in the mountains of Judah to avoid the fury of Saul (1 Sam. 22:5). We read also of the forest of Bethel (2 Kings 2:23, 24), and of that which the Israelites passed in their pursuit of the Philistines (1 Sam. 14:25), and of the forest of the cedars of Lebanon (1 Kings 4:33; 2 Kings 19:23; Hos. 14:5, 6).

"The house of the forest of Lebanon" (1 Kings 7:2; 10:17; 2 Chr. 9:16) was probably Solomon's armoury, and was so called because the wood of its many pillars came from Lebanon, and they had the appearance of a forest. (See BAALBEC.)

Heb. *ḥoresh*, denoting a thicket of trees, underwood, jungle, bushes, or trees entangled, and therefore affording a safe hiding-place. This word is rendered "forest" only in 2 Chr. 27:4. It is also rendered "wood"—the "wood" in the "wilderness of Ziph," in which David concealed himself (1 Sam. 23:15), which lay south-east of Hebron. In Isa. 17:9 this word is in Authorized Version rendered incorrectly "bough."

Heb. *pardês*, meaning an enclosed garden or plantation. Asaph is (Neh. 2:8) called the "keeper of the king's forest." The same Hebrew word is used Eccl. 2:5, where it is rendered in the plural "orchards" (R.V., "parks"), and Cant. 4:13, rendered "orchard" (R.V. marg., "a paradise").

"The forest of the vintage" (Zech. 11:2, "inaccessible forest," or R.V. "strong forest") is probably a figurative allusion to Jerusalem, or the verse may simply point to the devastation of the region referred to.

The forest is an image of unfruitfulness as contrasted with a cultivated field (Isa. 29:17; 32:15; Jer. 26:18; Hos. 2:12). Isaiah (10:19, 33, 34) likens the Assyrian host under Sennacherib (*q.v.*) to the trees of some huge forest, to be suddenly cut down by an unseen stroke.

Forgive'ness of sin, one of the constituent parts of justification. In pardoning sin, God absolves the sinner from the condemnation of the law, and that on account of the work of Christ—*i.e.*, he removes the guilt of sin, or the sinner's actual liability to eternal wrath on account of it. All sins are forgiven freely (Acts 5:31; 13:38; 1 John 1:6-9). The sinner is by this act of grace for ever freed from the guilt and penalty of his sins. This is the peculiar prerogative of God (Ps. 130:4; Mark 2:5). It is offered to all in the gospel. (See JUSTIFICATION.)

Fornica'tion in every form of it was sternly condemned by the Mosaic law (Lev. 21:9; 19:29; Deut. 22:20, 21, 23-29; 23:18; Ex. 22:16). (See ADULTERY.)

But this word is more frequently used in a symbolical than in its ordinary sense. It frequently means a forsaking of God or a following after idols (Isa. 1:2; Jer. 2:20; Ezek. 16; Hos. 1:2; 2:1-5; Jer. 3:8, 9).

Fortuna'tus—*fortunate*—a disciple of Corinth who visited Paul at Ephesus, and returned with Stephanas and Achaicus, the bearers of the apostle's first letter to the Corinthians (1 Cor. 16:17).

Fount'ain (Heb. *'ain; i.e.*, "eye" of the desert), a natural source of living water. Palestine was a "land of brooks of water, of fountains, and depths that spring out of valleys and hills" (Deut. 8:7; 11:11).

These fountains, bright sparkling "eyes" of the desert, are remarkable for their abundance and their beauty, especially on the west of Jordan. All the perennial rivers and streams of the country are supplied from fountains, and depend comparatively little on surface water. "Palestine is a country of mountains and hills, and it abounds in fountains of water. The murmur of these waters is heard in every dell, and the luxuriant foliage which surrounds them is seen in every plain." Besides its rain-water, its cisterns and fountains, Jerusalem had also an abundant supply of water in the magnificent reservoir called "Solomon's Pools" (*q.v.*), at the head of the Urtâs valley, whence it was conveyed to the city by subterranean channels some 10 miles in length. These have all been long ago destroyed, so that no water from the "Pools" now reaches Jerusalem. Only one fountain has been discovered at Jerusalem—the so-called "Virgin's Fountain," in the valley of Kidron; and only one well (Heb. *beer*), the Bîr Eyub, also in the valley of Kidron, south of the King's Gardens, which has been dug through the solid rock. The inhabitants of Jerusalem are now mainly dependent on the winter rains, which they store in cisterns. (See WELL.)

Fountain of the Virgin, the perennial source from which the Pool of Siloam (*q.v.*)

is supplied, the waters flowing in a copious stream to it through a tunnel cut through the rock, the actual length of which is 1,750 feet. The spring rises in a cave 20 feet by 7. A serpentine tunnel 67 feet long runs from it toward the left, off which the tunnel to the Pool of Siloam branches. It is the only unfailing fountain in Jerusalem.

The fountain received its name from the "fantastic legend" that here the virgin washed the swaddling-clothes of our Lord. This spring has the singular character-

FOUNTAIN OF THE VIRGIN.

istic of being intermittent, flowing from three to five times daily in winter, twice daily in summer, and only once daily in autumn. This peculiarity is accounted for by the supposition that the outlet from the reservoir is by a passage in the form of a siphon.

Fowler, the arts of, referred to Ps. 91: 3; 124:7; Prov. 6:5; Jer. 5:26; Hos. 9: 8; Ezek. 17:20; Eccl. 9:12. Birds of all kinds abound in Palestine, and the capture of these for the table and for other uses

formed the employment of many persons. The traps and snares used for this purpose are mentioned Hos. 5:1; Prov. 7:23; 22: 5; Amos 3:5; Ps. 69:22; comp. Deut. 22:6, 7.

Fox (Heb. *shu'âl,* a name derived from its digging or burrowing under ground), the *Vulpes thaleb,* or Syrian fox, the only species of this animal indigenous to Palestine. It burrows, is silent and solitary in its habits, is destructive to vineyards, being a plunderer of ripe grapes (Cant. 2:15).

The *Vulpes Niloticus*, or Egyptian dog-fox, and the *Vulpes vulgaris*, or common fox, are also found in Palestine.

The proverbial cunning of the fox is alluded to in Ezek. 13 : 4, and in Luke 13 : 32, where our Lord calls Herod "that fox." In Judg. 15 : 4, 5, the reference is in all probability to the jackal. The Hebrew word *shu‘âl* through the Persian *schagal* becomes our *jackal* (*Canis aureus*), so that the word may bear that signification here. The reasons for preferring the rendering "jackal" are (1) that it is more easily caught than the fox; (2) that the fox is shy and suspicious, and flies mankind, while the jackal does not; and (3) that foxes are difficult, jackals comparatively easy, to treat in the way here described. Jackals hunt in large numbers, and are still very numerous in Southern Palestine.

SYRIAN FOX.

Frankin'cense (Heb. *lebônah;* Gr. *libanos—i.e.,* "white"), an odorous resin imported from Arabia (Isa. 60 : 6; Jer. 6 : 20), yet also growing in Palestine (Cant. 4 : 14). It was one of the ingredients in the perfume of the sanctuary (Ex. 30 : 34), and was used as an accompaniment of the meat-offering (Lev. 2 : 1, 16; 6 : 15; 24 : 7). When burnt it emitted a fragrant odour, and hence the incense became a symbol of the Divine name (Mal. 1 : 11; Cant. 1 : 3) and an emblem of prayer (Ps. 141 : 2; Luke 1 : 10; Rev. 5 : 8; 8 : 3).

This frankincense, or *olibanum*, used by the Jews in the temple services is not to be confounded with the frankincense of modern commerce, which is an exudation of the Norway spruce fir, the *Pinus abies*. It was

FRANKINCENSE (BOSWELLIA THURIFERA).

probably a resin from the Indian tree known to botanists by the name of *Boswellia serrata* or *thurifera*, which grows to the height of forty feet.

Free'dom. The law of Moses pointed out the cases in which the servants of the Hebrews were to receive their freedom (Ex. 21 : 2–4, 7, 8; Lev. 25 : 39–41, 47–55; Deut. 15 : 12–17). Under the Roman law the "freeman" (*ingenuus*) was one born free; the "freedman" (*libertinus*) was a manumitted slave, and had not equal rights with the freeman (Acts 22 : 28; comp. Acts 16 : 37–39; 21 : 39; 22 : 25; 25 : 11, 12).

Free-will offering, a spontaneous gift (Ex. 35 : 29), a voluntary sacrifice (Lev. 22 : 23; Ezra 3 : 5), as opposed to one in consequence of a vow, or in expiation of some offence.

Frog (Heb. *tsepharde‘a,* meaning a "marsh-leaper"). This reptile is mentioned in the Old Testament only in connection with one of the plagues which fell on the land of Egypt (Ex. 8 : 2–14; Ps. 78 : 45; 105 : 30).

In the New Testament this word occurs only in Rev. 16 : 13, where it is referred to as a symbol of uncleanness. The only species of frog existing in Palestine is the green frog (*Rana esculenta*), the well-known edible frog of the Continent.

Front'lets occurs only in Ex. 13 : 16; Deut. 6 : 8, and 11 : 18. The meaning of the injunction to the Israelites, with regard to the statutes and precepts given them, that they should "bind them for a sign upon their hand, and have them as frontlets between their eyes," was that they should keep them distinctly in view and carefully attend to them. But soon after their return from Babylon they began to interpret this injunction literally, and had accordingly portions of the law written out and worn about their person. These they called *tephillin*—*i.e.*, "prayers." The passages so written out on strips of parchment were these—Ex. 12:2–10; 13:11–21; Deut. 6:4–9; 11:18–21. They were then "rolled up in a case of black calfskin, which was attached to a stiffer piece of leather, having a thong one finger broad and one cubit and a half long. Those worn on the forehead were written on four strips of parchment, and put into four little cells within a square case, which had on it the Hebrew letter called *shin*, the three points of which were

"THE TEPHILLAH ON THE HEAD."

regarded as an emblem of God." This case tied around the forehead in a particular way was called "the *tephillah* on the head." (See PHYLACTERY.)

Frost (Heb. *kerah*, from its *smoothness*) —Job 37:10 (R.V., "ice"); Gen. 31:40; Jer. 36:30; rendered "ice" in Job 6:16, 38:29; and "crystal" in Ezek. 1:22. "At the present day frost is entirely unknown in the lower portions of the valley of the Jordan, but slight frosts are sometimes felt on the sea-coast and near Lebanon." Throughout Western Asia cold frosty nights are frequently succeeded by warm days.

"*Hoar frost*" (Heb. *kephôr*, so called from its *covering* the ground) is mentioned in Ex. 16:14; Job 38:29; Ps. 147:16.

In Ps. 78:47 the word rendered "frost" (R.V. marg., "great hail-stones"), *hanamâl*, occurs only there. It is rendered by Gesenius, the Hebrew lexicographer, "ant," and so also by others, but the usual interpretation derived from the ancient versions may be maintained.

Fruit, a word as used in Scripture denoting produce in general, whether vegetable or animal. The Hebrews divided the fruits of the land into three classes:—

(1.) The fruit of the field, "corn-fruit" (Heb. *dagân*); all kinds of grain and pulse.

(2.) The fruit of the vine, "vintage-fruit" (Heb. *tirôsh*); grapes, whether moist or dried.

(3.) "Orchard-fruits" (Heb. *yitshâr*), as dates, figs, citrons, etc.

Injunctions concerning offerings and tithes were expressed by these Hebrew terms alone (Num. 18:12; Deut. 14:23).

This word "fruit" is also used of children or offspring (Gen. 30:2; Deut. 7:13; Luke 1:42; Ps. 21:10; 132:11); also of the progeny of beasts (Deut. 28:51; Isa. 14:29).

It is used metaphorically in a variety of forms (Ps. 104:13; Prov. 1:31; 11:30; 31:16; Isa. 3:10; 10:12; Matt. 3:8; 21:41; 26:29; Heb. 13:15; Rom. 7:4,5; 15:28).

The fruits of the Spirit (Gal. 5:22, 23; Eph. 5:9; James 3:17, 18) are those gracious dispositions and habits which the Spirit produces in those in whom he dwells and works.

Frying-pan (Heb. *marhĕsheth*, a "boiler"), a pot for boiling meat (Lev. 2:7; 7:9).

Fuel. Almost every kind of combustible matter was used for fuel, such as the withered stalks of herbs (Matt. 6:30), thorns (Ps. 58:9; Eccl. 7:6), animal excrements (Ezek. 4:12–15; 15:4, 6; 21:32). Wood or charcoal is much used still in all the towns of Syria and Egypt. It is largely brought from the region of Hebron to Jerusalem. (See COAL.)

Fugitive. Gen. 4:12, 14, a rover or wanderer (Heb. *n'â*); Judg. 12:4, a refugee, one who has escaped (Heb. *pâlit*); 2 Kings 25:11, a deserter, one who has fallen away to the enemy (Heb. *nophel*); Ezek. 17:21, one who has broken away in flight (Heb. *mibrah*); Isa. 15:5; 43:14, a breaker away, a fugitive (Heb. *beriah*), one who flees away.

Ful'ler. The word "full" is from the Anglo-Saxon *fullian*, meaning "to whiten." To full is to press or scour cloth in a mill. This art is one of great antiquity. Mention is made of "fuller's soap" (Mal. 3:2), and of "the fuller's field" (2 Kings 18:17). At his transfiguration our Lord's raiment is said to have been white "so as no fuller on earth could white them" (Mark 9:3). En-rogel (*q.v.*), meaning literally "foot-fountain," has been interpreted as the "fuller's fountain," because there the fullers trod the cloth with their feet.

Ful'ler's soap (Heb. *borîth mekabbeshîm —i.e.*, "alkali of those treading cloth"). Mention is made (Prov. 25:20; Jer. 2:22) of nitre and also (Mal. 3:2) of soap (Heb. *borîth*) used by the fuller in his operations. Nitre is found in Syria, and vegetable alkali was obtained from the ashes of certain plants. (See SOAP.)

Ful'ler's field, a spot near Jerusalem (2 Kings 18:17; Isa. 36:2; 7:3), on the side of the highway west of the city, not far distant from the "upper pool" at the head of the valley of Hinnom. Here the fullers pursued their occupation.

Ful'ness. (1.) Of time (Gal. 4:4), the time appointed by God, and foretold by the prophets, when Messiah should appear. (2.) Of Christ (John 1:16), the superabundance of grace with which he was filled. (3.) Of the Godhead bodily dwelling in Christ (Col. 2:9)—*i.e.*, the whole nature and attributes of God are in Christ. (4.) Eph. 1:23, the church as the fulness of Christ—*i.e.*, the church makes Christ a complete and perfect head.

Fu'neral. Burying was among the Jews the only mode of disposing of corpses (Gen. 23:19; 25:9; 35:8, 9, etc.).

The first traces of *burning* the dead are found in 1 Sam. 31:12. The burning of

the body was affixed by the law of Moses as a penalty to certain crimes (Lev. 20:14; 21:9).

To leave the dead unburied was regarded with horror (1 Kings 13:22; 14:11; 16:4; 21:24, etc.).

In the earliest times of which we have record kinsmen carried their dead to the grave (Gen. 25:9; 35:29; Judg. 16:31), but in later times this was done by others (Amos 5:16).

Immediately after decease the body was washed, and then wrapped in a large cloth (Acts 9:37; Matt. 27:59; Mark 15:46). In the case of persons of distinction, aromatics were laid on the folds of the cloth (John 19:39; comp. John 12:7).

As a rule the burial (*q.v.*) took place on the very day of the death (Acts 5:6, 10), and the body was removed to the grave in an open coffin or on a bier (Luke 7:14). After the burial a funeral meal was usually given (2 Sam. 3:35; Jer. 16:5, 7; Hos. 9:4).

Fur'long, a stadium, a Greek measure of distance equal to 606 feet and 9 inches (Luke 24:13; John 6:19; 11:18; Rev. 14:20; 21:16).

Fur'nace. (1.) Chald. *'attûn*, a large furnace with a wide open mouth, at the top of which materials were cast in (Dan. 3:22, 23; comp. Jer. 29:22). This furnace would be in constant requisition, for the Babylonians disposed of their dead by cremation, as did also the Accadians who invaded Mesopotamia.

(2.) Heb. *kibshân*, a smelting furnace (Gen. 19:28), also a lime-kiln (Isa. 33:12; Amos 2:1).

(3.) Heb. *kûr*, a refining furnace (Prov. 17:3; 27:21; Ezek. 22:18).

(4.) Heb. *'alîl*, a crucible; only used in Ps. 12:7.

(5.) Heb. *tannûr*, oven for baking bread (Gen. 15:17; Isa. 31:9; Neh. 3:11). It was a large pot, narrowing towards the top. When it was heated by a fire made within, the dough was spread over the heated surface, and thus was baked. "A smoking furnace and a burning lamp" (Gen. 15:17), the symbol of the presence of the Almighty, passed between the divided pieces of Abraham's sacrifice in ratification of the covenant God made with him. (See OVEN.)

(6.) Gr. *kamnos*, a furnace, kiln, or oven (Matt. 13:42, 50; Rev. 1:15; 9:2).

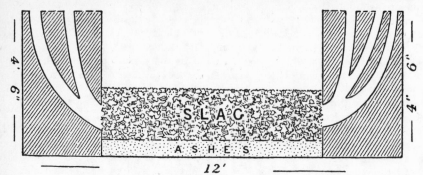

BLAST FURNACE FOUND IN MOUND AT LACHISH. (See p. 413.)
By permission of the Committee of the Palestine Exploration Fund.

Fur'row, an opening in the ground made by the plough (Isa. 65:10; Hos. 10:4, 16).

Fury, as attributed to God, is a figurative expression for dispensing afflictive judgments (Lev. 26:28; Job 20:23; Isa. 63:3; Jer. 4:4; Ezek. 5:13; Dan. 9:16; Zech. 8:2).

G

Ga'al—*loathing*—the son of Ebed, in whom the Shechemites "placed their confidence" when they became discontented with Abimelech. He headed the revolution, and led out the men of Shechem against Abimelech; but was defeated, and fled to his own home (Judg. 9:26-46). We hear no more of him after this battle.

Ga'ash—*a shaking*—a hill, on the north side of which Joshua was buried (Josh. 24:30; Judg. 2:9), in the territory of Ephraim. (See TIMNATH-SERAH.)

Gab'batha = *Gab Baitha*—i.e., "the ridge of the house" = "the temple-mound," on a part of which the fortress of Antonia was built. This "temple-mound" was covered with a tesselated "pavement" (Gr. *lithostrōton*—i.e., "stone-paved"). A judgment-seat (*bema*) was placed on this "pavement" outside the hall of the "prætorium" (*q.v.*), the judgment-hall (John 18:28; 19:13).

Ga'briel—*champion of God*—used as a proper name to designate the angel who was sent to Daniel (8:16) to explain the vision of the ram and the he-goat, and to communicate the prediction of the seventy weeks (Dan. 9:21-27).

He announced also the birth of John the Baptist (Luke 1:11), and of the Messiah (26). He describes himself in the words, "I am Gabriel, who stand in the presence of God" (1:19).

Gad—*fortune; luck.* (1.) Jacob's seventh son, by Zilpah, Leah's handmaid, and the brother of Asher (Gen. 30:11-13; 46:16, 18). In the Authorized Version of 30:11 the words, "A troop cometh: and she called," etc., should rather be rendered, "In fortune [R.V., 'Fortunate']: and she called," etc., or "Fortune cometh," etc.

The tribe of Gad during the march through the wilderness had their place with Simeon and Reuben on the south side of the tabernacle (Num. 2:14). The tribes of Reuben and Gad continued all through their history to follow the pastoral pursuits of the patriarchs (Num. 32:1-5).

The *portion* allotted to the tribe of Gad was on the east of Jordan, and comprehended the half of Gilead, a region of great beauty and fertility (Deut. 3:12), bounded on the east by the Arabian desert, on the west by the Jordan (Josh. 13 : 27), and on the north by the river Jabbok. It thus included the whole of the Jordan valley as far north as to the Sea of Galilee, where it narrowed almost to a point.

This tribe was fierce and warlike; they were "strong men of might, men of war for the battle, that could handle shield and buckler, their faces the faces of lions, and like roes upon the mountains for swiftness" (1 Chr. 12 : 8; 5 : 19–22). Barzillai (2 Sam. 17 : 27) and Elijah (1 Kings 17 : 1) were of this tribe. It was carried into captivity at the same time as the other tribes of the northern kingdom by Tiglath-pileser (1 Chr. 5 : 26), and in the time of Jeremiah (49 : 1) their cities were inhabited by the Ammonites.

(2.) A prophet who joined David in the "hold," and at whose advice he quitted it for the forest of Hareth (1 Chr. 29 : 29; 2 Chr. 29 : 25; 1 Sam. 22 : 5). Many years after we find mention made of him in connection with the punishment inflicted for numbering the people (2 Sam. 24 : 11–19; 1 Chr. 21 : 9–19). He wrote a book called the "Acts of David" (1 Chr. 29 : 29), and assisted in the arrangements for the musical services of the "house of God" (2 Chr. 29 : 25). He bore the title of "the king's seer" (2 Sam. 24 : 11, 13; 1 Chr. 21 : 9).

Gad'ara, the capital of the Roman province of Peræa. It stood on the summit of a mountain about 6 miles south-east of the Sea of Galilee. Mark (5 : 1) and Luke (8 : 27, 37) describe the miracle of the healing of the demoniac (Matthew [8 : 28–34] says two demoniacs) as having been wrought

RUINS OF UM-KEIS (GADARA).

"in the country of the Gadarenes," thus describing the scene *generally*. The miracle could not have been wrought at Gadara itself, for between the lake and this town there is the deep, almost impassable ravine of the Hieromax (Jarmûk). It is identified with the modern village of *Um-Keis*, which is surrounded by very extensive ruins, all bearing testimony to the splendour of ancient Gadara.

"The most interesting remains of Gadara are its *tombs*, which dot the cliffs for a considerable distance round the city, chiefly on the north-east declivity; but many beautifully sculptured sarcophagi are scattered over the surrounding heights. They are excavated in the limestone rock, and consist of chambers of various dimensions, some more than 20 feet square, with recesses in the sides for bodies......The present inhabitants of Um-Keis are all troglodytes, 'dwelling in tombs,' like the poor maniacs of old, and occasionally they are almost as dangerous to unprotected travellers."

Gad'arenes, the inhabitants of Gadara, in Revised Version "Gerasenes" (Matt. 5 : 1; Luke 8 : 26, 37). In Matt. 8 : 28 they are called Gergesenes, Revised Version "Gadarenes."

Gad'di—*fortunate*—the representative of the tribe of Manasseh among the twelve "spies" sent by Moses to spy the land (Num. 13 : 11).

Gad'diel—*fortune* (*i.e., sent*) *of God*—the representative of the tribe of Zebulun among the twelve spies (Num. 13 : 10).

Ga'har—*lurking-place*—one of the chief of the Nethinim, whose descendants returned to Jerusalem under Zerubbabel (Ezra 2 : 47).

Ga'ius. (1.) A Macedonian, Paul's fellow-traveller, and his host at Corinth when he wrote his Epistle to the Romans (16 : 23). He with his household were baptized by Paul (1 Cor. 1 : 16). During a heathen outbreak against Paul at Ephesus the mob seized Gaius and Aristarchus because they could not find Paul, and rushed with them into the theatre. Some have identified this Gaius with No. (2).

(2.) A man of Derbe who accompanied Paul into Asia on his last journey to Jerusalem (Acts 20 : 4).

(3.) A Christian of Asia Minor to whom John addressed his third epistle (3 John 1).

Gala'tia has been called the "Gallia" of the East, Roman writers calling its inhabitants Galli. They were an intermixture of Gauls and Greeks, and hence were called Gallo-Græci, and the country Gallo-Græcia. The Galatians were in their origin a part of that great Celtic migration which invaded Macedonia about B.C. 280. They were invited by the king of Bithynia to cross over into Asia Minor to assist him in his wars. There they ultimately settled, and being strengthened by fresh accessions of the same clan from Europe, they overran Bithynia, and supported themselves by plundering neighbouring countries. They were great warriors, and hired themselves out as mercenary soldiers, sometimes fighting on both sides in the great battles of the times. They were at length brought under the power of Rome in B.C. 189, and Galatia became a Roman province B.C. 25.

This province of Galatia, within the limits of which these Celtic tribes were confined, was the central region of Asia Minor.

During his second missionary journey Paul, accompanied by Silas and Timothy (Acts 16 : 6), visited the "region of Galatia," where he was detained by sickness (Gal. 4 : 13), and had thus the longer opportunity of preaching to them the gospel. On his third journey he went over "all the country of Galatia and Phrygia in order" (Acts 18 : 23). Crescens was sent thither by Paul toward the close of his life (2 Tim. 4 : 10).

Gala'tians, Epistle to. The *genuineness* of this epistle is not called in question. Its Pauline origin is universally acknowledged.

Occasion of. The churches of Galatia were founded by Paul himself (Acts 16 : 6; Gal. 1 : 8; 4 : 13, 19). They seem to have been composed mainly of converts from heathenism (4 : 8), but partly also of Jewish converts, who probably, under the influence of Judaizing teachers, sought to incorporate the rites of Judaism with Christianity, and by their active zeal had succeeded in inducing the majority of the churches to adopt their views (1 : 6; 3 : 1). This epistle was written for the purpose of counteracting this Judaizing tendency, and of recalling the Galatians to the simplicity of the gospel, and at the same time also of vindicating Paul's claim to be a divinely-commissioned apostle.

Time and place of writing. The epistle was probably written very soon after Paul's second visit to Galatia (Acts 18:23). The references of the epistle appear to agree with this conclusion. The visit to Jerusalem, mentioned in Gal. 2 : 1-10, was identical with that of Acts 15, and it is spoken of as a thing of the past, and consequently the epistle was written subsequently to the council of Jerusalem. The similarity between this epistle and that to the Romans has led to the conclusion that they were both written at the same time—namely, in the winter of A.D. 57-8, during Paul's stay in Corinth (Acts 20:2, 3). This to the Galatians is written on the urgency of the occasion, tidings having reached him of the state of matters; and that to the Romans in a more deliberate and systematic way, in exposition of the same great doctrines of the gospel.

Contents of. The great question discussed is, Was the Jewish law binding on Christians? The epistle is designed to prove against the Jews that men are justified by faith without the works of the law of Moses. After an introductory address (Gal. 1 : 1-10) the apostle discusses the subjects which had occasioned the epistle. (1) He defends his apostolic authority (1:11-19; 2:1-14); (2) shows the evil influence of the Judaizers in destroying the very essence of the gospel (3 and 4); (3) exhorts the Galatian believers to stand fast in the faith as it is in Jesus, and to abound in the fruits of the Spirit, and in a right use of their Christian freedom (5-6:1-10); (4) and then concludes with a summary of the topics discussed, and with the benediction.

The Epistle to the Galatians and that to the Romans taken together "form a complete proof that justification is not to be obtained meritoriously either by works of morality or by rites and ceremonies, though of divine appointment; but that it is a *free* gift, proceeding entirely from the mercy of God, to those who receive it by faith in Jesus our Lord."

In the conclusion of the epistle (6:11) Paul says, "Ye see how large a letter I have written with mine own hand." It is implied that this was different from his ordinary usage, which was simply to write the concluding salutation with his own hand, indicating that the rest of the epistle was written by another hand. Regarding this conclusion, Lightfoot, in his Commentary on the epistle, says: "At this point the apostle takes the pen from his amanuensis, and the concluding paragraph is written with his own hand. From the time when letters began to be forged in his name (2 Thess. 2:2; 3:17) it seems to have been his practice to close with a few words in his own handwriting, as a precaution against such forgeries......In the present case he writes a whole paragraph, summing up the main lessons of the epistle in terse, eager, disjointed sentences. He writes it, too, in large, bold characters (Gr. *pelikois grammasin*), that his hand-writing may reflect the energy and determination of his soul." (See JUSTIFICATION.)

Gal'banum—Heb. *ḥelbĕnâh*—(Ex. 30: 34), one of the ingredients in the holy incense. It is a gum, probably from the *Galbanum officinale.*

Ga'leed—*heap of witness*—the name of the pile of stones erected by Jacob and Laban to mark the league of friendship

into which they entered with each other (Gen. 31:47, 48). This was the name given to the "heap" by Jacob. It is Hebrew, while the name Jegar-sahadutha, given to it by Laban, is Aramaic (Chaldee or Syriac). Probably Nahor's family originally spoke Aramaic, and Abraham and his descendants learned Hebrew, a kindred dialect, in the land of Canaan.

Galile'an, an inhabitant or native of Galilee. This word was used as a name of contempt as applied to our Lord's disciples (Luke 22:59; Acts 2:7). All the apostles, with the exception of Judas Iscariot (Acts 1:11), were Galileans. Peter was detected by his Galilean accent (Matt. 26:69; Mark 14:70).

This was also one of the names of reproach given to the early Christians. Julian the Apostate, as he is called, not only used the epithet himself when referring to Christ and his apostles, but he made it a law that no one should ever call the Christians by any other name.

Gal'ilee—*circuit.* Solomon rewarded Hiram for certain services rendered him by the gift of an upland plain among the mountains of Naphtali. Hiram was dissatisfied with the gift, and called it "the land of Cabul" (*q.v.*). The Jews called it Galil. It continued long to be occupied by the original inhabitants, and hence came to be called "Galilee of the Gentiles" (Matt. 4:15), and also "Upper Galilee," to distinguish it from the extensive addition afterwards made to it toward the south, which was usually called "Lower Galilee." In the time of our Lord, Galilee embraced more than one-third of Western Palestine, extending "from Dan on the north, at the base of Mount Hermon, to the ridges of Carmel and Gilboa on the south, and from the Jordan valley on the east away across the splendid plains of Jezreel and Acre to the shores of the Mediterranean on the west." Palestine was divided into three provinces—Judea, Samaria, and Galilee, which comprehended the whole northern section of the country (Acts 9:31; 17:11), and was the largest of the three.

It was the scene of some of the most

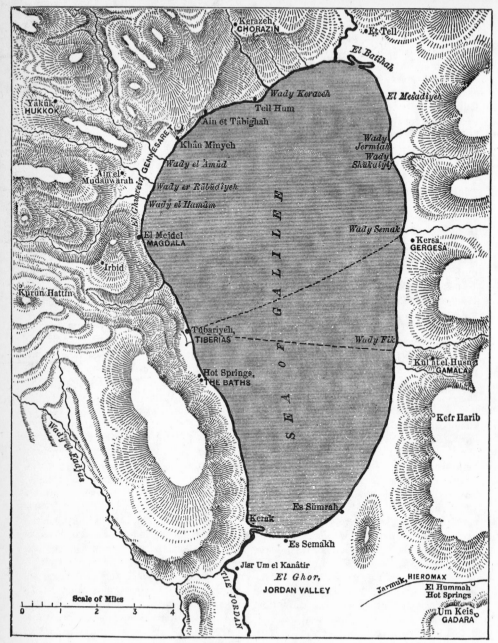

MAP OF THE SEA OF GALILEE.

memorable events of Jewish history. Galilee also was the home of our Lord during at least thirty years of his life. The first three Gospels are chiefly taken up with our Lord's public ministry in this province. "The entire province is encircled with a halo of holy associations connected with the life, works, and teachings of Jesus of

Nazareth.'' ''It is noteworthy that of his thirty-two beautiful parables, no less than nineteen were spoken in Galilee. And it is no less remarkable that of his entire thirty-three great miracles, twenty-five were wrought in this province. His first miracle was wrought at the wedding in Cana of Galilee, and his last, after his resurrection, on the shore of Galilee's sea. In Galilee our Lord delivered the 'sermon on the mount,' and the discourses on 'The Bread of Life,' on 'Purity,' on 'Forgiveness,' and on 'Humility.' In Galilee he called his first disciples; and there occurred the sublime scene of the 'Transfiguration'" (Porter's *Through Samaria*).

When the Sanhedrim were about to proceed with some plan for the condemnation of our Lord (John 7 : 45–52), Nicodemus interposed in his behalf. (Comp. Deut. 1 : 16, 17; 17 : 8.) They replied, "Art thou also of Galilee?...Out of Galilee ariseth no prophet." This saying of theirs was "not historically true; for two prophets at least had arisen from Galilee—Jonah of Gath-hepher, and the greatest of all the prophets, Elijah of Thisbe; and perhaps also Nahum and Hosea. Their contempt for Galilee made them lose sight of historical accuracy" (Alford, *Com.*).

The *Galilean accent* differed from that of Jerusalem in being broader and more guttural (Mark 14 : 70).

Gal'ilee, Sea of (Matt. 4 : 18; 15 : 29), is mentioned in the Bible under three other names. (1.) In the Old Testament it is called the "sea of Chinnereth" (Num. 34 : 11; Josh. 12 : 3; 13 : 27), as is supposed from its harp-like shape. (2.) The "lake of Gennesareth" once by Luke (5 : 1), from the flat district lying on its west coast. (3.) John (6 : 1; 21 : 1) calls it the "sea of Tiberias" (*q.v.*). The modern Arabs retain this name, *Bahr Tabarîyeh.*

This lake is $12\frac{1}{2}$ miles long, and from 4 to $7\frac{1}{2}$ broad. Its surface is 682 feet below the level of the Mediterranean. Its depth is from 80 to 160 feet. The Jordan enters it $10\frac{1}{2}$ miles below the southern extremity of the Huleh Lake, or about $26\frac{1}{2}$ miles from its source. In this distance of $26\frac{1}{2}$ miles there is a fall in the river of 1,682 feet, or

of more than 60 feet to the mile. It is 27 miles east of the Mediterranean coast, and about 60 miles north-east from Jerusalem. It is of an oval or pear-like shape, and abounds in fish.

Its present appearance is thus described: "The utter loneliness and absolute stillness of the scene are exceedingly impressive. It seems as if all nature had gone to rest, languishing under that scorching heat. How different it was in the days of our Lord! Then all was life and bustle along the shores; the cities and villages that thickly studded them resounded with the hum of a busy population; while from hill-side and corn-field came the cheerful cry of shepherd and ploughman. The lake, too, was dotted with dark fishing-boats and spangled with white sails. Now a mournful, solitary silence reigns over sea and shore. The cities are in ruins!"

This sea is chiefly of interest as associated with the public ministry of our Lord. Capernaum, "his own city" (Matt. 9 : 1), stood on its shores. From among the fishermen who plied their calling on its waters he chose Peter and his brother Andrew, and James and John, to be his disciples, and sent them forth to be "fishers of men" (Matt. 4 : 18, 22; Mark 1 : 16–20; Luke 5 : 1–11). He stilled its tempest, saying to the storm that swept over it, "Peace, be still" (Matt. 8 : 23–27; Mark 7 : 31–35); and here also he showed himself after his resurrection to his disciples (John 21).

Gall. (1.) Heb. *merêrâh*, meaning "bitterness" (Job 16 : 13); *i.e.*, the bile secreted in the liver. This word is also used of the poison of asps (20 : 14), and of the vitals, the seat of life (25).

(2.) Heb. *rôsh.* In Deut. 32 : 33 and Job 20 : 16 it denotes the poison of serpents. In Hos. 10 : 4 the Hebrew word is rendered "hemlock." The original probably denotes some bitter poisonous plant, most probably the poppy, which grows up quickly, and is therefore coupled with wormwood (Deut. 29 : 17; Jer. 9 : 15; Lam. 3 : 19). Comp. Jer. 8 : 14; 23 : 15, "water of gall," Gesenius, "poppy juice;" others "water of hemlock," "bitter water."

(3.) Gr. *cholē* (Matt. 27:34), the LXX. translation of the Hebrew *rôsh* in Ps. 69: 21, which foretells our Lord's sufferings. The drink offered to our Lord was vinegar (made of light wine rendered acid, the common drink of Roman soldiers) "mingled with gall," or, according to Mark (15:23), "mingled with myrrh;" both expressions meaning the same thing—namely, that the vinegar was made bitter by the infusion of wormwood or some other bitter substance, usually given, according to a merciful custom, as an anodyne to those who were crucified, to render them insensible to pain. Our Lord, knowing this, refuses to drink it. He would take nothing to cloud his faculties or blunt the pain of dying. He chooses to suffer every element of woe in the bitter cup of agony given him by the Father (John 18:11).

Gal'lery. (1.) Heb. *'attîk* (Ezek. 41:15, 16), a terrace; a projection; ledge.

(2.) Heb. *rahît* (Cant. 1:17), translated "rafters," marg. "galleries;" probably *panel*-work or fretted ceiling.

Gal'lim—*heaps*—(1 Sam. 25:44; Isa. 10:30). The native place of Phalti, to whom Michal was given by Saul. It was probably in Benjamin, to the north of Jerusalem.

Gal'lio, the elder brother of Seneca the philosopher, who was tutor and for some time minister of the emperor Nero. He was "deputy"—*i.e.*, proconsul, as in Revised Version—of Achaia, under the emperor Claudius, when Paul visited Corinth (Acts 18:12). The word used here by Luke in describing the rank of Gallio shows his accuracy. Achaia was a senatorial province under Claudius, and the governor of such a province was called a "proconsul." He is spoken of by his contemporaries as "sweet Gallio," and is described as a most popular and affectionate man. When the Jews brought Paul before his tribunal on the charge of persuading "men to worship contrary to the law" (18:13), he refused to listen to them, and "drave them from the judgment seat" (18:16).

Gal'lows—Heb. *'êts*, meaning "a tree" —(Esther 6:4), a post or gibbet. In Gen.

40:19 and Deut. 21:22 the word is rendered "tree."

Gama'liel—*reward of God.* (1.) A chief of the tribe of Manasseh at the census at Sinai (Num. 1:10; 2:20; 7:54, 59).

(2.) The son of rabbi Simeon, and grandson of the famous rabbi Hillel. He was a Pharisee, and therefore the opponent of the party of the Sadducees. He was noted for his learning, and was president of the Sanhedrim during the reigns of Tiberius, Caligula, and Claudius, and died, it is said, about eighteen years before the destruction of Jerusalem.

When the apostles were brought before the council, charged with preaching the resurrection of Jesus, as a zealous Pharisee Gamaliel counselled moderation and calmness. By a reference to well-known events, he advised them to "refrain from these men." If their work or counsel was of man, it would come to nothing; but if it was of God, they could not destroy it, and therefore ought to be on their guard lest they should be "found fighting against God" (Acts 5:34-40). Paul was one of his disciples (22:3).

Games. (1.) Of children (Zech. 8:5; Matt. 11:16). The Jewish youth were also apparently instructed in the use of the bow and the sling (Judg. 20:16; 1 Chr. 12:2).

(2.) Public games, such as were common among the Greeks and Romans, were foreign to the Jewish institutions and customs. Reference, however, is made to such games in two passages (Ps. 19:5; Eccl. 9:11).

(3.) Among the Greeks and Romans games entered largely into their social life.

(*a*) Reference in the New Testament is made to gladiatorial shows and fights with wild beasts (1 Cor. 15:22). These were common among the Romans, and sometimes on a large scale.

(*b*) Allusion is frequently made to the Grecian gymnastic contests (Gal. 2:2; 5:7; Phil. 2:16; 3:14; 1 Tim. 6:12; 2 Tim. 2:5; Heb. 12:1, 4, 12). These were very numerous. The Olympic, Pythian, Nemean, and Isthmian games were esteemed as of great national importance, and the victors at any of these games of wrestling, racing, etc., were esteemed as the noblest and the happiest of mortals.

Gam'madim (Ex. 27:11)—*brave warriors;* R.V. marg., "valorous men;" others interpret this word as meaning "short-swordsmen," or "daring ones"— the name of a class of men who were defenders of the towers of Tyre.

Ga'mul—*weaned*—the leader of one of the priestly courses (1 Chr. 24:17).

Gap, a rent or opening in a wall (Ezek. 13:5; comp. Amos 4:3). The false prophets did not stand in the gap (Ezek. 22:30)—*i.e.*, they did nothing to stop the outbreak of wickedness.

Gar'dens mentioned in Scripture—of Eden (Gen. 2:8, 9); Ahab's garden of herbs (1 Kings 21:2); the royal garden (2 Kings 21:18); the royal garden at Susa (Esther 1:5); the garden of Joseph of Arimathea (John 19:41); of Gethsemane (John 18:1).

The "king's garden" mentioned 2 Kings 25:4, Neh. 3:15, was near the Pool of Siloam.

Gardens were surrounded by hedges of thorns (Isa. 5:5) or by walls of stone (Prov. 24:31). "Watch-towers" or "lodges" were also built in them (Isa. 1:8; Mark 12:1), in which their keepers sat. On account of their retirement they were frequently used as places for secret prayer and communion with God (Gen. 24:63; Matt. 16:30; 26:36; John 2:48; 18:1, 2). The dead were sometimes buried in gardens (Gen. 23:19, 20; 2 Kings 21:4, 18, 26; 1 Sam. 25:1; Mark 15:46; John 19:41). (See PARADISE.)

Ga'reb—*scabby; itch.* (1.) One of David's warriors (2 Sam. 23:38), an Ithrite.

(2.) A hill near Jerusalem (Jer. 31:39), probably the hill of lepers, and consequently a place outside the boundary of the city.

Gar'lands (Acts 14:13). In heathen sacrifices the victims were adorned with fillets and garlands made of wool, with leaves and flowers interwoven. The altar and the priests and attendants were also in like manner adorned.

Gar'lic (Heb. *shûm,* from its strong odour), mentioned only once (Num. 11:5). The garlic common in Eastern countries is the *Allium sativum* or *Allium Ascalonicum,* so called from its having been brought into Europe from Ascalon by the Crusaders. It is now known by the name of "shallot" or "eschalot."

Gar'ner. (1.) Heb. *'otsâr,* a treasure; a store of goods laid up, and hence also the place where they are deposited (Joel 1:17; 2 Chr. 32:27, rendered "treasury").

(2.) Heb. *mezev,* a cell, storeroom (Ps. 144:13); Gr. *apothēkē,* a place for storing anything, a granary (Matt. 3:12; Luke 3:17).

Gar'nish, overlay with stones (2 Chr. 3:6), adorn (Rev. 21:19), deck with garlands (Matt. 23:29), furnish (12:44).

In Job 26:13 (Heb. *shiphrâh,* meaning "brightness"), "By his spirit the heavens are brightness"—*i.e.*, are bright, splendid, beautiful.

Gar'rison. (1.) Heb. *matstsâb,* a station; a place where one stands (1 Sam. 14:12); a military or fortified post (1 Sam. 13:23; 14:1, 4, 6, etc.).

(2.) Heb. *netsîb,* a præfect, superintendent; hence a military post (1 Sam. 10:5; 13:3, 4; 2 Sam. 8:6). This word has also been explained to denote a *pillar* set up to mark the Philistine conquest, or an *officer* appointed to collect taxes; but the idea of a military post seems to be the correct one.

(3.) Heb. *matstsêbah,* properly a monumental column; improperly rendered pl. "garrisons" in Ezek. 26:11; correctly in Revised Version "pillars," marg. "obelisks," probably an idolatrous image.

Gate. (1.) Of cities, as of Jerusalem (Jer. 37:13; Neh. 1:3; 2:3; 5:3), of Sodom (Gen. 19:1), of Gaza (Judg. 16:3).

(2.) Of royal palaces (Neh. 3:8).

(3.) Of the temple of Solomon (1 Kings 6:34, 35; 2 Kings 18:16); of the holy place (1 Kings 6:31, 32; Ezek. 41:23, 24); of the outer courts of the temple, the Beautiful gate (Acts 3:2).

(4.) Tombs (Matt. 27:60).

(5.) Prisons (Acts 12:10; 16:27).

(6.) Caverns (1 Kings 19:13).

(7.) Camps (Ex. 32:26, 27; Heb. 13:12).

The *materials* of which gates were made were,—

(1.) Iron and brass (Ps. 107 : 16 ; Isa. 45 : 2 ; Acts 12 : 10).

(2.) Stone and pearls (Isa. 54 : 12 ; Rev. 21 : 12).

(3.) Wood (Judg. 16 : 3) probably.

At the gates of cities courts of justice were frequently held, and hence "judges of the gate" are spoken of (Deut. 16 : 18 ; 17 : 8 ; 21 : 19 ; 25 : 6, 7, etc.). At the gates prophets also frequently delivered their messages (Prov. 1 : 21 ; 8 : 3 ; Isa. 29 : 21 ; Jer. 17 : 19, 20 ; 26 : 10). Criminals were punished without the gates (1 Kings 21 : 13 ; Acts 7 : 59). By the "gates of righteousness" we are probably to understand those of the temple (Ps. 118 : 19). "The gates of hell" (R.V., "gates of Hades") —Matt. 16 : 19—are generally interpreted as meaning the power of Satan, but probably they may mean the power of death, denoting that the Church of Christ shall never die.

Gath—*a wine-vat*—one of the five royal cities of the Philistines (Josh. 13 : 3) on which the ark brought calamity (1 Sam. 5 : 8, 9 ; 6 : 17). It was famous also as being the birthplace or residence of Goliath (1 Sam. 17 : 4). David fled from Saul to Achish, king of Gath (1 Sam. 21 : 10 ; 27 : 2–4 ; Ps. 56), and his connection with it will account for the words in 2 Sam. 1 : 20. It was afterwards conquered by David (2 Sam. 8 : 1). It occupied a strong position on the borders of Judah and Philistia (1 Sam. 21 : 10 ; 1 Chr. 18 : 1). Its site has been identified with the hill called *Tell es-Sâfieh*, the Alba Specula of the Middle Ages, which rises 695 feet above the plain on its east edge. It commanded the mouth of the valley of Elah. (See METHEG-AMMAH.)

Gath-he′pher—*wine-press of the well*—a town of Lower Galilee, about 5 miles from Nazareth ; the birthplace of Jonah (2 Kings 14 : 25) ; the same as Gittah-hepher (Josh. 19 : 13). It has been identified with the modern *el-Meshed*, a village on the top of a rocky hill. Here the supposed tomb of Jonah, *Neby Yûnas*, is still pointed out.

Gath-rim′mon—*press of the pomegranate.*

(1.) A Levitical city in the tribe of Dan (Josh. 19 : 45 ; 21 : 24 ; 1 Chr. 6 : 69).

(2.) Another city of the same name in Manasseh, west of the Jordan (Josh. 21 : 25), called also Bileam (1 Chr. 6 : 70).

Gaulani′tis, a name derived from "Golan" (*q.v.*), one of the cities of refuge in the territory of Manasseh (Josh. 20 : 8 ; 21 : 27 ; Deut. 4 : 43). This was one of the provinces ruled by Herod Antipas. It lay to the east of the Lake of Galilee, and included among its towns Bethsaida-Julias (Mark 8 : 22) and Seleucia.

Ga′za, called also Azzah, which is its Hebrew name (Deut. 2 : 23 ; 1 Kings 4 : 14 ; Jer. 25 : 20)—*strong*—a city on the Mediterranean shore, remarkable for its early importance as the chief centre of a great commercial traffic with Egypt. It is one of the oldest cities of the world (Gen. 10 : 19 ; Josh. 15 : 47). Its earliest inhabitants were the Avims, who were conquered and displaced by the Caphtorims (Deut. 2 : 23 ; Josh. 13 : 2, 3), a Philistine tribe. In the division of the land it fell to the lot of Judah (Josh. 15 : 47 ; Judg. 1 : 18). It was the southernmost of the five great Philistine cities which gave each a golden emerod as a trespass-offering unto the Lord (1 Sam. 6 : 17). Its gates were carried away by Samson (Judg. 16 : 1–3). Here he was afterwards a prisoner, and "did grind in the prison house." Here he also pulled down the temple of Dagon, and slew "all the lords of the Philistines," himself also perishing in the ruin (Judg. 16 : 21–30). The prophets denounce the judgments of God against it (Jer. 25 : 20 ; 47 : 5 ; Amos 1 : 6, 7 ; Zeph. 2 : 4). It is referred to in Acts 8 : 26. Philip is here told to take the road from Jerusalem to Gaza (about 6 miles south-west of Jerusalem), "which is desert"—*i.e.*, the "desert road," probably by Hebron, through the desert hills of Southern Judea. (See SAMSON.)

Its modern name is *Ghüzzeh*. It contains about ten thousand inhabitants, chiefly Mohammedans.

Ge′ba—*the hill*—(2 Sam. 5 : 25 [1 Chr. 14 : 16, "Gibeon"] ; 2 Kings 23 : 8 ; Neh. 11 : 31), a Levitical city of Benjamin (1 Kings 15 : 22 ; 1 Sam. 13 : 16 ; 14 : 5, wrongly "Gibeah" in the A.V.), on the north border of Judah near Gibeah (Isa. 10:29; Josh. 18:24, 28). "From Geba to Beersheba" expressed the whole extent of the kingdom of Judah, just as "from Dan to Beersheba" described the whole length of Palestine (2 Kings 23:8). It has been identified with Gaba (Josh. 18:24; Ezra 2:26; Neh. 7:30), now *Jeb'a*, about 3 miles north-east of Tell el-Fûl, and 5½ miles north of Jerusalem.

Some identify this town with Gibeah (*q.v.*), but these were probably different places.

Ge'bal—*a line* (or natural boundary, as a mountain range). (1.) A tract in the land of Edom south of the Dead Sea (Ps. 83:7); now called *Djebâl*.

(2.) A Phœnician city, not far from the sea coast, to the north of Beyrout (Ezek. 27:9); called by the Greeks Byblos. Now *Jibeil*. Mentioned in the Amarna tablets.

Ge'balites (1 Kings 5:18 R.V., in A.V. incorrectly rendered, after the Targum, "stone-squarers," but marg. "Giblites"), the inhabitants of Gebal (2).

Ge'ber—*a valiant man*—(1 Kings 4:19), one of Solomon's purveyors, having jurisdiction over a part of Gilead, comprising all the kingdom of Sihon and part of the kingdom of Og (Deut. 2; 3).

Ge'bim—*cisterns*—(rendered "pits," Jer. 14:3; "locusts," Isa. 33:4), a small place north of Jerusalem, whose inhabitants fled at the approach of the Assyrian army (Isa. 10:31). It is probably the modern *el-Isawiyeh*.

Gedali'ah — *made great by Jehovah.* (1.) The son of Jeduthun (1 Chr. 25:3, 9). (2.) The grandfather of the prophet Zephaniah, and the father of Cushi (Zeph. 1:1). (3.) One of the Jewish nobles who conspired against Jeremiah (Jer. 38:1). (4.) The son of Ahikam, and grandson of Shaphan, secretary of king Josiah (Jer. 26:24). After the destruction of Jerusalem (see ZEDEKIAH), Nebuchadnezzar left him to govern the country as tributary to him (1 Kings 25:22; Jer. 40:5; 52:16). Ishmael, however, at the head of a party of the royal family—"Jewish irreconcilables" —rose against him, and slew him and "all the Jews that were with him" (Jer. 41:2,

3) at Mizpah about three months after the destruction of Jerusalem. He and his band also plundered the town of Mizpah, and carried off many captives. He was, however, overtaken by Johanan and routed. He fled with such of his followers as escaped to the Ammonites (41:15). The little remnant of the Jews now fled to Egypt.

Ge'der—*a walled place*—(Josh. 12:13), perhaps the same as Gederah or Gedor (15:58).

Gede'rah—*the fortress; a fortified place*— a town in the plain (*shephêlah*) of Judah (Josh. 15:36). This is a very common Canaanite and Phœnician name. It is the feminine form of Geder (12:13); the plural form is Gederoth (41). This place has by some been identified with *Jedîreh*, a ruin 9 miles from Lydda, toward Eleutheropolis, and 4 miles north of Sur'ah (Zorah), in the valley of Elah.

Gede'rathite, an epithet applied to Josabad, one of David's warriors at Ziklag (1 Chr. 12:4), a native of Gederah.

Ge'dor—*a wall.* (1.) A city in the mountains or hill country of Judah (Josh. 15:58), identified with *Jedûr*, between Jerusalem and Hebron.

(2.) 1 Chr. 4:40, the Gederah of Josh. 15:36, or the well-known Gerar, as the LXX. read, where the patriarchs of old had sojourned and fed their flocks (Gen. 20:1, 14, 15; 26:1, 6, 14).

(3.) A town apparently in Benjamin (2 Chr. 12:7), the same probably as Geder (Josh. 12:13).

Geha'zi — *valley of vision* — Elisha's trusted servant (2 Kings 4:31; 5:25; 8:4, 5). He appears in connection with the history of the Shunammite (2 Kings 4:14, 31) and of Naaman the Syrian. On this latter occasion he was guilty of duplicity and dishonesty of conduct, causing Elisha to denounce his crime with righteous sternness, and pass on him the terrible doom that the leprosy of Naaman would cleave to him and his for ever (5:20-27).

He afterwards appeared before king Joram, to whom he recounted the great deeds of his master (2 Kings 8:1-6).

Gehen'na (originally *Ge bene Hinnom; i.e.,* "the valley of the sons of Hinnom"), a deep, narrow glen to the south of Jerusalem, where the idolatrous Jews offered their children in sacrifice to Molech (2 Chr. 28:3; 33:6; Jer. 7:31; 19:2-6). This valley afterwards became the common receptacle for all the refuse of the city. Here the dead bodies of animals and of criminals, and all kinds of filth, were cast and consumed by fire kept always burning. It thus in process of time became the image of the place of everlasting destruction. In this sense it is used by our Lord in Matt. 5:22, 29, 30; 10:28; 18:9; 23:15, 33; Mark 9:43, 45, 47; Luke 12:5. In these passages, and also in James 3:6, the word is uniformly rendered "hell," the Revised Version placing "Gehenna" in the margin. (See HELL; HINNOM.)

Geli'loth—*circles; regions*—a place in the border of Benjamin (Josh. 18:17); called Gilgal in 15:17.

Gemari'ah—*Jehovah has made perfect.* (1.) The son of Shaphan, and one of the Levites of the temple in the time of Jehoiakim (Jer. 36:10; 2 Kings 15:35). Baruch read aloud to the people from Gemariah's chamber, and again in the hearing of Gemariah and other scribes, the prophecies of Jeremiah (Jer. 36:11-20), which filled him with terror. He joined with others in entreating the king not to destroy the roll of the prophecies which Baruch had read (21-25).

(2.) The son of Hilkiah, who accompanied Shaphan with the tribute-money from Zedekiah to Nebuchadnezzar, and was the bearer at the same time of a letter from Jeremiah to the Jewish captives at Babylon (Jer. 29:3, 4).

Genera'tion. Gen. 2:4, "These are the generations," means the "history." 5:1, "The book of the generations," means a family register, or history of Adam. 37:2, "The generations of Jacob"=the history of Jacob and his descendants. 7:1, "In this generation"=in this age. Ps. 49:19, "The generation of his fathers" =the dwelling of his fathers—*i.e.*, the grave. Ps. 73:15, "The generation of thy children"=the contemporary race. Isa. 53:8, "Who shall declare his generation?"= His manner of life who shall declare? or

rather=His race, posterity, shall be so numerous that no one shall be able to declare it.

In Matt. 1:17, the word means a succession or series of persons from the same stock. Matt. 3:7, "Generation of vipers" =brood of vipers. 24:34, "This generation"=the persons then living contemporary with Christ. 1 Pet. 2:8, "A chosen generation"=a chosen people.

The Hebrews seem to have reckoned time by the generation. In the time of Abraham a generation was an hundred years, thus: Gen. 15:16, "In the fourth generation"=in four hundred years (comp. verse 13 and Ex. 12:10). In Deut. 1:35 and 2:14 a generation is a period of thirty-eight years.

Gen'esis. The five books of Moses were collectively called the *Pentateuch*, a word of Greek origin meaning "the five-fold book." The Jews called them the *Torah*—*i.e.*, "the law." It is probable that the division of the Torah into five books proceeded from the Greek translators of the Old Testament. The names by which these several books are generally known are Greek.

The first book of the Pentateuch (*q.v.*) is called by the Jews *Berêshith*—*i.e.*, "in the beginning"—because this is the first word of the book. It is generally known among Christians by the name of *Genesis*—*i.e.*, "creation" or "generation," being the name given to it in the LXX. as designating its character, because it gives an account of the origin of all things. It contains, according to the usual computation, the history of about two thousand three hundred and sixty-nine years.

Genesis is divided into two principal parts. The first part (1-11) gives a general history of mankind down to the time of the Dispersion. The second part presents the early history of Israel down to the death and burial of Joseph (12-50).

There are five principal persons brought in succession under our notice in this book, and around these persons the history of the successive periods is grouped—*viz.*, Adam (1-3), Noah (4-9), Abraham (10-25:18), Isaac (25:19-35:29), and Jacob (36-50).

In this book we have several prophecies

PLAIN OF GENNESARET.

concerning Christ (3 : 15 ; 12 : 3 ; 18 : 18 ;
22 : 18 ; 26 : 4 ; 28 : 14 ; 49 : 10). The *author*
of this book was Moses. Under divine
guidance he may indeed have been led to
make use of materials already existing in
primeval documents, or even of traditions
in a trustworthy form that had come down
to his time, purifying them from all that
was unworthy ; but the hand of Moses is
seen throughout in its composition.

Gennes′aret—*a garden of riches*. (1.) A
town of Naphtali called Chinnereth (Josh.
19 : 35), sometimes in the plural form Chinneroth (11 : 2). In later times the name
was gradually changed to Genezar and
Gennesaret (Luke 5 : 1). This city stood
on the western shore of the lake to which
it gave its name. No trace of it remains.
The plain of Gennesaret has been called,
from its fertility and beauty, "the paradise
of Galilee."

(2.) The Lake of Gennesaret, the Grecized
form of CHINNERETH (*q.v.*). (See GALILEE,
SEA OF.)

Gen′tiles (Heb., usually in plural, *goyîm*),
meaning in general all nations except the
Jews. In course of time, as the Jews began more and more to pride themselves on
their peculiar privileges, it acquired unpleasant associations, and was used as a
term of contempt.

In the New Testament the Greek word
Hellenes, meaning literally Greeks (as in
Acts 16 : 1, 3 ; 18 : 17 ; Rom. 1 : 14), gener-
ally denotes any non-Jewish nation.

Genu′bath—*theft*—the son of Hadad of
the Edomitish royal family. He was
brought up in Pharaoh's household. His
mother was a sister of Tahpenes, the king
of Egypt's wife (1 Kings 11 : 20).

Ge′ra—*grain*. (1.) The son of Bela and
grandson of Benjamin (1 Chr. 8 : 3, 5, 7).

(2.) The father of Ehud the judge (Judg.
3 : 15).

(3.) The father of Shimei, who so grossly
abused David (2 Sam. 16 : 5 ; 19 : 16,
18).

Ge′rah—*a bean*, probably of the carob
tree—the smallest weight, and also the
smallest piece of money, among the Hebrews, equal to the twentieth part of a
shekel (Ex. 30 : 13 ; Lev. 27 : 25 ; Num. 3 :

47). This word came into use in the same
way as our word "grain," from a grain of
wheat.

Ge′rar—*a region; lodging-place*—a very
ancient town and district in the south border of Palestine, which was ruled over by
a king named Abimelech (Gen. 10 : 19 ; 20 :
1, 2). Abraham sojourned here, and perhaps Isaac was born in this place. Both
of these patriarchs were guilty of the sin
of here denying their wives, and both of
them entered into a treaty with the king
before they departed to Beersheba (21 : 23-
34 ; 26). It seems to have been a rich
pastoral country (2 Chr. 14 : 12-18). Isaac
here reaped an hundred-fold (Gen. 26 : 12).
The "valley of Gerar" (17) was probably
the modern *Wâdy el-Jerâr.*

Ger′gesa=**Gerasa,** identified with the
modern *Khersa*, "over against Galilee,"
close to the lake. This was probably the
scene of the miracle, Mark 5 : 1-20, etc.
"From the base of the great plateau of
Bashan, 2,000 feet or more overhead, the
ground slopes down steeply, in places pre-
cipitously, to the shore. And at the foot
of the declivity a bold spur runs out to the
water's edge. By it the frantic swine
would rush on headlong into the lake and
perish."—Porter's *Through Samaria*. (See
GADARA.)

Ger′izim, a mountain of Samaria, about
3,000 feet above the Mediterranean. It
was on the left of the valley containing
the ancient town of Shechem (*q.v.*), on the
way to Jerusalem. It stood over against
Mount Ebal, the summits of these mountains being distant from each other about
2 miles (Deut. 27 ; Josh. 8 : 30-35). On the
slopes of this mountain the tribes descended
from the handmaids of Leah and Rachel,
together with the tribe of Reuben, were
gathered together, and gave the responses
to the blessings pronounced as the reward
of obedience, when Joshua in the valley below read the whole law in the hearing of
all the people ; as those gathered on Ebal
responded with a loud amen to the rehearsal
of the curses pronounced on the disobedient. It was probably at this time that the
coffin containing the embalmed body of
Joseph was laid in the "parcel of ground

which Jacob bought of the sons of Hamor" (Gen. 33:19; 50:25).

Josephus relates (*Ant.* 11:8, 2–4) that Sanballat built a temple for the Samaritans on this mountain, and instituted a priesthood, as rivals to those of the Jews at Jerusalem. This temple was destroyed after it had stood two hundred years. It was afterwards rebuilt by Herod the Great. There is a Samaritan tradition that it was the scene of the incident recorded in Gen. 22. There are many ruins on this mountain, some of which are evidently of Christian buildings. To this mountain the woman of Sychar referred in John 4:20. For centuries Gerizim was the centre of political outbreaks. The Samaritans (*q.v.*), a small but united body, still linger here, and keep up their ancient ceremonial worship.

Ger'shom—*expulsion.* (1.) The eldest son of Levi (1 Chr. 6:16, 17, 20, 43, 62, 71; 15:7)=GERSHON (*q.v.*).

(2.) The elder of the two sons of Moses born to him in Midian (Ex. 2:22; 18:4). On his way to Egypt with his family, in obedience to the command of the Lord, Moses was attacked by a sudden and dangerous illness (4:24–27), which Zipporah his wife believed to have been sent because he had neglected to circumcise his son. She accordingly took a "sharp stone" and circumcised her son Gershom, saying, "Surely a bloody husband art thou to me" —*i.e.*, by the blood of her child she had, as it were, purchased her husband—had won him back again.

(3.) A descendant of Phinehas who returned with Ezra from Babylon (Ezra 8:2).

(4.) The son of Manasseh (Judg. 18:30), in R.V. "of Moses."

Ger'shon=**Ger'shom**—*expulsion*—the eldest of Levi's three sons (Gen. 46:11; Ex. 6:16).

In the wilderness the sons of Gershon had charge of the fabrics of the tabernacle when it was moved from place to place— the curtains, veils, tent-hangings (Num. 4: 22–26). Thirteen Levitical cities fell to the lot of the Gershonites (Josh. 21:27–33).

Ge'shem or **Gashmu**—*firmness*—probably chief of the Arabs south of Palestine, one of the enemies of the Jews after the return from Babylon (Neh. 2:19; 6:1, 2). He united with Sanballat and Tobiah in opposing the rebuilding of the wall of Jerusalem.

Ge'shur—*bridge*—the name of a district or principality of Syria near Gilead, between Mount Hermon and the Lake of Tiberias (2 Sam. 15:8; 1 Chr. 2:23). The Geshurites probably inhabited the rocky fastness of Argob, the modern *Lejâh*, in the north-east corner of Bashan. In the time of David it was ruled by Talmai, whose daughter he married, and who was the mother of Absalom, who fled to Geshur after the murder of Amnon (2 Sam. 13: 37).

Gesh'urites. (1.) The inhabitants of Geshur. They maintained friendly relations with the Israelites on the east of Jordan (Josh. 12:5; 13:11, 13).

(2.) Another aboriginal people of Palestine who inhabited the south-west border of the land. Geshuri in Josh. 13:2 should be "the Geshurite," not the Geshurites mentioned in ver. 11, 13, but the tribe mentioned in 1 Sam. 27:8.

Gethsem'ane—*oil-press*—the name of an olive-yard at the foot of the Mount of Olives, to which Jesus was wont to retire (Luke 22:39) with his disciples, and which is specially memorable as being the scene of his agony (Mark 14:32; John 18:1; Luke 22:44). The plot of ground pointed out as Gethsemane is now surrounded by a wall, and is laid out as a modern European flower-garden. It contains eight venerable olive-trees, the age of which cannot, however, be determined. The exact site of Gethsemane is still in question. Dr. Thomson (*The Land and the Book*) says: "When I first came to Jerusalem, and for many years afterward, this plot of ground was open to all whenever they chose to come and meditate beneath its very old olive-trees. The Latins, however, have within the last few years succeeded in gaining sole possession, and have built a high wall around it......The Greeks have invented another site a little to the north of it...... My own impression is that both are wrong. The position is too near the city, and so close to what must have always been the great thoroughfare eastward, that our Lord would scarcely have selected it for *retirement* on that dangerous and dismal night ......I am inclined to place the garden in the secluded vale several hundred yards to the north-east of the present Gethsemane."

Ge'zer—*a precipice*—an ancient royal Canaanitish city (Josh. 10:33; 12:12). It was allotted with its suburbs to the Kohathite Levites (21:21; 1 Chr. 6:67). It stood between the lower Beth-horon and the sea (Josh. 16:3; 1 Kings 9:17). It was the last point to which David pursued the Philistines (2 Sam. 5:25; 1 Chr. 14:16) after the battle of Baal-perazim. The Canaanites retained possession of it till the time of Solomon, when the king of Egypt took it and gave it to Solomon as a part of the dowry of the Egyptian princess whom he married (1 Kings 9:13–16). It is identified with *Tell el-Jezer*, about 10 miles south-west of Beth-horon. It is mentioned in the Amarna tablets.

GETHSEMANE AT THE PRESENT DAY.

Ghost, an old Saxon word equivalent to soul or spirit. It is the translation of the Hebrew *nephesh* and the Greek *pneuma*, both meaning "breath," "life," "spirit," the "living principle" (Job 11:20; Jer. 15:9; Matt. 27:50; John 19:30). The expression "to give up the ghost" means to die (Lam. 1:19; Gen. 25:17; 35:29; 49:33; Job 3:11). (See HOLY GHOST.)

Gi'ants. (1.) Heb. *nephilim*, meaning "violent" or "causing to fall" (Gen. 6:4). These were the violent tyrants of those days, those who fell upon others. The word may also be derived from a root signifying "wonder," and hence "monsters" or "prodigies." In Num. 13:33 this name is given to a Canaanitish tribe, a race of large stature, "the sons of Anak." The Revised Version, in these passages, simply transliterates the original, and reads "Nephilim."

(2.) Heb. *rephaim*, a race of giants (Deut. 3:11) who lived on the east of Jordan, from whom Og was descended.

They were probably the original inhabitants of the land before the immigration of the Canaanites. They were conquered by Chedorlaomer (Gen. 14:5), and their territories were promised as a possession to Abraham (15:20). The Anakim, Zuzim, and Emim were branches of this stock.

In Job 26:5 (R.V., "they that are deceased;" marg., "the shades," the "Rephaim") and Isa. 14:9 this Hebrew word is rendered (A.V.) "dead." It means here "the shades," the departed spirits in Sheol. In 2 Sam. 21:16, 18, 20, 22, "the giant" is (A.V.) the rendering of the singular form *ha râphâh*, which may possibly be the name of the father of the four giants referred to here, or of the founder of the Rephaim. The Vulgate here reads "Arâpha," whence Milton (in *Samson Agonistes*) has borrowed the name "Harâpha." (See also 1 Chron. 20:5, 6, 8; Deut. 2:11, 20; 3:13; Josh. 15:8, etc., where the word is similarly rendered "giant.") It is rendered "dead" in (A.V.) Ps. 88:10; Prov. 2:18; 9:18; 21:16: in all these places the Revised Version marg. has "the shades." (See also Isa. 26:14.)

(3.) Heb. *'Anâkim* (Deut. 2:10, 11, 21; Josh. 11:21, 22; 14:12, 15; called "sons of Anak," Num. 13:33; "children of Anak," 13:22; Josh. 15:14), a nomad race of giants descended from Arba (Josh. 14:15), the father of Anak, that dwelt in the south of Palestine near Hebron (Gen. 23:2; Josh. 15:13). They were a Cushite tribe of the same race as the Philistines and the Egyptian shepherd kings. David on several occasions encountered them (2 Sam. 21:15–22). From this race sprung Goliath (1 Sam. 17:4).

(4.) Heb. *'emim*, a warlike tribe of the ancient Canaanites. They were "great, and many, and tall, as the Anakims" (Gen. 14:5; Deut. 2:10, 11).

(5.) Heb. *Zamzummim* (*q.v.*)—Deut. 2:20 —so called by the Amorites.

(6.) Heb. *gibbôr* (Job 16:14), *a mighty one—i.e.*, a champion or hero. In its plural form (*gibborîm*) it is rendered "mighty men" (2 Sam. 23:8–39; 1 Kings 1:8; 1 Chr. 11:9–47; 29:24.) The band of six hundred whom David gathered around him

when he was a fugitive were so designated. They were divided into three divisions of two hundred each, and thirty divisions of twenty each. The captains of the thirty divisions were called "the thirty," the captains of the two hundred "the three," and the captain over the whole was called "the captain of the mighty men."

The sons born of the marriages mentioned in Gen. 6:4 are also called by this Hebrew name.

Gib'bethon — *a height* — a city of the Philistines in the territory of Dan, given to the Kohathites (Josh. 19:44; 21:23). Nadab the king of Israel, while besieging it, was slain under its walls by Baasha, one of his own officers (1 Kings 15:27). It was in the possession of the Philistines after the secession of the ten tribes (2 Chr. 11:13, 14).

Gib'eah—*a hill* or *hill-town*—"of Benjamin" (1 Sam. 13:15), better known as "Gibeah of Saul" (11:4; Isa. 10:29). It was here that the terrible outrage was committed on the Levite's concubine which led to the almost utter extirpation of the tribe of Benjamin (Judg. 19; 20), only six hundred men surviving after a succession of disastrous battles. This was the birthplace of Saul, and continued to be his residence after he became king (1 Sam. 10:26; 11:4; 15:33). It was reckoned among the ancient sanctuaries of Palestine (10:56; 15:34; 23:19; 26:1; 2 Sam. 21:6–10), and hence it is called "Gibeah of God" (1 Sam. 10:4, R.V. marg.). It has been identified with the modern *Tell el-Fûl* (*i.e.*, "hill of the bean"), about 3 miles north of Jerusalem.

Gib'eah of Judah (Josh. 15:57), a city in the mountains of Judah, the modern *Jeba*, on a hill in the Wâdy Musurr, about 7½ miles west-south-west of Bethlehem.

Gib'eah of Phinehas (Josh. 15:57, R.V. marg.), a city on Mount Ephraim which had been given to Phinehas (24:33 "hill," A.V.; R.V. marg. and Heb., "Gibeah."). Here Eleazar the son of Aaron was buried. It has been identified with the modern *Khŭrbet Jibia*, 5 miles north of Guphna towards Shechem.

Gib'eah-haar'aloth (Josh. 5:3, marg.)

*—hill of the foreskins—*a place at Gilgal where those who had been born in the wilderness were circumcised. All the others—*i.e.*, those who were under twenty years old at the time of the sentence at Kadesh—had already been circumcised.

Gib'eon—*hill-city*—"one of the royal cities, greater than Ai, and all the men thereof were mighty" (Josh. 10:2). Its inhabitants were Hivites (11:19). It lay within the territory of Benjamin, and became a priest-city (18:25; 21:17). Here the tabernacle was set up after the destruction of Nob, and here it remained many years till the temple was built by Solomon. It is represented by the modern *el-Jîb*, to the south-west of Ai, and about 5½ miles north-north-west of Jerusalem.

A deputation of the Gibeonites, with their allies from three other cities (Josh. 9:17), visited the camp at Gilgal, and by false representations induced Joshua to enter into a league with them, although the Israelites had been specially warned against any league with the inhabitants of Canaan (Ex. 23:32; 34:12; Num. 33:55; Deut. 7:2). The deception practised on Joshua was detected three days later; but the oath rashly sworn "by Jehovah God of Israel" was kept, and the lives of the Gibeonites were spared. They were, however, made "bondmen" to the sanctuary (Josh. 9:23).

The most remarkable incident connected with this city was the victory Joshua gained over the kings of Palestine (Josh. 10:16-27). The battle here fought has been regarded as "one of the most important in the history of the world." The kings of southern Canaan entered into a confederacy against Gibeon (because it had entered into a league with Joshua) under the leadership of Adoni-zedec, king of Jerusalem, and marched upon Gibeon with the view of taking possession of it. The Gibeonites entreated Joshua to come to their aid with the utmost speed. His army came suddenly upon that of the Amorite kings as it lay encamped before the city. It was completely routed, and only broken remnants of their great host found refuge in the fenced cities. The five confederate kings who led the army were taken prison-

ers, and put to death at Makkedah (*q.v.*). This eventful battle of Beth-horon sealed the fate of all the cities of Southern Palestine. Among the Amarna tablets is a letter from Adoni-zedec (*q.v.*) to the king of Egypt, written probably at Makkedah after the defeat, showing that the kings contemplated flight into Egypt.

This place is again brought into notice as the scene of a battle between the army of Ish-bosheth under Abner and that of David led by Joab. At the suggestion of Abner, to spare the effusion of blood, twelve men on either side were chosen to decide the battle. The issue was unexpected; for each of the men slew his fellow, and thus they all perished. The two armies then engaged in battle, in which Abner and his host were routed and put to flight (2 Sam. 2:12-17). This battle led to a virtual truce between Judah and Israel—Judah, under David, increasing in power; and Israel, under Ish-bosheth, continually losing ground.

Soon after the death of Absalom and David's restoration to his throne his kingdom was visited by a grievous famine, which was found to be a punishment for Saul's violation (2 Sam. 21:2, 5) of the covenant with the Gibeonites (Josh. 9:3-27). The Gibeonites demanded blood for the wrong that had been done to them, and accordingly David gave up to them the two sons of Rizpah (*q.v.*) and the five sons of Michal, and these the Gibeonites took and hanged or crucified "in the hill before the Lord" (2 Sam. 21:9); and there the bodies hung for six months (21:10), and all the while Rizpah watched over the blackening corpses and "suffered neither the birds of the air to rest on them by day, nor the beasts of the field by night." David afterwards removed the remains, and had them buried with the bones of Saul and Jonathan at Jabesh-gilead (21:12, 13).

Here, "at the great stone," Amasa was put to death by Joab (2 Sam. 20:5-10). To the altar of burnt-offering which was at Gibeon, Joab (1 Kings 2:28-34), who had taken the side of Adonijah, fled for sanctuary in the beginning of Solomon's reign, and was there also slain by the hand of Benaiah.

Soon after he came to the throne, Solomon paid a visit of state to Gibeon, there to offer sacrifices (1 Kings 3:4; 2 Chr. 1:3). On this occasion the Lord appeared to him in a memorable dream, recorded in 1 Kings 3:5-15; 2 Chr. 1:7-12. When the temple was built "all the men of Israel assembled themselves" to king Solomon, and brought up from Gibeon the tabernacle and "all the holy vessels that were in the tabernacle" to Jerusalem, where they remained till they were carried away by Nebuchadnezzar (2 Kings 24:13).

Gid'eon, called also Jerubbaal (Judg. 6: 29, 32), was the first of the judges whose history is circumstantially narrated (Judg. 6-8). His calling is the commencement of the second period in the history of the judges. After the victory gained by Deborah and Barak over Jabin, Israel once more sank into idolatry, and the Midianites (*q.v.*) and Amalekites, with other "children of the east," crossed the Jordan each year for seven successive years for the purpose of plundering and desolating the land. Gideon received a direct call from God to undertake the task of delivering the land from these warlike invaders. He was of the family of Abiezer (Josh. 17:2; 1 Chr. 7:18), and of the little township of Ophrah (Judg. 6:11). First, with ten of his servants, he overthrew the altars of Baal and cut down the asherah which was upon it, and then blew the trumpet of alarm, and the people flocked to his standard on the crest of Mount Gilboa to the number of twenty-two thousand men. These were, however, reduced to only three hundred. These, strangely armed with torches and pitchers and trumpets, rushed in from three different points on the camp of Midian at midnight, in the valley to the north of Moreh, with the terrible war-cry, "For the Lord and for Gideon" (Judg. 7:18, R.V.). Terror-stricken, the Midianites were put into dire confusion, and in the darkness slew one another, so that only fifteen thousand out of the great army of one hundred and twenty thousand escaped alive. The

memory of this great deliverance impressed itself deeply on the mind of the nation (1 Sam. 12:11; Ps. 83:11; Isa. 9:4; 10:26; Heb. 11:32). The land had now rest for forty years. Gideon died in a good old age, and was buried in the sepulchre of his fathers. Soon after his death a change came over the people. They again forgot Jehovah, and turned to the worship of Baalim, "neither shewed they kindness to the house of Jerubbaal" (Judg. 8:35). Gideon left behind him seventy sons, a feeble, sadly degenerated race, with one exception—that of Abimelech, who seems to. have had much of the courage and energy of his father, yet of restless and unscrupulous ambition. He gathered around him a band who slaughtered all Gideon's sons, except Jotham, upon one stone. (See OPHRAH.)

Gier eagle (Heb. *râhâm* = "parental affection," Lev. 11:18; Deut. 14:17; R.V., "vulture"), a species of vulture living entirely on carrion. "It is about the size of a raven; has an almost triangular, bald, and wrinkled head, a strong pointed beak, black at the tip, large eyes and ears, the latter entirely on the outside, and long feet." It is common in Egypt, where it is popularly called "Pharaoh's chicken" (the *Neophron percnopterus*), and is found in Palestine only during summer. Tristram thinks that the Hebrew name, which is derived from a root meaning "to love," is given to it from the fact that the male and female bird never part company.

Gift. (1.) A gratuity (Prov. 19:6) to secure favour (18:16; 21:14), a thank-offering (Num. 18:11), or a dowry (Gen. 34:12).

(2.) An oblation or propitiatory gift (2 Sam. 8:2, 6; 1 Chr. 18:2, 6; 2 Chr. 26:8; Ps. 45:12; 72:10).

(3.) A bribe to a judge to obtain a favourable verdict (Ex. 23:8; Deut. 16:19).

(4.) Simply a thing given (Matt. 7:11; Luke 11:13; Eph. 4:8); sacrificial (Matt. 5:23, 24; 8:4); eleemosynary (Luke 21:1); a gratuity (John 4:10; Acts 8:20). In Acts 2:38 the generic word *dōrea* is rendered "gift." It differs from the *charisma* (1 Cor. 12:4) as denoting not miraculous powers but the working of a new spirit in men, and that spirit from God.

The giving of presents entered largely into the affairs of common life in the East. The nature of the presents was as various as were the occasions: food (1 Sam. 9:7; 16:20), sheep and cattle (Gen. 32:13-15), gold (2 Sam. 18:11), jewels (Gen. 24:53), furniture, and vessels for eating and drinking (2 Sam. 18:28); delicacies—as spices, honey, etc. (1 Kings 10:25; 2 Kings 5:22). The mode of presentation was with as much parade as possible: the presents were conveyed by the hands of servants (Judg. 3:18), or still better, on the backs of beasts of burden (2 Kings 8:9). The refusal of a present was regarded as a high indignity; and this constituted the aggravated insult noticed in Matt. 22:11, the marriage robe having been offered and refused.

Gifts, spiritual (Gr. *charismata*), gifts supernaturally bestowed on the early Christians, each having his own proper gift or gifts for the edification of the body of Christ. These were the result of the extraordinary operation of the Spirit, as on the day of Pentecost. They were the gifts of speaking with tongues, casting out devils, healing, etc. (Mark 16:17, 18), usually communicated by the medium of the

BIRKET EL-MAMILLA.

laying on of the hands of the apostles (Acts 8:17; 19:6; 1 Tim. 4:14). These *charismata* were enjoyed only for a time. They could not continue always in the church. They were suited to its infancy and to the necessities of those times.

Gi'hon—*a stream.* (1.) One of the four rivers of Eden (Gen. 2:13). It has been identified with the Nile. Others regard it as the Oxus, or the Araxes, or the Ganges. But as, according to the sacred narrative, all these rivers of Eden took their origin from the head-waters of the Euphrates and the Tigris, it is probable that the Gihon is the ancient Araxes, which, under the modern name of the Arras, discharges itself into the Caspian Sea. It was the Asiatic and not the African "Cush" which the Gihon compassed (Gen. 10:7-10). (See EDEN.)

(2.) The only natural spring of water in or near Jerusalem is the "Fountain of the Virgin" (*q.v.*), which rises outside the city walls on the west bank of the Kidron valley. On the occasion of the approach of the Assyrian army under Sennacherib, Hezekiah, in order to prevent the besiegers from finding water, "stopped the upper water course of Gihon, and brought it straight down to the west side of the city of David" (2 Chr. 32:30; 33:14). This "fountain" or spring is therefore to be regarded as the "upper water course of Gihon." From this "fountain" a tunnel cut through the ridge which forms the south part of the temple hill conveys the water to the Pool of Siloam, which lies on the opposite side of this ridge at the head of the Tyropœon ("cheesemakers'") valley, or valley of the son of Hinnom, now filled up by rubbish. The length of this tunnel is about 1,750 feet. In 1880 an inscription was accidentally discovered on the wall of the tunnel about nineteen feet from where it opens into the Pool of Siloam. This inscription was executed in all probability by Hezekiah's workmen. It briefly narrates the history of the excavation. It may, however, be possible that this tunnel was executed in the time of Solomon. If the "waters of Shiloah that go softly" (Isa. 8:6) refers to the gentle stream that still flows through the tunnel into the Pool of Siloam, then this excavation must have existed before the time of Hezekiah.

In the upper part of the Tyropœon valley there are two pools still existing—the first, called *Birket el-Mamilla*, to the west of the Jaffa gate; the second, to the south of the first, called *Birket es-Sultan*. It is the opinion of some that the former was the "upper" and the latter the "lower" Pool of Gihon (2 Kings 18:17; Isa. 7:3; 36:2; 22:9). (See CONDUIT; SILOAM.)

Gilbo'a — *boiling spring* — a mountain range, now *Jebel Fûkûa'*, memorable as the scene of Saul's disastrous defeat by the Philistines. Here also his three sons were slain, and he himself died by his own hand (1 Sam. 28:4; 31:1-8; 2 Sam. 1:6-21; 21:12; 1 Chr. 10:1, 8). It was a low barren range of mountains bounding the valley of Esdraelon (Jezreel) on the east, between it and the Jordan valley. When the tidings of this defeat were conveyed to David, he gave utterance to those pathetic words in the "Song of the Bow" (2 Sam. 1:19-27).

Gil'ead—*hill of testimony*—(Gen. 31:47), a mountainous region east of Jordan. From its mountainous character it is called "the mount of Gilead" (Gen. 31:25). It is called also "the land of Gilead" (Num.

32:1), and sometimes simply "Gilead" (Ps. 60:7; Gen. 37:25). It comprised the possessions of the tribes of Gad and Reuben and the south part of Manasseh (Deut. 3:13; Num. 32:40). It was bounded on the north by Bashan, and on the south by Moab and Ammon (Gen. 31:21; Deut. 3:12-17). "Half Gilead" was possessed by Sihon, and the other half, separated from it by the river Jabbok, by Og, king of Bashan. The deep ravine of the river Hieromax (the modern *Sheriat el-Mandhûr*) separated Bashan from Gilead, which was about 60 miles in length and 20 in breadth, extending from near the south end of the Lake of Gennesaret to the north end of the Dead Sea. Abarim, Pisgah, Nebo, and Peor are its mountains mentioned in Scripture.

Gil'ead, Balm of. The region of Gilead abounded in spices and aromatic gums, which were exported to Egypt and Tyre (Gen. 37:25; Jer. 8:22; 46:11; Ezek. 27:17). The word "balm" is a contracted form of "balsam," a word derived from the Greek *balsamon*, which was adopted as the representative of the Hebrew words *baal shemen*, meaning "lord" or "chief of oils."

The Hebrew name of this balm was *tsori*. The tree yielding this medicinal oil was probably the *Balsamodendron opobalsamum* of botanists, and the *Amyris opobalsamum* of Linnæus. It is an evergreen, rising to the height of about 14 feet. The oil or resin, exuding through an orifice made in its bark in very small quantities, is esteemed of great value for its supposed medicinal qualities. (See BALM.) It may be noted that Coverdale's version reads in Jer. 8:52, "There is no *triacle* in Galaad." The word "triacle" = "treacle" is used in the sense of ointment.

Gil'gal—*rolling*. (1.) From the solemn transaction of the reading of the law in the valley of Shechem between Ebal and Gerizim the Israelites moved forward to Gilgal, and there made a permanent camp (Josh. 9:6; 10:6). It was "beside the oaks of Moreh," near which Abraham erected his first altar (Gen. 12:6, 7). This was one of the three towns to which Samuel resorted for the administration of justice (1 Sam. 7:16), and here also he offered sacrifices when the ark was no longer in the tabernacle at Shiloh (1 Sam. 10 : 8 ; 13 : 7-9). To this place, as to a central sanctuary, all Israel gathered to renew their allegiance to Saul (11 : 14). At a later period it became the scene of idolatrous worship (Hos. 4 : 15 ; 9 : 15). It has been identified with the ruins of *Jiljilieh*, about 5 miles south-west of Shiloh and about the same distance from Bethel.

(2.) The place in "the plains of Jericho," "in the east border of Jericho," where the Israelites first encamped after crossing the Jordan (Josh. 4 : 19, 20). Here they kept their first Passover in the land of Canaan (5 : 10) and renewed the rite of circumcision, and so "rolled away the reproach" of their Egyptian slavery. Here the twelve memorial stones, taken from the bed of the Jordan, were set up; and here also the tabernacle remained till it was removed to Shiloh (18 : 1). It has been identified with *Tell Jiljûlieh*, about 5 miles from Jordan.

(3.) A place, probably in the hill country of Ephraim, where there was a school of the prophets (2 Kings 4 : 38), and whence Elijah and Elisha, who resided here, "went down" to Bethel (2 : 1, 2). It is mentioned also in Deut. 11 : 30. It is now known as *Jiljilia*, a place 8 miles north of Bethel.

Gi′loh—*exile*—a city in the south-west part of the hill-country of Judah (Josh. 15 : 51). It was the native place or residence of the traitor Ahithophel "the Gilonite" (Josh. 15 : 51 ; 2 Sam. 15 : 12), and where he committed suicide (17 : 23). It has been identified with *Kurbet Jâla*, about 7 miles north of Hebron.

Gim′zo—*a place fertile in sycamores*—a city in the plain of Judah, the villages of which were seized by the Philistines (2 Chr. 28 : 18). It is now called *Jimzû*, about 3 miles south-east of Ludd—*i.e.*, Lydda.

Gin—*a trap*. (1.) Ps. 140 : 6, 141 : 9, Amos 3 : 5, the Hebrew word used, *môkesh*, means a *noose* or "snare," as it is elsewhere rendered (Ps. 18 : 6 ; Prov. 13 : 14, etc.).

(2.) Job 18 : 9, Isa. 8 : 14—Heb. *paḥ*—a *plate* or thin layer; and hence a net, a snare, trap, especially of a fowler (Ps. 69 : 22, "Let their table before them become

a net ;" Amos 3 : 5, "Doth a bird fall into a net [*paḥ*] upon the ground where there is no trap-stick [*môkesh*] for her? doth the net [*paḥ*] spring up from the ground and take nothing at all ?"—Gesenius.)

Girdle. (1.) Heb. *ḥagor*, a girdle of any kind worn by soldiers (1 Sam. 18 : 4 ; 2 Sam. 20 : 8 ; 1 Kings 2 : 5 ; 2 Kings 3 : 21) or women (Isa. 3 : 24).

(2.) Heb. *'ezôr*, something "bound," worn by prophets (2 Kings 1 : 8 ; Jer. 13 : 1), soldiers (Isa. 5 : 27 ; 2 Sam. 20 : 8 ; Ezek. 23 : 15), kings (Job 12 : 18).

(3.) Heb. *mezaḥ*, a "band," a girdle worn by men alone (Ps. 109 : 19 ; Isa. 23 : 10).

(4.) Heb. *'abneṭ*, the girdle of sacerdotal and state officers (Ex. 28 : 4, 39, 40 ; 29 : 9 ; 39 : 29).

(5.) Heb. *ḥesheb*, the "curious girdle" (Ex. 28 : 8 ; R.V., "cunningly woven band") was attached to the ephod, and was made of the same material.

The common girdle was made of leather (2 Kings 1 : 8 ; Matt. 3 : 4); a finer sort of linen (Jer. 13 : 1 ; Ezek. 16 : 10 ; Dan. 10 : 5). Girdles of sackcloth were worn in token of sorrow (Isa. 3 : 24 ; 22 : 12). They were variously fastened to the wearer (Mark 1 : 4 ; Jer. 13 : 1 ; Ezek. 16 : 10).

The girdle was a symbol of strength and power (Job 12 : 18, 21 ; 30 : 11 ; Isa. 23 : 10 ; 45 : 15). "Righteousness and faithfulness" are the girdle of the Messiah (Isa. 11 : 5).

Girdles were used as purses or pockets (Matt. 10 : 9. A.V., "purses;" R.V. marg., "girdles." Also Mark 6 : 8).

Gir′gashite—*dwelling in clayey soil*—the descendants of the fifth son of Canaan (Gen. 10 : 16), one of the original tribes inhabiting the land of Canaan before the time of the Israelites (Gen. 15 : 21 ; Deut. 7 : 1). They were a branch of the great family of the Hivites. Of their geographical position nothing is certainly known. Probably they lived somewhere in the central part of Western Palestine.

Git′tah-hepher (Josh. 19 : 13). See GATH-HEPHER.

Git′taim—*two wine-presses*—(2 Sam. 4 : 3 ; Neh. 11 : 33), a town probably in Benjamin to which the Beerothites fled.

Git′tite, a native of the Philistine city

of Gath (Josh. 13:3). Obed-edom, in whose house the ark was placed, is so designated (2 Sam. 6 : 10). Six hundred Gittites came with David from Gath into Israel (15: 18, 19).

Git'tith, a stringed instrument of music. This word is found in the titles of Ps. 8, 81, 84. In these places the LXX. render the word by "on the wine-fats." The Targum explains by "on the harp which David brought from Gath." It is the only stringed instrument named in the titles of the Psalms.

Gi'zonite, a name given to Hashem, an inhabitant of Gizoh, a place somewhere in the mountains of Judah (1 Chr. 11:34; 2 Sam. 23:32, 34).

Glass was known to the Egyptians at a very early period of their national history, at least B.C. 1500. Various articles both useful and ornamental were made of it, as bottles, vases, etc. A glass bottle with the name of Sargon on it was found among the ruins of the north-west palace of Nimroud. The Hebrew word *zekûkîth* (Job 28:17), rendered in the Authorized Version "crystal," is rightly rendered in the Revised Version "glass." This is the only allusion to glass found in the Old Testament. It is referred to in the New Testament in Rev. 4:6; 15: 2; 21:18, 21. In Job 37:18, the word rendered "looking-glass" is in the Revised Version properly rendered "mirror," formed, *i.e.*, of some metal. (Comp. Ex. 38:8: "looking-glasses" are brazen mirrors —R.V.). A mirror is referred to also in James 1:23.

Glean. The corners of fields were not to be reaped, and the sheaf accidentally left behind was not to be fetched away, according to the law of Moses (Lev. 19:9; 23:22; Deut. 24:21). They were to be left for the poor to glean. Similar laws were given regarding vineyards and oliveyards. (Comp. Ruth 2:2.)

Glede, an Old English name for the common kite, mentioned only in Deut. 14:13 (Heb. *ra'âh*), the *Milvus ater* or black kite. The Hebrew word does not occur in the parallel passage in Leviticus (11:14, *da'âh*, rendered "vulture;" in R.V., "kite"). It was an unclean bird. The Hebrew name is

from a root meaning "to see," "to look," thus designating a bird with a keen sight. The bird intended is probably the buzzard, of which there are three species found in Palestine. (See VULTURE.)

Glo'rify. (1.) To make glorious, or cause so to appear (John 12:28; 13:31, 32; 17: 4, 5).

(2.) Spoken of God to "shew forth his praise" (1 Cor. 6:20; 10:31).

Glory (Heb. *kâbhod;* Gr. *doxa*). (1.) Abundance, wealth, treasure, and hence honour (Ps. 48:12); glory (Gen. 31:1; Matt. 4:8; Rev. 21:24, 26).

(2.) Honour, dignity (1 Kings 3:13; Heb. 2:7; 1 Pet. 1:24); of God (Ps. 19: 1; 29:1); of the mind or heart (Gen. 49: 6; Ps. 7:5; Acts 2:26).

(3.) Splendour, brightness, majesty (Gen. 45:13; Isa. 4:5; Acts 22:11; 2 Cor. 3:7); of Jehovah (Isa. 59:19; 60:1; 2 Thess. 1:9).

(4.) The glorious moral attributes, the infinite perfections of God (Isa. 40:5; Acts 7:2; Rom. 1:23; 9:23; Eph. 1:12). Jesus is the "brightness of the Father's glory" (Heb. 1:3; John 1:14; 2:11).

(5.) The bliss of heaven (Rom. 2:7, 10; 5:2; 8:18; Heb. 2:10; 1 Pet. 5:1, 10).

(6.) The phrase "Give glory to God" (Josh. 7:19; Jer. 13:16) is a Hebrew idiom meaning, "Confess your sins." The words of the Jews to the blind man, "Give God the praise" (John 9:24), are an adjuration to confess. They are equivalent to, "Confess that you are an impostor," "Give God the glory by speaking the truth;" for they denied that a miracle had been wrought.

Glut'ton (Deut. 21:20) — Heb. *zôlel,* from a word meaning "to shake out," "to squander;" and hence one who is prodigal, who wastes his means by indulgence. In Prov. 23:21, the word means debauchees or wasters of their own body. In Prov. 28:7, the word (pl.) is rendered Authorized Version "riotous men;" Revised Version, "gluttonous." Matt. 11:19, Luke 7:34, Greek *phagos*, given to eating, gluttonous.

Gnash—Heb. *hârak,* meaning "to grate the teeth"—(Job 16:9; Ps. 112:10; Lam. 2:16), denotes rage or sorrow. (See also Acts 7:54; Mark 9:18.)

Gnat, only in Matt. 23:24, a small two-winged stinging fly of the genus *Culex*, which includes mosquitoes. Our Lord alludes here to the gnat in a proverbial expression probably in common use, "who strain *out* a gnat;" the words in the Authorized Version, "strain *at* a gnat," being a mere typographical error, which has been corrected in the Revised Version. The custom of filtering wine for this purpose was common among the Jews. It was founded on Lev. 11:23. It is supposed that the "lice," Ex. 8:16 (marg. R.V., "sand-flies") were a species of gnat.

Goad (Heb. *malmâd*, only in Judg. 3:

IBEX.

31), an instrument used by ploughmen for guiding their oxen. Shamgar slew six hundred Philistines with an ox-goad. "The goad is a formidable weapon. It is sometimes ten feet long, and has a sharp point. We could now see that the feat of Shamgar was not so very wonderful as some have been accustomed to think."

In 1 Sam. 13:21, a different Hebrew word is used—*dŏrban*—meaning something pointed. The expression (Acts 9:5, omitted in the R.V.), "It is hard for thee to kick against the pricks"—*i.e.*, against the goad—was proverbial for unavailing resistance to superior power.

Goat. (1.) Heb. *'ez*, the she-goat (Gen.

15:9; 30:35; 31:38). This Hebrew word is also used for the he-goat (Ex. 12:5; Lev. 4:23; Num. 28:15). It is also used to denote a kid (Gen. 38:17, 20). Hence it may be regarded as the generic name of the animal as domesticated. It literally means "strength," and points to the superior strength of the goat as compared with the sheep.

(2.) Heb. 'attûd, only in plural; rendered "rams" (Gen. 31:10, 12); he-goats (Num. 7:17-88; Isa. 1:11); goats (Deut. 22:14; Ps. 50:13). They were used in sacrifice (Ps. 66:15). This word is used metaphorically for princes or chiefs in Isa. 14:9, and Zech. 10:3 as leaders. (Comp. Jer. 50:8.)

(3.) Heb. gedî, properly a kid. Its flesh was a delicacy among the Hebrews (Gen. 27:9, 14, 17; Judg. 6:19).

(4.) Heb. sa'ir, meaning the "shaggy," a hairy goat, a he-goat (2 Chr. 29:23); "a goat" (Lev. 4:24); "satyr" (Isa. 13:21); "devils" (Lev. 17:7). It is the goat of the sin-offering (Lev. 9:3, 15; 10:16).

(5.) Heb. tsaphir, a he-goat of the goats (2 Chr. 29:21). Dan. 8:5, 8, as a symbol of the Macedonian empire.

(6.) Heb. tayish, a "striker" or "butter," rendered "he-goat" (Gen. 30:35; 32:14).

(7.) Heb. 'azazel (q.v.), the "scapegoat" (Lev. 16:8, 10, 26).

(8.) There are two Hebrew words used to denote the undomesticated goat:—Yael, only in plural, mountain goats (1 Sam. 24:2; Job 39:1; Ps. 104:18). It is derived from a word meaning "to climb." It is the ibex, which abounded in the mountainous parts of Moab. And 'akko, only in Deut. 14:5, the wild goat.

Goats are mentioned in the New Testament in Matt. 25:32, 33; Heb. 9:12, 13, 19; 10:4. They represent oppressors and wicked men (Ezek. 34:17; 39:18; Matt. 25:33).

Several varieties of the goat were familiar to the Hebrews. They had an important place in their rural economy on account of the milk they afforded and the excellency of the flesh of the kid. They formed an important part of pastoral wealth (Gen. 31:10, 12; 32:14; 1 Sam. 25:2).

Go'ath—a lowing—a place near Jerusalem, mentioned only in Jer. 31:39.

Gob—a pit—a place mentioned in 2 Sam. 21:18, 19; called also Gezer in 1 Chr. 20:4.

Gob'let, a laver or trough for washing garments. In Cant. 7:2 a bowl or drinking vessel, a bowl for mixing wine; in Ex. 24:6 a sacrificial basin. (See CUP.)

God (A.S. and Dutch God; Dan. Gud; Ger. Gott), the name of the Divine Being. It is the rendering (1) of the Hebrew 'El, from a word meaning to be strong; (2) of 'Elôah, plural 'Elohim. The singular form, Eloah, is used only in poetry. The plural form is more commonly used in all parts of the Bible. The Hebrew word Jehovah (q.v.), the only other word generally employed to denote the Supreme Being, is uniformly rendered in the Authorized Version by "Lord," printed in small capitals. The existence of God is taken for granted in the Bible. There is nowhere any argument to prove it. He who disbelieves this truth is spoken of as one devoid of understanding (Ps. 14:1).

The arguments generally adduced by theologians in proof of the being of God are,—

(1.) The à priori argument, which is the testimony afforded by reason.

(2.) The à posteriori argument, by which we proceed logically from the facts of experience to causes. These arguments are,—

(a) The cosmological, by which it is proved that there must be a First Cause of all things, for every effect must have a cause.

(b) The teleological, or the argument from design. We see everywhere the operations of an intelligent Cause in nature.

(c) The moral argument, called also the anthropological argument, based on the moral consciousness and the history of mankind, which exhibits a moral order and purpose which can only be explained on the supposition of the existence of God. Conscience and human history testify that "verily there is a God that judgeth in the earth."

The attributes of God are set forth in

order by Moses in Ex. 34 : 6, 7. (See also Deut. 6 : 4; 10 : 17; 9 : 16; Num. 16 : 22; 33 : 19; Ex. 15 : 11; Isa. 44 : 6; Hab. 3 : 6; Ps. 102 : 26; Job 34 : 22.) They are also systematically classified in Rev. 5 : 12 and 7 : 12.

God's attributes are spoken of by some as *absolute*—*i.e.*, such as belong to his essence as Jehovah, Jah, etc.; and *relative*—*i.e.*, such as are ascribed to him with relation to his creatures. Others distinguish them into *communicable*—*i.e.*, those which can be imparted in degree to his creatures: goodness, holiness, wisdom, etc.; and *incommunicable*, which cannot be so imparted: independence, immutability, immensity, and eternity. They are by some also divided into *natural* attributes—eternity, immensity, etc.; and *moral*—holiness, goodness, etc.

God'head (Acts 17 : 29; Rom. 1 : 9; Col. 2 : 9), the essential being or the nature of God.

God'liness, the whole of practical piety (1 Tim. 4 : 8; 2 Pet. 1 : 6). "It supposes knowledge, veneration, affection, dependence, submission, gratitude, and obedience." In 1 Tim. 3 : 16 it denotes the substance of revealed religion.

Goel, in Hebrew the participle of the verb *gaal*, "to redeem." It is rendered in the Authorized Version "kinsman," Num. 5 : 8; Ruth 3 : 12; 4 : 1, 6, 8; "redeemer," Job 19 : 25; "avenger," Num. 35 : 12; Deut. 19 : 6, etc. The Jewish law gave the right of redeeming and repurchasing, as well as of avenging blood, to the next relative, who was accordingly called by this name. (See REDEEMER.)

Gog. (1.) A Reubenite (1 Chr. 5 : 4), the father of Shimei.

(2.) The name of the leader of the hostile party described in Ezek. 38, 39, as coming from the "north country" and assailing the people of Israel to their own destruction. This prophecy has been regarded as fulfilled in the conflicts of the Maccabees with Antiochus, the invasion and overthrow of the Chaldeans, and the temporary successes and destined overthrow of the Turks. But "all these interpretations are unsatisfactory and inadequate. The vision respect-

ing Gog and Magog in the Apocalypse (Rev. 20 : 8) is in substance a reannouncement of this prophecy of Ezekiel. But while Ezekiel contemplates the great conflict in a more general light as what was certainly to be connected with the times of the Messiah, and should come then to its last decisive issues, John, on the other hand, writing from the commencement of the Messiah's times, describes there the last struggles and victories of the cause of Christ. In both cases alike the vision describes the final workings of the world's evil and its results in connection with the kingdom of God, only the starting-point is placed further in advance in the one case than in the other."

It has been supposed to be the name of a district in the wild north-east steppes of Central Asia, north of the Hindoo-Kush, now a part of Turkestan—a region about 2,000 miles north-east of Nineveh.

Go'lan—*exile*—a city of Bashan (Deut. 4 : 23), one of the three cities of refuge east of the Jordan, about 12 miles north-east of the Sea of Galilee (1 Chr. 20 : 8). There are no further notices of it in Scripture. It became the head of the province of Gaulanitis, one of the four provinces into which Bashan was divided after the Babylonish captivity, and almost identical with the modern *Jaulân*, in Western Haurân, about 39 miles in length and 18 in breadth.

Gold. (1.) Heb. *zâhâb*, so called from its *yellow* colour, Ex. 25 : 11; 1 Chr. 28 : 18; 2 Chr. 3 : 5.

(2.) Heb. *segôr*, from its *compactness*, or as being enclosed or treasured up; thus precious or "fine gold," 1 Kings 6 : 20; 7 : 49.

(3.) Heb. *paz*, native or pure gold, Job 28 : 17; Ps. 19 : 10; 21 : 3, etc.

(4.) Heb. *betzer*, "ore of gold or silver" as dug out of the mine, Job 36 : 19, where it means simply riches.

(5.) Heb. *kéthem*—*i.e.*, something concealed or separated—Job 28 : 16, 19; Ps. 45 : 9; Prov. 25 : 12. Rendered "golden wedge" in Isa. 13 : 12.

(6.) Heb. *harûts*—*i.e.*, dug out; poetic for gold—Prov. 8 : 10; 16 : 16; Zech. 9 : 3.

Gold was known from the earliest times (Gen. 2 : 11). It was principally used for ornaments (Gen. 24 : 22). It was very abundant (1 Chr. 22 : 14; Nah. 2 : 9; Dan. 3 : 1). Many tons of it were used in connection with the temple (2 Chr. 1 : 15). It was found in Arabia, Sheba, and Ophir (1 Kings 9 : 28; 10 : 1; Job 28 : 16), but not in Palestine.

In Dan. 2 : 38, the Babylonian Empire is spoken of as a "head of gold" because of its great riches; and Babylon was called by Isaiah (14 : 4) the "golden city" (R.V. marg., "exactress," adopting the reading *marhêbah* instead of the usual word *madhêbah*).

Golden calf (Ex. 32 : 4, 8; Deut. 9 : 16; Neh. 9 : 19). This was a molten image of a calf which the idolatrous Israelites formed at Sinai. This symbol was borrowed from the custom of the Egyptians. It was destroyed at the command of Moses (Ex. 32 : 20). (See AARON; MOSES.)

Gold'smith (Neh. 3 : 8, 32; Isa. 40 : 19; 41 : 7; 46 : 6). The word so rendered means properly a *founder* or *finer*.

Gol'gotha, the common name of the spot where Jesus was crucified. It is in-

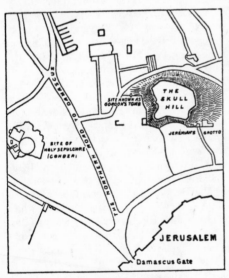

PLAN OF SKULL HILL.

terpreted by the evangelists as meaning "the place of a skull" (Matt. 27 : 33; Mark 15 : 21; John 19 : 17). This name represents in Greek letters the Aramaic word *Gulgaltha*, which is the Hebrew *Gûlgoleth*

(Num. 1 : 2; 1 Chr. 23 : 3, 24; 2 Kings 9 : 35), meaning "a skull." It is identical with the word "Calvary" (*q.v.*). It was a little knoll rounded like a bare skull. It is obvious from the evangelists that it was some well-known spot outside the gate (comp. Heb. 13 : 12), and near the city (Luke 23 : 26), containing a "garden" (John 19 : 41), and on a thoroughfare leading into the country. Hence it is an untenable idea that it is embraced within the present "Church of the Holy Sepulchre." The hillock above Jeremiah's Grotto, to the north of the city, is in all probability the true site of Calvary. The skull-like appearance of the rock in the southern precipice of the hillock is very remarkable.

Goli'ath—*great.* (1.) A famous giant of Gath, who for forty days openly defied the armies of Israel, but was at length slain by David with a stone from a sling (1 Sam. 17 : 4). He was probably descended from the Rephaim who found refuge among the Philistines after they were dispersed by the Ammonites (Deut. 20 : 20, 21). His height was "six cubits and a span," which, taking the cubit at 21 inches, is equal to 10½ feet. David cut off his head (1 Sam. 17 : 51) and brought it to Jerusalem, while he hung the armour which he took from him in his tent. His sword was preserved at Nob as a religious trophy (21 : 9). David's victory over Goliath was the turning-point in his life. He came into public notice now as the deliverer of Israel and the chief among Saul's men of war (18 : 5), and the devoted friend of Jonathan.

(2.) In 2 Sam. 21 : 19 there is another giant of the same name mentioned as slain by Elhanan. The staff of his spear "was like a weaver's beam." The Authorized Version interpolates the words "the brother of" from 1 Chr. 20 : 5, where this giant is called Lahmi.

Go'mer—*complete; vanishing.* (1.) The daughter of Diblaim, who (probably in vision only) became the wife of Hosea (1 : 3).

(2.) The eldest son of Japheth, and father of Ashkenaz, Riphath, and Togarmah (Gen. 10 : 2, 3), whose descendants formed the principal branch of the population of South-eastern Europe. He is generally regarded as the ancestor of the Celtæ and the Cimmerii, who in early times settled to the north of the Black Sea, and gave their name to the Crimea, the ancient Chersonesus Taurica. Traces of their presence are found in the names Cimmerian Bosphorus, Cimmerian Isthmus, etc. In the seventh century B.C. they were driven out of their original seat by the Scythians, and overran western Asia Minor, whence they were afterwards expelled. They subsequently reappear in the times of the Romans as the Cimbri of the north and west of Europe, whence they crossed to the British Isles, where their descendants are still found in the Gaels and Cymry. Thus the whole Celtic race may be regarded as descended from Gomer.

Gomor'rah—*submersion*—one of the five cities of the plain of Siddim (*q.v.*) which were destroyed by fire (Gen. 10:19; 13:10; 19:24, 28). These cities probably stood close together, and were near the northern extremity of what is now the Dead Sea. This city is always mentioned next after Sodom, both of which were types of impiety and wickedness (Gen. 18:20; Rom. 9:29). Their destruction is mentioned as an "ensample unto those that after should live ungodly" (2 Pet. 2:6; Jude 4–7). Their wickedness became proverbial (Deut. 32:32; Isa. 1:9, 10; Jer. 23:14). But that wickedness may be exceeded (Matt. 10:15; Mark 6:11). (See DEAD SEA.)

Good'ly trees, boughs of, were to be carried in festive procession on the first day of the feast of Tabernacles (Lev. 23:40). This was probably the olive tree (Neh. 8:15), although no special tree is mentioned.

Good'ness of God, a perfection of his character which he exercises towards his creatures according to their various circumstances and relations (Ps. 145:8, 9; 103:8; 1 John 4:8). Viewed generally, it is *benevolence;* as exercised with respect to the miseries of his creatures it is *mercy, pity, compassion,* and in the case of impenitent sinners, long-suffering *patience;* as exercised in communicating favour on the unworthy it is *grace.* "Goodness and justice are the several aspects of one unchangeable, infinitely wise, and sovereign

moral perfection. God is not sometimes merciful and sometimes just, but he is eternally infinitely just and merciful." God is infinitely and unchangeably good (Zeph. 3:17), and his goodness is incomprehensible by the finite mind (Rom. 11:35, 36). "God's goodness appears in two things—giving and forgiving."

Good'ness in man is not a mere passive quality, but the deliberate preference of right to wrong—the firm and persistent resistance of all moral evil, and the choosing and following of all moral good.

Go'pher, a tree from the wood of which Noah was directed to build the ark (Gen. 6:14). It is mentioned only there. The LXX. render this word by "squared beams," and the Vulgate by "planed wood." Other versions have rendered it "pine" and "cedar;" but the weight of authority is in favour of understanding by it the *cypress* tree, which grows abundantly in Chaldea and Armenia.

Go'shen. (1.) A district in Egypt where Jacob and his family settled, and in which they remained till the Exodus (Gen. 45:10; 46:28, 29, 31, etc.). It is called "the land of Goshen" (47:27), and also simply "Goshen" (46:28), and "the land of Rameses" (47:11; Ex. 12:37), for the towns Pithom and Rameses lay within its borders; also Zoan or Tanis (Ps. 78:12). It lay on the east of the Nile, and apparently not far from the royal residence. It was "the best of the land" (Gen. 47:6, 11), but is now a desert. It is first mentioned in Joseph's message to his father. It has been identified with the modern *Wâdy Tumilat,* lying between the eastern part of the Delta and the west border of Palestine. It was a pastoral district, where some of the king's cattle were kept (Gen. 47:6). The inhabitants were not exclusively Israelites (Ex. 3:22; 11:2; 12:35, 36).

(2.) A district in Palestine (Josh. 10:41; 11:16). It was a part of the maritime plain of Judah, and lay between Gaza and Gibeon.

(3.) A town in the mountains of Judah (Josh. 15:51).

Gos'pel, a word of Anglo-Saxon origin,

and meaning "God's spell"—*i.e.*, word of God, or rather, according to others, "good spell"—*i.e.*, good news. It is the rendering of the Greek *euangelion*—*i.e.*, "good message." It denotes (1) "the *welcome intelligence* of salvation to man as preached by our Lord and his followers. (2.) It was afterwards transitively applied to each of the four *histories of our Lord's life*, published by those who are therefore called 'Evangelists'—writers of the history of the gospel (the *euangelion*). (3.) The term is often used to express collectively the gospel *doctrines;* and 'preaching the gospel' is often used to include not only the proclaiming of the good tidings, but the teaching men how to *avail* themselves of the offer of salvation, the declaring of all the truths, precepts, promises, and threatenings of Christianity." It is termed "the gospel of the grace of God" (Acts 20:24), "the gospel of the kingdom" (Matt. 4:23), "the gospel of Christ" (Rom. 1:16), "the gospel of peace" (Eph. 4:15), "the glorious gospel," "the everlasting gospel," "the gospel of salvation" (Eph. 1:13).

Gos'pels. The central fact of Christian preaching was the intelligence that the Saviour had come into the world (Matt. 4:23; Rom. 10:15); and the first Christian preachers who called their account of the person and mission of Christ by the term *euangelion* (= good message) were called *euangelistai* (= evangelists) (Eph. 4:11; Acts 21:8).

There are four historical accounts of the person and work of Christ: "the first by Matthew, announcing the Redeemer as the promised King of the kingdom of God; the second by Mark, declaring him 'a prophet, mighty in deed and word;' the third by Luke, of whom it might be said that he represents Christ in the special character of the Saviour of sinners (Luke 7:36; 15:18); the fourth by John, who represents Christ as the Son of God, in whom deity and humanity become one. The ancient Church gave to Matthew the symbol of the lion, to Mark that of a man, to Luke that of the ox, and to John that of the eagle: these were the four faces of the cherubim" (Ezek. 1:10).

Date. The Gospels were all composed during the latter part of the first century, and there is distinct historical evidence to show that they were used and accepted as authentic before the end of the second century.

Mutual relation. "If the extent of all the coincidences be represented by 100, their proportionate distribution will be: Matthew, Mark, and Luke, 53; Matthew and Luke, 21; Matthew and Mark, 20; Mark and Luke, 6. Looking only at the general result, it may be said that of the contents of the synoptic Gospels [*i.e.*, the first three Gospels] about two-fifths are common to the three, and that the parts peculiar to one or other of them are little more than one-third of the whole."

Origin. Did the evangelists copy from one another? The opinion is well founded that the Gospels were published by the apostles orally before they were committed to writing, and that each had an independent origin. (See MATTHEW, GOSPEL OF.)

Gourd. (1.) Jonah's gourd (Jonah 4: 6–10), bearing the Hebrew name *kikayôn* (found only here), was probably the *kiki* of the Egyptians, the *croton*. This is the castor-oil plant, a species of *ricinus*, the *palma Christi*, so called from the palmate division of its leaves. Others with more probability regard it as the *cucurbita*— the *el-keroa* of the Arabs — a kind of pumpkin peculiar to the East. "It is grown in great abundance on the alluvial banks of the Tigris and on the plain between the river and the ruins of Nineveh." At the present day it is trained to run over structures of mud and brush to form booths to protect the gardeners from the heat of the noon-day sun. It grows with extraordinary rapidity, and when cut or injured withers away also with great rapidity.

(2.) Wild gourds (2 Kings 4:38–40)—Heb. *pakkuôth* — belong to the family of the cucumber-like plants, some of which are poisonous. The species here referred to is probably the colocynth (*Cucumis colocynthus*). The LXX. render the word by "wild pumpkin." It abounds in the desert parts of Syria, Egypt, and Arabia. There is, however, another species, called the *Cucumis prophetarum*, from the idea that it afforded the gourd which "the sons of the prophets" shred by mistake into their pottage.

Gov′ernment of God. See PROVI-DENCE.

Gov′ernments (1 Cor. 12:28), the powers which fit a man for a place of influence in the church; "the steersman's art; the art of guiding aright the vessel of church or state."

Gov′ernor. (1.) Heb. *nágîd*, a prominent, conspicuous person, whatever his capacity: as, chief of the royal palace (2 Chr. 28:7; comp. 1 Kings 4:6), chief of the temple (1 Chr. 9:11; Jer. 20:1), the leader of the Aaronites (1 Chr. 12:27), keeper of the sacred treasury (26:24), captain of the army (13:1), the king (1 Sam. 9:16), the Messiah (Dan. 9:25).

(2.) Heb. *nâsî*, raised; exalted. Used to denote the chiefs of families (Num. 3:24, 30, 32, 35); also of tribes (2:3; 7:2; 3:32). These dignities appear to have been elective, not hereditary.

(3.) Heb. *pakîd*, an officer or magistrate. It is used of the delegate of the high priest (2 Chr. 24:11), the Levites (Neh. 11:22), a military commander (2 Kings 25:19), Joseph's officers in Egypt (Gen. 41:34).

(4.) Heb. *shallit*, one who has power, who rules (Gen. 42:6; Ezra 4:20; Eccl. 8:8; Dan. 2:15; 5:29).

(5.) Heb. *'alûph*, literally one put over a thousand—*i.e.*, a clan or a subdivision of a tribe. Used of the "dukes" of Edom (Gen. 36), and of the Jewish chiefs (Zech. 9:7).

(6.) Heb. *môshêl*, one who rules, holds dominion. Used of many classes of rulers (Gen. 3:16; 24:2; 45:8; Ps. 105:20); of the Messiah (Micah 5:1); of God (1 Chr. 29:12; Ps. 103:19).

(7.) Heb. *sar*, a ruler or chief; a word of very general use. It is used of the chief baker of Pharaoh (Gen. 40:16); of the chief butler (40:2, etc. See also Gen. 47:6; Ex. 1:11; Dan. 1:7; Judg. 10:30; 1 Kings 22:26; 20:15; 2 Kings 1:19; 2 Sam. 24:2). It is used also of angels,

guardian angels (Dan. 10:13, 20, 21; 12:1; 10:13; 8:25).

(8.) *Peḥah*, whence *pasha*—*i.e.*, friend of the king; adjutant; governor of a province (2 Kings 18:24; Isa. 36:9; Jer. 51:57; Ezek. 23:6, 23; Dan. 3:2; Esther 3:12), or a prefect (Neh. 3:7; 5:14; Ezra 5:3; Hag. 1:1). This is a foreign word—Assyrian—which was early adopted into the Hebrew idiom (1 Kings 10:15).

(9.) The Chaldean word *ṣegan* is applied to the governors of the Babylonian satrapies (Dan. 3:2, 27; 6:8); the prefects over the Magi (2:48). The corresponding Hebrew word *ṣegan* is used of provincial rulers (Jer. 51:23, 28, 57); also of chiefs and rulers of the people of Jerusalem (Ezra 9:2; Neh. 2:16; 4:8, 13; 5:7, 17; 7:5; 12:40).

In the New Testament there are also different Greek words rendered thus.

(1.) Meaning an *ethnarch* (2 Cor. 11:32), which was an office distinct from military command, with considerable latitude of application.

(2.) The *procurator* of Judea under the Romans (Matt. 27:2). (Comp. Luke 2:2, where the verb from which the Greek word so rendered is derived is used.)

(3.) *Steward* (Gal. 4:2).

(4.) *Governor* of the feast (John 2:9), who appears here to have been merely an intimate friend of the bridegroom, and to have presided at the marriage banquet in his stead.

(5.) A *director*—*i.e.*, helmsman; Lat. *gubernator*—(James 3:4).

Go′zan, a region in Central Asia to which the Israelites were carried away captive (2 Kings 17:6; 1 Chr. 5:26; 2 Kings 19:12; Isa. 37:12). It was situated in Mesopotamia, on the river Habor (2 Kings 17:6; 18:11), the Khabûr, a tributary of the Euphrates. The "river of Gozan" (1 Chr. 5:26) is probably the upper part of the river flowing through the province of Gozan, now *Kizzel-Ozan*.

Grace. (1.) Of form or person (Prov. 1:9; 3:22; Ps. 45:2). (2.) Favour, kindness, friendship (Gen. 6:8; 18:3; 19:19; 2 Tim. 1:9). (3.) God's forgiving mercy (Rom. 11:6; Eph. 2:5). (4.) The gospel as distinguished from the law (John 1:17; Rom. 6:14; 1 Pet. 5:12). (5.) Gifts freely bestowed by God; as miracles, prophecy, tongues (Rom. 15:15; 1 Cor. 15:10; Eph. 3:8). (6.) Christian virtues (2 Cor. 8:7; 2 Pet. 3:18). (7.) The glory hereafter to be revealed (1 Pet. 1:13).

Grace, means of, an expression not used in Scripture, but employed (1) to denote those institutions ordained by God to be the ordinary channels of grace to the souls of men. These are the Word, Sacraments, and Prayer.

(2.) But in popular language the expression is used in a wider sense to denote those exercises in which we engage for the purpose of obtaining spiritual blessing; as hearing the gospel, reading the Word, meditation, self-examination, Christian conversation, etc.

Graft, the process of inoculating fruit-trees (Rom. 11:17-24). It is peculiarly appropriate to olive-trees. The union thus of branches to a stem is used to illustrate the union of true believers to the true Church.

Grain, used, in Amos 9:9, of a small stone or kernel; in Matt. 13:31, of an individual seed of mustard; in John 12:24, 1 Cor. 15:37, of wheat. The Hebrews sowed only wheat, barley, and spelt; rye and oats are not mentioned in Scripture.

Grape, the fruit of the vine, which was extensively cultivated in Palestine. Grapes are spoken of as "tender" (Cant. 2:13, 15), "unripe" (Job 15:33), "sour" (Isa. 18:5), "wild" (Isa. 5:2, 4). (See Rev. 14: 18; Micah 7:1; Jer. 6:9; Ezek. 18:2, for figurative use of the word.) (See VINE.)

Grass. (1.) Heb. *hâtsîr*, ripe grass fit for mowing (1 Kings 18:5; Job 40:5; Ps. 104:14). As the herbage rapidly fades under the scorching sun, it is used as an image of the brevity of human life (Isa. 40: 6, 7; Ps. 90:5). In Num. 11:5 this word is rendered "leeks."

(2.) Heb. *deshe'*, green grass (Gen. 1: 11, 12; Isa. 66:14; Deut. 32:2). "The sickly and forced blades of grass which spring up on the flat plastered roofs of houses in the East are used as an emblem of speedy destruction, because they are

small and weak, and because, under the scorching rays of the sun, they soon wither away" (2 Kings 19:26; Ps. 129:6; Isa. 37:27).

The dry stalks of grass were often used as fuel for the oven (Matt. 6:30; 13:30; Luke 12:28).

Grass'hopper belongs to the class of neuropterous insects called *Gryllidæ.* This insect is not unknown in Palestine.

In Judg. 6:5; 7:12; Job 39:20; Jer. 46:23, where the Authorized Version has "grasshopper," the Revised Version more correctly renders the Hebrew word (*'arbeh*) by "locust." This is the case also in Amos 7:1; Nah. 3:17, where the Hebrew word *gôb* is used; and in Lev. 11:22; Num. 13: 33; Eccl. 12:5; Isa. 11:22, where *hâgâb* is used. In all these instances the proper rendering is probably "locust" (*q.v.*).

Grate, a network of brass for the bottom of the great altar of sacrifice (Ex. 27:4; 35:16; 38:4, 5, 30).

Grave. Among the ancient Hebrews graves were outside of cities in the open field (Luke 7:12; John 11:30). Kings (1 Kings 2:10) and prophets (1 Sam. 25:1) were generally buried within cities. Graves were generally grottoes or caves, natural or hewn out in rocks (Isa. 22:16; Matt. 27:60). There were family cemeteries (Gen. 47:29; 50:5; 2 Sam. 19:37). Public burial-places were assigned to the poor (Jer. 26:23; 2 Kings 23:6). Graves were usually closed with stones, which were whitewashed, to warn strangers against contact with them (Matt. 23:27), which caused ceremonial pollution (Num. 19:16).

There were no graves in Jerusalem except those of the kings, and according to tradition that of the prophetess Huldah.

Gra'ven image—Deut. 27:25; Ps. 97:7 (Heb. *pesel*)—refers to the household gods of idolaters. "Every nation and city had its own gods......Yet every family had its separate household or tutelary god."

Gra'ving. (1.) Heb. *hâtsabh.* Job 19:24, rendered "graven," but generally means hewn stone or wood, in quarry or forest.

(2.) Heb. *hârush.* Jer. 17:1, rendered "engraving," and indicates generally artistic work in metal, wood, and stone, effected by fine instruments.

(3.) Heb. *ḥâqaq*. Ezek. 4:1, engraving a plan or map, rendered "pourtray;" Job 19:23, "written."

(4.) Heb. *paṣal* points rather to the sculptor's or the carver's art (Isa. 30:22; 40:19; 41:7; 44:12–15).

(5.) *Pathah* refers to *intaglio* work, the cutting and engraving of precious stones (Ex. 28:9–11, 21; Zech. 3:9; Cant. 1:10, 11).

(6.) *Hcreṭ.* In Ex. 32:4 rendered "graving tool;" and in Isa. 8:1, "a pen."

Greaves—only in 1 Sam. 17:6—a piece of defensive armour (*q.v.*) reaching from the foot to the knee; from French *grève*, "the shin." They were the Roman *cothurni.*

Gre'cians, *Hellenists*, Greek - Jews; Jews born in a foreign country, and thus did not speak Hebrew (Acts 6:1; 9:29), nor join in the Hebrew services of the Jews in Palestine, but had synagogues of their own in Jerusalem. Joel 3:6=Greeks.

Greece originally consisted of the four provinces of Macedonia, Epirus, Achaia, and Peleponnesus. In Acts 20:2 it designates only the Roman province of Macedonia. Greece was conquered by the Romans B.C. 146. After passing through various changes it was erected into an independent monarchy in 1831.

Moses makes mention of Greece under the name of Javan (Gen. 10:2–5); and this name does not again occur in the Old Testament till the time of Joel (3:6). Then the Greeks and Hebrews first came into contact in the Tyrian slave-market. Prophetic notice is taken of Greece in Dan. 8:21.

The cities of Greece were the special scenes of the labours of the apostle Paul.

Greek. Found only in the New Testament, where a distinction is observed between "Greek" and "Grecian" (*q.v.*). The former is (1) a Greek by race (Acts 16:1–3; 18:17; Rom. 1:14), or (2) a Gentile as opposed to a Jew (Rom. 2:9, 10). The latter, meaning properly "one who speaks Greek," is a foreign Jew opposed to a home Jew who dwelt in Palestine.

The word "Grecians" in Acts 11:20

should be "Greeks," denoting the heathen Greeks of that city, as rendered in the Revised Version according to the reading of the best manuscripts ("Hellenes").

Grey'hound (Prov. 30:31), the rendering of the Hebrew *zarzîr mothnayîm*, meaning literally "girded as to the loins." Some (Gesen.; R.V. marg.) render it "war-horse." The LXX. and Vulgate versions render it "cock." It has been by some interpreters rendered also "stag" and "warrior," as being girded about or panoplied, and "wrestler." The greyhound, however, was evidently known in ancient times, as appears from Egyptian monuments.

Grind (Ex. 32:20; Deut. 9:21; Judg. 16:21), to crush small (Heb. *ṭahan*); to oppress the poor (Isa. 3:5). The handmill was early used by the Hebrews (Num. 11:8). It consisted of two stones—the upper (Deut. 24:6; 2 Sam. 11:21) being movable and slightly concave, the lower being stationary.

The *grinders* mentioned Eccl. 12:3 are the teeth. (See MILL.)

Griz'zled, party-coloured, as goats (Gen. 31:10, 12), horses (Zech. 6:3, 6).

Grove. (1.) Heb. *'ashêrah*, properly a wooden image, or a pillar representing Ashtoreth, a sensual Canaanitish goddess, probably usually set up in a grove (2 Kings 21:7; 23:4). In the Revised Version the word "Ashêrah" (*q.v.*) is introduced as a proper noun, the name of the wooden symbol of a goddess, with the plurals Asherim (Ex. 34:13) and Asheroth (Judg. 3:13).

The LXX. have rendered *ashêrah* in 2 Chr. 15:16 by "Astarte." The Vulgate has done this also in Judg. 3:7.

(2.) Heb. *'eshel* (Gen. 21:33). In 1 Sam. 22:6 and 31:13 the Authorized Version renders this word by "tree." In all these passages the Revised Version renders by "tamarisk tree." It has been identified with the *Tamariscus orientalis*, five species of which are found in Palestine.

(3.) The Heb. word *'elon*, uniformly rendered in the Authorized Version by "plain," properly signifies a grove or plantation. In the Revised Version it is rendered, pl., "oaks" (Gen. 13:18; 14:13; 18:1; 12:6;

Deut. 11:30; Josh. 19:33). In the earliest times groves are mentioned in connection with religious worship. The heathen consecrated groves to particular gods, and for this reason they were forbidden to the Jews (Jer. 17:3; Ezek. 20:28).

Guard. (1.) Heb. *ṭabbaḥ* (properly a "cook," and in a secondary sense "executioner," because this office fell to the lot of the cook in Eastern countries), the bodyguard of the kings of Egypt (Gen. 37:36) and Babylon (2 Kings 25:8; Jer. 40:1; Dan. 2:14).

(2.) Heb. *râts*, properly a "courier," one whose office was to run before the king's chariot (2 Sam. 15:1; 1 Kings 1:5). The couriers were also military guards (1 Sam. 22:17; 2 Kings 10:25). They were probably the same who under David were called Pelethites (1 Kings 14:27; 2 Sam. 15:1).

(3.) Heb. *mishmĕrĕth*, one who watches (Neh. 4:22), or a watch-station (7:3; 12:9; Job 7:12).

In the New Testament (Mark 6:27) the Authorized Version renders the Greek *spekulator* by "executioner," earlier English versions by "hangman," the Revised Version by "soldier of his guard." The word properly means a "pikeman" or "halberdier," of whom the bodyguard of kings and princes was composed. In Matt.

27:65, 66; 28:11, the Authorized Version renders the Greek *kustodia* by "watch," and the Revised Version by "guard," the Roman guard, which consisted of four soldiers, who were relieved every three hours (Acts 12:4). The "captain of the guard" mentioned Acts 28:16 was the commander of the Prætorian troops, whose duty it was to receive and take charge of all prisoners from the provinces.

Guest-cham'ber, the spare room on the upper floor of an Eastern dwelling (Mark 14:14; Luke 22:11). In Luke 2:7 the word is translated "inn" (*q.v.*).

Gur—*a whelp*—a place near Ibleam where Jehu's servants overtook and mortally wounded king Ahaziah (2 Kings 9:27); an ascent from the plain of Jezreel.

Gur-ba'al—*sojourn of Baal*—a place in Arabia (2 Chr. 26:7) where there was probably a temple of Baal.

Gut'ter—Heb. *tsinnôr*—(2 Sam. 5:8). This Hebrew word occurs only elsewhere in Ps. 42:7 in the plural, where it is rendered "waterspouts." It denotes some passage through which water passed; a water-course.

In Gen. 30:38, 41 the Hebrew word rendered "gutters" is *raḥat*, and denotes vessels overflowing with water for cattle (Ex. 2:16); drinking-troughs.

H

Hab'akkuk—*embrace*—the eighth of the twelve minor prophets. Of his personal history we have no reliable information. He was probably a member of the Levitical choir. He was contemporary with Jeremiah and Zephaniah.

Hab'akkuk, Prophecies of, were probably written about B.C. 650-627, or, as some think, a few years later. This book consists of three chapters, the contents of which are thus comprehensively described: —"When the prophet in spirit saw the formidable power of the Chaldeans approaching and menacing his land, and saw the great evils they would cause in

Judea, he bore his complaints and doubts before Jehovah, the just and the pure (1:2-17). And on this occasion the future punishment of the Chaldeans was revealed to him (2). In the third chapter a presentiment of the destruction of his country, in the inspired heart of the prophet, contends with his hope that the enemy would be chastised." The third chapter is a sublime song dedicated "to the chief musician," and therefore intended apparently to be used in the worship of God. It is "unequalled in majesty and splendour of language and imagery."

The passage in 2:4, "The just shall live

by his faith," is quoted by the apostle in Rom. 1 : 17. (Comp. Gal. 3 : 12 ; Heb. 10 : 37, 38.)

Haber'geon, an Old English word for breastplate. In Job 41 : 26 (Heb. *shîryâh*) it is properly a "coat of mail ;" the Revised Version has "pointed shaft." In Ex. 28 : 32, 39 : 23, it denotes a military garment strongly and thickly woven and covered with mail round the neck and breast. Such linen corselets have been found in Egypt. The word used in these verses is *taḥra*, which is of Egyptian origin. The Revised Version, however, renders it by "coat of mail." (See ARMOUR.)

Habita'tion. God is the habitation of his people, who find rest and safety in him (Ps. 71 : 3 ; 91 : 9). Justice and judgment are the habitation of God's throne (Ps. 89 : 14, Heb. *měkhôn*, "foundation "), because all his acts are founded on justice and judgment. (See Ps. 132 : 5, 13 ; Eph. 2 : 22, of Canaan, Jerusalem, and the temple as God's habitation.) God inhabits eternity (Isa. 57 : 15)—*i.e.*, dwells not only among men, but in eternity, where time is unknown ; and "the praises of Israel" (Ps. 22 : 3)—*i.e.*, he dwells among those praises and is continually surrounded by them.

Ha'bor—the *united* stream, or, according to others, with *beautiful* banks—the name of a river in Assyria, and also of the district through which it flowed (1 Chr. 5 : 26). There is a river called Khabûr which rises in the central highlands of Kurdistan, and flows south-west till it falls into the Tigris, about 70 miles above Mosul. This was not, however, the Habor of Scripture. There is another river of the same name (the Chaboras) which, after a course of about 200 miles, flows into the Euphrates at Karkesia, the ancient Circesium. This was, there can be little doubt, the ancient Habor.

Hach'ilah—*the darksome hill*—one of the peaks of the long ridge of el-Kôlah, running out of the Ziph plateau, "on the south of Jeshimon" (*i.e.*, of the "waste "), the district to which one looks down from the plateau of Ziph (1 Sam. 23 : 19). After his reconciliation with Saul at Engedi (24 : 1–8), David returned to Hachilah, where

he had fixed his quarters. The Ziphites treacherously informed Saul of this, and he immediately (26 : 1–4) renewed his pursuit of David, and "pitched in the hill of Hachilah." David and his nephew Abishai stole at night into the midst of Saul's camp, when they were all asleep, and noiselessly removed the royal spear and the cruse from the side of the king, and then, crossing the intervening valley to the height on the other side, David cried to the people, and thus awoke the sleepers. He then addressed Saul, who recognized his voice, and expostulated with him. Saul professed to be penitent ; but David could not put confidence in him, and he now sought refuge at Ziklag. David and Saul never afterwards met (1 Sam. 26 : 13–25).

Ha'dad—*Adod, brave* (?)—the name of a Syrian god. (1.) An Edomite king who defeated the Midianites (Gen. 36 : 35 ; 1 Chr. 1 : 46).

(2.) Another Edomite king (1 Chr. 1 : 50, 51), called also Hadar (Gen. 36 : 39 ; 1 Chr. 1 : 51).

(3.) One of "the king's seed in Edom." He fled into Egypt, where he married the sister of Pharaoh's wife (1 Kings 11 : 14–22). He became one of Solomon's adversaries.

Ha'dad—*sharp*—(a different name in Hebrew from the preceding), one of the sons of Ishmael (1 Chr. 1 : 30). Called also Hadar (Gen. 25 : 15).

Hadade'zer — *Hadad is help ;* called also **Hadare'zer,** *Adod is his help*—the king of Zobah. Hanun, the king of the Ammonites, hired among others the army of Hadadezer to assist him in his war against David. Joab, who was sent against this confederate host, found them in double battle array—the Ammonites toward their capital of Rabbah, and the Syrian mercenaries near Medeba. In the battle which was fought the Syrians were scattered, and the Ammonites in alarm fled into their capital. After this Hadadezer went north "to recover his border " (2 Sam. 8 : 3, A.V.) ; but rather, as the Revised Version renders, " to recover his dominion"—*i.e.*, to recruit his forces. Then followed another battle with the Syrian army thus recruited, which resulted in its being totally routed at Helam (2 Sam. 10: 17). Shobach, the leader of the Syrian army, died on the field of battle. The Syrians of Damascus, who had come to help Hadadezer, were also routed, and Damascus was made tributary to David. All the spoils taken in this war—"shields of gold" and "exceeding much brass," from which afterwards the "brazen sea, and the pillars, and the vessels of brass" for the temple were made (1 Chr. 18:8)—were brought to Jerusalem and dedicated to Jehovah. Thus the power of the Ammonites and the Syrians was finally broken, and David's empire extended to the Euphrates (2 Sam. 10: 15–19; 2 Chr. 19:15–19).

Ha′dad - rim′mon (composed of the names of two Syrian idols), the name of a place in the valley of Megiddo. It is alluded to by the prophet Zechariah (12:11) in a proverbial expression derived from the lamentation for Josiah, who was mortally wounded near this place (2 Chr. 35 : 22–25). It has been identified with the modern *Rummâneh*, a village "at the foot of the Megiddo hills, in a notch or valley about an hour and a half south of Tell Metzellim."

Ha′dar—*Adod, brave* (?). (1.) A son of Ishmael (Gen. 25:15); in 1 Chr. 1:30 written Hadad.

(2.) One of the Edomitish kings (Gen. 36 : 39) about the time of Saul. Called also Hadad (1 Chr. 1 : 50, 51).

It is probable that in these cases Hadar may be an error simply of transcription for Hadad.

Hadare′zer—*Adod is his help*—the name given to Hadadezer (2 Sam. 8 : 3–12) in 2 Sam. 10.

Hada′shah—*new*—a city in the valley of Judah (Josh. 15 : 37).

Hadas′sah—*myrtle*—the Jewish name of Esther (*q.v.*)—Esther 2 : 7.

Hadat′tah—*new*—one of the towns in the extreme south of Judah (Josh. 15 : 25).

Ha′des—*that which is out of sight*—a Greek word used to denote the state or place of the dead. All the dead alike go into this place. To be buried, to go down to the grave, to descend into hades, are equivalent expressions. In the LXX. this word is the usual rendering of the Hebrew

sheôl, the common receptacle of the departed (Gen. 42 : 38; Ps. 139 : 8; Hos. 13 : 14; Isa. 14 : 9). This term is of comparatively rare occurrence in the Greek New Testament. Our Lord speaks of Capernaum as being "brought down to hell" (hades)—*i.e.*, simply to the lowest debasement—(Matt. 11 : 23). It is contemplated as a kind of kingdom which could never overturn the foundation of Christ's kingdom (16 : 18)—*i.e.*, Christ's church can never die.

In Luke 16 : 23 it is most distinctly associated with the doom and misery of the lost.

In Acts 2 : 27–31 Peter quotes the LXX. version of Ps. 16 : 8–11, plainly for the purpose of proving our Lord's resurrection from the dead. David was left in the place of the dead, and his body saw corruption. Not so with Christ. According to ancient prophecy (Ps. 30 : 3) he was recalled to life.

Ha′did—*pointed*—a place in the tribe of Benjamin near Lydda, or Lod, and Ono (Ezra 2 : 33; Neh. 7 : 37). It is identified with the modern *el-Hadîtheh*, 3 miles east of Lydda.

Had′lai—*resting*—an Ephraimite; the father of Amasa, mentioned in 2 Chr. 28 : 12.

Hado′ram—*is exalted*. (1.) The son of Tou, king of Hamath, sent by his father to congratulate David on his victory over Hadarezer, king of Syria (1 Chr. 18 : 10; called Joram 2 Sam. 8 : 10).

(2.) The fifth son of Joktan, the founder of an Arab tribe (Gen. 10 : 27; 1 Chr. 1 : 21).

(3.) One who was "over the tribute;" *i.e.*, "over the levy." He was stoned by the Israelites after they had revolted from Rehoboam (2 Chr. 10 : 18). Called also Adoram (2 Sam. 20 : 24) and Adoniram (1 Kings 4 : 6).

Ha′drach, the name of a country (Zech. 9 : 1) which cannot be identified. Rawlinson would identify it with Edessa. He mentions that in the Assyrian inscriptions it is recorded that "Shalmanezer III. made two expeditions—the first against Damascus B.C. 773, and the second against Hadrach B.C. 772; and again that Asshur-danin-il II. made expeditions against Hadrach in B.C. 765 and 755."

Hæm'orrhoids or **Emerods,** bleeding piles known to the ancient Romans as *mariscæ,* but more probably malignant boils of an infectious and fatal character. With this loathsome and infectious disease the men of Ashdod were smitten by the hand of the Lord. This calamity they attributed to the presence of the ark in their midst, and therefore they removed it to Gath (1 Sam. 5:6-8). But the same consequences followed from its presence in Gath, and therefore they had it removed to Ekron, 11 miles distant. The Ekronites were afflicted with the same dreadful malady, but more severely; and a panic seizing the people, they demanded that the ark should be sent back to the land of Israel (9-12; 6:1-9).

Haft, a handle as of a dagger (Judg. 3: 22).

Ha'gar—*flight,* or, according to others, *stranger*—an Egyptian, Sarah's handmaid (Gen. 16:1; 21:9, 10), whom she gave to Abraham (*q.v.*) as a secondary wife (16:2). When she was about to become a mother she fled from the cruelty of her mistress, intending apparently to return to her relatives in Egypt, through the desert of Shur, which lay between. Wearied and worn she had reached the place she distinguished by the name of Beer-lahai-roi ("the well of the visible God"), where the angel of the Lord appeared to her. In obedience to the heavenly visitor she returned to the tent of Abraham, where her son Ishmael was born, and where she remained (16) till after the birth of Isaac, the space of fourteen years. Sarah after this began to vent her dissatisfaction both on Hagar and her child. Ishmael's conduct was insulting to Sarah, and she insisted that he and his mother should be dismissed. This was accordingly done, although with reluctance on the part of Abraham (Gen. 21:14). They wandered out into the wilderness, where Ishmael, exhausted with his journey and faint from thirst, seemed about to die. Hagar "lifted up her voice and wept," and the angel of the·Lord, as before, appeared

unto her, and she was comforted and delivered out of her distresses (Gen. 21:18, 19).

Ishmael afterwards established himself in the wilderness of Paran, where he married an Egyptian (Gen. 21:20, 21).

"Hagar" allegorically represents the Jewish church (Gal. 4:24), in bondage to the ceremonial law; while "Sarah" represents the Christian church, which is free.

Hagare'ne or **Hag'arite.** (1.) One of David's mighty men (1 Chr. 11:38), the son of a foreigner.

(2.) Used of Jaziz (1 Chr. 27:31), who was over David's flocks. "A Hagarite had charge of David's flocks, and an Ishmaelite of his herds, because the animals were pastured in districts where these nomadic people were accustomed to feed their cattle."

(3.) In the reign of Saul a great war was waged between the trans-Jordanic tribes and the Hagarites (1 Chr. 5), who were overcome in battle. A great booty was captured by the two tribes and a half, and they took possession of the land of the Hagarites.

Subsequently the "Hagarenes," still residing in the land on the east of Jordan, entered into a conspiracy against Israel (comp. Ps. 83:6). They are distinguished from the Ishmaelites.

Hag'gai—*festive*—one of the twelve so-called minor prophets. He was the first of the three (Zechariah, his contemporary, and Malachi, who was about one hundred years later, being the other two) whose ministry belonged to the period of Jewish history which began after the return from captivity in Babylon. Scarcely anything is known of his personal history. He may have been one of the captives taken to Babylon by Nebuchadnezzar. He began his ministry about sixteen years after the Return. The work of rebuilding the temple had been put a stop to through the intrigues of the Samaritans. After having been suspended for fifteen years, the work was resumed through the efforts of Haggai and Zechariah (Ezra 6:14), who by their exhortations roused the people from their lethargy, and induced them to take advantage of the favourable opportunity that had arisen in a change in the policy of the Persian government. (See DARIUS [2].) Haggai's prophecies have thus been characterized:—"There is a ponderous and simple dignity in the emphatic reiteration addressed alike to every class of the community—prince, priest, and people—'*Be strong, be strong, be strong*' (2:4). 'Cleave, stick fast, to the work you have to do;' or again, '*Consider your ways, consider, consider, consider*' (1:5, 7; 2:15, 18). It is the Hebrew phrase for the endeavour, characteristic of the gifted seers of all times, to compel their hearers to turn the inside of their hearts outwards to their own view, to take the mask from off their consciences, to 'see life steadily, and to see it wholly.'"—Stanley's *Jewish Church*. (See SIGNET.)

Hag′gai, Book of, consists of two brief, comprehensive chapters. The object of the prophet was generally to urge the people to proceed with the rebuilding of the temple.

Chapter first comprehends the first address (2–11) and its effects (12–15).

Chapter second contains,—

(1.) The second prophecy (1–9), which was delivered a month after the first.

(2.) The third prophecy (10–19), delivered two months and three days after the second; and

(3.) The fourth prophecy (20–23), delivered on the same day as the third.

These discourses are referred to in Ezra 5:1; 6:14; Heb. 12:20. (Comp. Hag. 2:7, 8, 22.)

Hag′gith—*festive; the dancer*—a wife of David and the mother of Adonijah (2 Sam. 3:4; 1 Kings 1:5, 11; 2:13; 1 Chr. 3:2), who, like Absalom, was famed for his beauty.

Hagiog′rapha — *the holy writings* — a term which came early into use in the Christian church to denote the third division of the Old Testament scriptures, called by the Jews *Kethubim*—*i.e.,* "Writings." It consisted of five books—*viz.,* Job, Proverbs, and Psalms, and the two books of Chronicles. The ancient Jews classified their sacred books as the Law, the Prophets, and the *Kethubim*, or Writings. (See BIBLE.)

In the New Testament (Luke 24:44) we find three corresponding divisions—*viz.,* the Law, the Prophets, and the Psalms.

Hail! a salutation expressive of a wish for the welfare of the person addressed; the translation of the Greek *Chairè*, "Rejoice" (Luke 1:8). Used in mockery in Matt. 27:29.

Hail, frozen rain-drops; one of the plagues of Egypt (Ex. 9:23). It is mentioned by Haggai as a divine judgment (Hag. 2:17). A hail-storm destroyed the army of the Amorites when they fought against Joshua (Josh. 10:11). Ezekiel represents the wall daubed with untempered mortar as destroyed by great hail-stones (Ezek. 13:11). (See also 38:2; Rev. 20:9; 8:7.)

Hair. (1.) The Egyptians let the hair of their head and beard grow only when they were in mourning, shaving it off at other times. "So particular were they on this point that to have neglected it was a subject of reproach and ridicule; and whenever they intended to convey the idea of a man of low condition, or a slovenly person, the artists represented him with a beard." Joseph shaved himself before going in to Pharaoh (Gen. 41:14). The women of Egypt wore their hair long and plaited. Wigs were worn by priests and laymen to cover the shaven skull, and false beards were common. The great masses of hair seen in the portraits and statues of kings and priests are thus altogether artificial.

(2.) A precisely opposite practice, as regards men, prevailed among the Assyrians. In Assyrian sculptures the hair always appears long, and combed closely down upon the head. The beard also was allowed to grow to its full length.

(3.) Among the Greeks the custom in this respect varied at different times, as it did also among the Romans. In the time of the apostle, among the Greeks the men wore short hair, while that of the women was long (1 Cor. 11:14, 15). Paul reproves the Corinthians for falling in with a style of manners which so far confounded the distinction of the sexes and was hurtful to good morals. (See, however, 1 Tim. 2:9, and 1 Pet. 3:9, as regards women.)

(4.) Among the Hebrews the natural distinction between the sexes was preserved by the women wearing long hair (Luke 7:38; John 11:2; 1 Cor. 11:6), while the men preserved theirs as a rule at a moderate length by frequent clipping.

Baldness disqualified any one for the priest's office (Lev. 21).

Elijah is called a "hairy man" (2 Kings 1:8) from his flowing locks, or more probably from the shaggy cloak of hair which he wore. His raiment was of camel's hair.

Long hair is especially noticed in the description of Absalom's person (2 Sam. 14:26); but the wearing of long hair was unusual, and was only practised as an act of religious observance by Nazarites (Num. 6:5; Judg. 13:5) and others in token of special mercies (Acts 18:18).

In times of affliction the hair was cut off (Isa. 3:17, 24; 15:2; 22:12; Jer. 7:29; Amos 8:10). Tearing the hair and letting it go dishevelled were also tokens of grief (Ezra 9:3). "Cutting off the hair" is a figure of the entire destruction of a people (Isa. 7:20). The Hebrews anointed the hair profusely with fragrant ointments (Ruth 3:3; 2 Sam. 14:2; Ps. 23:5; 45:7, etc.), especially in seasons of rejoicing (Matt. 6:17; 26:7; Luke 7:46).

Hak'koz—*the thorn*—the head of one of the courses of the priests (1 Chr. 24:10).

Ha'lah, a district of Media to which captive Israelites were transported by the Assyrian kings (2 Kings 17:6; 18:11; 1 Chr. 5:26). It lay along the banks of the upper Khabûr, from its source to its junction with the Jerujer. Probably the district called by Ptolemy Chalcitis.

Ha'lak—*smooth; bald*—a hill at the southern extremity of Canaan (Josh. 11:17). It is referred to as if it were a landmark in that direction, being prominent and conspicuous from a distance. It has by some been identified with the modern Jebel el-Madura, on the south frontier of Judah, between the south end of the Dead Sea and the Wâdy Gaian.

Hal'hul—*full of hollows*—a town in the highlands of Judah (Josh. 15:58). It is now a small village of the same name, and is situated about 5 miles north-east of Hebron on the way to Jerusalem. There is an old Jewish tradition that Gad, David's seer (2 Sam. 24:11), was buried here.

Hall (Gr. *aulè*, Luke 22:55; R.V., "court"), the open court or quadrangle belonging to the high priest's house. In Matt. 26:69 and Mark 14:66 this word is incorrectly rendered "palace" in the Authorized Version, but correctly "court" in the Revised Version. In John 10:1, 16 it means a "sheep-fold." In Matt. 27:27 and Mark 15:16 (A.V., "common hall;" R.V., "palace") it refers to the *prætorium* or residence of the Roman governor at Jerusalem. The "porch" in Matt. 26:71 is the entrance-hall or passage leading into the central court, which is open to the sky.

Hal'lel—*praise*—the name given to the group of Psalms 113–118, which are preeminently psalms of praise. It is called "The Egyptian Hallel," because it was chanted in the temple whilst the Passover lambs were being slain. It was chanted also on other festival occasions—as at Pentecost, the feast of Tabernacles, and the feast of Dedication. The Levites, standing before the altar, chanted it verse by verse, the people responding by repeating the verses or by intoned hallelujahs. It was also chanted in private families at the feast of Passover. This was probably the hymn which our Saviour and his disciples sung at the conclusion of the Passover supper kept by them in the upper room at Jerusalem (Matt. 26:30; Mark 14:26).

There is also another group called "The Great Hallel," comprehending Psalms 118–136, which was recited on the first evening at the Passover supper and on occasions of great joy.

Hallelu'jah—*Praise ye Jehovah*—frequently rendered "Praise ye the Lord," stands at the beginning of ten of the psalms (106, 111–113, 135, 146–150), hence called "hallelujah psalms." From its frequent occurrence it grew into a formula of praise. The Greek form of the word (*alleluia*) is found in Rev. 19:1, 3, 4, 6.

Hal'low, to render sacred, to consecrate (Ex. 28:38; 29:1). This word is from the Saxon, and properly means "to make holy." The name of God is "hallowed"— *i.e.*, is reverenced as holy (Matt. 6 : 9).

Halt, lame on the feet (Gen. 32 : 31; Ps. 38 : 17). To "halt between two opinions" (1 Kings 18 : 21) is supposed by some to be an expression used in "allusion to birds, which hop from spray to spray, forwards and backwards." The LXX. render the expression "How long go ye lame on both knees?" The Hebrew verb rendered "halt" is used of the irregular dance ("leaped upon") around the altar (ver. 26). It indicates a lame, uncertain gait—going now in one direction, now in another, in the frenzy of wild leaping.

Ham—*warm*, *hot*, and hence the *south;* also an Egyptian word meaning "black"—the youngest son of Noah (Gen. 5 : 32; comp. 9 : 22, 24). The curse pronounced by Noah against Ham, properly against Canaan his fourth son, was accomplished when the Jews subsequently exterminated the Canaanites.

One of the most important facts recorded in Gen. 10 is the foundation of the earliest monarchy in Babylonia by Nimrod, the grandson of Ham (6, 8, 10). The primitive Babylonian empire was thus Hamitic, and of a cognate race with the primitive inhabitants of Arabia and of Ethiopia. (See ACCAD.)

TABLE OF THE DESCENDANTS OF HAM (Gen. 10 : 6-14).

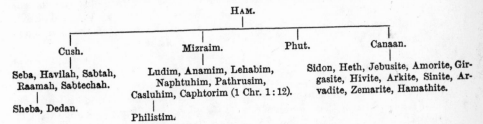

HAM.

Cush.	Mizraim.	Phut.	Canaan.
Seba, Havilah, Sabtah, Raamah, Sabtechah.	Ludim, Anamim, Lehabim, Naphtuhim, Pathrusim, Casluhim, Caphtorim (1 Chr. 1 : 12).		Sidon, Heth, Jebusite, Amorite, Girgasite, Hivite, Arkite, Sinite, Arvadite, Zemarite, Hamathite.
Sheba, Dedan.	Philistim.		

The race of Ham were the most energetic of all the descendants of Noah in the early times of the post-diluvian world.

Ha'man (of Persian origin)—*magnificent* —the name of the vizier (*i.e.*, the prime minister) of the Persian king Ahasuerus (Esther 3 : 1, etc.). He is called an "Agagite," which seems to denote that he was descended from the royal family of the Amalekites, the bitterest enemies of the Jews, as Agag was one of the titles of the Amalekite kings. He or his parents were brought to Persia as captives taken in war. He was hanged on the gallows which he had erected for Mordecai the Jew (Esther 7 : 10). (See ESTHER.)

Ha'math—*fortress*—the capital of one of the kingdoms of Upper Syria of the same name, on the Orontes, in the valley of Lebanon, at the northern boundary of Palestine (Num. 13 : 21; 34 : 8), at the foot of Hermon (Josh. 13 : 5) towards Damascus (Zech. 9 : 2; Jer. 49 : 20). It is called "Hamath the great" in Amos 6 : 2, and "Hamath-zobah" in 2 Chr. 8 : 3.

This is one of the oldest cities in the world. It was a place of importance when the Israelites first entered on the possession of the land of Canaan. Toi was king of Hamath in David's time. He sent an embassy to Jerusalem to congratulate David on the occasion of his victory over Hadadezer; also gifts "of all manner of vessels of gold, silver, and copper" (2 Sam. 8 : 9, 10; 1 Chr. 18 : 9-12). It was afterwards conquered by Solomon (2 Chr. 8 : 3); but on his death it regained its independence. It is frequently mentioned in subsequent times. In the time of Hezekiah it was conquered by the Assyrians (2 Kings 17 : 24; 18 : 34; 19 : 13; Isa. 10 : 9; 11 : 11), and remained under their rule till the time of Alexander the Great. It was called Epiphaneia by the Greeks in honour of Antiochus Epiphanes. This town, now called *Hamah*, is "beautifully situated on the Orontes, 32 miles north of Emesa, and 36 south of the ruins of Assamea."

The *kingdom of Hamath* comprehended

the great plain lying on both banks of the Orontes from the fountain near Riblah to Assamea on the north, and from Lebanon on the west to the desert on the east. The "entrance of Hamath" (Num. 34:8), which was the north boundary of Palestine, led from the west between the north end of Lebanon and the Nusairiyeh mountains.

Ha'math-zo'bah—*fortress of Zobah*—(2 Chr. 8:3) is supposed by some to be a different place from the foregoing; but this is quite uncertain.

Ham'math—*warm springs*—one of the "fenced cities" of Naphtali (Josh. 19:35). It is identified with the warm baths (the heat of the water ranging from 136° to 144°) still found on the shore a little to the south of Tiberias under the name of *Hŭmmam Tabarîyeh* ("Bath of Tiberias").

Hammeda'tha, father of Haman, designated usually "the Agagite" (Esther 3:1, 10; 8:5).

Hamme'lech—*the king's*—the father of Jerahmeel, mentioned in Jer. 36:26. Some take this word as a common noun—"the king"—and understand that Jerahmeel was Jehoiakim's son. Probably, however, it is to be taken as a proper name.

Ham'mer. (1.) Heb. *paṭṭish*, used by gold-beaters (Isa. 41:7) and by quarrymen (Jer. 23:29). Metaphorically of Babylon (Jer. 50:23) or Nebuchadnezzar.

(2.) Heb. *makâbâh*, a stone-cutter's mallet (1 Kings 6:7), or of any workman (Judg. 4:21; Isa. 44:12).

(3.) Heb. *halmûth*, a poetical word for a workman's hammer, found only in Judg. 5:26, where it denotes the mallet with which the pins of the tent of the nomad are driven into the ground.

(4.) Heb. *mappêts*, rendered "battle-axe" in Jer. 51:20. This was properly a "mace," which is thus described by Rawlinson: "The Assyrian mace was a short, thin weapon, and must either have been made of a very tough wood or (and this is more probable) of metal. It had an ornamented head, which was sometimes very beautifully modelled, and generally a strap or string at the lower end by which it could be grasped with greater firmness."

Hammol'eketh—*the queen*—the daughter of Machir and sister of Gilead (1 Chr. 7:17, 18). Abiezer was one of her three children.

Ham'mon—*warm springs.* (1.) A town in the tribe of Asher, near Zidon (Josh. 19:28), identified with ʿAin Hâmûl.

(2.) A Levitical city of Naphtali (1 Chr. 6:76).

Ham'moth-dor—*warm springs*—a Levitical city of Naphtali (Josh. 21:32); probably Hammath in 19:35.

Ha'mon. See BAAL-HAMON.

Hamo'nah—*multitude*—a name figuratively assigned to the place in which the slaughter and burial of the forces of Gog were to take place (Ezek. 39:16).

Ha'mon-gog — *multitude of Gog* — the name of the valley in which the slaughtered forces of Gog are to be buried (Ezek. 39:11, 15), "the valley of the passengers on the east of the sea."

Ha'mor—*he-ass*—a Hivite from whom Jacob purchased the plot of ground in which Joseph was afterwards buried (Gen. 33:19). He is called "Emmor" in Acts 7:16. His son Shechem founded the city of that name which Simeon and Levi destroyed because of his crime in the matter of Dinah, Jacob's daughter (Gen. 34:31). Hamor and Shechem were also slain (ver. 26).

Ha'mul — *spared* — one of the sons of Pharez, son of Judah (1 Chr. 2:5). His descendants are called Hamulites (Num. 26:21).

Hamu'tal — *kinsman of the dew* — the daughter of Jeremiah of Libnah, wife of king Josiah, and mother of king Jehoahaz (2 Kings 23:31), also of king Zedekiah (2 Kings 24:18).

Hanam'eel—*whom God has graciously given*—the cousin of Jeremiah, to whom he sold the field he possessed in Anathoth, before the siege of Jerusalem (Jer. 32:6-12).

Ha'nan — *merciful.* (1.) A Benjamite (1 Chr. 8:23). (2.) One of David's heroes (1 Chr. 11:43). (3.) Jer. 35:4. (4.) A descendant of Saul (1 Chr. 8:38). (5.) One of the Nethinim (Ezra 2:46). (6.) One of the Levites who assisted Ezra (Neh. 8:7).

(7.) One of the chiefs who subscribed the covenant (Neh. 10 : 22).

Hanan'eel—*God has graciously given*—a tower in the wall of Jerusalem (Neh. 3 : 1; 12 : 39). It is mentioned also in Jer. 31 : 38; Zech. 14 : 10.

Hana'ni—*God has gratified me*, or *is gracious*. (1.) One of the sons of Heman (1 Chr. 25 : 4, 25). (2.) A prophet who was sent to rebuke king Asa for entering into a league with Benhadad I., king of Syria, against Judah (2 Chr. 16 : 1-10). He was probably the father of the prophet Jehu (1 Kings 16 : 7). (3.) Probably a brother of Nehemiah (Neh. 1 : 2; 7 : 2), who reported to him the melancholy condition of Jerusalem. Nehemiah afterwards appointed him to have charge of the city gates.

Hanani'ah—*Jehovah has given*. (1.) A chief of the tribe of Benjamin (1 Chr. 8 : 24). (2.) One of the sons of Heman (1 Chr. 25 : 4, 23). (3.) One of Uzziah's military officers (2 Chr. 26 : 11). (4.) Grandfather of the captain who arrested Jeremiah (Jer. 37 : 13). (5.) Jer. 36 : 12. (6.) Jer. 38 : 1. (7.) Shadrach, one of the "three Hebrew children" (Dan. 1; 6 : 7). (8.) Son of Zerubbabel (1 Chr. 3 : 19, 21). (9.) Ezra 10 : 28. (10.) The "ruler of the palace; he was a faithful man, and feared God above many" (Neh. 7 : 2). (11.) Neh. 3 : 8. (12.) Neh. 3 : 30. (13.) A priest, son of Jeremiah (Neh. 12 : 12). (14.) A false prophet contemporary with Jeremiah (28 : 3, 17).

Hand. Called by Galen "the instrument of instruments." It is the symbol of human action (Ps. 9 : 17; Job 9 : 30; Isa. 1 : 15; 1 Tim. 2 : 8). Washing the hands was a symbol of innocence (Ps. 26 : 6; 73 : 13; Matt. 27 : 24), also of sanctification (1 Cor. 6 : 11; Isa. 50 : 16; Ps. 24 : 3, 4). In Ps. 77 : 2 the correct rendering is, as in the Revised Version, "My hand was stretched out," etc., instead of, as in the Authorized Version, "My sore ran in the night," etc.

The *right* hand denoted the *south*, and the *left* the *north* (Job 23 : 9; 1 Sam. 23 : 19). To give the right hand was a pledge of fidelity (2 Kings 10 : 15; Ezra 10 : 19); also of submission to the victors (Ezek. 17 : 18; Jer. 50 : 15). The right hand was lifted up in taking an oath (Gen. 14 : 22, etc.). The hand is frequently mentioned, particularly the right hand, as a symbol of power and strength (Ps. 66 : 5; Isa. 28 : 2). To kiss the hand is an act of homage (1 Kings 19 : 18; Job 31 : 27), and to pour water on one's hands is to serve him (2 Kings 3 : 11). The hand of God is the symbol of his power: its being upon one denotes favour (Ezra 7 : 6, 28; Isa. 1 : 25; Luke 1 : 66, etc.) or punishment (Ex. 9 : 3; Judg. 2 : 15; Acts 13 : 11, etc.). A position at the right hand was regarded as the chief place of honour and power (Ps. 45 : 9; 80 : 17; 110 : 1; Matt. 26 : 64).

Hand'breadth, a measure of four fingers, equal to about four inches (Ex. 25 : 25; 37 : 12; Ps. 39 : 5, etc.).

Hand'kerchief. Only once in Authorized Version (Acts 19 : 12). The Greek word (*sudarion*) so rendered means properly "a sweat-cloth." It is rendered in the plural "napkins" in John 11 : 44; 20 : 7; Luke 19 : 20.

Hand'maid, servant (Gen. 16 : 1; Ruth 3 : 9; Luke 1 : 48). It is probable that Hagar was Sarah's personal attendant while she was in the house of Pharaoh, and was among those maid-servants whom Abram had brought from Egypt.

Hand'writing (Col. 2 : 14). The "blotting out the handwriting" is the removal by the grace of the gospel of the condemnation of the law which we had broken.

Ha'nes, a place in Egypt mentioned only in Isa. 30 : 4 in connection with a reproof given to the Jews for trusting in Egypt. It was considered the same as Tahpanhes, a fortified town on the eastern frontier, but has been also identified as *Ahnas-el-Medeeneh*, 70 miles from Cairo.

Hanging (as a punishment), a mark of infamy inflicted on the dead bodies of criminals (Deut. 21 : 23) rather than our modern mode of punishment. Criminals were first strangled and then hanged (Num. 25 : 4; Deut. 21 : 22). (See 2 Sam. 21 : 6 for the practice of the Gibeonites.)

Hanging (as a curtain). (1.) Heb. *mâsâk*—(a) before the entrance to the court of the tabernacle (Ex. 35 : 17); (b) before the door of the tabernacle (26 : 36, 37);

(c) before the entrance to the most holy place, called "the veil of the *covering*" (35:12; 39:34), as the word properly means.

(2.) Heb. *kela'im*, tapestry covering the walls of the tabernacle (Ex. 27:9; 35:17; Num. 3:26) to the half of the height of the wall (27:18; comp. 26:16). These hangings were fastened to pillars.

(3.) Heb. *bottim* (2 Kings 23:7), "hangings for the grove" (R.V., "for the Asherah"); marg., instead of "hangings," has "tents" or "houses." Such curtained structures for idolatrous worship are also alluded to in Ezek. 16:16.

Han'nah — *favour, grace* — one of the wives of Elkanah the Levite, and the mother of Samuel (1 Sam. 1; 2). Her home was at Ramathaim-zophim, whence she was wont every year to go to Shiloh, where the tabernacle had been pitched by Joshua, to attend the offering of sacrifices there according to the law (Ex. 23:15; 34:20; Deut. 16:16), probably at the feast of the Passover (comp. Ex. 13:10). On occasion of one of these "yearly" visits, being grieved by reason of Peninnah's conduct toward her, she went forth alone, and kneeling before the Lord at the sanctuary she prayed inaudibly. Eli the high priest, who sat at the entrance to the holy place, observed her, and misunderstanding her character he harshly condemned her conduct (1 Sam. 1:14-16). After hearing her explanation he retracted his injurious charge and said to her, "Go in peace: and the God of Israel grant thee thy petition." Perhaps the story of the wife of Manoah was not unknown to her. Thereafter Elkanah and his family retired to their quiet home, and there, before another Passover, Hannah gave birth to a son, whom, in grateful memory of the Lord's goodness, she called Samuel—*i.e.*, "heard of God." After the child was weaned (probably in his third year) she brought him to Shiloh into the house of the Lord, and said to Eli the aged priest, "Oh my lord, I am the woman that stood by thee here, praying unto the Lord. For this child I prayed; and the Lord hath given me my petition which I asked of him: therefore I also

have granted him to the Lord; as long as he liveth he is granted to the Lord" (1 Sam. 1:27, 28, R.V.). Her gladness of heart then found vent in that remarkable prophetic song (2:1-11; comp. Luke 2:46-55) which contains the first designation of the Messiah under that name (1 Sam. 2:10, "Anointed" = "Messiah"). And so Samuel and his parents parted. He was left in Shiloh to minister "unto the Lord." And each year when they came up to Shiloh, Hannah brought to her absent child "a little coat" (Heb. *mĕīl*, a term used to denote the "robe" of the ephod worn by the high priest, Ex. 28:31), a priestly robe —a long upper tunic (1 Chr. 15:27) in which to minister in the tabernacle (1 Sam. 15:27; 2 Sam. 13:10; Job 2:12). "And the child Samuel grew before the Lord." After Samuel, Hannah had three sons and two daughters.

Han'niel—*grace of God*. (1.) A chief of the tribe of Manasseh (Num. 34:23). (2.) A chief of the tribe of Asher (1 Chr. 7:39).

Ha'nun—*graciously given*. (1.) The son and successor of Nahash, king of Moab. David's messengers, sent on an embassy of condolence to him to Rabbah Ammon, his capital, were so grossly insulted that he proclaimed war against Hanun. David's army, under the command of Joab, forthwith crossed the Jordan, and gained a complete victory over the Moabites and their allies (2 Sam. 10:1-14) at Medeba (*q.v.*).

(2.) Neh. 3:13. (3.) 3:30.

Ha'ra — *mountainous land* — a province of Assyria (1 Chr. 5:26), between the Tigris and the Euphrates, along the banks of the Khabûr, to which some of the Israelite captives were carried. It has not been identified. Some think the word a variation of Haran.

Har'adah — *fright; fear* — the twenty-fifth station of the Israelites in their wanderings (Num. 33:24).

Ha'ran. (1.) Heb. *harân; i.e.*, "mountaineer." The eldest son of Terah, brother of Abraham and Nahor, and father of Lot, Milcah, and Iscah. He died before his father (Gen. 11:27), in Ur of the Chaldees.

(2.) Heb. *harân, i.e.*, "parched;" or probably from the Accadian *charanâ*, meaning "a road." A celebrated city of Western Asia, now *Harran*, where Abram remained, after he left Ur of the Chaldees, till his father Terah died (Gen. 11:31, 38), when he continued his journey into the land of Canaan. It is called "Charran" in the LXX. and in Acts 7:2. It is called the "city of Nahor" (Gen. 24:10), and Jacob resided here with Laban (27:43). It stood on the river Belik, an affluent of the Euphrates, about 70 miles above where it joins that river in Upper Mesopotamia or Padan-aram, and about 600 miles north-west of Ur in a direct line. It was on the caravan route between the east and west. It is afterwards mentioned among the towns taken by the king of Assyria (1 Kings 19:12; Isa. 37:12). It was known to the Greeks and Romans under the name Carrhæ.

(3.) The son of Caleb of Judah (1 Chr. 2:46) by his concubine Ephah.

Harbo'na (a Persian word meaning "ass-driver"), one of the seven eunuchs or chamberlains of king Ahasuerus (Esther 1:10; 7:9).

Hare (Heb. *'arnĕbeth*) was prohibited as food according to the Mosaic law (Lev. 11:6; Deut. 14:7), "because he cheweth the cud, but divideth not the hoof." The habit of this animal is to grind its teeth and move its jaw *as if* it actually chewed the cud. But, like the cony (*q.v.*), it is not a ruminant with four stomachs, but a rodent like the squirrel, rat, etc. Moses speaks of it according to appearance. It is interdicted because, though apparently chewing the cud, it did not divide the hoof.

There are two species in Syria—(1) the *Lepus Syriacus* or Syrian hare, which is like the English hare; and (2) the *Lepus Sinaiticus*, or hare of the desert. No rabbits are found in Syria.

Ha'reth—*thicket*—a wood in the mountains of Judah where David hid when pursued by Saul (1 Sam. 22:5). It was possibly while he was here that the memorable incident narrated in 2 Sam. 23:14-17, 1 Chr. 11:16-19 occurred. This place has not been identified, but perhaps it may be the modern *Kharâs*, on the borders of the chain of mountains some 3 miles east of Keilah.

Harhai'ah—*zeal of Jehovah*—(Neh. 3:8) "of the goldsmiths," one whose son helped to repair the wall of Jerusalem.

Har'hur—*fever*—one of the Nethinim (Ezra 2:51).

Ha'rim—*flat-nosed*. (1.) The head of the second course of priests (1 Chr. 24:8). (2.) Ezra 2:32, 39; Neh. 7:35, 42. (3.) Neh. 3:11. (4.) 12:3. (5.) 10:5.

Har'iph—*autumnal rain*. (1.) Neh. 7:24. (2.) 10:19.

Har'lot. (1.) Heb. *zonâh* (Gen. 34:31; 38:15). In verses 21, 22 the Hebrew word used is *kedêshah*—*i.e.*, a woman consecrated or devoted to prostitution in connection with the abominable worship of Asherah or Astarte, the Syrian Venus. This word is also used in Deut. 23:17; Hos. 4:14. Thus Tamar sat by the wayside as a consecrated *kedêshah*.

It has been attempted to show that Rahab, usually called a "harlot" (Josh. 2:1; 6:17; Heb. 11:31; James 2:25), was only an innkeeper. This interpretation, however, cannot be maintained.

Jephthah's mother is called a "strange woman" (Judg. 11:2). This, however, merely denotes that she was of foreign extraction.

In the time of Solomon harlots appeared openly in the streets, and he solemnly warns against association with them (Prov. 7:12; 9:14. See also Jer. 3:2; Ezek. 16:24, 25, 31). The Revised Version, following the LXX., has "and the harlots washed," etc., instead of the rendering of the Authorized Version, "and they washed," of 1 Kings 22:38.

To commit fornication is metaphorically used for to practise idolatry (Jer. 3:1; Ezek. 16:15; Hos. throughout); hence Jerusalem is spoken of as a harlot (Isa. 1:22).

(2.) Heb. *nokrîyah*, the "strange woman" (1 Kings 11:1; Prov. 5:20; 7:5; 23:27). Those so designated were Canaanites and other Gentiles (Josh. 23:13). To the same class belonged the "foolish"—*i.e.*, the sinful—"woman."

In the New Testament the Greek *pornai*, plural, "harlots," occurs in Matt. 21:31, 32, where they are classed with publicans;

Luke 15:30; 1 Cor. 6:15, 16; Heb. 11:31; James 2:25. It is used symbolically in Rev. 17:1, 5, 15, 16; 19:2.

Har'nepher, a chief of the tribe of Asher (1 Chr. 7:36).

Har'ness. (1.) Heb. *'asâr*, "to bind;" hence the act of fastening animals to a cart (1 Sam. 6:7, 10; Jer. 46:4, etc.).

(2.) An Old English word for "armour;" Heb. *neshek* (2 Chr. 9:24).

(3.) Heb. *shiryan*, a coat of mail (1 Kings 22:34; 2 Chr. 18:33; rendered in the plural "breastplates" in Isa. 59:17).

(4.) The children of Israel passed out of Egypt "harnessed" (Ex. 13:18)—*i.e.*, in an orderly manner, and as if to meet a foe. The word so rendered is probably a derivative from Hebrew *hâmesh* (*i.e.*, "five"), and may denote that they went up in five divisions—*viz.*, the van, centre, two wings, and rear-guard.

Ha'rod—*palpitation*—a fountain near which Gideon and his army encamped on the morning of the day when they encountered and routed the Midianites (Judg. 7). It was south of the hill Moreh. The present *'Ain Jâlûd* ("Goliath's Fountain"), south of Jezreel and nearly opposite Shunem, is probably the fountain here referred to (7:4, 5).

Ha'rodite, an epithet applied to two of David's heroes (2 Sam. 23:25). (Comp. 1 Chr. 11:27.)

Haro'sheth of the Gentiles (Judg. 4:2) or **nations,** a city near Hazor in Galilee of the Gentiles, or Upper Galilee, in the north of Palestine. It was here that Jabin's great army was marshalled before it went forth into the great battlefield of Esdraelon to encounter the army of Israel, by which it was routed and put to flight (Judg. 4). It was situated "at the entrance of the pass to Esdraelon from the plain of Acre" at the base of Carmel. The name in the Hebrew is *Harosheth ha Gojim*—*i.e.*, "the smithy of the nations;" probably, as is supposed, so called because here Jabin's iron war-chariots, armed with scythes, were made. It is identified with *el-Hârithîyeh.*

Harp (Heb. *kinnôr*), the national instrument of the Hebrews. It was invented by Jubal (Gen. 4:21). Some think the word *kinnôr* denotes the whole class of stringed instruments. It was used as an accompaniment to songs of cheerfulness as well as of praise to God (Gen. 31:27; 1 Sam. 16:23; 2 Chr. 20:28; Ps. 33:2; 137:2).

In Solomon's time harps were made of almug-trees (1 Kings 10:11, 12). In 1 Chr. 15:21 mention is made of "harps on the Sheminith;" Revised Version, "harps set to the Sheminith;" better perhaps "harps of eight strings." The soothing effect of the music of the harp is referred to 1 Sam. 16:17, 24; 18:9; 19:9. The church in heaven is represented as celebrating the triumphs of the Redeemer "harping with their harps" (Rev. 14:2).

Har'row (Heb. *harîts*), a *tribulum* or sharp threshing sledge; a frame armed on the under side with rollers or sharp spikes (2 Sam. 12:31; 1 Chr. 20:3).

Heb. verb *sadad*, to harrow a field, break its clods (Job 39:10; Isa. 28:4; Hos. 10:11). Its form is unknown. It may have resembled the instrument still in use in Egypt.

Har'sha—*worker* or *enchanter*—one of the Nethinim (Ezra 2:52; Neh. 7:54).

Hart (Heb. *'ayal*), a stag or male deer. It is ranked among the clean animals (Deut. 12:15; 14:5; 15:22), and was commonly killed for food (1 Kings 4:23). The hart is frequently alluded to in the poetical and prophetical books (Isa. 35:6; Cant. 2:8, 9; Lam. 1:6; Ps. 42:1).

Ha'rum—*elevated*—(1 Chr. 4:8), a descendant of Judah.

Ha'ruphite, a native of Hariph; an epithet given to Shephatiah, one of those who joined David at Ziklag (1 Chr. 12:5).

Ha'ruz—*eager*—the father of Meshullemeth, the wife of king Manasseh (2 Kings 21:19) and mother of king Amon.

Har'vest, the season for gathering grain or fruit. On the 16th day of Abib (or April) a handful of ripe ears of corn was offered as a first-fruit before the Lord, and immediately after this the harvest commenced (Lev. 23:9-14; 2 Sam. 21:9, 10; Ruth 2:23). It began with the feast of Passover and ended with Pentecost, thus lasting for seven weeks (Ex. 23:16). The harvest was a season of joy (Ps. 126 : 1-6 ; Isa. 9 : 3). This word is used figuratively Matt. 9 : 37 ; 13 : 30 ; Luke 10 : 2 ; John 4 : 35. (See AGRICULTURE.)

Hasadi'ah—*favoured by Jehovah*—one of the sons of Pedaiah (1 Chr. 3 : 20), of the royal line of David.

Hasenu'ah—*bristling* or *hated*—a Benjamite (1 Chr. 9 : 7).

Hashabi'ah — *regarded by Jehovah.* (1.) Merarite Levite (1 Chr. 6 : 45 ; 9 : 14). (2.) A son of Jeduthun (25 : 3, 19). (3.) Son of Kemuel (26 : 30). (4.) One of the chief Levites (2 Chr. 35 : 9). (5.) A Levite (Neh. 11 : 22). (6.) One of the chief priests in the time of Ezra (Ezra 8 : 24). (7.) A chief of the Levites (Neh. 12 : 24). (8.) Ezra 8 : 19. (9.) Neh. 3 : 17.

Hashabni'ah. (1.) Neh. 3 : 10. (2.) One of the Levites whom Ezra appointed to interpret the law to the people (Neh. 9 : 5).

Hashbad'ana—*consideration in judging* —stood at Ezra's left hand when he read the law (Neh. 8 : 4).

Hashmo'nah — *fatness* — the thirtieth halting-place of the Israelites during their wanderings in the wilderness, not far from Mount Hor (Num. 33 : 29, 30).

Ha'shub—*intelligent.* (1.) A Levite of the family of Merari (Neh. 11 : 15 ; 1 Chr. 9 : 14). (2.) Neh. 3 : 21. (3.) 3 : 11.

Hashu'bah — *ibid.* — a descendant of David (1 Chr. 3 : 20).

Ha'shum — *opulent.* (1.) Ezra 2 : 19 ; Neh. 7 : 22. (2.) Stood on Ezra's left hand while he read the law (Neh. 8 : 4).

Has'rah—*poverty*—"keeper of the wardrobe," *i.e.*, of the sacerdotal vestments (2 Chr. 34 : 22) ; called Har'has 2 Kings 22 : 14. He was husband of the prophetess Huldah.

Hasu'pha—*uncovered*—one of the Nethinim (Ezra 2 : 43 ; Neh. 7 : 46).

Hat—Chald. *karb'elâ*—(Dan. 3 : 21), properly *mantle* or *pallium*. The Revised Version renders it "tunic."

Ha'tach—*verity*—one of the eunuchs or chamberlains in the palace of Ahasuerus (Esther 4 : 5, 6, 9, 10).

Ha'tred, among the works of the flesh (Gal. 5 : 20). Altogether different is the meaning of the word in Deut. 21 : 15 ; Matt.

6 : 24 ; 10 : 37 ; Luke 14 : 26 ; Rom. 9 : 13, where it denotes only a less degree of love.

Ha'thath—*terror*—son of Othniel (1 Chr. 4 : 13).

Hati'pha—*captured*—one of the Nethinim (Ezra 2 : 54).

Hat'ita—*exploration*—one of the temple porters or janitors (Ezra 2 : 42). He returned from Babylon with Zerubbabel.

Hat'tush—*assembled.* (1.) A priest who returned with Zerubbabel (Neh. 12 : 2). (2.) Ezra 8 : 2. (3.) Neh. 3 : 10. (4.) Neh. 10 : 4. (5.) 1 Chr. 3 : 22.

Hau'ran—*cave-land*—mentioned only in Ezek. 47 : 16, 18. It was one of the ancient divisions of Bashan (*q.v.*), and lay on the south-east of Gaulanitis or the Jaulân, and on the south of Lejah, extending from the Arnon to the Hieromax. It was the most fertile region in Syria, and to this day abounds in the ruins of towns, many of which have stone doors and massive walls. It retains its ancient name. It was known by the Greeks and Romans as "Auranitis."

Ha'ven, a harbour (Ps. 107 : 30 ; Acts 27 : 12). The most famous on the coast of Palestine was that of Tyre (Ezek. 27 : 3). That of Crete, called "Fair Havens," is mentioned Acts 27 : 8.

Havi'lah—*the sand region.* (1.) A land mentioned in Gen. 2 : 11 rich in gold and bdellium and onyx stone. The question as to the locality of this region has given rise to a great diversity of opinion. It may perhaps be identified with the sandy tract which skirts Babylonia along the whole of its western border, stretching from the lower Euphrates to the mountains of Edom.

(2.) A district in Arabia-Felix. It is uncertain whether the tribe gave its name to this region or derived its name from it, and whether it was originally a Cushite (Gen. 10 : 7) or a Joktanite tribe (10 : 29 ; comp. 25 : 18), or whether there were both a Cushite and a Joktanite Havilah. It is the opinion of Kalisch, however, that Havilah "in both instances designates the same country, extending at least from the Persian to the Arabian Gulf, and on account of its vast extent easily divided

into two distinct parts." This opinion may
be well vindicated.

(3.) One of the sons of Cush (Gen. 10:7).

(4.) A son of Joktan (Gen. 10:29; 1 Chr.
1:20).

Ha′voth-ja′ir—*hamlets of the enlightener*
—a district in the east of Jordan. (1.) Jair,
the son of Manasseh, took some villages of
Gilead and called them by this name (Num.
32:41).

(2.) Again, it is said that Jair "took all
the tract of Argob," and called it Bashan-
havoth-jair (Deut. 3:14). (See also Josh.
13:30; 1 Kings 4:13; 1 Chr. 2:22, 23.)

Hawk (Heb. *nêtz*, a word expressive of
strong and rapid flight, and hence appropriate to the hawk). It is an unclean bird
(Lev. 11:16; Deut. 14:15). It is common
in Syria and surrounding countries. The
Hebrew word includes various species of
Falconidæ, with special reference perhaps
to the kestrel (*Falco tinnunculus*), the hobby

KESTREL.

(*Hypotriorchis subbuteo*), and the lesser kestrel (*Tin. Cenchris*). The kestrel remains
all the year in Palestine, but some ten or
twelve other species are all migrants from
the south. Of those summer visitors to
Palestine special mention may be made of
the *Falco sacer* and the *Falco lanarius*.
(See NIGHT-HAWK.)

Hay, properly so called, was not in use
among the Hebrews; straw was used instead. They cut the grass green as it was
needed. The word rendered "hay" in

Prov. 27:25 means the first shoots of the
grass. In Isa. 15:6 the Revised Version
has correctly "grass," where the Authorized Version has "hay."

Ha′zael—*whom God beholds*—an officer
of Ben-hadad II., king of Syria, who ultimately came to the throne, according to
the word of the Lord to Elijah (1 Kings
19:15), after he had put the king to death
(2 Kings 8:15). His interview with Elisha
is mentioned in 2 Kings 8. The Assyrians
soon after his accession to the throne came
against him and defeated him with very
great loss; and three years afterwards again
invaded Syria, but on this occasion Hazael
submitted to them. He then turned his
arms against Israel, and ravaged "all the
land of Gilead," etc. (2 Kings 10:33), which
he held in a degree of subjection to him
(13:3–7, 22). He aimed at the subjugation
also of the kingdom of Judah, when Joash
obtained peace by giving him "all the gold
that was found in the treasures of the
house of the Lord, and in the king's house"
(2 Kings 12:18; 2 Chr. 24:24). He reigned
about forty-six years (B.C. 886–840), and
was succeeded on the throne by his son
Ben-hadad (2 Kings 13:22–25), who on
several occasions was defeated by Jehoash,
the king of Israel, and compelled to restore
all the land of Israel his father had taken.

Ha′zar-ad′dar—*village of Addar*—a
place in the southern boundary of Palestine
(Num. 34:4), in the desert to the west of
Kadesh-barnea. It is called Adar in Josh.
15:3.

Ha′zar-e′nan—*village of fountains*—a
place on the north-east frontier of Palestine (Num. 34:9, 10). Some have identified
it with *Ayûn ed-Dara* in the heart of the
central chain of Anti-Libanus. More probably, however, it has been identified with
Kuryetein, about 60 miles east-north-east
of Damascus. (Comp. Ezek. 47:17; 48:1.)

Ha′zar-gad′dah—*village of fortune*—a
city on the south border of Judah (Josh.
15:27), midway between the Mediterranean
and the Dead Sea.

Ha′zar-hat′ticon—*village of the midway*
—a place near Hamath in the confines of
Hauran (Ezek. 47:16), probably on the
north brow of Hermon,

Ha'zar-ma'veth—*court of death*—the third son of Joktan, and a region in Arabia-Felix settled by him (Gen. 10:26; 1 Chr. 1:20). It is probably the modern province of *Hadramaut*, situated on the Indian Ocean east of the modern Yemen.

Ha'zar-shu'al—*village or enclosure of the jackal*—a city on the south border of Judah (Josh. 15:28; Neh. 11:26). It has been identified with the ruins of *Saweh*, half-way between Beersheba and Moladah.

Ha'zar-su'sah—*village of the horse*—the same as Sansannah, one of Solomon's "chariot cities" (Josh. 15:31; 2 Chr. 1:14), a depôt in the south border of Judah.

Ha'zel—Heb. *lûz*—(Gen. 30:37), a nut-bearing tree. The Hebrew word is rendered in the Vulgate by *amygdalinus*, "the almond-tree," which is probably correct. That tree flourishes in Syria.

Haze'rim—*villages*—probably the name of the temporary villages in which the nomad Avites resided (Deut. 2:23).

Haze'roth, fenced enclosures consisting of "a low wall of stones in which thick bundles of thorny acacia are inserted, the tangled branches and long needle-like spikes forming a perfectly impenetrable hedge around the encampment" of tents and cattle which they sheltered. Such like enclosures abound in the wilderness of Paran, which the Israelites entered after leaving Sinai (Num. 11:35; 12:16; 33:17, 18). This third encampment of the Israelites has been identified with the modern *'Ain el-Hudhera*, some 40 miles north-east of Sinai. Here Miriam (*q.v.*), being displeased that Moses had married a Cushite wife (Num. 12:1), induced Aaron to join with her in rebelling against Moses. God vindicated the authority of his "servant Moses," and Miriam was smitten with leprosy. Moses interceded for her, and she was healed (Num. 12:4-16). From this encampment the Israelites marched northward across the plateau of et-Tih, and at length reached KADESH.

Ha'zezon-ta'mar—*pruning of the palm*—the original name of the place afterwards called ENGEDI (*q.v.*)—Gen. 14:7; called also HAZAZON-TAMAR (2 Chr. 20:2).

Ha'zo—*vision*—one of the sons of Nahor (Gen. 22:22).

Ha'zor—*enclosed; fortified.* (1.) A stronghold of the Canaanites in the mountains north of Lake Merom (Josh. 11:1-5). Jabin the king with his allied tribes here encountered Joshua in a great battle. Joshua gained a signal victory, which virtually completed his conquest of Canaan (11:10-13). This city was, however, afterwards rebuilt by the Canaanites, and was ruled by a king with the same hereditary name of Jabin. His army, under a noted leader of the name of Sisera, swept down upon the south, aiming at the complete subjugation of the country. This powerful army was met by the Israelites under Barak, who went forth by the advice of the prophetess Deborah. The result was one of the most remarkable victories for Israel recorded in the Old Testament (Josh. 19:36; Judg. 4:2; 1 Sam. 12:9). The city of Hazor was taken and occupied by the Israelites. It was fortified by Solomon to defend the entrance into the kingdom from Syria and Assyria. When Tiglath-pileser, the Assyrian king, invaded the land, this was one of the first cities he captured, carrying its inhabitants captive into Assyria (2 Kings 15:29). It has been identified with *Khŭrbet Harrah*, $2\frac{1}{2}$ miles south-east of Kedesh.

(2.) A city in the south of Judah (Josh. 15:23). The name here should probably be connected with the word following, Ithnan—HAZOR-ITHNAN instead of "Hazor and Ithnan."

(3.) A district in Arabia (Jer. 49:28-33), supposed by some to be Jetor—*i.e.*, Ituræa.

(4.) "Kerioth *and* Hezron" (Josh. 15:25) should be "Kerioth-hezron" (as in the R.V.), the two names being joined together as the name of one place (*e.g.*, like Kirjath-jearim)—"the same is Hazor" (R.V.). This place has been identified with *el-Kuryetein*, and has been supposed to be the home of Judas Iscariot. (See KERIOTH.)

Ha'zor-hadat'tah—*New Hazor*—a city in the south of Judah (Josh. 15:25). It is probably identified with the ruins of *el-Hazzârah*, near Beit Jebrin.

Head'-bands (Heb. *kishshŭrim*), properly girdles or belts for the waist (Isa. 3:20, R.V., "sashes;" Jer. 2:32, rendered "attire"—*i.e.*, a girdle round the waist).

Head'-dress. Not in common use among the Hebrews. It is first mentioned in Ex. 28:40 (A.V., "bonnets;" R.V., "head-tires"). It was used especially for purposes of ornament (Job 29:14; Isa. 3:23; 62:3). The Hebrew word here used, *tsaniph*, properly means a turban—folds of linen wound round the head. The Hebrew word *velr*,

used in Isa. 61:3, there rendered "beauty" (A.V.) and "garland" (R.V.), is a head-dress or turban worn by females (Isa. 3:20, "bonnets"), priests (Ex. 39:28), a bridegroom (Isa. 61:10, "ornament;" R.V., "garland"). Ezek. 16:10 and Jonah 2:5 are to be understood of the turban wrapped round the head. The Hebrew *shebîṣim* (Isa. 3:18), in the Authorized Version rendered "cauls," and marg. "networks," denotes probably a kind of netted head-dress. The "horn" (Heb. *kĕrĕn*) mentioned in 1 Sam.

HORNED HEAD-DRESS OF DRUSE LADIES.

2:1 is the head-dress called by the Druses of Mount Lebanon the *tantûra.*

Heap. When Joshua took the city of Ai (Josh. 8), he burned it and "made it an heap [Heb. *tel*] for ever" (8:28). The ruins of this city were for a long time sought for in vain. It has been at length, however, identified with the mound which simply bears the name of "*Tel.*" "There are many *Tels* in modern Palestine, that land of *Tels*, each *Tel* with some other name attached to it to mark the former site. But

the site of Ai has no other name 'unto this day.' It is simply *et-Tel*—'the heap' *par excellence.*"

Heart. According to the Bible, the heart is the centre not only of spiritual activity, but of all the operations of human life. "Heart" and "soul" are often used interchangeably (Deut. 6:5; 26:16; comp. Matt. 22:37; Mark 12:30, 33), but this is not generally the case.

The heart is the "home of the personal life," and hence a man is designated, according to his heart, wise (1 Kings 5:12, etc.), pure (Ps. 41:12; Matt. 5:8, etc.), upright and righteous (Gen. 20:5, 6; Ps. 11:2; 78:72), pious and good (Luke 8:15), etc. In these and such passages the word "soul" could not be substituted for "heart."

The heart is also the seat of the conscience (Rom. 2:15). It is naturally wicked (Gen. 8:21), and hence it contaminates the whole life and character (Matt. 12:34; 15:18; comp. Eccl. 8:11; Ps. 73:7). Hence the heart must be changed, regenerated (Ezek. 36:26; 11:19; Ps. 51:12-14), before a man can willingly obey God.

The process of salvation begins in the heart by the believing reception of the testimony of God, while the rejection of that testimony hardens the heart (Ps. 96:8; Prov. 28:14; 2 Chr. 36:13). "Hardness of heart evidences itself by light views of sin; partial acknowledgment and confession of it; pride and conceit; ingratitude; unconcern about the word and ordinances of God; inattention to divine providences; stifling convictions of conscience; shunning reproof; presumption, and general ignorance of divine things."

Hearth—Heb. *aḥ* (Jer. 36:22, 23; R.V., "brazier"), meaning a large pot like a brazier, a portable furnace in which fire was kept in the king's winter apartment.

Heb. *kiyôr* (Zech. 12:6; R.V., "pan"), a fire-pan.

Heb. *moqêd* (Ps. 102:3; R.V., "firebrand"), properly a fagot.

Heb. *yaqûd* (Isa. 30:14), a burning mass on a hearth.

He-ass—Heb. *ḥamôr*—(Gen. 12:16), the general designation of the donkey used for carrying burdens (Ex. 42:26) and for ploughing (Isa. 30:24). Is described in Gen. 49:14; 2 Sam. 19:27. (See Ass.)

Heath—Heb. *'arâr*—(Jer. 17:6; 48:6), a species of juniper called by the Arabs by the same name (*'arar*)—the *Juniperus sabina* or savin. "Its gloomy, stunted appearance, with its scale-like leaves pressed close to its gnarled stem, and cropped close by the wild goats, as it clings to the rocks about Petra, gives great force to the contrast suggested by the prophet, between him that trusteth in man, naked and destitute, and the man

that trusteth in the Lord, flourishing as a tree planted by the waters" (Tristram, *Natural History of the Bible*).

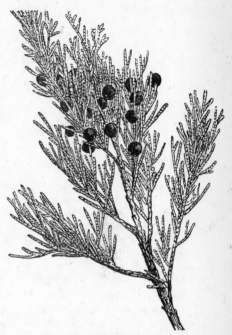

JUNIPERUS SABINA OR SAVIN.

Hea'then (Heb. plural *gôyim*). At first the word *gôyim* denoted generally all the nations of the world (Gen. 18:18; comp. Gal. 3:6). The Jews afterwards became a people distinguished in a marked manner from the other *gôyim*. They were a separate people (Lev. 20:23; 26:14-38; Deut. 28), and the other nations—the Amorites, Hittites, etc.—were the *gôyim*, the heathen, with whom the Jews were forbidden to be associated in any way (Josh. 23:7; 1 Kings 11:2). The practice of idolatry was the characteristic of these nations, and hence the word came to designate idolaters (Ps. 106:47; Jer. 46:28; Lam. 1:3; Isa. 36:18), the wicked (Ps. 9:5, 15, 17).

The corresponding Greek word in the New Testament, *ethnê*, has similar shades of meaning. In Acts 22:26, Gal. 3:14, it denotes the people of the earth generally; and in Matt. 6:7, an idolater.

In modern usage the word denotes all nations that are strangers to revealed religion.

Heav'en. (1.) *Definitions.*—The phrase "heaven and earth" is used to indicate the whole universe (Gen. 1:1; Jer. 23:24; Acts 17:24). According to the Jewish notion there were three heavens,—

(*a*) The firmament, as "fowls of the heaven" (Gen. 2:19; 7:3, 23; Ps. 8:8, etc.), "the eagles of heaven" (Lam. 4:19), etc.

(*b*) The starry heavens (Deut. 17:3; Jer. 8:2; Matt. 24:29).

(*c*) "The heaven of heavens," or "the third heaven" (Deut. 10:14; 1 Kings 8:27; Ps. 115:16; 148:4; 2 Cor. 12:2).

(2.) *Meaning of words in the original,*—

(*a*) The usual Hebrew word for "heavens" is *shâmayîm*, a plural form meaning "heights," "elevations" (Gen. 1:1; 2:1).

(*b*) The Hebrew word *marôm* is also used (Ps. 68:18; 93:4; 102:19, etc.) as equivalent to *shâmayîm*, "high places," "heights."

(*c*) Heb. *galyal*, literally a "wheel," is rendered "heaven" in Ps. 77:18 (R.V., "whirlwind").

(*d*) Heb. *shahak*, rendered "sky" (Deut. 33:26; Job 37:18; Ps. 18:11), plural "clouds" (Job 35:5; 36:28; Ps. 68:34, marg. "heavens"), means probably the firmament.

(*e*) Heb. *rakîa* is closely connected with (*d*), and is rendered "*firmamentum*" in the Vulgate, whence our "firmament" (Gen. 1:6; Deut. 33:26, etc.), regarded as a solid expanse.

(3.) *Metaphorical* meaning of term. Isa. 14:13, 14; "doors of heaven" (Ps. 78:23); heaven "shut" (1 Kings 8:35); "opened" (Ezek. 1:1). (See 1 Chr. 21:16.)

(4.) *Spiritual* meaning. The place of the everlasting blessedness of the righteous; the abode of departed spirits.

(*a*) Christ calls it his "Father's house" (John 14:2).

(*b*) It is called "paradise" (Luke 23:43; 2 Cor. 12:4; Rev. 2:7; 22:2).

(*c*) "The heavenly Jerusalem" (Gal. 4:26; Heb. 12:22; Rev. 3:12).

(*d*) The "kingdom of heaven" (Matt. 25:1; James 2:5).

(*e*) The "eternal kingdom" (2 Pet. 1:11).

(*f*) The "eternal inheritance" (1 Pet. 1:4; Heb. 9:15).

(*g*) The "better country" (Heb. 11:14, 16).

(*h*) The blessed are said to "sit down with Abraham, Isaac, and Jacob," and to be "in Abraham's bosom" (Luke 16:22; Matt. 8:11); to "reign with Christ" (2 Tim. 2:11); and to enjoy "rest" (Heb. 4:10, 11).

In heaven the blessedness of the righteous consists in the possession of "life everlasting," "an eternal weight of glory" (2 Cor. 4:17), an exemption from all sufferings for ever, a deliverance from all evils (2 Cor. 5:1, 2) and from the society of the wicked (2 Tim. 4:18), bliss without termination, the "fulness of joy" for ever (Luke 20:36; 2 Cor. 4:16, 18; 1 Pet. 1:4; 5:10; 1 John 3:2). The believer's heaven is not only a state of everlasting blessedness, but also a "place"—a place "prepared" for them (John 14:2).

Heave of'fering—Heb. *terûmah*—(Ex. 29:27) means simply an offering, a present, including all the offerings made by the Israelites as a present. This Hebrew word is frequently employed. Some of the rabbis attach to the word the meaning of elevation, and refer it to the *heave* offering, which consisted in presenting the offering by a motion up and down, distinguished from the *wave* offering, which consisted in a repeated movement in a horizontal direction—a "*wave offering* to the Lord as ruler of earth, a *heave offering* to the Lord as ruler of heaven." The right shoulder, which fell to the priests in presenting thank offerings, was called the *heave* shoulder (Lev. 7:34; Num. 6:20). The first fruits offered in harvest-time (Num. 15:20, 21) were heave offerings.

He'ber—*passing over*. (1.) Son of Beriah and grandson of Asher (Gen. 46:17; 1 Chr. 7:31, 32).

(2.) The Kenite (Judg. 4:11, 17; 5:24), a descendant of Hobab. His wife Jael received Sisera (*q.v.*) into her tent and then killed him.

(3.) 1 Chr. 4:18.

(4.) A Benjamite (1 Chr. 8:17).

(5.) A Gadite (5:13). (See EBER.)

He'brew, a name applied to the Israelites in Scripture only by one who is a foreigner

(Gen. 39:14, 17; 41:12, etc.), or by the Israelites when they speak of themselves to foreigners (40:15; Ex. 1:19), or when spoken of as contrasted with other peoples (Gen. 43:32; Ex. 1:3, 7, 15; Deut. 15:12). In the New Testament there is the same contrast between Hebrews and foreigners (Acts 6:1; Phil. 3:5).

Derivation. (1.) The name is derived, according to some, from Eber (Gen. 10:24), the ancestor of Abraham. The Hebrews are "sons of Eber" (10:21).

(2.) Others trace the name to a Hebrew root-word signifying "to pass over," and hence regard it as meaning "the man who passed over," *viz.*, the Euphrates; or to the Hebrew word meaning "the region" or "country beyond," *viz.*, the land of Chaldea. This latter view is preferred. It is the more probable origin of the designation given to Abraham coming among the Canaanites as a man from beyond the Euphrates (Gen. 14:13).

(3.) A third derivation of the word has been suggested—*viz.*, that it is from the Hebrew word *'abhar*, "to pass over," whence *'ebher*, in the sense of a "sojourner" or "passer through" as distinct from a "settler" in the land, and thus applies to the condition of Abraham (Heb. 11:13).

He'brew of the Hebrews, one whose parents are both Hebrews (Phil. 3:5; 2 Cor. 11:22); a genuine Hebrew.

He'brews (Acts 6:1) were the Hebrew-speaking Jews, as distinguished from those who spoke Greek. (See GREEKS.)

He'brew language, the language of the Hebrew nation, and that in which the Old Testament is written, with the exception of a few portions in Chaldee. In the Old Testament it is only spoken of as "Jewish" (2 Kings 18:26, 28; Isa. 36:11, 13; 2 Chr. 32:18). This name is first used by the Jews in times subsequent to the close of the Old Testament.

It is one of the class of languages called Semitic, because they were chiefly spoken among the descendants of Shem.

When Abraham entered Canaan it is obvious that he found the language of its inhabitants closely allied to his own. Isaiah (19:18) calls it "the language of Canaan." Whether this language, as seen in the earliest books of the Old Testament, was the very dialect which Abraham brought with him into Canaan, or whether it was the common tongue of the Canaanitish nations which he only *adopted*, is uncertain; probably the latter opinion is the correct one. For the thousand years between Moses and the Babylonian exile the Hebrew language underwent little or no modification. It preserves all through a remarkable uniformity of structure. From the first it appears in its full maturity of development. But through intercourse with Damascus, Assyria, and Babylon, from the time of David, and more particularly from the period of the Exile, it comes under the influence of the Aramaic idiom, and this is seen in the writings which date from this period. It was never spoken *in its purity* by the Jews after their return from Babylon. They now spoke Hebrew *with a large admixture of Aramaic or Chaldee,* which latterly became the predominant element in the national language.

The Hebrew of the Old Testament has only about six thousand words, all derived from about five hundred roots. Hence the same word has sometimes a great variety of meanings. So long as it was a living language, and for ages after, only the consonants of the words were written. This also has been a source of difficulty in interpreting certain words, for the meaning varies according to the vowels which may be supplied. The Hebrew is one of the oldest languages of which we have any knowledge. It is essentially identical with the Phœnician language. (See MOABITE STONE.) The Semitic languages, to which class the Hebrew and Phœnician belonged, were spoken over a very wide area: in Babylonia, Mesopotamia, Syria, Palestine, and Arabia—in all the countries from the Mediterranean to the borders of Assyria, and from the mountains of Armenia to the Indian Ocean. The rounded form of the letters, as seen in the Moabite stone, was probably that in which the ancient Hebrew was written down to the time of the Exile, when the present square or Chaldean form was adopted.

He'brews, Epistle to. (1.) *Its canon-*

icity. All the results of critical and historical research to which this epistle has been specially subjected abundantly vindicate its right to a place in the New Testament canon among the other inspired books.

(2.) *Its authorship.* A considerable variety of opinions on this subject has at different times been advanced. Some have maintained that its author was Silas, Paul's companion. Others have attributed it to Clement of Rome, or Luke, or Barnabas, or some unknown Alexandrian Christian, or Apollos; but the conclusion which we think is best supported, both from internal and external evidence, is that Paul was its author. There are, no doubt, many difficulties in the way of accepting it as Paul's; but we may at least argue with Calvin that there can be no difficulty in the way of "embracing it without controversy as one of the apostolical epistles."

(3.) *Date and place of writing.* It was in all probability written at Rome, near the close of Paul's two years' imprisonment (Heb. 13:19, 21). It was certainly written before the destruction of Jerusalem (13:10).

(4.) *To whom addressed.* Plainly it was intended for Jewish converts to the faith of the gospel—probably for the church at Jerusalem. The subscription of this epistle is, of course, without authority. In this case it is incorrect, for obviously Timothy could not be the bearer of it (13:23).

(5.) Its *design* was to show the true end and meaning of the Mosaic system, and its symbolical and transient character. It proves that the Levitical priesthood was a "shadow" of that of Christ, and that the legal sacrifices prefigured the great and all-perfect sacrifice he offered for us. It explains that the gospel was designed, not to modify the law of Moses, but to supersede and abolish it. Its teaching was fitted, as it was designed, to check that tendency to apostatize from Christianity and to return to Judaism which now showed itself among certain Jewish Christians. The supreme authority and the transcendent glory of the gospel are clearly set forth, and in such a way as to strengthen and confirm their allegiance to Christ.

(6.) It consists of two parts: (*a*) doctrinal (1–10:18), (*b*) and practical (10:19-ch. 13). There are found in it many references to portions of the Old Testament. It may be regarded as a treatise supplementary to the Epistles to the Romans and Galatians, and as an inspired commentary on the book of Leviticus.

He′bron—*a community; alliance.* (1.) A city in the south end of the valley of Eshcol, about midway between Jerusalem and Beersheba, from which it is distant about 20 miles in a straight line. It was built "seven years before Zoan in Egypt" (Gen. 13:18; Num. 13:22). It still exists under the same name, and is one of the most ancient cities in the world. Its earlier name was Kirjath-arba (Gen. 23:2; Josh. 14:15; 15:3). But "Hebron would appear to have been the original name of the city, and it was not till after Abraham's stay there that it received the name Kirjath-arba, who [*i.e.,* Arba] was not the founder but the conqueror of the city, having led thither the tribe of the Anakim, to which he belonged. It retained this name till it came into the possession of Caleb, when the Israelites restored the original name *Hebron*" (Keil, *Com.*). The name of this city does not occur in any of the prophets or in the New Testament. It is found about forty times in the Old. It was the favourite home of Abraham. Here he pitched his tent under the oaks of Mamre, by which name it came afterwards to be known; and here Sarah died, and was buried in the cave of Machpelah (Gen. 23:17–20), which he bought from Ephron the Hittite. From this place the patriarch departed for Egypt by way of Beersheba (37:14; 46:1). It was taken by Joshua and given to Caleb (Josh. 10:36, 37; 12:10; 14:13). It became a Levitical city and a city of refuge (20:7; 21:11). When David became king of Judah this was his royal residence, and he resided here for seven and a half years (2 Sam. 5:5); and here he was anointed as king over all Israel (1 Sam. 2:1–4, 11; 1 Kings 2:11). It became the residence also of the rebellious Absalom (2 Sam. 15:10), who probably expected to find his chief support in the tribe of Judah, now called *el-Khülîl.*

In one part of the modern city is a great mosque, which is built over the grave of Machpelah. The first European who was permitted to enter this mosque was the Prince of Wales in 1862. It was also visited by the Marquis of Bute in 1866, and by the late Emperor Frederick of Germany (then Crown-Prince of Prussia) in 1869.

One of the largest oaks in Palestine is found in the valley of Eshcol, about 3 miles north of the town. It is supposed by some to be the tree under which Abraham pitched his tent, and is called "Abraham's oak." (See OAK.)

(2.) The third son of Kohath the Levite (Ex. 6:18; 1 Chr. 6:2, 18).

HEBRON.

described in Num. 19:1-10; comp. Heb. 9:13.

Heir. Under the patriarchs the property of a father was divided among the sons of his legitimate wives (Gen. 21:10; 24:36; 25:5), the eldest son getting a larger portion than the rest. The Mosaic law made specific regulations regarding the transmission of real property, which are given in detail in Deut. 21:17; Num. 27:8; 36:6; 27:9-11. Succession to property was a matter of right and not of favour.

Christ is the "heir of all things" (Heb. 1:2; Col. 1:15). Believers are heirs of the "promise," "of righteousness," "of the kingdom," "of the world," "of God," "joint heirs" with Christ (Gal 3:29; Heb.

usually identifie
called *Haleb* b
more probably
villages in the
brated for its
Anti-Lebanon,
(Abana).

Hel'dai—*wo*
called also He
David's captai
(2.) Zech. 6:
Babylon.

Hel'eb—*fat*
(2 Sam. 23:29)

Hel'ed — *th*
called Heleb (2

Hel'ek—*a*
scended from

Hel'em—*a*
Asher (1 Chr.

Hel'eph—*ex*
border of Nap
19:33).

Hel'ez—*str*
Judah's poster
of David's war

He'li—*eleva*
line of our Lo

Hel'kai—*s*
chief priests i
12:15).

Hel'kath—
on the east b
called also Hu

Hel'kath-h
blades, or *the*
After the batt
and his house
took up his re
there anointe
the fugitives
the only sur
Abner, Saul'
dan to Maha
claimed king
forces at his
Gibeon, with
from David.
David's arm
camped on t
was on the e
town of Gib

with the modern Aleppo,
the native Arabs, but is
o be found in one of the
âdy Helbôn, which is cele-
apes, on the east slope of
orth of the river Barada

dly. (1.) 1 Chr. 27:15;
b (2 Sam. 23:29); one of

0, one who returned from

ss—one of David's warriors

world — (1 Chr. 11:30);
3am. 23:29).

rtion—(Josh. 17:2), de-
anasseh.

roke—great - grandson of
35).

hange—a city on the north
ali (Num. 18:21, 31; Josh.

g, or *loin* (?) (1.) One of
y (1 Chr. 2:39). (2.) One
ors (2 Sam. 23:26).

on—father of Joseph in the
's ancestry (Luke 3:23).

ooth - tongued—one of the
the time of Joiakim (Neh.

ioothness—a town of Asher,
der (Josh. 19:25; 21:31);
ok (1 Chr. 6:75).

z'zurim—*plot of the sharp
d of heroes*—(2 Sam. 2:16).
of Gilboa, so fatal to Saul
David, as divinely directed,
dence in Hebron, and was
king over Judah. Among
m Gilboa was Ish-bosheth,
ving son of Saul, whom
ncle, took across the Jor-
m, and there had him pro-
Abner gathered all the
ommand and marched to
e object of wresting Judah
Toab had the command of
of trained men, who en-
south of the pool, which
of the hill on which the
was built, while Abner's

army lay on the north of the pool. Abner
proposed that the conflict should be decided by twelve young men engaging
in personal combat on either side. So
fiercely did they encounter each other that
"they caught every man his fellow by the
head, and thrust his sword in his fellow's
side; so they fell down together: wherefore that place was called Helkath-hazzurim." The combat of the champions
was thus indecisive, and there followed a
severe general engagement between the
two armies, ending in the total rout of
the Israelites under Abner. The general
result of this battle was that "David
waxed stronger and stronger, and the
house of Saul waxed weaker and weaker"
(2 Sam. 3:1). (See GIBEON.)

Hell, derived from the Saxon *helan,* to
cover; hence the *covered* or the invisible
place. In Scripture there are three words
so rendered:—

(1.) *Sheôl,* occurring in the Old Testament sixty-five times. This word *sheôl* is
derived from a root-word meaning "to
ask," "demand;" hence insatiableness
(Prov. 30:15, 16). It is rendered "grave"
thirty-one times (Gen. 37:35; 42:38; 44:
29, 31; 1 Sam. 2:6, etc.). The Revisers
have retained this rendering in the historical books with the original word in
the margin, while in the poetical books
they have reversed this rule.

In thirty-one cases in the Authorized
Version this word is rendered "hell," the
place of disembodied spirits. The inhabitants of *sheôl* are "the congregation of the
dead" (Prov. 21:16). It is (*a*) the abode
of the wicked (Num. 16:33; Job 24:19;
Ps. 9:17; 31:17, etc.); (*b*) of the good
(Ps. 16:10; 30:3; 49:15; 86:13, etc.).

Sheôl is described as deep (Job 11:8),
dark (10:21, 22), with bars (17:16). The
dead "go down" to it (Num. 16:30, 33;
Ezek. 31:15, 16, 17).

(2.) The Greek word *hades* of the New
Testament has the same scope of signification as *sheôl* of the Old Testament. It is
a prison (1 Pet. 3:19), with gates and bars
and locks (Matt. 16:18; Rev. 1:18), and
it is downward (Matt. 11:23; Luke 10:15).
The righteous and the wicked are sepa-

rated. The blessed dead are in that part of *hades* called paradise (Luke 23 : 43). They are also said to be in Abraham's bosom (Luke 16 : 22).

(3.) *Gehenna*, in most of its occurrences in the Greek New Testament, designates the place of the lost (Matt. 23 : 33). The fearful nature of their condition there is described in various figurative expressions (Matt. 8 : 12; 13 : 42; 22 : 13; 25 : 30; Luke 16 : 24, etc.). (See HINNOM.)

Hel′met (Heb. *kôb'a*), a cap for the defence of the head (1 Sam. 17 : 5, 38). In the New Testament the Greek equivalent is used (Eph. 6 : 17; 1 Thess. 5 : 8). (See ARMS.)

He′lon—*strong*—father of Eliab, who was "captain of the children of Zebulun" (Num. 1 : 9; 2 : 7).

Help-meet (Heb. *'ezer ke-negdô; i.e.*, "a help as his counterpart"=a help suitable to him), a wife (Gen. 2 : 18–20).

Helps (1 Cor. 12 : 28) may refer to help (*i.e.*, by interpretation) given to him who speaks with tongues, or more probably simply help which Christians can render to one another, such as caring for the poor and needy, etc.

Hem *of a garment*, the fringe of a garment. The Jews attached much importance to these, because of the regulations in Num. 15 : 38, 39. These borders or fringes were in process of time enlarged so as to attract special notice (Matt. 23 : 5). The hem of Christ's garment touched (9 : 20; 14 : 36; Luke 8 : 44).

He′man—*faithful.* (1.) 1 Kings 4 : 31; 1 Chr. 2 : 6, a son of Zerah, noted for his wisdom.

(2.) Grandson of Samuel (1 Chr. 6 : 33; 15 : 17), to whom the 88th Psalm probably was inscribed. He was one of the "seers" named in 2 Chr. 29 : 14, 30, and took a leading part in the administration of the sacred services.

He′math, a Kenite (1 Chr. 2 : 55), the father of the house of Rechab.

Hem′lock. (1.) Heb. *rôsh* (Hos. 10 : 4; rendered "gall" in Deut. 29 : 18; 32 : 32; Ps. 69 : 21; Jer. 9 : 15; 23 : 15; "poison," Job 20 : 16; "venom," Deut. 32 : 33). "*Rôsh* is the name of some poisonous plant which grows quickly and luxuriantly; of

a bitter taste, and therefore coupled with wormwood (Deut. 29 : 17; Lam. 3 : 19). Hence it would seem to be not the hemlock *cicuta*, nor the *colocynth* or wild gourd, nor *lôlium* darnel, but the poppy so called from its heads" (Gesenius, *Lex.*).

(2.) Heb. *la'anâh*, generally rendered "wormwood" (*q.v.*)—Deut. 29 : 18, Text 17; Prov. 5 : 4; Jer. 9 : 15; 23 : 15. Once it is rendered "hemlock" (Amos 6 : 12; R.V., "wormwood"). This Hebrew word is from a root meaning "to curse," hence the *accursed.*

Hen, common in later times among the Jews in Palestine (Matt. 23 : 37; Luke 13 : 34). It is noticeable that this familiar bird is only mentioned in these passages in connection with our Lord's lamentation over the impenitence of Jerusalem.

He′na, one of the cities of Mesopotamia destroyed by Sennacherib (2 Kings 18 : 34; 19 : 33). It is identified with the modern *Anah*, lying on the right bank of the Euphrates, not far from Sepharvaim.

Hen′adad—*favour of Hadad*—the name of a Levite after the Captivity (Ezra 3 : 9).

He′noch. See ENOCH.

He′pher—*a well* or *stream.* (1.) A royal city of the Canaanites taken by Joshua (12 : 17).

(2.) The youngest son of Gilead (Num. 26 : 32; 27 : 1).

(3.) The second son of Asher (1 Chr. 4 : 6).

(4.) One of David's heroes (1 Chr. 11 : 36).

Heph′zibah—*my delight is in her.* (1.) The wife of Hezekiah and mother of king Manasseh (2 Kings 21 : 1).

(2.) A symbolical name of Zion, as representing the Lord's favour toward her (Isa. 62 : 4).

Herb. (1.) Heb. *'eseb*, any green plant; herbage (Gen. 1 : 11, 12, 29, 30; 2 : 5; 3 : 18, etc.); comprehending vegetables and all green herbage (Amos 7 : 1, 2).

(2.) *Yarak*, green; any green thing; foliage of trees (2 Kings 19 : 26; 37 : 27, etc.); a plant; herb (Deut. 11 : 10).

(3.) *Or*, meaning "light." In Isa. 26 : 19 it means "green herbs;" in 2 Kings 4 : 39 probably the fruit of some plant.

(4.) *Merorim*, plural, "bitter herbs," eaten

by the Israelites at the Passover (Ex. 12:8; Num. 9:11). They were bitter plants of various sorts, and referred symbolically to the oppression in Egypt.

Herd, Gen. 13:2; Deut. 7:14. (See CATTLE.)

Herds'man. In Egypt herdsmen were probably of the lowest caste. Some of Joseph's brethren were made rulers over Pharaoh's cattle (Gen. 47:6, 17). The Israelites were known in Egypt as "keepers of cattle;" and when they left it they took their flocks and herds with them (Ex. 12:38). Both David and Saul came from "following the herd" to occupy the throne (1 Sam. 9; 11:5; Ps. 78:70). David's herd-masters were among his chief officers of state. The daughters also of wealthy chiefs were wont to tend the flocks of the family (Gen. 29:9; Ex. 2:16). The "chief of the herdsmen" was in the time of the monarchy an officer of high rank (1 Sam. 21:7; comp. 1 Chr. 27:29). The herdsmen lived in tents (Isa. 38:12; Jer. 6:3); and there were folds for the cattle (Num. 32:16), and watch-towers for the herdsman, that he might therefrom observe any coming danger (Micah 4:8; Nah. 3:8).

He'res—*sun.* (1.) "Mount Heres" (Judg. 1:35), Heb. *Har-heres*—*i.e.*, "sun-mountain;" probably identical with Ir-shemesh in Josh. 19:41.

(2.) Isa. 19:18, marg. (See ON.)

Her'esy, from a Greek word signifying (1) a choice, (2) the opinion chosen, and (3) the sect holding the opinion. In the Acts of the Apostles (5:17; 15:4; 24:5; 26:5, etc.) it denotes a sect, without reference to its character. Elsewhere, however, in the New Testament it has a different meaning attached to it. Paul ranks "heresies" with crimes and seditions (Gal. 5:20). This word also denotes divisions or schisms in the church (1 Cor. 11:9). In Titus 3:10 a "heretical person" is one who follows his own self-willed "questions," and who is to be avoided. Heresies thus came to signify self-chosen doctrines not emanating from God (2 Pet. 2:1).

Her'mas—*Mercury*—a Roman Christian to whom Paul sends greetings (Rom. 16:14). Some suppose him to have been the author of the celebrated religious romance called *The Shepherd,* but it is very probable that that work is the production of a later generation.

Her'mes—*Mercury*—a Roman Christian (Rom. 16:14).

Hermog'enes — *Mercury-born* — at one time Paul's fellow-labourer in Asia Minor, who, however, afterwards abandoned him, along with one Phygellus, probably on account of the perils by which they were beset (2 Tim. 1:15).

Her'mon—*a peak*—the eastern prolongation of the Anti-Lebanon range, reaching to the height of about 9,200 feet above the Mediterranean. It marks the north boundary of Palestine (Deut. 3:8; 4:48; Josh. 11:3, 17; 13:11; 12:1), and is seen from a great distance. It is about 40 miles north of the Sea of Galilee. It is called "the Hermonites" (Ps. 42:7) because it has more than one summit. The Sidonians called it Sirion, and the Amorites Shenir (Deut. 3:9; Cant. 4:8). It is also called Baal-hermon (Deut. 3:3; 1 Chr. 5:23) and Sion (Deut. 4:48). There is every probability that one of its three summits was the scene of the transfiguration (*q.v.*). The "dew of Hermon" is referred to (Ps. 89:12). Its modern name is *Jebel-esh-Sheikh,* "the chief mountain." It is one of the most conspicuous mountains in Palestine or Syria. "In whatever part of Palestine the Israelite turned his eye northward, Hermon was there, terminating the view. From the plain along the coast, from the Jordan valley, from the heights of Moab and Gilead, from the plateau of Bashan, the pale, blue, snow-capped cone forms the one feature in the northern horizon."

Our Lord and his disciples climbed this "high mountain apart" one day, and remained on its summit all night, "weary after their long and toilsome ascent." During the night "he was transfigured before them; and his face did shine as the sun." The next day they descended to Cæsarea Philippi.

Her'monites, the (Ps. 42:6, 7)="the Hermons"—*i.e.*, the three peaks or summits of Hermon, which are about a quarter of a mile apart.

JEBEL-ESH-SHEIKH (HERMON) FROM TEMPLE AT THELTHATHA.

Her'od the Great (Matt. 2:1–22; Luke 1:5; Acts 23:35), the son of Antipater, an Idumæan, and Cypros, an Arabian of noble descent. In the year B.C. 47 Julius Cæsar made Antipater, a "wily Idumæan," procurator of Judea, who divided his territories between his four sons, Galilee falling to the lot of Herod, who was afterwards appointed tetrarch of Judea by Mark Antony (B.C. 40), and also king of Judea by the Roman senate.

He was of a stern and cruel disposition. "He was brutish and a stranger to all humanity." Alarmed by the tidings of One "born King of the Jews," he sent forth and "slew all the children that were in Bethlehem, and in all the coasts thereof, from two years old and under" (Matt. 2:16). He was fond of splendour, and lavished great sums in rebuilding and adorning the cities of his empire. He rebuilt the city of Cæsarea (q.v.) on the coast, and also the city of Samaria (q.v.), which he called Sebaste, in honour of Augustus. He restored the ruined temple of Jerusalem; a work which was begun B.C. 20, but was not finished till after Herod's death, probably not till about A.D. 50 (John 2:20). After a troubled reign of thirty-seven years, he died at Jericho amid great agonies both of body and mind, B.C. 4—i.e., according to the common chronology, in the year in which Jesus was born.

After his death his kingdom was divided among his sons.

GENEALOGICAL TABLE OF THE HERODIAN FAMILY.

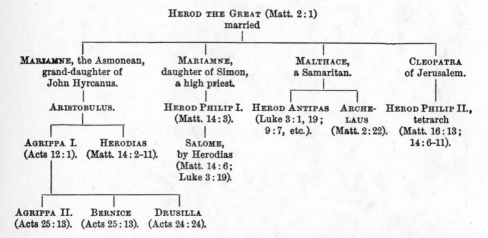

HEROD THE GREAT (Matt. 2:1)
married

MARIAMNE, the Asmonean, grand-daughter of John Hyrcanus.

MARIAMNE, daughter of Simon, a high priest.

MALTHACE, a Samaritan.

CLEOPATRA of Jerusalem.

ARISTOBULUS.

HEROD PHILIP I. (Matt. 14:3).

HEROD ANTIPAS (Luke 3:1, 19; 9:7, etc.).

ARCHELAUS (Matt. 2:22).

HEROD PHILIP II., tetrarch (Matt. 16:13; 14:6–11).

AGRIPPA I. (Acts 12:1).

HERODIAS (Matt. 14:2–11).

SALOME, by Herodias (Matt. 14:6; Luke 3:19).

AGRIPPA II. (Acts 25:13).

BERNICE (Acts 25:13).

DRUSILLA (Acts 24:24).

Her'od An'tipas, Herod's son by Malthace (Matt. 14:1; Luke 3:1, 19; 9:7; Acts 13:1). (See ANTIPAS.)

Her'od Archela'us (Matt. 2:22), the brother of Antipas (q.v.).

Her'od Philip I. (Mark 6:17), the son of Herod the Great by Mariamne, the daughter of Simon, the high priest. He is distinguished from another Philip called "the tetrarch." He lived at Rome as a private person with his wife Herodias and his daughter Salome.

Hero'dias (Matt. 14:1–11; Mark 6:14–16; Luke 3:19), the daughter of Aristobulus and Bernice. While residing at Rome with her husband Herod Philip I. and her daughter, Herod Antipas fell in with her during one of his journeys to Rome. She consented to leave her husband and become his wife. Some time after, Herod met John the Baptist, who boldly declared the marriage to be unlawful. For this he was "cast into prison," in the castle probably of Machærus (q.v.), and was there subsequently beheaded.

Her'od Philip II., the son of Herod the Great and Cleopatra of Jerusalem. He was "tetrarch" of Batanea, Iturea, usually identified with the modern Aleppo, called *Haleb* by the native Arabs, but is more probably to be found in one of the villages in the Wâdy Helbôn, which is celebrated for its grapes, on the east slope of Anti-Lebanon, north of the river Barada (Abana).

Hel'dai—*worldly.* (1.) 1 Chr. 27 : 15 ; called also Heleb (2 Sam. 23 : 29) ; one of David's captains.

(2.) Zech. 6 : 10, one who returned from Babylon.

He'leb—*fatness*—one of David's warriors (2 Sam. 23 : 29).

Hel'ed — *this world* — (1 Chr. 11 : 30) ; called Heleb (2 Sam. 23 : 29).

He'lek—*a portion*—(Josh. 17 : 2), descended from Manasseh.

He'lem—*a stroke*—great - grandson of Asher (1 Chr. 7 : 35).

He'leph—*exchange*—a city on the north border of Naphtali (Num. 18 : 21, 31 ; Josh. 19 : 33).

He'lez—*strong,* or *loin*(?) (1.) One of Judah's posterity (1 Chr. 2 : 39). (2.) One of David's warriors (2 Sam. 23 : 26).

He'li—*elevation*—father of Joseph in the line of our Lord's ancestry (Luke 3 : 23).

Hel'kai — *smooth - tongued* — one of the chief priests in the time of Joiakim (Neh. 12 : 15).

Hel'kath—*smoothness*—a town of Asher, on the east border (Josh. 19 : 25 ; 21 : 31) ; called also Hukok (1 Chr. 6 : 75).

Hel'kath-haz'zurim—*plot of the sharp blades,* or *the field of heroes*—(2 Sam. 2 : 16). After the battle of Gilboa, so fatal to Saul and his house, David, as divinely directed, took up his residence in Hebron, and was there anointed king over Judah. Among the fugitives from Gilboa was Ish-bosheth, the only surviving son of Saul, whom Abner, Saul's uncle, took across the Jordan to Mahanaim, and there had him proclaimed king. Abner gathered all the forces at his command and marched to Gibeon, with the object of wresting Judah from David. Joab had the command of David's army of trained men, who encamped on the south of the pool, which was on the east of the hill on which the town of Gibeon was built, while Abner's

army lay on the north of the pool. Abner proposed that the conflict should be decided by twelve young men engaging in personal combat on either side. So fiercely did they encounter each other that "they caught every man his fellow by the head, and thrust his sword in his fellow's side ; so they fell down together : wherefore that place was called Helkath-hazzurim." The combat of the champions was thus indecisive, and there followed a severe general engagement between the two armies, ending in the total rout of the Israelites under Abner. The general result of this battle was that "David waxed stronger and stronger, and the house of Saul waxed weaker and weaker" (2 Sam. 3 : 1). (See GIBEON.)

Hell, derived from the Saxon *helan,* to cover ; hence the *covered* or the invisible place. In Scripture there are three words so rendered :—

(1.) *Sheôl,* occurring in the Old Testament sixty-five times. This word *sheôl* is derived from a root-word meaning "to ask," "demand ;" hence insatiableness (Prov. 30 : 15, 16). It is rendered "grave" thirty-one times (Gen. 37 : 35 ; 42 : 38 ; 44 : 29, 31 ; 1 Sam. 2 : 6, etc.). The Revisers have retained this rendering in the historical books with the original word in the margin, while in the poetical books they have reversed this rule.

In thirty-one cases in the Authorized Version this word is rendered "hell," the place of disembodied spirits. The inhabitants of *sheôl* are "the congregation of the dead" (Prov. 21 : 16). It is (*a*) the abode of the wicked (Num. 16 : 33 ; Job 24 : 19 ; Ps. 9 : 17 ; 31 : 17, etc.) ; (*b*) of the good (Ps. 16 : 10 ; 30 : 3 ; 49 : 15 ; 86 : 13, etc.).

Sheôl is described as deep (Job 11 : 8), dark (10 : 21, 22), with bars (17 : 16). The dead "go down" to it (Num. 16 : 30, 33 ; Ezek. 31 : 15, 16, 17).

(2.) The Greek word *hades* of the New Testament has the same scope of signification as *sheôl* of the Old Testament. It is a prison (1 Pet. 3 : 19), with gates and bars and locks (Matt. 16 : 18 ; Rev. 1 : 18), and it is downward (Matt. 11 : 23 ; Luke 10 : 15).

The righteous and the wicked are sepa-

In one part of the modern city is a great mosque, which is built over the grave of Machpelah. The first European who was permitted to enter this mosque was the Prince of Wales in 1862. It was also visited by the Marquis of Bute in 1866, and by the late Emperor Frederick of Germany (then Crown-Prince of Prussia) in 1869.

One of the largest oaks in Palestine is found in the valley of Eshcol, about 3 miles north of the town. It is supposed by some to be the tree under which Abraham pitched his tent, and is called "Abraham's oak." (See OAK.)

(2.) The third son of Kohath the Levite (Ex. 6:18; 1 Chr. 6:2, 18).

(3.) 1 Chr. 2:42, 43.

(4.) A town in the north border of Asher (Josh. 19:28).

He′gai—*eunuch*—had charge of the harem of Ahasuerus (Esther 2:3).

Heif′er—Heb. *'eglâh*—(Deut. 21:4, 6; Jer. 46:20). Untrained to the yoke (Hos. 10:11); giving milk (Isa. 7:21); ploughing (Judg. 14:18); treading out grain (Jer. 50:11); unsubdued to the yoke an emblem of Judah (Isa. 15:5; Jer. 48:34).

Heb. *parâh* (Gen. 41:2; Num. 19:2). Bearing the yoke (Hos. 4:16); "heifers of Bashan" (Amos 4:1), metaphorical for the voluptuous females of Samaria. The ordinance of sacrifice of the "red heifer"

HEBRON.

described in Num. 19:1-10; comp. Heb. 9:13.

Heir. Under the patriarchs the property of a father was divided among the sons of his legitimate wives (Gen. 21:10; 24:36; 25:5), the eldest son getting a larger portion than the rest. The Mosaic law made specific regulations regarding the transmission of real property, which are given in detail in Deut. 21:17; Num. 27:8; 36:6; 27:9-11. Succession to property was a matter of right and not of favour.

Christ is the "heir of all things" (Heb. 1:2; Col. 1:15). Believers are heirs of the "promise," "of righteousness," "of the kingdom," "of the world," "of God," "joint heirs" with Christ (Gal 3:29; Heb.

6:17; 11:7; James 2:5; Rom. 4:13; 8:17).

He′lah—*rust*—(1 Chr. 4:5, 7), one of the wives of Ashur.

He′lam—*place of abundance*—a place on the east of Jordan and west of the Euphrates where David gained a great victory over the Syrian army (2 Sam. 10:16), which was under the command of Shobach. Some would identify it with *Alamata*, near Nicephorium.

Hel′bah—*fatness*—a town of the tribe of Asher (Judg. 1:31), in the plain of Phœnicia.

Hel′bon—*fat; i.e.*, "fertile"—(Ezek. 27:18 only), a place whence wine was brought to the great market of Tyre. It has been

Trachonitis, and Auranitis. He rebuilt the city of Cæsarea Philippi, calling it by his own name to distinguish it from the Cæsarea on the sea-coast which was the seat of the Roman government. He married Salome, the daughter of Herodias (Matt. 16 : 13 ; Mark 8 : 27 ; Luke 3 : 1).

Her'od Agrip'pa I., son of Aristobulus and Bernice, and grandson of Herod the Great. He was made tetrarch of the provinces formerly held by Lysanias II., and ultimately possessed the entire kingdom of his grandfather, Herod the Great, with the title of king. He put the apostle James the elder to death, and cast Peter into prison (Luke 3 : 1 ; Acts 12 : 1–19). On the second day of a festival held in honour of the emperor Claudius, he appeared in the great theatre of Cæsarea. "The king came in clothed in magnificent robes, of which silver was the costly brilliant material. It was early in the day, and the sun's rays fell on the king, so that the eyes of the beholders were dazzled with the brightness which surrounded him. Voices from the crowd here and there exclaimed that it was the apparition of something divine. And when he spoke and made an oration to them, they gave a shout, saying, 'It is the voice of a god, and not of a man.' But in the midst of this idolatrous ostentation an angel of God suddenly smote him. He was carried out of the theatre a dying man." He died (A.D. 44) of the same loathsome malady which slew his grandfather (Acts 12 : 21–23), in the fifty-fourth year of his age, having reigned four years as tetrarch and three as king over the whole of Palestine. After his death his kingdom came under the control of the prefect of Syria, and Palestine was now fully incorporated with the empire.

Her'od Agrip'pa II., the son of Herod Agrippa I. and Cypros. The emperor Claudius made him tetrarch of the provinces of Philip and Lysanias, with the title of king (Acts 25 : 13 ; 26 : 2, 7). He enlarged the city of Cæsarea Philippi, and called it Neronias, in honour of Nero. It was before him and his sister that Paul made his defence at Cæsarea (25 : 12–27).

He died at Rome A.D. 100, in the third year of the emperor Trajan.

Hero'dians, a Jewish political party who sympathized with (Mark 3 : 6 ; 12 : 13 ; Matt. 22 : 16 ; Luke 20 : 20) the Herodian rulers in their general policy of government, and in the social customs which they introduced from Rome. They were at one with the Sadducees in holding the duty of submission to Rome, and of supporting the Herods on the throne. (Comp. Mark 8 : 15 ; Matt. 16 : 6.)

Hero'dion, a Christian at Rome whom Paul salutes and calls his "kinsman" (Rom. 16 : 11).

Heron (Lev. 11 : 19 ; Deut. 14 : 18), ranked among the unclean birds. The Hebrew name is *'anâphah*, and indicates that the bird so named is remarkable for its *angry* disposition. "The herons are wading-birds, peculiarly irritable, remark-

HERON.

able for their voracity, frequenting marshes and oozy rivers, and spread over the regions of the East." The *Ardea russeta*, or little golden egret, is the commonest species in Asia.

Hesh'bon — *intelligence* — a city ruled over by Sihon, king of the Amorites (Josh. 3 : 10 ; 13 : 17). It was taken by Moses

(Num. 21:23–26), and became afterwards a Levitical city (Josh. 21:39) in the tribe of Reuben (Num. 32:37). After the Exile it was taken possession of by the Moabites (Isa. 15:4; Jer. 48:2, 34, 45). The ruins of this town are still seen about 20 miles east of Jordan from the north end of the Dead Sea. There are reservoirs in this district, which are probably the "fish-pools" referred to in Cant. 7:4.

Hesh'mon—*fatness*—a town in the south of Judah (Josh. 15:27).

Heth—*dread*—a descendant of Canaan, and the ancestor of the Hittites (Gen. 5:20; Deut. 7:1), who dwelt in the vicinity of Hebron (Gen. 23:3, 7). The Hittites were a Hamitic race. They are called "the sons of Heth" (23:3, 5, 7, 10, 16, 18, 20).

Heth'lon—*wrapped up*—a place on the north border of Palestine. The "way of Hethlon" (Ezek. 47:15; 48:1) is probably the pass at the end of Lebanon from the Mediterranean to the great plain of Hamath (*q.v.*), or the "entrance of Hamath."

Hezeki'ah—*whom Jehovah has strengthened.* (1.) Son of Ahaz (2 Kings 18:2; 2 Chr. 29:1), whom he succeeded on the throne of the kingdom of Judah. He reigned twenty-nine years (B.C. 726–697). The history of this king is contained in 2 Kings 18:20, Isa. 36–39, and 2 Chr. 29–32. He is spoken of as a great and good king. In public life he followed the example of his great-grandfather Uzziah. He set himself to abolish idolatry from his kingdom, and among other things which he did for this end, he destroyed the "brazen serpent," which had been removed to Jerusalem, and had become an object of idolatrous worship (Num. 21:9). A great reformation was wrought in the kingdom in his day (2 Kings 18:4; 2 Chr. 29:20–36). On the death of Sargon and the accession of his son Sennacherib to the throne of Assyria, Hezekiah refused to pay the tribute which his father had paid, and "rebelled against the king of Assyria, and served him not," but entered into a league with Egypt (Isa. 30; 31; 36:6–9). This led to the invasion of Judea by Sennacherib (2 Kings 18:13–16), who took forty

cities, and besieged Jerusalem with mounds. Hezekiah yielded to the demands of the Assyrian king, and agreed to pay him 800 talents of silver and 30 of gold (18:14). But Sennacherib dealt treacherously with Hezekiah (Isa. 33:1), and a second time within two years invaded his kingdom (2 Kings 18:17; 2 Chr. 32:9; Isa. 36). This invasion issued in the destruction of Sennacherib's army. Hezekiah prayed to God, and "that night the angel of the Lord went out, and smote in the camp of the Assyrians 185,000 men." Sennacherib fled with the shattered remnant of his forces to Nineveh, where, seventeen years after, he was assassinated by his sons Adrammelech and Sharezer (2 Kings 19:37). (See SENNACHERIB.)

The narrative of Hezekiah's sickness and miraculous recovery is found in 2 Kings 20:1, 2 Chr. 32:24, Isa. 38:1. Various ambassadors came to congratulate him on his recovery, and among them Merodach-baladan, the viceroy of Babylon (2 Chr. 32:23; 2 Kings 20:12). He closed his days in peace and prosperity, and was succeeded by his son Manasseh. He was buried in the "chiefest of the sepulchres of the sons of David" (2 Chr. 32:27–33). He had "after him none like him among all the kings of Judah, nor any that were before him" (2 Kings 18:5). (See ISAIAH.)

Hez'ion—*vision*—the father of Tabrimon, and grandfather of Ben-hadad, king of Syria (1 Kings 15:18).

He'zir—*swine* or *strong*. (1.) The head of the seventeenth course of the priests (1 Chr. 24:15). (2.) Neh. 10:20, one who sealed Nehemiah's covenant.

Hez'ro, a Carmelite, one of David's warriors (1 Chr. 11:37).

Hez'ron—*enclosed*. (1.) One of the sons of Reuben (Gen. 46:9; Ex. 6:14). (2.) The older of the two sons of Pharez (Gen. 46:12). (3.) A plain in the south of Judah, west of Kadesh-barnea (Josh. 15:3).

Hid'dai—*rejoicing of Jehovah*—one of David's thirty-seven guards (2 Sam. 23:30).

Hid'dekel—called by the Accadians *id Idikla*; i.e., "the river of Idikla"—the third of the four rivers of Paradise (Gen. 2:14). Gesenius interprets the word as meaning "the rapid Tigris." The Tigris rises in the mountains of Armenia, 15 miles south of the source of the Euphrates, which, after pursuing a south-east course, it joins at Kurnah, about 50 miles above Bassorah. Its whole length is about 1,150 miles.

Hi'el—*life of* (*i.e.*, *from*) *God*—a native of Bethel, who built (*i.e.*, fortified) Jericho some seven hundred years after its destruction by the Israelites. There fell on him for such an act the imprecation of Joshua (6:26). He laid the foundation in his first-born, and set up the gates in his youngest son (1 Kings 16:34)—*i.e.*, during the progress of the work all his children died.

Hierap'olis—*sacred city*—a city of Phrygia, where was a Christian church under the care of Epaphras (Col. 4:12, 13). This church was founded at the same time as that of Colosse. It now bears the name of *Pambûk-Kalek*—*i.e.*, "Cotton Castle"—from the white appearance of the cliffs at the base of which the ruins are found.

Higgai'on in Ps. 92:3 means the *murmuring tone* of the harp. In Ps. 9:17 it is a musical sign, denoting probably a pause in the instrumental interlude. In Ps. 19:14 the word is rendered "meditation;" and in Lam. 3:62, "device" (R.V., "imagination").

High place, an eminence, natural or artificial, where worship by sacrifice or offerings was made (1 Kings 13:32; 2 Kings 16:29). The first altar after the Flood was built on a mountain (Gen. 8:20). Abraham also built an altar on a mountain (12:7, 8). It was on a mountain in Gilead that Laban and Jacob offered sacrifices (31:54). After the Israelites entered the Promised Land they were strictly enjoined to overthrow the high places of the Canaanites (Ex. 34:13; Deut. 7:5; 12:2, 3), and they were forbidden to worship the Lord on high places (Deut. 12:11–14), and were enjoined to use but *one* altar for sacrifices (Lev. 17:3, 4; Deut. 12; 16:21). The injunction against high places was, however, very imperfectly obeyed, and we find again and again mention made of them (2 Kings 14:4; 15:5, 35; 2 Chr. 15:17, etc.).

High priest. Aaron was the first who was solemnly set apart to this office (Ex. 29:7; 30:23; Lev. 8:12). He wore a peculiar dress, which on his death passed to his successor in office (Ex. 29:29, 30). Besides those garments which he wore in common with all priests, there were four that were peculiar to himself as high priest:

(1.) The "robe" of the ephod, all of blue, of "woven work," worn immediately under the ephod. It was without seam or sleeves. The hem or skirt was ornamented with pomegranates and golden bells, seventy-two of each in alternate order. The sounding of the bells intimated to the people in the outer court the time when the high priest entered into the holy place to burn incense before the Lord (Ex. 28).

(2.) The "ephod" consisted of two parts, one of which covered the back and the other the breast, which were united by the "curious girdle." It was made of fine twined linen, and ornamented with gold and purple. Each of the shoulder-straps was adorned with a precious stone, on which the names of the twelve tribes were engraven. This was the high priest's distinctive vestment (1 Sam. 2:28; 14:3; 21:9; 23:6, 9; 30:7).

(3.) The "breastplate of judgment" (Ex. 28:6–12, 25–28; 39:2–7) of "cunning work." It was a piece of cloth doubled, of one span square. It bore twelve precious stones, set in four rows of three in a row, which constituted the Urim and Thummim (*q.v.*). These stones had engraven on them the names of the twelve tribes. When the high priest, clothed with the ephod and the breastplate, inquired of the Lord, answers were given in some mysterious way by the Urim and Thummim (1 Sam. 14:3, 18, 19; 23:2, 4, 9, 11, 12; 28:6; 2 Sam. 5:23).

(4.) The "mitre," or upper turban, a twisted band of eight yards of fine linen coiled into a cap, with a gold plate in front, engraved with "Holiness to the Lord," fastened to it by a ribbon of blue.

To the high priest alone it was permitted to enter the holy of holies, which he did only once a year, on the great Day of Atonement, for "the way into the holiest of all was not yet made manifest" (Heb. 9; 10). Wearing his gorgeous priestly vestments, he entered the temple before all the people, and then, laying them aside and assuming only his *linen* garments in secret, he entered the holy of holies alone, and made expiation, sprinkling the blood of the sin offering on the mercy seat, and offering up incense. Then resuming his splendid robes, he reappeared before the people (Lev. 16). Thus the wearing of these robes came to be identified with the Day of Atonement.

The office, dress, and ministration of the high priest were typical of the priesthood of our Lord (Heb. 4 : 14 ; 7 : 25 ; 9 : 12, etc.).

It is supposed that there were in all eighty-three high priests, beginning with

PART OF AN ASSYRIAN CYLINDER CONTAINING HEZEKIAH'S NAME.
(*Original in the British Museum.*)

Aaron (B.C. 1657) and ending with Phannias (A.D. 70). At its first institution the office of high priest was held for life (but comp. 1 Kings 2 : 27), and was hereditary in the family of Aaron (Num. 3 : 10). The office continued in the line of Eleazar, Aaron's eldest son, for two hundred and ninety-six years, when it passed to Eli, the first of the line of Ithamar, who was the fourth son of Aaron. In this line it continued to Abiathar, whom Solomon deposed, and appointed Zadok, of the family of Eleazar, in his stead (1 Kings 2 : 35), in which it remained till the time of the Captivity. After the Return, Joshua, the son of Josedek, of the family of Eleazar, was appointed to this office. After him the succession was changed from time to time under priestly or political influences.

High′way, a raised road for public use. Such roads were not found in Palestine; hence the force of the language used to describe the return of the captives and the advent of the Messiah (Isa. 11:16; 35:8; 40:3; 62:16) under the figure of the preparation of a grand thoroughfare for their march.

During their possession of Palestine the Romans constructed several important highways, as they did in all countries which they ruled.

Hilki′ah—*portion of Jehovah.* (1.) 1 Chr. 6:54.

(2.) 26:11.

(3.) The father of Eliakim (2 Kings 18: 18, 26, 37).

(4.) The father of Gemariah (Jer. 29:3).

(5.) The father of the prophet Jeremiah (1:1).

(6.) The high priest in the reign of Josiah (1 Chr. 6:13; Ezra 7:1). To him and his deputy (2 Kings 23:5), along with the ordinary priests and the Levites who had charge of the gates, was intrusted the purification of the temple in Jerusalem. While this was in progress, he discovered in some hidden corner of the building a book called the "book of the law" (2 Kings 22:8) and the "book of the covenant" (23:2). Some have supposed that this "book" was nothing else than the original autograph copy of the Pentateuch written by Moses (Deut. 31:9-26). This remarkable discovery occurred in the eighteenth year of Josiah's reign (B.C. 624)—a discovery which permanently affected the whole subsequent history of Israel. (See JOSIAH; SHAPHAN.)

(7.) Neh. 12:7.

(8.) Neh. 8:4.

Hill. (1.) Heb. *gibʻeah,* a curved or rounded hill, such as are common to Palestine (Ps. 65:12; 72:3; 114:4, 6).

(2.) Heb. *hâr,* properly a mountain range rather than an individual eminence (Ex. 24:4, 12, 13, 18; Num. 14:40, 44, 45). In Deut. 1:7; Josh. 9:1; 10:40; 11:16, it denotes the elevated district of Judah,

Benjamin, and Ephraim, which forms the water-shed between the Mediterranean and the Dead Sea.

(3.) Heb. *maʻaleh* in 1 Sam. 9:11. Authorized Version "hill" is correctly rendered in the Revised Version "ascent."

(4.) In Luke 9:37 the "hill" is the Mount of Transfiguration.

Hill of E′vil Coun′sel, on the south of the Valley of Hinnom. It is so called from a tradition that the house of the high priest Caiaphas, when the rulers of the Jews resolved to put Christ to death, stood here.

Hil′lel—*praising*—a Pirathonite, father of the judge Abdon (Judg. 12:13, 15).

Hind. Heb. *'ayalâh* (2 Sam. 22:34; Ps. 18:33, etc.) and *'ayeleth* (Ps. 22, title), the female of the hart or stag. It is referred to as an emblem of activity (Gen. 49:21), gentleness (Prov. 5:19), feminine modesty (Cant. 2:7; 3:5), earnest longing (Ps. 42:1), timidity (Ps. 29:9). In the title of Ps. 22, the word probably refers to some tune bearing that name.

Hinge (Heb. *tsîr*), that on which a door revolves. "Doors in the East turn rather on pivots than on what we term hinges. In Syria, and especially in the Haurân, there are many ancient doors, consisting of stone slabs with pivots carved out of the same piece inserted in sockets above and below, and fixed during the building of the house" (Prov. 26:14).

Hin′nom, a deep, narrow ravine separating Mount Zion from the so-called "Hill of Evil Counsel." It took its name from "some ancient hero, the son of Hinnom." It is first mentioned in Josh. 15:8. It had been the place where the idolatrous Jews burned their children alive to Moloch and Baal. A particular part of the valley was called Tophet, or the "fire-stove," where the children were burned. After the Exile, in order to show their abhorrence of the locality, the Jews made this valley the receptacle of the offal of the city, for the destruction of which a fire was, as is supposed, kept constantly burning there.

The Jews associated with this valley these two ideas—(1) that of the sufferings of the victims that had there been sacrificed; and (2) that of filth and corruption. It became thus to the popular mind a symbol of the abode of the wicked hereafter. It came to signify hell as the place of the wicked. "It might be shown by infinite examples that the Jews expressed hell, or the place of the damned, by this word. The word *Gehenna* [the Greek contraction of Hinnom] was never used in the time of Christ in any other sense than to denote the place of future punishment." About this fact there can be no question. In this sense the word is used eleven times in our Lord's discourses (Matt. 23:33; Luke 12: 15; Matt. 5:22, etc.).

Hi′ram—*high-born.* (1.) Generally "Huram," one of the sons of Bela (1 Chr. 8:5).

(2.) Also "Huram" and "Horam," king of Tyre. He entered into an alliance with David, and assisted him in building his palace by sending him able workmen, and also cedar-trees and fir-trees from Lebanon (2 Sam. 5:11; 1 Chr. 14:1). After the death of David he entered into a similar alliance with Solomon, and assisted him greatly in building the temple (1 Kings 5:1; 9:10; 1 Chr. 2:3). He also took part in Solomon's traffic to the Eastern Seas (1 Kings 9:27; 10:11; 2 Chr. 8:18; 9:10).

(3.) The "master workman" whom Hiram sent to Solomon. He was the son of a widow of Dan, and of a Tyrian father. In 2 Chr. 2:13 "Huram my father" should be Huram Abi—the word "Abi" (rendered here "my father") being regarded as a proper name, or it may perhaps be a title of distinction given to Huram, and equivalent to "master." (Comp. 1 Kings 7:14; 2 Chr. 4:16.) He cast the magnificent brazen works for Solomon's temple in clay-beds in the valley of Jordan, between Succoth and Zarthan.

Hire′ling, a labourer employed on hire for a limited time (Job 12:1; 14:6; Mark 1:20). His wages were paid as soon as his work was over (Lev. 19:13). In the time of our Lord a day's wage was a "penny" (*q.v.*) —*i.e.,* a Roman *denarius* (Matt. 20:1-14).

Hiss, to express contempt (Job 27:23). The destruction of the temple is thus spoken of (1 Kings 9:8). Zechariah (10:8)

speaks of the Lord gathering the house of Judah as it were with a hiss: "I will hiss for them." This expression may be " derived from the noise made to attract bees in hiving, or from the sound naturally made to attract a person's attention."

Hit′tites. Palestine and Syria appear to have been originally inhabited by three different tribes. (1.) The Semites, living on the east of the isthmus of Suez. They were nomadic and pastoral tribes. (2.) The Phœnicians, who were merchants and traders; and (3.) the Hittites, who were the warlike element of this confederation of tribes. They inhabited the whole region between the Euphrates and Damascus, their chief cities being Carchemish on the Euphrates, and Kadesh, now Tell Neby Mendeh, in the Orontes valley, about six miles south of the Lake of Homs. These Hittites seem to have risen to great power as a nation, as for a long time they were formidable rivals of the Egyptian and Assyrian empires. In the book of Joshua they always appear as the dominant race to the north of Galilee.

Somewhere about the twenty-third century B.C. the Syrian confederation, led probably by the Hittites, marched against Lower Egypt, which they took possession of, making Zoan their capital. Their rulers were the Hyksos, or shepherd kings. They were at length finally driven out of Egypt. Rameses II. sought vengeance against the "vile Kheta," as he called them, and encountered and defeated them in the great battle of Kadesh, four centuries after Abraham. (See JOSHUA.)

They are first referred to in Scripture in the history of Abraham, who bought from Ephron the Hittite the field and the cave of Machpelah (Gen. 15:20; 23:3-18). They were then settled at Kirjath-arba. From this tribe Esau took his first two wives (26: 34; 36:2).

They are afterwards mentioned in the usual way among the inhabitants of the Promised Land (Ex. 23:28). They were closely allied to the Amorites, and are frequently mentioned along with them as inhabiting the mountains of Palestine. When the spies entered the land they seem to have occupied with the Amorites the mountain region of Judah (Num. 13:29). They took part with the other Canaanites against the Israelites (Josh. 9:1; 11:3).

After this there are few references to them in Scripture. Mention is made of "Ahimelech the Hittite" (1 Sam. 26:6), and of "Uriah the Hittite," one of David's chief officers (2 Sam. 23:39; 1 Chr. 11:41). In the days of Solomon they were a powerful confederation in the north of Syria, and were ruled by "kings." They are met with after the Exile still a distinct people (Ezra 9:1; comp. Neh. 13:23-28).

The Hebrew merchants exported horses from Egypt not only for the kings of Israel, but also for the Hittites (1 Kings 10:28, 29). From the Egyptian monuments we learn that "the Hittites were a people with yellow skins and 'Mongoloid' features, whose receding foreheads, oblique eyes, and protruding upper jaws are represented as faithfully on their own monuments as they are on those of Egypt, so that we cannot accuse the Egyptian artists of caricaturing their enemies. The Amorites, on the contrary, were a tall and handsome people. They are depicted with white skins, blue eyes, and reddish hair—all the characteristics, in fact, of the white race" (Sayce's *The Hittites*). The original seat of the Hittite tribes was the mountain ranges of Taurus. They belonged to Asia Minor, and not to Syria. They pushed their way southward, and thus were found in Syria and Palestine. The Hittite empire was not like that of Rome, whose several provinces were consolidated under one great central authority. It consisted of a number of provinces whose inhabitants paid tribute and did homage to the king as a great conqueror whom they could not resist. They were not held together by any bond.

Hi'vites, one of the original tribes scattered over Palestine, from Hermon to Gibeon in the south. The name is interpreted as "midlanders" or "villagers" (Gen. 10:17; 1 Chr. 1:15). They were probably a branch of the Hittites. At the time of Jacob's return to Canaan, Hamor the Hivite was the "prince of the land" (Gen. 24:2-28).

They are next mentioned during the Conquest (Josh. 9:7; 11:19). They principally inhabited the northern confines of Western Palestine (Josh. 11:3; Judg. 3:3). A remnant of them still existed in the time of Solomon (1 Kings 9:20).

Hizki'ah, an ancestor of the prophet Zephaniah (1:1).

Hizki'jah (Neh. 10:17), one who sealed the covenant.

Ho'bab—*beloved*—the Kenite, has been usually identified with Jethro (*q.v.*)—Ex. 18:5, 27; comp. Num. 10:29, 30. In Judg. 4:11, the word rendered "father-in-law" means properly any male relative by marriage (comp. Gen. 19:14, "son-in-law," A.V.), and should be rendered "brother-in-law," as in the R.V. His descendants followed Israel to Canaan (Num. 10:29), and at first pitched their tents near Jericho, but afterwards settled in the south in the borders of Arad (Judg. 1:8-11, 16).

Ho'bah—*hiding-place*—a place to the north of Damascus, to which Abraham pursued Chedorlaomer and his confederates (Gen. 14:15).

Hodi'jah—*majesty of Jehovah*. (1.) One of the Levites who assisted Ezra in expounding the law (Neh. 8:7; 9:5). (2.) Neh. 10:18, a Levite who sealed the covenant.

Hog'lah—*partridge*—one of the daughters of Zelophehad the Gileadite, to whom portions were assigned by Moses (Num. 26:33; 27:1; 36:11).

Ho'ham—*Jehovah impels*—the king of Hebron who joined the league against Gibeon. He and his allies were defeated (Josh. 10:3, 5, 16-27).

Hold—*a fortress*—the name given to David's lurking-places (1 Sam. 22:4, 5; 24:22).

Ho'liness in the highest sense belongs to God (Isa. 6:3; Rev. 15:4), and to Christians as consecrated to God's service, and in so far as they are conformed in all things to the will of God (Rom. 6:19, 22; Eph. 1:4; Titus 1:8; 1 Pet. 1:15). Personal holiness is a work of gradual development. It is carried on under many hindrances, hence the frequent admonitions to watchfulness, prayer, and perseverance (1 Cor. 1:30; 2 Cor. 7:1; Eph. 4:23, 24). (See SANCTIFICATION.)

Holy Ghost, the third Person of the adorable Trinity.

His *personality* is proved (1) from the fact that the attributes of personality, as intelligence and volition, are ascribed to him (John 14:17, 26; 15:26; 1 Cor. 2:10, 11; 12:11). He reproves, helps, glorifies, intercedes (John 16:7–13; Rom. 8:26). (2) He executes the offices peculiar only to a person. The very nature of these offices involves personal distinction (Luke 12:12; Acts 5:32; 15:28; 16:6; 28:25; 1 Cor. 2:13; Heb. 2:4; 3:7; 2 Pet. 1:21).

His *divinity* is established (1) from the fact that the names of God are ascribed to him (Ex. 17:7; Ps. 95:7; comp. Heb. 3:7–11); and (2) that divine attributes are also ascribed to him—omnipresence (Ps. 139:7; Eph. 2:17, 18; 1 Cor. 12:13); omniscience (1 Cor. 2:10, 11); omnipotence (Luke 1:35; Rom. 8:11); eternity (Heb. 9:4). (3) Creation is ascribed to him (Gen. 1:2; Job 26:13; Ps. 104:30), and the working of miracles (Matt. 12:28; 1 Cor. 12:9–11). (4) Worship is required and ascribed to him (Isa. 6:3; Acts 28:25; Rom. 9:1; Rev. 1:4; Matt. 28:19).

Holy place, one of the two portions into which the tabernacle was divided (Ex. 25:31; 37:17–25; Heb. 9:2). It was 20 cubits long and 10 in height and breadth. It was illuminated by the golden candlestick, as it had no opening to admit the light. It contained the table of showbread (Ex. 25:23–29) and the golden altar of incense (30:1–11). It was divided from the holy of holies by a veil of the most costly materials and the brightest colours.

The arrangement of the temple (*q.v.*) was the same in this respect. In it the walls of hewn stone were wainscotted with cedar and overlaid with gold, and adorned with beautiful carvings. It was entered from the porch by folding doors overlaid with gold and richly embossed. Outside the holy place stood the great tank or "sea" of molten brass, supported by twelve oxen, three turned each way, capable of containing two thousand baths of water. Besides this there were ten lavers and the brazen altar of burnt sacrifice.

Holy of holies, the second or interior portion of the tabernacle. It was left in total darkness. No one was permitted to enter it except [the high priest, and that only once a year. It contained the ark of the covenant only (Ex. 25:10–16). It was in the form of a perfect cube of 20 cubits. (See TABERNACLE.)

Ho′mer — *heap* — the largest of dry measures, containing about 8 bushels or 1 quarter English = 10 ephahs (Lev. 27:16; Num. 11:32) = a COR. (See OMER.)

"Half a homer," a grain measure mentioned only in Hos. 3:3.

Honey. (1.) Heb. *ya'ar*, occurs only 1 Sam. 14:25, 27, 29; Cant. 5:1, where it denotes the honey of bees. Properly the word signifies a forest or copse, and refers to honey found in woods.

(2.) *Nôpheth*, honey that drops (Ps. 19:10; Prov. 5:3; Cant. 4:11).

(3.) *Debash* denotes bee-honey (Judg. 14:8); but also frequently a vegetable honey distilled from trees (Gen. 43:11; Ezek. 27:17). In these passages it may probably mean "dibs," or syrup of grapes, *i.e.*, the juice of ripe grapes boiled down to one-third of its bulk.

(4.) *Tsûph*, the cells of the honey-comb full of honey (Prov. 16:24; Ps. 19:11).

(5.) "Wild honey" (Matt. 3:4) may have been the vegetable honey distilled from trees, but rather was honey stored by bees in rocks or in trees (Deut. 22:13; Ps. 81:17; 1 Sam. 14:24–32).

Canaan was a "land flowing with milk and honey" (Ex. 3:8). Milk and honey were among the chief dainties in the earlier ages, as they are now among the Bedawin; and butter and honey are also mentioned among articles of food (Isa. 7:15). The ancients used honey instead of sugar (Ps. 119:103; Prov. 24:13); but when taken in great quantities it caused nausea—a fact referred to in Prov. 25:16, 17 to inculcate moderation in pleasures. Honey and milk also are put for sweet discourse (Cant. 4:11).

Hood (Heb. *tsaniph*), a tiara round the head (Isa. 3:23; R.V., pl., "turbans"). Rendered "diadem," Job 29:14; high priest's "mitre," Zech. 3:5; "royal diadem," Isa. 62:3.

Hoof, a cleft hoof as of neat cattle (Ex. 10:26; Ezek. 22, etc.); hence also of the horse, though not cloven (Isa. 5:28). The "parting of the hoof" is one of the distinctions between clean and unclean animals (Lev. 11:3; Deut. 4:5).

Hook. (1.) Heb. *ḥaḥ*, a "ring" inserted in the nostrils of animals to which a cord was fastened for the purpose of restraining them (2 Kings 19:28; Isa. 37:28, 29; Ezek. 29:4; 38:4). "The Orientals make use of this contrivance for curbing their work-beasts......When a beast becomes unruly they have only to draw the cord on one side, which, by stopping his breath, punishes him so effectually that after a few repetitions he fails not to become quite tractable whenever he begins to feel it" (Michaelis). So God's agents are never beyond his control.

(2.) *Hakkâh*, a fish "hook" (Job 41:2—Heb. Text, 40:25; Isa. 19:8; Hab. 1:15).

(3.) *Vav*, a "peg" on which the curtains of the tabernacle were hung (Ex. 26:32).

(4.) *Tsinnâh*, a fish-hook (Amos 4:2).

(5.) *Mazlêg*, flesh-hooks (1 Sam. 2:13, 14), a kind of fork with three teeth for turning the sacrifices on the fire, etc.

(6.) *Mazmerôth*, pruning-hooks (Isa. 2:4; Joel 3:10).

(7.) *'Agmôn* (Job 41:2—Heb. Text 40:26), incorrectly rendered in the Authorized Version. Properly a rush-rope for binding animals, as in Revised Version margin.

Hope, one of the three main elements of Christian character (1 Cor. 13:13). It is joined to faith and love, and is opposed to seeing or possessing (Rom. 8:24; 1 John 3:2). "Hope is an essential and fundamental element of Christian life, so essential indeed, that, like faith and love, it can itself designate the essence of Christianity (1 Pet. 3:15; Heb. 10:23). In it the whole glory of the Christian vocation is centred (Eph. 1:18; 4:4)." Unbelievers are without this hope (Eph. 2:12; 1 Thess. 4:13). Christ is the actual object of the believer's hope, because it is in his second coming that the hope of glory will be fulfilled (1 Tim. 1:1; Col. 1:27; Titus 2:13). It is spoken of as "lively"—*i.e.*, a living—hope, a hope not frail and perishable, but having a perennial life (1 Pet. 1:3). In Rom. 5:2 the "hope" spoken of is probably objective, *i.e.*, "the hope set before us"—namely, eternal life (comp. 12:12). In 1 John 3:3 the expression "hope in him" ought rather to be, as in the Revised Version, "hope on him," *i.e.*, a hope based on God.

Hoph'ni—*pugilist* or *client*—one of the two sons of Eli, the high priest (1 Sam. 1:3; 2:34), who, because he was "very old," resigned to them the active duties of his office. By their scandalous conduct they brought down a curse on their father's house (2:22, 12-17, 27-36; 3:11-14). For their wickedness they were called "sons of Belial," *i.e.*, worthless men (2:12). They both perished in the disastrous battle with the Philistines at Aphek (4:11). (See PHINEHAS.)

Hoph'ra—*i.e.*, PHARAOH-HOPHRA (called Apries by the Greek historian Herodotus)—king of Egypt (B.C. 591-572) in the time of Zedekiah, king of Judah (Jer. 37:5; 44:30; Ezek. 39:6, 7).

Hor—*mountain.* (1.) One of the mountains of the chain of Seir or Edom, on the confines of Idumea (Num. 20:22-29; 23:37). It was one of the stations of the Israelites in the wilderness (33:37), which they reached in the circuitous route they were obliged to take because the Edomites refused them a passage through their territory. It was during the encampment here that Aaron died (Num. 33:37-41). (See AARON.) The Israelites passed this mountain several times in their wanderings. It bears the modern name of *Jebel Harûn*, and is the highest and most conspicuous of the whole range. It stands about midway between the Dead Sea and the Elanitic gulf. It has two summits, in the hollow between which it is supposed that Aaron died. Others, however, suppose that this mountain is the modern *Jebel Madurah*, or the opposite—*i.e.*, the western—side of the Arabah.

(2.) One of the marks of the northern

boundary of Palestine (Num. 34:7, 8). Nowhere else mentioned. Perhaps it is one of the peaks of Lebanon.

Ho'reb—*desert* or *mountain of the dried-up ground*—a general name for the whole mountain range of which Sinai was one of the summits (Ex. 3:1; 17:6; 33:6; Ps. 106:19, etc.). The modern name of the whole range is *Jebel Mûsa*. It is a huge mountain block, about 2 miles long by about 1 in breadth, with a very spacious plain at its north-east end, called the Er Râhah, in which the Israelites encamped for nearly a whole year. (See SINAI.)

Ho'rem—*consecrated*—one of the fenced cities of Naphtali (Josh. 19:38).

Ho'rites—*cave-men*—a race of Troglo-dytes who dwelt in the limestone caves which abounded in Edom. Their ancestor was "Seir," who probably gave his name to the district where he lived. They were a branch of the Hivites (Gen. 14:6; 36:20–36; 1 Chr. 38:42). They were dispossessed by the descendants of Esau, and as a people gradually became extinct (Deut. 2:12–22).

Hor'mah—*banning; i.e.*, placing under a "ban," or devoting to utter destruction. After the manifestation of God's anger against the Israelites, on account of their rebellion and their murmurings when the spies returned to the camp at Kadesh, in the wilderness of Paran, with an evil report of the land, they quickly repented of

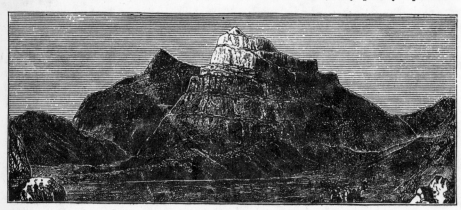

MOUNT HOR.

their conduct, and presumed to go up " to the head of the mountain," seeking to enter the Promised Land, but without the presence of the Lord, without the ark of the covenant, and without Moses. The Amalekites and the Canaanites came down and "smote and discomfited them even unto Hormah" (Num. 14:45). This place, or perhaps the watch-tower commanding it, was originally called Zephath (Judg. 1:17), the modern *Sebaiteh*. Afterwards (Num. 21:1-3) Arad, the king of the Canaanites, at the close of the wanderings, when the Israelites were a second time encamped at Kadesh, "fought against them, and took some of them prisoners." But Israel vowed a vow unto the Lord utterly to destroy the cities of the Canaanites; they "banned" them, and hence the place was now called Hormah. But this "ban" was not fully executed till the time of Joshua, who finally conquered the king of this district, so that the ancient name Zephath became "Hormah" (Josh. 12:14; Judg. 1:17).

Horn. *Trumpets* were at first horns perforated at the tip, used for various purposes (Josh. 6:4, 5).

Flasks or vessels were made of horn (1 Sam. 16:1, 13; 1 Kings 1:39).

But the word is used also *metaphorically* to denote the projecting corners of the altar of burnt offerings (Ex. 27:2) and of incense (30:2). The horns of the altar of burnt offerings were to be smeared with the blood of the slain bullock (29:12; Lev. 4:7-18). The criminal, when his crime was accidental, found an asylum by laying hold of the horns of the altar (1 Kings 1: 50; 2:28).

The word also denotes the peak or summit of a hill (Isa. 5:1, where the word "hill" is the rendering of the same Hebrew word).

This word is used metaphorically also for *strength* (Deut. 32:17) and *honour* (Job 16:15; Lam. 2:3). Horns are emblems of power, dominion, glory, and fierceness, as they are the chief means of attack and defence with the animals endowed with them (Dan. 8:5, 9; 1 Sam. 2:1; 16:1, 13; 1 Kings 1:39; 22:11; Josh. 6:4, 5; Ps. 75:5, 10; 132:17; Luke 1:69, etc.). The expression "horn of salvation," applied to Christ, means a salvation of strength, or a strong Saviour (Luke 1:69). To have the horn "exalted" denotes prosperity and triumph (Ps. 89:17, 24). To "lift up" the horn is to act proudly (Zech. 1:21).

Horns are also the symbol of royal dignity and power (Jer. 48:25; Zech. 1:18; Dan. 8:24).

Hor′net—Heb. *tsir‘âh*, "stinging"— (Ex. 23:28; Deut. 7:20; Josh. 24:12). The word is used in these passages as referring to some means by which the Canaanites were to be driven out from before the Israelites. Some have supposed that the word is used in a metaphorical sense as the symbol of some panic which would seize the people as a "terror of God" (Gen. 35:5)—the consternation with which God would inspire the Canaanites. In Palestine there are four species of hornets, differing from our hornets, being larger in size, and they are very abundant. They "attack human beings in a very furious manner." "The furious attack of a swarm of hornets drives cattle and horses to madness, and has even caused the death of the animals."

Horona′im—*two caverns*—a city of Moab to the south of the Arnon, built, apparently, upon an eminence, and a place of some importance (Isa. 15:5; Jer. 48:3, 5, 34).

Hor′onite, the designation of Sanballat (Neh. 2:10, 19), a native of Horonaim, or of one of the two Beth-horons, the "upper" or the "nether," mentioned in Josh. 16:3, 5.

Horse, always referred to in the Bible in connection with warlike operations, except Isa. 28:28. The war-horse is described Job 39:19-25. For a long period after their settlement in Canaan the Israelites made no use of horses, according to the prohibition, Deut. 17:16. David was the first to form a force of cavalry (2 Sam. 8:4). But Solomon, from his connection with Egypt, greatly multiplied their number (1 Kings 4:26; 10:26, 29). After this, horses were freely used in Israel (1 Kings 22:4; 2 Kings 3:7; 9:21, 33; 11:16). The furniture of the horse consisted simply of a bridle (Isa. 30:28) and a curb (Ps. 32:9).

Horse′-gate, a gate in the wall of Jerusalem, at the west end of the bridge, leading from Zion to the temple (Neh. 3:28; Jer. 31:40).

Horse′-leech occurs only in Prov. 30: 15 (Heb. *’alûkah*); the generic name for any blood-sucking annelid. There are various species in the marshes and pools of Palestine. That here referred to, the *Hæmopis*, is remarkable for the coarseness of its bite, and is therefore not used for medical purposes. They are spoken of in the East with feelings of aversion and horror, because of their propensity to fasten on the tongue and nostrils of horses when they come to drink out of the pools. The medicinal leech (*Hirudo medicinalis*), besides other species of leeches, are common in the waters of Syria.

Horse′man—Heb. *ba‘al parâsh*, "master of a horse." The "horsemen" mentioned Ex. 14:9 were "mounted men"—*i.e.*, men who rode in chariots. The army of Pharaoh consisted of a chariot and infantry force. We find that at a later period, however, the Egyptians had cavalry (2 Chr. 12:3). (See HORSE.)

Hosan′na—*Save now!* or *Save, we beseech*—(Matt. 21:9). This was a customary form of acclamation at the feast of Tabernacles. (Comp. Ps. 118:25.)

Hose (Dan. 3:21), a tunic or undergarment.

Hose′a—*salvation*—the son of Beêri, and author of the book of prophecies bearing his name. He belonged to the kingdom of

Israel. "His Israelitish origin is attested by the peculiar, rough, Aramäizing diction, pointing to the northern part of Palestine; by the intimate acquaintance he evinces with the localities of Ephraim (5:1; 6:8, 9; 12:12; 14:6, etc.); by passages like 1:2, where the kingdom is styled *the land*, and 7:5, where the Israelitish king is designated as *our* king." The period of his ministry (extending to some sixty years) is indicated in the superscription (Hos. 1:1, 2). He is the only prophet of Israel who has left any written prophecy.

Hose'a, Prophecies of. This book stands first in order among the "Minor Prophets." "The probable cause of the location of Hosea may be the thoroughly national character of his oracles, their length, their earnest tone, and vivid representations." This was the longest of the prophetic books written before the Captivity. Hosea prophesied in a dark and melancholy period of Israel's history—the period of Israel's decline and fall. Their sins had brought upon them great national disasters. "Their homicides and fornication, their perjury and theft, their idolatry and impiety, are censured and satirized with a faithful severity." He was a contemporary of Isaiah.

The book may be divided into two parts, the first containing chapters 1–3, and symbolically representing the idolatry of Israel under imagery borrowed from the matrimonial relation. The figures of marriage and adultery are common in the Old Testament writings to represent the spiritual relations between Jehovah and the people of Israel. Here we see the apostasy of Israel and their punishment, with their future repentance, forgiveness, and restoration.

The second part, containing 4-14, is a summary of Hosea's discourses, filled with denunciations, threatenings, exhortations, promises, and revelations of mercy.

Quotations from Hosea are found in Matt. 2:15; 9:15; 12:7; Rom. 9:25, 26. There are, in addition, various allusions to it in other places (Luke 23:30; Rev. 6:16, comp. Hos. 10:18; Rom. 9:25, 26; 1 Pet. 2:10, comp. Hos. 1:10, etc.).

As regards the style of this writer, it has been said that "each verse forms a whole for itself, like one heavy toll in a funeral knell." "Inversions (7:8; 9:11, 13; 12:8), anacolutha (9:6; 12:8, etc.), ellipses (9:4; 13:9, etc.), paranomasias, and plays upon words, are very characteristic of Hosea (8:7; 9:15; 10:5; 11:5; 12:11)."

Ho'shah—*refuge*. (1.) A place on the border of the tribe of Asher (Josh. 19:29), a little to the south of Zidon.

(2.) A Levite of the family of Merari (1 Chr. 16:38).

Hoshe'a—*salvation*. (1.) The original name of the son of Nun, afterwards called Joshua (Num. 13:8, 16; Deut. 32:44).

(2.) 1 Chr. 27:20. The ruler of Ephraim in David's time.

(3.) The last king of Israel. He conspired against and slew his predecessor, Pekah (Isa. 7:16), but did not ascend the throne till after an interregnum of warfare of eight years (2 Kings 17:1, 2). Soon after this he submitted to Shalmaneser, the Assyrian king, who a second time invaded the land to punish Hoshea, because of his withholding tribute which he had promised to pay. A second revolt brought back the Assyrian king Sargon, who besieged Samaria, and carried the ten tribes away beyond the Euphrates, B.C. 720 (2 Kings 17:5, 6; 18:9-12). No more is heard of Hoshea. He disappeared like "foam upon the water" (Hos. 10:7; 13:11).

Host, an entertainer (Rom. 16:23); a tavern-keeper, the keeper of a caravansary (Luke 10:35).

In warfare, a troop or military force. This consisted at first only of infantry. Solomon afterwards added cavalry (1 Kings 4:26; 10:26). Every male Israelite from twenty to fifty years of age was bound by the law to bear arms when necessary (Num. 1:3; 26:2; 2 Chr. 25:5).

Saul was the first to form a standing army (1 Sam. 13:2; 24:3). This example was followed by David (1 Chr. 27:1), and Solomon (1 Kings 4:26), and by the kings of Israel and Judah (2 Chr. 17:14; 26:11; 2 Kings 11:4, etc.).

Host of heaven. The sun, moon, and stars are so designated (Gen. 2:1). When the Jews fell into idolatry they worshipped these (Deut. 4:19; 2 Kings 17:16; 21:3,

5; 23:5; Jer. 19:13; Zeph. 1:5; Acts 7:42).

Hos'tage, a person delivered into the hands of another as a security for the performance of some promise, etc. (2 Kings 14:14; 2 Chr. 25:24).

Hough, to hamstring—*i.e.*, sever the "tendon of Achilles" of the hinder legs of captured horses (Josh. 11:6; 2 Sam. 8:4; 1 Chr. 18:4), so as to render them useless.

Hour. First found in Dan. 3:6; 4:19, 33; 5:5. It is the rendering of the Chaldee *shâdh*, meaning a "moment," a "look." It is used in the New Testament frequently to denote some determinate season (Matt. 8:13; Luke 12:39).

With the ancient Hebrews the divisions of the day were "morning, evening, and noon-day" (Ps. 55:17, etc.). The Greeks, following the Babylonians, divided the day into twelve hours. The Jews, during the Captivity, learned also from the Babylonians this method of dividing time. When Judea became subject to the Romans, the Jews adopted the Roman mode of reckoning time. The night was divided into four watches (Luke 12:38; Matt. 14:25; 13:35). Frequent allusion is also made to hours (Matt. 25:13; 26:40, etc.). (See DAY.)

An hour was the twelfth part of the day, reckoning from sunrise to sunset, and consequently it perpetually varied in length.

House. Till their sojourn in Egypt the Hebrews dwelt in tents. They then for the first time inhabited cities (Gen. 47:3; Ex. 12:7; Heb. 11:9). From the earliest times the Assyrians and the Canaanites were builders of cities. The Hebrews after the Conquest took possession of the captured cities, and seem to have followed the methods of building that had been pursued by the Canaanites. Reference is made to the stone (1 Kings 7:9; Isa. 9:10) and marble (1 Chr. 29:2) used in building, and to the internal wood-work of the houses (1 Kings 6:15; 7:2; 10:11, 12; 2 Chr. 3:5; Jer. 22:14). "Ceiled houses" were such as had beams inlaid in the walls to which wainscotting was fastened (Ezra 6:4; Jer. 22:14; Hag. 1:4). "Ivory houses" had the upper parts of the walls adorned with figures in stucco with gold

and ivory (1 Kings 22:39; 2 Chr. 3:6; Ps. 45:8).

The *roofs* of the dwelling-houses were flat, and are often alluded to in Scripture (2 Sam. 11:2; Isa. 22:1; Matt. 24:17). Sometimes tents or booths were erected on them (2 Sam. 16:22). They were protected by parapets or low walls (Deut. 22:8). On the house-tops grass sometimes grew (Prov. 19:13; 27:15; Ps. 129:6, 7). They were used, not only as places of recreation in the evening, but also sometimes as sleeping-places at night (1 Sam. 9:25, 26; 2 Sam. 11:2; 16:22; Dan. 4:29; Job 27:18; Prov. 21:9), and as places of devotion (Jer. 32:29; 19:13).

Huk'kok—*decreed*—a town near Zebulun, not far from Jordan, on the border of Naphtali (Josh. 19:24). (See HELKATH.)

Hul—*circle*—the second son of Aram (Gen. 10:23), and grandson of Shem.

Hul'dah—*weasel*—a prophetess; the wife of Shallum. She was consulted regarding the "book of the law" discovered by the high priest Hilkiah (2 Kings 22:14-20; 2 Chr. 34:22-28). She resided in that part of Jerusalem called the Mishneh (A.V., "the college;" R.V., "the second quarter"), supposed by some to be the suburb between the inner and the outer wall, the second or lower city, Akra. Miriam (Ex. 15:20) and Deborah (Judg. 4:4) are the only others who bear the title of "prophetess," for the word in Isa. 8;3 means only the prophet's wife.

Humilia'tion of Christ (Phil. 2:8), seen in (1) his birth (Gal. 4:4; Luke 2:7; John 1:46; Heb. 2:9), (2) his circumstances, (3) his reputation (Isa. 53; Matt. 26:59, 67; Ps. 22:6; Matt. 22:68), (4) his soul (Ps. 21:1; Matt. 4:1-11; Luke 22:43; Heb. 2:17, 18; 4:15), (5) his death (Luke 23; John 19; Mark 15:24, 25), (6) and his burial (Isa. 53:10; Matt. 13:46).

His humiliation was necessary (1) to execute the purpose of God (Acts 2:23, 24; Ps. 40:6-8), (2) fulfil the Old Testament types and prophecies, (3) satisfy the law in the room of the guilty (Isa. 53; Heb. 9:12, 15), procure for them eternal redemption, (4) and to show us an example.

Humil'ity, a prominent Christian grace (Rom. 12:3; 15:17, 18; 1 Cor. 3:5-7; 2 Cor. 3:5; Phil. 4:11-13). It is a state of mind well pleasing to God (1 Pet. 3:4); it preserves the soul in tranquillity (Ps. 69:32, 33), and makes us patient under trials (Job 1:22).

Christ has set us an example of humility (Phil. 2:6-8). We should be led thereto by a remembrance of our sins (Lam. 3:39), and by the thought that it is the way to honour (Prov. 16:18), and that the greatest promises are made to the humble (Ps. 147:6; Isa. 57:15; 56:2; 1 Pet. 5:5). It is a "great paradox in Christianity that it makes humility the avenue to glory."

Hunt'ing, mentioned first in Gen. 10:9 in connection with Nimrod. Esau was "a cunning hunter" (Gen. 25:27). Hunting was practised by the Hebrews after their settlement in the "Land of Promise" (Lev. 17:15; Prov. 12:27). The lion and other ravenous beasts were found in Palestine (1 Sam. 17:34; 2 Sam. 23:20; 1 Kings 13:24; Ezek. 19:3-8), and it must have been necessary to hunt and destroy them. Various snares and gins were used in hunting (Ps. 91:3; Amos 3:5; 2 Sam. 23:20).

War is referred to under the idea of hunting (Jer. 16:16; Ezek. 32:30).

Hur—*a hole,* as of a viper, etc. (1.) A son of Caleb (1 Chr. 2:19, 50; 4:1, 4; comp. 2 Chr. 1:5).

(2.) The husband of Miriam, Moses' sister (Ex. 17:10-12). He was associated with Aaron in charge of the people when Moses was absent on Sinai (Ex. 25:14). He was probably of the tribe of Judah, and grandfather of Bezaleel (Ex. 31:2; 35:20; 1 Chr. 2:19).

(3.) One of the five princes of Midian who were defeated and slain by the Israelites under the command of Phinehas (Num. 31:8).

Hu'rai—*linen - worker*—one of David's heroes, a native of the valley of Mount Gaash (1 Chr. 11:32).

Hus'band, *i.e.,* the "house-band," connecting and keeping together the whole family. A man when betrothed was esteemed from that time a husband (Matt. 1:16, 20; Luke 2:5). A recently married man was exempt from going to war for "one year" (Deut. 20:7; 24:5).

Hus'bandman, one whose business it is to cultivate the ground. It was one of the first occupations, and was esteemed most honourable (Gen. 9:20; 26:12, 14; 37:7, etc.). All the Hebrews, except those engaged in religious services, were husbandmen. (See AGRICULTURE.)

Hu'shai—*quick*—"the Archite," "the king's friend" (1 Chr. 27:33). When David fled from Jerusalem, on account of the rebellion of Absalom, and had reached the summit of Olivet, he there met Hushai, whom he sent back to Jerusalem for the purpose of counteracting the influence of Ahithophel, who had joined the ranks of Absalom (2 Sam. 15:32, 37; 16:16-18). It was by his advice that Absalom refrained from immediately pursuing after David. By this delay the cause of Absalom was ruined, for it gave David time to muster his forces.

Husk. In Num. 6:4 (Heb. *zâg*) it means the "skin" of a grape. In 2 Kings 4:42 (Heb. *tsiqlôn*) it means a "sack" for grain, as rendered in the Revised Version. In Luke 15:16, in the parable of the Prodigal Son, it designates the beans of the carob tree, or *Ceratonia siliqua.* From

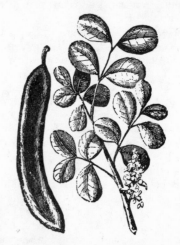

POD, LEAVES, AND FLOWER OF CAROB TREE

the supposition—mistaken, however—that it was on the husks of this tree that John the Baptist fed, it is called "St. John's bread" and "locust tree." This tree is in " February covered with innumerable purple-red pendent blossoms, which ripen in April and May into large crops of pods from 6 to 10 inches long—flat, brown, narrow, and bent like a horn (whence the Greek name *keratia*, meaning 'little horns'), with a sweetish taste when still unripe. Enormous quantities of these are gathered for sale in various towns and for exportation." "They were eaten as food, though only by the poorest of the poor, in the time of our Lord." The bean is called a "gerah," which is used as the name of the smallest Hebrew weight, twenty of these making a shekel.

Hymn, occurs only Eph. 5 : 19 and Col. 3 : 16. The verb to "sing an hymn" occurs Matt. 26 : 30 and Mark 14 : 26. The same Greek word is rendered to "sing praises" Acts 16 : 25 (R.V., "sing hymns") and Heb. 2 : 12. The "hymn" which our Lord sang with his disciples at the last Supper is generally supposed to have been the latter part of the *Hallel*, comprehending Ps. 113–118. It was thus a name given to a number of psalms taken together and forming a devotional exercise.

The noun *hymn* is used only with reference to the services of the Greeks, and was distinguished from the psalm. The Greek tunes required Greek hymns. Our information regarding the hymnology of the early Christians is very limited.

Hyp′ocrite, one who puts on a mask and feigns himself to be what he is not ; a dissembler in religion. Our Lord severely rebuked the scribes and Pharisees for their hypocrisy (Matt. 6 : 2, 5, 16). "The hypocrite's hope shall perish" (Job 8 : 13). The Hebrew word here rendered "hypocrite" rather means the "godless" or "profane," as it is rendered in Jer. 23 : 11—*i.e.*, polluted with crimes.

Hys′sop (Heb. *′ēzôb ;* LXX. *hyssōpos*), first mentioned in Ex. 12 : 22 in connection with the institution of the Passover. We find it afterwards mentioned in Lev. 14 : 4, 6, 52 ; Num. 19 : 6, 18 ; Heb. 9 : 19. It is spoken of as a plant "springing out of the wall" (1 Kings 4 : 33). Many conjectures have been formed as to what this plant really was. Some contend that it was a species of marjoram (*origanum*), six species of which are found in Palestine. Others with more probability think that it was the caper plant, the *Capparis spinosa* of Linnæus. This plant grew in Egypt, in the desert of Sinai, and in Palestine. It was capable of producing a stem three or four feet in length (Matt. 27 : 48 ; Mark 15 : 36. Comp. John 19 : 29).

I

Ib′har—*chosen*—one of David's sons (1 Chr. 3 : 6 ; 2 Sam. 5 : 15).

Ib′leam—*people-waster*—a city assigned to Manasseh (Josh. 17 : 11), from which the Israelites, however, could not expel the Canaanites (Judg. 1 : 27). It is also called Bileam (1 Chr. 6 : 70). It was probably the modern *Jelamah*, a village 2½ miles north of Jenin.

Ib′zan—*illustrious*—the tenth judge of Israel (Judg. 12 : 8–10). He ruled seven years.

Ice, frequently mentioned (Job 6 : 16 ; 38 : 29 ; Ps. 147 : 17, etc.). (See CRYSTAL.)

Ich′abod. When the tidings of the disastrous defeat of the Israelites in the battle against the Philistines near to Mizpeh were carried to Shiloh, the wife of Phinehas " was near to be delivered. And when she heard the tidings that the ark of God was taken, and that her father-in-law and her husband were dead, she bowed herself and travailed" (1 Sam. 4 : 19–22). . In her great distress she regarded not "the women that stood by her," but named the child that was born "Ichabod" —*i.e.*, *no glory*—saying, "The glory is departed from Israel ;" and with that word on her lips she expired.

Ico′nium, the capital of ancient Lyca

onia. It was first visited by Paul and Barnabas from Antioch-in-Pisidia during the apostle's first missionary journey (Acts 13 : 50, 51). Here they were persecuted by the Jews, and being driven from the city, they fled to Lystra. They afterwards returned to Iconium, and encouraged the church which had been founded there (14 : 21, 22). It was probably again visited by Paul during his third missionary journey along with Silas (18 : 23). It is the modern *Konieh*, at the foot of Mount Taurus, about 120 miles inland from the Mediterranean.

Id'alah—*snares* (?)—a city near the west border of Zebulun (Josh. 19 : 15). It has been identified with the modern *Jeida*, in the valley of Kishon.

Id'do. (1.) *Timely* (1 Chr. 6 : 21). A Gershonite Levite.

(2.) *Lovely.* The son of Zechariah (1 Chr. 27 : 21), the ruler of Manasseh in David's time.

(3.) *Timely.* The father of Ahinadab, who was one of Solomon's purveyors (1 Kings 4 : 14).

(4.) *Lovely.* A prophet of Judah who wrote the history of Rehoboam and Abijah (2 Chr. 12 : 15). He has been identified with Oded (2 Chr. 15 : 1).

(5.) *Lovely.* The father of Berachiah, and grandfather of the prophet Zechariah (Zech. 1 : 1, 7). He returned from Babylon (Neh. 12 : 4).

Idol. (1.) Heb. *âven*, "nothingness;" "vanity" (Isa. 66 : 3; 41 : 29; Deut. 32 : 21; 1 Kings 16 : 13; Ps. 31 : 6; Jer. 8 : 19, etc.).

(2.) *'Elil*, "a thing of naught" (Ps. 97 : 7; Isa. 19 : 3); a word of contempt, used of the gods of Noph (Ezek. 30 : 13).

(3.) *'Emâh*, "terror," in allusion to the hideous form of idols (Jer. 50 : 38).

(4.) *Miphletzeth*, "a fright;" "horror" (1 Kings 15 : 13; 2 Chr. 15 : 16).

(5.) *Bôsheth*, "shame;" "shameful thing" (Jer. 11 : 13; Hos. 9 : 10); as characterizing the obscenity of the worship of Baal.

(6.) *Gillûlim*, also a word of contempt, "dung;" "refuse" (Ezek. 16 : 36; 20 : 8; Deut. 29 : 17, marg.).

(7.) *Shikkûts*, "filth;" "impurity" (Ezek. 37 : 23; Nah. 3 : 6).

(8.) *Sêmĕl*, "likeness;" "a carved image" (Deut. 4 : 16).

(9.) *Tsĕlĕm*, "a shadow" (Dan. 3 : 1; 1 Sam. 6 : 5), as distinguished from the "likeness," or the exact counterpart.

(10.) *Temûnâh*, "similitude" (Deut. 4 : 12–19). Here Moses forbids the several forms of Gentile idolatry.

(11.) *'Atsab*, "a figure;" from the root "to fashion," "to labour;" denoting that idols are the result of man's labour (Isa. 48 : 5; Ps. 139 : 24, "wicked way;" literally, as some translate, "way of an idol").

(12.) *Tsîr*, "a form;" "shape" (Isa. 45 : 16).

(13.) *Matztzêbâh*, a "statue" set up (Jer. 43 : 13); a memorial stone like that erected by Jacob (Gen. 28 : 18; 31 : 45; 35 : 14, 20), by Joshua (4 : 9), and by Samuel (1 Sam. 7 : 12). It is the name given to the statues of Baal (2 Kings 3 : 2; 10 : 27).

(14.) *Hammânîm*, "sun-images." *Hamman* is a synonym of Baal, the sun-god of the Phœnicians (2 Chr. 34 : 4, 7; 14 : 3, 5; Isa. 17 : 8).

(15.) *Maskîth*, "device" (Lev. 26 : 1; Num. 33 : 52). In Lev. 26 : 1, the words "image of stone" (A.V.) denote "a stone or cippus with the image of an idol, as Baal, Astarte, etc." In Ezek. 8 : 12, "chambers of imagery" (*maskith*), are "chambers of which the walls are painted with the figures of idols;" comp. ver. 10, 11.

(16.) *Pĕsĕl*, "a graven" or "carved image" (Isa. 44 : 10–20). It denotes also a figure cast in metal (Deut. 7 : 25; 27 : 15; Isa. 40 : 19; 44 : 10).

(17.) *Massekah*, "a molten image" (Deut. 9 : 12; Judg. 17 : 3, 4).

(18.) *Terâphîm*, pl., "images," family gods (*penates*) worshipped by Abram's kindred (Josh. 24 : 14). Put by Michal in David's bed (Judg. 17 : 5; 18 : 14, 17, 18, 20; 1 Sam. 19 : 13).

"Nothing can be more instructive and significant than this multiplicity and variety of words designating the instruments and inventions of idolatry."

Idol'atry, image-worship or divine honour paid to any created object. Paul describes the origin of idolatry in Rom.

1 : 21-25 : men forsook God, and sank into ignorance and moral corruption (1 : 28).

The *forms* of idolatry are—(1.) *Fetishism*, or the worship of trees, rivers, hills, stones, etc.

(2.) *Nature worship*, the worship of the sun, moon, and stars, as the supposed powers of nature.

(3.) *Hero worship*, the worship of deceased ancestors, or of heroes.

In Scripture, idolatry is regarded as of heathen origin, and as being imported among the Hebrews through contact with heathen nations. The first allusion to idolatry is in the account of Rachel stealing her father's teraphim (Gen. 31 : 19), which were the relics of the worship of other gods by Laban's progenitors "on the other side of the river in old time" (Josh. 24 : 2). During their long residence in Egypt the Hebrews fell into idolatry, and it was long before they were delivered from it (Josh. 24 : 14 ; Ezek. 20 : 7). Many a token of God's displeasure fell upon them because of this sin.

The idolatry learned in Egypt was probably rooted out from among the people during the forty years' wanderings; but when the Jews entered Palestine, they came into contact with the monuments and associations of the idolatry of the old Canaanitish races, and showed a constant tendency to depart from the living God and follow the idolatrous practices of those heathen nations. It was their great national sin, which was only effectually rebuked by the Babylonian exile. That exile finally purified the Jews of all idolatrous tendencies.

The first and second commandments are directed against idolatry of every form. Individuals and communities were equally amenable to the rigorous code. The individual offender was devoted to destruction (Ex. 22 : 20). His nearest relatives were not only bound to denounce him and deliver him up to punishment (Deut. 13 : 2-10), but their hands were to strike the first blow when, on the evidence of two witnesses at least, he was stoned (Deut. 17 : 2-5). To attempt to seduce others to false worship was a crime of equal enormity (13 :

6-10). An idolatrous nation shared the same fate. No facts are more strongly declared in the Old Testament than that the extermination of the Canaanites was the punishment of their idolatry (Ex. 34 : 15, 16 ; Deut. 7 ; 12 : 29-31 ; 20 : 17), and that the calamities of the Israelites were due to the same cause (Jer. 2 : 17). "A city guilty of idolatry was looked upon as a cancer in the state; it was considered to be in rebellion, and treated according to the laws of war. Its inhabitants and all their cattle were put to death." Jehovah was the theocratic King of Israel, the civil Head of the commonwealth, and therefore to an Israelite idolatry was a state offence (1 Sam. 15 : 23), high treason. On taking possession of the land, the Jews were commanded to destroy all traces of every kind of the existing idolatry of the Canaanites (Ex. 23 : 24, 32 ; 34 : 13 ; Deut. 7 : 5, 25 ; 12 : 1-3).

In the New Testament the term idolatry is used to designate covetousness (Matt. 6 : 24 ; Luke 16 : 13 ; Col. 3 : 5 ; Eph. 5 : 5).

Idumæ′a, the Greek form of Edom (Isa. 34 : 5, 6 ; Ezek. 35 : 15 ; 36 : 5, but in R.V. "Edom"). (See EDOM.)

I′gal—*avengers.* (1.) Num. 13 : 7, one of the spies of the tribe of Issachar. (2.) Son of Nathan of Zobah, and one of David's warriors (2 Sam. 23 : 36). (3.) 1 Chr. 3 : 22.

I′im—*ruins.* (1.) A city in the south of Judah (Josh. 15 : 29).

(2.) One of the stations of the Israelites in the wilderness (Num. 33 : 45).

I′je-ab′arim — *ruins of Abarim* — the forty-seventh station of the Israelites in the wilderness, "in the border of Moab" (Num. 33 : 44).

I′jon—*a ruin*—a city of Naphtali, captured by Ben-hadad of Syria at the instance of Asa (1 Kings 15 : 20), and afterwards by Tiglath-pileser of Assyria (2 Kings 15 : 29) in the reign of Pekah ; now *el-Khîam.*

I′lai, an Ahohite, one of David's chief warriors (1 Chr. 11 : 29); called also Zalmon (2 Sam. 23 : 28).

Illyr′icum, a country to the north-west of Macedonia, on the eastern shores of the Adriatic, now almost wholly comprehended in Dalmatia, a name formerly given to the southern part of Illyricum (2 Tim. 4:10). It was traversed by Paul in his third missionary journey (Rom. 15:19). It was the farthest district he had reached in preaching the gospel of Christ. This reference to Illyricum is in harmony with Acts 20:2, inasmuch as the apostle's journey over the parts of Macedonia would bring him to the borders of Illyricum.

Im'agery, only in the phrase "chambers of his imagery" (Ezek. 8:12). (See CHAMBER.)

Im'la—*replenisher*—the father of Micaiah the prophet (2 Chr. 18:7, 8).

Imman'uel—*God with us.* In the Old Testament it occurs only in Isa. 7:14 and 8:8. Most Christian interpreters have regarded these words as directly and exclusively a prophecy of our Saviour—an interpretation borne out by the words of the evangelist Matthew (1:23).

Im'mer—*talkative.* (1.) The head of the sixteenth priestly order (1 Chr. 24:14).

(2.) Jer. 20:1.

(3.) Ezra 2:37; Neh. 7:40.

(4.) Ezra 2:59; Neh. 7:61.

(5.) The father of Zadok (Neh. 3:29).

Immortal'ity, perpetuity of existence. The doctrine of immortality is taught in the Old Testament. It is plainly implied in the writings of Moses (Gen. 5:22, 24; 25:8; 37:35; 47:9; 49:29, comp. Heb. 11:13–16; Ex. 3:6, comp. Matt. 22:23). It is more clearly and fully taught in the later books (Isa. 14:9; Ps. 17:15; 49:15; 73:24). It was thus a doctrine obviously well known to the Jews.

With the full revelation of the gospel this doctrine was "brought to light" (2 Tim. 1:10; 1 Cor. 15; 2 Cor. 5:1–6; 1 Thess. 4:13–18).

Imputa'tion is used to designate any action or word or thing as reckoned to a person. Thus in doctrinal language (1) the sin of Adam is imputed to all his descendants—*i.e.*, it is reckoned as theirs, and they are dealt with therefore as guilty; (2) the righteousness of Christ is imputed to them that believe in him, or so attributed to them as to be considered their own; and (3) our sins are imputed to Christ—*i.e.*, he assumed our "law-place," undertook to answer the

demands of justice for our sins. In all these cases the nature of imputation is the same (Rom. 5:12–19; comp. Philemon 18, 19).

Incarna'tion, that act of grace whereby Christ took our human nature into union with his Divine Person—became man. Christ is both God and man. Human attributes and actions are predicated of him, and he of whom they are predicated is God. A Divine Person was united to a human nature (Acts 20:28; Rom. 8:32; 1 Cor. 2:8; Heb. 2:11–14; 1 Tim. 3:16; Gal. 4:4, etc.). The union is hypostatical—*i.e.*, is personal; the two natures are not mixed or confounded—and it is perpetual.

In'cense, a fragrant composition prepared by the "art of the apothecary." It consisted of four ingredients "beaten small" (Ex. 30:34–36). That which was not thus prepared was called "strange incense" (30:9). It was offered along with every meat-offering; and besides was daily offered on the golden altar in the holy place, and on the great day of atonement was burnt by the high priest in the holy of holies (30:7, 8). It was the symbol of prayer (Ps. 141:1, 2; Rev. 5:8; 8:3, 4).

In'dia occurs only in Esther 1:1 and 8:9, where the extent of the dominion of the Persian king is described. The country so designated here is not the peninsula of Hindustan, but the country surrounding the Indus—the Punjâb.

The people and the products of India were well known to the Jews, who seem to have carried on an active trade with that country (Ezek. 27:15, 24).

Inn, in the modern sense, unknown in the East. The khans or caravanserais, which correspond to the European inn, are not alluded to in the Old Testament. The "inn" mentioned in Ex. 4:24 was just the halting-place of the caravan. In later times khans were erected for the accommodation of travellers. In Luke 2:7 the word there so rendered denotes a place for *loosing* the beasts of their burdens. It is rendered "guest-chamber" in Mark 14:14 and Luke 22:11. In Luke 10:34 the word so rendered is different. That inn had an "inn-keeper," who attended to the wants of travellers.

Ink'horn. The Hebrew word so rendered means simply a round vessel or cup for containing ink, which was generally worn by writers in the girdle (Ezek. 9 : 2, 3, 11). The word "inkhorn" was used by

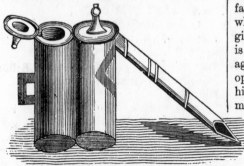

INKHORN AND REED PEN.

the translators, because in former times in this country horns were used for containing ink.

Inspira'tion, that extraordinary or supernatural divine influence vouchsafed to those who wrote the Holy Scriptures, rendering their writings infallible. "All scripture is given by inspiration of God " (R. V., "Every scripture inspired of God "), 2 Tim. 3 : 16. This is true of all the "sacred writings," not in the sense of their being works of genius or of supernatural insight, but as "theopneustic," *i.e.,* "breathed into by God " in such a sense that the writers were supernaturally guided to express exactly what God intended them to express as a revelation of his mind and will. The testimony of the sacred writers themselves abundantly demonstrates this truth; and if they are infallible as teachers of doctrine, then the doctrine of *plenary* inspiration must be accepted. There are no errors in the Bible as it came from God—none have been *proved* to exist. Difficulties and phenomena we cannot explain are not errors. All these books of the Old and New Testaments are inspired. We do not say that they *contain,* but that they *are,* the Word of God. The gift of inspiration rendered the writers the organs of God, for the infallible communication of his mind and will, in the very

manner and *words* in which it was originally given.

As to the *nature* of inspiration, we have no information. This only we know, it rendered the writers infallible. They were all equally inspired, and are all equally infallible. There are other divine influences which operate among men from which this gift is to be distinguished. Thus (1) it is distinguished from God's providential agency, which is always and everywhere operative; (2) it is distinguished also from his gracious operation on the hearts of men. Inspiration is a supernatural agency, only rendering those who are the subjects of it infallible in their character as teachers—infallible *only* when thus acting as the spokesmen of God. Their inspiration was limited to the work to which they were specially called—namely, the communication, of God's will to men; and in this they were infallible and perfect, so that the books they wrote constitute the very Word of God.

The inspiration of the sacred writers "did not change their characters. It did not make them more refined or cultivated, more intellectual or logical, more impassioned and eloquent. They retained all their peculiarities as thinkers or writers. If the writer was a Hebrew, he wrote in the Hebrew language; if a Greek, he wrote in that language. If he lived in the time of Moses or Isaiah, he wrote Hebrew in its purity. If he belonged to the time of the Captivity, he wrote Hebrew with all the idiomatic and grammatical peculiarities which the language had at that time assumed. If he wrote Greek, it was the Greek which he and his contemporaries were accustomed to use. If the subject of inspiration was a shepherd, he wrote as a shepherd; if a man of education, he wrote as an educated man. If his mind was logical and his style of writing argumentative, he retained this characteristic when writing under the guidance of the Spirit. And so of other mental qualities and peculiarities. Hence it is that the Bible, containing as it does the writings of about forty different writers, presents the same diversity of style and manner as the productions of any like number of un-inspired men. The effect of inspiration was *only* to preserve the writers from error —to make them infallible as teachers." (See BIBLE; WORD OF GOD.)

Interces'sion of Christ. Christ's priestly office consists of these two parts— (1) the offering up of himself as a sacrifice, and (2) making continual intercession for us.

When on earth he made intercession for his people (Luke 23 : 34; John 17 : 20; Heb. 5 : 7); but now he exercises this function of his priesthood in heaven, where he is said to appear in the presence of God for us (Heb. 9 : 12, 24).

His advocacy with the Father for his people rests on the basis of his own all-perfect sacrifice. Thus he pleads for and obtains the fulfilment of all the promises of the everlasting covenant (1 John 2 : 1; John 17 : 24; Heb. 7 : 25). He can be "touched with the feeling of our infirmi-ties," and is both a merciful and a faith-ful high priest (Heb. 2 : 17, 18; 4 : 15, 16).

This intercession is an essential part of his mediatorial work. Through him we have "access" to the Father (John 14 : 6; Eph. 2 : 18; 3 : 12). "The communion of his people with the Father will ever be sustained through him as mediatorial Priest" (Ps. 110 : 4; Rev. 7 : 17).

Interces'sion of the Spirit (Rom. 8 : 26, 27; John 14 : 26). "Christ is a royal Priest (Zech. 6 : 13). From the same throne, as King, he dispenses his Spirit to all the objects of his care, while as Priest he intercedes for them. The Spirit acts for him, taking only of his things. They both act with one consent—Christ as prin-cipal, the Spirit as his agent. Christ inter-cedes for us, without us, as our advocate in heaven, according to the provisions of the everlasting covenant. The Holy Spirit works upon our minds and hearts, en-lightening and quickening, and thus de-termining our desires 'according to the will of God,' as our advocate within us. The work of the one is complementary to that of the other, and together they form a complete whole."—Hodge's *Outlines of Theology.*

Iphedei'ah—*set free by Jehovah*—a chief of the tribe of Benjamin (1 Chr. 8 : 25).

I'ra—*citizen; wakeful.* (1.) A Tekoite, one of David's thirty warriors (2 Sam. 23 : 26).

(2.) An Ithrite, also one of David's heroes (2 Sam. 23 : 38).

(3.) A Jairite and priest, a royal chap-lain (2 Sam. 20 : 26) or confidential adviser (comp. 2 Sam. 8 : 18; 1 Chr. 18 : 17).

I'rad—*runner; wild ass*—one of the antediluvian patriarchs, the father of Me-hujael (Gen. 4 : 18), and grandson of Cain.

I'ram—*citizen*—chief of an Edomite tribe in Mount Seir (Gen. 36 : 43).

'Ir'ha-he'res—according to some MSS., meaning "city of destruction." Other MSS. read *'Irhaḥâres;* rendered "city of the sun"—Isa. 19 : 18, where alone the word occurs. This name may probably refer to Heliopolis. The prophecy here points to a time when the Jews would so increase in number there as that the city would fall under their influence. This might be in the time of the Ptolemies. (See ON.)

I'ron. Tubal-Cain is the first-mentioned worker in iron (Gen. 4 : 22). The Egyptians wrought it at Sinai before the Exodus. David prepared it in great abundance for the temple (1 Chr. 22 : 3 : 29 : 7). The merchants of Dan and Javan brought it to the market of Tyre (Ezek. 27 : 19). Various instruments are mentioned as made of iron (Deut. 27 : 5; 19 : 5; Josh. 17 : 16, 18; 1 Sam. 17 : 7; 2 Sam. 12 : 31; 2 Kings 6 : 5, 6; 1 Chr. 22 : 3; Isa. 10 : 34).

Figuratively, a yoke of iron (Deut. 28 : 48) denotes hard service; a rod of iron (Ps. 2 : 9), a stern government; a pillar of iron (Jer. 1 : 18), a strong support; a fur-nace of iron (Deut. 4 : 20), severe labour; a bar of iron (Job 40 : 18), strength; fetters of iron (Ps. 107 : 10), affliction; giving silver for iron (Isa. 60 : 17), prosperity.

Irriga'tion. As streams were few in Palestine, water was generally stored up in winter in reservoirs, and distributed through gardens in numerous rills, which could easily be turned or diverted by the foot (Deut. 11 : 10).

For purposes of irrigation, water was raised from streams or pools by water-wheels, or by a *shadûf*, commonly used on the banks of the Nile to the present day.

I'saac—*laughter*. (1.) Israel, or the kingdom of the ten tribes (Amos 7 : 9, 16).

(2.) The only son of Abraham by Sarah. He was the longest lived of the three patriarchs (Gen. 21 : 1-3). He was circumcised when eight days old (4-7); and when he was probably two years old a great feast was held in connection with his being weaned.

The next memorable event in his life is that connected with the command of God given to Abraham to offer him up as a sacrifice on a mountain in the land of Moriah (Gen. 22). (See ABRAHAM.) When he was forty years of age Rebekah was chosen for his wife (Gen. 24). After the death and burial of his father he took up his residence at Beer-lahai-roi (25 : 7-11), where his two sons, Esau and Jacob, were born (21-26), the former of whom seems to have been his favourite son (27, 28).

In consequence of a famine (Gen. 26 : 1) Isaac went to Gerar, where he practised deception as to his relation to Rebekah, imitating the conduct of his father in Egypt (12 : 12-20) and in Gerar (20 : 2). The Philistine king rebuked him for his prevarication.

After sojourning for some time in the land of the Philistines, he returned to Beersheba, where God gave him fresh assurance of covenant blessing, and where Abimelech entered into a covenant of peace with him.

The next chief event in his life was the blessing of his sons (Gen. 27 : 1). He died at **Mamre,** "being old and full of days" (35 : 27-29)—one hundred and eighty years old—and was buried in the cave of Machpelah.

In the New Testament reference is made to his having been "offered up" by his father (Heb. 11 : 17; James 2 : 21), and to his blessing his sons (Heb. 11 : 20). As the child of promise, he is contrasted with Ishmael (Rom. 9 : 7, 10; Gal. 4 : 28; Heb. 11 : 18).

Isaac is "at once a counterpart of his father in simple devoutness and purity of life, and a contrast in his passive weakness of character, which in part, at least, may

have sprung from his relations to his mother and wife. After the expulsion of Ishmael and Hagar, Isaac had no competitor, and grew up in the shade of Sarah's tent, moulded into feminine softness by habitual submission to her strong, loving will." His life was so quiet and uneventful that it was spent "within the circle of a few miles; so guileless that he let Jacob overreach him rather than disbelieve his assurance; so tender that his mother's death was the poignant sorrow of years; so patient and gentle that peace with his neighbours was dearer than even such a coveted possession as a well of living water dug by his own men; so grandly obedient that he put his life at his father's disposal; so firm in his reliance on God that his greatest concern through life was to honour the divine promise given to his race."—Geikie's *Hours, etc.*

Isa'iah (Heb. *Yesha'yâhu*—*i.e.*, "the salvation of Jehovah"). (1.) The son of Amoz (Isa. 1 : 1; 2 : 1), who was apparently a man of humble rank. His wife was called "the prophetess" (8 : 3), either because she was endowed with the prophetic gift, like Deborah (Judg. 4 : 4) and Huldah (2 Kings 22 : 14-20), or simply because she was the wife of "the prophet" (Isa. 38 : 1). He had two sons, who bore symbolical names.

He exercised the functions of his office during the reigns of Uzziah (or Azariah), Jotham, Ahaz, and Hezekiah (1 : 1). Uzziah reigned fifty-two years (B.C. 810-759), and Isaiah must have begun his career a few years before Uzziah's death — probably B.C. 762. He lived till the fourteenth year of Hezekiah, and in all likelihood outlived that monarch (who died B.C. 698), and may have been contemporary for some years with Manasseh. Thus Isaiah may have prophesied for the long period of at least sixty-four years.

His first call to the prophetical office is not recorded. A second call came to him "in the year that King Uzziah died" (Isa. 6 : 1). He exercised his ministry in a spirit of uncompromising firmness and boldness in regard to all that bore on the interests of religion. He conceals nothing and keeps nothing back from fear of man. He was also noted for his spirituality and for his deep-toned reverence toward "the holy One of Israel."

In early youth Isaiah must have been moved by the invasion of Israel by the Assyrian monarch Pul (*q.v.*)—2 Kings 15 : 19; and again, twenty years later, when he had already entered on his office, by the invasion of Tiglath-pileser and his career of conquest. Ahaz, king of Judah, at this crisis refused to co-operate with the kings of Israel and Syria in opposition to the Assyrians, and was on that account attacked and defeated by Rezin of Damascus and Pekah of Samaria (2 Kings 16 : 5; 2 Chr. 28 : 5, 6). Ahaz, thus humbled, sided with Assyria, and sought the aid of Tiglath-pileser against Israel and Syria. The consequence was that Rezin and Pekah were conquered and many of the people carried captive to Assyria (2 Kings 15 : 29; 16 : 9; 1 Chr. 5 : 26). Soon after this Shalmaneser determined wholly to subdue the kingdom of Israel. Samaria was taken and destroyed (B.C. 722). So long as Ahaz reigned, the kingdom of Judah was unmolested by the Assyrian power; but on his accession to the throne, Hezekiah (B.C. 726), who "rebelled against the king of Assyria" (2 Kings 18 : 7), in which he was encouraged by Isaiah, who exhorted the people to place all their dependence on Jehovah (Isa. 10 : 24; 37 : 6), entered into an alliance with the king of Egypt (Isa. 30 : 2–4). This led the king of Assyria to threaten the king of Judah, and at length to invade the land. Sennacherib (B.C. 701) led a powerful army into Palestine. Hezekiah was reduced to despair, and submitted to the Assyrians (2 Kings 18 : 14–16). But after a brief interval war broke out again, and again Sennacherib (*q.v.*) led an army into Palestine, one detachment of which threatened Jerusalem (Isa. 36 : 2–22; 37 : 8). Isaiah on that occasion encouraged Hezekiah to resist the Assyrians (37 : 1–7), whereupon Sennacherib sent a threatening letter to Hezekiah, which he "spread before the Lord" (37 : 14). The judgment of God now fell on the Assyrian host. "Like Xerxes in Greece, Sennacherib never recovered from the shock of the disaster in

Judah. He made no more expeditions against either Southern Palestine or Egypt." The remaining years of Hezekiah's reign were peaceful (2 Chr. 32 : 23 27–29). Isaiah probably lived to its close, and possibly into the reign of Manasseh, but the time and manner of his death are unknown. There is a tradition that he suffered martyrdom in the heathen reaction in the time of Manasseh (*q.v.*).

(2.) One of the heads of the singers in the time of David (1 Chr. 25 : 3, 15, "Jeshaiah").

(3.) A Levite (1 Chr. 26 : 25).

(4.) Ezra 8 : 7.

(5.) Neh. 11 : 7.

Isaiah, The Book of, consists of prophecies delivered (Isa. 1) in the reign of Uzziah (1–5), (2) of Jotham (6), (3) Ahaz (7–14 : 27), (4) the first half of Hezekiah's reign (14 : 28–35), (5) the second half of Hezekiah's reign (36–66). Thus, counting from the fourth year before Uzziah's death (B.C. 762) to the last year of Hezekiah (B.C. 698), Isaiah's ministry extended over a period of sixty-four years. He may, however, have survived Hezekiah, and may have perished in the way indicated above.

The book, as a whole, has been divided into three main parts : (1.) The first thirty-five chapters, almost wholly prophetic—Israel's enemy Assyria—present the Messiah as a mighty Ruler and King. (2.) Four chapters are historical (36–39), relating to the times of Hezekiah. (3.) Prophetical (40–66)—Israel's enemy Babylon—describing the Messiah as a suffering victim, meek and lowly.

The genuineness of the section Isa. 40–66 has been keenly opposed by able critics. They assert that it must be the production of a deutero-Isaiah, who lived toward the close of the Babylonian captivity. This theory was originated by Koppe, a German writer at the close of the last century. There are other portions of the book also (*e.g.*, ch. 13; 24–27; and certain verses in ch. 14 and 21) which they attribute to some other prophet than Isaiah. Thus they say that some five or seven, or even more, unknown prophets had a hand in the production of this book. The considerations which have led to such a result are various :—(1.) They cannot, as some say, conceive it possible that Isaiah, living in B.C. 700, could foretell the appearance and the exploits of a prince called Cyrus, who would set the Jews free from captivity one hundred and seventy years after. (2.) It is alleged that the prophet takes the time of the Captivity as his standpoint, and speaks of it as then present ; and (3) that there is such a difference between the style and language of the closing section (40–66) and those of the preceding chapters as to necessitate a different authorship, and lead to the conclusion that there were at least two Isaiahs. But even granting the fact of a great diversity of style and language, this will not necessitate the conclusion attempted to be drawn from it. The diversity of subjects treated of and the peculiarities of the prophet's position at the time the prophecies were uttered will sufficiently account for this.

The arguments in favour of the unity of the book are quite conclusive. When the LXX. version was made (about B.C. 250) the entire contents of the book were ascribed to Isaiah, the son of Amoz. It is not called in question, moreover, that in the time of our Lord the book existed in the form in which we now have it. Many prophecies in the disputed portions are quoted in the New Testament as the words of Isaiah (Matt. 3:3; Luke 3:4–6; 4: 16–20; John 12:38; Acts 8:28; Rom. 10:16–21). Universal and persistent tradition has ascribed the whole book to one author.

Besides this, the internal evidence—the similarity in the language and style, in the thoughts and images and rhetorical ornaments—all points to the same conclusion ; and its local colouring and allusions show that it is obviously of Palestinian origin. The theory therefore of a double authorship of the book, much less of a manifold authorship, cannot be maintained. The book, with all the diversity of its contents, is one, and is, we believe, the production of the great prophet whose name it bears.

Is'cah—*spy*—the daughter of Haran and sister of Milcah and Lot (Gen. 11:29, 31).

Iscar'iot. (See JUDAS.)

Ish'bak—*leaving*—one of Abraham's sons by Keturah (Gen. 25:2).

Ish'bi-be'nob—*my seat at Nob*—one of the Rephaim, whose spear was three hundred shekels in weight. He was slain by Abishai (2 Sam. 21:16, 17).

Ish-bo'sheth—*man of shame* or *humiliation*—the youngest of Saul's four sons, and the only one who survived him (2 Sam. 2–4). His name was originally Eshbaal (1 Chr. 8:33; 9:39). He was about forty years of age when his father and three brothers fell at the battle of Gilboa. Through the influence of Abner, Saul's cousin, he was acknowledged as successor to the throne of Saul, and ruled over all Israel, except the tribe of Judah (over whom David was king), for two years, having Mahanaim, on the east of Jordan, as his capital (2 Sam. 2:9). After a troubled and uncertain reign he was murdered by his guard, who stabbed him while he was asleep on his couch at mid-day (2 Sam. 4:5–7); and having cut off his head, presented it to David, who sternly rebuked them for this cold-blooded murder, and ordered them to be immediately executed (9–12).

I'shi—*my husband*—a symbolical name used in Hos. 2:16. (See BAALI.)

Ish'mael—*God hears.* (1.) Abraham's eldest son, by Hagar the concubine (Gen. 16:15; 17:23). He was born at Mamre, when Abraham was eighty-six years of age, eleven years after his arrival in Canaan (16:3; 21:5). At the age of thirteen he was circumcised (17:25). He grew up a true child of the desert, wild and wayward. On the occasion of the weaning of Isaac his rude and wayward spirit broke out in expressions of insult and mockery (21: 9, 10); and Sarah, discovering this, said to Abraham, "Expel this slave and her son." Influenced by a divine admonition, Abraham dismissed Hagar and her son with no more than a skin of water and some bread. The narrative describing this act is one of the most beautiful and touching incidents of patriarchal life (Gen. 21:14–16). (See HAGAR.)

Ishmael settled in the land of Paran, a region lying between Canaan and the mountains of Sinai; and "God was with him, and he became a great archer" (Gen. 21: 9–21). He became a great desert chief, but of his history little is recorded. He was about ninety years of age when his father Abraham died, in connection with whose burial he once more for a moment re-appears. On this occasion the two brothers met after being long separated. "Isaac with his hundreds of household slaves, Ishmael with his troops of wild retainers and half-savage allies, in all the state of a Bedouin prince, gathered before the cave of Machpelah, in the midst of the men of Heth, to pay the last duties to the 'father of the faithful,' would make a notable sub-ject for an artist" (Gen. 25:9). Of the after events of his life but little is known. He died at the age of one hundred and thirty-seven years, but where and when are unknown (25:17). He had twelve sons, who became the founders of so many Arab tribes or colonies—the Ishmaelites—who spread over the wide desert spaces of Nor-thern Arabia from the Red Sea to the Eu-phrates (Gen. 37:25, 27, 28; 39:1), "their hand against every man, and every man's hand against them."

(2.) The son of Nethaniah, "of the seed royal" (Jer. 40:8, 15). He plotted against Gedaliah, and treacherously put him and others to death. He carried off many captives, "and departed to go over to the Ammonites."

Ishma′iah—*heard by Jehovah.* (1.) A Gibeonite who joined David at Ziklag, "a hero among the thirty and over the thirty" (1 Chr. 12:4).

(2.) Son of Obadiah, and viceroy of Zebu-lun under David and Solomon (1 Chr. 27:19).

Ish′meelites (Gen. 37:28; 39:1, A.V.) should be "Ishmaelites," as in the Revised Version.

Ish′tob—*man of Tob*—one of the small Syrian kingdoms which together consti-tuted Aram (2 Sam. 10:6, 8).

Island (Heb. *′i*, "dry land," as opposed to water) occurs in its usual signification (Isa. 42:4, 10, 12, 15, comp. Jer. 47:4), but more frequently simply denotes a maritime region or sea-coast (Isa. 20:6, R.V., "coast-land;" 23:2, 6; Jer. 2:10; Ezek. 27:6, 7). (See CHITTIM.) The shores of the Medi-

terranean are called the "islands of the sea" (Isa. 11:11), or the "isles of the Gen-tiles" (Gen. 10:5), and sometimes simply "isles" (Ps. 72:10; Ezek. 26:15, 18; 27: 3, 35; Dan. 11:18).

Is′rael, the name conferred on Jacob after the great prayer-struggle at Peniel (Gen. 32:28), because "as a prince he had power with God and prevailed." (See JACOB.) This is the common name given to Jacob's descendants. The whole people of the twelve tribes are called "Israelites," the "children of Israel" (Josh. 3:17; 7: 25; Judg. 8:27; Jer. 3:21), and the "house of Israel" (Ex. 16:31; 40:38).

This name Israel is sometimes used em-phatically for the *true* Israel (Ps. 73:1; Isa. 45:17; 49:3; John 1:47; Rom. 9:6; 11:26).

After the death of Saul the ten tribes arrogated to themselves this name, as if they were the whole nation (2 Sam. 2:9, 10, 17, 28; 3:10, 17; 19:40–43), and the kings of the ten tribes were called "kings of Israel," while the kings of the two tribes were called "kings of Judah."

After the Exile the name Israel was as-sumed as designating the entire nation.

Is′rael, Kingdom of (B.C. 975–B.C. 722). Soon after the death of Solomon, Ahijah's prophecy (1 Kings 11:31–35) was fulfilled, and the kingdom was rent in twain. Reho-boam, the son and successor of Solomon, was scarcely seated on his throne when the old jealousies between Judah and the other tribes broke out anew, and Jeroboam was sent for from Egypt by the malcontents (12:2, 3). Rehoboam insolently refused to lighten the burdensome taxation and ser-vices which his father had imposed on his subjects (12:4), and the rebellion became complete. Ephraim and all Israel raised the old cry, "Every man to his tents, O Israel" (2 Sam. 20:1). Rehoboam fled to Jerusalem (1 Kings 12:1–18; 2 Chr. 10), and Jeroboam was proclaimed king over all Israel at Shechem, Judah and Benja-min remaining faithful to Solomon's son. War, with varying success, was carried on between the two kingdoms for about sixty years, till Jehoshaphat entered into an alliance with the house of Ahab.

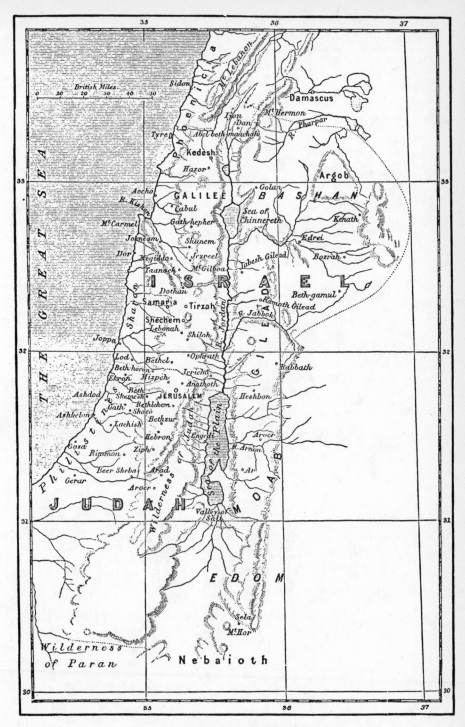

THE KINGDOMS OF JUDAH AND ISRAEL.

Dura-tion of Reign	KINGS OF ISRAEL.	Commence-ment of Reign.		KINGS OF JUDAH.	Dura-tion of Reign
		Margin of A.V.	Ussher		
22	Jeroboam (1 Kings 12:20, 25-33; 13:1-34; 14:1-20).	975	976	Rehoboam (1 Kings 12:21-24; 14:21-31; 2 Chr. 10:17-ch. 12).	17
		958	959	Abijah (1 Kings 15:1-8; 2 Chr. 13).	3
		955	956	Asa (1 Kings 15:9-24; 2 Chr. 14:1 to 16:14).	41
2	Nadab (1 Kings 15:25-27, 31).	954	955		
24	Baasha (1 Kings 15:28-34; 16:1-7).	953	954		
2	Elah (1 Kings 16:8-14).	930	930		
0	Zimri (1 Kings 16:11, 12, 15-20).	929	930		
12	Omri (1 Kings 16:23-28).	929	930		
22	Ahab (1 Kings 16:29 to 22:40).	918	919		
		914	915	Jehoshaphat (1 Kings 22:41-50; 2 Chr. 17:1 to 21:1).	25
2	Ahaziah (1 Kings 22:51-53; 2 Kings 1).	898	896		
12	Jehoram (2 Kings 3:1 to 9:26).	896	895		
		892	891	Jehoram (2 Kings 8:16-24; 2 Chr. 21).	8
		885	884	Ahaziah (2 Kings 8:25-29; 9:16-29; 2 Chr. 22:1-9).	1
28	Jehu (2 Kings 9:1-37; 10:1-36).	884	883	Athaliah (2 Kings 11:1-3; 2 Chr. 22:10-12).	6
		878	877	Jehoash (2 Kings 11:4-ch. 12; 2 Chr. 23, 24).	40
17	Jehoahaz (2 Kings 13:1-9).	856	855		
16	Jehoash (2 Kings 13:10-25; 14:8-16).	841	839		
		839	837	Amaziah (2 Kings 14:1-20; 2 Chr. 25).	29
41	Jeroboam II. (2 Kin. 14:23-29).	825	823		
		810	808	Uzziah or Azariah (2 Kings 14:21, 22; 15:1-7; 2 Chr. 26).	52
11	Interregnum.				
0	Zachariah (2 Kings 15:8-12).	773	771		
0	Shallum (2 Kings 15:13-15).	772	770		
10	Menahem (2 Kings 15:16-22).	772	770		
2	Pekahiah (2 Kings 15:23-26).	761	759		
20	Pekah (2 Kin. 15:27-31; 16:5).	759	757		
		758	756	Jotham (2 Kings 15:32-38; 2 Chr. 27).	16
		742	741	Ahaz (2 Kings 16; 2 Chr. 28).	16
9	Second Interregnum.				
9	Hoshea (2 Kings 17:1-6).	730	730		
		726	726	Hezekiah (2 Kings 18:1 to 20:21; 2 Chr. 29:1 to 32:33).	29
	Samaria taken (2 Kings 17, 18).	721	721		
		698	697	Manasseh (2 Kings 21:1-18; 2 Chr. 33:1-20).	55
		643	642	Amon (2 Kings 21:19-26; 2 Chr. 33:21-25).	2
		641	640	Josiah (2 Kings 22:1-20; 23:1-30; 2 Chr. 34, 35).	31
		610	609	Jehoahaz (2 Kings 23:31-33; 2 Chr. 36:1-4).	0
		610	609	Jehoiachim (2 Kings 23:34-37; 24:1-6; 2 Chr. 36:5-8).	11
		606	606	Captivity of two tribes (2 Kin. 24)	
		599	599	Jehoiachin or Coniah (2 Kings 24:8-16; 2 Chr. 36:9, 10).	0
		599	599	Zedekiah (2 Kings 24:17-20; 25:1-7; 2 Chr. 36:11-21).	11
		588	588	Jerusalem destroyed (2 Kin. 25)	

Extent of the kingdom. In the time of Solomon the area of Palestine, excluding the Phœnician territories on the shore of the Mediterranean, did not much exceed 13,000 square miles. The kingdom of Israel comprehended about 9,375 square miles. Shechem was the first capital of this kingdom (1 Kings 12 : 25), afterwards Tirza (14 : 17). Samaria was subsequently chosen as the capital. (16 : 24), and continued to be so till the destruction of the kingdom by the Assyrians (2 Kings 17 : 5). During the siege of Samaria (which lasted for three years) by the Assyrians, Shalmaneser died and was succeeded by Sargon, who himself thus records the capture of that city :—"Samaria I looked at, I captured ; 27,280 men who dwelt in it I carried away" (2 Kings 17 : 6) into Assyria. Thus after a duration of two hundred and fifty-three years the kingdom of the ten tribes came to an end. They were scattered throughout the East. (See CAPTIVITY.)

"Judah held its ground against Assyria for yet one hundred and twenty - three years, and became the rallying-point of the dispersed of every tribe, and eventually gave its name to the whole race. Those of the people who in the last struggle escaped into the territories of Judah or other neighbouring countries naturally looked to Judah as the head and home of their race. And when Judah itself was carried off to Babylon, many of the exiled Israelites joined them from Assyria, and swelled that immense population which made Babylonia a second Palestine."

After the deportation of the ten tribes, the deserted land was colonized by various eastern tribes, whom the king of Assyria sent thither (Ezra 4 : 2, 10 ; 2 Kings 17 : 24–29). (See KINGS.)

In contrast with the kingdom of Judah is that of Israel. (1.) "There was no fixed capital and no religious centre. (2.) The army was often insubordinate. (3.) The succession was constantly interrupted, so that out of nineteen kings there were no less than nine dynasties, each ushered in by a revolution. (4.) The authorized priests left the kingdom in a body, and the priesthood established by Jeroboam had no divine sanction and no promise ; it was corrupt at its very source." — (Maclean's *O. T. Hist.*)

Is'sachar—*hired*—(Gen. 30 : 18). "God hath given me," said Leah, "my hire (Heb. *sĕkhâri*)......and she called his name Issachar." He was Jacob's ninth son, and was born in Padan-aram (comp. 29 : 35). He had four sons at the going down into Egypt (46 : 13 ; Num. 26 : 23, 25).

Issachar, Tribe of, during the journey through the wilderness, along with Judah and Zebulun (Num. 2 : 5), marched on the east of the tabernacle. This tribe contained 54,400 fighting men when the census was taken at Sinai. After the entrance into the Promised Land, this tribe was one of the six which stood on Gerizim during the ceremony of the blessing and cursing (Deut. 27 : 12). The allotment of Issachar is described in Josh. 19 : 17-23. It included the plain of Esdraelon (=Jezreel), which was and still is the richest portion of Palestine (Deut. 33 : 18, 19 ; 1 Chr. 12 : 40).

The prophetic blessing pronounced by Jacob on Issachar corresponds with that of Moses (Gen. 49 : 14, 15 ; comp. Deut. 33 : 18, 19).

Ital'ian band, the name of the Roman cohort to which Cornelius belonged (Acts 10 : 1), so called probably because it consisted of men recruited in Italy.

It'aly (Acts 18 : 2 ; 27 : 1, 6 ; Heb. 13 : 24), like most geographical names, was differently used at different periods of history. As the power of Rome advanced, nations were successively conquered and added to it till it came to designate the whole country to the south of the Alps. There was constant intercourse between Palestine and Italy in the time of the Romans.

Ith'amar—*palm isle*—the fourth and youngest son of Aaron (1 Chr. 6 : 3). He was consecrated to the priesthood along with his brothers (Ex. 6 : 23) ; and after the death of Nadab and Abihu, he and Eleazar alone discharged the functions of that office (Lev. 10 : 6, 12 ; Num. 3 : 4). He and his family occupied the position of common priests till the high priesthood passed into his family in the person of Eli (1 Kings 2 :

27), the reasons for which are not recorded. (See Zadok.)

Ith'rite, two of David's warriors so designated (2 Sam. 23 : 38 ; 1 Chr. 11 : 40).

It'tai—*near; timely;* or, *with the Lord.* (1.) A Benjamite, one of David's thirty heroes (2 Sam. 23 : 29).

(2.) A native of Gath, a Philistine, who had apparently the command of the six hundred heroes who formed David's band during his wanderings (2 Sam. 15 : 19–22 ; comp. 1 Sam. 23 : 13 ; 27 : 2 ; 30 : 9, 10). He is afterwards with David at Mahanaim, holding in the army equal rank with Joab and Abishai (2 Sam. 18 : 2, 5, 12). He then passes from view.

Ituræ'a, a district in the north-east of Palestine, forming, along with the adjacent territory of Trachonitis, the tetrarchy of Philip (Luke 3 : 1). The present *Jedur* comprehends the chief part of Ituræa. It is bounded on the east by Trachonitis, on the south by Gaulanitis, on the west by Hermon, and on the north by the plain of Damascus.

I'vah—*overturning*—a city of the Assyrians, whence colonists were brought to Samaria (2 Kings 18 : 34 ; 19 : 13). It lay on the Euphrates, between Sepharvaim and Henah, and is supposed by some to have been the Ahava of Ezra (8 : 15).

I'vory (Heb. pl. *shĕnhabbĭm*, the "tusks of elephants") was early used in decorations by the Egyptians, and a great trade in it was carried on by the Assyrians (Ezek. 27 : 6 ; Rev. 18 : 12). It was used by the Phœnicians to ornament the box-wood rowing-benches of their galleys, and Hiram's skilled workmen made Solomon's throne of ivory (1 Kings 10 : 18). It was brought by the caravans of Dedan (Isa. 21 : 13), and from the East Indies by the navy of Tarshish (1 Kings 10 : 22). Many specimens of ancient Egyptian and Assyrian ivory-work have been preserved. The word *habbĭm* is derived from the Sanscrit *ibhas*, meaning "elephant," preceded by the Hebrew article (*ha*) ; and hence it is argued that Ophir, from which it and the other articles mentioned in 1 Kings 10 : 22 were brought, was in India.

Iz'har—*oil*—one of the sons of Kohath, and grandson of Levi (Ex. 6 : 18, 21 ; Num. 16 : 1).

Iz'rahite, the designation of one of David's officers (1 Chr. 27 : 8).

J

Ja'akăn—*he twists*—one of the sons of Ezer, the son of Seir the Horite (1 Chr. 1 : 42).

Jaako'bah—*heel-catcher*—a form of the name Jacob, one of the descendants of Simeon (1 Chr. 4 : 36).

Ja'ala—*a wild she-goat*—one of the Nethinim, whose descendants returned from the Captivity (Neh. 7 : 58).

Ja'alam—*concealer*—the second of Esau's three sons by Aholibamah (Gen. 36 : 5, 14).

Ja'anai—*mourner*—one of the chief Gadites (1 Chr. 5 : 12).

Ja'are-or'egim—*forests of the weavers*—a Bethlehemite (2 Sam. 21 : 19), and the father of Elhanan, who slew Goliath. In 1 Chr. 20 : 5 called Jair.

Ja'asau—*fabricator*—an Israelite who renounced his Gentile wife after the Return (Ezra 10 : 37).

Ja'asiel—*made by God*—one of David's body-guard, the son of Abner (1 Chr. 27 : 21), called Jasiel in 1 Chr. 11 : 47.

Jaaz-ani'ah—*heard by Jehovah.* (1.) The son of Jeremiah, and one of the chief Rechabites (Jer. 35 : 3).

(2.) The son of Shaphan (Ezek. 8 : 11).

(3.) The son of Azur, one of the twenty-five men seen by Ezekiel (11 : 1) at the east gate of the temple.

(4.) A Maachathite (2 Kings 25 : 23 ; Jer. 40 : 8 ; 42 : 1). He is also called Azariah (Jer. 43 : 2).

Ja'azer—*he* (God) *helps*—a city of the Amorites on the east of Jordan, and assigned, with neighbouring places in Gilead, to Gad (Num. 32 : 1, 3, 35 ; Josh. 13 : 25). It was allotted to the Merarite Levites (21 : 39). In David's time it was occupied by the Hebronites—*i.e.*, the descendants of Kohath (1 Chr. 26 : 31). It is mentioned in the "burdens" proclaimed over Moab (Isa. 16 : 8, 9 ; Jer. 48 : 32). Its site is marked by the modern ruin called *Sar* or *Seir*, about 10 miles west of Ammân, and 12 from Heshbon. "The vineyards that once covered the hill-sides are gone; and the wild Bedawîn from the eastern desert make cultivation of any kind impossible."

Jaazi′ah—*comforted by Jehovah*—a descendant of 'Merari the Levite (1 Chr. 24 : 26, 27).

Jaazi′el—*comforted by God*—a Levitical musician (1 Chr. 15 : 18).

Ja′bal—*a stream*—a descendant of Cain, and brother of Jubal; "the father of such as dwell in tents and have cattle" (Gen. 4 : 20). This description indicates that he led a wandering life.

Jab′bok—a *pouring out*, or a *wrestling*—one of the streams on the east of Jordan, into which it falls about midway between the Sea of Galilee and the Dead Sea, or about 45 miles below the Sea of Galilee. It rises on the eastern side of the mountains of Gilead, and runs a course of about 65 miles in a wild and deep ravine. It was the boundary between the territory of the Ammonites and that of Og, king of Bashan (Josh. 12 : 1-5; Num. 21 : 24); also between the tribe of Reuben and the half tribe of Manasseh (21 : 24; Deut. 3 : 16). In its course westward across the plains it 'passes more than once underground. "The scenery along its banks is probably the most picturesque in Palestine; and the ruins of town and village and fortress which stud the surrounding mountain-side render the country as interesting as it is beautiful." This river is now called the *Zerka*, or blue river.

Ja′besh—*dry*. (1.) For **Jabesh-Gilead** (1 Sam. 11 : 3, 9, 10).

(2.) The father of Shallum (2 Kings 15 : 10, 13, 14), who usurped the throne of Israel on the death of Zachariah.

Ja′besh-Gil′ead, a town on the east of Jordan, on the top of one of the green hills of Gilead, within the limits of the half tribe of Manasseh, and in full view of Beth-shan. It is first mentioned in connection with the vengeance taken on its inhabitants because they had refused to come up to Mizpeh to take part with Israel against the tribe of Benjamin (Judg. 21 : 8-14). After the battles at Gibeah, that tribe was almost extinguished, only six hundred men remaining. An expedition went against Jabesh-Gilead, the whole of whose inhabitants were put to the sword, except four hundred maidens, whom they brought as prisoners and sent to "proclaim peace" to the Benjamites who had fled to the crag Rimmon. These captives were given to them as wives, that the tribe might be preserved from extinction (1-25).

This city was afterwards taken by Nahash, king of the Ammonites, but was delivered by Saul, the newly-elected king of Israel. In gratitude for this deliverance, forty years after this, the men of Jabesh-Gilead took down the bodies of Saul and of his three sons from the walls of Beth-shan, and after burning them, buried the bones under a tree near the city (1 Sam. 31 : 11-13). David thanked them for this act of piety (2 Sam. 2 : 4-6), and afterwards transferred the remains to the royal sepulchre (21 : 14). It is identified with the ruins of *ed-Deir*, about 6 miles south of Pella, on the north of the Wâdy Yabis.

Ja′bez—*affliction*. (1.) A descendant of Judah, of whom it is recorded that "God granted him that which he requested" (1 Chr. 4 : 9, 10).

(2.) A place inhabited by several families of the scribes (1 Chr. 2 : 55).

Ja′bin—*discerner; the wise*. (1.) A king of Hazor, at the time of the entrance of Israel into Canaan (Josh. 11 : 1-14), whose overthrow and that of the northern chief with whom he had entered into a confederacy against Joshua was the crowning act in the conquest of the land (11 : 21-23; comp. 14 : 6-15). This great battle, fought at Lake Merom, was the last of Joshua's battles of which we have any record. Here for the first time the Israelites encountered the iron chariots and horses of the Canaanites.

(2.) Another king of Hazor, called "the king of Canaan," who overpowered the Israelites of the north one hundred and sixty years after Joshua's death, and for twenty years held them in painful subjection. The whole population were paralyzed with fear, and gave way to hopeless despondency (Judg. 5 : 6–11), till Deborah and Barak aroused the national spirit, and gathering together ten thousand men, gained a great and decisive victory over Jabin in the plain of Esdraelon (Judg. 4 : 10–16; comp. Ps. 83 : 9). This was the first great victory Israel had gained since the days of Joshua. They never needed to fight another battle with the Canaanites (Judg. 5 : 31).

Jab'neel—*built by God*. (1.) A town in the north boundary of Judah (Josh. 15 : 11), called afterwards by the Greeks Jamnia, the modern *Yebna*, 11 miles south of Jaffa. After the fall of Jerusalem (A.D. 70), it became one of the most populous cities of Judea, and the seat of a celebrated school. (2.) A town on the border of Naphtali (Josh. 19 : 33). Its later name was *Kĕfr Yemmah*, "the village by the sea," on the south shore of Lake Merom.

Jab'neh—*building*—(2 Chr. 26 : 6), identical with Jabneel (Josh. 15 : 11).

Ja'chan—*mourner*—one of the chief Gadite "brothers" in Bashan (1 Chr. 5 : 13).

Ja'chin—*firm*. (1.) The fourth son of Simeon (Gen. 46 : 10), called also Jarib (1 Chr. 4 : 24). (2.) The head of one of the courses (the twenty-first) of priests (1 Chr. 24 : 17). (3.) One of the priests who returned from the Exile (1 Chr. 9 : 10).

Ja'chin and Boaz, the names of two brazen columns set up in Solomon's temple (1 Kings 7 : 15–22). Each was eighteen cubits high and twelve in circumference (Jer. 52 : 21, 23; 1 Kings 7 : 17–21). They had doubtless a symbolical import.

Ja'cinth, properly a flower of a reddish blue or deep purple (*hyacinth*), and hence a precious stone of that colour (Rev. 21 : 20). It has been supposed to designate the same stone as the ligure (Heb. *lĕshĕm*) mentioned in Ex. 28 : 19 as the first stone of the third row in the high priest's breastplate. In Rev. 9 : 17 the word is simply descriptive of colour.

Ja'cob—*one who follows on another's heels; supplanter*—(Gen. 25 : 26; 27 : 36; Hos. 12 : 2–4), the second born of the twin sons of Isaac by Rebekah. He was born probably at Lahai-roi, when his father was fifty-nine and Abraham one hundred and fifty-nine years old. Like his father, he was of a quiet and gentle disposition, and when he grew up followed the life of a shepherd, while his brother Esau became an enterprising hunter. His dealing with Esau, however, showed much mean selfishness and cunning (Gen. 25 : 29–34).

When Isaac was near the end of his life, Jacob and his mother conspired to deceive the aged patriarch (Gen. 27), with the view of procuring the transfer of the birthright to himself. The birthright secured to him who possessed it (1) superior rank in his family (Gen. 49 : 3); (2) a double portion of the paternal inheritance (Deut. 21 : 17); (3) the priestly office in the family (Num. 8 : 17–19); and (4) the promise of the Seed in which all nations of the earth were to be blessed (Gen. 22 : 18).

Soon after his acquisition of his father's blessing (Gen. 27), Jacob became conscious of his guilt; and afraid of the anger of Esau, at the suggestion of Rebekah Isaac sent him away to Haran, 400 miles or more, to find a wife among his cousins, the family of Laban, the Syrian (28). There he met with Rachel (29). Laban would not consent to give him his daughter in marriage till he had served seven years; but to Jacob these years "seemed but a few days, for the love he had to her." But when the seven years were expired, Laban craftily deceived Jacob, and gave him his daughter Leah. Other seven years of service had to be completed probably before he obtained the beloved Rachel. But "lifelong sorrow, disgrace, and trials, in the retributive providence of God, followed as a consequence of this double union."

At the close of the fourteen years of service, Jacob desired to return to his parents, but at the entreaty of Laban he tarried yet six years with him, tending his flocks (31 :

41). He then set out with his family and property "to go to Isaac his father in the land of Canaan" (Gen. 31). Laban was angry when he heard that Jacob had set out on his journey, and pursued after him, overtaking him in seven days. The meeting was of a painful kind. After much recrimination and reproach directed against Jacob, Laban is at length pacified, and taking an affectionate farewell of his daughters, returns to his home in Padan-aram. And now all connection of the Israelites with Mesopotamia is at an end.

Soon after parting with Laban he is met by a company of angels, as if to greet him on his return and welcome him back to the Land of Promise (32 : 1, 2). He called the name of the place Mahanaim, i.e., "the double camp," probably his own camp and that of the angels. The vision of angels was the counterpart of that he had formerly seen at Bethel, when, twenty years before, the weary, solitary traveller, on his way to Padan-aram, saw the angels of God ascending and descending on the ladder whose top reached to heaven (28 : 12).

He now hears with dismay of the approach of his brother Esau with a band of 400 men to meet him. In great agony of mind he prepares for the worst. He feels that he must now depend only on God, and he betakes himself to him in earnest prayer, and sends on before him a munificent present to Esau—"a present to my lord Esau from thy servant Jacob." Jacob's family were then transported across the Jabbok; but he himself remained behind, spending the night in communion with God. While thus engaged, there appeared one in the form of a man who wrestled with him. In this mysterious contest Jacob prevailed, and as a memorial of it his name was changed to Israel (*wrestler with God*); and the place where this occurred he called Peniel, "for," said he, "I have seen God face to face, and my life is preserved" (32 : 25-31).

After this anxious night, Jacob went on his way, halting, mysteriously weakened by the conflict, but strong in the assurance of the divine favour. Esau came forth and met him; but his spirit of revenge was appeased, and the brothers met as friends, and during the remainder of their lives they maintained friendly relations. After a brief sojourn at Succoth, Jacob moved forward and pitched his tent near Shechem (*q.v.*)—33 : 18; but at length, under divine directions, he moved to Bethel, where he made an altar unto God (35 : 6, 7), and where God appeared to him and renewed the Abrahamic covenant. While journeying from Bethel to Ephrath (the Canaanitish name of Bethlehem), Rachel died in giving birth to her second son Benjamin (35 : 16-20), fifteen or sixteen years after the birth of Joseph. He then reached the old family residence at Mamre, to wait on the dying bed of his father Isaac. The complete reconciliation between Esau and Jacob was shown by their uniting in the burial of the patriarch (35 : 27-29).

Jacob was soon after this deeply grieved by the loss of his beloved son Joseph through the jealousy of his brothers (37 : 33). Then follows the story of the famine, and the successive goings down into Egypt to buy corn (42), which led to the discovery of the long-lost Joseph, and the patriarch's going down with all his household, numbering about seventy souls (Ex. 1 : 5; Num. 26 : 28-37), to sojourn in the land of Goshen. Here Jacob, "after being strangely tossed about on a very rough ocean, found at last a tranquil harbour, where all the best affections of his nature were gently exercised and largely unfolded" (Gen. 48). At length the end of his checkered course draws nigh, and he summons his sons to his bedside that he may bless them. Among his last words he repeats the story of Rachel's death, although forty years had passed away since that event took place, as tenderly as if it had happened only yesterday; and when "he had made an end of charging his sons, he gathered up his feet into the bed, and yielded up the ghost" (49 : 33). His body was embalmed and carried with great pomp into the land of Canaan, and buried beside his wife Leah in the cave of Machpelah, according to his dying charge. There, probably, his embalmed body remains to this day (50 : 1-13). (See HEBRON.)

The history of Jacob is referred to by the prophets Hosea (12 : 3, 4, 12) and Malachi (1 : 2). In Micah 1 : 5 the name is a poetic synonym for Israel, the kingdom

JACOB'S WELL.

of the ten tribes. There are, besides the mention of his name along with those of the other patriarchs, distinct references to events of his life in Paul's epistles (Rom.

9 : 11–13; Heb. 12 : 16; 11 : 21). See references to his vision at Bethel and his possession of land at Shechem, in John 1 : 51; 4 : 5, 12; also to the famine which was the occasion of his going down into Egypt, in Acts 7 : 12. (See Luz; Bethel.)

Jacob's Well (John 4 : 5, 6). This is one of the few sites in Palestine about which there is no dispute. It was dug by Jacob, and hence its name, in the "parcel of ground" which he purchased from the sons of Hamor (Gen. 33 : 19). It still exists, but although after copious rains it contains a little water, it is now usually quite dry. It is at the entrance to the valley between Ebal and Gerizim, about 2 miles south-east of Shechem. It is about 9 feet in diameter and about 75 feet in depth, though in ancient times it was no doubt much deeper, probably twice as deep. The digging of such a well must have been a very laborious and costly undertaking.

Jad'dua—*known.* (1.) One of the chiefs who subscribed the covenant (Neh. 10 : 21).

(2.) The last high priest mentioned in the Old Testament (Neh. 12 : 11, 22), the son of Jonathan.

Ja'don—*judge*—a Meronothite who assisted in rebuilding the walls of Jerusalem (Neh. 3 : 7).

Ja'el—*mountain-goat*—the wife of Heber the Kenite (Judg. 4 : 17-22). When the Canaanites were defeated by Barak, Sisera, the captain of Jabin's army, fled and sought refuge with the friendly tribe of Heber, beneath the oaks of Zaanaim. As he drew near, Jael invited him to enter her tent. He did so, and as he lay wearily on the floor he fell into a deep sleep. She then took in her left hand one of the great wooden pins ("nail") which fastened down the cords of the tent, and in her right hand the mallet, or "hammer," used for driving it into the ground, and stealthily approaching her sleeping guest, with one well-directed blow drove the nail through his temples into the earth (Judg. 5 : 27). She then led Barak, who was in pursuit, into her tent, and boastfully showed him what she had done. (See SISERA ; DEBORAH.)

Ja'gur—*place of sojourn*—a city on the southern border of Judah (Josh. 15 : 21).

Jah, a contraction for *Jehovah* (Ps. 68 : 4).

Ja'hath—*union.* (1.) A son of Shimei, and grandson of Gershom (1 Chr. 23 : 10).

(2.) One of the sons of Shelomoth, of the family of Kohath (1 Chr. 24 : 22).

(3.) A Levite of the family of Merari, one of the overseers of the repairs of the temple under Josiah (2 Chr. 34 : 12).

Ja'haz—*trodden down* (called also Jahaza, Josh. 13 : 18; Jahazah, 21 : 36; Jahzah, 1 Chr. 6 : 78)—a town where Sihon was defeated, in the borders of Moab and in the land of the Ammonites beyond Jordan, and north of the river Arnon (Num. 21 : 23; Deut. 2 : 32). It was situated in the tribe of Reuben, and was assigned to the Merarite Levites (Josh. 13 : 18; 21 : 36). Here was fought the decisive battle in which Sihon (*q.v.*) was completely routed, and his territory (the modern *Belka*) came into the possession of Israel. This town is mentioned in the denunciations of the prophets against Moab (Isa. 15 : 4; Jer. 48 : 34).

Jaha'ziel—*beheld by God.* (1.) The third son of Hebron (1 Chr. 23 : 19).

(2.) A Benjamite chief who joined David at Ziklag (1 Chr. 12 : 4).

(3.) A priest who accompanied the removal of the ark to Jerusalem (1 Chr. 16 : 6).

(4.) The son of Zechariah, a Levite of the family of Asaph (2 Chr. 20 : 14–17). He encouraged Jehoshaphat against the Moabites and Ammonites.

Jah'dai—*grasper*—a descendant of Caleb, of the family of Hezron (1 Chr. 2 : 47).

Jah'zeel—*allotted by God*—the first of the sons of Naphtali (Gen. 46 : 24).

Jah'zerah—*returner*—the son of Meshullam, and father of Adiel (1 Chr. 9 : 12).

Jailer (of Philippi)—Acts 16 : 23. The conversion of the Roman jailer, a man belonging to a class "insensible as a rule and hardened by habit, and also disposed to despise the Jews, who were the bearers of the message of the gospel," is one of those cases which illustrate its universality and power.

Ja'ir—*enlightener.* (1.) The son of Segub. He was brought up with his mother in Gilead, where he had possessions (1 Chr. 2 : 22). He distinguished himself in an expedition against Bashan, and settled in the part of Argob on the borders of Gilead. The small towns taken by him there are called Havoth-jair—*i.e.,* "Jair's villages" (Num. 32 : 41; Deut. 3 : 14; Josh. 13 : 30).

(2.) The eighth judge of Israel, which he ruled for twenty-two years. His opulence is described in Judg. 10 : 3–5. He had thirty sons, each riding on "ass colts." They had possession of thirty of the sixty cities (1 Kings 4 : 13; 1 Chr. 2 : 23) which formed the ancient Havoth-jair.

(3.) A Benjamite, the father of Mordecai, Esther's uncle (Esther 2 : 5).

(4.) The father of Elhanan, who slew Lachmi, the brother of Goliath (1 Chr. 20 : 5).

Jai'rus, a ruler of the synagogue at Capernaum, whose only daughter Jesus restored to life (Mark 5 : 22; Luke 8 : 41). Entering into the chamber of death, accompanied by Peter and James and John and the father and mother of the maiden, he went forward to the bed whereon the corpse lay, and said, *Talitha cumi—i.e.,* "Maid, arise," and immediately the spirit of the maiden came to her again, and she arose straightway ; and "at once to strengthen that life which had come back to her, and to prove that she was indeed no ghost, but had returned to the realities of a mortal existence, 'he commanded to give her meat'" (Mark 5 : 43).

Ja'keh—*pious*—the father of Agur (Prov. 30 : 1). Nothing is known of him.

Ja'kim—*establisher.* (1.) Chief of the twelfth priestly order (1 Chr. 24 : 12).

(2.) A Benjamite (1 Chr. 8 : 19).

(3.) Margin in Matt. 1 : 11 means Jehoiakim.

Ja'lon—*lodger*—the last of the four sons of Ezra, of the tribe of Judah (1 Chr. 4 : 17).

Jam'bres, one of those who opposed Moses in Egypt (2 Tim. 3 : 8). (See JANNES.)

James. (1.) The son of Zebedee and Salome; an elder brother of John the apostle. He was one of the twelve. He was by trade a fisherman, in partnership with Peter (Matt. 20 : 20; 27 : 56). With John and Peter he was present at the transfiguration (Matt. 17 : 1; Mark 9 : 2), at the raising of Jairus's daughter (Mark 5 : 37-43), and in the garden with our Lord (14 : 33). Because, probably, of their boldness and energy, he and John were called Boanerges—*i.e.,* "sons of thunder." He was the first martyr among the apostles, having been beheaded by King Herod Agrippa (Acts 12 : 1, 2), A.D. 44. (Comp. Matt. 4 : 21; 20 : 20-23.)

(2.) The son of Alphæus, or Cleopas, "the brother" or near kinsman or cousin of our Lord (Gal. 1 : 18, 19), called James "the Less," or "the Little," probably because he was of low stature. He is mentioned along with the other apostles (Matt. 10 : 3; Mark 3 : 18; Luke 6 : 15). He had a separate interview with our Lord after his resurrection (1 Cor. 15 : 7), and is mentioned as one of the apostles of the circumcision (Acts 1 : 13). He appears to have occupied the position of head of the Church at Jerusalem, where he presided at the council held to consider the case of the Gentiles (Acts 12 : 17; 15 : 13-29; 21 : 18-24). This James was the author of the epistle which bears his name.

James, Epistle of. (1.) *Author of,* was James the Less, the Lord's brother, one of the twelve apostles. He was one of the three pillars of the Church (Gal. 2 : 9).

(2.) It was *addressed* to the Jews of the dispersion—"the twelve tribes scattered abroad."

(3.) The *place and time* of the writing of the epistle were Jerusalem, where James was residing, and, from internal evidence, the period between Paul's two imprisonments at Rome, probably about A.D. 62.

(4.) The *object* of the writer was to enforce the practical duties of the Christian life. "The Jewish vices against which he warns them are—formalism, which made the service of God consist in washings and outward ceremonies, whereas he reminds them (1 : 27) that it consists rather in active love and purity; fanaticism, which, under the cloak of religious zeal, was tearing Jerusalem in pieces (1 : 20); fatalism, which threw its sins on God (1 : 13); meanness, which crouched upon the rich (2 : 2); falsehood, which had made words and oaths playthings (3 : 2-12); partisanship (3 : 14); evil speaking (4 : 11); boasting (4 : 16); oppression (5 : 4). The great lesson which he teaches them as Christians is patience—patience in trial (1 : 2), patience in good works (1 : 22-25), patience under provocation (3 : 17), patience under oppression (5 : 7), patience under persecution (5 : 10); and the ground of their patience is that the coming of the Lord draweth nigh, which is to right all wrong (5 : 8)."

"Justification by works," which James contends for, is justification before man—the justification of our profession of faith by a consistent life. Paul contends for the doctrine of "justification by faith;" but that is justification before God—a being regarded and accepted as just by virtue of the righteousness of Christ, which is received by faith.

Jan'nes, one of the Egyptians who "withstood Moses" (2 Tim. 3 : 8).

Jano'ah or **Jano'hah**—*rest.* (1.) A town on the north-eastern border of Ephraim, in the Jordan valley (Josh. 16 : 6, 7). Identified with the modern *Yânûn,* 8 miles south-east of Nablûs.

(2.) A town of Northern Palestine, within the boundaries of Naphtali. It was taken by the king of Assyria (2 Kings 15 : 29).

Ja'num—*slumber*—a town in the mountains of Judah (Josh. 15 : 53).

Ja'pheth—*wide spreading:* "God shall enlarge Japheth" (Heb. *Yaphat Elohim le-Yĕphĕt* — Gen. 9 : 27. Some, however, derive the name from *yaphah,* "to be beautiful;" hence *white*)—one of the sons of Noah, mentioned last in order (Gen. 5 : 32; 6 : 10; 7 : 13), perhaps first by birth (10 :

21; comp. 9:24). He and his wife were two of the eight saved in the ark (1 Pet. 3:20). He was the progenitor of many tribes inhabiting the east of Europe and the north of Asia (Gen. 10:2-5). An act of filial piety (9:20-27) was the occasion of Noah's prophecy of the extension of his posterity.

After the Flood the earth was re-peopled by the descendants of Noah—"the sons of Japheth" (Gen. 10:2), "the sons of Ham" (6), and "the sons of Shem" (22). It is important to notice that modern ethnological science, reasoning from a careful analysis of facts, has arrived at the conclusion that there is a three-fold division of the human family, corresponding in a remarkable way with the great ethnological chapter of the book of Genesis (10). The three great races thus distinguished are called the Semitic, Aryan, and Turanian (Allophylian). "Setting aside the cases where the ethnic names employed are of doubtful application, it cannot reasonably be questioned that the author [of Gen. 10]

has in his account of the sons of Japheth classed together the Cymry or Celts (Gomer), the Medes (Madai), and the Ionians or Greeks (Javan), thereby anticipating what has become known in modern times as the 'Indo-European Theory,' or the essential unity of the Aryan (Asiatic) race with the principal races of Europe, indicated by the Celts and the Ionians. Nor can it be doubted that he has thrown together under the one head of 'children of Shem' the Assyrians (Asshur), the Syrians (Aram), the Hebrews (Eber), and the Joktanian Arabs (Joktan)—four of the principal races which modern ethnology recognizes under the heading of 'Semitic.' Again, under the heading of 'sons of Ham,' the author has arranged 'Cush'—*i.e.*, the Ethiopians; 'Mizraim,' the people of Egypt; 'Sheba and Dedan,' or certain of the Southern Arabs; and 'Nimrod,' or the ancient people of Babylon,—four races between which the latest linguistic researches have established a close affinity" (Rawlinson's *Hist. Illustrations*).

DESCENDANTS OF JAPHETH (Gen. 10:1-5).

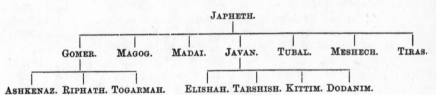

Japhi'a—*splendid*. (1.) The king of Lachish, who joined in the confederacy against Joshua (Josh. 10:3), and was defeated and slain. In one of the Amarna tablets he speaks of himself as king of Gezer. Called also Horam (Josh. 10:33).

(2.) One of the sons of David (2 Sam. 5:15), born in Jerusalem.

(3.) A town in the southern boundary of Zebulun (Josh. 19:12); now *Yafa*, 2 miles south-west of Nazareth.

Ja'pho—*beauty*—a sea-port in Dan (Josh. 19:46); called Joppa (*q.v.*) in 2 Chr. 2:16; Ezra 3:7; Jonah 1:3; and in New Testament.

Ja'red—*descent*. (1.) The fourth ante-

diluvian patriarch in descent from Seth (Gen. 5:15-20; Luke 3:37), the father of Enoch; called Jered in 1 Chr. 1:2.

(2.) A son of Ezra probably (1 Chr. 4:18).

Ja'rib—*an adversary*. (1.) A son of Simeon (1 Chr. 4:24).

(2.) One of the chiefs sent by Ezra to bring up the priests to Jerusalem (Ezra 8:16).

(3.) Ezra 10:18.

Jar'muth—*height*. (1.) A town in the plain of Judah (Josh. 15:35), originally the residence of one of the Canaanitish kings (10:3, 5, 23). It has been identified with the modern *Yarmûk*, a village about 7 miles north-east of Beit-Jibrîn.

(2.) A Levitical city of the tribe of Issachar (Josh. 21 : 29), supposed by some to be the Ramah of Samuel (1 Sam. 19 : 22).

Ja'shen—*sleeping*—called also Hashem (1 Chr. 11 : 34); a person, several of whose sons were in David's body-guard (2 Sam. 23 : 32).

Ja'sher — *upright.* "The Book of Jasher," rendered in the LXX. "the Book of the Upright One," by the Vulgate "the Book of Just Ones," was probably a kind of national sacred song-book—a collection of songs in praise of the heroes of Israel, a "book of golden deeds," a national anthology. We have only two specimens from the book—(1) the words of Joshua which he spake to the Lord at the crisis of the battle of Beth-horon (Josh. 10 : 12, 13); and (2) "the Song of the Bow," that beautiful and touching mournful elegy which David composed on the occasion of the death of Saul and Jonathan (2 Sam. 1 : 18–27).

Jasho'beam—*dweller among the people;* or *to whom the people turn*—the Hachmonite (1 Chr. 11 : 11), one of David's chief heroes who joined him at Ziklag (12 : 6). He was the first of the three who broke through the host of the Philistines to fetch water to David from the well of Bethlehem (2 Sam. 23 : 13–17). He is also called Adino the Eznite (8).

Jash'ub—*returner.* (1.) The third of Issachar's four sons (1 Chr. 7 : 1); called also Job (Gen. 46 : 13).

(2.) Ezra 10 : 29.

Ja'son—*he that will cure*—the host of Paul and Silas in Thessalonica. The Jews assaulted his house in order to seize Paul, but failing to find him, they dragged Jason before the ruler of the city (Acts 17 : 5–9). He was apparently one of the kinsmen of Paul (Rom. 16 : 21), and accompanied him from Thessalonica to Corinth.

Jas'per (Heb. *yashphêh*, "glittering"), a gem of various colours, one of the twelve inserted in the high priest's breast-plate (Ex. 28 : 20). It is named in the building of the New Jerusalem (Rev. 21 : 18, 19). It was "most precious," "like crystal" (21 : 11). It was emblematical of the glory of God (4 : 3).

Jat'tir — *pre-eminent* — a city in the mountains of Judah (Josh. 15 : 48; 21 : 14).

Ja'van. (1.) The fourth "son" of Japheth (Gen. 10 : 2), whose descendants settled in Greece—*i.e.,* Ionia, which bears the name of Javan in Hebrew. Alexander the Great is called the "king of Javan" (rendered "Græcia," Dan. 8 : 21; 10 : 20; comp. 11 : 2; Zech. 9 : 13). This word was universally used by the nations of the East as the generic name of the Greek race.

(2.) A town or district of Arabia Felix, from which the Syrians obtained iron, cassia, and calamus (Ezek. 27 : 19).

Jav'elin. (1.) Heb. *hanîth,* a lance, from its *flexibility* (1 Sam. 18 : 10, 11; 19 : 9, 10; 20 : 33).

(2.) Heb. *rómah,* a lance for heavy-armed troops, so called from its *piercing* (Num. 25 : 7). (See Arms.)

Jaw-bone of an ass afforded Samson a weapon for the great slaughter of the Philistines (Judg. 15 . 15), in which he slew a thousand men. In verse 19 the Authorized Version reads, "God clave a hollow place that was in the jaw, and there came water thereout." This is a mistranslation of the words. The rendering should be as in the Revised Version, "God clave the hollow place that is in Lehi," etc., Lehi (*q.v.*) being the name of the hill where this conflict was waged, possibly so called because it was in shape like a jaw-bone.

Jeal'ousy, suspicion of a wife's purity, one of the strongest passions (Num. 5 : 14; Prov. 6 : 34; Cant. 8 : 6); also an intense interest for another's honour or prosperity (Ps. 79 : 5; 1 Cor. 10 : 22; Zech. 1 : 14).

Jeal'ousy, Image of, an idolatrous object, seen in vision by Ezekiel (Ezek. 8 : 3, 5), which stood in the priests' or inner court of the temple. Probably identical with the statue of Astarte (2 Kings 21 : 7).

Jeal'ousy offering, the name of the offering the husband was to bring when he charged his wife with adultery (Num. 5 : 11–15).

Jeal'ousy, Waters of, water which the suspected wife was required to drink, so that the result might prove her guilt or innocence (Num. 5 : 12–17, 27). We have no record of this form of trial having been actually resorted to.

Je'arim—*forests*—a mountain on the border of Judah (Josh. 15 : 10).

Je'bus—*trodden hard*, or *fastness*, or "*the waterless hill*"—the name of the Canaanitish city which stood on Mount Zion (Josh. 15 : 8 ; 18 : 16, 28). It is identified with Jerusalem (*q.v.*) in Judg. 19 : 10, and with the castle or city of David (1 Chr. 11 : 4, 5). It was a place of great natural strength, and its capture was one of David's most brilliant achievements (2 Sam. 5 : 8).

Jeb'usites, the name of the original inhabitants of Jebus, mentioned frequently among the seven nations doomed to destruction (Gen. 10 : 16 ; 15 : 21 ; Ex. 3 : 8, 17 ; 13 : 5, etc.). At the time of the arrival of the Israelites in Palestine they were ruled by Adonizedek (Josh. 10 : 1, 23). They were defeated by Joshua, and their king was slain ; but they were not entirely driven out of Jebus till the time of David, who made it the capital of his kingdom instead of Hebron. The site on which the temple was afterwards built belonged to Araunah, a Jebusite, from whom it was purchased by David, who refused to accept it as a free gift (2 Sam. 24 : 16-25 ; 1 Chr. 21 : 24, 25).

Jecoli'ah — *able through Jehovah* — the wife of King Amaziah, and mother of King Uzziah (2 Chr. 26 : 3).

Jedai'ah. (1.) *Invoker of Jehovah.* The son of Shimri, a chief Simeonite (1 Chr. 4 : 37).

(2.) One of those who repaired the walls of Jerusalem after the return from Babylon (Neh. 3 : 10).

(3.) *Knowing Jehovah.* The chief of one of the courses of the priests (1 Chr. 24 : 7).

(4.) A priest in Jerusalem after the Exile (1 Chr. 9 : 10).

Jedi'ael—*known by God.* (1.) One of the sons of Benjamin, whose descendants numbered 17,200 warriors (1 Chr. 7 : 6, 10, 11).

(2.) A Shimrite, one of David's body-guard (1 Chr. 11 : 45). Probably same as in 12 : 20.

(3.) A Korhite of the family of Ebiasaph, and one of the gate-keepers to the temple (1 Chr. 26 : 2).

Jedidi'ah—*beloved by Jehovah*—the name which, by the mouth of Nathan, the Lord gave to Solomon at his birth as a token of the divine favour (2 Sam. 12 : 25).

Jedu'thun—*lauder ; praising*—a Levite of the family of Merari, and one of the three masters of music appointed by David (1 Chr. 16 : 41, 42 ; 25 : 1-6). He is called in 2 Chr. 35 : 15 "the king's seer." His descendants are mentioned as singers and players on instruments (Neh. 11 : 17). He was probably the same as Ethan (1 Chr. 15 : 17, 19). In the superscriptions to Ps. 39, 62, and 77, the words "upon Jeduthun" probably denote a musical instrument ; or they may denote the style or tune invented or introduced by Jeduthun, or that the psalm was to be sung by his choir.

Je'gar-sahadu'tha—*pile of testimony*—the Aramaic or Syriac name which Laban gave to the pile of stones erected as a memorial of the covenant between him and Jacob (Gen. 31 : 47), who, however, called it in Hebrew by an equivalent name —Galeed (*q.v.*).

Jehal'eleel—*praiser of God.* (1.) A descendant of Judah (1 Chr. 4 : 16).

(2.) A Levite of the family of Merari (2 Chr. 29 : 12).

Jehdei'ah—*rejoicer in Jehovah.* (1.) One of the Levitical attendants at the temple, a descendant of Shubael (1 Chr. 24 : 20).

(2.) A Meronothite, herdsman of the asses under David and Solomon (1 Chr. 27 : 30).

Jehi'el—*God's living one.* (1.) The father of Gibeon (1 Chr. 9 : 35).

(2.) One of David's guard (1 Chr. 11 : 44).

(3.) One of the Levites "of the second degree," appointed to conduct the music on the occasion of the ark's being removed to Jerusalem (1 Chr. 15 : 18, 20).

(4.) A Hachmonite, a tutor in the family of David toward the close of his reign (1 Chr. 27 : 32).

(5.) The second of Jehoshaphat's six sons (2 Chr. 21 : 2).

(6.) One of the Levites of the family of Heman who assisted Hezekiah in his work of reformation (2 Chr. 29 : 14).

(7.) A "prince" and "ruler of the house of God" who contributed liberally to the renewal of the temple sacrifices under Josiah (2 Chr. 35 : 8).

(8.) The father of Obadiah (Ezra 8 : 9).

(9.) One of the "sons" of Elam (Ezra 10 : 26).

(10.) Ezra 10 : 21.

Jehizki'ah—*Jehovah strengthens*—one of the chiefs of Ephraim (2 Chr. 28 : 12).

Jehoad'dan—*Jehovah his ornament*—the wife of King Jehoash, and mother of King Amaziah (2 Kings 14 : 2).

Jeho'ahaz—*Jehovah his sustainer*, or *he whom Jehovah holdeth*. (1.) The youngest son of Jehoram, king of Judah (2 Chr. 21 : 17 ; 22 : 1, 6, 8, 9) ; usually Ahaziah (*q.v.*).

(2.) The son and successor of Jehu, king of Israel (2 Kings 10 : 35). He reigned seventeen years, and followed the evil ways of the house of Jeroboam. The Syrians, under Hazael and Benhadad, prevailed over him, but were at length driven out of the land by his son Jehoash (13 : 1–9, 25).

(3.) Josiah's third son, usually called Shallum (1 Chr. 3 : 15). He succeeded his father on the throne, and reigned over Judah for three months (2 Kings 23 : 31, 34). He fell into the idolatrous ways of his predecessors (23 : 32), was deposed by Pharaoh-Necho from the throne, and carried away prisoner into Egypt, where he died in captivity (23 : 33, 34 ; Jer. 22 : 10–12 ; 2 Chr. 36 : 1–4).

Jeho'ash—*Jehovah-given*. (1.) The son of King Ahaziah. While yet an infant, he was saved from the general massacre of the family by his aunt Jehosheba, and was apparently the only surviving descendant of Solomon (2 Chr. 21 : 4, 17). His uncle, the high priest Jehoiada, brought him forth to public notice when he was eight years of age, and crowned and anointed him king of Judah with the usual ceremonies. Athaliah was taken by surprise when she heard the shout of the people, "Long live the king ;" and when she appeared in the temple, Jehoiada commanded her to be led forth to death (2 Kings 11 : 13–20). While the high priest lived, Jehoash favoured the worship of God and observed the law ; but on his death he fell away into evil courses, and the land was defiled with idolatry. Zechariah, the son and successor of the high priest, was put to death. These

evil deeds brought down on the land the judgment of God, and it was oppressed by the Syrian invaders. He is one of the three kings omitted by Matthew (1 : 8) in the genealogy of Christ, the other two being Ahaziah and Amaziah. He was buried in the city of David (2 Kings 12 : 21). (See JOASH [4].)

(2.) The son and successor of Jehoahaz, king of Israel (2 Kings 14 : 1 ; comp. 12 : 1 ; 13 : 10). When he ascended the throne the kingdom was suffering from the invasion of the Syrians. Hazael "was cutting Israel short." He tolerated the worship of the golden calves, yet seems to have manifested a character of sincere devotion to the God of his fathers. He held the prophet Elisha in honour, and wept by his bedside when he was dying, addressing him in the words Elisha himself had used when Elijah was carried up into heaven : "O my father, my father, the chariot of Israel and the horsemen thereof." He was afterwards involved in war with Amaziah, the king of Judah (2 Chr. 25 : 23–24), whom he utterly defeated at Beth-shemesh, on the borders of Dan and Philistia, and advancing on Jerusalem, broke down a portion of the wall, and carried away the treasures of the temple and the palace. He soon after died (B.C. 825), and was buried in Samaria (2 Kings 14 : 1–17, 19, 20). He was succeeded by his son. (See JOASH [5].)

Jeho'hanan—*Jehovah-granted*—Jeroboam II. (1.) A Korhite, the head of one of the divisions of the temple porters (1 Chr. 26 : 3).

(2.) One of Jehoshaphat's "captains" (2 Chr. 17 : 15).

(3.) The father of Azariah (2 Chr. 28 : 12).

(4.) The son of Tobiah, an enemy of the Jews (Neh. 6 : 18).

(5.) Neh. 12 : 42.

(6.) Neh. 12 : 13.

Jehoi'ada — *Jehovah-known*. (1.) The father of Benaiah, who was one of David's chief warriors (2 Sam. 8 : 18 ; 20 : 23).

(2.) The high priest at the time of Athaliah's usurpation of the throne of Judah. He married Jehosheba, or Jehoshabeath, the daughter of king Jehoram (2 Chr. 22 : 11), and took an active part along with his wife in the preservation and training of Jehoash when Athaliah slew all the royal family of Judah.

The plans he adopted in replacing Jehoash on the throne of his ancestors are described in 1 Kings 14:26, 27; 1 Chr. 18: 7-11; 26:20-28. He was among the foremost of the benefactors of the kingdom, and at his death was buried in the city of David among the kings of Judah (2 Chr. 24:15, 16). He is said to have been one hundred and thirty years old.

Jehoi′akim—*he whom Jehovah has set up* —the second son of Josiah, and eighteenth king of Judah, which he ruled over for eleven years (B.C. 610–599). His original name was Eliakim (*q.v.*).

On the death of his father his younger brother Jehoahaz (= Shallum, Jer. 22:11), who favoured the Chaldeans against the Egyptians, was made king by the people; but the king of Egypt, Pharaoh-Necho, invaded the land and deposed Jehoahaz (2 Kings 23:33, 34; Jer. 22:10–12), setting Eliakim on the throne in his stead, changing his name to Jehoiakim.

After this the king of Egypt took no part in Jewish politics, having been defeated by the Chaldeans at Carchemish (2 Kings 24:7; Jer. 46:2). Palestine was now invaded and conquered by Nebuchadnezzar. Jehoiakim was taken prisoner and carried captive to Babylon (2 Chr. 36:6, 7). It was at this time that Daniel also and his three companions were taken captive to Babylon (Dan. 1:1, 2).

Nebuchadnezzar reinstated Jehoiakim on his throne, but treated him as a vassal king. In the year after this Jeremiah caused his prophecies to be read by Baruch in the court of the temple. Jehoiakim, hearing of this, had them also read in the royal palace before himself. The words displeased him, and taking the roll from the hands of Baruch he cut it in pieces and threw it into the fire (Jer. 36:23). During his disastrous reign there was a return to the old idolatry and corruption of the days of Manasseh.

After three years of subjection to Babylon, Jehoiakim withheld his tribute, and threw off the yoke (2 Kings 24:2), hoping to make himself independent. Nebuchad-

nezzar sent bands of Chaldeans, Syrians, and Ammonites (2 Kings 24:7) to chastise his rebellious vassal. They cruelly harassed the whole country (comp. Jer. 49:1-6). The king came to a violent death, and his body having been thrown over the wall of Jerusalem, to convince the besieging army that he was dead, after having been dragged away, was buried beyond the gates of Jerusalem "with the burial of an ass," B.C. 599 (Jer. 22:18, 19; 36:30). Nebuchadnezzar placed his son Jehoiakin on the throne, wishing still to retain the kingdom of Judah as tributary to him.

Jehoi′akin succeeded his father Jehoiakim (B.C. 599) when only eighteen years of age, and reigned for one hundred days (2 Chr. 36:9). He is also called Jeconiah (Jer. 24:1; 27:20, etc.), and Coniah (22: 24; 37:1). He was succeeded by his uncle, Mattaniah = Zedekiah (*q.v.*). He was the last direct heir to the Jewish crown. He was carried captive to Babylon by Nebuchadnezzar, along with the flower of the nobility, all the leading men in Jerusalem, and a great body of the general population, some thirteen thousand in all (2 Kings 24: 12–16; Jer. 52:28). After an imprisonment of thirty-seven years (Jer. 52:31, 33) he was liberated by Evil-Merodach, and permitted to occupy a place in the king's household and sit at his table, receiving "every day a portion until the day of his death, all the days of his life" (52:32–34).

Jehoia′rib—*Jehovah defends*—a priest at Jerusalem, head of one of the sacerdotal courses (1 Chr. 9:10; 24:7). His "course" went up from Babylon after the Exile (Ezra 2:36–39; Neh. 7:39–42).

Jehon′adab—*Jehovah is liberal;* or, *whom Jehovah impels.* (1.) A son of Shimeah, and nephew of David. It was he that gave the fatal wicked advice to Amnon, the heir to the throne (2 Sam. 13:3–6). He was very "subtil," but unprincipled.

(2.) A son of Rechab, the founder of a tribe who bound themselves by a vow to abstain from wine (Jer. 35:6–19). There were different settlements of Rechabites (Judg. 4:11; 1:16; 1 Chr. 2:55). (See RECHABITE.) His interview and alliance with Jehu are mentioned in 2 Kings 10:

15-23. He went with Jehu in his chariot to Samaria.

Jehon'athan—*whom Jehovah gave.* (1.) One of the stewards of David's store-houses (1 Chr. 27 : 25).

(2.) A Levite who taught the law to the people of Judah (2 Chr. 17 : 8).

(3.) Neh. 10 : 18.

Jeho'ram—*Jehovah-exalted.* (1.) Son of Toi, king of Hamath, sent by his father to congratulate David on the occasion of his victory over Hadadezer (2 Sam. 8 : 10).

(2.) A Levite of the family of Gershom (1 Chr. 26 : 25).

(3.) A priest sent by Jehoshaphat to instruct the people in Judah (2 Chr. 17 : 8).

(4.) The son of Ahab and Jezebel, and successor to his brother Ahaziah on the throne of Israel. He reigned twelve years —B.C. 896–884 (2 Kings 1 : 17; 3 : 1). His first work was to reduce to subjection the Moabites, who had asserted their independence in the reign of his brother. Jehoshaphat, king of Judah, assisted Jehoram in this effort. He was further helped by his ally the king of Edom. Elisha went forth with the confederated army (2 Kings 3 : 1–19), and at the solicitation of Jehoshaphat encouraged the army with the assurance from the Lord of a speedy victory. The Moabites under Mesha their king were utterly routed and their cities destroyed. At Kir-haraseth Mesha made a final stand. The Israelites refrained from pressing their victory further, and returned to their own land.

Elisha afterwards again befriended Jehoram when a war broke out between the Syrians and Israel, and in a remarkable way brought that war to a bloodless close (2 Kings 6 : 23). But Jehoram, becoming confident in his own power, sank into idolatry, and brought upon himself and his land another Syrian invasion, which led to great suffering and distress in Samaria (2 Kings 6 : 30, 33). By a remarkable providential interposition the city was saved from utter destruction, and the Syrians were put to flight (2 Kings 7 : 6–15).

Jehoram was wounded in a battle with the Syrians at Ramah, and obliged to return to Jezreel (2 Kings 8 : 29; 9 : 14, 15),

and soon after the army proclaimed their leader Jehu king of Israel, and revolted from their allegiance to Jehoram (2 Kings 9). Jehoram was pierced by an arrow from Jehu's bow on the piece of ground at Jezreel which Ahab had taken from Naboth, and there he died (2 Kings 21 : 21-29).

(5.) The eldest son and successor of Jehoshaphat, king of Judah. He reigned eight years (B.C. 892–885) alone as king of Judah, having been previously for some years associated with his father (2 Chr. 21 : 5, 20; 2 Kings 8 : 16). His wife was Athaliah, the daughter of Ahab and Jezebel. His daughter Jehosheba was married to the high priest Jehoiada. He sank into gross idolatry, and brought upon himself and his kingdom the anger of Jehovah. The Edomites revolted from under his yoke, and the Philistines and the Arabians and Cushites invaded the land, and carried away great spoil, along with Jehoram's wives and all his children, except Ahaziah. He died a painful death from a fearful malady, and was refused a place in the sepulchre of the kings (2 Kings 8 : 16-24; 2 Chr. 21).

Jehosh'aphat — *Jehovah-judged.* (1.) One of David's body-guard (1 Chr. 11 : 43).

(2.) One of the priests who accompanied the removal of the ark to Jerusalem (1 Chr. 15 : 24).

(3.) Son of Ahilud, "recorder" or annalist under David and Solomon (2 Sam. 8 : 16), a state officer of high rank, chancellor or vizier of the kingdom.

(4.) Solomon's purveyor in Issachar (1 Kings 4 : 17).

(5.) The son and successor of Asa, king of Judah. After fortifying his kingdom against Israel (2 Chr. 17 : 1, 2), he set himself to cleanse the land of idolatry (1 Kings 22 : 43). In the third year of his reign he sent out priests and Levites over the land to instruct the people in the law (2 Chr. 17 : 7-9). He enjoyed a great measure of peace and prosperity, the blessing of God resting on the people "in their basket and their store."

The great mistake of his reign was his entering into an alliance with Ahab, the king of Israel, which involved him in much disgrace, and brought disaster on his kingdom (1 Kings 22 : 1–33). Escaping from the bloody battle of Ramoth-gilead, the prophet Jehu (2 Chr. 19 : 1–3) reproached him for the course he had been pursuing, whereupon he entered with rigour on his former course of opposition to all idolatry, and of deepening interest in the worship of God and in the righteous government of the people (2 Chr. 19 : 4–11).

Again he entered into an alliance with Ahaziah, the king of Israel, for the purpose of carrying on maritime commerce with Ophir. But the fleet that was then equipped at Ezion-gaber was speedily wrecked. A new fleet was fitted out without the co-operation of the king of Israel, and although it was successful, the trade was not prosecuted (2 Chr. 20 : 35–37 ; 1 Kings 22 : 48–49).

He subsequently joined Jehoram, king of Israel, in a war against the Moabites, who were under tribute to Israel. This war was successful. The Moabites were subdued ; but the dreadful act of Mesha in offering his own son a sacrifice on the walls of Kir-haresheth in the sight of the armies of Israel filled him with horror, and he withdrew and returned to his own land (2 Kings 3 : 4–27).

The last most notable event of his reign was that recorded in 2 Chr. 20. The Moabites formed a great and powerful confederacy with the surrounding nations, and came against Jehoshaphat. The allied forces were encamped at Engedi. The king and his people were filled with alarm, and betook themselves to God in prayer. The king prayed in the court of the temple —"O our God, wilt thou not judge them ? for we have no might against this great company that cometh against us." Amid the silence that followed, the voice of Jahaziel the Levite was heard announcing that on the morrow all this great host would be overthrown. So it was, for they quarrelled among themselves, and slew one another, leaving to the people of Judah only to gather the rich spoils of the slain. This was recognized as a great deliverance wrought for them by God (B.C. 890). Soon after this Jehoshaphat died, after a reign

of twenty-five years, being sixty years of age, and was succeeded by his son Jehoram (2 Kings 22 : 50). He had this testimony, that "he sought the Lord with all his heart" (2 Chr. 22 : 9). The kingdom of Judah was never more prosperous than under his reign.

(6.) The son of Nimshi, and father of Jehu, king of Israel (2 Kings 9 : 2, 14).

Jehosh′aphat, Valley of, mentioned in Scripture only in Joel 3 : 2, 12. This is the name given in modern times to the valley between Jerusalem and the Mount of Olives, and the Kidron flows through it. Here Jehoshaphat overthrew the confederated enemies of Israel (Ps. 83 : 6–8) ; and in this valley also God was to overthrow the Tyrians, Zidonians, etc. (Joel 3 : 4, 19), with an utter overthrow. This has been fulfilled ; but Joel speaks of the final conflict, when God would destroy all Jerusalem's enemies, of whom Tyre and Zidon, etc., were types. The "valley of Jehoshaphat" may therefore be simply regarded as a general term for the theatre of God's final judgments on the enemies of Israel.

This valley has from ancient times been used by the Jews as a burial-ground. It is all over paved with flat stones as tombstones, bearing on them Hebrew inscriptions.

Jehosh′eba — *Jehovah-swearing* — the daughter of Jehoram, the king of Israel. She is called Jehoshabeath in 2 Chr. 22 : 11. She was the only princess of the royal house who was married to a high priest— Jehoiada (2 Chr. 22 : 11).

Jeho′vah, the special and significant name (not merely an appellative title such as Lord) by which God revealed himself to the ancient Hebrews (Ex. 6 : 2, 3). This name, the Tetragrammaton of the Greeks, was held by the later Jews to be so sacred that it was never pronounced except by the high priest on the great Day of Atonement, when he entered into the most holy place. Whenever this name occurred in the sacred books they pronounced it, as they still do, "Adônâi" (*i.e.*, Lord), thus using another word in its stead. The Massorets gave to it the vowel-points appropriate to this word. This Jewish practice was founded on a false interpretation of Lev. 24:16. The meaning of the word appears from Ex. 3:14 to be "the unchanging, eternal, self-existent God," the "I am that I am," a covenant-keeping God. (Comp. Mal. 3:6; Hos. 12: 6; Rev. 1:4, 8.)

The Hebrew name "Jehovah" is generally translated in the Authorized Version (and the Revised Version has not departed from this rule) by the word LORD printed in small capitals, to distinguish it from the rendering of the Hebrew *Adônâi* and the Greek *Kurios*, which are also rendered Lord, but printed in the usual type. The Hebrew word is translated "Jehovah" only in Ex. 6:3; Ps. 83:18; Isa. 12:2; 26:4, and in the compound names mentioned below.

It is worthy of notice that this name is never used in the LXX., the Samaritan Pentateuch, the Apocrypha, or in the New Testament. It is found, however, on the "Moabite stone" (*q.v.*), and consequently it must have been in the days of Mesha so commonly pronounced by the Hebrews as to be familiar to their heathen neighbours.

Jeho'vah-ji'reh—*Jehovah will see; i.e., will provide*—the name given by Abraham to the scene of his offering up the ram which was caught in the thicket on Mount Moriah. The expression used in Gen. 22:14, "in the mount of the Lord it shall be seen," has been regarded as equivalent to the saying, "Man's extremity is God's opportunity."

Jeho'vah-nis'si—*Jehovah my banner*—the title given by Moses to the altar which he erected on the hill on the top of which he stood with uplifted hands while Israel prevailed over their enemies the Amalekites (Ex. 17:15).

Jeho'vah-sha'lom—*Jehovah send peace*—the name which Gideon gave to the altar he erected on the spot at Ophrah where the angel appeared to him (Judg. 6:24).

Jeho'vah-sham'mah—*Jehovah is there*—the symbolical title given by Ezekiel to Jerusalem, which was seen by him in vision (Ezek. 48:35). It was a type of the gospel Church.

Jeho'vah-tsidke'nu—*Jehovah our righteousness*—rendered in the Authorized Version, "The Lord our righteousness," a title given to the Messiah (Jer. 23:6, marg.), and also to Jerusalem (23:16, marg.).

Jehoz'abad—*Jehovah-given*. (1.) The son of Obed-edom (1 Chr. 26:4), one of the Levite porters.

(2.) The son of Shomer, one of the two conspirators who put king Jehoash to death in Millo in Jerusalem (2 Kings 12:21).

(3.) 2 Chr. 17:18.

Jehoz'adak—*Jehovah-justified*—the son of the high priest Seraiah at the time of the Babylonian exile (1 Chr. 6:14, 15). He was carried into captivity by Nebuchadnezzar, and probably died in Babylon. He was the father of Jeshua, or Joshua, who returned with Zerubbabel.

Je'hu—*Jehovah is he*. (1.) The son of Obed, and father of Azariah (1 Chr. 2:38).

(2.) One of the Benjamite slingers that joined David at Ziklag (1 Chr. 12:3).

(3.) The son of Hanani, a prophet of Judah (1 Kings 16:1, 7; 2 Chr. 19:2; 20: 34), who pronounced the sentence of God against Baasha, the king of Israel.

(4.) King of Israel, the son of Jehoshaphat (2 Kings 9:2), and grandson of Nimshi. The story of his exaltation to the throne is deeply interesting. During the progress of a war against the Syrians, who were becoming more and more troublesome to Israel, in a battle at Ramoth-gilead Jehoram, the king of Israel, had been wounded; and leaving his army there, had returned to Jezreel, whither his ally, Ahaziah, king of Judah, had also gone on a visit of sympathy with him (2 Kings 8:28, 29). The commanders, being left in charge of the conduct of the war, met in council; and while engaged in their deliberations, a messenger from Elisha appeared in the camp, and taking Jehu from the council, led him into a secret chamber, and there anointed him king over Israel, and immediately retired and disappeared (2 Kings 9:5, 6). On being interrogated by his companions as to the object of this mysterious visitor, he informed them of what had been done, when immediately, with the utmost enthusiasm, they blew their trumpets and proclaimed him king (2 Kings 9:11-14). He then with a chosen band set forth with all speed to Jezreel, where, with his own hand, he slew Jehoram, shooting him through the heart with an arrow (9:24). The king of Judah, when trying to escape, was fatally wounded by one of Jehu's soldiers at Beth-gan. On entering the city, Jehu commanded the eunuchs of the royal palace to cast down Jezebel into the street, where her mangled body was trodden under foot by the horses. Jehu was now master of Jezreel, whence he communicated with the persons in authority in Samaria the capital, commanding them to appear before him on the morrow with the heads of all the royal princes of Samaria. Accordingly on the morrow seventy heads were piled up in two heaps at his gate. At "the shearing-house" (2 Kings 10: 12–14) other forty-two connected with the house of Ahab were put to death (2 Kings 10:14). As Jehu rode on toward Samaria, he met Jehonadab (*q.v.*), whom he took into his chariot, and they entered the capital together. By a cunning stratagem he cut off all the worshippers of Baal found in Samaria (2 Kings 10:19–25), and destroyed the temple of the idol (2 Kings 10:27).

Notwithstanding all this apparent zeal for the worship of Jehovah, Jehu yet tolerated the worship of the golden calves at Dan and Bethel. For this the divine displeasure rested upon him, and his kingdom suffered disaster in war with the Syrians (2 Kings 10:29–33). He died after a reign of twenty-eight years (B.C. 884–856), and was buried in Samaria (10:34–36). "He was one of those decisive, terrible, and ambitious, yet prudent, calculating, and passionless men whom God from time to time raises up to change the fate of empires and execute his judgments on the earth." He was the first Jewish king who came in contact with the Assyrian power in the time of Shalmaneser II.

Jehu'cal—*able*—the son of Shelemiah. He is also called Jucal (Jer. 38:1). He was one of the two persons whom Zedekiah sent to request the prophet Jeremiah to pray for the kingdom (Jer. 37:3) during the time of its final siege by Nebuchadnezzar. He was accompanied by Zephaniah (*q.v.*).

Jehu'di—*a Jew*—son of Nethaniah. He was sent by the princes to invite Baruch to read Jeremiah's roll to them (Jer. 36: 14, 21).

Jei'el—*snatched away by God.* (1.) A descendant of Benjamin (1 Chr. 9:35; 8: 29).

(2.) One of the Levites who took part in praising God on the removal of the ark to Jerusalem (1 Chr. 16:5).

(3.) 2 Chr. 29:13. A Levite of the sons of Asaph.

(4.) 2 Chr. 26:11. A scribe.

(5.) 1 Chr. 5:7. A Reubenite chief.

(6.) One of the chief Levites, who made an offering for the restoration of the Passover by Josiah (2 Chr. 35:9).

(7.) Ezra 8:13.

(8.) Ezra 10:43.

Jemi'ma—*dove*—the eldest of Job's three daughters born after his time of trial (Job 42:14).

Jeph'thah—*whom God sets free*, or *the breaker through*—a "mighty man of valour" who delivered Israel from the oppression of the Ammonites (Judg. 11:1–33), and judged Israel six years (12:7). He has been described as "a wild, daring, Gilead mountaineer—a sort of warrior Elijah." After forty-five years of comparative quiet Israel again apostatized, and in "process of time the children of Ammon made war against Israel" (11:5). In their distress the elders of Gilead went to fetch Jephthah out of the land of Tob, to which he had fled when driven out wrongfully by his brothers from his father's inheritance (2), and the people made him their head and captain. The "elders of Gilead" in their extremity summoned him to their aid, and he at once undertook the conduct of the war against Ammon. Twice he sent an embassy to the king of Ammon, but in vain. War was inevitable. The people obeyed his summons, and "the spirit of the Lord came upon him." Before engaging in war he vowed that if successful he would offer as a "burnt-offering" whatever would come out of the door of his house first to meet him on his return. The defeat of the Ammonites was complete. "He smote them from Aroer, even until thou come to Minnith, even twenty cities, and unto the plain of the vineyards [Heb. *'Abel Kerâmim*], with a very great slaughter" (Judg. 11 : 33). The men of Ephraim regarded themselves as insulted in not having been called by Jephthah to go with him to war against Ammon. This led to a war between the men of Gilead and Ephraim (12 : 4), in which many of the Ephraimites perished. (See SHIBBOLETH.) "Then died Jephthah the Gileadite, and was buried in one of the cities of Gilead" (7).

Jeph'thah's vow (Judg. 11 : 30, 31). After a crushing defeat of the Ammonites, Jephthah returned to his own house, and the first to welcome him was his own daughter. This was a terrible blow to the victor, and in his despair he cried out, "Alas, my daughter! thou hast brought me very low......I have opened my mouth unto the Lord, and cannot go back." With singular nobleness of spirit she answered, "Do to me according to that which hath proceeded out of thy mouth." She only asked two months to bewail her maidenhood with her companions upon the mountains. She utters no reproach against her father's rashness, and is content to yield her life since her father has returned a conqueror. But was it so? Did Jephthah offer up his daughter as a "burnt-offering"? This question has been much debated, and there are many able commentators who argue that such a sacrifice was actually offered. We are constrained, however, by a consideration of Jephthah's known piety as a true worshipper of Jehovah, his evident acquaintance with the law of Moses, to which such sacrifices were abhorrent (Lev. 18 : 21 ; 20 : 2-5 ; Deut. 12 : 31), and the place he holds in the roll of the heroes of the faith in the Epistle to the Hebrews (11 : 32), to conclude that she was only doomed to a life of perpetual celibacy.

Jephun'neh — *nimble*, or *a beholder*. (1.) The father of Caleb, who was Joshua's companion in exploring Canaan (Num. 13 : 6), a Kenezite (Josh. 14 : 14).

(2.) One of the descendants of Asher (1 Chr. 7 : 38).

Jerah'meel—*loving God*. (1.) The son of Hezron, the brother of Caleb (1 Chr. 2 : 9, 25, 26, etc.).

(2.) The son of Kish, a Levite (1 Chr. 24 : 29).

(3.) Son of Hammelech (Jer. 36 : 26).

Jeremi'ah — *raised up* or *appointed by Jehovah*. (1.) A Gadite who joined David in the wilderness (1 Chr. 12 : 10).

(2.) A Gadite warrior (1 Chr. 12 : 13).

(3.) A Benjamite slinger who joined David at Ziklag (1 Chr. 12 : 4).

(4.) One of the chiefs of the tribe of Manasseh on the east of Jordan (1 Chr. 5 : 24).

(5.) The father of Hamutal (2 Kings 23 : 31), the wife of Josiah.

(6.) One of the "greater prophets" of the Old Testament, son of Hilkiah (*q.v.*), a priest of Anathoth (Jer. 1 : 1 ; 32 : 6). He was called to the prophetical office when still young (1 : 6), in the thirteenth year of Josiah (B.C. 628). He left his native place, and went to reside in Jerusalem, where he greatly assisted Josiah in his work of reformation (2 Kings 23 : 1-25). The death of this pious king was bewailed by the prophet as a national calamity (2 Chr. 35 : 25).

During the three years of the reign of Jehoahaz we find no reference to Jeremiah, but in the beginning of the reign of Jehoiakim the enmity of the people against him broke out in bitter persecution, and he was placed apparently under restraint (Jer. 36:5). In the fourth year of Jehoiakim he was commanded to write the predictions given to him, and to read them to the people on the fast-day. This was done by Baruch his servant in his stead, and produced much public excitement. The roll was read to the king. In his recklessness he seized the roll, and cut it to pieces, and cast it into the fire, and ordered both Baruch and Jeremiah to be apprehended. Jeremiah procured another roll, and wrote in it the words of the roll the king had destroyed, and "many like words" besides (Jer. 36 : 32).

He remained in Jerusalem, uttering from time to time his words of warning, but without effect. He was there when Nebuchadnezzar besieged the city (Jer. 37 : 4, 5), B.C. 589. The rumour of the approach of the Egyptians to aid the Jews in this crisis induced the Chaldeans to withdraw and return to their own land. This, however, was only for a time. The prophet, in answer to his prayer, received a message from God announcing that the Chaldeans would come again and take the city, and burn it with fire (37 : 7, 8). The princes, in their anger at such a message by Jeremiah, cast him into prison (37 : 15–38 : 13). He was still in confinement when the city was taken (B.C. 588). The Chaldeans released him, and showed him great kindness, allowing him to choose the place of his residence. He accordingly went to Mizpah with Gedaliah, who had been made governor of Judea. Johanan succeeded Gedaliah, and refusing to listen to Jeremiah's counsels, went down into Egypt, taking Jeremiah and Baruch with him (Jer. 43 : 6). There probably the prophet spent the remainder of his life, in vain seeking still to turn the people to the Lord, from whom they had so long revolted (44). He lived till the reign of Evil-Merodach, son of Nebuchadnezzar, and must have been about ninety years of age at his death. We have no authentic record of his death. He may have died at Tahpanhes, or, according to a tradition, may have gone to Babylon with the army of Nebuchadnezzar; but of this there is nothing certain.

Jeremi'ah, Book of, consists of twenty-three separate and independent sections, arranged in five books. I. The introduction, ch. 1. II. Reproofs of the sins of the Jews, consisting of seven sections— (1.) ch. 2; (2.) ch. 3–6; (3.) ch. 7–10; (4.) ch. 11–13; (5.) ch. 14–17 : 18; (6.) ch. 17 : 19–ch. 20; (7.) ch. 21–24. III. A general review of all nations, in two sections— (1.) ch. 46–49; (2.) ch. 25; with an historical appendix of three sections—(1.) ch. 26; (2.) ch. 27; (3.) ch. 28, 29. IV. Two sections picturing the hopes of better times— (1.) ch. 30, 31; (2.) ch. 32, 33; to which is added an historical appendix in three sections—(1.) ch. 34 : 1–7; (2.) ch. 34 : 8–22; (3.) ch. 35. V. The conclusion, in two sections—(1.) ch. 36; (2.) ch. 45.

In Egypt, after an interval, Jeremiah is supposed to have added three sections— viz., ch. 37–39; 40–43; and 44.

The principal Messianic prophecies are found in 23 : 1–8; 30 : 31–40; and 33 : 14–26.

Jeremiah's prophecies are noted for the frequent repetitions found in them of the same words and phrases and imagery. They cover the period of about 30 years. They are not recorded in the order of time. When and under what circumstances this book assumed its present form we know not.

The LXX. Version of this book is, in its arrangement and in other particulars, singularly at variance with the original. The LXX. omits 10 : 6–8; 27 : 19–22; 29 : 16–20; 33 : 14–26; 39 : 4–13; 52 : 2, 3, 15, 28–30, etc. About 2,700 words in all of the original are omitted. These omissions, etc., are capricious and arbitrary, and render the version unreliable.

Jer'icho—*place of fragrance*—a fenced city in the midst of a vast grove of palm trees, in the plain of Jordan, over against the place where that river was crossed by the Israelites (Josh. 3 : 16). Its site was near the 'Ain es-Sultan—Elisha's Fountain (2 Kings 2 : 19–22)—about 5 miles west of Jordan. It was the most important city in the Jordan valley (Num. 22 : 1; 34 : 15), and the strongest fortress in all the land of Canaan. It was the key to Western Palestine.

This city was taken in a very remarkable manner by the Israelites (Josh. 6). God gave it into their hands. The city was "accursed" (Heb. *ḥerem*, "devoted" to Jehovah), and accordingly (Josh. 6 : 17; comp. Lev. 27 : 28, 29; Deut. 13 : 16) all the inhabitants and all the spoil of the city were to be destroyed, "only the silver, and the gold, and the vessels of brass and of iron" were reserved and "put into the treasury of the house of Jehovah" (Josh. 6 : 24; comp. Num. 31 : 22, 23, 50–54). Only Rahab "and her father's household, and all that she had," were preserved from destruction, according to the promise of the spies (Josh. 2 : 14). In one of the Amarna tablets Adoni-zedec (*q.v.*) writes to the king of Egypt informing him that the 'Abiri (Hebrews) had prevailed, and had taken the fortress of Jericho, and were plundering "all the king's lands." It would seem that the Egyptian troops had before this been withdrawn from Palestine.

This city was given to the tribe of Benjamin (Josh. 18:21), and it was inhabited in the time of the Judges (Judg. 3:13; 2 Sam. 10:5). It is not again mentioned till the time of David (2 Sam. 10:5). "Children of Jericho" were among the captives who returned under Zerubbabel (Ezra 2:34; Neh. 7:36). Hiel (*q.v.*) the Bethelite attempted to make it once more a fortified city (1 Kings 16:34). Between the beginning and the end of his undertaking all his children were cut off.

In New Testament times Jericho stood some distance to the south-east of the ancient one, and near the opening of the Valley of Achor. It was a rich and flourishing town, having a considerable trade, and celebrated for its palm trees, which adorned the plain around. It was visited by our Lord on his last journey to Jerusa-

ER-RIHA (THE JERICHO OF THE CRUSADES).

lem. Here he gave sight to two blind men (Matt. 20:29-34; Mark 10:46-52), and brought salvation to the house of Zacchæus the publican (Luke 19:2-10).

The poor hamlet of *Er-Rîha*, the representative of modern Jericho, is situated some two miles farther to the east. It is in a ruinous condition, having been destroyed by the Turks in 1840. "The soil of the plain," about the middle of which the ancient city stood, "is unsurpassed in fertility; there is abundance of water for irrigation, and many of the old aqueducts are about perfect; yet nearly the whole plain is waste and desolate......The climate of Jericho is exceedingly hot and unhealthy. This is accounted for by the depression of the plain, which is about 1,200 feet below the level of the sea."

Jer'imoth—*heights*. (1.) One of the sons of Bela (1 Chr. 7:7).

(2.) 1 Chr. 24:30, a Merarite Levite.

(3.) A Benjamite slinger who joined David at Ziklag (1 Chr. 12:5).

(4.) A Levitical musician under Heman his father (1 Chr. 25:4).

(5.) 1 Chr. 27:19, ruler of Naphtali.

(6.) One of David's sons (2 Chr. 11:18).

(7.) A Levite, one of the overseers of the temple offerings (2 Chr. 31:13) in the reign of Hezekiah.

Jerobo'am — *increase of the people.* (1.) The son of Nebat (1 Kings 11:26–39), "an Ephrathite," the first king of the ten tribes, over whom he reigned twenty-two years (B.C. 976–954). He was the son of a widow of Zereda, and while still young was promoted by Solomon to be chief superintendent of the "burden"—*i.e.*, of the bands of forced labourers. Influenced by the words of the prophet Ahijah, he began to form conspiracies with the view of becoming king of the ten tribes; but these having been discovered, he fled to Egypt (1 Kings 11:29–40), where he remained for a length of time under the protection of Shishak I. On the death of Solomon, the ten tribes, having revolted, sent to invite him to become their king. The conduct of Rehoboam favoured the designs of Jeroboam, and he was accordingly proclaimed "king of Israel" (1 Kings 12:1–20). He rebuilt and fortified Shechem as the capital of his kingdom. He at once adopted means to perpetuate the division thus made between the two parts of the kingdom, and erected at Dan and Bethel, the two extremities of his kingdom, "golden calves," which he set up as symbols of Jehovah, enjoining the people not any more to go up to worship at Jerusalem, but to bring their offerings to the shrines he had erected. Thus he became distinguished as the man "who made Israel to sin." This policy was followed by all the succeeding kings of Israel.

While he was engaged in offering incense at Bethel, a prophet from Judah appeared before him with a warning message from the Lord. Attempting to arrest the prophet for his bold words of defiance, his hand was "dried up," and the altar before which he stood was rent asunder. At his urgent entreaty his "hand was restored him again" (1 Kings 13:1-6, 9; comp. 2 Kings 23:15); but the miracle made no abiding impression on him. His reign was one of constant war with the house of Judah. He died soon after his son Abijah (1 Kings 14:1–18).

(2.) Jeroboam II., the son and successor of Jehoash, and the fourteenth king of Israel, over which he ruled for forty-one years, B.C. 825–784 (2 Kings 14:23). He followed the example of the first Jeroboam in keeping up the worship of the golden calves (2 Kings 14:24). His reign was contemporary with those of Amaziah (2 Kings 14:23) and Uzziah (15:1), kings of Judah. He was victorious over the Syrians (13:4; 14:26, 27), and extended Israel to its former limits, from "the entering of Hamath to the sea of the plain" (14:25; Amos 6:14). His reign of forty-one years was the most prosperous that Israel had ever known as yet. With all this outward prosperity, however, iniquity widely prevailed in the land (Amos 2:6-8; 4:1; 6:6; Hos. 4:12-14). The prophets Hosea (1:1), Joel (3:16; Amos 1:12), Amos (1:1), and Jonah (2 Kings 14:25) lived during his reign. He died, and was buried with his ancestors (14:29). He was succeeded by his son Zachariah (*q.v.*).

His name occurs in Scripture only in 2 Kings 13:13; 14:16, 23, 27, 28, 29; 15:1, 8; 1 Chr. 5:17; Hos. 1:1; Amos 1:1; 7:9, 10, 11. In all other passages it is Jeroboam the son of Nebat that is meant.

Jero'ham—*cherished; who finds mercy.* (1.) Father of Elkanah, and grandfather of the prophet Samuel (1 Sam. 1:1).

(2.) The father of Azareel, the "captain" of the tribe of Dan (1 Chr. 27:22).

(3.) 1 Chr. 12:7; a Benjamite.

(4.) 1 Chr. 23:1; one whose son assisted in placing Joash on the throne.

(5.) 1 Chr. 9:8; a Benjamite.

(6.) 1 Chr. 9:12; a priest, perhaps the same as in Neh. 11:12.

Jerub'baal—*contender with Baal;* or, *let Baal plead*—a surname of Gideon; a name given to him because he destroyed the altar of Baal (Judg. 6:32; 7:1; 8:29; 35:9).

Jerub'besheth—*contender with the*

shame; i.e., idol—a surname also of Gideon (2 Sam. 11 : 21).

Jeru'el—*founded by God*—a "desert" on the ascent from the valley of the Dead Sea towards Jerusalem. It lay beyond the wilderness of Tekoa, in the direction of Engedi (1 Chr. 20 : 16, 20). It corresponds with the tract of country now called *el-Hasasah.*

Jeru'salem, called also Salem, Ariel, Jebus, the "city of God," the "holy city;" by the modern Arabs *el-Khuds,* meaning "the holy;" once "the city of Judah" (2 Chr. 25 : 28). This name is in the original in the dual form, and means "possession of peace," or "foundation of peace." The dual form probably refers to the two mountains on which it was built— *viz.,* Zion and Moriah ; or, as some suppose, to the two parts of the city, the "upper" and the "lower city." Jerusalem is a "mountain city enthroned on a mountain fastness" (comp. Ps. 68 : 15, 16; 87 : 1; 125 : 1; 76 : 1, 2; 66 : 4). It stands on the edge of one of the highest tablelands in Palestine, and is surrounded on the south-eastern, the southern, and the western sides by deep and precipitous ravines.

It is first mentioned in Scripture under the name Salem (Gen. 14 : 18; comp. Ps. 76 : 2). When first mentioned under the name Jerusalem, Adonizedek was its king (Josh. 10 : 1). It is afterwards named among the cities of Benjamin (Judg. 19 : 10; 1 Chr. 11 : 4); but in the time of David it was divided between Benjamin and Judah. After the death of Joshua the city was taken and set on fire by the men of Judah (Judg. 1 : 1–8); but the Jebusites were not wholly driven out of it. The city is not again mentioned till we are told that David brought the head of Goliath thither (1 Sam. 17 : 54). David afterwards led his forces against the Jebusites still residing within its walls, and drove them out, fixing his own dwelling on Zion, which he called "the city of David" (1 Sam. 5 : 5–9; 1 Chr. 12 : 4–8). Here he built an altar to the Lord on the threshing-floor of Araunah the Jebusite (2 Sam. 24 : 15–25), and thither he brought up the ark of the covenant and placed it in the new tabernacle which he had prepared for it. Jerusalem now became the capital of the kingdom.

After the death of David, Solomon built the temple, a house for the name of the Lord, on Mount Moriah (B.C. 1010). He also greatly strengthened and adorned the city, and it became the great centre of all the civil and religious affairs of the nation (Deut. 12 : 5; comp. 13 : 14; 14 : 23; 16 : 11–16; Ps. 122).

After the disruption of the kingdom on the accession to the throne of Rehoboam, the son of Solomon, Jerusalem became the capital of the kingdom of the two tribes. It was subsequently often taken and retaken by the Egyptians, the Assyrians, and by the kings of Israel (2 Kings 14 : 13; 14; 18 : 15, 16; 23 : 33–35; 24 : 14; 2 Chr. 12 : 9; 26 : 9; 27 : 3, 4; 29 : 3; 32 : 30; 33 : 11), till finally, for the abounding iniquities of the nation, after a siege of three years, it was taken and utterly destroyed, its walls razed to the ground, and its temple and palaces consumed by fire, by Nebuchadnezzar, the king of Babylon (2 Kings 25; 2 Chr. 36; Jer. 39), B.C. 588. The desolation of the city and the land was completed by the retreat of the principal Jews into Egypt (Jer. 40–44), and by the final carrying captive into Babylon of all that still remained in the land (52 : 3), so that it was left without an inhabitant (B.C. 582). Compare the predictions, Deut. 28; Lev. 26 : 14–39.

But the streets and walls of Jerusalem were again to be built, in troublous times (Dan. 9 : 16, 19, 25), after a captivity of seventy years. This restoration was begun B.C. 536, "in the first year of Cyrus" (Ezra 1 : 2, 3, 5–11). The Books of Ezra and Nehemiah contain the history of the re-building of the city and temple, and the restoration of the kingdom of the Jews, consisting of a portion of all the tribes. The kingdom thus constituted was for two centuries under the dominion of Persia, till B.C. 331; and thereafter, for about a century and a half, under the rulers of the Greek empire in Asia, till B.C. 167. For a century the Jews maintained their independence under native rulers, the Asmonean

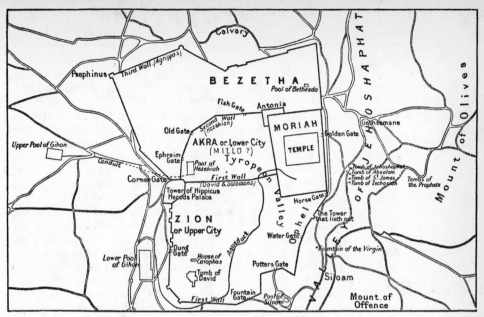

PLAN OF ANCIENT JERUSALEM.

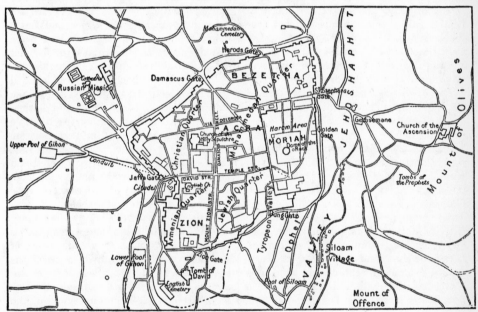

PLAN OF MODERN JERUSALEM.

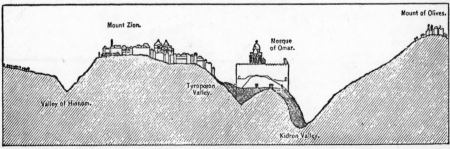

SECTION ACROSS JERUSALEM—WEST TO EAST.

princes. At the close of this period they fell under the rule of Herod and of members of his family, but practically under Rome, till the time of the destruction of Jerusalem, A.D. 70. The city was then laid in ruins.

The modern Jerusalem by-and-by began to be built over the immense beds of rubbish resulting from the overthrow of the ancient city; and whilst it occupies certainly the same site, there are no evidences that even the lines of its streets are now what they were in the ancient city. Till A.D. 131 the Jews who still lingered about Jerusalem quietly submitted to the Roman sway. But in that year the emperor (Hadrian), in order to hold them in subjection, rebuilt and fortified the city. The Jews, however, took possession of it, having risen under the leadership of one Bar-Chohaba (*i.e.*, "the son of the star") in revolt against the Romans. Some four years afterwards (A.D. 135), however, they were driven out of it with great slaughter, and the city was again destroyed; and over its ruins was built a Roman city called *Aelia Capitolina*, a name which it retained till it fell under the dominion of the Mohammedans, when it was called *el-Khuds*— *i.e.*, "the holy."

In A.D. 326 Helena, mother of the emperor Constantine, made a pilgrimage to Jerusalem with the view of discovering the places mentioned in the life of our Lord. She caused a church to be built on what was then supposed to be the place of the nativity at Bethlehem. Constantine, animated by her example, searched for the holy sepulchre, and built over the supposed site a magnificent church, which was completed and dedicated A.D. 335. He relaxed the laws against the Jews till this time in force, and permitted them once a year to visit the city and wail over the desolation of "the holy and beautiful house."

In A.D. 614 the Persians, after defeating the Roman forces of the emperor Heraclius, took Jerusalem by storm, and retained it till A.D. 637, when it was taken by the Arabians under the Khalif Omar. It remained in their possession till it passed, in A.D. 960, under the dominion of the

Fatimite khalifs of Egypt, and in A.D. 1073 under the Turcomans. In A.D. 1099 the crusader Godfrey of Bouillon took the city from the Moslems with great slaughter, and was elected king of Jerusalem. He converted the Mosque of Omar into a Christian cathedral. During the eighty-eight years which followed, many churches and convents were erected in the holy city. The Church of the Holy Sepulchre was rebuilt during this period, and it alone remains to this day. In A.D. 1187 the sultan Saladin wrested the city from the Christians. From that time to the present day, with few intervals, Jerusalem has remained in the hands of the Moslems. It has, however, during that period been again and again taken and retaken, demolished in great part and rebuilt, no city in the world having passed through so many vicissitudes.

In the year 1850 the Greek and Latin monks residing in Jerusalem had a fierce dispute about the guardianship of what are called the "holy places." In this dispute the emperor Nicholas of Russia sided with the Greeks, and Louis Napoleon, the emperor of the French, with the Latins. This led the Turkish authorities to settle the question in a way unsatisfactory to Russia. Out of this there sprang the Crimean War, which was protracted and sanguinary, but which had important consequences in the way of breaking down the barriers of Turkish exclusiveness.

Modern Jerusalem "lies near the summit of a broad mountain-ridge, which extends without interruption from the plain of Esdraelon to a line drawn between the southern end of the Dead Sea and the south-eastern corner of the Mediterranean." This high, uneven table-land is everywhere from 20 to 25 geographical miles in breadth. It was anciently known as the mountains of Ephraim and Judah.

"Jerusalem is a city of contrasts, and differs widely from Damascus, not merely because it is a stone town in mountains, whilst the latter is a mud city in a plain, but because while in Damascus Moslem religion and Oriental custom are unmixed with any foreign element, in Jerusalem

JERUSALEM FROM THE MOUNT OF OLIVES.

every form of religion, every nationality of East and West, is represented at one time.

"Jerusalem is quite a small town, the circumference of its walls being only 2¾ miles; yet within this space it contains a population of 20,000 [now above 45,000]. Ten sects or religions are established in it, and if their various sub-divisions are counted, they amount to a total of twenty-four, more than half of which are Christian. Prophets and missionaries of no particular sect are also not wanting at any time in the holy city......The city as a whole is not beautiful; its flat-roofed houses and dirty lanes are neither pleasing nor healthy, and the surrounding chalk hills are barren and shapeless. Shechem is a fine, well-watered city; Damascus is bedded in gardens and bristles with minarets; but there is nothing in the site or architecture of Jerusalem as a whole which can save it from the imputation of ugliness."—Conder's *Tent Work in Palestine.* (See QUARRIES.)

Jeru'sha—*possession,* or *possessed; i.e.,* "by a husband"—the wife of Uzziah, and mother of king Jotham (2 Kings 15 : 33).

Jeshai'ah—*deliverance of Jehovah.* (1.) A Kohathite Levite, the father of Joram, of the family of Eliezer (1 Chr. 26 : 25); called also Isshiah (24 : 21).

(2.) One of the sons of Jeduthun (1 Chr. 25 : 3, 15).

(3.) One of the three sons of Hananiah (1 Chr. 3 : 21).

(4.) Son of Athaliah (Ezra 8 : 7).

(5.) A Levite of the family of Merari (8:19).

Jesha'nah, a city of the kingdom of Israel (2 Chr. 13 : 19).

Jeshar'elah—*upright towards God*—the head of the seventh division of Levitical musicians (1 Chr. 25 : 14).

Jesheb'eab—*seat of his father*—the head of the fourteenth division of priests (1 Chr. 24 : 13).

Je'sher—*uprightness*—the first of the three sons of Caleb by Azubah (1 Chr. 2 : 18).

Jesh'imon—*the waste*—probably some high waste land to the south of the Dead Sea (Num. 21 : 20; 23 : 28; 1 Sam. 23 : 19, 24); or rather not a proper name at all, but simply "the waste" or "wilderness," the district on which the plateau of Ziph (*q.v.*) looks down.

Jesh'ua. (1.) Head of the ninth priestly order (Ezra 2 : 36); called also Jeshuah (1 Chr. 24 : 11).

(2.) A Levite appointed by Hezekiah to distribute offerings in the priestly cities (2 Chr. 31 : 15).

(3.) Ezra 2 : 6; Neh. 7 : 11.

(4.) Ezra 2 : 40; Neh. 7 : 43.

(5.) The son of Jozadak, and high priest of the Jews under Zerubbabel (Neh. 7 : 7; 12 : 1, 7, 10, 26); called Joshua (Hag. 1 : 1, 12; 2 : 2, 4; Zech. 3 : 1, 3, 6, 8, 9).

(6.) A Levite (Ezra 8 : 33).

(7.) Neh. 3 : 19.

(8.) A Levite who assisted in the reformation under Nehemiah (8 : 7; 9 : 4, 5).

(9.) Son of Kadmiel (Neh. 12 : 24).

(10.) A city of Judah (Neh. 11 : 26).

(11.) Neh. 8 : 17; Joshua, the son of Nun.

Jesh'urun, a poetical name for the people of Israel, used in token of affection, meaning, "the dear upright people" (Deut. 32 : 15; 33 : 5, 26; Isa. 44 : 2).

Jes'se—*firm,* or *a gift*—a son of Obed, the son of Boaz and Ruth (Ruth 4 : 17, 22; Matt. 1 : 5, 6; Luke 3 : 32). He was the father of eight sons, the youngest of whom was David (1 Sam. 17 : 12). The phrase "stem of Jesse" is used for the family of David (Isa. 11 : 1), and "root of Jesse" for the Messiah (Isa. 11 : 10; Rev. 5 : 5). Jesse was a man apparently of wealth and position at Bethlehem (1 Sam. 17 : 17, 18, 20; Ps. 78 : 71). The last reference to him is of David's procuring for him an asylum with the king of Moab (1 Sam. 22 : 3).

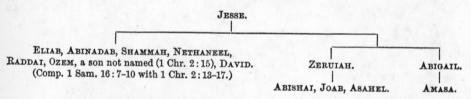

JESSE.

ELIAB, ABINADAB, SHAMMAH, NETHANEEL, RADDAI, OZEM, a son not named (1 Chr. 2 : 15), DAVID. (Comp. 1 Sam. 16 : 7-10 with 1 Chr. 2 : 13-17.)

ZERUIAH.

ABISHAI, JOAB, ASAHEL.

ABIGAIL.

AMASA.

Je'sus. (1.) Joshua, the son of Nun (Acts 7 : 45; Heb. 4 : 8; R.V., "Joshua").

(2.) A Jewish Christian surnamed Justus (Col. 4 : 11).

Je'sus, the proper, as *Christ* is the official, name of our Lord. To distinguish him from others so called, he is spoken of as "Jesus of Nazareth" (John 18 : 7), and "Jesus the son of Joseph" (John 6 : 42).

This is the Greek form of the Hebrew name Joshua, which was originally Hoshea (Num. 13 : 8, 16), but changed by Moses into Jehoshua (Num. 13 : 16; 1 Chr. 7 : 27), or Joshua. After the Exile it assumed the form Jeshua, whence the Greek form Jesus. It was given to our Lord to denote the object of his mission—to *save* (Matt. 1 : 21).

The life of Jesus on earth may be divided into two great periods—(1) that of his private life, till he was about thirty years of age; and (2) that of his public life, which lasted about three years.

In the "fulness of time" he was born at Bethlehem, in the reign of the emperor Augustus, of Mary, who was betrothed to Joseph, a carpenter (Matt. 1 : 1; Luke 3 : 23; comp. John 7 : 42). His birth was announced to the shepherds (Luke 2 : 8–20). Wise men from the east came to Bethlehem to see him who was born "King of the Jews," bringing gifts with them (Matt. 2 : 1–12). Herod's cruel jealousy led to Joseph's flight into Egypt with Mary and the infant Jesus, where they tarried till the death of this king (Matt. 2 : 13–23), when they returned and settled in Nazareth, in Lower Galilee (2 : 23; comp. Luke 4 : 16; John 1 : 46, etc.). At the age of twelve years he went up to Jerusalem to the Passover with his parents. There, in the temple, "in the midst of the doctors," all that heard him were "astonished at his understanding and answers" (Luke 2 : 41, etc.).

Eighteen years pass, of which we have no record beyond this, that he returned to Nazareth and "increased in wisdom and stature, and in favour with God and man" (Luke 2 : 52).

He entered on his public ministry when he was about thirty years of age. It is generally reckoned to have extended to about three years. "Each of these years had peculiar features of its own. (1.) The first year may be called the year of *obscurity*, both because the records of it which we possess are very scanty, and because he seems during it to have been only slowly emerging into public notice. It was spent for the most part in Judea. (2.) The second year was the year of *public favour*, during which the country had become thoroughly aware of him; his activity was incessant, and his fame rang through the length and breadth of the land. It was almost wholly passed in Galilee. (3.) The third was the year of *opposition*, when the public favour ebbed away. His enemies multiplied and assailed him with more and more pertinacity, and at last he fell a victim to their hatred. The first six months of this final year were passed in Galilee, and the last six in other parts of the land."—Stalker's *Life of Jesus Christ*, p. 45.

The only *reliable sources of information* regarding the life of Christ on earth are the Gospels, which present in historical detail the words and the work of Christ in so many different aspects. (See CHRIST.)

Je'ther—*surplus; excellence.* (1.) Father-in-law of Moses (Ex. 4 : 18 marg.), called elsewhere Jethro (*q.v.*).

(2.) The oldest of Gideon's seventy sons (Judg. 8 : 20).

(3.) The father of Amasa, David's general (1 Kings 2 : 5, 32); called Ithra (2 Sam. 17 : 25).

(4.) 1 Chr. 7 : 38.

(5.) 1 Chr. 2 : 32; one of Judah's posterity.

(6.) 1 Chr. 4 : 17.

Je'theth—*a peg,* or *a prince*—one of the Edomitish kings of Mount Seir (Gen. 36 : 40).

Jeth'lah—*suspended; high*—a city on the borders of Dan (Josh. 19 : 42).

Jeth'ro—*his excellence,* or *gain*—a prince or priest of Midian, who succeeded his father Reuel. Moses spent forty years after his exile from the Egyptian court as keeper of Jethro's flocks. While the Israelites were encamped at Sinai, and soon after their victory over Amalek, Jethro came to meet Moses, bringing with him Zipporah and her two sons. They met at the "mount of God," and "Moses told him all that the Lord had done unto Pharaoh" (Ex. 18 : 8).

On the following day Jethro, observing the multiplicity of the duties devolving on Moses, advised him to appoint subordinate judges—rulers of thousands, of hundreds, of fifties, and of tens—to decide smaller matters, leaving only the weightier matters to be referred to Moses, to be laid before the Lord. This advice Moses adopted (Ex. 18). He was also called Hobab (*q.v.*), which was probably his personal name, while Jethro was an official name. (See MOSES.)

Je'tur—*an enclosure*—one of the twelve sons of Ishmael (Gen. 25:15).

Jeu'el—*snatched away by God*—a descendant of Zerah (1 Chr. 9:6).

Je'ush—*assembler*. (1.) The oldest of Esau's three sons by Aholibamah (Gen. 36:5, 14, 18).

(2.) A son of Bilhan, grandson of Benjamin (1 Chr. 7:10).

(3.) A Levite, one of the sons of Shimei (1 Chr. 23:10, 11).

(4.) One of the three sons of Rehoboam (2 Chr. 11:19).

(5.) 1 Chr. 8:39.

Jew, the name derived from the patriarch Judah, at first given to one belonging to the tribe of Judah or to the separate kingdom of Judah (2 Kings 16:6; 25:25; Jer. 32:12; 38:19; 40:11; 41:3), in contradistinction from those belonging to the kingdom of the ten tribes, who were called Israelites.

During the Captivity, and after the Restoration, the name, however, was extended to all the Hebrew nation without distinction (Esther 3:6, 10; Dan. 3:8, 12; Ezra 4:12; 5:1, 5).

Originally this people were called *Hebrews* (Gen. 39:14; 40:15; Ex. 2:7; 3:18; 5:3; 1 Sam. 4:6, 9, etc.), but after the Exile this name fell into disuse. But Paul was styled a Hebrew (2 Cor. 11:22; Phil. 3:5).

The *history* of the Jewish nation is interwoven with the history of Palestine and with the narratives of the lives of their rulers and chief men. They are now dispersed over all lands, and to this day remain a separate people, "without a king, and without a prince, and without a sacrifice, and without an image [R.V. 'pillar,'

marg. 'obelisk'], and without an ephod, and without teraphim" (Hos. 3:4). Till about the beginning of the present century they were everywhere greatly oppressed, and often cruelly persecuted; but now their condition is greatly improved, and they are admitted in most European countries to all the rights of free citizens. In 1860 the "Jewish disabilities" were removed, and they were admitted to a seat in the British Parliament. Their number in all is estimated at about six millions, about four millions being in Europe.

There are three names used in the New Testament to designate this people—(1.) Jews, as regards their nationality, to distinguish them from Gentiles. (2.) Hebrews, with regard to their language and education, to distinguish them from Hellenists —*i.e.*, Jews who spoke the Greek language. (3.) Israelites, as respects their sacred privileges as the chosen people of God. "To other races we owe the splendid inheritance of modern civilization and secular culture; but the religious education of mankind has been the gift of the Jew alone."

Jew'ess, a woman of Hebrew birth, as Eunice, the mother of Timothy (Acts 16:1; 2 Tim. 1:5), and Drusilla (24:24), the wife of Felix, and daughter of Herod Agrippa I.

Jez'ebel—*chaste*—the daughter of Ethbaal, the king of the Zidonians, and the wife of Ahab, the king of Israel (1 Kings 16:31). This was the "first time that a king of Israel had allied himself by marriage with a heathen princess; and the alliance was in this case of a peculiarly disastrous kind. Jezebel has stamped her name on history as the representative of all that is designing, crafty, malicious, revengeful, and cruel. She is the first great instigator of persecution against the saints of God. Guided by no principle, restrained by no fear of either God or man, passionate in her attachment to her heathen worship, she spared no pains to maintain idolatry around her in all its splendour. Four hundred and fifty prophets ministered under her care to Baal, besides four hundred prophets of the groves [R.V., 'prophets of the Asherah'], which ate at her table (1 Kings 18:19). The idolatry, too, was of the most debased and sensual kind." Her conduct was in many respects very disastrous to the kingdom both of Israel and Judah (21:1-29). At length she came to an untimely end. As Jehu rode into the gates of Jezreel, she looked out at the window of the palace, and said, "Had Zimri peace, who slew his master?" He looked up and called to her chamberlains, who instantly threw her from the window, so that she was dashed in pieces on the street, and his horses trod her under their feet. She was immediately consumed by the dogs of the street (2 Kings 9:7-37), according to the word of Elijah the Tishbite (1 Kings 21:19).

Her name afterwards came to be used as the synonym for a wicked woman (Rev. 2:20).

It may be noted that she is said to have been the grand-aunt of Dido, the founder of Carthage.

Je'ziel—*assembled by God*—a son of Azmaveth. He was one of the Benjamite archers who joined David at Ziklag (1 Chr. 12:3).

Jez'reel—*God scatters.* (1.) A town of Issachar (Josh. 19:18), where the kings of Israel often resided (1 Kings 18:45; 21:1; 2 Kings 9:30). Here Elijah met Ahab, Jehu, and Bidkar; and here Jehu executed his dreadful commission against the house of Ahab (2 Kings 9:14-37; 10:1-11). It has been identified with the modern *Zerin,* on the most western point of the range of Gilboa, reaching down into the great and fertile valley of Jezreel, to which it gave its name.

(2.) A town in Judah (Josh. 15:56), to the south-east of Hebron. Ahinoam, one of David's wives, probably belonged to this place (1 Sam. 27:3).

(3.) A symbolical name given by Hosea to his oldest son (Hos. 1:4), in token of a great slaughter predicted by him, like that which had formerly taken place in the plain of Esdraelon (comp. Hos. 2:2, 3).

Jez'reel, Blood of, the murder perpetrated here by Ahab and Jehu (Hos. 1:4; comp. 1 Kings 18:4; 2 Kings 9:6-10).

Jez'reel, Day of, the time predicted for the execution of vengeance for the deeds of blood committed there (Hos. 1:5).

Jez'reel, Ditch of (1 Kings 21:23; comp. 13), the fortification surrounding the city, outside of which Naboth was executed.

Jez'reel, Fountain of, where Saul encamped before the battle of Gilboa (1 Sam. 29:1). In the valley under Zerin there are two considerable springs, one of which, perhaps that here referred to, "flows from under a sort of cavern in the wall of conglomerate rock which here forms the base of Gilboa. The water is excellent; and issuing from crevices in the rocks, it spreads out at once into a fine limpid pool forty or fifty feet in diameter, full of fish" (Robinson). This may be identical with the "well of Harod" (Judg. 7:1; comp. 2 Sam. 23:25), probably the *'Ain Jâlûd*—*i.e.,* the "spring of Goliath."

Jez'reel, Portion of, the field adjoining the city (2 Kings 9:10, 21, 36, 37). Here Naboth was stoned to death (1 Kings 21:13).

Jez'reel, Tower of, one of the turrets which guarded the entrance to the city (2 Kings 9:17).

Jez'reel, Valley of, lying on the northern side of the city, between the ridges of Gilboa and Moreh, an offshoot of Esdraelon, running east to the Jordan (Josh. 17:16; Judg. 6:33; Hos. 1:5). It was the scene of the signal victory gained by the Israelites under Gideon over the Midianites, the Amalekites, and the "children of the east" (Judg. 6:3). Two centuries after this the Israelites were here defeated by the Philistines, and Saul and Jonathan, with the flower of the army of Israel, fell (1 Sam. 31:1-6).

This name was in after ages extended to the whole of the plain of Esdraelon (*q.v.*). It was only this plain of Jezreel and that north of Lake Huleh that were then accessible to the chariots of the Canaanites (comp. 2 Kings 9:21; 10:15).

Jo'ab—*Jehovah is his father.* (1.) One of the three sons of Zeruiah, David's sister, and "captain of the host" during the whole of David's reign (2 Sam. 2:13; 10:7; 11:1; 1 Kings 11:15). His father's name is nowhere mentioned, although his sepulchre at Bethlehem is mentioned (2

Sam. 2:32). His two brothers were Abishai and Asahel, the swift of foot, who was killed by Abner (2 Sam. 2:13–32), whom Joab afterwards treacherously murdered (3:22–27). He afterwards led the assault at the storming of the fortress on Mount Zion, and for this service was raised to the rank of "prince of the king's army" (2 Sam. 5:6–10; 1 Chr. 27:34). His chief military achievements were—(1) against the allied forces of Syria and Ammon; (2) against Edom (1 Kings 11:15, 16); and (3) against the Ammonites (2 Sam. 10:7–19; 11:1, 11). His character is deeply stained by the part he willingly took in the murder of Uriah (11:14–25). He acted apparently from a sense of duty in putting Absalom to death (18:1–14). David was unmindful of the many services Joab had rendered to him, and afterwards gave the command of the army to Amasa, Joab's cousin (2 Sam. 20:1–13; 19:13). When David was dying Joab espoused the cause of Adonijah in preference to that of Solomon. He was afterwards slain by Benaiah, by the command of Solomon, in accordance with his father's injunction (2 Sam. 3:29; 19:5–7), at the altar to which he had fled for refuge. Thus this hoary conspirator died without one to lift up a voice in his favour. He was buried in his own property in the "wilderness," probably in the north-east of Jerusalem (1 Kings 2:5, 28–34). Benaiah succeeded him as commander-in-chief of the army.

(2.) 1 Chr. 4:14.

(3.) Ezra 2:6.

Jo'ah—*Jehovah his brother; i.e., helper*. (1.) One of the sons of Obed-edom (1 Chr. 26:4), a Korhite porter.

(2.) A Levite of the family of Gershom (1 Chr. 6:21), probably the same as Ethan (42).

(3.) The son of Asah, and "recorder" (*q.v.*) or chronicler to King Hezekiah (2 Kings 18:18, 26, 37).

(4.) Son of Joahaz, and "recorder" (*q.v.*) or keeper of the state archives under King Josiah (2 Chr. 34:8).

Jo'ahaz (2 Chr. 34:8), a contracted form of **Jehoahaz** (*q.v.*).

Joan'na—*whom Jehovah has graciously given*. (1.) The grandson of Zerubbabel,

in the lineage of Christ (Luke 3:27); the same as Hananiah (1 Chr. 3:19).

(2.) The wife of Chuza, the steward of Herod Antipas, tetrarch of Galilee (Luke 8:3). She was one of the women who ministered to our Lord, and to whom he appeared after his resurrection (Luke 8:3; 24:10).

Jo'ash—*whom Jehovah bestowed*. (1.) A contracted form of **Jehoash**, the father of Gideon (Judg. 6:11, 29; 2 Kings 12:1; 13:1).

(2.) One of the Benjamite archers who joined David at Ziklag (1 Chr. 12:3).

(3.) One of King Ahab's sons (1 Kings 22:26).

(4.) King of Judah (2 Kings 11:2; 12:19, 20). (See JEHOASH [1].)

(5.) King of Israel (2 Kings 13:9, 12, 13, 25). (See JEHOASH [2].)

(6.) 1 Chr. 7:8.

(7.) One who had charge of the royal stores of oil under David and Solomon (1 Chr. 27:28).

Jôb—*persecuted*—an Arabian patriarch who resided in the land of Uz (*q.v.*). While living in the midst of great prosperity, he was suddenly overwhelmed by a series of sore trials that fell upon him. Amid all his sufferings he maintained his integrity. Once more God visited him with the rich tokens of his goodness and even greater prosperity than he had enjoyed before. He survived the period of trial for one hundred and forty years, and died in a good old age, an example to succeeding generations of integrity (Ezek. 14:14, 20) and of submissive patience under the sorest calamities (James 5:11). His history, so far as it is known, is recorded in his book.

Jôb, Book of. A great diversity of opinion exists as to the authorship of this book. From internal evidence—such as the similarity of sentiment and language to those in the Psalms and Proverbs (see Ps. 88 and 89), the prevalence of the idea of "wisdom," and the style and character of the composition—it is supposed by some to have been written in the time of David and Solomon. Others argue that it was written by Job himself, or by Elihu, or Isaiah, or perhaps more probably by Moses, who was "learned in all the wisdom of the Egyptians, and mighty in words and deeds" (Acts 7 : 22). He had opportunities in Midian for obtaining the knowledge of the facts related. But the authorship is altogether uncertain.

As to the *character* of the book, it is a historical poem—one of the greatest and sublimest poems in all literature. Job was a historical person, and the localities and names were real and not fictitious. It is "one of the grandest portions of the inspired Scriptures, a heavenly-replenished storehouse of comfort and instruction, the patriarchal Bible, and a precious monument of primitive theology. It is to the Old Testament what the Epistle to the Romans is to the New." It is a didactic narrative in a dramatic form.

This book was apparently well known in the days of Ezekiel, B.C. 600 (Ezek. 14 : 14). It formed a part of the sacred Scriptures used by our Lord and his apostles, and is referred to as a part of the inspired Word (Heb. 12 : 5 ; 1 Cor. 3 : 19).

The *subject* of the book is the trial of Job—its occasion, nature, endurance, and issue. It exhibits the harmony of the truths of revelation and the dealings of Providence, which are seen to be at once inscrutable, just, and merciful. It shows the blessedness of the truly pious, even amid sore afflictions, and thus ministers comfort and hope to tried believers of every age. It is a book of manifold instruction, and is profitable for doctrine, for reproof, for correction, and for instruction in righteousness (2 Tim. 3 : 16).

It consists of—

(1.) An historical introduction in prose (ch. 1, 2).

(2.) The controversy and its solution, in poetry (ch. 3–42 : 6).

Job's desponding lamentation (ch. 3) is the occasion of the controversy which is carried on in three courses of dialogues between Job and his three friends. The first course gives the commencement of the controversy (ch. 4–14) ; the second the growth of the controversy (15–21) ; and the third the height of the controversy (22–27). This is followed by the solution of the controversy in the speeches of Elihu and the address of Jehovah, followed by Job's humble confession (42 : 1–6) of his own fault and folly.

(3.) The third division is the historical conclusion, in prose (42 : 7–15).

Sir J. W. Dawson in "The Expositor" says : "It would now seem that the language and theology of the book of Job can be better explained by supposing it to be a portion of Minean [Southern Arabia] literature obtained by Moses in Midian than in any other way. This view also agrees better than any other with its references to natural objects, the art of mining, and other matters."

Jo'bab—*dweller in the desert.* (1.) One of the sons of Joktan, and founder of an Arabian tribe (Gen. 10 : 29). (2.) King of Edom, succeeded Bela (Gen. 36 : 33, 34). (3.) A Canaanitish king (Josh. 11 : 1) who joined the confederacy against Joshua.

Joch'ebed—*Jehovah is her glory*—the wife of Amram, and the mother of Miriam, Aaron, and Moses (Num. 26 : 59). She is spoken of as the sister of Kohath, Amram's father (Ex. 6 : 20 ; comp. 16, 18 ; 2 : 1–10).

Jo'el—*Jehovah is his God.* (1.) The oldest of Samuel's two sons appointed by him as judges in Beersheba (1 Sam. 8 : 2). (See VASHNI.) (2.) A descendant of Reuben (1 Chr. 5 : 4, 8). (3.) One of David's famous warriors (1 Chr. 11 : 38). (4.) A Levite of the family of Gershom (1 Chr. 15 : 7, 11). (5.) 1 Chr. 7 : 3. (6.) 1 Chr. 27 : 20. (7.) The second of the twelve minor prophets. He was the son of Pethuel. His personal history is only known from his book.

Jo'el, Book of. Joel was probably a resident in Judah, as his commission was to that people. He makes frequent mention of Judah and Jerusalem (1 : 14 ; 2 : 1, 15, 32 ; 3 : 1, 12, 17, 20, 21).

He probably flourished in the reign of Uzziah (about B.C. 800), and was contemporary with Amos and Isaiah.

The *contents* of this book are—(1.) A prophecy of a great public calamity then impending over the land, consisting of a want of water and an extraordinary plague of locusts (1 : 1–2 : 11). (2.) The prophet then calls on his countrymen to repent and to turn to God, assuring them of his readiness to forgive (2:12-17), and foretelling the restoration of the land to its accustomed fruitfulness (18-26). (3.) Then follows a Messianic prophecy, quoted by Peter (Acts 2:39). (4.) Finally, the prophet foretells portents and judgments as destined to fall on the enemies of God (ch. 3, but in the Hebrew text 4).

Joe′lah, a Benjamite who joined David at Ziklag (1 Chr. 12:7).

Jo′ezer—*Jehovah is his help*—one of the Korhites who became part of David's bodyguard (1 Chr. 12:6).

Joha′nan—*whom Jehovah graciously bestows.* (1.) One of the Gadite heroes who joined David in the desert of Judah (1 Chr. 12:12).

(2.) The oldest of King Josiah's sons (1 Chr. 3:15).

(3.) Son of Careah, one of the Jewish chiefs who rallied round Gedaliah, whom Nebuchadnezzar had made governor in Jerusalem (2 Kings 25:23; Jer. 40:8). He warned Gedaliah of the plans of Ishmael against him, a warning which was unheeded (Jer. 40:13, 16). He afterwards pursued the murderer of the governor, and rescued the captives (41:8, 13, 15, 16). He and his associates subsequently fled to Tahpanhes in Egypt (43:2, 4, 5), taking Jeremiah with them. "The flight of Gedaliah's community to Egypt extinguished the last remaining spark of life in the Jewish state. The work of the ten centuries since Joshua crossed the Jordan had been undone."

John. (1.) One who, with Annas and Caiaphas, sat in judgment on the apostles Peter and John (Acts 4:6). He was of the kindred of the high priest; otherwise unknown.

(2.) The Hebrew name of Mark (*q.v.*). He is designated by this name in the Acts of the Apostles (12:12, 25; 13:5, 13; 15:37).

(3.) THE APOSTLE, brother of James the "Greater" (Matt. 4:21; 10:2; Mark 1:19; 3:17; 10:35). He was one, probably the younger, of the sons of Zebedee (Matt. 4:21) and Salome (Matt. 27:56; comp. Mark 15:40), and was born at Bethsaida. His father was apparently a man of some wealth (comp. Mark 1:20; Luke 8:3; John 19:27). He was doubtless trained in all that constituted the ordinary education of Jewish youth. When he grew up he followed the occupation of a fisherman on the Lake of Galilee. When John the Baptist began his ministry in the wilderness of Judea, John, with many others, gathered round him, and was deeply influenced by his teaching. There he heard the announcement, "Behold the Lamb of God," and forthwith, on the invitation of Jesus, became a disciple and ranked among his followers (John 1:36, 37) for a time. He and his brother then returned to their former avocation, for how long is uncertain. Jesus again called them (Matt. 4:21; Luke 5:1-11), and now they left all and permanently attached themselves to the company of his disciples. He became one of the innermost circle (Mark 5:37; Matt. 17:1; 26:37; Mark 13:3). He was the disciple whom Jesus loved. In zeal and intensity of character he was a "Boanerges" (Mark 3:17). This spirit once and again broke out (Matt. 20:20-24; Mark 10:35-41; Luke 9:49, 54). At the betrayal he and Peter follow Christ afar off, while the others betake themselves to hasty flight (John 18:15). At the trial he follows Christ into the council chamber, and thence to the prætorium (18:16, 19, 28) and to the place of crucifixion (19:26, 27). To him and Peter, Mary first conveys tidings of the resurrection (20:2), and they are the first to go and see what her strange words mean. After the resurrection he and Peter again return to the Sea of Galilee, where the Lord reveals himself to them (21:1, 7). We find Peter and John frequently after this together (Acts 3:1; 4:13). John remained apparently in Jerusalem as the leader of the church there (Acts 15:6; Gal. 2:9). His subsequent history is unrecorded. He was not there, however, at the time of Paul's last visit (Acts 21:15-40). He appears to have retired to Ephesus, but at what time is unknown. The seven churches of Asia were the objects of his special care (Rev. 1:11). He suffered under persecution, and was banished to Patmos (1:9); whence he again returned to Ephesus, where he died, probably about A.D. 98, having outlived all or nearly all the friends and companions even of his maturer years. There are many interesting traditions regarding John during his residence at Ephesus, but these cannot claim the character of historical truth.

John, Gospel of. The *genuineness* of this Gospel—*i.e.*, the fact that the apostle John was its author—is beyond all reasonable doubt. In recent times, from about 1820, many attempts have been made to impugn its genuineness, but without success.

The *design* of John in writing this Gospel is stated by himself (John 20 : 31). It was at one time supposed that he wrote for the purpose of supplying the omissions of the synoptical—*i.e.*, of the first three—Gospels, but there is no evidence for this. "There is here no history of Jesus and his teaching after the manner of the other evangelists. But there is in historical form a representation of the Christian faith in relation to the person of Christ as its central point ; and in this representation there is a picture on the one hand of the antagonism of the world to the truth revealed in him, and on the other of the spiritual blessedness of the few who yield themselves to him as the Light of life" (Reuss).

After the prologue (1 : 1-5), the historical part of the book begins with verse 6, and consists of two parts. The first part (1 : 6-ch. 12) contains the history of our Lord's public ministry from the time of his introduction to it by John the Baptist to its close. The second part (ch. 13-21) presents our Lord in the retirement of private life and in his intercourse with his immediate followers (13-17), and gives an account of his sufferings and of his appearances to the disciples after his resurrection (18-21).

The peculiarities of this Gospel are the place it gives (1) to the mystical relation of the Son to the Father, and (2) of the Redeemer to believers ; (3) the announcement of the Holy Ghost as the Comforter ; (4) the prominence given to love as an element in the Christian character. It was obviously addressed primarily to Christians.

It was probably written at Ephesus, which, after the destruction of Jerusalem (A.D. 70), became the centre of Christian life and activity in the East, about A.D. 90.

John, First Epistle of, the fourth of the catholic or "general" epistles. It was evidently written by John the evangelist, and probably also at Ephesus, and when the writer was in advanced age. The purpose of the apostle (1 : 1-4) is to declare the Word of Life to those to whom he writes, in order that they might be united in fellowship with the Father and his Son Jesus Christ. He shows that the means of union with God are—(1) on the part of Christ, his atoning work (1 : 7 ; 2 : 2 ; 3 : 5 ; 4 : 10, 14 ; 5 : 11, 12) and his advocacy (2 : 1) ; and (2), on the part of man, holiness (1 : 6), obedience (2 : 3), purity (3 : 3), faith (3 : 23 ; 4 : 3 ; 5 : 5), and love (2 : 7, 8 ; 3 : 14 ; 4 : 7 ; 5 : 1).

John, Second Epistle of, is addressed to "the elect lady," and closes with the words, "The children of thy elect sister greet thee ; " but some would read instead of " lady " the proper name Kyria. Of the thirteen verses composing this epistle seven are in the First Epistle. The person addressed is commended for her piety, and is warned against false teachers.

John, Third Epistle of, is addressed to Caius, or Gaius, but whether to the Christian of that name in Macedonia (Acts 19 : 29) or in Corinth (Rom. 16 : 23) or in Derbe (Acts 20 : 4) is uncertain. It was written for the purpose of commending to Gaius some Christians who were strangers in the place where he lived, and who had gone thither for the purpose of preaching the gospel (ver. 7).

The Second and Third Epistles were probably written soon after the First, and from Ephesus.

John the Baptist, the "forerunner of our Lord." We have but fragmentary and imperfect accounts of him in the Gospels. He was of priestly descent. His father, Zacharias, was a priest of the course of Abia (1 Chr. 24 : 10), and his mother, Elisabeth, was of the daughters of Aaron (Luke 1 : 5). The mission of John was the subject of prophecy (Matt. 3:3; Isa. 40:3; Mal. 3:1). His birth, which took place six months before that of Jesus, was foretold by an angel. Zacharias, deprived of the power of speech as a token of God's truth and a reproof of his own incredulity with reference to the birth of his son, had the power of speech restored to him on the occasion of his circumcision (Luke 1:64). After this no more is recorded of him for thirty years than what is mentioned in Luke 1:80. John was a Nazarite from his birth (Luke 1:15; Num. 6:1–12). He spent his early years in the mountainous tract of Judah lying between Jerusalem and the Dead Sea (Matt. 3:1–12).

At length he came forth into public life, and great multitudes from "every quarter" were attracted to him. The sum of his preaching was the necessity of repentance. He denounced the Sadducees and Pharisees as a "generation of vipers," and warned them of the folly of trusting to external privileges (Luke 3:8). "As a preacher, John was eminently practical and discriminating. Self-love and covetousness were the prevalent sins of the people at large. On them, therefore, he enjoined charity and consideration for others. The publicans he cautioned against extortion, the soldiers against crime and plunder." His doctrine and manner of life roused the entire south of Palestine, and the people from all parts flocked to the place where he was, on the banks of the Jordan. There he baptized thousands unto repentance.

The fame of John reached the ears of Jesus in Nazareth (Matt. 3:5), and he came from Galilee to Jordan to be baptized of John, on the special ground that it became him to "fulfil all righteousness" (3:15). John's special office ceased with the baptism of Jesus, who must now "increase as the King come to his kingdom. He continued, however, for a while to bear testimony to the Messiahship of Jesus. He pointed him out to his disciples, saying, "Behold the Lamb of God." His public ministry was suddenly (after about six months probably) brought to a close by his being cast into prison by Herod, whom he had reproved for the sin of having taken

to himself the wife of his brother Philip (Luke 3:19). He was shut up in the castle of Machærus (q.v.), a fortress on the southern extremity of Peræa, 9 miles east of the Dead Sea, and here he was beheaded. His disciples, having consigned the headless body to the grave, went and told Jesus all that had occurred (Matt. 14:3–12). John's death occurred apparently just before the third Passover of our Lord's ministry. Our Lord himself testified regarding him that he was a "burning and a shining light" (John 5:35).

Joi′ada (*whom Jehovah favours*) = Jehoiada. (1.) Neh. 3:6. (2.) One of the high priests (12:10, 11, 22).

Joi′akim (*whom Jehovah has set up*) = Jehoiakim, a high priest, the son and successor of Jeshua (Neh. 12:10, 12, 26).

Joi′arib (*whom Jehovah defends*) = Jehoiarib. (1.) The founder of one of the courses of the priests (Neh. 11:10).

(2.) Neh. 11:5; a descendant of Judah.

(3.) Neh. 12:6.

(4.) Ezra 8:16, a "man of understanding" whom Ezra sent to "bring ministers for the house of God."

Jok′deam, a city in the mountains of Judah (Josh. 15:56).

Jo′kim—*whom Jehovah has set up*—one of the descendants of Shelah (1 Chr. 4:22).

Jok′meam—*gathering of the people*—a city of Ephraim, which was given with its suburbs to the Levites (1 Chr. 6:68). It lay somewhere in the Jordan valley (1 Kings 4:12, R.V.; but in A.V. incorrectly "Jokneam").

Jok′neam—*gathered by the people*—(Josh. 19:11; 21:34), a city "of Carmel" (12:22)—*i.e.*, on Carmel, allotted with its suburbs to the Merarite Levites. It is the modern *Tell Kaimôn*, about 12 miles southwest of Nazareth, on the south of the river Kishon.

Jok′shan—*snarer*—the second son of Abraham and Keturah (Gen. 25:2, 3; 1 Chr. 1:32).

Jok′tan—*little*—the second of the two sons of Eber (Gen. 10:25; 1 Chr. 1:19). There is an Arab tradition that Joktan (Arab. *Kahtân*) was the progenitor of all the purest tribes of Central and Southern Arabia.

Jok'theel—*subdued by God.* (1.) A city of Judah near Lachish (Josh. 15, 38). Perhaps the ruin *Kutlâneh*, south of Gezer.

(2.) Amaziah, king of Judah, undertook a great expedition against Edom (2 Chr. 25:5-10), which was completely successful. He routed the Edomites and slew vast numbers of them. So wonderful did this victory appear to him that he acknowledged that it could have been achieved only by the special help of God, and therefore he called Selah (*q.v.*), their great fortress city, by the name of Joktheel (2 Kings 14:7).

Jon'adab=Jehon'adab. (1.) The son of Rechab, and founder of the Rechabites (*q.v.*)—2 Kings 10:15; Jer. 35:6, 10.

(2.) The son of Shimeah, David's brother (2 Sam, 13:3). He was "a very subtil man."

Jo'nah—*a dove*—the son of Amittai of Gath-hepher. He was a prophet of Israel, and predicted the restoration of the ancient boundaries (2 Kings 14:25-27) of the kingdom. He exercised his ministry very early in the reign of Jeroboam II., and thus was contemporary with Hosea and Amos; or possibly he preceded them, and consequently may have been the very oldest of all the prophets whose writings we possess. His personal history is mainly to be gathered from the book which bears his name. It is chiefly interesting from the two-fold character in which he appears—(1) as a missionary to heathen Nineveh, and (2) as a type of the "Son of man."

Jo'nah, Book of. This book professes to give an account of what actually took place in the experience of the prophet. Some critics have sought to interpret the book as a parable or allegory, and not as a history. They have done so for various reasons. Thus (1) some reject it on the ground that the miraculous element enters so largely into it, and that it is not prophetical but narrative in its form; (2) others, denying the possibility of miracles altogether, hold that therefore it cannot be true history.

Jonah and his story is referred to by our Lord (Matt. 12:39, 40; Luke 11:29), a fact to which the greatest weight must be attached. It is impossible to interpret this reference on any other theory. This one argument is of sufficient importance to settle the whole question. No theories devised for the purpose of getting rid of difficulties can stand against such a proof that the book is a veritable history.

There is every reason to believe that this book was written by Jonah himself. It gives an account of (1) his divine commission to go to Nineveh, his disobedience, and the punishment following (1:1-17); (2) his prayer and miraculous deliverance (1:17-2:10); (3) the second commission given to him, and his prompt obedience in delivering the message from God, and its results in the repentance of the Ninevites, and God's long-sparing mercy toward them (ch. 3); (4) Jonah's displeasure at God's merciful decision, and the rebuke tendered to the impatient prophet (ch. 4). Nineveh was spared after Jonah's mission for more than a century. The history of Jonah may well be regarded "as a part of that great onward movement which was before the Law and under the Law; which gained strength and volume as the fulness of the times drew near."—Perowne's *Jonah.*

Jonas. (1.) Greek form of Jonah (Matt. 12:39, 40, 41, etc.).

(2.) The father of the apostles Peter (John 21:15-17) and Andrew; but the reading should be (also in 1:42), as in the Revised Version, "John," instead of Jonas.

Jon'athan—*whom Jehovah gave*—the name of fifteen or more persons that are mentioned in Scripture. The chief of these are—(1.) A Levite descended from Gershom (Judg. 18:30). His history is recorded in 17:7-13 and 18:30. The Rabbins changed this name into Manasseh "to screen the memory of the great lawgiver from the stain of having so unworthy an apostate among his near descendants." He became priest of the idol image at Dan, and this office continued in his family till the Captivity.

(2.) The eldest son of king Saul, and the bosom friend of David. He is first men-

JAFFA FROM THE HARBOUR.

tioned when he was about thirty years of age, some time after his father's accession to the throne (1 Sam. 13:2). Like his father, he was a man of great strength and activity (2 Sam. 1:23), and excelled in archery and slinging (1 Chr. 12:2; 2 Sam. 1:22). The affection that evidently subsisted between him and his father was interrupted by the growth of Saul's insanity. At length, "in fierce anger," he left his father's presence and cast in his lot with the cause of David (1 Sam. 20:34). After an eventful career, interwoven to a great

extent with that of David, he fell, along with his father and his two brothers, on the fatal field of Gilboa (1 Sam. 31:2, 8). He was first buried at Jabesh-gilead, but his remains were afterwards removed with those of his father to Zelah, in Benjamin (2 Sam. 21:12–14). His death was the occasion of David's famous elegy of "the Song of the Bow" (2 Sam. 1:22–26). He left one son five years old, Merib-baal, or Mephibosheth (2 Sam. 4:4; comp. 1 Chr. 8:34).

(3.) Son of the high priest Abiathar, and

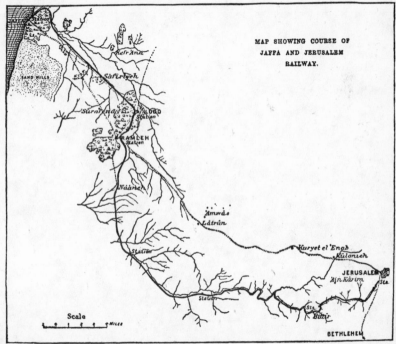

MAP SHOWING COURSE OF
JAFFA AND JERUSALEM
RAILWAY.

(By permission of the Committee of the Palestine Exploration Fund.)

one who adhered to David at the time of Absalom's rebellion (2 Sam. 15:27, 36). He is the last descendant of Eli of whom there is any record.

(4.) Son of Shammah, and David's nephew, and also one of his chief warriors (2 Sam. 21:21). He slew a giant in Gath.

Jo'nath-e'lem-recho'kim—*dove of the dumbness of the distance; i.e.,* "the silent dove in distant places"—title of Ps. 56. This was probably the name of some well-known tune or melody to which the psalm was to be sung.

Jop'pa—*beauty*—a town in the portion of Dan (Josh. 19:46; A.V., "Japho"), on a sandy promontory between Cæsarea and Gaza, and at a distance of 30 miles northwest from Jerusalem. It is one of the oldest towns in Asia. It was and still is the chief sea-port of Judea. It was never wrested from the Phœnicians. It became a Jewish town only in the second century B.C. It was from this port that Jonah "took ship to flee from the presence of the Lord" (Jonah 1:3). To this place also the wood cut in Lebanon by Hiram's men for

Solomon was brought in floats (2 Chr. 2: 16); and here the material for the building of the second temple was also landed (Ezra 3:7). At Joppa, in the house of Simon the tanner, "by the sea-side," Peter resided "many days," and here, "on the house-top," he had his "vision of tolerance" (Acts 9:36–43). It bears the modern name of *Jaffa*, and exhibits all the decrepitude and squalor of cities ruled over by the Turks. "Scarcely any other town has been so often overthrown, sacked, pillaged, burned, and rebuilt." Its present popula-

tion is said to be about 16,000. It was taken by the French under Napoleon in 1799, who gave orders for the massacre here of 4,000 prisoners. It is connected with Jerusalem by the only carriage road that exists in the country, and also by a railway completed in 1892.

Jo′ram = Jeho′ram. (1.) One of the kings of Israel (2 Kings 8:16, 25, 28). He was the son of Ahab.

(2.) Jehoram, the son and successor of Jehoshaphat on the throne of Judah (2 Kings 8:24).

SOURCE OF THE JORDAN NEAR BANIAS.

Jordan—Heb. *Yardên*, "the descender;" Arab. *Nahr-esh-Sherîah*, "the watering-place"—the chief river of Palestine. It flows from north to south down a deep valley in the centre of the country. The name *descender* is significant of the fact that there is along its whole course a descent to its banks; or it may simply denote the rapidity with which it "descends" to the Dead Sea.

It originates in the snows of Hermon, which feed its perennial fountains. Two sources are generally spoken of. (1.) From

the western base of a hill on which once stood the city of Dan, the northern border-city of Palestine, there gushes forth a considerable fountain called the Leddân, which is the largest fountain in Syria and the principal source of the Jordan. (2.) Beside the ruins of Banias, the ancient Cæsarea-Philippi and the yet more ancient Panium, is a lofty cliff of limestone, at the base of which is a fountain. This is the other source of the Jordan, and has always been regarded by the Jews as its true source. It rushes down to the plain in a foaming torrent, and joins the Leddân about 5 miles south of Dan (*Tell-el-Kâdy*). (3.) But besides these two historical fountains there is a third, called the *Hasbâny*, which rises in the bottom of a valley at the western base of Hermon, 12 miles north of Tell-el-Kâdy. It joins the main stream about a mile below the junction of the Leddân and the Banias. The river thus formed is at this point about 45 feet wide, and flows in a channel from 12 to 20 feet below the plain.

After this it flows, "with a swift current and a much-twisted course," through a marshy plain for some 6 miles, when it falls into the Lake Hûleh, "the waters of Merom" (*q.v.*). During this part of its course the Jordan has descended about 1,100 feet. At Banias it is 1,080 feet above sea-level. Flowing from the southern extremity of Lake Hûleh, here almost on a level with the sea, it flows for 2 miles "through a waste of islets and papyrus," and then for 9 miles through a narrow gorge in a foaming torrent onward to the Sea of Galilee (*q.v.*).

"In the whole valley of the Jordan, from the Lake Hûleh to the Sea of Galilee, there is not a single settled inhabitant. Along the whole eastern bank of the river and the lakes, from the base of Hermon to the ravine of Hieromax—a region of great fertility, 30 miles long by 7 or 8 wide—there are only some three inhabited villages. The western bank is almost as desolate. Ruins are numerous enough. Every mile or two is an old site of town or village, now well-nigh hid beneath a dense jungle of thorns and thistles. The words of Scripture here recur to us with peculiar force: 'I will make your cities waste, and bring your sanctuaries unto desolation...... And I will bring the land into desolation: and your enemies which dwell therein shall be astonished at it......And your land shall be desolate, and your cities waste. Then shall the land enjoy her sabbaths, as long as it lieth desolate' (Lev. 26:31–34)."—Dr. Porter's *Handbook, etc.*

From the Sea of Galilee, at the level of 682 feet below the Mediterranean, the river flows through a long, low plain called "the region of Jordan" (Matt. 3:5), and by the modern Arabs the *Ghôr* or "sunken plain." This section is properly the Jordan of Scripture. Down through the midst of the "plain of Jordan," there winds a ravine varying in breadth from 200 yards to half a mile, and in depth from 40 to 150 feet. Through it the Jordan flows in a rapid, rugged, tortuous course down to the Dead Sea. The whole distance from the southern extremity of the Sea of Galilee to the Dead Sea is in a straight line about 65 miles, but following the windings of the river about 200 miles, during which it falls 618 feet. The total length of the Jordan from Banias is about 104 miles in a straight line, during which it falls 2,380 feet.

There are two considerable affluents which enter the river between the Sea of Galilee and the Dead Sea, both from the east. (1.) The *Wâdy Mandhûr*, called the Yarmûk by the Rabbins and the Hieromax by the Greeks. It formed the boundary between Bashan and Gilead. It drains the plateau of the Haurân. (2.) The Jabbok or *Wâdy Zerka*, formerly the northern boundary of Ammon. It enters the Jordan about 20 miles north of Jericho.

The *first historical notice* of the Jordan is in the account of the separation of Abraham and Lot (Gen. 13:10). "Lot beheld the plain of Jordan as the garden of the Lord." Jacob crossed and re-crossed "this Jordan" (32:10). The Israelites passed over it as "on dry ground" (Josh. 3:17; Ps. 114:3). Twice afterwards its waters were miraculously divided at the same spot by Elijah and Elisha (2 Kings 2:8, 14).

The Jordan is mentioned in the Old Testament about one hundred and eighty times, and in the New Testament fifteen times. The chief events in gospel history connected with it are (1) John the Baptist's ministry; when "there went out to him Jerusalem, and all Judea, and were baptized of him in Jordan" (Matt. 3:6). (2.) Jesus also "was baptized of John in Jordan" (Mark 1:9).

Jo'seph—*remover* or *increaser*. (1.) The elder of the two sons of Jacob by Rachel (Gen. 30:23, 24), who, on the occasion of his birth, said, "God hath taken away [Heb. *'dsaph*] my reproach." "The Lord shall add [Heb. *yoseph*] to me another son" (Gen. 30:24). He was a child of probably six years of age when his father returned from Haran to Canaan and took up his residence in the old patriarchal town of Hebron. "Now Israel loved Joseph more than all his children, because he was the son of his old age," and he "made him a long garment with sleeves" (Gen. 37:3, R.V. marg.)—*i.e.*, a garment long and full, such as was worn by the children of nobles. This seems to be the correct rendering of the words. The phrase, however, may also be rendered, "a coat of many pieces"—*i.e.*, a patchwork of many small pieces of divers colours.

When he was about seventeen years old Joseph incurred the jealous hatred of his brothers (Gen. 37:4). They "hated him, and could not speak peaceably unto him." Their anger was increased when he told them his dreams (37:11).

Jacob desiring to hear tidings of his sons, who had gone to Shechem with their flocks—some 60 miles from Hebron—sent Joseph as his messenger to make inquiry regarding them. Joseph found that they had left Shechem for Dothan, whither he followed them. As soon as they saw him coming they began to plot against him, and would have killed him had not Reuben interposed. They ultimately sold him to a company of Ishmaelite merchants for twenty pieces (shekels) of silver (about £2, 10s.)—ten pieces less than the current value of a slave, for "they cared little what they had for him, if so be they were rid of him." These merchants were going down with a varied assortment of merchandise to the Egyptian market, and thither they conveyed him, and ultimately sold him as a slave to Potiphar, an "officer of Pharaoh's, and captain of the guard" (Gen. 37:36). "The Lord blessed the Egyptian's house for Joseph's sake," and Potiphar made him overseer over his house. At length a false charge having been brought against him by Potiphar's wife, he was at once cast into the state prison (39; 40), where he remained for at least two years.

After a while the "chief of the cup-bearers" and the "chief of the bakers" of Pharaoh's household were cast into the same prison (40:2). Each of these new prisoners dreamed a dream in the same night, which Joseph interpreted, the event occurring as he had said.

This led to Joseph's being remembered subsequently by the chief butler when Pharaoh also dreamed. At his suggestion Joseph was brought from prison to interpret the king's dreams. Pharaoh was well pleased with Joseph's wisdom in interpreting his dreams, and with his counsel with reference to the events then predicted; and he set him over all the land of Egypt (Gen. 41:46), and gave him the name of Zaphnath-paaneah. He was married to Asenath, the daughter of the priest of On, and thus became a member of the priestly class. Joseph was now about thirty years of age.

As Joseph had interpreted, seven years of plenty came, during which he stored up great abundance of corn in granaries built for the purpose. These years were followed by seven years of famine "over all the face of the earth," when "all countries came into Egypt to Joseph to buy corn" (Gen. 41:56, 57; 47:13, 14). Thus "Joseph gathered up all the money that was in the land of Egypt, and in the land of Canaan, for the corn which they bought." Afterwards all the cattle and all the land, and at last the Egyptians themselves, became the property of Pharaoh.

During this period of famine Joseph's brethren also came down to Egypt to buy corn. The history of his dealings with them, and of the manner in which he at length made himself known to them, is one of the most interesting narratives that can be read (Gen. 42–44). Joseph directed his brethren to return and bring Jacob and his family to the land of Egypt, saying, "I will give you the good of the land of Egypt, and ye shall eat the fat of the land. Regard not your stuff; for the good of all the land is yours." Accordingly Jacob and his family, to the number of threescore and ten souls, together with "all that they had," went down to Egypt. They were settled in the land of Goshen, where Joseph met his father, and "fell on his neck, and wept on his neck a good while" (Gen. 46:29).

Jacob at length died, and in fulfilment of a promise which he had exacted, Joseph went up to Canaan to bury his father in "the field of Ephron the Hittite" (Gen. 47:29-31; 50:1-14). This was the last recorded act of Joseph, who again returned to Egypt.

HEAD OF SPHINX OF ZOAN.
(Believed to represent Apepi.)

By his wife Asenath, Joseph had two sons—Manasseh and Ephraim (Gen. 41:50). Joseph having obtained a promise from his brethren that when the time should come that God would "bring them unto the land which he sware to Abraham, to Isaac, and to Jacob," they would carry up his bones out of Egypt, at length died, at the age of one hundred and ten years; and "they embalmed him, and he was put in a coffin" (Gen. 50:26). This promise was faithfully observed. Their descendants, long after, when the Exodus came, carried the body about with them during their forty years' wanderings, and at length buried it in Shechem, in the parcel of ground which Jacob bought from the sons of Hamor (Josh. 24:32; comp. Gen. 33:19). With the death of Joseph the patriarchal age of the history of Israel came to a close.

The Pharaoh of *Joseph's elevation* was probably Apepi, or Apôpis, the last of the Hyksôs kings. Some, however, think that Joseph came to Egypt in the reign of Thothmes III. (see page 539), long after the expulsion of the Hyksôs.

The name Joseph denotes the two tribes of Ephraim and Manasseh in Deut. 33:13-17; the kingdom of Israel in Ezek. 37:16, 19, Amos 5:6; and the whole covenant people of Israel in Ps. 81:4.

(2.) One of the sons of Asaph, head of the first division of sacred musicians (1 Chr. 25:2, 9).

(3.) The son of Judah, and father of Semei (Luke 3:26). Other two of the same name in the ancestry of Christ are also mentioned (3:24, 30).

(4.) The foster-father of our Lord (Matt. 1:16; Luke 3:23). He lived at Nazareth in Galilee (Luke 2:4). He is called a "just man.". He was by trade a carpenter (Matt. 13:55). He is last mentioned in connection with the journey to Jerusalem, when Jesus was twelve years old. It is probable that he died before Jesus entered on his public ministry. This is concluded from the fact that Mary only was present at the marriage feast in Cana of Galilee. His name does not appear in connection with the scenes of the crucifixion along with that of Mary (*q.v.*)—John 19:25.

(5.) A native of Arimathea, probably the Ramah of the Old Testament (1 Sam. 1:19), a man of wealth, and a member of the Sanhedrim (Matt. 27:57; Luke 23:50), an "honourable counsellor, who waited for the kingdom of God." As soon as he heard the tidings of Christ's death, he "went in boldly" (*lit.* "having summoned courage, he went") "unto Pilate, and craved the body of Jesus." Pilate having ascertained from the centurion that the death had really taken place, granted Joseph's request, who immediately, having purchased fine linen (Mark 15:45), proceeded to Golgotha to take the body down from the cross. There, assisted by Nicodemus, he took down the body and wrapped it in the fine linen, sprinkling it with the myrrh and aloes which Nicodemus had brought (John 19:39), and then conveyed the body to the new tomb hewn by Joseph himself out of a rock in his garden hard by. There they laid it, in the presence of Mary Magdalene, Mary the mother of Joses, and other women, and rolled a great stone to the entrance, and departed (Luke 23:53, 54). This was done in haste, "for the Sabbath was drawing on" (comp. Isa. 53:9).

(6.) Surnamed **Bar'sabas** (Acts 1:23); also called Justus. He was one of those who "companied with the apostles all the time that the Lord Jesus went out and in among them" (Acts 1:15), and was one of the candidates for the place of Judas.

Josh'ua—*Jehovah is his help*, or *Jehovah the Saviour*. The son of Nun, of the tribe of Ephraim, the successor of Moses as the leader of Israel. He is called Jehoshua in Num. 13:16 (A.V.), and Jesus in Acts 7:45 and Heb. 4:8 (R.V., Joshua).

He was born in Egypt, and was probably of the age of Caleb, with whom he is generally associated. He shared in all the events of the Exodus, and held the place of commander of the host of the Israelites at their great battle against the Amalekites in Rephidim (Ex. 17:8-16). He became Moses' minister or servant, and accompanied him part of the way when he ascended Mount Sinai to receive the two tables (Ex. 32:17). He was also one of the twelve who were sent on by Moses to explore the land of Canaan (Num. 13:16, 17), and only he and Caleb gave an encouraging report. Under the direction of God, Moses, before his death, invested Joshua in a public and solemn manner with authority over the people as his successor (Deut. 3:28). The people were encamped at Shittim when he assumed the command (Josh. 1:1); and crossing the Jordan, they encamped at Gilgal, where, having circumcised the people, he kept the Passover, and was visited by the Captain of the Lord's host, who spoke to him encouraging words (1:1-9).

Now began the wars of conquest which Joshua carried on for many years, the record of which is in the book which bears his name. Six nations and thirty-one kings were conquered by him (Josh. 11:18-23; 12:24). Having thus subdued the Canaanites, Joshua divided the land among the tribes, Timnath-serah in Mount Ephraim being assigned to himself as his own inheritance. (See SHILOH; PRIEST.)

His work being done, he died, at the age of one hundred and ten years, twenty-five years after having crossed the Jordan. He was buried in his own city of Timnath-serah (Josh. 24); and "the light of Israel for the time faded away."

Joshua has been regarded as a type of Christ (Heb. 4:8) in the following particulars:—(1) In the name common to both; (2) Joshua brings the people into the possession of the Promised Land, as Jesus brings his people to the heavenly Canaan; and (3) as Joshua succeeded Moses, so the Gospel succeeds the Law.

The character of Joshua is thus well sketched by Edersheim:—"Born a slave in Egypt, he must have been about forty years old at the time of the Exodus. Attached to the person of Moses, he led Israel in the first decisive battle against Amalek (Ex. 17:9, 13), while Moses in the prayer of faith held up to heaven the God-given 'rod.' It was no doubt on that occasion that his name was changed from *Oshea*, 'help,' to *Jehoshua*, 'Jehovah is help' (Num. 13:16). And this name is the key to his life and work. Alike in bringing the people into Canaan, in his wars, and in the distribution of the land among the tribes — from the miraculous crossing of Jordan and taking of Jericho to his last address—he was the embodiment of his new name, 'Jehovah is help.' To this outward calling his character also corresponded. It is marked by singleness of purpose, directness, and decision......He sets an object before him, and unswervingly follows it" (*Bible Hist.*, iii. 103).

Josh'ua, The Book of, contains a history of the Israelites from the death of Moses to that of Joshua. It consists of three parts:—(1.) The history of the conquest of the land (1-12). (2.) The allotment of the land to the different tribes, with the appointment of cities of refuge, the provision for the Levites (13–22), and the dismissal of the eastern tribes to their homes. This section has been compared to the Domesday Book of the Norman conquest. (3.) The farewell addresses of Joshua, with an account of his death (23, 24).

This book stands first in the second of the three sections—(1) the Law, (2) the Prophets, (3) the "other writings" = Hagiographa — into which the Jewish Church divided the Old Testament. There is every reason for concluding that the uniform tradition of the Jews is correct when they assign the *authorship* of the book to Joshua, all except the concluding section; the last verses (24 : 29–33) were added by some other hand.

There are two difficulties connected with this book which have given rise to much discussion—(1.) The miracle of the standing still of the sun and moon on Gibeon. The record of it occurs in Joshua's impassioned prayer of faith, as quoted (Josh. 10 : 12–15) from the "Book of Jasher" (*q.v.*). There are many explanations given of these words. They need, however, present no difficulty if we believe in the possibility of God's miraculous interposition in behalf of his people. Whether it was caused by the refraction of the light, or how, we know not.

(2.) Another difficulty arises out of the command given by God utterly to exterminate the Canaanites. "Shall not the Judge of all the earth do right?" It is enough that Joshua clearly knew that this was the will of God, who employs his terrible agencies, famine, pestilence, and war, in the righteous government of this world. The Canaanites had sunk into a state of immorality and corruption so foul and degrading that they had to be rooted out of the land with the edge of the sword. "The Israelites' sword, in its bloodiest executions, wrought a work of mercy for all the countries of the earth to the very end of the world."

This book resembles the Acts of the Apostles in the number and variety of historical incidents it records, and in its many references to persons and places;

and as in the latter case the epistles of Paul (see Paley's *Horæ Paul.*) confirm its historical accuracy by their incidental allusions and "undesigned coincidences," so in the former modern discoveries confirm its historicity. The Amarna tablets (see ADONI-ZEDEC) are among the most remarkable discoveries of the age. Dating from about B.C. 1480 down to the time of Joshua, and consisting of official communications from Amorite, Phœnician, and Philistine chiefs to the king of Egypt, they afford a glimpse into the actual condition of Palestine prior to the Hebrew invasion, and illustrate and confirm the history of the conquest. A letter, also still extant, from a military officer, "master of the captains of Egypt," dating from near the end of the reign of Rameses II., gives a curious account of a journey, probably official, which he undertook through Palestine as far north as to Aleppo, and an insight into the social condition of the country at that time. Among the things brought to light by this letter and the Amarna tablets is the state of confusion and decay that had now fallen on Egypt. The Egyptian garrisons that had held possession of Palestine from the time of Thothmes III., some two hundred years before, had now been withdrawn. The way was thus opened for the Hebrews. In the history of the conquest there is no mention of Joshua having encountered any Egyptian force. The tablets contain many appeals to the king of Egypt for help against the inroads of the Hebrews, but no help seems ever to have been sent. Is not this just such a state of things as might have been anticipated as the result of the disaster of the Exodus? In many points, as shown under various articles, the progress of the conquest is remarkably illustrated by the tablets. The value of modern discoveries in their relation to Old Testament history has been thus well described :—

"The difficulty of establishing the charge of lack of historical credibility, as against the testimony of the Old Testament, has of late years greatly increased. The outcome of recent excavations and explorations is altogether against it. As long as these books contained, in the main, the only known accounts of the events they mention, there was some plausibility in the theory that perhaps these accounts were written rather to teach moral lessons than to preserve an exact knowledge of events. It was easy to say in those times men had not the historic sense. But the recent discoveries touch the events recorded in the Bible at very many different points in many different generations, mentioning the same persons, countries, peoples, events that are mentioned in the Bible, and showing beyond question that these were strictly historic. The point is not that the discoveries confirm the correctness of the Biblical statements, though that is commonly the case, but that the discoveries show that the peoples of those ages had the historic sense, and, specifically, that the Biblical narratives they touch are narratives of actual occurrences."

Josi'ah—*healed by Jehovah,* or *Jehovah will support.* (1.) The son of Amon, and his successor on the throne of Judah (2 Kings 22:1; 2 Chr. 34:1). His history is contained in 2 Kings 22–24. He stands foremost among all the kings of the line of David for unswerving loyalty to Jehovah (23:25). He "did that which was right in the sight of the Lord, and walked in all the ways of David his father." He ascended the throne at the early age of eight years, and it appears that not till eight years afterwards did he begin "to seek after the God of David his father." At that age he devoted himself to God. He distinguished himself by beginning a war of extermination against the prevailing idolatry, which had practically been the state religion for some seventy years (2 Chr. 34:3; comp. Jer. 25:3, 11, 29).

In the eighteenth year of his reign he proceeded to repair and beautify the temple, which by time and violence had become sorely dilapidated (2 Kings 22:3, 5, 6; 23:23; 2 Chr. 34:11). While this work was being carried on, Hilkiah, the high priest, discovered a roll, which was probably the original copy of the law—the entire Pentateuch—written by Moses. When this book was read to him, the king was alarmed by the things it contained, and sent for Huldah, the "prophetess," for her counsel. She spoke to him words of encouragement, telling him that he would be gathered to his fathers in peace before the threatened days of judgment came. Josiah immediately gathered the people together, and engaged them in a renewal of their ancient national covenant with God. The Passover was then celebrated, as in the days of his great predecessor, Hezekiah, with unusual magnificence. Nevertheless, "the Lord turned not from the fierceness of his great wrath wherewith his anger was kindled against Judah" (2 Kings 22:3-20; 23:21-27; 2 Chr. 35:1-19). During the progress of this great religious revolution Jeremiah helped it on by his earnest exhortations.

Soon after this, Pharaoh-Necho II. (*q.v.*), king of Egypt, in an expedition against the king of Assyria, with the view of gaining possession of Carchemish, sought a passage through the territory of Judah for his army. This Josiah refused to permit. He had probably entered into some new alliance with the king of Assyria, and faithful to his word he sought to oppose the progress of Necho.

The army of Judah went out and encountered that of Egypt at Megiddo, on the verge of the plain of Esdraelon. Josiah went into the field in disguise, and was fatally wounded by a random arrow. His attendants conveyed him toward Jerusalem, but had only reached Hadadrimmon, a few miles south of Megiddo, when he died (2 Kings 23:28, 30; comp. 2 Chr. 35:20-27), after a reign of thirty-one years. He was buried with the greatest honours in fulfilment of Huldah's prophecy (2 Kings 22:20; comp. Jer. 34:5). Jeremiah composed a funeral elegy on this the best of the kings of Israel (Lam. 4:20; 2 Chr. 35:25). The outburst of national grief on account of his death became proverbial (Zech. 12:11; comp. Rev. 16:16).

Jot or **Iota,** the smallest letter of the Greek alphabet, used metaphorically or proverbially for the smallest thing (Matt. 5:18); or it may be = *yod,* which is the smallest of the Hebrew letters.

Jo′tham—*Jehovah is perfect.* (1.) The youngest of Gideon's seventy sons. He escaped when the rest were put to death by the order of Abimelech (Judg. 9:5). When "the citizens of Shechem and the whole house of Millo" were gathered together "by the plain of the pillar" (*i.e.*, the stone set up by Joshua—24:26; comp. Gen. 35:4) "that was in Shechem, to make Abimelech king," from one of the heights of Mount Gerizim he protested against their doing so in the earliest parable, that of the bramble-king. His words then spoken were prophetic. There came a recoil in the feelings of the people toward Abimelech, and then a terrible revenge, in which many were slain and the city of Shechem was destroyed by Abimelech (Judg. 9:45). Having delivered his warning, Jotham fled to Beer from the vengeance of Abimelech (9:7–21).

(2.) The son and successor of Uzziah on the throne of Judah. As during his last years Uzziah was excluded from public life on account of his leprosy, his son, then twenty-five years of age, administered for seven years the affairs of the kingdom in his father's stead (2 Chr. 26:21, 23; 27:1). After his father's death he became sole monarch, and reigned for sixteen years (B.C. 759–743). He ruled in the fear of God, and his reign was prosperous. He was contemporary with the prophets Isaiah, Hosea, and Micah, by whose ministrations he profited. He was buried in the sepulchre of the kings, greatly lamented by the people (2 Kings 15:38; 2 Chr. 17:3–9).

Jour′ney. (1.) A *day's journey* in the East is from 16 to 20 miles (Num. 11:31).

(2.) A *Sabbath-day's journey* is 2,000 paces or yards from the city walls (Acts 1:12). According to Jewish tradition, it was the distance one might travel without violating the law of Ex. 16:29. (See SABBATH.)

Joz′abad—*whom Jehovah bestows.* (1.) One of the Benjamite archers who joined David at Ziklag (1 Chr. 12:4). (2.) A chief of the tribe of Manasseh (1 Chr. 12:20).

Joz′achar—*Jehovah-remembered*—one of the two servants who assassinated Je-

hoash, the king of Judah, in Millo (2 Kings 12:21). He is called also Zabad (2 Chr. 24:26).

Ju′bal—*jubilee, music*—Lamech's second son by Adah, of the line of Cain. He was the inventor of "the harp" (Heb. *kinnôr*, properly "lyre") and "the organ" (Heb. *'ugâb*, properly "mouth-organ" or Pan's pipe)—Gen. 4:21.

Ju′bilee—a joyful *shout* or *clangour* of trumpets—the name of the great semi-centennial festival of the Hebrews. It lasted for a year. During this year the land was to be fallow, and the Israelites were only permitted to gather the spontaneous produce of the fields (Lev. 25:11, 12). All landed property during that year reverted to its original owner (13–34; 27:16–24), and all who were slaves were set free (25:39–54), and all debts were remitted.

The return of the jubilee year was proclaimed by a blast of trumpets which sounded throughout the land. There is no record in Scripture of the actual observance of this festival, but there are numerous allusions (Isa. 5:7, 8, 9, 10; 61:1, 2; Ezek. 7:12, 13; Neh. 5:1–19; 2 Chr. 36:24) which place it beyond a doubt that it was observed.

The advantages of this institution were manifold. "1. It would prevent the accumulation of land on the part of a few to the detriment of the community at large. 2. It would render it impossible for any one to be born to absolute poverty, since every one had his hereditary land. 3. It would preclude those inequalities which are produced by extremes of riches and poverty, and which make one man domineer over another. 4. It would utterly do away with slavery. 5. It would afford a fresh opportunity to those who were reduced by adverse circumstances to begin again their career of industry in the patrimony which they had temporarily forfeited. 6. It would periodically rectify the disorders which crept into the state in the course of time, preclude the division of the people into nobles and plebeians, and preserve the theocracy inviolate."

Ju′da. (1.) The patriarch Judah, son

of Jacob (Luke 3:33; Heb. 7:14). In Luke 1:39; Heb. 7:14; Rev. 5:5; 7:5, the word refers to the tribe of Judah.

(2.) The father of Simeon in Christ's maternal ancestry (Luke 3:30).

(3.) Son of Joanna, and father of Joseph in Christ's maternal ancestry (26), probably identical with Abiud (Matt. 1:13), and with Obadiah (1 Chr. 3:21).

(4.) One of the Lord's "brethren" (Mark 6:3).

Ju'dah—*praise*—the fourth son of Jacob by Leah. The name originated in Leah's words of praise to the Lord on account of his birth: "Now will I praise [Heb. *ôdeh*] Jehovah, and she called his name *Yehûdah*" (Gen. 29:35).

It was Judah that interposed in behalf of Joseph, so that his life was spared (Gen. 37:26, 27). He took a lead in the affairs of the family, and "prevailed above his brethren" (Gen. 43:3-10; 44:14, 16-34; 46:28; 1 Chr. 5:2).

Soon after the sale of Joseph to the Ishmaelites, Judah went to reside at Adullam, where he married a woman of Canaan. (See ONAN and TAMAR.) After the death of his wife Shuah, he returned to his father's house, and there exercised much influence over the patriarch, taking a principal part in the events which led to the whole family at length going down into Egypt. We hear nothing more of him till he received his father's blessing (Gen. 49:8-12).

Ju'dah, Tribe of. Judah and his three surviving sons went down with Jacob into Egypt (Gen. 46:12; Ex. 1:2). At the time of the Exodus, when we meet with the family of Judah again, they have increased to the number of 74,000 males (Num. 1:26, 27). Its number increased in the wilderness (26:22). Caleb, the son of Jephunneh, represented the tribe as one of the spies (13:6; 34:19). This tribe marched at the van on the east of the tabernacle (Num. 2:3-9; 10:14), its standard, as is supposed, being a lion's whelp. Under Caleb, during the wars of conquest, they conquered that portion of the country which was afterwards assigned to them as their inheritance. This was the only case in which any tribe had its inheritance thus determined (Josh. 14:6-15; 15:13-19).

The *inheritance* of the tribe of Judah was at first fully one-third of the whole country west of Jordan, in all about 2,300 square miles (Josh. 15). But there was a second distribution, when Simeon received an allotment, about 1,000 square miles, out of the portion of Judah (Josh. 19:9). That which remained to Judah was still very large in proportion to the inheritance of the other tribes. The boundaries of the territory are described in Josh. 15:20-63.

This territory given to Judah was divided into four sections. (1.) The south (Heb. *nĕgĕb*), the undulating pasture-ground between the hills and the desert to the south (Josh. 15:21.) This extent of pasture-land became famous as the favourite camping-ground of the old patriarchs. (2.) The "valley" (15:33) or lowland (Heb. *shephêlah*), a broad strip lying between the central highlands and the Mediterranean. This tract was the garden as well as the granary of the tribe. (3.) The "hill-country," or the mountains of Judah, an elevated plateau stretching from below Hebron northward to Jerusalem. "The towns and villages were generally perched on the tops of hills or on rocky slopes. The resources of the soil were great. The country was rich in corn, wine, oil, and fruit; and the daring shepherds were able to lead their flocks far out over the neighbouring plains and through the mountains." The number of towns in this district was thirty-eight (Josh. 15:48-60). (4.) The "wilderness," the sunken district next the Dead Sea (Josh. 15:6), "averaging 10 miles in breadth, a wild, barren, uninhabitable region, fit only to afford scanty pasturage for sheep and goats and a secure home for leopards, bears, wild goats, and outlaws" (1 Sam. 17:34; 22:1; Mark 1:13). It was divided into the "wilderness of En-gedi" (1 Sam. 24:1), the "wilderness of Judah" (Judg. 1:16; Matt. 3:1), between the Hebron mountain range and the Dead Sea, the "wilderness of Maon" (1 Sam. 23:24). It contained only six cities.

Nine of the cities of Judah were assigned to the priests (Josh. 21 : 9–19).

Ju'dah upon Jordan. The Authorized Version, following the Vulgate, has this rendering in Josh. 19 : 34. It has been suggested that, following the Masoretic punctuation, the expression should read thus, "and Judah; the Jordan was toward the sun-rising." The sixty cities (Havoth-jair, Num. 32 : 41) on the east of Jordan were reckoned as belonging to Judah, because Jair, their founder, was a Manassite only on his mother's side, but on his father's side of the tribe of Judah (1 Chr. 2 : 5, 21–23).

Ju'dah, Kingdom of. When the disruption took place at Shechem, at first only the tribe of Judah followed the house of David. But very soon after the tribe of Benjamin joined the tribe of Judah, and Jerusalem became the capital of the new kingdom (Josh. 18 : 28), which was called the kingdom of Judah. It was very small in extent, being only about the size of the Scottish county of Perth.

For the first sixty years the kings of Judah aimed at re-establishing their authority over the kingdom of the other ten tribes, so that there was a state of perpetual war between them. For the next eighty years there was no open war between them. For the most part they were in friendly alliance, co-operating against their common enemies, especially against Damascus. For about another century and a half Judah had a somewhat checkered existence after the termination of the kingdom of Israel till its final overthrow in the destruction of the temple (B.C. 588) by Nebuzar-adan, who was captain of Nebuchadnezzar's body-guard (2 Kings 25 : 8–21).

The kingdom maintained a separate existence for three hundred and eighty-nine years. It occupied an area of 3,435 square miles. (See ISRAEL, KINGDOM OF.)

Ju'das, the Græcized form of **Judah.** (1.) The patriarch (Matt. 1 : 2, 3).

(2.) Son of Simon (John 6 : 71; 13 : 2, 26), surnamed **Iscariot**—*i.e.,* a man of Kerioth (Josh. 15 : 25). His name is uniformly the last in the list of the apostles, as given in the synoptic (*i.e.,* the first three)

Gospels. The evil of his nature probably gradually unfolded itself till "Satan entered into him" (John 13 : 27), and he betrayed our Lord (18 : 3). Afterwards he owned his sin with "an exceeding bitter cry," and cast the money he had received as the wages of his iniquity down on the floor of the sanctuary, and "departed and went and hanged himself" (Matt. 27 : 5). He perished in his guilt, and "went unto his own place" (Acts 1 : 25). The statement in Acts 1 : 18 that he "fell headlong and burst asunder in the midst, and all his bowels gushed out," is in no way contrary to that in Matt. 27 : 5. The suicide first hanged himself, perhaps over the valley of Hinnom, "and the rope giving way, or the branch to which he hung breaking, he fell down headlong on his face, and was crushed and mangled on the rocky pavement below."

Why such a man was chosen to be an apostle we know not, but it is written that "Jesus knew from the beginning who should betray him" (John 6 : 64). Nor can any answer be satisfactorily given to the question as to the motives that led Judas to betray his Master. "Of the motives that have been assigned we need not care to fix on any one as that which simply led him on. Crime is, for the most part, the result of a hundred motives rushing with bewildering fury through the mind of the criminal."

(3.) A Jew of Damascus (Acts 9 : 11), to whose house Ananias was sent. The street called "Straight" in which it was situated is identified with the modern "street of bazaars," where is still pointed out the so-called "house of Judas."

(4.) A Christian teacher, surnamed **Barsabas.** He was sent from Jerusalem to Antioch along with Paul and Barnabas with the decision of the council (Acts 15 : 22, 27, 32). He was a "prophet" and a "chief man among the brethren."

Jude = Judas. Among the apostles there were two who bore this name—(1) Judas (Jude 1; Matt. 13 : 55; John 14 : 22; Acts 1 : 13), called also Lebbæus or Thaddæus (Matt. 10 : 3; Mark 3 : 18); and (2) Judas Iscariot (Matt. 10 : 4; Mark 3 : 19).

He who is called "the brother of James" (Luke 6 : 16), may be the same with the Judas surnamed Lebbæus. The only thing recorded regarding him is in John 14 : 22.

Jude, Epistle of. The author was "Judas, the brother of James" the Less (Jude 1), called also Lebbæus (Matt. 10 : 3) and Thaddæus (Mark 3 : 18). The *genuineness* of this epistle was early questioned, and doubts regarding it were revived at the time of the Reformation; but the evidences in support of its claims are complete. It has all the marks of having proceeded from the writer whose name it bears.

There is nothing very definite to determine the *time* and *place* at which it was written. It was apparently written in the later period of the apostolic age, for when it was written there were persons still alive who had heard the apostles preach (ver. 17). It may thus have been written about A.D. 66 or 70, and apparently in Palestine.

The epistle is addressed to Christians in general (ver. 1), and its *design* is to put them on their guard against the misleading efforts of a certain class of errorists to which they were exposed. The *style* of the epistle is that of an "impassioned invective, in the impetuous whirlwind of which the writer is hurried along, collecting example after example of divine vengeance on the ungodly; heaping epithet upon epithet, and piling image upon image, and, as it were, labouring for words and images strong enough to depict the polluted character of the licentious apostates against whom he is warning the Church; returning again and again to the subject, as though all language was insufficient to give an adequate idea of their profligacy, and to express his burning hatred of their perversion of the doctrines of the gospel."

The striking resemblance this epistle bears to 2 Peter suggests the idea that the author of the one had seen the epistle of the other.

The doxology with which the epistle concludes is regarded as the finest in the New Testament.

Jude'a. After the Captivity this name was applied to the whole of the country west of the Jordan (Hag. 1 : 1, 14; 2 : 2).

But under the Romans, in the time of Christ, it denoted the southernmost of the three divisions of Palestine (Matt. 2 : 1, 5; 3 : 1; 4 : 25), although it was also sometimes used for Palestine generally (Acts 28 : 21).

The province of Judea, as distinguished from Galilee and Samaria, included the territories of the tribes of Judah, Benjamin, Dan, Simeon, and part of Ephraim. Under the Romans it was a part of the province of Syria, and was governed by a procurator.

Judge (Heb. *shôphet*, pl. *shôphetîm*), properly a magistrate or ruler, rather than one who judges in the sense of trying a cause. This is the name given to those rulers who presided over the affairs of the Israelites during the interval between the death of Joshua and the accession of Saul (Judg. 2 : 18)—a period of general anarchy and confusion. "The office of judges or regents was held during life, but it was not hereditary, neither could they appoint their successors. Their authority was limited by the law alone, and in doubtful cases they were directed to consult the divine King through the priest by Urim and Thummim (Num. 27 : 21). Their authority extended only over those tribes by whom they had been elected or acknowledged. There was no income attached to their office, and they bore no external marks of dignity. The only cases of direct divine appointment are those of Gideon and Samson, and the latter stood in the peculiar position of having been from before his birth ordained 'to begin to deliver Israel.' Deborah was called to deliver Israel, but was already a judge. Samuel was called by the Lord to be a prophet but not a judge, which ensued from the high gifts the people recognized as dwelling in him; and as to Eli, the office of judge seems to have devolved naturally or rather *ex officio* upon him." Of five of the judges—Tola (Judg. 10 : 1), Jair (3), Ibzan, Elon, and Abdon (12 : 8-15) —we have no record at all beyond the bare fact that they were judges. Sacred history is not the history of individuals but of the kingdom of God in its onward progress.

In Ex. 2 : 14 Moses is so styled. This fact may indicate that while for revenue purposes the "taskmasters" were over the people, they were yet, just as at a later time when under the Romans, governed by their own rulers.

Judges, Book of, is so called because it contains the history of the deliverance and government of Israel by the men who bore the title of the "judges." The book of Ruth originally formed part of this book, but about A.D. 450 it was separated from it and placed in the Hebrew scriptures immediately after the Song of Solomon.

The book contains—(1.) An introduction (1–3 : 6), connecting it with the previous narrative in Joshua, as a "link in the chain of books." (2.) The history of the thirteen judges (3 : 7–ch. 16 : 31) in the following order:—

FIRST PERIOD (3 : 7–ch. 5).

	Years.
I. *Servitude* under Chushan-rishathaim of Mesopotamia	8
1. OTHNIEL delivers Israel—rest	40
II. *Servitude* under Eglon of Moab: Ammon, Amalek	18
2. EHUD's deliverance—rest	80
3. SHAMGAR	Unknown.
III. *Servitude* under Jabin of Hazor in Canaan	20
4. DEBORAH ⎱	40
5. BARAK ⎰	
	——
	206

SECOND PERIOD (6–10 : 5).

IV. *Servitude* under Midian, Amalek, and children of the east	7
6. GIDEON	40
ABIMELECH, Gideon's son, reigns as king over Israel	3
7. TOLA	23
8. JAIR	22
	——
	95

THIRD PERIOD (10 : 6–ch. 12).

V. *Servitude* under Ammonites with the Philistines	18
9. JEPHTHAH	6
10. IBZAN	7
11. ELON	10
12. ABDON	8
	——
	49

FOURTH PERIOD (13–16).

VI. *Servitude* under Philistines	40
13. SAMSON	20
	——
	60
In all	410

Samson's exploits probably synchronize with the period immediately preceding the national repentance and reformation under Samuel (1 Sam. 7 : 2-6).

After Samson came Eli, who was both high priest and judge. He directed the civil and religious affairs of the people for forty years, at the close of which the Philistines again invaded the land and oppressed it for twenty years. Samuel was raised up to deliver the people from this oppression, and he judged Israel for some twelve years, when the direction of affairs fell into the hands of Saul, who was anointed king. If Eli and Samuel are included, there were then fifteen judges. But the chronology of this whole period is uncertain.

(3.) The historic section of the book is followed by an appendix (17-21), which has no formal connection with that which goes before. It records (*a*) the conquest (17, 18) of Laish by a portion of the tribe of Dan; and (*b*) the almost total extinction of the tribe of Benjamin by the other tribes, in consequence of their assisting the men of Gibeah (19-21). This section properly belongs to the period only a few years after the death of Joshua. It shows the religious and moral degeneracy of the people.

The *author* of this book was most probably Samuel. The internal evidence both of the first sixteen chapters and of the appendix warrants this conclusion. It was probably composed during Saul's reign, or at the very beginning of David's. The words in 18 : 30, 31, imply that it was written after the taking of the ark by the Philistines, and after it was set up at Nob (1 Sam. 21). In David's reign the ark was at Gibeon (1 Chr. 16 : 39).

Judg'ment hall—Gr. *praitōrion* (John 18 : 28, 33 ; 19 : 9 ; Matt. 27 : 27)—"common hall." In all these passages the Revised Version renders "palace." In Mark 15 : 16 the word is rendered "Prætorium" (*q.v.*), which is a Latin word, meaning literally the residence of the prætor, and then the governor's residence in general, though not a prætor. Throughout the Gospels the word "praitorion" has this meaning (comp. Acts 23 : 35). Pilate's official residence when he was in Jerusalem was probably a part of the fortress of Antonia.

The trial of our Lord was carried on in a room or office of the palace. The "whole band" spoken of by Mark were gathered together in the palace court.

Judg'ment, The final, the sentence that will be passed on our actions at the last day (Matt. 25; Rom. 14:10, 11; 2 Cor. 5: 10; 2 Thess. 1:7-10).

The *judge* is Jesus Christ, as mediator. All judgment is committed to him (Acts 17:31; John 5:22, 27; Rev. 1:7). "It pertains to him as mediator to complete and publicly manifest the salvation of his people and the overthrow of his enemies, together with the glorious righteousness of his work in both respects."

The *persons* to be judged are—(1) the whole race of Adam without a single exception (Matt. 25:31-46; 1 Cor. 15:51, 52; Rev. 20:11-15); and (2) the fallen angels (2 Pet. 2:4; Jude 6).

The *rule* of judgment is the standard of God's law as revealed to men—the heathen by the law as written on their hearts (Luke 12:47, 48; Rom. 2:12-16); the Jew who "sinned in the law shall be judged by the law" (Rom. 2:12); the Christian enjoying the light of revelation, by the will of God as made known to him (Matt. 11:20-24; John 3:19). Then the secrets of all hearts will be brought to light (1 Cor. 4:5; Luke 8:17; 12:2, 3) to vindicate the justice of the sentence pronounced.

The *time* of the judgment will be after the resurrection (Heb. 9:27; Acts 17: 31).

As the Scriptures represent the final judgment "as certain [Eccl. 11:9], universal [2 Cor. 5:10], righteous [Rom. 2:5], decisive [1 Cor. 15:52], and eternal as to its consequences [Heb. 6:2], let us be concerned for the welfare of our immortal interests, flee to the refuge set before us, improve our precious time, depend on the merits of the Redeemer, and adhere to the dictates of the divine word, that we may be found of him in peace."

Judg'ments of God. (1.) The secret decisions of God's will (Ps. 110:5; 36:6).

(2.) The revelations of his will (Ex. 21:1; Deut. 6:12; Ps. 119:7-175). (3.) The infliction of punishment on the wicked (Ex. 6:6; 12:12; Ezek. 25:11; Rev. 16:7), such as is mentioned in Gen. 7; 19:24, 25; Judg. 1:6, 7; Acts 5:1-10, etc.

Judg'ment seat (Matt. 27:19), a portable tribunal (Gr. *bēma*) which was placed according as the magistrate might direct, and from which judgment was pronounced. In this case it was placed on a tesselated pavement, probably in front of the procurator's residence. (See GABBATHA.)

Ju'dith—*Jewess*—the daughter of Beeri the Hittite, and one of Esau's wives (Gen. 26:34), elsewhere called Aholibamah (36: 2-14).

Ju'lia, a Christian woman at Rome to whom Paul sent his salutations (Rom. 16: 15), supposed to be the wife of Philologus.

Ju'lius, the centurion of the Augustan cohort, or the emperor's body-guard, in whose charge Paul was sent prisoner to Rome (Acts 27:1, 3, 43). He entreated Paul "courteously," showing in many ways a friendly regard for him.

Ju'nia (Rom. 16:7), a Christian at Rome to whom Paul sends salutations along with Andronicus.

Ju'niper (Heb. *rôthem*), called by the Arabs *rētem*, and known as *Spanish broom;* ranked under the genus *genista*. It is a

JUNIPER.

desert shrub, and abounds in many parts of Palestine. In the account of his journey from Akabah to Jerusalem, Dr. Robinson says: "This is the largest and most conspicuous shrub of these deserts, growing thickly in the water-courses and valleys. Our Arabs always selected the place of encampment, if possible, in a spot where it grew, in order to be sheltered by it at night from the wind; and during the day, when they often went on in advance of the camels, we found them not unfrequently sitting or sleeping under a bush of *rētem* to shelter them from the sun. It was in this very desert, a day's journey from Beersheba, that the prophet Elijah lay down and slept beneath the same shrub" (1 Kings 19:4, 5). It afforded material for fuel, and also in cases of extremity for human food (Ps. 120:4; Job 30:4). One of the encampments in the wilderness of Paran is called Rithmah—*i.e.*, "place of broom" (Num. 33:18).

"The Bedawîn of Sinai still burn this very plant into a charcoal which throws out the most intense heat."

Ju′piter, the principal deity of the ancient Greeks and Romans. He was worshipped by them under various epithets. Barnabas was identified with this god by the Lycaonians (Acts 14:12), because he was of stately and commanding presence, as they supposed Jupiter to be. There was a temple dedicated to this god outside the gates of Lystra (14:13).

Jus′tice is rendering to every one that which is his due. It has been distinguished from equity in this respect, that while justice means merely the doing what positive law demands, equity means the doing of what is fair and right in every separate case.

Jus′tice of God, that perfection of his nature whereby he is infinitely righteous in himself and in all he does—the righteousness of the divine nature exercised in his moral government. At first God imposes righteous laws on his creatures and executes them righteously. Justice is not an optional product of his will, but an unchangeable principle of his very nature. His *legislative* justice is his requiring of his rational creatures conformity in all respects to the moral law. His *rectoral* or *distributive* justice is his dealing with his accountable creatures according to the requirements of the law in rewarding or punishing them (Ps. 89:14). In *remunerative* justice he distributes rewards (James 1:12; 2 Tim. 4:8); in *vindictive* or *punitive* justice he inflicts punishment on account of transgression (2 Thess. 1:6). He cannot, as being infinitely righteous, do otherwise than regard and hate sin as intrinsically hateful and deserving of punishment. "He cannot deny himself" (2 Tim. 2:13). His essential and eternal righteousness immutably determines him to visit every sin as such with merited punishment.

Justifica′tion, a forensic term, opposed to condemnation.

As regards its *nature*, it is the judicial act of God, by which he pardons all the sins of those who believe in Christ, and accounts, accepts, and treats them as righteous in the eye of the law—*i.e.*, as conformed to all its demands. In addition to the pardon (*q.v.*) of sin, justification declares that all the claims of the law are satisfied in respect of the justified. It is the act of a judge and not of a sovereign. The law is not relaxed or set aside, but is declared to be fulfilled in the strictest sense; and so the person justified is declared to be entitled to all the advantages and rewards arising from perfect obedience to the law (Rom. 5:1-10).

It proceeds on the imputing or crediting to the believer by God himself of the perfect righteousness, active and passive, of his Representative and Surety, Jesus Christ (Rom. 10:3-9). Justification is not the forgiveness of a man without righteousness, but a declaration that he possesses a righteousness which perfectly and for ever satisfies the law—namely, Christ's righteousness (2 Cor. 5:21; Rom. 4:6-8).

The *sole condition* on which this righteousness is imputed or credited to the believer is faith in or on the Lord Jesus Christ. Faith is called a "condition," not because it possesses any merit, but only because it is the instrument, the only instrument, by which the soul appropriates or apprehends Christ and his righteousness (Rom. 1:17; 3:25, 26; 4:20, 22; Phil. 3:8-11; Gal. 2:16).

The act of faith which thus secures our justification secures also at the same time our sanctification (*q.v.*); and thus the doctrine of justification by faith does not lead to licentiousness (Rom. 6:2-7). Good works, while not the ground, are the certain consequence of justification (6:14; 7:6). (See GALATIANS, EPISTLE TO.)

Jus′tus. (1.) Another name for Joseph, surnamed Barsabas. He and Matthias are mentioned only in Acts 1:23. "They must have been among the earliest disciples of Jesus, and must have been faithful to the end; they must have been well known and esteemed among the brethren. What became of them afterwards, and what work they did, are entirely unknown" (Lindsay's *Acts of the Apostles*).

(2.) A Jewish proselyte at Corinth, in whose house, next door to the synagogue, Paul held meetings and preached after he left the synagogue (Acts 18:7).

(3.) A Jewish Christian, called Jesus, Paul's only fellow-labourer at Rome, where he wrote his Epistle to the Colossians (Col. 4:11).

Jut′tah—*extended*—a Levitical city in the mountains or hill-country of Judah (Josh. 15:55; 21:16). Its modern name is *Yûtta*, a place about 5½ miles south of Hebron. It is supposed to have been the residence of Zacharias and Elisabeth, and the birthplace of John the Baptist, and on this account is annually visited by thousands of pilgrims belonging to the Greek Church (Luke 1:39). (See MARY.)

K

Kab′zeel—*gathering of God*—a city in the extreme south of Judah, near to Idumæa (Josh. 15:21), the birthplace of Benaiah, one of David's chief warriors (2 Sam. 23:20; 1 Chr. 11:22). It was called also Jekabzeel (Neh. 11:25), after the Captivity.

Ka′desh—*holy*—or **Kadesh-Barnea**—*sacred desert of wandering*—a place on the south-eastern border of Palestine, about 165 miles from Horeb. It lay in the "wilderness" or "desert of Zin" (Gen. 14:7; Num. 13:3-26; 14:29-33; 20:1; 27:14), on the border of Edom (20:16). From this place, in compliance with the desire of the people, Moses sent forth "twelve spies" to spy the land. After examining it in all its districts, the spies brought back an evil report, Joshua and Caleb alone giving a good report of the land (13: 18-31). Influenced by the discouraging report, the people abandoned all hope of entering into the Promised Land. They remained a considerable time in the camp at Kadesh. (See HORMAH, KORAH.) Because of their unbelief, they were condemned by God to an aimless wandering for thirty-eight years in the wilderness,

till all that guilty generation had perished. They took their journey from Kadesh into the deserts of Paran, "by way of the Red Sea" (Deut. 2:1).

At the end of these years of wanderings, the tribes were a second time gathered together at Kadesh. During their stay here at this time Miriam died and was buried. Here the people murmured for want of water, as their forefathers had done formerly at Rephidim; and Moses, irritated by their chidings, "with his rod smote the rock twice," instead of "speaking to the rock before their eyes," as the Lord had commanded him (comp. Num. 27:14; Deut. 9:23; Ps. 106:32, 33). Because of this act of his, in which Aaron too was involved, neither of them was to be permitted to set foot within the Promised Land (Num. 20:12, 24). The king of Edom would not permit them to pass on through his territory, and therefore they commenced an eastward march, and "came unto Mount Hor" (20:22).

This place has been identified with *'Ain el-Kadeis*, about 12 miles east-south-east of Beersheba. (See SPIES.)

Ka′desh, the sacred city of the Hittites,

on the left bank of the Orontes, about 4 miles south of the Lake of Homs. It is identified with the great mound *Tell Neby Mendeh*, some 50 to 100 feet high, and 400 yards long. On the ruins of the temple of Karnak, in Egypt, has been found an inscription recording the capture of this city by Rameses II. (See PHARAOH.) Here the sculptor "has chiselled in deep work on the stone, with a bold execution of the several parts, the procession of the warriors, the battle before Kadesh, the storming of the fortress, the overthrow of the enemy, and the camp life of the Egyptians." (See HITTITES.)

Kad'miel—*before God; i.e.*, his servant —one of the Levites who returned with Zerubbabel from the Captivity (Neh. 9:4; 10:9; 12:8).

Kad'monites—*Orientals*—the name of a Canaanitish tribe which inhabited the north-eastern part of Palestine in the time of Abraham (Gen. 15:19). Probably they were identical with the "children of the east," who inhabited the country between Palestine and the Euphrates.

Ka'nah—*reedy; brook of reeds.* (1.) A stream forming the boundary between Ephraim and Manasseh, from the Mediterranean eastward to Tappuah (Josh. 16:8). It has been identified with the sedgy streams that constitute the *Wâdy Talaik*, which enters the sea between Joppa and Cæsarea. Others identify it with the river *'Aujeh*.

(2.) A town in the north of Asher (Josh. 19:28). It has been identified with *'Ain-Kana*, a village on the brow of a valley some 7 miles south-east of Tyre. About a mile north of this place are many colossal ruins strown about. And in the side of a neighbouring ravine are figures of men, women, and children cut in the face of the rock. These are supposed to be of Phœnician origin.

Kare'ah—*bald*—the father of Johanan and Jonathan, who for a time were loyal to Gedaliah, the Babylonian governor of Jerusalem (Jer. 40:8, 13, 15, 16).

Karka'a—*a floor; bottom*—a place between Adar and Azmon, about midway between the Mediterranean and the Dead Sea (Josh. 15:3).

Kar'kor—*foundation*—a place in the open desert wastes on the east of Jordan (Judg. 8:10), not far beyond Succoth and Penuel, to the south. Here Gideon overtook and routed a fugitive band of Midianites under Zeba and Zalmunna, whom he took captive.

Kar'tah—*city*—a town in the tribe of Zebulun assigned to the Levites of the family of Merari (Josh. 21:34). It is identical with Kattath (19:15), and perhaps also with Kitron (Judg. 1:30).

Kar'tan—*double city*—a town of Naphtali, assigned to the Gershonite Levites, and one of the cities of refuge (Josh. 21:32). It is called also Kirjathaim (1 Chr. 6:76). It was probably near the north-western shore of the Sea of Tiberias, identical with the ruined village *el-Katanah*.

Kat'ta (Josh. 19:15), a town of Asher, has been identified with *Kana el Jelil*. (See CANA.)

Ke'dar—*dark-skinned*—the second son of Ishmael (Gen. 25:13).

It is the name for the nomadic tribes of Arabs, the Bedouins generally (Isa. 21:16; 42:11; 60:7; Jer. 2:10; Ezek. 27:21), who dwelt in the north-west of Arabia. They lived in black hair-tents (Cant. 1:5). To "dwell in the tents of Kedar" was to be cut off from the worship of the true God (Ps. 120:5). The Kedarites suffered at the hands of Nebuchadnezzar (Jer. 49:28-33).

Ked'emah—*eastward*—the last-named of the sons of Ishmael (Gen. 25:15).

Ked'emoth—*beginnings; easternmost*—a city of Reuben, assigned to the Levites of the family of Merari (Josh. 13:18). It lay not far north-east of Dibon-gad, east of the Dead Sea.

Ked'esh—*sanctuary.* (1.) A place in the extreme south of Judah (Josh. 15:23). Probably the same as Kadesh-barnea (*q.v.*).

(2.) A city of Issachar (1 Chr. 6:72). Possibly *Tell Abu Kadeis*, near Lejjûn.

(3.) A "fenced city" of Naphtali, one of the cities of refuge (Josh. 19:37; Judg. 4:6). It was assigned to the Gershonite Levites (Josh. 21:32). It was originally a Canaanite royal city (Josh. 12:22), and was the residence of Barak (Judg. 4:6);

and here he and Deborah assembled the tribes of Zebulun and Naphtali before the commencement of the conflict with Sisera in the plain of Esdraelon, "for Jehovah among the mighty" (9, 10). In the reign of Pekah it was taken by Tiglath-Pileser (2 Kings 15 : 29). It was situated near the "plain" (rather "the oak") of Zaanaim, and has been identified with the modern *Kedes*, on the hills fully four miles north-west of Lake El Hûleh.

It has been supposed by some that the Kedesh of the narrative, where Barak assembled his troops, was not the place in Upper Galilee so named, which was 30 miles distant from the plain of Esdraelon, but *Kedish*, on the shore of the Sea of Galilee, 12 miles from Tabor.

Ke′dron, the valley, now quite narrow, between the Mount of Olives and Mount Moriah. The upper part of it is called the Valley of Jehoshaphat. The LXX., in 1 Kings 15 : 13, translate "of the cedar." The word means "black," and may refer to the colour of the water or the gloom of the ravine, or the black green of the cedars which grew there. John 18 : 1, "Cedron," only here in New Testament. (See KID-RON.)

Kehel′athah — *assembly* — one of the stations of the Israelites in the desert (Num. 33 : 22, 23).

Kei′lah—*citadel*—a city in the lowlands of Judah (Josh. 15 : 44). David rescued it from the attack of the Philistines (1 Sam. 23 : 7); but the inhabitants proving unfaithful to him, in that they sought to deliver him up to Saul (13), he and his men "departed from Keilah, and went whithersoever they could go." They fled to the hill Hareth, about 3 miles to the east, and thence through Hebron to Ziph (*q.v.*). "And David was in the wilderness of Ziph, in a wood" (1 Sam. 23 : 15). Here Jonathan sought him out, "and strengthened his hand in God." This was the last interview between David and Jonathan (23:16–18). It is the modern *Khŭrbet Kîla.* Others identify it with *Khuweilfeh*, between *Beit Jibrîn* (Eleutheropolis) and Beersheba, mentioned in the Amarna tablets.

Kel′ita—*dwarf*—a Levite who assisted Ezra in expounding the law to the people (Neh. 8 : 7 ; 10 : 10).

Kemu′el—*helper of God,* or *assembly of God.* (1.) The third son of Nahor (Gen. 22 : 21).

(2.) Son of Shiphtan, appointed on behalf of the tribe of Ephraim to partition the land of Canaan (Num. 34 : 24).

(3.) A Levite (1 Chr. 27 : 17).

Ke′nath—*possession*—a city of Gilead. It was captured by Nobah, who called it by his own name (Num. 32 : 42). It has been identified with *Kunawât*, on the slopes of Jebel Haûrân (Mount Bashan), 60 miles east from the south end of the Sea of Galilee.

Ke′naz—*hunter.* (1.) One of the sons of Eliphaz, the son of Esau. He became the chief of an Edomitish tribe (Gen. 36 : 11 ; 15 : 42).

(2.) Caleb's younger brother, and father of Othniel (Josh. 15 : 17), whose family was of importance in Israel down to the time of David (1 Chr. 27 : 15). Some think that Othniel (Judg. 1 : 13), and not Kenaz, was Caleb's brother.

(3.) Caleb's grandson (1 Chr. 4 : 15).

Ken′ites—*smiths*—the name of a tribe inhabiting the desert lying between southern Palestine and the mountains of Sinai. Jethro was of this tribe (Judg. 1 : 16). He is called a "Midianite" (Num. 10 : 29), and hence it is concluded that the Midianites and the Kenites were the same tribe. They were wandering smiths, "the gipsies and travelling tinkers of the old Oriental world. They formed an important guild in an age when the art of metallurgy was confined to a few" (Sayce's *Races,* etc.). They showed kindness to Israel in their journey through the wilderness. They accompanied them in their march as far as Jericho (Judg. 1 : 16), and then returned to their old haunts among the Amalekites, in the desert to the south of Judah. They sustained afterwards friendly relations with the Israelites when settled in Canaan (Judg. 4 : 11, 17–21 ; 1 Sam. 27 : 10 ; 30 : 29). The Rechabites belonged to this tribe (1 Chr. 2 : 55) and in the days of Jeremiah (35 : 7–10) are referred to as following their nomad habits. Saul bade them depart from the Amalekites (1 Sam. 15 : 6) when, in obedience to the divine commission, he was about to "smite Amalek." And his reason is, "for ye showed kindness to all the children of Israel when they came up out of Egypt." Thus "God is not unrighteous to forget the kindnesses shown to his people; but they shall be remembered another day, at the farthest in the great day, and recompensed in the resurrection of the just" (M. Henry's *Commentary*). They are mentioned for the last time in Scripture in 1 Sam. 27:10; comp. 30:20.

Ken'izzite. (1.) The name of a tribe referred to in the covenant God made with Abraham (Gen. 15:19). They are not mentioned among the original inhabitants of Canaan (Ex. 3:8; Josh. 3:10), and probably they inhabited some part of Arabia, in the confines of Syria.

(2.) A designation given to Caleb (R.V., Num. 32:12; A.V., Kenezite).

Ker'chief, mentioned only Ezek. 13:18, 21, as an article of apparel or ornament applied to the head of the idolatrous women of Israel. The precise meaning of the word is uncertain. It appears to have been a long loose shawl, such as Oriental women wrap themselves in (Ruth 3:15; Isa. 3:22). Some think that it was a long veil or head-dress, denoting by its form the position of those who wore it.

Ke'ren-hap'puch — *horn of the face-paint* = cosmetic-box—the name of Job's third daughter (Job 42:14), born after prosperity had returned to him.

Ker'ioth—*cities.* (1.) A town in the south of Judah (Josh. 15:25). Judas the traitor was probably a native of this place, and hence his name *Iscariot.* It has been identified with the ruins of *el-Kureitein,* about 10 miles south of Hebron. (See HAZOR [4]).

(2.) A city of Moab (Jer. 48:24, 41), called Kirioth (Amos 2:2).

Kesi'tah (Gen. 33:19, R.V., marg., a Hebrew word, rendered, A.V., pl. "pieces of money," marg., "lambs;" Josh. 24:32, "pieces of silver;" Job 42:11, "piece of money"). The *kesitah* was probably a piece of money of a particular weight, cast in the form of a lamb. The monuments of Egypt show that such weights were used. (See PIECES.)

Ket'tle, a large pot for cooking. The same Hebrew word (*dŭd,* "boiling") is rendered also "pot" (Ps. 81:6), "caldron" (2 Chr. 35:13), "basket" (Jer. 24:2). It was used for preparing the peace-offerings (1 Sam. 2:13, 14).

Ketu'rah—*incense*—the wife of Abraham, whom he married probably after Sarah's death (Gen. 25:1-6), by whom he had six sons, whom he sent away into the east country. Her nationality is unknown. She is styled "Abraham's concubine" (1 Chr. 1:32). Through the offshoots of the Keturah line Abraham became the "father of many nations."

Key, frequently mentioned in Scripture. It is called in Hebrew *maphtêah*—*i.e.,* the *opener* (Judg. 3:25); and in the Greek New Testament *kleis,* from its use in *shutting* (Matt. 16:19; Luke 11:52; Rev. 1:18, etc.). Figures of ancient Egyptian keys are frequently found on the monuments, also of Assyrian locks and keys of wood, and of a large size (comp. Isa. 22:22).

The word is used figuratively of *power* or *authority* or *office* (Isa. 22:22; Rev. 3:7; Rev. 1:8; comp. 9:1; 20:1; comp. also Matt. 16:19; 18:18). The "key of knowledge" (Luke 11:52; comp. Matt. 23:13) is the means of attaining the knowledge regarding the kingdom of God. The "power of the keys" is a phrase in general use to denote the extent of ecclesiastical authority.

Kezi'a — *cassia* — the name of Job's second daughter (42:14), born after prosperity had returned to him.

Ke'ziz—*abrupt; cut off*—a city of the tribe of Judah (Josh. 18:21).

Kib'roth-hatta'avah—*the graves of the longing* or of *lust*—one of the stations of the Israelites in the wilderness. It was probably in the Wâdy Murrah, and has been identified with the *Erweis el-Ebeirig,* where the remains of an ancient encampment have been found, about 30 miles north-east of Sinai, and exactly a day's journey from 'Ain Hudherah.

"Here began the troubles of the journey.

First, complaints broke out among the
people, probably at the heat, the toil, and
the privations of the march; and then God
at once punished them by lightning, which
fell on the hinder part of the camp, and
killed many persons, but ceased at the intercession of Moses (Num. 11:1, 2). Then
a disgust fell on the multitude at having
nothing to eat but the manna day after
day—no change, no flesh, no fish, no high-
flavoured vegetables, no luscious fruits......
The people loathed the 'light food,' and
cried out to Moses, 'Give us flesh, give us
flesh, that we may eat.'" In this emergency Moses, in despair, cried unto God.
An answer came. God sent "a prodigious
flight of quails, on which the people
satiated their gluttonous appetite for a
full month. Then punishment fell on
them: they loathed the food which they
had desired; it bred disease in them; the
divine anger aggravated the disease into a
plague, and a heavy mortality was the consequence. The dead were buried without
the camp; and in memory of man's sin
and of the divine wrath this name, *Kibroth-
hattaavah*—the Graves of Lust—was given
to the place of their sepulchre" (Num. 11:
34, 35; 33:16, 17; Deut. 9:22; comp. Ps.
78:30, 31).—Rawlinson's *Moses, etc.*, p. 175.
From this encampment they journeyed in
a north-eastern direction to Hazeroth.

Kib'zaim—*two heaps*—a city of Ephraim, assigned to the Kohathite Levites,
and appointed as a city of refuge (Josh. 21:
22). It is also called Jokmeam (1 Chr.
6:68).

Kid, the young of the goat. It was
much used for food (Gen. 27:9; 38:17;
Judg. 6:19; 14:6). The Mosaic law forbade to dress a kid in the milk of its dam
—a law which is thrice repeated (Ex. 23:
19; 34:26; Deut. 14:21). Among the
various reasons assigned for this law, that
appears to be the most satisfactory which
regards it as "a protest against cruelty
and outraging the order of nature." A
kid cooked in its mother's milk is "a
gross, unwholesome dish, and calculated
to kindle up animal and ferocious passions,
and on this account Moses may have forbidden it. Besides, it is even yet associ-

ated with immoderate feasting; and originally, I suspect," says Dr. Thomson (*Land
and the Book*), "was connected with idolatrous sacrifices."

Ki'dron = **Kedron** = **Cedron**—*turbid*—
the winter torrent which flows through the
Valley of Jehoshaphat, on the eastern side
of Jerusalem, between the city and the
Mount of Olives. This valley is known
in Scripture only by the name "the brook
Kidron." David crossed this brook barefoot and weeping, when fleeing from Absalom (2 Sam. 15:23, 30), and it was
frequently crossed by our Lord in his journeyings to and fro (John 18:1). Here Asa
burnt the obscene idols of his mother (1
Kings 15:13), and here Athaliah was executed (2 Kings 11:16). It afterwards became the receptacle for all manner of
impurities (2 Chr. 29:16; 30:14); and in
the time of Josiah this valley was the common cemetery of the city (2 Kings 23:6;
comp. Jer. 26:23).

Through this mountain ravine no water
runs, except after heavy rains in the mountains round about Jerusalem. Its length
from its head to en-Rogel is 2¾ miles.
Its precipitous, rocky banks are filled with
ancient tombs, especially the left bank
opposite the temple area. The greatest
desire of the Jews is to be buried there,
from the idea that the Kidron is the
"Valley of Jehoshaphat" mentioned in
Joel 3:2.

Below en-Rogel the Kidron has no historical or sacred interest. It runs on in a
winding course through the wilderness of
Judea to the north-western shore of the
Dead Sea. Its whole length, in a straight
line, is only some 20 miles, but in this
space its descent is about 3,912 feet. (See
KEDRON.)

Recent excavations have brought to light
the fact that the true bed of the Kidron is
about 40 feet lower than its present bed,
and about 70 feet nearer the sanctuary
wall.

Ki'nah—an *elegy*—a city in the extreme
south of Judah (Josh. 15:22). It was probably not far from the Dead Sea, in the
Wâdy Fikreh.

Kine (Heb. sing. *pârâh*—*i.e.*, "fruitful"),

Absalom's Tomb.   TOMBS IN THE KIDRON VALLEY.

mentioned in Pharaoh's dream (Gen. 41: 18). Here the word denotes "buffaloes," which fed on the reeds and sedge by the river's brink.

King is in Scripture very generally used to denote one invested with authority, whether extensive or only limited. There were thirty-one kings in Canaan (Josh. 12: 9, 24), whom Joshua subdued. Adoni-bezek subdued seventy kings (Judg. 1: 7). In the New Testament the Roman emperor is spoken of as a king (1 Pet. 2: 13, 17);

and Herod Antipas, who was only a tetrarch, is also called a king (Matt. 14: 9; Mark 6: 22).

This title is applied to God (1 Tim. 1: 17), and to Christ, the Son of God (1 Tim. 6: 15, 16; Matt. 27: 11). The people of God are also called "kings" (Dan. 7: 22, 27; Matt. 19: 28; Rev. 1: 6, etc.). Death is called the "king of terrors" (Job 18: 14).

Jehovah was the sole King of the Jewish nation (1 Sam. 8: 7; Isa. 33: 22). But there came a time in the history of that people when a king was demanded, that they might be like other nations (1 Sam. 8 : 5). The prophet Samuel remonstrated with them, but the people cried out, "Nay, but we will have a king over us." The misconduct of Samuel's sons was the immediate cause of this demand.

The *Hebrew kings* did not rule in their own right, nor in name of the people who had chosen them, but partly as servants and partly as representatives of Jehovah, the true King of Israel (1 Sam. 10 : 1). The limits of the king's power were pre- scribed (1 Sam. 10 : 25). The *officers* of his court were—(1) the recorder or remembran- cer (2 Sam. 8 : 16 ; 1 Kings 4 : 3) ; (2) the scribe (2 Sam. 8 : 17 ; 20 : 25) ; (3) the officer over the house, the chief steward (Isa. 22 : 15) ; (4) the "king's friend," a confidential companion (1 Kings 4 : 5) ; (5) the keeper of the wardrobe (2 Kings 22 : 14) ; (6) captain of the body-guard (2 Sam. 20 : 23) ; (7) offi- cers over the king's treasures, etc. (1 Chr. 27 : 25-31) ; (8) commander-in-chief of the army (1 Chr. 27 : 34) ; (9) the royal coun- sellor (1 Chr. 27 : 32 ; 2 Sam. 16 : 20-23).

(For catalogue of kings of Israel and Judah see chronological table in Appendix.)

King'dom of God (Matt. 6 : 33 ; Mark 1 : 14, 15 ; Luke 4 : 43) = "kingdom of Christ" (Matt. 13 : 41 ; 20 : 21) = "king- dom of Christ and of God" (Eph. 5 : 5) = "kingdom of David" (Mark 11 : 10) = "the kingdom" (Matt. 8 : 12 ; 13 : 19) = "kingdom of heaven" (Matt. 3 : 2 ; 4 : 17 ; 13 : 41), all denote the same thing under different aspects—viz. : (1) Christ's media- torial authority, or his rule on the earth ; (2) the blessings and advantages of all kinds that flow from this rule ; (3) the sub- jects of this kingdom taken collectively, or the Church.

Kingly office of Christ, one of the three special relations in which Christ stands to his people. Christ's office as mediator comprehends three different func- tions—viz., those of a prophet, priest, and king. These are not three distinct offices, but three functions of the *one* office of mediator.

Christ is King and sovereign Head over his Church and over all things to his Church

(Eph. 1 : 22 ; 4 : 15 ; Col. 1 : 18 ; 2 : 19). He executes this mediatorial kingship in his Church, and over his Church, and over all things in behalf of his Church. This roy- alty differs from that which essentially be- longs to him as God, for it is *given* to him by the Father as the reward of his obedi- ence and sufferings (Phil. 2 : 6-11), and has as its especial object the upbuilding and the glory of his redeemed Church. It attaches, moreover, not to his divine nature as such, but to his person as God-man.

Christ's mediatorial kingdom may be re- garded as comprehending—(1) his kingdom of *power*, or his providential government of the universe ; (2) his kingdom of *grace*, which is wholly spiritual in its subjects and administration ; and (3) his kingdom of *glory*, which is the consummation of all his providential and gracious administra- tion.

Christ sustained and exercised the func- tion of mediatorial King as well as of Prophet and Priest, from the time of the fall of man, when he entered on his media- torial work ; yet it may be said that he was publicly and formally enthroned when he ascended up on high and sat down at the Father's right hand (Ps. 2 : 6 ; Jer. 23 : 5 ; Isa. 9 : 6), after his work of humiliation and suffering on earth was "finished."

Kings, The Books of. The two books of Kings formed originally but one book in the Hebrew Scriptures. The present division into two books was first made by the LXX., which now, with the Vulgate, numbers them as the third and fourth books of Kings—the two books of Samuel being the first and second books of Kings.

They contain the annals of the Jewish commonwealth from the accession of Solo- mon till the subjugation of the kingdom by Nebuchadnezzar and the Babylonians (apparently a period of about four hundred and fifty-three years). The books of Chron- icles (*q.v.*) are more comprehensive in their contents than those of Kings. The latter synchronize with 1 Chr. 28-2 Chr. 36 : 22. While in the Chronicles greater promi- nence is given to the priestly or Levitical office, in the Kings greater prominence is given to the kingly.

The *authorship* of these books is uncertain. There are some portions of them and of Jeremiah that are almost identical—*e.g.*, 2 Kings 24 : 18-25 and Jer. 52 ; 39 : 1-10 ; 40 : 7-41 : 10. There are also many undesigned coincidences between Jeremiah and Kings (2 Kings 21-23 and Jer. 7 : 15 ; 15 : 4 ; 19 : 3, etc.), and events recorded in Kings of which Jeremiah had personal knowledge. These facts countenance in some degree the tradition that Jeremiah was the author of the books of Kings. But the more probable supposition is that Ezra, after the Captivity, compiled them from documents written perhaps by David, Solomon, Nathan, Gad, and Iddo, and that he arranged them in the order in which they now exist.

In the threefold division of the Scriptures by the Jews, these books are ranked among the "Prophets." They are frequently quoted or alluded to by our Lord and his apostles (Matt. 6 : 29 ; 12 : 42 ; Luke 4 : 25, 26 ; 10 : 4 ; comp. 2 Kings 4 : 29 ; Mark 1 : 6 ; comp. 2 Kings 1 : 8 ; Matt. 3 : 4, etc.).

The *sources* of the narrative are referred to (1) "the book of the acts of Solomon" (1 Kings 11 : 41) ; (2) the "book of the chronicles of the kings of Judah" (14 : 29 ; 15 : 7, 23, etc.) ; (3) the "book of the chronicles of the kings of Israel" (14 : 19 ; 15 : 31 ; 16 : 14, 20, 27, etc.).

The *date* of its composition was some time between B.C. 561, the date of the last chapter (2 Kings 25), when Jehoiachin was released from captivity by Evil-merodach, and B.C. 538, the date of the decree of deliverance by Cyrus.

King's dale, mentioned only in Gen. 14 : 17 ; 2 Sam. 18 : 18, the name given to "the valley of Shaveh," where the king of Sodom met Abram.

Kins'man—Heb. *goël*, from root meaning to *redeem*. The *goël* among the Hebrews was the nearest male blood relation alive. Certain important obligations devolved upon him toward his next of kin. (1.) If any one from poverty was unable to redeem his inheritance, it was the duty of the kinsman to redeem it (Lev. 25 : 25-28 ; Ruth 3 : 9, 12). He was also required to re-deem his relation who had sold himself into slavery (Lev. 25 : 48, 49).

God is the *Goël* of his people because he redeems them (Ex. 6 : 6 ; Isa. 43 : 1 ; 41 : 14 ; 44 : 6, 22 ; 48 : 20 ; Ps. 103 : 4 ; Job 19 : 25, etc.).

(2.) The *goël* also was the avenger (*q.v.*) of blood (Num. 35 : 31) in the case of the murder of the next of kin.

Kir—a *wall* or *fortress*—a place to which Tiglath-pileser carried the Syrians captive after he had taken the city of Damascus (2 Kings 16 : 9 ; Amos 1 : 5 ; 9 : 7). Isaiah (22 : 6), who also was contemporary with these events, mentions it along with Elam. Some have supposed that Kir is a variant of Cush (Susiana), on the south of Elam.

Kir of Moab, Isa. 15 : 1. The two strongholds of Moab were Ar and Kir, which latter is probably the Kir-haraseth (16 : 7) following.

Kir-har'aseth— *built fortress* — a city and fortress of Moab, the modern *Kerak*, a small town on the brow of a steep hill about 6 miles from Rabbath-Moab and 10 miles from the Dead Sea ; called also Kir-haresh, Kir-hareseth, Kir-heres (Isa. 16 : 7, 11 ; Jer. 48 : 31, 36). After the death of Ahab, Mesha, king of Moab (see MOABITE STONE), threw off allegiance to the king of Israel, and fought successfully for the independence of his kingdom. After this Jehoram, king of Israel, in seeking to regain his supremacy over Moab, entered into an alliance with Jehoshaphat, king of Judah, and with the king of Edom. The three kings led their armies against Mesha, who was driven back to seek refuge in Kir-haraseth. The Moabites were driven to despair. Mesha then took his eldest son, who would have reigned in his stead, and offered him as a burnt-offering on the wall of the fortress in the sight of the allied armies. "There was great indignation against Israel : and they departed from him, and returned to their own land." The invaders evacuated the land of Moab, and Mesha achieved the independence of his country (2 Kings 3 : 20-27).

Kir'jath—*city*—a city belonging to Benjamin (Josh. 18 : 28), the modern *Kŭriet el-*

'Enab—*i.e.*, "city of grapes"—about 7½ miles west-north-west of Jerusalem.

Kir'jatha'im—*two cities; a double city.* (1.) A city of refuge in Naphtali (1 Chr. 6:76).

(2.) A town on the east of Jordan (Gen. 14:5; Deut. 2:9, 10). It was assigned to the tribe of Reuben (Num. 32:37). In the time of Ezekiel (25:9) it was one of the four cities which formed the "glory of Moab" (comp. Jer. 48:1, 23). It has been identified with *el-Kureiyat*, 11 miles south-west of Medeba, on the south slope of *Jebel Attarûs*, the ancient Ataroth.

Kir'jath-ar'ba—*city of Arba*—the original name of Hebron (*q.v.*), so called from the name of its founder, one of the Anakim (Gen. 23:2; 35:27; Josh. 15:13). It was given to Caleb by Joshua as his portion. The Jews interpret the name as meaning "the city of the four"—*i.e.*, of Abraham, Isaac, Jacob, and Adam, who were all, as they allege, buried there.

Kir'jath-hu'zoth—*city of streets*—Num. 22:39, a Moabite city, which some identify with Kirjathaim. Balak here received and entertained Balaam, whom he had invited from Pethor, among the "mountains of the east," beyond the Euphrates, to lay his ban upon the Israelites, whose progress he had no hope otherwise of arresting. It was probably from the summit of Attarûs, the high place near the city, that the soothsayer first saw the encampments of Israel.

Kir'jath-je'arim—*city of jaars; i.e.*, of *woods* or *forests*—a Gibeonite town (Josh. 9:17) on the border of Benjamin, to which tribe it was assigned (18:15, 28). The ark was brought to this place (1 Sam. 7:1, 2) from Beth-shemesh and put in charge of Abinadab, a Levite. Here it remained till it was removed by David to Jerusalem (2 Sam. 6:2, 3, 12; 1 Chr. 15:1–29; comp. Ps. 132). It was also called Baalah (Josh. 15:9) and Kirjath-baal (60). It has been usually identified with *Kŭriet el-'Enab* (*i.e.*, "city of grapes"), among the hills, about 8 miles north-east of 'Ain Shems (*i.e.*, Beth-shemesh). The opinion, however, that it is to be identified with *'Erma*, 4 miles east of 'Ain Shems, on the edge of the valley of

Sorek, seems to be better supported. (See KIRJATH.)

The words of Ps. 132:6, "We found it in the fields of the wood," refer to the sojourn of the ark at Kirjath-jearim. "Wood" is here the rendering of the Hebrew word *jaar*, which is the singular of *jearim*.

Kir'jath-san'nah—*city of the sannah; i.e.*, of *the palm* (?)—Josh. 15:49; the same as Kirjath-sepher (15:16; Judg. 1:11) and Debir (*q.v.*), a Canaanitish royal city included in Judah (Josh. 10:38; 15:49), and probably the chief seat of learning among the Hittites. It was about 12 miles to the south-west of Hebron.

Kir'jath-se'pher—*city of books*—Josh. 15:15; same as Kirjath-sannah (*q.v.*), now represented by the valley of *ed-Dhâberîych*, south-west of Hebron. The name of this town is an evidence that the Canaanites were acquainted with writing and books. "The town probably contained a noted school, or was the site of an oracle and the residence of some learned priest." The "books" were probably engraved stones or bricks.

Kish—*a bow*. (1.) A Levite of the family of Merari (1 Chr. 23:21; 24:29).

(2.) A Benjamite of Jerusalem (1 Chr. 8:30; 9:36).

(3.) A Levite in the time of Hezekiah (2 Chr. 29:12).

(4.) The great-grandfather of Mordecai (Esther 2:5).

(5.) A Benjamite, the son of Abiel, and father of king Saul (1 Sam. 9:1, 3; 10:11, 21; 14:51; 2 Sam. 21:14). All that is recorded of him is that he sent his son Saul in search of his asses that had strayed, and that he was buried in Zelah. Called Cis, Acts 13:21 (R.V., Kish).

Kish'ion—*hardness*—a city of Issachar assigned to the Gershonite Levites (Josh. 19:20), the same as Kishon (21:28).

Ki'shon—*winding*—a winter torrent of Central Palestine, which rises about the roots of Tabor and Gilboa, and passing in a northerly direction through the plains of Esdraelon and Acre, falls into the Mediterranean at the north-eastern corner of the bay of Acre, at the foot of Carmel. It is the drain by which the waters of the plain of

Esdraelon and of the mountains that surround it find their way to the sea. It bears the modern name of *Nahr el-Mokattah* —i.e., "the river of slaughter" (comp. 1 Kings 18:40). In the triumphal song of Deborah (Judg. 5:21) it is spoken of as "that ancient river," either (1) because it had flowed on for ages, or (2), according to the Targum, because it was "the torrent in which were shown signs and wonders to Israel of old;" or (3) probably the reference is to the exploits in that region among the ancient Canaanites, for the adjoining plain of Esdraelon was the great battle-field of Palestine.

This was the scene of the defeat of Sisera (Judg. 4:7, 13), and of the destruction of the prophets of Baal by Elijah (1 Kings 18:40). "When the Kishon was at its height, it would be, partly on account of its quicksands, as impassable as the ocean itself to a retreating army." (See DEBORAH.)

Kiss of affection (Gen. 27:26, 27; 29:13; Luke 7:38, 45); reconciliation (Gen. 33:4; 2 Sam. 14:33); leave-taking (Gen. 31:28, 55; Ruth 1:14; 2 Sam. 19:39); homage (Ps. 2:12; 1 Sam. 10:1); spoken of as between parents and children (Gen. 27:26; 31:28, 55; 48:10; 50:1; Ex. 18:7; Ruth 1:9, 14); between male relatives (Gen. 29:13; 33:4; 45:15). It accompanied social worship as a symbol of brotherly love (Rom. 16:16; 1 Cor. 16:20; 2 Cor. 13:12; 1 Thess. 5:26; 1 Pet. 5:14). The worship of idols was by kissing the image or the hand toward the image (1 Kings 19:18; Hos. 13:2).

Kite, an unclean and keen-sighted bird of prey (Lev. 11:14; Deut. 14:13). The Hebrew word used—*'ayeṭ*—is rendered "vulture" in Job 28:7 in Authorized Version, "falcon" in Revised Version. It is probably the red kite (*Milvus regalis*), a bird of piercing sight and of soaring habits found all over Palestine.

Kith'lish—*a man's wall*—a town in the plain of Judah (Josh. 15:40). It has been identified with *Jelameh.*

Kit'ron — *knotty* — a city of Zebulun (Judg. 1:30), called also Kattath (Josh. 19:15); supposed to be "Cana of Galilee."

Kit'tim (Gen. 10:4). (See CHITTIM.)

Knead, to prepare dough in the process of baking (Gen. 18:6; 1 Sam. 28:24; Hos. 7:4).

Knead'ing-trough, the vessel in which the dough, after being mixed and leavened, was left to swell or ferment (Ex. 8:3; 12:34; Deut. 28:5, 7). The dough in the vessels at the time of the Exodus was still unleavened, because the people were compelled to withdraw in haste.

Knife. (1.) Heb. *ḥereb*, "the waster," a sharp instrument for circumcision (Josh. 5:2, 3, *lit.* "knives of flint;" comp. Ex. 4:25); a razor (Ezek. 5:1); a graving tool (Ex. 20:25); an axe (Ezek. 26:9).

(2.) Heb. *maakĕleth*, a large knife for slaughtering and cutting up food (Gen. 22:6, 10; Prov. 30:14).

(3.) Heb. *sakkin*, a knife for any purpose, a table knife (Prov. 23:2).

(4.) Heb. *maḥalâph*, a butcher's knife for slaughtering the victims offered in sacrifice (Ezra 1:9).

(5.) Smaller knives (Heb. *ta'ar*, Jer. 36:23) were used for sharpening pens. The pruning-knives mentioned in Isa. 18:5 (Heb. *mizmaroth*) were probably curved knives.

Knock. "Though Orientals are very jealous of their privacy, they never knock when about to enter your room, but walk in without warning or ceremony. It is nearly impossible to teach an Arab servant to knock at your door. They give warning at the outer gate either by calling or knocking. To stand and *call* is a very common and respectful mode. Thus Moses commanded the holder of a pledge to stand without and call to the owner to come forth (Deut. 24:10). This was to avoid the violent intrusion of cruel creditors. Peter stood knocking at the outer door (Acts 12:13, 16), and so did the three men sent to Joppa by Cornelius (10:17, 18). The idea is that the guard over your privacy is to be placed at the entrance" (Thomson's *Land and the Book*).

Knocking is used as a sign of importunity (Matt. 7:7, 8; Luke 13:25), and of the coming of Christ (Luke 12:36; Rev. 3:20).

Knop, some architectural ornament. (1.) Heb. *kaphtôr* (Ex. 25:31-36), occurring in the description of the candlestick. It was an ornamental swell beneath the cups of the candlestick, probably an imitation of the fruit of the almond.

(2.) Heb. *pekâ'im*—found only in 1 Kings 6:18 and 7:24—an ornament resembling a small gourd or an egg, on the cedar wainscot in the temple and on the castings on the brim of the brazen sea.

Ko'a—*he-camel*—occurs only in Ezek. 23:23, some province or place in the Babylonian empire, used in this passage along with Shoa (*q.v.*).

Ko'hath—*assembly*—the second son of Levi, and father of Amram (Gen. 46:11). He came down to Egypt with Jacob, and lived to the age of one hundred and thirty-three years (Ex. 6:18).

Ko'hathites, the descendants of Kohath. They formed the first of the three divisions of the Levites (Ex. 6:16, 18; Num. 3:17). In the journeyings of the Israelites they had the charge of the most holy portion of the vessels of the tabernacle, including the ark (Num. 4). Their place in the marching and encampment was south of the tabernacle (Num. 3:29, 31). Their numbers at different times are specified (3:28; 4:36; 26:57, 62). Samuel was of this division.

Ko'rah—*ice, hail.* (1.) The third son of Esau, by Aholibamah (Gen. 36:14; 1 Chr. 1:35).

(2.) A Levite, the son of Izhar, the brother of Amram, the father of Moses and Aaron (Ex. 6:21). The institution of the Aaronic priesthood and the Levitical service at Sinai was a great religious revolution. The old priesthood of the heads of families passed away. This gave rise to murmurings and discontent—while the Israelites were encamped at Kadesh for the first time—which came to a head in a rebellion against Moses and Aaron, headed by Korah, Dathan, and Abiram. Two hundred and fifty princes, "men of renown"—*i.e.*, well-known men from among the other tribes—joined this conspiracy. The whole company demanded of Moses and Aaron that the old state of things should be restored, alleging that "they took too much upon them" (Num. 16:1-3). On the morn-

ing after the outbreak, Korah and his associates presented themselves at the door of the tabernacle, and "took every man his censer, and put fire in them, and laid incense thereon." But immediately "fire from the Lord" burst forth and destroyed them all (Num. 16:35). Dathan and Abiram "came out and stood in the door of their tents, and their wives, and their sons, and their little children," and it came to pass "that the ground clave asunder that was under them; and the earth opened her mouth and swallowed them up." A plague thereafter began among the people who sympathized in the rebellion, and was only stayed by Aaron's appearing between the living and the dead, and making "an atonement for the people" (16:47).

The descendants of the sons of Korah who did not participate in the rebellion afterwards rose to eminence in the Levitical service.

Ko'rahites, that portion of the Kohathites that descended from Korah.

(1.) They were an important branch of the singers of the Kohathite division (2 Chr. 20:19). There are eleven psalms (42-49; 84; 85; 87; 88) dedicated to the sons of Korah.

(2.) Some of the sons of Korah also were "porters" of the temple (1 Chr. 9:17-19); one of them was over "things that were made in the pans" (31)—*i.e.*, the baking in pans for the meat-offering (Lev. 2:5).

Ko're—*partridge.* (1.) A Levite and temple-warder of the Korahites, the son of Asaph. He was father of Shallum and Meshelemiah, temple-porters (1 Chr. 9:19; 26:1).

(2.) A Levitical porter at the east gate of the temple (2 Chr. 31:14).

(3.) In 1 Chr. 26:19 the word should be "Korehites," as in the Revised Version.

Kor'hites, a Levitical family descended from Korah (Ex. 6:24; 1 Chr. 12:6; 26:1; 2 Chr. 20:19).

Koz—*thorn.* (1.) A descendant of Judah. 1 Chr. 4:8, "Coz;" R.V., "Hakkoz."

(2.) A priest, the head of the seventh division of the priests (Ezra 2:61; Neh. 3:4, 21; 7:63). In 1 Chr. 24:10 the word has the article prefixed, and it is taken as a part of the word "Hakkoz."

L

La'ban—*white.* (1.) The son of Bethuel, who was the son of Nahor, Abraham's brother. He lived at Haran in Mesopotamia. His sister Rebekah was Isaac's wife (Gen. 24). Jacob, one of the sons of this marriage, fled to the house of Laban, whose daughters Leah and Rachel (ch. 29) he eventually married. (See JACOB.)

(2.) A city in the Arabian desert in the route of the Israelites (Deut. 1:1), probably identical with Libnah (Num. 33:20).

La'chish—*impregnable*—a royal Canaanitish city in the Shephelah or maritime plain of Palestine (Josh. 10:3, 5; 12:11). It was taken and destroyed by the Israelites (Josh. 10:31-35). It afterwards became, under Rehoboam, one of the strongest fortresses of Judah (2 Chr. 10:32-35). It was assaulted and probably taken by Sennacherib (2 Kings 18:14, 17; 19:8; Isa. 36:2). An account of this siege is given on some slabs found in the chambers of the palace of Kouyunjik, and now in the British Museum. The inscription has been deciphered as follows:—"Sennacherib, the mighty king, king of the country of Assyria, sitting on the throne of judgment before the city of Lachish: I gave permission for its slaughter."

Lachish has been identified with *Tell el-Hesy,* where a cuneiform tablet has been found, containing a letter supposed to be from Amenophis at Amarna in reply to one of the Amarna tablets (see page 214) sent by Zimridi from Lachish. This letter is from the chief of Atim (=Etam, 1 Chr. 4:32) to the chief of Lachish (see Illustration, p. 20), in which the writer expresses great alarm at the approach of marauders from the Hebron hills. "They have entered the land," he says, "to lay waste...strong is he who has come down. He lays waste." This letter shows that "the communication by tablets in cuneiform script was not only usual in writing to Egypt, but in the internal correspondence of the country. The letter, though not so important in some ways as the Moabite stone and Siloam text, is one of the most valuable discoveries ever made in Palestine" (Conder's *Tell Amarna Tablets,* p. 134).

Excavations at Lachish are still going on, and among other discoveries is that of an iron blast-furnace, with slag and ashes, which is supposed to have existed 1500 B.C. If the theories of experts are correct, the use of the hot-air blast instead of cold air (an improvement in iron manufacture patented by Neilson in 1828) was known fifteen hundred years before Christ. (See FURNACE, p. 270.)

Lad'der occurs only once, in the account of Jacob's vision (Gen. 28:12).

La'ish—*a lion.* (1.) A city of the Sidonians, in the extreme north of Palestine (Judg. 18:7, 14); called also Leshem (Josh. 19:47) and Dan (Judg. 18:7, 29; Jer. 8:16). It lay near the sources of the Jordan, about 4 miles from Paneas. The restless and warlike tribe of Dan (*q.v.*), looking out for larger possessions, invaded this country and took Laish with its territory. It is identified with the ruin *Tell el-Kâdy,* "the mound of the judge," to the north of the Waters of Merom (Josh. 11:5).

(2.) A place mentioned in Isa. 10:30. It has been supposed to be the modern *el-Isawîyeh,* about a mile north-east of Jerusalem.

(3.) The father of Phalti (1 Sam. 25:44).

La'ma (Matt. 27:46), a Hebrew word meaning *why,* quoted from Ps. 22:2.

Lamb. (1.) Heb. *kĕbĕs,* a male lamb from the first to the third year. Offered daily at the morning and the evening sacrifice (Ex. 29:38-41), on the Sabbath day (Num. 28:9), at the feast of the New Moon (11), of Trumpets (29:2), of Tabernacles (13-40), of Pentecost (Lev. 23:18-20), and of the Passover (Ex. 12:5), and on many other occasions (1 Chr. 29:21; 2 Chr. 29:21; Lev. 9:3; 14:10-25).

(2.) Heb. *ṭâleh,* a young sucking lamb (1 Sam. 7:9; Isa. 65:25).

In the symbolical language of Scripture the lamb is the type of meekness and innocence (Isa. 11:6; 65:25; Luke 10:3; John 21:15).

The lamb was the symbol of Christ (Gen. 4:4; Ex. 12:3; 29:38; Isa. 16:1; 53:7; John 1:36; Rev. 13:8).

Christ is called the *Lamb of God* (John 1:29, 36), as the great sacrifice of which the former sacrifices were only types (Num. 6:12; Lev. 14:12–17; Isa. 53:7; 1 Cor. 5:7).

La'mech—*the striker down; the wild man.* (1.) The fifth in descent from Cain. He was the first to violate the primeval ordinance of marriage (Gen. 4:18–24). His address to his two wives Adah and Zillah (4:23, 24) is the only extant example of antediluvian poetry. It has been called "Lamech's sword-song." He was "rude and ruffianly," fearing neither God nor man. With him the curtain falls on the race of Cain. We know nothing of his descendants.

(2.) The seventh in descent from Seth, being the only son of Methuselah. Noah was the oldest of his several sons (Gen. 5: 25–31; Luke 3:36).

Lamenta'tion (Heb. *qînah*), an elegy or dirge. The first example of this form of poetry is the lament of David over Saul and Jonathan (2 Sam. 1:17–27). It was a frequent accompaniment of mourning (Amos 8:10). In 2 Sam. 3:33, 34 is recorded David's lament over Abner. Prophecy sometimes took the form of a lament when it predicted calamity (Ezek. 27:2, 32; 28:12; 32:2, 16).

Lamenta'tions, Book of, called in the Hebrew canon *'Ekhâh*, meaning "how," being the formula for the commencement of a song of wailing. It is the first word of the book (see 2 Sam. 1:19–27). The LXX. adopted the name rendered "Lamentations" (Gr. *thrênoi* = Heb. *qinôth*) now in common use, to denote the character of the book, in which the prophet mourns over the desolations brought on the city and the holy land by Chaldeans. In the Hebrew Bible it is placed among the *Khethubim.* (See BIBLE.)

As to its *authorship*, there is no room for hesitancy in following the LXX. and the Targum in ascribing it to Jeremiah. The spirit, tone, language, and subject-matter are in accord with the testimony of tradition in assigning it to him. According to tradition, he retired after the destruction of Jerusalem by Nebuchadnezzar to a cavern outside the Damascus gate, where he wrote this book. That cavern is still pointed out. "In the face of a rocky hill, on the western side of the city, the local belief has placed 'the grotto of Jeremiah.' There, in that fixed attitude of grief which Michael Angelo has immortalized, the prophet may well be supposed to have mourned the fall of his country" (Stanley, *Jewish Church*).

The book *consists* of five separate poems. In chapter 1 the prophet dwells on the manifold miseries oppressed by which the city sits as a solitary widow weeping sorely. In chapter 2 these miseries are described in connection with the national sins that had caused them. Chapter 3 speaks of hope for the people of God. The chastisement would only be for their good; a better day would dawn for them. Chapter 4 laments the ruin and desolation that had come upon the city and temple, but traces it only to the people's sins. Chapter 5 is a prayer that Zion's reproach may be taken away in the repentance and recovery of the people.

The first four poems (chapters) are acrostics, like some of the Psalms (25, 34, 37, 119)—*i.e.*, each verse begins with a letter of the Hebrew alphabet taken in order. The first, second, and fourth have each twenty-two verses, the number of the letters in the Hebrew alphabet. The third has sixty-six verses, in which each three successive verses begin with the same letter. The fifth is not acrostic.

Speaking of the "Wailing-place (*q.v.*) of the Jews" at Jerusalem—a portion of the old wall of the temple of Solomon—Schaff says: "There the Jews assemble every Friday afternoon to bewail the downfall of the holy city, kissing the stone wall and watering it with their tears. They repeat from their well-worn Hebrew Bibles and prayer-books the Lamentations of Jeremiah and suitable Psalms. The key-note of all these laments and prayers was struck by Jeremiah, the most pathetic and tender-hearted of prophets, in the Lamentations, that funeral dirge of Jerusalem and the theocracy. Every year, on the 9th of the month Ab, it is read with loud weeping in all the synagogues of the Jews, and especially at Jerusalem. It keeps alive the memory of their deepest humiliation and guilt, and the hope of final deliverance" (*Through Bible Lands*).

Lamp. (1.) That part of the candlesticks of the tabernacle and the temple which bore the light (Ex. 25 : 37; 1 Kings 7 : 49; 2 Chr. 4 : 20; 13 : 11; Zech. 4 : 2). Their form is not described. Olive oil was generally burned in them (Ex. 27 : 20).

(2.) A torch carried by the soldiers of Gideon (Judg. 7 : 16, 20).

(3.) Domestic lamps (A.V., "candles") were in common use among the Hebrews (Matt. 5 : 15; Mark 4 : 21, etc.).

(4.) Lamps or torches were used in connection with marriage ceremonies (Matt. 25 : 1).

This word is also frequently metaphorically used to denote life, welfare, guidance, etc. (2 Sam. 21 : 17; Ps. 119 : 105; Prov. 6 : 23; 13 : 9).

Land law (Num. 26 : 53). "Every peasant was made a land-owner, but rather in trust for his descendants than as a freeholder. Jehovah himself remained absolute owner-in-chief (Lev. 25 : 23), the occupants being only his stewards (Luke 16 : 2, 3; 1 Cor. 4 : 2; 1 Pet. 4 : 10), holding possession under stringent conditions. The first-fruits, the first-born of all farm stock, the tenth of all produce, must be paid in the name of God to the priests, the Levites, and the poor. Every seventh year the land must lie fallow, trusting to his bounty in the preceding harvests (Ex. 23 : 10, 11; Lev. 25 : 3, 4; 26 : 34, 35, 43; 2 Chr. 36 : 21). The soil was held, in fact, for the Crown, subject to certain payments and duties; but the Crown was that of Heaven. These conditions honourably satisfied, the title of the land-owner was indefeasible" (Geikie's *Hours, etc.*, v.)

Land'mark, a boundary line indicated by a stone, stake, etc. (Deut. 19 : 14; 27 : 17; Prov. 22 : 28; 23 : 10; Job 24 : 2). Landmarks could not be removed without incurring the severe displeasure of God.

Laodice'a. The city of this name mentioned in Scripture lay on the confines of Phrygia and Lydia, about 40 miles east of Ephesus (Rev. 3 : 14), on the banks of the Lycus. It was originally called Diospolis and then Rhoas, but afterwards Laodicea, from Laodice, the wife of Antiochus II., king of Syria, who rebuilt it. It was one of the most important and flourishing cities of Asia Minor. At a very early period it became one of the chief seats of Christianity (Col. 2 : 1; 4 : 15; Rev. 1 : 11, etc.). It is now a deserted place, called by the Turks *Eski-hissar* or "old castle."

Laodice'a, Epistle from (Col. 4:16), was probably the Epistle to the Ephesians, as designed for general circulation. It would reach the Colossians by way of Laodicea.

Lap'idoth—*torches*. Deborah is called "the wife of Lapidoth" (Judg. 4 : 4). Some have rendered the expression "a woman of a fiery spirit," under the supposition that Lapidoth is not a proper name—a woman of a torch-like spirit.

Lap'ping of water like a dog—*i.e.*, by putting the hand filled with water to the mouth. The dog drinks by shaping the end of his long thin tongue into the form of a spoon, thus rapidly lifting up water, which he throws into his mouth. The three hundred men that went with Gideon thus employed their hands and lapped the water out of their hands (Judg. 7 : 7).

Lap'wing, the name of an unclean bird, mentioned only in Lev. 11 : 19 and Deut. 14 : 18. The Hebrew name of this bird, *dukiphath*, has been generally regarded as denoting the *hoopoe* (*Upupa epops*), an onomatopöetic word derived from the cry of the bird, which resembles the word "hoop;" a bird not uncommon in Palestine. Others identify it with the English *peewit*.

Lasæ'a, a city in the island of Crete (Acts 27 : 8). Its ruins are still found near Cape Leonda, about 5 miles east of "Fair Havens."

La'sha—*fissure*—a place apparently east of the Dead Sea (Gen. 10 : 19). It was afterwards known as *Callirhoë*, a place famous for its hot springs.

Latch′et, a thong (Acts 22 : 25), cord, or strap fastening the sandal on the foot (Isa. 5 : 27; Mark 1 : 7; Luke 3 : 16).

LATCHET.

Lat′in, the vernacular language of the ancient Romans (John 19 : 20).

Lat′tice. (1.) Heb. *'eshnâbh,* a latticed opening through which the cool breeze passes (Judg. 5 : 28). The flat roofs of the houses were sometimes enclosed with a parapet of lattice-work on wooden frames, to screen the women of the house from the gaze of the neighbourhood.

(2.) Heb. *harakim,* the network or lattice of a window (Cant. 2 : 9).

(3.) Heb. *sebâkhâh,* the latticed balustrade before a window or balcony (2 Kings 1 : 2). The lattice window is frequently used in Eastern countries.

La′ver (Heb. *kiyôr*), a "basin" for boiling in, a "pan" for cooking (1 Sam.

LAVER.

2 : 14), a "fire-pan" or hearth (Zech. 12 : 6), the sacred wash-bowl of the tabernacle and temple (Ex. 30 : 18, 28; 31 : 9; 35 : 16; 38 : 8; 39 : 39; 40 : 7, 11, 30, etc.), a basin for the water used by the priests in their ablutions.

That which was originally used in the tabernacle was of brass (rather copper; Heb. *nihsheth*), made from the metal mirrors the women brought out of Egypt (Ex. 38 : 8). It contained water wherewith the priests washed their hands and feet when they entered the tabernacle (40 : 32). It stood in the court between the altar and the door of the tabernacle (30 : 19, 21).

In the temple there were ten lavers used for the sacrifices, and the molten sea for the ablutions of the priests (2 Chr. 4 : 6). The position and uses of these are described 1 Kings 7 : 27-39; 2 Chr. 4 : 6. The "molten sea" was made of copper, taken from Tibhath and Chun, cities of Hadarezer, king of Zobah (1 Chr. 18 : 8; 1 Kings 7 : 23-26).

No lavers are mentioned in the second temple.

Law, a rule of action. (1.) The *Law of Nature* is the will of God as to human conduct, founded on the moral difference of things, and discoverable by natural light (Rom. 1 : 20; 2 : 14, 15). This law binds all men at all times. It is generally designated by the term *conscience,* or the capacity of being influenced by the moral relations of things.

(2.) The *Ceremonial Law* prescribes under the Old Testament the rites and ceremonies of worship. This law was obligatory only till Christ, of whom these rites were typical, had finished his work (Heb. 7 : 9, 11 : 10 : 1; Eph. 2 : 16). It was fulfilled rather than abrogated by the gospel.

(3.) The *Judicial Law,* the law which directed the civil policy of the Hebrew nation.

(4.) The *Moral Law* is the revealed will of God as to human conduct, binding on all men to the end of time. It was promulgated at Sinai. It is perfect (Ps. 19 : 7), perpetual (Matt. 5 : 17, 18), holy (Rom. 7 : 12), good, spiritual (14), and exceeding broad (Ps. 119 : 96). Although binding on all, we are not under it as a covenant of works (Gal. 3 : 15). (See COMMANDMENTS.)

(5.) *Positive Laws* are precepts founded only on the will of God. They are right because God commands them.

(6.) *Moral positive laws* are commanded by God because they are right.

Law of Moses is the whole body of the Mosaic legislation (1 Kings 2:3; 2 Kings 23:25; Ezra 3:2). It is called by way of eminence simply "the Law" (Heb. *Tôrah*, Deut. 1:5; 4:8, 44; 17:18, 19; 27:3, 8). As a written code it is called the "book of the law of Moses" (2 Kings 14:6; Isa. 8:20), the "book of the law of the Lord" (Josh. 24:26).

The great leading principle of the Mosaic law is that it is essentially theocratic; *i.e.*, it refers at once to the commandment of God as the foundation of all human duty.

Law'yer, among the Jews, was one versed in the laws of Moses, which he expounded in the schools and synagogues (Matt. 22:35; Luke 10:25). The functions of the "lawyer" and "scribe" were identical. (See DOCTOR.)

Laz'arus, an abbreviation of **Eleazar**— *whom God helps.* (1.) The brother of Mary and Martha of Bethany. He was raised from the dead after he had lain four days in the tomb (John 12:1-17). This miracle so excited the wrath of the Jews that they sought to put both Jesus and Lazarus to death.

(2.) A beggar named in the parable recorded Luke 16:19-31.

Leaf *of a tree.* The olive-leaf mentioned Gen. 8:11. The barren fig-tree had nothing but leaves (Matt. 21:19; Mark 11:13). The oak-leaf is mentioned Isa. 1:30; 6:13. There are numerous allusions to leaves— their flourishing, their decay, and their restoration (Lev. 26:36; Isa. 34:4; Jer. 8:13; Dan. 4:12, 14, 21; Mark 11:13; 13:28). The fresh leaf is a symbol of prosperity (Ps. 1:3; Jer. 17:8; Ezek. 47:12); the faded, of decay (Job 13:25; Isa. 1:30; 64:6; Jer. 8:13).

Leaf of a door (1 Kings 6:34), the valve of a folding door.

Leaf of a book (Jer. 36:23), perhaps a fold of a roll.

League, a treaty or confederacy. The Jews were forbidden to enter into an alliance of any kind (1) with the Canaanites (Ex. 23:32, 33; 34:12-16); (2) with the Amalekites (Ex. 17:8, 14; Deut. 25:17-19); (3) with the Moabites and Ammonites (Deut. 2:9, 19). Treaties were permitted to be entered into with all other nations. Thus David maintained friendly intercourse with the kings of Tyre and Hamath, and Solomon with the kings of Tyre and Egypt.

Le'ah—*weary*—the eldest daughter of Laban, and sister of Rachel (Gen. 29:16). Jacob took her to wife through a deceit of her father (Gen. 29:23). She was "tendereyed" (17). She bore to Jacob six sons (32-35), also one daughter, Dinah (30:21). She accompanied Jacob into Canaan, and died there before the time of the going down into Egypt (Gen. 31), and was buried in the cave of Machpelah (49:31).

Lean'noth—*for answering; i.e.*, in singing—occurs in the title to Ps. 88. The title "Mahalath (*q.v.*) Leannoth" may be rendered "concerning sickness, to be sung" —*i.e.*, perhaps, to be sung in sickness.

Leas'ing (Ps. 4:2; 5:6) an Old English word meaning lies, or lying, as the Hebrew word *kâzâbh* is generally rendered.

Leath'er, a girdle of, worn by Elijah (2 Kings 1:8) and John the Baptist (Matt. 3:4). Leather was employed both for clothing (Job 31:20; Heb. 11:37) and for writing upon. The trade of a tanner is mentioned (Acts 9:43; 10:6, 32). It was probably learned in Egypt.

Leav'en. (1.) Heb. *seôr* (Ex. 12:15, 19; 13:7; Lev. 2:11), the remnant of dough from the preceding baking which had fermented and become acid.

(2.) Heb. *ḥamets*, properly "ferment." In Num. 6:3, "vinegar of wine" is more correctly "*fermented* wine." In Ex. 13:7, the proper rendering would be, "Unfermented things [Heb. *matstsôth*] shall be consumed during the seven days; and there shall not be seen with thee fermented things [*ḥamets*], and there shall not be seen with thee leavened mass [*seôr*] in all thy borders." The chemical definition of ferment or yeast is "a substance in a state of putrefaction, the atoms of which are in a continual motion."

The use of leaven was strictly forbidden in all offerings made to the Lord by fire (Lev. 2:11; 7:12; 8:2; Num. 6:15). Its secretly penetrating and diffusive power is referred to in 1 Cor. 5:6. In this respect it is used to illustrate the growth of the kingdom of heaven both in the individual heart and in the world (Matt. 13:33). It is a figure also of corruptness and of perverseness of heart and life (Matt. 16:6, 11; Mark 8:15; 1 Cor. 5:7, 8).

Leb'anon—*white*—"the white mountain of Syria," is the loftiest and most celebrated mountain range in Syria. It is a branch running southward from the Caucasus, and at its lower end forking into two parallel ranges—the eastern or Anti-Lebanon, and the western or Lebanon proper. They enclose a long valley (Josh. 11:17) of from 5 to 8 miles in width, called by Roman writers Cœle-Syria, now called *el-Buka'a*, "the valley," a prolongation of the valley of the Jordan.

Lebanon proper, *Jebel es-Sharki*, commences at its southern extremity in the gorge of the Leontes, the ancient Litâny, and extends north-east, parallel to the Mediterranean coast, as far as the river Eleutherus, at the plain of Emesa, "the entering of Hamath" (Num. 34:8; 1 Kings 8:65), in all about 90 geographical miles in extent. The average height of this range is from 6,000 to 8,000 feet; the peak of *Jebel Mukhmel* is about 10,200 feet, and the *Sannîn* about 9,000. The highest peaks are covered with perpetual snow and ice. In the recesses of the range wild beasts as of old still abound (2 Kings 14:9; Cant. 4:8). The scenes of the Lebanon are remarkable for their grandeur and beauty, and supplied the sacred writers with many expressive similes (Ps. 29:5, 6; 72:16; 104:16–18; Cant. 4:15; Isa. 2:13; 35:2; 60:13; Hos. 14:5). It is famous for its cedars (Cant. 5:15), its wines (Hos. 14:7), and its cool waters (Jer. 18:14). The ancient inhabitants were Giblites and Hivites (Josh. 13:5; Judg. 3:3). It was part of the Phœnician kingdom (1 Kings 5:2-6).

The eastern range, or Anti-Lebanon, or "Lebanon towards the sunrising," runs nearly parallel with the western from the plain of Emesa till it connects with the hills of Galilee in the south. The height of this range is about 5,000 feet. Its highest peak is Hermon (*q.v.*), from which a number of lesser ranges radiate.

Lebanon is first mentioned in the description of the boundary of Palestine (Deut. 1:7; 11:24). It was assigned to Israel, but was never conquered (Josh. 13:2-6; Judg. 3:1-3).

The Lebanon range is now inhabited by a population of about 300,000 Christians, Maronites, and Druses, and is ruled by a Christian governor. The Anti-Lebanon is inhabited by Mohammedans, and is under a Turkish ruler.

Lebbæ'us—*courageous*—a surname of Judas (Jude), one of the twelve (Matt. 10:3), called also Thaddæus, not to be confounded with the Judas who was the brother of our Lord.

Lebo'nah—*frankincense*—a town near Shiloh, on the north side of Bethel (Judg. 21:19). It has been identified with *el-Lubban*, to the south of Nablûs.

Leek (Heb. *hatsîr*; the *Allium porrum*), rendered "grass" in 1 Kings 18:5, 2 Kings 19:26, Job 40:15, etc.; "herb" in Job 8:12; "hay" in Prov. 27:25, and Isa. 15:6; "leeks" only in Num. 11:5. This Hebrew word seems to denote in this last passage simply herbs, such as lettuce or savoury herbs cooked as kitchen vegetables, and not necessarily what are now called leeks. The leek was a favourite vegetable in Egypt, and is still largely cultivated there and in Palestine.

Lees (Heb. *shemârîm*), from a word meaning to keep or preserve. It was applied to "lees" from the custom of allowing wine to stand on the lees that it might thereby be better preserved (Isa. 25:6). "Men settled on their lees" (Zeph. 1:12) are men "hardened or crusted." The image is derived from the crust formed at the bottom of wines long left undisturbed (Jer. 48:11). The effect of wealthy undisturbed ease on the ungodly is hardening. They become stupidly secure (comp. Ps. 55:19; Amos 6:1). To drink the lees (Ps. 75:8) denotes severe suffering.

Left hand, among the Hebrews, denoted

the north (Job 23:9; Gen. 14:15), the face of the person being supposed to be toward the east.

Left-handed (Judg. 3:15; 20:16), one unable to use the right hand skilfully, and who therefore uses the left; and also one who uses the left as well as the right—ambidexter. Such a condition of the hands is due to physical causes. This quality was common apparently in the tribe of Benjamin.

Le'gion, a regiment of the Roman army, the number of men composing which differed at different times. It originally consisted of three thousand men, but in the time of Christ consisted of six thousand, exclusive of horsemen, who were in number a tenth of the foot-men. The word is used (Matt. 26:53; Mark 5:9) to express simply a great multitude.

Le'hi—*a jawbone*—a place in the tribe of Judah where Samson achieved a victory over the Philistines (Judg. 15:9, 14, 16), slaying a thousand of them with the jawbone of an ass. The words in 15:19, "a hollow place that was in the jaw" (A.V.), should be, as in Revised Version, "the hollow place that is in Lehi."

Lem'uel — *dedicated to God* — a king whom his mother instructed (Prov. 31:1–6). Nothing is certainly known concerning him. The rabbis identified him with Solomon.

LENTIL.

Len'tiles (Heb. *'adâshim*), a species of vetch (Gen. 25:34; 2 Sam. 23:11), common in Syria under the name *addas.* The *red* pottage made by Jacob was of lentils (Gen. 25:29–34). They were among the provisions brought to David when he fled from Absalom (2 Sam. 17:28). It is the *Ervum lens* of Linnæus, a leguminous plant which produces a fruit resembling a bean.

Leop'ard (Heb. *nâmêr,* so called because *spotted*—Cant. 4:8), was that great spotted feline which anciently infested the mountains of Syria, more appropriately called a panther (*Felis pardus*). Its fierceness (Isa. 11:6), its watching for its prey (Jer. 5:6), its swiftness (Hab. 1:8), and the spots of its skin (Jer. 13:23), are noticed. This word is used symbolically (Dan. 7:6; Rev. 13:2).

Lep'rosy (Heb. *tsâra'ath,* a "smiting," a "stroke," because the disease was regarded as a direct providential infliction). This name is from the Greek *lepra,* by which the Greek physicians designated the disease from its *scaliness.* We have the description of the disease, as well as the regulations connected with it, in Lev. 13, 14; Num. 12:10–15, etc. There were reckoned six different circumstances under which it might develop itself—(1) without any apparent cause (Lev. 13:2–8); (2) its reappearance (9–17); (3) from an inflammation (18–28); (4) on the head or chin (29–37); (5) in white polished spots (38, 39); (6) at the back or in the front of the head (40–44).

Lepers were required to live outside the camp or city (Num. 5:1–4; 12:10–15, etc.). This disease was regarded as an awful punishment from the Lord (2 Kings 5:7; 2 Chr. 26:20). (See MIRIAM; GEHAZI; UZZIAH.)

This disease "begins with specks on the eyelids and on the palms, gradually spreading over the body, bleaching the hair white wherever they appear, crusting the affected parts with white scales, and causing terrible sores and swellings. From the skin the disease eats inward to the bones, rotting the whole body piecemeal." "In Christ's day no leper could live in a walled town, though he might in an open village. But wherever he was he was required to have his outer garment rent as a sign of deep grief, to go bareheaded, and to cover his beard with his mantle, as if in lamentation at his own virtual death. He had further to warn passers-by to keep away from him, by calling out, 'Unclean! unclean!' nor could he speak to any one, or receive or return a salutation, since in the East this involves an embrace."

That the disease was not contagious is evident from the regulations regarding it (Lev. 13:12, 13, 36; 2 Kings 5:1). Leprosy was "the outward and visible sign of the innermost spiritual corruption; a meet emblem in its small beginnings, its gradual spread, its internal disfigurement, its dissolution little by little of the whole body, of that which corrupts, degrades, and defiles man's inner nature, and renders him unmeet to enter the presence of a pure and holy God" (Maclear's *Handbook O. T*). Our Lord cured lepers (Matt. 8:2, 3; Mark 1:40–42). This divine power so manifested illustrates his gracious dealings with men in curing the leprosy of the soul —the fatal taint of sin.

Let'ter in Rom. 2:27, 29 means the outward form. The "oldness of the letter" (7:6) is a phrase which denotes the old way of literal outward obedience to the law as a system of mere external rules of conduct. In 2 Cor. 3:6, "the letter" means the Mosaic law as a *written* law. (See WRITING.)

Leum'mim—*peoples; nations*—the last mentioned of the three sons of Dedan, and head of an Arabian tribe (Gen. 25:3).

Le'vi—*adhesion.* (1.) The third son of Jacob by Leah. The origin of the name is found in Leah's words (Gen. 29:34), "This time will my husband *be joined* [Heb. *yillâveh*] unto me." He is mentioned as taking a prominent part in avenging his sister Dinah (Gen. 34:25–31). He and his three sons went down with Jacob (46:11) into Egypt, where he died at the age of one hundred and thirty-seven years (Ex. 6:16).

(2.) The father of Matthat, and son of Simeon, of the ancestors of Christ (Luke 3:29).

(3.) Luke 3:24.

(4.) One of the apostles, the son of Alphæus (Mark 2:14; Luke 5:27, 29), called also Matthew (Matt. 9:9).

Levi'athan, a transliterated Hebrew word (*livyâthân*), meaning "twisted," "coiled." In Job 3:8, Revised Version, and marg. of Authorized Version, it denotes the dragon which, according to Eastern tradition, is an enemy of light; in ver. 41 the crocodile is meant; in Ps. 104:26 it "denotes any large animal that moves by writhing or wriggling the body—the whale, the monsters of the deep." This word is also used figuratively for a cruel enemy, as some think "the Egyptian host, crushed by the divine power, and cast on the shores of the Red Sea" (Ps. 74:14). As used in Isa. 27:1, "leviathan the piercing [R.V. 'swift'] serpent, even leviathan that crooked [R.V. marg. 'winding'] serpent," the word may probably denote the two empires, the Assyrian and the Babylonian.

Lev'irate Law, from Latin *levir*, "a husband's brother," the name of an ancient custom ordained by Moses, by which, when an Israelite died without issue, his surviving brother was required to marry the widow, so as to continue his brother's family through the son that might be born of that marriage (Gen. 38:8; Deut. 25:5–10; comp. Ruth 3; 4:10). Its object was "to raise up seed to the departed brother."

Le'vite, a descendant of the tribe of Levi (Ex. 6:25; Lev. 25:32; Num. 35:2; Josh. 21:3, 41). This name is, however, generally used as the title of that portion of the tribe which was set apart for the subordinate offices of the sanctuary service (1 Kings 8:4; Ezra 2:70), as assistants to the priests.

When the Israelites left Egypt, the ancient manner of worship was still observed by them, the eldest son of each house inheriting the priest's office. At Sinai the first change in this ancient practice was made. A hereditary priesthood in the family of Aaron was then instituted (Ex. 28:1). But it was not till that terrible scene in connection with the sin of the golden calf that the tribe of Levi stood apart and began to occupy a distinct position (Ex. 32). The religious primogeniture was then conferred on this tribe, which henceforth was devoted to the service of the sanctuary (Num. 3:11–13). They were selected for this purpose because of their zeal for the glory of God (Ex. 32 : 26), and because, as the tribe to which Moses and Aaron belonged, they would naturally stand by the lawgiver in his work.

The Levitical order consisted of all the descendants of Levi's three sons, Gershon, Kohath, and Merari; whilst Aaron, Amram's son (Amram, son of Kohath), and his issue constituted the priestly order.

The *age and qualification* for Levitical service are specified in Num. 4 : 3, 23, 30, 39, 43, 47.

They were not included among the armies of Israel (Num. 1 : 47 ; 2 : 33 ; 26 : 62), but were reckoned by themselves. They were the special guardians of the tabernacle (Num. 1 : 51 ; 18 : 22-24). The Gershonites pitched their tents on the west of the tabernacle (3 : 23), the Kohathites on the south (3 : 29), the Merarites on the north (3 : 35), and the priests on the east (3 : 38). It was their duty to move the tent and carry the parts of the sacred structure from place to place. They were given to Aaron and his sons the priests to wait upon them and do work for them at the sanctuary services (Num. 8 : 19 ; 18 : 2-6).

As being wholly consecrated to the service of the Lord, they had no territorial possessions. Jehovah was their inheritance (Num. 18 : 20 ; 26 : 62 ; Deut. 10 : 9 ; 18 : 1, 2), and for their support it was ordained that they should receive from the other tribes the tithes of the produce of the land. Forty-eight cities also were assigned to them, thirteen of which were for the priests "to dwell in "—*i.e.*, along with their other inhabitants. Along with their dwellings they had "suburbs "—*i.e.*, "commons "—for their herds and flocks, and also fields and vineyards (Num. 35 : 2-5). Nine of these cities were in Judah, three in Naphtali, and four in each of the other tribes (Josh. 21). Six of the Levitical cities were set apart as "cities of refuge " (*q.v.*). Thus the Levites were scattered among the tribes to keep alive among them the knowledge and service of God. (See PRIEST.)

Levit'icus, the third book of the Pentateuch ; so called in the Vulgate, after the LXX., because it treats chiefly of the Levitical service.

In the first section of the book (1–17), which exhibits the worship itself, there is —(1.) A series of laws (1–7) regarding sacrifices, burnt-offerings, meat-offerings, and thank-offerings (1–3), sin-offerings and trespass-offerings (4 ; 5), followed by the law of the priestly duties in connection with the offering of sacrifices (6 ; 7). (2.) An historical section (8–10), giving an account of the consecration of Aaron and his sons (8) ; Aaron's first offering for himself and the people (9) ; Nadab and Abihu's presumption in offering "strange fire before Jehovah," and their punishment (10). (3.) Laws concerning purity, and the sacrifices and ordinances for putting away impurity (11–16). An interesting fact may be noted here. Canon Tristram, speaking of the remarkable discoveries regarding the flora and fauna of the Holy Land by the Palestine Exploration officers, makes the following statement :— "Take these two catalogues of the clean and unclean animals in the books of Leviticus [11] and Deuteronomy [14]. There are eleven in Deuteronomy which do not occur in Leviticus, and these are nearly all animals and birds which are not found in Egypt or the Holy Land, but which are numerous in the Arabian desert. They are not named in Leviticus a few weeks after the departure from Egypt ; but after the people were thirty-nine years in the desert they are named—a strong proof that the list in Deuteronomy was written at the end of the journey, and the list in Leviticus at the beginning. It fixes the writing of that catalogue to one time and period only— *viz.*, that when the children of Israel were familiar with the fauna and the flora of the desert " (*Palest. Expl. Quart., Jan. 1887*). (4.) Laws marking the separation between Israel and the heathen (17–20). (5.) Laws about the personal purity of the priests, and their eating of the holy things (20 ; 21) ; about the offerings of Israel—that they were to be without blemish (22 : 17–33) ; and about the due celebration of the great festivals (23 ; 25). (6.) Then follow promises and warnings to the people regarding obedience to these commandments, closing with a section on vows.

The various ordinances contained in this book were all delivered in the space of a month (comp. Ex. 40:17; Num. 1:1), the first month of the second year after the Exodus. It is the third book of Moses.

No book contains more of the very words of God. He is almost throughout the whole of it the direct speaker. This book is a prophecy of things to come—a shadow whereof the substance is Christ and his kingdom. The principles on which it is to be interpreted are laid down in the Epistle to the Hebrews. It contains in its complicated ceremonial the gospel of the grace of God.

Levy (1 Kings 4:6, R.V.; 5:13), forced service. The service of tributaries was often thus exacted by kings. Solomon raised a "great levy" of 30,000 men, about two per cent. of the population, to work for him by courses on Lebanon. Adoram (12:18) presided over this forced labour service (Ger. *Frohndienst;* Fr. *corvée*).

Lewd'ness (Acts 18:14), villany or wickedness, not lewdness in the modern sense of the word. The word "lewd" is from the Saxon, and means properly "ignorant," "unlearned," and hence low, vicious (Acts 17:5).

Lib'ertine, found only Acts 6:9, one who once had been a slave, but who had been set at liberty, or the child of such a person. In this case the name probably denotes those descendants of Jews who had been carried captives to Rome as prisoners of war by Pompey and other Roman generals in the Syrian wars, and had afterwards been liberated. In A.D. 19 these manumitted Jews were banished from Rome. Many of them found their way to Jerusalem, and there established a synagogue.

Lib'nah—*transparency; whiteness.* (1.) One of the stations of the Israelites in the wilderness (Num. 33:20, 21).

(2.) One of the royal cities of the Canaanites taken by Joshua (Josh. 10:29–32; 12:15). It became one of the Levitical towns in the tribe of Judah (21:13), and was strongly fortified. Sennacherib laid siege to

it (2 Kings 19:8; Isa. 37:8). It was the native place of Hamutal, the queen of Josiah (2 Kings 23:31). It stood near Lachish, and has been identified with the modern *Arâk el-Menshîyeh.*

Lib'ni—*white*—one of the two sons of Gershon, the son of Levi (Ex. 6:17; Num. 3:18, 21). (See LAADAN.)

Lib'ya, the country of the *Lubim* (Gen. 10:13), Northern Africa, a large tract lying along the Mediterranean, to the west of Egypt (Acts 2:10). Cyrene was one of its five cities.

Lice (Heb. *kinnîm*), the creatures employed in the third plague sent upon Egypt (Ex. 8:16–18). They were miraculously produced from the dust of the land. "The entomologists Kirby and Spence place these minute but disgusting insects in the very front rank of those which inflict injury upon man. A terrible list of examples they have collected of the ravages of this and closely allied parasitic pests." The plague of lice is referred to in Ps. 105:31.

Some have supposed that the word denotes not lice properly, but gnats. Others, with greater probability, take it to mean the "tick," which is much larger than lice.

Lie, an intentional violation of the truth. Lies are emphatically condemned in Scripture (John 8:44; 1 Tim. 1:9, 10; Rev. 21:27; 22:15). Mention is made of the lies told by good men, as by Abraham (Gen. 12:12, 13; 20:2), Isaac (26:7), and Jacob (27:24); also by the Hebrew midwives (Ex. 1:15–19), by Michal (1 Sam. 19:14), and by David (1 Sam. 20:6). (See ANANIAS.)

Lieuten'ant (only in A.V. Esther 3:12; 8:9; 9:3; Ezra 8:36), a governor or viceroy of a Persian province having both military and civil power. Correctly rendered in the Revised Version "satrap."

Life, generally of physical life (Gen. 2:7; Luke 16:25, etc.); also used figuratively (1) for immortality (Heb. 7:16); (2) conduct or manner of life (Rom. 6:4); (3) spiritual life or salvation (John 3:16, 17, 18, 36); (4) eternal life (Matt. 19:16, 17; John 3:15); of God and Christ as the absolute source and cause of all life (John 1:4; 5:26, 39; 11:25; 12:50).

Light, the offspring of the divine command (Gen. 1 : 3). "All the more joyous emotions of the mind, all the pleasing sensations of the frame, all the happy hours of domestic intercourse were habitually described among the Hebrews under imagery derived from light" (1 Kings 11 : 36 ; Isa. 58 : 8 ; Esther 8 : 16 ; Ps. 97 : 11). Light came also naturally to typify true religion and the felicity it imparts (Ps. 119 : 105 ; Isa. 8 : 20 ; Matt. 4 : 16, etc.), and the glorious inheritance of the redeemed (Col. 1 : 12 ; Rev. 21 : 23-25). God is said to dwell in light inaccessible (1 Tim. 6 : 16). It frequently signifies instruction (Matt. 5 : 16 ; John 5 : 35). In its highest sense it is applied to Christ as the "Sun of righteousness" (Mal. 4 : 2 ; Luke 2 : 32 ; John 1 : 7-9). God is styled "the Father of lights" (James 1 : 17). It is used of angels (2 Cor. 11 : 14), and of John the Baptist, who was a "burning and a shining light" (John 5 : 35), and of all true disciples, who are styled "the light of the world" (Matt. 5 : 14).

Light'ning, frequently referred to by the sacred writers (Nah. 1 : 3-6). Thunder and lightning are spoken of as tokens of God's wrath (2 Sam. 22 : 15 ; Job 28 : 26 ; 37 : 4 ; Ps. 135 : 7 ; 144 : 6 ; Zech. 9 : 14). They represent God's glorious and awful majesty (Rev. 4 : 5), or some judgment of God on the world (20 : 9).

Lign-al'oes (only in pl., Heb. *'ahălim*), a perfume derived from some Oriental tree (Num. 24 : 6), probably the *agallochum* or *aloe-wood.* (See ALOES.)

Lig'ure (Heb. *lĕshĕm*) occurs only in Ex. 28 : 19 and 39 : 12, as the name of a stone in the third row on the high priest's breastplate. Some have supposed that this stone was the same as the jacinth (*q.v.*), others that it was the opal. There is now no mineral bearing this name. The "ligurite" is so named from Liguria in Italy, where it was found.

Lil'y. The Hebrew name *shûshân* or *shôshân*—*i.e.,* "whiteness"—was used as the general name of several plants common to Syria, such as the tulip, iris, anemone, gladiolus, ranunculus, etc. Some interpret it, with much probability, as denoting in the Old Testament the water-lily (*Nymphœa lotus* of Linn.), or lotus (Cant. 2 : 1, 2 ; 2 : 16 ; 4 : 5 ; 5 : 13 ; 6 : 2, 3 ; 7 : 2). "Its flowers are large, and they are of a white colour, with streaks of pink. They supplied models for the ornaments of the pillars and the molten sea" (1 Kings 7 : 19, 22, 26 ; 2 Chr. 4 : 5). In the Canticles its beauty and fragrance shadow forth the preciousness of Christ to the Church. Groser, however (*Scrip. Nat. Hist.*), strongly argues that the word, both in the Old and New Testaments, denotes liliaceous plants in general, or if one genus is to be selected, that it must be the genus Iris, which is "large, vigorous, elegant in form, and gorgeous in colouring."

The lilies (Gr. *krinia*) spoken of in the New Testament (Matt. 6 : 28 ; Luke 12 : 27) were probably the scarlet martagon (*Lilium Chalcedonicum*) or "red Turk's-cap

LILIUM CHALCEDONICUM.

lily," which "comes into flower at the season of the year when our Lord's sermon on the mount is supposed to have been delivered. It is abundant in the district of Galilee ; and its fine scarlet flowers render it a very conspicuous and showy object, which would naturally attract the attention of the hearers" (Balfour's *Plants of the Bible*).

Of the true "floral glories of Palestine" the pheasant's eye (*Adonis Palestina*), the ranunculus (*R. Asiaticus*), and the anemone

(*A. coronaria*), the last named is, however, with the greatest probability regarded as the "lily of the field" to which our Lord refers. "Certainly," says Tristram (*Nat. Hist. of the Bible*), "if, in the wondrous richness of bloom which characterizes the land of Israel in spring, any one plant can claim pre-eminence, it is the anemone, the most natural flower for our

ANEMONE CORONARIA.

Lord to pluck and seize upon as an illustration, whether walking in the fields or sitting on the hill-side." "The white water-lily (*Nymphœa alba*) and the yellow water-lily (*Nuphar lutea*) are both abundant in the marshes of the Upper Jordan, but have no connection with the lily of Scripture."

Lime. The Hebrew word so rendered means "boiling" or "effervescing." From Isa. 33 : 12 it appears that lime was made in a kiln lighted by thorn-bushes. In Amos 2 : 1 it is recorded that the king of Moab "burned the bones of the king of Edom with lime." The same Hebrew word is used in Deut. 27 : 2–4, and is there rendered "plaster." Limestone is the chief constituent of the mountains of Syria.

Lines were used for measuring and dividing land; and hence the word came to denote a portion or inheritance measured out; a possession (Ps. 16 : 6).

Lin′en. (1.) Heb. *pishet, pishtah*, denotes "flax," of which linen is made (Isa. 19 : 9); wrought flax—*i.e.,* "linen cloth"—Lev. 13 : 47, 48, 52, 59; Deut. 22 : 11.

Flax was early cultivated in Egypt (Ex. 9 : 31), and also in Palestine (Josh. 2 : 6; Hos. 2 : 9). Various articles were made of it : garments (2 Sam. 6 : 14), girdles (Jer. 13 : 1), ropes and thread (Ezek. 40 : 3), napkins (Luke 24 : 12; John 20 : 7), turbans (Ezek. 44 : 18), and lamp-wicks (Isa. 42 : 3).

(2.) Heb. *bûts*, "whiteness;" rendered "fine linen" in 1 Chr. 4 : 21; 15 : 27; 2 Chr. 2 : 14; 3 : 14; Esther 1 : 6; 8 : 15, and "white linen" 2 Chr. 5 : 12. It is not certain whether this word means cotton or linen.

(3.) Heb. *bad*; rendered "linen" Ex. 28 : 42; 39 : 28; Lev. 6 : 10; 16 : 4, 23, 32; 1 Sam. 2 : 18; 2 Sam. 6 : 14, etc. It is uniformly used of the sacred vestments worn by the priests. The word is from a root signifying "separation."

(4.) Heb. *shêsh;* rendered "fine linen" Ex. 25 : 4; 26 : 1, 31, 36, etc. In Prov. 31 : 22 it is rendered in Authorized Version "silk," and in Revised Version "fine linen." The word denotes Egyptian linen of peculiar *whiteness* and fineness (*byssus*). The finest Indian linen—the finest now made—has in an inch one hundred threads of warp and eighty-four of woof; while the Egyptian had sometimes one hundred and forty in the warp and sixty-four in the woof. This was the usual dress of the Egyptian priest. Pharaoh arrayed Joseph in a dress of linen (Gen. 41 : 42).

(5.) Heb. *'etûn.* Prov. 7 : 16, "fine linen of Egypt;" in Revised Version, "the yarn of Egypt."

(6.) Heb. *sâdin.* Prov. 31 : 24, "fine linen;" in Revised Version, "linen garments" (Judg. 14 : 12, 13; Isa. 3 : 23). From this Hebrew word is probably derived the Greek word *sindon*, rendered "linen" in Mark 14 : 51, 52; 15 : 46; Matt. 27 : 59.

The word "linen" is used as an emblem of moral purity (Rev. 15 : 6). In Luke 16 : 19 it is mentioned as a mark of luxury.

Lin′en-yarn. (See YARN.)

Lin′tel. (1.) Heb. *mashkôph*, a projecting cover (Ex. 12 : 22, 23; ver. 7, "upper door post," but R.V. "lintel"); the head-piece of a door, which the Israelites were commanded to mark with the blood of the paschal lamb.

(2.) Heb. *kaphtâr.* Amos 9 : 1; Zech.

2:14 (R.V. correctly "chapiters," as in A.V. marg.).

Li'ons, the most powerful of all carnivorous animals. Although not now found in Palestine, they must have been in ancient times very numerous there. They had their lairs in the forests (Jer. 5:6; 12:8; Amos 3:4), in the caves of the mountains (Cant. 4:8; Nah. 2:12), and in the canebrakes on the banks of the Jordan (Jer. 49:19; 50:44; Zech. 11:3).

No fewer than at least six different words are used in the Old Testament for the lion. (1.) *Gôr* (i.e., a "suckling"), the lion's whelp (Gen. 49:9; Jer. 51:38, etc.). (2.) *Kĕphir* (i.e., "shaggy"), the young lion (Judg. 14: 5; Job 4:10; Ps. 91:13; 104:21), a term which is also used figuratively of cruel enemies (Ps. 34:10; 35:17; 58:6; Jer. 2: 15). (3.) *'Arî* (i.e., the "puller" in pieces), denoting the lion in general, without reference to age or sex (Num. 23:24; 2 Sam. 17:10, etc.). (4.) *Shahal* (the "roarer"), the mature lion (Job 4:10; Ps. 91:13; Prov. 26:13; Hos. 5:14). (5.) *Laish,* so called from its strength and bravery (Job 4:11; Prov. 30:30; Isa. 30:6). The capital of Northern Dan received its name from this word. (6.) *Lâbî,* from a root meaning "to roar," a grown lion or lioness (Gen. 49:9; Num. 23:24; 24:9; Jer. 19:2; Nah. 2: 11).

The lion of Palestine was properly of the Asiatic variety, distinguished from the African variety, which is larger. Yet it not only attacked flocks in the presence of the shepherd, but also laid waste towns and villages (2 Kings 17:25, 26) and devoured men (1 Kings 13:24, 25). Shepherds sometimes, single-handed, encountered lions and slew them (1 Sam. 17:34, 35; Amos 3:12). Samson seized a young lion with his hands and "rent him as he would have rent a kid" (Judg. 14:5, 6). The strength (Judg. 14:18), courage (2 Sam. 17:10), and ferocity (Gen. 49:9) of the lion were proverbial.

Lip, besides its literal sense (Isa. 37:29, etc.), is used in the original (*sâphâh*) metaphorically for an edge or border, as of a cup (1 Kings 7:26), a garment (Ex. 28:32), a curtain (26:4), the sea (Gen. 22:17), the

Jordan (2 Kings 2:13). To "open the lips" is to begin to speak (Job 11:5); to "refrain the lips" is to keep silence (Ps. 40:9). The "fruit of the lips" (Heb. 13: 15; 1 Pet. 3:10) is praise, and the "calves of the lips" thank-offerings (Hos. 14:2). To "shoot out the lips" is to manifest scorn and defiance (Ps. 22:7). Many similar forms of expression are found in Scripture.

Lit'ter (Heb. *tsâb,* as being lightly and gently borne), a sedan or palanquin for the conveyance of persons of rank (Isa. 66:20). In Num. 7:3, the words "covered wagons" are more literally "carts of the litter kind." There they denote large and commodious vehicles drawn by oxen, and fitted for transporting the furniture of the temple.

Liv'er (Heb. *kâbhêd,* "heavy;" hence the liver, as being the *heaviest* of the viscera—Ex. 29:13, 22; Lev. 3:4, 10, 15) was burnt upon the altar, and not used as sacrificial food. In Ezek. 21:21 there is allusion, in the statement that the king of Babylon "looked upon the liver," to one of the most ancient of all modes of divination. The first recorded instance of divination (*q.v.*) is that of the teraphim of Laban. By the teraphim the LXX. and Josephus understood "the liver of goats." By the "caul above the liver," in Lev. 4:9; 7:4, etc., some understand the great lobe of the liver itself.

Liv'ing crea'tures, as represented by Ezekiel (1–10) and John (Rev. 4, etc.), are the cherubim. They are distinguished from angels (Rev. 15:7); they join the elders in the "new song" (5:8, 9); they warn of danger from divine justice (Isa. 6:3–5), and deliver the commission to those who execute it (Ezek. 10:2, 7); they associate with the elders in their sympathy with the hundred and forty-four thousand who sing the new song (Rev. 14:3), and with the Church in the overthrow of her enemies (19:4).

They are supposed to represent mercy, as distinguished from justice—mercy in its various instrumentalities, and especially as connected with the throne of God, the "throne of grace."

Liz'ard. Only in Lev. 11:30, as rendering of Hebrew *letâ'âh,* so called from its "hiding." Supposed to be the *Lacerta gecko* or fan-foot lizard, from the toes of which poison exudes. (See CHAMELEON.)

Lo-am′mi—*not my people*—a symbolical name given by God's command to Hosea's second son in token of Jehovah's rejection of his people (Hos. 1 : 9, 10), his treatment of them as a foreign people. This Hebrew word is rendered by "not my people" in ver. 10; 2 : 23.

Loan. The Mosaic law required that when an Israelite needed to borrow, what he asked was to be freely lent to him, and no interest was to be charged, although interest might be taken of a foreigner (Ex. 22 : 25; Deut. 23 : 19, 20; Lev. 25 : 35–38). At the end of seven years all debts were remitted. Of a foreigner the loan might, however, be exacted. At a later period of the Hebrew commonwealth, when commerce increased, the practice of exacting usury or interest on loans, and of suretiship in the commercial sense, grew up. Yet the exaction of it from a Hebrew was regarded as discreditable (Ps. 15 : 5; 27 : 13; Prov. 6 : 1, 4; 11 : 15; 17 : 18; 20 : 16; Jer. 15 : 10).

Limitations are prescribed by the law to the taking of a pledge from the borrower. The outer garment in which a man slept at night, if taken in pledge, was to be returned before sunset (Ex. 22 : 26, 27; Deut. 24 : 12, 13). A widow's garment (Deut. 24 : 17) and a millstone (6) could not be taken. A creditor could not enter the house to reclaim a pledge, but must remain outside till the borrower brought it (10, 11). The Hebrew debtor could not be retained in bondage longer than the seventh year, or at farthest the year of jubilee (Ex. 21 : 2; Lev. 25 : 39, 42), but foreign sojourners were to be "bondmen for ever" (Lev. 25 : 44–54).

Lock. The Hebrews usually secured their doors by bars of wood or iron (Isa. 45 : 2; 1 Kings 4 : 3). These were the locks originally used, and were opened and shut by large keys applied through an opening in the outside (Judg. 3 : 24). (See KEY.)

Lock of hair (Judg. 16 : 13, 19; Ezek. 8 : 3; Num. 6 : 5, etc.).

Lo′cust. There are ten Hebrew words used in Scripture to signify locust. In the New Testament locusts are mentioned as forming part of the food of John the Baptist (Matt. 3 : 4; Mark 1 : 6). By the Mosaic law they were reckoned "clean," so that he could lawfully eat them. The name also occurs in Rev. 9 : 3, 7, in allusion to this Oriental devastating insect.

Locusts belong to the class of the *Orthoptera*—*i.e.*, straight-winged. They are of many species. The ordinary Syrian locust resembles the grasshopper, but is larger and more destructive. "The legs and thighs of these insects are so powerful that they can leap to a height of two hundred times the length of their bodies. When so raised they spread their wings and fly so close together as to appear like one compact moving mass." Locusts are prepared as food in various ways. Sometimes they are pounded, and then mixed with flour and water, and baked into cakes;

LOCUST.

"sometimes boiled, roasted, or stewed in butter, and then eaten." They were eaten in a preserved state by the ancient Assyrians. The devastations they make in Eastern lands are often very appalling.

The invasions of locusts are the heaviest calamities that can befall a country. "Their numbers exceed computation : the Hebrews called them 'the countless,' and the Arabs knew them as 'the darkeners of the sun.' Unable to guide their own flight, though capable of crossing large spaces, they are at the mercy of the wind, which bears them as blind instruments of Providence to the doomed region given over to them for the time. Innumerable as the drops of water or the sands of the seashore, their flight obscures the sun and casts a thick shadow on the earth (Ex. 10 : 15; Judg. 6 : 5; 7 : 12; Jer. 46 : 23; Joel 2 : 10). It seems indeed as if a great aerial mountain, many miles in breadth, were advancing with a slow, unresting progress. Woe to the countries beneath them if the wind fall and let them alight! They descend unnumbered as flakes of snow and hide the ground. It may be 'like the garden of Eden before them, but behind them is a desolate wilderness. At their approach the people are in anguish; all faces lose their colour' (Joel 2:6). No walls can stop them; no ditches arrest them; fires kindled in their path are forthwith extinguished by the myriads of their dead, and the countless armies march on (Joel 2:8, 9). If a door or a window be open, they enter and destroy everything of wood in the house. Every terrace, court, and inner chamber is filled with them in a moment. Such an awful visitation swept over Egypt (Ex. 10: 1-19), consuming before it every green thing, and stripping the trees, till the land was bared of all signs of vegetation. A strong north-west wind from the Mediterranean swept the locusts into the Red Sea." —Geikie's *Hours, etc.*, ii., 149.

Lo-de'bar—*no pasture*—(2 Sam. 17:27), a town in Gilead not far from Mahanaim, north of the Jabbok (9:4, 5). It is probably identical with Debir (Josh. 13:26).

Lodge, a shed for a watchman in a garden (Isa. 1:8). The Hebrew name *mĕlûnâh* is rendered "cottage" (*q.v.*) in Isa. 24:20. It also denotes a hammock or hanging-bed.

Log, the smallest measure for liquids used by the Hebrews (Lev. 14:10, 12, 15, 21, 24), called in the Vulgate *sextarius*. It is the Hebrew unit of measure of capacity, and is equal to the contents of six ordinary hen's eggs=the twelfth part of a hin, or nearly a pint.

Lo'is, the maternal grandmother of Timothy. She is commended by Paul for her faith (2 Tim. 1:5).

Loop, a knotted "eye" of cord, corresponding to the "taches" or knobs in the edges of the curtains of the tabernacle, for joining them into a continuous circuit, fifty to a curtain (Ex. 26:4, 5, 10, 11).

Lord. There are various Hebrew and Greek words so rendered.

(1.) Heb. *Jehôvah*, has been rendered in the English Bible LORD, printed in small capitals. This is the proper name of the God of the Hebrews. The form "Jehovah" is retained only in Ex. 6:3; Ps. 83:18; Isa. 12:2; 26:4, both in the Authorized and the Revised Version.

(2.) Heb. *'adôn*, means one possessed of absolute control. It denotes a master, as of slaves (Gen. 24:14, 27), or a ruler of his subjects (45:8), or a husband, as lord of his wife (18:12).

The old plural form of this Hebrew word is *'adônai.* From a superstitious reverence for the name "Jehovah," the Jews, in reading their Scriptures, whenever that name occurred, always pronounced it *'Adônai.*

(3.) Greek *kurios*, a supreme master, etc. In the LXX. this is invariably used for "Jehovah" and "'Adonai."

(4.) Heb. *ba'al*, a master, as having domination. This word is applied to human relations, as that of husband, to persons skilled in some art or profession, and to heathen deities. "The men of Shechem," literally "the baals of Shechem" (Judg. 9:2, 3). These were the Israelite inhabitants who had reduced the Canaanites to a condition of vassalage (Josh. 16:10; 17:13).

(5.) Heb. *sĕrĕn*, applied exclusively to the "lords of the Philistines" (Judg. 3:3). The LXX. render it by *satrapies*. At this period the Philistines were not, as at a later period (1 Sam. 21:10), under a kingly government. (See Josh. 13:3; 1 Sam. 6:17.) There were five such lordships—*viz.*, Gath, Ashdod, Gaza, Ashkelon, and Ekron.

Lord's day—only once, in Rev. 1:10— was in the early Christian ages used to denote the first day of the week, which commemorated the Lord's resurrection. There is every reason to conclude that John thus used the name. (See SABBATH.)

Lord's Prayer, the name given to the only form of prayer Christ taught his disciples (Matt. 6:9-13). The closing doxology of the prayer is omitted by Luke (11: 2-4), also in the R.V. of Matt. 6:13. This prayer contains no allusion to the atonement of Christ, nor to the offices of the Holy Spirit. "All Christian prayer is based on the Lord's Prayer, but its spirit is also guided by that of His prayer in Gethsemane and of the prayer recorded John 17. The Lord's Prayer is the comprehensive type of the simplest and most universal prayer."

Lord's Supper (1 Cor. 11 : 20), called also "the Lord's table" (10 : 21), "communion," "cup of blessing" (10 : 16), and "breaking of bread" (Acts 2 : 42).

In the early Church it was called also "eucharist," or giving of thanks (comp. Matt. 26 : 27), and generally by the Latin Church "mass," a name derived from the formula of dismission, *Ite, missa est—i.e.,* "Go, it is discharged."

The account of the institution of this ordinance is given in Matt. 26 : 26-29, Mark 14 : 22-25, Luke 22 : 19, 20, and 1 Cor. 11 : 24-26. It is not mentioned by John.

It was designed—(1.) To commemorate the death of Christ : "This do in remembrance of me." (2.) To signify, seal, and apply to believers all the benefits of the new covenant. In this ordinance Christ ratifies his promises to his people, and they on their part solemnly consecrate themselves to him and to his entire service. (3.) To be a badge of the Christian profession. (4.) To indicate and to promote the communion of believers with Christ. (5.) To represent the mutual communion of believers with each other.

The *elements* used to represent Christ's body and blood are bread and wine. The kind of bread, whether leavened or unleavened, is not specified. Christ used unleavened bread simply because it was at that moment on the paschal table. Wine, and no other liquid, is to be used (Matt. 26 : 26-29). Believers "feed" on Christ's body and blood, (1) not with the mouth in any manner, but (2) by the soul alone, and (3) by faith, which is the mouth or hand of the soul. This they do (4) by the power of the Holy Ghost. This "feeding" on Christ, however, takes place not in the Lord's Supper alone, but whenever faith in him is exercised.

This is a permanent ordinance in the Church of Christ, and is to be observed "till he come" again.

Lo-ruha'mah—*not pitied*—the name of the prophet Hosea's first daughter, a type of Jehovah's temporary rejection of his people (Hos. 1 : 6 ; 2 : 23).

Lot (Heb. *gôrâl*, a "pebble"), a small stone used in casting lots (Num. 33 : 54 ; Jonah 1 : 7). The lot was always resorted to by the Hebrews with strictest reference to the interposition of God, and as a method of ascertaining the divine will (Prov. 16 : 33), and in serious cases of doubt (Esther 3 : 7). Thus the lot was used at the division of the land of Canaan among the several tribes (Num. 26 : 55 ; 34 : 13), at the detection of Achan (Josh. 7 : 14, 18), the election of Saul to be king (1 Sam. 10 : 20, 21), the distribution of the priestly offices of the temple service (1 Chr. 24 : 3, 5, 19 ; Luke 1 : 9), and over the two goats at the feast of Atonement (Lev. 16 : 8). Matthias, who was "numbered with the eleven" (Acts 1 : 24-26), was chosen by lot.

This word also denotes a *portion* or an inheritance (Josh. 15 : 1 ; Ps. 125 : 3 ; Isa. 17 : 4), and a *destiny,* as assigned by God (Ps. 16 : 5 ; Dan. 12 : 13).

Lot (Heb. *lôṭ*)—*a covering ; veil*—the son of Haran, and nephew of Abraham (Gen. 11 : 27). On the death of his father, he was left in charge of his grandfather Terah (31), after whose death he accompanied his uncle Abraham into Canaan (12 : 5), thence into Egypt (10), and back again to Canaan (13 : 1). After this he separated from him and settled in Sodom (13 : 5-13). There his righteous soul was "vexed" from day to day (2 Pet. 2 : 7), and he had great cause to regret this act. Not many years after the separation he was taken captive by Chedorlaomer, and was rescued by Abraham (Gen. 14). At length, when the judgment of God descended on the guilty cities of the plain (Gen. 19 : 1-20), Lot was miraculously delivered. When fleeing from the doomed city his wife "looked back from behind him, and became a pillar of salt." There is to this day a peculiar crag at the south end of the Dead Sea, near Kumrân, which the Arabs call *Bint Sheik Lot—i.e.,* Lot's wife. It is "a tall, isolated needle of rock, which really does bear a curious resemblance to an Arab woman with a child upon her shoulder." From the words of warning in Luke 17 : 32, "Remember

Lot's wife," it would seem as if she had gone back, or tarried so long behind in the desire to save some of her goods, that she became involved in the destruction which fell on the city, and became a stiffened corpse—fixed for a time in the saline incrustations. She became "a pillar of salt" —*i.e.*, as some think, of asphalt. (See SALT.)

Lot and his daughters sought refuge first in Zoar, and then, fearing to remain there longer, retired to a cave in the neighbouring mountains (Gen. 19 : 30). There, through an act of the vilest wickedness, his two daughters became the mothers of two sons, Moab and Ammon (31–38). Nothing more is recorded of Lot.

Love. This word seems to require explanation only in the case of its use by our Lord in his interview with "Simon, the son of Jonas," after his resurrection (John 21 : 16, 17). When our Lord says, "Lovest thou me?" he uses the Greek word *agapās;* and when Simon answers, he uses the Greek word *philō*—*i.e.*, "I love." This is the usage in the first and second questions put by our Lord; but in the third our Lord uses Simon's word. The distinction between these two Greek words is thus fitly described by Trench :—"*Agapān* has more of judgment and deliberate choice; *philein* has more of attachment and peculiar personal affection. Thus the 'Lovest thou' (Gr. *agapās*) on the lips of the Lord seems to Peter at this moment too cold a word, as though his Lord were keeping him at a distance, or at least not inviting him to draw near, as in the passionate yearning of his heart he desired now to do. Therefore he puts by the word and substitutes his own stronger 'I love' (Gr. *philō*) in its room. A second time he does the same. And now he has conquered; for when the Lord demands a third time whether he loves him, he does it in the word which alone will satisfy Peter ('Lovest thou,' Gr. *phileis*), which alone claims from him that personal attachment and affection with which indeed he knows that his heart is full."

In 1 Cor. 13 the apostle sets forth the excellency of love, as the word "charity" there is rendered in the Revised Version.

Lo′tan—*coverer*—one of the sons of Seir, the Horite (Gen. 36 : 20, 29).

Lu′bims, the inhabitants of a *thirsty* or *scorched* land; the Lybians, an African nation under tribute to Egypt (2 Chr. 12 : 3; 16 : 8). Their territory was apparently near Egypt. They were probably the Mizraite Lehabim.

Lu′cas, a friend and companion of Paul during his imprisonment at Rome; Luke (*q.v.*), the beloved physician (Philemon 24; Col. 4 : 14).

Lu′cifer—*brilliant star*—a title given to the king of Babylon (Isa. 14 : 12) to denote his glory.

Lu′cius of Cyrene, a Christian teacher at Antioch (Acts 13 : 1), and Paul's kinsman (Rom. 16 : 21). His name is Latin, but his birthplace seems to indicate that he was one of the Jews of Cyrene, in North Africa.

Lu′cre—from the Lat. *lucrum*, "gain." 1 Tim. 3 : 3, "not given to filthy lucre." Some MSS. have not the word so rendered, and the expression has been omitted in the Revised Version.

Lud. (1.) The fourth son of Shem (Gen. 10 : 22; 1 Chr. 1 : 17), ancestor of the Lydians probably.

(2.) One of the Hamitic tribes descended from Mizraim (Gen. 10 : 13), a people of Africa (Ezek. 27 : 10; 30 : 5), on the west of Egypt. The people called Lud were noted archers (Isa. 66 : 19; comp. Jer. 46 : 9).

Lu′dim, probably the same as Lud (2) (comp. Gen. 10 : 13; 1 Chr. 1 : 11). They are associated (Jer. 46 : 9) with African nations as mercenaries of the king of Egypt.

Lu′hith—*made of boards*—a Moabitish place between Zoar and Horonaim (Isa. 15 : 5; Jer. 48 : 5).

Luke, the evangelist, was a Gentile. The date and circumstances of his conversion are unknown. According to his own statement (Luke 1 : 2), he was not an "eyewitness and minister of the word from the beginning." It is probable that he was a physician in Troas, and was there converted by Paul, to whom he attached himself. He accompanied him to Philippi, but did not there share his imprisonment, nor did he accompany him further after his release in his missionary journey at this time (Acts 17 : 1). On Paul's third visit to Philippi (20 : 5, 6) we again meet with Luke, who probably had spent all the intervening time in that city, a period of seven or eight years. From this time Luke was Paul's constant companion during his journey to Jerusalem (20 : 6–21 : 18). He again disappears from view during Paul's imprisonment at Jerusalem and Cæsarea, and only reappears when Paul sets out for Rome (27 : 1), whither he accompanies him (28 : 2, 12–16), and where he remains with him till the close of his first imprisonment (Philemon 24; Col. 4 : 14). The last notice of the "beloved physician" is in 2 Tim. 4 : 11.

There are many passages in Paul's epistles, as well as in the writings of Luke, which show the extent and accuracy of his medical knowledge.

Luke, Gospel according to, was written by Luke. He does not claim to have been an eye-witness of our Lord's ministry, but to have gone to the best sources of information within his reach, and to have written an orderly narrative of the facts (Luke 1 : 1–4). The authors of the first three Gospels—the synoptics—wrote independently of each other. Each wrote his independent narrative under the guidance of the Holy Spirit.

Each writer has some things, both in matter and style, peculiar to himself, yet all the three have much in common. Luke's Gospel has been called "the Gospel of the nations, full of mercy and hope, assured to the world by the love of a suffering Saviour;" "the Gospel of the saintly life;" "the Gospel for the Greeks; the Gospel of the future; the Gospel of progressive Christianity, of the universality and gratuitousness of the gospel; the historic Gospel; the Gospel of Jesus as the good Physician and the Saviour of mankind;" the "Gospel of the Fatherhood of God and the brotherhood of man;" "the Gospel of womanhood;" "the Gospel of the outcast, of the Samaritan, the publican, the harlot, and the prodigal;" "the Gospel of tolerance." The main characteristic of this Gospel, as Farrar (*Cambridge Bible,*

Luke, Introd.) remarks, is fitly expressed in the motto, "Who went about doing good, and healing all that were oppressed of the devil " (Acts 10 : 38; comp. Luke 4 : 18). Luke wrote for the "Hellenic world." This Gospel is indeed "rich and precious."

"Out of a total of 1151 verses, Luke has 389 in common with Matthew and Mark, 176 in common with Matthew alone, 41 in common with Mark alone, leaving 544 peculiar to himself. In many instances all three use identical language." (See MATTHEW; MARK; GOSPELS.)

There are seventeen of our Lord's parables peculiar to this Gospel. (See List of Parables in Appendix.)

Luke also records seven of our Lord's miracles which are omitted by Matthew and Mark. (See List of Miracles in Appendix.)

The synoptical Gospels are related to each other after the following scheme. If the contents of each Gospel be represented by 100, then when compared this result is obtained:—

> Mark has 7 peculiarities, 93 coincidences.
> Matthew 42 peculiarities, 58 coincidences.
> Luke   59 peculiarities, 41 coincidences.

That is, thirteen-fourteenths of Mark, four-sevenths of Matthew, and two-fifths of Luke are taken up in describing the same things in very similar language.

Luke's *style* is more finished and classical than that of Matthew and Mark. There is less in it of the Hebrew idiom. He uses a few Latin words (Luke 12 : 6; 7 : 41; 8 : 30; 11 : 33; 19 : 20), but no Syriac or Hebrew words except *sikera*, an exciting drink of the nature of wine, but not made of grapes (from Heb. *shakar,* "he is intoxicated"—Lev. 10 : 9), probably palm wine.

This Gospel contains twenty-eight distinct references to the Old Testament.

The *date* of its composition is uncertain. It must have been written before the Acts, the date of the composition of which is generally fixed at about 63 or 64 A.D. This Gospel was written, therefore, probably about 60 or 63, when Luke may have been at Cæsarea in attendance on Paul, who was then a prisoner. Others have conjectured that it was written at Rome during Paul's imprisonment there. But on this point no positive certainty can be attained.

It is commonly supposed that Luke wrote under the direction, if not at the dictation of Paul. Many words and phrases are common to both; e.g.—

Compare	with
Luke 4 : 22	Col. 4 : 6.
,, 4 : 32	1 Cor. 2 : 4.
,, 6 : 36	2 Cor. 1 : 3.
,, 6 : 39	Rom. 2 : 19.
,, 9 : 56	2 Cor. 10 : 8.
,, 10 : 8	1 Cor. 10 : 27.
,, 11 : 41	Titus 1 : 15.
,, 18 : 1	2 Thess. 1 : 11.
,, 21 : 36	Eph. 6 : 18.
,, 22 : 19, 20	1 Cor. 11 : 23-29.
,, 24 : 46	Acts 17 : 3.
,, 24 : 34	1 Cor. 15 : 5.

Lu'natic, probably the same as epileptic, the symptoms of which disease were supposed to be more aggravated as the moon increased. In Matt. 4 : 24 "lunatics" are distinguished from demoniacs. In 17 : 15 the name "lunatic" is applied to one who is declared to have been possessed. (See DEMONIAC.)

Lust, sinful longing; the inward sin which leads to the falling away from God (Rom. 1 : 21). "Lust, the origin of sin, has its place in the heart, not of necessity, but because it is the centre of all moral forces and impulses and of spiritual activity." In Mark 4 : 19 "lusts" are objects of desire.

Luz—a nut-bearing tree, the almond. (1.) The ancient name of a royal Canaanitish city near the site of Bethel (Gen. 28 : 19; 35 : 6), on the border of Benjamin (Josh. 18 : 13). Here Jacob halted, and had a prophetic vision. (See BETHEL.)

(2.) A place in the land of the Hittites, founded (Judg. 1 : 26) by "a man who came forth out of the city of Luz." It is identified with Luweizîyeh, 4 miles northwest of Banias.

Lycao'nia, an inland province of Asia Minor, on the west of Cappadocia and the south of Galatia. It was a Roman province, and its chief towns were Iconium, Lystra, and Derbe. The "speech of Lycaonia" (Acts 14 : 11) was probably the ancient Assyrian language, or perhaps, as others think, a corrupt Greek intermingled with Syriac words. Paul preached in this region, and revisited it (Acts 16 : 1-6; 18 : 23; 19 : 1).

Ly'cia—a wolf—a province in the southwest of Asia Minor, opposite the island of Rhodes. It forms part of the region now called Tekeh. It was a province of the Roman empire when visited by Paul (Acts 21 : 1; 27 : 5). Two of its towns are mentioned—Patara (21 : 1, 2) and Myra (27 : 5).

Lyd'da, a town in the tribe of Ephraim, mentioned only in the New Testament (Acts 9 : 32, 35, 38) as the scene of Peter's miracle in healing the paralytic Æneas. It lay about 9 miles east of Joppa, on the road from that sea-port to Jerusalem. In the Old Testament (1 Chr. 8 : 12) it is called Lod. It was burned by the Romans, but was afterwards rebuilt, and was known by the name of Diospolis. Its modern name is Ludd. The so-called patron saint of England, St. George, is said to have been born here.

Lyd'ia. (1.) Ezek. 30 : 5 (Heb. Lud), a province in the west of Asia Minor, which derived its name from the fourth son of Shem (Gen. 10 : 22). It was bounded on the east by the greater Phrygia, and on the west by Ionia and the Ægean Sea.

(2.) A woman of Thyatira, a "seller of purple," who dwelt in Philippi (Acts 16 : 14, 15). She was not a Jewess but a proselyte. The Lord opened her heart as she heard the gospel from the lips of Paul (16 : 13). She thus became the first in Europe who embraced Christianity. She was a person apparently of considerable wealth, for she could afford to give a home to Paul and his companions. (See THYATIRA.)

Lysa'nias, tetrarch of Abilene (Luke 3 : 1), on the eastern slope of Anti-Lebanon, near the city of Damascus.

Lys'ias, Clau'dius, the chief captain (chiliarch) who commanded the Roman troops in Jerusalem, and sent Paul under guard to the procurator Felix at Cæsarea (Acts 21 : 31-38; 22 : 24-30). His letter to his superior officer is an interesting specimen of Roman military correspondence (23 : 26-30). He obtained his Roman citizenship by purchase, and was therefore probably a Greek. (See CLAUDIUS.)

Lys'tra, a town of Lycaonia, in Asia Minor, in a wild district and among a rude population. Here Paul preached the gospel after he had been driven by persecution from Iconium (Acts 14 : 2–7). Here also he healed a lame man (8), and thus so impressed the ignorant and superstitious people that they took him for Mercury, because he was the "chief speaker," and his companion Barnabas for Jupiter, probably in consequence of his stately, venerable appearance ; and were proceeding to offer sacrifices to them (13), when Paul earnestly addressed them and turned their attention to the true source of all blessings. But soon after, through the influence of the Jews from Antioch in Pisidia and Iconium, they stoned Paul and left him for dead (14 : 19). On recovering, Paul left for Derbe ; but soon returned again, through Lystra, encouraging the disciples there to steadfastness. He in all likelihood visited this city again on his third missionary tour (Acts 18 : 23). Timothy, who was probably born here (2 Tim. 3 : 10, 11), was no doubt one of those who were on this occasion witnesses of Paul's persecution and his courage in Lystra.

M

Ma'achah—*oppression*—a small Syrian kingdom near Geshur, east of the Haurân, the district of Batanea (Josh. 13 : 13; 2 Sam. 10 : 6, 8; 1 Chr. 19 : 7).

(2.) A daughter of Talmai, king of the old native population of Geshur. She became one of David's wives, and was the mother of Absalom (2 Sam. 3 : 3).

(3.) The father of Hanan, who was one of David's body-guard (1 Chr. 11 : 43).

(4.) The daughter of Abishalom (called Absalom, 2 Chr. 11 : 20-22), the third wife of Rehoboam, and mother of Abijam (1 Kings 15 : 2). She is called "Michaiah the daughter of Uriel," who was the husband of Absalom's daughter Tamar (2 Chr. 13 : 2). Her son Abijah or Abijam was heir to the throne.

(5.) The father of Achish, the king of Gath (1 Kings 2 : 39), called also Maoch (1 Sam. 27 : 2).

Ma'aleh-acrab'bim—*ascent of the scorpions; i.e.,* "scorpion-hill"—a pass on the south-eastern border of Palestine (Num. 34 : 4; Josh. 15 : 3). It is identified with the pass of *Sufâh,* entering Palestine from the great Wâdy el-Fikreh, south of the Dead Sea. (See AKRABBIM.)

Ma'arath—*desolation*—a place in the mountains of Judah (Josh. 15 : 59), probably the modern village *Beit Ummar,* 6 miles north of Hebron.

Maase'iah—*the work of Jehovah.* (1.) One of the Levites whom David appointed as porter for the ark (1 Chr. 15 : 18, 20).

(2.) One of the "captains of hundreds" associated with Jehoiada in restoring king Jehoash to the throne (2 Chr. 23 : 1).

(3.) The "king's son," probably one of the sons of king Ahaz, killed by Zichri in the invasion of Judah by Pekah, king of Israel (2 Chr. 28 : 7).

(4.) One who was sent by king Josiah to repair the temple (2 Chr. 34 : 8). He was governor (Heb. *sar,* rendered elsewhere in the Authorized Version "prince," "chief captain," "chief ruler") of Jerusalem.

(5.) The father of the priest Zephaniah (Jer. 21 : 1; 37 : 3).

(6.) The father of the false prophet Zedekiah (Jer. 29 : 21).

Maase'iah—*refuge is Jehovah*—a priest, the father of Neriah (Jer. 32 : 12; 51 : 59).

Maasi'ai—*work of Jehovah*—one of the priests resident at Jerusalem at the Captivity (1 Chr. 9 : 12).

Ma'ath—*small*—a person named in our Lord's ancestry (Luke 3 : 26).

Maazi'ah—*strength* or *consolation of Jehovah.* (1.) The head of the twenty-fourth priestly course (1 Chr. 24 : 18) in David's reign.

(2.) A priest (Neh. 10 : 8).

Mac'cabees. This word does not occur in Scripture. It was the name given to the leaders of the national party among the Jews who suffered in the persecution under Antiochus Epiphanes, who succeeded to the Syrian throne B.C. 175. It is supposed to have been derived from the Hebrew word (*makkâbâh*) meaning "hammer," as suggestive of the heroism and power of this Jewish family, who are, however, more properly called Asmoneans or Hasmonæans, the origin of which is much disputed.

After the expulsion of Antiochus Epiphanes from Egypt by the Romans, he gave vent to his indignation on the Jews, great numbers of whom he mercilessly put to death in Jerusalem. He oppressed them in every way, and tried to abolish altogether the Jewish worship. Mattathias, an aged priest, then residing at Modin, a city to the west of Jerusalem, became now the courageous leader of the national party; and having fled to the mountains, rallied round him a large band of men prepared to fight and die for their country and for their religion, which was now violently suppressed. In 1 Macc. 2: 60 is recorded his dying counsels to his sons with reference to the war they were now to carry on. His son Judas, "the Maccabee," succeeded him (B.C. 166) as the leader in directing the war of independence, which was carried on with great heroism on the part of the Jews, and was terminated in the defeat of the Syrians.

Mac'cabees, Books of the. There were originally five books of the Maccabees. The *first* contains a history of the war of independence, commencing (B.C. 175) in a series of patriotic struggles against the tyranny of Antiochus Epiphanes, and terminating B.C. 135. It became part of the Vulgate Version of the Bible, and was thus retained among the Apocrypha.

The *second* gives a history of the Maccabees' struggle from B.C. 176 to B.C. 161. Its object is to encourage and admonish the Jews to be faithful to the religion of their fathers.

The *third* does not hold a place in the Apocrypha, but is read in the Greek Church. Its design is to comfort the Alexandrian Jews in their persecution. Its writer was evidently an Alexandrian Jew.

The *fourth* was found in the Library of Lyons, but was afterwards burned. The *fifth* contains a history of the Jews from B.C. 184 to B.C. 86. It is a compilation made by a Jew after the destruction of Jerusalem, from ancient memoirs, to which he had access. It need scarcely be added that none of these books has any divine authority.

Macedo'nia, in New Testament times, was a Roman province lying north of Greece. It was governed by a proprætor with the title of proconsul. Paul was summoned by the vision of the "man of Macedonia" to preach the gospel there (Acts 16:9). Frequent allusion is made to this event (18:5; 19:21; Rom. 15:26; 2 Cor. 1:16; 11:9; Phil. 4:15). The history of Paul's first journey through Macedonia is given in detail in Acts 16:10-17:15. At the close of this journey he returned from Corinth to Syria. He again passed through this country (20:1-6), although the details of the route are not given. After many years he probably visited it for a third time (Phil. 2:24; 1 Tim. 1:3). The first convert made by Paul in Europe was (Acts 16:13-15) Lydia (*q.v.*), a "seller of purple," residing in Philippi, the chief city of the eastern division of Macedonia.

Machæ'rus — *the Black Fortress* — was built by Herod the Great in the gorge of Callirhoë, one of the wâdies 9 miles east of the Dead Sea, as a frontier rampart against Arab marauders. John the Baptist was probably cast into the prison connected with this castle by Herod Antipas, whom he had reproved for his adulterous marriage with Herodias. Here Herod "made a supper" on his birthday. He was at this time marching against Aretas, king of Perea, to whose daughter he had been married. During the revelry of the banquet held in the border fortress, to please Salome, who danced before him, he sent an executioner, who beheaded John, and "brought his head in a charger, and gave it to the damsel" (Mark 6 : 14–29). This castle stood "starkly bold and clear" 3,860 feet above the Dead Sea, and 2,546 above the Mediterranean. Its ruins, now called *M'khaur*, are still visible on the northern end of Jebel Attarûs.

Machban'ai—*clad with a mantle*, or *bond of the Lord*—one of the Gadite heroes who joined David in the wilderness (1 Chr. 12 : 13).

Ma'chir—*sold*. (1.) Manasseh's oldest son (Josh. 17 : 1), or probably his only son (see 1 Chr. 7 : 14, 15; comp. Num. 26 : 29– 33; Josh. 13 : 31). His descendants are referred to under the name of Machirites, being the offspring of Gilead (Num. 26 : 29). They settled in land taken from the Amorites (32 : 39, 40; Deut. 3 : 15) by a special enactment (Num. 36 : 1–3; Josh. 17 : 3, 4). He is once mentioned as the representative of the tribe of Manasseh east of Jordan (Judg. 5 : 14).

(2.) A descendant of the preceding, residing at Lo-debar, where he maintained Jonathan's son, Mephibosheth, till he was taken under the care of David (2 Sam. 9 : 4), and where he afterwards gave shelter to David himself when he was a fugitive (17 : 27).

Machpe'lah—*portion; double cave*—the cave which Abraham bought, together with the field in which it stood, from Ephron the Hittite, for a family burying-place (Gen. 23). It is one of those Bible localities about the identification of which there can be no doubt. It was on the slope of a hill on the east of Hebron "before Mamre." Here were laid the bodies of Abraham and Sarah, Isaac and Rebekah, Jacob and Leah (Gen. 23 : 19; 25 : 9; 49 : 31; 50 : 13). Over the cave an ancient Christian church was erected, probably in the time of Justinian, the Roman emperor. This church has been converted into a Mohammedan mosque. The whole is surrounded by the *el-Haram* —*i.e.*, "the sacred enclosure"—about 200 feet long, 115 broad, and of an average height of about 50. This building, from the immense size of some of its stones, and the manner in which they are fitted together, is supposed by some to have been erected in the days of David or Solomon,

while others ascribe it to the time of Herod. It is looked upon as the most ancient and the finest relic of Jewish architecture.

On the floor of the mosque are erected six large cenotaphs as monuments to the dead who are buried in the cave beneath. Between the cenotaphs of Isaac and Rebekah there is a circular opening in the floor into the cavern below, the cave of Machpelah. Here it may be that the body of Jacob, which was embalmed in Egypt, is still preserved (much older embalmed bodies have recently been found in the cave of *Deir el-Bahari* in Egypt—see PHARAOH), though those of the others there buried may have long ago mouldered into dust. The interior of the mosque was visited by the Prince of Wales in 1862 by a special favour of the Mohammedan authorities. An interesting account of this visit is given in Dean Stanley's *Lectures on the Jewish Church*. It was also visited in 1866 by the Marquis of Bute, and in 1869 by the late Emperor (Frederick) of Germany, then the Crown Prince of Prussia. In 1881 it was visited by the two sons of the Prince of Wales, accompanied by Sir C. Wilson and others. (See Palestine *Quarterly Statement*, October 1882.)

Mad'ai—*middle land*—the third "son" of Japheth (Gen. 10 : 2), the name by which the Medes are known on the Assyrian monuments.

Madman'nah—*dunghill*—the modern *el-Minyây*, 15 miles south-south-west of Gaza (Josh. 15 : 31; 1 Chr. 2 : 49), in the south of Judah. The *Pal. Mem.*, however, suggest *Umm Deimneh*, 12 miles north-east of Beersheba, as the site.

Mad'men—*ibid.*—a Moabite town threatened with the sword of the Babylonians (Jer. 48 : 2).

Madme'nah—*ibid.*—a town in Benjamin, not far from Jerusalem, towards the north (Isa. 10 : 31). The same Hebrew word occurs in Isa. 25 : 10, where it is rendered "dunghill." This verse has, however, been interpreted as meaning "that Moab will be trodden down by Jehovah as *teben* [broken straw] is trodden to fragments on the threshing-floors of Madmenah."

Mad'ness. This word is used in its proper sense in Deut. 28 : 34, John 10 : 20,

EL HARAM (MACHPELAH), HEBRON.

1 Cor. 14:23. It also denotes a reckless state of mind arising from various causes, as over-study (Eccl. 1:17; 2:12), blind rage (Luke 6:11), or a depraved temper (Eccl. 7:25; 9:3; 2 Pet. 2:16). David feigned madness (1 Sam. 21:13) at Gath because he "was sore afraid of Achish."

Ma'don—*strife*—a Canaanitish city in the north of Palestine (Josh. 11:1; 12:19) whose king was slain by Joshua; perhaps the ruin *Madin*, near Hattin, some 5 miles west of Tiberias.

Mag'dala—*a tower*—a town in Galilee, mentioned only in Matt. 15:39. In the parallel passage in Mark 8:10 this place is called Dalmanutha. It was the birthplace of Mary called the Magdalen, or Mary Magdalene. It was on the west shore of the Lake of Tiberias, and is now probably the small obscure village called *el-Mejdel*, about 3 miles north-west of Tiberias. In the Talmud this city is called "the city of colour," and a particular district of it was called "the tower of dyers." The indigo plant was much cultivated here.

Magdale'ne, a surname derived from Magdala, the place of her nativity, given to one of the Maries of the Gospel to distinguish her from the other Maries (Matt. 27:56, 61; 28:1, etc.). A mistaken notion has prevailed that this Mary was a woman of bad character—that she was the woman who is emphatically called "a sinner" (Luke 7:36–50). (See MARY.)

Magic. The Jews seem early to have consulted the teraphim (*q.v.*) for oracular answers (Judg. 18:5, 6; Zech. 10:2). There is a remarkable illustration of this divining by teraphim in Ezek. 21:19–22. We read also of the divining cup of Joseph (Gen. 44:5). The magicians of Egypt are frequently referred to in the history of the Exodus. Magic was an inherent part of the ancient Egyptian religion, and entered largely into their daily life.

All magical arts were distinctly prohibited under penalty of death in the Mosaic law. The Jews were commanded not to learn the "abomination" of the people of the Promised Land (Lev. 19:31; Deut. 18:9–14). The history of Saul's consulting the witch of Endor (1 Sam. 28:3–20) gives no warrant for attributing supernatural power to magicians. From the first the witch is here only a bystander. The practice of magic lingered among the people till after the Captivity, when they gradually abandoned it.

It is not much referred to in the New Testament. The Magi mentioned in Matt. 2:1–12 were not magicians in the ordinary sense of the word. They belonged to a religious caste, the followers of Zoroaster, the astrologers of the East. Simon, a magician, was found by Philip at Samaria (Acts 8:9–24), and Paul and Barnabas encountered Elymas, a Jewish sorcerer, at Paphos (13:6–12). At Ephesus there was a great destruction of magical books (Acts 19:18, 19).

Magi'cians—Heb. *ḥartumim*—(Dan. 1:20) were sacred scribes who acted as interpreters of omens or "revealers of secret things."

Mag'istrate, a public civil officer invested with authority. The Hebrew *shôphetim*, or *judges*, were magistrates having authority in the land (Deut. 1:16, 17). In Judg. 18:7 the word "magistrate" (A. V.) is rendered in the Revised Version "possessing authority"—*i.e.*, having power to do them harm by invasion. In the time of Ezra (9:2) and Nehemiah (2:16; 4:14; 13:11) the Jewish magistrates were called *segânim*, properly meaning "nobles." In the New Testament the Greek word *archon*, rendered "magistrate" (Luke 12:58; Titus 3:1), means one *first* in power, and hence a prince, as in Matt. 20:25, 1 Cor. 2:6, 8. This term is used of the Messiah, "Prince of the kings of the earth" (Rev. 1:5). In Acts 16:20, 22, 35, 36, 38, the Greek term *stratēgos*, rendered "magistrate," properly signifies the leader of an army, a general, one having military authority. The *strategoi* were the *duumviri*, the two prætors appointed to preside over the administration of justice in the colonies of the Romans. They were attended by the sergeants (properly *lictors* or "rod bearers").

Ma'gog—*region of Gog*—the second of the "sons" of Japheth (Gen. 10:2; 1 Chr. 1:5). In Ezekiel (38:2; 39:6) it is the

MAGDALA.

name of a nation, probably some Scythian or Tartar tribe descended from Japheth. They are described as skilled horsemen, and expert in the use of the bow. The Latin father Jerome says that this word denotes "Scythian nations, fierce and innumerable, who live beyond the Caucasus and the Lake Mæotis, and near the Caspian Sea, and spread out even onward to India." Perhaps the name "represents the Assyrian *Mat Gugi*, or ' country of Gugu,' the Gyges of the Greeks " (Sayce's *Races*, etc.).

Ma'gor-missa'bib—*fear on every side*—(Jer. 20:3), a symbolical name given to the priest Pashur, expressive of the fate announced by the prophet as about to come upon him. Pashur was to be carried to Babylon, and there to die.

Maha'laleel—*praise of God.* (1.) The son of Cainan, of the line of Seth (Gen. 5: 12–17), called Malaleel (Luke 3 : 37).

(2.) Neh. 11 : 4, a descendant of Perez.

Ma'halath—*a lute; lyre.* (1.) The daughter of Ishmael, and third wife of Esau (Gen. 28 : 9); called also Bashemath (Gen. 36 : 3).

(2.) The daughter of Jerimoth, who was one of David's sons. She was one of Rehoboam's wives (2 Chr. 11 : 18).

Ma'halath Maschil, in the title of Ps. 53, denoting that this was a didactic psalm, to be sung to the accompaniment of the *lute* or *guitar*. Others regard this word "mahalath " as the name simply of an old *air* to which the psalm was to be sung. Others again take the word as meaning "sickness," and regard it as alluding to the contents of the psalm.

Ma'halath Lean'noth Maschil. This word *leannoth* seems to point to some kind of instrument unknown (Ps. 88, title). The whole phrase has by others been rendered, "On the sickness of affliction : a lesson ; " or, "Concerning afflictive sickness : a didactic psalm."

Mahana'im—*two camps*—a place near the Jabbok, beyond Jordan, where Jacob was met by the "angels of God," and where he divided his retinue into "two hosts " on his return from Padan-aram (Gen. 32:2). This name was afterwards given to the town which was built at that place. It was the southern boundary of Bashan (Josh. 13:26, 30), and became a city of the Levites (21 : 38). Here Saul's son Ishbosheth reigned (2 Sam. 2 : 8, 12), while David reigned at Hebron. Here also, after a troubled reign, Ishbosheth was murdered by two of his own body-guard (2 Sam. 4 : 5–7), who brought his head to David at Hebron, but were, instead of being rewarded, put to death by him for their cold-blooded murder. Many years after this, when he fled from Jerusalem on the rebellion of his son Absalom, David made Mahanaim, where Barzillai entertained him, his head-quarters, and here he mustered his forces which were led against the army that had gathered around Absalom. It was while sitting at the gate of this town that tidings of the great and decisive battle between the two hosts and of the death of his son Absalom reached him, when he gave way to the most violent grief (2 Sam. 17 : 24–27).

The only other reference to Mahanaim is as a station of one of Solomon's purveyors (1 Kings 4 : 14). It has been identified with the modern *Mukhumah*, a ruin found in a depressed plain called *el-Bukie'a*, "the little vale," near Penuel, south of the Jabbok, and north-east of *es-Salt*.

Ma'haneh-dan—Judg. 18:12,= "camp of Dan " 13 : 25 (R.V., "Mahaneh-dan ")—a place behind (*i.e.*, west of) Kirjath-jearim, where the six'hundred Danites from Zorah and Eshtaol encamped on their way to capture the city of Laish, which they rebuilt and called "Dan, after the name of their father " (18 : 11–31). The Palestine Explorers point to a ruin called 'Erma, situated about 3 miles from the great corn valley on the east of Samson's home.

Ma'hath—*grasping.* (1.) A Kohathite Levite, father of Elkanah (1 Chr. 6 : 35).

(2.) Another Kohathite Levite, of the time of Hezekiah (2 Chr. 29 : 12).

Maha'zioth—*visions*—a Kohathite Levite, chief of the twenty-third course of musicians (1 Chr. 25 : 4, 30).

Ma'her-sha'lal-hash'-baz—*plunder speedeth; spoil hasteth*—(Isa. 8 : 1–3 ; comp. Zeph. 1 : 14), a name Isaiah was commanded first to write in large characters on a tablet, and afterwards to give as a symbolical name to a son that was to be born to him (Isa. 8 : 1, 3), as denoting the sudden attack on Damascus and Syria by the Assyrian army.

Mah'lah—*disease*—one of the five daughters of Zelophehad (Num. 27 : 1–11) who had their father's inheritance, the law of inheritance having been altered in their favour.

Mah'lon—*sickly*—the elder of Elimelech the Bethlehemite's two sons by Naomi. He married Ruth, and died childless (Ruth 1 : 2, 5 ; 4 : 9, 10) in the land of Moab.

Ma'hol—*dance*—the father of four sons (1 Kings 4 : 31) who were inferior in wisdom only to Solomon.

Mail, Coat of, "a corselet of scales," a cuirass formed of pieces of metal overlapping each other, like fish-scales (1 Sam. 17 : 5); also (38) a corselet or garment thus encased.

Main-sail (Gr. *artĕmôn*), answering to the modern "mizzen-sail," as some suppose. Others understand the "jib," near the prow, or the "fore-sail," as likely to be most useful in bringing a ship's head to the wind in the circumstances described (Acts 27 : 40).

Makhe'loth—*assemblies*—a station of the Israelites in the desert (Num. 33 : 25, 26).

Mak'kedah—*herdsman's place*—one of the royal cities of the Canaanites (Josh. 12 : 16), near which was a cave where the five kings who had confederated against Israel sought refuge (10 : 10–29). They were put to death by Joshua, who afterwards suspended their bodies upon five trees. It has been identified with the modern village called *Sumeil*, standing on a low hill about 7 miles to the north-west of Eleutheropolis (Beit Jibrin), where are ancient remains and a great cave. The Palestine Exploration surveyors have, however, identified it with *el-Mŭghâr*, or "the caves," 3 miles from Jabneh and 2½ south-west of Ekron, because, they say, "at this site only of all possible sites for Makkedah in the Palestine plain do caves still exist." (See ADONI-ZEDEC.)

Mak'tesh—*mortar*—a place in or near Jerusalem inhabited by silver-merchants (Zeph. 1 : 11). It has been conjectured that it was the "Phœnician quarter" of the city, where the traders of that nation resided, after the Oriental custom.

Mal'achi—*messenger* or *angel*—the last of the minor prophets, and the writer of the last book of the Old Testament canon (Mal. 4 : 4, 5, 6). Nothing is known of him beyond what is contained in his book of prophecies. Some have supposed that the name is simply a title descriptive of his character as a messenger of Jehovah, and not a proper name. There is reason, however, to conclude that Malachi was the ordinary name of the prophet.

He was contemporary with Nehemiah (comp. Mal. 2 : 8 with Neh. 13 : 15; Mal. 2 : 10–16 with Neh. 13 : 23). No allusion is made to him by Ezra, and he does not mention the restoration of the temple, and hence it is inferred that he prophesied after Haggai and Zechariah, and when the temple services were in existence (Mal. 1 : 10 ; 3 : 1, 10). It is probable that he delivered his prophecies about B.C. 420, after the second return of Nehemiah from Persia (Neh. 13 : 6), or possibly before his return.

Mal'achi, Prophecies of. The *contents* of the book are comprised in four chapters. In the Hebrew text the third and fourth chapters (of the A. V.) form but one. The whole consists of three sections, preceded by an introduction (Mal. 1 : 1–5), in which the prophet reminds Israel of Jehovah's love to them. The first section (1 : 6–2 : 9) contains a stern rebuke addressed to the priests who had despised the name of Jehovah, and been leaders in a departure from his worship and from the covenant, and for their partiality in administering the law. In the second (2 : 9–16) the people are rebuked for their intermarriages with idolatrous heathen. In the third (2 : 17–4 : 6) he addresses the people as a whole, and warns them of the coming of the God of judgment, preceded by the advent of the Messiah.

This book is frequently referred to in the New Testament (Matt. 11 : 10; 17 : 12; Mark 1 : 2; 9 : 11, 12; Luke 1 : 17; Rom. 9 : 13).

Mal'cam (2 Sam. 12 : 30, Heb., R.V., "their king;" Jer. 49 : 1, 3, R.V.; Zeph. 1 : 5), the national idol of the Ammonites.

When Rabbah was taken by David, the crown of this idol was among the spoils. The weight is said to have been "a talent of gold" (above 100 lbs.). The expression probably denotes its value rather than its weight. It was adorned with precious stones.

Malchi'ah — *Jehovah's king*. (1.) The head of the fifth division of the priests in the time of David (1 Chr. 24 : 9).

(2.) A priest, the father of Pashur (1 Chr. 9 : 12 ; Jer. 38 : 1).

(3.) One of the priests appointed as musicians to celebrate the completion of the walls of Jerusalem (Neh. 12 : 42).

(4.) A priest who stood by Ezra when he "read in the book of the law of God" (Neh. 8 : 4).

(5.) Neh. 3 : 11.

(6.) Neh. 3 : 31.

(7.) Neh. 3 : 14.

Malchi-shu'a—*king of help*—one of the four sons of Saul (1 Chr. 8 : 33). He perished along with his father in the battle of Gilboa (1 Sam. 31 : 2).

Mal'chus—*reigning*—the personal servant or slave of the high priest Caiaphas. He is mentioned only by John. Peter cut off his right ear in the garden of Gethsemane (John 18 : 10). But our Lord cured it with a touch (Matt. 26 : 51 ; Mark 14 : 47 ; Luke 22 : 51). This was the last miracle of bodily cure wrought by our Lord. It is not mentioned by John.

Mallo'thi — *my fulness* — a Kohathite Levite, one of the sons of Heman the Levite (1 Chr. 25 : 4), and chief of the nineteenth division of the temple musicians (26).

Mal'lows occurs only in Job 30 : 4 (R. V., "saltwort"). The word so rendered (*malluah*, from *melah*, "salt") most probably denotes the *Atriplex halimus* of Linnæus, a species of sea purslane found on the shores of the Dead Sea, as also of the Mediterranean, and in salt marshes. It is a tall shrubby orach, growing to the height sometimes of 10 feet. Its buds and leaves, with those of other saline plants, are eaten by the poor in Palestine.

Mal'luch — *reigned over*, or *reigning*. (1.) A Levite of the family of Merari (1 Chr. 6 : 44).

(2.) A priest who returned from Babylon (Neh. 12 : 2).

(3.) Ezra 10 : 29. (4.) Ezra 10 : 32.

Mam'mon, a Chaldee or Syriac word meaning "wealth" or "riches" (Luke 16 : 9–11); also, by personification, the god of riches (Matt. 6 : 24 ; Luke 16 : 9–11).

Mam're—*manliness*. (1.) An Amoritish chief in alliance with Abraham (Gen. 14 : 13, 24).

(2.) The name of the place in the neighbourhood of Hebron (*q.v.*) where Abraham dwelt (Gen. 23 : 17, 19 ; 35 : 27); called also in Authorized Version (13 : 18) the "plain of Mamre," but in Revised Version more correctly "the oaks [marg., 'terebinths'] of Mamre." The name probably denotes the "oak grove" or the "wood of Mamre," thus designated after Abraham's ally.

This "grove" must have been within sight of or "facing" Machpelah (*q.v.*). The site of Mamre has been identified with *Ballatet Selta*—*i.e.*, "the oak of rest"—where there is a tree called "Abraham's oak," about a mile and a half west of Hebron. Others identify it with *er-Râmeh*, 2 miles north of Hebron.

Man. (1.) Heb. '*Adam*, used as the proper name of the first man. The name is derived from a word meaning "to be red," and thus the first man was called Adam because he was formed from the red earth. It is also the generic name of the human race (Gen. 1 : 26, 27 ; 5 : 2 ; 8 : 21 ; Deut. 8 : 3). Its equivalents are the Latin *homo* and the Greek *anthrôpos* (Matt. 5 : 13, 16). It denotes also man in opposition to woman (Gen. 3 : 12 ; Matt. 19 : 10).

(2.) Heb. '*ish*, like the Latin *vir* and Greek *aner*, denotes properly a man in opposition to a woman (1 Sam. 17 : 33 ; Matt. 14 : 21); a husband (Gen. 3 : 16 ; Hos. 2 : 16); man with reference to excellent mental qualities.

(3.) Heb. '*enosh*, man as mortal, transient, perishable (2 Chr. 14 : 11 ; Isa. 8 : 1 ; Job 15 : 14 ; Ps. 8 : 4 ; 9 : 19, 20 ; 103 : 15). It is applied to women (Josh. 8 : 25).

(4.) Heb. *gĕbĕr*, man with reference to his strength, as distinguished from woman (Deut. 22 : 5) and from children (Ex. 12 : 37); a husband (Prov. 6 : 34).

(5.) Heb. *methîm*, men as mortal (Isa. 41:14), and as opposed to women and children (Deut. 3:6; Job 11:3; Isa. 3:25).

Man was *created* by the immediate hand of God, and is generically different from all other creatures (Gen. 1:26, 27; 2:7).

His complex nature is composed of two elements, two distinct substances — *viz.*, body and soul (Gen. 2:7; Eccl. 12:7; 2 Cor. 5:1–8).

The words translated "spirit" and "soul," in 1 Thess. 5:23, Heb. 4:12, are habitually used interchangeably (Matt. 10:28; 16:26; 1 Pet. 1:22). The "spirit" (Gr. *pneuma*) is the soul as rational; the "soul" (Gr. *psuchè*) is the same, considered as the animating and vital principle of the body.

Man was created in the likeness of God as to the perfection of his nature, in knowledge (Col. 3:10), righteousness, and holiness (Eph. 4:24), and as having dominion over all the inferior creatures (Gen. 1:28). He had in his original state God's law written on his heart, and had power to obey it, and yet was capable of disobeying, being left to the freedom of his own will. He was created with holy dispositions, prompting him to holy actions; but he was fallible, and did fall from his integrity (3:1–6). (See FALL.)

Man of sin, a designation of Antichrist given in 2 Thess. 2:3–10, usually regarded as descriptive of the Papal power; but "in whomsoever these distinctive features are found—whoever wields temporal and spiritual power in any degree similar to that in which the man of sin is here described as wielding it—he, be he pope or potentate, is beyond all doubt a distinct type of Antichrist."

Man'aen—*consoler*—a Christian teacher at Antioch. Nothing else is known of him beyond what is stated in Acts 13:1, where he is spoken of as having been brought up with (Gr. *syntröphos;* rendered in R.V. "foster brother" of) Herod—*i.e.*, Herod Antipas, the tetrarch, who, with his brother Archelaus, was educated at Rome.

Manas'seh—*who makes to forget.* "God hath made me forget" (Heb. *nashshani*), Gen. 41:51. (1.) The elder of the two sons of Joseph. He and his brother Ephraim were afterwards adopted by Jacob as his own sons (48:1). There is an account of his marriage to a Syrian (1 Chr. 7:14); and the only thing afterwards recorded of him is, that his grandchildren were "brought up upon Joseph's knees" (Gen. 50:23; R.V., "born upon Joseph's knees") —*i.e.*, were from their birth adopted by Joseph as his own children.

The tribe of Manasseh was associated with that of Ephraim and Benjamin during the wanderings in the wilderness. They encamped on the west side of the tabernacle. According to the census taken at Sinai, this tribe then numbered 32,200 (Num. 1:10, 35; 2:20, 21). Forty years afterwards its numbers had increased to 52,700 (26:34, 37), and it was at this time the most distinguished of all the tribes.

The half of this tribe, along with Reuben and Gad, had their territory assigned them by Moses on the east of the Jordan (Josh. 13:7–14); but it was left for Joshua to define the limits of each tribe. This territory on the east of Jordan was more valuable, and of larger extent, than all that was allotted to the nine and a half tribes in the land of Palestine. It is called sometimes "the land of Gilead," and is also spoken of as "on the other side of Jordan." The portion given to the half tribe of Manasseh was the largest on the east of Jordan. It embraced the whole of Bashan. It was bounded on the south by Mahanaim, and extended north to the foot of Lebanon. Argob, with its sixty cities, that "ocean of basaltic rocks and boulders tossed about in the wildest confusion," lay in the midst of this territory.

The whole "land of Gilead" having been conquered, the two and a half tribes left their wives and families in the fortified cities there, and accompanied the other tribes across the Jordan, and took part with them in the wars of conquest. The allotment of the land having been completed, Joshua dismissed the two and a half tribes, commending them for their heroic service (Josh. 22:1–34). Thus dismissed, they returned over Jordan to their own inheritance. (See ED.)

On the west of Jordan the other half of the tribe of Manasseh was associated with Ephraim, and they had their portion in the very centre of Palestine—an area of about 1,300 square miles—the most valuable part of the whole country, abounding in springs of water. Manasseh's portion was immediately to the north of that of Ephraim (Josh. 16). Thus the western Manasseh defended the passes of Esdraelon as the eastern kept the passes of the Haûran.

(2.) The only son and successor of Hezekiah on the throne of Judah. He was twelve years old when he began to reign (2 Kings 21 : 1), and he reigned fifty-five years (B.C. 698–643). Though he reigned so long, yet comparatively little is known of this king. His reign was a continuation of that of Ahaz, both in religion and national polity. He early fell under the influence of the heathen court circle, and his reign was characterized by a sad relapse into idolatry with all its vices, showing that the reformation under his father had been to a large extent only superficial (Isa. 1 : 10 ; 2 Kings 21 : 10–15). A systematic and persistent attempt was made, and all too successfully, to banish the worship of Jehovah out of the land. Amid this wide-spread idolatry there were not wanting, however, faithful prophets (Isaiah, Micah) who lifted up their voice in reproof and in warning. But their fidelity only aroused bitter hatred, and a period of cruel persecution against all the friends of the old religion began. "The days of Alva in Holland, of Charles IX. in France, or of the Covenanters under Charles II. in Scotland, were anticipated in the Jewish capital. The streets were red with blood." There is an old Jewish tradition that Isaiah was put to death at this time (2 Kings 21 : 16 ; 24 : 3, 4 ; Jer. 2 : 30), having been sawn asunder in the trunk of a tree. Psalms 49, 73, 77, 140, and 141 seem to express the feelings of the pious amid the fiery trials of this great persecution. He has been called the "Nero of Palestine."

Esarhaddon, Sennacherib's successor on the Assyrian throne, who had his residence in Babylon for thirteen years (the only Assyrian monarch who ever reigned in Babylon), took Manasseh prisoner (B.C. 681) to Babylon. Such captive kings were usually treated with great cruelty. They were brought before the conqueror with a hook or ring passed through their lips or their jaws, having a cord attached to it, by which they were led. This is referred to in 2 Chr. 33 : 11, where the Authorized Version reads that Esarhaddon "took Manasseh among the thorns ; " while the Revised Version renders the words "took Manasseh in chains ; " or literally, as in the margin, "with hooks." (Comp. 2 Kings 19 : 28.)

The severity of Manasseh's imprisonment brought him to repentance. God heard his cry, and he was restored to his kingdom (2 Chr. 33 : 11–13). He abandoned his idolatrous ways and enjoined the people to worship Jehovah ; but there was no thorough reformation. After a lengthened reign extending through fifty-five years—the longest in the history of Judah —he died, and was buried in the garden of Uzza, the "garden of his own house" (2 Kings 21 : 17, 18 ; 2 Chr. 33 : 20), and not in the city of David, among his ancestors. He was succeeded by his son Amon.

In Judg. 18 : 30 the correct reading is "Moses," and not "Manasseh." The name "Manasseh" is supposed to have been introduced by some transcriber to avoid the scandal of naming the grandson of Moses the great lawgiver as the founder of an idolatrous religion.

Man′drakes — Hebrew *dudâim ; i.e.,* "love-plants"—occurs only in Gen. 30 : 14–16 and Cant. 7 : 13. Many interpretations have been given to this word *dudâim.* It has been rendered "violets," "lilies," "jasmines," "truffles or mushrooms," "flowers," the "citron," etc. The weight of authority is in favour of its being regarded as the *Mandragora officinalis* of botanists—"a near relative of the nightshades, the 'apple of Sodom' and the potato plant." It possesses stimulating and narcotic properties (Gen. 30 : 14–16). The fruit of this plant resembles the potato-apple in size, and is of a pale orange colour. It has been called the "love-

MANDRAKE (MANDRAGORA OFFICINALIS).

apple." The Arabs call it "Satan's apple." It still grows near Jerusalem, and in other parts of Palestine.

Ma′neh—*portion* (Ezek. 45 : 12), rendered "pound" (1 Kings 10 : 17; Ezra 2 : 69; Neh. 7 : 21, 22)—a weight variously estimated, probably about 2½ or 3 lbs. A maneh of gold consisted of a hundred common shekels (*q.v.*). (Comp. 1 Kings 10 : 17, and 2 Chr. 9 : 16). ◦

Man′ger (Luke 2 : 7, 12, 16), the name (Gr. *phatnē*, rendered "stall" in Luke 13 : 15) given to the place where the infant Redeemer was laid. It seems to have been a stall or crib for feeding cattle. Stables and mangers in our modern sense were in ancient times unknown in the East. The word here properly denotes "the ledge or projection in the end of the room used as a stall on which the hay or other food of the animals of travellers was placed." (See INN.)

Man′na—Heb. *mân-hu*, "What is that?" —the name given by the Israelites to the food miraculously supplied to them during their wanderings in the wilderness (Ex. 16 : 15–35). The name is commonly taken as derived from *man*, an expression of surprise, "What is it?" but more probably it is derived from *mânan*, meaning "to allot," and hence denoting an "allotment" or a "gift." This "gift" from God is described as "a small round thing," like the "hoar-frost on the ground," and "like coriander seed," "of the colour of bdellium," and in taste "like wafers made with honey." It was capable of being baked and boiled, ground in mills, or beaten in a mortar (Ex. 16 : 23; Num. 11 : 7). If any was kept over till the following morning, it became corrupt with worms; but as on the Sabbath none fell, on the preceding day a double portion was given, and that could be kept over to supply the wants of the Sabbath without becoming corrupt. Directions concerning the gathering of it are fully given (Ex. 16 : 16–18, 33; Deut. 8 : 3, 16). It fell for the first time after the eighth encampment in the desert of Sin, and was daily furnished, except on the Sabbath, for all the years of the wanderings, till they encamped at Gilgal, after crossing the Jordan, when it suddenly ceased, and where they "did eat of the old corn of the land; neither had the children of Israel manna any more" (Josh. 5 : 12). They now no longer needed the "bread of the wilderness."

This manna was evidently altogether

FLOWER OF MANNA ASH.

a miraculous gift, wholly different from any natural product with which we are acquainted, and which bears this name. The manna of European commerce comes chiefly from Calabria and Sicily. It drops from the twigs of a species of ash during the months of June and July. At night it is fluid and resembles dew, but in the morning it begins to harden. The manna of the Sinaitic peninsula is an exudation from the "manna-tamarisk" tree (*Tamarix mannifera*), the *el-tarfah* of the Arabs.

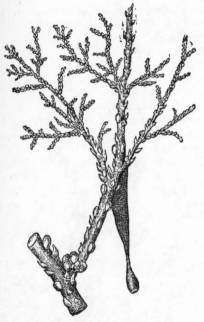

BRANCH OF MANNA-TAMARISK TREE
(TAMARIX MANNIFERA.)

This tree is found at the present day in certain well-watered valleys in the peninsula of Sinai. The manna with which the people of Israel were fed for forty years differs in many particulars from all these natural products.

Our Lord refers to the manna when he calls himself the "true bread from heaven" (John 6:31-35; 48-51). He is also the "hidden manna" (Rev. 2:17; comp. John 6:49, 51).

Mano'ah—*rest*—a Danite, the father of Samson (Judg. 13:1-22, and 14:2-4).

Man'slayer, one who was guilty of accidental homicide, and was entitled to flee to a city of refuge (Num. 35:6, 12, 22, 23), his compulsory residence in which terminated with the death of the high priest. (See CITY OF REFUGE.)

Man'tle. (1.) Heb. '*addĕrĕth*, a large over-garment. This word is used of Elijah's mantle (1 Kings 19:13, 19; 2 Kings 2:8, 13, etc.), which was probably a sheepskin. It appears to have been his only garment, a strip of skin or leather binding it to his loins. '*Addereth* twice occurs with the epithet "hairy" (Gen. 25:25; Zech. 13:4, R.V.). It is the word denoting the "goodly Babylonish garment" which Achan coveted (Josh. 7:21).

(2.) Heb. *mĕ'il*, frequently applied to the "*robe* of the ephod" (Ex. 28:4, 31; Lev. 8:7), which was a splendid under tunic wholly of blue, reaching to below the knees. It was woven without seam, and was put on by being drawn over the head. It was worn not only by priests but by kings (1 Sam. 24:4), prophets (15:27), and rich men (Job 1:20; 2:12). This was the "little coat" which Samuel's mother brought to him from year to year to Shiloh (1 Sam. 2:19), a miniature of the official priestly robe.

(3.) *Semîkah*, "a rug," the garment which Jael threw as a covering over Sisera (Judg. 4:18). The Hebrew word occurs nowhere else in Scripture.

(4.) *Maatâphoth*, plural, only in Isa. 3:22, denoting a large exterior tunic worn by females. (See DRESS.)

Ma'och—*compressed*—the father of Achish, king of Gath (1 Sam. 27:2). Called also Maachah (1 Kings 2:39).

Ma'on — *habitation* — a town in the tribe of Judah, about 7 miles south of Hebron, which gave its name to the wilderness, the district round the conical hill on which the town stood. Here David hid from Saul, and here Nabal had his possessions and his home (1 Sam. 23:24, 25; 25:2). "Only some small foundations of hewn stone, a square enclosure, and several cisterns are now to be seen at Maon. Are they the remains of Nabal's great establishment?" The hill is now called *Tell M'ain*.

Ma'ra —*bitter; sad*—a symbolical name

which Naomi gave to herself because of her misfortunes (Ruth 1 : 20).

Ma′rah—*bitterness*—a fountain at the sixth station of the Israelites (Ex. 15 : 23, 24; Num. 33 : 8) whose waters were so bitter that they could not drink them. On this account they murmured against Moses, who, under divine direction, cast into the fountain "a certain tree" which took away its bitterness, so that the people drank of it. This was probably the *'Ain Hawârah*, where there are still several springs of water that are very "bitter," distant some 47 miles from *'Ayûn Mousa*.

Mar′alah—*trembling*—a place on the southern boundary of Zebulun (Josh. 19 : 11). It has been identified with the modern *M'alûl*, about 4 miles south - west of Nazareth.

Maran′atha (1 Cor. 16 : 22) consists of two Aramean words, *Maran′ athah*, meaning, "our Lord comes," or is "coming." If the latter interpretation is adopted, the meaning of the phrase is, "Our Lord is coming, and he will judge those who have set him at nought." (Comp. Phil. 4 : 5; James 5 : 8, 9.)

Mar′ble, as a mineral, consists of carbonate of lime, its texture varying from the highly crystalline to the compact. In Esther 1 : 6 there are four Hebrew words which are rendered marble :—(1.) *Shêsh*, "pillars of marble." But this word probably designates dark-blue limestone rather than marble. (2.) *Dar* some regard as Parian marble. It is here rendered "white marble." But nothing is certainly known of it. (3.) *Bahaṭ*, "red marble," probably the *verd-antique* or half-porphyry of Egypt. (4.) *Sohâreth*, "black marble," probably some spotted variety of marble. "The marble pillars and tesseræ of various colours of the palace at Susa came doubtless from Persia itself, where marble of various colours is found, especially in the province of Hamadan Susiana." The marble of Solomon's architectural works may have been limestone from near Jerusalem, or from Lebanon, or possibly white marble from Arabia. Herod employed Parian marble in the temple, and marble columns still exist in great abundance at Jerusalem.

Marchesh′van, the post-biblical name of the month which was the eighth of the sacred and the second of the civil year of the Jews. It began with the new moon of our November. It is once called Bul (1 Kings 6 : 38). Assyrian, *Arah Samna*, "eighth month."

Mar′cus, Col. 4 : 10; Philemon 24; 1 Pet. 5 : 13; R.V., "Mark" (*q.v.*).

Mare′shah—*possession*—a city in the plain of Judah (Josh. 15 : 44). Here Asa defeated Zerah the Ethiopian (2 Chr. 14 : 9, 10). It is identified with the ruin *el-Mer′ash*, about 1½ mile south of Beit Jibrin.

Mark, the evangelist ; "John, whose surname was Mark " (Acts 12 : 12, 25). Mark (*Marcus*, Col. 4 : 10, etc.) was his Roman name, which gradually came to supersede his Jewish name John. He is called John in Acts 13 : 5, 13, and Mark in 15 : 39, 2 Tim. 4 : 11, etc.

He was the son of Mary, a woman apparently of some means and influence, and was probably born in Jerusalem, where his mother resided (Acts 12 : 12). Of his father we know nothing. He was cousin of Barnabas (Col. 4 : 10). It was in his mother's house that Peter found "many gathered together praying" when he was released from prison; and it is probable that it was here that he was converted by Peter, who calls him his "son" (1 Pet. 5 : 13). It is probable that the "young man" spoken of in Mark 14 : 51, 52 was Mark himself. He is first mentioned in Acts 12 : 25. He went with Paul and Barnabas on their first journey (about A.D. 47) as their "minister," but from some cause turned back when they reached Perga in Pamphylia (Acts 12 : 25; 13 : 13). Three years afterwards a "sharp contention" arose between Paul and Barnabas (15 : 36–40), because Paul would not take Mark with him. He, however, was evidently at length reconciled to the apostle, for he was with him in his first imprisonment at Rome (Col. 4 : 10; Philemon 24). At a later period he was with Peter in Babylon (1 Pet. 5 : 13), then, and for some centuries afterwards, one of the chief seats of Jewish learning ; and he was with Timothy in Ephesus when Paul wrote him during his second imprisonment (2 Tim. 4:11). He then disappears from view.

Mark, Gospel according to. It is the current and apparently well-founded tradition that Mark derived his information mainly from the discourses of Peter. In his mother's house he would have abundant opportunities of obtaining information from the other apostles and their coadjutors, yet he was "the disciple and interpreter of Peter" specially.

As to the *time* when it was written, the Gospel furnishes us with no definite information. Mark makes no mention of the destruction of Jerusalem, hence it must have been written before that event, and probably about A.D. 63.

The *place* where it was written was probably Rome. Some have supposed Antioch (comp. Mark 15:21 with Acts 11:20).

It was intended primarily for Romans. This appears probable when it is considered that it makes no reference to the Jewish law, and that the writer takes care to interpret words which a Gentile would be likely to misunderstand—such as, "Boanerges" (3:17); "Talitha cumi" (5:41); "Corban" (7:11); "Bartimæus" (10:46); "Abba" (14:36); "Eloi," etc. (15:34). Jewish usages are also explained (7:3; 13:3; 14:12; 15:42). Mark also uses certain Latin words not found in any of the other Gospels, as "speculator" (6:27, rendered, A.V., "executioner;" R.V. "soldier of the guard"), "xestes" (a corruption of *sextarius*, rendered "pots," 7:4, 8), "quadrans" (12:42, rendered "a farthing"), "centurion" (15:39, 44, 45). He only twice quotes from the Old Testament (1:2; 15:28).

The *characteristics* of this Gospel are—(1) the absence of the genealogy of our Lord, (2) whom he represents as clothed with power, the "lion of the tribe of Judah." (3.) Mark also records with wonderful minuteness the very words (3:17; 5:41; 7:11, 34; 14:36) as well as the position (9:35) and gestures (3:5, 34; 5:32; 9:36; 10:16) of our Lord. (4.) He is also careful to record particulars of person (1:29, 36; 3:6, 22, etc.), number (5:13; 6:7, etc.), place (2:13; 4:1; 7:31, etc.), and time (1:35; 2:1; 4:35, etc.), which the other evangelists omit. (5.) The phrase "and straightway" occurs nearly forty times in this Gospel; while in Luke's Gospel, which is much longer, it is used only seven times, and in John only four times.

"The Gospel of Mark," says Westcott, "is essentially a transcript from life. The course and issue of facts are imaged in it with the clearest outline." "In Mark we have no attempt to draw up a continuous narrative. His Gospel is a rapid succession of vivid pictures loosely strung together without much attempt to bind them into a whole or give the events in their natural sequence. This pictorial power is that which specially characterizes this evangelist, so that 'if any one desires to know an evangelical fact, not only in its main features and grand results, but also in its most minute and so to speak more graphic delineation, he must betake himself to Mark.'" The leading principle running through this Gospel may be expressed in the motto : "Jesus came......preaching the gospel of the kingdom" (Mark 1:14).

"Out of a total of 662 verses, Mark has 406 in common with Matthew and Luke, 145 with Matthew, 60 with Luke, and at most 51 peculiar to itself." (See MATTHEW.)

Mar′ket-place, any place of public resort, and hence a public place or broad street (Matt. 11:16; 20:3), as well as a forum or market-place proper, where goods were exposed for sale, and where public assemblies and trials were held (Acts 16:19; 17:17). This word occurs in the Old Testament only in Ezek. 27:3.

In early times markets were held at the gates of cities, where commodities were exposed for sale (2 Kings 7:18). In large towns the sale of particular articles seems to have been confined to certain streets, as we may infer from such expressions as "the bakers' street" (Jer. 37:21), and from the circumstance that in the time of Josephus the valley between Mounts Zion and Moriah was called the Tyropœon or the "valley of the cheesemakers."

Ma′roth — *bitternesses ; i.e.,* "perfect

grief "—a place not far from Jerusalem; mentioned in connection with the invasion of the Assyrian army (Micah 1:12).

Mar′riage was instituted in Paradise when man was in innocence (Gen. 2:18-24). Here we have its original charter, which was confirmed by our Lord, as the basis on which all regulations are to be framed (Matt. 19:4, 5). It is evident that monogamy was the original law of marriage (Matt. 19:5; 1 Cor. 6:16). This law was violated in after times, when corrupt usages began to be introduced (Gen. 4:19; 6:2). We meet with the prevalence of polygamy and concubinage in the patriarchal age (Gen. 16:1-4; 22:21-24; 28:8, 9; 29:23-30, etc.). Polygamy was acknowledged in the Mosaic law and made the basis of legislation, and continued to be practised all down through the period of Jewish history to the Captivity, after which there is no instance of it on record.

It seems to have been the practice from the beginning for fathers to select wives for their sons (Gen. 24:3; 38:6). Sometimes also proposals were initiated by the father of the maiden (Ex. 2:21). The brothers of the maiden were also sometimes consulted (Gen. 24:51; 34:11), but her own consent was not required. The young man was bound to give a price to the father of the maiden (31:15; 34:12; Ex. 22:15, 16; 1 Sam. 18:23, 25; Ruth 4:10; Hos. 3:2) On these patriarchal customs the Mosaic law made no change.

In the pre-Mosaic times, when the proposals were accepted and the marriage price given, the bridegroom could come at once and take away his bride to his own house (Gen. 24:63-67). But in general the marriage was celebrated by a feast in the house of the bride's parents, to which all friends were invited (29:22, 27); and on the day of the marriage the bride, concealed under a thick veil, was conducted to her future husband's home.

Our Lord corrected many false notions then existing on the subject of marriage (Matt. 22:23-30), and placed it as a divine institution on the highest grounds. The apostles state clearly and enforce the nuptial duties of husband and wife (Eph.

5:22-33; Col. 3:18, 19; 1 Pet. 3:1-7). Marriage is said to be "honourable" (Heb. 13:4), and the prohibition of it is noted as one of the marks of degenerate times (1 Tim. 4:20).

The marriage relation is used to represent the union between God and his people (Isa. 54:5; Jer. 3:1-14; Hos. 2:9, 20). In the New Testament the same figure is employed in representing the love of Christ to his saints (Eph. 5:25-27). The Church of the redeemed is the "Bride, the Lamb's wife" (Rev. 19:7-9).

Mar′riage-feasts (John 2:1-11) "lasted usually for a whole week; but the cost of such prolonged rejoicing is very small in the East. The guests sit round the great bowl or bowls on the floor, the meal usually consisting of a lamb or kid stewed in rice or barley. The most honoured guests sit nearest, others behind; and all in eating dip their hand into the one smoking mound, pieces of the thin bread, bent together, serving for spoons when necessary. After the first circle have satisfied themselves, those lower in honour sit down to the rest—the whole company being men, for women are never seen at a feast. Water is poured on the hands before eating; and this is repeated when the meal closes, the fingers having first been wiped on pieces of bread, which, after serving the same purpose as table-napkins with us, are thrown on the ground to be eaten by any dog that may have stolen in from the streets through the ever-open door, or picked up by those outside when gathered and tossed out to them (Matt. 15:27; Mark 7:28). Rising from the ground and retiring to the seats round the walls, the guests then sit down cross-legged and gossip, or listen to recitals, or puzzle over riddles, light being scantily supplied by a small lamp or two, or if the night be chilly, by a smouldering fire of weeds kindled in the middle of the room, perhaps in a brazier, often in a hole in the floor. As to the smoke, it escapes as it best may; but indeed there is little of it, though enough to blacken the water or wine or milk skins hung up on pegs on the wall. (Comp. Ps. 119:83.) To some

such marriage-feast Jesus and his five disciples were invited at Cana of Galilee."—
Geikie's *Life of Christ*. (See CANA.)

Mars' Hill, the Areopagus or rocky hill
in Athens, north-west of the Acropolis,
where the Athenian supreme tribunal and
court of morals was held. From some
part of this hill Paul delivered the address
recorded in Acts 17 : 22–31. (See AREO-
PAGUS.)

Mar'tha—*bitterness*—the sister of Lazarus and Mary, and probably the eldest
of the family, who all resided at Bethany
(Luke 10 : 38, 40, 41; John 11 : 1–39). From
the residence being called "her house,"
some have supposed that she was a widow,
and that her brother and sister lodged with
her. She seems to have been of an anxious,
bustling spirit, anxious to be helpful in
providing the best things for the Master's
use, in contrast to the quiet earnestness
of Mary, who was more concerned to avail
herself of the opportunity of sitting at his
feet and learning of him. Afterwards at
a supper given to Christ and his disciples
in her house "Martha served." Nothing
further is known of her.

"Mary and Martha are representatives
of two orders of human character. One
was absorbed, preoccupied, abstracted;
the other was concentrated and single-
hearted. Her own world was the all of
Martha; Christ was the first thought with
Mary. To Martha life was 'a succession
of particular businesses;' to Mary life 'was
rather the flow of one spirit.' Martha was
Petrine, Mary was Johannine. The one
was a well-meaning, bustling busybody;
the other was a reverent disciple, a wistful
listener." Paul had such a picture as that
of Martha in his mind when he spoke of
serving the Lord "without distraction"
(1 Cor. 7 : 35).

Mar'tyr, one who bears witness of the
truth, and suffers death in the cause of
Christ (Acts 22 : 20; Rev. 2 : 13; 17 : 6).
In this sense Stephen was the first martyr.
The Greek word so rendered in all other
cases is translated "witness." (1.) In a
court of justice (Matt. 18 : 16; 26 : 65;
Acts 6 : 13; 7 : 58; Heb. 10 : 28; 1 Tim. 5 :
19). (2.) As of one bearing testimony to

the truth of what he has seen or known
(Luke 24 : 48; Acts 1 : 8, 22; Rom. 1 : 9;
2 Cor. 1 : 22; 1 Thess. 2 : 5, 10).

Ma'ry—Hebrew *Miriam*. (1.) The wife
of Joseph, the mother of Jesus, called the
"Virgin Mary," though never so designated
in Scripture (Matt. 2 : 11; Acts 1 : 14).
Little is known of her personal history.
Her genealogy is given in Luke 3. She
was of the tribe of Judah and the lineage
of David (Ps. 132 : 11; Luke 1 : 32). She
was connected by marriage with Elisabeth,
who was of the lineage of Aaron (Luke
1 : 36).

While she resided at Nazareth with her
parents, before she became the wife of
Joseph, the angel Gabriel announced to
her that she was to be the mother of the
promised Messiah (Luke 1 : 35). After this
she went to visit her cousin Elisabeth, who
was living with her husband Zacharias
(probably at Juttah, Josh. 15 : 55; 21 : 16,
in the neighbourhood of Maon), at a considerable distance, about 100 miles, from
Nazareth. Immediately on entering the
house she was saluted by Elisabeth as the
mother of her Lord, and then forthwith
gave utterance to her hymn of thanksgiving (Luke 1 : 46–56; comp. 1 Sam. 2 :
1–10). After three months Mary returned
to Nazareth to her own home. Joseph
was supernaturally made aware (Matt. 1 :
18–25) of her condition, and took her to his
own home. Soon after this the decree of
Augustus (Luke 2 : 1) required that they
should proceed to Bethlehem (Micah 5 : 2),
some 80 or 90 miles from Nazareth; and
while they were there they found shelter
in the inn or *khan* provided for strangers
(Luke 2 : 6, 7). But as the inn was crowded,
Mary had to retire to a place among the
cattle, and there she brought forth her son,
who was called Jesus (Matt. 1 : 21), because
he was to save his people from their sins.
This was followed by the presentation in
the temple, the flight into Egypt, and their
return in the following year and residence
at Nazareth (Matt. 2). There for thirty
years Mary, the wife of Joseph the carpenter, resides, filling her own humble
sphere, and pondering over the strange
things that had happened to her. During

these years only one event in the history of Jesus is recorded—*viz.*, his going up to Jerusalem when twelve years of age, and his being found among the doctors in the temple (Luke 2:41–52). Probably also during this period Joseph died, for he is not again mentioned.

After the commencement of our Lord's public ministry little notice is taken of Mary. She was present at the marriage in Cana. A year and a half after this we find her at Capernaum (Matt. 12:46, 48, 49), where Christ uttered the memorable words, "Who is my mother? and who are my brethren? And he stretched forth his hand toward his disciples, and said, Behold my mother and my brethren!" The next time we find her is at the cross along with her sister Mary, and Mary Magdalene, and Salome, and other women (John 19:26). From that hour John took her to his own abode. She was with the little company in the upper room after the Ascension (Acts 1:14). From this time she wholly disappears from public notice. The time and manner of her death are unknown.

(2.) *Mary Magdalene*—*i.e.*, Mary of Magdala, a town on the western shore of the Lake of Tiberias. She is for the first time noticed in Luke 8:3 as one of the women who "ministered to Christ of their substance." Their motive was that of gratitude for deliverances he had wrought for them. Out of Mary were cast seven demons. Gratitude to her great Deliverer prompted her to become his follower. These women accompanied him also on his last journey to Jerusalem (Matt. 27:55; Mark 15:41; Luke 23:55). They stood near the cross. There Mary remained till all was over, and the body was taken down and laid in Joseph's tomb. Again, in the earliest dawn of the first day of the week she, with Salome and Mary the mother of James (Matt. 28:1; Mark 16:2), came to the sepulchre, bringing with them sweet spices, that they might anoint the body of Jesus. They found the sepulchre empty, but saw the "vision of angels" (Matt. 28:5). She hastens to tell Peter and John, who were probably living together at this time (John 20:1, 2), and again immediately returns to the sepulchre. There she lingers thoughtfully, weeping at the door of the tomb. The risen Lord appears to her, but at first she knows him not. His utterance of her name "Mary" recalls her to consciousness, and she utters the joyful, reverent cry, "Rabboni." She would fain cling to him, but he forbids her, saying, "Touch me not; for I am not yet ascended to my Father." This is the last record regarding Mary of Magdala, who now returned to Jerusalem. The idea that this Mary was "the woman who was a sinner," or that she was unchaste, is altogether groundless.

(3.) *Mary the sister of Lazarus* is brought to our notice in connection with the visits of our Lord to Bethany. She is contrasted with her sister Martha, who was "cumbered about many things" while Jesus was their guest, while Mary had chosen "the good part." Her character also appears in connection with the death of her brother (John 11:20, 31, 33). On the occasion of our Lord's last visit to Bethany, Mary brought "a pound of ointment of spikenard, very costly, and anointed the feet of Jesus" as he reclined at table in the house of one Simon, who had been a leper (Matt. 26:6; Mark 14:3; John 12:2, 3). This was an evidence of her overflowing love to the Lord. Nothing is known of her subsequent history. It would appear from this act of Mary's, and from the circumstance that they possessed a family vault (11:38), and that a large number of Jews from Jerusalem came to condole with them on the death of Lazarus (11:19), that this family at Bethany belonged to the wealthier class of the people. (See MARTHA.)

(4.) *Mary the wife of Cleopas* is mentioned (John 19:25) as standing at the cross in company with Mary of Magdala and Mary the mother of Jesus. By comparing Matt. 27:56 and Mark 15:40, we find that this Mary and "Mary the mother of James the little" are one and the same person, and that she was the sister of our Lord's mother. She was that "other Mary" who was present with Mary of Magdala at the burial of our Lord (Matt. 27:61; Mark 15:47); and she was one of those who went early in the morning of the first day of the week to anoint the body, and thus became the first witness of the resurrection (Matt. 28:1; Mark 16:1; Luke 24:1).

(5.) *Mary the mother of John Mark* was one of the earliest of our Lord's disciples. She was the sister of Barnabas (Col. 4:10), and joined with him in disposing of their land and giving the proceeds of the sale into the treasury of the Church (Acts 4:37; 12:12). Her house in Jerusalem was the common meeting-place for the disciples there.

(6.) A Christian at Rome who treated Paul with special kindness (Rom. 16:6).

Mas′chil — *instructing* — occurs in the title of thirteen Psalms (32, 42, 44, etc.). It denotes a song enforcing some lesson of wisdom or piety, a didactic song. In Ps. 47:7 it is rendered, Authorized Version, "with understanding;" Revised Version, marg., "in a skilful psalm."

Mash (= **Meshech,** 1 Chr. 1:17), one of the four sons of Aram, and the name of a tribe descended from him (Gen. 10:23) inhabiting some part probably of Mesopotamia. Some have supposed that they were the inhabitants of Mount Masius, the present *Karja Baghlar*, which forms part of the chain of Taurus.

Ma′shal — *entreaty* — a Levitical town in the tribe of Asher (1 Chr. 6:74); called Mishal (Josh. 21:30).

Ma′son, an artificer in stone. The Tyrians seem to have been specially skilled in architecture (1 Kings 5:17, 18; 2 Sam. 5:11). This art the Hebrews no doubt learned in Egypt (Ex. 1:11, 14), where ruins of temples and palaces fill the traveller with wonder at the present day.

Mas′rekah — *vineyard of noble vines* — a place in Idumea, the native place of Samlah, one of the Edomitish kings (Gen. 36:36; 1 Chr. 1:47).

Mas′sa — *a lifting up, gift* — one of the sons of Ishmael, the founder of an Arabian tribe (Gen. 25:14); a nomad tribe inhabiting the Arabian desert toward Babylonia.

Mas′sah — *trial, temptation* — a name given to the place where the Israelites, by their murmuring for want of water, provoked Jehovah to anger against them. It is also called Meribah (Ex. 17:7; Deut. 6:16; Ps. 95:8, 9; Heb. 3:8).

Mat′tan — *gift.* (1.) A priest of Baal, slain before his altar during the reformation under Jehoiada (2 Kings 11:18).

(2.) The son of Eleazar, and father of Jacob, who was the father of Joseph, the husband of the Virgin Mary (Matt. 1:15).

(3.) The father of Shephatiah (Jer. 38:1).

Mat′tanah — *a gift* — a station of the Israelites (Num. 21:18, 19) between the desert and the borders of Moab, in the Wâdy Wâleh.

Mattani′ah — *gift of Jehovah.* (1.) A Levite, son of Heman, the chief of the ninth class of temple singers (1 Chr. 25:4, 16).

(2.) A Levite who assisted in purifying the temple at the reformation under Hezekiah (2 Chr. 29:13).

(3.) The original name of Zedekiah (*q.v.*), the last of the kings of Judah (2 Kings 24:17). He was the third son of Josiah, who fell at Megiddo. He succeeded his nephew Jehoiakin.

Mattathi′as — *ibid.* (1.) The son of Amos, in the genealogy of our Lord (Luke 3:25).

(2.) The son of Semei, in the same genealogy (Luke 3:26).

Mat′than — *gift* — one of our Lord's ancestry (Matt. 1:15).

Mat′that — *gift of God.* (1.) The son of Levi, and father of Eli (Luke 3:29).

(2.) Son of another Levi (Luke 3:24).

Mat′thew — *gift of God* — a common Jewish name after the Exile. He was the son of Alphæus, and was a publican or taxgatherer at Capernaum. On one occasion Jesus, coming up from the side of the lake, passed the custom-house where Matthew was seated, and said to him, "Follow me." Matthew arose and followed him, and became his disciple (Matt. 9:9). Formerly the name by which he was known was Levi (Mark 2:14; Luke 5:27); he now changed it, possibly in grateful memory of his call, to Matthew. The same day on which Jesus called him he made a "great feast" (Luke 5:29), a farewell feast, to which he invited Jesus and his disciples, and probably also many of his old associates. He was afterwards selected as one of the twelve

(6:15). His name does not occur again in the Gospel history except in the lists of the apostles. The last notice of him is in Acts 1:13. The time and manner of his death are unknown.

Mat'thew, Gospel according to. The *author* of this book was beyond a doubt the Matthew, an apostle of our Lord, whose name it bears. He wrote the Gospel of Christ according to his own plans and aims, and from his own point of view, as did also the other "evangelists."

As to the *time* of its composition, there is little in the Gospel itself to indicate. It was evidently written before the destruction of Jerusalem (Matt. 24), and some time after the events it records. The probability is that it was written between the years A.D. 60 and 65.

The cast of thought and the forms of expression employed by the writer show that this Gospel was written for Jewish Christians of Palestine. His great object is to prove that Jesus of Nazareth was the promised Messiah, and that in him the ancient prophecies had their fulfilment. The Gospel is full of allusions to those passages of the Old Testament in which Christ is predicted and foreshadowed. The one aim pervading the whole book is to show that Jesus is he "of whom Moses in the law and the prophets did write." This Gospel contains no fewer than sixty-five references to the Old Testament, forty-three of these being direct verbal citations, thus greatly outnumbering those found in the other Gospels. The main feature of this Gospel may be expressed in the motto, "I am not come to destroy, but to fulfil."

As to the *language* in which this Gospel was written there is much controversy. Many hold, in accordance with old tradition, that it was originally written in Hebrew (*i.e.*, the Aramaic or Syro-Chaldee dialect, then the vernacular of the inhabitants of Palestine), and afterwards translated into Greek, either by Matthew himself or by some person unknown. This theory, though earnestly maintained by able critics, we cannot see any ground for adopting. From the first this Gospel in Greek was received as of authority in the Church. There is nothing in it to show that it is a translation. Though Matthew wrote mainly for the Jews, yet they were everywhere familiar with the Greek language. The same reasons which would have suggested the necessity of a translation into Greek would have led the evangelist to write in Greek at first. It is confessed that this Gospel has never been found in any other form than that in which we now possess it.

The leading *characteristic* of this Gospel is that it sets forth the kingly glory of Christ, and shows him to be the true heir to David's throne. It is the Gospel of the kingdom. Matthew uses the expression "kingdom of heaven" (thirty-two times), while Luke uses the expression "kingdom of God" (thirty-three times). Some Latinized forms occur in this Gospel, as *kodrantes* (Matt. 5:26), for the Latin *quadrans*, and *phragello* (27:26), for the Latin *flagello*. It must be remembered that Matthew was a tax-gatherer for the Roman government, and hence in contact with those using the Latin language.

As to the *relation* of the Gospels to each other, we must maintain that each writer of the synoptics (the first three) wrote independently of the other two, Matthew being probably first in point of time.

"Out of a total of 1071 verses, Matthew has 387 in common with Mark and Luke, 130 with Mark, 184 with Luke; only 387 being peculiar to itself." (See MARK; LUKE; GOSPELS.)

The book is fitly divided into these four parts:—

(1.) Containing the genealogy, the birth, and the infancy of Jesus (1; 2).

(2.) The discourses and actions of John the Baptist preparatory to Christ's public ministry (3; 4:11).

(3.) The discourses and actions of Christ in Galilee (4:12–20:16).

(4.) The sufferings, death, and resurrection of our Lord (20:17-28).

Matthi'as—*gift of God.* Acts 1:23.

Mattithi'ah—*gift of Jehovah.* (1.) One of the sons of Jeduthun (1 Chr. 25:3, 21).

(2.) The eldest son of Shallum, of the family of Korah (1 Chr. 9:31).

(3.) One who stood by Ezra while reading the law (Neh. 8 : 4).

(4.) The son of Amos, and father of Joseph, in the genealogy of our Lord (Luke 3 : 25).

Mat'tock. (1.) Heb. *ma'ĕdêr*, an instrument for dressing or pruning a vineyard (Isa. 7 : 25); a weeding-hoe.

(2.) Heb. *maḥarêshâh* (1 Sam. 13 : 1), perhaps the ploughshare or coulter.

(3.) Heb. *ḥerebh*, marg. of text (2 Chr. 34 : 6). Authorized Version, "with their mattocks," marg. "mauls." The Revised Version renders "in their ruins," marg. "with their axes." The Hebrew text is probably corrupt.

Maul, an old name for a mallet, the rendering of the Hebrew *mephîts* (Prov. 25 : 18), properly a war-club.

Maz'zaroth — *prognostications* — found only Job 38 : 32, probably meaning "the twelve signs" (of the zodiac), as in the margin (comp. 2 Kings 23 : 5).

Mead'ow. (1.) Heb. *ha-'âḥu* (Gen. 41 : 2, 18), probably an Egyptian word transferred to the Hebrew; some kind of reed or water-plant. In the Revised Version it is rendered "reed-grass"—*i.e.*, the sedge or rank grass by the river side.

(2.) Heb. *ma'arêh* (Judg. 20 : 33), pl., "meadows of Gibeah" (R.V., after the LXX., "Maareh-geba"). Some have adopted the rendering "after Gibeah had been left open." The Vulgate translates the word "from the west."

Me'ah—*an hundred*—a tower in Jerusalem on the east wall (Neh. 3 : 1) in the time of Nehemiah.

Meals are at the present day "eaten from a round table little higher than a stool, guests sitting cross-legged on mats or small carpets in a circle, and dipping their fingers into one large dish heaped with a mixture of boiled rice and other grain and meat. But in the time of our Lord, and perhaps even from the days of Amos (6 : 4, 7), the foreign custom had been largely introduced of having broad couches, forming three sides of a small square, the guests reclining at ease on their elbows during meals, with their faces to the space within, up and down which servants passed offering various dishes, or in the absence of servants, helping themselves from dishes laid on a table set be-

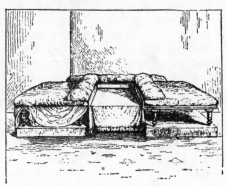

THE ROMAN TRICLINIUM.

tween the couches."—Geikie's *Life of Christ*. (Comp. Luke 7 : 36-50.) (See ABRAHAM'S BOSOM; BANQUET; FEAST.)

Mea'rah—*a cave*—a place in the northern boundary of Palestine (Josh. 13 : 4). This may be the cave of *Jezzîn* in Lebanon, 10 miles east of Sidon, on the Damascus road; or probably, as others think, *Mogheirîzch*, north-east of Sidon.

Meas'ure. Several words are so rendered in the Authorized Version.

(1.) Those which are indefinite. (*a*) *Hôk*, Isa. 5 : 14, elsewhere "statute." (*b*) *Mad*, Job 11 : 3; Jer. 13 : 25, elsewhere "garment." (*c*) *Middâh*, the word most frequently thus translated, Ex. 26 : 2, 8, etc. (*d*) *Mesurâh*, Lev. 19 : 35; 1 Chr. 23 : 39. (*e*) *Mishpat*, Jer. 30 : 2, elsewhere "judgment." (*f*) *Mithkôneth* and *tôken*, Ezek. 45 : 11. (*g*) In New Testament *metron*, the usual Greek word thus rendered (Matt. 7 : 2; 23 : 32; Mark 4 : 24).

(2.) Those which are definite. (*a*) '*Eyphâh*, Deut. 25 : 14, 15, usually "ephah." (*b*) *Ammâh*, Jer. 51 : 13, usually "cubit." (*c*) *Kor*, 1 Kings 4 : 22, elsewhere "cor;" Greek *koros*, Luke 16 : 7. (*d*) *Seâh*, Gen. 18 : 6; 1 Sam. 25 : 18, a seah; Greek *saton*, Matt. 13 : 33; Luke 13 : 21. (*e*) *Shalîsh*, "a great measure," Isa. 11 : 12; literally a *third*— *i.e.*, of an ephah. (*f*) In New Testament *batos*, Luke 16 : 6, the Hebrew "bath;" and *choinix*, Rev. 6 : 6, the *choenix*, equal in dry commodities to one-eighth of a modius.

Meat-offering (Heb. *minḥâh*), originally a gift of any kind. This Hebrew word came latterly to denote an "unbloody" sacrifice, as opposed to a "bloody" sacrifice. A "drink-offering" generally accompanied it. The law regarding it is given in Lev. 2, and 6:14–23. It was a recognition of the sovereignty of God and of his bounty in giving all earthly blessings (1 Chr. 29:10–14; Deut. 26:5–11). It was an offering which took for granted and was based on the offering for sin. It followed the sacrifice of blood. It was presented every day with the burnt-offering (Ex. 29:40, 41), and consisted of flour or of cakes prepared in a special way with oil and frankincense.

Mebun'nai—*construction, building of Jehovah*—one of David's bodyguard (2 Sam. 23:27; comp. 21:18); called Sibbechai and Sibbecai (1 Chr. 11:29; 27:11).

Me'dad—*love*—one of the elders nominated to assist Moses in the government of the people. He and Eldad "prophesied in the camp" (Num. 11:24–29).

Me'dan—*contention*—the third son of Abraham by Keturah (Gen. 25:2).

Mede (Heb. *Madai*), a Median or inhabitant of Media (Dan. 11:1). In Gen. 10:2 the Hebrew word occurs in the list of the sons of Japheth. But probably this is an ethnic and not a personal name, and denotes simply the Medes as descended from Japheth.

Med'eba—*waters of quiet*—an ancient Moabite town (Num. 21:30). It was assigned to the tribe of Reuben (Josh. 13:16). Here was fought the great battle in which Joab defeated the Ammonites and their allies (1 Chr. 19:7–15; comp. 2 Sam. 10:6–14). In the time of Isaiah (15:2) the Moabites regained possession of it from the Ammonites. (See HANUN.)

The ruins of this important city, now *Mâdeba* or *Madiyabah*, are seen about 8 miles south-west of Heshbon, and 14 east of the Dead Sea. Among these are the ruins of what must have been a large temple, and of three cisterns of considerable extent, which are now dry. These cisterns may have originated the name Medeba, "waters of quiet." (See OMRI.)

Me'dia—Heb. *Madai*—which is rendered in the Authorized Version (1) "Madai," Gen. 10:2; (2) "Medes," 2 Kings 17:6; 18:11; (3) "Media," Esther 1:3; 10:2; Isa. 21:2; Dan. 8:20; (4) "Mede," only in Dan. 11:1.

We first hear of this people in the Assyrian cuneiform records, under the name of Amadâ, about B.C. 840. They appear to have been a branch of the Aryans, who came from the east bank of the Indus, and were probably the predominant race for a while in the Mesopotamian valley. They consisted for three or four centuries of a number of tribes, each ruled by its own chief, who at length were brought under the Assyrian yoke (2 Kings 17:6). From this subjection they achieved deliverance, and formed themselves into an empire under Cyaxares (B.C. 633). This monarch entered into an alliance with the king of Babylon, and invaded Assyria, capturing and destroying the city of Nineveh (B.C. 625), thus putting an end to the Assyrian monarchy (Nah. 1:8; 2:5,6; 3:13,14).

Media now rose to a place of great power, vastly extending its boundaries. But it did not long exist as an independent kingdom. It rose with Cyaxares, its first king, and it passed away with him; for during the reign of his son and successor Astyages, the Persians waged war against the Medes and conquered them, the two nations being united under one monarch, Cyrus the Persian (B.C. 558).

The "cities of the Medes" are first mentioned in connection with the deportation of the Israelites on the destruction of Samaria (2 Kings 17:6; 18:11). Soon afterwards Isaiah (13:17; 21:2) speaks of the part taken by the Medes in the destruction of Babylon (comp. Jer. 51:11, 28). Daniel gives an account of the reign of Darius the Mede, who was made viceroy by Cyrus (Dan. 6:1–28). The decree of Cyrus, Ezra informs us (6:2–5), was found in "the palace that is in the province of the Medes," Achmetha or Ecbatana of the Greeks, which is the only Median city mentioned in Scripture.

Media'tor, one who intervenes between two persons who are at variance, with a view to reconcile them. This word is not found in the Old Testament; but the idea it expresses is found in Job 9:33, in the word "daysman" (*q.v.*)—marg., "umpire."

This word is used in the New Testament to denote simply an *internuncius*, an ambassador, one who acts as a medium of communication between two contracting parties. In this sense Moses is called a mediator in Gal. 3:19.

Christ is the one and only mediator between God and man (1 Tim. 2:5; Heb. 8:6; 9:15; 12:24). He makes reconciliation between God and man by his all-perfect atoning sacrifice. Such a mediator must be at once divine and human—divine, that his obedience and his sufferings might possess infinite worth, and that he might possess infinite wisdom and knowledge and power to direct all things in the kingdoms of providence and grace which are committed to his hands (Matt. 28:18; John 5:22, 25, 26, 27); and human, that in his work he might represent man, and be capable of rendering obedience to the law and satisfying the claims of justice (Heb. 2:17, 18; 4:15, 16), and that in his glorified humanity he might be the head of a glorified Church (Rom. 8:29).

This office involves the three functions of prophet, priest, and king, all of which are discharged by Christ both in his estate of humiliation and exaltation. These functions are so inherent in the one office that the quality appertaining to each gives character to every mediatorial act. They are never separated in the exercise of the office of mediator.

Meek'ness, a calm temper of mind, not easily provoked (James 3:7, 8). Peculiar promises are made to the meek (Matt. 5:5; Isa. 66:2). The cultivation of this spirit is enjoined (Col. 3:12; 1 Tim. 6:11; Zeph. 2:3) and exemplified in Christ (Matt. 11:28), Abraham (Gen. 13; 16:5, 8), Moses (Num. 12:3), David (Zech. 12:8; 2 Sam. 16:10, 12), and Paul (1 Cor. 9:19).

Megid'do—*place of troops*—originally one of the royal cities of the Canaanites (Josh. 12:21), belonged to the tribe of Manasseh (Judg. 1:27), but does not seem to have been fully occupied by the Israelites till the time of Solomon (1 Kings 4:12; 9:15).

The valley or plain of Megiddo was part of the plain of Esdraelon, the great battle-field of Palestine. It was here Barak gained a notable victory over Jabin, the king of Hazor, whose general, Sisera, led on the hostile army. Barak rallied the warriors of the northern tribes, and under the encouragement of Deborah (*q.v.*), the prophetess, attacked the Canaanites in the great plain. The army of Sisera was thrown into complete confusion, and was engulfed in the waters of the Kishon, which had risen and overflowed its banks (Judg. 4:5).

Many years after this (B.C. 610), Pharaoh-necho II., on his march against the king of Assyria, passed through the plains of Philistia and Sharon; and King Josiah, attempting to bar his progress in the plain of Megiddo, was defeated by the Egyptians. He was wounded in battle, and died as they bore him away in his chariot towards Jerusalem (2 Kings 23:29; 2 Chr. 35:22-24), and all Israel mourned for him. So general and bitter was this mourning that it became a proverb, to which Zechariah (12:11, 12) alludes. Megiddo has been identified with the modern *el-Lejjûn*, at the head of the Kishon, under the north-eastern brow of Carmel, on the south-western edge of the plain of Esdraelon, and 9 miles west of Jezreel. Others identify it with *Mujedd'a*, 4 miles south-west of Bethshean, but the question of its site is still undetermined.

Mehet'abeel—*whose benefactor is God*—the father of Delaiah, and grandfather of Shemaiah, who joined Sanballat against Nehemiah (Neh. 6:10).

Mehet'abel, wife of Hadad, one of the kings of Edom (Gen. 36:39).

Mehu'jael—*smitten by God*—the son of Irad, and father of Methusael (Gen. 4:18).

Mehu'man—*faithful*—one of the eunuchs whom Ahasuerus (Xerxes) commanded to bring in Vashti (Esther 1:10).

Mehu'nims—*habitations*—(2 Chr. 26:7; R.V. "Meunim," Vulg. *Ammonitæ*), a people against whom Uzziah waged a successful war. This word is in Hebrew the plural of *Mâ'ôn*, and thus denotes the Maonites who inhabited the country on the eastern side of the Wady el-Arabah. They are again mentioned in 1 Chr. 4:41 (R.V.), in the reign of King Hezekiah, as a Hamite people, settled in the eastern end of the valley of Gedor, in the wilderness south of Palestine. In this passage the Authorized Version has "habitation," erroneously following the translation of Luther.

They are mentioned in the list of those from whom the Nethinim were made up (Ezra 2:50; Neh. 7:52).

Me-jar'kon—*waters of yellowness*, or *clear waters*—a river in the tribe of Dan (Josh. 19:46). It has been identified with the river '*Aûjeh*, which rises at Antipatris.

Mek'onah—*a base* or *foundation*—a town in the south of Judah (Neh. 11:28), near Ziklag.

Mel'chi—*my king*. (1.) The son of Addi, and father of Neri (Luke 3:28). (2.) Luke 3:24, 28.

Melchiz'edek—*king of righteousness*—the king of Salem (*q.v.*). All we know of him is recorded in Gen. 14:18–20. He is subsequently mentioned only once in the Old Testament, in Ps. 110:4. The typical significance of his history is set forth in detail in the Epistle to the Hebrews, ch. 7. The apostle there points out the superiority of his priesthood to that of Aaron in these several respects—(1) Even Abraham paid him tithes; (2) he blessed Abraham; (3) he is the type of a Priest who lives for ever; (4) Levi, yet unborn, paid him tithes in the person of Abraham; (5) the permanence of his priesthood in Christ implied the abrogation of the Levitical system; (6) he was made priest not without an oath; and (7) his priesthood can

MAP OF MALTA.

neither be transmitted nor interrupted by death: "this man, because he continueth ever, hath an unchangeable priesthood."

The question as to who this mysterious personage was has given rise to a great deal of modern speculation. It is an old tradition among the Jews that he was Shem, the son of Noah, who may have survived to this time. Melchizedek was a Canaanitish prince, a worshipper of the true God, and in his peculiar history and character an instructive type of our Lord, the great High Priest (Heb. 5:6, 7; 6:20). One of the Amarna tablets is from Ebed-Tob, king of Jerusalem, the successor of Melchizedek, in which he claims the very attributes and dignity given to Melchizedek in the Epistle to the Hebrews.

Me'lea—*fulness*—the son of Menan and father of Eliakim, in the genealogy of our Lord (Luke 3:31).

Me'lech—*king*—the second of Micah's four sons (1 Chr. 8:35), and thus grandson of Mephibosheth.

Meli'ta (Acts 27:28), an island in the Mediterranean, the modern Malta. Here the ship in which Paul was being conveyed a prisoner to Rome was wrecked. The bay in which it was wrecked now bears the name of "St. Paul's Bay"—"a certain creek with a shore." It is about 2 miles deep and 1 broad, and the whole physical condition of the scene answers the description of the shipwreck given in Acts 28. It was originally colonized by Phœnicians ("barbarians," 28:2). It came into the possession of the Greeks (B.C. 736), from whom it was taken by the Carthaginians (B.C. 528). In B.C. 242 it was conquered by the Romans, and was governed by a Roman propraetor at the time of the shipwreck (Acts 28 : 7). Since 1800, when the French garrison surrendered to the English force, it has been a British dependency. The island is about 17 miles long and 9 wide, and about 60 in circumference. After a stay of three months on this island, during which the "barbarians" showed them no little kindness, Julius procured for himself and his company a passage in another Alexandrian corn-ship which had wintered in the island, in which they proceeded on their voyage to Rome (Acts 28 : 13, 14).

Mel′ons, only in Num. 11 : 5, the translation of the Hebrew *abaṭṭihîm*, the LXX. and Vulgate *pepones*, Arabic *britikh*. Of this plant there are various kinds—the Egyptian melon, the *Cucumus chate*, which has been called "the queen of cucumbers;" the water melon, the *Cucurbita citrullus;* and the common or flesh melon, the *Cucumus melo*. "A traveller in the East who

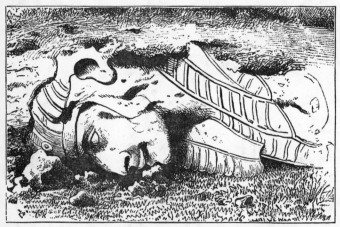

PROSTRATE STATUE OF RAMESES THE GREAT AT MEMPHIS.

recollects the intense gratitude which a gift of a slice of melon inspired while journeying over the hot and dry plains, will readily comprehend the regret with which the Hebrews in the Arabian desert looked back upon the melons of Egypt " (Kitto).

Mel′zar, probably a Persian word mean-

ing *master of wine—i.e.,* chief butler; the title of an officer at the Babylonian court (Dan. 1 : 11, 16) who had charge of the diet of the Hebrew youths.

Mem′phis, only in Hos. 9 : 6—Hebrew *Môph*. In Isa. 19 : 13; Jer. 2 : 16; 46 : 14, 19; Ezek. 30 : 13, 16, it is mentioned under the name Noph. It was the capital of Lower, *i.e.,* of Northern Egypt. From certain remains found half buried in the sand, the site of this ancient city has been discovered near the modern village of *Minyet Rahineh,* or *Mitraheny,* about 16 miles above the ancient head of the Delta, and 9 miles south of Cairo, on the west bank of the Nile. It is said to have been founded by Menes, the first king of Egypt, and to have been in circumference about 19 miles. "There are few remains above ground," says Manning (*The Land of the Pharaohs*), "of the splendour of ancient Memphis. The city has utterly disappeared. If any traces yet exist, they are buried beneath the vast mounds of crumbling bricks and broken pottery which meet the eye in every direction. Near the village of Mitraheny is a colossal statue of Rameses the Great. It is apparently one of the two described by Herodotus and Diodorus as standing in front of the temple of Ptah. They were originally 50 feet in height. The one which remains, though mutilated, measures 48 feet. It is finely carved in limestone, which takes a high polish, and is evidently a portrait. It lies in a pit, which, during the inundation, is filled with water. As we gaze on this fallen and battered statue of the mighty conqueror who was probably contemporaneous with Moses, it is impossible not to remember the words of the prophet Isaiah, 19 : 13; 44 : 16-19, and Jeremiah, 46 : 19."

Memu′can—*dignified*—one of the royal counsellors at the court of Ahasuerus, by whose suggestion Vashti was divorced (Esther 1 : 14, 16, 21).

Men'ahem—*comforting*—the son of Gadi, and successor of Shallum, king of Israel, whom he slew. After a reign of about ten years (B.C. 771–760) he died, leaving the throne to his son Pekahiah. His reign was one of cruelty and oppression (2 Kings 15 : 14–22). During his reign, Pul (*q.v.*), king of Assyria, came with a powerful force against Israel, but was induced to retire by a gift from Menahem of 1,000 talents of silver.

Me'ne (Dan. 5 : 25, 26)—*numbered*—one of the words of the mysterious inscription written "upon the plaister of the wall" in Belshazzar's palace at Babylon. The writing was explained by Daniel. (See BELSHAZZAR.)

Me'ni, Isa. 65 : 11, marg. (A.V., "that number;" R.V., "destiny"), probably an idol which the captive Israelites worshipped after the example of the Babylonians. It may have been a symbol of destiny. LXX., *tuché*.

Meo'nenim (Judg. 9 : 37; A.V., "the plain of Meonenim;" R.V., "the oak of Meonenim") means properly "soothsayers" or "sorcerers," "wizards" (Deut. 18 : 10, 14; 2 Kings 21 : 6; Micah 5 : 12). This may be the oak at Shechem under which Abram pitched his tent (see SHECHEM), the "enchanter's oak," so called, perhaps, from Jacob's hiding the "strange gods" under it (Gen. 35 : 4).

Mepha'ath—*splendour*—a Levitical city (Josh. 21 : 37) of the tribe of Reuben (13 : 18).

Mephib'osheth—*exterminator of shame; i.e., of idols.* (1.) The name of Saul's son by the concubine Rizpah (*q.v.*), the daughter of Aiah. He and his brother Armoni were with five others "hanged on a hill before the Lord" by the Gibeonites, and their bodies exposed in the sun for five months (2 Sam. 21 : 8–10). (2.) The son of Jonathan, and grandson of Saul (2 Sam. 4 : 4). He was but five years old when his father and grandfather fell on Mount Gilboa. The child's nurse hearing of this calamity, fled with him from Gibeah, the royal residence, and stumbling in her haste, the child was thrown to the ground and maimed in both his feet, and ever after was unable to walk (19 : 26). He was carried to the land of Gilead, where he found a refuge in the house of Machir, the son of Ammiel, at Lo-debar, by whom he was brought up.

Some years after this, when David had subdued all the adversaries of Israel, he began to think of the family of Jonathan, and discovered that Mephibosheth was residing in the house of Machir. Thither he sent royal messengers, and brought him and his infant son to Jerusalem, where he ever afterwards resided (2 Sam. 9).

When David was a fugitive, according to the story of Ziba (2 Sam. 16 : 1–4) Mephibosheth proved unfaithful to him, and was consequently deprived of half of his estates; but according to his own story, however (19 : 24–30), he had remained loyal to his friend. After this incident he is only mentioned as having been protected by David against the vengeance the Gibeonites were permitted to execute on the house of Saul (21 : 7). He is also called Merib-baal (1 Chr. 8 : 34; 9 : 40). (See ZIBA.)

Me'rab—*increase*—the eldest of Saul's two daughters (1 Sam. 14 : 49). She was betrothed to David after his victory over Goliath, but does not seem to have entered heartily into this arrangement (18 : 2, 17, 19). She was at length, however, married to Adriel of Abel-Meholah, a town in the Jordan valley, about 10 miles south of Bethshean, with whom the house of Saul maintained alliance. She had five sons, who were all put to death by the Gibeonites on the hill of Gibeah (2 Sam. 21 : 8).

Merai'ah—*resistance*—a chief priest, a contemporary of the high priest Joiakim (Neh. 12 : 12).

Merai'oth—*rebellions.* (1.) Father of Amariah, a high priest of the line of Eleazar (1 Chr. 6 : 6, 7, 52).

(2.) Neh. 12 : 15, a priest who went to Jerusalem with Zerubbabel. He is called Meremoth in Neh. 12 : 3.

Mera'ri—*sad; bitter*—the youngest son of Levi, born before the descent of Jacob into Egypt, and one of the seventy who accompanied him thither (Gen. 46 : 11; Ex. 6 : 16). He became the head of one of the great divisions of the Levites (Ex. 6:19). (See MERARITES.)

Mera'rites, the descendants of Merari (Num. 26:57). They with the Gershonites and the Kohathites had charge of the tabernacle, which they had to carry from place to place (Num. 3:20, 33–37; 4:29–38). In the distribution of the oxen and waggons offered by the princes (Num. 7), Moses gave twice as many to the Merarites (four waggons and eight oxen) as he gave to the Gershonites, because the latter had to carry only the lighter furniture of the tabernacle, such as the curtains, hangings, etc., while the former had to carry the heavier portion, as the boards, bars, sockets, pillars, etc., and consequently needed a greater supply of oxen and waggons. This is a coincidence illustrative of the truth of the narrative. Their place in marching and in the camp was on the north of the tabernacle. The Merarites afterwards took part with the other Levitical families in the various functions of their office (1 Chr. 23: 6, 21–23; 2 Chr. 29:12, 13). Twelve cities with their suburbs were assigned to them (Josh. 21:7, 34–40).

Meratha'im—*double rebellion*—probably a symbolical name given to Babylon (Jer. 50:21), denoting rebellion exceeding that of other nations.

Mer'chant. The Hebrew word so rendered is from a root meaning "to travel about," "to migrate," and hence "a traveller." In the East, in ancient times, merchants travelled about with their merchandise from place to place (Gen. 37:25; Job 6: 18), and carried on their trade mainly by bartering (Gen. 37:28; 39:1). After the Hebrews became settled in Palestine they began to engage in commercial pursuits, which gradually expanded (49:13; Deut. 33: 18; Judg. 5:17), till in the time of Solomon they are found in the chief marts of the world (1 Kings 9:26; 10:11, 26, 28; 22: 48; 2 Chr. 1:16; 9:10, 21). After Solomon's time their trade with foreign nations began to decline. After the Exile it again expanded into wider foreign relations, because now the Jews were scattered in many lands.

Mercu'rius, the *Hermes* (*i.e.,* "the

speaker") of the Greeks (Acts 14:12), a heathen God represented as the constant attendant of Jupiter, and the god of eloquence. The inhabitants of Lystra took Paul for this god because he was the "chief speaker."

Mer'cy, compassion for the miserable. Its object is misery. By the atoning sacrifice of Christ a way is open for the exercise of mercy towards the sons of men, in harmony with the demands of truth and righteousness (Gen. 19:19; Ex. 20:6; 34:6, 7; Ps. 85:10; 86:15, 16). In Christ mercy and truth meet together. Mercy is also a Christian grace (Matt. 5:7; 18:33–35).

Mer'cy-seat (Heb. *kappôreth,* a "covering;" LXX. and N.T., *hilasterion;* Vulg., *propitiatorium*), the covering or lid of the ark of the covenant (*q.v.*). It was of acacia wood, overlaid with gold, or perhaps rather a plate of solid gold, 2½ cubits long and 1½ broad (Ex. 25:17; 30:6; 31:7). It is compared to the throne of grace (Heb. 9: 5; Rom. 3:25). The holy of holies is called the "place of the mercy-seat" (1 Chr. 28: 11: Lev. 16:2).

It has been conjectured that the censer (*thumiatērion,* meaning "anything having regard to or employed in the burning of incense") mentioned in Heb. 9:4 was the "mercy-seat," at which the incense was burned by the high priest on the great day of atonement, and upon or toward which the blood of the goat was sprinkled (Lev. 16:11–16; comp. Num. 7:89 and Ex. 25: 22).

Me'red—*rebellion*—one of the sons of Ezra, of the tribe of Judah (1 Chr. 4:17).

Mer'emoth—*exaltations, heights*—a priest who returned from Babylon with Zerubbabel (Neh. 12:3), to whom were sent the sacred vessels (Ezra 8:33) belonging to the temple. He took part in rebuilding the walls of Jerusalem (Neh. 3:4).

Mer'ibah—*quarrel* or *strife.* (1.) One of the names given by Moses to the fountain in the desert of Sin, near Rephidim, which issued from the rock in Horeb, which he smote by the divine command, "because of the chiding of the children of Israel" (Ex. 17:1–7). It was also called

Massah (q.v.). It was probably in Wâdy Feirân, near Mount Serbal.

(2.) Another fountain having a similar origin in the desert of Zin, near to Kadesh (Num. 27:14). The two places are mentioned together in Deut. 33:8. Only once is it called simply by this name (Ps. 81:7). In smiting the rock at this place Moses showed the same impatience as the people (Num. 20:10-12). This took place near the close of the wanderings in the desert (Num. 20:1-24; Deut. 32:51).

Me'rib-ba'al—*contender with Baal*—(1 Chr. 8:34; 9:40), elsewhere called Mephibosheth (2 Sam. 4:4), the son of Jonathan.

Mero'dach—*death; slaughter*—the name of a Babylonian god, probably the planet Mars (Jer. 50:2), or it may be another name of Bel, the guardian divinity of Babylon. This name frequently occurs as a surname to the kings of Assyria and Babylon.

Mero'dach-bal'adan—*Merodach has given a son*—(Isa. 39:1), "the hereditary chief of the Chaldeans, a small tribe at that time settled in the marshes at the mouth of the Euphrates, but in consequence of his conquest of Babylon afterwards, they became the dominant caste in Babylonia itself." One bearing this name sent ambassadors to Hezekiah (B.C. 721). He is also called Berodach-baladan (2 Kings 20:12; 2 Chr. 20:31). (See HEZEKIAH.)

Me'rom—*height*—a lake in Northern Palestine through which the Jordan flows. It was the scene of the third and last great victory gained by Joshua over the Canaanites (Josh. 11:5-7). It is not again mentioned in Scripture. Its modern name is *Bakrat el-Hûleh*. "The Ard el-Hûleh, the centre of which the lake occupies, is a nearly level plain of 16 miles in length from north to south, and its breadth from east to west is from 7 to 8 miles. On the west it is walled in by the steep and lofty range of the hills of Kedesh-Naphtali; on the east it is bounded by the lower and more gradually ascending slopes of Bashan; on the north it is shut in by a line of hills hummocky and irregular in shape and of no great height, and stretching across from the mountains of Naphtali to the roots of Mount Hermon, which towers up at the north-eastern angle of the plain to a height of 10,000 feet. At its southern extremity the plain is similarly traversed by elevated and broken ground, through which, by deep and narrow clefts, the Jordan, after passing through Lake Hûleh, makes its rapid descent to the Sea of Galilee."

The lake is triangular in form, about 4½ miles in length by 3½ at its greatest breadth. Its surface is 7 feet above that of the Mediterranean. It is surrounded by a morass, which is thickly covered with canes and papyrus reeds, which are impenetrable. Macgregor with his canoe, the *Rob Roy*, was the first that ever, in modern times, sailed on its waters. (See JORDAN.)

Meron'othite, a name given to Jehdeiah, the herdsman of the royal asses in the time of David and Solomon (1 Chr. 27:30), probably as one being a native of some unknown town called Meronoth.

Me'roz, a plain in the north of Palestine, the inhabitants of which were severely condemned because they came not to help Barak against Sisera (Judg. 5:23; comp. 21:8-10; 1 Sam. 11:7). It has been identified with *Marassus*, on a knoll to the north of Wâdy Jâlûd, but nothing certainly is known of it. Like Chorazin, it is only mentioned in Scripture in connection with the curse pronounced upon it.

Me'sha—*middle district*—Vulgate, Messa. (1.) A plain in that part of the boundaries of Arabia inhabited by the descendants of Joktan (Gen. 10:30).

(2.) Heb. *meysh'a*, "deliverance," the eldest son of Caleb (1 Chr. 2:42), and brother of Jerahmeel.

(3.) Heb. *id*, a king of Moab, the son of Chemosh-Gad, a man of great wealth in flocks and herds (2 Kings 3:4). After the death of Ahab at Ramoth-Gilead, Mesha shook off the yoke of Israel; but on the ascension of Jehoram to the throne of Israel, that king sought the help of Jehoshaphat in an attempt to reduce the Moabites again to their former condition. The united armies of the two kings came unexpectedly on the army of the Moabites, and gained over them an easy victory. The whole land was devastated by the conquering armies, and Mesha sought refuge in his last stronghold, Kir-harasheth (*q.v.*). Reduced to despair, he ascended the wall of the city, and there, in the sight of the allied armies, offered his first-born son a sacrifice to Chemosh, the fire-god of the Moabites. This fearful spectacle filled the beholders with horror, and they retired from before the besieged city, and recrossed the Jordan laden with spoil (2 Kings 3: 25–27).

The exploits of Mesha are recorded in the Phœnician inscription on a block of black basalt found at Dibon, in Moab, usually called the "Moabite stone" (*q.v.*).

Me′shach, the title given to Mishael, one of the three Hebrew youths who were under training at the Babylonian court for the rank of Magi (Dan. 1 : 7; 2 : 49; 3 : 12–30). This was probably the name of some Chaldean god.

Me′shech—*drawing out*—the sixth son of Japheth (Gen. 10 : 2), the founder of a tribe (1 Chr. 1 : 5; Ezek. 27 : 13; 38 : 2, 3). They were in all probability the *Moschi,* a people inhabiting the Moschian Mountains, between the Black and the Caspian Seas. In Ps. 120 : 5 the name occurs as simply a synonym for foreigners or barbarians. "During the ascendency of the Babylonians and Persians in Western Asia, the Moschi were subdued; but it seems probable that a large number of them crossed the Caucasus range and spread over the northern steppes, mingling with the Scythians. There they became known as *Muscovs,* and gave that name to the Russian nation and its ancient capital by which they are still generally known throughout the East."

Meshelemi′ah—*friendship of Jehovah*—a Levite of the family of the Korhites, called also Shelemiah (1 Chr. 9 : 21; 26 : 1, 2, 9, 14). He was a temple gate-keeper in the time of David.

Meshil′lemoth—*requitals.* (1.) The father of Berechiah (2 Chr. 28 : 12).

(2.) A priest, the son of Immer (Neh. 11 : 13).

Meshul′lam—*befriended.* (1.) One of the chief Gadites in Bashan in the time of Jotham (1 Chr. 5 : 13).

(2.) Grandfather of Shaphan, "the

scribe," in the reign of Josiah (2 Kings 22 : 3).

(3.) A priest, father of Hilkiah (1 Chr. 9 : 11; Neh. 11 : 11), in the reign of Ammon; called Shallum in 1 Chr. 6 : 12.

(4.) A Levite of the family of Kohath (2 Chr. 34 : 12), in the reign of Josiah.

(5.) 1 Chr. 8 : 17.

(6.) 1 Chr. 3 : 19.

(7.) Neh. 12 : 13.

(8.) A chief priest (Neh. 12 : 16).

(9.) One of the leading Levites in the time of Ezra (8 : 16).

(10.) A priest (1 Chr. 9 : 12).

(11.) One of the principal Israelites who supported Ezra when expounding the law to the people (Neh. 8 : 4).

Meshul′lemeth—*friend*—the wife of Manasseh, and the mother of Amon (2 Kings 21 : 19), kings of Judah.

Mesopota′mia—*the country between the two rivers* (Heb. *Aram-naharaîm; i.e.,* "Syria of the two rivers")—the name given by the Greeks and Romans to the region between the Euphrates and the Tigris (Gen. 24 : 10; Deut. 23 : 4; Judg. 3 : 8, 10). In the Old Testament it is mentioned also under the name "Padan-aram;" *i.e.,* the plain of Aram, or Syria (Gen. 25 : 20). The northern portion of this fertile plateau was the original home of the ancestors of the Hebrews (Gen. 11; Acts 7 : 2). From this region Isaac obtained his wife Rebecca (Gen. 24 : 10, 15), and here also Jacob sojourned (28 : 2–7) and obtained his wives, and here most of his sons were born (35 : 26; 46 : 15). The petty, independent tribes of this region, each under its own prince, were warlike, and used chariots in battle. They maintained their independence till after the time of David, when they fell under the dominion of Assyria, and were absorbed into the empire (2 Kings 19 : 13).

Mess, a portion of food given to a guest (Gen. 43 : 34; 2 Sam. 11 : 8).

Mes′senger (Heb. *mal′âk,* Gr. *angelos*), an angel, a messenger who runs on foot, the bearer of despatches (Job 1 : 14; 1 Sam. 11 : 7; 2 Chr. 36 : 22); swift of foot (2 Kings 9 : 18).

Messi′ah (Heb. *mâshîah*), in all the

thirty-nine instances of its occurring in the Old Testament, is rendered by the LXX. "Christos." It means *anointed.* Thus *priests* (Ex. 28:41; 40:15; Num. 3:3), *prophets* (1 Kings 19:16), and *kings* (1 Sam. 9:16; 16:3; 2 Sam. 12:7) were anointed with oil, and so consecrated to their respective offices. The great Messiah is anointed "above his fellows" (Ps. 45:7); *i.e.,* he embraces in himself all the three offices. The Greek form "Messias" is only twice used in the New Testament—in John 1:41 and 4:25 (R.V., "Messiah"), and in the Old Testament the word Messiah, as the rendering of the Hebrew, occurs only twice (Dan 9:25, 26; R.V., "the anointed one").

The first great promise (Gen. 3:15) contains in it the germ of all the prophecies recorded in the Old Testament regarding the coming of the Messiah and the great work he was to accomplish on earth. The prophecies became more definite and fuller as the ages rolled on; the light shone more and more unto the perfect day. Different periods of prophetic revelation have been pointed out—(1) the patriarchal; (2) the Mosaic; (3) the period of David; (4) the period of prophetism—*i.e.,* of those prophets whose works form a part of the Old Testament canon. The expectations of the Jews were thus kept alive from generation to generation, till the "fulness of the times," when Messiah came, "made of a woman, made under the law, to redeem them that were under the law." In him all these ancient prophecies have their fulfilment. Jesus of Nazareth is the Messiah, the great Deliverer who was to come. (Comp. Matt. 26:54; Mark 9:12; Luke 18:31; 22:37; John 5:39; Acts 2;16:31; 26:22, 23.)

Me′theg-am′mah—*bridle of the mother* —a figurative name for a chief city, as in 2 Sam. 8:1, "David took Metheg-ammah out of the hand of the Philistines" (R.V., "took the bridle of the mother-city"); *i.e.,* subdued their capital or strongest city, viz., Gath (1 Chr. 18:1).

Methu′sael—*champion of El; man of God*—a descendant of Cain (Gen. 4:18), so called, perhaps, to denote that even among the descendants of Cain God had not left himself without a witness.

Methu′selah—*man of the dart*—the son of Enoch, and grandfather of Noah. He was the oldest man of whom we have any record, dying at the age of nine hundred and sixty-nine years, in the year of the Flood (Gen. 5:21-27; 1 Chr. 1:3).

Mez′ahab—*water of gold*—the father of Matred (Gen. 36:39; 1 Chr. 1:50), and grandfather of Mehetabel, wife of Hadar, the last king of Edom.

Mi′amin = Mijamin—*from the right hand.* (1.) The head of one of the divisions of the priests (1 Chr. 24:9).

(2.) A chief priest who returned from Babylon with Zerubbabel (Neh. 12:5), called Mijamin (10:7) and Miniamin (12:17).

Mib′har—*choice*—a Hagarene, one of David's warriors (1 Chr. 11:38); called also Bani the Gadite (2 Sam. 23:36).

Mib′sam—*fragrance.* (1.) One of Ishmael's twelve sons, and head of an Arab tribe (Gen. 25:13).

(2.) A son of Simeon (1 Chr. 4:25).

Mib′zar—*fortress*—one of the Edomitish "dukes" descended from Esau (Gen. 36:42; 1 Chr. 1:53).

Mi′cah, a shortened form of **Micaiah**—*who is like Jehovah?* (1.) A man of Mount Ephraim, whose history so far is introduced in Judg. 17, apparently for the purpose of leading to an account of the settlement of the tribe of Dan in Northern Palestine, and for the purpose also of illustrating the lawlessness of the times in which he lived (Judg. 18; 19:1-29; 21:25).

(2.) The son of Merib-baal (Mephibosheth)—1 Chr. 8:34, 35.

(3.) The first in rank of the priests of the family of Kohathites (1 Chr. 23:20).

(4.) A descendant of Joel the Reubenite (1 Chr. 5:5).

(5.) "The Morasthite," so called to distinguish him from Micaiah, the son of Imlah (1 Kings 22:8). He was a prophet of Judah, a contemporary of Isaiah (Micah 1:1), a native of Moresheth of Gath (1:14, 15). Very little is known of the circumstances of his life (comp. Jer. 26:18-24).

Mi′cah, Book of, the sixth in order of

the so-called minor prophets. The super-scription to this book states that the pro-phet exercised his office in the reigns of Jotham, Ahaz, and Hezekiah. If we reckon from the beginning of Jotham's reign to the end of Hezekiah's (B.C. 759–698), then he ministered for about fifty-nine years; but if we reckon from the death of Jotham to the accession of Hezekiah (B.C. 743–726), his ministry lasted only six-teen years. It has been noticed as re-markable that this book commences with the last words of another prophet, "Mi-caiah the son of Imlah" (1 Kings 22:28): "Hearken, O people, every one of you."

The book *consists of* three sections, each commencing with a rebuke, "Hear ye," etc., and closing with a promise—(1) ch. 1; 2; (2) ch. 3–5, especially addressed to the princes and heads of the people; (3) ch. 6–7, in which Jehovah is represented as holding a controversy with his people: the whole concluding with a song of triumph at the great deliverance which the Lord will achieve for his people. The closing verse is quoted in the song of Zacharias (Luke 1:72, 73). The prediction regard-ing the place "where Christ should be born," one of the most remarkable Mes-sianic prophecies (Micah 5:2), is quoted in Matt. 2:6.

There are the following references to this book in the New Testament:—

5:2, comp. Matt. 2:6; John 7:42.

7:6, comp. Matt. 10:21, 35, 36.

7:20, comp. Luke 1:72, 73.

Micai'ah—*who is like Jehovah?*—the son of Imlah, a faithful prophet of Samaria (1 Kings 22:8–28). Three years after the great battle with Ben-hadad (20:29–34), Ahab proposed to Jehoshaphat, king of Judah, that they should go up against Ramoth-Gilead to do battle again with Ben-hadad. Jehoshaphat agreed, but suggested that inquiry should be first made "at the word of Jehovah." Ahab's prophets approved of the expedition; but Jehoshaphat, still dis-satisfied, asked if there was no other prophet besides the four hundred that had appeared, and was informed of this Micaiah. He was sent for from prison, where he had been confined, probably on account of some pre-

diction disagreeable to Ahab; and he con-demned the expedition, and prophesied that it would end, as it did, in disaster. We hear nothing further of this prophet. Some have supposed that he was the unnamed prophet referred to in 1 Kings 20:35–42.

Mi'cha. (1.) 2 Sam. 9:12 = MICAH (2).

(2.) The son of Zabdi, a Levite of the family of Asaph (Neh. 11:17, 22).

Mi'chael—*who is like God?* (1.) The title given to one of the chief angels (Dan. 10:13, 21; 12:1). He had special charge of Israel as a nation. He disputed with Satan (Jude 9) about the body of Moses. He is also represented as warring against "that old serpent, called the Devil, and Satan, which deceiveth the whole world" (Rev. 12:7–9).

(2.) The father of Sethur, the spy selected to represent Asher (Num. 13:13).

(3.) 1 Chr. 7:3, a chief of the tribe of Issachar.

(4.) 1 Chr. 8:16, a Benjamite.

(5.) A chief Gadite in Bashan (1 Chr. 5:13).

(6.) A Manassite, "a captain of thou-sands" who joined David at Ziklag (1 Chr. 12:20).

(7.) A Gershonite Levite (1 Chr. 6:40).

(8.) The father of Omri (1 Chr. 27:18).

(9.) One of the sons of king Jehoshaphat (2 Chr. 21:2, 4). He was murdered by his brother Jehoram.

Michai'ah. (1.) The queen-mother of King Abijah (2 Chr. 13:2). (See MAACAH [4]).

(2.) One of those sent out by Jehoshaphat to instruct the people in the law (2 Chr. 17:7).

(3.) 2 Kings 22:12.

(4.) The son of Gemariah. He reported to the king's officers Jeremiah's prediction, which he had heard Baruch read (Jer. 36:11, 13) from his father Gemariah's chamber in the temple.

(5.) A Levite (Neh. 12:35).

(6.) A priest (Neh. 12:41).

Mi'chal—*rivulet*, or *who as God?*—the younger of Saul's two daughters by his wife Ahinoam (1 Sam. 14:49, 50). "Attracted by the graces of his person and the gallantry of his conduct, she fell in love with David and became his wife" (18:20–28). She showed her affection for him by promoting his escape to Naioth when Saul sought his life (1 Sam. 19:12–17. Comp. Ps. 59. See TERAPHIM). After this she did not see David for many years. Meanwhile she was given in marriage to another man—Phalti or Phaltiel of Gallim (1 Sam. 25:44)—but David afterwards formally reclaimed her as his lawful wife (2 Sam. 3:12–16). The relation between her and David soon after this was altered. They became alienated from each other. This happened on that memorable day when the ark was brought up in great triumph from its temporary resting-place to the Holy City. In David's conduct on that occasion she saw nothing but a needless humiliation of the royal dignity (1 Chr. 15:27). She remained childless, and thus the races of David and Saul were not mixed. In 2 Sam. 21:8 her name again occurs, but the name Merab should probably be here substituted for Michal (comp. 1 Sam. 18:19).

Mich'mash—*something hidden*—a town of Benjamin (Ezra 2:27), east of Bethel and south of Migron, on the road to Jerusalem (Isa. 10:28). It lay on the line of march of an invading army from the north, on the north side of the steep and precipitous Wâdy es-Suweinît ("valley of the little thorn-tree" or "the acacia"), and now bears the name of *Mŭkhmâs*. This wâdy is called "the passage of Michmash" (1 Sam. 13:23). Immediately facing Mŭkhmâs, on the opposite side of the ravine, is the modern representative of Geba, and behind this again are Ramah and Gibeah. This was the scene of a great battle fought between the army of Saul and the Philistines, who were utterly routed and pursued for some 16 miles towards Philistia as far as the valley of Aijalon. "The freedom of Benjamin secured at Michmash led through long years of conflict to the freedom of all its kindred tribes." The power of Benjamin and its king now steadily increased. A new spirit and a new hope were now at work in Israel. (See SAUL.)

Mich'methah—*hiding-place*—a town in the northern border of Ephraim and Manasseh, and not far west of Jordan (Josh. 16:6; 17:7).

Mich'ri—*prize of Jehovah*—a Benjamite, the father of Uzzi (1 Chr. 9:8).

Mich'tam—*writing; i.e.*, a poem or song —found in the titles of Ps. 16; 56–60. Some translate the word "golden"—*i.e.*, precious. It is rendered in the LXX. by a word meaning "tablet inscription" or a "stelograph." The root of the word means to stamp or grave, and hence it is regarded as denoting a composition so precious as to be worthy to be engraven on a durable tablet for preservation; or, as others render, "a psalm precious as *stamped gold*," from the word *kĕthĕm*, "fine or stamped gold."

Mid'din—*measures*—one of the six cities "in the wilderness," on the west of the Dead Sea, mentioned along with En-gedi (Josh. 15:61).

Mid'ian—*strife*—the fourth son of Abraham by Keturah, the father of the Midianites (Gen. 25:2; 1 Chr. 1:32).

Mid'ianite, an Arabian tribe descended from Midian. They inhabited principally the desert north of the peninsula of Arabia. The peninsula of Sinai was the pasture-ground for their flocks. They were virtually the rulers of Arabia, being the dominant tribe. Like all Arabians, they were a nomad people. They early engaged in commercial pursuits. It was to one of their caravans that Joseph was sold (Gen. 37:25, 27). The next notice of them is in connection with Moses' flight from Egypt (Ex. 2:15–21). Here in Midian Moses became the servant and afterwards the son-in-law of Reuel or Jethro, the priest. After the Exodus, the Midianites were friendly to the Israelites so long as they traversed only their outlying pasture-ground on the west of the Arabah; but when, having passed the southern end of Edom, they entered into the land of Midian proper, they joined with Balak, the king of Moab, in a conspiracy against them (Num. 22:4–7). Balaam, who had been sent for to curse Israel, having utterly failed to do so, was dismissed by the king of Moab; nevertheless he still tarried among the Midianites, and induced them to enter into correspondence with the Israelites, so as to bring them into association with them in the licentious orgies connected with the worship of Baal-Peor. This crafty counsel prevailed. The Israelites took part in the heathen festival, and so brought upon themselves a curse indeed. Their apostasy brought upon them a severe punishment. A plague broke out amongst them, and more than twenty-four thousand of the people perished (Num. 25:9). But the Midianites were not to be left unpunished. A terrible vengeance was denounced against them. A thousand warriors from each tribe, under the leadership of Phinehas, went forth against them. The Midianites were utterly routed. Their cities were consumed by fire, five of their kings were put to death, and the whole nation was destroyed (Josh. 13:22–35). Balaam also perished by the sword, receiving the "wages of his unrighteousness" (Num. 31:8; 2 Pet. 2:15). The whole of the country on the east of Jordan, now conquered by the Israelites (see SIHON; OG), was divided between the two tribes of Reuben and Gad and the half tribe of Manasseh.

Some two hundred and fifty years after this the Midianites had regained their ancient power, and in confederation with the Amalekites and the "children of the east" they made war against their old enemies the Israelites, whom for seven years they oppressed and held in subjection. They were at length assailed by Gideon in that ever-memorable battle in the great plain of Esdraelon, and utterly destroyed (Judg. 6: 1-ch. 7). Frequent allusions are afterwards made to this great victory (Ps. 83:10, 12; Isa. 9:4; 10:6). They now wholly pass away from the page of history both sacred and profane.

Mid'wife. The two midwives mentioned in Ex. 1:15 were probably the superintendents of the whole class.

Mig'dal-E'dar — *tower of the flock* — a place 2 miles south of Jerusalem, near the Bethlehem road (Gen. 35:21). (See EDAR.)

Mig'dal-el—*tower of God*—a fortified city of Naphtali (Josh. 19:38), supposed by some to be identical with Magdala (*q.v.*).

Mig'dal-gad—*tower of fortune*—a town in the plains of Judah, probably the modern *el-Mejdel*, a little to the north-east of Ascalon (Josh. 15:37).

Mig'dol—*tower.* (1.) A strongly-fortified place 12 miles from Pelusium, in the north of Egypt (Jer. 44:1; 46:14). This word

is rendered "tower" in Ezek. 29:10, but the margin correctly retains the name Migdol—"from Migdol to Syene;" *i.e.*, from Migdol in the north to Syene in the south —in other words, the whole of Egypt.

(2.) A place mentioned in the passage of the Red Sea (Ex. 14:2; Num. 33:7, 8). It is probably to be identified with *Bir Suweis*, about 2 miles from Suez.

Mig'ron—*precipice* or *landslip*—a place between Aiath and Michmash (Isa. 10:28). The town of the same name mentioned in 1 Sam. 14:2 was to the south of this.

Mik'loth—*staves.* (1.) An officer under Dodai, in the time of David and Solomon (1 Chr. 27:4).

(2.) A Benjamite (1 Chr. 8:32; 9:37, 38).

Milala'i—*eloquent*—a Levitical musician (Neh. 12:36) who took part in the dedication of the wall of Jerusalem.

Mil'dew (the rendering of a Hebrew word meaning "to be yellow," yellowness), the result of cutting east winds blighting and thus rendering the grain unproductive (Deut. 28:22; 1 Kings 8:37; 2 Chr. 6:28).

Mile (from Lat. *mille*, "a thousand;" Matt. 5:41), a Roman measure of 1,000 paces of 5 feet each. Thus the Roman mile has 1618 yards, being 142 yards shorter than the English mile.

Mile'tus (Miletum, 2 Tim. 4:20), a seaport town and the ancient capital of Ionia, about 36 miles south of Ephesus. On his voyage from Greece to Syria, Paul touched at this port, and delivered that noble and pathetic address to the elders ("presbyters," ver. 28) of Ephesus recorded in Acts 20:15-35. The site of Miletus is now some 10 miles from the coast. (See EPHESIANS, EPISTLE TO.)

Milk. (1.) Hebrew *hâlâbh*, "new milk"— milk in its fresh state (Judg. 4:19). It is frequently mentioned in connection with honey (Ex. 3:8; 13:5; Josh. 5:6; Isa. 7:15, 22; Jer. 11:5). Sheep (Deut. 32:14) and goats (Prov. 27:27) and camels (Gen. 32:15), as well as cows, are made to give their milk for the use of man. Milk is used figuratively as a sign of abundance (Gen. 49:12; Ezek. 25:4; Joel 3:18). It is also a symbol of the rudiments of doctrine (1

Cor. 3 : 2 ; Heb. 5 : 12, 13), and of the un-adulterated word of God (1 Pet. 2 : 2).

(2.) Heb. *hĕm'ăh*, always rendered "but-ter" in the Authorized Version. It means "butter," but also more frequently "cream," or perhaps, as some think, "curdled milk," such as that which Abraham set before the angels (Gen. 18 : 8), and which Jael gave to Sisera (Judg. 5 : 25). In this state milk was used by travellers (2 Sam. 17 : 29). If

kept long enough, it acquired a slightly in-toxicating or soporific power.

This Hebrew word is also sometimes used for milk in general (Deut. 32 : 14; Job 20 : 17).

Mill, for grinding corn, mentioned as used in the time of Abraham (Gen. 18 : 6). That used by the Hebrews consisted of two circular stones, each 2 feet in diameter and half a foot thick, the lower of which was

WOMEN GRINDING AT THE MILL.

called the "nether millstone" (Job 41 : 24) and the upper the "rider." The upper stone was turned round by a stick fixed in it as a handle. There were then no public mills, and thus each family required to be provided with a hand-mill. The corn was ground daily, generally by the women of the house (Isa. 47 : 1, 2 ; Matt. 24 : 41). It was with the upper stone of a hand-mill that "a certain woman" at Thebez broke Abime-lech's skull (Judg. 9 : 53, "a *piece* of a mill-

stone ;" literally, "a millstone rider "—*i. e.*, the "runner," the stone which revolves. Comp. 2 Sam. 11 : 21). Millstones could not be pledged (Deut. 24 : 6), as they were necessary in every family.

Millen'nium, a thousand years ; the name given to the era mentioned in Rev. 20 : 1–7. Some maintain that Christ will personally appear on earth for the purpose of estab-lishing his kingdom at the beginning of this millennium. Those holding this view are usually called "millenarians." On the other hand, it is maintained, more in accordance with the teaching of Scripture, we think, that Christ's second advent will not be pre-millennial, and that the right conception of the prospects and destiny of his kingdom is that which is taught, *e.g.*, in the parables of the leaven and the mustard-seed. The triumph of the gospel, it is held, must be looked for by the wider and more efficient operation of the very forces that are now at work in extending the gospel; and that Christ will only come again at the close of this dispensation to judge the world at the "last day." The millennium will thus precede his coming.

Mil′let (Heb. *dôḥan;* only in Ezek. 4:9), a small grain, the produce of the *Panicum miliaceum* of botanists. It is universally

MILLET (PANICUM MILIACEUM).

cultivated in the East as one of the smaller corn-grasses. This seed is the *cenchros* of the Greeks. It is called in India *warree*, and by the Arabs *dukhân*, and is extensively used for food, being often mixed with other grain. In this country it is only used for feeding birds.

Mil′lo (Heb. always with the article, "the"

Millo). (1.) Probably the Canaanite name of some fortification, consisting of walls filled in with earth and stones, which protected Jerusalem on the north as its outermost defence. It is always rendered *Akra* —*i.e.*, "the citadel"—in the LXX. It was already existing when David conquered Jerusalem (2 Sam. 5:9). He extended it to the right and left, thus completing the defence of the city. It was rebuilt by Solomon (1 Kings 9:15, 24; 11:27) and repaired by Hezekiah (2 Chr. 32:5).

(2.) In Judg. 9:6, 20 it is the name of a rampart in Shechem, probably the "tower of Shechem" (9:46, 49).

Min′cing (Heb. *ṭâphôph*, Isa. 3:16), taking affectedly short and quick steps. Luther renders the word by "wag" or "waggle," thus representing "the affected gait of coquettish females."

Mine. The process of mining is described in Job 28:1–11. Moses speaks of the mineral wealth of Palestine (Deut. 8:9). Job 28:4 is rightly thus rendered in the Revised Version, "He breaketh open a shaft away from where men sojourn; they are forgotten of the foot [that passeth by]; they hang afar from men, they swing to and fro." These words illustrate ancient mining operations.

Min′ister, one who serves, as distinguished from the master. (1.) Heb. *meshêreth*, applied to an attendant on one of superior rank, as to Joshua, the servant of Moses (Ex. 33:11), and to the servant of Elisha (2 Kings 4:43). This name is also given to attendants at court (2 Chr. 22:8), and to the priests and Levites (Jer. 33:21; Ezek. 44:11).

(2.) Heb. *pelâh* (Ezra 7:24), a "minister" of religion. Here used of that class of sanctuary servants called "Solomon's servants" in Ezra 2:55–58 and Neh. 7:57–60.

(3.) Greek *leitourgos*, a subordinate public administrator, and in this sense applied to magistrates (Rom. 13:6). It is applied also to our Lord (Heb. 8:2), and to Paul in relation to Christ (Rom. 15:16).

(4.) Greek *hypērétēs* (literally, "under-rower"), a personal attendant on a superior, thus of the person who waited on the officiating priest in the synagogue (Luke

4:20). It is applied also to John Mark, the attendant on Paul and Barnabas (Acts 13:5).

(5.) Greek *diacŏnos*, usually a subordinate officer or assistant employed in relation to the ministry of the gospel, as to Paul and Apollos (1 Cor. 3:5), Tychicus (Eph. 6:21), Epaphras (Col. 1:7), Timothy (1 Thess. 3:2), and also to Christ (Rom. 15:8).

Min'ni, only in Jer. 51:27, as the name of a province in Armenia, which was at this time under the Median kings. Armenia is regarded by some as = Har-minni —*i.e.*, the mountainous country of Minni. (See ARMENIA.)

Min'nith—*distribution*—an Ammonitish town (Judg. 11:33) from which wheat was exported to Tyre (Ezek. 27:17). It was probably somewhere in the Mishor or table-land on the east of Jordan. There is a gentle valley running for about 4 miles east of Dhibân called *Kurm Dhibân,* "the vineyards of Dibon." Tristram supposes that this may be the "vineyards" mentioned in Judg. (*l.c.*).

Min'strel (Matt. 9:23), a flute-player. Such music was a usual accompaniment of funerals. In 2 Kings 3:15 it denotes a player on a stringed instrument.

Mint (Gr. *hēduosmon*—*i.e.,* "having a sweet smell"), one of the garden herbs of which the Pharisees paid tithes (Matt. 23:23; Luke 11:42). It belongs to the labiate family of plants. The species most common in Syria is the *Mentha sylvestris,* the wild mint, which grows much larger than the garden mint (*M. sativa*). It was much used in domestic economy as a condiment, and also as a medicine. The paying of tithes of mint was in accordance with the Mosaic law (Deut. 14:22), but the error of the Pharisees lay in their being more careful about this little matter of the mint than about weightier matters.

Mir'acle, an event in the external world brought about by the immediate agency or the simple volition of God, operating without the use of means capable of being discerned by the senses, and designed to authenticate the divine commission of a religious teacher and the truth of his message (John 2:18; Matt. 12:38). It is

MINT (MENTHA SYLVESTRIS).

an occurrence at once above nature and above man. It shows the intervention of a power that is not limited by the laws either of matter or of mind, a power interrupting the fixed laws which govern their movements, a supernatural power.

"The suspension or violation of the laws of nature involved in miracles is nothing more than is constantly taking place around us. One force counteracts another: vital force keeps the chemical laws of matter in abeyance; and muscular force can control the action of physical force. When a man raises a weight from the ground, the law of gravity is neither suspended nor violated, but counteracted by a stronger force. The same is true as to the walking of Christ on the water and the swimming of iron at the command of the prophet. The simple and grand truth that the universe is not under the exclusive control of physical forces, but that everywhere and always there is above, separate from and superior to all else, an infinite personal will, not superseding, but directing and controlling all physical causes, acting with or without them." God ordinarily effects his purpose through the agency of second causes; but he has the power also of effecting his purpose immediately and without the intervention of second causes—*i.e.*, of invading the fixed order, and thus of working miracles. Thus we affirm the *possibility* of miracles—the possibility of a higher hand intervening to control or reverse nature's ordinary movements.

In the New Testament these four Greek words are principally used to designate miracles:—(1.) *Sēmeion*, a "sign"—*i.e.*, an evidence of a divine commission; an attestation of a divine message (Matt. 12:38, 39; 16:1, 4; Mark 8:11; Luke 11:16; 23:8; John 2:11, 18, 23; Acts 6:8, etc.); a token of the presence and working of God; the seal of a higher power.

(2.) *Terata*, "wonders;" wonder-causing events; portents; producing astonishment in the beholder (Acts 2:19).

(3.) *Dunameis*, "mighty works;" works of superhuman power (Acts 2:22; Rom. 15:19; 2 Thess. 2:9); of a new and higher power.

(4.) *Erga*, "works;" the works of Him who is "wonderful in working" (John 5:20, 36).

Miracles are seals of a divine mission. The sacred writers appealed to them as proofs that they were messengers of God. Our Lord also appealed to miracles as a conclusive proof of his divine mission (John 5:20, 36; 10:25, 38). Thus, being out of the common course of nature and beyond the power of man, they are fitted to convey the impression of the presence and power of God. Where miracles are there certainly God is. The man, therefore, who works a miracle affords thereby clear proof that he comes with the authority of God; they are his credentials that he is God's messenger. The teacher points to these credentials, and they are a proof that he speaks with the authority of God. He boldly says, "God bears me witness, both with signs and wonders, and with divers miracles."

The *credibility* of miracles is established by the evidence of the senses on the part of those who are witnesses of them, and to all others by the testimony of such witnesses. The witnesses were competent, and their testimony is trustworthy. Unbelievers, following Hume, deny that any testimony can prove a miracle, because they say miracles are impossible. We have shown that miracles are possible, and surely they can be borne witness to. Surely they are credible when we have abundant and trustworthy evidence of their occurrence. They are credible just as any facts of history well authenticated are credible. Miracles, it is said, are contrary to experience. Of course they are contrary to our experience, but that does not prove that they were contrary to the experience of those who witnessed them. We believe a thousand facts, both of history and of science, that are contrary to our experience, but we believe them on the ground of competent testimony. An atheist or a pantheist must, as a matter of course, deny the possibility of miracles; but to one who believes in a personal God, who in his wisdom may see fit to interfere with the ordinary processes of nature, miracles are not impossible, nor are they incredible. (See LIST OF MIRACLES, Appendix.)

Mir'iam—*their rebellion*. (1.) The sister of Moses and Aaron (Ex. 2:4–10; 1 Chr. 6:3). Her name is prominent in the history of the Exodus. She is called "the prophetess" (Ex. 15:20). She took the lead in the song of triumph after the passage of the Red Sea. She died at Kadesh during the second encampment at that place, toward the close of the wanderings in the wilderness, and was buried there (Num. 20:1). (See AARON; MOSES.)

(2.) 1 Chr. 4:17, one of the descendants of Judah.

Misdeem' (Deut. 32:27, R.V.). The Authorized Version reads—"should behave themselves strangely;" *i.e.*, not recognize the truth, misunderstand or mistake the cause of Israel's ruin, which was due to the fact that God had forsaken them on account of their apostasy.

Mis'gab—*height*—a town of Moab, or simply, the height=the citadel, some fortress so called; or perhaps a general name for the highlands of Moab, as some think (Jer. 48:1). In Isa. 25:12, the word is rendered "high fort."

Mish'ael—*who is like God?* (1.) A

Levite; the eldest of the three sons of Uzziel (Ex. 6 : 22).

(2.) One of the three Hebrew youths who were trained with Daniel in Babylon (Dan. 1 : 11, 19), and promoted to the rank of Magi. He and his companions were afterwards cast into the burning fiery furnace for refusing to worship the idol the king had set up, from which they were miraculously delivered (3 : 13-30). His Chaldean name was Meshach (*q.v.*).

Mi'shal, a city of the tribe of Asher (Josh. 21 : 30; 1 Chr. 6 : 74). It is probably the modern *Misalli*, on the shore near Carmel.

Mi'sham—*their cleansing* or *their beholding*—a Benjamite, one of the sons of Elpaal (1 Chr. 8 : 12).

Mi'sheal (Josh. 19 : 26), a town of Asher, probably the same as Mishal.

Mish'ma—*hearing.* (1.) One of the sons of Ishmael (Gen. 25 : 14), and founder of an Arab tribe.

(2.) A Simeonite (1 Chr. 4 : 25, 26).

Mishman'nah—*fatness*—one of the Gadite heroes who gathered to David at Ziklag (1 Chr. 12 : 10).

Mis'rephoth-ma'im—*burning of waters*—supposed to be salt-pans, or lime-kilns, or glass-factories, a place to which Joshua pursued a party of Canaanites after the defeat of Jabin (Josh. 11 : 8). It is identified with the ruin *Musheirifeh*, at the promontory of en-Nâkhûrah, some 11 miles north of Acre.

Mite, contraction of *minute*, from the Latin *minūtum*, the translation of the Greek word *lepton*, the very smallest bronze or copper coin (Luke 12 : 59; 21 : 2). Two mites made one *quadrans*—*i.e.*, the fourth part of a Roman *as*, which was in value nearly a halfpenny. (See FARTHING.)

Mith'cah—*sweetness*—one of the stations of the Israelites in the wilderness (Num. 33 : 28, 29).

Mith'redath—*given by Mithra*, or *dedicated to Mithra, i.e.*, the sun—the Hebrew form of the Greek name Mithridates. (1.) The "treasurer" of King Cyrus (Ezra 1 : 8).

(2.) Ezra 4 : 7, a Persian officer in Samaria.

Mitre (Heb. *mîtsnĕphĕth*), something *rolled* round the head; the turban or headdress of the high priest (Ex. 28 : 4, 37, 39;

29 : 6, etc.). In the Authorized Version of Ezek. 21 : 26, this Hebrew word is rendered "diadem," but in the Revised Version, "mitre." It was a twisted band of fine linen, 8 yards in length, coiled into the form of a cap, and worn on official occasions (Lev. 8 : 9; 16 : 4; Zech. 3 : 5). On the front of it was a golden plate with the inscription, "Holiness to the Lord." The *mitsncpheth* differed from the mitre or head-dress (*migbâ'âh*) of the common priest. (See BONNET.)

Mityle'ne, the chief city of the island of Lesbos, on its east coast, in the Ægean Sea. Paul, during his third missionary journey, touched at this place on his way from Corinth to Judea (Acts 20 : 14), and here tarried for a night. It lies between Assos and Chios. It is now under the Turkish rule, and bears the name of *Metelin*.

Mixed mul'titude (Ex. 12 : 38), a class who accompanied the Israelites as they journeyed from Rameses to Succoth, the first stage of the Exodus. These were probably miscellaneous hangers-on to the Hebrews, whether Egyptians of the lower orders, or the remains of the Hyksos (see EGYPT; MOSES), as some think. The same thing happened on the return of the Jews from Babylon (Neh. 13 : 3)—a "mixed multitude" accompanied them so far.

Mi'zar—*smallness*—a summit on the eastern ridge of Lebanon, near which David lay after escaping from Absalom (Ps. 42 : 6). It may, perhaps, be the present *Jebel Ajlûn*, thus named—"the little"—in contrast with the greater elevation of Lebanon and Hermon.

Miz'pah or **Miz'peh**—*watch-tower; the look-out.* (1.) A place in Gilead, so named by Laban, who overtook Jacob at this spot (Gen. 31 : 49) on his return to Palestine from Padan-aram. Here Jacob and Laban set up their memorial cairn of stones. It is the same as Ramath-mizpeh (Josh. 13 : 26).

(2.) A town in Gilead, where Jephthah resided, and where he assumed the command of the Israelites in a time of national danger. Here he made his rash vow; and here his daughter submitted to her mysterious fate (Judg. 10 : 17; 11 : 11, 34). It may be the same as Ramoth-Gilead (Josh.

20 : 8), but it is more likely that it is identical with the foregoing, the Mizpeh of Gen. 31 : 23, 25, 48, 49.

(3.) Another place in Gilead, at the foot of Mount Hermon, inhabited by Hivites (Josh. 11 : 3, 8). The name in Hebrew here has the article before it—"the Mizpeh," "the watch-tower." The modern village of *Metullah*, meaning also "the look-out," probably occupies the site so called.

(4.) A town of Moab to which David removed his parents for safety during his persecution by Saul (1 Sam. 22 : 3). This was probably the citadel known as Kir-

Moab, now *Kerak*. While David resided here he was visited by the prophet Gad, here mentioned for the first time, who was probably sent by Samuel to bid him leave the land of Moab and betake himself to the land of Judah. He accordingly removed to the forest of Hareth (*q. v.*), on the edge of the mountain chain of Hebron.

(5.) A city of Benjamin—"the watch-tower "—where the people were accustomed to meet in great national emergencies (Josh. 18 : 26 ; Judg. 20 : 1, 3 ; 21 : 1, 5 ; 1 Sam. 7 : 5–16). It has been supposed to be the same as Nob (1 Sam. 21 : 1 ; 22 : 9–19).

NEBY SAMWÎL.

It was some 4 miles north-west of Jerusalem, and was situated on the loftiest hill in the neighbourhood, some 600 feet above the plain of Gibeon. This village has the modern name of *Neby Samwil* — *i.e.*, the prophet Samuel—from a tradition that Samuel's tomb is here. (See Nob.)

Samuel inaugurated the reformation that characterized his time by convening a great assembly of all Israel at Mizpeh, now the politico - religious centre of the nation. There, in deep humiliation on account of their sins, they renewed their vows and entered again into covenant with the God

of their fathers. It was a period of great religious awakening and of revived national life. The Philistines heard of this assembly, and came up against Israel. The Hebrews charged the Philistine host with great fury, and they were totally routed. Samuel commemorated this signal victory by erecting a memorial - stone, which he called "Ebenezer" (*q.v.*), saying, "Hitherto hath the Lord helped us " (1 Sam. 10 : 1–13).

Miz′par — *number* — one of the Jews who accompanied Zerubbabel from Babylon (Ezra 2 : 2); called also Mispereth (Neh. 7 : 7).

Miz′raim, the dual form of *matzor,* meaning a "mound" or "fortress," the name of a people descended from Ham (Gen. 10:6, 13; 1 Chr. 1:8, 11). It was the name generally given by the Hebrews to the land of Egypt (*q.v.*), and may denote the two Egypts, the Upper and the Lower. The modern Arabic name for Egypt is *Muzr.*

Miz′zah—*despair*—one of the four sons of Reuel, the son of Esau (Gen. 36:13, 17).

Mna′son—*reminding,* or *remembrancer* —a Christian of Jerusalem with whom Paul lodged (Acts 21:16). He was apparently a native of Cyprus, like Barnabas (11:19, 20), and was well known to the Christians of Cæsarea (4:36). He was an "old disciple" (R.V., "early disciple") — *i.e.,* he had become a Christian in the beginning of the formation of the Church in Jerusalem.

Mo′ab—*the seed of the father,* or, according to others, *the desirable land*—the eldest son of Lot (Gen. 19:37), of incestuous birth.

(2.) Used to denote the people of Moab (Num. 22:3–14; Judg. 3:30; 2 Sam. 8:2; Jer. 48:11, 13).

(3.) The land of Moab (Jer. 48:24), called also the "country of Moab" (Ruth 1:2, 6; 2:6), on the east of Jordan and the Dead Sea, and south of the Arnon (Num. 21:13, 26). In a wider sense it included the whole region that had been occupied by the Amorites. It bears the modern name of *Kerak.*

In the *Plains of Moab,* opposite Jericho (Num. 22:1; 26:63; Josh. 13:32), the children of Israel had their last encampment before they entered the land of Canaan. It was at that time in the possession of the Amorites (Num. 21:22). "Moses went up from the plains of Moab unto the mountain of Nebo, to the top of Pisgah," and "died there in the land of Moab, according to the word of the Lord" (Deut. 34:5, 6). "Surely if we had nothing else to interest us in the land of Moab, the fact that it was from the top of Pisgah, its noblest height, this mightiest of the prophets looked out with eye undimmed upon the Promised Land; that it was here on Nebo, its loftiest mountain, that he died his solitary death; that it was here, in the valley

over against Beth-peor, he found his mysterious sepulchre, we have enough to enshrine the memory in our hearts."

Moa′bite, the designation of a tribe descended from Moab, the son of Lot (Gen. 19:37). From Zoar, the cradle of this tribe, on the south-eastern border of the Dead Sea, they gradually spread over the region on the east of Jordan. Shortly before the Exodus, the warlike Amorites crossed the Jordan under Sihon their king and drove the Moabites (Num. 21:26–30) out of the region between the Arnon and the Jabbok, and occupied it, making Heshbon their capital. They were then confined to the territory to the south of the Arnon, along the southern half of the high table-land on the eastern shore of the Dead Sea, extending to the Wady Zered on the south.

On their journey the Israelites did not pass through Moab, but through the "wilderness" to the east (Deut. 2:8; Judg. 11:18), at length reaching the country to the north of the Arnon. Here they remained for some time till they had conquered Bashan (see SIHON; OG). The Moabites were alarmed, and their king, Balak, sought aid from the Midianites (Num. 22:2–4). It was while they were here that the visit of Balaam (*q.v.*) to Balak took place. (See MOSES.)

After the Conquest, the Moabites maintained hostile relations with the Israelites, and frequently harassed them in war (Judg. 3:12–30; 1 Sam. 11). The story of Ruth, however, shows the existence of friendly relations between Moab and Bethlehem. By his descent from Ruth, David may be said to have had Moabite blood in his veins. Yet there was war between David and the Moabites (2 Sam. 8:2; 23: 20; 1 Chr. 18:2), from whom he took great spoil (2 Sam. 8:2, 11, 12; 1 Chr. 11:22; 18:11).

During the one hundred and fifty years which followed the defeat of the Moabites, after the death of Ahab (see MESHA), they regained, apparently, much of their former prosperity. At this time Isaiah (15:1) delivered his "burden of Moab," predicting the coming of judgment on that land (comp. 2 Kings 17:3; 18:9; 1 Chr.

5:25, 26). Between the time of Isaiah and the commencement of the Babylonian captivity we have very seldom any reference to Moab (Jer. 25:21; 27:3; 40:11; Zeph. 2:8-10).

After the Return, it was Sanballat, a Moabite, who took chief part in seeking to prevent the rebuilding of Jerusalem (Neh. 2:19; 4:1; 6:1).

Moa'bite Stone, a basalt stone, bearing an inscription by King Mesha, which was discovered at Dibon by Klein, a German missionary at Jerusalem, in 1868. It was

MOABITE STONE.

3½ feet high and 2 in breadth and in thickness, rounded at the top. Through tribal jealousies it was broken in pieces by the Arabs, by lighting a fire round it and throwing cold water on it when it was hot, but not before an impression (a "splash," or "squeeze") of the inscription had been obtained by M. Ganneau. Other impressions, and also most of the fragments of the stone, which are now in the Louvre at Paris, were afterwards secured. It consisted of thirty-four lines, written in Hebrew-Phœnician characters. It was set up

by Mesha as a record and memorial of his victories. It records (1) Mesha's wars with Omri, (2) his public buildings, and (3) his wars against Horonaim. This inscription in a remarkable degree supplements and corroborates the history of King Mesha recorded in 2 Kings 3:4-27.

With the exception of a very few variations, the Moabite language in which the inscription is written is identical with the Hebrew. The form of the letters here used supplies very important and interesting information regarding the history of the formation of the alphabet, as well as, incidentally, regarding the arts of civilized life of those times in the land of Moab.

This ancient monument, recording the heroic struggles of King Mesha with Omri and Ahab, was erected about B.C. 900. Here "we have the identical slab on which the workmen of the old world carved the history of their own times, and from which the eye of their contemporaries read thousands of years ago the record of events of which they themselves had been the witnesses." It is the oldest inscription written in alphabetic characters, and hence is, apart from its value in the domain of Hebrew antiquities, of great linguistic importance.

Mol'adah—*birth*—a city in the south of Judah which fell to Simeon (Josh. 15:21-26; 19:2). It has been identified with the modern *el-Milh*, 10 miles east of Beersheba.

Mole—Heb. *tinshâmeth* (Lev. 11:30)—probably signifies some species of lizard (rendered in R.V., "chameleon"). In Lev. 11:18; Deut. 14:16, it is rendered, in Authorized Version, "swan" (R.V., "horned owl").

The Heb. *hôled* (Lev. 11:29), rendered "weasel," was probably the mole-rat. The true mole (*Talpa Europæa*) is not found in Palestine. The mole-rat (*Spalax typhlus*) "is twice the size of our mole, with no external eyes, and with only faint traces within of the rudimentary organ; no apparent ears, but, like the mole, with great internal organs of hearing; a strong, bare snout, and with large gnawing teeth; its colour a pale slate; its feet short, and provided with strong nails; its tail only rudimentary."

In Isa. 2:20, this word is the rendering of two words *haphar perôth*, which are rendered by Gesenius "*into the digging of rats*"—*i.e.*, rats' holes. But these two Hebrew words ought probably to be combined into one (*lahporpêrôth*) and translated "to the moles"—*i.e.*, the rat-moles. This animal "lives in underground communities, making large subterranean chambers for its young and for storehouses, with many runs connected with them, and is decidedly partial to the loose *débris* among ruins and stone-heaps, where it can form its chambers with least trouble."

Mo'loch—*king*—the name of the national god of the Ammonites, to whom children were sacrificed by fire. He was the consuming and destroying and also at the same time the purifying fire. In Amos 5:26, "your Moloch" of the Authorized Version is "your king" in the Revised Version (comp. Acts 7:43). Solomon (1 Kings 11:7) erected a high place for this idol on the Mount of Olives, and from that time till the days of Josiah his worship continued (2 Kings 23:10, 13). In the days of Jehoahaz it was partially restored, but after the Captivity wholly disappeared. He is also called Molech (Lev. 18:21; 20:2-5, etc.), Milcom (1 Kings 11:5, 33, etc.), and Malcham (Zeph. 1:5). This god became Chemosh among the Moabites.

Mon'ey. Of *uncoined* money the first notice we have is in the history of Abraham (Gen. 13:2; 20:16; 24:35). Next, this word is used in connection with the purchase of the cave of Machpelah (23:16), and again in connection with Jacob's purchase of a field at Shalem (Gen. 33:18, 19) for "an hundred pieces of money "=an hundred Hebrew *kesîtahs* (*q.v.*)—*i.e.*, probably pieces of money, as is supposed, bearing the figure of a lamb.

The history of Joseph affords evidence of the constant use of money—silver of a fixed weight. This appears also in all the subsequent history of the Jewish people, in all their internal as well as foreign transactions. There were in common use in trade silver pieces of a definite weight—shekels, half-shekels, and quarter-shekels. But these were not properly *coins*, which are pieces of metal authoritatively issued, and bearing a stamp.

Of the use of *coined* money we have no early notice among the Hebrews. The first mentioned is of Persian coinage—the *daric* (Ezra 2:69; Neh. 7:70) and the *'adarkon* (Ezra 8:27). The daric (*q.v.*) was a gold piece current in Palestine in the time of Cyrus. As long as the Jews, after the Exile, lived under Persian rule, they used Persian coins. These gave place to Greek coins when Palestine came under the dominion of the Greeks (B.C. 331), the coins consisting of gold, silver, and copper pieces. The usual gold pieces were *staters*

ATHENIAN TETRADRACHM.

(*q.v.*), and the silver coins *tetradrachms* and *drachms*.

In the year B.C. 140, Antiochus VII. gave permission to Simon the Maccabee to coin Jewish money. Shekels (*q.v.*) were then coined bearing the figure of the almond rod and the pot of manna.

Mon'ey-chan'ger (Matt. 21:12; Mark 11:15; John 2:15). Every Israelite from twenty years and upwards had to pay (Ex. 30:13-15) into the sacred treasury half a shekel every year as an offering to Jehovah, and that in the exact Hebrew half-shekel piece. There was a class of men, who frequented the temple courts, who exchanged at a certain premium foreign moneys for these half-shekels to the Jews who came up to Jerusalem from all parts of the world. (See PASSOVER.) When our Lord drove the traffickers out of the temple, these money-changers fared worst. Their tables were overturned and they themselves were expelled.

Month. Among the Egyptians the month of thirty days each was in use long before the time of the Exodus, and formed the basis of their calculations. From the time of the institution of the Mosaic law the month among the Jews was lunar. The cycle of religious feasts depended on the moon. The commencement of a month was determined by the observation of the new moon. The number of months in the year was usually twelve (1 Kings 4:7; 1 Chr. 27:1-15); but every third year an additional month (ve-Adar) was inserted, so as to make the months coincide with the seasons.

"The Hebrews and Phœnicians had no word for month save 'moon,' and only saved their calendar from becoming vague like that of the Moslems by the interpolation of an additional month. There is no evidence at all that they ever used a true solar year such as the Egyptians possessed. The latter had twelve months of thirty days and five epagomenac or odd days."— *Palestine Quarterly*, January 1889.

TABLE OF HEBREW MONTHS AND SACRED FESTIVALS.

Months.	Beginning with new moon.	Sacred	Civil	Seasons.	Festivals.
NISAN, or ABIB (30 days), Ex. 12:2, 18; Esther 3:7.	March. April.	1	7	Harvest.	14. Paschal lamb killed. 15. Passover. 16. First-fruits of barley harvest. 21. Passover ended.
ZIF (29 days), 1 Kings 6:1.	April. May.	2	8	Harvest.	14. The second Passover (Num. 9:10, 11).
SIVAN (30 days), Esther 8:9.	May. June.	3	9	Summer.	6. Pentecost. First-fruits of wheat harvest.
TAMMUZ (29 days), Ezek. 8:14.	June. July.	4	10	Summer.	
AB (30 days).	July. August.	5	11	Hot season.	
ELUL (29 days), Neh. 6:15.	August. September.	6	12	Hot season.	
ETHANIM, TISRI (30 days), 1 Kings 8:2.	September. October.	7	1	Seed-time.	1. Feast of Trumpets. 10. Day of Atonement. 15. Feast of Tabernacles. First-fruits of wine and oil.
MARCHESVAN, BUL (29 days), 1 Kings 6:38.	October. November.	8	2	Seed-time.	
CHISLEU (30 days), Zech. 7:1.	November. December.	9	3	Winter.	25. Feast of the Dedication of the Temple.
TEBETH (29 days), Esther 2:16.	December. January.	10	4	Winter.	
SEBAT, SEVET (30 days), Zech. 1:7.	January. February.	11	5	Cold season.	
ADAR (29 days), Esther 3:7. VE-ADAR was added to this month when necessary.		12	6	Cold season.	14, 15. Feast of Purim.

Moon—Heb. *yarêah*, from its paleness (Ezra 6:15), and *lebânâh*, the "white" (Cant. 6:10; Isa. 24:23)—was appointed by the Creator to be with the sun "for signs, and for seasons, and for days, and years" (Gen. 1:14–16). A lunation was among the Jews the period of a month, and several of their festivals were on the day of the new moon. It is frequently referred to along with the sun (Josh. 10:12; Ps. 72:5, 7, 17; Eccl. 12:2; 24:23, etc.), and also by itself (Ps. 8:3; 89:37; 121:6).

The great brilliance of the moon in Eastern countries led to its being early an object of idolatrous worship (Deut. 4:19; 17:3; Job 31:26),—a form of idolatry against which the Jews were warned (Deut. 4:19; 17:3). They, however, fell into this idolatry, and offered incense (2 Kings 23:5; Jer. 8:2), and also cakes of honey, to the moon (Jer. 7:18; 44:17–19, 25).

Mor'al law, the all-perfect, unchangeable, perpetual law under which man was created as a moral and accountable being. This law, notwithstanding the Fall, remains as the revealed expression of the divine will, and as binding on the consciences of all men as a rule of life. It has its ground in the all-perfect moral nature of God. The principle on which all duty is founded finds its root in the unchangeable nature of God, of which his will is the outward expression. This law is absolutely immutable and permanent.

In its essential principles this law was at first revealed in the very constitution of our nature, and so much of it yet remains written on the heart and conscience as to make the heathen, who have not the Bible to guide them, inexcusable before God (Rom. 1:19, 20; 2:14, 15).

But God has been pleased to give a summary of this law in the ten commandments (*q.v.*)—Ex. 20:1–17—the first four of which contain our duty to God, and the other six our duty to man. The Scripture, however, taken as a whole, is our rule, our only rule, of faith and practice, and, as a revelation of God's will, is binding on the consciences of all Christian men.

Christ's great atoning work as our surety has fulfilled the law in its relation of a covenant of works, but as a rule of conduct and a standard of character that law remains unchangeable, unrelaxable, personally binding on all. (See LAW.)

Mor'decai, the son of Jair, of the tribe of Benjamin. It has been alleged that he was carried into captivity with Jeconiah, and hence that he must have been at least one hundred and twenty-nine years old in the twelfth year of Ahasuerus (Xerxes). But the words of Esther (2:19) do not necessarily lead to this conclusion. It was probably Kish of whom it is said (ver. 6) that he "had been carried away with the captivity."

He resided at Susa, the metropolis of Persia. He adopted his cousin Hadassah (Esther), an orphan child, whom he tenderly brought up as his own daughter. When she was brought into the king's harem and made queen in the room of the deposed queen Vashti, he was promoted to some office in the court of Ahasuerus, and was one of those who "sat in the king's gate" (Esther 2:41). While holding this office he discovered a plot of the eunuchs to put the king to death, which, by his vigilance, was defeated. His services to the king in this matter were duly recorded in the royal chronicles.

Haman (*q.v.*) the Agagite had been raised to the highest position at court. Mordecai refused to bow down before him; and Haman, being stung to the quick by the conduct of Mordecai, resolved to accomplish his death in a wholesale destruction of the Jewish exiles throughout the Persian empire (Esther 3:8–15). Tidings of this cruel scheme soon reached the ears of Mordecai, who communicated with queen Esther regarding it, and by her wise and bold intervention the scheme was frustrated. The Jews were delivered from destruction, Mordecai was raised to a high rank, and Haman was executed on the gallows he had by anticipation erected for Mordecai (6:2–11). In memory of the signal deliverance thus wrought for them, the Jews to this day celebrate the feast (9:26–32) of Purim (*q.v.*).

Mo'reh—*an archer, teacher; fruitful.* (1.) A Canaanite probably who inhabited the district south of Shechem, between Mount Ebal and Gerizim, and gave his name to the "plain" there (Gen. 12:6). Here at this "plain," or rather (R.V.) "oak," of Moreh, Abraham built his first altar in the land of Palestine; and here the Lord appeared unto him. He afterwards left this plain and moved southward, and pitched his tent between Bethel on the west and Hai on the east (12:7, 8).

Mo'reh, the Hill of, probably identical with "little Hermon," the modern *Jebel ed-Duhy,* or perhaps one of the lower spurs of this mountain. It is a gray ridge parallel to Gilboa on the north; and between the two lay the battle-field, the plain of Jezreel (*q.v.*), where Gideon overthrew the Midianites (Judg. 7:1–12).

Mo'resheth-gath—*possession of the wine-press*—the birthplace of the prophet Micah (1:14), who is called the "Morasthite" (Jer. 26:18). This place was probably a suburb of Gath.

Mori'ah—*the chosen of Jehovah.* Some contend that Mount Gerizim is meant, but most probably we are to regard this as one of the hills of Jerusalem. Here Solomon's temple was built, on the spot that had been the thrashing-floor of Ornan the Jebusite (2 Sam. 24:24, 25; 2 Chr. 3:1). It is usually included in Zion, to the north-east of which it lay, and from which it was separated by the Tyropœan valley. This was "the land of Moriah" to which Abraham went to offer up his son Isaac (Gen. 22:2). It has been supposed that the highest point of the temple hill, which is now covered by the Mohammedan *Kubbet es Sakhrah,* or "Dome of the Rock," is the actual site of Araunah's thrashing-floor. Here also, one thousand years after Abraham, David built an altar and offered sacrifices to God. (See JERUSALEM; NUMBERING THE PEOPLE.)

Mor'tar (Heb. *ḥomer*), *cement* of lime and sand (Gen. 11:3; Ex. 1:14); also potter's *clay* (Isa. 41:25; Nah. 3:14). Also Heb. *'âphâr,* usually rendered "dust," clay or mud used for cement in building (Lev. 14:42, 45).

Mor'tar, for pulverizing (Prov. 27:22) grain or other substances by means of a pestle instead of by a mill. Mortars were used in the wilderness for pounding the manna (Num. 11:8). It is commonly used in Palestine at the present day to pound wheat, from which the Arabs make a favourite dish called *kibby.*

Mose'ra—*a bond*—one of the stations of the Israelites in the wilderness (Deut. 10:6), at the foot of Mount Hor. (Comp. Num. 33:37, 38). It has been identified with *el-Tayibeh,* a small fountain at the bottom of the pass leading to the ascent of Mount Hor.

Mose'roth—*bonds*—one of the stations in the wilderness (Num. 33:30, 31), probably the same as Mosera.

Mos'es—*drawn* (or Egypt. *mesu,* "son;" hence Rameses, royal son). On the invitation of Pharaoh (Gen. 45:17–25), Jacob and his sons went down into Egypt. This immigration took place probably about 350 years before the birth of Moses. Some centuries before Joseph, Egypt had been conquered by a pastoral Semitic race from Asia, the Hyksos, who brought into cruel subjection the native Egyptians, who were an African race. Jacob and his retinue were accustomed to a shepherd's life, and on their arrival in Egypt were received with favour by the king, who assigned them the "best of the land"—the land of Goshen—to dwell in. The Hyksos or "Shepherd" king who thus showed favour to Joseph and his family was in all probability the Pharaoh Apepi (or Apophis).

Thus favoured, the Israelites began to "multiply exceedingly" (Gen. 47:27), and extended to the west and south. At length the supremacy of the Hyksos came to an end. The descendants of Jacob were allowed to retain their possession of Goshen undisturbed, but after the death of Joseph their position was not so favourable. The Egyptians began to despise them, and the period of their "affliction" (15:13) commenced. They were sorely oppressed. They continued, however, to increase in numbers, and "the land was filled with them" (Ex. 1:7). The native Egyptians regarded them with suspicion, so that they felt all the hardship of a struggle for existence.

In process of time "a king [probably

Seti I.] arose who knew not Joseph" (Ex. 1:8). (See PHARAOH.) The circumstances of the country were such that this king thought it necessary to weaken his Israelite subjects by oppressing them, and by degrees reducing their number. They were accordingly made public slaves, and were employed in connection with his numerous buildings, especially in the erection of store-cities, temples, and palaces. The children of Israel were made to serve with rigour. Their lives were made bitter with hard bondage, and "all their service, wherein they were made to serve, was with rigour" (Ex. 1:13, 14). But this cruel oppression had not the result expected of reducing their number. On the contrary, "the more the Egyptians afflicted them, the more they multiplied and grew" (Ex. 1:12).

The king next tried, through a compact secretly made with the guild of midwives, to bring about the destruction of all the Hebrew male children that might be born. But the king's wish was not rigorously enforced; the male children were spared by the midwives, so that "the people multiplied" more than ever. Thus baffled, the king issued a public proclamation calling on the people to put to death all the Hebrew male children by casting them into the river (Ex. 1:22). But neither by this edict was the king's purpose effected.

One of the Hebrew households into which this cruel edict of the king brought great alarm was that of Amram, of the family of the Kohathites (Ex. 6:16-20), who, with his wife Jochebed and two children, Miriam, a girl of perhaps fifteen years of age, and Aaron, a boy of three years, resided in or near Memphis, the capital city of that time. In this quiet home a male child was born (B.C. 1571). His mother concealed him in the house for three months from the knowledge of the civic authorities. But when the task of concealment became difficult, Jochebed contrived to bring her child under the notice of the daughter of the king by constructing for him an ark of bulrushes, which she laid among the flags which grew on the edge of the river at the spot where the princess was wont to come down and bathe. Her plan was successful.

The king's daughter "saw the child; and behold the child wept." The princess (see PHARAOH'S DAUGHTER [2]) sent Miriam, who was standing by, to fetch a nurse. She went and brought the mother of the child, to whom the princess said, "Take this child away, and nurse it for me, and I will give thee thy wages." Thus Jochebed's child, whom the princess called "Moses"—i.e., "Saved from the water" (Ex. 2:10)—was ultimately restored to her.

As soon as the natural time for weaning the child had come, he was transferred from the humble abode of his father to the royal palace, where he was brought up as the adopted son of the princess, his mother probably accompanying him and caring still for him. He grew up amid all the grandeur and excitement of the Egyptian court, maintaining, however, probably a constant fellowship with his mother, which was of the highest importance as to his religious belief and his interest in his "brethren." His education would doubtless be carefully attended to, and he would enjoy all the advantages of training both as to his body and his mind. He at length became "learned in all the wisdom of the Egyptians" (Acts 7:22). Egypt had then two chief seats of learning, or universities, at one of which, probably that of Heliopolis, his education was completed. Moses, being now about twenty years of age, spent over twenty more before he came into prominence in Bible history. These twenty years were probably spent in military service. There is a tradition recorded by Josephus that he took a lead in the war which was then waged between Egypt and Ethiopia, in which he gained renown as a skilful general, and became "mighty in deeds" (Acts 7:22).

After the termination of the war in Ethiopia, Moses returned to the Egyptian court, where he might reasonably have expected to be loaded with honours and enriched with wealth. But "beneath the smooth current of his life hitherto—a life of alternate luxury at the court and comparative hardness in the camp and in the discharge of his military duties—there had lurked from childhood to youth, and from youth to manhood, a secret discontent, perhaps a secret ambition. Moses, amid all his Egyptian surroundings, had never forgotten, had never wished to forget, that he was a Hebrew." He now resolved to make himself acquainted with the condition of his countrymen, and "went out unto his brethren, and looked upon their burdens" (Ex. 2 : 11). This tour of inspection revealed to him the cruel oppression and bondage under which they everywhere groaned, and could not fail to press on him the serious consideration of his duty regarding them. The time had arrived for his making common cause with them, that he might thereby help to break their yoke of bondage. He made his choice accordingly (Heb. 11 : 25–27), assured that God would bless his resolution for the welfare of his people. He now left the palace of the king and took up his abode, probably in his father's house, as one of the Hebrew people who had for forty years been suffering cruel wrong at the hands of the Egyptians.

He could not remain indifferent to the state of things around him, and going out one day among the people, his indignation was roused against an Egyptian who was maltreating a Hebrew. He rashly lifted up his hand and slew the Egyptian, and hid his body in the sand. Next day he went out again and found two Hebrews striving together. He speedily found that the deed of the previous day was known. It reached the ears of Pharaoh (the "great Rameses," Rameses II.), who "sought to slay Moses" (Ex. 2 : 15). Moved by fear, Moses fled from Egypt, and betook himself to the land of Midian, the southern part of the peninsula of Sinai, probably by much the same route as that by which, forty years afterwards, he led the Israelites to Sinai. He was providentially led to find a new home with the family of Reuel, where he remained for forty years (Acts 7 : 30), under training unconsciously for his great life's work.

Suddenly the angel of the Lord appeared to him in the burning bush (Ex. 3), and commissioned him to go down to Egypt and "bring forth the children of Israel" out of bondage. He was at first unwilling to go, but at length he was obedient to the heavenly vision, and left the land of Midian (4 : 18–26). On the way he was met by Aaron (q.v.) and the elders of Israel (27–31). He and Aaron had a hard task before them; but the Lord was with them (ch. 7–12), and the ransomed host went forth in triumph. (See EXODUS.) After an eventful journey to and fro in the wilderness, we see them at length encamped in the plains of Moab, ready to cross over the Jordan into the Promised Land. There Moses addresses the assembled elders (Deut. 1 : 1–4 : 40; 5 : 1–26 : 19; 27 : 11–30 : 20), and gives the people his last counsels, and then rehearses the great song (Deut. 32), clothing in fitting words the deep emotions of his heart at such a time, and in review of such a marvellous history as that in which he had acted so conspicuous a part. Then, after blessing the tribes (33), he ascends to "the mountain of Nebo (q.v.), to the top of Pisgah, that is over against Jericho" (34 : 1), and from thence he surveys the land. "Jehovah shewed him all the land of Gilead, unto Dan, and all Naphtali, and the land of Ephraim, and Manasseh, and all the land of Judah, unto the utmost sea, and the south, and the plain of the valley of Jericho, the city of palm trees, unto Zoar" (Deut. 34 : 2–3), the magnificent inheritance of the tribes of whom he had been so long the leader; and there he died, being one hundred and twenty years old, according to the word of the Lord, and was buried by the Lord "in a valley in the land of Moab, over against Beth-peor" (34 : 6). The people mourned for him during thirty days.

Thus died "Moses the man of God"(Deut. 33 : 1; Josh. 14 : 6). He was distinguished for his meekness and patience and firmness, and "he endured as seeing him who is invisible." "There arose not a prophet since in Israel like unto Moses, whom the Lord knew face to face, in all the signs and the wonders, which the Lord sent him to do in the land of Egypt to Pharaoh, and to all his servants, and to all his land, and in all that mighty hand, and in all the great terror which Moses shewed in the sight of all Israel" (Deut. 34 : 10–12).

The name of Moses occurs frequently in the Psalms and Prophets as the chief of the prophets.

In the New Testament he is referred to as the representative of the law and as a type of Christ (John 1:17; 2 Cor. 3:13–18; Heb. 3:5, 6). Moses is the only character in the Old Testament to whom Christ likens himself (John 5:46; comp. Deut. 18:15, 18, 19; Acts 7:37). In Heb. 3: 1–19 this likeness to Moses is set forth in various particulars.

In Jude 9 mention is made of a contention between Michael and the devil about the body of Moses. This dispute is supposed to have had reference to the concealment of the body of Moses so as to prevent idolatry.

Mote (Gr. *karphos*, something dry, hence a particle of wood or chaff, etc.). A slight moral defect is likened to a mote (Matt. 7:3–5; Luke 6:41, 42).

Moth. Heb. *'âsh*, from a root meaning "to fall away," as moth-eaten garments fall to pieces (Job 4:19; 13:28; Isa. 50:9; 51:6, 8; Hos. 5:12).

Gr. *sês*, thus rendered in Matt. 6:19, 20; Luke 12:33. Allusion is thus made to the destruction of clothing by the larvæ of the clothes-moth. This is the only lepidopterous insect referred to in Scripture.

Moul'dy. Of the Gibeonites it is said that "all the bread of their provision was dry and mouldy" (Josh. 9:5, 12). The Hebrew word here rendered "mouldy" (*nikuddîm*) is rendered "cracknels" in 1 Kings 14:3, and denotes a kind of crisp cake. The meaning is that the bread of the Gibeonites had become dry and hard—hard as biscuits—and thus was an evidence of the length of the journey they had travelled.

Mount. Palestine is a hilly country (Deut. 3:25; 11:11; Ezek. 34:13). *West* of Jordan the mountains stretch from Lebanon far down into Galilee, terminating in Carmel. The isolated peak of Tabor rises from the elevated plain of Esdraelon, which, in the south, is shut in by hills spreading over the greater part of Samaria. The mountains of Western and Middle Palestine do not extend to the sea, but gently slope into plains, and toward the Jordan fall down into the Ghor.

East of the Jordan the Anti-Lebanon, stretching south, terminates in the hilly district called *Jebel Heish*, which reaches down to the Sea of Gennesareth. South of the river Hieromax there is again a succession of hills, which are traversed by wâdies running toward the Jordan. These gradually descend to a level at the river Arnon, which was the boundary of the ancient trans-Jordanic territory toward the south.

The composition of the Palestinian hills is limestone, with occasional strata of chalk, and hence the numerous caves, some of large extent, found there.

Mount of the Amalekites, a place near Pirathon (*q.v.*), in the tribe of Ephraim (Judg. 12:15).

Mount of the Amorites, the range of hills which rises abruptly in the wilderness of *et-Tîh* ("the wandering"), mentioned Deut. 1:19, 20—"that great and terrible wilderness."

Mount of the congregation, only in Isa. 14:13, a mythic mountain of the Babylonians, regarded by them as the seat of the gods. It was situated in the far north, and in Babylonian inscriptions is described as a mountain called Im-Kharasak, "the mighty mountain of Bel, whose head reaches heaven, whose root is the holy deep." In their geography they are said to have identified it with mount Elwend, near Ecbatana.

Mount of the valley (Josh. 13:19), a district in the east of Jordan, in the territory of Reuben. The "valley" here was probably the Ghor or valley of the Jordan, and hence the "mount" would be the hilly region in the north end of the Dead Sea. (See ZARETH-SHAHAR.)

Mount of corruption (2 Kings 23:13; Vulg., "mount of offence"), the name given to a part of the Mount of Olives, so called because idol temples were there erected in the time of Solomon—temples to the Zidonian Ashtoreth and to the "abominations" of Moab and Ammon.

Mount of beatitudes. See SERMON.

Mourn. Frequent references are found

in Scripture to—(1.) *Mourning for the dead.*
Abraham mourned for Sarah (Gen. 23 : 2);
Jacob for Joseph (37 : 34, 35); the Egyptians for Jacob (50 : 3–10); Israel for Aaron
(Num. 20 : 29), for Moses (Deut. 34 : 8), and
for Samuel (1 Sam. 25 : 1); David for Abner
(2 Sam. 3 : 31, 35); Mary and Martha for
Lazarus (John 11); devout men for Stephen (Acts 8 : 2), etc.

(2.) *For calamities*—Job (1 : 20, 21; 2 : 8);
Israel (Ex. 33 : 4); the Ninevites (Jonah 3 :
5); Israel, when defeated by Benjamin
(Judg. 20 : 26), etc.

(3.) *Penitential mourning*—by the Israelites on the day of atonement (Lev. 23 : 27;
Acts 27 : 9); under Samuel's ministry (1
Sam. 7 : 6); predicted in Zechariah (Zech.
12 : 10, 11); in many of the psalms (51,
etc.).

Mourning was expressed—(1) by weeping
(Gen. 35 : 8, marg.; Luke 7 : 38, etc.); (2) by
loud lamentation (Ruth 1 : 9; 1 Sam. 6 : 19;
2 Sam. 3 : 31); (3) by the disfigurement of
the person, as rending the clothes (Gen.
37 : 29, 34; Matt. 26 : 65), wearing sackcloth (Gen. 37 : 34; Ps. 35 : 13), sprinkling
dust or ashes on the person (2 Sam. 13 : 19;
Jer. 6 : 26; Job 2 : 12), shaving the head
and plucking out the hair of the head or
beard (Lev. 10 : 6; 2 Sam. 19 : 24; Job 1 :
20), neglect of the person or the removal
of ornaments (Deut. 21 : 12, 13; Ex. 33 : 4;
2 Sam. 14 : 2; Matt. 6 : 16, 17), fasting (2
Sam. 1 : 12), covering the upper lip (Lev.
13 : 45; 2 Sam. 15 : 20), cutting the flesh
(Jer. 16 : 6, 7), and sitting in silence (Judg.
20 : 26; 2 Sam. 12 : 16; 13 : 31; Job 1 : 20).

In the later times we find a class of
mourners who could be hired to give by
their loud lamentation the external
tokens of sorrow (2 Chr. 35 : 25; Jer. 9 :
17; Matt. 9 : 23).

The period of mourning for the dead
varied. For Jacob it was seventy days
(Gen. 50 : 3); for Aaron (Num. 20 : 29)
and Moses (Deut. 34 : 8) thirty days;
and for Saul only seven days (1 Sam.
31 : 13). In 2 Sam. 3 : 31–35, we have a
description of the great mourning for
the death of Abner.

Mouse (Heb. *'akhbâr,* "swift digger"),
properly the dormouse, the field-mouse (1
Sam. 6 : 4). In Lev. 11 : 29, Isa. 66 : 17
this word is used generically, and includes
the jerboa (*Mus jaculus*), rat, hamster
(*Cricetus*), which, though declared to be
unclean animals, were eaten by the Arabs,
and are still eaten by the Bedouins. It
is said that no fewer than twenty-three
species of this group ('*akhbâr* = Arab. *ferâh*)
of animals inhabit Palestine. God "laid
waste" the people of Ashdod by the terrible visitation of field-mice, which are like
locusts in their destructive effects (1 Sam.
6 : 4,11,18). Herodotus, the Greek historian,
accounts for the destruction of the army of
Sennacherib (2 Kings 19 : 35) by saying that
in the night thousands of mice invaded the
camp and gnawed through the bow-strings,
quivers, and shields, and thus left the Assyrians helpless. (See SENNACHERIB.)

Mow'ing (Heb. *gez*), rendered in Ps. 72 :
6 "mown grass." The expression "king's
mowings" (Amos 7 : 1) refers to some royal
right of early pasturage, the first crop of
grass for the cavalry (comp. 1 Kings 18 : 5).

Mo'za—*a going forth.* (1.) One of the
sons of Caleb (1 Chr. 2 : 46).

(2.) The son of Zimri, of the posterity
of Saul (1 Chr. 8 : 36, 37; 9 : 42, 43).

Mo'zah—*an issuing of water*—a city of
Benjamin (Josh. 18 : 26).

Muff'lers (Isa. 3 : 19)—*veils*—light and
tremulous. Margin, "spangled ornaments."

Mul'berry—Heb. *bâkâh,* "to weep;" rendered "Baca" (R.V., "weeping") in Ps.
84 : 6. The plural form of the Hebrew
bekâîm is rendered "mulberry trees" in 2
Sam. 5 : 23, 24 and 1 Chr. 14 : 14, 15. The
tree here alluded to was probably the
aspen or trembling poplar. "We know
with certainty that the black poplar, the
aspen, and the Lombardy poplar grew in
Palestine. The aspen, whose long leaf-
stalks cause the leaves to tremble with
every breath of wind, unites with the willow and the oak to overshadow the water-
courses of the Lebanon, and with the
oleander and the acacia to adorn the ravines of Southern Palestine" (Kitto). By
"the sound of a going in the tops of the
mulberry trees" we are to understand a
rustling among the trees like the marching
of an army. This was the signal that the

Lord himself would lead forth David's army to victory. (See SYCAMINE.)

THE ASPEN, OR TREMBLING POPLAR.

Mule (Heb. *pĕrĕd*), so called from the *quick* step of the animal or its power of *carrying* loads. It is not probable that the Hebrews bred mules, as this was strictly forbidden in the law (Lev. 19 : 19), although their use was not forbidden. We find them in common use even by kings and nobles (2 Sam. 18 : 9; 1 Kings 1 : 33; 2 Kings 5 : 17; Ps. 32 : 9). They are not mentioned, however, till the time of David, for the word rendered "mules" (R.V. correctly, "hot springs") in Gen. 36 : 24 (*yêmîm*) properly denotes the warm springs of Callirhoë, on the eastern shore of the Dead Sea. In David's reign they became very common (2 Sam. 13 : 29; 1 Kings 10 : 25).

Mules are not mentioned in the New Testament. Perhaps they had by that time ceased to be used in Palestine.

Mur'der. Wilful murder was distinguished from accidental homicide, and was invariably visited with capital punishment (Num. 35 : 16, 18, 21, 31; Lev. 24 : 17). This law in its principle is founded on the fact of man's having been made in the likeness of God (Gen. 9 : 5, 6; John 8 : 44; 1 John 3 : 12, 15). The Mosaic law prohibited any compensation for murder or the reprieve of the murderer (Ex. 21 : 12, 14; Deut. 19 : 11, 13; 2 Sam. 17 : 25; 20 : 10). Two witnesses were required in any capital case (Num. 35 : 19-30; Deut. 17 : 6-12). If the murderer could not be discovered, the city nearest the scene of the murder was required to make expiation for the crime committed (Deut. 21 : 1-9). These offences also were to be punished with death—(1) striking a parent; (2) cursing a parent; (3) kidnapping (Ex. 21 : 15-17; Deut. 27 : 16).

Mur'muring, of the Hebrews in the wilderness, called forth the displeasure of God, which was only averted by the earnest prayer of Moses (Num. 11 : 33, 34; 12; 14 : 27, 30, 31; 16 : 3; 21 : 4-6; Ps. 106 : 25). Forbidden by Paul (1 Cor. 10 : 10).

Mur'rain—Heb. *dĕbĕr*, "destruction," a "great mortality "—the fifth plague that fell upon the Egyptians (Ex. 9 : 3). It was some distemper that resulted in the sudden and widespread death of the cattle. It was confined to the cattle of the Egyptians that were in the field (9 : 6).

Mu'shi—*receding*—the second of the two sons of Merari (Ex. 6 : 19; Num. 3 : 20). His sons were called *Mushites* (Num. 3 : 33; 26 : 58).

Mu'sic. Jubal was the inventor of musical instruments (Gen. 4 : 21). The Hebrews were much given to the cultivation of music. Their whole history and literature afford abundant evidence of this.

After the Deluge, the first mention of music is in the account of Laban's interview with Jacob (Gen. 31 : 27). After their triumphal passage of the Red Sea, Moses and the children of Israel sang their song of deliverance (Ex. 15).

But the period of Samuel, David, and Solomon was the golden age of Hebrew music, as it was of Hebrew poetry. Music was now for the first time systematically cultivated. It was an essential part of training in the schools of the prophets (1 Sam. 10 : 5; 19 : 19-24; 2 Kings 3 : 15; 1 Chr. 25 : 6). There now arose also a class of professional singers (2 Sam. 19 : 35; Eccl. 2 : 8). The temple, however, was the great school of music. In the conducting of its services large bands of trained singers and players on instruments were constantly employed (2 Sam. 6:5; 1 Chr. 15; 16; 23: 5; 25:1-6).

In private life also music seems to have held an important place among the Hebrews (Eccl. 2:8; Amos 6:4-6; Isa. 5:11, 12; 24:8, 9; Ps. 137; Jer. 48:33; Luke 15:25).

Mu'sic, Instrumental. Among instruments of music used by the Hebrews a principal place is given to *stringed instruments.* These were—(1.) The *kinnôr,* the "harp." (2.) The *nĕbĕl,* "a skin bottle," rendered "psaltery." (3.) The *sabbekâ,* or "sackbut," a lute or lyre. (4.) The *gittith,* occurring in the title of Ps. 8; 81; 84. (5.)

ANCIENT MUSICAL INSTRUMENTS.

Minnim (Ps. 150:4), rendered "stringed instruments;" in Ps. 45:8, in the form *minni,* probably the apocopated (*i.e.,* shortened) plural, rendered, Authorized Version, "whereby," and in the Revised Version "stringed instruments." (6.) *Machalath,* in the titles of Ps. 53 and 88; supposed to be a kind of lute or guitar.

Of *wind instruments* mention is made of —(1.) The *'ûgab* (Gen. 4:21; Job 21:12; 30:31), probably the so-called Pan's pipes or *syrinx.* (2.) The *qĕrĕn* or "horn" (Josh. 6:5; 1 Chr. 25:5). (3.) The *shophâr,* rendered "trumpet" (Josh. 6:4, 6, 8). The word means "bright," and may have been so called from the clear, shrill sound it emitted. It was often used (Ex. 19:13; Num. 10:10; Judg. 7:16, 18; 1 Sam. 13:3). (4.) The *hatsotsĕrâh,* or straight

trumpet (Ps. 98:6; Num. 10:1-10). This name is supposed by some to be an onomatopoetic word, intended to imitate the pulse-like sound of the trumpet, like the Latin *taratantara.* Some have identified it with the modern *trombone.* (5.) The *halil, i.e.,* "bored through," a flute or pipe (1 Sam. 10:5; 1 Kings 1:40; Isa. 5:12; Jer. 48:36) which is still used in Palestine. (6.) The *sumponyâh,* rendered "dulcimer" (Dan. 3:5), probably a sort of bagpipe. (7.) The *maskrokith'a* (Dan. 3:5), rendered "flute," but its precise nature is unknown.

Of *instruments of percussion* mention is made of—(1.) The *tôph,* an instrument of the drum kind, rendered "timbrel" (Ex. 15:20; Job 21:12; Ps. 68:25); also "tabret" (Gen. 31:27; Isa. 24:8; 1 Sam. 10: 5). (2.) The *paamôn,* the "bells" on the robe of the high priest (Ex. 28: 33; 39:25). (3.) The *tsĕltselim,* "cymbals" (2 Sam. 6:5; Ps. 150:5), which are struck together and produce a loud, clanging sound. *Metsillôth,* "bells" on horses and camels for ornament, and *metsiltayim,* "cymbals" (1 Chr. 13:8; Ezra 3:10, etc.). These words are all derived from the same root, *tsalal,* meaning "to tinkle." (4.) The *menaan'im,* used only in 2 Sam. 6:5, rendered "cornets" (R.V., "castanets"); in the Vulgate, "sistra," an instrument of agitation. (5.) The *shalishim,* mentioned only in 1 Sam. 18:6, rendered "instruments of music" (marg. of R.V., "triangles or three-stringed instruments").

The words in Eccl. 2:8, "musical instruments, and that of all sorts," Authorized Version, are in the Revised Version "concubines very many."

Musi'cian, Chief (Heb. *menatstsêah*), the precentor of the Levitical choir or orchestra in the temple, mentioned in the titles of fifty-five psalms, and in Hab. 3:19, Revised Version. The first who held this office was Jeduthun (1 Chr. 16:41), and the office appears to have been hereditary. Heman and Asaph were his two colleagues (2 Chr. 35:15).

Mus'tard, a plant of the genus *sinapis,* a pod-bearing, shrub-like plant, growing wild, and also cultivated in gardens. The little round seeds were an emblem of any small insignificant object. It is not mentioned in the Old Testament; and in each of the three instances of its occurrence in the New Testament (Matt. 13:31, 32; Mark 4:31, 32; Luke 13:18, 19) it is spoken of only with reference to the smallness of its seed. The common mustard of Palestine is the *Sinapis nigra*. This garden herb sometimes grows to a considerable height, so as to be spoken of as "a tree," as compared with garden herbs.

Muth-lab′ben, occurring only in the title of Psalm 9. Some interpret the words as meaning "on the death of Labben," some unknown person. Others render the word, "on the death of the son;" *i.e.*, of Absalom (2 Sam. 18:33). Others again have taken the word as the name of a musical instrument, or as the name of an air to which the psalm was sung.

Muz′zle. Grain in the East is usually thrashed by the sheaves being spread out on a floor, over which oxen and cattle are driven to and fro, till the grain is trodden out. Moses ordained that the ox was not to be muzzled while thrashing. It was to be allowed to eat both the grain and the straw (Deut. 25:4). (See AGRICULTURE.)

My′ra, one of the chief towns of Lycia, in Asia Minor, about 2½ miles from the coast (Acts 27:5). Here Paul removed from the Adramyttian ship in which he had sailed from Cæsarea, and entered into the Alexandrian ship, which was afterwards wrecked at Melita (27:39–44).

Myrrh—Heb. *môr.* (1.) First mentioned as a principal ingredient in the holy anointing oil (Ex. 30:23). It formed part of the gifts brought by the wise men from the east, who came to worship the infant Jesus (Matt. 2:11). It was used in embalming (John 19:39), also as a perfume (Esther 2:12; Ps. 45:8; Prov. 7:17). It was a custom of the Jews to give those who were condemned to death by crucifixion "wine mingled with myrrh" to produce insensibility. This drugged wine was probably partaken of by the two malefactors, but when the Roman soldiers pressed it

upon Jesus "he received it not" (Mark 15:23). (See GALL.)

This was the gum or viscid white liquid which flows from a tree resembling the acacia, found in Africa and Arabia, the *Balsamodendron myrrha* of botanists. The

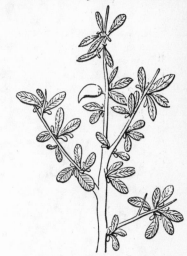

BALSAMODENDRON MYRRHA.

"bundle of myrrh" in Cant. 1:13 is rather a "bag" of myrrh or a scent-bag.

(2.) Another word *lôt* is also translated

LOT OR LADANUM.

"myrrh" (Gen. 37:25; 43:11; R.V., marg., "or *ladanum*"). What was meant

by this word is uncertain. It has been thought to be the chestnut, mastich, stacte, balsam, turpentine, pistachio nut, or the lotus. It is probably correctly rendered by the Latin word *ladanum*, the Arabic *ladan*, an aromatic juice of a shrub called the *Cistus* or rock rose, which has the same qualities, though in a slight degree, of opium, whence a decoction of opium is called laudanum. This plant was indigenous to Syria and Arabia.

Myrtle (Isa. 41:19; Neh. 8:15; Zech. 1:8), Hebrew *hadâs*, known in the East

MYRTLE.

by the name *as*, the *Myrtus communis* of the botanist. "Although no myrtles are now found on the mount [of Olives], ex-cepting in the gardens, yet they still exist in many of the glens about Jerusalem, where we have often seen its dark shining leaves and white flowers. There are many near Bethlehem and about Hebron, especially near Dewir Dan, the ancient Debir. It also sheds its fragrance on the sides of Carmel and of Tabor, and fringes the clefts of the Leontes in its course through Galilee. We meet with it all through Central Palestine" (Tristram).

Mys'ia, a province in the north-west of Asia Minor. On his first voyage to Europe (Acts 16:7, 8) Paul passed through this province and embarked at its chief port Troas.

Mys'tery, the calling of the Gentiles into the Christian Church, so designated (Eph. 1:9, 10; 3:8–11; Col. 1:25–27); a truth undiscoverable except by revelation, long hid, now made manifest. The resurrection of the dead (1 Cor. 15:51), and other doctrines which need to be explained but which cannot be fully understood by finite intelligence (Matt. 13:11; Rom. 11:25; 1 Cor. 13:2); the union between Christ and his people symbolized by the marriage union (Eph. 5:31, 32; comp. 6:19); the seven stars and the seven candlesticks (Rev. 1:20); and the woman clothed in scarlet (17:7), are also in this sense mysteries. The anti-Christian power working in his day is called by the apostle (2 Thess. 2:7) the "mystery of iniquity."

N

Na'am—*pleasantness*—one of the three sons of Caleb, the son of Jephunneh (1 Chr. 4:15).

Na'amah — *the beautiful.* (1.) The daughter of Lamech and Zillah (Gen. 4:22).

(2.) The daughter of the king of Ammon, one of the wives of Solomon, the only one who appears to have borne him a son, *viz.,* Rehoboam (1 Kings 14:21, 31).

(3.) A city in the plain of Judah (Josh. 15:41), supposed by some to be identified with *Na'aneh,* some 5 miles south-east of Makkedah.

Na'aman—*pleasantness*—a Syrian, the commander of the armies of Benhadad II. in the time of Joram, king of Israel. He was afflicted with leprosy; and when the little Hebrew slave-girl that waited on his wife told her of a prophet in Samaria who could cure her master, he obtained a letter from Benhadad and proceeded with it to Joram. The king of Israel suspected in this some evil design against him, and rent his clothes. Elisha the prophet hearing of this, sent for Naaman, and the strange interview which took place is recorded in 2 Kings 5. The narrative contains all that is known of the Syrian commander. He was cured of his leprosy by dipping himself seven times in the Jordan, according to the word of Elisha. His cure is alluded to by our Lord (Luke 4 : 27).

Na'amathite, the designation of Zophar, one of Job's three friends (Job 2 : 11; 11 : 1), so called from some place in Arabia, called Naamah probably.

Na'arah—*a girl*—the second of Ashur's two wives, of the tribe of Judah (1 Chr. 4 : 5, 6).

Na'arai—*youthful*—a military chief in David's army (1 Chr. 11 : 37), called also Paarai (2 Sam. 23 : 35).

Na'aran—*boyish, juvenile*—a town in Ephraim between Bethel and Jericho (1 Chr. 7 : 28).

Na'arath—*girl*—a town on the boundary between Ephraim and Benjamin (Josh. 16 : 7), not far probably from Jericho, to the north (1 Chr. 7 : 28).

Na'bal—*foolish*—a descendant of Caleb who dwelt at Maon (1 Sam. 25), the modern *Main*, 7 miles south-east of Hebron. He was "very great, and he had 3,000 sheep and 1,000 goats......but the man was churlish and evil in his doings." During his wanderings David came into that district, and hearing that Nabal was about to shear his sheep, he sent ten of his young men to ask "whatsoever cometh unto thy hand for thy servants." Nabal insultingly resented the demand, saying, "Who is David, and who is the son of Jesse?" (1 Sam. 25 : 10, 11). One of the shepherds that stood by and saw the reception David's messengers had met with, informed Abigail, Nabal's wife, who at once realized the danger that threatened her household. She forthwith proceeded to the camp of David, bringing with her ample stores of provisions (25 : 18). She so courteously and persuasively pled her cause that David's anger was appeased, and he said to her, "Blessed be the Lord God of Israel which sent thee this day to meet me."

On her return she found her husband incapable from drunkenness of understanding the state of matters, and not till the following day did she explain to him what had happened. He was stunned by a sense of the danger to which his conduct had exposed him. "His heart within him died, and he became a stone," and about ten days after "the Lord smote Nabal that he died" (1 Sam. 25 : 37, 38).

Not long after David married Abigail (*q.v.*).

Na'both—*fruits*—"the Jezreelite," was the owner of a portion of ground on the eastern slope of the hill of Jezreel (2 Kings 9 : 25, 26). This small "plat of ground" seems to have been all he possessed. It was a vineyard, and lay "hard by the palace of Ahab" (1 Kings 21 : 1, 2), who greatly coveted it. Naboth, however, refused on any terms to part with it to the king. He had inherited it from his fathers, and no Israelite could lawfully sell his property (Lev. 25 : 23). Jezebel, Ahab's wife, was grievously offended at Naboth's refusal to part with his vineyard. By a crafty and cruel plot she compassed his death. His sons also shared his fate (2 Kings 9 : 26; 1 Kings 21 : 19). She then came to Ahab and said, "Arise, take possession of the vineyard; for Naboth is not alive, but dead." Ahab arose and went forth into the garden which had so treacherously and cruelly been acquired, seemingly enjoying his new possession, when, lo, Elijah suddenly appeared before him and pronounced against him a fearful doom (1 Kings 21 : 17-24). Jehu and Bidcar were with Ahab at this time, and so deeply were the words of Elijah imprinted on Jehu's memory that many years afterwards he refers to them (2 Kings 9 : 26), and he was the chief instrument in inflicting this sentence on Ahab and Jezebel and all their house (9 : 30-37). The house of Ahab was extinguished by him. Not one of all his great men and his kinsfolk and his priests did Jehu spare (10 : 11).

Ahab humbled himself at Elijah's words (1 Kings 21 : 28, 29), and therefore the prophecy was fulfilled not in his fate but in that of his son Joram (2 Kings 9 : 25).

The history of Naboth, compared with

that of Ahab and Jezebel, furnishes a remarkable illustration of the law of a retributive providence — a law which runs through all history (comp. Ps. 109:17, 18).

Na'chon—*prepared*—the owner of a thrashing-floor near which Uzzah was slain (2 Sam. 6:6); called also Chidon (1 Chr. 13:9).

Na'dab—*liberal, generous.* (1.) The eldest of Aaron's four sons (Ex. 6:23; Num. 3:2). He with his brothers and their father were consecrated as priests of Jehovah (Ex. 28:1). He afterwards perished with Abihu for the sin of offering strange fire on the altar of burnt-offering (Lev. 10:1, 2; Num. 3:4; 26:60).

(2.) The son and successor of Jeroboam, the king of Israel (1 Kings 14:20). While engaged with all Israel in laying siege to Gibbethon, a town of southern Dan (Josh. 19:44), a conspiracy broke out in his army, and he was slain by Baasha (1 Kings 15: 25–28), after a reign of two years (B.C. 955– 953). The assassination of Nadab was followed by that of his whole house, and thus this great Ephraimite family became extinct (2 Chr. 34:5).

(3.) One of the sons of Shammai in the tribe of Judah (1 Chr. 2:28, 30).

Nag'ge—*illuminating*—one of the ancestors of Christ in the maternal line (Luke 3:25).

Naha'liel—*possession*, or *valley of God* —one of the encampments of the Israelites in the wilderness (Num. 21:19), on the confines of Moab. This is identified with the ravine of the *Zerka M'ain*, the ancient Callirhoë, the hot springs on the east of the Jordan, not far from the Dead Sea.

Na'hallal—*pasture*—a city in Zebulun on the border of Issachar (Josh. 19:15), the same as Nahalol (Judg. 1:30). It was given to the Levites. It has been by some identified with *Malûl* in the plain of Esdraelon, 4 miles from Nazareth.

Na'harai—*snorer*—a Berothite, one of David's heroes, and armour-bearer of Joab (1 Chr. 11:39).

Na'hash—*serpent.* (1.) King of the Ammonites in the time of Saul. The inhabitants of Jabesh-Gilead having been exposed to great danger from Nahash, sent messengers

to Gibeah to inform Saul of their extremity. He promptly responded to the call, and gathering together an army he marched against Nahash. "And it came to pass that they which remained were scattered, so that two of them [the Ammonites] were not left together" (1 Sam. 11:1–11).

(2.) Another king of the Ammonites of the same name is mentioned, who "showed kindness to David during his wanderings" (2 Sam. 10:2). On his death David sent an embassy of sympathy to Hanun, his son and successor, at Rabbah Ammon, his capital. The grievous insult which was put upon these ambassadors led to a war against the Ammonites, who, with their allies the Syrians, were completely routed in a battle fought at "the entering in of the gate," probably of Medeba (2 Sam. 10:6–14). Again Hadarezer rallied the Syrian host, which was totally destroyed by the Israelite army under Joab in a decisive battle fought at Helam (2 Sam. 10:17), near to Hamath (1 Chr. 18:3). "So the Syrians feared to help the children of Ammon any more" (2 Sam. 10:19).

(3.) The father of Amasa, who was commander-in-chief of Absalom's army (2 Sam. 17:25). Jesse's wife had apparently been first married to this man, to whom she bore Abigail and Zeruiah, who were thus David's sisters, but only on the mother's side (1 Chr. 2:16).

Na'hath—*rest.* (1.) One of the four sons of Reuel, the son of Esau (Gen. 36: 13, 17).

(2.) A Kohathite Levite (1 Chr. 6:26).

(3.) A Levite, one of the overseers of the sacred offerings of the temple (2 Chr. 31:13).

Nah'bi—*hidden*—one of the twelve spies sent out to explore the land of Canaan (Num. 13:14).

Na'hor—*snorting.* (1.) The father of Terah, who was the father of Abraham (Gen. 11:22–25; Luke 3:34).

(2.) A son of Terah, and elder brother of Abraham (Gen. 11:26, 27; Josh. 24:2, R.V.). He married Milcah, the daughter of his brother Haran, and remained in the land of his nativity on the east of the river Euphrates at Haran (Gen. 11:27–32). A correspondence was maintained between the family of Abraham in Canaan and the relatives in the old ancestral home at Haran till the time of Jacob. When Jacob fled from Haran all intercourse between the two branches of the family came to an end (Gen. 31 : 46). His grand-daughter Rebekah became Isaac's wife (24 : 67).

Nah'shon—*sorcerer*—the son of Aminadab, and prince of the children of Judah at the time of the first numbering of the tribes in the wilderness (Ex. 6 : 23). His sister Elisheba was the wife of Aaron. He died in the wilderness (Num. 26 : 64, 65). His name occurs in the Greek form Naasson in the genealogy of Christ (Matt. 1 : 4; Luke 3 : 32).

Na'hum—*consolation*—the seventh of the so-called minor prophets, an Elkoshite. All we know of him is recorded in the book of his prophecies. He was probably a native of Galilee, and after the deportation of the ten tribes took up his residence in Jerusalem. Others think that Elkosh was the name of a place on the east bank of the Tigris, and that Nahum dwelt there.

Na'hum, Book of. Nahum prophesied, according to some, in the beginning of the reign of Ahaz (B.C. 743). Others, however, think that his prophecies are to be referred to the latter half of the reign of Hezekiah (about B.C. 709). This is the more probable opinion, internal evidences leading to that conclusion. Probably the book was written in Jerusalem (soon after B.C. 709), where he witnessed the invasion of Sennacherib and the destruction of his host (2 Kings 19 : 35).

The *subject* of this prophecy is the approaching complete and final destruction of Nineveh, the capital of the great and at that time flourishing Assyrian empire. Assur-bani-pal was at the height of his glory. Nineveh was a city of vast extent, and was then the centre of the civilization and commerce of the world—a "bloody city all full of lies and robbery" (Nah. 3 : 1), for it had robbed and plundered all the neighbouring nations. It was strongly fortified on every side, bidding defiance to every enemy; yet it was to be utterly destroyed as a punishment for the great wickedness of its inhabitants.

Jonah had already uttered his message of warning, and Nahum was followed by Zephaniah, who also predicted (Zeph. 2 : 4-15) the destruction of the city—predictions which were remarkably fulfilled (B.C. 625) when Nineveh was destroyed apparently by fire, and the Assyrian empire came to an end, an event which changed the face of Asia. (See NINEVEH.)

Nail, for fastening. (1.) Hebrew *yâthêd*, "piercing," a peg or nail of any material (Ezek. 15 : 3), more especially a tent-peg (Ex. 27 : 19; 35 : 18; 38 : 20), with one of which Jael (*q.v.*) pierced the temples of Sisera (Judg. 4 : 21, 22). This word is also used metaphorically (Zech. 10 : 4) for a prince or counsellor, just as "the battle-bow" represents a warrior.

(2.) *Masmêr*, a "point," the usual word for a nail. The words of the wise are compared to "nails fastened by the masters of assemblies" (Eccl. 12 : 11, A.V.). The Revised Version reads, "as nails well fastened are the words of the masters," etc. Others (as Plumptre) read, "as nails fastened are the masters of assemblies" (comp. Isa. 22 : 23; Ezra 9 : 8).

David prepared nails for the temple (1 Chr. 22 : 3; 2 Chr. 3 : 9). The nails by which our Lord was fixed to the cross are mentioned (John 20 : 25; Col. 2 : 14).

Nail, of the finger (Heb. *tsippôrĕn*, "scraping"). To "pare the nails" is in Deut. 21 : 12 (marg., "make," or "dress," or "suffer to grow") one of the signs of purification, separation from former heathenism (comp. Lev. 14 : 8; Num. 8 : 7). In Jer. 17 : 1 this word is rendered "point."

Na'in (from Heb. *nain*, "green pastures," "lovely"), the name of a town near the gate of which Jesus raised to life a widow's son (Luke 7 : 11-17). It is identified with the village called *Nein*, standing on the north-western slope of Jebel ed-Dûhy (= the "hill Moreh" = "Little Hermon"), about 4 miles from Tabor and 25 southwest of Capernaum. At the foot of the slope on which it stands is the great plain of Esdraelon.

This was the first miracle of raising the dead our Lord had wrought, and it excited

NEIN (NAIN).

great awe and astonishment among the people.

Na'ioth—*dwellings*—the name given to the prophetical college established by Samuel near Ramah. It consisted of a cluster of separate dwellings, and hence its name. David took refuge here when he fled from Saul (1 Sam. 19:18, 19, 22, 23), and here he passed a few weeks in peace (comp. Ps. 11). It was probably the common residence of the "sons of the prophets."

Na'ked. This word denotes (1) absolute nakedness (Gen. 2:25; Job 1:21; Eccl. 5:15; Micah 1:8; Amos 2:16); (2) being poorly clad (Isa. 58:7; James 2:15). It denotes also (3) the state of one who has laid aside his loose outer garment (Lat. *nudus*), and appears clothed only in a long tunic or under robe worn next the skin (1 Sam. 19:24; Isa. 47:3; comp. John 21:7). It is used figuratively, meaning "being discovered" or "made manifest" (Job 26:6; Mark 14:52; Heb. 4:13). In Ex. 32:25 the expression "the people were naked" (A.V.) is more correctly rendered in the Revised Version "the people were broken loose"—*i.e.*, had

fallen into a state of lawlessness and insubordination. In 2 Chr. 28:19 the words "he made Judah naked" (A.V.), but Revised Version "he had dealt wantonly in Judah," mean "he had permitted Judah to break loose from all the restraints of religion."

Na'omi—*the lovable; my delight*—the wife of Elimelech, and mother of Mahlon and Chilion, and mother-in-law of Ruth (1:2, 20, 21; 2:1). Elimelech and his wife left the district of Bethlehem-Judah, and found a new home in the uplands of Moab. In course of time he died, as also his two sons Mahlon and Chilion, who had married women of Moab, and three widows were left mourning the loss of their husbands. Naomi longs to return now to her own land, to Bethlehem. One of her widowed daughters-in-law, Ruth, accompanies her, and is at length married to Boaz (*q.v.*).

Na'phish—*refresher*—one of the sons of Ishmael (Gen. 25:15; 1 Chr. 1:31). He was the father of an Arab tribe.

Naph'tali—*my wrestling*—the fifth son of Jacob. His mother was Bilhah, Rachel's handmaid (Gen. 30:8). When Jacob went down into Egypt, Naphtali had four sons (Gen. 46 : 24). Little is known of him as an individual.

Naph'tali, Tribe of. On this tribe Jacob pronounced the patriarchal blessing, "Naphtali is a hind let loose: he giveth goodly words" (Gen. 49 : 21). It was intended thus to set forth under poetic imagery the future character and history of the tribe.

At the time of the Exodus this tribe numbered 53,400 adult males (Num. 1 ; 43), but at the close of the wanderings they numbered only 45,400 (26 : 48–50). Along with Dan and Asher they formed "the camp of Dan," under a common standard (2 : 25–31), occupying a place during the march on the north side of the tabernacle.

The possession assigned to this tribe is set forth in Josh. 19 ; 32–39. It lay in the north-eastern corner of the land, bounded on the east by the Jordan and the lakes of Merom and Galilee, and on the north it extended far into Cœle-Syria, the valley between the two Lebanon ranges. It comprehended a greater variety of rich and beautiful scenery and of soil and climate than fell to the lot of any other tribe. The territory of Naphtali extended to about 800 square miles, being the double of that of Issachar. The region around Kedesh, one of its towns, was originally called *Galil*, a name afterwards given to the whole northern division of Canaan. A large number of foreigners settled here among the mountains, and hence it was called "Galilee of the Gentiles" (*q.v.*)—Matt. 4 : 15, 16. The southern portion of Naphtali has been called the "Garden of Palestine." It was of unrivalled fertility. It was the principal scene of our Lord's public ministry. Here most of his parables were spoken and his miracles wrought.

This tribe was the first to suffer from the invasion of Benhadad, king of Syria, in the reigns of Baasha, king of Israel, and Asa, king of Judah (1 Kings 15 : 20; 2 Chr. 16 : 4). In the reign of Pekah, king of Israel, the Assyrians under Tiglath-pileser swept over the whole north of Israel, and carried the people into captivity (2 Kings 15 : 29). Thus the kingdom of Israel came to an end (B.C. 722).

Naphtali is now almost wholly a desert, the towns of Tiberias, on the shore of the Lake of Galilee, and Safed being the only places in it of any importance.

Naph'tali, Mount, the mountainous district of Naphtali (Josh. 20 : 7).

Naph'tuhim, a Hamitic tribe descended from Mizraim (Gen. 10 : 13). Others identify this word with *Napata*, the name of the city and territory on the southern frontier of Mizraim, the modern *Meroë*, at the great bend of the Nile at Soudan. This city was the royal residence, it is said, of Queen Candace (Acts 8 : 27). Here there are extensive and splendid ruins.

Nap'kin (Gr. *soudarion*, John 11 : 44; 20 : 7 ; Lat. *sudarium*, a "sweat-cloth"), a cloth for wiping the sweat from the face. But the word is used of a wrapper to fold money in (Luke 19 : 20), and as an article of dress, a "handkerchief" worn on the head (Acts 19 : 12).

Narcis'sus—*daffodil*—a Roman whom Paul salutes (Rom. 16 : 11). He is supposed to have been the private secretary of the emperor Claudius. This is, however, quite uncertain.

Na'than—*given*. (1.) A prophet in the reigns of David and Solomon (2 Chr. 9 : 29). He is first spoken of in connection with the arrangements David made for the building of the temple (2 Sam. 7 : 2, 3, 17), and next appears as the reprover of David on account of his sin with Bathsheba (12 : 1–14). He was charged with the education of Solomon (12 : 25), at whose inauguration to the throne he took a prominent part (1 Kings 1 : 8, 10, 11, 22–45). His two sons, Zabad (1 Chr. 2 : 36) and Azariah (1 Kings 4 : 5) occupied places of honour at the king's court. He last appears in assisting David in reorganizing the public worship (2 Chr. 29 : 25). He seems to have written a life of David, and also a life of Solomon (1 Chr. 29 : 29 ; 2 Chr. 9 : 29).

(2.) A son of David, by Bathsheba (2 Sam. 5 : 14), whose name appears in the genealogy of Mary, the mother of our Lord (Luke 3 : 31).

(3.) Ezra 8 : 16.

Nathan'ael—*given* or *gift of God*—one of our Lord's disciples, "of Cana in Galilee" (John 21 : 2). He was "an Israelite indeed, in whom was no guile" (1 : 47, 48). His name occurs only in the Gospel of John, who in his list of the disciples never mentions Bartholomew, with whom he has consequently been identified. He was one of those to whom the Lord showed himself alive after his resurrection, at the Sea of Tiberias.

Nativ'ity of Christ. The birth of our Lord took place at the time and place predicted by the prophets (Gen. 49 : 10 ; Isa. 7 : 14 ; Jer. 31 : 15 ; Micah 5 : 2 ; Hag. 2 : 6–9 ; Dan. 9 : 24, 25). Joseph and Mary were providentially led to go up to Bethlehem at this period, and there Christ was born (Matt. 2 : 1, 6 ; Luke 2 : 1, 7). The exact year or month or day of his birth cannot, however, now be exactly ascertained. We know, however, that it took place in the "fulness of the time" (Gal. 4 : 4)—*i.e.*, at the fittest time in the world's history. Chronologists are now generally agreed that the year 4 before the Christian era was the year of Christ's nativity, and consequently that he was about four years old in the year 1 A.D.

Naught'y figs (Jer. 24 : 2). "The bad figs may have been such either from having decayed, and thus been reduced to a rotten condition, or as being the fruit of the sycamore, which contains a bitter juice" (Tristram, *Nat. Hist.*). The inferiority of the fruit is here referred to as an emblem of the rejected Zedekiah and his people.

Naz'arene. This epithet (Gr. *Nazaraios*) is applied to Christ only once (Matt. 2 : 23). In all other cases the word is rendered "of Nazareth" (Mark 1 : 24 ; 10 : 47 ; 14 : 67, etc.). When this Greek designation was at first applied to our Lord, it was meant simply to denote the place of his residence. In course of time the word became a term of reproach. Thus the word "Nazarene" carries with it an allusion to those prophecies which speak of Christ as "despised of men" (Isa. 53 : 3). Some, however, think that in this name there is an allusion to the Hebrew *netser*, which signifies a branch or sprout. It is so applied to the Messiah

(Isa. 11 : 1)—*i.e.*, he whom the prophets called the *Nêtsĕr*, the "Branch."

The followers of Christ were called "the sect of Nazarenes" (Acts 24 : 5). All over Palestine and Syria this name is still given to Christians. (See NAZARETH.)

Naz'areth—*separated*—generally supposed to be the Greek form of the Hebrew *nêtsĕr*, a "shoot" or "sprout." Some, however, think that the name of the city must be connected with the name of the hill behind it, from which one of the finest prospects in Palestine is obtained, and accordingly they derive it from the Hebrew *notsĕrâh'*—*i.e.*, one guarding or watching, thus designating the hill which overlooks and thus guards an extensive region.

This city is not mentioned in the Old Testament. It was the home of Joseph and Mary (Luke 2 : 39), and here the angel announced to the Virgin the birth of the Messiah (1 : 26–28). Here Jesus grew up from his infancy to manhood (4 : 16) ; and here he began his public ministry in the synagogue (Matt. 13 : 54), at which the people were so offended that they sought to cast him down from the precipice whereon their city was built (Luke 4 : 29). Twice they expelled him from their borders (4 : 16–29 ; Matt. 13 : 54–58) ; and he finally retired from the city, where he did not many mighty works because of their unbelief (Matt. 13 : 58), and took up his residence in Capernaum.

Nazareth is situated among the southern ridges of Lebanon, on the steep slope of a hill, about 14 miles from the Sea of Galilee, and about 6 west from Mount Tabor. It is identified with the modern village *en-Nâzirah*, of six or ten thousand inhabitants. It lies "as in a hollow cup" lower down upon the hill than the ancient city. The main road for traffic between Egypt and the interior of Asia passed by Nazareth near the foot of Tabor, and thence northward to Damascus.

It is supposed from the words of Nathanael in John 1 : 47 that the city of Nazareth was held in great disrepute, either because, it is said, the people of Galilee were a rude and less cultivated class, and were largely influenced by the Gentiles

NAZARETH.

who mingled with them, or because of their lower type of moral and religious character. But there seems to be no sufficient reason for these suppositions. The Jews believed that, according to Micah 5:2, the birth of the Messiah would take place at Bethlehem, and nowhere else. Nathanael had the same opinion as his countrymen, and believed that the great "good" which they were all expecting could not come from Nazareth. This is probably what Nathanael meant. Moreover there does not seem to be any evidence that the inhabitants of Galilee were in any respect inferior, or that a Galilean was held in contempt, in the time of our Lord. (See Dr. Merrill's *Galilee in the Time of Christ.*)

The population of this city (now about 10,000) in the time of Christ probably amounted to 15,000 or 20,000 souls.

Naz′arite (Heb. form *Nazirite*), the name of such Israelites as took on them the vow prescribed in Num. 6:2–21. The word denotes generally one who is separated from others, and consecrated to God. Although there is no mention of any Nazarite before Samson, yet it is evident that they existed before the time of Moses. The vow of a Nazarite involved these three things— (1) abstinence from wine and strong drink, (2) refraining from cutting the hair off the head during the whole period of the continuance of the vow, and (3) the avoidance of contact with the dead.

When the period of the continuance of the vow came to an end, the Nazarite had to present himself at the door of the sanctuary with (1) a he-lamb of the first year for a burnt-offering, (2) a ewe-lamb of the first year for a sin-offering, and (3) a ram for a peace-offering. After these sacrifices were offered by the priest, the Nazarite cut off his hair at the door and threw it into the fire under the peace-offering.

For some reason, probably in the midst of his work at Corinth, Paul took on himself the Nazarite vow. This could only be terminated by his going up to Jerusalem to offer up the hair which till then was to be left uncut. But it seems to have been allowable for persons at a distance to cut the hair, which was to be brought up to Jerusalem, where the ceremony was completed. This Paul did at Cenchrea just before setting out on his voyage into Syria (Acts 18:18).

On another occasion (Acts 21:23–26), at the feast of Pentecost, Paul took on himself again the Nazarite vow. "The ceremonies involved took a longer time than Paul had at his disposal, but the law permitted a man to share the vow if he could find companions who had gone through the prescribed ceremonies, and who permitted him to join their company. This permission was commonly granted if the newcomer paid all the fees required from the whole company (fee to the Levite for cutting the hair and fees for sacrifices), and finished the vow along with the others. Four Jewish Christians were performing the vow, and would admit Paul to their company, provided he paid their expenses. Paul consented, paid the charges, and when the last seven days of the vow began he went with them to live in the temple, giving the usual notice to the priests that he had joined in regular fashion, was a sharer with the four men, and that his vow would end with theirs. Nazarites retired to the temple during the last period of seven days, because they could be secure there against any accidental defilement" (Lindsay's *Acts*).

As to the duration of a Nazarite's vow, every one was left at liberty to fix his own time. There is mention made in Scripture of only three who were Nazarites for life— Samson, Samuel, and John the Baptist (Judg. 13:4, 5; 1 Sam. 1:11; Luke 1:15). In its ordinary form, however, the Nazarite's vow lasted only thirty, and at most one hundred days. (See RECHABITES.)

This institution was a symbol of a life devoted to God, and separated from all sin —a holy life.

Ne′ah—*shaking,* or *settlement,* or *descent* —a town on the east side of Zebulun, not far from Rimmon (Josh. 19:13).

Neap′olis—*new city*—a town in Thrace at which Paul first landed in Europe (Acts 16:11). It was the sea-port of the inland town of Philippi, which was distant about

10 miles. From this port Paul embarked on his last journey to Jerusalem (Acts 20:6). It is identified with the modern Turko-Grecian *Kavalla*.

Nebai'oth—*height*. (1.) Ishmael's eldest son (Gen. 25:13), and the prince of an Israelitish tribe (16). He had a sister, Mahalath, who was one of Esau's wives (Gen. 28:9; 36:3).

(2.) The name of the Ishmaelite tribe descended from the above (Gen. 25:18; 21:12). The "rams of Nebaioth" (Isa. 60:7) are the gifts which these wandering tribes of the desert would consecrate to God.

Nebal'lat—*wickedness in secret*—(Neh. 11:34), probably the village of *Beit Nebâla*, about 4 miles north of Lydda.

Ne'bat—*sight; aspect*—the father of Jeroboam, the king of Israel (1 Kings 11:26, etc.).

Ne'bo—*proclaimer; prophet*. (1.) A Chaldean god, whose worship was introduced into Assyria by Pul (Isa. 46:1; Jer. 48:1). To this idol was dedicated the great temple whose ruins are still seen at Birs Nimrûd. A statue of Nebo found at Calah, where it was set up by Pul, king of Assyria, is now in the British Museum.

(2.) A mountain in the land of Moab from which Moses looked for the first and the last time on the Promised Land (Deut. 32:49; 34:1). It has been identified with *Jebel Nebâh*, on the eastern shore of the Dead Sea, near its northern end, and about 5 miles south-west of Heshbon. It was the summit of the ridge of Pisgah (*q.v.*), which was a part of the range of the "mountains of Abarim." It is about 2,643 feet in height, but from its position it commands a view of Western Palestine. Close below it are the plains of Moab, where Baalam and afterwards Moses saw the tents of Israel spread along.

(3.) A town on the east of Jordan which was taken possession of and rebuilt by the tribe of Reuben (Num. 32:3, 38; 1 Chr. 5:8). It was about 8 miles south of Heshbon.

(4.) The "children of Nebo" (Ezra 2:29; Neh. 7:33) were of those who returned from Babylon. It was a town in Benjamin,

probably the modern *Beit-Nûbah*, about 7 miles north-west of Hebron.

NEBO.
(From statue in British Museum.)

Nebuchadnez'zar, in the Babylonian orthography *Nabu-kuduri-utsur*, which means "Nebo, protect the crown!" or the "frontiers." In an inscription he styles himself "Nebo's favourite." He was the son and successor of Nabopolassar, who delivered Babylon from its dependence on Assyria and laid Nineveh in ruins. He was the greatest and most powerful of all the Babylonian kings. He married the daughter of Cyaxares, and thus the Median and Babylonian dynasties were united.

Necho II., the king of Egypt, gained a victory over the Assyrians at Carchemish. (See JOSIAH; MEGIDDO.) This secured to Egypt the possession of the Syrian provinces of Assyria, including Palestine. The remaining provinces of the Assyrian empire were divided between Babylonia and Media. But Nabopolassar was ambitious of reconquering from Necho the western provinces of Syria, and for this purpose he sent his son with a powerful army westward (Dan. 1:1). The Egyptians met him at Carchemish, where a furious battle was fought, resulting in the complete rout of the Egyptians, who were driven back (Jer. 46:2-12), and Syria and Phœnicia brought under the sway of Babylon (B.C. 606). "From that time the king of Egypt came not again any more out of his land" (2 Kings 24:7). Nebuchadnezzar also subdued the whole of Palestine, and took Jerusalem, carrying away captive a great multitude of the Jews, among whom were Daniel and his companions (Dan. 1:1, 2; Jer. 4:1).

Three years after this Jehoiakim, who had reigned in Jerusalem as a Babylonian vassal, rebelled against the oppressor, trusting to help from Egypt (2 Kings 24:1). This led Nebuchadnezzar to march an army again to the conquest of Jerusalem, which at once yielded to him (B.C. 598). A third time he came against it, and deposed Jehoiakin, whom he carried into Babylon, with a large portion of the population of the city, and the sacred vessels of the temple, placing Zedekiah on the throne of Judah in his stead. He also, heedless of the warnings of the prophet, entered into an alliance with Egypt, and rebelled against Babylon. This brought about the final siege of the city, which was at length taken and utterly destroyed (B.C. 586). Zedekiah was taken captive, and had his eyes put out by order of the king of Babylon, who made him a prisoner for the remainder of his life.

An onyx cameo, now in the museum of Florence, bears on it an arrow-headed inscription, which is certainly ancient and genuine. The helmeted profile is said (Schrader) to be genuine also, but it is more probable that it is the portrait of a usurper in the time of Darius (Hystaspes) called Nidinta-Bel, who took the name of "Nebuchadrezzar." The inscription has been

thus translated:—"In honour of Merodach, his lord, Nebuchadnezzar, king of Babylon, in his life-time had this made."

CAMEO OF THE NEBUCHADNEZZARS.

A clay tablet, now in the British Museum, bears the following inscription, the only one as yet found which refers to his wars:—"In the thirty-seventh year of Nebuchadnezzar, king of the country of Babylon, he went to Egypt (Misr) to make war. Amasis, king of Egypt, collected (his army), and marched and spread abroad." Thus were fulfilled the words of the prophet (Jer. 46:13-26; Ezek. 29:2-20). Having completed the subjugation of Phœnicia, and inflicted chastisement on Egypt, Nebuchadnezzar now set himself to rebuild and adorn the city of Babylon (Dan. 4:30), and to add to the greatness and prosperity of his kingdom by constructing canals and aqueducts and reservoirs, surpassing in grandeur and magnificence everything of the kind mentioned in history (Dan. 2:37). He is represented as a "king of kings," ruling over a vast kingdom of many provinces, with a long list of officers and rulers under him, "princes, governors, captains," etc. (3:2, 3, 27). He may indeed be said to have created the mighty empire over which he ruled.

"Modern research has shown that Nebuchadnezzar was the greatest monarch that Babylon, or perhaps the East generally, ever produced. He must have possessed an enormous command of human labour—nine-tenths of Babylon itself, and nineteen-twentieths of all the other ruins that in almost countless profusion cover the land, are composed of bricks stamped with his name. He appears to have built or restored almost every city and temple in the whole country. His inscriptions give an elaborate account of the immense works which he constructed in and about Babylon itself, abundantly illustrating the boast, 'Is not this great Babylon which I have built?'" —Rawlinson, *Hist. Illustrations.*

After the incident of the "burning fiery furnace" (Dan. 7) into which the three Hebrew confessors were cast, Nebuchadnezzar was afflicted with some peculiar mental aberration as a punishment for his pride and vanity, probably the form of madness known as lycanthropy (*i.e.*, "the change of a man into a wolf"). A remark· able confirmation of the Scripture narrative is afforded by the recent discovery of a bronze door-step, which bears an inscription to the effect that it was presented by Nebuchadnezzar to the great temple at Borsippa as a votive offering on account of his recovery from a terrible illness. (See DANIEL.)

He survived his recovery for some years, and died B.C. 562, in the eighty-third or eighty-fourth year of his age, after a reign of forty-three years, and was succeeded by his son Evil-merodach, who, after a reign of two years, was succeeded by Neriglissar (559-555), who was succeeded by Nabonadius (555-538), at the close of whose reign (less than a quarter of a century after the death of Nebuchadnezzar) Babylon fell under Cyrus at the head of the combined armies of Media and Persia.

"I have examined," says Sir H. Rawlinson, "the bricks belonging perhaps to a hundred different towns and cities in the neighbourhood of Baghdad, and I never found any other legend than that of Nebuchadnezzar, son of Nabopolassar, king of Babylon." Nine-tenths of all the bricks amid the ruins of Babylon are stamped with his name.

Nebuchadrez'zar = Nebuchadnezzar (Jer. 21:2, 7; 22:25; 24:1, etc.), a nearer approach to the correct spelling of the word.

Nebushas'ban—*adorer of Nebo*, or *Nebo saves me*—the "Rabsaris," or chief chamberlain, of the court of Babylon. He was one of those whom the king sent to release Jeremiah from prison in Jerusalem (Jer. 39:13).

Nebuzara'dan, "the captain of the guard," in rank next to the king, who appears prominent in directing affairs at the capture of Jerusalem (2 Kings 25:8-21; Jer. 39:11; 40:2-5). He showed kindness toward Jeremiah, as commanded by Nebuchadnezzar (40:1). Five years after this he again came to Jerusalem and carried captive seven hundred and forty-five more Jews.

Necho II., an Egyptian king, the son and successor of Psammetichus (B.C. 610-594), the contemporary of Josiah, king of Judah. For some reason he proclaimed war against the king of Assyria. He led forth a powerful army and marched northward, but was met by the king of Judah at Megiddo, who refused him a passage through his territory. Here a fierce battle was fought and Josiah was slain (2 Chr. 35:20-24). Possibly, as some suppose, Necho may have brought his army by sea to some port to the north of Dor (comp. Josh. 11:2; 12:23), a Phœnician town at no great distance from Megiddo. After this battle Necho marched on to Carchemish (*q.v.*), where he met and conquered the Assyrian army, and thus all the Syrian provinces, including Palestine, came under his dominion.

On his return march he deposed Jehoahaz, who had succeeded his father Josiah, and made Eliakim, Josiah's eldest son, whose name he changed into Jehoiakim, king. Jehoahaz he carried down into Egypt, where he died (2 Kings 23:31; 2 Chr. 36:1-4). Four years after this conquest Necho again marched to the Euphrates; but here he was met and his army routed by the Chaldeans (B.C. 606) under Nebuchadnezzar, who drove the Egyptians back, and took from them all the territory they had conquered, from the Euphrates unto the "river of Egypt" (Jer. 46:2; 2 Kings 24:7, 8). Soon after this Necho died, and was succeeded by his son, Psammetichus II. (See NEBUCHADNEZZAR.)

Neck, used sometimes figuratively. To

"lay down the neck" (Rom. 16:4) is to hazard one's life. Threatenings of coming judgments are represented by the prophets by their laying bands upon the people's necks (Deut. 28:48; Isa. 10:27; Jer. 27:2). Conquerors put their feet on the necks of their enemies as a sign of their subjection (Josh. 10:24; 2 Sam. 22:41).

Nec'romancer (Deut. 18:11)—*i.e.*, "one who interrogates the dead," as the word literally means, with the view of discovering the secrets of futurity (comp. 1 Sam. 28:7). (See DIVINATION.)

Nedabi'ah—*moved of Jehovah*—one of the sons of Jeconiah (1 Chr. 3:18).

Needle, used only in the proverb, "to pass through a needle's eye" (Matt. 19:24; Mark 10:25; Luke 18:25). Some interpret the expression as referring to the side gate, close to the principal gate, usually called the "eye of a needle" in the East; but it is rather to be taken literally.

The Hebrew females were skilled in the use of the needle (Ex. 28:39; 26:36; Judg. 5:30).

Neg'inah, in the title of Ps. 61, denotes the music of *stringed instruments* (1 Sam. 16:16; Isa. 38:20). It is the singular form of Neginoth.

Neg'inoth—*i.e.*, songs with instrumental accompaniment, found in the titles of Ps. 4; 6; 54; 55; 67; 76; rendered "stringed instruments," Hab. 3:19, A.V. It denotes all kinds of stringed instruments, as the "harp," "psaltery," "viol," etc. The "chief musician on Neginoth" is the leader of that part of the temple choir which played on stringed instruments.

Nehel'amite, the name given to a false prophet Shemaiah, who went with the captives to Babylon (Jer. 29:24, 31, 32). The origin of the name is unknown. It is rendered in the marg. "dreamer."

Nehemi'ah—*comforted by Jehovah*. (1.) Ezra 2:2; Neh. 7:7.

(2.) Neh. 3:16.

(3.) The son of Hachaliah (Neh. 1:1), and probably of the tribe of Judah. His family must have belonged to Jerusalem (Neh. 2:3). He was one of the "Jews of the dispersion," and in his youth was appointed to the important office of royal cup-bearer at the palace of Shushan. The king, Artaxerxes Longimanus, seems to have been on terms of friendly familiarity with his attendant. Through his brother Hanani, and perhaps from other sources (Neh. 1:2; 2:3), he heard of the mournful and desolate condition of the Holy City, and was filled with sadness of heart. For many days he fasted and mourned and prayed for the place of his fathers' sepulchres. At length the king observed his sadness of countenance and asked the reason of it. Nehemiah explained it all to the king, and obtained his permission to go up to Jerusalem and there to act as tirshatha, or governor of Judea. He went up in the spring of B.C. 446 (eleven years after Ezra), with a strong escort supplied by the king, and with letters to all the pashas of the provinces through which he had to pass, as also to Asaph, keeper of the royal forests, directing him to assist Nehemiah. On his arrival he set himself to survey the city, and to form a plan for its restoration; a plan which he carried out with great skill and energy, so that the whole was completed in about six months. He remained in Judea for thirteen years as governor, carrying out many reforms, notwithstanding much opposition that he encountered (Neh. 13:11). He built up the state on the old lines, "supplementing and completing the work of Ezra," and making all arrangements for the safety and good government of the city. At the close of this important period of his public life, he returned to Persia to the service of his royal master at Shushan or Ecbatana. Very soon after this the old corrupt state of things returned, showing the worthlessness to a large extent of the professions that had been made at the feast of the dedication of the walls of the city (Neh. 12. See EZRA). Malachi now appeared among the people with words of stern reproof and solemn warning; and Nehemiah again returned from Persia (after an absence of some two years), and was grieved to see the widespread moral degeneracy that had taken place during his absence. He set himself with vigour to rectify the flagrant abuses that had sprung up, and restored the orderly administration of public worship and the outward observance of the law of Moses. Of his subsequent history we know nothing. Probably he remained at his post as governor till his death (about B.C. 413) in a good old age. The place of his death and burial is, however, unknown. "He resembled Ezra in his fiery zeal, in his active spirit of enterprise, and in the piety of his life: but he was of a bluffer and a fiercer mood; he had less patience with transgressors; he was a man of action rather than a man of thought, and more inclined to use force than persuasion. His practical sagacity and high courage were very markedly shown in the arrangement with which he carried through the rebuilding of the wall and balked the cunning plans · of the 'adversaries.' The piety of his heart, his deeply religious spirit and constant sense of communion with and absolute dependence upon God, are strikingly exhibited, first in the long prayer recorded in ch. 1:5-11, and secondly and most remarkably in what have been called his 'interjectional prayers'—those short but moving addresses to Almighty God which occur so frequently in his writings—the instinctive outpouring of a heart deeply moved, but ever resting itself upon God, and looking to God alone for aid in trouble, for the frustration of evil designs, and for final reward and acceptance" (Rawlinson). Nehemiah was the last of the governors sent from the Persian court. Judea after this was annexed to the satrapy of Cœle-Syria, and was governed by the high priest under the jurisdiction of the governor of Syria, and the internal government of the country became more and more a hierarchy.

Nehemi'ah, Book of. The *author* of this book was no doubt Nehemiah himself. There are portions of the book written in the first person (ch. 1-7; 12:27-47, and 13). But there are also portions of it in which Nehemiah is spoken of in the third person (ch. 8; 9; 10). It is supposed that these portions may have been written by Ezra; of this, however, there is no distinct evidence. These portions had their place assigned them in the book, there can be no

doubt, by Nehemiah. He was the responsible author of the whole book, with the exception of ch. 12:11, 22, 23.

The *date* at which the book was written was probably about B.C. 431-430, when Nehemiah had returned the second time to Jerusalem after his visit to Persia.

The book, which may historically be regarded as a continuation of the book of Ezra, consists of four parts. (1.) An account of the rebuilding of the wall of Jerusalem, and of the register Nehemiah had found of those who had returned from Babylon (ch. 1-7). (2.) An account of the state of religion among the Jews during this time (8-10). (3.) Increase of the inhabitants of Jerusalem; the census of the adult male population, and names of the chiefs, together with lists of priests and Levites (11-12:1-26). (4.) Dedication of the wall of Jerusalem, the arrangement of the temple officers, and the reforms carried out by Nehemiah (12:27-ch. 13).

This book closes the history of the Old Testament. Malachi the prophet was contemporary with Nehemiah.

Ne'hiloth, only in the title of Ps. 5. It is probably derived from a root meaning "to bore," "perforate," and hence denotes perforated wind instruments of all kinds. The psalm may be thus regarded as addressed to the conductor of the temple choir which played on flutes and such-like instruments.

Nehush'ta—*copper*—the daughter of Elnathan of Jerusalem, and the wife of Jehoiakin (2 Kings 24:8), king of Judah.

Nehush'tan—*of copper; a brazen thing*—a name of contempt given to the serpent Moses had made in the wilderness (Num. 21:8), and which Hezekiah destroyed because the children of Israel began to regard it as an idol and "burn incense to it." The lapse of nearly one thousand years had invested the "brazen serpent" with a mysterious sanctity; and in order to deliver the people from their infatuation, and impress them with the idea of its worthlessness, Hezekiah called it, in contempt, "Nehushtan," a brazen thing—a mere piece of brass (2 Kings 18:4).

Nei'el—*dwelling-place of God*—a town in

the territory of Asher, near its southern border (Josh. 19:27). It has been identified with the ruin Y'anîn, near the outlet of the Wâdy esh Shâ-ghûr, less than 2 miles north of Kâbûl, and 16 miles east of Cæsarea.

Ne'keb—*cavern*—a town on the boundary of Naphtali (Josh. 19:33). It has, with probability, been identified with *Seiyâdeh*, nearly 2 miles east of Bessum, a ruin half way between Tiberias and Mount Tabor.

Nem'uel — *day of God*. (1.) One of Simeon's five sons (1 Chr. 4:24), called also Jemuel (Gen. 46:10).

(2.) A Reubenite, a son of Eliab, and brother of Dathan and Abiram (Num. 26:9).

Nephi'lim (Gen. 6:4; Num. 13:33, R.V.)—*giants*—the Hebrew word left untranslated by the Revisers, the name of one of the Canaanitish tribes. The Revisers have, however, translated the Hebrew *gibbôrim*, in Gen. 6:4, "mighty men."

Nephto'ah—*opened*—a fountain and a stream issuing from it on the border between Judah and Benjamin (Josh. 15:8, 9; 18:15). It has been identified with '*Ain Lifta*, a spring about 2½ miles north-west of Jerusalem. Others, however, have identified it with '*Ain 'Atân*, on the south-west of Bethlehem, whence water is conveyed through "Pilate's aqueduct" to the Haram area at Jerusalem.

Ner—*light*—the father of Kish (1 Chr. 8:33). 1 Sam. 14:51 should be read, "Kish, the father of Saul, and Ner, the father of Abner, were the sons of Abiel." And hence this Kish and Ner were brothers, and Saul and Abner were first cousins (comp. 1 Chr. 9:36).

Ne'reus, a Christian at Rome to whom Paul sent his salutation (Rom. 16:15).

Ner'gal—*the great dog; that is, lion*—one of the chief gods of the Assyrians and Babylonians (2 Kings 17:30), the god of war and hunting. He is connected with Cutha as its tutelary deity.

Ner'gal-share'zer—*Nergal, protect the king!* (1.) One of the "princes of the king of Babylon who accompanied him in his last expedition against Jerusalem" (Jer. 39:3, 13).

(2.) Another of the "princes," who bore the title of "Rabmag." He was one of those who were sent to release Jeremiah from prison (Jer. 39:13) by "the captain of the guard." He was a Babylonian grandee of high rank. From profane history and the inscriptions, we are led to conclude that he was the Neriglissar who murdered Evil-merodach, the son of Nebuchadnezzar, and succeeded him on the throne of Babylon (B.C. 559–556). He was married to a daughter of Nebuchadnezzar. The ruins of a palace, the only one on the right bank of the Euphrates, bear inscriptions denoting that it was built by this king. He was succeeded by his son, a mere boy, who was murdered after a reign of some nine months by a conspiracy of the nobles, one of whom, Nabonadius, ascended the vacant throne, and reigned for a period of seventeen years (B.C. 555–538), at the close of which period Babylon was taken by Cyrus. Belshazzar, who comes into notice in connection with the taking of Babylon, was by some supposed to have been the same as Nabonadius, who was called Nebuchadnezzar's son (Dan. 5:11, 18, 22), because he had married his daughter. But it is known from the inscriptions that Nabonadius had a son called Belshazzar, who may have been his father's associate on the throne at the time of the fall of Babylon, and who therefore would be the grandson of Nebuchadnezzar. The Jews had only one word, usually rendered "father," to represent also such a relationship as that of "grandfather" or "great-grandfather."

Ne'ro occurs only in the superscription (which is probably spurious, and is altogether omitted in the R.V.) to the Second Epistle to Timothy. He became emperor of Rome when he was about seventeen years of age (A.D. 54), and soon began to exhibit the character of a cruel tyrant and heathen debauchee. In May A.D. 64, a terrible conflagration broke out in Rome, which raged for six days and seven nights, and totally destroyed a great part of the city. The guilt of this fire was attached to him at the time, and the general verdict of history accuses him of the crime. "Hence, to suppress the rumour," says Tacitus (*Annals*, xv. 44), "he falsely charged with the guilt, and punished with the most exquisite tortures, the persons commonly called Christians, who are hated for their enormities. Christus, the founder of that name, was put to death as a criminal by Pontius Pilate, procurator of Judea, in the reign of Tiberius; but the pernicious superstition, repressed for a time, broke out again, not only throughout Judea, where the mischief originated, but through the city of Rome also, whither all things horrible and disgraceful flow, from all quarters, as to a common receptacle, and where they are encouraged. Accordingly, first three were seized, who confessed they were Christians. Next, on their information, a vast multitude were convicted, not so much on the charge of burning the city as of hating the human race. And in their deaths they were also made the subjects of sport; for they were covered with the hides of wild beasts and worried to death by dogs, or nailed to crosses, or set fire to, and, when day declined, burned to serve for nocturnal lights. Nero offered his own gardens for that spectacle, and exhibited a Circensian game, indiscriminately mingling with the common people in the habit of a charioteer, or else standing in his chariot; whence a feeling of compassion arose toward the sufferers, though guilty and deserving to be made examples of by capital punishment, because they seemed not to be cut off for the public good, but victims to the ferocity of one man." Another Roman historian, Suetonius (*Nero*, xvi.), says of him: "He likewise inflicted punishments on the Christians, a sort of people who hold a new and impious superstition" (Forbes's *Footsteps of St. Paul*, p. 59).

Nero was the emperor before whom Paul was brought on his first imprisonment at Rome, and the apostle is supposed to have suffered martyrdom during this persecution. He is repeatedly alluded to in Scripture (Acts 25:11; Phil. 1:12, 13; 4:22). He died A.D. 68.

Net, in use among the Hebrews for fishing, hunting, and fowling.

The *fishing-net* was probably constructed after the form of that used by the Egyptians (Isa. 19:8). There were three kinds of nets. (1.) The *drag-net* or *hauling-net* (Gr. *sagēnē*), of great size, and requiring many men to work it. It was usually let down from the fishing-boat, and then drawn to the shore or into the boat, as circumstances might require (Matt. 13:47, 48). (2.) The *hand-net* or *casting-net* (Gr. *amphiblēstron*), which was thrown from a rock or a boat at any fish that might be seen (Matt. 4:18; Mark 1:16). It was called by the Latins *funda*. It was of circular form, "like the top of a tent." (3.) The *bag-net* (Gr. *diktyon*), used for enclosing fish in deep water (Luke 5:4-9).

The *fowling-nets* were (1) the trap, consisting of a net spread over a frame, and supported by a stick in such a way that it fell with the slightest touch (Amos 3:5, "gin;" Ps. 69:22; Job 18:9; Eccl. 9:12). (2.) The snare, consisting of a cord to catch birds by the leg (Job 18:10; Ps. 18:5; 116:3; 140:5). (3.) The decoy, a cage filled with birds as decoys (Jer. 5:26, 27).

Hunting-nets were much in use among the Hebrews.

Nethan'eel—*given of God.* (1.) The son of Zuar, chief of the tribe of Issachar at the Exodus (Num. 1:8; 2:5).

(2.) One of David's brothers (1 Chr. 2:14).

(3.) A priest who blew the trumpet before the ark when it was brought up to Jerusalem (1 Chr. 15:24).

(4.) A Levite (1 Chr. 24:6).

(5.) A temple porter, of the family of the Korhites (1 Chr. 26:4).

(6.) One of the "princes" appointed by Jehoshaphat to teach the law through the cities of Judah (2 Chr. 17:7).

(7.) A chief Levite in the time of Josiah (2 Chr. 35:9).

(8.) Ezra 10:22.

(9.) Neh. 12:21.

(10.) A priest's son who bore a trumpet at the dedication of the walls of Jerusalem (Neh. 12:36).

Nethani'ah—*given of Jehovah.* (1.) One of Asaph's sons, appointed by David to minister in the temple (1 Chr. 25:2, 12).

(2.) A Levite sent by Jehoshaphat to teach the law (2 Chr. 17:8).

(3.) Jer. 36 : 14.

(4.) 2 Kings 25 : 23, 25.

Neth'inim, the name given to the hereditary temple servants in all the post-Exilian books of Scripture. The word means *given—i.e.,* "those set apart"—*viz.,* to the menial work of the sanctuary for the Levites. The name occurs seventeen times, and in each case in the Authorized Version incorrectly terminates in *s*—"Nethinims;" in the Revised Version, correctly without the *s* (Ezra 2 : 70; 7 : 7, 24; 8 : 20, etc.). The tradition is that the Gibeonites (Josh. 9 : 27) were the original caste, afterwards called Nethinim. Their numbers were added to afterwards from captives taken in battle; and they were formally given by David to the Levites (Ezra 8 : 20), and so were called Nethinim — *i.e.,* the *given ones*—given to the Levites to be their servants. Only 612 Nethinim returned from Babylon (Ezra 2 : 58; 8 : 20). They were under the control of a chief from among themselves (2 : 43; Neh. 7 : 46).

No reference to them appears in the New Testament, because it is probable that they became merged in the general body of the Jewish people.

Neto'phah—*distillation; dropping*—a town in Judah, in the neighbourhood, probably, of Bethlehem (Neh. 7 : 26; 1 Chr. 2 : 54). Two of David's guards were Netophathites (1 Chr. 27 : 13, 15). It has been identified with the ruins of *Metoba,* or *Um Tôba,* to the north-east of Bethlehem.

Net'tle. (1.) Heb. *hârûl,* "pricking" or "burning," Prov. 24 : 30, 31 (R.V. marg., "wild vetches"); Job 30 : 7; Zeph. 2 : 9. Many have supposed that some thorny or prickly plant is intended by this word— such as the bramble, the thistle, the wild plum, the cactus or prickly pear, etc. It may probably be a species of mustard, the *Sinapis arvensis,* which is a pernicious weed abounding in corn-fields. Tristram thinks that this word "designates the prickly acanthus (*Acanthus spinosus*), a very common and troublesome weed in the plains of Palestine."

(2.) Heb. *qimmôsh,* Isa. 34 : 13 (R.V., "thorns"); Hos. 9 : 6; Prov. 24 : 31 (in both versions, "thorns"). This word has been regarded as denoting thorns, thistles, wild camomile; but probably it is correctly rendered "nettle," the *Urtica pilulifera,* "a tall and vigorous plant, often 6 feet high, the sting of which is much more severe and irritating than that of our common nettle."

New Moon, Feast of. Special services were appointed for the commencement of a month (Num. 28 : 11–15; 10 : 10). (See FESTIVALS.)

New Test'ament (Luke 22 : 20), rather "New Covenant," in contrast to the old covenant of works, which is superseded. "The covenant of grace is called *new;* it succeeds to the old broken covenant of works. It is ever fresh, flourishing, and excellent; and under the gospel it is dispensed in a more clear, spiritual, extensive, and powerful manner than of old" (Brown of Haddington). Hence is derived the name given to the latter portion of the Bible. (See TESTAMENT.)

Nezi'ah—*victory; pure*—Ezra 2 : 54; Neh. 7 : 56.

Ne'zib, a town in the "plain" of Judah. It has been identified with *Beit Nûzib,* about 14 miles south-west of Jerusalem, in the Wâdy Sûr (Josh. 15 : 43).

Nib'haz—*barker*—the name of an idol, supposed to be an evil demon of the Zabians. It was set up in Samaria by the Avites (2 Kings 17 : 31), probably in the form of a dog.

Nib'shan — *fertile; light soil* — a city somewhere "in the wilderness" of Judah (Josh. 15 : 62), probably near Engedi.

Nica'nor—*conqueror*—one of the seven deacons appointed in the apostolic Church (Acts 6 : 1–6). Nothing further is known of him.

Nicode'mus — *the people is victor*—a Pharisee and a member of the Sanhedrin. He is first noticed as visiting Jesus by night (John 3 : 1–21) for the purpose of learning more of his doctrines, which our Lord then unfolded to him, giving prominence to the necessity of being "born again." He is next met with in the Sanhedrin (7 : 50–52), where he protested against the course they were taking in plotting against Christ. Once more he is mentioned as taking part in the preparation for the anointing and burial of the body of Christ (John 19 : 39). We hear nothing more of him. There can be little doubt that he became a true disciple.

Nicola'itanes. The church at Ephesus (Rev. 2:6) is commended for hating the "deeds" of the Nicolaitanes, and the church of Pergamos is blamed for having them who hold their "doctrines" (15). They were seemingly a class of professing Christians, who sought to introduce into the church a false freedom or licentiousness, thus abusing Paul's doctrine of grace (comp. 2 Pet. 2:15, 16, 19), and were probably identical with those who held the doctrine of Baalam (*q.v.*)—Rev. 2:14.

Nic'olas—*the victory of the people*—a proselyte of Antioch, one of the seven deacons (Acts 6 : 5).

Nicop'olis—*city of victory*—where Paul intended to winter (Titus 3:12). There were several cities of this name. The one here referred to was most probably that in Epirus, which was built by Augustus Cæsar to commemorate his victory at the battle of Actium (B.C. 31). It is the modern *Paleoprevesa*—*i.e.*, "Old Prevesa." The subscription to the epistle to Titus calls it "Nicopolis of Macedonia"—*i.e.*, of Thrace. This is, however, probably incorrect.

Ni'ger—*black*—a surname of Simeon (Acts 13:1). He was probably so called from his dark complexion.

Night-hawk (Heb. *tahmâs*) occurs only in the list of unclean birds (Lev. 11:16; Deut. 14:15). This was supposed to be the night-jar (*Caprimulgus*), allied to the swifts. The Hebrew word is derived from a root meaning "to scratch or tear the face," and may be best rendered, in accordance with the ancient versions, "an owl" (*Strix flammea*). The Revised Version renders "night-hawk."

Nile—*dark; blue*—not found in Scripture, but frequently referred to in the Old Testament under the name of Sihor—*i.e.*, "the black stream" (Isa. 23:3; Jer. 2:18) —or simply "the river" (Gen. 41:1; Ex. 1:22, etc.) and the "flood of Egypt"

(Amos 8 : 8). It consists of two rivers— the White Nile, which takes its rise in the Victoria Nyanza, and the Blue Nile, which rises in the Abyssinian Mountains. These unite at the town of Khartoum, whence it pursues its course for 1,800 miles, and falls into the Mediterranean through its two branches, into which it is divided a few miles north of Cairo, the Rosetta and the Damietta branch. (See EGYPT.)

Nim'rah—*pure*—a city on the east of Jordan (Num. 32:3); probably the same as Beth-nimrah (Josh. 13:27). It has been identified with the *Nahr Nimrîn*, at one of the fords of Jordan, not far from Jericho.

Nim'rim, Waters of—*the stream of the leopards*—a stream in Moab (Isa. 15:6; Jer. 48:34); probably the modern *Wâdy en-Nemeirah*, a rich, verdant spot at the south-eastern end of the Dead Sea.

Nim'rod—*firm*—a descendant of Cush, the son of Ham. He was the first who claimed to be a "mighty one in the earth." Babel was the beginning of his kingdom, which he gradually enlarged (Gen. 10:8-10). The "land of Nimrod" (Micah 5:6) is a designation of Assyria or of Shinar, which is a part of it.

Nim'shi—*saved*. Jehu was "the son of Jehoshaphat, the son of Nimshi" (2 Kings 9:2; comp. 1 Kings 19:16).

Nin'eveh. First mentioned in Gen. 10: 11, which is rendered in the Revised Version, "He [*i.e.*, Nimrod] went forth into Assyria and builded Nineveh." It is not again noticed till the days of Jonah, when it is described (Jonah 3:3; 4:11) as a great and populous city, the flourishing capital of the Assyrian empire (2 Kings 19:36; Isa. 37:37). The book of the prophet Nahum is almost exclusively taken up with prophetic denunciations against this city. Its ruin and utter desolation are foretold (Nah. 1:14; 3:19, etc.). Zephaniah also (2:13-15) predicts its destruction along with the fall of the empire of which it was the capital. From this time there is no mention of it in Scripture till it is named in gospel history (Matt. 12:41; Luke 11:32).

This "exceeding great city" lay on the eastern or left bank of the river Tigris, along which it stretched for some 30 miles, having an average breadth of 10 miles or more from the river back toward the eastern hills. This whole extensive space is now one immense area of ruins. Occupying a central position on the great highway between the Mediterranean and the Indian Ocean, thus uniting the East and the West, wealth flowed into it from many sources, so that it became the greatest of all ancient cities.

About B.C. 633 the Assyrian empire began to show signs of weakness, and Nine-

veh was attacked by the Medes, who subsequently—about B.C. 625—being joined by the Babylonians and Susianians, again attacked it, when it fell, and was razed to the ground. The Assyrian empire then came to an end, the Medes and Babylonians dividing its provinces between them. "After having ruled for more than six hundred years with hideous tyranny and violence, from the Caucasus and the Caspian to the Persian Gulf, and from beyond the Tigris to Asia Minor and Egypt, it vanished like a dream" (Nah.

SCULPTURED SLAB FROM NINEVEH.

2 : 6–11). Its end was strange, sudden, tragic. It was God's doing — his judgment on Assyria's pride (Isa. 10 : 5–19).

Forty years ago our knowledge of the great Assyrian empire and of its magnificent capital was almost wholly a blank. Vague memories had indeed survived of its power and greatness, but very little was definitely known about it. Other cities which had perished—as Palmyra, Persepolis, and Thebes—had left ruins to mark their sites and tell of their former greatness; but of this city, imperial Nine-

veh, not a single vestige seemed to remain, and the very place on which it had stood was only matter of conjecture. In fulfilment of prophecy, God made "an utter end of the place." It became a "desolation."

In the days of the Greek historian Herodotus, B.C. 400, it had become a thing of the past; and when Xenophon the historian passed the place in the "Retreat of the Ten Thousand," the very memory of its name had been lost. It was buried out of sight, and no one knew its grave. It is never again to rise from its ruins.

At length, after being lost for more than two thousand years, the city was disentombed. A little more than forty years ago the French consul at Mosul began to search the vast mounds that lay along the opposite bank of the river. The Arabs whom he employed in these excavations, to their great surprise, came upon the ruins of a building at the mound of Khorsabad, which, on further exploration, turned out to be the royal palace of Sargon, one of the Assyrian kings. They found their way into its extensive courts and chambers, and brought forth from its hidden depths many wonderful sculptures and other relics of those ancient times.

The work of exploration has been carried on almost continuously by M. Botta, Sir Henry Layard, George Smith, and others, in the mounds of Nebi-Yunus, Nimrud, Kouyunjik, and Khorsabad, and a vast treasury of specimens of old Assyrian art have been exhumed. Palace after palace has been discovered, with their decorations

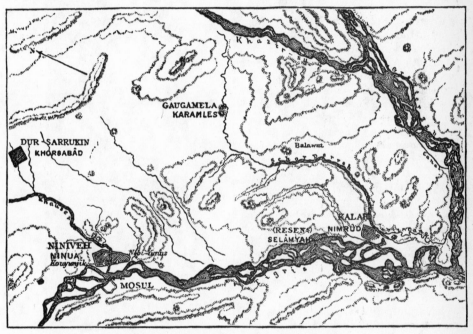

MAP OF NINEVEH AND THE NEIGHBOURHOOD.

and their sculptured slabs, revealing the life and manners of this ancient people, their arts of war and peace, the forms of their religion and the style of their architecture, and the magnificence of their monarchs. The streets of the city have been explored, the inscriptions on the bricks and tablets and sculptured figures have been read, and now the secrets of their history have been brought to light.

One of the most remarkable of recent discoveries is that of the library of King Assur-bani-pal, or, as the Greek historians call him, Sardanapalus, the grandson of Sennacherib (q.v.). (See ASNAPPER.) This library consists of about ten thousand flat bricks or tablets, all written over with Assyrian characters. They contain a record of the history, the laws, and the religion of Assyria, of the greatest value. These strange clay leaves found in the royal library form the most valuable of all the treasuries of the literature of the old world. It contains also old Accadian documents, which are the very oldest extant documents in the world, dating as far back as probably about the time of Abraham. (See SAR-GON.)

"The Assyrian royalty is, perhaps, the most luxurious of our century [reign of As-sur-bani-pal]. Its victories and conquests, uninterrupted for one hundred years, have enriched it with the spoil of twenty peoples. Sargon has taken what remained to the Hittites; Sennacherib overcame Chaldea, and the treasures of Babylon were trans-ferred to his coffers; Esarhaddon and Assur-bani-pal himself have pillaged Egypt and her great cities—Sais, Memphis, and Thebes of the hundred gates......Now for-eign merchants flock into Nineveh, bring-ing with them the most valuable produc-tions from all countries—gold and perfume from South Arabia and the Chaldean Sea, Egyptian linen and glass-work, carved enamels, goldsmiths' work, tin, silver, Phœnician purple; cedar wood from Leba-non, unassailable by worms; furs and iron from Asia Minor and Armenia" (*Ancient Egypt and Assyria*, by G. Maspero, page 271).

The bas-reliefs, alabaster slabs, and sculp-tured monuments found in these recovered palaces serve in a remarkable manner to confirm the Old Testament history of the kings of Israel. The appearance of the ruins shows that the destruction of the city was due not only to the assailing foe but also to the flood and the fire, thus confirming the ancient prophecies con-cerning it. "The recent excavations," says Rawlinson, "have shown that fire was a great instrument in the destruction of the Nineveh palaces. Calcined ala-baster, charred wood, and charcoal, colos-sal statues split through with heat, are met with in parts of the Nineveh mounds, and attest the veracity of prophecy."

Nineveh in its glory was (Jonah 3:4) an "exceeding great city of three days' jour-ney"—*i.e.*, probably in circuit. This would give a circumference of about 60 miles. At the four corners of an irregular quadrangle are the ruins of Kouyunjik, Nimrud, Kar-amless, and Khorsabad. These four great masses of ruins, with the whole area in-cluded within the parallelogram they form by lines drawn from the one to the other,

are generally regarded as composing the whole ruins of Nineveh.

Ni'san—*month of flowers*—(Neh. 2:1) the first month of the Jewish sacred year. (See ABIB.) Assyrian *nisannu*, "beginning."

Nis'roch, probably connected with the Hebrew word *nĕshĕr*, an eagle. An As-syrian god, supposed to be that represented with the head of an eagle. Sennacherib was killed in the temple of this idol (2 Kings 19:37; Isa. 37:38).

NISROCH.

Ni'tre (Prov. 25:20; R. V. marg., "soda"), properly "natron," a substance so called because, rising from the bottom of the Lake Natron in Egypt, it becomes dry and hard in the sun, and is the *soda* which effervesces when vinegar is poured on it. It is a carbon-ate of soda—not saltpetre, which the word generally denotes (Jer. 2:22; R. V. "lye").

No or **No-A'mon**—*the home of Amon*—the name of Thebes, the ancient capital of what is called the Middle Empire, in Upper or Southern Egypt. "The multitude of No" (Jer. 46 : 25) is more correctly rendered, as in the Revised Version, "Amon of No"— *i.e.*, No, where Jupiter Amon had his temple. In Ezek. 30 : 14, 16 it is simply called "No ; " but in ver. 15 the name has the Hebrew *Hamon* prefixed to it, "Hamon No." This prefix is probably the name simply of the god usually styled Amon or Ammon. In Nah. 3 : 8 the "populous No" of the Authorized Version is in the Revised Version correctly rendered "No Amon."

It was the Diospolis or Thebes of the Greeks, celebrated for its hundred gates and its vast population. It stood on both sides of the Nile, and is by some supposed to have included Karnak and Luxor. In grandeur and extent it can only be compared to Nineveh. It is mentioned only in the prophecies referred to, which point to its total destruction. It was first taken by the Assyrians in the time of Sargon (Isa. 20). It was afterwards "delivered into the hand" of Nebuchadnezzar and Assurbani-pal (Jer. 46 : 25, 26). Cambyses, king of the Persians (B.C. 525), further laid it waste by fire. Its ruin was completed (B.C. 81) by Ptolemy Lathyrus. The ruins of this city are still among the most notable in the valley of the Nile. They have formed a great storehouse of interesting historic remains for more than two thousand years. "As I wandered day after day with ever-growing amazement amongst these relics of ancient magnificence, I felt that if all the ruins in Europe—classical, Celtic, and medieval—were brought together into one centre, they would fall far short both in extent and grandeur of those of this single Egyptian city."—Manning, *The Land of the Pharaohs.*

Noadi'ah—*meeting with the Lord.* (1.) A Levite who returned from Babylon (Ezra 8 : 33).

(2.) A false prophetess who assisted Tobiah and Sanballat against the Jews (Neh. 6 : 14). Being bribed by them, she tried to stir up discontent among the inhabitants of Jerusalem, and so to embarrass Nehemiah in his great work of rebuilding the ruined walls of the city.

No'ah—*rest*—(Heb. *Noah*) the grandson of Methuselah (Gen. 5 : 25–29), who was for two hundred and fifty years contemporary with Adam, and the son of Lamech, who was about fifty years old at the time of Adam's death. This patriarch is rightly regarded as the connecting link between the old and the new world. He is the second great progenitor of the human family.

The words of his father Lamech at his birth (Gen. 5 : 29) have been regarded as in a sense prophetical, designating Noah as a type of Him who is the true "rest and comfort" of men under the burden of life (Matt. 11 : 28).

He lived five hundred years, and then there were born unto him three sons— Shem, Ham, and Japheth (Gen. 5 : 32). He was a "just man and perfect in his generation," and "walked with God" (comp. Ezek. 14 : 14, 20). But now the descendants of Cain and of Seth began to intermarry, and then there sprang up a race distinguished for their ungodliness. Men became more and more corrupt, and God determined to sweep the earth of its wicked population (Gen. 6 : 7). But with Noah God entered into a covenant, with a promise of deliverance from the threatened deluge (18). He was accordingly commanded to build an ark (6 : 14–16) for the saving of himself and his house. An interval of one hundred and twenty years elapsed while the ark was being built (6 : 3), during which Noah bore constant testimony against the unbelief and wickedness of that generation (1 Pet. 3 : 18–20 ; 2 Pet. 2 : 5).

When the ark of "gopher-wood" (mentioned only here) was at length completed according to the command of the Lord, the living creatures that were to be preserved entered into it ; and then Noah and his wife and sons and daughters-in-law entered it, and the "Lord shut him in" (Gen. 7 : 16). The judgment threatened now fell on the guilty world—"the world that then was, being overflowed with water, perished" (2 Pet. 3 : 6). The ark floated on the waters for one hundred and fifty days, and then rested on the mountains of Ararat (Gen. 8 : 3, 4) ; but not for a considerable time after this was divine permission given him to leave the ark, so that he and his family were a whole year shut up within it (Gen. 6-14).

On leaving the ark Noah's first act was to erect an altar, the first of which there is any mention, and offer the sacrifices of adoring thanks and praise to God, who entered into a covenant with him—the first covenant between God and man—granting him possession of the earth by a new and special charter, which remains in force to the present time (Gen. 8:21-9:17). As a sign and witness of this covenant, the rainbow was adopted and set apart by God, as a sure pledge that never again would the earth be destroyed by a flood.

But, alas! Noah after this fell into grievous sin (Gen. 9:21); and the conduct of Ham on this sad occasion led to the memorable prediction regarding his three sons and their descendants. Noah "lived after the flood three hundred and fifty years, and he died" (28:29). (See DELUGE.)

No'ah—*motion*—(Heb. *No'ah*) one of the five daughters of Zelophehad (Num. 26:33; 27:1; 36:11; Josh. 17:3).

Nob—*high place*—a city of the priests, first mentioned in the history of David's wanderings (1 Sam. 21:1). Here the tabernacle was then standing, and here Ahimelech the priest resided. (See AHIMELECH.) From Isa. 10:28-32 it seems to have been near Jerusalem. It has been identified by some with *el-Isawiyeh*, one mile and a half to the north-east of Jerusalem. But according to Isa. 10:28-32 it was on the south of Geba, on the road to Jerusalem, and within sight of the city. This identification does not meet these conditions, and hence others (as Dean Stanley) think that it was the northern summit of Mount Olivet, the place where David "worshipped God" when fleeing from Absalom (2 Sam. 15:32), or more probably (Conder) that it was the same as Mizpeh (*q.v.*)—Judg. 20:1; Josh. 18:26; 1 Sam. 7:16—at *Nebi Samwil*, about 5 miles north-west of Jerusalem.

After being supplied with the sacred loaves of showbread, and girding on the sword of Goliath, which was brought forth from behind the ephod, David fled from

Nob and sought refuge at the court of Achish, the king of Gath, where he was cast into prison. (Comp. titles of Ps. 34 and 56.)

No'bah—*howling*. (1.) Num. 32:42.

(2.) The name given to Kenath (*q.v.*) by Nobah when he conquered it. It was on the east of Gilead (Judg. 8:11).

No'bleman (Gr. *basilikos*—i.e., "king's man")—an officer of state (John 4:49) in the service of Herod Antipas. He is supposed to have been the Chuza, Herod's steward, whose wife was one of those women who "ministered unto the Lord of their substance" (Luke 8:3). This officer came to Jesus at Cana and besought him to go down to Capernaum and heal his son, who lay there at the point of death. Our Lord sent him away with the joyful assurance that his son was alive.

Nod—*exile; wandering; unrest*—a name given to the country to which Cain fled (Gen. 4:16). It lay on the east of Eden.

No'dab—*noble*—probably a tribe descended from one of the sons of Ishmael, with whom the trans-Jordanic tribes made war (1 Chr. 5:19).

No'gah—*splendour*—one of David's sons, born at Jerusalem (1 Chr. 3:7).

Noph, the Hebrew name of an Egyptian city (Isa. 19:13; Jer. 2:16; 44:1; 46:14, 19; Ezek. 30:13, 16). In Hos. 9:6 the Hebrew name is Moph, and is translated "Memphis," which is its Greek and Latin form. It was one of the most ancient and important cities of Egypt, and stood a little to the south of the modern Cairo, on the western bank of the Nile. It was the capital of Lower Egypt. Among the ruins found at this place is a colossal statue of Rameses the Great. (See MEMPHIS.)

No'phah—*blast*—a city of Moab which was occupied by the Amorites (Num. 21:30).

North country, a general name for the countries that lay north of Palestine. Most of the invading armies entered Palestine from the north (Isa. 41:25; Jer. 1:14, 15; 50:3, 9, 41; 51:48; Ezek. 26:7).

North'ward (Heb. *tsâphôn*), a "hidden" or "dark place," as opposed to the sunny south (Deut. 3:27). A Hebrew in speaking of the points of the compass was considered as always having his face to the east, and hence "the left hand" (Gen. 14 : 15; Job 23 : 9) denotes the north. The "kingdoms of the north" are Chaldea, Assyria, Media, etc.

Nose-jew'els. Only mentioned in Isa. 3 : 21, although referred to in Gen. 24 : 47, Prov. 11 : 22, Hos. 2 : 13. They were among the most valued of ancient female ornaments. They "were made of ivory or metal, and occasionally jewelled. They were more than an inch in diameter, and hung upon the mouth. Eliezer gave one to Rebekah which was of gold and weighed half a shekel......At the present day the women in the country and in the desert wear these ornaments in one of the sides of the nostrils, which droop like the ears in consequence."

Numbering of the people. Besides the numbering of the tribes mentioned in the history of the wanderings in the wilderness, we have an account of a general census of the whole nation from Dan to Beersheba, which David gave directions to Joab to make (1 Chr. 21 : 1). Joab very reluctantly began to carry out the king's command.

This act of David in ordering a numbering of the people arose from pride and a self-glorifying spirit. It indicated a reliance on his part on an arm of flesh, an estimating of his power not by the divine favour but by the material resources of his kingdom. He thought of military achievement and of conquest, and forgot that he was God's vicegerent. In all this he sinned against God. While Joab was engaged in the census, David's heart smote him, and he became deeply conscious of his fault; and in profound humiliation he confessed, "I have sinned greatly in what I have done." The prophet Gad was sent to him to put before him three dreadful alternatives (2 Sam. 24 : 13; for "seven years" in this verse, the LXX. and 1 Chr. 21 : 12 have "three years"), three of Jehovah's four sore judgments (Ezek. 14 : 21). Two of these David had already experienced. He had fled for some months before Absalom, and had suffered three years' famine on account of the slaughter of the Gibeon-

ites. In his "strait" David said, "Let me fall into the hands of the Lord." A pestilence broke out among the people, and in three days swept away 70,000. At David's intercession the plague was stayed, and at the threshing-floor of Araunah (q.v.), where the destroying angel was arrested in his progress, David erected an altar, and there offered up sacrifices to God (2 Chr. 3 : 1).

The census, so far as completed, showed that there were at least 1,300,000 fighting men in the kingdom, indicating at that time a population of about six or seven millions in all. (See CENSUS.)

Num'bers, Book of, the fourth of the books of the Pentateuch, called in the Hebrew be-midbar—i.e., "in the wilderness." In the LXX. version it is called "Numbers," and this name is now the usual title of the book. It is so called because it contains a record of the numbering of the people in the wilderness of Sinai (1-4), and of their numbering afterwards on the plain of Moab (26).

This book is of special historical interest as furnishing us with details as to the route of the Israelites in the wilderness and their principal encampments. It may be divided into three parts :—

1. The numbering of the people at Sinai, and preparations for their resuming their march (1-10 : 10). The sixth chapter gives an account of the vow of a Nazarite.

2. An account of the journey from Sinai to Moab, the sending out of the spies and the report they brought back, and the murmurings (eight times) of the people at the hardships by the way (10 : 11-21 : 20).

3. The transactions in the plain of Moab before crossing the Jordan (21 : 21-ch. 36).

The period comprehended in the history extends from the second month of the second year after the Exodus to the beginning of the eleventh month of the fortieth year—in all about thirty-eight years and ten months; a dreary period of wanderings, during which that disobedient generation all died in the wilderness. They were fewer in number at the end of their wanderings than when they left the land of Egypt. We see in this history, on the one hand, the unceasing care of the Almighty over his chosen people during their wanderings ; and, on the other hand, the murmurings and rebellions by which they offended their heavenly Protector, drew down repeated marks of his displeasure, and provoked him to say that they should "not enter into his rest" because of their unbelief (Heb. 3:19).

This, like the other books of the Pentateuch, bears evidence of having been written by Moses.

The expression "the book of the wars of the Lord," occurring in 21:14, has given rise to much discussion. But, after all, "what this book was is uncertain—whether some writing of Israel not now extant, or some writing of the Amorites which contained songs and triumphs of their king Sihon's victories, out of which Moses may cite this testimony, as Paul sometimes does out of heathen poets (Acts 17:28; Titus 1:12)."

Nun. Beyond the fact that he was the father of Joshua nothing more is known of him (Ex. 33:11).

Nuts were among the presents Jacob sent into Egypt for the purpose of conciliating Joseph (Gen. 43:11). This was the fruit of the pistachio tree, which resembles the sumac. It is of the size of an olive. In Cant. 6:11 a different Hebrew word (*'egôz*), which means "walnuts," is used.

Nym'phas—*nymph*—saluted by Paul in his Epistle to the Colossians as a member of the church of Laodicea (Col. 4:15).

O

Oak. There are six Hebrew words rendered "oak."

(1.) *'El* occurs only in the word El-paran (Gen. 14:6). The LXX. renders by "terebinth." In the plural form this word occurs in Isa. 1:29; 57:5 (A.V. marg. and R.V., "among the oaks"); 61:3 ("trees"). The word properly means strong, mighty, and hence a strong tree.

(2.) *'Elâh*, Gen. 35:4, "under the oak which was by Shechem" (R.V. marg., "terebinth"). Isa. 6:13, A.V., "teil-tree;" R.V., "terebinth." Isa. 1:30, R.V. marg., "terebinth." Absalom in his flight was caught in the branches of a "great oak" (2 Sam. 18:9; R.V. marg., "terebinth").

(3.) *'Elôn*, Judg. 4:11; 9:6 (R.V., "oak;" A.V., following the Targum, "plain") properly the deciduous species of oak shedding its foliage in autumn.

(4.) *'Elân*, only in Dan. 4:11, 14, 20, rendered "tree" in Nebuchadnezzar's dream. Probably some species of the oak is intended.

(5.) *'Allâh*, Josh. 24:26. The place here referred to is called *Allôn-moreh* ("the oak of Moreh," as in R.V.) in Gen. 12:6 and 35:4.

(6.) *'Allôn*, always rendered "oak." Probably the evergreen oak (called also ilex and holm oak) is intended. The oak woods of Bashan are frequently alluded to (Isa. 2:13; Ezek. 27:6). Three species of oaks are found in Palestine, of which the "prickly evergreen oak" (*Quercus coccifera*) is the most abundant. "It covers the rocky hills of Palestine with a dense brushwood of trees from 8 to 12 feet high, branching from the base, thickly covered with small evergreen rigid leaves, and bearing acorns copiously." The so-called Abraham's oak at Hebron is of this species. Tristram says that this oak near Hebron "has for several centuries taken the place of the once renowned terebinth which marked the site of Mamre on the other side of the city. The terebinth existed at Mamre in the time of Vespasian, and under it the captive Jews were sold as slaves. It disappeared about A.D. 330, and no tree now marks the grove of Mamre. The present oak is the noblest tree in Southern Palestine, being 23 feet in girth, and the diameter of the foliage, which is unsymmetrical, being about 90 feet." (See HEBRON ; TEIL-TREE.)

Oath, a solemn appeal to God, permitted

on fitting occasions (Deut. 6 : 13 ; Jer. 4 : 2), in various forms (Gen. 16 : 5 ; 2 Sam. 12 : 5 ; Ruth 1 : 17 ; Hos. 4 : 15 ; Rom. 1 : 9), and taken in different ways (Gen. 14 : 22 ; 24 : 2 ; 2 Chr. 6 : 22). God is represented as taking an oath (Heb. 6 : 16–18), so also Christ (Matt. 26 : 64), and Paul (Rom. 9 : 1 ; Gal. 1 : 20 ; Phil. 1 : 8). The precept, "Swear not at all," refers probably to ordinary conversation between man and man (Matt. 5 : 34, 37). But if the words are taken as referring to oaths, then their intention may have been to show " that the proper state of Christians is to require no oaths ; that when evil is expelled from among them every yea and nay will be as decisive as an oath, every promise as binding as a vow."

Obadi′ah—*servant of the Lord.* (1.) An Israelite who was chief in the household of King Ahab (1 Kings 18 : 3). Amid great spiritual degeneracy he maintained his fidelity to God, and interposed to protect the Lord's prophets, an hundred of whom he hid at great personal risk in a cave (4, 13). Ahab seems to have held Obadiah in great honour, although he had no sympathy with his piety (5, 6, 7). The last notice of him is his bringing back tidings to Ahab that Elijah, whom he had so long sought for, was at hand (9–16). "Go," said Elijah to him, when he met him in the way—" go tell thy lord, Behold, Elijah is here."

(2.) A chief of the tribe of Issachar (1 Chr. 7 : 3).

(3.) A descendant of Saul (1 Chr. 8 : 38).

(4.) A Levite, after the Captivity (1 Chr. 9 : 16).

(5.) A Gadite who joined David at Ziklag (1 Chr. 12 : 9).

(6.) A prince of Zebulun in the time of David (1 Chr. 27 : 19).

(7.) One of the princes sent by Jehoshaphat to instruct the people in the law (2 Chr. 17 : 7).

(8.) A Levite who superintended the repairs of the temple under Josiah (2 Chr. 34 : 12).

(9.) One who accompanied Ezra on the return from Babylon (Ezra 8 : 9).

(10.) A prophet, fourth of the minor prophets in the Hebrew canon, and fifth in the LXX. He was probably contemporary

with Jeremiah and Ezekiel. Of his personal history nothing is known.

Obadi′ah, Book of, consists of one chapter, "concerning Edom,"its impending doom (1–16), and the restoration of Israel (17–21). This is the shortest book of the Old Testament.

There are on record the account of four captures of Jerusalem—(1) by Shishak in the reign of Rehoboam (1 Kings 14 : 25) ; (2) by the Philistines and Arabians in the reign of Jehoram (2 Chr. 21 : 16) ; (3) by Joash, the king of Israel, in the reign of Amaziah (2 Kings 14 : 13) ; and (4) by the Babylonians, when Jerusalem was taken and destroyed by Nebuchadnezzar (B.C. 586). Obadiah (11–14) speaks of this capture as a thing past. He sees the calamity as having already come on Jerusalem, and the Edomites as joining their forces with those of the Chaldeans in bringing about the degradation and ruin of Israel. We do not indeed read that the Edomites actually took part with the Chaldeans, but the probabilities are that they did so, and this explains the words of Obadiah in denouncing against Edom the judgments of God. The date of his prophecies was thus in or about the year of the destruction of Jerusalem.

Edom is the type of Israel's and of God's last foe (Isa. 62 : 1-4). These will finally all be vanquished, and the kingdom will be the Lord's (comp. Ps. 22 : 28).

O′bal—*stripped*—the eighth son of Joktan (Gen. 10 : 28) ; called also Ebal (1 Chr. 1 : 22).

O′bed—*serving ; worshipping.* (1.) A son of Boaz and Ruth (Ruth 4 : 21, 22), and the grandfather of David (Matt. 1 : 5).

(2.) 1 Chr. 2 : 34–38.

(3.) 1 Chr. 26 : 7.

(4.) 2 Chr. 23 : 1.

O′bed-E′dom—*servant of Edom.* (1.) "The Gittite " (probably so called because he was a native of Gath-rimmon), a Levite of the family of the Korahites (1 Chr. 26 : 1, 4–8), to whom was specially intrusted the custody of the ark (1 Chr. 15 : 18). When David was bringing up the ark " from the house of Abinadab, that was in Gibeah " (probably some hill or eminence near Kirjath-jearim), and had reached

Nachon's threshing-floor, he became afraid because of the "breach upon Uzzah," and carried it aside into the house of Obed-edom (2 Sam. 6 : 1–12). There it remained for six months, and was to him and his house the occasion of great blessing. David then removed it with great rejoicing to Jerusalem, and set it in the midst of the tabernacle he had pitched for it.

(2.) A Merarite Levite, a temple porter, who with his eight sons guarded the southern gate (1 Chr. 15 : 18, 21 ; 26 : 4, 8, 15).

(3.) One who had charge of the temple treasures (2 Chr. 25 : 24).

Obei'sance, homage or reverence to any one (Gen. 37 : 7 ; 43 : 28).

O'bil—*a keeper of camels*—an Ishmaelite who was "over the camels" in the time of David (1 Chr. 27 : 30).

O'both—*bottles*—an encampment of the Israelites during the wanderings in the wilderness (Num. 33 : 43)—the first after the setting up of the brazen serpent.

O'ded—*restoring*, or *setting up*. (1.) Father of the prophet Azariah (2 Chr. 15 : 1, 8). (2.) A prophet in the time of Ahaz and Pekah (2 Chr. 28 : 9–15).

Offence'. (1.) An injury or wrong done to one (1 Sam. 25 : 31 ; Rom. 5 : 15).

(2.) A stumbling-block or cause of temptation (Isa. 8 : 14 ; Matt. 16 : 23 ; 18 : 7). Greek *skandalon*, properly that at which one stumbles or takes offence. The "offence of the cross" (Gal. 5 : 11) is the offence the Jews took at the teaching that salvation was by the crucified One, and by him alone. Salvation by the cross was a stumbling-block to their national pride.

Of'fering, an oblation, dedicated to God. Thus Cain consecrated to God of the first-fruits of the earth, and Abel of the first-lings of the flock (Gen. 4 : 3, 4).

Under the Levitical system different kinds of offerings are specified, and laws laid down as to their presentation. These are described under their distinctive names.

Og—*gigantic*—the king of Bashan, who was defeated by Moses in a pitched battle at Edrei, and was slain along with his sons (Deut. 1 : 4), and whose kingdom was given to the tribes of Reuben and Gad and half the tribe of Manasseh (Num. 21 : 32–35 ;

Deut. 3 : 1–13). His bedstead (or rather sarcophagus) was of iron (or ironstone), 9 cubits in length and 4 cubits in breadth. His overthrow was afterwards celebrated in song (Ps. 135 : 11 ; 136 : 20). (See SIHON.)

O'had—*united*, or *power*—the third son of Simeon (Gen. 46 : 10).

O'hel—*a house ; tent*—the fourth son of Zerubbabel (1 Chr. 3 : 20).

Oil. Only olive oil seems to have been used among the Hebrews. It was used for many purposes : for anointing the body or the hair (Ex. 29 : 7 ; 2 Sam. 14 : 2 ; Ps. 23 : 5 ; 92 : 10 ; 104 : 15 ; Luke 7 : 46) ; in some of the offerings (Ex. 29 : 40 ; Lev. 7 : 12 ; Num. 6 : 15 ; 15 : 14), but was excluded from the sin-offering (Lev. 5 : 11) and the jealousy-offering (Num. 5 : 15) ; for burning in lamps (Ex. 25 : 6 ; 27 : 20 ; Matt. 25 : 3) ; for medicinal purposes (Isa. 1 : 6 ; Luke 10 : 34 ; James 5 : 14) ; and for anointing the dead (Matt. 26 : 12 ; Luke 23 : 56).

It was one of the most valuable products of the country (Deut. 32 : 13 ; Ezek. 16 : 13), and formed an article of extensive commerce with Tyre (27 : 17).

The use of it was a sign of gladness (Ps. 92 : 10 ; Isa. 61 : 3), and its omission a token of sorrow (2 Sam. 14 : 2 ; Matt. 6 : 17). It was very abundant in Galilee. (See OLIVE.)

Oil-tree (Isa. 41 : 19 ; R.V. marg., "ole-aster ") — Heb. *'êtz shemen* — rendered "olive tree" in 1 Kings 6 : 23, 31, 32, 33 (R.V., "olive wood") and "pine branches" in Neh. 8 : 15 (R.V., "branches of wild olive"), was some tree distinct from the olive. It was probably the oleaster (*Eleagnus angustifolius*), which grows abundantly in almost all parts of Palestine, especially about Hebron and Samaria. "It has a fine hard wood," says Tristram, "and yields an inferior oil, but it has no relationship to the olive, which, however, it resembles in general appearance."

Oint'ment. Various fragrant preparations, also compounds for medical purposes, are so called (Ex. 30 : 25 ; Ps. 133 : 2 ; Isa. 1 : 6 ; Amos 6 : 6 ; John 12 : 3 ; Rev. 18 : 13).

Old gate, one of the gates in the north wall of Jerusalem, so called because built by the Jebusites (Neh. 3 : 6 ; 12 : 39).

Ol′ive, the fruit of the olive-tree. This tree yielded oil which was highly valued. The best oil was from olives that were plucked before being fully ripe, and then beaten or squeezed (Deut. 24:20; Isa. 17:6; 24:13). It was called "beaten," or "fresh oil" (Ex. 27:20). There were also oil-presses, in which the oil was trodden out by the feet (Micah 6:15). James (3: 12) calls the fruit "olive berries." The phrase "vineyards and olives" (Judg. 15:5, A.V.) should be simply "olive-yard," or "olive-garden," as in the Revised Version. (See OIL.)

Ol′ive-tree is frequently mentioned in Scripture. The dove from the ark brought an olive-branch to Noah (Gen. 8:11). It is mentioned among the most notable trees of Palestine, where it was cultivated long before the time of the Hebrews (Deut. 6: 11; 8:8). It is mentioned in the first Old Testament parable, that of Jotham (Judg. 9:9), and is named among the blessings of the "good land," and is at the present day

Branch.   OLIVE-TREE.   *Fruit.*

the one characteristic tree of Palestine. The oldest olive-trees in the country are those which are enclosed in the Garden of Gethsemane. It is referred to as an emblem of prosperity and beauty and religious privilege (Ps. 52:8; Jer. 11:16; Hos. 14: 6). The two "witnesses" mentioned in Rev. 11:4 are spoken of as "two olive trees standing before the God of the earth." (Comp. Zech. 4:3, 11–14.)

The "olive-tree, wild by nature" (Rom. 11:24), is the shoot or cutting of the good olive-tree which, left ungrafted, grows up to be a "wild olive." In Rom. 11:17 Paul refers to the practice of grafting shoots of the wild olive into a "good" olive which has become unfruitful. By such a process the sap of the good olive, by pervading the branch which is "graffed in," makes it a good branch, bearing good olives. Thus the Gentiles, being a "wild olive," but now "graffed in," yield fruit, but only through the sap of the tree into which they have been graffed. This is a process "contrary to nature" (11:24).

Ol′ives, Mount of, so called from the

olive trees with which its sides are clothed, is a mountain ridge on the east of Jerusalem (1 Kings 11 : 7 ; Ezek. 11 : 23 ; Zech. 14 : 4), from which it is separated by the valley of Kidron. It is first mentioned in connection with David's flight from Jerusalem through the rebellion of Absalom (2 Sam. 15 : 20), and is only once again mentioned in the Old Testament, in Zech. 14 : 4. It is, however, frequently alluded to (1 Kings 11 : 7 ; 2 Kings 23 : 13 ; Neh. 8 : 15 ; Ezek. 11 : 23).

It is frequently mentioned in the New Testament (Matt. 21 : 1 ; 26 : 30, etc.). It now bears the name of *Jebel et-Tûr—i.e.*, "Mount of the Summit ; " also sometimes called *Jebel ez-Zeitun—i.e.*, "Mount of Olives." It is about 200 feet above the level of the city. The road from Jerusalem to Bethany runs as of old over this mount. It was on this mount that Jesus stood when he wept over Jerusalem. "No name in Scripture," says Dr. Porter, "calls up associations at once so sacred and so pleasing as that of Olivet. The 'mount' is so intimately connected with the private, the devotional life of the Saviour, that we read of it and look at it with feelings of deepest interest and affection. Here he often sat with his disciples, telling them of wondrous events yet to come—of the destruction of the Holy City ; of the sufferings, the persecution, and the final triumph of his followers (Matt. 24). Here he gave them the beautiful parables of the ten virgins and the five talents (25) ; here he was wont to retire on each evening for meditation, and prayer, and rest of body, when weary and harassed by the labours and trials of the day (Luke 21 : 37) ; and here he came on the night of his betrayal to utter that wonderful prayer, 'O my Father, if it be possible, let this cup pass from me : nevertheless not as I will, but as thou wilt' (Matt. 26 : 39). And when the cup of God's wrath had been drunk, and death and the grave conquered, he led his disciples out again over Olivet as far as to Bethany, and after a parting blessing ascended to heaven (Luke 24 : 50, 51 ; Acts 1 : 12)."

This mount, or rather mountain range, has four summits or peaks : (1) the "Galilee " peak, so called from a tradition that the angels stood here when they spoke to the disciples (Acts 1 : 11) ; (2) the "Mount of Ascension," the supposed site of that event, which was, however, somewhere probably nearer Bethany (Luke 24 : 51, 52) ; (3) the "Prophets,"from the catacombs on its side, called "the prophets' tombs ; " and (4) the "Mount of Corruption," so called because of the "high places"erected there by Solomon for the idolatrous worship of his foreign wives (1 Kings 11 : 7, 8 ; 2 Kings 23 : 13 ; Vulg., "Mount of Offence ").

Olym'pas, a Roman Christian whom Paul salutes (Rom. 16 : 15).

O'mar—*eloquent*—the son of Eliphaz, who was Esau's eldest son (Gen. 36 : 11-15).

O'mega (Rev. 1 : 8), the last letter in the Greek alphabet. (See ALPHA.)

O'mer—*a handful*—one-tenth of an ephah =half a gallon dry measure (Ex. 16 : 22, 32, 33, 36)= "tenth deal."

Om'ri—*servant of Jehovah.* (1.) When Elah was murdered by Zimri at Tirzah (1 Kings 16 : 15-27), Omri, his captain, was made king (B.C. 931). For four years there was continued opposition to his reign, Tibni, another claimant to the throne, leading the opposing party ; but at the close of that period all his rivals were defeated, and he became king of Israel— "Tibni died and Omri reigned " (B.C. 927). By his vigour and power he gained great eminence and consolidated the kingdom. He fixed his dynasty on the throne so firmly that it continued during four succeeding reigns. Tirza was for six years the seat of his government. He then removed the capital to Samaria (*q.v.*), where he died, and was succeeded by his son Ahab. "He wrought evil in the eyes of the Lord, and did worse than all that were before him."

Beth-omri, "the house" or "city of Omri," is the name usually found on Assyrian inscriptions for Samaria. In the *stèle* of Mesha (the "Moabite stone"), which was erected in Moab about twenty or thirty years after Omri's death, it is recorded that Omri oppressed Moab till Mesha delivered the land : "Omri, king of Israel, oppressed Moab many days, for Chemosh was angry with his land. His son succeeded him, and he also said, I will oppress Moab" (comp. 2 Kings 1:1; 3:4, 5). The "Moabite stone" also records that "Omri took the land of Medeba, and occupied it in his day and in the days of his son forty years."

On—*light; the sun*—(Gen. 41:45, 50), the great seat of sun-worship, called also Beth-shemesh (Jer. 43:13) and Aven (Ezek. 30:17), stood on the east bank of the Nile, a few miles north of Memphis, and near Cairo, in the north-east. The Vulgate and the LXX. Versions have "Heliopolis" ("city of the sun") instead of On in Genesis and of Aven in Ezekiel. The "city of destruction" Isaiah speaks of (19:18, marg. "of Heres;" Heb. *'Ir-ha-hĕrĕs*, which some MSS. read *Ir-ha-heres*—*i.e.*, "city of the sun") may be the name given to On, the prophecy being that the time will come when that city which was known as the "city of the sun-god" shall become the "city of destruction" of the sun-god—*i.e.*, when idolatry shall cease, and the worship of the true God be established.

In ancient times this city was full of obelisks dedicated to the sun. Of these only one now remains standing. "Cleopatra's Needle" was one of those which stood in this city in front of the Temple of Tum—*i.e.*, "the sun." It is now erected on the Thames Embankment, London.

"It was at On that Joseph wooed and won the dark-skinned Asenath, the daughter of the high priest of its great temple." This was a noted university town, and here Moses gained his acquaintance with "all the wisdom of the Egyptians."

O'nan—*strong*—the second son of Judah (Gen. 38:4-10; comp. Deut. 25:5; Matt. 22:24). He died before the going down of Jacob and his family into Egypt.

Ones'imus—*useful*—a slave who, after robbing his master Philemon (*q.v.*) at Colosse, fled to Rome, where he was converted by the apostle Paul, who sent him back to his master with the epistle which bears his name. In it he beseeches Philemon to receive his slave as a "faithful and beloved brother." Paul offers to pay to Philemon anything his slave had taken, and to bear the wrong he had done him. He was accompanied on his return by Tychicus, the bearer of the Epistle to the Colossians (Philemon 16, 18).

The story of this fugitive Colossian slave is a remarkable evidence of the freedom of access to the prisoner which was granted to all, and "a beautiful illustration both of the character of St. Paul and the transfiguring power and righteous principles of the gospel."

Onesiph'orus — *bringing profit* — an Ephesian Christian who showed great kindness to Paul at Rome. He served him in many things, and had oft refreshed him. Paul expresses a warm interest in him and his household (2 Tim. 1:16-18; 4:19).

On'ion. The Israelites in the wilderness longed for the "onions and garlick of Egypt" (Num. 11:5). This was the *bĕtsĕl* of the Hebrews, the *Allium cepe* of botanists, of which it is said that there are some thirty or forty species now growing in Palestine. The onion is "the 'undivided' leek—*unio, unus*, one."

O'no, a town of Benjamin, in the "plain of Ono" (1 Chr. 8:12; Ezra 2:33); now *Kefr 'Ana*, 5 miles north of Lydda, and about 30 miles north-west of Jerusalem. Not succeeding in their attempts to deter Nehemiah from rebuilding the walls of Jerusalem, Sanballat and Tobiah resorted to stratagem, and pretending to wish a conference with him, they invited him to meet them at Ono. Four times they made the request, and every time Nehemiah refused to come. Their object was to take him prisoner.

On'ycha—*a nail; claw; hoof*—(Heb. *shehĕleth;* Ex. 30:34), a Latin word applied to the *operculum*—*i.e.*, the claw or nail of the strombus or wing-shell, a univalve common in the Red Sea. The *opercula* of these shell-fish when burned emit a strong odour "like castoreum." This was an ingredient in the sacred incense.

O'nyx — *a nail; claw; hoof* — (Heb. *shôham*), a precious stone adorning the breast-plate of the high priest and the shoulders of the ephod (Ex. 28:9-12, 20;

35:27; Job 28:16; Ezek. 28:13). It was found in the land of Havilah (Gen. 2:12). The LXX. translates the Hebrew word by *smaragdos,* an emerald. Some think that the sardonyx is meant. But the onyx differs from the sardonyx in this, that while the latter has two layers (black and white) the former has three (black, white, and red).

Open place. Gen. 38:14, 21, marg. Enaim; the same probably as Enam (Josh. 15:34), a city in the lowland or Shephêlah.

O'phel—*hill; mound*—the long, narrow, rounded promontory on the southern slope of the temple hill, between the Tyropœon and the Kedron valley (2 Chr. 27:3; 33:14; Neh. 3:26, 27). It was surrounded by a separate wall, and was occupied by the Nethinim after the Captivity. This wall has been discovered by the engineers of the Palestine Exploration Fund at the south-eastern angle of the temple area. It is 4 feet below the present surface.

In 2 Kings 5:24 this word is translated "tower" (R.V., "hill"), denoting probably some eminence near Elisha's house.

O'phir. (1.) One of the sons of Joktan (Gen. 10:29).

(2.) Some region famous for its gold (1 Kings 9:28; 10:11; 22:48; Job 22:24; 28:10; Isa. 45:9). In the LXX. this word is rendered "Sophir," and "Sofir" is the Coptic name for India, which is the rendering of the Arabic version, as also of the Vulgate. Josephus has identified it with the Golden Chersonese—*i.e.*, the Malay peninsula. It is now generally identified with *Abhíra,* at the mouth of the Indus. Much may be said, however, in favour of the opinion that it was somewhere in Arabia.

Oph'ni—*mouldy*—a city of Benjamin (Josh. 18:24).

Oph'rah—*a fawn.* 1 Chr. 4:14.

Oph'rah—*id.* (1.) A city of Benjamin (Josh. 18:23); probably identical with Ephron (2 Chr. 13:19) and Ephraim (John 11:54).

(2.) "Of the Abi-ezrites." A city of Manasseh, 6 miles south-west of Shechem, the residence of Gideon (Judg. 6:11; 8:27, 32). After his great victory over the Midianites, he slew at this place the cap-

tive kings (8:18–21). He then assumed the function of high priest, and sought to make Ophrah what Shiloh should have been. This thing "became a snare" to Gideon and his house. After Gideon's death his family resided here till they were put to death by Abimelech (Judg. 9:5). It is identified with *Ferâta.*

Or'acle. In the Old Testament used in every case, except 2 Sam. 16:23, to denote the most holy place in the temple (1 Kings 6:5, 19–23; 8:6). In 2 Sam. 16:23 it means the Word of God. A man inquired "at the oracle of God" by means of the Urim and Thummim in the breastplate on the high priest's ephod.

In the New Testament it is used only in the plural, and always denotes the Word of God (Rom. 3:2; Heb. 5:12, etc.). The Scriptures are called "living oracles" (comp. Heb. 4:12) because of their quickening power (Acts 7:38).

O'reb—*raven*—a prince of Midian, who, being defeated by Gideon and put to straits, was slain along with Zeeb (Judg. 7:20–25). Many of the Midianites perished along with him (Ps. 83:9; Isa. 10:26).

O'reb, The rock of, the place where Gideon slew Oreb after the defeat of the Midianites (Judg. 7:25; Isa. 10:26). It was probably the place now called *Orbo,* on the east of Jordan, near Bethshean.

O'ren—*ash* or *pine*—the son of Jerahmeel (1 Chr. 2:25).

Or'gan, some kind of wind instrument, probably a kind of Pan's pipes (Gen. 4:21; Job 21:12; Ps. 150:4), which consisted of seven or eight reeds of unequal length.

Ori'on—Heb. *kĕsîl; i.e.,* "the fool"—the name of a constellation (Job 9:9; 38:31; Amos 5:8) consisting of about eighty stars. The Vulgate renders thus, but the LXX. renders by Hesperus—*i.e.,* "the evening-star," Venus. The Orientals "appear to have conceived of this constellation under the figure of an impious giant bound upon the sky." This giant was, according to tradition, Nimrod, the type of the folly that contends against God. In Isa. 13:10 the plural form of the Hebrew word is rendered "constellations."

Or'nan. 1 Chr. 21:15. (See ARAUNAH.)

Or'pah—*forelock* or *fawn*—a Moabitess, the wife of Chilion (Ruth 1:4; 4:10). On the death of her husband she accompanied Naomi, her mother-in-law, part of the way to Bethlehem, and then returned to Moab.

Or'phans (Lam. 5:3) — *i.e.*, desolate and without protectors. The word occurs only here. In John 14:18 the word there rendered "comfortless" (R.V., "desolate;" marg., "orphans") properly means "orphans." The same Greek word is rendered "fatherless" in James 1:27.

Os'prey—Heb. *'ozniyyâh*—an unclean bird according to the Mosaic law (Lev. 11: 13; Deut. 14:12); the fish-eating eagle (*Pandion haliaëtus*); one of the lesser eagles. But the Hebrew word may be taken to denote the short-toed eagle (*Circaëtus gallicus* of Southern Europe), one of the most abundant of the eagle tribe found in Palestine.

Os'sifrage—Heb. *pĕrĕs* = to "break" or "crush"—the *lammer-geier*, or bearded vulture, the largest of the whole vulture tribe. It was an unclean bird (Lev. 11:13; Deut. 14:12). It is not a gregarious bird, and is found but rarely in Palestine. "When the other vultures have picked the flesh off any animal, he comes in at the end of the feast, and swallows the bones, or breaks them, and swallows the pieces if he cannot otherwise extract the marrow. The bones he cracks [hence the appropriateness of the name ossifrage—*i.e.*, "bone-breaker"] by letting them fall on a rock from a great height. He does not, however, confine himself to these delicacies, but whenever he has an opportunity will devour lambs, kids, or hares. These he generally obtains by pushing them over cliffs, when he has watched his opportunity; and he has been known to attack men while climbing rocks, and dash them against the bottom. But tortoises and serpents are his ordinary food. ......No doubt it was a lammer-geier that mistook the bald head of the poet Æschylus for a stone, and dropped on it the tortoise which killed him" (Tristram's *Nat. Hist.*).

Os'trich (Lam. 4:3), the rendering of Hebrew pl. *'ênîm;* so called from its greediness and gluttony. The allusion here is to the habit of the ostrich with reference to its eggs, which is thus described: "The outer layer of eggs is generally so ill covered that they are destroyed in quantities by jackals, wild-cats, etc., and that the natives carry them away, only taking care not to leave the marks of their footsteps, since, when the ostrich comes and finds that her nest is discovered, she crushes the whole brood, and builds a nest elsewhere." In Job 39:13 this word in the Authorized Version is the rendering of a Hebrew word (*notsâh*) which means "feathers," as in the Revised Version. In the same verse the word "peacocks" of the Authorized Version is the rendering of the Hebrew pl. *rĕnânîm*, properly meaning "ostriches," as in the Revised Version. (See OWL [1].)

Oth'ni — *a lion of Jehovah* — a son of Shemaiah, and one of the temple porters in the time of David (1 Chr. 26:7). He was a "mighty man of valour."

Oth'niel—*lion of God*—the first of the judges. His wife Achsah was the daughter of Caleb (Josh. 15:16, 17; Judg. 1:13). He gained her hand as a reward for his bravery in leading a successful expedition against Debir (*q.v.*) Some thirty years after the death of Joshua, the Israelites fell under the subjection of Chushan-rishathaim (*q.v.*), the king of Mesopotamia. He oppressed them for full eight years, when they "cried" unto Jehovah, and Othniel was raised up to be their deliverer. He was the younger brother of Caleb (Judg. 3:6, 9-11). He is the only judge mentioned connected with the tribe of Judah. Under him the land had rest forty years.

Ouch'es, an Old English word denoting cavities or sockets in which gems were set (Ex. 28:11).

Ov'en—Heb. *tannûr*—(Hos. 7:4). In towns there appear to have been public ovens. There was a street in Jerusalem (Jer. 37:21) called "bakers' street" (the only case in which the name of a street in Jerusalem is preserved). The words "tower of the furnaces" (Neh. 3:11; 12:38) is more properly "tower of the ovens" (Heb. *tannûrîm*). These resemble the ovens in use among ourselves.

There were other private ovens of different kinds. Some were like large jars made of earthenware or copper, which were heated inside with wood (1 Kings 17 : 12 ; Isa. 44 : 15 ; Jer. 7 : 18) or grass (Matt. 6 : 30), and when the fire had burned out, small pieces of dough were placed inside or spread in thin layers on the outside, and were thus baked. (See FURNACE.)

Pits were also formed for the same purposes, and lined with cement. These were used after the same manner.

Heated stones, or sand heated by a fire heaped over it, and also flat iron pans, all served as ovens for the preparation of bread. (See Gen. 18 : 6 ; 1 Kings 19 : 6.)

Owl. (1.) Heb. *bath - haya'anâh,* "daughter of greediness" or of "shouting."

GREAT EAGLE OWL (BUBO MAXIMUS).

In the list of unclean birds (Lev. 11 : 16 ; Deut. 14 : 15) ; also mentioned in Job 30 : 29 ; Isa. 13 : 21 ; 34 : 13 ; 43 : 20 ; Jer. 50 : 39 ; Micah 1 : 8. In all these passages the Revised Version translates "ostrich" (*q.v.*), which is the correct rendering.

(2.) Heb. *yanshûph,* rendered "great owl" in Lev. 11 : 17 ; Deut. 14 : 16, and "owl" in Isa. 34 : 11. This is supposed to be the Egyptian eagle - owl (*Bubo ascalaphus*), which takes the place of the eagle - owl (*Bubo maximus*) found in Southern Europe. It is found frequenting the ruins of Egypt and also of the Holy Land. "Its cry is a loud, prolonged, and very powerful hoot. I know nothing which more vividly brought to my mind the sense of desolation and loneliness than the re-echoing hoot of two or three of these great owls as I stood at midnight among the ruined temples of Baalbek" (Tristram).

The LXX. and Vulgate render this word by "ibis"—*i.e.,* the Egyptian heron.

(3.) Heb. *kôs,* rendered "little owl" in Lev. 11 : 17 ; Deut. 14 : 16, and "owl" in Ps. 102 : 6. The Arabs call this bird "the mother of ruins." It is by far the most common of all the owls of Palestine. It is the *Athene persica,* the bird of Minerva, the symbol of ancient Athens.

(4.) Heb. *kippôz,* the "great owl" (Isa. 34 : 15) ; Revised Version, "arrow-snake ; " LXX. and Vulgate, "hedgehog," reading in the text, *kippôd,* instead of *kippôz.* There is no reason to doubt the correctness of the rendering of the Authorized Version. Tristram says : "The word [*i.e., kippôz*] is very possibly an imitation of the cry of the scops owl (*Scops giu*), which is very common among ruins, caves, and old walls of towns......It is a migrant, returning to Palestine in spring."

(5.) Heb. *lilith,* "screech owl" (Isa. 34 : 14—marg. and R.V., "night monster"). The Hebrew word is from a root signifying "night." Some species of the owl is obviously intended by this word. It may be the hooting or tawny owl (*Syrnium aluco*), which is common in Egypt and in many parts of Palestine. This verse in Isaiah is "descriptive of utter and perpetual desolation—of a land that should be full of ruins, and inhabited by the animals that usually make such ruins their abode."

Ox — Heb. *bâkâr,* "cattle ; " "neat cattle"—(Gen. 12 : 16 ; 34 : 28 ; Job 1 : 3, 14 ; 42 : 12, etc.) ; not to be muzzled when treading the corn (Deut. 25 : 4). Referred to by our Lord in his reproof to the Pharisees (Luke 13 : 15 ; 14 : 5).

Ox goad—mentioned only in Judg. 3 : 31 —the weapon with which Shamgar (*q.v.*) slew six hundred Philistines. "The ploughman still carries his goad—a weapon apparently more fitted for the hand of the soldier than the peaceful husbandman. The one I saw was of the 'oak of Bashan,' and measured upwards of ten feet in length. At one end was an iron spear, and at the other a piece of the same metal flattened. One can well understand how a warrior might use such a weapon with effect in the battle-field" (Porter's *Syria, etc.*). (See GOAD.)

O'zem—*strong.* (1.) One of David's brothers; the sixth son of Jesse (1 Chr. 2:15).

(2.) A son of Jerahmeel (1 Chr. 2:25).

Ozi'as, son of Joram (Matt. 1:8); called also Uzziah (2 Kings 15:32, 34).

Oz'ni—*hearing*—one of the sons of Gad; also called Elzon (Gen. 46:16; Num. 26:16).

P

Pa'ari—*opening of the Lord*—"the Arbite," one of David's heroes (2 Sam. 23:35); called also Naarai, 1 Chr. 11:37.

Pa'dan—*a plain*—occurring only in Gen. 48:7, where it designates Padan-aram.

Pa'dan-a'ram—*the plain of Aram*, or *the plain of the highlands*—(Gen. 25:20; 28:2, 5–7; 31:18, etc.), commonly regarded as the district of Mesopotamia (*q.v.*) lying around Haran.

Pagi'el—*God allots*—a prince of the tribe of Asher (Num. 1:13), in the wilderness.

Pa'hath-mo'ab—*governor of Moab*—a person whose descendants returned from the Captivity and assisted in rebuilding Jerusalem (Ezra 2:6; 8:4; 10:30).

Paint. Jezebel "painted her face" (2 Kings 9:30); and the practice of painting the face and the eyes seems to have been common (Jer. 4:30; Ezek. 23:40). An allusion to this practice is found in the name of Job's daughter (42:14) Keren-happuch (*q.v.*). Paintings in the modern sense of the word were unknown to the ancient Jews.

Pal'ace. Used now only of royal dwellings, although originally meaning simply (as the Latin word *palatium*, from which it is derived, shows) a building surrounded by a fence or a paling. In the Authorized Version there are many different words so rendered, presenting different ideas, such as that of citadel or lofty fortress or royal residence (Neh. 1:1; Dan. 8:2). It is the name given to the temple fortress (Neh. 2:8) and to the temple itself (1 Kings 29:1).

It denotes also a spacious building or a great house (Dan. 1:4; 4:4, 29; Esther 1:5; 7:7), and a fortified place or an enclosure (Ezek. 25:4). Solomon's palace is described in 1 Kings 7:1–12 as a series of buildings rather than a single great structure. Thirteen years were spent in their erection. This palace stood on the eastern hill, adjoining the temple on the south.

In the New Testament it designates the official residence of Pilate or that of the high priest (Matt. 26:3, 58, 69; Mark 14:54, 66; John 18:15). In Phil. 1:13 this word is the rendering of the Greek *praitōrion*, meaning the prætorian cohorts at Rome (the life-guard of the Cæsars). Paul was continually chained to a soldier of that corps (Acts 28:16), and hence his name and sufferings became known in all the *prætorium*. The "soldiers that kept" him would, on relieving one another on guard, naturally spread the tidings regarding him among their comrades. Some, however, regard the *prætorium* (*q.v.*) as the barrack within the palace (the *palatium*) of the Cæsars in Rome where a detachment of these prætorian guards was stationed, or as the camp of the guards placed outside the eastern walls of Rome.

"In the chambers which were occupied as guard-rooms," says Dr. Manning, "by the prætorian troops on duty in the palace, a number of rude caricatures are found roughly scratched upon the walls, just such as may be seen upon barrack walls in every part of the world. Amongst these is one of a human figure nailed upon a cross. To add to the 'offence of the cross,' the cruci-fied one is represented with the head of an animal, probably that of an ass. Before it stands the figure of a Roman legionary with one hand upraised in the attitude of wor-ship. Underneath is the rude, misspelt, ungrammatical inscription, *Alexamenos worships his god*. It can scarcely be doubted that we have here a contemporary caricature, executed by one of the præ-torian guard, ridiculing the faith of a Christian comrade."

Pal'estine originally denoted only the sea-coast of the land of Canaan inhabited by the Philistines (Ex. 15 : 14 ; Isa. 14 : 29, 31 ; Joel 3 : 4), and in this sense exclusively the Hebrew name *Pelĕshĕth* (rendered "Philistia" in Ps. 60 : 8 ; 83 : 7 ; 87 : 4 ; 109 : 9) occurs in the Old Testament.

Not till a late period in Jewish history was this name used to denote "the land of the Hebrews" in general (Gen. 40 : 15). It is also called "the holy land" (Zech. 2 : 12), the "land of Jehovah" (Hos. 9 : 3 ; Ps. 85 : 1), the "land of promise" (Heb. 11 : 9), be-cause promised to Abraham (Gen. 12 : 7 ; 24 : 7), the "land of Canaan" (Gen. 12 : 5), the "land of Israel" (1 Sam. 13 : 19), and the "land of Judah" (Isa. 19 : 17).

The territory promised as an inheritance to the seed of Abraham (Gen. 15 : 18–21 ; Num. 34 : 1–12) was bounded on the east by the river Euphrates, on the west by the Mediterranean, on the north by the "en-trance of Hamath," and on the south by the "river of Egypt." This extent of territory, about 60,000 square miles, was at length conquered by David, and was ruled over also by his son Solomon (2 Sam. 8 ; 1 Chr. 18 ; 1 Kings 4 : 1, 21). This vast empire was the Promised Land ; but Pales-tine was only a part of it, terminating in the north at the southern extremity of the Lebanon range, and in the south in the wilderness of Paran—thus extending in all to about 144 miles in length. Its average breadth was about 60 miles from the Medi-terranean on the west to beyond the Jordan. It has fittingly been designated "the least of all lands." Western Palestine, on the south of Gaza, is only about 40 miles in breadth from the Mediterranean to the Dead Sea, narrowing gradually toward the north, where it is only 20 miles from the sea-coast to the Jordan.

Palestine, "set in the midst" (Ezek. 5 : 5) of all other lands, is the most remarkable country on the face of the earth. No single country of such an extent has so great a variety of climate, and hence also of plant and animal life. Moses describes it as "a good land, a land of brooks of water, of fountains and depths that spring out of valleys and hills ; a land of wheat, and barley, and vines, and fig trees, and pome-granates ; a land of oil olive, and honey ; a land wherein thou shalt eat bread without scarceness, thou shalt not lack any thing in it ; a land whose stones are iron, and out of whose hills thou mayest dig brass" (Deut. 8 : 7–9).

"In the time of Christ the country looked, in all probability, much as now. The whole land consists of rounded limestone hills, fretted into countless stony valleys, offering but rarely level tracts, of which Esdraelon alone, below Nazareth, is large enough to be seen on the map. The original woods had for ages disappeared, though the slopes were dotted, as now, with figs, olives, and other fruit-trees where there was any soil. Permanent streams were even then un-known, the passing rush of winter torrents being all that was seen among the hills. The autumn and spring rains, caught in deep cisterns hewn out like huge under-ground jars in the soft limestone, with arti-ficial mud-banked ponds still found near all villages, furnished water. Hills now bare, or at best rough with stunted growth, were then terraced, so as to grow vines, olives, and grain. To-day almost desolate, the country then teemed with population. Wine-presses cut in the rocks, endless ter-races, and the ruins of old vineyard towers are now found amidst solitudes overgrown for ages with thorns and thistles, or with wild shrubs and poor gnarled scrub" (Geikie's *Life of Christ*).

From an early period the land was in-habited by the descendants of Canaan, who retained possession of the whole land "from Sidon to Gaza" till the time of the conquest by Joshua, when it was occupied by the

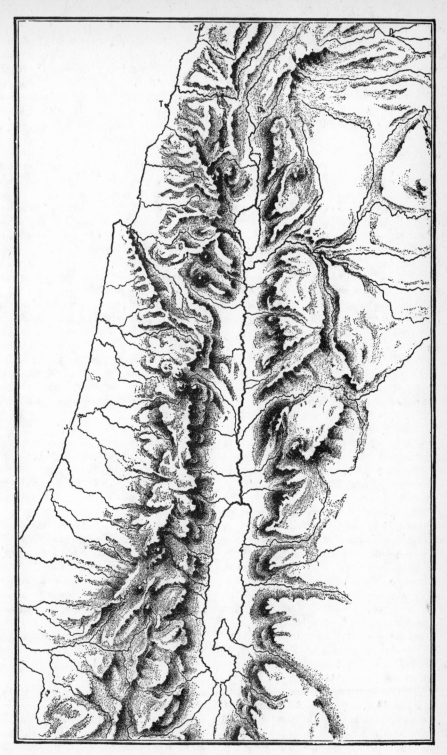

PHYSICAL MAP OF PALESTINE.

twelve tribes. Two tribes and a half had their allotments given them by Moses on the east of the Jordan (Deut. 3 : 12-20; comp. Num. 1 : 17-46; Josh. 4 : 12-13). The remaining tribes had their portion on the west of Jordan.

From the conquest till the time of Saul—about four hundred years—the people were governed by judges. For a period of one hundred and twenty years the kingdom retained its unity while it was ruled by Saul and David and Solomon. On the death of Solomon, his son Rehoboam ascended the throne; but his conduct was such that ten of the tribes revolted, and formed an independent monarchy, called the kingdom of Israel, or the northern kingdom, the capital of which was first Shechem and afterwards Samaria. This kingdom was destroyed. The Israelites were carried captive by Shalmanezer, king of Assyria, B.C. 722, after an independent existence of two hundred and fifty-three years. The place of the captives carried away was supplied by tribes brought from the east, and thus was formed the Samaritan nation (2 Kings 17 : 24-29).

Nebuchadnezzar came up against the kingdom of the two tribes, the kingdom of Judah, the capital of which was Jerusalem, one hundred and thirty-four years after the overthrow of the kingdom of Israel. He overthrew the city, plundered the temple, and carried the people into captivity to Babylon (B.C. 587), where they remained seventy years. At the close of the period of the Captivity, they returned to their own land, under the edict of Cyrus (Ezra 1 : 1-4). They rebuilt the city and temple, and restored the old Jewish commonwealth.

For a while after the Restoration the Jews were ruled by Zerubbabel, Ezra, and Nehemiah, and afterwards by the high priests, assisted by the Sanhedrin. After the death of Alexander the Great at Babylon (B.C. 323), his vast empire was divided between his four generals. Egypt, Arabia, Palestine, and Cœle-Syria fell to the lot of Ptolemy Lagus. Ptolemy took possession of Palestine in B.C. 320, and carried nearly one hundred thousand of the inhabitants of Jerusalem into Egypt. He

made Alexandria the capital of his kingdom, and treated the Jews with consideration, confirming them in the enjoyment of many privileges.

After suffering persecution at the hands of Ptolemy's successors, the Jews threw off the Egyptian yoke, and became subject to Antiochus the Great, the king of Syria. The cruelty and oppression of the successors of Antiochus at length led to the revolt under the Maccabees (B.C. 163), when they threw off the Syrian yoke.

In the year B.C. 68, Palestine was reduced by Pompey the Great to a Roman province. He laid the walls of the city in ruins, and massacred some twelve thousand of the inhabitants. He left the temple, however, uninjured. About twenty-five years after this the Jews revolted and cast off the Roman yoke. They were, however, subdued by Herod the Great (q.v.). The city and the temple were destroyed, and many of the inhabitants were put to death. About B.C. 20, Herod proceeded to rebuild the city and restore the ruined temple, which in about nine years and a half was so far completed that the sacred services could be resumed in it (comp. John 2 : 20). He was succeeded by his son Archelaus, who was deprived of his power, however, by Augustus, A.D. 6, when Palestine became a Roman province, ruled by Roman governors or procurators. Pontius Pilate was the fifth of these procurators. He was appointed to his office A.D. 25.

Exclusive of Idumea, the kingdom of Herod the Great comprehended the whole of the country originally divided among the twelve tribes, which he divided into four provinces or districts. This division was recognized so long as Palestine was under the Roman dominion. These four provinces were—(1) Judea, the southern portion of the country; (2) Samaria, the middle province, the northern boundary of which ran along the hills to the south of the plain of Esdraelon; (3) Galilee, the northern province; and (4) Peræa (a Greek name meaning the "opposite country"), the country lying east of the Jordan and the Dead Sea. This province was subdivided into these districts—(1) Peræa proper, lying between the

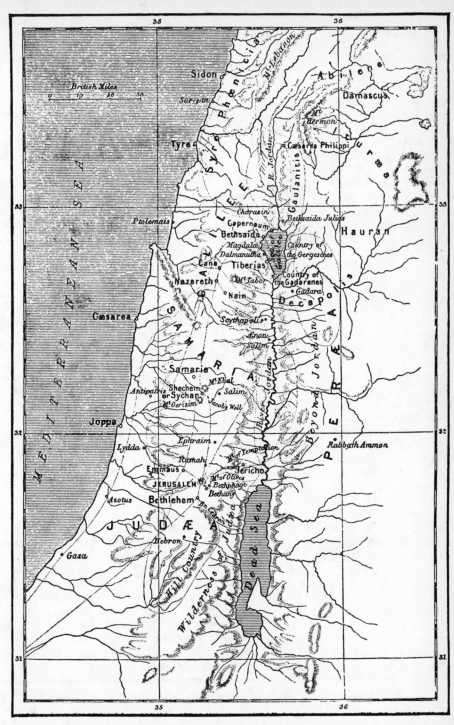

PALESTINE UNDER HEROD.
(The dotted lines indicate the Journeys of Christ.)

rivers Arnon and Jabbok; (2) *Galaaditis* (Gilead); (3) *Batanæa;* (4) *Gaulonitis* (Jaulân); (5) *Ituræa* or *Auranitis*, the ancient Bashan; (6) *Trachonitis;* (7) *Abilene;* (8) *Decapolis*—*i.e.*, the region of the ten cities. The whole territory of Palestine, including the portions allotted to the trans-Jordan tribes, extended to about eleven thousand square miles. Recent exploration has shown the territory on the west of Jordan alone to be six thousand square miles in extent, the size of the principality of Wales.

Pal'lu—*separated*—the second son of Reuben (1 Chr. 5:3); called Phallu, Gen. 46:9. He was the father of the Palluites (Ex. 6:14; Num. 26:5, 8).

Palm tree (Heb. *tâmâr*), the date-palm characteristic of Palestine. It is described as "flourishing" (Ps. 92:12), tall (Cant. 7:7), "upright" (Jer. 10:5). Its branches are a symbol of victory (Rev. 7:9). "Rising with slender stem 40 or 50, at times even 80, feet aloft, its only branches, the feathery, snow-like, pale-green fronds from 6 to 12 feet long, bending from its top, the palm attracts the eye wherever it is seen." The whole land of Palestine was called by the Greeks and Romans Phœnicia—*i.e.*, "the land of palms." Tadmor in the desert was called by the Greeks and Romans Palmyra—*i.e.*, "the city of palms." The finest specimens of this tree grew at Jericho (Deut. 34:3) and Engedi and along the banks of the Jordan. Branches of the palm tree were carried at the feast of Tabernacles (Lev. 23:40). At our Lord's triumphal entrance into Jerusalem the crowds took palm branches, and went forth to meet him, crying, "Hosanna: Blessed is the King of Israel that cometh in the name of the Lord" (Matt. 21:8; John 12:13). (See DATE.)

Palm trees, The city of, the name given to Jericho (*q.v.*)—Deut. 34:3; Judg. 1:16; 3:13.

Palm'er-worm (Heb. *gâzâm*). The English word may denote either a caterpillar (as rendered by the LXX.)—which wanders like a palmer or pilgrim, or which travels like pilgrims in bands (Joel 1:4; 2:25)—the wingless locust, or the migratory locust in its larva state.

Pal'sy, a shorter form of "paralysis." Many persons thus afflicted were cured by our Lord (Matt. 4:24; 8:5-13; 9:2-7; Mark 2:3-11; Luke 7:2-10; John 5:5-7) and the apostles (Acts 8:7; 9:33, 34).

Pal'ti—*deliverance from the Lord*—one of the spies representing the tribe of Benjamin (Num. 13:9).

Pal'tiel—*deliverance of God*—the prince of Issachar who assisted "to divide the land by inheritance" (Num. 34:26).

Pal'tite, the designation of one of David's heroes (2 Sam. 23:26); called also the Pelonite (1 Chr. 11:27).

Pamphyl'ia. Paul and his company, loosing from Paphos, sailed north-west and came to Perga, the capital of Pamphylia (Acts 13:13, 14), a province about the middle of the southern sea-board of Asia Minor. It lay between Lycia on the west and Cilicia on the east. There were strangers from Pamphylia at Jerusalem on the day of Pentecost (2:10).

Pan, a vessel of metal or earthenware used in culinary operations; a cooking-pan or frying-pan frequently referred to in the Old Testament (Lev. 2:5; 6:21; Num. 11:8; 1 Sam. 2:14, etc.).

The "ash-pans" mentioned in Ex. 27:3 were made of copper, and were used in connection with the altar of burnt-offering. The "iron pan" mentioned in Ezek. 4:3 (marg., "flat plate" or "slice") was probably a mere plate of iron used for baking. The "fire-pans" of Ex. 27:3 were fire-shovels used for taking up coals. The same Hebrew word is rendered "snuff-dishes" (25:38; 37:23) and "censers" (Lev. 10:1; 16:12; Num. 4:14, etc.). These were probably simply metal vessels employed for carrying burning embers from the brazen altar to the altar of incense.

The "frying-pan" mentioned in Lev. 2:7, 7:9 was a pot for boiling.

Pan'nag (Ezek. 27:17; marg. R.V., "perhaps a kind of confection") the Jews explain as the name of a kind of sweet pastry. Others take it as the name of some place, identifying it with Pingi, on the road between Damascus and Baalbec. "Pannaga" is the Sanscrit name of an aromatic plant (comp. Gen. 43:11).

Pa'per. The expression in the Authorized Version (Isa. 19:7), "the paper reeds by the brooks," is in the Revised Version more correctly "the meadows by the Nile." The words undoubtedly refer to a grassy place on the banks of the Nile fit for pasturage.

In 2 John 12 the word is used in its proper sense. The material so referred to was manufactured from the papyrus, and hence its name. The papyrus (Heb. *gōmĕ*) was a kind of bulrush (*q.v.*). It is mentioned by Job (8:11) and Isaiah (35:7). It was used for many purposes. This plant (*Papyrus Nilotica*) is now unknown in Egypt; no trace of it can be found. The unaccountable disappearance of this plant from Egypt was foretold by Isaiah (19:6, 7) as a part of the divine judgment on that land. The most extensive papyrus growths now known are in the marshes at the northern end of the lake of Merom.

Pa'phos, the capital of the island of Cyprus, and therefore the residence of the Roman governor. It was visited by Paul and Barnabas on their first missionary tour (Acts 13:6). It is new Paphos which is here meant. It lay on the west coast of the island, about 8 miles north of old Paphos. Its modern name is *Baffa*.

Par'able (Gr. *parabolē*), a placing beside; a comparison; equivalent to the Heb. *mâshâl*, a similitude. In the Old Testament this is used to denote (1) a proverb (1 Sam. 10:12; 24:13; 2 Chr. 7:20), (2) a prophetic utterance (Num. 23:7; Ezek. 20:49), (3) an enigmatic saying (Ps. 78:2; Prov. 1:6). In the New Testament, (1) a proverb (Mark 7:17; Luke 4:23), (2) a typical emblem (Heb. 9:9; 11:19), (3) a similitude or allegory (Matt. 15:15; 24:32; Mark 3:23; Luke 5:36; 14:7); (4) ordinarily, in a more restricted sense, a comparison of earthly with heavenly things, "an earthly story with a heavenly meaning," as in the parables of our Lord.

Instruction by parables has been in use from the earliest times. A large portion of our Lord's public teaching consisted of parables. He himself explains his reasons for this in his answer to the inquiry of the disciples, "Why speakest thou to them in parables?" (Matt. 13:13–15; Mark 4:11, 12; Luke 8:9, 10). He followed in so doing the rule of the divine procedure, as recorded in Matt. 13:12.

The parables uttered by our Lord are all recorded in the synoptical (*i.e.*, the first three) Gospels. The fourth Gospel contains no parable properly so called, although the illustration of the good shepherd (John 10:1–10) has all the essential features of a parable. (See List of Parables in Appendix.)

Par'adise, a Persian word (*pardes*), properly meaning a "pleasure-ground" or "park" or "king's garden." (See EDEN.) It came in course of time to be used as a name for the world of happiness and rest hereafter (Luke 23:43; 2 Cor. 12:4; Rev. 2:7). For "garden" in Gen. 2:8 the LXX. has "paradise."

Pa'rah—*the heifer*—a town in Benjamin (Josh. 18:23), supposed to be identical with the ruins called *Fâr'ah*—about 6 miles north-east of Jerusalem—in the Wâdy Fâr'ah, which is a branch of the Wâdy Kelt.

Pa'ran—*abounding in foliage*, or *abounding in caverns*—(Gen. 21:21), a desert tract forming the north-eastern division of the peninsula of Sinai, lying between the 'Arabah on the east and the wilderness of Shur on the west. It is intersected in a north-western direction by the Wâdy el-'Arîsh. It bears the modern name of *Bâdiet et-Tîh*—*i.e.*, "the desert of the wanderings." This district, through which the children of Israel wandered, lay three days' march from Sinai (Num. 10:12, 33). From Kadesh, in this wilderness, spies (*q.v.*) were sent to spy the land (13:3, 26). Here, long afterwards, David found refuge from Saul (1 Sam. 25:1, 4).

Pa'ran, Mount, probably the hilly region or upland wilderness on the north of the desert of Paran forming the southern boundary of the Promised Land (Deut. 33:2; Hab. 3:3).

Par'bar (1 Chr. 26:18), a place apparently connected with the temple, probably a "suburb" (*q.v.*), as the word is rendered in 2 Kings 23:11; a space between the temple wall and the wall of the court;

an open portico into which the chambers of the official persons opened (1 Chr. 26: 18).

Parch'ed ground (Isa. 35:7) — Heb. *shârâb*, a "mirage"—a phenomenon caused by the refraction of the rays of the sun on the glowing sands of the desert, causing them suddenly to assume the appearance of a beautiful lake. It is called by the modern Arabs by the same Hebrew name *serâb*.

Parch'ment, a skin prepared for writing on; so called from Pergamos (*q.v.*), where this was first done (2 Tim. 4: 13).

Par'don, the forgiveness of sins granted freely (Isa. 43:25), readily (Neh. 9:17; Ps. 86:5), abundantly (Isa. 55:7; Rom. 5:20). Pardon is an act of a sovereign, in pure sovereignty, granting simply a remission of the penalty due to sin, but securing neither honour nor reward to the pardoned. Justification (*q.v.*), on the other hand, is the act of a judge, and not of a sovereign, and includes pardon and, at the same time, a title to all the rewards and blessings promised in the covenant of life.

Par'lour (from the Fr. *parler*, "to speak") denotes an "audience chamber," but that is not the import of the Hebrew word so rendered. It corresponds to what the Turks call a kiosk, as in Judg. 3:20 (the "summer parlour"), or as in the margin of the Revised Version ("the upper chamber of cooling"), a small room built on the roof of the house, with open windows to catch the breeze, and having a door communicating with the outside by which persons seeking an audience may be admitted. While Eglon was resting in such a parlour, Ehud, under pretence of having a message from God to him, was admitted into his presence, and murderously plunged his dagger into his body (21, 22).

The "inner parlours" in 1 Chr. 28:11 were the small rooms or chambers which Solomon built all round two sides and one end of the temple (1 Kings 6:5), "side chambers;" or they may have been, as some think, the porch and the holy place.

In 1 Sam. 9:22 the Revised Version reads "guest chamber," a chamber at the high place specially used for sacrificial feasts.

Parmash'ta—*strong-fisted*—a son of Haman, slain in Shushan (Esther 9:9).

Par'menas—*constant*—one of the seven "deacons" (Acts 6:5).

Parshan'datha — *an interpreter of the law*—the eldest of Haman's sons, slain in Shushan (Esther 9:7).

Par'thians were present in Jerusalem at Pentecost (Acts 2:9). Parthia lay on the east of Media and south of Hyrcania, which separated it from the Caspian Sea. It corresponded with the western half of the modern Khorasan, and now forms a part of Persia.

Par'tridge (Heb. *kôrê*—*i.c.*, "caller"). This bird, unlike our own partridge, is distinguished by "its ringing call-note, which in early morning echoes from cliff to cliff amidst the barrenness of the wilderness of Judea and the glens of the forest of Carmel" —hence its Hebrew name. This name occurs only twice in Scripture.

In 1 Sam. 26:20 "David alludes to the mode of chase practised now, as of old, when the partridge, continuously chased, was at length, when fatigued, knocked down by sticks thrown along the ground." It endeavours to save itself "by running, in preference to flight, unless when suddenly started. It is not an inhabitant of the plain or the corn-field, but of rocky hillsides" (Tristram's *Nat. Hist.*).

In Jer. 17:11 the prophet is illustrating the fact that riches unlawfully acquired are precarious and short-lived. The exact nature of the illustration cannot be precisely determined. Some interpret the words as meaning that the covetous man will be as surely disappointed as the partridge which gathers in eggs, not of her own laying, and is unable to hatch them; others (Tristram), with more probability, as denoting that the man who enriches himself by unjust means "will as surely be disappointed as the partridge which commences to sit, but is speedily robbed of her hopes of a brood" by her eggs being stolen away from her.

The commonest partridge in Palestine is the *Caccabis saxatilis*, the Greek partridge.

The partridge of the wilderness (*Ammoperdix heyi*) is a smaller species.

DESERT PARTRIDGE (AMMOPERDIX HEYI).

Paru'ah—*flourishing*—the father of Jehoshaphat, appointed to provide monthly supplies for Solomon from the tribe of Issachar (1 Kings 4 : 17).

Parva'im, the name of a country from which Solomon obtained gold for the temple (2 Chr. 3 : 6). Some have identified it with Ophir, but it is uncertain whether it is even the name of a place. It may simply, as some think, denote "Oriental regions."

Pa'sach—*clearing*—one of the sons of Japhlet, of the tribe of Asher (1 Chr. 7 : 33).

Pas-dam'mim—*the border of blood* = Ephes-dammim (*q.v.*)—between Shochoh and Azekah (1 Sam. 17 : 1; 1 Chr. 11 : 13).

Pash'ur—*release*. (1.) The son of Immer (probably the same as Amariah—Neh. 10 : 3; 12 : 2), the head of one of the priestly courses, was "chief governor [Heb. *paqîd nagîd*, meaning "deputy governor"] of the temple" (Jer. 20 : 1, 2). At this time the *nagîd*, or "governor," of the temple was Seraiah the high priest (1 Chr. 6 : 14), and Pashur was his *paqîd*, or "deputy." Enraged at the plainness with which Jeremiah uttered his solemn warnings of coming judgments, because of the abounding iniquity of the times, Pashur ordered the temple police to seize him, and after inflicting on him corporal punishment (forty stripes save one—Deut. 25 : 3; comp. 2 Cor. 11 : 24), to put him in the stocks in the high gate of Benjamin, where he remained all night. On being set free in the morning, Jeremiah went to Pashur (Jer. 20 : 3, 5), and announced to him that God had changed his name to Magor-missabib—*i.e.*, "terror on every side." The punishment that fell upon him was probably remorse, when he saw the ruin he had brought upon his country by advising a close alliance with Egypt in opposition to the counsels of Jeremiah (20 : 4–6). He was carried captive to Babylon, and died there.

(2.) A priest sent by king Zedekiah to Jeremiah to inquire of the Lord (1 Chr. 24 : 9; Jer. 21 : 1; 38 : 1–6). He advised that the prophet should be put to death.

(3.) The father of Gedaliah. He was probably the same as (1).

Pass'age denotes in Josh. 22 : 11, as is generally understood, the place where the children of Israel passed over Jordan. The words "the passage of" are, however, more correctly rendered "by the side of," or "at the other side of," thus designating the position of the great altar erected by the eastern tribes on their return home. This word also designates the fords of the Jordan to the south of the Sea of Galilee (Judg. 12 : 5, 6), and a pass or rocky defile (1 Sam. 13 : 23; 14 : 4). "Passages" in Jer. 22 : 20 is in the Revised Version more correctly "Abarim" (*q.v.*), a proper name.

Pas'sion. Only once found, in Acts 1 : 3, meaning suffering, referring to the sufferings of our Lord.

Pass'over, the name given to the chief of the three great historical annual festivals of the Jews. It was kept in remembrance of the Lord's passing over the houses of the Israelites (Ex. 12 : 13) when the first born of all the Egyptians were destroyed. It is called also the "feast of unleavened bread" (Ex. 23 : 15; Mark 14 : 1; Acts 12 : 3), because during its celebration no leavened bread was to be eaten or even kept in the household (Ex. 12 : 15). The word afterwards came to denote the lamb that was slain at the feast (Mark 14 : 12–14 ; 1 Cor. 5 : 7).

A detailed account of the institution of this feast is given in Ex. 12 and 13. It was afterwards incorporated in the ceremonial law (Lev. 23 : 4–8) as one of the great festivals of the nation. In after times many changes seem to have taken place as to the mode of its celebration as compared with its first celebration (comp. Deut. 16 : 2, 5, 6; 2 Chr. 30 : 16; Lev. 23 : 10–14; Num. 9 : 10, 11; 28 : 16–24). Again, the use of wine (Luke 22 : 17, 20), of sauce with the bitter herbs (John 13 : 26), and the service of praise were introduced.

There is recorded only one celebration of this feast between the Exodus and the entrance into Canaan — namely, that mentioned in Num. 9 : 5. (See JOSIAH.) It was primarily a commemorative ordinance, reminding the children of Israel of their deliverance out of Egypt; but it was, no doubt, also a type of the great deliverance wrought by the Messiah for all his people from the doom of death on account of sin, and from the bondage of sin itself, a worse than Egyptian bondage (1 Cor. 5 : 7; John 1 : 29; 19 : 32–36; 1 Pet. 1 : 19; Gal. 4 : 4, 5). The appearance of Jerusalem on the occasion of the Passover in the time of our Lord is thus fittingly described :—"The city itself and the neighbourhood became more and more crowded as the feast approached, the narrow streets and dark arched bazaars showing the same throng of men of all nations as when Jesus had first visited Jerusalem as a boy. Even the temple offered a strange sight at this season, for in parts of the outer courts a wide space was covered with pens for sheep, goats, and cattle to be used for offerings. Sellers shouted the merits of their beasts, sheep bleated, oxen lowed. Sellers of doves also had a place set apart for them. Potters offered a choice from huge stacks of clay dishes and ovens for roasting and eating the Passover lamb. Booths for wine, oil, salt, and all else needed for sacrifices invited customers. Persons going to and from the city shortened their journey by crossing the temple grounds, often carrying burdens......Stalls to change foreign money

into the shekel of the temple, which alone could be paid to the priests, were numerous, the whole confusion making the sanctuary like a noisy market " (Geikie's *Life of Christ*).

Pat'ara, a city on the south-west coast of Lycia at which Paul landed on his return from his third missionary journey (Acts 21 : 1, 2). Here he found a larger vessel, which was about to sail across the open sea to the coast of Phœnicia. In this vessel he set forth, and reached the city of Tyre in perhaps two or three days.

Path'ros, the name generally given to Upper Egypt (the Thebaid of the Greeks), as distinguished from Matsor, or Lower Egypt (Isa. 11 : 11 ; Jer. 44 : 1, 15 ; Ezek. 30 : 14), the two forming Mizraim. After the destruction of Jerusalem by Nebuchadnezzar, colonies of Jews settled "in the country of Pathros " and other parts of Egypt.

Pat'mos, a small rocky and barren island, one of the group called the "Sporădes," in the Ægean Sea. It is mentioned in Scripture only in Rev. 1 : 9. It was on this island, to which John was banished by the emperor Domitian (A.D. 95), that he received from God the wondrous revelation recorded in his book. This has naturally invested it with the deepest interest for all time. It is now called *Patmo*. (See JOHN.)

Pa'triarch, a name employed in the New Testament with reference to Abraham (Heb. 7 : 4), the sons of Jacob (Acts 7 : 8, 9), and to David (2 : 29). This name is generally applied to the progenitors of families or "heads of the fathers " (Josh. 14 : 1) mentioned in Scripture, and they are spoken of as antediluvian (from Adam to Noah) and post-diluvian (from Noah to Jacob) patriarchs. But the expression "the patriarchs," by way of eminence, is applied to the twelve sons of Jacob, or to Abraham, Isaac, and Jacob.

"Patriarchal longevity presents itself as one of the most striking of the facts concerning mankind which the early history of the Book of Genesis places before us...... There is a large amount of consentient tradition to the effect that the life of man

PATMOS.

was originally far more prolonged than it is at present, extending to at least several hundred years. The Babylonians, Egyptians, and Chinese exaggerated these hundreds into thousands. The Greeks and Romans, with more moderation, limited human life within a thousand or eight hundred years. The Hindus still farther shortened the term. Their books taught that in the first age of the world man was free from diseases, and lived ordinarily four hundred years; in the second age the term of life was reduced from four hundred to three hundred; in the third it became two hundred; in the fourth and last it was brought down to one hundred" (Rawlinson's *Historical Illustrations*).

Pat′robas, a Christian at Rome to whom Paul sent salutations (Rom. 16 : 14).

Pa′u (Gen. 36 : 39) or **Pai** (1 Chr. 1 : 50) —*bleating*—an Edomitish city ruled over by Hadar.

Paul = Saul (*q.v.*) was born about the same time as our Lord. His circumcision-name was Saul, and probably the name Paul was also given to him in infancy "for use in the Gentile world," as "Saul" would be his Hebrew home-name. He was a native of Tarsus, the capital of Cilicia, a Roman province in the south-east of Asia Minor. That city stood on the banks of the river Cydnus, which was navigable thus far; hence it became a centre of extensive commercial traffic with many countries along the shores of the Mediterranean, as well as with the countries of central Asia Minor. It thus became a city distinguished for the wealth of its inhabitants.

Tarsus was also the seat of a famous university, higher in reputation even than the universities of Athens and Alexandria, the only others that then existed. Here Saul was born, and here he spent his youth, doubtless enjoying the best education his native city could afford. His father was of the straitest sect of the Jews—a Pharisee —of the tribe of Benjamin, of pure and unmixed Jewish blood (Acts 23 : 6; Phil. 3 : 5). We learn nothing regarding his mother; but there is reason to conclude that she was a pious woman, and that, like-minded with her husband, she exercised all a mother's influence in moulding the character of her son, so that he could afterwards speak of himself as being, from his youth up, "touching the righteousness which is in the law, blameless" (Phil. 3 : 6).

We read of his sister and his sister's son

(Acts 23:16), and of other relatives (Rom. 16:7, 11, 12). Though a Jew, his father was a Roman citizen. How he obtained this privilege we are not informed. "It might be bought, or won by distinguished service to the state, or acquired in several other ways; at all events, his son was free-born. It was a valuable privilege, and one that was to prove of great use to Paul, although not in the way in which his father might have been expected to desire him to make use of it." Perhaps the most natural career for the youth to follow was that of a merchant. "But it was decided that......he should go to college and become a rabbi—that is, a minister, a teacher, and a lawyer all in one."

According to Jewish custom, however, he learned a trade before entering on the more direct preparation for the sacred profession. The trade he acquired was the making of tents from goats' hair cloth, a trade which was one of the commonest in Tarsus.

His preliminary education having been completed, Saul was sent, when about thirteen years of age probably, to the great Jewish school of sacred learning at Jerusalem as a student of the law. Here he became a pupil of the celebrated rabbi Gamaliel, and here he spent many years in an elaborate study of the Scriptures and of the many questions concerning them with which the rabbis exercised themselves. During these years of diligent study he lived "in all good conscience," unstained by the vices of that great city.

After the period of his student-life expired, he probably left Jerusalem for Tarsus, where he may have been engaged in connection with some synagogue for some years. But we find him back again at Jerusalem very soon after the death of our Lord. Here he now learned the particulars regarding the crucifixion, and the rise of the new sect of the "Nazarenes."

For some two years after Pentecost, Christianity was quietly spreading its influence in Jerusalem. At length Stephen, one of the seven deacons, gave forth more public and aggressive testimony that Jesus was the Messiah, and this led to much ex-citement among the Jews and much disputation in their synagogues. Persecution arose against Stephen and the followers of Christ generally, in which Saul of Tarsus took a prominent part. He was at this time probably a member of the great Sanhedrin, and became the active leader in the furious persecution by which the rulers then sought to exterminate Christianity.

But the object of this persecution also failed. "They that were scattered abroad went everywhere preaching the word." The anger of the persecutor was thereby kindled into a fiercer flame. Hearing that fugitives had taken refuge in Damascus, he obtained from the chief priest letters authorizing him to proceed thither on his persecuting career. This was a long journey of about 130 miles, which would occupy perhaps six days, during which, with his few attendants, he steadily went onward, "breathing out threatenings and slaughter." But the crisis of his life was at hand. He had reached the last stage of his journey, and was within sight of Damascus. As he and his companions rode on, suddenly at mid-day a brilliant light shone round them, and Saul was laid prostrate in terror on the ground, a voice sounding in his ears, "Saul, Saul, why persecutest thou me?" The risen Saviour was there, clothed in the vesture of his glorified humanity. In answer to the anxious inquiry of the stricken persecutor, "Who art thou, Lord?" he said, "I am Jesus whom thou persecutest" (Acts 9:5; 22:8; 26:15).

This was the moment of his *conversion*, the most solemn in all his life. Blinded by the dazzling light (Acts 9:8), his companions led him into the city, where, absorbed in deep thought for three days, he neither ate nor drank (9:11). Ananias, a disciple living in Damascus, was informed by a vision of the change that had happened to Saul, and was sent to him to open his eyes and admit him by baptism into the Christian church (9:11-16). The whole purpose of his life was now permanently changed.

Immediately after his conversion he retired into the solitudes of Arabia (Gal. 1:17), perhaps of "Sinai in Arabia," for the purpose, probably, of devout study and meditation on the marvellous revelation that had been made to him. "A veil of thick darkness hangs over this visit to Arabia. Of the scenes among which he moved, of the thoughts and occupations which engaged him while there, of all the circumstances of a crisis which must have shaped the whole tenor of his after-life, absolutely nothing is known. 'Immediately,' says St. Paul, 'I went away into Arabia.' The historian passes over the incident [comp. Acts 9:23 and 1 Kings 11: 38, 39]. It is a mysterious pause, a moment of suspense, in the apostle's history, a breathless calm, which ushers in the tumultuous storm of his active missionary life." Coming back, after three years, to Damascus, he began to preach the gospel "boldly in the name of Jesus" (Acts 9:27), but was soon obliged to flee (9:25; 2 Cor. 11:33) from the Jews and betake himself to Jerusalem. Here he tarried for three weeks, but was again forced to flee (Acts 9:28, 29) from persecution. He now returned to his native Tarsus (Gal. 1:21), where, for probably about three years, we lose sight of him. The time had not yet come for his entering on his great life-work of preaching the gospel to the Gentiles.

At length the city of Antioch, the capital of Syria, became the scene of great Christian activity. There the gospel gained a firm footing, and the cause of Christ prospered. Barnabas (q.v.), who had been sent from Jerusalem to superintend the work at Antioch, found it too much for him, and remembering Saul, he set out to Tarsus to seek for him. He readily responded to the call thus addressed to him, and came down to Antioch, which for "a whole year" became the scene of his labours, which were crowned with great success. The disciples now, for the first time, were called "Christians" (Acts 11:26).

The church at Antioch now proposed to send out missionaries to the Gentiles, and Saul and Barnabas, with John Mark as their attendant, were chosen for this work. This was a great epoch in the history of the church. Now the disciples began to give effect to the Master's command: "Go ye into all the world, and preach the gospel to every creature."

The three missionaries went forth on the *first missionary tour*. They sailed from Seleucia, the seaport of Antioch, across to Cyprus, some 80 miles to the south-west. Here at Paphos, Sergius Paulus, the Roman proconsul, was converted, and now Saul took the lead, and was ever afterwards called Paul. The missionaries now crossed to the mainland, and then proceeded 6 or 7 miles up the river Cestrus to Perga (Acts 13:13), where John Mark deserted the work and returned to Jerusalem. The two then proceeded about 100 miles inland, passing through Pamphylia, Pisidia, and Lycaonia. The towns mentioned in this tour are the Pisidian Antioch—where Paul delivered his first address of which we have any record (13:16–31; comp. 10:30–43)— Iconium, Lystra, and Derbe. They returned by the same route to see and encourage the converts they had made, and ordain elders in every city to watch over the churches which had been gathered. From Perga they sailed direct for Antioch, from which they had set out.

After remaining "a long time"—probably till A.D. 50 or 51—in Antioch, a great controversy broke out in the church there regarding the relation of the Gentiles to the Mosaic law. For the purpose of obtaining a settlement of this question, Paul and Barnabas were sent as deputies to consult the church at Jerusalem. The council or synod which was there held (Acts 15) decided against the Judaizing party; and the deputies, accompanied by Judas and Silas, returned to Antioch, bringing with them the decree of the council.

After a short rest at Antioch, Paul said to Barnabas: "Let us go again and visit our brethren in every city where we have preached the word of the Lord, and see how they do." Mark proposed again to accompany them; but Paul refused to allow him to go. Barnabas was resolved to take Mark, and thus he and Paul had a sharp contention. They separated, and never again met. Paul, however, afterwards speaks with honour of Barnabas, and sends for Mark to come to him at Rome (Col. 4 : 10 ; 2 Tim. 4 : 11).

Paul took with him Silas, instead of Barnabas, and began his *second missionary journey* about A.D. 51. This time he went by land, revisiting the churches he had already founded in Asia. But he longed to enter into "regions beyond," and still went forward through Phrygia and Galatia (16 : 6). Contrary to his intention, he was constrained to linger in Galatia (*q.v.*), on account of some bodily affliction (Gal. 4 : 13, 14). Bithynia, a populous province on the shore of the Black Sea, lay now before him, and he wished to enter it ; but the way was shut, the Spirit in some manner guiding him in another direction, till he came down to the shores of the Ægean and arrived at Troas, on the north-western coast of Asia Minor (Acts 16 : 8). Of this long journey from Antioch to Troas we have no account except some references to it in his Epistle to the Galatians (4 : 13).

As he waited at Troas for indications of the will of God as to his future movements, he saw, in the vision of the night, a man from the opposite shores of Macedonia standing before him, and heard him cry, "Come over, and help us" (Acts 16 : 9). Paul recognized in this vision a message from the Lord, and the very next day set sail across the Hellespont, which separated him from Europe, and carried the tidings of the gospel into the Western world. In Macedonia, churches were planted in Philippi, Thessalonica, and Berea. Leaving this province, Paul passed into Achaia, "the paradise of genius and renown." He reached Athens, but quitted it after, probably, a brief sojourn (17 : 17-31). The Athenians had received him with cold disdain, and he never visited that city again. He passed over to Corinth, the seat of the Roman government of Achaia, and remained there a year and a half, labouring with much success. While at Corinth, he wrote his two epistles to the church of Thessalonica—his earliest apostolic letters—and then sailed for Syria, that he might be in time to keep the feast of Pentecost at Jerusalem. He was accompanied by Aquila and Priscilla. whom he left at Ephesus, at which he touched, after a voyage of thirteen or fifteen days. He landed at Cæsarea, and went up to Jerusalem, and having "saluted the church" there, and kept the feast, he left for Antioch, where he abode "some time" (Acts 18 : 20-23).

He then began his *third missionary tour.* He journeyed by land in the "upper coasts" (the more eastern parts) of Asia Minor, and at length made his way to Ephesus, where he tarried for no less than three years, engaged in ceaseless Christian labour. "This city was at that time the Liverpool of the Mediterranean. It possessed a splendid harbour, in which was concentrated the traffic of the sea which was then the highway of the nations ; and as Liverpool has behind her the great towns of Lancashire, so had Ephesus behind and around her such cities as those mentioned along with her in the epistles to the churches in the book of Revelation—Smyrna, Pergamos, Thyatira, Sardis, Philadelphia, and Laodicea. It was a city of vast wealth, and it was given over to every kind of pleasure, the fame of its theatres and race-course being world-wide" (Stalker's *Life of St. Paul*). Here a "great door and effectual" was opened to the apostle. His fellow-labourers aided him in his work, carrying the gospel to Colosse and Laodicea and other places which they could reach.

Very shortly before his departure from Ephesus, the apostle wrote his First Epistle to the Corinthians (*q.v.*). The silversmiths, whose traffic in the little images which they made was in danger (see DEMETRIUS), organized a riot against Paul, and he left the city, and proceeded to Troas (2 Cor. 2 : 12), whence after some time he went to meet Titus in Macedonia. Here, in consequence of the report Titus brought from Corinth, he wrote his second epistle to that church. Having spent probably most of the summer and autumn in Macedonia, visiting the churches there, specially the churches of Philippi, Thessalonica, and Berea, probably penetrating into the interior, to the shores of the Adriatic (Rom. 15 : 19), he then came into Greece, where he abode three months, spending probably the greater part of this time in Corinth

PAUL'S FIRST MISSIONARY JOURNEY.

PAUL'S SECOND MISSIONARY JOURNEY.

(Acts 20 : 2). During his stay in this city he wrote his Epistle to the Galatians, and also the great Epistle to the Romans. At the end of the three months he left Achaia for Macedonia, thence crossed into Asia Minor, and touching at Miletus, there addressed the Ephesian presbyters, whom he had sent for to meet him (Acts 20 : 17), and then sailed for Tyre, finally reaching Jerusalem, probably in the spring of A.D. 58.

While at Jerusalem, at the feast of Pentecost, he was almost murdered by a Jewish mob in the temple. (See TEMPLE, HEROD'S.) Rescued from their violence by the Roman commandant, he was conveyed as a prisoner to Cæsarea, where, from various causes, he was detained a prisoner for two years in Herod's prætorium (Acts 23 : 35). "Paul was not kept in close confinement; he had at least the range of the barracks in which he was detained. There we can imagine him pacing the ramparts on the edge of the Mediterranean, and gazing wistfully across the blue waters in the direction of Macedonia, Achaia, and Ephesus, where his spiritual children were pining for him, or perhaps encountering dangers in which they sorely needed his presence. It was a mysterious providence which thus arrested his energies and condemned the ardent worker to inactivity; yet we can now see the reason for it. Paul was needing rest. After twenty years of incessant evangelization, he required leisure to garner the harvest of experience......During these two years he wrote nothing; it was a time of internal mental activity and silent progress" (Stalker's *Life of St. Paul*).

At the end of these two years Felix (*q.v.*) was succeeded in the governorship of Palestine by Porcius Festus, before whom the apostle was again heard. But judging it right at this crisis to claim the privilege of a Roman citizen, he appealed to the emperor (Acts 25 : 11). Such an appeal could not be disregarded, and Paul was at once sent on to Rome under the charge of one Julius, a centurion of the "Augustan cohort." After a long and perilous voyage, he at length reached the imperial city in the early spring, probably, of A.D. 61. Here he was permitted to occupy his own hired

house, under constant military custody. This privilege was accorded to him, no doubt, because he was a Roman citizen, and as such could not be put into prison without a trial. The soldiers who kept guard over Paul were of course changed at frequent intervals, and thus he had the opportunity of preaching the gospel to many of them during these "two whole years," and with the blessed result of spreading among the imperial guards, and even in Cæsar's household, an interest in the truth (Phil. 1 : 13). His rooms were resorted to by many anxious inquirers, both Jews and Gentiles (Acts 28 : 23, 30, 31), and thus his imprisonment "turned rather to the furtherance of the gospel," and his "hired house" became the centre of a gracious influence which spread over the whole city. According to a Jewish tradition, it was situated on the borders of the modern Ghetto, which has been the Jewish quarters in Rome from the time of Pompey to the present day. During this period the apostle wrote his epistles to the Colossians, Ephesians, Philippians, and to Philemon, and probably also to the Hebrews.

This first imprisonment came at length to a close, Paul having been acquitted, probably because no witnesses appeared against him. Once more he set out on his missionary labours, probably visiting western and eastern Europe and Asia Minor. During this period of freedom he wrote his First Epistle to Timothy and his Epistle to Titus. The year of his release was signalized by the burning of Rome, which Nero saw fit to attribute to the Christians. A fierce persecution now broke out against the Christians. Paul was seized, and once more conveyed to Rome a prisoner. During this imprisonment he probably wrote the Second Epistle to Timothy, the last he ever wrote. "There can be little doubt that he appeared again at Nero's bar, and this time the charge did not break down. In all history there is not a more startling illustration of the irony of human life than this scene of Paul at the bar of Nero. On the judgment-seat, clad in the imperial purple, sat a man who, in a

PAUL'S THIRD MISSIONARY JOURNEY.

PAUL'S VOYAGE TO ROME.

bad world, had attained the eminence of being the very worst and meanest being in it—a man stained with every crime—a man whose whole being was so steeped in every nameable and unnameable vice, that body and soul of him were, as some one said at the time, nothing but a compound of mud and blood; and in the prisoner's dock stood the best man the world possessed, his hair whitened with labours for the good of men and the glory of God. The trial ended: Paul was condemned, and delivered over to the executioner. He was led out of the city, with a crowd of the lowest rabble at his heels. The fatal spot was reached; he knelt beside the block; the headsman's axe gleamed in the sun and fell; and the head of the apostle of the world rolled down in the dust" (probably A.D. 66), four years before the fall of Jerusalem.

Pave'ment. It was the custom of the Roman governors to erect their tribunals in open places, as the market-place, the circus, or even the highway. Pilate caused his seat of judgment to be set down in a place called "the Pavement" (John 19:13) —i.e., a place paved with a mosaic of coloured stones. It was probably a place thus prepared in front of the "judgment hall." (See GABBATHA.)

Pavil'ion, a tent or tabernacle (2 Sam. 22:12; 1 Kings 20:12–16), or enclosure (Ps. 18:11; 27:5). In Jer. 43:10 it probably denotes the canopy suspended over the judgment-seat of the king.

Peace offerings (Heb. shelâmîm), detailed regulations regarding given in Lev. 3; 7:11–21, 29–34. They were of three kinds — (1) eucharistic or thanksgiving offerings, expressive of gratitude for blessings received; (2) in fulfilment of a vow, but expressive also of thanks for benefits received; and (3) free-will offerings, something spontaneously devoted to God.

Pea'cock (Heb. tûk, apparently borrowed from the Tamil tôkei). This bird is indigenous to India. It was brought to Solomon by his ships from Tarshish (1 Kings 10:22; 2 Chr. 9:21), which in this case was probably a district on the Malabar coast of India, or in Ceylon. The word so rendered in Job 39:13 literally means wild,

tumultuous crying, and properly denotes the female ostrich (q.v.).

Pearl (Heb. gâbîsh — Job 28:18; Gr. margarītes—Matt. 7:6; 13:46; Rev. 21:21). The pearl oyster is found in the Persian Gulf and the Red Sea. Its shell is the "mother of pearl," which is of great value for ornamental purposes (1 Tim. 2:9; Rev. 17:4). Each shell contains eight or ten pearls of various sizes.

Pecu'liar, as used in the phrase "peculiar people" in 1 Pet. 2:9, is derived from the Lat. peculium, and denotes, as rendered in the Revised Version ("a people for God's own possession"), a special possession or property. The church is the "property" of God, his "purchased possession" (Eph. 1:14; R.V., "God's own possession").

Peda'hel—redeemed of God—the son of Ammihud, a prince of Naphtali (Num. 34:28).

Pedah'zur — rock of redemption — the father of Gamaliel and prince of Manasseh at the time of the Exodus (Num. 1:10; 2:20).

Pedai'ah—redemption of the Lord. (1.) The father of Zebudah, who was the wife of Josiah and mother of king Jehoiakim (2 Kings 23:36).

(2.) The father of Zerubbabel (1 Chr. 3:17–19).

(3.) The father of Joel, ruler of the half-tribe of Manasseh (1 Chr. 27:20).

(4.) Neh. 3:25.

(5.) A Levite (8:4).

(6.) A Benjamite (11:7).

(7.) A Levite (13:13).

Pe'kah—open-eyed—the son of Remaliah, a captain in the army of Pekahiah, king of Israel, whom he slew, with the aid of a band of Gileadites, and succeeded (B.C. 758) on the throne (2 Kings 15:25). Seventeen years after this he entered into an alliance with Rezin, king of Syria, and took part with him in besieging Jerusalem (2 Kings 15:37; 16:5). But Tiglath-pileser, who was in alliance with Ahaz, king of Judah, came up against Pekah, and carried away captive many of the inhabitants of his kingdom (2 Kings 15:29). This was the beginning of the "Captivity." Soon after this Pekah was put to death by Hoshea, the son of Elah, who usurped the throne (2 Kings 15 : 30 ; 16 : 1–9. Comp. Isa. 7 : 16 ; 8 : 4 ; 9 : 12). He is supposed by some to have been the "shepherd" mentioned in Zech. 11 : 16.

Pekahi'ah—*the Lord opened his eyes*—the son and successor of Menahem on the throne of Israel. He was murdered in the royal palace of Samaria by Pekah, one of the captains of his army (2 Kings 15 : 23–26), after a reign of two years (B.C. 761–759). He "did that which was evil in the sight of the Lord."

Pe'kod, probably a place in Babylonia (Jer. 50 : 21 ; Ezek. 23 : 23). It is the opinion, however, of some that this word signifies "visitation," "punishment," and allegorically "designates Babylon as the city which was to be destroyed."

Pelai'ah—*distinguished of the Lord.* (1.) One of David's posterity (1 Chr. 3 : 24).

(2.) A Levite who expounded the law (Neh. 8 : 7).

Pelati'ah—*deliverance of the Lord.* (1.) A son of Hananiah and grandson of Zerubbabel (1 Chr. 3 : 21).

(2.) A captain of "the sons of Simeon" (4 : 42, 43).

(3.) Neh. 10 : 22.

(4.) One of the twenty-five princes of the people against whom Ezekiel prophesied on account of their wicked counsel (Ezek. 11 : 1–13).

Pe'leg—*division*—one of the sons of Eber ; so called because "in his days was the earth divided" (Gen. 10 : 25). Possibly he may have lived at the time of the dispersion from Babel. But more probably the reference is to the dispersion of the two races which sprang from Eber—the one spreading towards Mesopotamia and Syria, and the other southward into Arabia.

Pe'let—*deliverance.* (1.) A descendant of Judah (1 Chr. 2 : 47).

(2.) A Benjamite who joined David at Ziklag (1 Chr. 12 : 3).

Pe'leth—*swiftness.* (1.) A Reubenite whose son was one of the conspirators against Moses and Aaron (Num. 16 : 1).

(2.) One of the sons of Jonathan (1 Chr. 2 : 33).

Pel'ethites, mentioned always along with the Cherethites, and only in the time of David. The word probably means "runners" or "couriers," and may denote that while forming part of David's body-guard, they were also sometimes employed as couriers (2 Sam. 8 : 18 ; 20 : 7, 23 ; 1 Kings 1 : 38, 41 ; 1 Chr. 18 : 17). Some, however, think that these are the names simply of two Philistine tribes from which David selected his body-guard. They are mentioned along with the Gittites (2 Sam. 15 : 18), another body of foreign troops whom David gathered round him.

Pel'icans are frequently met with at the waters of Merom and the Sea of Galilee. The pelican is ranked among unclean birds (Lev. 11 : 18 ; Deut. 14 : 17). It is of an enormous size, being about 6 feet long, with wings stretching out óver 12 feet. The Hebrew name (*kâath*—*i.e.*, "vomiter") of this bird is incorrectly rendered "cormorant" in the Authorized Version of Isa. 34 : 11 and Zeph. 2 : 14, but correctly in the Revised Version. It receives its Hebrew name from its habit of storing in its pouch large quantities of fish, which it disgorges when it feeds its young. Two species are found on the Syrian coast—the *Pelicanus onocrotalus*, or white pelican, and the *Pelicanus crispus*, or Dalmatian pelican.

Pen'ny (Gr. *denarion*), a silver coin of the value of about 7½d. or 8d. of our present money. It is thus rendered in the New Testament, and is more frequently men-

DENARIUS.

tioned than any other coin (Matt. 18 : 28 ; 20 : 2, 9, 13 ; Mark 6 : 37 ; 14 : 5, etc.). It was the daily pay of a Roman soldier in the time of Christ. In the reign of Edward III. an English penny was a labourer's day's wages. This was the "tribute money" with reference to which our Lord said, "Whose image and superscription is this?" When they answered, "Cæsar's," he replied, "Render therefore to Cæsar the things that are Cæsar's; and to God the things that are God's" (Matt. 22:19; Mark 12:15).

Pen'tateuch, the five-fold volume, consisting of the first five books of the Old Testament. This word does not occur in Scripture, nor is it certainly known when the roll was thus divided into five portions—Genesis, Exodus, Leviticus, Numbers, Deuteronomy. Probably that was done by the LXX. translators. Some modern critics speak of a *Hexateuch*, introducing the Book of Joshua as one of the group. But this book is of an entirely different character from the other books, and has a different author. It stands by itself as the first of a series of historical books beginning with the entrance of the Israelites into Canaan. (See JOSHUA.)

The books composing the Pentateuch are properly but *one* book—the "Law of Moses," the "Book of the Law of Moses," the "Book of Moses," or, as the Jews designate it, the "Torah" or "Law." That in its present form it "proceeds from a single author is proved by its plan and aim, according to which its whole contents refer to the covenant concluded between Jehovah and his people, by the instrumentality of Moses, in such a way that everything before his time is perceived to be preparatory to this fact, and all the rest to be the development of it. Nevertheless, this unity has not been stamped upon it as a matter of necessity by the latest redactor: it has been there from the beginning, and is visible in the first plan and in the whole execution of the work."—Keil, *Einl. i. d. A. T.*

A certain school of critics have set themselves to reconstruct the books of the Old Testament. By a process of "scientific study" they have discovered that the so-called historical books of the Old Testament are not history at all, but a miscellaneous collection of stories, the inventions of many different writers, patched together by a variety of editors! As regards the Pentateuch, they are not ashamed to attribute fraud, and even conspiracy, to its authors, who sought to find acceptance to their work

—which was composed partly in the age of Josiah, and partly in that of Ezra and Nehemiah—by giving it out to be the work of Moses! This is not the place to enter into the details of this controversy. We may say frankly, however, that we have no faith in this "higher criticism." It degrades the books of the Old Testament below the level of fallible human writings, and the arguments on which its speculations are built are altogether untenable.

The evidences in favour of the Mosaic authorship of the Pentateuch are conclusive. We may thus state some of them briefly:—

(1.) These books profess to have been written by Moses in the name of God (Ex. 17:14; 24:3, 4, 7; 32:7–10, 30–34; 34:27; Lev. 26:46; 27:34; Deut. 31:9, 24, 25).

(2.) This also is the uniform and persistent testimony of the Jews of all sects in all ages and countries (comp. Josh. 8:31, 32; 1 Kings 2:3; Jer. 7:22; Ezra 6:18; Neh. 8:1; Mal. 4:4; Matt. 22:24; Acts 15:21).

(3.) Our Lord plainly taught the Mosaic authorship of these books (Matt. 5:17, 18; 19:8; 22:31, 32; 23:2; Mark 10:9; 12:26; Luke 16:31; 20:37; 24:26, 27, 44; John 3:14; 5:45, 46, 47; 6:32, 49; 7:19, 22). In the face of this fact, will any one venture to allege either that Christ was ignorant of the composition of the Bible, or that, knowing the true state of the case, he yet encouraged the people in the delusion they clung to?

(4.) From the time of Joshua down to the time of Ezra there is, in the intermediate historical books, a constant reference to the Pentateuch as the "Book of the Law of Moses." This is a point of much importance, inasmuch as the critics deny that there is any such reference; and hence they deny the historical character of the Pentateuch. As regards the Passover, *e.g.*, we find it frequently spoken of or alluded to in the historical books following the Pentateuch, showing that the "Law of Moses" was then certainly known. It was celebrated in the time of Joshua (Josh. 5:10, *cf.* 4:19), Hezekiah (2 Chr. 30), Josiah (2 Kings 23; 2 Chr. 35), and Zerubbabel (Ezra 6:19–22), and is referred to in such passages as 2 Kings 23:22; 2 Chr. 35:18;

1 Kings 9 : 25 ("three times a year"); 28 : 13. Similarly we might show frequent references to the Feast of Tabernacles and other Jewish institutions, although we do not admit that any valid argument can be drawn from the silence of Scripture in such a case. An examination of the following texts, 1 Kings 2 : 9; 2 Kings 14 : 6; 2 Chr. 23 : 18; 25 : 4; 34 : 11; Ezra 3 : 2; 7 : 6; Dan. 9 : 11, 13, will also plainly show that the "Law of Moses" was known during all these centuries.

Granting that in the time of Moses there existed certain oral traditions or written records and documents which he was divinely led to make use of in his history, and that his writing was revised by inspired successors, this will fully account for certain peculiarities of expression which critics have called "anachronisms" and "contradictions," but in no way militates against the doctrine that Moses was the original author of the whole of the Pentateuch. It is not necessary for us to affirm that the whole is an original composition; but we affirm that the evidences clearly demonstrate that Moses was the author of those books which have come down to us bearing his name. The Pentateuch is certainly the basis and necessary preliminary of the whole of the Old Testament history and literature. (See DEUTERONOMY.)

Pen'tecost—*i.e.*, "fiftieth"—found only in the New Testament (Acts 2 : 1; 20 : 16; 1 Cor. 16 : 8). The festival so named is first spoken of in Ex. 23 : 16 as "the feast of harvest," and again in Ex. 34 : 22 as "the feast of weeks." It is called also "the day of the firstfruits" (Num. 28 : 26). From the sixteenth of the month of Nisan (the second day of the Passover), seven complete weeks—*i.e.*, forty-nine days—were to be reckoned, and this feast was held on the fiftieth day. The manner in which it was to be kept is described in Lev. 23 : 15–19; Num. 28 : 27–29. Besides the sacrifices prescribed for the occasion, every one was to bring to the Lord his "tribute of a freewill offering" (Deut. 16 : 9–11). The purpose of this feast was to commemorate the completion of the grain harvest. Its distinguishing feature was the offering of "two

leavened loaves" made from the new corn of the completed harvest, which, with two lambs, were waved before the Lord as a thank offering.

The day of Pentecost is noted in the Christian Church as the day on which the Spirit descended upon the apostles, and on which, under Peter's preaching, so many thousands were converted in Jerusalem (Acts 2).

Penu'el—*face of God*—a place not far from Succoth, on the east of the Jordan and north of the river Jabbok. It is also called "Peniel." Here Jacob wrestled (Gen. 32 : 24–32) "with a man" ("the angel"—Hos. 12 : 4. Jacob says of him, "I have seen God face to face") "till the break of day."

A town was afterwards built there (Judg. 8 : 8; 1 Kings 12 : 25). The men of this place refused to succour Gideon and his little army when they were in pursuit of the Midianites (Judg. 8 : 1–21). On his return, Gideon slew the men of this city and razed its lofty watch-tower to the ground.

Pe'or—*opening*. (1.) A mountain peak (Num. 23 : 28) to which Balak led Balaam as a last effort to induce him to pronounce a curse upon Israel. When he looked on the tribes encamped in the acacia groves below him, he could not refrain from giving utterance to a remarkable benediction (24 : 1–9). Balak was more than ever enraged at Balaam, and bade him flee for his life. But before he went he gave expression to that wonderful prediction regarding the future of this mysterious people, whose "goodly tents" were spread out before him, and the coming of a "Star" out of Jacob and a "Sceptre" out of Israel (24 : 14–17).

(2.) A Moabite divinity, called also "Baal-peor" (Num. 25 : 3, 5, 18; comp. Deut. 3 : 29).

Pera'zim, Mount—*mount of breaches*—only in Isa. 28 : 21. It is the same as BAAL-PERAZIM (*q.v.*), where David gained a victory over the Philistines (2 Sam. 5 : 20).

Pe'res—*divided*—one of the mysterious words "written over against the candlestick upon the plaster of the wall" of king Belshazzar's palace (Dan. 5 : 28). (See MENE.)

Pe′rez = Pharez (*q.v.*)—*breach*—the son of Judah (Neh. 11:4). "The chief of all the captains of the host for the first month" in the reign of David was taken from his family (1 Chr. 27:3). Four hundred and sixty-eight of his "sons" came back from captivity with Zerubbabel, who himself was one of them (1 Chr. 9:4; Neh. 11:6).

Pe′rez-uz′zah—*the breach of Uzzah*—a place where God "burst forth upon Uzzah, so that he died," when he rashly "took hold" of the ark (2 Sam. 6:6-8). It was not far from Kirjath-jearim (*q.v.*).

Perfec′tion. See SANCTIFICATION.

Per′fumes were used in religious worship and for personal and domestic enjoyment (Ex. 30:35-37; Prov. 7:17; Cant. 3:6; Isa. 57:9), and also in embalming the dead, and in other funeral ceremonies (Mark 14:8; Luke 24:1; John 19:39).

Per′ga, the capital of Pamphylia, on the coast of Asia Minor. Paul and his companions landed at this place from Cyprus on their first missionary journey (Acts 13:13, 14), and here Mark forsook the party and returned to Jerusalem. Some time afterwards Paul and Barnabas again visited this city and "preached the word" (14:25). It stood on the banks of the river Cestrus, some 7 miles from its mouth, and was a place of some commercial importance. It is now a ruin, called *Eski Kalessi.*

Per′gamos, the chief city of Mysia, in Asia Minor. One of the "seven churches" was planted here (Rev. 1:11; 2:17). It was noted for its wickedness, insomuch that our Lord says "Satan's seat" was there. The church of Pergamos was rebuked for swerving from the truth and embracing the doctrines of Balaam and the Nicolaitanes. Antipas, Christ's "faithful martyr," here sealed his testimony with his blood.

This city stood on the banks of the river Caicus, about 20 miles from the sea. It is now called *Bergama*, and has a population of some twenty thousand, of whom about two thousand profess to be Christians. Parchment (*q.v.*) was first made here, and was called by the Greeks *pergamēnē*, from the name of the city.

Peri′da — *kernel* — Neh. 7:57. (See PERUDA.)

Per′izzites—*villagers; dwellers in the open country*—the Canaanitish nation inhabiting the fertile regions south and southwest of Carmel. "They were the graziers, farmers, and peasants of the time." They were to be driven out of the land by the descendants of Abraham (Gen. 15:20; Ex. 3:8, 17; 23:23; 33:2; 34:11). They are afterwards named among the conquered tribes (Josh. 24:11). Still lingering in the land, however, they were reduced to servitude by Solomon (1 Kings 9:20).

Persecu′tion. The first great persecution for religious opinion of which we have any record was that which broke out against the worshippers of God among the Jews in the days of Ahab, when that king, at the instigation of his wife Jezebel—"a woman in whom, with the reckless and licentious habits of an Oriental queen, were united the fiercest and sternest qualities inherent in the old Semitic race"—sought in the most relentless manner to extirpate the worship of Jehovah and substitute in its place the worship of Ashtoreth and Baal. Ahab's example in this respect was followed by Manasseh, who "shed innocent blood very much, till he filled Jerusalem from one end to another" (2 Kings 21:16; comp. 24:4). In all ages, in one form or another, the people of God have had to suffer persecution. In its earliest history the Christian church passed through many bloody persecutions. Of subsequent centuries in our own and in other lands the same sad record may be made.

Christians are forbidden to seek the propagation of the gospel by force (Matt. 7:1; Luke 9:54-56; Rom. 14:4; James 4:11, 12). The words of Ps. 7:13, "He ordaineth his arrows against the persecutors," ought rather to be, as in the Revised Version, "He maketh his arrows fiery [shafts] against," etc.

Persever′ance of the saints, their certain continuance in a state of grace. Once justified and regenerated, the believer can neither totally nor finally fall away from grace, but will certainly persevere therein and attain everlasting life.

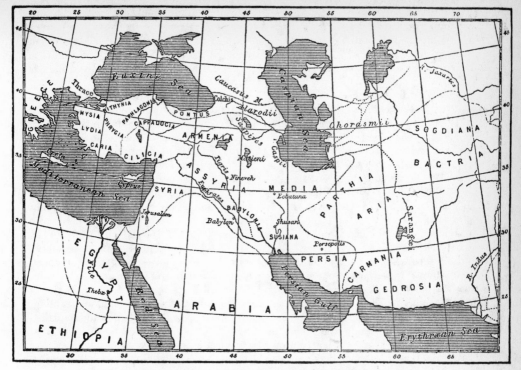

THE PERSIAN EMPIRE IN ITS GREATEST EXTENT.

See page 535.

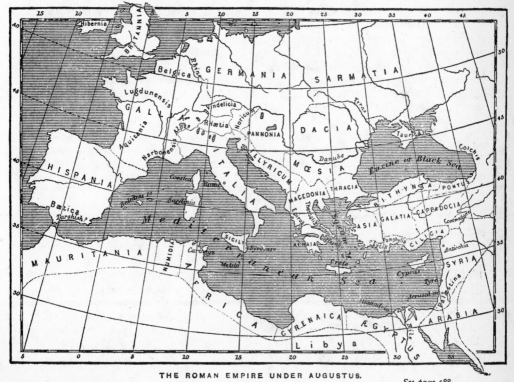

THE ROMAN EMPIRE UNDER AUGUSTUS.

See page 588.

This doctrine is clearly taught in these passages—John 10:28, 29; Rom. 11:29; Phil. 1:6; 1 Pet. 1:5. It, moreover, follows from a consideration of (1) the immutability of the divine decrees (Jer. 31:3; Matt. 24:22-24; Acts 13:48; Rom. 8:30); (2) the provisions of the covenant of grace (Jer. 32:40; John 10:29; 17:2-6); (3) the atonement and intercession of Christ (Isa. 53:6, 11; Matt. 20:28; 1 Pet. 2:24; John 11:42; 17:11, 15, 20; Rom. 8:34); and (4) the indwelling of the Holy Ghost (John 14:16; 2 Cor. 1:21, 22; 5:5; Eph. 1:14; 1 John 3:9).

This doctrine is not inconsistent with the truth that the believer may nevertheless fall into grievous sin, and continue therein for some time. (See BACKSLIDE.)

Per'sia, an ancient empire, extending from the Indus to Thrace and from the Caspian Sea to the Red Sea and the Persian Gulf,—thus including the whole of Western Asia and a portion of both Europe and Africa. The country of Persia proper (Ezek. 38:5)—now called *Fars* or *Farsistan* —however, was only a part of this empire. It was bounded on the north by Media, from which it was separated by a mountain range, on the west by Susiana (Elam), and on the south by the Persian Gulf. Till the time of Cyrus, Persia seems to have been in a state of subjection to Media. Cyrus (*q.v.*) secured its independence (about B.C. 558), and extended his conquests far and wide, till Persia became a great empire, which held sway in Asia for about two hundred years, when it was conquered by Alexander the Great (B.C. 330) in the days of Darius, the only successor of Cyrus who is mentioned in Scripture (Neh. 12:22). Modern Persia is still an important Asiatic power, embracing a territory of about 500,000 square miles, with a population of about nine million. (See MEDIA.)

Per'sis, a female Christian at Rome whom Paul salutes (Rom. 16:12). She is spoken of as "beloved," and as having "laboured much in the Lord."

Peru'da, one whose descendants returned with Zerubbabel (Ezra 2:55); called also Perida (Neh. 7:57).

Pe'ter, originally called Simon (=Simeon —*i.e.,* "hearing"), a very common Jewish name in the New Testament. He was the son of Jona (Matt. 16:17). His mother is nowhere named in Scripture. He had a younger brother called Andrew, who first brought him to Jesus (John 1:40-42). His native town was Bethsaida, on the western coast of the Sea of Galilee, to which also Philip belonged. Here he was brought up by the shores of the Sea of Galilee, and was trained to the occupation of a fisher. His father had probably died while he was still young, and he and his brother were brought up under the care of Zebedee and his wife Salome (Matt. 27:56; Mark 15:40; 16:1). There the four youths—Simon, Andrew, James, and John—spent their boyhood and early manhood in constant fellowship. Simon and his brother doubtless enjoyed all the advantages of a religious training, and were early instructed in an acquaintance with the Scriptures and with the great prophecies regarding the coming of the Messiah. They did not probably enjoy, however, any special training in the study of the law under any of the rabbis. When Peter appeared before the Sanhedrin, he looked like an "unlearned man" (Acts 4:13).

"Simon was a Galilean, and he was that out and out......The Galileans had a marked character of their own. They had a reputation for an independence and energy which often ran out into turbulence. They were at the same time of a franker and more transparent disposition than their brethren in the south. In all these respects— in bluntness, impetuosity, headiness, and simplicity—Simon was a genuine Galilean. They spoke a peculiar dialect. They had a difficulty with the guttural sounds and some others, and their pronunciation was reckoned harsh in Judea. The Galilean accent stuck to Simon all through his career. It betrayed him as a follower of Christ when he stood within the judgment-hall (Mark 14:70). It betrayed his own nationality and that of those conjoined with him on the day of Pentecost (Acts 2:7)."

It would seem that Simon was married before he became an apostle. His wife's mother is referred to (Matt. 8:14; Mark

ANCIENT PERSIAN KINGS, PERSEPOLIS.

STATUE OF CYRUS.

See "Persia."

1 : 30 ; Luke 4 : 38). He was in all probability accompanied by his wife on his missionary journeys (1 Cor. 9 : 5 ; comp. 1 Pet. 5 : 13).

He appears to have been settled at Capernaum when Christ entered on his public ministry, and may have reached beyond the age of thirty. His house was large enough to give a home to his brother Andrew, his wife's mother, and also to Christ, who seems to have lived with him (Mark 1 : 29–35 ; 2 : 1), as well as to his own family. It was apparently two stories high (2 : 4).

At Bethabara (R. V., John 1 : 28, "Bethany"), beyond Jordan, John the Baptist had borne testimony concerning Jesus as the "Lamb of God" (John 1 : 29–36). Andrew and John hearing it, followed Jesus, and abode with him where he was. They were convinced, by his gracious words and by the authority with which he spoke, that he was the Messiah (Luke 4 : 22 ; Matt. 7 : 29) ; and Andrew went forth and found Simon and brought him to Jesus (John 1 : 41).

Jesus at once recognized Simon, and declared that hereafter he would be called *Cephas*, an Aramaic name corresponding to the Greek *Petros*, which means "a mass of rock detached from the living rock." The Aramaic name does not occur again, but the name Peter gradually displaces the old name Simon, though our Lord himself always uses the name Simon when addressing him (Matt. 17 : 25 ; Mark 14 : 37 ; Luke 22 : 31, comp. 21 : 15–17). We are not told what impression the first interview with Jesus produced on the mind of Simon. When we next meet him it is by the Lake of Galilee (Matt. 4 : 18–22). There the four (Simon and Andrew, James and John) had had an unsuccessful night's fishing. Jesus appeared suddenly, and entering into Simon's boat, bade him launch forth and let down the nets. He did so, and enclosed a great multitude of fishes. This was plainly a miracle wrought before Simon's eyes. The awe-stricken disciple cast himself at the feet of Jesus, with the cry, "Depart from me ; for I am a sinful man, O Lord." Jesus addressed him with the assuring words, "Fear not," and announced to him his life's

work. Simon responded at once to the call to become a disciple, and after this we find him in constant attendance on our Lord.

He is next called into the rank of the apostleship, and becomes a "fisher of men" in the stormy seas of the world of human life (Matt. 10 : 2–4 ; Mark 3 : 13–19 ; Luke 6 : 12–19), and takes a more and more prominent part in all the leading events of our Lord's life. It is he who utters that notable profession of faith at Capernaum (John 6 : 66–69), and again at Cæsarea Philippi (Matt. 16 : 13–20 ; Mark 8 : 27–30 ; Luke 9 : 18–21). This profession at Cæsarea was one of supreme importance, and our Lord in response used these memorable words : "Thou art Peter, and upon this rock I will build my church."

"From this time forth" Jesus began to speak of his sufferings. For this Peter rebuked him. But our Lord in return rebuked Peter, speaking to him in sterner words than he ever used to any other of his disciples (Matt. 16 : 21–28 ; Mark 8 : 31). At the close of his brief sojourn at Cæsarea our Lord took Peter and James and John with him into "an high mountain apart," and was transfigured before them. Peter on that occasion, under the impression the scene produced on his mind, exclaimed, "Lord, it is good to be here : let us make three tabernacles" (Matt. 17 : 1–13).

On his return to Capernaum the collectors of the temple-tax (a *didrachma*, half a sacred shekel), which every Israelite of twenty years old and upwards had to pay (Ex. 30 : 15), came to Peter and reminded him that Jesus had not paid it (Matt. 17 : 24–27). Our Lord instructed Peter to go and catch a fish in the lake and take from its mouth the exact amount needed for the tax—*viz.*, a *stater*, or two half-shekels. "That take," said our Lord, "and give unto them for me and thee."

As the end was drawing nigh, our Lord sent Peter and John (Luke 22 : 7–13) into the city to prepare a place where he should keep the feast with his disciples. There he was forewarned of the fearful sin into which he afterwards fell (22 : 31–34). He accompanied our Lord from the guest-chamber to the garden of Gethsemane (Luke

22:39-46), which he and the other two who had been witnesses of the transfiguration were permitted to enter with our Lord, while the rest were left without. Here he passed through a strange experience. Under a sudden impulse he cut off the ear of Malchus (47-51), one of the band that had come forth to take Jesus. Then follow the scenes of the judgment-hall (54-62) and of his bitter grief (Luke 24:9-12).

He is found in John's company early on the morning of the resurrection. He boldly entered into the empty grave (John 20:1-10), and saw the "linen clothes laid by themselves." To him, the first of the apostles, our risen Lord revealed himself—thus conferring on him a signal honour, and showing how fully he was restored to his favour (John 21:1-19; Luke 24:34; 1 Cor. 15:5). We next read of our Lord's singular interview with Peter on the shores of the Sea of Galilee, where he thrice asked him, "Simon, son of Jonas, lovest thou me?" (See LOVE.)

After this scene at the lake we hear nothing of Peter till he again appears with the others at the ascension (Acts 1:15-26). It was he who proposed that the vacancy caused by the apostasy of Judas should be filled up. He is prominent on the day of Pentecost (2:14-40). The events of that day "completed the change in Peter himself which the painful discipline of his fall and all the lengthened process of previous training had been slowly making. He is now no more the unreliable, changeful, self-confident man, ever swaying between rash courage and weak timidity, but the steadfast, trusted guide and director of the fellowship of believers, the intrepid preacher of Christ in Jerusalem and abroad. And now that he is become Cephas indeed, we hear almost nothing of the name Simon (only in Acts 10:5, 32; 15:14), and he is known to us finally as *Peter*."

After the miracle at the temple-gate (Acts 4) persecution arose against the Christians, and Peter was cast into prison. He boldly defended himself and his companions at the bar of the council (4:19, 20). A fresh outburst of violence against the Christians (5:17-28) led to the whole body of the

apostles being cast into prison; but during the night they were wonderfully delivered, and were found in the morning teaching in the temple. A second time Peter defended them before the council (Acts 5:29-33), who, "when they had called the apostles and beaten them, let them go."

The time had come for Peter to leave Jerusalem. After labouring for some time in Samaria, he returned to Jerusalem, and reported to the church there the results of his work (Acts 8:14-25). Here he remained for a period, during which he met Paul for the first time since his conversion (9:26-30; Gal. 1:18). Leaving Jerusalem again, he went forth on a missionary journey to Lydda and Joppa (Acts 9:32-43). He is next called on to open the door of the Christian church to the Gentiles by the admission of Cornelius of Cæsarea (ch. 10).

After remaining for some time at Cæsarea, he returned to Jerusalem (Acts 11:1-18), where he defended his conduct with reference to the Gentiles. Next we hear of his being cast into prison by Herod Agrippa (12:1-19); but in the night an angel of the Lord opened the prison gates, and he went forth and found refuge in the house of Mary.

He took part in the deliberations at the council in Jerusalem (Acts 15:1-31; Gal. 2:1-10) regarding the relation of the Gentiles to the church. This subject had awakened new interest at Antioch, and for its settlement was referred to the council of the apostles and elders at Jerusalem. Here Paul and Peter met again.

We have no further mention of Peter in the Acts of the Apostles. He seems to have gone down to Antioch after the council at Jerusalem, and there to have been guilty of dissembling, for which he was severely reprimanded by Paul (Gal. 2:11-16), who "rebuked him to his face."

After this he appears to have carried the gospel to the east, and to have laboured for a while at Babylon, on the Euphrates (1 Pet. 5:13). There is no satisfactory evidence that he was ever at Rome. Where or when he died is not certainly known. Probably he died between A.D. 64 and 67.

Pe'ter, First Epistle of. This epistle

is addressed to "the strangers scattered abroad"—*i.e.*, to the Jews of the Dispersion (the *Diaspora*).

Its object is to confirm its readers in the doctrines they had been already taught. Peter has been called "the apostle of hope," because this epistle abounds with words of comfort and encouragement fitted to sustain a "lively hope." It contains about thirty-five references to the Old Testament.

It was written from Babylon, on the Euphrates, which was at this time one of the chief seats of Jewish learning, and a fitting centre for labour among the Jews. It has been noticed that in the beginning of his epistle Peter names the provinces of Asia Minor in the order in which they would naturally occur to one writing from Babylon. He counsels (1) to steadfastness and perseverance under persecution (1–2: 10); (2) to the practical duties of a holy life (2:11–3:13); (3) he adduces the example of Christ and other motives to patience and holiness (3:14–4:19); and (4) concludes with counsels to pastors and people (5).

Pe'ter, Second Epistle of. The question of the authenticity of this epistle has been much discussed, but the weight of evidence is wholly in favour of its claim to be the production of the apostle whose name it bears. It appears to have been written shortly before the apostle's death (1:14). This epistle contains eleven references to the Old Testament. It also contains (3:15, 16) a remarkable reference to Paul's epistles. Some think this reference is to 1 Thess. 4: 13–5:11. A few years ago, among other documents, a parchment fragment, called the "Gospel of Peter," was discovered in a Christian tomb at Akhmîm in Upper Egypt. Origen (*obiit* 254 A.D.), Eusebius (*obiit* 340), and Jerome (*obiit* 420) refer to such a work, and hence it has been concluded that it was probably written about the middle of the second century. It professes to give a history of our Lord's resurrection and ascension. While differing in not a few particulars from the canonical gospels, the writer shows plainly that he was acquainted both with the synoptics and with the Gospel of John. Though apocryphal, it is of considerable value as showing that the main facts of the history of our Lord were then widely known.

Pethahi'ah—*loosed of the Lord.* (1.) The chief of one of the priestly courses (the nineteenth) in the time of David (1 Chr. 24:16). (2.) A Levite (Ezra 10:23). (3.) Neh. 9:5. (4.) A descendant of Judah who had some office at the court of Persia (Neh. 11:24).

Pe'thor—*interpretation of dreams*—identified with *Pitru*, on the west bank of the Euphrates, a few miles south of the Hittite capital of Carchemish (Num. 22:5, "which is by the river of the land of the children of [the god] Ammo "). (See BALAAM.)

Pethu'el—*vision of God*—the father of Joel the prophet (Joel 1:1).

Pe'tra—*rock*—Isa. 16:1, marg. (See SELA.)

Peul'thai—*wages of the Lord*—one of the sons of Obed-edom, a Levite porter (1 Chr. 26:5).

Pha'lec (Luke 3:35) = **Peleg** (*q.v.*)—Gen. 11:16.

Phal'lu—*separated*—the second son of Reuben (Gen. 46:9).

Phal'ti—*deliverance of the Lord*—the son of Laish of Gallim (1 Sam. 25:44)= **Phalti'el** (2 Sam. 3:15). Michal, David's wife, was given to him.

Phanu'el—*face of God*—father of the prophetess Anna (*q.v.*)—Luke 2:36.

Pha'raoh, the official title borne by the Egyptian kings down to the time when that country was conquered by the Greeks. (See EGYPT.) The name is a compound, as some think, of the words *Ra*, the "sun" or "sun-god," and the article *phe*, "the," prefixed; hence *phera*, "the sun," or "the sun-god." But others, perhaps more correctly, think the name derived from *Perāo*, "the great house"=his majesty=in Turkish, "the Sublime Porte."

(1.) The Pharaoh who was on the throne when Abram went down into Egypt (Gen. 12:10–20) was probably one of the Hyksôs, or "shepherd kings." The Egyptians called the nomad tribes of Syria *Shasu*, "plunderers," their king or chief *Hyk*, and hence the name of these invaders who conquered the native kings and established a strong government, with Zoan or Tanis as their capital. They were of Semitic origin, and of kindred blood accordingly with Abram.

They were probably driven forward by the pressure of the Hittites. The name they bear on the monuments is "Mentiu."

(2.) The Pharaoh of Joseph's days (Gen. 41) was probably Apopi, or Apôpis, the last of the Hyksôs kings. To the old native Egyptians, who were an African race, shepherds were "an abomination;" but to the Hyksôs kings these Asiatic shepherds who now appeared with Jacob at their head were congenial, and being akin to their own race, had a warm welcome (Gen. 47:5, 6). Some argue that Joseph came to Egypt in the reign of Thothmes III., long after the expulsion of the Hyksôs, and that his influence is to be seen in the rise and progress of the religious revolution in the direction of monotheism which characterized the middle of the eighteenth dynasty. The wife of Amenophis III., of that dynasty, was a Semite. Is this singular fact to be explained from the presence of some of Joseph's kindred at the Egyptian court? Pharaoh said to Joseph, "Thy father and thy brethren are come unto thee: the land of Egypt is before thee; in the best of the land make thy father and brethren to dwell" (Gen. 47:5,6).

(3.) The "new king who knew not Joseph" (Ex. 1:8-22) has been generally supposed to have been Aahmes I., or Amôsis, as he is called by Josephus. Recent discoveries, however, have led to the conclusion that Seti was the "new king."

During about seventy years the Hebrews in Egypt were under the powerful protection of Joseph. After his death their condition was probably very slowly and gradually changed. The invaders, the Hyksôs, who for some five centuries had been masters of Egypt, were driven out, and the old dynasty restored. The Israelites now began to be looked down upon. They began to be afflicted and tyrannized over. In process of time a change appears to have taken place in the government of Egypt. A new dynasty—the nineteenth, as it is called—came into power under Seti I., who was its founder. He associated with him in his government his son, Rameses II., when he was yet young, probably ten or twelve years of age.

Note.—Professor Maspero, keeper of the museum of Bûlâk, near Cairo, had his attention in 1870 directed to the fact that scarabs—*i.e.*, stone and metal imitations of the beetle (symbols of immortality), originally worn as amulets by royal personages—which were evidently genuine relics of the time of the ancient Pharaohs, were being sold at Thebes and different places along the Nile. This led him to suspect that some hitherto undiscovered burial-place of the Pharaohs had been opened, and that these and other relics, now secretly sold, were a part of the treasure found there. For a long time he failed, with all his ingenuity, to find the source of these rare treasures. At length one of those in the secret volunteered to give information regarding this burial-place. The result was that a party was conducted in 1881 to Deir-el-Baharî, near Thebes, when the wonderful discovery was made of thirty-six mummies of kings, queens, princes, and high priests hidden away in a cavern prepared for them, where they had lain undisturbed for thirty centuries. "The temple of Deir-el-Baharî stands in the middle of a natural amphitheatre of cliffs, which is only one of a number of smaller amphitheatres into which the limestone mountains of the tombs are broken up. In the wall of rock separating this basin from the one next to it some ancient Egyptian engineers had constructed the hiding-place, whose secret had been kept for nearly three thousand years." The exploring party being guided to the place, found behind a great rock a shaft 6 feet square and about 40 feet deep, sunk into the limestone. At the bottom of this a passage led westward for 25 feet, and then turned sharply northward into the very heart of the mountain, where in a chamber 23 feet by 13, and 6 feet in height, they came upon the wonderful treasures of antiquity. The mummies were all carefully secured and brought down to Bûlâk, where they were deposited in the royal museum, which has now been removed to Ghizeh.

Among the most notable of the ancient kings of Egypt thus discovered were Thothmes III., Seti I., and Rameses II. Thothmes III. was the most distinguished monarch of the brilliant eighteenth dynasty. When this mummy was unwound "once more, after an interval of thirty-six centuries, human eyes gazed on the features of the man who had conquered Syria and Cyprus and Ethiopia, and had raised

Egypt to the highest pinnacle of her power. The spectacle, however, was of brief duration. The remains proved to be in so fragile a state that there was only time to take a hasty photograph, and then the features crumbled to pieces and vanished like an apparition, and so passed away from human view for ever." "It seems strange that though the body of this man," who overran Palestine with his armies two hundred years before the birth of

THOTHMES III.

Moses, "mouldered to dust, the flowers with which it had been wreathed were so wonderfully preserved that even their colour could be distinguished" (Manning's *Land of the Pharaohs*).

Seti I. (his throne name Merenptah), the father of Rameses II., was a great and successful warrior, also a great builder. The mummy of this Pharaoh, when unrolled, brought to view "the most beautiful mummy-head ever seen within the walls of the museum. The sculptors of Thebes and Abydos did not flatter this Pharaoh when they gave him that delicate, sweet, and smiling profile which is the admiration of travellers. After a lapse of thirty-two centuries, the mummy retains the same expression which characterized the features of the living man. Most remarkable of all, when compared with the mummy of Rameses II., is the striking resemblance

between the father and the son. Seti I. is, as it were, the idealized type of Rameses II. He must have died at an advanced age. The head is shaven, the eyebrows are white, the condition of the body points to considerably more than threescore years of life, thus confirming the opinions of the learned, who have attributed a long reign to this king."

(4.) Rameses II., the son of Seti I., is probably the Pharaoh of the oppression. During his forty years' residence at the court of Egypt, Moses must have known this ruler well. During his sojourn in Midian, however, Rameses died, after a reign of sixty-seven years, and his body was embalmed and laid in the royal sepulchre in the Valley of the Tombs of Kings beside that of his father. Like the other mummies found hidden in the cave of Deir-el-Baharî, it had been for some reason removed from its original tomb, and probably carried from place to place till finally deposited in the cave where it was so recently discovered.

In 1886, the mummy of this king, the "great Rameses," the "Sesostris" of the Greeks, was unwound, and showed the body of what must have been a robust old man. The features revealed to view are thus described by Maspero: "The head is long and small in proportion to the body. The top of the skull is quite bare. On the temple there are a few sparse hairs, but at the poll the hair is quite thick, forming smooth, straight locks about two inches in length.

MUMMY HEAD OF SETI I.

White at the time of death, they have been dyed a light yellow by the spices used in

STATUE OF RAMESES II., THE PHARAOH OF THE OPPRESSION.
(*Found at Tanis.*)

embalmment. The forehead is low and narrow; the brow-ridge prominent; the eyebrows are thick and white; the eyes are small and close together; the nose is long, thin, arched like the noses of the Bourbons; the temples are sunken; the cheek-bones very prominent; the ears round, standing far out from the head, and pierced, like those of a woman, for the wearing of ear-rings; the jaw-bone is massive and strong; the chin very prominent; the mouth small, but thick-lipped; the teeth worn and very brittle, but white and well preserved. The moustache and beard are thin. They seem to have been kept shaven during life, but were probably allowed to grow during the king's last illness,

MUMMY HEAD OF RAMESES II.

or they may have grown after death. The hairs are white, like those of the head and eyebrows, but are harsh and bristly, and a tenth of an inch in length. The skin is of an earthy-brown, streaked with black. Finally, it may be said the face of the mummy gives a fair idea of the face of the living king. The expression is unintellectual, perhaps slightly animal; but even under the somewhat grotesque disguise of mummification there is plainly to be seen an air of sovereign majesty, of resolve, and of pride."

Both on his father's and mother's side it has been pretty clearly shown that Rameses had Chaldean or Mesopotamian blood in his veins to such a degree that he might be called an Assyrian. This fact is thought to throw light on Isa. 52:4.

(5.) The Pharaoh of the Exodus was probably Menephtah I., the fourteenth and eldest surviving son of Rameses II. He resided at Zoan, where he had the various interviews with Moses and Aaron recorded in the book of Exodus. His mummy was not among those found at Deir-el-Bahari. It is still a question, however, whether Seti II. or his father Menephtah was the Pharaoh of the Exodus. Some think the balance of evidence to be in favour of the former, whose reign it is known began peacefully, but came to a sudden and disastrous end. The "Harris papyrus," found at Medinet-Abou in Upper Egypt in 1856, a state document written by Rameses III., the second king of the twentieth dynasty, gives at length an account of a great exodus from Egypt, followed by widespread confusion and anarchy. This, there is great reason to believe, was the Hebrew exodus, with which the nineteenth dynasty of the Pharaohs came to an end. This period of anarchy was brought to a close by Setnekht, the founder of the twentieth dynasty.

(6.) The Pharaoh mentioned in 1 Kings 11:18–22.

(7.) So, king of Egypt (2 Kings 17:4, 7).

(8.) The Pharaoh of 1 Chr. 4:18.

(9.) Pharaoh, whose daughter Solomon married (1 Kings 3:1; 7:8).

(10.) Pharaoh, in whom Hezekiah put his trust in his war against Sennacherib (2 Kings 18:21).

(11.) The Pharaoh by whom Josiah was defeated and slain at the great battle of Megiddo (2 Chr. 35:20–24; 2 Kings 23:29, 30). (See NECHO.)

(12.) Pharaoh-hophra, who in vain sought to relieve Jerusalem when it was besieged by Nebuchadnezzar (q.v.)—2 Kings 25:1–4; comp. Jer. 37:5–8; Ezek. 17:11–13. (See ZEDEKIAH.)

Pharaoh's daughters. Three princesses are thus mentioned in Scripture:—

(1.) The princess who adopted the infant Moses (q.v.)—Ex. 2:10. She is twice mentioned in the New Testament (Acts 7:21; Heb. 11:24). It would seem that she was alive and in some position of influence about the court when Moses was compelled to flee from Egypt, and thus for forty years he had in some way been under her influence.

She was in all probability the sister of Rameses, and the daughter of Seti I. Josephus calls her Thermuthis. It is supposed by some that she was Nefert-ari, the wife as well as sister of Rameses. The mummy of this queen was among the treasures found at Deir-el-Bahari.

HEAD OF NEFERT-ARI.
(From a Sculpture at Abu-Simbel.)

(2.) "Bithiah the daughter of Pharaoh, which Mered took" (1 Chr. 4:18).

(3.) The wife of Solomon (1 Kings 3:1). This is the first reference since the Exodus to any connection of Israel with Egypt.

Pha'rez—*breach*—the elder of the twin sons of Judah (Gen. 38:29). From him the royal line of David sprang (Ruth 4: 18–22). "The chief of all the captains of the host" was of the children of Perez (1 Chr. 27:3; Matt. 1:3).

Phar'isees—*separatists* (Heb. *persahin*, from *parash*, "to separate"). They were probably the successors of the Assideans (*i.e.*, the "pious"), a party that originated in the time of Antiochus Epiphanes in revolt against his heathenizing policy. The first mention of them is in a description by Josephus of the three sects or schools into which the Jews were divided (B.C. 145). The other two sects were the Essenes and the Sadducees. In the time of our Lord they were the popular party (John 7:48). They were extremely accurate and minute in all matters appertaining to the law of Moses (Matt. 9:14; 23:15; Luke 11:39; 18:12). Paul, when brought before the council of Jerusalem, professed himself a Pharisee (Acts 23:6–8; 26:4, 5).

There was much that was sound in their creed, yet their system of religion was a form and nothing more. Theirs was a very lax morality (Matt. 5:20; 15:4, 8; 23:3, 14, 23, 25; John 8:7). On the first notice of them in the New Testament (Matt. 3:7), they are ranked by our Lord with the Sadducees as a "generation of vipers." They were noted for their self-righteousness and their pride (Matt. 9:11; Luke 7: 44–46; 18:11). They were frequently rebuked by our Lord (Matt. 12:39; 16:1–4).

From the very beginning of his ministry the Pharisees showed themselves bitter and persistent enemies of our Lord. They could not bear his doctrines, and they sought by every means to destroy his influence among the people.

Phar'par—*swift*—one of the rivers of Damascus (2 Kings 5:12). It has been identified with the *'Awaj*, "a small lively river." The whole of the district watered by the 'Awaj is called the Wâdy el-'Ajam— *i.e.*, "the valley of the Persians"—so called for some unknown reason. This river empties itself into the lake or marsh Bahret Hijaneh, on the east of Damascus. One of its branches bears the modern name of *Wâdy Barbar*, which is probably a corruption of Pharpar.

Phe'be, a "deaconess of the church at Cenchrea," the port of Corinth. She was probably the bearer of Paul's epistle to the Romans. Paul commended her to the Christians at Rome; "for she hath been," says he, "a succourer of many, and of myself also" (Rom. 16:1, 2).

Pheni'ce, properly **Phœ'nix**—*a palm-tree* (as in the R.V.)—a town with a harbour on the southern side of Crete (Acts

27 : 12), west of the Fair Havens. It is now called *Lutro*.

Pheni'cia (Acts 21 : 2) = **Pheni'ce** (11 : 19 ; 15 : 3 ; R. V., Phœnicia) — Gr. *phoinix*, "a palm"—the *land of palm-trees;* a strip of land of an average breadth of about 20 miles along the shores of the Mediterranean, from the river Eleutherus in the north to the promontory of Carmel in the south, about 120 miles in length. This name is not found in the Old Testament, and in the New Testament it is mentioned only in the passages above referred to.

"In the Egyptian inscriptions Phœnicia is called Keft, the inhabitants being Kefa ; and since Keft-ur, or 'Greater Phœnicia,' was the name given to the delta of the Nile from the Phœnician colonies settled upon it, the Philistines who came from Caphtor or Keft-ur must have been of Phœnician origin" (comp. Deut. 2 : 23 ; Jer. 47 : 4 ; Amos 9 : 7).—Sayce's *Bible and the Monuments.*

Phœnicia lay in the very centre of the old world, and was the natural *entrepôt* for commerce with foreign nations. It was the "England of antiquity." "The trade routes from all Asia converged on the Phœnician coast ; the centres of commerce on the Euphrates and Tigris forwarding their goods by way of Tyre to the Nile, to Arabia, and to the west ; and, on the other hand, the productions of the vast regions bordering the Mediterranean passing through the Canaanite capital to the eastern world." It was "situate at the entry of the sea, a merchant of the people for many isles " (Ezek. 27 : 3, 4). The far-reaching commercial activity of the Phœnicians, especially with Tarshish and the western world, enriched them with vast wealth, which introduced boundless luxury and developed among them a great activity in all manner of arts and manufactures. (See TYRE.)

The Phœnicians were the most enterprising merchants of the old world, establishing colonies at various places, of which Carthage was the chief. They were a Canaanite branch of the race of Ham, and are frequently called Sidonians, from their principal city of Sidon. None could "skill to hew timber like unto the Sidonians"

(1 Kings 5 : 6). King Hiram rendered important service to Solomon in connection with the planning and building of the temple, casting for him all the vessels for the temple service, and the two pillars which stood in the front of the porch, and "the molten sea" (1 Kings 7 : 21-23). Singular marks have been found by recent exploration on the great stones that form the substructure of the temple. These marks, both painted and engraved, have been regarded as made by the workmen in the quarries, and as probably intended to indicate the place of these stones in the building. "The Biblical account (1 Kings 5 : 17, 18) is accurately descriptive of the massive masonry now existing at the southeastern angle (of the temple area), and standing on the native rock 80 feet below the present surface. The Royal Engineers found, buried deeply among the rubbish of many centuries, great stones, costly and hewed stones, forming the foundation of the sanctuary wall ; while Phœnician fragments of pottery and Phœnician marks painted on the massive blocks seem to proclaim that the stones were prepared in the quarry by the cunning workmen of Hiram, the king of Tyre." (See TEMPLE.)

The Phœnicians have been usually regarded as the inventors of alphabetic writing. The Egyptians expressed their thoughts by certain symbols, called "hieroglyphics "—*i.e.*, sacred carvings—so styled because used almost exclusively on sacred subjects. The recent discovery, however, of inscriptions in Southern Arabia (Yemen and Hadramaut), known as Hemyaritic, in connection with various philological considerations, has led some to the conclusion that the Phœnician alphabet was derived from the Mineans (admitting the antiquity of the kingdom of Ma'in—Judg. 10 : 12 ; 2 Chr. 26 : 7). Thus the Phœnician alphabet ceases to be the mother alphabet. Sayce thinks "it is more than possible that the Egyptians themselves were emigrants from Southern Arabia." (See MOABITE STONE.)

"The Phœnicians were renowned in ancient times for the manufacture of glass, and some of the specimens of this work that have been preserved are still the wonder of mankind......In the matter of shipping, whether ship-building be thought of or traffic upon the sea, the Phœnicians surpassed all other nations. Their ships went to all parts of the world as then known; and news of remote peoples, conquests, and discoveries would be brought first to Phœnicia and disseminated among themselves and their immediate neighbours."

Phi'col—*great*—the chief captain of the army of Abimelech, the Philistine king of Gerar. He entered into an alliance with Abraham with reference to a certain well which, from this circumstance, was called Beersheba (*q.v.*), "the well of the oath" (Gen. 21:22, 32; 26:26).

Philadel'phia—*brotherly love*—a city of Lydia in Asia Minor, about 25 miles southeast of Sardis. It was the seat of one of the "seven churches" (Rev. 3:7–12). It came into the possession of the Turks in A.D. 1392. It has several times been nearly destroyed by earthquakes. It is still a town of considerable size, called *Allahshehr*, "the city of God."

PHILADELPHIA (ALLAH-SHEHR).

Phile'mon, an inhabitant of Colosse, and apparently a person of some note among the citizens (Col. 4:9; Philemon 2). He was brought to a knowledge of the gospel through the instrumentality of Paul (19), and held a prominent place in the Christian community for his piety and beneficence (4–7). He is called in the epistle a "fellow-labourer," and therefore probably held some office in the church at Colosse; at all events, the title denotes that he took part in the work of spreading a knowledge of the gospel.

Phile'mon, Epistle to, was written from Rome at the same time as the epistles to the Colossians and Ephesians, and was sent also by Onesimus. It was addressed to Philemon and the members of his family.

It was written for the purpose of interceding for Onesimus (*q.v.*), who had deserted his master Philemon and been "unprofitable" to him. Paul had found Onesimus at Rome, and had there been instrumental in his conversion, and now he sends him back to his master with this letter.

This epistle has the character of a strictly private letter, and is the only one of such epistles preserved to us. "It exhibits the apostle in a new light. He throws off as far as possible his apostolic dignity and his fatherly authority over his converts. He speaks simply as Christian to Christian. He speaks, therefore, with that peculiar grace of humility and courtesy which has, under the reign of Christianity, developed the spirit of chivalry and what is called 'the character of a gentleman,' certainly very little known in the old Greek and Roman civilization" (Dr. Barry). (See SLAVE.)

Phile'tus—*amiable*—with Hymenæus, at Ephesus, said that the "resurrection was past already" (2 Tim. 2:17, 18). This was a Gnostic heresy held by the Nicolaitanes. (See ALEXANDER [4].)

Phil'ip—*lover of horses*. (1.) One of the twelve apostles; a native of Bethsaida, "the city of Andrew and Peter" (John 1:44). He readily responded to the call of Jesus when first addressed to him (43), and forthwith brought Nathanael also to Jesus (45, 46). He seems to have held a prominent place among the apostles (Matt. 10:3; Mark 3:18; John 6:5-7; 12:21, 22; 14:8, 9; Acts 1:13). Of his later life nothing is certainly known. He is said to have preached in Phrygia, and to have met his death at Hierapolis.

(2.) One of the "seven" (Acts 6:5), called also "the evangelist" (21:8, 9). He was one of those who were "scattered abroad" by the persecution that arose on the death of Stephen. He went first to Samaria, where he laboured as an evangelist with much success (8:5-13). While he was there he received a divine command to proceed toward the south, along the road leading from Jerusalem to Gaza. These towns were connected by two roads. The one Philip was directed to take was that which led through Hebron, and thence through a district little inhabited, and hence called "desert." As he travelled along this road he was overtaken by a chariot in which sat a man of Ethiopia, the eunuch or chief officer of Queen Candace, who was at that moment reading—probably from the Septuagint version—a portion of the prophecies of Isaiah (53:6, 7). Philip entered into conversation with him, and expounded these verses, preaching to him the glad tidings of the Saviour. The eunuch received the

message and believed, and was forthwith baptized, and then "went on his way rejoicing." Philip was instantly caught away by the Spirit after the baptism, and the eunuch saw him no more. He was next found at Azotus, whence he went forth in his evangelistic work till he came to Cæsarea. He is not mentioned again for about twenty years, when he is still found at Cæsarea (Acts 21:8) when Paul and his companions were on the way to Jerusalem. He then finally disappears from the page of history.

(3.) Mentioned only in connection with the imprisonment of John the Baptist (Matt. 14:3; Mark 6:17; Luke 3:19). He was the son of Herod the Great, and the first husband of Herodias, and the father of Salome. (See HEROD PHILIP I.)

(4.) The "tetrarch of Ituræa" (Luke 3:1); a son of Herod the Great, and brother of Herod Antipas. The city of Cæsarea-Philippi was named partly after him (Matt. 16:13; Mark 8:27). (See HEROD PHILIP II.)

Philip'pi. (1.) Formerly *Crenîdes*, "the fountain," the capital of the province of Macedonia. It stood near the head of the Ægean Sea, about 8 miles north-west of Kavalla. It is now a ruined village, called *Philibedjik*. Philip of Macedonia fortified the old Thracian town of Crenîdes, and called it after his own name Philippi (B.C. 359-336). In the time of the Emperor Augustus this city became a Roman colony —*i.e.*, a military settlement of Roman soldiers, there planted for the purpose of controlling the district recently conquered. It was a "miniature Rome," under the municipal law of Rome, and governed by military officers, called *duumviri*, who were appointed directly from Rome. Having been providentially guided thither, here Paul and his companion Silas preached the gospel and formed the first church in Europe. (See LYDIA.) This success stirred up the enmity of the people, and they were "shamefully entreated" (Acts 16:9-40; 1 Thess. 2:2). Paul and Silas at length left this city and proceeded to Amphipolis (*q.v.*).

(2.) When Philip the tetrarch, the son of Herod, succeeded to the government of the northern portion of his kingdom, he enlarged the city of Paneas, and called it Cæsarea, in honour of the emperor. But in order to distinguish it from the Cæsarea on the sea coast, he added to it subsequently his own name, and called it Cæsarea-Philippi (*q.v.*).

Philip'pians, Epistle to, was written by Paul during the two years when he was "in bonds" in Rome (Phil. 1 : 7–13), probably early in the year A.D. 62 or in the end of 61.

The Philippians had sent Epaphroditus, their messenger, with contributions to meet the necessities of the apostle; and on his return Paul sent back with him this letter. With this precious communication Epaphroditus sets out on his homeward journey. "The joy caused by his return, and the effect of this wonderful letter when first read in the church of Philippi, are hidden from us. And we may almost say that with this letter the church itself passes from our view. To-day, in silent meadows, quiet cattle browse among the ruins which mark the site of what was once the flourishing Roman colony of Philippi, the home of the most attractive church of the apostolic age. But the name and fame and spiritual influence of that church will never pass. To myriads of men and women in every age and nation the letter written in a dungeon at Rome, and carried along the Egnatian Way by an obscure Christian messenger, has been a light divine and a cheerful guide along the most rugged paths of life" (Professor Beet).

The church at Philippi was the first-fruits of European Christianity. Their attachment to the apostle was very fervent, and so also was his affection for them. They alone of all the churches helped him by their contributions, which he gratefully acknowledges (Acts 20 : 33–35 ; 2 Cor. 11 : 7–12 ; 2 Thess. 3 : 8). The pecuniary liberality of the Philippians comes out very conspicuously (Phil. 4 : 15). "This was a characteristic of the Macedonian missions, as 2 Cor. 8 and 9 amply and beautifully prove. It is remarkable that the Macedonian converts were, as a class, very poor (2 Cor. 8 : 2); and the parallel facts—their poverty and their open-handed support of the great missionary and his work—are

deeply harmonious. At the present day the missionary liberality of poor Christians is, in proportion, really greater than that of the rich" (Moule's *Philippians, Introd.*).

The *contents* of this epistle give an interesting insight into the condition of the church at Rome at the time it was written. Paul's imprisonment, we are informed, was no hindrance to his preaching the gospel, but rather "turned out to the furtherance of the gospel." The gospel spread very extensively among the Roman soldiers, with whom he was in constant contact, and the Christians grew into a "vast multitude." It is plain that Christianity was at this time making rapid advancement in Rome.

The doctrinal statements of this epistle bear a close relation to those of the Epistle to the Romans. Compare also Phil. 3 : 20 with Eph. 2 : 12, 19, where the church is presented under the idea of a city or commonwealth for the first time in Paul's writings. The personal glory of Christ is also set forth in almost parallel forms of expression in Phil. 2 : 5–11, compared with Eph. 1 : 17–23 ; 2 : 8 ; and Col. 1 : 15–20. "This exposition of the grace and wonder of His personal majesty, personal self-abasement, and personal exaltation after it," found in these epistles, "is, in a great measure, a new development in the revelations given through St. Paul" (Moule). Other minuter analogies in forms of expression and of thought are also found in these epistles of the Captivity.

Philis'tia = **Palestine** (*q.v.*), "the land of the Philistines" (Ps. 60 : 8 ; 87 : 4 ; 108 : 9). The word is supposed to mean "the land of wanderers" or "of strangers."

Philis'tines (Gen. 10 : 14, R.V. ; but in A.V., "Philistim"), a tribe allied to the Phœnicians. They were a branch of the primitive race which spread over the whole district of the Lebanon and the valley of the Jordan, and Crete and other Mediterranean islands. Some suppose them to have been a branch of the Rephaim (2 Sam. 21 : 16–22). In the time of Abraham they inherited the south-west of Judea, Abimelech of Gerar being their king (Gen. 21 : 32, 34 ; 26 : 1). They are, however, not noticed among the Canaanitish tribes mentioned in the Pentateuch. They are spoken of by Amos (9 : 7) and Jeremiah (47 : 4) as from Caphtor—*i.e.*, probably Crete, or, as some think, the Delta of Egypt. In the whole record from Exodus to Samuel they are represented as inhabiting the tract of country which lay between Judea and Egypt (Ex. 13 : 17; 15 : 14, 15; Josh. 13 : 3; 1 Sam. 4).

This powerful tribe made frequent incursions against the Hebrews. There was almost perpetual war between them. They sometimes held the tribes, especially the southern tribes, in degrading servitude (Judg. 15 : 11; 1 Sam. 13 : 19–22); at other times they were defeated with great slaughter (1 Sam. 14 : 1–47; 17). These hostilities did not cease till the time of Hezekiah (2 Kings 18 : 8), when they were entirely subdued. They still, however, occupied their territory, and always showed their old hatred to Israel (Ezek. 25 : 15–17). They were finally conquered by the Romans.

Little is known of their language. It is supposed to have been Semitic, and accordingly akin to the language of the Hebrews.

They had five principal cities, with their surrounding districts — Ekron, Ashdod, Gath, Ashkelon, and Gaza—which were so many centres of government, under the sway of separate kings, who in time of war, however, acted in concert. They are said to have been tall and strong men, lighter in complexion than the Egyptians. They shaved all the hair entirely off their faces. Some think that they were of the same stock as the Hittites—the Mongolian.

Philol'ogus—*fond of learning*—a Roman Christian to whom Paul sent salutations (Rom. 16 : 15).

Philos'ophy—*the love of wisdom*—the pursuit of wisdom, or sometimes science in general. The word is found only once in Scripture (Col. 2 : 8, 18–23), where the apostle warns the Colossians against false philosophy. Here the warning may be—(1.) Against regarding Christianity as a mere philosophy—*i.e.*, as only a speculative search after truth. It is, indeed, in the highest sense a philosophy. But it is the "wisdom of God;" it is not the result of human thought or speculation; it is a direct revelation from God. (2.) Or the warning may

be against that form of philosophy which then began to influence society, known by the name of Gnosticism, with its many forms, some of them having a leaven of Judaism.

Phin'ehas—*mouth of brass*, or from old Egypt. *the negro*. (1.) Son of Eleazar, the high priest (Ex. 6 : 25). While yet a youth he distinguished himself at Shittim by his zeal against the immorality into which the Moabites had tempted the people (Num. 25 : 1–9), and thus "stayed the plague" that had broken out among the people, and by which twenty-four thousand of them perished. For his faithfulness on that occasion he received the divine approbation (10–13). He afterwards commanded the army that went out against the Midianites (31 : 6–8). When representatives of the people were sent to expostulate with the two and a half tribes who, just after crossing Jordan, built an altar and departed without giving any explanation, Phinehas was their leader, and addressed them in the words recorded in Josh. 22 : 16–20. Their explanation follows. This great altar was intended to be to all ages only a witness that they still formed a part of Israel. Phinehas was afterwards the chief adviser in the war with the Benjamites. He is commemorated in Ps. 106 : 30, 31. (See ED.)

(2.) One of the sons of Eli, the high priest (1 Sam. 1 : 3; 2 : 12). He and his brother Hophni were guilty of great crimes, for which destruction came on the house of Eli (31). He died in battle with the Philistines (1 Sam. 4 : 4, 11); and his wife, on hearing of his death, gave birth to a son, whom she called "Ichabod," and then she died (19–22).

Phle'gon—*burning*—a Roman Christian to whom Paul sent salutations (Rom. 16 : 14).

Phœni'cia (Acts 21 : 2). (See PHENICIA.)

Phry'gia—*dry*—an irregular and ill-defined district in Asia Minor. It was divided into two parts—the Greater Phrygia on the south, and the Lesser Phrygia on the west. It is the Greater Phrygia that is spoken of in the New Testament. The towns of Antioch in Pisidia (Acts 13 : 14), Colosse, Hierapolis, Iconium, and Laodicea were situated in it.

There were Phrygians at Jerusalem on the day of Pentecost, and Paul twice travelled through their country, preaching the gospel (Acts 2:10; 16:6; 18:23).

Phu′rah—*wine-press*—Gideon's armour-bearer, who accompanied him when he visited the camp of the Midianites (Judg. 7:10, 11).

Phygel′lus—*fugitive*—a Christian of Asia, who "turned away" from Paul during his second imprisonment at Rome (2 Tim. 1:15). Nothing more is known of him.

Phylac′teries (Gr. *phulakteria; i.e.,* "defences" or "protections"), called by modern Jews *tephillin* (*i.e.,* "prayers") are mentioned only in Matt. 23:5. They consisted of strips of parchment on which were inscribed these four texts:—(1.) Ex. 13:1-10; (2.) 11-16; (3.) Deut. 6:4-9; (4.) 11:18-21—and which were enclosed in a square leather case, on one side of which was inscribed the Hebrew letter *shin*, to which the rabbis attached some significance. This case was fastened by certain straps to the forehead just between the eyes. The "making broad the phylacteries" refers to the enlarging of the case so as to make it conspicuous. (See FRONTLETS.)

Another form of the phylactery consisted of two rolls of parchment, on which

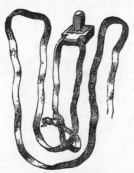

TEPHILLAH ON THE ARM.

the same texts were written, enclosed in a case of black calfskin. This was worn on the left arm near the elbow, to which it was bound by a thong. It was called the "*Tephillah on the arm.*"

Physi′cian. Asa, afflicted with some bodily malady, "sought not unto the Lord but unto the physicians" (2 Chr. 16:12). The "physicians" were those who "practised heathen arts of magic, disavowing recognized methods of cure, and dissociating the healing art from dependence on the God of Israel. The sin of Asa was not, therefore, in seeking medical advice, as we understand the phrase, but in forgetting Jehovah."

Pi-be′seth (Ezek. 30:17), supposed to mean "a cat," or a deity in the form of a cat, worshipped by the Egyptians. It was called by the Greeks Bubastis. The hieroglyphic name is "Pe-bast"—*i.e.,* the house of Bast, the Artemis of the Egyptians. The town of Bubastis was situated on the Pelusian branch — *i.e.,* the easternmost branch—of the Delta. It was the seat of one of the chief annual festivals of the Egyptians. Its ruins bear the modern name of *Tel-Basta.*

Pieces (1) of silver. In Ps. 68:30 denotes "fragments," and not properly money. In 1 Sam. 2:36 (Heb. *agôrah*), properly a "small sum" as wages, weighed rather than coined. Josh. 24:32 (Heb. *kesîtâh*—*q.v.*), supposed by some to have been a piece of money bearing the figure of a lamb, but rather simply a certain amount. (Comp. Gen. 33:19).

(2.) The word pieces is omitted in many passages, as Gen. 20:16; 37:28; 45:22, etc. The passage in Zech. 11:12, 13 is quoted in the Gospel (Matt. 26:15), and from this we know that the word to be supplied is "shekels." In all these omissions we may thus warrantably supply this word.

(3.) The "piece of money" mentioned in Matt. 17:27 is a *stater*=a Hebrew shekel, or four Greek drachmæ; and that in Luke 15:8, 9, Acts 19:19, a Greek *drachma*=a *denarius*. (See PENNY.)

Pi′ety=Lat. *pietas*, properly honour and respect toward parents (1 Tim. 5:4). In Acts 17:23 the Greek verb is rendered "ye worship," as applicable to God.

Pi′geon. Pigeons are mentioned as among the offerings which, by divine appointment, Abram presented unto the Lord (Gen. 15:9). They were afterwards enumerated among the sin-offerings (Lev.

1:14; 12:6), and the law provided that those who could not offer a lamb might offer two young pigeons (5:7; comp. Luke 2:24). (See Dove.)

Pi-hahi'roth—*place where the reeds grow* (LXX. and Copt. read "farmstead")—the name of a place in Egypt where the children of Israel encamped (Ex. 14:2, 9), how long is uncertain. Some have identified it with *Ajrûd*, a fortress between Etham and Suez. The condition of the Isthmus of Suez at the time of the Exodus is not exactly known, and hence this, with the other places mentioned as encampments of Israel in Egypt, cannot be definitely ascertained. The isthmus has been formed by the Nile deposits. This increase of deposit still goes on, and so rapidly that within the last fifty years the mouth of the Nile has advanced northward about four geographical miles. In the maps of Ptolemy (of the second and third centuries A.D.) the mouths of the Nile are forty miles further south than at present. (See Exodus.)

Pi'late, Pon'tius, probably connected with the Roman family of the Pontii, and called "Pilate" from the Latin *pileatus*— *i.c.*, "wearing the *pileus*"—which was the "cap or badge of a manumitted slave," as indicating that he was a "freedman," or the descendant of one. He was the sixth in the order of the Roman procurators of Judea (A.D. 26–36). His headquarters were at Cæsarea, but he frequently went up to Jerusalem. His reign extended over the period of the ministry of John the Baptist and of Jesus Christ, in connection with whose trial his name comes into prominent notice. Pilate was a "typical Roman, not of the antique, simple stamp, but of the imperial period, a man not without some remains of the ancient Roman justice in his soul, yet pleasure-loving, imperious, and corrupt. He hated the Jews whom he ruled, and in times of irritation freely shed their blood. They returned his hatred with cordiality, and accused him of every crime—maladministration, cruelty, and robbery. He visited Jerusalem as seldom as possible; for, indeed, to one accustomed to the pleasures of Rome, with its theatres, baths, games,

and gay society, Jerusalem, with its religiousness and ever-smouldering revolt, was a dreary residence. When he did visit it he stayed in the palace of Herod the Great, it being common for the officers sent by Rome into conquered countries to occupy the palaces of the displaced sovereigns."

After his trial before the Sanhedrin, Jesus was brought to the Roman procurator, Pilate, who had come up to Jerusalem as usual to preserve order during the Passover, and was now residing, perhaps, in the castle of Antonia, or it may be in Herod's palace. Pilate came forth from his palace and met the deputation from the Sanhedrin, who, in answer to his inquiry as to the nature of the accusation they had to prefer against Jesus, accused him of being a "malefactor." Pilate was not satisfied with this, and they further accused him (1) of sedition, (2) preventing the payment of the tribute to Cæsar, and (3) of assuming the title of king (Luke 23:2). Pilate now withdrew with Jesus into the palace (John 18:33) and examined him in private (37, 38); and then going out to the deputation still standing before the gate, he declared that he could find no fault in Jesus (Luke 23:4). This only aroused them to more furious clamour, and they cried that he excited the populace "throughout all Jewry, beginning from Galilee." When Pilate heard of Galilee, he sent the accused to Herod Antipas, who had jurisdiction over that province, thus hoping to escape the difficulty in which he found himself. But Herod, with his men of war, set Jesus at nought, and sent him back again to Pilate, clad in a purple robe of mockery (23:11, 12).

Pilate now proposed that as he and Herod had found no fault in him, they should release Jesus; and anticipating that they would consent to this proposal, he ascended the judgment-seat as if ready to ratify the decision (Matt. 27:19). But at this moment his wife (Claudia Procula) sent a message to him imploring him to have nothing to do with the "just person." Pilate's feelings of perplexity and awe were deepened by this incident, while the crowd vehemently cried out, "Not this man, but Barabbas." Pilate answered, "What then shall I do with Jesus?" The fierce cry immediately followed, "Let him be crucified." Pilate, apparently vexed, and not knowing what to do, said, "Why, what evil hath he done?" but with yet fiercer fanaticism the crowd yelled out, "Away with him! crucify him, crucify him!" Pilate yielded, and sent Jesus away to be scourged. This scourging was usually inflicted by lictors; but as Pilate was only a procurator he had no lictor, and hence his soldiers inflicted this terrible punishment. This done, the soldiers began to deride the sufferer, and they threw around him a purple robe, probably some old cast-off robe of state (Matt. 27:28; John 19:2), and putting a reed in his right hand, and a crown of thorns on his head, bowed the knee before him in mockery, and saluted him, saying, "Hail, King of the Jews!" They took also the reed and smote him with it on the head and face, and spat in his face, heaping upon him every indignity.

Pilate then led forth Jesus from within the Prætorium (Matt. 27:27) before the people, wearing the crown of thorns and the purple robe, saying, "Behold the man!" But the sight of Jesus, now scourged and crowned and bleeding, only stirred their hatred the more, and again they cried out, "Crucify him, crucify him!" and brought forth this additional charge against him, that he professed to be "the Son of God." Pilate heard this accusation with a superstitious awe, and taking him once more within the Prætorium, asked him, "Whence art thou?" Jesus gave him no answer. Pilate was irritated by his continued silence, and said, "Knowest thou not that I have power to crucify thee?" Jesus, with calm dignity, answered the Roman, "Thou couldest have no power at all against me, except it were given thee from above."

After this Pilate seemed more resolved than ever to let Jesus go. The crowd perceiving this cried out, "If thou let this man go, thou art not Cæsar's friend." This settled the matter. He was afraid of being accused to the emperor. Calling for water, he washed his hands in the sight of the people, saying, "I am innocent of the blood of this just person." The mob, again scorning his scruples, cried, "His blood be on us, and on our children." Pilate was stung to the heart by their insults, and putting forth Jesus before them, said, "Shall I crucify your King?" The fatal moment had now come. They madly exclaimed, "We have no king but Cæsar;" and now Jesus is given up to them, and led away to be crucified.

By the direction of Pilate an inscription was placed, according to the Roman custom, over the cross, stating the crime for which he was crucified. Having ascertained from the centurion that he was dead, he gave up the body to Joseph of Arimathea to be buried. Pilate's name now disappears from the Gospel history. References to him, however, are found in the Acts of the Apostles (3:13; 4:27; 13:28), and in 1 Tim. 6:13. In A.D. 36 the governor of Syria brought serious accusations against Pilate, and he was banished to Vienne in Gaul, where, according to tradition, he committed suicide.

Pil'lar, used to support a building (Judg. 16:26, 29); as a trophy or memorial (Gen. 28:18; 35:20; Ex. 24:4; 1 Sam. 15:12—A.V., "place," more correctly "monument," or "trophy of victory," as in 2 Sam. 18:18); of fire, by which the Divine Presence was manifested (Ex. 13:2). The "plain of the pillar" in Judg. 9:6 ought to be, as in the Revised Version, the "oak of the pillar"—*i.e.*, of the monument or stone set up by Joshua (24:26).

Pine tree—Heb. *tidhâr* — mentioned along with the fir-tree in Isa. 41:19; 60:13. This is probably the cypress; or it may be the stone-pine, which is common on the northern slopes of Lebanon. Some suppose that the elm, others that the oak, or holm, or ilex, is meant by the Hebrew word. In Neh. 8:15 the Revised Version has "wild olive" instead of "pine." (See FIR.)

Pin'nacle—*a little wing*—(Matt. 4:5; Luke 4:9). On the southern side of the temple court was a range of porches or cloisters forming three arcades. At the south-eastern corner the roof of this cloister was some 300 feet above the Kidron valley. The pinnacle—some parapet or wing-like projection—was above this roof, and hence at a great height—probably 350 feet or more above the valley.

Pipe (1 Sam. 10:5; 1 Kings 1:40; Isa. 5:12; 30:29). The Hebrew word *hâlîl*, so rendered, means "bored through," and is the name given to various kinds of wind instruments, as the fife, flute, Pan-pipes, etc. In Amos 6:5 this word is rendered "instrument of music." This instrument is mentioned also in the New Testament (Matt. 11:17; 1 Cor. 14:7). It is still used in Palestine, and is, as in ancient times, made of different materials, as reed, copper, bronze, etc.

Pir'am—*like a wild ass*—a king of Jarmuth, a royal city of the Canaanites, who was conquered and put to death by Joshua (10:3, 23, 26).

Pir'athon—*prince*, or *summit*—a place "in the land of Ephraim" (Judg. 12:15), now *Fer'ôn*, some 10 miles south-west of Shechem. This was the home of Abdon the judge.

Pir'athonite. (1.) Abdon, the son of Hillel, so called, Judg. 12:13, 15.

(2.) Benaiah the Ephraimite (2 Sam. 23:30), one of David's thirty heroes.

Pis'gah—*a part*—a mountain summit in the land of Moab, in the territory of Reuben, where Balak offered up sacrifices (Num. 21:20; 23:14), and from which Moses viewed the promised land (Deut. 3:27). It is probably the modern *Jebel Siâghah*. (See NEBO.)

Pisid'ia, a district in Asia Minor, to the north of Pamphylia. The Taurus range of mountains extends through it. Antioch, one of its chief cities, was twice visited by Paul (Acts 13:14; 14:21–24).

Pi'son—Babylonian, the *current, broad-flowing*—one of the "four heads" into which the river which watered the garden of Eden was divided (Gen. 2:11). Some identify it with the modern Phasis, others with the Halys, others the Jorak or Acampis, others the Jaab, the Indus, the Ganges, etc.

Pit, a hole in the ground (Ex. 21:33, 34),

a cistern for water (Gen. 37:24; Jer. 14:3), a vault (41:9), a grave (Ps. 30:3). It is used as a figure for mischief (Ps. 9:15), and is the name given to the unseen place of woe (Rev. 20:1, 3). The slime-pits in the vale of Siddim were wells which yielded asphalt (Gen. 14:10).

Pitch (Gen. 6:14), asphalt or bitumen in its soft state, called "slime" (Gen. 11:3; 14:10; Ex. 2:3), found in pits near the Dead Sea (*q.v.*). It was used for various purposes, as the coating of the outside of vessels and in building. Allusion is made in Isa. 34:9 to its inflammable character. (See SLIME.)

Pitch'er, a vessel for containing liquids. In the East pitchers were usually carried on the head or shoulders (Gen. 24:15–20; Judg. 7:16, 19; Mark 14:13).

Pi'thom—Egyptian, *Pa-Tûm*, "house of Tûm," the sun-god—one of the "treasure" cities built for Pharaoh Rameses II. by the Israelites (Ex. 1:11). It was probably the *Patûmos* of the Greek historian Herodotus. It has now been satisfactorily identified with *Tell-el-Maskhuta*, about 12 miles west of Ismailia, and 20 east of Tell-el-Kebir, on the southern bank of the present Suez Canal. Here have recently (1883) been discovered the ruins of supposed grain-chambers, and other evidences to show that this was a great "store city." Its immense ruin-heaps show that it was built of bricks, and partly also of bricks without straw. Succoth (Ex. 12:37) is supposed by some to be the secular name of this city, Pithom being its sacred name. This was the first halting-place of the Israelites in their exodus. It has been argued (Dr. Lansing) that these "store" cities "were residence cities, royal dwellings, such as the Pharaohs of old, the Kings of Israel, and our modern Khedives have ever loved to build, thus giving employment to the superabundant muscle of their enslaved peoples, and making a name for themselves."

Plague, a "stroke" of affliction, or disease. Sent as a divine chastisement (Num. 11:33; 14:37; 16:46–49; 2 Sam. 24:21). Painful afflictions or diseases, (Lev. 13:3, 5, 30; 1 Kings 8:37), or severe calamity (Mark 5:29; Luke 7:21), or the judgment of God, so called (Ex. 9:14).

Plagues of Egypt were ten in number. (1.) The river Nile was turned into blood, and the fish died, and the river stank, so that the Egyptians loathed to drink of the river (Ex. 7 : 14–25).

(2.) The plague of frogs (Ex. 8 : 1–15).

(3.) The plague of lice (Heb. *kinnîm,* properly *gnats* or *mosquitoes; comp.* Ps. 78 : 45; 105 : 31), "out of the dust of the land" (Ex. 8 : 16–19).

(4.) The plague of flies (Heb. *'arôb,* rendered by the LXX. *dog-fly)*—Ex. 8 : 21–24.

(5.) The murrain (Ex. 9 : 1–7), or epidemic pestilence which carried off vast numbers of cattle in the field. Warning was given of its coming.

(6.) The sixth plague, of "boils and blains," like the third, was sent without warning (Ex. 9 : 8–12). It is called (Deut. 28 : 27) "the botch of Egypt," A. V.; but in R. V., "the boil of Egypt." "The magicians could not stand before Moses" because of it.

(7.) The plague of hail, with fire and thunder (Ex. 9 : 13–33). Warning was given of its coming. (Comp. Ps. 18 : 13; 105 : 33).

(8.) The plague of locusts, which covered the whole face of the earth, so that the land was darkened with them (Ex. 10 : 12–15). The Hebrew name of this insect, *arbĕh,* points to the "multitudinous" character of this visitation. Warning was given before this plague came.

(9.) After a short interval the plague of darkness succeeded that of the locusts; and it came without any special warning (Ex. 10 : 21–29). The darkness covered "all the land of Egypt" to such an extent that "they saw not one another." It did not, however, extend to the land of Goshen.

(10.) The last and most fearful of these plagues was the death of the first-born of man and of beast (Ex. 11 : 4, 5; 12 : 29, 30). The exact time of the visitation was announced—"about midnight"—which would add to the horror of the infliction. Its extent also is specified—from the first-born of the king to the first-born of the humblest slave, and all the first-born of beasts. But from this plague the Hebrews were com-

pletely exempted. The Lord "put a difference" between them and the Egyptians. (See PASSOVER.)

Plain. (1.) Heb. *'abêl* (Judg. 11 : 33), a "grassy plain" or "meadow." Instead of "plains of the vineyards," as in the Authorized Version, the Revised Version has "Abel-cheramim" (*q.v.*)—comp. Judg. 11 : 22; 2 Chr. 16 : 4.

(2.) Heb. *'elôn* (Gen. 12 : 6; 13 : 18; 14 : 13; 18 : 1; Deut. 11 : 30; Judg. 9 : 6), more correctly "oak," as in the Revised Version; margin, "terebinth."

(3.) Heb. *bik'âh* (Gen. 11 : 2; Neh. 6 : 2; Ezek. 3 : 23; Dan. 3 : 1), properly a valley, as rendered in Isa. 40 : 4, a broad plain between mountains. In Amos 1 : 5 the margin of Authorized Version has "Bikathaven."

(4.) Heb. *kikar,* "the circle," used only of the Ghôr, or the low ground along the Jordan (Gen. 13 : 10–12; 19 : 17, 25, 28, 29; Deut. 34 : 3; 2 Sam. 18 : 23; 1 Kings 7 : 46; 2 Chr. 4 : 17; Neh. 3 : 22; 12 : 28), the floor of the valley through which it flows. This name is applied to the Jordan valley as far north as Succoth.

(5.) Heb. *mishôr,* "level ground," smooth, grassy table-land (Deut. 3 : 10; 4 : 43; Josh. 13 : 9, 16, 17, 21; 20 : 8; Jer. 48 : 21), an expanse of rolling downs without rock or stone. In these passages, with the article prefixed, it denotes the plain in the tribe of Reuben. In 2 Chr. 26 : 10 the plain of Judah is meant. Jerusalem is called "the rock of the plain" in Jer. 21 : 13, because the hills on which it is built rise high above the plain.

(6.) Heb. *'arâbâh,* the valley from the Sea of Galilee southward to the Dead Sea (the "sea of the plain," 2 Kings 14 : 25; Deut. 1 : 1; 2 : 8), a distance of about 70 miles. It is called by the modern Arabs the *Ghôr.* This Hebrew name is found in Authorized Version (Josh. 18 : 18), and is uniformly used in the Revised Version. Down through the centre of this plain is a ravine, from 200 to 300 yards wide, and from 50 to 100 feet deep, through which the Jordan flows in a winding course. This ravine is called the "lower plain."

The name *Arabah* is also applied to the

whole Jordan valley from Mount Hermon to the eastern branch of the Red Sea, a distance of about 200 miles, as well as to that portion of the valley which stretches from the Sea of Galilee to the same branch of the Red Sea—*i.e.*, to the Gulf of Akabah —about 100 miles in all.

(7.) Heb. *shephêlâh*, "low ground," "low hill-land," rendered "vale" or "valley" in Authorized Version (Josh. 9 : 1 ; 10 : 40 ; 11 : 2 ; 12 : 8 ; Judg. 1 : 9 ; 1 Kings 10 : 27). In Authorized Version (1 Chr. 27 : 28 ; 2 Chr. 26 : 10) it is also rendered "low country." In Jer. 17 : 26, Obad. 19, Zech. 7 : 7, "plain." The Revised Version renders it uniformly "low land." When it is preceded by the article, as in Deut. 1 : 7, Josh. 11 : 16 ; 15 : 33, Jer. 32 : 44 ; 33 : 13, Zech. 7 : 7, "*the* shephelah," it denotes the plain along the Mediterranean from Joppa to Gaza, "the plain of the Philistines." (See VALLEY.)

Plain of Mamre (Gen. 13 : 18 ; 14 : 13 ; R.V., "oaks of Mamre ;" marg., "terebinths"). (See MAMRE ; TEIL-TREE.)

Plane tree. Heb. *'armôn* (Gen. 30 : 37 ; Ezek. 31 : 8), rendered "chesnut" in the Authorized Version, but correctly "plane tree" in the Revised Version and the LXX. This tree is frequently found in Palestine, both on the coast and in the north. It usually sheds its outer bark, and hence its Hebrew name, which means "naked." (See CHESTNUT.)

Pledge. See LOAN.

Plei′ades — Heb. *kîmâh*, "a cluster" (Job 9 : 9 ; 38 : 31 ; Amos 5 : 8 — A.V., "seven stars ;" R.V., "Pleiades ") — a name given to the cluster of stars seen in the shoulder of the constellation Taurus.

Plough, first referred to in Gen. 45 : 6, where the Authorized Version has "earing," but the Revised Version "ploughing ;" next in Ex. 34 : 21 and Deut. 21 : 4. The plough was originally drawn by oxen, but sometimes also by asses and by men. (See AGRICULTURE.)

Po′etry has been well defined as "the measured language of emotion." Hebrew poetry deals almost exclusively with the great question of man's relation to God. "Guilt, condemnation, punishment, par-

don, redemption, repentance are the awful themes of this heaven-born poetry."

In the Hebrew scriptures there are found three distinct kinds of poetry—(1) that of the Book of Job and the Song of Solomon, which is dramatic; (2) that of the Book of Psalms, which is lyrical ; and (3) that of the Book of Ecclesiastes, which is didactic and sententious.

Hebrew poetry has nothing akin to that of Western nations. It has neither metre nor rhyme. Its great peculiarity consists in the mutual correspondence of sentences or clauses, called parallelism, or "thoughtrhyme." Various kinds of this parallelism have been pointed out :—

(1.) Synonymous or cognate parallelism, where the same idea is repeated in the same words (Ps. 93 : 3 ; 94 : 1 ; Prov. 6 : 2), or in different words (Ps. 22, 23, 28, 114, etc.); or where it is expressed in a positive form in the one clause and in a negative in the other (Ps. 40 : 12 ; Prov. 6 : 26); or where the same idea is expressed in three successive clauses (Ps. 40 : 15, 16) ; or in a double parallelism, the first and second clauses corresponding to the third and fourth (Isa. 9 : 1 ; 61 : 10, 11).

(2.) Antithetic parallelism, where the idea of the second clause is the converse of that of the first (Ps. 20 : 9 ; 27 : 6, 7 ; 34 : 11 ; 37 : 9, 17, 21, 22). This is the common form of gnomic or proverbial poetry. (See Prov. 10-15.)

(3.) Synthetic or constructive or compound parallelism, where each clause or sentence contains some accessory idea enforcing the main idea (Ps. 19 : 7-10 ; 85 : 12 ; Job 3 : 3-9 ; Isa. 1 : 5-9).

(4.) Introverted parallelism, in which of four clauses the first answers to the fourth and the second to the third (Ps. 135 : 15-18 ; Prov. 23 : 15, 16), or where the second line reverses the order of words in the first (Ps. 86 : 2).

Hebrew poetry sometimes assumes other forms than these. (1.) An alphabetical arrangement is sometimes adopted for the purpose of connecting clauses or sentences. Thus in the following the initial words of the respective verses begin with the letters of the alphabet in regular succession :—

Prov. 31:10–31; Lam. 1, 2, 3, 4; Ps. 25, 34, 37, 145. Ps. 119 has a letter of the alphabet in regular order beginning every eighth verse.

(2.) The repetition of the same verse or of some emphatic expression at intervals (Ps. 42, 107, where the refrain is in verses 8, 15, 21, 31). (Comp. also Isa. 9:8–10: 4; Amos 1:3, 6, 9, 11, 13; 2:1, 4, 6.)

(3.) Gradation, in which the thought of one verse is resumed in another (Ps. 121).

Several odes of great poetical beauty are found in the historical books of the Old Testament, such as the song of Moses (Ex. 15), the song of Deborah (Judg. 5), of Hannah (1 Sam. 2), of Hezekiah (Isa. 38: 9–20), of Habakkuk (Hab. 3), and David's "song of the bow" (2 Sam. 1:19–27).

Poi′son. (1.) Heb. *ḥemâh*, "heat," the poison of certain venomous reptiles (Deut. 32:24, 33; Job 6:4; Ps. 58:4), causing inflammation.

(2.) Heb. *rôsh*, "a head," a poisonous plant (Deut. 29:18), growing luxuriantly (Hos. 10:4), of a bitter taste (Ps. 69:21; Lam. 3:5), and coupled with wormwood; probably the poppy. This word is rendered "gall"—*q.v.*— (Deut. 29:18; 32:33; Ps. 69:21; Jer. 8:14, etc.), "hemlock" (Hos. 10:4; Amos 6:12), and "poison" (Job 20:16), "the poison of asps," showing that the *rôsh* was not exclusively a vegetable poison.

(3.) In Rom. 3:13 (comp. Job 20:16; Ps. 140:3), James 3:8, as the rendering of the Greek *ios*.

Pome′granate—*i.e.*, "grained apple" (*pomum granatum*)—Heb. *rimmôn*. Common in Egypt (Num. 20:5) and Palestine (13:23; Deut. 8:8). The Romans called it *Punicum malum*—*i.e.*, Carthaginian apple—because they received it from Carthage. It belongs to the myrtle family of trees. The withering of the pomegranate tree is mentioned among the judgments of God (Joel 1:12). It is frequently mentioned in the Song of Solomon (Cant. 4:

3, 13, etc.). The skirt of the high priest's blue robe and ephod was adorned with the representation of pomegranates, alternating with golden bells (Ex. 28:33, 34), as also were the "chapiters upon the two pillars" (1 Kings 7:20) which "stood before the house."

Pom′mels (2 Chr. 4:12, 13), or bowls (1 Kings 7:41), were balls or "rounded knobs" on the top of the chapiters (*q.v.*).

Pontius Pilate. See PILATE.

Pon′tus, a province of Asia Minor,

POMEGRANATE BRANCH AND FRUIT.

stretching along the southern coast of the Euxine Sea, corresponding nearly to the modern province of Trebizond. In the time of the apostles it was a Roman province. Strangers from this province were at Jerusalem at Pentecost (Acts 2:9), and to "strangers scattered throughout Pontus," among others, Peter addresses his first epistle (1 Pet. 1:1). It was evidently the resort of many Jews of the Dispersion. Aquila was a native of Pontus (Acts 18:2).

Pool, a pond, or reservoir, for holding water (Heb. *berêkhâh ;* modern Arabic, *birket*), an artificial cistern or tank. Mention is made of the pool of Gibeon (2 Sam. 2:13); the pool of Hebron (4:12); the upper pool at Jerusalem (2 Kings 18:17; 20:20); the pool of Samaria (1 Kings 22:38); the king's pool (Neh. 2:14); the pool of Siloah (Neh. 3:15; Eccles. 2:6); the fishpools of Heshbon (Cant. 7:4); the "lower pool," and the "old pool" (Isa. 22:9, 11).

The "pool of Bethesda" (John 5:2, 4, 7) and the "pool of Siloam" (John 9:7, 11) are also mentioned. Isaiah (35:7) says, "The parched ground shall become a pool." This is rendered in the Revised Version "the thirsty ground," etc. (marg. "the mirage," etc.). The Arabs call the mirage "*sĕrab,*" plainly the same as the Hebrew word *sarab,* here rendered "parched ground." "The mirage shall become a pool"—*i.e.,* the mock-lake of the burning desert shall become a real lake, "the pledge of refreshment and joy." The "pools" spoken of in Isa. 14:23 are the marshes caused by the ruin of the canals of the

POOLS OF SOLOMON.

Euphrates in the neighbourhood of Babylon.

The cisterns or pools of the Holy City are for the most part excavations beneath the surface. Such are the vast cisterns in the temple hill that have recently been discovered by the engineers of the Palestine Exploration Fund. These underground caverns are about thirty-five in number, and are capable of storing about ten million gallons of water. They are connected with one another by passages and tunnels.

Pools of Solomon, the name given to three large open cisterns at Etam, at the head of the Wâdy Urtâs, having an average length of 400 feet by 220 in breadth, and 20 to 30 in depth. These pools derive their chief supply of water from a spring called "the sealed fountain," about 200 yards to the north-west of the upper pool, to which it is conveyed by a large subterranean passage. They are 150 feet distant from each other, and each pool is 20 feet lower than that above it, the conduits being so arranged that the lowest, which is the largest and finest of the three, is filled first, and then in succession the others. It has been estimated that these pools cover in all a space of about 7 acres, and are capable of containing three million gallons of water. They were, as is generally supposed, constructed in the days of Solomon. They are probably referred to in Eccles. 2 : 6. On the fourth day after his victory over the Ammonites, etc., in the wilderness of Tekoa, Jehoshaphat assembled his army in the valley of Berachah ("blessing"), and there blessed the Lord. Berachah has been identified with the modern *Bereikût*, some 5 miles south of Wâdy Urtâs, and hence the "valley of Berachah" may be this valley of pools, for the word means both "blessing" and "pools;" and it has been supposed, therefore, that this victory was celebrated beside Solomon's pools (2 Chr. 20 : 26).

These pools were primarily designed to supply Jerusalem with water. From the lower pool an aqueduct has been traced conveying the water through Bethlehem and across the valley of Gihon, and along the west slope of the Tyropœon valley, till it finds its way into the great cisterns underneath the temple hill. The water, however, from the pools reaches now only to Bethlehem. The aqueduct beyond this has been destroyed.

Poor. The Mosaic legislation regarding the poor is specially important.

(1.) They had the right of gleaning the fields (Lev. 19 : 9, 10; Deut. 24 : 19, 21).

(2.) In the sabbatical year they were to have their share of the produce of the fields and the vineyards (Ex. 23 : 11; Lev. 25 : 6).

(3.) In the year of jubilee they recovered their property (Lev. 25 : 25–30).

(4.) Usury was forbidden, and the pledged raiment was to be returned before the sun went down (Ex. 22 : 25–27; Deut. 24 : 10–13). The rich were to be generous to the poor (Deut. 15 : 7–11).

(5.) In the sabbatical and jubilee years the bond-servant was to go free (Deut. 15 : 12–15; Lev. 25 : 39–42, 47–54).

(6.) Certain portions from the tithes were assigned to the poor (Deut. 14 : 28, 29; 26 : 12, 13).

(7.) They shared in the feasts (Deut. 16 : 11, 14; Neh. 8 : 10).

(8.) Wages were to be paid at the close of each day (Lev. 19 : 13).

In the New Testament (Luke 3 : 11; 14 : 13; Acts 6 : 1; Gal. 2 : 10; James 2 : 15, 16) we have similar injunctions given with reference to the poor. Begging was not common under the Old Testament, while it was so in the New Testament times (Luke 16 : 20, 21, etc.). But begging in the case of those who are able to work is forbidden, and all such are enjoined to "work with their own hands" as a Christian duty (1 Thess. 4 : 11; 2 Thess. 3 : 7–13; Eph. 4 : 28).

This word is used figuratively in Matt. 5 : 3; Luke 6 : 20; 2 Cor. 8 : 9; Rev. 3 : 17.

Pop'lar—Heb. *libneh*, "white"—(Gen. 30 : 37; Hos. 4 : 13), in all probability the storax tree (*Styrax officinalis*) or white poplar, distinguished by its white blossoms and pale leaves. It is common in the Anti-Libanus. Other species of the poplar are found in Palestine, such as the white poplar (*P. alba*) of our own country, the black poplar (*P. nigra*), and the aspen (*P. tremula*). (See WILLOW.)

Porch, Solomon's, a colonnade on the east of the temple, so called from a tradition that it was a relic of Solomon's temple left standing after the destruction of Jerusalem by the Babylonians. (Comp. 1 Kings 7 : 6.) The word "porch" is in the New Testament the rendering of three different Greek words :—

(1.) *Stoa*, meaning a portico or veranda (John 5 : 2; 10 : 23; Acts 3 : 11; 5 : 12).

(2.) *Pulon*, a gateway (Matt. 26 : 71).

(3.) *Proaulion*, the entrance to the inner court (Mark 14 : 68).

Porcius Festus. See FESTUS.

Por'ter, a gate-keeper (2 Sam. 18 : 26; 2 Kings 7 : 10; 1 Chr. 9 : 21; 2 Chr. 8 : 14). Of the Levites, 4,000 were appointed as porters by David (1 Chr. 23 : 5), who were arranged according to their families (26 : 1–19) to take charge of the doors and gates of the temple. They were sometimes employed as musicians (1 Chr. 15 : 18).

Post. (1.) A runner, or courier, for the rapid transmission of letters, etc. (2 Chr. 30 : 6; Esther 3 : 13, 15; 8 : 10, 14; Job 9 : 25; Jer. 51 : 31). Such messengers were used from very early times. Those employed by the Hebrew kings had a military character (1 Sam. 22:17; 2 Kings 10:25, "guard," marg. "runners").

The modern system of postal communication was first established by Louis XI. of France in A.D. 1464.

(2.) This word sometimes also is used for lintel or threshold (Isa. 6:4).

Pot'iphar—*dedicated to Ra; i.e.,* to the sun-god—the Egyptian to whom the Ishmaelites sold Joseph (Gen. 39:1). He was "captain of the guard"—*i.e.,* chief, probably, of the state police, who, while they formed part of the Egyptian army, were also largely employed in civil duties (37:36; marg., "chief of the executioners"). Joseph, though a foreigner, gradually gained his confidence, and became overseer over all his possessions. Believing the false accusation which his profligate wife brought against Joseph, Potiphar cast him into prison, where he remained for some years. (See JOSEPH.)

Potiphe'rah, a priest of On, whose daughter Asenath became Joseph's wife (Gen. 41:45).

Pot'sherd, a "sherd"—*i.e.,* anything severed, as a fragment of earthenware (Job 2:8; Prov. 26:23; Isa. 45:9).

Pot'tage—Heb. *nazid,* "boiled"—a dish of boiled food, as of lentils (Gen. 25:29; 2 Kings 4:38).

Pot'ters' field, the name given to the piece of ground which was afterwards bought with the money that had been given to Judas. It was called the "field of blood" (Matt. 27:7-10). Tradition places it in the valley of Hinnom. (See ACELDAMA.)

Pot'tery, the art of, was early practised among all nations. Various materials seem to have been employed by the potter. Earthenware is mentioned in connection with the history of Melchizedek (Gen. 14:18), of Abraham (18:4-8), of Rebekah (27:14), of Rachel (29:2, 3, 8, 10). The potter's wheel is mentioned by Jeremiah (18:3). See also 1 Chr. 4:23; Ps. 2:9; Isa. 45:9; 64:8; Jer. 19:1; Lam. 4:2; Zech. 11:13; Rom. 9:21.

Pound. (1.) A weight. Heb. *maneh,* equal to 100 shekels (1 Kings 10:17; Ezra 2:69; Neh. 7:71, 72). Gr. *litra,* equal to about 12 oz. avoirdupois (John 12:3; 19:39).

(2.) A sum of money; the Gr. *mna* or *mina* (Luke 19:13, 16, 18, 20, 24, 25). It was equal to 100 drachmas, and was of the value of about £3, 6s. 8d. of our money. (See MONEY.)

Præto'rium. The Greek word (*praitōrion*) thus rendered in Mark 15:16 is rendered "common hall" (Matt. 27:27—marg., "governor's house"), "judgment hall," (John 18:28, 33—marg., "Pilate's house"—19:9; Acts 23:35), "palace" (Phil. 1:13). This is properly a military word. It denotes (1) the general's tent or headquarters; (2) the governor's residence, as in Acts 23:35 (R.V., "palace"); and (3) the prætorian guard (see PALACE), or the camp or quarters of the prætorian cohorts (Acts 28:16), the imperial guards in immediate attendance on the emperor, who was "prætor" or commander-in-chief.

Pray'er is converse with God; the intercourse of the soul with God, not in contemplation or meditation, but in direct address to him. Prayer may be oral or mental, occasional or constant, ejaculatory or formal. It is a "beseeching the Lord" (Ex. 32:11); "pouring out the soul before the Lord" (1 Sam. 1:15); "praying and crying to heaven" (2 Chr. 32:20); "seeking unto God and making supplication" (Job 8:5); "drawing near to God" (Ps. 73:28); "bowing the knees" (Eph. 3:14).

Prayer presupposes a belief in the personality of God, his ability and willingness to hold intercourse with us, his personal control of all things and of all his creatures and all their actions.

Acceptable prayer must be sincere (Heb. 10:22), offered with reverence and godly fear, with a humble sense of our own insignificance as creatures and of our own unworthiness as sinners, with earnest importunity, and with unhesitating submission to the divine will. Prayer must also be offered in the faith that God is, and is the hearer and answerer of prayer, and that he will fulfil his word, "Ask, and ye shall receive" (Matt. 7:7, 8; 21:22; Mark 11:24;

John 14 : 13, 14), and in the name of Christ (16 : 23, 24 ; 15 : 16 ; Eph. 2 : 18 ; 5 : 20 ; Col. 3 : 17 ; 1 Pet. 2 : 5).

Prayer is of different kinds—*secret* (Matt. 6 : 6); *social*, as family prayers, and in social worship; and *public*, in the service of the sanctuary.

Intercessory prayer is enjoined (Num. 6 : 23 ; Job 42 : 8 ; Isa. 62 : 6 ; Ps. 122 : 6 ; 1 Tim. 2 : 1 ; James 5 : 14), and there are many instances on record of answers having been given to such prayers—*e.g.*, of Abraham (Gen. 17 : 18, 20 ; 18 : 23–32 ; 20 : 7, 17, 18), of Moses for Pharaoh (Ex. 8 : 12, 13, 30, 31 ; Ex. 9 : 33), for the Israelites (Ex. 17 : 11, 13 ; 32 : 11–14, 31–34 ; Num. 21 : 7, 8 ; Deut. 9 : 18, 19, 25), for Miriam (Num. 12 : 13), for Aaron (Deut. 9 : 20), of Samuel (1 Sam. 7 : 5–12), of Solomon (1 Kings 8 ; 2 Chr. 6), Elijah (1 Kings 17 : 20–23), Elisha (2 Kings 4 : 33–36), Isaiah (2 Kings 19), Jeremiah (42 : 2–10), Peter (Acts 9 : 40), the church (12 : 5–12), Paul (28 : 8).

No rules are anywhere in Scripture laid down for the manner of prayer or the attitude to be assumed by the suppliant. There is mention made of kneeling in prayer (1 Kings 8 : 54 ; 2 Chr. 6 : 13 ; Ps. 95 : 6 ; Isa. 45 : 23 ; Luke 22 : 41 ; Acts 7 : 60 ; 9 : 40 ; Eph. 3 : 14, etc.); of bowing and falling prostrate (Gen. 24 : 26, 52 ; Ex. 4 : 31 ; 12 : 27 ; Matt. 26 : 39 ; Mark 14 : 35, etc.); of spreading out the hands (1 Kings 8 : 22, 38, 54 ; Ps. 28 : 2 ; 63 : 4 ; 88 : 9 ; 1 Tim. 2 : 8, etc.); and of standing (1 Sam. 1 : 26 ; 1 Kings 8 : 14, 55 ; 2 Chr. 20 : 9 ; Mark 11 : 25 ; Luke 18 : 11, 13).

If we except the "Lord's Prayer" (Matt. 6 : 9–13), which is, however, rather a model or pattern of prayer than a set prayer to be offered up, we have no special form of prayer for general use given us in Scripture.

Prayer is frequently enjoined in Scripture (Ex. 22 : 23, 27 ; 1 Kings 3 : 5 ; 2 Chr. 7 : 14 ; Ps. 37 : 4 ; Isa. 55 : 6 ; Joel 2 : 32 ; Ezek. 36 : 37, etc), and we have very many testimonies that it has been answered (Ps. 3 : 4 ; 4 : 1 ; 6 : 8 ; 18 : 6 ; 28 : 6 ; 30 : 2 ; 34 : 4 ; 118 : 5 ; James 5 : 16–18, etc.).

"Abraham's servant prayed to God, and God directed him to the person who should be wife to his master's son and heir (Gen. 24 : 10–20).

"Jacob prayed to God, and God inclined the heart of his irritated brother, so that they met in peace and friendship (Gen. 32 : 24–30 ; 33 : 1–4).

"Samson prayed to God, and God showed him a well where he quenched his burning thirst, and so lived to judge Israel (Judg. 15 : 18–20).

"David prayed, and God defeated the counsel of Ahithophel (2 Sam. 15 : 31 ; 16 : 20–23 ; 17 : 14–23).

"Daniel prayed, and God enabled him both to tell Nebuchadnezzar his dream and to give the interpretation of it (Dan. 2 : 16–23).

"Nehemiah prayed, and God inclined the heart of the king of Persia to grant him leave of absence to visit and rebuild Jerusalem (Neh. 1 : 11 ; 2 : 1–6).

"Esther and Mordecai prayed, and God defeated the purpose of Haman, and saved the Jews from destruction (Esther 4 : 15–17 ; 6 : 7, 8).

"The believers in Jerusalem prayed, and God opened the prison doors and set Peter at liberty, when Herod had resolved upon his death (Acts 12 : 1–12).

"Paul prayed that the thorn in the flesh might be removed, and his prayer brought a large increase of spiritual strength, while the thorn perhaps remained (2 Cor. 12 : 7–10).

"Prayer is like the dove that Noah sent forth, which blessed him not only when it returned with an olive-leaf in its mouth, but when it never returned at all."—Robinson's *Job*.

Predestina'tion. This word is properly used only with reference to God's plan or purpose of salvation. The Greek word rendered "predestinate" is found only in these six passages, Acts 4 : 28 ; Rom. 8 : 29, 30 ; 1 Cor. 2 : 7 ; Eph. 1 : 5, 11 ; and in all of them it has the same meaning. They teach that the eternal, sovereign, immutable, and unconditional decree or "determinate purpose" of God governs all events.

This doctrine of predestination or election is beset with many difficulties. It belongs to the "secret things" of God. But if we take the revealed word of God as our guide, we must accept this doctrine with all its mysteriousness, and settle all our questionings in the humble, devout acknowledgment, "Even so, Father: for so it seemed good in thy sight."

For the teaching of Scripture on this subject let the following passages be examined in addition to those referred to above:—Gen. 21:12; Ex. 9:16; 33:19; Deut. 10:15; 32:8; Josh. 11:20; 1 Sam. 12:22; 2 Chr. 6:6; Ps. 33:12; 65:4; 78: 68; 135:4; Isa. 41:1-10; Jer. 1:5; Mark 13:20; Luke 22:22; John 6:37; 15:16; 17:2, 6, 9; Acts 2:28; 3:18; 4:28; 13: 48; 17:26; Rom. 9:11, 18, 21; 11:5; Eph. 3:11; 1 Thess. 1:4; 2 Thess. 2:13; 2 Tim. 1:9; Titus 1:2; 1 Pet. 1:2. (See DECREES OF GOD; ELECTION.)

Hodge has well remarked that, "rightly understood, this doctrine (1) exalts the majesty and absolute sovereignty of God, while it illustrates the riches of his free grace and his just displeasure with sin. (2.) It enforces upon us the essential truth that salvation is entirely of grace. That no one can either complain if passed over, or boast himself if saved. (3.) It brings the inquirer to absolute self-despair and the cordial embrace of the free offer of Christ. (4.) In the case of the believer who has the witness in himself, this doctrine at once deepens his humility and elevates his confidence to the full assurance of hope" (*Outlines*).

Pre′sidents. Three presidents are mentioned, of whom Daniel was the first (Dan. 6:2-7). The name in the original is *sârkhîn*, probably a Persian word meaning prefects or ministers.

Priest. The Heb. *kôhen*, Gr. *hierus*, Lat. *sacerdos*, always denote one who offers sacrifices.

At first every man was his own priest, and presented his own sacrifices before God. Afterwards that office devolved on the head of the family, as in the cases of Noah (Gen. 8:20), Abraham (12:7; 13:4), Isaac (26:25), Jacob (31:54), and Job (Job 1:5).

The name first occurs as applied to Melchizedek (Gen. 14:18). Under the Levitical arrangements the office of the priesthood was limited to the tribe of Levi, and to only one family of that tribe, the family of Aaron. Certain laws respecting the qualifications of priests are given in Lev. 21:16-23. There are ordinances also regarding the priests' dress (Ex. 28:40-43) and the manner of their consecration to the office (29:1-37).

Their duties were manifold (Ex. 27:20, 21; 29:38-44; Lev. 6:12; 10:11; 24:8; Num. 10:1-10; Deut. 17:8-13; 33:10; Mal. 2:7). They represented the people before God, and offered the various sacrifices prescribed in the law.

In the time of David the priests were divided into twenty-four courses or classes (1 Chr. 24:7-18). This number was retained after the Captivity (Ezra 2:36-39; Neh. 7:39-42).

"The priests were not distributed over the country, but lived together in certain cities [forty-eight in number, of which six were cities of refuge, *q.v.*], which had been assigned to their use. From thence they went up by turns to minister in the temple at Jerusalem. Thus the religious instruction of the people in the country generally was left to the heads of families, until the establishment of synagogues—an event which did not take place till the return from the Captivity, and which was the main source of the freedom from idolatry that became as marked a feature of the Jewish people thenceforward as its practice had been hitherto their great national sin."

The whole priestly system of the Jews was typical. It was a shadow of which the body is Christ. The priests all prefigured the great Priest who offered "one sacrifice for sins" "once for all" (Heb. 10: 10, 12). There is now no human priesthood. (See Epistle to the Hebrews throughou) The term "priest" is indeed applied to believers (1 Pet. 2:9; Rev. 1:6), but in these cases it implies no sacerdotal functions. All true believers are now "kings and priests unto God." As priests they have free access into the holiest of all, and offer up the sacrifices of praise and thanksgiving, and the sacrifices of grateful service from day to day.

Prince, the title generally applied to the chief men of the state. The "princes of the provinces" (1 Kings 20:14) were the governors or lord-lieutenants of the provinces. So also the "princes" mentioned in Dan. 6:1, 3, 4, 6, 7 were the officers who administered the affairs of the provinces; the "satraps" (as rendered in R. V.). These are also called "lieutenants" (Esther 3:12; 8:9; R. V., "satraps"). The promised Saviour is called by Daniel (9:25) "Messiah the Prince" (Heb. *nagíd*); compare Acts 3:15; 5:31. The angel Michael is called (Dan. 12:1) a "prince" (Heb. *sar*, whence "Sarah," the "princess").

Priscil'la, the wife of Aquila (Acts 18:2), who is never mentioned without her. Her name sometimes takes the precedence of his (Rom. 16:3; 2 Tim. 4:19). She took part with Aquila (*q.v.*) in instructing Apollos (Acts 18:26).

Pri'son. The first occasion on which we read of a prison is in the history of Joseph in Egypt. Then Potiphar, "Joseph's master, took him, and put him into the prison, a place where the king's prisoners were bound" (Gen. 39:20–23). The Heb. word here used (*çohar*) means properly a round tower or fortress. It seems to have been a part of Potiphar's house, a place in which state prisoners were kept.

The Mosaic law made no provision for imprisonment as a punishment. In the wilderness two persons were "put in ward" (Lev. 24:12; Num. 15:34), but it was only till the mind of God concerning them should be ascertained. Prisons and prisoners are mentioned in the book of Psalms (69:33; 79:11; 142:7). Samson was confined in a Philistine prison (Judg. 16:21, 25). In the subsequent history of Israel frequent references are made to prisons (1 Kings 22:27; 2 Kings 17:4; 25:27, 29; 2 Chr. 16:10; Isa. 42:7; Jer. 32:2). Prisons seem to have been common in New Testament times (Matt. 11:2; 25:36, 43). The apostles were put into the "common prison" at the instance of the Jewish council (Acts 5:18, 23; 8:3); and at Philippi Paul and Silas were thrust into the "inner prison" (16:24; comp. 4:3; 12:4, 5).

Pro'phecy, or *prediction*, was one of the functions of the prophet. It has been defined as a "miracle of knowledge, a declaration or description or representation of something future, beyond the power of human sagacity to foresee, discern, or conjecture." (See PROPHET.)

The great prediction which runs like a golden thread through the whole contents of the Old Testament is that regarding the coming and work of the Messiah; and the great use of prophecy was to perpetuate faith in his coming, and to prepare the world for that event. But there are many subordinate and intermediate prophecies also which hold an important place in the great chain of events which illustrate the sovereignty and all-wise overruling providence of God.

Then there are many prophecies regarding the Jewish nation, its founder Abraham (Gen. 12:1–3; 13:16; 15:5; 17:2, 4–6, etc.), and his posterity, Isaac and Jacob and their descendants (12:7; 13:14, 15, 17; 15:18–21; Ex. 3:8, 17), which have all been fulfilled. The twenty-eighth chapter of Deuteronomy contains a series of predictions which are even now in the present day being fulfilled. In the writings of the prophets Isaiah (2:18–21), Jeremiah (27:3–7; 29:11–14), Ezekiel (5:12; 8), Daniel (8; 9:26, 27), Hosea (9:17), there are also many prophecies regarding the events which were to befall that people.

There is in like manner a large number of prophecies relating to those nations with which the Jews came into contact—as Tyre (Ezek. 26:3–5, 14–21), Egypt (Ezek. 29:10, 15; 30:6, 12, 13), Ethiopia (Nahum 3:8–10), Nineveh (Nahum 1:10; 2:8–13; 3:17–19), Babylon (Isa. 13:4; Jer. 51:7; Isa. 44:27; Jer. 50:38; 51:36, 39, 57), the land of the Philistines (Jer. 47:4–7; Ezek. 25:15–17; Amos 1:6–8; Zeph. 2:4–7; Zech. 9:5–8), and of the four great monarchies (Dan. 2:39, 40; 7–17:24; 8; 9).

But the great body of Old Testament prophecy relates directly to the advent of the Messiah, beginning with Gen. 3:15—

the first great promise—and extending in ever-increasing fulness and clearness all through to the very close of the canon. The Messianic prophecies are too numerous to be quoted. "To him gave all the prophets witness." (Comp. Micah 5:2; Hag. 2:6–9; Isa. 7:14; 9:6, 7; 11:1, 2; 53; 60:10, 13; Ps. 16:11; 68:18.)

Many predictions also were delivered by Jesus and his apostles. Those of Christ were very numerous. (Comp. Matt. 10:23:24; 11:23; 19:28; 21:43, 44; 24; 25:31–46; 26:17–35, 46, 64; Mark 9:1; 10:30; 13; 11:1–6, 14; 14:12–31, 42, 62; 16:17, etc.)

Pro'phet (Heb. *nâbi'*, from a root meaning "to bubble forth, as from a fountain," hence "to utter"—comp. Ps. 45:1). This Hebrew word is the first and the most generally used for a prophet. In the time of Samuel another word—*ro'eh*, "seer"—began to be used (1 Sam. 9:9). It occurs seven times in reference to Samuel. Afterwards another word—*hozeh*, "seer" (2 Sam. 24:11)—was employed. In 1 Chr. 29:29 all these three words are used: "Samuel the seer (*ro'eh*), Nathan the prophet (*nâbi'*), Gad the seer" (*hozeh*). In Josh. 13:22 Balaam is called (Heb.) a *kosêm* = "diviner," a word used only of a false prophet.

The "prophet" proclaimed the message given to him, as the "seer" beheld the vision of God. (See Num. 12:6, 8.) Thus a prophet was a spokesman for God; he spake in God's name and by his authority (Ex. 7:1). He is the mouth by which God speaks to men (Jer. 1:9; Isa. 51:16), and hence what the prophet says is not of man but of God (2 Pet. 1:20, 21; comp. Heb. 3:7; Acts 4:25; 28:25). Prophets were the immediate organs of God for the communication of his mind and will to men (Deut. 18:18, 19). The whole Word of God may in this general sense be spoken of as prophetic, inasmuch as it was written by men who received the revelation they communicated from God, no matter what its nature might be. The foretelling of future events was not a necessary but only an incidental part of the prophetic office. The great task assigned to the prophets whom God raised up among the people was

"to correct moral and religious abuses, to proclaim the great moral and religious truths which are connected with the character of God, and which lie at the foundation of his government."

Any one being a spokesman for God to man might thus be called a prophet. Thus Enoch, Abraham, and the patriarchs, as bearers of God's message (Gen. 20:7; Ex. 7:1; Ps. 105:15), as also Moses (Deut. 18:15; 34:10; Hos. 12:13), are ranked among the prophets. The seventy elders of Israel (Num. 11:16–29), "when the spirit rested upon them, prophesied;" Asaph and Jeduthun "prophesied with the harp" (1 Chr. 25:3). Miriam and Deborah were prophetesses (Ex. 15:20; Judg. 4:4). The title thus has a general application to all who have messages from God to men.

But while the prophetic gift was thus exercised from the beginning, the *prophetical order* as such began with Samuel. Colleges—"schools of the prophets"—were instituted for the training of prophets, who were constituted a distinct order (1 Sam. 19:18–24; 2 Kings 2:3, 15; 4:38), which continued to the close of the Old Testament. Such "schools" were established at Ramah, Bethel, Gilgal, Gibeah, and Jericho. The "sons" or "disciples" of the prophets were young men (2 Kings 5:22; 9:1, 4) who lived together at these different "schools" (4:38–41). These young men were taught not only the rudiments of secular knowledge, but they were brought up to exercise the office of prophet, "to preach pure morality and the heart-felt worship of Jehovah, and to act along and co-ordinately with the priesthood and monarchy in guiding the state aright and checking all attempts at illegality and tyranny."

In New Testament times the prophetical office was continued. Our Lord is frequently spoken of as a prophet (Luke 13:33; 24:19). He was and is the great Prophet of the Church. There was also in the Church a distinct order of prophets (1 Cor. 12:28; Eph. 2:20; 3:5), who made new revelations from God. They differed from the "teacher," whose office it was to impart truths already revealed.

Of the Old Testament prophets there are

sixteen, whose prophecies form part of the inspired canon. These are divided into four groups:—

(1.) The prophets of the northern kingdom (Israel)—*viz.*, Hosea, Amos, Joel, Jonah.

(2.) The prophets of Judah—*viz.*, Isaiah, Jeremiah, Obadiah, Micah, Nahum, Habakkuk, Zephaniah.

(3.) The prophets of the Captivity—*viz.*, Ezekiel and Daniel.

(4.) The prophets of the Restoration—*viz.*, Haggai, Zechariah, and Malachi.

Propitia′tion, that by which God is rendered propitious—*i.e.*, by which it becomes consistent with his character and government to pardon and bless the sinner. The propitiation does not procure his love or make him loving; it only renders it consistent for him to exercise his love towards sinners.

In Rom. 3:25 and Heb. 9:5 (A.V., "mercy-seat") the Greek word *hilasterion* is used. It is the word employed by the LXX. translators in Ex. 25:17 and elsewhere as the equivalent for the Hebrew *kappôreth*, which means "covering," and is used of the lid of the ark of the covenant (Ex. 25:21; 30:6). This Greek word (*hilasterion*) came to denote not only the mercy-seat or lid of the ark, but also propitiation or reconciliation by blood. On the great day of atonement the high priest carried the blood of the sacrifice he offered for all the people within the veil and sprinkled with it the "mercy-seat," and so made propitiation.

In 1 John 2:2; 4:10, Christ is called the "propitiation for our sins." Here a different Greek word is used (*hilasmos*). Christ is "the propitiation," because by his becoming our substitute and assuming our obligations he expiated our guilt, covered it, by the vicarious punishment which he endured. (Comp. Heb. 2:17, where the expression "make reconciliation" of the A.V. is more correctly in the R.V. "make propitiation.")

Proportion of faith (Rom. 12:6). Paul says here that each one was to exercise his gift of prophecy—*i.e.*, of teaching—"according to the proportion of faith." The meaning is, that the utterances of the "prophet" were not to fluctuate according to his own impulses or independent thoughts, but were to be adjusted to the truth revealed to him as a believer—*i.e.*, were to be in accordance with it.

In post-Reformation times this phrase was used as meaning that all Scripture was to be interpreted with reference to all other Scripture—*i.e.*, that no words or expressions were to be isolated or interpreted in a way contrary to its general teaching. This was also called the "analogy of faith."

Pro′selyte is used in the LXX. for "stranger" (1 Chr. 22:2)—*i.e.*, a comer to Palestine; a sojourner in the land (Ex. 12:48; 20:10; 22:21)—and in the New Testament for a convert to Judaism. There were such converts from early times (Isa. 56:3; Neh. 10:28; Esther 8:17). The law of Moses made specific regulations regarding the admission into the Jewish church of such as were not born Israelites (Ex. 20:10; 23:12; 12:19, 48; Deut. 5:14; 16:11, 14, etc.). The Kenites, the Gibeonites, the Cherethites, and the Pelethites were thus admitted to the privileges of Israelites. Thus also we hear of individual proselytes who rose to positions of prominence in Israel—as of Doeg the Edomite, Uriah the Hittite, Araunah the Jebusite, Zelek the Ammonite, Ithmah and Ebedmelech the Ethiopians.

In the time of Solomon there were one hundred and fifty-three thousand six hundred strangers in the land of Israel (1 Chr. 22:2; 2 Chr. 2:17, 18). And the prophets speak of the time as coming when the strangers shall share in all the privileges of Israel (Ezek. 47:22; Isa. 2:2; 11:10; 56:3-6; Micah 4:1). Accordingly, in New Testament times, we read of proselytes in the synagogues (Acts 10:2, 7; 13:42, 43, 50; 17:4; 18:7; Luke 7:5). The "religious proselytes" here spoken of were proselytes of righteousness, as distinguished from proselytes of the gate.

The distinction between "proselytes of the gate" (Ex. 20:10) and "proselytes of righteousness" originated only with the rabbis. According to them, the "proselytes of the gate" (half proselytes) were not required to be circumcised nor to comply with the Mosaic ceremonial law. They were bound only to conform to the so-called seven precepts of Noah—*viz.*, to abstain from idolatry, blasphemy, bloodshed, uncleanness, the eating of blood, theft, and to yield obedience to the authorities. Besides these laws, however, they were required to abstain from work on the Sabbath, and to refrain from the use of leavened bread during the time of the Passover.

The "proselytes of righteousness"—religious or devout proselytes (Acts 13 : 43)—were bound to all the doctrines and precepts of the Jewish economy, and were members of the synagogue in full communion.

The name "proselyte" occurs in the New Testament only in Matt. 23 : 15; Acts 2 : 10; 6 : 5; 13 : 43. The name by which they are commonly designated is that of "devout men," or men "fearing God" or "worshipping God."

Pro'verb, a trite maxim; a similitude; a parable. The Hebrew word thus rendered (*mashâl*) has a wide signification. It comes from a root meaning "to be like," and is sometimes rendered "by-word," "parable." Rendered "proverb" in Isa. 14 : 4, Hab. 2 : 6; "dark saying" in Ps. 49 : 4, Num. 12 : 8. Ahab's defiant words in answer to the insolent demands of Benhadad, "Let not him that girdeth on his harness boast himself as he that putteth it off," is a well-known instance of a proverbial saying (1 Kings 20 : 11).

Proverbs, Book of, a collection of moral and philosophical maxims of a wide range of subjects presented in a poetic form. This book sets forth the "philosophy of practical life. It is the sign to us that the Bible does not despise common sense and discretion. It impresses upon us in the most forcible manner the value of intelligence and prudence and of a good education. The whole strength of the Hebrew language and of the sacred authority of the book is thrown upon these homely truths. It deals, too, in that refined, discriminating, careful view of the finer shades of human character so often overlooked by theologians, but so necessary to any true estimate of human life" (Stanley's *Jewish Church*).

As to the *origin* of this book, "it is probable that Solomon gathered and recast many proverbs which sprang from human experience in preceding ages and were floating past him on the tide of time, and that he also elaborated many new ones from the material of his own experience. Towards the close of the book, indeed, are preserved some of Solomon's own sayings that seem to have fallen from his lips in later life and been gathered by other hands' (Arnot's *Laws from Heaven, etc.*).

This book is usually divided into three parts :—

(1.) Consisting of ch. 1–9, which contain an exhibition of wisdom as the highest good.

(2.) Consisting of ch. 10–24.

(3.) Containing proverbs of Solomon "which the men of Hezekiah, the king of Judah, collected" (ch. 25–29).

These are followed by two supplements—(1) "The words of Agur" (ch. 30); and (2) "The words of Lemuel" (ch. 31).

Solomon is said to have written three thousand proverbs, and those contained in this book may be a selection from these (1 Kings 4 : 32). In the New Testament there are thirty-five direct quotations from this book or allusions to it.

Pro'vidence literally means *foresight*, but is generally used to denote God's preserving and governing all things by means of second causes (Ps. 18 : 35; 63 : 8; Acts 17 : 28; Col. 1 : 17; Heb. 1 : 3). God's providence *extends* to the natural world (Ps. 104 : 14; 135 : 5–7; Acts 14 : 17), the brute creation (Ps. 104 : 21–29; Matt. 6 : 26; 10 : 29), and the affairs of men (1 Chr. 16 : 31; Ps. 47 : 7; Prov. 21 : 1; Job 12 : 23; Dan. 2 : 21; 4 : 25), and of individuals (1 Sam. 2 : 6; Ps. 18 : 30; Luke 1 : 53; James 4 : 13–15). It extends also to the free actions of men (Ex. 12 : 36; 1 Sam. 24 : 9–15; Ps. 33 : 14, 15; Prov. 16 : 1; 19 : 21; 20 : 24; 21 : 1), and things sinful (2 Sam. 16 : 10; 24 : 1; Rom. 11 : 32; Acts 4 : 27, 28), as well as to their good actions (Phil. 2 : 13; 4 : 13; 2 Cor. 12 : 9, 10; Eph. 2 : 10; Gal. 5 : 22–25).

As regards *sinful* actions of men, they are represented as occurring by God's permission (Gen. 45:5; 50:20. Comp. 1 Sam. 6:6; Ex. 7:13; 14:17; Acts 2:3; 3:18; 4:27, 28), and as controlled (Ps. 76:10) and overruled for good (Gen. 50:20; Acts 3:13). God does not cause or approve of sin, but only limits, restrains, overrules it for good.

The *mode* of God's providential government is altogether unexplained. We only know that it is a fact that God does govern all his creatures and all their actions; that this government is universal (Ps. 103:17-19), particular (Matt. 10:29-31), efficacious (Ps. 33:11; Job 23:13), embraces events apparently contingent (Prov. 16:9, 33; 19:21; 21:1), is consistent with his own perfection (2 Tim. 2:13), and to his own glory (Rom. 9:17; 11:36).

Psalms. The psalms are the production of various authors. "Only a portion of the Book of Psalms claims David as its author. Other inspired poets in successive generations added now one now another contribution to the sacred collection, and thus in the wisdom of Providence it more completely reflects every phase of human emotion and circumstances than it otherwise could." But it is specially to David and his contemporaries that we owe this precious book. In the "titles" of the psalms, the genuineness of which there is no sufficient reason to doubt, 73 are ascribed to David. Peter and John (Acts 4:25) ascribe to him also the second psalm, which is one of the 50 that are anonymous. About two-thirds of the whole collection have been ascribed to David.

Psalms 29, 62, and 77 are addressed to Jeduthun, to be sung after his manner or in his choir. Psalms 50 and 73-84 are addressed to Asaph, as the master of his choir, to be sung in the worship of God. The "sons of Korah," who formed a leading part of the Kohathite singers (2 Chr. 20:19), were intrusted with the arranging and singing of Ps. 42, 44-49, 84, 85, 87, and 88.

In Luke 24:44 the word "psalms" means the Hagiographa—*i.e.*, the holy writings, one of the sections into which the Jews divided the Old Testament. (See BIBLE.)

None of the psalms can be *proved* to have been of a later date than the time of Ezra and Nehemiah, hence the whole collection extends over a period of about 1,000 years. There are in the New Testament 116 direct quotations from the Psalter.

The Psalter is divided, after the analogy of the Pentateuch, into five books, each closing with a doxology or benediction:—

(1.) The first book comprises the first 41 psalms, all of which are ascribed to David except 1, 2, and 33, which, though anonymous, may also be ascribed to him.

(2.) Book second consists of the next 31 psalms (42-72), 18 of which are ascribed to David and 1 to Solomon (the 72nd). The rest are anonymous.

(3.) The third book contains 17 psalms (73-89), of which the 86th is ascribed to David, the 88th to Heman the Ezrahite, and the 89th to Ethan the Ezrahite.

(4.) The fourth book also contains 17 psalms (90-106), of which the 90th is ascribed to Moses, and the 101st and 103rd to David.

(5.) The fifth book contains the remaining psalms, 44 in number. Of these, 15 are ascribed to David, and the 127th to Solomon.

Ps. 136 is generally called "the great hallel." But the Talmud includes also Ps. 120-135. Ps. 113-118, inclusive, constitute the "hallel" recited at the three great feasts, at the new moon, and on the eight days of the feast of dedication.

"It is presumed that these several collections were made at times of high religious life: the first, probably, near the close of David's life; the second in the days of Solomon; the third by the singers of Jehoshaphat (2 Chr. 20:19); the fourth by the men of Hezekiah (29, 30, 31); and the fifth in the days of Ezra."

The Mosaic ritual makes no provision for the service of song in the worship of God. David first taught the Church to sing the praises of the Lord. He first introduced into the ritual of the tabernacle music and song.

Divers names are given to the psalms. (1.) Some bear the Hebrew designation *shîr* (Gr. *odē*, a song). Thirteen have this title. It means the flow of speech, as it were, in a straight line or in a regular strain. This title includes secular as well as sacred song.

(2.) Fifty-seven psalms bear the designation (Heb.) *mitsmôr* (Gr. *psalmos*, a psalm), a lyric ode, or a song set to music; a sacred song accompanied with a musical instrument.

(3.) Ps. 145, and many others, have the designation (Heb.) *tehillâh* (Gr. *hymnos*, a hymn), meaning a song of praise; a song the prominent thought of which is the praise of God.

(4.) Six psalms (16, 56-60) have the title (Heb.) *michtam* (*q.v.*).

(5.) Ps. 7 and Hab. 3 bear the title (Heb.) *shiggaion* (*q.v.*).

Psal′tery, a musical instrument, supposed to have been a kind of lyre, or a harp with twelve strings. The Hebrew word *nĕbhêl*, so rendered, is translated "viol" in Isa. 5 : 12 (R.V., "lute"); 14 : 11. In Dan. 3 : 5, 7, ·10, 15, the word thus rendered is Chaldaic, *pĕṣanterîn*, which is supposed to be a word of Greek origin denoting an instrument of the harp kind.

Ptolema′is, a maritime city of Galilee (Acts 21 : 7). It was originally called "Accho" (*q.v.*), and received the name Ptolemais from Ptolemy Soter when he was in possession of Cœle-Syria.

Pu′ah—*splendid*. (1.) One of the two midwives who feared God, and refused to kill the Hebrew male children at their birth (Ex. 1 : 15–21).

(2.) A descendant of Issachar (Judg. 10 : 1).

Pub′lican, one who farmed the taxes (*e.g.*, Zacchæus, Luke 19 : 2) to be levied from a town or district, and thus undertook to pay to the supreme government a certain amount. In order to collect the taxes, the publicans employed subordinates (5 : 27 ; 15 : 1 ; 18 : 10), who, for their own ends, were often guilty of extortion and peculation. In New Testament times these taxes were paid to the Romans, and hence were regarded by the Jews as a very heavy burden, and hence also the collectors of taxes, who were frequently Jews, were hated, and were usually spoken of in very opprobrious terms. Jesus was ac-

cused of being a "friend of publicans and sinners" (Luke 7 : 34).

Pub′lius, "the chief man of the island" of Malta (Acts 28 : 7), who courteously entertained Paul and his shipwrecked companions for three days, till they found a more permanent place of residence; for they remained on the island for three months, till the stormy season had passed. The word here rendered "chief man" (*prôtos*) is supposed by some to be properly a Maltese term, the official title of the governor.

Pu′dens—*bashful*—a Christian at Rome, who sent his greetings to Timothy (2 Tim. 4 : 21). (See CLAUDIA.)

Pul. (1.) An Assyrian king. It has been a question whether he was identical with Tiglath-pileser III. (*q.v.*), or was his predecessor. The weight of evidence is certainly in favour of their identity. Pul was the throne-name he bore in Babylonia as king of Babylon, and Tiglath-pileser the throne-name he bore as king of Assyria. He was the founder of what is called the second Assyrian empire. He consolidated and organized his conquests on a large scale. He subdued Northern Syria and Hamath, and the kings of Syria rendered him homage and paid him tribute. His ambition was to found in Western Asia a kingdom which should embrace the whole civilized world, having Nineveh as its centre. Menahem, king of Israel, gave him the enormous tribute of a thousand talents of silver, "that his hand might be with him" (2 Kings 15 : 19 ; 1 Chr. 5 : 26). The fact that this tribute could be paid showed the wealthy condition of the little kingdom of Israel even in this age of disorder and misgovernment. Having reduced Syria, he turned his arms against Babylon, which he subdued. The Babylonian king was slain, and Babylon and other Chaldean cities were taken, and Pul assumed the title of "King of Sumer [*i.e.*, Shinar] and Accad." He was succeeded by Shalmanezer IV.

(2.) A geographical name in Isa. 66 : 19. Probably=Phut (Gen. 10 : 6 ; Jer. 46 : 9, R.V. "Put;" Ezek. 27 : 10).

Pul′pit (Neh. 8 : 4). (See EZRA.)

Pulse (Dan. 1:12, 16), R.V. "herbs," vegetable food in general.

Pun'ishment. The New Testament lays down the general principles of good government, but contains no code of laws for the punishment of offenders. Punishment proceeds on the principle that there is an eternal distinction between right and wrong, and that this distinction must be maintained *for its own sake.* It is not primarily intended for the reformation of criminals, nor for the purpose of deterring others from sin. These results may be gained, but crime in itself demands punishment. (See MURDER; THEFT.) *Endless*—of the impenitent and unbelieving. The rejection of this doctrine "cuts the ground from under the gospel...blots out the attribute of retributive justice; transmutes sin into misfortune instead of guilt; turns all suffering into chastisement; converts the piacular work of Christ into moral influence ...The attempt to retain the evangelical theology in connection with it is futile" (*Shedd*).

Pur, Pu'rim—*a lot, lots*—a festival instituted by the Jews (Esther 9:24–32) in ironical commemoration of Haman's consultation of the Pur (a Persian word), for

THE QUAY AT PUTEOLI.

the purpose of ascertaining the auspicious day for executing his cruel plot against their nation. It became a national institution by the common consent of the Jews, and is observed by them to the present day, on the 14th and 15th of the month Adar, a month before the Passover.

Purifica'tion, the process by which a person unclean, according to the Levitical law, and thereby cut off from the sanctuary and the festivals, was restored to the enjoyment of all these privileges.

The great annual purification of the people was on the Day of Atonement (*q.v.*).

But in the details of daily life there were special causes of ceremonial uncleanness which were severally provided for by ceremonial laws enacted for each separate case. For example, the case of the leper (Lev. 13, 14), and of the house defiled by leprosy (14:49–53; see also Matt. 8:2–4). Uncleanness from touching a dead body (Num. 19:11; Hos. 9:4; Hag. 2:13; Matt. 23:27; Luke 11:44). The case of the high priest and of the Nazarite (Lev.

21:1-4, 10, 11; Num. 6:6, 7; Ezek. 44:
25). Purification was effected by bathing
and washing the clothes (Lev. 14:8, 9);
by washing the hands (Deut. 21:6; Matt.
27:24); washing the hands and feet (Ex.
30:18-21; Heb. 6:2, "baptisms"—R.V.
marg.,"washings;" 9:10); sprinkling with
blood and water (Ex. 24:5-8; Heb. 9:19),
etc. Allusions to this rite are found in Ps.
26:6; 51:7; Ezek. 36:25; Heb. 10:22.

Purse. (1.) Gr. *balantion*, a bag (Luke
10:4; 22:35, 36).

(2.) Gr. *zōnē*, properly a girdle (Matt.
10:9; Mark 6:8), a money-belt. As to
our Lord's sending forth his disciples without money in their purses, the remark has
been made that in this "there was no departure from the simple manners of the
country. At this day the farmer sets out
on excursions quite as extensive without a
para in his purse; and a modern Moslem
prophet of Tarshīsha thus sends forth his
apostles over this identical region. No
traveller in the East would hesitate to
throw himself on the hospitality of any
village."—Thomson's *Land and the Book.*
(See SCRIP.)

Put, Phut. (1.) One of the sons of
Ham (Gen. 10:6).

(2.) A land or people from among whom
came a portion of the mercenary troops of
Egypt—Jer. 46:9 (A.V., "Libyans," but
correctly, R.V., "Put"); Ezek. 27:10;
30:5 (A.V., "Libya;" R.V., "Put");
38:5; Nahum 3:9.

Pute'oli, a city on the coast of Cam-
pania, on the north shore of a bay running
north from the Bay of Naples, at which
Paul landed on his way to Rome, from
which it was distant 170 miles. Here he
tarried for seven days (Acts 28:13, 14).
This was the great emporium for the Alexandrian corn ships. Here Paul and his
companions began their journey, by the
"Appian Way," to Rome. It is now
called *Pozzuoli.* The remains of the quay,
at which Paul landed, may still be seen
here.

Py'garg—Heb. *dishôn,* "springing"—
(Deut. 14:5), one of the animals permitted
for food. It is supposed to be the *Antelope
addax.* It is described as "a large animal,
over 3½ feet high at the shoulder, and, with
its gently-twisted horns, 2½ feet long. Its
colour is pure white, with the exception of
a short black mane, and a tinge of tawny
on the shoulders and back."— Tristram's
Natural History.

Q

Quails. The Israelites were twice relieved in their privation by a miraculous
supply of quails—(1) in the wilderness of
sin (Ex. 16:13), and (2) again at Kibroth-
hattaavah (*q.v.*) — Num. 11:31. God
"rained flesh upon them as dust, and
feathered fowls like as the sand of the sea"
(Ps. 78:27). The words in Num. 11:31,
according to the Authorized Version, appear to denote that the quails lay one above
another to the thickness of two cubits
above the ground. The Revised Version,
however, reads, "about two cubits above
the face of the earth"—*i.e.,* the quails
flew at this height, and were easily killed
or caught by the hand. Being thus secured in vast numbers by the people, they

"spread them all abroad" (11:32) in order
to salt and dry them.

These birds (the *Coturnix vulgaris* of
naturalists) are found in countless numbers
on the shores of the Mediterranean, and
their annual migration is an event causing
great excitement.

Quaranta'nia, a mountain some 1,200
feet high, about 7 miles north-west of
Jericho, the traditional scene of our Lord's
temptation (Matt. 4:8).

Quar'ries. (1.) The "Royal Quarries"
(not found in Scripture) is the name given
to the vast caverns stretching far underneath the northern hill, Bezetha, on which
Jerusalem is built. Out of these mammoth
caverns stones—a hard lime-stone—have

been quarried in ancient times for the buildings in the city, and for the temples of Solomon, Zerubbabel, and Herod. Huge

QUAIL (COTURNIX VULGARIS).

blocks of stone are still found in these caves bearing the marks of pick and chisel. The general appearance of the whole suggests to the explorer the idea that the Phœnician quarrymen have just suspended their work. The supposition that the polished blocks of stone for Solomon's temple were sent by Hiram from Lebanon or Tyre is not supported by any evidence (comp. 1 Kings 5 : 8). Hiram sent masons and stone-squarers to Jerusalem to assist Solomon's workmen in their great undertaking, but did not send stones to Jerusalem, where, indeed, they were not needed, as these royal quarries abundantly testify.

(2.) The "quarries" (Heb. *peṣilîm*) by Gilgal (Judg. 3 : 19), from which Ehud turned back for the purpose of carrying out his design to put Eglon king of Moab to death, were probably the "graven images" (as the word is rendered by the LXX. and the Vulgate and in the marg. A.V. and R.V.), or the idol temples the Moabites had erected at Gilgal, where the children of Israel first encamped after crossing the Jordan. The Hebrew word

is rendered "graven images" in Deut. 7 : 25, and is not elsewhere translated "quarries."

Quar′tus—*fourth*—a Corinthian Christian who sent by Paul his salutations to friends at Rome (Rom. 16 : 23).

Quater′nion, a band of four soldiers. Peter was committed by Herod to the custody of four quaternions—*i.e.*, one quaternion for each watch of the night (Acts 12 : 4). Thus every precaution was taken against his escape from prison. Two of each quaternion were in turn stationed at the door (12 : 6), and to two the apostle was chained according to Roman custom.

Queen. No explicit mention of queens is made till we read of the "queen of Sheba." The wives of the kings of Israel are not so designated. In Ps. 45 : 9, the Hebrew for "queen" is not *malkâh*, one actually ruling like the Queen of Sheba, but *shegâl*, which simply means the king's wife. In 1 Kings 11 : 19, Pharaoh's wife is called "the queen," but the Hebrew word so rendered (*g′bîrâh*) is simply a title of honour, denoting a royal lady, used sometimes for "queen-mother" (1 Kings 15 : 13; 2 Chron. 15 : 16). In Cant. 6 : 8, 9, the king's wives are styled "queens" (Heb. *melâkhôth*).

In the New Testament we read of the "queen of the south"—*i.e.*, Southern Arabia, Sheba (Matt. 12 : 42; Luke 11 : 31) —and the "queen of the Ethiopians" (Acts 8 : 27), Candace.

Queen of heaven (Jer. 7 : 18; 44 : 17, 25), the moon, worshipped by the Assyrians as the receptive power in nature.

Quick′sands, found only in Acts 27 : 17, the rendering of the Greek *Syrtis.* On the north coast of Africa were two localities dangerous to sailors, called the Greater and Lesser Syrtis. The former of these is probably here meant. It lies between Tripoli and Barca, and near Cyrene. The Lesser Syrtis lay farther to the west.

Quiv′er, the sheath for arrows. The Hebrew word (*ashpâh*) thus commonly rendered is found in Job 39 : 23; Ps. 127 : 5; Isa. 22 : 6; 49 : 2; Jer. 5 : 16; Lam. 3 : 13. In Gen. 27 : 3 this word is the rendering of the Hebrew *tĕlî*, which is supposed rather to mean a suspended weapon, literally "that which hangs from one"—*i.e.*, is suspended from the shoulder or girdle.

Quota'tions from the Old Testament in the New, which are very numerous, are not made according to any uniform method.

When the New Testament was written, the Old was not divided, as it now is, into chapters and verses, and hence such peculiarities as these:—When Luke (20:37) refers to Ex. 3:6, he quotes from "Moses at the bush"—*i.e.*, the section containing the record of Moses at the bush. So also Mark (2:26) refers to 1 Sam. 21:1-6, in the words, "in the days of Abiathar;" and Paul (Rom. 11:2) refers to 1 Kings ch. 17-19, in the words, "in Elias"—*i.e.*, in the portion of the history regarding Elias.

In general, the New Testament writers quote from the Septuagint (*q.v.*) version of the Old Testament, as it was then in common use among the Jews. But it is noticeable that these quotations are not made in any uniform manner. Sometimes, *e.g.*, the quotation does not agree literally either with the LXX. or the Hebrew text. This occurs in about one hundred instances. Sometimes the LXX. is literally quoted (in about ninety instances), and sometimes it is corrected or altered in the quotations (in over eighty instances).

Quotations are sometimes made also directly from the Hebrew text (Matt. 4:15, 16; John 19:37; 1 Cor. 15:54).

Besides the quotations made directly, there are found numberless allusions, more or less distinct, showing that the minds of the New Testament writers were filled with the expressions and ideas as well as historical facts recorded in the Old.

There are in all two hundred and eighty-three *direct* quotations from the Old Testament in the New, but not one clear and certain case of quotation from the Apocrypha (*q.v.*).

Besides quotations in the New from the Old Testament, there are in Paul's writings three quotations from certain Greek poets—Acts 17:28; 1 Cor. 15:33; Titus 1:12. These quotations are memorials of his early classical education.

R

Ra'amah—*thunder*. (1.) One of the sons of Cush (Gen. 10:7).

(2.) A country which traded with Tyre (Ezek. 27:22).

Raami'ah—*thunder of the Lord*—one of the princes who returned from the Exile (Neh. 7:7); called also Reelaiah (Ezra 2:2).

Raam'ses (Ex. 1:11). (See RAMESES.)

Rab'bah or **Rab'bath**—*great*. (1.) "Rabbath of the children of Ammon," the chief city of the Ammonites, among the eastern hills, some 20 miles east of the Jordan, on the southern of the two streams which united with the Jabbok. Here the bedstead of Og was preserved (Deut. 3:11), perhaps as a trophy of some victory gained by the Ammonites over the king of Bashan. After David had subdued all their allies in a great war, he sent Joab with a strong force to take their city. For two years it held out against its assailants. It was while his army was engaged in this protracted siege that David was guilty of that deed of shame which left a blot on his character and cast a gloom over the rest of his life. At length, having taken the "royal city" (or the "city of waters," 2 Sam. 12:27—*i.e.*, the lower city on the river, as distinguished from the citadel), Joab sent for David to direct the final assault (11:1; 12:26-31). The city was given up to plunder, and the people were ruthlessly put to death, and "thus did he with all the cities of the children of Ammon." The destruction of Rabbath was the last of David's conquests. His kingdom now reached its farthest limits (2 Sam. 8:1-15; 1 Chr. 18:1-15). The capture of this city is referred to by

Amos (1:14), Jeremiah (49:2, 3), and Ezekiel (21:20; 25:5).

(2.) A city in the hill country of Judah (Josh. 15:60), possibly the ruin *Rubba*, six miles north-east of Beit-Jibrîn.

Rab′bi—*my master*—a title of dignity given by the Jews to their doctors of the law and their distinguished teachers. It is sometimes applied to Christ (Matt. 23: 7, 8; Mark 9:5 (R.V.); John 1:38, 49; 3:2; 6:25, etc.); also to John (3:26).

Rabbo′ni (*id.*) occurs only twice in the New Testament (Mark 10:51—A.V., "Lord," R.V., "Rabboni;" John 20: 16). It was the most honourable of all the titles.

Rab′mag—Assyrian *Rab-mugi*, "chief physician," who was attached to the king (Jer. 39:3, 13)—the title of one of Sennacherib's officers sent with messages to Hezekiah and the people of Jerusalem (2 Kings 18:17-19:13; Isa. 36:12-37:13) demanding the surrender of the city. He was accompanied by a "great army;" but his mission was unsuccessful.

Rab′saris—*chief of the Heads*—one of the three officers whom Sennacherib sent from Lachish with a threatening message to Jerusalem (2 Kings 18:17; Jer. 39:3, 13).

Rab shakeh—*chief of the princes*—the name given to the chief cup-bearer or the vizier of the Assyrian court; one of Sennacherib's messengers to Hezekiah. See the speech he delivered, in the Hebrew language, in the hearing of all the people, as he stood near the wall on the north side of the city (2 Kings 18:17-37). He and the other envoys returned to their master and reported that Hezekiah and his people were obdurate, and would not submit.

Ra′ca—*vain, empty, worthless*—only found in Matt. 5:22. The Jews used it as a word of contempt. It is derived from a root meaning "to spit."

Ra′chab=**Rahab**, a name found in the genealogy of our Lord (Matt. 1:5).

Ra′chal—*traffic*—a town in the tribe of Judah, to which David sent presents from the spoils of his enemies (1 Sam. 30:29).

Ra′chel—*ewe*, "the daughter"—"the somewhat petulant, peevish, and self-willed though beautiful younger daughter" of Laban, and one of Jacob's wives (Gen. 29: 6, 28). He served Laban fourteen years for her, so deep was Jacob's affection for her. She was the mother of Joseph (Gen. 30:22–24). Afterwards, on Jacob's departure from Mesopotamia, she took with her her father's teraphim (31:34, 35). As they journeyed on from Bethel, Rachel died in giving birth to Benjamin (35:18, 19), and was buried "in the way to Ephrath, which is Bethlehem. And Jacob set up a pillar upon her grave." Her sepulchre is still regarded with great veneration by the Jews. Its traditional site is about half a mile from Jerusalem.

This name is used poetically by Jeremiah (31:15–17) to denote God's people mourning under their calamities. This passage is also quoted by Matthew as fulfilled in the lamentation at Bethlehem on account of the slaughter of the infants there at the command of Herod (Matt. 2: 17, 18).

Ragu′el—*friend of God*—(Num. 10:29)== **Reuel** (*q.v.*)—Ex. 2:18—the father-in-law of Moses, and probably identical with Jethro (*q.v.*).

Râ′hab—*insolence; pride*—a poetical name applied to Egypt in Ps. 87:4; 89: 10; Isa. 51:9, as "the proud one."

Ra′hab (Heb. *Râḥâb; i.e.*, "broad," "large"). When the Hebrews were encamped at Shittim, in the "Arabah" or Jordan valley opposite Jericho, ready to cross the river, Joshua, as a final preparation, sent out two spies to "spy the land." After five days they returned, having swum across the river, which at this season—the month Abib—overflowed its banks from the melting of the snow on Lebanon. The spies reported how it had fared with them (Josh. 2:1-7). They had been exposed to danger in Jericho, and had been saved by the fidelity of Rahab the harlot, to whose house they had gone for protection. When the city of Jericho fell (6:17-25), Rahab and her whole family were preserved according to the promise of the spies, and were incorporated among the Jewish people. She afterwards became the wife of Salmon, a prince of the tribe of Judah (Ruth 4:21; 1 Chr.

2 : 11; Matt. 1 : 5). "Rahab's being asked to bring out the spies to the soldiers (Josh. 2 : 3) sent for them, is in strict keeping with Eastern manners, which would not permit any man to enter a woman's house without her permission. The fact of her covering the spies with bundles of flax which lay on her house-roof (2 : 6) is an 'undesigned coincidence' which strictly corroborates the narrative. It was the time of the barley harvest, and flax and barley are ripe at the same time in the Jordan valley, so that the bundles of flax stalks might have been expected to be drying just then" (Geikie's *Hours, etc.*, ii., 390).

Ra'ham—*merciful*—one of the descendants of Caleb, the son of Hezron (1 Chr. 2 : 44).

Rain. There are three Hebrew words used to denote the rains of different seasons—(1.) *Yôreh* (Hos. 6 : 3), or *môreh* (Joel 2 : 23), denoting the former or the early rain. (2.) *Melqosh*, the "latter rain" (Prov. 16 : 15). (3.) *Geshem*, the winter rain, "the rains." The heavy winter rain is mentioned in Gen. 7 : 12; Ezra 10 : 9; Cant. 2 : 11. The "early" or "former" rains commence in autumn in the latter part of October or beginning of November (Deut. 11 : 14; Joel 2 : 23; comp. Jer. 3 : 3), and continue to fall heavily for two months. Then the heavy "winter rains" fall from the middle of December to March. There is no prolonged fair weather in Palestine between October and March. The "latter" or spring rains fall in March and April, and serve to swell the grain then coming to maturity (Deut. 11 : 14; Hos. 6 : 3). After this there is ordinarily no rain, the sky being bright and cloudless till October or November.

Rain is referred to symbolically in Deut. 32 : 2; Ps. 72 : 6; Isa. 44 : 3, 4; Hos. 10 : 12.

Rain'bow, caused by the reflection and refraction of the rays of the sun shining on falling rain. It was appointed as a witness of the divine faithfulness (Gen. 9 : 12–17). It existed indeed before, but it was then constituted as a sign of the covenant. Others, however (as Delitzsch, *Commentary on Pentateuch*), think that it "appeared then for the first time in the vault and

clouds of heaven." It is argued by those holding this opinion that the atmosphere was differently constituted before the Flood. It is referred to three other times in Scripture (Ezek. 1 : 27, 28; Rev. 4 : 1–3; 10 : 1).

Rai'sins, dried grapes; mentioned 1 Sam. 25 : 18; 30 : 12; 2 Sam. 16 : 1; 1 Chr. 12 : 40.

Rak'kath—*shore-town*—a "fenced city" of the tribe of Naphtali (Josh. 19 : 35). The old name of Tiberias, according to the Rabbins.

Rak'kon—*a place upon the shore*—a town belonging to Dan (Josh. 19 : 46). It is now *Tell er-Rakkeit*, 6 miles north of Joppa, on the sea-shore, near the mouth of the river *'Aujeh*—*i.e.*, "yellow water." (See KANAH.)

Ram—*exalted*. (1.) The son of Hezron, and one of the ancestors of the royal line (Ruth 4 : 19). The margin of 1 Chr. 2 : 9, also Matt. 1 : 3, 4 and Luke 3 : 33, have "Aram."

(2.) One of the sons of Jerahmeel (1 Chr. 2 : 25, 27).

(3.) A person mentioned in Job 32 : 2 as founder of a clan to which Elihu belonged. The same as Aram of Gen. 22 : 21.

Ra'ma (Matt. 2 : 18), the Greek form of **Ra'mah.** (1.) A city first mentioned in Josh. 18 : 25, near Gibeah of Benjamin. It was fortified by Baasha, king of Israel (1 Kings 15 : 17–22; 2 Chr. 16 : 1–6). Asa, king of Judah, employed Benhadad the Syrian king to drive Baasha from this city (1 Kings 15 : 18, 20). Isaiah (10 : 29) refers to it, and also Jeremiah, who was once a prisoner there among the other captives of Jerusalem when it was taken by Nebuchadnezzar (Jer. 39 : 8–12; 40 : 1). Rachel, whose tomb lies close to Bethlehem, is represented as weeping in Ramah (Jer. 31 : 15) for her slaughtered children. This prophecy is illustrated and fulfilled in the re-awakening of Rachel's grief at the slaughter of the infants in Bethlehem (Matt. 2 : 18). It is identified with the modern village of *er-Râm*, between Gibeon and Beeroth, about 5 miles due north of Jerusalem. (See SAMUEL.)

(2.) A town identified with *Râmeh*, on the

border of Asher, about 13 miles south-east of Tyre, "on a solitary hill in the midst of a basin of green fields" (Josh. 19:29).

(3.) One of the "fenced cities" of Naphtali (Josh. 19:36), on a mountain slope, about seven and a half miles west-south-west of Safed, and 15 miles west of the north end of the Sea of Galilee, the present large and well-built village of *Râmeh*.

(4.) The same as Ramathaim-zophim (*q.v.*), a town of Mount Ephraim (1 Sam. 1:1, 19).

(5.) The same as Ramoth-gilead (*q.v.*)— 2 Kings 8:29; 2 Chr. 22:6.

Ramatha′im-zo′phim—*the two heights of the Zophites* or *of the watchers* (only in 1 Sam. 1:1)—"in the land of Zuph" (9:5). Ramathaim is another name for Ramah (4).

One of the Levitical families descended from Kohath, that of Zuph or Zophai (1 Chr. 6:26, 35), had a district assigned to them in Ephraim, which from this circumstance was called "the land of Zuph," and hence the name of the town, "Zophim." It was the birth-place of Samuel and the seat of his authority (1 Sam. 2:11; 7:17). It is frequently mentioned in the history of that prophet and of David (15:34; 16:13; 19:18-23). Here Samuel died and was buried (25:1).

This town has been identified with the modern *Neby Samwil* ("the prophet Samuel"), about 4 or 5 miles north-west of Jerusalem. But there is no certainty as to its precise locality. Some have supposed that it may be identical with Arimathea of the New Testament. (See MIZPAH.)

Ra′math-le′hi—*elevation of Lehi*, or *the jawbone height; i.e.*, the Ramah of Lehi (Judg. 15:15-17). The phrase "in the jaw," ver. 19, Authorized Version, is in the margin, also in the Revised Version, "in Lehi." Here Samson slew a thousand Philistines with a jawbone.

Ra′math-miz′peh—*the height of Mizpeh* or *of the watch-tower* (Josh. 13:26)—a place mentioned as one of the limits of Gad. There were two Mizpehs on the east of the Jordan. This was the Mizpeh where Jacob and Laban made a covenant, "Mizpeh of Gilead," called also Galeed and Jegar-sahadutha. It has been identified

with the modern *es-Salt*, where the roads from Jericho and from Shechem to Damascus unite, about 25 miles east of the Jordan and 13 south of the Jabbok.

Ra′math of the south (Heb. *Ramath-něgeb*). The Heb. *něgeb* is the general designation for the south or south-west of Judah. This was one of the towns of Simeon (Josh. 19:8). It is the same as "south Ramoth" (1 Sam. 30:27; R.V., "Ramoth of the south"). Its site is doubtful. Some have thought it another name for Baalath-beer.

Ra′mathite, the designation given to Shimei, the manager of David's vineyard (1 Chr. 27:27).

Rame′ses, "the land of" (Gen. 47:11), was probably "the land of Goshen" (*q.v.*) —45:10. After the Hebrews had built Rameses, one of the "treasure cities," it came to be known as the "land" in which that city was built.

The city bearing this name (Ex. 12:37) was probably identical with Zoan, which Rameses II. ("son of the sun") rebuilt. It became his special residence, and ranked next in importance and magnificence to Thebes. Huge masses of bricks, made of Nile mud, sun-dried, some of them mixed with stubble, possibly moulded by Jewish hands, still mark the site of Rameses. This was the general rendezvous of the Israelites before they began their march out of Egypt. Called also Raamses (Ex. 1: 11).

BRICK OF SUN-DRIED CLAY AND STRAW, WITH CARTOUCHE OF RAMESES II.

Ra′moth—*heights.* A Levitical city in the tribe of Issachar (1 Sam. 30:27; 1 Chr. 6:73), the same as Jarmuth (Josh. 21:29) and Remeth (*q.v.*)—19:21.

Ra′moth-gil′ead—*heights of Gilead*—a

city of refuge on the east of Jordan; called "Ramoth in Gilead" (Deut. 4:43; Josh. 20:8; 21:38). Here Ahab, who joined Jehoshaphat in an endeavour to rescue it from the hands of the king of Syria, was mortally wounded (1 Kings 22:1-36). A similar attempt was afterwards made by Ahaziah and Joram, when the latter was wounded (2 Kings 8:28). In this city Jehu, the son of Jehoshaphat, was anointed by one of the sons of the prophets (9:1, 4).

It has with probability been identified with *Reimûn*, on the northern slope of the Jabbok, about 5 miles west of Jerâsh or Gerasa, one of the cities of Decapolis. Others identify it with *Gerosh*, about 25 miles north-east of es-Salt, with which also many have identified it. (See RAMATH-MIZPEH.)

Ran'ges. (1.) Lev. 11:35. Probably a cooking furnace for two or more pots, as the Hebrew word here is in the dual number; or perhaps a fire-place fitted to receive a pair of ovens.

(2.) 2 Kings 11:8. A Hebrew word is here used different from the preceding, meaning "ranks of soldiers." The Levites were appointed to guard the king's person within the temple (2 Chr. 23:7), while the soldiers were his guard in the court, and in going from the temple to the palace. The soldiers are here commanded to slay any one who should break through the "ranks" (as rendered in the R.V.) to come near the king. In 2 Kings 11:15 the expression, "Have her forth without the ranges," is in the Revised Version, "Have her forth between the ranks;" *i.e.*, Jehoiada orders that Athaliah should be kept surrounded by his own guards, and at the same time conveyed beyond the precincts of the temple.

Ran'som, the price or payment made for our redemption, as when it is said that the Son of man "gave his life a ransom for many" (Matt. 20:28; comp. Acts 20:28; Rom. 3:23, 24; 1 Cor. 6:19, 20; Gal. 3:13; 4:4, 5: Eph. 1:7; Col. 1:14; 1 Tim. 2:6; Titus 2:14; 1 Pet. 1:18, 19. In all these passages the same idea is expressed). This word is derived from the Fr. *rançon;* Lat. *redemptio.* The debt is represented not as cancelled but as fully paid. The

slave or captive is not liberated by a mere gratuitous favour, but a ransom price has been paid, in consideration of which he is set free. The original owner receives back his alienated and lost possession because he has bought it back "with a price." This price or ransom (Gr. *lutron*) is always said to be Christ, his blood, his death. He secures our redemption by the payment of a ransom. (See REDEMPTION.)

Ra'pha—*tall*. (1.) A Benjamite, the son of Binea (1 Chr. 8:2, 37), a descendant of Saul.

(2.) Margin of 1 Chr. 20:4, 6, where "giant" is given in the text.

Ra'phu—*healed*—a Benjamite, whose son Palti was one of the twelve spies (Num. 13:9).

Ra'ven. Heb. ʻ*orebh*, from a root meaning "to be black" (comp. Cant. 5:11); first mentioned as "sent forth" by Noah from the ark (Gen. 8:7). "Every raven after his kind" was forbidden as food (Lev. 11:15; Deut. 14:14). Ravens feed mostly on carrion, and hence their food is procured with difficulty (Job 38:41; Ps. 147:9). When they attack kids or lambs or weak animals, it is said that they first pick out the eyes of their victims (Prov. 30:17). When Elijah was concealed by the brook Cherith, God commanded the ravens to bring him "bread and flesh in the morning, and bread and flesh in the evening" (1 Kings 17:3-6). (See ELIJAH.)

There are eight species of ravens in Palestine, and they are everywhere very numerous in that land.

Ra'zor. The Nazarites were forbidden to make use of the razor (Num. 6:5; Judg. 13:5). At their consecration the Levites were shaved all over with a razor (Num. 8:7; comp. Ps. 52:2; Ezek. 5:1).

Re'ba—*fourth*—one of the Midianite chiefs slain by the Israelites in the wilderness (Num. 31:8; Josh. 13:21).

Rebek'ah—*a noose*—the daughter of Bethuel, and the wife of Isaac (Gen. 22:23; 24:67). The circumstances under which Abraham's "steward" found her at the "city of Nahor," in Padan-aram, are narrated in Gen. 24-27. "She can hardly be regarded as an amiable woman. When we first see her she is ready to leave her father's house for ever at an hour's notice; and her future life showed not only a full share of her brother Laban's duplicity, but the grave fault of partiality in her relations to her children, and a strong will, which soon controlled the gentler nature of her husband." The time and circumstances of her death are not recorded, but it is said that she was buried in the cave of Machpelah (Gen. 49 : 31).

Re'chab — *horseman,* or *chariot.* (1.) One of Ishbosheth's "captains of bands" or leaders of predatory troops (2 Sam. 4 : 2).

(2.) The father of Jehonadab, who was the father of the Rechabites (2 Kings 10 : 15, 23; Jer. 35 : 6-19).

Re'chabites, the descendants of Rechab through Jonadab or Jehonadab. They belonged to the Kenites, who accompanied the children of Israel into Palestine, and dwelt among them. Moses married a Kenite wife (Judg. 1 : 16), and Jael was the wife of "Heber the Kenite" (4 : 17). Saul also showed kindness to the Kenites (1 Sam. 15 : 6). The main body of the Kenites dwelt in cities, and adopted settled habits of life (30 : 29); but Jehonadab forbade his descendants to drink wine or to live in cities. They were commanded to lead always a nomad life. They adhered to the law laid down by Jonadab, and were noted for their fidelity to the old-established custom of their family in the days of Jeremiah (35); and this feature of their character is referred to by the prophet for the purpose of giving point to his own exhortation. They are referred to in Neh. 3 : 14 and 1 Chr. 2 : 55. Dr. Wolff (1839) found in Arabia, near Mecca, a tribe claiming to be descendants of Jehonadab; and recently a Bedouin tribe has been found near the Dead Sea who also profess to be descendants of the same Kenite chief.

Reconcilia'tion, a change from enmity to friendship. It is mutual—*i.e.,* it is a change wrought in both parties who have been at enmity.

(1.) In Col. 1 : 21, 22, the word there used refers to a change wrought in the personal character of the sinner who ceases to be an enemy to God by wicked works, and yields up to him his full confidence and love. In 2 Cor. 5 : 20 the apostle beseeches the Corinthians to be "reconciled to God" —*i.e.,* to lay aside their enmity.

(2.) Rom. 5 : 10 refers not to any change in our disposition toward God, but to God himself, as the party reconciled. Romans 5 : 11 teaches the same truth. From God we have received "the reconciliation" (R.V.)—*i.e.,* he has conferred on us the token of his friendship. So also 2 Cor. 5 : 18, 19 speaks of a reconciliation originating with God, and consisting in the removal of his merited wrath. In Eph. 2 : 16 it is clear that the apostle does not refer to the winning back of the sinner in love and loyalty to God, but to the restoration of God's forfeited favour. This is effected by his justice being satisfied, so that he can, in consistency with his own nature, be favourable toward sinners. Justice demands the punishment of sinners. The death of Christ satisfies justice, and so reconciles God to us. This reconciliation makes God our friend, and enables him to pardon and save us. (See ATONEMENT.)

Record'er (Heb. *mazkir* — *i.e.,* "the mentioner," "remembrancer"), the office first held by Jehoshaphat in the court of David (2 Sam. 8 : 16), also in the court of Solomon (1 Kings 4 : 3). The next recorder mentioned is Joah, in the reign of Hezekiah (2 Kings 18 : 18, 37; Isa. 36 : 11, 22). In the reign of Josiah another of the name of Joah filled this office (2 Chr. 34 : 8). The "recorder" was the chancellor or vizier of the kingdom. He brought all weighty matters under the notice of the king, "such as complaints, petitions, and wishes of subjects or foreigners. He also drew up papers for the king's guidance, and prepared drafts of the royal will for the scribes. All treaties came under his oversight; and he had the care of the national archives or records, to which, as royal historiographer, like the same state officer in Assyria and Egypt, he added the current annals of the kingdom."

Red Sea. The sea so called extends along the west coast of Arabia for about 1,400 miles, and separates Asia from Africa. It is connected with the Indian

Ocean, of which it is an arm, by the Strait of Bab-el-Mandeb. At a point (Ras Mohammed) about 200 miles from its northern extremity it is divided into two arms—that on the east called the Ælanitic Gulf, now the *Bahr el-'Akabah*, about 100 miles long by 15 broad, and that on the west the Gulf of Suez, about 150 miles long by about 20 broad. This branch is now connected with the Mediterranean by the Suez Canal. Between these two arms lies the Sinaitic Peninsula.

The Hebrew name generally given to this sea is *Yam Sûph*. This word *sûph* means a woolly kind of sea-weed, which the sea casts up in great abundance on its shores. In these passages, Ex. 10:19; 13:18; 15:4, 22; 23:31; Num. 14:25, etc., the Hebrew name is always translated "Red Sea," which was the name given to it by the Greeks. The origin of this name (Red Sea), is uncertain. Some think it is derived from the red colour of the mountains on the western shore; others from the red coral found in the sea, or the red appearance sometimes given to the water by certain zoophytes floating in it. In the New Testament (Acts 7:36; Heb. 11:29) this name is given to the Gulf of Suez.

This sea was also called by the Hebrews *Yam-mitsraim*, *i.e.*, "the Egyptian sea" (Isa. 11:15), and simply *Ha-yam*, "the sea" (Ex. 14:2, 9, 16, 21, 28; Josh. 24:6, 7; Isa. 10:26, etc.).

The great historical event connected with the Red Sea is the passage of the children of Israel, and the overthrow of the Egyptians, to which there is frequent reference in Scripture (Ex. 14–16; Num. 33:8; Deut. 11:4; Josh. 2:10; Judg. 11:16; 2 Sam. 22:16; Neh. 9:9–11; Ps. 66:6; Isa. 10:26; Acts 7:36, etc.).

Red Sea, Passage of. The account of the march of the Israelites through the Red Sea is given in Ex. 14:22–31. There has been great diversity of opinion as to the precise place where this occurred. The difficulty of arriving at any definite conclusion on the matter is much increased by the consideration that the head of the Gulf of Suez, which was the branch of the sea that was crossed, must have extended at the time of the Exodus probably 50 miles farther north than it does at present. Some have argued that the crossing took place opposite the Wâdy Tawârik, where the sea is at present some 7 miles broad. But the opinion that seems to be best supported is that which points to the neighbourhood of Suez. This position perfectly satisfies all the conditions of the stupendous miracle as recorded in the sacred narrative. (See EXODUS.)

Redeem'er—Heb. *goël; i.e.*, one charged with the duty of restoring the rights of another and avenging his wrongs (Lev. 25:48, 49; Num. 5:8; Ruth 4:1; Job 19:25; Ps. 19:14; 78:35, etc.). This title is peculiarly applied to Christ. He redeems us from all evil by the payment of a ransom (*q.v.*). (See REDEMPTION.)

Redemp'tion, the purchase back of something that had been lost, by the payment of a ransom. The Greek word so rendered is *apolutrōsis*, a word occurring nine times in Scripture, and always with the idea of a ransom or price paid—*i.e.*, redemption by a *lutron* (see Matt. 20:28; Mark 10:45). There are instances in the LXX. Version of the Old Testament of the use of *lutron* in man's relation to man (Lev. 19:20; 25:51; Ex. 21:30; Num. 35:31, 32; Isa. 45:13; Prov. 6:35), and in the same sense of man's relation to God (Num. 3:49; 18:15).

There are many passages in the New Testament which represent Christ's sufferings under the idea of a ransom or price, and the result thereby secured is a purchase or *redemption* (comp. Acts 20:28; 1 Cor. 6:19, 20; Gal. 3:13; 4:4, 5; Eph. 1:7; Col. 1:14; 1 Tim. 2:5, 6; Titus 2:14; Heb. 9:12; 1 Pet. 1:18, 19; Rev. 5:9). The idea running through all these texts, however various their reference, is that of *payment* made for our redemption. The debt against us is not viewed as simply cancelled, but is fully paid. Christ's blood or life, which he surrendered for them, is the "ransom" by which the deliverance of his people from the servitude of sin and from its penal consequences is secured. It is the plain doctrine of Scripture that "Christ saves us neither by the mere exercise of power, nor by his doctrine, nor by his example, nor by the moral influence which he exerted, nor by any subjective influence on his people, whether natural or mystical, but as a satisfaction to divine justice, as an expiation for sin, and as a ransom from the curse and authority of the law, thus reconciling us to God by making it consistent with his perfection to exercise mercy toward sinners" (Hodge's *Systematic Theology*).

Reed. (1.) "Paper reeds" (Isa. 19:7; R.V., "reeds"). Heb. *'arôth*, properly green herbage growing in marshy places.

(2.) Heb. *kâneh* (1 Kings 14:15; Job 40:21; Isa. 19:6), whence the Gr. *kanna*, a "cane," a generic name for a reed of any kind.

The reed of Egypt and Palestine is the *Arundo donax*, which grows to the height of 12 feet, its stalk jointed like the bamboo, "with a magnificent panicle of blossom at the top, and so slender and yielding that it will lie perfectly flat under a gust of wind, and immediately resume its upright position." It is used to illustrate weakness (2 Kings 18:21; Ezek. 19:6), also fickleness or instability (Matt. 11:7; comp. Eph. 4:14).

A "bruised reed" (Isa. 42:3; Matt. 12:20) is an emblem of a believer weak in grace. A reed was put into our Lord's hands in derision (Matt. 27:29); and "they took the reed and smote him on the head" (30). The "reed" on which they put the sponge filled with vinegar (Matt. 27:48) was, according to John (19:29), a hyssop stalk, which must have been of some length, or perhaps a bunch of hyssop twigs fastened to a rod with the sponge. (See CANE.)

Refin'er. The process of refining metals is referred to by way of illustration in Isa. 1:25; Jer. 6:29; Zech. 13:9; Mal. 3:2, 3.

Re'fuge, Cities of, were six in number (Num. 35). 1. On the west of Jordan were—(1) Kadesh, in Naphtali; (2) Shechem, in Mount Ephraim; (3) Hebron, in Judah. 2. On the east of Jordan were—(1) Golan, in Bashan; (2) Ramoth-Gilead, in Gad; and (3) Bezer, in Reuben. (See under each of these names.)

Re'gem-mel'ech—*friend of the king*—one of the two messengers sent by the exiled Jews to Jerusalem in the time of Darius (Zech. 7:2) to make inquiries at the temple.

Regenera'tion, only found in Matt. 19:28 and Titus 3:5. This word literally means a "new birth." The Greek word so rendered (*palingenesia*) is used by classical writers with reference to the changes produced by the return of spring. In Matt. 19:28 the word is equivalent to the "restitution of all things" (Acts 3:21). In Titus 3:5 it denotes that change of heart elsewhere spoken of as a passing from death to life (1 John 3:14); becoming a new creature in Christ Jesus (2 Cor. 5:17); being born again (John 3:5); a renewal of the mind (Rom. 12:2); a resurrection from the dead (Eph. 2:6); a being quickened (2:1, 5).

This change is *ascribed* to the Holy Spirit. It originates not with man but with God (John 1:12, 13; 1 John 2:29; 5:1, 4).

As to the *nature* of the change, it consists in the implanting of a new principle or disposition in the soul. When God created Adam, the disposition of his heart was created holy. Regeneration is the recreating of the governing disposition; the impartation of spiritual life to those who are by nature "dead in trespasses and sins."

The *necessity* of such a change is emphatically affirmed in Scripture (John 3:3; Rom. 7:18; 8:7-9; 1 Cor. 2:14; Eph. 2:1; 4:21-24).

It is distinguished from conversion, as the implantation of the gracious principle is different from its exercise. The former, regeneration, is the act of God; the latter, conversion, is the consequent act of man in his turning under the guidance of this new principle from sin to God through Jesus Christ. Conversion is the beginning of a holy living. The first and instant act of the regenerated man is faith in the person and work of Christ, and hence there is a change of *relation* to God, in that the believer is instantly justified. Sanctification is the progressive growth of the new spiritual life in the heart implanted in regeneration.

Rehabi'ah—*enlargement of the Lord*—the son of Eliezer, and grandson of Moses (1 Chr. 23:17; 24:21).

Re'hob—*street; broad place.* (1.) The father of Hadadezer, king of Tobah (2 Sam. 8:3, 12).

(2.) Neh. 10:11.

(3.) The same, probably, as Beth-rehob (2 Sam. 10:6, 8; Judg. 18:28), a place in the north of Palestine (Num. 13:21). It is now supposed to be represented by the castle of *Hûnin*, south-west of Dan, on the road from Hamath into Cœle-Syria.

(4.) A town of Asher (Josh. 19:28), to the east of Zidon.

(5.) Another town of Asher (Josh. 19:30), kept possession of by the Canaanites (Judg. 1:31).

Rehobo'am—*he enlarges the people*—the successor of Solomon on the throne, and apparently his only son. He was the son of Naamah "*the* Ammonitess," some well-known Ammonitish princess (1 Kings 14:21; 2 Chr. 12:13). He was forty-one years old when he ascended the throne, and he reigned seventeen years (B.C. 975–958). Although he was acknowledged at once as the rightful heir to the throne, yet there was a strongly felt desire to modify the character of the government. The burden of taxation to which they had been subjected during Solomon's reign was very oppressive, and therefore the people assembled at Shechem and demanded from the king an alleviation of their burdens. He went to meet them at Shechem, and heard their demands for relief (1 Kings 12:4). After three days, having consulted with a younger generation of courtiers that had grown up around him, instead of following the advice of the elders, he answered the people haughtily (9–11). "The king hearkened not unto the people; for the cause was from the Lord" (comp. 11:31). This brought matters speedily to a crisis. The terrible cry was heard (comp. 2 Sam. 20:1): "What portion have we in David?

Neither have we inheritance in the son of Jesse:

To your tents, O Israel:

Now see to thine own house, David" (1 Kings 12:16).

And now at once the kingdom was rent in twain. Rehoboam was appalled, and tried concessions, but it was too late (18). The tribe of Judah, Rehoboam's own tribe, alone remained faithful to him. Benjamin was reckoned along with Judah, and these two tribes formed the southern kingdom, with Jerusalem as its capital; while the northern ten tribes formed themselves into a separate kingdom, choosing Jeroboam as their king. Rehoboam tried to win back the revolted ten tribes by making war against them, but he was forbidden by the prophet Shemaiah (24; 2 Chr. 11:1–4) from carrying out his purpose. (See JERO-BOAM.)

In the fifth year of Rehoboam's reign, Shishak (*q.v.*), one of the kings of Egypt of the Assyrian dynasty, stirred up no doubt by Jeroboam his son-in-law, made war against him. Jerusalem submitted to the invader, who plundered the temple and virtually reduced the kingdom to the position of a vassal of Egypt (1 Kings 14:25, 26; 2 Chr. 12:8). A remarkable memorial of this invasion has been discovered at Karnac, in Upper Egypt, in certain sculptures on the walls of a small temple there. These sculptures represent the king, Shishak, holding in his hand a train of prisoners and other figures, with the names of the captured towns of Judah—the towns which Rehoboam had fortified (2 Chr. 11:5–12).

The kingdom of Judah, under Rehoboam, sank more and more in moral and spiritual decay. "There was war between Rehoboam and Jeroboam all their days." At length, in the fifty-eighth year of his age, Rehoboam "slept with his fathers, and was buried with his fathers in the city of David" (1 Kings 14:31). He was succeeded by his son Abijah. (See EGYPT.)

Reho'both—*broad places.* (1.) A well in Gerar dug by Isaac (Gen. 26:22), supposed to be in Wâdy er-Ruheibeh, about 20 miles south of Beersheba.

(2.) An ancient city on the Euphrates (Gen. 36:37; 1 Chr. 1:48), "Rehoboth by the river."

(3.) Named among the cities of Asshur (Gen. 10:11). Probably, however, the words "*rehôboth'ir*" are to be translated as in the Vulgate and the margin of A.V., "the streets of the city," or rather "the public square of the city"—*i.e.*, of Nineveh.

Re'hum—*merciful.* (1.) One of "the children of the province" who returned from the Captivity (Ezra 2:2); the same as "Nehum" (Neh. 7:7).

(2.) The "chancellor" of Artaxerxes, who sought to stir him up against the Jews (Ezra 4:8–24) and prevent the rebuilding of the walls and the temple of Jerusalem.

(3.) A Levite (Neh. 3:17).

(4.) Neh. 10:25.

(5.) A priest (Neh. 12:3).

Re'i—*friendly*—one who maintained true allegiance to king David (1 Kings 1:8) when Adonijah rebelled.

Reins, the kidneys, the supposed seat of the desires and affections; used metaphorically for "heart." The "reins" and the "heart" are often mentioned together, as denoting the whole moral constitution of man (Ps. 7:9; 16:7; 26:2; 139:13; Jer. 17:10, etc.).

Re'kem—*embroidered; variegated.* (1.) One of the five Midianite kings whom the Israelites destroyed (Num. 31:8).

(2.) One of the sons of Hebron (1 Chr. 2:43, 44).

(3.) A town of Benjamin (Josh. 18:27).

Remali'ah—*adorned by the Lord*—the father of Pekah, who conspired successfully against Pekahiah (2 Kings 15:25, 27, 30, 32, 37; Isa. 7:1, 4, 5, 9; 8:6).

Re'meth, another form of Ramah (*q.v.*) or Ramoth (1 Chr. 6:73; Josh. 19:21), and probably also of Jarmuth (Josh. 21:29).

Rem'mon-metho'ar (Josh. 19:13), rendered correctly in the Revised Version, "Remmon, which is stretched unto Neah," a landmark of Zebulun; called also Rimmon (1 Chr. 6:77).

Rem'phan (Acts 7:43; R.V., "Rephan"). In Amos 5:26 the Heb. *Chiun* (*q.v.*) is rendered by the LXX. "Rephan," and this name is adopted by Luke in his narrative of the Acts. These names represent the star-god Saturn or Moloch.

Rent (Isa. 3:24), probably a *rope*, as rendered in the LXX. and Vulgate and Revised Version, or as some prefer interpreting the phrase, "girdle and robe are torn [*i.e.*, are 'a rent'] by the hand of violence."

Repent'ance. There are three Greek words used in the New Testament to denote repentance. (1.) The verb *metamelomai* is used of a change of mind, such as to produce regret or even remorse on account of sin, but not necessarily a change of heart. This word is used with reference to the repentance of Judas (Matt. 27:3).

(2.) *Metanoeo*, meaning to change one's mind and purpose, as the result of after knowledge. This verb, with (3) the cognate noun *metanoia*, is used of true repentance—a change of mind and purpose and life, to which remission of sin is promised.

Evangelical repentance consists of (1) a true sense of one's own guilt and sinfulness; (2) an apprehension of God's mercy in Christ; (3) an actual hatred of sin (Ps. 119:128; Job 42:5, 6; 2 Cor. 7:10) and turning from it to God; and (4) a persistent endeavour after a holy life in a walking with God in the way of his commandments.

It differs from conversion in these particulars—(1.) Conversion is the more general term, including the first exercise of faith, as well as the various results which flow from it; while repentance is the more specific term, denoting that turning from sin to God which accompanies faith. (2.) Conversion further properly denotes only the first turning to God, the first actings of the new nature implanted in regeneration; while repentance is that constant hatred of sin and turning from it which characterizes the whole Christian life (Ps. 19:12, 13; Luke 9:23; Gal. 6:14).

The true penitent is conscious of guilt (Ps. 51:4, 9), of pollution (51:5, 7, 10), and of helplessness (51:11; 109:21, 22). Thus he apprehends himself to be just what God has always seen him to be and declares him to be. But repentance comprehends not only such a sense of sin, but also an apprehension of mercy, without which there can be no true repentance (Ps. 51:1; 130:4).

The *evidences* of genuine repentance are (1) such a sense of guilt and helplessness and sinfulness as leads to shame and self-loathing in the presence of God; (2) humble confession of sin (Ps. 32:5, 6; Prov. 28: 13; James 5:16; 1 John 1:9); and (3) an earnest and constant desire to be delivered from it—a hating and forsaking of all sin, secret as well as open. "True repentance is not only *from* sin, but *for* sin." The true penitent is self-convicted and self-condemned. He acquiesces in the truth of every charge the law of God brings against him. He renounces every personal ground of acceptance in the sight of God, and looks for forgiveness only "for Christ's sake." Repentance is *necessary*, in that none who are impenitent are pardoned. But it is not to be rested in as in any sense the cause of pardon. It is necessary, as the natural result of regeneration and the fruit of faith. Like faith, it is a duty as well as a grace (Luke 24:47; Acts 20:21).

Re'phael—*healed of God*—one of Shemaiah's sons. He and his brethren, on account of their "strength for service," formed one of the divisions of the temple porters (1 Chr. 26:7, 8).

Repha'im—*lofty men; giants*—(Gen. 14:5; 2 Sam. 21:16, 18; Deut. 3:13, R.V.). The aborigines of Palestine, afterwards conquered and dispossessed by the Canaanite tribes, are classed under this general title. They were known to the Moabites as Emim—*i.e.,* "fearful"—(Deut. 2:11), and to the Ammonites as Zamzummim. Some of them found refuge among the Philistines, and were still existing in the days of David (2 Sam. 21: 16, "sons of the giant," A.V.; but R.V., "sons of Rephah"). We know nothing of their origin. They were not necessarily connected with the "giants" (R.V., "Nephilim") of Gen. 6:4. (See GIANTS.)

Repha'im, Valley of (Josh. 15:8; 18:16, R.V.). When David became king over all Israel, the Philistines, judging that he would now become their uncompromising enemy, made a sudden attack upon Hebron, compelling David to retire from it. He sought refuge in "the hold" at Adullam (2 Sam. 5:17-22), and the Philistines took up their position in the valley of Rephaim, on the west and south-west of Jerusalem. Thus all communication between Bethlehem and Jerusalem was intercepted. While David and his army were encamped here there occurred that incident narrated in 2 Sam. 23:15-17. Having obtained divine direction, David led his army against the Philistines, and gained a complete victory over them. The scene of this victory was afterwards called Baal-perazim (*q.v.*).

A second time, however, the Philistines rallied their forces in this valley (2 Sam. 5:22). Again warned by a divine oracle, David led his army to Gibeon, and attacked the Philistines from the south, inflicting on them another severe defeat, and chasing them with great slaughter to Gezer (*q.v.*). There David kept in check these enemies of Israel. This valley is now called *el-Bukei'a*.

Reph'idim—*supports*—one of the stations of the Israelites, situated in the Wâdy Feirân, near its junction with the Wâdy esh-Sheikh. Here no water could be found for the people to drink, and in their impatience they were ready to stone Moses, as if he were the cause of their distress. At the command of God Moses smote "the rock in Horeb," and a copious stream flowed forth, enough for all the people. After this the Amalekites attacked the Israelites while they were here encamped, but they were utterly defeated (Ex. 17:1, 8-16). They were the "first of the nations" to make war against Israel (Num. 24:20).

Leaving Rephidim, the Israelites advanced into the wilderness of Sinai (Ex. 19:1, 2; Num. 33:14-16), marching probably through the two passes of the Wâdy Solaf and the Wâdy esh-Sheikh, which converge at the entrance to the plain er-Rahah, the "desert of Sinai," which is two miles long and about half a mile broad. (See SINAI; MERIBAH.)

Re'probate, that which is rejected on account of its own worthlessness (Jer. 6: 30; Heb. 6:8; Gr. *adokimos*, "rejected"). This word is also used with reference to persons cast away or rejected because they have failed to make use of opportunities offered them (1 Cor. 9:27; 2 Cor. 13: 5-7).

Rere'ward (Josh. 6:9), the troops in the rear of an army on the march—the rear-guard. This word is a corruption of the French *arrière-garde*. During the wilderness march the tribe of Dan formed the rear-guard (Num. 10:25; comp. 1 Sam. 29:2; Isa. 52:12; 58:8).

Re'sen—*head of the stream; bridle*—one of Nimrod's cities (Gen. 10:12), "between Nineveh and Calah." It has been supposed that the four cities named in this verse were afterwards combined into one under the name of Nineveh (*q.v.*). Resen was on the east side of the Tigris. It is probably identified with the mound of ruins called *Karamless*.

Rest. (1.) Gr. *katapausis*, equivalent to the Hebrew word *noaḥ* (Heb. 4:1).

(2.) Gr. *anapausis*, "rest from weariness" (Matt. 11:28).

(3.) Gr. *anĕsis*, "relaxation" (2 Thess. 1:7).

(4.) Gr. *sabbatismos*, a Sabbath rest, a rest from all work (Heb. 4:9; R. v., "sabbath"), a rest like that of God when he had finished the work of creation.

Resurrec'tion of Christ, one of the cardinal facts and doctrines of the gospel. If Christ be not risen, our faith is vain (1 Cor. 15:14). The whole of the New Testament revelation rests on this as an historical fact. On the day of Pentecost Peter argued the necessity of Christ's resurrection from the prediction in Ps. 16 (Acts 2:22-36). In his own discourses, also, our Lord clearly intimates his resurrection (Matt. 20:19; Mark 9:9; 14:28; Luke 18:33; John 2:19-22).

The evangelists give circumstantial accounts of the facts connected with that event, and the apostles, also, in their public teaching largely insist upon it.

Ten different appearances of our risen Lord are recorded in the New Testament. They may be arranged as follows:—

(1.) To Mary Magdalene at the sepulchre alone. This is recorded at length only by John (20:11-18), and alluded to by Mark (16:9-11).

(2.) To certain women, "the other Mary," Salome, Joanna, and others, as they returned from the sepulchre. Mat-thew (28:1-10) alone gives an account of this. (Comp. Mark 16:1-8, and Luke 24:1-11.)

(3.) To Simon Peter alone on the day of the resurrection. (See Luke 24:34; 1 Cor. 15:5.)

(4.) To the two disciples on the way to Emmaus on the day of the resurrection, recorded fully only by Luke (24:13-35. Comp. Mark 16:12, 13).

(5.) To the ten disciples (Thomas being absent) and others "with them," at Jerusalem on the evening of the resurrection day. Three of the evangelists give an account of this appearance — Mark (16:14-18), Luke (24:36-40), John (20:19-23). (See also 1 Cor. 15:5.)

(6.) To the disciples again (Thomas being present) at Jerusalem. Of this appearance John alone (20:26-28) gives an account.

(7.) To the disciples when fishing at the Sea of Galilee. Of this appearance also John (21:1-23) alone gives an account.

(8.) To the eleven, and above 500 brethren at once, at an appointed place in Galilee (1 Cor. 15:6; comp. Matt. 28:16-20).

(9.) To James, but under what circumstances we are not informed (1 Cor. 15:7).

(10.) To the apostles immediately before the ascension. They accompanied him from Jerusalem to Mount Olivet, and there they saw him ascend "till a cloud received him out of their sight" (Mark 16:19; Luke 24:50-52; Acts 1:3-8).

It is worthy of note that it is distinctly related that on most of these occasions our Lord afforded his disciples the amplest opportunity of testing the fact of his resurrection. He conversed with them face to face. They touched him (Matt. 28:9; Luke 24:39; John 20:27), and he ate bread with them (Luke 24:42, 43; John 21:12, 13).

(11.) In addition to the above, mention might be made of Christ's manifestation of himself to Paul at Damascus, who speaks of it as an appearance of the risen Saviour (Acts 9:3-9, 17; 1 Cor. 15:8; 9:1).

It is implied in the words of Luke (Acts 1:3) that there may have been other appearances of which we have no record.

The resurrection is spoken of as the act

(1) of God the Father (Ps. 16 : 10; Acts 2 : 24; 3 : 15; Rom. 8 : 11; Eph. 1 : 20; Col. 2 : 12; Heb. 13 : 20); (2) of Christ himself (John 2 : 19; 10 : 18); and (3) of the Holy Spirit (1 Peter 3 : 18).

The resurrection is a public testimony of Christ's release from his undertaking as surety, and an evidence of the Father's acceptance of his work of redemption. It is a victory over death and the grave for all his followers.

The *importance* of Christ's resurrection will be seen when we consider that if he rose the gospel is true, and if he rose not it is false. His resurrection from the dead makes it manifest that his sacrifice was accepted. Our justification was secured by his obedience to the death, and *therefore* he was raised from the dead (Rom. 4 : 25). His resurrection is a proof that he made a full atonement for our sins, that his sacrifice was accepted as a satisfaction to divine justice, and his blood a ransom for sinners. It is also a pledge and an earnest of the resurrection of all believers (Rom. 8 : 11; 1 Cor. 6 : 14, 15; 15 : 49; Phil. 3 : 21; 1 John 3 : 2). As he lives, they shall live also.

It proved him to be the Son of God, inasmuch as it authenticated all his claims (John 2 : 19; 10 : 17). "If Christ did not rise, the whole scheme of redemption is a failure, and all the predictions and anticipations of its glorious results for time and for eternity, for men and for angels of every rank and order, are proved to be chimeras. 'But now is Christ risen from the dead, and become the first-fruits of them that slept.' Therefore the Bible is true from Genesis to Revelation. The kingdom of darkness has been overthrown, Satan has fallen as lightning from heaven, and the triumph of truth over error, of good over evil, of happiness over misery is for ever secured."—Hodge.

With reference to the report which the Roman soldiers were bribed (Matt. 28 : 12–14) to circulate concerning Christ's resurrection, "his disciples came by night and stole him away while we slept," Matthew Henry in his "Commentary," under John 20 : 1-10, fittingly remarks,

"The grave-clothes in which Christ had been buried were found in very good order, which serves for an evidence that his body was not 'stolen away while men slept.' Robbers of tombs have been known to take away 'the clothes' and leave the body; but none ever took away 'the body' and left the clothes, especially when they were 'fine linen' and new (Mark 15 : 46). Any one would rather choose to carry a dead body in its clothes than naked. Or if they that were supposed to have stolen it would have left the grave-clothes behind, yet it cannot be supposed they would find leisure to 'fold up the linen.'"

Resurrec'tion of the dead will be simultaneous both of the just and the unjust (Dan. 12 : 2; John 5 : 28, 29; Rom. 2 : 6–16; 2 Thess. 1 : 6-10). The qualities of the resurrection body will be different from those of the body laid in the grave (1 Cor. 15 : 53, 54; Phil. 3 : 21); but its identity will nevertheless be preserved. It will still be the same body (1 Cor. 15 : 42–44) which rises again.

As to the *nature* of the resurrection body, (1) it will be spiritual (1 Cor. 15 : 44)—*i.e.*, a body adapted to the use of the soul in its glorified state, and to all the conditions of the heavenly state; (2) glorious, incorruptible, and powerful (54); (3) like unto the glorified body of Christ (Phil. 3 : 21); and (4) immortal (Rev. 21 : 4).

Christ's resurrection secures and illustrates that of his people. "(1.) Because his resurrection seals and consummates his redemptive power; and the redemption of our persons involves the redemption of our bodies (Rom. 8 : 23). (2.) Because of our federal and vital union with Christ (1 Cor. 15 : 21, 22; 1 Thess. 4 : 14). (3.) Because of his Spirit which dwells in us making our bodies his members (1 Cor. 6 : 15; Rom. 8 : 11). (4.) Because Christ by covenant is Lord both of the living and the dead (Rom. 14 : 9). This same federal and vital union of the Christian with Christ likewise causes the resurrection of the believer to be similar to as well as consequent upon that of Christ (1 Cor. 15 : 49; Phil. 3 : 21; 1 John 3 : 2)."—Hodge's *Outlines of Theology*.

Reu'ben—*behold a son!*—the eldest son of Jacob and Leah (Gen. 29:32). His sinful conduct, referred to in Gen. 35:22, brought down upon him his dying father's malediction (49:4). He showed kindness to Joseph, and was the means of saving his life when his other brothers would have put him to death (37:21, 22). It was he also who pledged his life and the life of his sons when Jacob was unwilling to let Benjamin go down into Egypt. After Jacob and his family went down into Egypt (46:8) no further mention is made of Reuben beyond what is recorded in ch. 49:3, 4.

Reu'ben, Tribe of, at the Exodus numbered 46,500 male adults, from twenty years old and upwards (Num. 1:20, 21), and at the close of the wilderness wanderings they numbered only 43,730 (26:7). This tribe united with that of Gad in asking permission to settle in the "land of Gilead," "on the other side of Jordan" (32:1-5). The lot assigned to Reuben was the smallest of the lots given to the trans-Jordanic tribes. It extended from the Arnon, in the south, along the coast of the Dead Sea to its northern end, where the Jordan flows into it (Josh. 13:15-21, 23). It thus embraced the original kingdom of Sihon. Reuben is "to the eastern tribes what Simeon is to the western. 'Unstable as water,' he vanishes away into a mere Arabian tribe. 'His men are few;' it is all he can do 'to live and not die.' We hear of nothing beyond the multiplication of their cattle in the land of Gilead, their spoils of 'camels fifty thousand, and of asses two thousand' (1 Chr. 5:9, 10, 20, 21). In the great struggles of the nation he never took part. The complaint against him in the song of Deborah is the summary of his whole history. 'By the streams of Reuben'—*i.e.*, by the fresh streams which descend from the eastern hills into the Jordan and the Dead Sea, on whose banks the Bedouin chiefs met then as now to debate—in the 'streams' of Reuben great were the 'desires'"—*i.e.*, resolutions which were never carried out, the people idly resting among their flocks as if it were a time of peace (Judg. 5:15, 16). — Stanley's *Sinai and Palestine.*

All the three tribes on the east of Jordan at length fell into complete apostasy, and the time of retribution came. God "stirred up the spirit of Pul, king of Assyria, and the spirit of Tiglath-pileser, king of Assyria," to carry them away — the first of the tribes—into captivity (1 Chr. 5:25, 26).

Reu'el—*friend of God.* (1.) A son of Esau and Bashemath (Gen. 36:4, 10; 1 Chr. 1:35). (2.) "The priest of Midian," Moses' father-in-law (Ex. 2:18)=Raguel (Num. 10:29). If he be identified with Jethro (*q.v.*), then this may be regarded as his proper name, and Jether or Jethro (*i.e.*, "excellency") as his official title. (3.) Num. 2:14, called also Deuel (1:14; 7:42).

Revela'tion, an uncovering, a bringing to light of that which had been previously wholly hidden or only obscurely seen. God has been pleased in various ways and at different times (Heb. 1:1) to make a supernatural revelation of himself and his purposes and plans, which, under the guidance of his Spirit, has been committed to writing. (See WORD OF GOD.) The Scriptures are not merely the "record" of revelation; they are the revelation itself in a written form, in order to the accurate preservation and propagation of the truth.

Revelation and inspiration differ. Revelation is the supernatural communication of truth to the mind; inspiration (*q.v.*) secures to the teacher or writer infallibility in communicating that truth to others. It renders its subject the spokesman or prophet of God in such a sense that everything he asserts to be true, whether fact or doctrine or moral principle, is true—infallibly true.

Revela'tion, Book of = **The Apocalypse,** the closing book and the only prophetical book of the New Testament canon.

The *author* of this book was undoubtedly John the apostle. His name occurs four times in the book itself (1:1, 4, 9; 22:8), and there is every reason to conclude that the "John" here mentioned was the apostle. In a manuscript of about the twelfth century he is called "John the divine," but no reason can be assigned for this appellation.

The *date* of the writing of this book has generally been fixed at A.D. 96, in the reign of Domitian. There are some, however, who contend for an earlier date, A.D. 68 or 69, in the reign of Nero. Those who are in favour of the later date appeal to the testimony of the Christian father Irenæus, who received information relative to this book from those who had seen John face to face. He says that the Apocalypse "was seen no long time ago."

As to the relation between this book and the Gospel of John, it has been well observed that "the leading ideas of both are the same. The one gives us in a magnificent vision, the other in a great historic drama, the supreme conflict between good and evil and its issue. In both Jesus Christ is the central figure, whose victory through defeat is the issue of the conflict. In both the Jewish dispensation is the preparation for the gospel, and the warfare and triumph of the Christ is described in language saturated with the Old Testament... The difference of date will go a long way toward explaining the difference of style." —Plummer's *Gospel of St. John, Introd.*

Revela'tion of Christ, the second advent of Christ. Three different Greek words are used by the apostles to express this—(1) *apokalupsis* (1 Cor. 1:7; 2 Thess. 1:7; 1 Pet. 1:7, 13); (2) *parousia* (Matt. 24:3, 27; 1 Thess. 2:19; James 5:7, 8); (3) *epiphaneia* (1 Tim. 6:14; 2 Tim. 1:10; 4:1-8; Titus 2:13). There existed among Christians a wide expectation, founded on Matt. 24:29, 30, 34, of the speedy return of Christ. (See MILLENNIUM.)

Re'zeph—*solid; a stone*—(2 Kings 19:12; Isa. 37:12), a fortress near Haran, probably on the west of the Euphrates, conquered by Sennacherib.

Re'zin—*firm; a prince*—a king of Syria, who joined Pekah (*q.v.*) in an invasion of the kingdom of Judah (2 Kings 15:37; 16:5-9; Isa. 7:1-8). Ahaz induced Tiglath-pileser III. to attack Damascus, and this caused Rezin to withdraw for the purpose of defending his own kingdom. Damascus was taken, and Rezin was slain in battle by the Assyrian king, and his people carried into captivity, B.C. 732 (2 Kings 16:9).

Re'zon—*prince*—son of Eliadah. Abandoning the service of Hadadezer, the king of Zobah, on the occasion of his being defeated by David, he became the "captain over a band" of marauders, and took Damascus, and became king of Syria (1 Kings 11:23-25; 2 Sam. 8:3-8). For centuries after this the Syrians were the foes of Israel. He "became an adversary to Israel all the days of Solomon."

Rhe'gium—*breach*—a town in the south of Italy, on the Strait of Messina, at which Paul touched on his way to Rome (Acts 28:13). It is now called *Rheggio*.

Rhe'sa—*affection*—son of Zorobabel, mentioned in the genealogy of our Lord (Luke 3:27).

Rho'da—*a rose*—the damsel in the house of Mary, the mother of John Mark. She came to hearken when Peter knocked at the door of the gate (Acts 12:12-15).

Rhodes—*a rose*—an island to the south of the western extremity of Asia Minor, between Coos and Patara, about 46 miles long and 18 miles broad. Here the apostle probably landed on his way from Greece to Syria (Acts 21:1), on returning from his third missionary journey.

Rib'lah—*fruitful*—an ancient town on the northern frontier of Palestine, 35 miles north-east of Baalbec, and 10 or 12 south of Lake Homs, on the eastern bank of the Orontes, in a wide and fertile plain. Here Nebuchadnezzar had his head-quarters in his campaign against Jerusalem, and here also Necho fixed his camp after he had routed Josiah's army at Megiddo (2 Kings 23:29-35; 25:6, 20, 21; Jer. 39:5; 52:10). It was on the great caravan road from Palestine to Carchemish, on the Euphrates. It is described (Num. 34:11) as "on the eastern side of Ain." A place still called *el-Ain*—i.e., "the fountain"—is found in such a position about 10 miles distant. (See JERUSALEM.)

Rid'dle (Heb. *ḥodah*). The oldest and, strictly speaking, the only example of a riddle was that propounded by Samson (Judg. 14:12-18). The parabolic prophecy in Ezek. 17:2-18 is there called a "riddle." It was rather, however, an allegory. The word "darkly" in 1 Cor. 13:12 is the rendering of the Greek *enigma*; marg., "in a riddle."

Right'eousness. See JUSTIFICATION.

Rim'mon—*pomegranate.* (1.) A man of Beeroth (2 Sam. 4 : 2), one of the four Gibeonite cities. (See Josh. 9 : 17.)

(2.) A Syrian idol, mentioned only in 2 Kings 5 : 18.

(3.) One of the "uttermost cities" of Judah, afterwards given to Simeon (Josh. 15 : 21, 32 ; 19 : 7 ; 1 Chr. 4 : 32). In Josh. 15 : 32 Ain and Rimmon are mentioned separately, but in 19 : 7 and 1 Chr. 4 : 32 (comp. Neh. 11 : 29) the two words are probably to be combined, as forming together the name of one place, Ain-Rimmon=*the spring of the pomegranate.* It has been identified with *Um er-Rûmâmin*, about 13 miles south-west of Hebron.

(4.) "Rock of," to which the Benjamites fled (Judg. 20 : 45, 47 ; 21 : 13), and where they maintained themselves for four months after the fearful battle at Gibeah, in which they were almost exterminated, 600 only surviving out of about 27,000. It is the present village of *Rümmôn*, "on the very edge of the hill country, with a precipitous descent toward the Jordan valley," supposed to be the site of Ai.

Rim'mon-pa'rez—*a pomegranate breach,* or *Rimmon of the breach*—one of the stations of the Israelites in the wilderness (Num. 33 : 19, 20).

Ring. Used as an ornament to decorate the fingers, arms, wrists, and also the ears and the nose. Rings were used as a signet (Gen. 38 : 18). They were given as a token of investment with authority (Gen. 41 : 42 ; Esther 3 : 8–10 ; 8 : 2), and of favour and dignity (Luke 15 : 22). They were generally worn by rich men (James 2 : 2). They are mentioned by Isaiah (3 : 21) among the adornments of Hebrew women.

Ri'phath—*a crusher*—Gomer's second son (Gen. 10 : 3), supposed to have been the ancestor of the Paphlagonians.

Ris'sah—*heap of ruins ; dew*—a station of the Israelites in the wilderness (Num. 33 : 21, 22).

Rith'mah—*wild broom*—a station in the wilderness (Num. 33 : 18, 19), the "broom valley," or "valley of broom-bushes," the place apparently of the original encampment of Israel, near Kadesh.

Riv'er. (1.) Heb. *'aphîk,* properly the channel or ravine that holds water (2 Sam. 22 : 16), translated "brook," "river," "stream," but not necessarily a perennial stream (Ezek. 6 : 3 ; 31 : 12 ; 32 : 6 ; 34 : 13).

(2.) Heb. *nâhal,* in winter a "torrent," in summer a "wâdy " or valley (Gen. 32 : 23 ; Deut. 2 : 24 ; 3 : 16 ; Isa. 30 : 28 ; Lam. 2 : 18 ; Ezek. 47 : 9).

These winter torrents sometimes come down with great suddenness and with desolating force. A distinguished traveller thus describes his experience in this matter : — "I was encamped in Wâdy Feiran, near the base of Jebel Serbal, when a tremendous thunderstorm burst upon us. After little more than an hour's rain, the water rose so rapidly in the previously dry wâdy that I had to run for my life, and with great difficulty succeeded in saving my tent and goods ; my boots, which I had not time to pick up, were washed away. In less than two hours a dry desert wâdy upwards of 300 yards broad was turned into a foaming torrent from 8 to 10 feet deep, roaring and tearing down and bearing everything upon it—tangled masses of tamarisks, hundreds of beautiful palm-trees, scores of sheep and goats, camels and donkeys, and even men, women, and children, for a whole encampment of Arabs was washed away a few miles above me. The storm commenced at five in the evening ; at half-past nine the waters were rapidly subsiding, and it was evident that the flood had spent its force." (Comp. Matt. 7 : 26 ; Luke 6 : 49.)

(3.) *Nâhâr,* a "river" continuous and full, a perennial stream, as the Jordan, the Euphrates (Gen. 2 : 10 ; 15 : 18 ; Deut. 1 : 7 ; Ps. 66 : 6 ; Ezek. 10 : 15).

(4.) *Têl'âlâh,* a conduit, or water-course (1 Kings 18 : 32 ; 2 Kings 18 : 17 ; 20 : 20 ; Job 38 : 25 ; Ezek. 31 : 4).

(5.) *Peleg,* properly "waters divided"—*i.e.,* streams divided—throughout the land (Ps. 1 : 3) ; "the rivers [*i.e.,* 'divisions'] of waters" (Job 20 : 17 ; 29 : 6 ; Prov. 5 : 16).

(6.) *Ye'or*—*i.e.,* "great river"—probably from an Egyptian word (*Aur*), commonly applied to the Nile (Gen. 41 : 1–3), but also to other rivers (Job 28 : 10 ; Isa. 33 : 21).

(7.) *Yubhal*, "a river" (Jer. 17 : 8), a full flowing stream.

(8.) *'Ubhal*, "a river" (Dan. 8 : 2).

River of E'gypt. (1.) Heb. *nâhâr mitsraim*, denotes in Gen. 15 : 18 the Nile, or its eastern branch (2 Chr. 9 : 26). (2.) In Num. 34:5 (R.V., "brook of Egypt") the Hebrew word is *nahal*, denoting a stream flowing rapidly in winter, or in the rainy season. This is a desert stream on the borders of Egypt. It is now called the *Wâdy el-'Arîsh*. The present boundary between Egypt and Palestine is about midway between this *wâdy* and Gaza. (See Num. 34:5; Josh. 15: 4, 47 ; 1 Kings 8 :65; 2 Kings 24:7 ; Isa. 27 : 12 ; Ezek. 47 : 19. In all these passages the R.V. has "brook" and the A.V. "river.")

River of Gad, probably the Arno (2 Sam. 24 : 5).

River of God (Ps. 65 : 9), as opposed to earthly streams, denoting that the divine resources are inexhaustible, or the sum of all fertilizing streams that water the earth (Gen. 2 : 10).

Rivers of Bab'ylon (Ps. 137 : 1), *i.e.*, of the whole country of Babylonia—*e.g.*, the Tigris, Euphrates, Chalonas, the Ulai, and the numerous canals.

Rivers of Damas'cus, the Abana and Pharpar (2 Kings 5 : 12).

Rivers of Ju'dah (Joel 3 :18), the watercourses of Judea.

Riz'pah—*coal; hot stone*—the daughter of Aiah, and one of Saul's concubines. She was the mother of Armoni and Mephibosheth (2 Sam. 3 : 7 ; 21 : 8, 10, 11).

It happened that a grievous famine, which lasted for three years, fell upon the land during the earlier half of David's reign at Jerusalem. This calamity was sent "for Saul and for his bloody house, because he slew the Gibeonites." David inquired of the Gibeonites what satisfaction they demanded, and was answered that nothing would compensate for the wrong Saul had done to them but the death of seven of Saul's sons. David accordingly delivered up to them the two sons of Rizpah and five of the sons of Merab (*q.v.*), Saul's eldest daughter, whom she bore to Adriel. These the Gibeonites put to death, and hung up their bodies before the Lord at the sanctuary at Gibeah. Rizpah thereupon took her place on the rock of Gibeah (*q.v.*), and for five months watched the suspended bodies of her children, to prevent them from being devoured by the beasts and birds of prey, till they were at length taken down and buried by David.

Her marriage to Abner was the occasion of a quarrel between him and Ishbosheth, which led to Abner's going over to the side of David (2 Sam. 3 : 17–21).

Road (1 Sam. 27 : 10; R.V., "raid"), an inroad, an incursion. This word is never used in Scripture in the sense of a way or path.

Rob'bery. Practised by the Ishmaelites (Gen. 16 : 12), the Chaldeans and Sabeans (Job 1 : 15, 17), and the men of Shechem (Judg. 9 : 25. See also 1 Sam. 27 : 6–10; 30 ; Hos. 4 : 2 ; 6 : 9). Robbers infested Judea in our Lord's time (Luke 10 : 30 ; John 18 : 40 ; Acts 5 : 36, 37 ; 21 : 38 ; 2 Cor. 11 : 26). The words of the Authorized Version, "counted it not robbery to be equal," etc. (Phil. 2 : 6, 7), are better rendered in the Revised Version, "counted it not a prize to be on an equality," etc.—*i.e.*, "did not look upon equality with God as a prize which must not slip from his grasp" = "did not cling with avidity to the prerogatives of his divine majesty ; did not ambitiously display his equality with God."

"Robbers of churches" should be rendered, as in the Revised Version, "of temples." In the temple at Ephesus there was a great treasure-chamber, and as all that was laid up there was under the guardianship of the goddess Diana, to steal from such a place would be sacrilege (Acts 19 : 37).

Rock (Heb. *tsûr*), employed as a symbol of God in the Old Testament (1 Sam. 2 : 2 ; 2 Sam. 22 : 3 ; Isa. 17 : 10 ; Ps. 28 : 1 ; 31 : 2, 3 ; 89 : 26 ; 95 : 1) ; also in the New Testament (Matt. 16 : 18 ; Rom. 9 : 33 ; 1 Cor. 10 : 4). In Dan. 2 : 45 the Chaldaic form of the Hebrew word is translated "mountain." It ought to be translated "rock," as in the margin of the Revised Version. The "rock" from which the stone is cut there signifies the divine origin of Christ. (See STONE.)

Roe (Heb. *tsĕbi*), properly the gazelle (Arab. *ghâzal*), permitted for food (Deut. 14:5; comp. Deut. 12:15, 22; 15:22; 1 Kings 4:23), noted for its swiftness and beauty and grace of form (2 Sam. 2:18; 1 Chr. 12:8; Cant. 2:9; 7:3; 8:14).

The gazelle (*Gazella dorcas*) is found in great numbers in Palestine. "Among the gray hills of Galilee it is still 'the roe upon the mountains of Bether,' and I have seen a little troop of gazelles feeding on the Mount of Olives close to Jerusalem itself" (Tristram).

The Hebrew word (*'ayyâlâh*) in Prov. 5:19 thus rendered (R.V., "doe"), is properly the "wild she-goat," the mountain goat, the ibex. (See 1 Sam 24:3; Ps. 104:18; Job 39:3.)

Roge'lim—*fullers*—a town of Gilead, the residence of Barzillai the Gileadite (2 Sam. 17:27; 19:31), probably near to Mahanaim.

Roll, the common form of ancient books. The Hebrew word rendered "roll" or "volume" is *mĕghîllah*, found in Ezra 6:2; Ps. 40:7; Jer. 36:2, 6, 23, 28, 29; Ezek. 2:9; 3:1-3; Zech. 5:1, 2. "Rolls"

GAZELLES.

(Chald. pl. of *sĕphar*, corresponding to Heb. *sĕpher*) in Ezra 6:1 is rendered in the Revised Version "archives."

In the New Testament the word "volume" (Heb. 10:7; R.V., "roll") occurs as the rendering of the Greek *kephalis*, meaning the head or top of the stick or cylinder on which the manuscript was rolled, and hence the manuscript itself. (See BOOK.)

Ro'mamti-e'zer—*elevation of help*—one of the sons of Heman, "the king's seer in the words of God, to lift up the horn." He was head of the "four-and-twentieth" course of singers (1 Chr. 25:4, 31).

Ro'mans, Epistle to the. This epistle was probably written at Corinth. Phœbe

(Rom. 16:1) of Cenchrea conveyed it to Rome, and Gaius of Corinth entertained the apostle at the time of his writing it (16:23; 1 Cor. 1:14), and Erastus was chamberlain of the city—*i.e.*, of Corinth (2 Tim. 4:20).

The precise *time* at which it was written is not mentioned in the epistle, but it was obviously written when the apostle was about to "go unto Jerusalem to minister unto the saints"—*i.e.*, at the close of his second visit to Greece, during the winter preceding his last visit to that city (Rom. 15:25; comp. Acts 19:21; 20:2, 3, 16; 1 Cor. 16:1-4), early in A.D. 58.

It is highly probable that Christianity

was planted in Rome by some of those who had been at Jerusalem on the day of Pentecost (Acts 2 : 11). At this time the Jews were very numerous in Rome, and their synagogues were probably resorted to by Romans also, who in this way became acquainted with the great facts regarding Jesus as these were reported among the Jews. Thus a church composed of both Jews and Gentiles was formed at Rome. Many of the brethren went out to meet Paul on his approach to Rome. There are evidences that Christians were then in Rome in considerable numbers, and had probably more than one place of meeting (Rom. 16 : 14, 15).

The *object* of the apostle in writing to this church was to explain to them the great doctrines of the gospel. His epistle was a "word in season." Himself deeply impressed with a sense of the value of the doctrines of salvation, he opens up in a clear and connected form the whole system of the gospel in its relation both to Jew and Gentile. This epistle is peculiar in this, that it is a systematic exposition of the gospel of universal application. The subject is here treated argumentatively, and is a plea for Gentiles addressed to Jews. In the Epistle to the Galatians, the same subject is discussed, but there the apostle pleads his own authority, because the church in Galatia had been founded by him.

After the introduction (1 : 1–15), the apostle presents in its divers aspects and relations the doctrine of justification by faith (1 : 16–11 : 36) on the ground of the imputed righteousness of Christ. He shows that salvation is all of grace, and only of grace. This main section of his letter is followed by various practical exhortations (12 : 1–15 : 13), which are followed by a conclusion containing personal explanations and salutations, which contain the names of twenty-four Christians at Rome, a benediction, and a doxology (Rom. 15 : 14–ch. 16).

Rome, the most celebrated city in the world at the time of Christ. It is said to have been founded B.C. 753. When the New Testament was written, Rome was enriched and adorned with the spoils of the world, and contained a population estimated

INSCRIPTIONS FROM THE CATACOMBS (ROME).

at 1,200,000, of which the half were slaves. It was distinguished for its wealth and luxury and profligacy. The empire of which it was the capital had then reached its greatest prosperity. (See Map facing page 534.)

On the day of Pentecost there were in Jerusalem "strangers from Rome," who doubtless carried with them back to Rome tidings of that great day, and were instrumental in founding the church there. Paul was brought to this city a prisoner, where he remained for two years (Acts 28 : 30, 31) "in his own hired house." While here, Paul wrote his epistles to the Philippians, to the Ephesians, to the Colossians, to Philemon, and probably also to the Hebrews. He had during these years for companions Luke and Aristarchus (Acts 27 : 2), Timothy (Phil. 1 : 1; Col. 1 : 1), Tychicus (Eph. 6 : 21), Epaphroditus (Phil. 4 : 18), and John Mark (Col. 4 : 10). (See PAUL.)

Beneath this city are extensive galleries, called "catacombs," which were used from about the time of the apostles (one of the inscriptions found in them bears the date A.D. 71) for some three hundred years as places of refuge in the time of persecution, and also of worship and burial. About four thousand inscriptions have been found in the catacombs. These give an interesting insight into the history of the church at Rome down to the time of Constantine.

Rose. Many varieties of the rose proper are indigenous to Syria. The famed rose of Damascus is white, but there are also red and yellow roses. In Cant. 2 : 1 and Isa. 35 : 1 the Hebrew word *ḥabatstsĕleth* (found only in these passages), rendered "rose" (R.V. marg., "autumn crocus"), is supposed by some to mean the oleander, by others the sweet-scented narcissus (a native of Palestine), the tulip, or the daisy; but nothing definite can be affirmed regarding it.

The "rose of Sharon" is probably the cistus or rock-rose, several species of which abound in Palestine. "Mount Carmel especially abounds in the cistus, which in April covers some of the barer parts of the mountain with a glow not inferior to that of the Scottish heather." (See MYRRH [2].)

Rosh (Ezek. 38 : 2, 3; 39 : 1) is rendered "chief" in the Authorized Version. It is left untranslated as a proper name in the Revised Version. Some have supposed that the Russians are here meant, as one of the three Scythian tribes of whom Magog was the prince. They invaded the land of Judah in the days of Josiah. Herodotus, the Greek historian, says: "For twenty-eight years the Scythians ruled over Asia, and things were turned upside down by their violence and contempt." (See BETHSHEAN.)

Ros'in, found only in Authorized Version, margin, Ezek. 27 : 17—Heb. *tsorî*, uniformly rendered elsewhere "balm" (*q.v.*), as here in the text. The Vulgate has *resinam*, rendered "rosin" in the Douay Version. As used, however, by Jerome, the Lat. *resina* denotes some odoriferous gum or oil.

Ru'by (Heb. *pĕnînîm*), only in plural (Lam. 4 : 7). The ruby was one of the stones in the high priest's breastplate (Ex. 28 : 17). A comparison is made between the value of wisdom and rubies (Job 28 : 18; Prov. 3 : 15; 8 : 11). The price of a virtuous woman is said to be "far above rubies" (Prov. 31 : 10).

The exact meaning of the Hebrew word is uncertain. Some render it "red coral;" others, "pearl" or "mother-of-pearl."

Rud'der bands. Ancient ships had two great broad-bladed oars for rudders. These, when not in use, were lifted out of the water and bound or tied up. When required for use, these bands were unloosed and the rudders allowed to drop into the water (Acts 27 : 40).

Rue, a garden herb (*Ruta graveolens*) which the Pharisees were careful to tithe

RUE (RUTA GRAVEOLENS).

(Luke 11 : 42), neglecting weightier matters. It is omitted in the parallel passage of

Matt. 23 : 23. There are several species growing wild in Palestine. It is used for medicinal and culinary purposes. It has a powerful scent, and is a stimulant. (See MINT.)

Ru'fus—*red*—the son of Simon the Cyrenian (Mark 15 : 21), whom the Roman soldiers compelled to carry the cross on which our Lord was crucified. Probably it is the same person who is again mentioned in Rom. 16 : 13 as a disciple at Rome, whose mother also was a Christian held in esteem by the apostle. Mark mentions him along with his brother Alexander as persons well known to his readers (Mark 15 : 21).

Ruha'mah—*having obtained mercy*—a symbolical name given to the daughter of Hosea (2 : 1).

Ru'mah—*elevation*—probably the same as Arumah (Judg. 9 : 41 ; 2 Kings 23 : 36), near Shechem. Others identify it with *Tell Rûmeh*, in Galilee, about 6 miles north of Nazareth.

Rush, the papyrus (Job 8 : 11). (See BULRUSH.) The expression "branch and rush" in Isa. 9 : 14 ; 19 : 15 means "utterly."

Ruth—*a friend*—a Moabitess, the wife of Mahlon, whose father, Elimelech, had settled in the land of Moab. On the death of Elimelech and Mahlon, Naomi came with Ruth, her daughter-in-law, who refused to leave her, to Bethlehem, the old home from which Elimelech had migrated. There she had a rich relative, Boaz, to whom Ruth was eventually married. She became the mother of Obed, the grandfather of David. Thus Ruth, a Gentile, is among the maternal progenitors of our Lord (Matt. 1 : 5). The story of "the gleaner Ruth illustrates the friendly relations between the good Boaz and his reapers, the Jewish

land system, the method of transferring property from one person to another, the working of the Mosaic law for the relief of distressed and ruined families ; but, above all, handing down the unselfishness, the brave love, the unshaken trustfulness of her who, though not of the chosen race, was, like the Canaanitess Tamar (Gen. 38 : 29 ; Matt. 1 : 3) and the Canaanitess Rahab (Matt. 1 : 5), privileged to become the ancestress of David, and so of ' great David's greater Son ' " (Ruth 4 : 18–22).

Ruth, The Book of, was originally a part of the Book of Judges, but it now forms one of the twenty-four separate books of the Hebrew Bible.

The history it contains refers to a period perhaps about one hundred and twenty-six years before the birth of David. It gives (1) an account of Naomi's going to Moab with her husband, Elimelech, and of her subsequent return to Bethlehem with her daughter-in-law ; (2) the marriage of Boaz and Ruth ; and (3) the birth of Obed, of whom David sprang.

The author of this book was probably Samuel, according to Jewish tradition.

"Brief as this book is, and simple as is its story, it is remarkably rich in examples of faith, patience, industry, and kindness, nor less so in indications of the care which God takes of those who put their trust in him."

Rye = Rie (Heb. *kussĕmeth*), found in Ex. 9 : 32 ; Isa. 28 : 25, in all of which the margins of the Authorized and of the Revised Versions have "spelt." This Hebrew word also occurs in Ezek. 4 : 9, where the Authorized Version has "fitches" (*q.v.*) and the Revised Version "spelt." This, there can be no doubt, was the *Triticum spelta*, a species of hard, rough-grained wheat.

S

Sabachtha'ni—*thou hast forsaken me*—one of the Aramaic words uttered by our Lord on the cross (Matt. 27 : 46 ; Mark 15 : 34).

Saba'oth, the transliteration of the Hebrew word *tsĕbhâ'oth*, meaning "hosts," "armies" (Rom. 9 : 29 ; James 5 : 4). In the LXX. the Hebrew word is rendered by

"Almighty." (See Rev. 4:8; comp. Isa. 6:3.) It may designate Jehovah as either (1) God of the armies of earth, or (2) God of the armies of the stars, or (3) God of the unseen armies of angels; or perhaps it may include all these ideas.

Sab′bath (Heb. verb *shábbath*, meaning "to rest from labour"), the day of rest. It is first mentioned as having been instituted in Paradise, when man was in innocence (Gen. 2:2). "The sabbath was made for man," as a day of rest and refreshment for the body and of blessing to the soul.

It is next referred to in connection with the gift of manna to the children of Israel in the wilderness (Ex. 16:23); and afterwards, when the law was given from Sinai (20:11), the people were solemnly charged to "remember the sabbath day, to keep it holy." Thus it is spoken of as an institution already existing.

In the Mosaic law strict regulations were laid down regarding its observance (Ex. 35:2, 3; Lev. 23:3; 26:34). These were peculiar to that dispensation.

In the subsequent history of the Jews frequent references are made to the sanctity of the Sabbath (Isa. 56:2, 4, 6, 7; 58:13, 14; Jer. 17:20-22; Neh. 13:19). In later times they perverted the Sabbath by their traditions. Our Lord rescued it from their perversions, and recalled to them its true nature and intent (Matt. 12:10-13; Mark 2:27; Luke 13:10-17).

The Sabbath, originally instituted for man at his creation, is of *permanent* and *universal obligation*. The physical necessities of man require a Sabbath of rest. He is so constituted that his bodily welfare needs at least one day in seven for rest from ordinary labour. Experience also proves that the moral and spiritual necessities of men also demand a Sabbath of rest. "I am more and more sure by experience that the reason for the observance of the Sabbath lies deep in the everlasting necessities of human nature, and that as long as man is man the blessedness of keeping it, not as a day of rest only, but as a day of spiritual rest, will never be annulled. I certainly do feel by experience the eternal obligation, because of the eternal necessity, of the Sabbath.

The soul withers without it. It thrives in proportion to its observance. The Sabbath was made for man. God made it for men in a certain spiritual state because they needed it. The need, therefore, is deeply hidden in human nature. He who can dispense with it must be holy and spiritual indeed. And he who, still unholy and unspiritual, would yet dispense with it is a man that would fain be wiser than his Maker" (F. W. Robertson).

The ancient Babylonian calendar, as seen from recently recovered inscriptions on the bricks among the ruins of the royal palace, was based on the division of time into weeks of seven days. The Sabbath is in these inscriptions designated *Sabattu*, and defined as "a day of rest for the heart" and "a day of completion of labour."

The *change* of the day. Originally at creation the seventh day of the week was set apart and consecrated as the Sabbath. The first day of the week is now observed as the Sabbath. Has God authorized this change? There is an obvious distinction between the Sabbath as an institution and the particular day set apart for its observance. The question, therefore, as to the change of the day in no way affects the perpetual obligation of the Sabbath as an institution. Change of the day or no change, the Sabbath remains as a sacred institution the same. It cannot be abrogated.

If any change of the day has been made, it must have been by Christ or by his authority. Christ has a right to make such a change (Mark 2:23-28). As Creator, Christ was the original Lord of the Sabbath (John i. 3; Heb. 1:10). It was originally a memorial of creation. A work vastly greater than that of creation has now been accomplished by him—the work of redemption. We would naturally expect just such a change as would make the Sabbath a memorial of that greater work.

True, we can give no text authorizing the change in so many words. We have no express law declaring the change. But there are evidences of another kind. We know for a fact that the first day of the week has been observed from apostolic times, and the necessary conclusion is, that it was observed by the apostles and their immediate disciples. This, we may be sure, they never would have done without the permission or the authority of their Lord.

After his resurrection—which took place on the first day of the week (Matt. 28:1; Mark 16:2; Luke 24:1; John 20:1)—we never find Christ meeting with his disciples on the seventh day. But he specially honoured the first day by manifesting himself to them on four separate occasions (Matt. 28:9; Luke 24:34, 18–33; John 20:19–23). Again, on the next first day of the week, Jesus appeared to his disciples (John 20:26).

Some have calculated that Christ's ascension took place on the first day of the week. And there can be no doubt that the descent of the Holy Ghost at Pentecost was on that day (Acts 2:1). Thus Christ appears as instituting a new day to be observed by his people as the Sabbath—a day to be henceforth known amongst them as the "Lord's day." The observance of this "Lord's day" as the Sabbath was the general custom of the primitive churches, and must have had apostolic sanction (comp. Acts 20:3–7; 1 Cor. 16:1, 2) and authority, and so the sanction and authority of Jesus Christ.

The words "at her sabbaths" (Lam. 1:7, A.V.) ought probably to be, as in the Revised Version, "at her desolations."

Sab'bath day's journey, supposed to be a distance of 2,000 cubits, or less than half-a-mile, the distance to which, according to Jewish tradition, it was allowable to travel on the Sabbath day without violating the law (Acts 1:12; comp. Ex. 16:29; Num. 35:5; Josh. 3:4).

Sabbat'ical year, every seventh year, during which the land, according to the law of Moses, had to remain uncultivated (Lev. 25:2–7; comp. Ex. 23:10, 11, 12; Lev. 26:34, 35). Whatever grew of itself during that year was not for the owner of the land, but for the poor and the stranger and the beasts of the field. All debts, except those of foreigners, were to be remitted (Deut. 15:1–11). There is little notice of the observance of this year in Biblical his-

tory. It appears to have been much neglected (2 Chr. 36:20, 21).

Sabe'ans, descendants of Seba (Gen. 10:7); Africans (Isa. 40:3). They were "men of stature," and engaged in merchandise (Isa. 45:14). Their conversion to the Lord was predicted (Ps. 72:10). This word, in Ezek. 23:42, should be read, as in the margin of the Authorized Version, and in the Revised Version, "drunkards." Another tribe, apparently given to war, is mentioned in Job 1:15.

Sab'tah—*rest*—the third son of Cush (Gen. 10:7; 1 Chr. 1:9).

Sab'techa, the fifth son of Cush (*id.*).

Sa'char—*hire.* (1.) One of David's heroes (1 Chr. 11:35); called also Sharar (2 Sam. 23:33).

(2.) A son of Obed-edom the Gittite, and a temple porter (1 Chr. 26:4).

Sack'but (Chald. *ṣabkha;* Gr. *sambukē*), a Syrian stringed instrument resembling a harp (Dan. 3:5, 7, 10, 15); not the modern sackbut, which is a wind instrument.

Sack'cloth, cloth made of black goats' hair—coarse, rough, and thick—used for sacks, and also worn by mourners (Gen. 37:34; 42:25; 2 Sam. 3:31; Esther 4:1, 2; Ps. 30:11, etc.), and as a sign of repentance (Matt. 11:21). It was put upon animals by the people of Nineveh (Jonah 3:8).

Sac'rifice. The offering up of sacrifices is to be regarded as a divine institution. It did not originate with man. God himself appointed it as the mode in which acceptable worship was to be offered to him by guilty man. The language and the idea of sacrifice pervade the whole Bible.

Sacrifices were offered in the *antediluvian age.* The Lord clothed Adam and Eve with the skins of animals, which in all probability had been offered in sacrifice (Gen. 3:21). Abel offered a sacrifice "of the firstlings of his flock" (4:4; Heb. 11:4). A distinction also was made between clean and unclean animals, which there is every reason to believe had reference to the offering up of sacrifices (Gen. 7:2, 8), because animals were not given to man as food till after the Flood.

The same practice is continued down

through the *patriarchal age* (Gen. 8:20;
12:7; 13:4, 18; 15:9-11; 22:1-18, etc.).

In the *Mosaic period* of Old Testament
history definite laws were prescribed by God
regarding the different kinds of sacrifices
that were to be offered and the manner in
which the offering was to be made. The
offering of stated sacrifices became indeed
a prominent and distinctive feature of the
whole period (Ex. 12:3-27; Lev. 23:5-8;
Num. 9:2-14). (See ALTAR.)

We learn from the Epistle to the Hebrews that sacrifices had in themselves no
value or efficacy. They were only the
"shadow of good things to come," and
pointed the worshippers forward to the
coming of the great High Priest, who, in
the fulness of the time, "was offered once
for all to bear the sin of many." Sacrifices belonged to a temporary economy, to a
system of types and emblems which served
their purposes and have now passed away.
The "one sacrifice for sins" hath "perfected for ever them that are sanctified."

Sacrifices were of two kinds:—1. Unbloody—such as (1) first-fruits and tithes;
(2) meat and drink-offerings; and (3) incense. 2. Bloody—such as (1) burnt-
offerings; (2) peace-offerings; and (3) sin
and trespass offerings. (See OFFERINGS.)

Sad'ducees. The origin of this Jewish
sect cannot definitely be traced. It was
probably the outcome of the influence of
Grecian customs and philosophy during
the period of Greek domination. The first
time they are met with is in connection
with John the Baptist's ministry. They
came out to him when on the banks of the
Jordan, and he said to them, "O generation of vipers, who hath warned you to flee
from the wrath to come?" (Matt. 3:7.)
The next time they are spoken of they are
represented as coming to our Lord tempting him. He calls them "hypocrites" and
"a wicked and adulterous generation"
(Matt. 16:1-4; 22:23). The only reference to them in the Gospels of Mark (12:
18-27) and Luke (20:27-38) is their attempting to ridicule the doctrine of the
resurrection, which they denied, as they
also denied the existence of angels. They
are never mentioned in John's Gospel.

There were many Sadducees among the
"elders" of the Sanhedrin. They seem,
indeed, to have been as numerous as the
Pharisees (Acts 23:6). They showed their
hatred of Jesus in taking part in his condemnation (Matt. 16:21; 26:1-3, 59;
Mark 8:31; 15:1; Luke 9:22; 22:66).
They endeavoured to prohibit the apostles
from preaching the resurrection of Christ
(Acts 2:24, 31, 32; 4:1, 2; 5:17, 24-28).
They were the deists or sceptics of that
age. They do not appear as a separate
sect after the destruction of Jerusalem.

Sa'doc—*just*—mentioned in the genealogy of our Lord (Matt. 1:14).

Saf'fron—Heb. *karkôm*, Arab. *zafran*
(*i.e.*, "yellow")—mentioned only in Cant.
4:13, 14; the *Crocus sativus*. Many species
of the crocus are found in Palestine. The

SAFFRON (CROCUS SATIVUS).

pistils and stigmata, from the centre of its
flowers, are pressed into "saffron cakes,"
common in the East. "We found," says

Tristram, "saffron a very useful condiment in travelling cookery, a very small pinch of it giving not only a rich yellow colour but an agreeable flavour to a dish of rice or to an insipid stew."

Saint, one separated from the world and consecrated to God; one holy by profession and by covenant; a believer in Christ (Ps. 16:3; Rom. 1:7; 8:27; Phil. 1:1; Heb. 6:10).

The "saints" spoken of in Jude 14 are probably not the disciples of Christ, but the "innumerable company of angels" (Heb. 12:22; Ps. 68:17), with reference to Deut. 33:2.

This word is also used of the holy dead (Matt. 27:52; Rev. 18:24). It was not used as a distinctive title of the apostles and evangelists and of a "spiritual nobility" till the fourth century. In that sense it is not a scriptural title.

Sa'la—*a shoot*—a descendant of Arphaxad (Luke 3:35, 36); called also Shelah (1 Chr. 1:18, 24).

Sal'amis, a city on the south-east coast of Cyprus (Acts 13:5), where Saul and Barnabas, on their first missionary journey, preached the word in one of the Jewish synagogues, of which there seem to have been several in that place. It is now called *Famagusta.*

Sala'thiel—*whom I asked of God*—the son of Jeconiah (Matt. 1:12; 1 Chr. 3:17); also called the son of Neri (Luke 3:27). The probable explanation of the apparent discrepancy is that he was the son of Neri, the descendant of Nathan, and thus heir to the throne of David on the death of Jeconiah (comp. Jer. 22:30).

Sal'cah—*wandering*—a city of Bashan assigned to the half tribe of Manasseh (Deut. 3:10; Josh. 12:5; 13:11), identified with *Salkhad,* about 56 miles east of Jordan.

Sa'lem—*peace*—commonly supposed to be another name of Jerusalem (Gen. 14:18; Ps. 76:2; Heb. 7:1, 2).

Sa'lim—*peaceful*—a place near Ænon (*q.v.*), on the west of Jordan, where John baptized (John 3:23). It was probably the Shalem mentioned in Gen. 33:18, about 7 miles south of Ænon, at the head

of the great Wâdy Fâr'ah, which formed the northern boundary of Judea in the Jordan valley.

Sal'lai—*basket-maker.* (1.) A Benjamite (Neh. 11:8).

(2.) A priest in the days of Joshua and Zerubbabel (Neh. 12:20).

Sal'lu—*weighed.* (1.) A priest (Neh. 12:7).

(2.) A Benjamite (1 Chr. 9:7; Neh. 11:7).

Sal'mon—*garment*—the son of Nashon (Ruth 4:20; Matt. 1:4, 5), possibly the same as Salma in 1 Chr. 2:51.

Sal'mon—*shady;* or **Zalmon** (*q.v.*)—a hill covered with dark forests, south of Shechem, from which Abimelech and his men gathered wood to burn that city (Judg. 9:48). In Ps. 68:14 the change from war to peace is likened to snow on the dark mountain, as some interpret the expression. Others suppose the words here mean that the bones of the slain left unburied covered the land, so that it seemed to be white as if covered with snow. The reference, however, of the psalm is probably to Josh. 11 and 12. The scattering of the kings and their followers is fitly likened unto the snow-flakes rapidly falling on the dark Salmon. It is the modern *Jebel Suleimán.*

Salmo'ne, a promontory on the east of Crete, under which Paul sailed on his voyage to Rome (Acts 27:7); the modern *Cape Sidero.*

Salo'me—*perfect.* (1.) The wife of Zebedee and mother of James and John (Matt. 27:56), and probably the sister of Mary, the mother of our Lord (John 19:25). She sought for her sons places of honour in Christ's kingdom (Matt. 20:20, 21; comp. 19:28). She witnessed the crucifixion (Mark 15:40), and was present with the other women at the sepulchre (Matt. 27:56).

(2.) "The daughter of Herodias," not named in the New Testament. On the occasion of the birthday festival held by Herod Antipas, who had married her mother Herodias, in the fortress of Machærus, she "came in and danced, and pleased Herod" (Mark 6:14-29). John the Baptist, at that time a prisoner in the dungeons underneath the castle, was at her request beheaded by order of Herod, and his head given to the damsel in a charger, "and the damsel gave it to her mother," whose revengeful spirit was thus gratified. "A luxurious feast of the period" (says Farrar, *Life of Christ*) "was not regarded as complete unless it closed with some gross pantomimic representation; and doubtless Herod had adopted the evil fashion of his day. But he had not anticipated for his guests the rare luxury of seeing a princess,—his own niece, a grand-daughter of Herod the Great and of Mariamne, a descendant, therefore, of Simon the high priest and the great line of Maccabean princes—a princess who afterwards became the wife of a tetrarch [Philip, tetrarch of Trachonitis] and the mother of a king,—honouring them by degrading herself into a scenic dancer."

Salt, used to season food (Job 6 : 6), and mixed with the fodder of cattle (Isa. 30 : 24, "clean ;" in marg. of R.V. "salted"). All meat-offerings were seasoned with salt (Lev. 2 : 13). To eat salt with one is to partake of his hospitality—to derive subsistence from him ; and hence he who did so was bound to look after his host's interests (Ezra 4 : 14, "We have maintenance from the king's palace ;" A.V. marg., "We are salted with the salt of the palace ;" R.V., "We eat the salt of the palace").

A "covenant of salt" (Num. 18 : 19 ; 2 Chr. 13 : 5) was a covenant of perpetual obligation. New-born children were rubbed with salt (Ezek. 16 : 4). Disciples are likened unto salt, with reference to its cleansing and preserving uses (Matt. 5 : 13). When Abimelech took the city of Shechem, he sowed the place with salt, that it might always remain a barren soil (Judg. 9 : 45). Sir Lyon Playfair argues, on scientific grounds, that under the generic name of "salt," in certain passages, we are to understand petroleum or its residue asphalt. Thus in Gen. 19 : 26 he would read "pillar of asphalt ;" and in Matt. 5 : 13, instead of "salt," "petroleum," which loses its essence by exposure, as salt does not, and becomes asphalt, with which pavements were made.

The *Jebel Usdum*, to the south of the Dead Sea, is a mountain of rock salt about 7 miles long and from 2 to 3 miles wide and some hundreds of feet high.

Salt Sea (Josh. 3 : 16). See DEAD SEA.

Salt, The city of, one of the cities of Judah (Josh. 15 : 62), probably in the Valley of Salt, at the southern end of the Dead Sea.

Salt, Valley of, a place where it is said David smote the Syrians (2 Sam. 8 : 13). This valley (the 'Arabah) is between Judah and Edom on the south of the Dead Sea. Hence some interpreters would insert the words, "and he smote Edom," after the word "Syrians" in the above text. It is conjectured that while David was leading his army against the Ammonites and Syrians, the Edomites invaded the south of Judah, and that David sent Joab or Abishai against them, who drove them back and finally subdued Edom. (Comp. title to Ps. 60.)

Here also Amaziah "slew of Edom ten thousand men" (2 Kings 14 : 7 ; comp. 8 : 20–22 and 2 Chr. 25 : 5–11).

Saluta′tion. "Eastern modes of salutation are not unfrequently so prolonged as to become wearisome and a positive waste of time. The profusely polite Arab asks so many questions after your health, your happiness, your welfare, your house, and other things, that a person ignorant of the habits of the country would imagine there must be some secret ailment or mysterious sorrow oppressing you, which you wished to conceal, so as to spare the feelings of a dear, sympathizing friend, but which he, in the depth of his anxiety, would desire to hear of. I have often listened to these prolonged salutations in the house, the street, and the highway, and not unfrequently I have experienced their tedious monotony, and I have bitterly lamented useless waste of time" (Porter, *Through Samaria, etc.*). The work on which the disciples were sent forth was one of urgency, which left no time for empty compliments and prolonged greetings (Luke 10 : 4).

Salva′tion. This word is used of the deliverance of the Israelites from the Egyptians (Ex. 14 : 13), and of deliverance generally from evil or danger. In the New Testament it is specially used with reference to the great deliverance from the guilt and the pollution of sin wrought out by Jesus Christ—"the great salvation" (Heb. 2:3). (See REDEMPTION; REGENERATION.)

Sama′ria—*a watch-mountain* or *a watch-tower*. In the heart of the mountains of Israel, a few miles north-west of Shechem, stands the "hill of Shomĕrôn," a solitary mountain, a great "*mamelon.*" It is an oblong hill, with steep but not inaccessible sides, and a long flat top. Omri, the king of Israel, purchased this hill from Shemer its owner for two talents of silver, and built on its broad summit the city to which he gave the name of "Shomĕrôn"—*i.e.,* Samaria, as the new capital of his kingdom instead of Tirzah (1 Kings 16:24). As such it possessed many advantages. Here Omri resided during the last six years of his reign. As the result of an unsuccessful war with Syria, he appears to have been obliged to grant to the Syrians the right to "make streets in Samaria"— *i.e.,* probably permission to the Syrian merchants to carry on their trade in the

COLONNADE OF HEROD THE GREAT (SAMARIA—SEBASTE).

Israelite capital. This would imply the existence of a considerable Syrian population. "It was the only great city of Palestine created by the sovereign. All the others had been already consecrated by patriarchal tradition or previous possession. But Samaria was the choice of Omri alone. He, indeed, gave to the city which he had built the name of its former owner, but its especial connection with himself as its founder is proved by the designation which it seems Samaria bears in Assyrian inscriptions, *Beth-khumri* ('the house or palace of Omri')."—*Stanley.*

Samaria was frequently besieged. In the days of Ahab, Benhadad II. came up against it with thirty-two vassal kings, but was defeated with a great slaughter (1 Kings 20:1-22). A second time, next year, he assailed it; but was again utterly routed, and was compelled to surrender to Ahab (20:28-34), whose army, as compared with that of Benhadad, was no more than "two little flocks of kids."

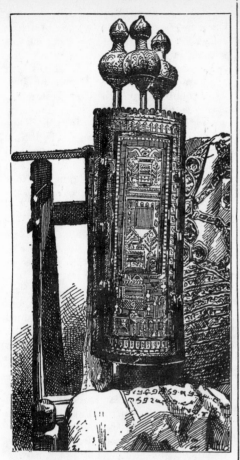

MANUSCRIPT OF SAMARITAN PENTATEUCH.

In the days of Jehoram this Benhadad again laid siege to Samaria, during which the city was reduced to the direst extremities. But just when success seemed to be within their reach, they suddenly broke up the siege, alarmed by a mysterious noise of chariots and horses and a great army, and fled, leaving their camp with all its contents behind them. The famishing inhabitants of the city were soon relieved with the abundance of the spoil of the Syrian camp; and it came to pass, according to the word of Elisha, that "a measure of fine flour was sold for a shekel, and two measures of barley for a shekel, in the gates of Samaria" (2 Kings 7 : 1–20).

Shalmaneser invaded Israel in the days of Hoshea, and reduced it to vassalage. He laid siege to Samaria (B.C. 723), which held out for three years, and was at length captured by Sargon, who completed the conquest Shalmaneser had begun (2 Kings 18 : 9–12 ; 17 : 3), and removed vast numbers of the tribes into captivity. (See SARGON.)

This city, after passing through various vicissitudes, was given by the emperor Augustus to Herod the Great, who rebuilt it, and called it *Sebaste* (Gr. form of *Augusta*) in honour of the emperor. In the New Testament the only mention of it is in Acts 8 : 5–13, where it is recorded that Philip went down to the city of Samaria and preached there.

It is now represented by the hamlet of *Sebustieh*, containing about three hundred inhabitants. The ruins of the ancient town are all scattered over the hill, down the sides of which they have rolled. The shafts of about one hundred of what must have been grand Corinthian columns are still standing, and attract much attention, although nothing definite is known regarding them. (Comp. Micah 1 : 6.)

In the time of Christ, Western Palestine was divided into three provinces—Judea, Samaria, and Galilee. Samaria occupied the centre of Palestine (John 4 : 4). It is called in the Talmud the "land of the Cuthim," and is not regarded as a part of the Holy Land at all.

It may be noticed that the distance between Samaria and Jerusalem — the respective capitals of the two kingdoms—is only 35 miles in a direct line.

Samar′itans, the name given to the new and mixed inhabitants whom Esarhaddon (B.C. 677), the king of Assyria, brought from Babylon and other places and settled in the cities of Samaria, instead of the original inhabitants whom Sargon (B.C. 721) had removed into captivity (2 Kings 17 : 24 ; comp. Ezra 4 : 2, 9, 10). These strangers (comp. Luke 17 : 18) amalgamated with the Jews still remaining in the land, and gradually abandoned their old idolatry and adopted partly the Jewish religion.

After the return from the Captivity, the Jews in Jerusalem refused to allow them to take part with them in rebuilding the temple, and hence sprang up an open enmity between them. They erected a rival temple on Mount Gerizim, which was, however, destroyed by a Jewish king (B.C. 130). They then built another at Shechem. The bitter enmity between the Jews and Samaritans continued in the time of our Lord: the Jews "had no dealings with the Samaritans" (John 4:9; comp. Luke 9:52, 53). Our Lord was in contempt called "a Samaritan" (John 8:48). Many of the Samaritans early embraced the gospel (John 4:5-42; Acts 8:25; 9:31; 15:3). Of these Samaritans there still remains a small population of about one hundred and sixty, who all reside in Shechem, where they carefully observe the religious customs of their fathers. They are the "smallest and oldest sect in the world."

Samar′itan Pen′tateuch. On the return from the Exile, the Jews refused the Samaritans participation with them in the worship at Jerusalem, and the latter separated from all fellowship with them, and built a temple for themselves on Mount Gerizim. This temple was razed to the ground more than one hundred years B.C. Then a system of worship was instituted similar to that of the temple at Jerusalem. It was founded on the Law, copies of which had been multiplied in Israel as well as in Judah. Thus the Pentateuch was preserved among the Samaritans, although they never called it by this name, but always "the Law," which they read as one book. The division into five books, as we now have it, however, was adopted by the Samaritans, as it was by the Jews, in all their priests' copies of "the Law," for the sake of convenience. This was the only portion of the Old Testament which was accepted by the Samaritans as of divine authority.

The *form* of the letters in the manuscript copies of the Samaritan Pentateuch is different from that of the Hebrew copies, and is probably the same as that which was in general use before the Captivity. There are other peculiarities in the writing which need not here be specified.

There are important differences between the Hebrew and the Samaritan copies of the Pentateuch in the readings of many sentences. In about two thousand instances in which the Samaritan and the Jewish texts differ, the LXX. agrees with the former. The New Testament also, when quoting from the Old Testament, agrees as a rule with the Samaritan text, where that differs from the Jewish. Thus Ex. 12:40 in the Samaritan reads, "Now the sojourning of the children of Israel and of their fathers which they had dwelt in the land of Canaan and in Egypt was four hundred and thirty years" (comp. Gal. 3:17). It may be noted that the LXX. has the same reading of this text.

Sam′gar-ne′bo—*be gracious, O Nebo!* or *a cup-bearer of Nebo*—probably the title of Nergal-sharezer, one of the princes of Babylon (Jer. 39:3).

Sa′mos, an island in the Ægean Sea, which Paul passed on his voyage from Assos to Miletus (Acts 20:15), on his third missionary journey. It is about 27 miles long and 20 broad, and lies about 42 miles south-west of Smyrna.

Samothra′cia, an island in the Ægean Sea, off the coast of Thracia, about 32 miles distant. This Thracian Samos was passed by Paul on his voyage from Troas to Neapolis (Acts 16:11) on his first missionary journey. It is about 8 miles long and 6 miles broad. Its modern name is *Samothraki*.

Sam′son—*of the sun*—the son of Manoah, born at Zorah. The narrative of his life is given in Judg. 13-16. He was a "Nazarite unto God" from his birth—the first Nazarite mentioned in Scripture (Judg. 13:3-5; comp. Num. 6:1-21). The first recorded event of his life was his marriage with a Philistine woman of Timnath (Judg. 14:1-4). Such a marriage was not forbidden by the law of Moses, as the Philistines did not form one of the seven doomed Canaanite nations (Ex. 34:11-16; Deut. 7:1-4). It was, however, an ill-assorted and unblessed marriage. His wife was soon taken from him and given "to his companion" (Judg. 14:20). For this Samson took revenge by burning the "standing corn of the Philistines" (15:1-8), who, in their turn, in revenge "burnt her and her father with fire." Her death he terribly avenged (15 : 7–19). During the twenty years following this he judged Israel; but we have no record of his life. Probably these twenty years may have been simultaneous with the last twenty years of Eli's life. After this we have an account of his exploits at Gaza (16 : 1–3), and of his infatuation for Delilah, and her treachery (16 : 4–20), and then of his melancholy death (16 : 21–31). He perished in the last terrible destruction he brought upon his enemies. "So the dead which he slew at his death were more [in social and political importance = the *élite* of the people] than they which he slew in his life."

"Straining all his nerves, he bowed:
As with the force of winds and waters pent,
When mountains tremble, those two massy pillars
With horrible convulsion to and fro
He tugged, he shook, till down they came, and drew
The whole roof after them, with burst of thunder
Upon the heads of all who sat beneath—
Lords, ladies, captains, counsellors, or priests,
Their choice nobility and flower."
Milton's *Samson Agonistes.*

Sam′uel—*heard of God.* The peculiar circumstances connected with his birth are recorded in 1 Sam. 1 : 20. Hannah, one of the two wives of Elkanah, who came up to Shiloh to worship before the Lord, earnestly prayed to God that she might become the mother of a son. Her prayer was graciously granted; and after the child was weaned she brought him to Shiloh and consecrated him to the Lord as a perpetual Nazarite (1 : 23–2 : 11). Here his bodily wants and training were attended to by the women who served in the tabernacle, while Eli cared for his religious culture. Thus, probably, twelve years of his life passed away. "The child Samuel grew on, and was in favour both with the Lord, and also with men" (2 : 26 ; comp. Luke 2 : 52). It was a time of great and growing degeneracy in Israel (Judg. 21 : 19–21 ; 1 Sam. 2 : 12-17, 22). The Philistines, who of late had greatly increased in number and in power, were practically masters of the country, and kept the people in subjection (1 Sam. 10 : 5 ; 13 : 3).

At this time *new communications from God* began to be made to the pious child. A mysterious voice came to him in the night season, calling him by name, and, instructed by Eli, he answered, "Speak, Lord ; for thy servant heareth." The message that came from the Lord was one of woe and ruin to Eli and his profligate sons. Samuel told it all to Eli, whose only answer to the terrible denunciations (1 Sam. 3 : 11–18) was, "It is the Lord; let him do what seemeth him good"—the passive submission of a weak character, not, in his case, the expression of the highest trust and faith. The Lord revealed himself now in divers manners to Samuel, and his fame and his influence increased throughout the land as of one divinely called to the prophetical office. A new period in the history of the kingdom of God now commenced.

The Philistine yoke was heavy, and the people, groaning under the wide-spread oppression, suddenly rose in revolt, and "went out against the Philistines to battle." A fierce and disastrous battle was fought at Aphek, near to Ebenezer (1 Sam. 4 : 1, 2). The Israelites were defeated, leaving 4,000 dead "in the field." The chiefs of the people thought to repair this great disaster by carrying with them the ark of the covenant as the symbol of Jehovah's presence. They accordingly, without consulting Samuel, fetched it out of Shiloh to the camp near Aphek. At the sight of the ark among them the people "shouted with a great shout, so that the earth rang again." A second battle was fought, and again the Philistines defeated the Israelites, stormed their camp, slew 30,000 men, and took the sacred ark. The tidings of this fatal battle was speedily conveyed to Shiloh ; and so soon as the aged Eli heard that the ark of God was taken, he fell backward from his seat at the entrance of the sanctuary, and his neck brake, and he died. The tabernacle with its furniture was probably, by the advice of Samuel, now about twenty years of age, removed from Shiloh to some place of safety, and finally to Nob, where it remained many years (21 : 1).

The Philistines followed up their advantage, and marched upon Shiloh, which they plundered and destroyed (comp. Jer. 7:12; Ps. 78:59). This was a great epoch in the history of Israel. For twenty years after this fatal battle at Aphek the whole land lay under the oppression of the Philistines. During all these dreary years Samuel was a spiritual power in the land. From Ramah, his native place, where he resided, his influence went forth on every side among the people. With unwearied zeal he went up and down from place to place, reproving, rebuking, and exhorting the people, endeavouring to awaken in them a sense of their sinfulness, and to lead them to repentance. His labours were so far successful that "all the house of Israel lamented after the Lord." Samuel summoned the people to Mizpeh, one of the loftiest hills in Central Palestine, where they fasted and prayed, and prepared themselves there, under his direction, for a great war against the Philistines, who now marched their whole force toward Mizpeh, in order to crush the Israelites once for all. At the intercession of Samuel God interposed in behalf of Israel. Samuel himself was their leader—the only occasion in which he acted as a leader in war. The Philistines were utterly routed. They fled in terror before the army of Israel, and a great slaughter ensued. This battle, fought probably about B.C. 1095, put an end to the forty years of Philistine oppression. In memory of this great deliverance, and in token of gratitude for the help vouchsafed, Samuel set up a great stone in the battlefield, and called it "Ebenezer," saying, "Hitherto hath the Lord helped us" (1 Sam. 7:1-12). This was the spot where, twenty years before, the Israelites had suffered a great defeat, when the ark of God was taken.

This victory over the Philistines was followed by a *long period of peace for Israel* (1 Sam. 7:13, 14), during which Samuel exercised the functions of judge, going "from year to year in circuit" from his home in Ramah to Bethel, thence to Gilgal (not that in the Jordan valley, but that which lay to the west of Ebal and Gerizim), and returning by Mizpeh to Ramah.

He established regular services at Shiloh, where he built an altar; and at Ramah he gathered a company of young men around him and established a school of the prophets. The schools of the prophets, thus originated, and afterwards established also at Gibeah, Bethel, Gilgal, and Jericho, exercised an important influence on the national character and history of the people in maintaining pure religion in the midst of growing corruption. They continued to the end of the Jewish commonwealth.

Many years now passed, during which Samuel exercised the functions of his judicial office, being the friend and counsellor of the people in all matters of private and public interest. He was a great statesman as well as a reformer, and all regarded him with veneration as the "seer," the prophet of the Lord. At the close of this period, when he was now an old man, the elders of Israel came to him at Ramah (1 Sam. 8:4, 5, 19-22); and feeling how great was the danger to which the nation was exposed from the misconduct of Samuel's sons, whom he had invested with judicial functions as his assistants, and had placed at Beersheba on the Philistine border, and also from a threatened invasion of the Ammonites, they demanded that a king should be set over them. This request was very displeasing to Samuel. He remonstrated with them, and warned them of the consequences of such a step. At length, however, referring the matter to God, he acceded to their desires, and anointed Saul (*q.v.*) to be their king (11:15). Before retiring from public life he convened an assembly of the people at Gilgal (ch. 12), and there solemnly addressed them with reference to his own relation to them as judge and prophet.

The remainder of his life he spent in retirement at Ramah, only occasionally and in special circumstances appearing again in public (1 Sam. 13, 15) with communications from God to king Saul. While mourning over the many evils which now fell upon the nation, he is suddenly summoned (ch. 16) to go to Bethlehem and anoint David, the son of Jesse, as king over Israel instead of Saul. After this little is known of him till the time of his death, which took place at Ramah when he was probably about eighty years of age. "And all Israel gathered themselves together, and lamented him, and buried him in his house at Ramah" (25:1)—not in the house itself, but in the court or garden of his house. (Comp. 2 Kings 21:18; 2 Chr. 33:20; 1 Kings 2:34; John 19:41.)

Samuel's devotion to God, and the special favour with which God regarded him, are referred to in Jer. 15:1 and Ps. 99:6.

"It is difficult to realize the greatness of a historic figure after three thousand years; but Samuel must have been more than the Luther of his day. Uniting in himself all the highest offices of his nation— its supreme prophet, its virtual high priest, and its acknowledged ruler—his influence was intensified by the lofty singleness of his life and aim. Men could not forget, as his age increased, how Jehovah had chosen to make revelations through him while he was yet a child; how he had grown up in the sacred shadow of the tabernacle; how he had been a Nazarite from his birth; how fearless and loyal had been his enthusiasm for Jehovah; how incorruptible he had been as a judge; and how well his life had illustrated the high morality and godliness he had enforced. They had seen the religious revolution he had accomplished. The state, as a whole, in its great characteristics, owed, in fact, its noble future to his work; for he had in effect founded the order of prophets, he had prepared the way for the kings, and his revival of the Mosaic religion brought with it the future temple and its priesthood. Before his time Israel had had no real national existence, and seemed likely to perish entirely; yet he left it proud of its dignity as the people of God, and on the threshold of its highest glory under David."—Geikie's *Hours with the Bible*.

Sam'uel, Books of. The LXX. translators regarded the books of Samuel and of Kings as forming one continuous history, which they divided into four books, which they called "Books of the Kingdom." The Vulgate version followed this division, but styled them "Books of the Kings."

These books of Samuel they accordingly called the "First" and "Second" Books of Kings, and not, as in the modern Protestant versions, the "First" and "Second" Books of Samuel.

The *authors* of the books of Samuel were probably Samuel, Gad, and Nathan. Samuel penned the first twenty-four chapters of the first book. Gad, the companion of David (1 Sam. 22:5), continued the history thus commenced; and Nathan completed it, probably arranging the whole in the form in which we now have it (1 Chr. 29:29).

The *contents* of the books. The first book comprises a period of about a hundred years, and nearly coincides with the life of Samuel. It contains (1) the history of Eli (1–4); (2) the history of Samuel (5–12); (3) the history of Saul and of David in exile (13–31). The second book, comprising a period of perhaps fifty years, contains a history of the reign of David (1) over Judah (1–4), and (2) over all Israel (5–24), mainly in its political aspects. The last four chapters of Second Samuel may be regarded as a sort of appendix recording various events, but not chronologically. These books do not contain complete histories. Frequent gaps are met with in the record, because their object is to present a history of the kingdom of God in its gradual development, and not of the events of the reigns of the successive rulers. It is noticeable that the section (2 Sam. 11:2–12:29) containing an account of David's sin in the matter of Bathsheba is omitted in the corresponding passage in 1 Chr. 20.

Sanbal'lat held some place of authority in Samaria when Nehemiah went up to Jerusalem to rebuild its ruined walls. He vainly attempted to hinder this work (Neh. 2:10, 19; 4:1–12; 6). His daughter became the wife of one of the sons of Joiada, a son of the high priest, much to the grief of Nehemiah (13:28).

Sanc'tification involves more than a mere moral reformation of character, brought about by the power of the truth: it is the work of the Holy Spirit bringing the whole nature more and more under the influences of the new gracious principles implanted in the soul in regeneration. In other words, sanctification is the carrying on to perfection the work begun in regeneration, and it extends to the whole man (Rom. 6 : 13 ; 2 Cor. 4 : 6 ; Col. 3 : 10 ; 1 John 4 : 7 ; 1 Cor. 6 : 19). It is the special office of the Holy Spirit in the plan of redemption to carry on this work (1 Cor. 6 : 11 ; 2 Thess. 2 : 13).

Faith is instrumental in securing sanctification, inasmuch as it (1) secures union to Christ (1 Cor. 13 ; Gal. 2 : 20), and (2) brings the believer into living contact with the truth, whereby he is led to yield obedience "to the commands, trembling at the threatenings, and embracing the promises of God for this life and that which is to come."

Perfect sanctification is not attainable in this life (1 Kings 8 : 46 ; Prov. 20 : 9 ; Eccl. 7 : 20 ; James 3 : 2 ; 1 John 1 : 8). See Paul's account of himself in Rom. 7 : 14–25 ; Phil. 3 : 12–14 ; and 1 Tim. 1 : 15 ; also the confessions of David (Ps. 19 : 12 ; 51), of Moses (90 : 8), of Job (42 : 5, 6), and of Daniel (9 : 20). "The more holy a man is, the more humble, self-renouncing, self-abhorring, and the more sensitive to every sin, he becomes, and the more closely he clings to Christ. The moral imperfections which cling to him he feels to be sins, which he laments and strives to overcome. Believers find that their life is a constant warfare, and they need to take the kingdom of heaven by storm, and watch while they pray. They are always subject to the constant chastisement of their Father's loving hand, which can only be designed to correct their imperfections and to confirm their graces. And it has been notoriously the fact that the best Christians have been those who have been the least prone to claim the attainment of perfection for themselves."—Hodge's *Outlines*.

Sanc′tuary denotes—(1) the Holy Land (Ex. 15 : 17 ; comp. Ps. 114 : 2) ; (2) the temple (1 Chr. 22 : 19 ; 2 Chr. 29 : 21) ; (3) the tabernacle (Ex. 25 : 8 ; Lev. 12 : 4 ; 21 : 12) ; (4) the holy place, the place of the Presence (Gr. *hiëron*, the temple-*house; not the nâos,* which is the temple area, with its courts and porches)—Lev. 4 : 6 ; Num. 10 : 21 ; Eph. 2 : 21, R.V., marg. ; (5) God's

holy habitation in heaven (Ps. 102 : 19). In the final state there is properly "no sanctuary" (Rev. 21 : 22), for God and the Lamb "are the sanctuary." All is there hallowed by the Divine Presence ; all is sanctuary.

San′dals. Mentioned only in Mark 6 : 9 and Acts 12 : 8. The sandal was simply a sole, made of wood or palm-bark, fastened to the foot by leathern straps. Sandals

SANDALS.

were also made of seal-skin (Ezek. 16 : 10 ; lit. *tahash,* "leather ;" A.V., "badger's skin"). (See SHOE.)

San′hedrim, more correctly **San′hedrin** (Gr. *synedrion*), meaning "a sitting together," or a "council." This word (rendered "council," A.V.) is frequently used in the New Testament (Matt. 5 : 22 ; 26 : 59 ; Mark 15 : 1, etc.) to denote the supreme judicial and administrative council of the Jews, which, it is said, was first instituted by Moses, and was composed of seventy men (Num. 11 : 16, 17). But that seems to have been only a temporary arrangement which Moses made. This council is with greater probability supposed to have originated among the Jews when they were under the domination of the Syrian kings in the time of the Maccabees. The name is first employed by the Jewish historian Josephus. This "council" is referred to simply as the "chief priests and elders of the people" (Matt. 26 : 3, 47, 57, 59 ; 27 : 1, 3, 12, 20, etc.), before whom Christ was tried on the charge of claiming to be the Messiah. Peter and John were also brought before it for promulgating heresy (Acts 4: 1-23; 5:17-41); as was also Stephen on a charge of blasphemy (6:12-15), and Paul for violating a temple by-law (22:30; 23: 1-10).

The Sanhedrin is said to have consisted of seventy-one members, the high priest being president. They were of three classes —(1) the chief priests, or heads of the twenty-four priestly courses (1 Chr. 24), (2) the scribes, and (3) the elders. As the highest court of judicature, "in all causes and over all persons, ecclesiastical and civil, supreme," its decrees were binding, not only on the Jews in Palestine, but on all Jews wherever scattered abroad. Its jurisdiction was greatly curtailed by Herod, and afterwards by the Romans.

Its usual place of meeting was within the precincts of the temple, in the hall "Gazith," but it sometimes met also in the house of the high priest (Matt. 26:3), who was assisted by two vice-presidents.

Sansan′nah—*a palm branch*, or *a thorn bush*—a town in the south (the *negeb*) of Judah (Josh. 15:31); called also Hazar-susah (19:5), or Hazar-susim (1 Chr. 4:31).

Saph—*extension*—the son of the giant whom Sibbechai slew (2 Sam. 21:18); called also Sippai (1 Chr. 20:4).

Saph′ir—*beautiful*—a town of Judah (Micah 1:11), identified with *es-Suâfir*, 5 miles south-east of Ashdod.

Sapph′ira—*beautiful*—the wife of Ananias (*q.v.*). She was a partner in his guilt and also in his punishment (Acts 5:1-11).

Sapph′ire. Associated with diamonds (Ex. 28:18) and emeralds (Ezek. 28:13); one of the stones in the high priest's breast-plate. It is a precious stone of a sky-blue colour, probably the *lapis lazuli*, brought from Babylon. The throne of God is described as of the colour of a sapphire (Ex. 24:10; comp. Ezek. 1:26).

Sa′rah—*princess*—the wife and at the same time the half-sister of Abraham (Gen. 11:29; 20:12). This name was given to her at the time that it was announced to Abraham that she should be the mother of the promised child. Her story is from her marriage identified with that of the patriarch till the time of her death. Her death at

the age of one hundred and twenty-seven years (the only instance in Scripture where the age of a woman is recorded) was the occasion of Abraham's purchasing the cave of Machpelah as a family burying-place.

In the allegory of Gal. 4:22-31 she is the type of the "Jerusalem which is above." She is also mentioned in Heb. 11:11 among the Old Testament worthies, who "all died in faith." (See ABRAHAM.)

Sa′rai—*my princess*—the name originally borne by Sarah (Gen. 11:31; 17:15).

Sar′dine stone (Rev. 4:3—R.V., "sardius;" Heb. *'odhem*; LXX., Gr. *sardion*, from a root meaning "red"), a gem of a blood-red colour. It was called "sardius" because obtained from Sardis in Lydia. It is enumerated among the precious stones in the high priest's breastplate (Ex. 28: 17; 39:10). It is our red carnelian.

Sar′dis, the metropolis of Lydia in Asia Minor. It stood on the river Pactolus, at the foot of mount Tmolus. Here was one of the seven Asiatic churches (Rev. 3:1-6). It is now a ruin called *Sert-Kalessi*.

Sar′donyx (Rev. 21:20), a species of the carnelian combining the sard and the onyx, having three layers of opaque spots or stripes on a transparent red basis. Like the sardine, it is a variety of the chalcedony.

Sarep′ta (Luke 4:26). See ZAREPHATH.

Sar′gon. (In the inscriptions, "Sarra-yukin" [*the god*] *has appointed the king;* also "Sarru-kinu," *the legitimate king.*) On the death of Shalmaneser (B.C. 723) one of the Assyrian generals established himself on the vacant throne, taking the name of "Sargon," after that of the famous monarch, the Sargon of Accad, founder of the first Semitic empire, as well as of one of the most famous libraries of Chaldea. He forthwith began a conquering career, and became one of the most powerful of the Assyrian monarchs. He is mentioned by name in the Bible only in connection with the siege of Ashdod (Isa. 20:1).

At the very beginning of his reign he besieged and took the city of Samaria (2 Kings 17:6; 18:9-21). On an inscription found in the palace he built at

Khorsabad, near Nineveh, he says, "The city of Samaria I besieged, I took; 27,280 of its inhabitants I carried away; fifty chariots that were among them I collected," etc. The northern kingdom he changed into an Assyrian satrapy. He afterwards drove Merodach-baladan (*q.v.*), who kept

him at bay for twelve years, out of Babylon, which he entered in triumph. By a succession of victories he gradually enlarged and consolidated the empire, which now extended from the frontiers of Egypt in the west to the mountains of Elam in the east, and thus carried almost to completion the ambitious designs of Tiglath-pileser (*q.v.*). He was murdered by one of his own soldiers (B.C. 705) in his palace at Khorsabad, after a reign of sixteen years, and was succeeded by his son Sennacherib.

CYLINDER RECORDING THE CONQUEST OF SAMARIA BY SARGON.

Sa'tan—*adversary; accuser.* When used as a proper name, the Hebrew word so rendered has the article "*the* adversary" (Job 1:6-12; 2:1-7). In the New Testament it is used as interchangeable with *Diabolos*, or the devil, and is so used more than thirty times.

He is also called "the dragon" and "the serpent" (Rev. 12:9; 20:2); "the prince of this world" (John 12:31; 14:30); "the prince of the power of the air" (Eph. 2:2); "the god of this world" (2 Cor. 4:4); and "the spirit that worketh in the children of disobedience" (Eph. 2:2). The distinct personality of Satan and his activity among men are thus obviously recognized. He tempted our Lord in the wilderness (Matt. 4:1-11). He is "Beelzebub, the prince of the devils" (12:24). He is "the constant enemy of God, of Christ, of the divine kingdom, of the followers of Christ, and of all truth; full of falsehood and all malice, and exciting and seducing to evil in every possible way." His power is very great in

the world. He is a "roaring lion, seeking whom he may devour" (1 Pet. 5:8). Men are said to be "taken captive by him" (2 Tim. 2:26). Christians are warned against his "devices" (2 Cor. 2:11), and called on to "resist" him (James 4:7).

Christ redeems his people from "him that hath the power of death, that is, the devil" (Heb. 2:14). Satan has the "power of death," not as lord, but simply as executioner.

Sa'tyr—*hairy one.* Mentioned in Greek mythology as a creature composed of a man and a goat, supposed to inhabit wild and desolate regions. The Hebrew word is rendered also "goat" (Lev. 4:24) and "devil"—*i.e.*, an idol in the form of a goat (17:7; 2 Chr. 11:15). When it is said (Isa. 13:21; comp. 34:14) "the satyrs shall dance there," the meaning is that the place referred to shall become a desolate waste. Some render the Hebrew word "baboon," a species of which is found in Babylonia.

Saul—*asked for.* (1.) A king of Edom (Gen. 36:37, 38); called Shaul in 1 Chr. 1:48.

(2.) The son of Kish (probably his only son, and a child of prayer—"asked for"), of the tribe of Benjamin, the first king of the Jewish nation. The singular providential circumstances connected with his election as king are recorded in 1 Sam. 8-10. His father's she-asses had strayed, and Saul was sent with a servant to seek for them. Leaving his home at Gibeah (10:5, "the hill of God," A.V.; lit., "Gibeah of God"), Saul and his servant went toward the north-west over Mount Ephraim, and then turning north-east they came to "the land of Shalisha," and thence eastward to the land of Shalim, and at length came to the district of Zuph, near Samuel's home at Ramah (9:3-10). At this point Saul proposed to return from the three days' fruitless search, but his servant suggested that they should first consult the "seer." Hearing that he was about to offer sacrifice, the two hastened into Ramah, and "behold Samuel was coming out to meet them," on his way to the "*bamah*"—*i.e.*, the "height"—where sacrifice was to be offered; and in answer to Saul's question, "Tell me, I pray thee, where the seer's house is," Samuel made himself known to him. Samuel had been divinely prepared for his coming (9:15-17), and received Saul as his guest. He took him with him to the sacrifice, and then after the feast "communed with Saul upon the top of the house" of all that was in his heart. On the morrow Samuel "took a vial of oil and poured it on his head," and anointed Saul as king over Israel (9:25-10:8), giving him three signs in confirmation of his call to be king. When Saul reached his home in Gibeah the last of these signs was fulfilled, and the Spirit of God came upon him, and "he was turned into another man." The simple countryman was transformed into the king of Israel, a remarkable change suddenly took place in his whole demeanour, and the people said in their astonishment, as they looked on the stalwart son of Kish, "Is Saul also among the prophets?"—a saying which passed into a "proverb." (Comp. 19:24.)

The intercourse between Saul and Samuel was as yet unknown to the people. The "anointing" had been in secret. But now the time had come when the transaction must be confirmed by the nation. Samuel accordingly summoned the people to a solemn assembly "before the Lord" at Mizpeh. Here the lot was drawn (10:17-27), and it fell upon Saul, and when he was presented before them, the stateliest man in all Israel, the air was rent for the first time in Israel by the loud cry, "God save the king!" He now returned to his home in Gibeah, attended by a kind of body-guard—"a band of men whose hearts God had touched." On reaching his home he dismissed them, and resumed the quiet toils of his former life.

Soon after this, on hearing of the conduct of Nahash the Ammonite at Jabesh-gilead (q.v.), an army out of all the tribes of Israel rallied at his summons to the trysting-place at Bezek, and he led them forth a great army to battle, gaining a complete victory over the Ammonite invaders at Jabesh (11:1-11). Amid the universal joy occasioned by this victory he

was now fully recognized as the king of Israel. At the invitation of Samuel "all the people went to Gilgal, and there they made Saul king before the Lord in Gilgal." Samuel now officially anointed him as king (11:15). Although Samuel never ceased to be a judge in Israel, yet now his work in that capacity practically came to an end.

Saul now undertook the great and difficult enterprise of freeing the land from its hereditary enemies the Philistines, and for this end he gathered together an army of 3,000 men (1 Sam. 13:1, 2). The Philistines were encamped at Geba. Saul, with 2,000 men, occupied Michmash and Mount Bethel; while his son Jonathan, with 1,000 men, occupied Gibeah, to the south of Geba, and seemingly without any direction from his father "smote" the Philistines in Geba. Thus roused, the Philistines, who gathered an army of 30,000 chariots and 6,000 horsemen, and "people as the sand which is on the sea-shore in multitude," encamped in Michmash, which Saul had evacuated for Gilgal. Saul now tarried for seven days in Gilgal before making any movement, as Samuel had appointed (10:8); but becoming impatient on the seventh day, as it was drawing to a close, when he had made an end of offering the burnt offering, Samuel appeared and warned him of the fatal consequences of his act of disobedience, for he had not waited long enough (13:13, 14).

When Saul, after Samuel's departure, went out from Gilgal with his 600 men, his followers having decreased to that number (13:15), against the Philistines at Michmash (q.v.), he had his head-quarters under a pomegranate tree at Migron, over against Michmash, the Wâdy es-Suweinit alone intervening. Here at Gibeah-Geba Saul and his army rested, uncertain what to do. Jonathan became impatient, and with his armour-bearer planned an assault against the Philistines, unknown to Saul and the army (14:1-15). Jonathan and his armour-bearer went down into the wâdy, and on their hands and knees climbed to the top of the narrow rocky ridge called Bozez, where was the outpost of the Philistine army. They surprised and then slew twenty of the Philistines, and immediately the whole host of the Philistines was thrown into disorder and fled in great terror. "It was a very great trembling;" a supernatural panic seized the host. Saul and his 600 men—a band which speedily increased to 10,000—perceiving the confusion, pursued the army of the Philistines, and the tide of battle rolled on as far as to Bethaven, halfway between Michmash and Bethel. The Philistines were totally routed. "So the Lord saved Israel that day." While pursuing the Philistines, Saul rashly adjured the people, saying, "Cursed be the man that eateth any food until evening." But though faint and weary, the Israelites "smote the Philistines that day from Michmash to Aijalon" (a distance of from 15 to 20 miles). Jonathan had, while passing through the wood in pursuit of the Philistines, tasted a little of the honeycomb which was abundant there (14:27). This was afterwards discovered by Saul (ver. 42), and he threatened to put his son to death. The people, however, interposed, saying, "There shall not one hair of his head fall to the ground." He whom God had so signally owned, who had "wrought this great salvation in Israel," must not die. "Then Saul went up from following the Philistines: and the Philistines went to their own place" (1 Sam. 14:24-46); and thus the campaign against the Philistines came to an end. This was Saul's second great military success.

Saul's reign, however, continued to be one of almost constant war against his enemies round about (14:47, 48), in all of which he proved victorious. The war against the Amalekites is the only one which is recorded at length (1 Sam. 15). These oldest and hereditary (Ex. 17:8; Num. 14:43-45) enemies of Israel occupied the territory to the south and south-west of Palestine. Samuel summoned Saul to execute the "ban" which God had pronounced (Deut. 25:17-19) on this cruel and relentless foe of Israel. The cup of their iniquity was now full. This command was "the test of his moral qualification for being king." Saul proceeded to

execute the divine command; and gathering the people together, marched from Telaim (1 Sam. 15:4) against the Amalekites, whom he "smote from Havilah until thou comest to Shur," utterly destroying "all the people with the edge of the sword"—i.e., all that fell into his hands. He was, however, guilty of rebellion and disobedience in sparing Agag their king, and in conniving at his soldiers' sparing the best of the sheep and cattle; and Samuel, following Saul to Gilgal, in the Jordan valley, said unto him, "Because thou hast rejected the word of the Lord, he also hath rejected thee from being king" (15:23). The kingdom was rent from Saul and was given to another, even to David, whom the Lord chose to be Saul's successor, and whom Samuel anointed (16:1-13). From that day "the spirit of the Lord departed from Saul, and an evil spirit from the Lord troubled him." He and Samuel parted only to meet once again at one of the schools of the prophets.

David was now sent for as a "cunning player on the harp" (1 Sam. 16:16, 18), to play before Saul when the evil spirit troubled him, and thus was introduced to the court of Saul. He became a great favourite with the king. At length David returned to his father's house and to his wonted avocation as a shepherd for perhaps some three years. The Philistines once more invaded the land, and gathered their army between Shochoh and Azekah, in Ephes-dammim, on the southern slope of the valley of Elah. Saul and the men of Israel went forth to meet them, and encamped on the northern slope of the same valley which lay between the two armies. It was here that David slew Goliath of Gath, the champion of the Philistines (17:32-40), an exploit which led to the flight and utter defeat of the Philistine army. Saul now took David permanently into his service (18:2); but he became jealous of him (ver. 9), and on many occasions showed his enmity toward him (ver. 10, 11), his enmity ripening into a purpose of murder which at different times he tried in vain to carry out.

After some time the Philistines "gathered themselves together" in the plain of Esdraelon, and pitched their camp at Shunem, on the slope of Little Hermon; and Saul "gathered all Israel together," and "pitched in Gilboa" (1 Sam. 28 : 3-14). Being unable to discover the mind of the Lord, Saul, accompanied by two of his retinue, betook himself to the "witch of Endor," some 7 or 8 miles distant. Here he was overwhelmed by the startling communication that was mysteriously made to him by Samuel (ver. 16-19), who appeared to him. "He fell straightway all along on the earth, and was sore afraid, because of the words of Samuel" (ver. 20). The Philistine host "fought against Israel: and the men of Israel fled before the Philistines, and fell down slain in Mount Gilboa" (31 : 1). In his despair at the disaster that had befallen his army, Saul "took a sword and fell upon it." And the Philistines on the morrow "found Saul and his three sons fallen in Mount Gilboa." Having cut off his head, they sent it with his weapons to Philistia, and hung up the skull in the temple of Dagon at Ashdod. They suspended his headless body, with that of Jonathan, from the walls of Bethshan. The men of Jabesh-gilead afterwards removed the bodies from this position; and having burnt the flesh, they buried the bodies under a tree at Jabesh. The remains were, however, afterwards removed to the family sepulchre at Zelah (2 Sam. 21 : 13, 14). (See DAVID.)

(3.) "Who is also called Paul" (*q.v.*), the circumcision name of the apostle, given to him, perhaps, in memory of King Saul (Acts 7 : 58; 8 : 1; 9 : 1).

Sav'iour, one who saves from any form or degree of evil. In its highest sense the word indicates the relation sustained by our Lord to his redeemed ones—he is their Saviour. The great message of the gospel is about salvation and the Saviour. It is the "gospel of salvation." Faith in the Lord Jesus Christ secures to the sinner a personal interest in the work of redemption. Salvation is redemption made effectual to the individual by the power of the Holy Spirit.

Scape'goat—Lev. 16 : 8-26; R.V., "the goat for Azazel" (*q.v.*)—the name given to the goat which was taken away into the wilderness on the day of Atonement (16 : 20-22). The priest made atonement over the scapegoat, laying Israel's guilt upon it, and then sent it away, the goat bearing "upon him all their iniquities unto a land not inhabited."

At a later period an evasion or modification of the law of Moses was introduced by the Jews. "The goat was conducted to a mountain named Tzuk, situated at a distance of ten Sabbath days' journey, or about six and a half English miles, from Jerusalem. At this place the Judean desert was supposed to commence; and the man in whose charge the goat was sent out, while setting him free, was instructed to push the unhappy beast down the slope of the mountain side, which was so steep as to insure the death of the goat, whose bones were broken by the fall. The reason of this barbarous custom was that on one occasion the scapegoat returned to Jerusalem after being set free, which was considered such an evil omen that its recurrence was prevented for the future by the death of the goat" (*Twenty-one Years' Work in the Holy Land*). This mountain is now called *el-Muntâr.*

Scar'let. This dye was obtained by the Egyptians from the shell-fish *Carthamus tinctorius;* and by the Hebrews from the *Coccus ilicis,* an insect which infests oak trees, called *kermes* by the Arabians.

This colour was early known (Gen. 38 : 28). It was one of the colours of the ephod (Ex. 28 : 6), the girdle (8), and the breastplate (15) of the high priest. It is also mentioned in various other connections (Josh. 2 : 18; 2 Sam. 1 : 24; Lam. 4 : 5; Nahum 2 : 3). A scarlet robe was in mockery placed on our Lord (Matt. 27 : 28; Luke 23 : 11). "Sins as scarlet" (Isa. 1 : 18)—*i.e.,* as scarlet robes "glaring and habitual." Scarlet and crimson were the *firmest* of dyes, and thus not easily washed out.

Scep'tre (Heb. *shêbeṭ* = Gr. *skeptron*), properly a staff or rod. As a symbol of authority, the use of the sceptre originated in the idea that the ruler was as a shepherd of his people (Gen. 49:10; Num. 24: 17; Ps. 45:6; Isa. 14:5). There is no example on record of a sceptre having ever been actually handled by a Jewish king.

Sce′va—*an implement*—a Jew, chief of the priests at Ephesus (Acts 19:13-16); *i.e.*, the head of one of the twenty-four courses of the house of Levi. He had seven sons, who "took upon them to call over them which had evil spirits the name of the Lord Jesus," in imitation of Paul. They tried their method of exorcism on a fierce demoniac, and failed. His answer to them was to this effect (19:15): "The Jesus whom you invoke is One whose authority I acknowledge; and the Paul whom you name I recognize to be a servant or messenger of God; but what sort of men are ye who have been empowered to act as you do by neither?" (Lindsay on the *Acts of the Apostles*.)

Schism—*a separation*—an alienation causing divisions among Christians, who ought to be united (1 Cor. 12:25).

School′master, the law so designated by Paul (Gal. 3:24, 25). As so used, the word does not mean teacher, but pedagogue (shortened into the modern *page*)—*i.e.*, one who was intrusted with the supervision of a family, taking them to and from the school, being responsible for their safety and manners. Hence the pedagogue was stern and severe in his discipline. Thus the law was a pedagogue to the Jews, with a view to Christ—*i.e.*, to prepare for faith in Christ by producing convictions of guilt and helplessness. The office of the pedagogue ceased when "faith came"—*i.e.*, the object of that faith, the seed, which is Christ.

Schools of the Prophets (1 Sam. 19: 18-24; 2 Kings 2:3, 5, 7, 12, 15) were instituted for the purpose of training young men for the prophetical and priestly offices. (See PROPHET; SAMUEL.)

Scor′pions, mentioned along with serpents (Deut. 8:15). Used also figuratively to denote wicked persons (Ezek. 2:6; Luke 10:19); also a particular kind of scourge or whip (1 Kings 12:11). Scorpions were a species of spider. They abounded in the Jordan valley.

SCORPION.

Scourg′ing (1 Kings 12:11). Variously administered. In no case were the stripes to exceed forty (Deut. 25:3; comp. 2 Cor. 11:24). In the time of the apostles, in consequence of the passing of what was called the Porcian law, no Roman citizen could be scourged in any case (Acts 16: 22-37). (See BASTINADO.) In the scourging of our Lord (Matt. 27:26; Mark 15: 15) the words of prophecy (Isa. 53:5) were fulfilled.

Scribes anciently held various important offices in the public affairs of the nation. The Hebrew word so rendered (*sopher*) is first used to designate the holder of some military office (Judg. 5:14; A.V., "pen of the writer;" R.V., "the marshal's staff;" marg., "the staff of the scribe"). The scribes acted as secretaries of state, whose business it was to prepare and issue decrees in the name of the king (2 Sam. 8:17; 20:25; 1 Chr. 18:16; 24:6; 1 Kings 4:3; 2 Kings 12:9-11; 18:18-37, etc.). They discharged various other important public duties as men of high authority and influence in the affairs of state.

There was also a subordinate class of scribes, most of whom were Levites. They were engaged in various ways as writers. Such, for example, was Baruch, who "wrote from the mouth of Jeremiah all the words of the Lord" (Jer. 36:4, 32).

In later times, after the Captivity, when the nation lost its independence, the scribes turned their attention to the law, gaining for themselves distinction by their intimate acquaintance with its contents. On them devolved the duty of multiplying copies of the law and of teaching it to others (Ezra 7:6, 10–12; Neh. 8:1, 4, 9, 13). It is evident that in New Testament times the scribes belonged to the sect of the Pharisees, who supplemented the ancient written law by their traditions (Matt. 23), thereby obscuring it and rendering it of none effect. The titles "scribes" and "lawyers" (*q.v.*) are in the Gospels interchangeable (Matt. 22:35; Mark 12:28; Luke 20:39, etc.). They were in the time of our Lord the public teachers of the people, and frequently came into collision with him. They afterwards showed themselves greatly hostile to the apostles (Acts 4:5; 6:12).

Some of the scribes, however, were men of a different spirit, and showed themselves friendly to the gospel and its preachers. Thus Gamaliel advised the Sanhedrin, when the apostles were before them charged with "teaching in this name," to "refrain from these men and let them alone" (Acts 5:34–39; comp. 23:9).

Scrip, a small bag or wallet usually fastened to the girdle (1 Sam. 17:40); "a shepherd's bag."

In the New Testament it is the rendering of Gr. *pĕra,* which was a bag carried by travellers and shepherds, generally made of skin (Matt. 10:10; Mark 6:8; Luke 9:3; 10:4). The name "scrip" is meant to denote that the bag was intended to hold scraps, fragments, as if scraped off from larger articles, trifles.

Scrip'ture invariably in the New Testament denotes that definite collection of sacred books, regarded as given by inspiration of God, which we usually call the Old Testament (2 Tim. 3:15, 16; John 20:9; Gal. 3:22; 2 Pet. 1:20). It was God's purpose thus to perpetuate his revealed will. From time to time he raised up men to commit to writing in an infallible record the revelation he gave. The "Scripture," or collection of sacred writings, was thus enlarged from time to time as God saw necessary. We have now a completed "Scripture," consisting of the Old and New Testaments. The Old Testament canon in the time of our Lord was precisely the same as that which we now possess under that name. He placed the seal of his own authority on this collection of writings, as all equally given by inspiration (Matt. 5:17; 7:12; 22:40; Luke 16:29, 31). (See BIBLE; CANON.)

Scyth'ian. The Scythians consisted of "all the pastoral tribes who dwelt to the north of the Black Sea and the Caspian, and were scattered far away toward the east. Of this vast country but little was anciently known. Its modern representative is Russia, which, to a great extent, includes the same territories." They were the descendants of Japheth (Gen. 9:27). It appears that in apostolic times there were some of this people that embraced Christianity (Col. 3:11).

Sea, The (Heb. *yam*), signifies (1) "the gathering together of waters," the ocean (Gen. 1:10); (2) a river, as the Nile (Isa. 19:5), the Euphrates (Isa. 21:1; Jer. 51:36); (3) the Red Sea (Ex. 14:16, 27; 15:4, etc.); (4) the Mediterranean (Ex. 23:31; Num. 34:6, 7; Josh. 15:47; Ps. 80:11, etc.); (5) the "sea of Galilee," an inland fresh-water lake, and the Dead Sea or "salt sea" (Gen. 14:3; Num. 34:3, 12, etc.). The word "sea" is used symbolically in Isa. 60:5, where it probably means the nations around the Mediterranean. In Dan. 7:3, Rev. 13:1 it may mean the tumultuous changes among the nations of the earth.

Sea of Ja'zer (Jer. 48:32), a lake, now represented by some ponds in the high valley in which the Ammonite city of Jazer lies, the ruins of which are called *Sar*.

Sea, The molten, the great laver made by Solomon for the use of the priests in the temple, described in 1 Kings 7:23–26; 2 Chr. 4:2–5. It stood in the south-eastern corner of the inner court. It was 5 cubits high, 10 in diameter from brim to brim, and 30 in circumference. It was placed on the backs of twelve oxen, standing with their faces outward. It was capable of containing two or three thousand baths of

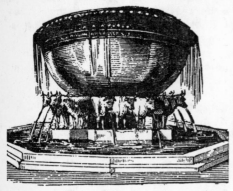

SUPPOSED FORM OF THE MOLTEN SEA.

water (comp. 2 Chr. 4 : 5), which was originally supplied by the Gibeonites, but was afterwards brought by a conduit from the pools of Bethlehem. It was made of "brass" (copper), which Solomon had taken from the captured cities of Hadarezer, the king of Zobah (1 Chr. 18 : 8). Ahaz afterwards removed this laver from the oxen, and placed it on a stone pavement (2 Kings 16 : 17). It was destroyed by the Chaldeans (25 : 13).

Sea of glass, a figurative expression used in Rev. 4 : 6 and 15 : 2. According to the interpretation of some, "this calm, glass-like sea, which is never in storm, but only interfused with flame, represents the counsels of God, those purposes of righteousness and love which are often fathomless but never obscure—always the same, though sometimes glowing with holy anger." (Comp. Ps. 36 : 6 ; 77 : 19 ; Rom. 11 : 33–36.)

Se'ah. In land measure, a space of 50 cubits long by 50 broad. In measure of capacity, a seah was a little over one peck. (See MEASURE.)

Seal, commonly a ring engraved with some device (Gen. 38 : 18, 25). Jezebel "wrote letters in Ahab's name, and sealed them with his seal" (1 Kings 21 : 8). Seals are frequently mentioned in Jewish history (1 Kings 8 : 6 ; Neh. 9 : 38 ; 10 : 1 ; Esther 3 : 12 ; Cant. 8 : 6 ; Isa. 8 : 16 ; Jer. 22 : 24 ; 32 : 44, etc.). Sealing a document was

equivalent to the signature of the owner of the seal. "The use of a signet-ring by the

ANCIENT JEWISH SEALS.

monarch has recently received a remarkable illustration by the discovery of an impression of such a signet on fine clay at Koyunjik, the site of the ancient Nineveh. This seal appears to have been impressed from the bezel of a metallic finger-ring. It is an oval, 2 inches in length by 1 inch wide, and bears the image, name, and titles of the Egyptian king Sabaco" (Rawlinson's *Hist. Illus. of the O.T.*, p. 46). The actual signet-rings of two Egyptian kings (Cheops and Horus) have been discovered.

EGYPTIAN SIGNET-RINGS.

The use of seals is mentioned in the New Testament only in connection with the record of our Lord's burial (Matt. 27 : 66). The tomb was sealed by the Pharisees and chief priests for the purpose of making sure that the disciples would not come and steal the body away (ver. 63, 64). The mode of doing this was probably by stretching a cord across the stone and sealing it at both ends with sealing-clay. When God is said to have sealed the Redeemer, the meaning is, that he has attested his divine mission (John 6:27). Circumcision is a seal, an attestation of the covenant (Rom. 4:11). Believers are sealed with the Spirit, as God's mark put upon them (Eph. 1:13; 4:30). Converts are by Paul styled the seal of his apostleship—*i.e.*, they are its attestation (1 Cor. 9:2). Seals and sealing are frequently mentioned in the book of Revelation (5:1; 6:1; 7:3; 10:4; 22:10).

Sea'sons (Gen. 8:22). See AGRICULTURE; MONTH.

Se'ba. (1.) One of the sons of Cush (Gen. 10:7).

(2.) The name of a country and nation (Isa. 43:3; 5:14) mentioned along with Egypt and E hiopia, and therefore probably in north-eastern Africa. The ancient name of Meroë. The kings of Sheba and Seba are mentioned together in Ps. 72:10.

Se'bat, the eleventh month of the Hebrew year, extending from the new moon of February to that of March (Zech. 1:7). Assyrian *sabatu*, "storm." (See MONTH.)

Seca'cah—*enclosure*—one of the six cities in the wilderness of Judah, noted for its "great cistern" (Josh. 15:61). It has been identified with the ruin *Sikkeh*, east of Bethany.

Se'chu—*a hill* or *watch-tower*—a place between Gibeah and Ramah noted for its "great well" (1 Sam. 19:22); probably the modern *Suweikeh*, south of Beeroth.

Sect (Gr. *hairĕsis*, usually rendered "heresy"—Acts 24:14; 1 Cor. 11:19; Gal. 5:20, etc.), meaning properly "a choice," then "a chosen manner of life," and then "a religious party," as the "sect" of the Sadducees (Acts 5:17), of the Pharisees (15:5), the Nazarenes—*i.e.*, Christians—(24:5). It afterwards came to be used in a bad sense, of those holding pernicious error, divergent forms of belief (2 Pet. 2:1; Gal. 5:20).

Secun'dus—*second*—a Christian of Thessalonica who accompanied Paul into Asia (Acts 20:4).

Seer, a name sometimes applied to the prophets because of the *visions* granted to them. It is first found in 1 Sam. 9:9. It is afterwards applied to Zadok, Gad, etc. (2 Sam. 15:27; 24:11; 1 Chr. 9:22; 25:5;

2 Chr. 9:29; Amos 7:12; Micah 3:7). The "sayings of the seers",(2 Chr. 33:18, 19) is rendered in the Revised Version "the history of Hozai" (marg., *the seers;* so the LXX.), of whom, however, nothing is known. (See PROPHET.)

Seethe, to boil (Ex. 16:23).

Seeth'ing pot, a vessel for boiling provisions in (Job 41:20; Jer. 1:13).

Se'gub—*elevated.* (1.) The youngest son of Hiel the Bethelite. His death is recorded in 1 Kings 16:34 (comp. Josh. 6:26).

(2.) A descendant of Judah (1 Chr. 2:21, 22).

Se'ir—*rough; hairy.* (1.) A Horite; one of the "dukes" of Edom (Gen. 36:20-30).

(2.) The name of a mountainous region occupied by the Edomites, extending along the eastern side of the Arabah from the south-eastern extremity of the Dead Sea to near the Akabah, or the eastern branch of the Red Sea. It was originally occupied by the Horites (Gen. 14:6), who were afterwards driven out by the Edomites (Gen. 32:3; 33:14, 16). It was allotted to the descendants of Esau (Deut. 2:4, 22; Josh. 24:4; 2 Chr. 20:10; Isa. 21:11; Ezek. 25:8).

(3.) A mountain range (not the Edomite range, Gen. 32:3) lying between the Wâdy Aly and the Wâdy Ghurab (Josh. 15:10).

Sei'rath—*woody district; shaggy*—a place among the mountains of Ephraim, bordering on Benjamin, to which Ehud fled after he had assassinated Eglon at Jericho (Judg. 3:26, 27).

Se'la = **Se'lah**—*rock*—the capital of Edom, situated in the great valley extending from the Dead Sea to the Red Sea (2 Kings 14:7). It was near Mount Hor, close by the desert of Zin. It is called "the rock" (Judg. 1:36). When Amaziah took it he called it Joktheel (*q.v.*). It is mentioned by the prophets (Isa. 16:1; Obad. 3) as doomed to destruction.

It appears in later history and in the Vulgate Version under the name of Petra. "The caravans from all ages, from the interior of Arabia and from the Gulf of Persia, from Hadramaut on the ocean, and even from Sabea or Yemen, appear to have

ROCK TEMPLE, PETRA.

pointed to Petra as a common centre; and from Petra the tide seems again to have branched out in every direction—to Egypt, Palestine, and Syria, through Arsinoë, Gaza, Tyre, Jerusalem, and Damascus, and by other routes, terminating at the Mediterranean." (See EDOM [2].)

Se'la-hammahle'koth—*cliff of divisions*—the name of the great gorge which lies between Hachilah and Maon, south-east of Hebron. This gorge is now called the *Wâdy Malâky*. This was the scene of the interview between David and Saul mentioned in 1 Sam. 26:13. Each stood on an opposing cliff, with this deep chasm between.

Se'lah, a word frequently found in the book of Psalms, and also in Hab. 3:9, 13—about seventy-four times in all in Scripture. Its meaning is doubtful. Some interpret it as meaning "silence" or "pause;" others, "end," "a louder strain," "piano," etc.

The LXX. render the word by *daplusma*—*i.e.*, "a division."

Seleu'cia, the sea-port of Antioch, near the mouth of the Orontes. Paul and his companions sailed from this port on their first missionary journey (Acts 13:4). This city was built by Seleucus Nicator, the "king of Syria." It is said of him that "few princes have ever lived with so great a passion for the building of cities. He is reputed to have built in all nine Seleucias, sixteen Antiochs, and six Laodiceas." Seleucia became a city of great importance, and was made a "free city" by Pompey. It is now a small village, called *el-Kalusi.*

Sem'ei, mentioned in the genealogy of our Lord (Luke 3:26).

Sena'ah—*thorny*—a place many of the inhabitants of which returned from Babylon with Zerubbabel (Ezra 2:35; Neh. 7:38).

Sen'ate (Acts 5:21), the "elders of

Israel" who formed a component part of the Sanhedrin.

Se′neh—*the acacia; rock-thorn*—the southern cliff in the Wâdy es-Suweinît, a valley south of Michmash, which Jonathan climbed with his armour-bearer (1 Sam. 14 : 4, 5). The rock opposite, on the other side of the wâdy, was called Bozez.

Se′nir = Shenir, the name given to Hermon by the Amorites (Deut. 3 : 9). It means "coat of mail" or "breastplate," and is equivalent to "Sirion." Some interpret the word as meaning "the prominent" or "the snowy mountain." It is properly the name of the central of the three summits of Hermon (*q.v.*)

Sennach′erib—*Sin* (the god) *sends many brothers*—son of Sargon, whom he succeeded on the throne of Assyria (B.C. 705), in the 23rd year of Hezekiah. "Like the Persian Xerxes, he was weak and vainglorious, cowardly under reverse, and cruel and boastful in success." He first set himself to break up the powerful combination of princes who were in league against him. Among these was Hezekiah, who had entered into an alliance with Egypt against Assyria. He accordingly led a very powerful army of at least 200,000 men into Judea, and devastated the land on every side, taking and destroying many cities (2 Kings 18 : 13-16 ; comp. Isa. 22, 24, 29, and 2 Chr. 32 : 1-8). His own account of this invasion, as given in the Assyrian annals, is in these words: "Because Hezekiah, king of Judah, would not submit to my yoke, I came up against him, and by force of arms and by the might of my power I took forty-six of his strong fenced cities ; and of the smaller towns which were scattered about, I took and plundered a countless number. From these places I took and carried off 200,156 persons, old and young, male and female, together with horses and mules, asses and camels, oxen and sheep, a countless multitude ; and Hezekiah himself I shut up in

Jerusalem, his capital city, like a bird in a cage, building towers round the city to hem him in, and raising banks of earth against the gates, so as to prevent escape......Then upon Hezekiah there fell the fear of the power of my arms, and he sent out to me the chiefs and the elders of Jerusalem with 30 talents of gold and 800 talents of silver, and divers treasures, a rich and immense booty......All these things were brought to me at Nineveh, the seat of my government." (Comp. Isa. 22 : 1-13 for description of the feelings of the inhabitants of Jerusalem at such a crisis.)

SENNACHERIB IN CHARIOT.
(From Koyunjik.)

Hezekiah was not disposed to become an Assyrian feudatory. He accordingly at once sought help from Egypt (2 Kings 18 : 20-24). Sennacherib, hearing of this, marched a second time into Palestine (2 Kings 18 : 17-37 ; 19 ; 2 Chr. 32 : 9-23 ; Isa. 36 : 2-22. Isa. 37 : 25 should be rendered "dried up all the Nile-arms of Matsor," *i.e.*, of Egypt, so called from the "Matsor" or great fortification across the isthmus of Suez, which protected it from invasions from the east). Sennacherib sent envoys to try to persuade Hezekiah to surrender, but in vain. (See TIRHAKAH.) He next sent a threatening letter (2 Kings 19 : 10–14), which Hezekiah carried into the temple and spread before the Lord. Isaiah again brought an encouraging message to the pious king (2 Kings 19 : 20–34). "In that night" the angel of the Lord went forth and smote the camp of the Assyrians. In the morning, "behold, they were all dead corpses." The Assyrian army was annihilated.

This great disaster is not, as was to be expected, taken notice of in the Assyrian annals.

The scene is thus depicted by the English poet :—

"The Assyrian came down like the wolf on the fold,
And his cohorts were gleaming with purple and gold....
Like the leaves of the forest when summer is
/ green,
That host with their banners at sunset were seen :
Like the leaves of the forest when autumn hath blown,
That host on the morrow lay withered and strown.
For the Angel of Death spread his wings on the blast,
And breathed in the face of the foe as he passed ;
And the eyes of the sleepers waxed deadly and chill,
And their hearts but once heaved, and for ever grew still."—Byron's *Hebrew Melodies.*

Though Sennacherib survived this disaster some twenty years, he never again renewed his attempt against Jerusalem. He was murdered by two of his own sons (Adrammelech and Sharezer), and was succeeded by another son, Esarhaddon (B.C. 681), after a reign of twenty-four years.

Seo'rim—*barley*—the chief of the fourth priestly course (1 Chr. 24 : 8).

Se'phar—*numbering*—(Gen. 10 : 30), supposed by some to be the ancient Himyaritic capital, "Shaphar," *Zaphar*, on the Indian Ocean, between the Persian Gulf and the Red Sea.

Seph'arad (Obad. 20), some locality unknown. The modern Jews think that Spain is meant, and hence they designate the Spanish Jews "Sephardim," as they do the German Jews by the name "Ash-

kenazim," because the rabbis call Germany Ashkenaz. Others identify it with Sardis, the capital of Lydia. The Latin father Jerome regarded it as an Assyrian word, meaning "boundary," and interpreted the sentence, "which is in Sepharad," by "who are scattered abroad in all the boundaries and regions of the earth." Perowne says : "Whatever uncertainty attaches to the word *Sepharad*, the drift of the prophecy is clear—*viz.*, that not only the exiles from Babylon, but Jewish captives from other and distant regions, shall be brought back to live prosperously within the enlarged borders of their own land."

Sepharva'im, taken by Sargon, king of Assyria (2 Kings 17 : 24 ; 18 : 34 ; 19 : 13 ; Isa. 37 : 13). It was a double city, and received the common name Sepharvaim—*i.e.*, "the two Sipparas," or "the two booktowns." The Sippara on the east bank of the Euphrates is now called Abu-Habba ; that on the other bank was Accad, the old capital of Sargon I., where he established a great library. (See SARGON.) The recent discovery of cuneiform inscriptions at Tel el-Amarna in Egypt, consisting of official despatches to Pharaoh Amenophis IV. and his predecessor from their agents in Palestine, proves that in the century before the Exodus an active literary intercourse was carried on between these nations, and that the medium of the correspondence was the Babylonian language and script. (See KIRJATH-SEPHER.)

Sep'tuagint. See VERSIONS.

Sep'ulchre, first mentioned as purchased by Abraham for Sarah from Ephron the Hittite (Gen. 23 : 20). This was the "cave of the field of Machpelah," where also Abraham and Rebekah and Jacob and Leah were buried (49 : 29–32). In Acts 7 : 16 it is said that Jacob was "laid in the sepulchre that Abraham bought for a sum of money of the sons of Emmor the father of Sychem." It has been proposed, as a mode of reconciling the apparent discrepancy between this verse and Gen. 23 : 20, to read Acts 7 : 16 thus : "And they [*i.e., our fathers*] were carried over into Sychem, and laid in the sepulchre that Abraham bought for a sum of money of the sons of Emmor [*the* *son*] of Sychem." In this way the purchase made by Abraham is not to be confounded with the purchase made by Jacob subsequently in the same district. Of this purchase by Abraham there is no direct record in the Old Testament. (See Tomb.)

Se′rah—*abundance; princess*—the daughter of Asher and grand-daughter of Jacob (Gen. 46 : 17) ; called also Sarah (Num. 26 : 46 ; R.V., "Serah ").

Sera′iah—*soldier of Jehovah.* (1.) The father of Joab (1 Chr. 4 : 13, 14).

(2.) The grand-daughter of Jehu (1 Chr. 4 : 35).

(3.) One of David's scribes or secretaries (2 Sam. 8 : 17).

(4.) A Netophathite (Jer. 40 : 8).

(5.) Ezra 2 : 2.

(6.) Father of Ezra the scribe (7 : 1).

(7.) A ruler of the temple (Neh. 11 : 11).

(8.) A priest of the days of Jehoiakim (Neh. 12 : 1, 12).

(9.) A chief priest of the time of Zedekiah. He was carried captive by Nebuchadnezzar to Babylon, and there put to death (2 Kings 25 : 18, 23 ; 1 Chr. 6 : 14).

(10.) The son of Neriah. When Zedekiah made a journey to Babylon to do homage to Nebuchadnezzar, Seraiah had charge of the royal gifts to be presented on that occasion. Jeremiah took advantage of the occasion, and sent with Seraiah a word of cheer to the exiles in Babylon, and an announcement of the doom in store for that guilty city. The roll containing this message (Jer. 50 : 1-8) Seraiah was to read to the exiles, and then, after fixing a stone to it, was to throw it into the Euphrates, uttering, as it sank, the prayer recorded in Jer. 51 : 59-64. Babylon was at this time in the height of its glory, the greatest and most powerful monarchy in the world. Scarcely seventy years elapsed when the words of the prophet were all fulfilled. Jer. 51 : 59 is rendered in the Revised Version, "Now Seraiah was chief chamberlain," instead of "was a quiet prince," as in the Authorized Version.

Ser′aphim, mentioned in Isa. 6 : 2, 3, 6, 7. This word means *fiery ones*, in allusion, as is supposed, to their burning love. They are represented as "standing" above the King as he sat upon his throne, ready at once to minister unto him. Their form appears to have been human, with the addition of wings. (See Angels.) This word, in the original, is used elsewhere only of the "fiery serpents "(Num. 21 : 6, 8 ; Deut. 8 : 15 ; comp. Isa. 14 : 29 ; 30 : 6) sent by God as his instruments to inflict on the people the righteous penalty of sin.

Se′red—*fear*—one of the sons of Zebulun (Gen. 46 : 14).

Ser′geants—Acts 16 : 35, 38 (R.V., "lictors ")—officers who attended the magistrates and assisted them in the execution of justice.

Ser′gius Pau′lus, a "prudent man" (R.V., "man of understanding "), the deputy (R.V., "proconsul ") of Cyprus (Acts 13 : 6-13). He became a convert to Christianity under Paul, who visited this island on his first mission to the heathen.

A remarkable memorial of this proconsul was recently (1887) discovered at Rome. On a boundary stone of Claudius his name is found, among others, as having been appointed (A.D. 47) one of the curators of the banks and the channel of the river Tiber. After serving his three years as proconsul at Cyprus, he returned to Rome, where he held the office referred to. As he is not saluted in Paul's letter to the Romans, he probably died before it was written.

Sermon on the mount. After spending a night in solemn meditation and prayer in the lonely mountain-range to the west of the Lake of Galilee (Luke 6 : 12), on the following morning our Lord called to him his disciples, and from among them chose twelve, who were to be henceforth trained to be his apostles (Mark 3 : 14, 15). After this solemn consecration of the twelve, he descended from the mountain-peak to a more, level spot (Luke 6 : 17), and there he sat down and delivered the "sermon on the mount " (Matt. 5-7 ; Luke 6 : 20-49) to the assembled multitude. The mountain here spoken of was probably that known by the name of the "Horns of Hattin " (*Kurûn Hattîn*), a ridge running east and west, not far from Capernaum. It was afterwards called the "Mount of Beatitudes."

Ser′pent (Heb. *nahash ;* Gr. *ophis*), frequently noticed in Scripture. More than forty species are found in Syria and Arabia. The poisonous character of the serpent is alluded to in Jacob's blessing on Dan (Gen. 49:17; see Prov. 30:18, 19; James 3:7; Jer. 8:17). (See ADDER.)

This word is used symbolically of a deadly, subtle, malicious enemy (Luke 10:19).

The serpent is first mentioned in connection with the history of the temptation and fall of our first parents (Gen. 3). It has been well remarked regarding this temptation: "A real serpent was the agent of the temptation, as is plain from what is said of the natural characteristic of the serpent in the first verse of the chapter (3:1), and from the curse pronounced upon the animal itself. But that Satan was the actual tempter, and that he used the serpent merely as his instrument, is evident (1) from the nature of the transaction; for although the serpent may be the most subtle of all the beasts of the field, yet he has not the high intellectual faculties which the tempter here displayed. (2.) In the New Testament it is both directly asserted and in various forms assumed that Satan seduced our first parents into sin (John 8:44; Rom. 16:20; 2 Cor. 11:3, 14; Rev. 12:9; 20:2)." —Hodge's *System. Theol.*, ii. 127.

Ser′pent, Fiery (LXX. "deadly," Vulg. "burning")—Num. 21:6—probably the *naja haje* of Egypt; some swift-springing, deadly snake (Isa. 14:29). After setting out from their encampment at Ezion-geber, the Israelites entered on a wide sandy desert, which stretches from the mountains of Edom as far as the Persian Gulf. While traversing this region, the people began to murmur and utter loud complaints against Moses. As a punishment, the Lord sent serpents among them, and much people of Israel died. Moses interceded on their behalf, and by divine direction he made a "brazen serpent," and raised it on a pole in the midst of the camp, and all the wounded Israelites who looked on it were at once healed. (Comp. John 3:14, 15.) (See ASP.) This "brazen serpent" was preserved by the Israelites till the days of Hezekiah, when it was destroyed (2 Kings 18:4). (See BRASS.)

Se′rug—*branch*—the father of Nahor (Gen. 11:20-23); called Saruch in Luke 3:35.

Serv′itor occurs only in 2 Kings 4:43, Authorized Version (R.V., "servant"). The Hebrew word there rendered "servitor" is elsewhere rendered "minister," "servant" (Ex. 24:13; 33:11). Probably Gehazi, the personal attendant on Elisha, is here meant.

Seth—*appointed; a substitute*—the third son of Adam and Eve (Gen. 4:25; 5:3). His mother gave him this name, "for God," said she, "hath appointed me [*i.e.*, compensated me with] another seed instead of Abel, whom Cain slew."

Se′thur—*hidden*—one of the spies sent to search the Promised Land. He was of the tribe of Asher (Num. 13:13).

Sev′en. This number occurs frequently in Scripture, and in such connections as lead to the supposition that it has some typical meaning. On the seventh day God rested, and hallowed it (Gen. 2:2, 3). The division of time into weeks of seven days each accounts for many instances of the occurrence of this number. This number has been called the symbol of perfection, and also the symbol of rest. "Jacob's seven years' service to Laban; Pharaoh's seven fat oxen and seven lean ones; the seven branches of the golden candlestick; the seven trumpets and the seven priests who sounded them; the seven days' siege of Jericho; the seven churches, seven spirits, seven stars, seven seals, seven vials, and many others, sufficiently prove the importance of this sacred number" (see Lev. 25:4; 1 Sam. 2:5; Ps. 12:6; 79:12; Prov. 26:16; Isa. 4:1; Matt. 18:21, 22; Luke 17:4). The feast of Passover (Ex. 12:15, 16), the feast of Weeks (Deut. 16:9), of Tabernacles (13:15), and the Jubilee (Lev. 25:8), were all ordered by seven. Seven is the number of sacrifice (2 Chr. 29:21; Job 42:8), of purification and consecration (Lev. 4:6, 17; 8:11, 33; 14:9, 51), of forgiveness (Matt. 18:21, 22; Luke 17:4), of reward (Deut. 28:7; 1 Sam. 2:5), and of punishment (Lev. 26:21, 24, 28; Deut. 28:25). It is used for any round number in such passages as Job 5:19;

Prov. 26 : 16, 25; Isa. 4 : 1; Matt. 12 : 45. It is used also to mean "abundantly" (Gen. 4 : 15, 24; Lev. 26 : 24; Ps. 79 : 12).

Sev'enty weeks, a prophetic period mentioned in Dan. 9 : 24, and usually interpreted on the "year-day" theory—*i.e.*, reckoning each day for a year. This period will thus represent 490 years. This is regarded as the period which would elapse till the time of the coming of the Messiah, dating "from the going forth of the commandment to restore and rebuild Jerusalem"—*i.e.*, from the close of the Captivity.

Shaalab'bin or **Shaal'bim**—*a place of foxes*—a town of the tribe of Dan (Josh. 19 : 42; Judg. 1 : 35). It was one of the chief towns from which Solomon drew his supplies (1 Kings 4 : 9). It is probably the modern village of *Selbît*, 3 miles north of Ajalon.

Shaara'im—*two gates.* (1.) A city in the plain of Judah (1 Sam. 17 : 52); called also Sharaim (Josh. 15 : 36).

(2.) A town in Simeon (1 Chr. 4 : 31).

Shaash'gaz—*servant of the beautiful*—a chief eunuch in the second house of the harem of king Ahasuerus (Esther 2 : 14).

Shabbeth'ai—*Sabbath-born*—a Levite who assisted in expounding the law and investigating into the illegal marriages of the Jews (Ezra 10 : 15; Neh. 8 : 7; 11 : 16).

Shad'dai—*the Omnipotent*—the name of God in frequent use in the Hebrew Scriptures, generally translated "the Almighty."

Shad'ow, used in Col. 2 : 17; Heb. 8 : 5; 10 : 1 to denote the typical relation of the Jewish to the Christian dispensation.

Shad'rach—*Aku's command*—the Chaldean name given to Hananiah, one of the Hebrew youths whom Nebuchadnezzar carried captive to Babylon (Dan. 1 : 6, 7; 3 : 12-30). He and his two companions refused to bow down before the image which Nebuchadnezzar had set up on the plains of Dura. Their conduct filled the king with the greatest fury, and he commanded them to be cast into the burning fiery furnace. Here, amid the fiery flames, they were miraculously preserved from harm. Over them the fire had no power, "neither was a hair of their head singed, neither

had the smell of fire passed on them." Thus Nebuchadnezzar learned the greatness of the God of Israel. (See ABEDNEGO.)

Sha'lem—*perfect*—a place (probably the village of *Salim*) some 2 miles east of Jacob's well. There is an abundant supply of water, which may have been the reason for Jacob's settling at this place (Gen. 33 : 18-20). The Revised Version translates this word, and reads, "Jacob came in peace to the city of Shechem," thus not regarding it as a proper name at all.

Sha'lim, Land of—*land of foxes*—a place apparently to the north-west of Jerusalem (1 Sam. 9 : 4), perhaps in the neighbourhood of Shaalabbin in Dan (Josh. 19 : 42).

Shali'sha, Land of, probably the district of Baal-shalisha (2 Kings 4 : 42), lying about 12 miles north of Lydda (1 Sam. 9 : 4).

Shal'lecheth, The gate of—*i.e.*, "the gate of casting out," hence supposed to be the refuse gate; one of the gates of the house of the Lord, "by the causeway of the going up"—*i.e.*, the causeway rising up from the Tyropœon valley = valley of the cheesemakers (1 Chr. 26 : 16).

Shal'lum—*retribution.* (1.) The son of Jabesh, otherwise unknown. He "conspired against Zachariah, and smote him before the people, and slew him, and reigned in his stead" (2 Kings 15 : 9, 10). He reigned only "a month of days in Samaria." Menahem rose up against Shallum and put him to death (1 Kings 14 : 17; 16 : 6, 9, 23; 2 Kings 15 : 14), and became king in his stead.

(2.) Keeper of the temple vestments in the reign of Josiah (2 Kings 22 : 14).

(3.) One of the posterity of Judah (1 Chr. 2 : 40, 41).

(4.) A descendant of Simeon (1 Chr. 4 : 25).

(5.) One of the line of the high priests (1 Chr. 6 : 13).

(6.) 1 Chr. 7 : 13.

(7.) A keeper of the gate in the reign of David (1 Chr. 9 : 17).

(8.) A Levite porter (1 Chr. 9 : 19, 31; Jer. 35 : 4).

(9.) An Ephraimite chief (2 Chr. 28 : 12).

(10.) The uncle of the prophet Jeremiah (Jer. 32 : 7).

(11.) A son of king Josiah (1 Chr. 3: 15; Jer. 22:11), who was elected to succeed his father on the throne, although he was two years younger than his brother Eliakim. He assumed the crown under the name of Jehoahaz (*q.v.*). He did not imitate the example of his father (2 Kings 23:32), but was "a young lion that had learned to catch his prey, to devour men" (Ezek. 19:3). His policy was anti-Egyptian therefore. Necho, at that time at Riblah, sent an army against Jerusalem, which at once yielded, and Jehoahaz was carried captive to the Egyptian camp, Eliakim being appointed king in his stead. He remained a captive in Egypt till his death, and was the first king of Judah that died in exile.

Shal'man, an Assyrian king (Hos. 10: 14), identified with Shalmanezer II. (Sayce) or IV. (Lenormant), the successor of Pul on the throne of Assyria (B.C. 728). He made war against Hoshea, the king of Israel, whom he subdued and compelled to pay an annual tribute. Hoshea, however, soon after rebelled against his Assyrian conqueror. Shalmanezer again marched against Samaria, which, after a siege of three years, was taken (2 Kings 17:3-5; 18:9) by Sargon (*q.v.*). A revolution meantime had broken out in Assyria, and Shalmanezer was deposed. Sargon usurped the vacant throne. Schrader thinks that this is probably the name of a king of Moab mentioned on an inscription of Tiglath-pileser as *Salamanu.*

Sham'gar. The Philistines from the maritime plain had made incursions into the Hebrew upland for the purposes of plunder, when one of this name, the son of Anath, otherwise unknown, headed a rising for the purpose of freeing the land from this oppression. He repelled the invasion, slaying 600 men with an "ox goad" (*q.v.*). The goad was a formidable sharp-pointed instrument, sometimes ten feet long. He was probably contemporary for a time with Deborah and Barak (Judg. 3: 31; 5:6).

Sha'mir—*a sharp thorn.* (1.) One of the sons of Michah (1 Chr. 24:24).

(2.) A town among the mountains of

Judah (Josh. 15:48); probably *Sômerah,* 2½ miles north-west of Debir.

(3.) The residence of Tola, one of the judges, on Mount Ephraim (Judg. 10:1, 2).

Sham'mah—*desert.* (1.) One of the "dukes" of Edom (Gen. 36:13, 17).

(2.) One of the sons of Jesse (1 Sam. 16: 9). He is also called Shimeah (2 Sam. 13: 3) and Shimma (1 Chr. 2:13).

(3.) One of David's three mighty men (2 Sam. 23:11, 12).

(4.) One of David's mighties (2 Sam. 23: 25); called also Shammoth (1 Chr. 11:27) and Shamhuth (27:8).

Shammu'a—*heard.* (1.) One of the spies sent out by Moses to search the land (Num. 13:4). He represented the tribe of Reuben.

(2.) One of David's sons (1 Chr. 14:4; 3:5, "Shimea;" 2 Sam. 5:14).

(3.) A Levite under Nehemiah (11:17).

Sha'phan—*a coney*—a scribe or secretary of king Josiah (2 Kings 22:3-7). He consulted Huldah concerning the newly-discovered copy of the law which was delivered to him by Hilkiah the priest (8-14). His grandson Gedaliah was governor of Judea (25:22).

Sha'phat—*judge.* (1.) One of the spies. He represented the tribe of Simeon (Num. 13:5).

(2.) The father of Elisha (1 Kings 19: 16-19).

(3.) One of David's chief herdsmen (1 Chr. 27:29).

Sha'pher—*brightness*—one of the stations where Israel encamped in the wilderness (Num. 33:23, 24).

Shar'aim—*two gates* (Josh. 15:36)— more correctly Shaaraim (1 Sam. 17:52), probably *Tell Zakarîya* and *Kefr Zakarîya,* in the valley of Elah, 3½ miles north-west of Socoh.

Share'zer—*(god) protect the king!*—a son of Sennacherib, king of Assyria. He and his brother Adrammelech murdered their father and then fled into the land of Armenia (2 Kings 19:37).

Sha'ron, Sa'ron—*a plain*—a level tract extending from the Mediterranean to the hill country to the west of Jerusalem, about 30 miles long and from 8 to 15 miles

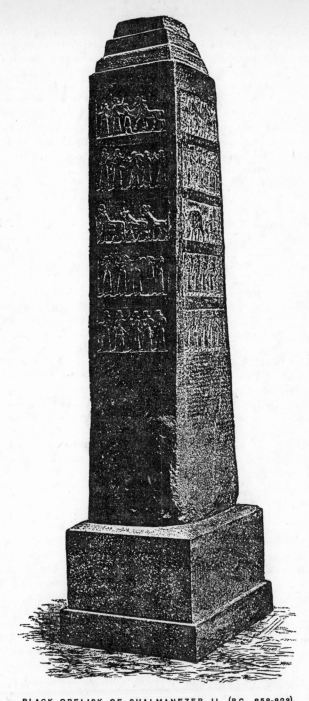

BLACK OBELISK OF SHALMANEZER II. (B.C. 858-823).
In the British Museum.
With inscription giving an account of his victories, which, says Sayce, "is strictly in accordance with the Book of Kings."

broad, celebrated for its beauty and fertility (1 Chr. 27 : 29 ; Isa. 33 : 9 ; 35 : 2 ; 65 : 10). The "rose of Sharon" is celebrated (Cant. 2 : 1). It is called Lasharon (the article *la* being here a part of the word) in Josh. 12:18.

Sha'veh, Valley of—*valley of the plain* —the ancient name of the "king's dale" (*q.v.*), or Kidron, on the north side of Jerusalem (Gen. 14 : 17).

Sha'veh-Kiriatha'im—*plain of Kirjathaim*—where Chedorlaomer defeated the Emims, the original inhabitants (Gen. 14 : 5). Now *Kureiyât*, north of Dibon, in the land of Moab.

Shav'sha ("Seraiah," 2 Sam. 8 : 17; "Shisha," 1 Kings 4 : 3), one of David's secretaries (1 Chr. 18 : 16).

Sheal'tiel—*asked for of God*—father of Zerubbabel (Ezra 3 : 2, 8; Neh. 12 : 1).

Shear'ing-house (2 Kings 10 : 12, 14; marg., "house of shepherds binding sheep." R.V., "the shearing-house of the shepherds ;" marg., "house of gathering "), some place between Samaria and Jezreel, where Jehu slew "two and fifty men" of the royal family of Judah. The Heb. word *Beth-eked* so rendered is supposed by some to be a proper name.

She'ar-Ja'shub—*a remnant shall escape or return* (*i.e.*, to God)—a symbolical name which the prophet Isaiah gave to his son (Isa. 7 : 3), perhaps his eldest son.

She'ba — *an oath, seven*. (1.) Heb. *shĕbhâ'*, the son of Raamah (Gen. 10 : 7), whose descendants settled with those of Dedan on the Persian Gulf.

(2.) Heb. *id.* A son of Joktan (Gen. 10 : 28), probably the founder of the Sabeans.

(3.) Heb. *id.* A son of Jokshan, who was a son of Abraham by Keturah (Gen. 25 : 3).

(4.) Heb. *id.* A kingdom in Arabia Felix. The queen of Sheba brought gold, spices, and precious stones to Solomon (1 Kings 10 : 1, 2). She is called by our Lord the "queen of the south" (Matt. 12 : 42).

(5.) Heb. *shĕbha'*—"seven" or "an oak." A town of Simeon (Josh. 19 : 2).

(6.) Heb. *id.* A "son of Bichri," of the family of Becher, the son of Benjamin, and thus of the stem from which Saul was descended (2 Sam. 20 : 1-22).

When David was returning to Jerusalem after the defeat of Absalom, a strife arose between the ten tribes and the tribe of Judah, because the latter took the lead in bringing back the king. Sheba took advantage of this state of things, and raised the standard of revolt, proclaiming, "We have no part in David." With his followers he proceeded northward. David seeing it necessary to check this revolt, ordered Abishai to take the *gibborim*, "mighty men," and the body-guard and such troops as he could gather, and pursue Sheba. Joab joined the expedition, and having treacherously put Amasa to death, assumed the command of the army. Sheba took refuge in Abel - Bethmaachah, a fortified town some miles north of Lake Merom. While Joab was engaged in laying siege to this city, Sheba's head was, at the instigation of a "wise woman" who had held a parley with him from the city walls, thrown over the wall to the besiegers, and thus the revolt came to an end.

Shebani'ah—*whom Jehovah hides*, or *has made grow up*. (1.) A Levite appointed to blow the trumpet before the ark of God (1 Chr. 15 : 17, 24).

(2.) Another Levite (Neh. 9 : 4, 5).

(3.) A priest (Neh. 10 : 12).

(4.) A Levite (Neh. 10 : 4).

Sheb'arim—*breaks; ruins*—a place near Ai (Josh. 7 : 5; R.V. marg., "the quarries ").

Sheb'na — *tender youth* — "treasurer" over the house in the reign of Hezekiah— *i.e.*, comptroller or governor of the palace. On account of his pride he was ejected from this office, and Eliakim was promoted to it (Isa. 22 : 15-25). He appears to have been the leader of the party who favoured an alliance with Egypt against Assyria. It is conjectured that "Shebna the scribe," who was one of those whom the king sent to confer with the Assyrian ambassador (2 Kings 18 : 18, 26, 37 ; 19 : 2; Isa. 36 : 3, 11, 22; 37 : 2), was a different person.

Sheb'uel—*captive of God*. (1.) One of the descendants of Gershom, who had charge of the temple treasures in the time of David (1 Chr. 23 : 16; 26 : 24).

(2.) One of the sons of Heman; one of those whose duty it was to "lift up the

See page 622

NÂBLUS OR SHECHEM.

horn" in the temple service (1 Chr. 25:4); called also Shubael (ver. 20).

Shecani'ah—*one intimate with Jehovah.* (1.) A priest to whom the tenth lot came forth when David divided the priests (1 Chr. 24:11).

(2.) One of the priests who were "set to give to their brethren by courses" of the daily portion (2 Chr. 31:15, 16).

Shechani'ah—*id.* (1.) A priest whose sons are mentioned in 1 Chr. 3:21, 22.

(2.) Ezra 8:5.

(3.) Ezra 10:2, 3.

(4.) The father of Shemaiah, who repaired the wall of Jerusalem (Neh. 3:29).

(5.) The father-in-law of Tobiah (Neh. 6:18).

(6.) A priest who returned from the Captivity with Zerubbabel (Neh. 12:3).

She'chem—*shoulder.* (1.) The son of Hamor the Hivite (Gen. 33:19; 34).

(2.) A descendant of Manasseh (Num. 26:31; Josh. 17:2).

(3.) A city in Samaria (Gen. 33:18), called also Sichem (12:6), Sychem (Acts 7:16). It stood in the narrow sheltered valley between Ebal on the north and Gerizim on the south, these mountains at their base being only some 500 yards apart. Here Abraham pitched his tent and built his first altar in the Promised Land, and received the first divine promise (Gen. 12:6, 7). Here also Jacob "bought a parcel of a field at the hands of the children of Hamor" after his return from Mesopotamia, and settled with his household, which he purged from idolatry by burying the teraphim of his followers under an oak tree, which was afterwards called "the oak of the sorcerer" (Gen. 33:19; 35:4; Judg. 9:37). (See MEONENIM.) Here too after a while he dug a well, which bears his name to this day (John 4:5, 39–42). To Shechem Joshua gathered all Israel "before God," and delivered to them his second parting address (Josh. 24:1–15). He "made a covenant with the people that day" at the very place where, on first entering the land, they had responded to the law from Ebal and Gerizim (Josh. 24:25), the terms of which were recorded "in the book of the law of God"—*i.e.*, in the roll of the law of Moses;

and in memory of this solemn transaction a great stone was set up "under an oak" (comp. Gen. 28:18; 31:44–46; Ex. 24:4; Josh. 4:3), possibly the old "oak of Moreh," as a silent witness of the transaction to all coming time.

Shechem became one of the cities of refuge, the central city of refuge for Western Palestine (Josh. 20:7), and here the bones of Joseph were buried (24:32). Rehoboam was appointed king in Shechem (1 Kings 12:1, 19), but Jeroboam afterwards took up his residence here. This city is mentioned in connection with our Lord's conversation with the woman of Samaria (John 4:5); and thus, remaining as it does to the present day, it is one of the oldest cities of the world. It is the modern *Nâblus*, a contraction for Neapolis, the name given to it by Vespasian. It lies about a mile and a half up the valley on its southern slope, and on the north of Gerizim, which rises about 1,100 feet above it, and is about 34 miles north of Jerusalem. It contains about 10,000 inhabitants, of whom about 160 are Samaritans and 100 Jews, the rest being Christians and Mohammedans.

The site of Shechem is said to be of unrivalled beauty. Stanley says it is "the most beautiful, perhaps the only very beautiful, spot in Central Palestine."

Gaza, near Shechem, only mentioned 1 Chr. 7:28, has entirely disappeared. It was destroyed at the time of the Conquest, and its place was taken by Shechem. (See SYCHAR.)

Shechi'nah, a Chaldee word meaning *resting-place*, not found in Scripture, but used by the later Jews to designate the visible symbol of God's presence in the tabernacle, and afterwards in Solomon's temple. When the Lord led Israel out of Egypt he went before them "in a pillar of a cloud." This was the symbol of his presence with his people. For references made to it during the wilderness wanderings, see Ex. 14:20; 40:34–38; Lev. 9:23, 24; Num. 14:10; 16:19, 42.

It is probable that after the entrance into Canaan this glory-cloud settled in the tabernacle upon the ark of the covenant in the most holy place. We have, however, no special reference to it till the consecration of the temple by Solomon, when it filled the whole house with its glory, so that the priests could not stand to minister (1 Kings 8 : 10–13 ; 2 Chr. 5 : 13, 14 ; 7 : 1–3). Probably it remained in the first temple in the holy of holies as the symbol of Jehovah's presence so long as that temple stood. It afterwards disappeared. (See CLOUD.)

Sheep are of different varieties. Probably the flocks of Abraham and Isaac were of the wild species found still in the mountain regions of Persia and Kurdistan. After the Exodus, and as a result of intercourse with surrounding nations, other species were no doubt introduced into the herds of the people of Israel. They are frequently mentioned in Scripture. The care of a shepherd over his flock is referred to as illustrating God's care over his people (Ps. 23 : 1, 2 ; 74 : 1 ; 77 : 20 ; Isa. 40 : 11 ; 53 : 6 ; John 10 : 1–5, 7–16).

"The sheep of Palestine are longer in the head than ours, and have tails from 5 inches broad at the narrowest part to 15 inches at the widest, the weight being in proportion, and ranging generally from 10 to 14 lbs., but sometimes extending to 30 lbs. The tails are indeed huge masses of fat" (Geikie's *Holy Land, etc.*). The tail was no doubt the "rump" so frequently referred to in the Levitical sacrifices (Ex. 29 : 22 ; Lev. 3 : 9 ; 7 : 3 ; 9 : 19).

Sheep-shearing was generally an occasion of great festivity (Gen. 31 : 19 ; 38 : 12, 13 ; 1 Sam. 25 : 4–8, 36 ; 2 Sam. 13 : 23–28).

Sheep'-fold, a strong fenced enclosure for the protection of the sheep gathered within it (Num. 32 : 24 ; 1 Chr. 17 : 7 ; Ps. 50 : 9 ; 78 : 70). In John 10 : 16 the Authorized Version renders by "fold" two distinct Greek words, *aulē* and *poimnē*, the latter of which properly means a "flock," and is so rendered in the Revised Version. (See also Matt. 26 : 31 ; Luke 2 : 8 ; 1 Cor. 9 : 7.)

Sheep'-gate, one of the gates of Jerusalem mentioned by Nehemiah (3 : 1, 32 ; 12 : 39). It was in the eastern wall of the city.

Sheep'-market occurs only in John 5 : 2

(marg., also R.V., "sheep-gate"). The word so rendered is an adjective, and it is uncertain whether the noun to be supplied should be "gate" or, following the Vulgate Version, "pool."

She'kel—*weight*—the common standard both of weight and value among the Hebrews. It is estimated at 220 English grains, or a little more than half an ounce avoirdupois. The "shekel of the sanctuary" (Ex. 30 : 13 ; Num. 3 : 47) was equal to twenty gerahs (Ezek. 45 : 12). There were shekels of gold (1 Chr. 21 : 25), of silver (1 Sam. 9 : 8), of brass (17 : 5), and of iron (7). When it became a coined piece of money, the shekel of gold was equivalent to about £2 of our money. Six gold shekels, according to the later Jewish system, were equal in value to fifty silver ones.

The temple contribution, with which the public sacrifices were bought (Ex. 30 : 13 ; 2 Chr. 24 : 6), consisted of one common shekel, or a sanctuary half-shekel, equal to

THE SANCTUARY HALF-SHEKEL.

two Attic drachmas. The coin, a stater (*q.v.*), which Peter found in the fish's mouth paid this contribution for both him and Christ (Matt. 17 : 24, 27).

A zuza, or quarter of a shekel, was given by Saul to Samuel (1 Sam. 9 : 8).

ZUZA, OR QUARTER-SHEKEL.

She'lah—*petition*. (1.) Judah's third son (Gen. 38 : 2, 5, 11, 14).

(2.) A son of Arphaxad (1 Chr. 1 : 18).

Shelemi'ah—*whom Jehovah repays.* (1.) Ezra 10 : 39.

(2.) The father of Hananiah (Neh. 3 : 30).

(3.) A priest in the time of Nehemiah (13 : 13).

(4.) Father of one of those who accused Jeremiah to Zedekiah (Jer. 37 : 3 ; 38 : 1).

(5.) Father of a captain of the ward (Jer. 37 : 13).

(6.) Jer. 36 : 14.

Shem—*a name; renown*—the first mentioned of the sons of Noah (Gen. 5 : 32 ; 6 : 10). He was probably the eldest of Noah's sons. The words "brother of Japheth the elder" in Gen. 10 : 21 are more correctly rendered "the elder brother of Japheth," as in the Revised Version. Shem's name is generally mentioned first in the list of Noah's sons. He and his wife were saved in the ark (11 : 11). Noah foretold his preeminence over Canaan (9 : 23-27). He died at the age of six hundred years, having been for many years contemporary with Abraham, according to the usual chronology. The Israelitish nation sprang from him (Gen. 11 : 10-26 ; 1 Chr. 1 : 24-27).

She'ma—*rumour.* (1.) A Reubenite (1 Chr. 5 : 8).

(2.) A Benjamite (1 Chr. 8 : 13).

(3.) One who stood by Ezra when he read the law (Neh. 8 : 4).

(4.) A town in the south of Judah (Josh. 15 : 26); the same as Sheba (ver. 5).

Shema'ah—*rumour*—a Benjamite whose sons "came to David to Ziklag" (1 Chr. 12 : 3).

Shema'iah—*whom Jehovah heard.* (1.) A prophet in the reign of Rehoboam (1 Kings 12 : 22-24).

(2.) Neh. 3 : 29.

(3.) A Simeonite (1 Chr. 4 : 37).

(4.) A priest (Neh. 12 : 42).

(5.) A Levite (1 Chr. 9 : 14).

(6.) 1 Chr. 9 : 16 ; Neh. 11 : 15.

(7.) A Levite in the time of David, who with 200 of his brethren took part in the bringing up of the ark from Obed-edom to Hebron (1 Chr. 15 : 8).

(8.) A Levite (1 Chr. 24 : 6).

(9.) The eldest son of Obed-edom (1 Chr. 26 : 4-8).

(10.) A Levite (2 Chr. 29 : 14).

(11.) A false prophet who hindered the rebuilding of Jerusalem (Neh. 6 : 10).

(12.) A prince of Judah who assisted at the dedication of the wall of Jerusalem (Neh. 12 : 34-36).

(13.) A false prophet who opposed Jeremiah (Jer. 29 : 24-32).

(14.) One of the Levites whom Jehoshaphat appointed to teach the law (2 Chr. 17 : 8).

(15.) A Levite appointed to "distribute the oblations of the Lord" (2 Chr. 31 : 15).

(16.) A Levite (2 Chr. 35 : 9).

(17.) The father of Urijah the prophet (Jer. 26 : 20).

(18.) The father of a prince in the reign of Jehoiakim (Jer. 36 : 12).

Shemari'ah — *whom Jehovah guards.* (1.) One who joined David at Ziklag (1 Chr. 12 : 5).

(2.) Ezra 10 : 32, 41.

Shem'eber—*soaring on high*—the king of Zeboiim, who joined with the other kings in casting off the yoke of Chedorlaomer. After having been reconquered by him, he was rescued by Abraham (Gen. 14 : 2).

Shem'inith—*eighth; octave*—a musical term, supposed to denote the lowest note sung by men's voices (1 Chr. 15 : 21 ; Ps. 6 ; 12, title).

Shemir'amoth—*most high name.* (1.) A Levite in the reign of Jehoshaphat (2 Chr. 17 : 8).

(2.) A Levite in David's time (1 Chr. 15 : 18, 20).

Shemu'el—*heard of God.* (1.) The son of Ammihud. He represented Simeon in the division of the land (Num. 34 : 20).

(2.) Used for "Samuel" (1 Chr. 6 : 33, R.V.).

(3.) A prince of the tribe of Issachar (1 Chr. 7 : 2).

Shen—*a tooth*—probably some conspicuous tooth-shaped rock or crag (1 Sam. 7 : 12), a place between which and Mizpeh Samuel set up his "Ebenezer." In the Hebrew the word has the article prefixed, "*the* Shen." The site is unknown.

She'nir = **Senir** (Deut. 3 : 9 ; Cant. 4 : 8), the name given to Mount Hermon (*q.v.*) by the Sidonians.

EASTERN SHEEP AND SHEPHERD.

Page 621.

She′ol (Heb., "the all-demanding world" = Gr. *Hades*, "the unknown region"), the invisible world of departed souls. (See HELL.)

She′phar (Gen. 10:30), a mount on the coast of Hadramaut, in the south of Arabia.

Shephati′ah—*judged of the Lord*. (1.) One of the sons of David by Abital (2 Sam. 3:4).

(2.) A Benjamite who joined David at Ziklag (1 Chr. 12:5).

(3.) A Simeonite prince in David's time (1 Chr. 27:16).

(4.) One of Jehoshaphat's sons (2 Chr. 21:2).

(5.) Ezra 2:4.

(6.) Ezra 2:57; Neh. 7:59.

(7.) One of the princes who urged the putting of Jeremiah to death (Jer. 38:1-4).

Shep′herd, a word naturally of frequent occurrence in Scripture. Sometimes the word "pastor" is used instead (Jer. 2:8; 3:15; 10:21; 12:10; 17:16).

This word is used figuratively to represent the relation of rulers to their subjects and of God to his people (Ps. 23:1; 80:1; Isa. 40:11; 44:28; Jer. 25:34, 35; Nahum 3:18; John 10:11, 14; Heb. 13:20; 1 Pet. 2:25; 5:4).

The duties of a shepherd in an unenclosed country like Palestine were very onerous. "In early morning he led forth the flock from the fold, marching at its head to the spot where they were to be pastured. Here he watched them all day, taking care that none of the sheep strayed, and if any for a time eluded his watch and wandered away from the rest, seeking diligently till he found and brought it back. In those lands sheep require to be supplied regularly with water, and the shepherd for this purpose has to guide them either to some running stream or to wells dug in the wilderness and furnished with troughs. At night he brought the flock home to the fold, counting them as they passed under the rod at the door to assure himself that none were missing. Nor did his labours always end with sunset. Often he had to guard the fold through the dark hours from the attack of wild beasts, or the wily attempts

of the prowling thief (see 1 Sam. 17:34)." —Deane's *David*.

Sherebi′ah—*flame of the Lord*—a priest whose name is prominent in connection with the work carried on by Ezra and Nehemiah at Jerusalem (Ezra 8:17, 18, 24-30; Neh. 8:7; 9:4, 5; 10:12).

She′resh—*root*—a descendant of Manasseh (1 Chr. 7:16).

Shere′zer, one of the messengers whom the children of the Captivity sent to Jerusalem "to pray for them before the Lord" (Zech. 7:2).

Sher′iffs (Dan. 3:2), Babylonian officers.

She′shach (Jer. 25:26), supposed to be equivalent to Babel (Babylon), according to a secret (cabalistic) mode of writing among the Jews of unknown antiquity, which consisted in substituting the last letter of the Hebrew alphabet for the first, the last but one for the second, and so on. Thus the letters *sh, sh, ch* become *b, b, l* —*i.e., Babel*. This is supposed to be confirmed by a reference to Jer. 51:41, where Sheshach and Babylon are in parallel clauses. There seems to be no reason to doubt that Babylon is here intended by this name. (See Streane's *Jeremiah, l.c.*)

She′shai—*whitish*—one of the sons of Anak (Num. 13:22). When the Israelites obtained possession of the country the sons of Anak were expelled and slain (Josh. 15:14; Judg. 1:10).

Sheshbaz′zar—*O sun-god, defend the lord!* —(Ezra 1:8, 11), probably another name for Zerubbabel (*q.v.*)—Ezra 2:2; Hag. 1:12, 14; Zech. 4:6, 10.

Sheth—*tumult*. (1.) "The children of Sheth" (Num. 24:17); R.V., "the sons of tumult," which is probably the correct rendering, as there is no evidence that this is a proper name here.

(2.) The antediluvian patriarch (1 Chr. 1:1).

She′thar—*a star*—a prince at the court of Ahasuerus (Esther 1:14).

She′thar-boz′nai—*star of splendour*—a Persian officer who vainly attempted to hinder the rebuilding of the temple (Ezra 5:3, 6; 6:6, 13).

She′va—Heb. *Shĕbhĕr*. (1.) The son of Caleb (1 Chr. 2:49). (2.) Heb. *Sheva′*, one of David's scribes (2 Sam. 20:25).

Shew'bread—Ex. 25:30 (R.V. marg., "presence bread"); 1 Chr. 9:32 (marg., "bread of ordering"); Num. 4:7: called "hallowed bread" (R.V., "holy bread") in 1 Sam. 21:1-6.

This bread consisted of twelve loaves made of the finest flour. They were flat and thin, and were placed in two rows of six each on a table in the holy place before the Lord. They were renewed every Sabbath (Lev. 24:5-17), and those that were removed to give place to the new ones were to be eaten by the priests only in the holy place (see 1 Sam. 21:3-6; comp. Matt. 12:3, 4).

The number of the loaves represented the twelve tribes of Israel, and also the entire spiritual Israel, "the true Israel;" and the placing of them on the table sym-

TABLE WITH SHEWBREAD.

bolized the entire consecration of Israel to the Lord, and their acceptance of God as their God. The table for the bread was made of acacia wood, 3 feet long, 18 inches broad, and 2 feet 3 inches high. It was plated with pure gold. Two staves, plated with gold, passed through golden rings, were used for carrying it.

Shib'boleth—*river*, or *an ear of corn.* The tribes living on the east of Jordan, separated from their brethren on the west by the deep ravines and the rapid river, gradually came to adopt peculiar customs, and from mixing largely with the Moabites, Ishmaelites, and Ammonites to pronounce certain letters in such a manner as to distinguish them from the other tribes. Thus when the Ephraimites from the west invaded Gilead, and were defeated by the Gileadites under the leadership of Jephthah, and tried to escape by the "passages of the Jordan," the Gileadites seized the fords and would allow none to pass who could not pronounce "shibboleth" with a strong aspirate. This the fugitives were unable to do. They said "sibboleth," as the word was pronounced by the tribes on the west, and thus they were detected (Judg. 12:1-7). Forty-two thousand were thus detected, and

" Without reprieve, adjudged to death,
  For want of well-pronouncing *shibboleth.*"

Shib'mah—*fragrance*—a town of Reuben, east of Jordan (Num. 32:38).

Shield, used in defensive warfare, varying at different times and under different circumstances in size, form, and material (1 Sam. 17:7; 2 Sam. 1:21; 1 Kings 10:17; 1 Chr. 12:8, 24, 34; Isa. 22:6; Ezek. 39:9; Nahum 2:3).

Used figuratively of God and of earthly princes as the defenders of their people (Gen. 15:1; Deut. 33:29; Ps. 33:20; 84:11). Faith is compared to a shield (Eph. 6:16).

Shields were usually "anointed" (Isa. 21:5), in order to preserve them, and at the same time make the missiles of the enemy glide off them more easily.

Shigg'aion, from the verb *shâgâh,* "to reel about through drink," occurs in the title of Ps. 7. The plural form, *shigionoth,* is found in Hab. 3:1. The word denotes a lyrical poem composed under strong mental emotion; a song of impassioned imagination accompanied with suitable music; a dithyrambic ode.

Shi'hon—*overturning*—a town of Issachar (Josh. 19:19).

Shi'hor—*dark*—(1 Chr. 13:5), the southwestern boundary of Canaan, the *Wâdy el-'Arîsh.* (See SIHOR; NILE.)

Shi′hor - Lib′nath — *black - white* — a stream on the borders of Asher, probably the modern *Nahr Zerka*—*i.e.*, the "crocodile brook," or "blue river"—which rises in the Carmel range and enters the Mediterranean a little to the north of Cæsarea (Josh. 19 : 26). Crocodiles are still found in the Zerka. Thomson suspects "that long ages ago some Egyptians, accustomed to worship this ugly creature, settled here (*viz.*, at Cæsarea), and brought their gods with them. Once here they would not easily be exterminated" (*The Land and the Book*).

Shil′him—*aqueducts*—a town in the south of Judah (Josh. 15 : 32); called also Sharuhen and Shaarim (19 : 6; 1 Chr. 4 : 31).

Shilo′ah, The waters of=Siloah (Neh. 3 : 15) and **Siloam** (*q.v.*).

Shi′loh, generally understood as denoting the Messiah, "the peaceful one," as the word signifies (Gen. 49 : 10). The Vulgate Version translates the word, "he who is to be sent," in allusion to the Messiah; the Revised Version, margin, "till he come to Shiloh;" and the LXX., "until that which is his shall come to Shiloh." It is most simple and natural to render the expression, as in the Authorized Version, "till Shiloh come," interpreting it as a proper name (comp. Isa. 9 : 5).

Shi′loh—*a place of rest*—a city of Ephraim, "on the north side of Bethel," from which it is distant 10 miles (Judg. 21 : 19); the modern *Seilûn* (the Arabic for Shiloh), a "mass of shapeless ruins." Here the tabernacle was set up after the Conquest (Josh. 18 : 1–10), where it remained during all the period of the judges till the ark fell into the hands of the Philistines. "No spot in Central Palestine could be more secluded than this early sanctuary, nothing more featureless than the landscape around; so featureless, indeed, the landscape and so secluded the spot that from the time of St. Jerome till its re-discovery by Dr. Robinson in 1838 the very site was forgotten and unknown." It is referred to by Jeremiah (7 : 12, 14; 26 : 4–9) five hundred years after its destruction.

Shi′lonite. Ahijah the prophet, whose home was in Shiloh, is so designated (1 Kings 11 : 29; 15 : 29). The plural form occurs (1 Chr. 9 : 5), denoting the descendants of Shelah, Judah's youngest son.

Shim′ea—*the hearing prayer*. (1.) One of David's sons by Bathsheba (1 Chr. 3 : 5); called also Shammua (14 : 4).

(2.) A Levite of the family of Merari (1 Chr. 6 : 30).

(3.) Another Levite of the family of Gershon (1 Chr. 6 : 39); called also Shimeam (9 : 38).

(4.) One of David's brothers (1 Sam. 16 : 9, marg.).

Shim′eah. (1.) One of David's brothers (2 Sam. 21 : 21); same as Shimea (4).

(2.) A Benjamite, a descendant of Gibeon (1 Chr. 8 : 32).

Shim′ei—*famous*. (1.) A son of Gershon, and grandson of Levi (Num. 3 : 18; 1 Chr. 6 : 17, 29); called Shimi in Ex. 6 : 17.

(2.) A Benjamite of the house of Saul, who stoned and cursed David when he reached Bahurim in his flight from Jerusalem on the occasion of the rebellion of Absalom (2 Sam. 16 : 5–13). After the defeat of Absalom he "came cringing to the king, humbly suing for pardon, bringing with him a thousand of his Benjamite tribesmen, and representing that he was heartily sorry for his crime, and had hurried the first of all the house of Israel to offer homage to the king" (19 : 16–23). David forgave him; but on his death-bed he gave Solomon special instructions regarding Shimei, of whose fidelity he seems to have been in doubt (1 Kings 2 : 8, 9). He was put to death at the command of Solomon, because he had violated his word by leaving Jerusalem and going to Gath to recover two of his servants who had escaped (36–46).

(3.) One of David's mighty men who refused to acknowledge Adonijah as David's successor (1 Kings 1 : 8). He is probably the same person who is called elsewhere (4 : 18) "the son of Elah."

(4.) A son of Pedaiah, the brother of Zerubbabel (1 Chr. 3 : 19).

(5.) A Simeonite (1 Chr. 4 : 26, 27).

(6.) A Reubenite (1 Chr. 5 : 4).

(7.) A Levite of the family of Gershon (1 Chr. 6 : 42).

(8.) A Ramathite who was "over the vineyards" of David (1 Chr. 27 : 27).

(9.) One of the sons of Heman, who assisted in the purification of the temple (2 Chr. 29 : 14).

(10.) A Levite (2 Chr. 31 : 12, 13).

(11.) Another Levite (Ezra 10 : 23).

"The family of Shimei" (Zech. 12 : 13; R.V., "the family of the Shimeites") were the descendants of Shimei (1).

Shim'eon—*hearkening.* Ezra 10 : 31.

Shim'hi—*famous*—a Benjamite (1 Chr. 8 : 21).

Shim'rath—*guardian*—a Benjamite, one of Shimhi's sons (*id.*).

Shim'ri—*watchman.* (1.) A Simeonite (1 Chr. 4 : 37).

(2.) The father of one of the "valiant men" of David's armies (1 Chr. 11 : 45).

(3.) Assisted at the purification of the temple in the time of Hezekiah (2 Chr. 29 : 13).

Shim'rom—*watchman*—the fourth son of Issachar (Gen. 14 : 13; 1 Chr. 7 : 1; R.V., correctly, "Shimron").

Shim'ron—*watch-post*—an ancient city of the Canaanites; with its villages, allotted to Zebulun (Josh. 19 : 15); now probably *Semûnieh,* on the northern edge of the plain of Esdraelon, 5 miles west of Naza-reth.

Shim'ron-mer'on, the same, probably, as Shimron (Josh. 12 : 20).

Shim'shai—*the shining one,* or *sunny*—the secretary of Rehum the chancellor, who took part in opposing the rebuilding of the temple after the Captivity (Ezra 4 : 8, 9, 17–23).

Shin'ab—*cooling*—the king of Admah, in the valley of Siddim, who with his confederates was conquered by Chedorlaomer (Gen. 14 : 2).

Shi'nar, The Land of. LXX. and Vulgate "Senaar;" in the inscriptions, "Shumir;" probably identical with Babylonia or Southern Mesopotamia, extending almost to the Persian Gulf. Here the tower of Babel was built (Gen. 11 : 1-6), and the city of Babylon. The name occurs later in Jewish history (Isa. 11 : 11; Zech. 5 : 11). Shinar was apparently first peopled by Turanian tribes, who tilled the land and made bricks and built cities. Then tribes of Semites invaded the land and settled in it,

and became its rulers. This was followed in course of time by an Elamite invasion; from which the land was finally delivered by Hammurabi, the son of Amarpel (perhaps "Amraphel, king of Shinar"), who became the founder of the new empire of Chaldea.

Ships, early used in foreign commerce by the Phœnicians (Gen. 49 : 13). Moses (Deut. 28 : 68) and Job (9 : 26) make reference to them, and Balaam speaks of the "ships of Chittim" (Num. 24 : 24). Solomon constructed a navy at Ezion-geber by the assistance of Hiram's sailors (1 Kings 9 : 26-28; 2 Chr. 8 : 18). Afterwards, Jehoshaphat sought to provide himself with a navy at the same port, but his ships appear to have been wrecked before they set sail (1 Kings 22 : 48, 49; 2 Chr. 20 : 35-37).

In our Lord's time fishermen's boats on the Sea of Galilee were called "ships." Much may be learned regarding the construction of ancient merchant ships and navigation from the record in Acts 27, 28.

Shiph'mite, probably the designation of Zabdi, who had charge of David's vineyards (1 Chr. 27 : 27).

Shiph'rah—*beauty*—one of the Egyptian midwives (Ex. 1 : 15).

Shiph'tan—*judicial*—an Ephraimite prince at the time of the division of Canaan (Num. 34 : 24).

Shi'shak I.=Sheshonk I., king of Egypt. His reign was one of great national success, and a record of his wars and conquests adorns the portico of what are called the "Bubastite kings" at Karnak, the ancient Thebes. Among these conquests is a record of that of Judea. In the fifth year of Rehoboam's reign Shishak came up against the kingdom of Judah with a powerful army. He took the fenced cities and came to Jerusalem. He pillaged the treasures of the temple and of the royal palace, and carried away the shields of gold which Solomon had made (1 Kings 11 : 40; 14 : 25; 2 Chr. 12 : 2). (See REHOBOAM.) This expedition of the Egyptian king was undertaken at the instigation of Jeroboam for the purpose of humbling Judah. Hostilities between the two kingdoms still continued; but during Rehoboam's reign there was not again the intervention of a third party.

Shit'tah-tree. Shittah wood was employed in making the various parts of the tabernacle in the wilderness, and must therefore have been indigenous in the desert in which the Israelites wandered. It was the acacia or mimosa (*Acacia Nilotica* and *A. seyal*). "The wild acacia (*Mimosa Nilotica*), under the name of *sŭnt*, everywhere represents the *seneh*, or *senna*, of the burning bush. A slightly different form of the tree, equally common under the name of *seyal*, is the ancient 'shittah,' or, as more usually expressed in the plural form, the 'shittim,' of which the tabernacle was made."—Stanley's *Sinai, etc.* (Ex. 25 : 10, 13, 23, 28).

Shit'tim—*acacias*—also called "Abel-shittim" (Num. 33 : 49), a plain or valley in the land of Moab where the Israelites were encamped after their two victories over Sihon and Og, at the close of their desert wanderings, and from which Joshua sent forth two spies (*q.v.*) "secretly" to "view" the land and Jericho (Josh. 2 : 1).

Sho'a—*opulent*—the mountain district lying to the north-east of Babylonia, anciently the land of the Guti, or Kuti, the modern *Kurdistan*. The plain lying between these mountains and the Tigris was called su-Edina—*i.e.*, "the border of the plain." This name was sometimes shortened into Suti and Su, and has been regarded as = Shoa (Ezek. 23 : 23). Some think it denotes a place in Babylon. (See PEKOD.)

Sho'bab—*apostate*. (1.) One of David's sons by Bathsheba (2 Sam. 5 : 14).

(2.) One of the sons of Caleb (1 Chr. 2 : 18), the son of Hezron.

Sho'bach—*poured out*—the "captain of the host of Hadarezer" when he mustered his vassals and tributaries from beyond "the river Euphrates" (2 Sam. 10 : 15–18); called also Shophach (1 Chr. 19 : 16).

Sho'bai—*captors* (Ezra 2 : 42).

Sho'bal—*pilgrim*. (1.) The second son of Seir the Horite; one of the Horite "dukes" (Gen. 36 : 20).

(2.) One of the sons of Caleb, and grandson of Hur (1 Chr. 2 : 50, 52 ; 4 : 1, 2).

Sho'bi—*captor*—son of Nahash of Rab-bah, the Ammonite. He showed kindness to David when he fled from Jerusalem to Mahanaim (2 Sam. 17 : 27).

Sho'cho (2 Chr. 28 : 18) = **Shochoh** (1 Sam. 17 : 1) = **Shoco** (2 Chr. 11 : 7). See SOCOH.

Shoe. Of various forms, from the mere sandal (*q.v.*) to the complete covering of the foot. The word so rendered (A.V.) in Deut. 33 : 25, *min'al*, "a bar," is derived from a root meaning "to bolt" or "shut fast," and hence a fastness or fortress. The verse has accordingly been rendered "iron and brass shall be thy fortress," or, as in the Revised Version, "thy bars shall be iron and brass."

Sho'mer—*watchman*. (1.) The father of Jehozabad, who murdered Joash (2 Kings 12 : 21); called also Shimrith (2 Chr. 24 : 26).

(2.) A man of Asher (1 Chr. 7 : 32); called also Shamer (34).

Sho'phan—*hidden*, or *hollow*—a town east of Jordan (Num. 32 : 35), "built by the children of Gad." This word should probably be joined with the word preceding it in this passage, Atroth-Shophan, as in the Revised Version.

Shoshan'nim—*lilies*—the name of some musical instrument, probably resembling in shape a lily (Ps. 45 ; 69—title). Some think that an instrument of six strings is meant.

Shoshan'nim-E'duth, in title of Ps. 80 (R.V. marg., "lilies, a testimony"), probably the name of the melody to which the psalm was to be sung.

Shrines, Silver, little models and medallions of the temple and image of Diana of Ephesus (Acts 19 : 24). The manufacture of these was a very large and profitable business.

Shu'a—*wealth*. (1.) A Canaanite whose daughter was married to Judah (1 Chr. 2 : 3).

(2.) A daughter of Heber the Asherite (1 Chr. 7 : 32).

Shu'ah—*prostration; a pit*. (1.) One of Abraham's sons by Keturah (Gen. 25 : 2 ; 1 Chr. 1 : 32). (2.) 1 Chr. 4 : 11.

Shu'al, The land of—*land of the fox*—a district in the tribe of Benjamin (1 Sam. 13 : 17); possibly the same as Shalim (9 : 4), in the neighbourhood of Shaalabbin (Josh. 19 : 42).

Shu'hite, a designation of Bildad (Job 2 : 11), probably because he was a descendant of Shuah.

Shu'lamite, the same, as some think, with "Shunammite," from "Shunem;" otherwise, the origin and import of the word are unknown (Cant. 6 : 13).

Shu'nammite, a person of Shunem (1 Kings 1 : 3 ; 2 Kings 4 : 12). The Syr. and Arab. read "Sulamite."

Shu'nem—*two resting-places*—a little village in the tribe of Issachar, to the north of Jezreel and south of Mount Gilboa (Josh. 19 : 18), where the Philistines encamped when they came against Saul (1 Sam. 28 : 4), and where Elisha was hospitably entertained by a rich woman of the place. On the sudden death of this woman's son she hastened to Carmel, 20 miles distant across the plain, to tell Elisha and to bring him with her to Shunem. There, in the "prophet's chamber," the dead child lay ; and Elisha entering it, shut the door and prayed earnestly : and the boy was restored to life (2 Kings 4 : 8–37). This woman afterwards retired during the famine to the low land of the Philistines ; and on returning a few years afterwards, found her house and fields in the possession of a stranger. She appealed to the king at Samaria, and had them in a somewhat remarkable manner restored to her (comp. 2 Kings 8 : 1-6).

Shur—*an enclosure; a wall*—a part, probably, of the Arabian desert, on the north-eastern border of Egypt, giving its name to a wilderness extending from Egypt toward Philistia (Gen. 16 : 7 ; 20 : 1 ; 25 : 18 ; Ex. 15 : 22). The name was probably given to it from the wall which the Egyptians built to defend their frontier on the north-east from the desert tribes. This wall or line of fortifications extended from Pelusium to Heliopolis.

Shu'shan—*a lily*—the Susa of Greek and Roman writers, once the capital of Elam. It lay in the uplands of Susiana, on the east of the Tigris, about 150 miles to the north of the head of the Persian Gulf. It is the modern *Shush*, on the north-west of Shuster. Once a magnificent city, it is now an immense mass of ruins. Here Daniel saw one of his visions (Dan. 8); and here also Nehemiah (Neh. 1) began his public life. Most of the events recorded in the Book of Esther took place here. Modern explorers have brought to light numerous relics, and the ground-plan of the splendid palace of Shushan, one of the residences of the great king, together with numerous specimens of ancient art, which illustrate the statements of Scripture regarding it (Dan. 8 : 2). The great hall of this palace (Esther 1) "consisted of several magnificent groups of columns, together with a frontage of 343 feet 9 inches, and a depth of 244 feet. These groups were arranged into a central phalanx of thirty-six columns (six rows of six each), flanked on the west, north, and east by an equal number, disposed in double rows of six each, and distant from them 64 feet 2 inches." The inscriptions on the ruins represent that the palace was founded by Darius and completed by Artaxerxes.

Shu'shan-E'duth—*lily of the testimony* —the title of Ps. 80. (See SHOSHANNIM.)

Sib'becai—*the Lord sustains*—one of David's heroes (1 Chr. 11 : 29), general of the eighth division of the army (27 : 11). He slew the giant Saph in the battle of Gob (2 Sam. 21 : 18). Called also Mebunnai (23 : 27).

Sib'mah—*coolness; fragrance*—a town in Reuben, in the territory of Moab, on the east of Jordan (Josh. 13 : 19); called also Shebam and Shibmah (Num. 32 : 3, 38). It was famous for its vines (Isa. 16 : 9 ; Jer. 48 : 32). It has been identified with the ruin of *Sûmieh*, where there are rock-cut wine-presses. This fact explains the words of the prophets referred to above. It was about 5 miles east of Heshbon.

Si'chem = She'chem (*q.v.*), Gen. 12 : 6.

Sickle of the Egyptians resembled that in modern use. The ears of corn were cut with it near the top of the straw. There was also a sickle used for warlike purposes, more correctly, however, called a pruning-kook (Deut. 16 : 9 ; Jer. 50 : 16 ; Joel 3 : 13 ; Mark 4 : 29).

Sid'dim, Vale of—*valley of the broad plains*—"which is the salt sea" (Gen. 14 : 3, 8, 10), between Engedi and the cities of the plain, at the south end of the Dead Sea. It was "full of slime-pits"—*i.e.*, bitumen springs. Here Chedorlaomer and the confederate kings overthrew the kings of Sodom and the cities of the plain. God afterwards, on account of their wickedness, "overthrew those cities, and all the plain, and all the inhabitants of the cities;" and the smoke of their destruction "went up as the smoke of a furnace" (19:24-28), and was visible from Mamre, where Abraham dwelt.

Some, however, contend that the "cities of the plain" were somewhere at the north of the Dead Sea. (See SODOM.)

Si'don—*fishing; fishery*—Gen. 10:15, 19 (R.V., Zidon); Matt. 11:21, 22; Luke 6:17. (See ZIDON.)

Sig'net, a seal used to attest documents (Dan. 6:8-10, 12). In 6:17, this word properly denotes a ring. The impression of a signet ring on fine clay has recently been discovered among the ruins at Nineveh. It bears the name and title of an Egyptian king. Two actual signet rings of ancient Egyptian monarchs (Cheops and Horus) have also been discovered.

When digging a shaft close to the south wall of the temple area, the engineers of the Palestine Exploration Fund, at a depth of 12 feet below the surface, came upon a pavement of polished stones, formerly one of the streets of the city. Under this pavement they found a stratum of 16 feet of concrete, and among this concrete, 10 feet down, they found a signet stone bearing the inscription, in Old Hebrew characters, "Haggai, son of Shebaniah." It has been asked, Might not this be the actual seal of Haggai the prophet? We know that he was in Jerusalem after the Captivity; and it is somewhat singular that he alone of all the minor prophets makes mention of a signet (Hag. 2:23). (See SEAL.)

HAGGAI'S SEAL.

Si'hon — *striking down.* The whole country on the east of Jordan, from the Arnon to the Jabbok, was possessed by the Amorites, whose king, Sihon, refused to permit the Israelites to pass through his territory, and put his army in array against them. The Israelites went forth against him to battle, and gained a complete victory. The Amorites were defeated; Sihon, his sons, and all his people, were smitten with the sword, his walled towns were captured, and the entire country occupied by the Amorites was taken possession of by the Israelites (Num. 21:21-30; Deut. 2:24-37).

The country from the Jabbok to Hermon was at this time ruled by Og, the last of the Rephaim. He also tried to prevent the progress of the Israelites, but was utterly routed, and all his cities and territory fell into the hands of the Israelites (comp. Num. 21:34; Deut. 3:3, 4, 14; Ps. 135:10-12; 136:15-21).

These two victories gave the Israelites possession of the country on the east of Jordan, from the Arnon to the foot of Hermon.

The kingdom of Sihon embraced about 1,500 square miles, while that of Og was more than 3,000 square miles.

Si'hor (correctly **Shi'hor**)—*black; dark*—the name given to the river Nile in Isa. 23:3; Jer. 2:18. In Josh. 13:3 it is probably "the river of Egypt"—*i.e.*, the *Wâdy el-Arish* (1 Chr. 13:5)—which flows "before Egypt"—*i.e.*, in a north-easterly direction from Egypt—and enters the sea about 50 miles south-west of Gaza.

Si'las—*wood*—a prominent member of the church at Jerusalem; also called Silvanus. He and Judas, surnamed Barsabas, were chosen by the church there to accompany Paul and Barnabas on their return to Antioch from the council of the apostles and elders (Acts 15:22), as bearers of the decree adopted by the council. He assisted Paul there in his evangelistic labours, and was also chosen by him to be his companion on his second missionary tour (Acts 16:19-24). He is referred to in the epistles under the name of Silvanus (2 Cor. 1:19; 1 Thess. 1:1; 2 Thess. 1:1; 1 Pet. 5:12). There is no record of the time or place of his death.

Silk — Heb. *demĕshĕk*, "damask," silk cloth manufactured at Damascus—Amos 3:12, A.V., "in the corner of a bed, and in Damascus in a couch," is more correctly in the R.V., "in the corner of a couch and on the silken cushions of a bed."

Heb. *meshi*—(Ezek. 16:10, 13, rendered "silk"). In Gen. 41:42 (marg. A.V.), Prov. 31:22 (R.V., "fine linen"), the word "silk" ought to be "fine linen."

Silk was common in New Testament times (Rev. 18:12).

Sil'la—*a highway; a twig*—only in 2 Kings 12:20. If taken as a proper name (as in the LXX. and other versions), the locality is unknown.

Silo'ah, The pool of—Heb. *shĕlah; i.e.,* "the dart"—Neh. 3:15; with the art.

shiloah, "sending," Isa. 8:6 (comp. 7:3) = **Siloam** (*q.v.*).

Silo'am, Pool of—*sent* or *sending*. Here a notable miracle was wrought by our Lord in giving sight to the blind (John 9:7–11). It has been identified with the *Birket Silwân* in the lower Tyropœon valley, to the south-east of the hill of Zion.

The water which flows into this pool intermittingly by a subterranean channel springs from the "Fountain of the Virgin" (*q.v.*). The length of this channel, which has several windings, is 1,750 feet, though the direct distance is only 1,100 feet. The pool is 53 feet in length from north to south, 18 feet wide, and 19 deep. The water passes from it by a channel cut

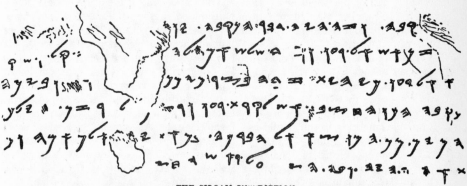

THE SILOAM INSCRIPTION.

(Tracing from a squeeze, taken 15th July, 1881, by Lieuts. Conder and Mantell, R.E.)

in the rock into the gardens below. (See EN-ROGEL.)

A few years ago (1880) a youth, while wading up the conduit by which the water enters the pool, accidentally discovered an inscription cut in the rock, on the eastern side, about 19 feet from the pool. This is the oldest extant Hebrew record of the kind. It has with great care been deciphered by scholars, and has been found to be an account of the manner in which the tunnel was constructed. Its whole length is said to be "twelve hundred cubits;" and the inscription further notes that the workmen, like the excavators of the Mont Cenis Tunnel, excavated from both ends, meeting in the middle.

Some have argued that the inscription

was cut in the time of Solomon; others, with more probability, refer it to the reign of Hezekiah. A more ancient tunnel was discovered in 1889 some 20 feet below the ground. It is of smaller dimensions, but more direct in its course. It is to this tunnel that Isaiah (8:6) probably refers.

The Siloam inscription above referred to was surreptitiously cut from the wall of the tunnel in 1891 and broken into fragments. These were, however, recovered by the efforts of the British Consul at Jerusalem, and have been restored to their original place.

Silo'am, Tower of, mentioned only Luke 13:4. The place here spoken of is the village now called *Silwân,* or *Kefr Silwân,* on the east of the valley of Kidron, and to the north-east of the pool. It stands on the west slope of the Mount of Olives.

As illustrative of the movement of small bands of Canaanites from place to place, and the intermingling of Canaanites and Israelites even in small towns in earlier times, M. C. Ganneau records the following curious fact: "Among the inhabitants of the village (of Siloam) there are a hundred or so domiciled for the most part in the lower quarter, and forming a group apart from the rest, called Dhiàbryè—*i.e.*, men of Dhiban. It appears that at some remote period a colony from the capital of king Mesha (Dibon-Moab) crossed the Jordan and fixed itself at the gates of Jerusalem at Silwan. The memory of this migration is still preserved; and I am assured by the people themselves that many of their number are installed in other villages round Jerusalem" (quoted by Henderson, *Palestine*).

Sil'ver, used for a great variety of purposes, as may be judged from the frequent references to it in Scripture. It first appears in commerce in Gen. 13:2; 23:15, 16. It was largely employed for making vessels for the sanctuary in the wilderness (Ex. 26:19; 27:17; Num. 7:13, 19; 10:2). There is no record of its having been found in Syria or Palestine. It was brought in large quantities by foreign merchants from abroad, from Spain and India and other countries probably.

Sil'verling (Isa. 7:23). Literally the words are "at a thousand of silver"—*i.e.*, "pieces of silver," or shekels.

Sim'eon—*hearing.* (1.) The second son of Jacob by Leah (Gen. 29:33). He was associated with Levi in the terrible act of vengeance against Hamor and the Shechemites (34:25, 26). He was detained by Joseph in Egypt as a hostage (42:24). His father, when dying, pronounced a malediction against him (49:5-7). The words in the Authorized Version (49:6), "they digged down a wall," ought to be, as correctly rendered in the Revised Version, "they houghed an ox."

(2.) An aged saint who visited the temple when Jesus was being presented before the Lord, and uttered lofty words of thanksgiving and of prophecy (Luke 2:29-35).

(3.) One of the ancestors of Joseph (Luke 3:30).

(4.) Surnamed Niger—*i.e.*, "black," perhaps from his dark complexion—a teacher of some distinction in the church of Antioch (Acts 13:1-3). It has been supposed that this was the Simon of Cyrene who bore Christ's cross. Note the number of nationalities represented in the church at Antioch.

(5.) James (Acts 15:14) thus designates the apostle Peter (*q.v.*).

Sim'eon, The tribe of, was "divided and scattered" according to the prediction in Gen. 49:5-7. They gradually dwindled in number, and sank into a position of insignificance among the other tribes. They decreased in the wilderness by about two-thirds (comp. Num. 1:23; 26:14). Moses pronounces no blessing on this tribe. It is passed by in silence (Deut. 33).

This tribe received as their portion a part of the territory already allotted to Judah (Josh. 19:1-9). It lay in the southwest of the land, with Judah on the east and Dan on the north; but whether it was a compact territory or not cannot be determined. The subsequent notices of this tribe are but few (1 Chr. 4:24-43). Like Reuben on the east of Jordan, this tribe had little influence on the history of Israel.

Si'mon, the abbreviated form of Simeon. (1.) One of the twelve apostles, called the Canaanite (Matt. 10:4; Mark 3:18). This word "Canaanite" does not mean a native of Canaan, but is derived from the Syriac word *Kanean* or *Kaneniah*, which was the name of a Jewish sect. The Revised Version has "Cananæan;" marg., "or Zealot" He is also called "Zelotes" (Luke 6:15; Acts 1:13; R.V., "the Zealot"), because previous to his call to the apostleship he had been a member of the fanatical sect of the Zealots. There is no record regarding him.

(2.) The father of Judas Iscariot (John 6:71; 13:2, 26).

(3.) One of the brothers of our Lord (Matt. 13:55; Mark 6:3).

(4.) A Pharisee in whose house "a woman of the city which was a sinner" anointed our Lord's feet with ointment (Luke 7: 36-38).

(5.) A leper of Bethany, in whose house Mary anointed our Lord's head with ointment "as he sat at meat" (Matt. 26:6-13; Mark 14:3-9).

(6.) A Jew of Cyrene, in North Africa, then a province of Libya. A hundred thousand Jews from Palestine had been settled in this province by Ptolemy Soter (B.C. 323-285), where by this time they had greatly increased in number. They had a synagogue in Jerusalem for such of their number as went thither to the annual feasts. Simon was seized by the soldiers as the procession wended its way to the place of crucifixion as he was passing by, and the heavy cross which Christ from failing strength could no longer bear was laid on his shoulders. Perhaps they seized him because he showed sympathy with Jesus. He was the "father of Alexander and Rufus" (Matt. 27:32). Possibly this Simon may have been one of the "men of Cyrene" who preached the word to the Greeks (Acts 11:20).

(7.) A sorcerer of great repute for his magical arts among the Samaritans (Acts 8:9-11). He afterwards became a professed convert to the faith under the preaching of Philip the deacon and evangelist (12, 13). His profession was, however, soon found to be hollow. His conduct called forth from Peter a stern rebuke (8:18-23). From this moment he disappears from the Church's history. The term "Simony," as denoting the purchase for money of spiritual offices, is derived from him.

(8.) A Christian at Joppa, a tanner by trade, with whom Peter on one occasion lodged (Acts 9:43).

(9.) Simon Peter (Matt. 4:18). See PETER.

Sim'ri—*watchman*—a Levite of the family of Merari (1 Chr. 26:10).

Sin is "any want of conformity unto or transgression of the law of God" (1 John 3:4; Rom. 4:15), in the inward state and habit of the soul, as well as in the outward conduct of the life, whether by omission or commission (Rom. 6:12-17; 7:5-24). It is "not a mere violation of the law of our constitution, nor of the system of things, but an offence against a personal lawgiver and moral governor who vindicates his law with penalties. The soul that sins is always conscious that his sin is (1) intrinsically vile and polluting, and (2) that it justly deserves punishment, and calls down the righteous wrath of God. Hence sin carries with it two inalienable characters—(1) ill-desert, guilt (*reatus*); and (2) pollution (*macula*)."—Hodge's *Outlines*.

The moral character of a man's actions is determined by the moral state of his heart. The disposition to sin, or the habit of the soul that leads to the sinful act, is itself also sin (Rom. 6:12-17; Gal. 5:17; James 1:14, 15).

The origin of sin is a mystery, and must for ever remain such to us. It is plain that for some reason God has permitted sin to enter this world, and that is all we know. His permitting it, however, in no way makes God the author of sin.

Adam's sin (Gen. 3:1-6) consisted in his yielding to the assaults of temptation and eating the forbidden fruit. It involved in it—(1) the sin of unbelief, virtually making God a liar; and (2) the guilt of disobedience to a positive command. By this sin he became an apostate from God, a rebel in arms against his Creator. He lost the favour of God and communion with him; his whole nature became depraved, and he incurred the penalty involved in the covenant of works.

Original sin. "Our first parents being the root of all mankind, the guilt of their sin was imputed, and the same death in sin and corrupted nature were conveyed to all their posterity, descending from them by ordinary generation." Adam was constituted by God the federal head and representative of all his posterity, as he was also their natural head, and therefore when he fell they fell with him (Rom. 5:12-21; 1 Cor. 15:22-45). His probation was their probation, and his fall their fall. Because of Adam's first sin all his posterity came into the world in a state of sin and condemnation—*i.e.*, (1) a state of moral corruption, and (2) of guilt, as having judicially imputed to them the guilt of Adam's first sin.

"Original sin" is frequently and properly used to denote only the moral corruption of their whole nature inherited by all men from Adam. This inherited moral corruption consists in—(1) the loss of original righteousness; and (2) the presence of a constant proneness to evil, which is the root and origin of all actual sin. It is called "sin" (Rom. 6 : 12, 14, 17; 7 : 5-17), the "flesh" (Gal. 5 : 17, 24), "lust" (James 1 : 14, 15), the "body of sin" (Rom. 6 : 6), "ignorance," "blindness of heart," "alienation from the life of God" (Eph. 4 : 18, 19). It influences and depraves the whole man, and its tendency is still downward to deeper and deeper corruption, there remaining no recuperative element in the soul. It is a total depravity, and it is also universally inherited by all the natural descendants of Adam (Rom. 3 : 10-23; 5 : 12-21; 8 : 7). Pelagians deny original sin, and regard man as by nature morally and spiritually well; semi-Pelagians regard him as morally sick ; Augustinians, or, as they are also called, Calvinists, regard man as described above, spiritually dead (Eph. 2 : 1; 1 John 3 : 14).

The doctrine of original sin is proved—(1.) From the fact of the universal sinfulness of men. "There is no man that sinneth not" (1 Kings 8 : 46; Isa. 53 : 6; Ps. 130 : 3; Rom. 3 : 19, 22, 23; Gal. 3 : 22). (2.) From the total depravity of man. All men are declared to be destitute of any principle of spiritual life; man's apostasy from God is total and complete (Job 15 : 14-16; Gen. 6 : 5, 6). (3.) From its early manifestation (Ps. 58 : 3; Prov. 22 : 15). (4.) It is proved also from the necessity, absolutely and universally, of regeneration (John 3 : 3; 2 Cor. 5 : 17). (5.) From the universality of death (Rom. 5 : 12-20).

Various *kinds* of sin are mentioned—(1.) "Presumptuous sins," or as literally rendered, "sins with an uplifted hand"—*i.e.*, defiant acts of sin, in contrast with "errors" or "inadvertencies" (Ps. 19 : 13). (2.) "Secret"—*i.e.*, hidden sins (19 : 12); sins which escape the notice of the soul. (3.) "Sin against the Holy Ghost" (*q.v.*), or a "sin unto death" (Matt. 12 : 31, 32; 1 John 5 : 16), which amounts to a wilful rejection of grace.

Sin, a city in Egypt, called by the Greeks Pelusium, which means, as does also the Hebrew name, "clayey" or "muddy," so called from the abundance of clay found there. It is called by Ezekiel (Ezek. 30 : 15) "the strength of Egypt," thus denoting its importance as a fortified city. It has been identified with the modern *Tineh*, "a miry place," where its ruins are to be found. Of its boasted magnificence only four red granite columns remain, and some few fragments of others.

Sin-offering (Heb. *ḥaṭṭāth*), the law of, is given in detail in Lev. 4-6 : 13; 9 : 7-11, 22-24; 12 : 6-8; 15 : 2, 14, 25-30; 14 : 19, 31; Num. 6 : 10-14. On the day of Atonement it was made with special solemnity (Lev. 16 : 5, 11, 15). The blood was then carried into the holy of holies and sprinkled on the mercy-seat. Sin-offerings were also presented at the five annual festivals (Num. 28, 29), and on the occasion of the consecration of the priests (Ex. 29 : 10-14, 36). As each individual—even the most private member of the congregation, as well as the congregation at large, and the high priest—was obliged, on being convicted by his conscience of any particular sin, to come with a sin-offering, we see thus impressively disclosed the need in which every sinner stands of the salvation of Christ, and the necessity of making application to it as often as the guilt of sin renews itself upon his conscience. This resort of faith to the perfect sacrifice of Christ is the one way that lies open for the sinner's attainment of pardon and restoration to peace. And then in the sacrifice itself there is the reality of that incomparable worth and preciousness which were so significantly represented in the sin-offering by the sacredness of its blood and the hallowed destination of its flesh. With reference to this the blood of Christ is called emphatically "the precious blood," and the blood that "cleanseth from all sin" (1 John 1 : 7).

Sin, Wilderness of, lying between Elim

and Sinai (Ex. 16:1; comp. Num. 33:11, 12). This was probably the narrow plain of *el-Markha*, which stretches along the eastern shore of the Red Sea for several miles toward the promontory of *Râs Mohammed*, the southern extremity of the Sinaitic Peninsula. While the Israelites rested here for some days they began to murmur on account of the want of nourishment, as they had by this time consumed all the corn they had brought with them out of Egypt. God heard their murmurings, and gave them "manna" and then quails in abundance.

Si'nai—*of Sin* (the moon god)—called also Horeb, the name of the mountain district which was reached by the Hebrews in the third month after the Exodus. Here they remained encamped for about a whole year. Their journey from the Red Sea to this encampment, including all the windings of the route, was about 150 miles. The last twenty-two chapters of Exodus, together with the whole of Leviticus and Num. 1-6:11, contain a record of all the transactions which occurred while they were here. From Rephidim (Ex. 17:8-13) the Israelites journeyed forward through the Wâdy Solaf and Wâdy esh-Sheikh into the plain of er-Râhah, "the desert of Sinai," about 2 miles long and half a mile broad, and encamped there "before the mountain." The part of the mountain range, a protruding lower bluff, known as the Râs Sasâfeh (Sufsâfeh), rises almost perpendicularly from this plain, and is in all probability the Sinai of history. Dean Stanley thus describes the scene:—"The plain itself is not broken and uneven and narrowly shut in, like almost all others in the range, but presents a long retiring sweep, within which the people could remove and stand afar off. The cliff, rising like a huge altar in front of the whole congregation, and visible against the sky in lonely grandeur from end to end of the whole plain, is the very image of the 'mount that might be touched,' and from which the voice of God might be heard far and wide over the plain below." This was the scene of the giving of the law. From the Ras Sufsâfeh the law was proclaimed

to the people encamped below in the plain of er-Râhah. During the lengthened period of their encampment here the Israelites passed through a very memorable experience. An immense change passed over them. They are now an organized nation, bound by covenant engagements to serve the Lord their God, their ever-present divine Leader and Protector. At length, in the second month of the second year of the Exodus, they move their camp and march forward according to a prescribed order. After three days they reach the "wilderness of Paran," the "et-Tih "—*i.e.*, "the desert"—and here they make their first encampment. At this time a spirit of discontent broke out amongst them, and the Lord manifested his displeasure by a fire which fell on the encampment and inflicted injury on them. Moses called the place Taberah (*q.v.*)—Num. 11: 1-3. The journey between Sinai and the southern boundary of the Promised Land (about 150 miles) at Kadesh was accomplished in about a year (Deut. 1:2). (See MAP facing page 198.)

Sinait'icus codex, usually designated by the first letter of the Hebrew alphabet, is one of the most valuable of ancient MSS. of the Greek New Testament. On the occasion of a third visit to the convent of St. Catherine, on Mount Sinai, in 1859, it was discovered by Dr. Tischendorf. He had on a previous visit in 1844 obtained forty-three parchment leaves of the LXX., which he deposited in the university library of Leipsic, under the title of the Codex Frederico-Augustanus, after his royal patron the king of Saxony. In the year referred to (1859) the emperor of Russia sent him to prosecute his search for MSS., which he was convinced were still to be found in the Sinai convent. The story of his finding the manuscript of the New Testament has all the interest of a romance. He reached the convent on 31st January; but his inquiries appeared to be fruitless. On the 4th February he had resolved to return home without having gained his object. "On that day, when walking with the provisor of the convent, he spoke with much regret of his ill-success. Returning from their promenade, Tischendorf accompanied the monk to his room, and there had displayed to him what his companion called a copy of the LXX., which he, the ghostly brother, owned. The MS. was wrapped up in a piece of cloth, and on its being unrolled, to the surprise and delight of the critic the very document presented itself which he had given up all hope of seeing. His object had been to complete the fragmentary LXX. of 1844, which he had declared to be the most ancient of all Greek codices on vellum that are extant; but he found not only that, but a copy of the Greek New Testament attached, of the same age, and perfectly complete, not wanting a single page or paragraph." This precious fragment, after some negotiations, he obtained possession of, and conveyed it to the Emperor Alexander, who fully appreciated its importance, and caused it to be published as nearly as possible in facsimile, so as to exhibit correctly the ancient handwriting. The entire codex consists of 346½ folios. Of these 199 belong to the Old Testament and 147½ to the New, along with two ancient documents called the Epistle of Barnabas and the Shepherd of Hermas. The books of the New Testament stand thus:—the four Gospels, the epistles of Paul, the Acts of the Apostles, the Catholic Epistles, the Apocalypse of John. It is shown by Tischendorf that this codex was written in the fourth century, and is thus of about the same age as the Vatican codex; but while the latter wants the greater part of Matthew and sundry leaves here and there besides, the Sinaiticus is the only copy of the New Testament in uncial characters which is complete. Thus it is the oldest extant MS. copy of the New Testament. Both the Vatican and the Sinai codices were probably written in Egypt. (See VATICANUS.)

Si'nim, The land of (Isa. 49:12), supposed by some to mean China, but more probably Phœnicia (Gen. 10:17) is intended.

Si'nite, an inhabitant of Sin, near Arka (Gen. 10:17; 1 Chr. 1:15). (See ARKITE.)

Si'on—*elevated.* (1.) Denotes Mount Hermon in Deut. 4:48; called Sirion by the Sidonians, and by the Amorites Shenir (Deut. 3:9). (See HERMON.)

(2.) The Greek form of Zion (*q.v.*) in Matt. 21:5; John 12:15.

Siph'moth—*fruitful places*—some unknown place in the south, where David found friends when he fled from Saul (1 Sam. 30:28).

Si'rah—*retiring*—a well from which Joab's messenger brought back Abner (2 Sam. 3:26). It is now called '*Ain Sârah*, and is situated about a mile from Hebron, on the road to the north.

Sir'ion — *a breastplate* — the Sidonian name of Hermon (*q.v.*)—Deut. 3:9; Ps. 29:6.

Sis'era (Egypt. *Ses-Ra*, "servant of Ra"). (1.) The captain of Jabin's army (Judg. 4:2), which was routed and destroyed by the army of Barak on the plain of Esdraelon. After all was lost he fled to the settlement of Heber the Kenite in the plain of Zaanaim. Jael, Heber's wife, received him into her tent with apparent hospitality, and "gave him butter" (*i.e.*, lebben, or curdled milk) "in a lordly dish." Having drunk the refreshing beverage, he lay down, and soon sank into the sleep of the weary. While he lay asleep Jael crept stealthily up to him, and taking in her hand one of the tent pegs, with a mallet she drove it with such force through his temples that it entered into the ground where he lay, and "at her feet he bowed, he fell; where he bowed, there he fell down dead."

The part of Deborah's song (Judg. 5:24–27) referring to the death of Sisera (which is a "mere patriotic outburst," and "is no proof that purer eyes would have failed to see gross sin mingling with Jael's service to Israel") is thus rendered by Professor Roberts (*Old Testament Revision*):—

" Extolled above women be Jael,
The wife of Heber the Kenite,
Extolled above women in the tent.
He asked for water, she gave him milk;
She brought him cream in a lordly dish.
She stretched forth her hand to the nail,
Her right hand to the workman's hammer,
And she smote Sisera: she crushed his head,
She crashed through and transfixed his temples.
At her feet he curled himself, he fell, he lay still;
At her feet he curled himself, he fell;
And where he curled himself, there he fell dead."

Facsimile columns (Codex Sinaiticus, uncial)

Column 1

ΤΟΥΠΩΠΟΤΕΛΛΗ
ΚΟΛΛΕΟΥΤΕΕΔΟϹ
ΑΥΤΟΥΕΩΡΑΚΑΤ
ΚΑΙΤΟΝΛΟΓΟΝΑΥ
ΤΟΥΟΥΚΕΧΕΤΕΕΝ
ΜΙΝΜΕΝΟΝΤΑ
ΤΙΟΝΑΠΕϹΤΙΛΕΝ
ΕΚΙΝΟϹΤΟΥΤΩ
ΜΙϹΟΥΠΙϹΤΕΥΕΤ
ΕΡΑΥΝΑΤΕΤΑϹΓΡΑ
ΦΑϹΟΤΙΥΜΕΙϹΔ
ΚΕΙΤΑΙΕΝΑΥΤΑΙϹ
ΗΝΑΙΩΝΙΟΝΕΧΙ
ΚΑΙΕΚΕΙΝΑΙΕΙϹ
ΑΙΜΑΡΤΥΡΟΥϹΑΙΠ
ΡΙΕΜΟΥΚΑΙΟΥΘΕ
ΛΕΤΕΕΛΘΕΙΝΠ
ΜΕΙΝΑΖΩΗΝΕΧΗ
ΤΕΔΟΞΑΝΠΑΡΑΛΛ
ΝΩΝΟΥΛΑΜ
ΥΜΑϹΟΤΙΟΥΚΕΧ
ΤΕΤΗΝΑΓΑΠΗΝΤ
ΘΥΟΥΚΕΧΕΤΕΕΝ
ΑΥΤΟΙϹΕΓΩΕΛΗ
ΛΥΘΕΝΤΩΟΝΟ
ΜΑΤΙΤΟΥΠΑΤΡΟ
ΜΟΥΚΑΙΟΥΛΑΜΒ
ΝΕΤΕΜΕΕΑΝΑΛ
ΕΛΘΗΤΩΟΝΟΜΑ
ΤΙΤΩΙΔΙΩΕΚΕΙ
ΝΟΝΛΗΜΨΕϹΘΕ
ΠΩϹΔΥΝΑϹΘΕ
ΥΜΙϹΠΙϹΤΕΥϹΑΙ
ΔΟΞΑΝΠΑΡΑΛΛΗ
ΛΩΝΛΑΜΒΑΝΟΝ
ΤΕϹΚΑΙΤΗΝΔΟΞ
ΤΗΝΠΑΡΑΤΟΥΜ
ΝΟΥΘΥΟΥΖΗΤΟΙΤ
ΤΕϹΜΗΔΟΚΕΙΤΑΙ
ΟΤΙΕΓΩΚΑΤΗΓΟΡ
ϹΩΥΜΩΝΠΡΟϹ
ΠΡΑΕϹΤΙΝΟΚΑΤΗ
ΓΟΡΩΝΥΜΩΝΜΩΝ
ΥϹΕΗϹΕΙϹΟΝΥΜ
ΠΙΚΑϹΤΕΙΓΑΡϹΠ
ϹΤΕΥΕΤΕΜΩϹΕΙ
ϹΠΙϹΤΕΥΕΤΕΑΝΕΜ

Column 2

ΠΕΡΙΓΑΡΕΜΟΥΕΚ
ΝΟϹΕΓΡΑΦΕΝΕΙ
ΔΕΤΟΙϹΕΚΕΙΝΟΥ
ΓΡΑΜΜΑϹΙΝΟΥΠΙ
ϹΤΕΥΤΑΙΠΩϹΤ
ΕΜΟΙϹΡΗΜΑϹΙΝ
ΠΙϹΤΕΥϹΕΤΕΜΕ
ΤΑΤΑΥΤΑΑΠΗΛΘ
ΟΙϹΠΕΡΑΝΤΗϹΘΑ
ΛΑϹϹΗϹΤΗϹΓΑΛΙΛΑ
ΑϹΤΗϹΤΙΒΕΡΙΑϹ
ΗΚΟΛΟΥΘΕΙΔΕΑΥ
ΟΤΙΕΩΡΩΝΤΑϹΗ
ΜΕΙΑΛΕΠΟΙΕΙΕΠ
ΤΩΝΑϹΘΕΝΟΥΝ
ΕΙϹΤΟΟΡΟϹ ΙϹ
ΚΑΙΕΚΑΘΕΖΕΤΟ
ΜΕΤΑΤΩΝΜΑΘΗ
ΤΩΝΑΥΤΟΥ ΗΝ
ΕΓΓΥϹΤΟΠΑϹΧΑ
ΗΕΟΡΤΗΤΩΝΙΟΥ
ΔΑΙΩΝ·
ΕΠΑΡΑϹΟΥΝΤΟΥϹΟ
ΦΘΑΛΜΟΥϹΙϹΚΑΙ
ΘΕΑϹΑΜΕΝΟϹΟΤΙ
ΟΧΛΟϹΠΟΛΥϹΕΡ
ΧΕΤΑΙΠΡΟϹΑΥΤΟΝ
ΛΕΓΕΙΠΡΟϹΦΙΛΙΠ
ΠΟΘΕΝΑΓΟΡΑϹΩ
ΜΕΝΑΡΤΟΥϹΙΝΑ
ΟΥΤΟΙΦΑΓΩϹΙΝ
ΤΟΥΤΟΔΕΕΛΕΓΕΝ
ΠΙΡΑΖΩΝΑΥΤΟΝ
ΑΥΤΟϹΔΕΗΔΕΙΤΙ
ΕΜΕΛΛΕΠΟΙΕΙΝ
ΑΠΟΚΡΙΝΕΤΑΙΟΥΝ
ΟΦΙΛΙΠΠΟϹΔΙΑ
ΚΟϹΙΩΝΔΗΝΑΡΙ
ΩΝΑΡΤΟΙΟΥΚΑΡ
ΚΟΥϹΙΝΙΝΑΕΚΑϹ
ΒΡΑΧΥΤΙΩϹΕΙϹΕΚΤ
ΓΕΙΑΥΤΩϹΕΙϹΕΚΤ
ΜΑΘΗΤΩΝΑΥΤΟΥ
ΑΝΔΡΕΑϹΟΑΔ
ΦΟϹϹΙΜΩΝΟϹΠΕ
ΤΡΟΥΕϹΤΙΝΠΑΙΔΑ

Column 3

ΡΙΟΝΩΔΕΟϹΕΧΕΙ
ΠΕΝΤΕΑΡΤΟΥϹΚΡΙ
ΘΙΝΟΥϹΚΑΙΔΥΟ
ΨΑΡΙΑΛΛΑΤΑΥΤΑ
ΤΙΕϹΤΙΝΕΙϹΤΟϹΥ
ΤΟϹΕΙΠΕΝΟΙϹ
ΠΟΙΗϹΑΤΕΤΟΥϹΑΝ
ΘΡΩΠΟΥϹΑΝΑΠ
ϹΙΝΗΝΔΕΧΟΡΤΟ
ΠΟΛΥϹΕΝΤΩΤΟΠ
ΑΝΕΠΕϹΑΝΟΥΝ
ΑΝΔΡΕϹΤΟΝΑΡΙ
ΟΜΟΝΩϹΠΕΝΤΑ
ΚΙϹΧΙΛΙΟΙΕΛΑΒΕΝ ΧϹΤ
ΑΡΤΟΥϹΟΙϹΚΑΙΕ
ΧΑΡΙϹΤΗϹΕΝΚΑΙ
ΕΔΩΚΕΝΤΟΙϹΑΝΑ
ΚΙΜΕΝΟΙϹΟΜΟΙ
ΩϹΚΑΙΕΚΤΩΝΟ
ΨΑΡΙΩΝΟϹΟΝΗ
ΛΟΝΩϹΔΕΕΝΕ
ΠΛΗϹΘΗϹΑΝΛΕ
ΤΟΙϹΜΑΘΗΤΑΙϹΑΥ
ΤΟΥϹΥΝΑΓΑΓΕΤΑΙ
ΤΑΠΕΡΙϹϹΕΥϹΑΝ
ΤΑΚΛΑϹΜΑΤΑΙΝΑΜ
ΤΙΑΠΟΛΗΤΑΙϹΥΝ
ΓΑΓΟΝΟΥΝΚΑΙΕ
ΜΙϹΑΝΔΩΔΕΚΑΚ
ΦΙΝΟΥϹΚΛΑϹΜΑ
ΕΚΤΩΝΠΕΝΤΕΑ
ΤΩΝΤΩΝΚΡΙΘΙΝ
ΛΕΠΕΡΙϹϹΕΥϹΕΝ
ΤΟΙϹΕΒΡΩΚΟϹΙΝ
ΟΙΟΥΝΑΝΘΡΩΠΟ
ΙΔΟΝΤΕϹΟΕΠΟΙ
ΗϹΕΝϹΗΜΕΙΟΝ
ΓΟΝΟΥΤΟϹΕϹΤΙΝ
ΑΛΗΘΩϹΟΠΡΟΦΗ
ΤΗϹΟΕΙϹΤΟΝΚ
ΕΡΧΟΜΕΝΟϹ
ΙϹΟΥΝΓΝΟΥϹΟΤΙ
ΜΕΛΛΟΥϹΙΝΕΡΧε
ϹΘΑΙΚΑΙΑΡΠΑΖΕΙΝ
ΑΥΤΟΝΚΑΙΑΝΑΔΙΝΑΠΟΙΗ
ΚΝΥΝΑΙΒΑϹΙΛΕΑ ϹΩϹΙΝ
ΦΕΥΓΕΙΠΑΛΙΝΕΙϹΤ
ΟΡΟϹΜΟΝΟϹΑΥΤ

Column 4

ΩϹΔΕΟΨΙΑϹΕΓΕΝΤ
ΚΑΤΕΒΗϹΑΝΟΙΜΑ
ΘΗΤΑΙΑΥΤΟΥΕΠΙ
ΤΗΝΘΑΛΑϹϹΑΝΚΑΙ
ΕΜΒΑΝΤΕϹΕΙϹΠΛΟΙ
ΟΝΕΡΧΟΝΤΑΠΕ
ΡΑΝΤΗϹΘΑΛΑϹϹΗϹ
ΕΙϹΚΑΦΑΡΝΑΟΥΜ
ΚΑΤΕΛΑΒΕΝΛΕΑΥ
ΤΟΥϹΗϹΚΟΤΙΑΚΝ
ΟΥΠΩΛΕΛΗΛΥΘΕΙ
ΙϹΠΡΟϹΑΥΤΟΥϹΗ
ΤΕΘΑΛΑϹϹΑΑΝΕ
ΜΟΥΜΕΓΑΛΟΥΠΝ
ΟΝΤΟϹΔΙΗΓΕΙΡ
ΤΟΕΛΗΛΑϹΟΤΕϹ
ΩϹϹΤΑΔΙΑΕΙΚΟϹΙ
ΠΕΝΤΕΗΤΡΙΑΚΝ
ΤΑΘΕΩΡΟΥϹΙΝΤ
ΙΝΠΕΡΙΠΑΤΟΥΝΤΑ
ΕΠΙΤΗϹΘΑΛΑϹϹ
ΚΑΙΕΓΓΥϹΤΟΥΠΛΟΙ
ΟΥΓΙΝΟΜΕΝΟΝΕ
ΕΦΟΒΗΘΗϹΑΝ
ΟΔΕΛΕΓΕΙΑΥΤΟΙϹ
ΕΓΩΕΙΜΙΜΗΦΟΒ
ϹΘΑΙΗΛΘΟΝΟΥΝ
ΛΑΒΙΝΑΥΤΟΝΕΙϹΤ
ΠΛΟΙΟΝΚΑΙΕΥΘ
ΩϹΤΟΠΛΟΙΟΝΕΓΝ
ΤΟΕΠΙΤΗΝΓΗΝΕΙϹ
ΥΠΗΝΘϹΕΝΤΗ
ΕΠΑΥΡΙΟΝΟΟΧ
ΟΕϹΤΩϹΠΕΡΑΝΤΗ
ΘΑΛΑϹϹΗϹΕΙΔΑ
ΟΤΙΠΛΟΙΑΡΙΟΝΑ
ΛΟΟΥΚΗΝΕΚΕΙ
ΜΗΕΝΕΚΕΙΝΟΕΙ
ϹΟΕΝΕΒΗϹΑΝΟΙ
ΜΑΘΗΤΑΙΤΟΥΙϹ
ΟΤΙΟΥϹΥΝΕΧΗΙϹ
ΘϹΛΥΤΟΙϹΟΙϹΕΙϹ
ΤΟΙΠΛΟΙΟΝΑΛΛΑ
ΝΟΙΟΙΜΑΘΗΤΑΙϹ
ΤΟΥϹΗΛΘΟΝΑΛΛΑ
ΕΠΕΛΘΟΝΤΩΝΟΥ
ΤΩΝΠΛΟΙΩΝΕΚΤΙ
ΒΕΡΙΑΔΟϹΕΓΓΥϹ

FACSIMILE FROM CODEX SINAITICUS (*reduced one-ninth of original*).
John v. 37 to end, and vi. 1-23.

(εποι)

HCENCHMEION ΔΕ	ησεν σημειον ελε
ΓΟΝΟΥΤΟϹΕϹΤΙΝ	γον· ουτος εστιν
ΑΛΗΘΩϹΟΠΡΟΦΗ	αληθως ο προφη
ΤΗϹΟΕΙϹΤΟΝΚ°ϲΜ°	της ο εις τον κοσμον
ΕΡΧΟΜΕΝΟϹ·	ερχομενος.
ΙϹΟΥΝΓΝΟΥϹΟΤΙ	Ιϲ [Ἰησοῦς] ουν γνους οτι
ΜΕΛΛΟΥϹΙΝΕΡΧε	μελλουσιν ερχε
ϹΘΑΙΚΑΙΑΡΠΑΖΕΙΝ	σθαι και αρπαζειν
ΑΥΤΟΝΚΑΙΑΝΑΔΙΝΑΠΟΙΗ	αυτον καὶ ἀνὰ δὶ να ποιη [Correction]
ΚΝΥΝΑΙΒΑϹΙΛΕΑ ϲΩϲΙΝ	κννᾶι βασιλεα σωσιν
ΝΑ ΑΝΕΧΩΡΗϹΕΝ	*ΝΑ ανεχωρησεν [Interpol. correction]
Δ ΦΕΥΓΕΙΠΑΛΙΝΕΙϹΤ°	φευγει παλιν εις το
ΟΡΟϹΜΟΝΟϹΑΥΤοϲ·	†Δ ορος μονος αυτος.

FACSIMILE FROM CODEX SINAITICUS (*exact size*).—John vi. 2, 3.

* NA=51, the beginning of the 51st Ammonian Section. These sections are numbered consecutively throughout the gospel.——† Δ=4, the fourth Eusebian Canon, showing that the passage following is found in the three gospels, Matthew, Mark, and John.

(2.) The ancestor of some of the Nethinim who returned with Zerubbabel (Ezra 2 : 53 ; Neh. 7 : 55).

Sit'nah—*strife*—the second of the two wells dug by Isaac, whose servants here contended with the Philistines (Gen. 26 : 21). It has been identified with the modern *Shutneh*, in the valley of Gerar, to the west of Rehoboth, about 20 miles south of Beersheba.

Sit'ting, the attitude generally assumed in Palestine by those who were engaged in any kind of work. "The carpenter saws, planes, and hews with his hand-adze, sitting on the ground or upon the plank he is planing. The washerwoman sits by the tub ; and, in a word, no one stands when it is possible to sit. Shopkeepers always sit, and Levi sitting at the receipt of custom (Matt. 9 : 9) is the exact way to state the case."—Thomson, *Land and Book.*

Si'van, a Persian word (Assyr. *sivanu,* "bricks"), used after the Captivity as the name of the third month of the Jewish year, extending from the new moon in June to the new moon in July (Esther 8 : 9).

Skin, Coats made of (Gen. 3 : 21). Skins of rams and badgers were used as a covering for the tabernacle (Ex. 25 : 5 ; Num. 4 : 8–14).

Skull, The place of a. See GOLGOTHA.

Slave, Jer. 2 : 14 (A.V.), but not there found in the original. In Rev. 18 : 13 the word "slaves" is the rendering of a Greek word meaning "bodies." The Hebrew and Greek words for slave are usually rendered simply "servant," "bondman," or "bondservant." Slavery as it existed under the Mosaic law has no modern parallel. That law did not originate but only regulated the already existing custom of slavery (Ex. 21 : 20, 21, 26, 27 ; Lev. 25 : 44–46 ; Josh. 9 : 6–18). The gospel in its spirit and genius is hostile to slavery in every form, which under its influence is gradually disappearing from among men.

Slime (Gen. 11 : 3 ; LXX., "asphalt ;" R.V. marg., "bitumen"). The vale of Siddim was full of slime pits (14 : 10). Jochebed daubed the "ark of bulrushes" with slime (Ex. 2 : 3). (See PITCH.)

Sling. With a sling and a stone David smote the Philistine giant (1 Sam. 17 : 40, 49). There were 700 Benjamites who were so skilled in its use that with the left hand they "could sling stones at a hair breadth, and not miss" (Judg. 20 : 16 ; 1 Chr. 12 : 2). It was used by the Israelites in war (2 Kings 3 : 25). (See ARMS.)

The words in Prov. 26 : 8, "As he that bindeth a stone in a sling," etc. (Authorized Version), should rather, as in the Revised Version, be "As a bag of gems in a heap of stones," etc.

Smith. The Hebrews were not permitted by the Philistines in the days of Samuel to have a smith amongst them, lest they should make them swords and spears (1 Sam. 13 : 19). Thus the Philistines sought to make their conquests permanent (comp. 2 Kings 24 : 16).

Smyr'na—*myrrh*—an ancient city of Ionia, on the western coast of Asia Minor, about 40 miles to the north of Ephesus. It is now the chief city of Anatolia, having a mixed population of about 200,000, of whom about one-third are professed Christians. The church founded here was one of the seven addressed by our Lord (Rev. 2 : 8–11). The celebrated Polycarp, a pupil of the apostle John, was in the second century a prominent leader in the church of Smyrna. Here he suffered martyrdom, A.D. 155.

Snail. (1.) Heb. *ḥomiṭ,* among the unclean creeping things (Lev. 11 : 30). This was probably the sand-lizard, of which there are many species in the wilderness of Judea and the Sinai peninsula.

(2.) Heb. *shablul* (Ps. 58 : 9), the snail or slug proper. Tristram explains the allusions of this passage by a reference to the heat and drought by which the moisture of the snail is evaporated. "We find," he says, "in all parts of the Holy Land myriads of snail-shells in fissures still adhering by the calcareous exudation round their orifice to the surface of the rock, but the animal of which is utterly shrivelled and wasted—'melted away.'"

Snare. The expression (Amos 3 : 5), "Shall one take up a snare from the earth ?" etc. (Authorized Version), ought

JEBEL USDUM

Page 637.

to be, as in the Revised Version, "Shall a snare spring up from the ground?" etc. (See GIN.)

Snow. Common in Palestine in winter (Ps. 147 : 16). The snow on the tops of the Lebanon range is almost always within view throughout the whole year. The word is frequently used figuratively by the sacred writers (Job 24 : 19 ; Ps. 51 : 7 ; 68 : 14 ; Isa. 1 : 18). It is mentioned only once in the historical books (2 Sam. 23 : 20). It was "carried to Tyre, Sidon, and Damascus as a luxury, and labourers sweltering in the hot harvest-fields used it for the purpose of cooling the water which they drank (Prov. 25 : 13 ; Jer. 18 : 14). No doubt Herod Antipas, at his feasts in Tiberias, enjoyed also from this very source the modern luxury of ice-water."

So (Nubian, *Sabako*), an Ethiopian king who brought Egypt under his sway. He was bribed by Hoshea to help him against the Assyrian monarch Shalmaneser (2 Kings 17 : 4). This was a return to the policy that had been successful in the reign of Jeroboam I. (1 Kings 12 : 20).

Soap (Jer. 2 : 22 ; Mal. 3 : 2 ; Heb. *bôrith*), properly a vegetable alkali, obtained from the ashes of certain plants, particularly the *salsola kali* (saltwort), which abounds on the shores of the Dead Sea and of the Mediterranean. It does not appear that the Hebrews were acquainted with what is now called "soap," which is a compound of alkaline carbonates with oleaginous matter. The word "purely" in Isa. 1 : 25 (R.V., "throughly ;" marg., "as with lye") is lit. "as with *bôr*." This word means "clearness," and hence also that which makes clear, or pure, *alkali*. "The ancients made use of alkali mingled with oil, instead of soap (Job 9 : 30), and also in smelting metals, to make them melt and flow more readily and purely."—Gesenius, *Lex. Heb.*

So'cho—*a fence ; hedge*—(1 Chr. 4 : 18) = **So'choh** (1 Kings 4 : 10), **Sho'choh** (1 Sam. 17 : 1), **Sho'co** (2 Chr. 11 : 7), **Sho'cho** (2 Chr. 28 : 18)—a city in the plain or lowland of Judah, where the Philistines encamped when they invaded Judah after their defeat at Michmash. It lay on the

northern side of the valley of Elah (Wâdy es-Sûnt). It has been identified with the modern *Khûrbet Shûweikeh*, about 14 miles south-west of Jerusalem. In this campaign Goliath was slain, and the Philistines were completely routed.

Sod'om—*burning ; the walled*—a city in the vale of Siddim (Gen. 13 : 10 ; 14 : 1-16). The wickedness of its inhabitants brought down upon it fire from heaven, by which it was destroyed (18 : 16-33 ; 19 : 1-29 ; Deut. 23 : 17). This city and its awful destruction are frequently alluded to in Scripture (Deut. 29 : 23 ; 32 : 32 ; Isa. 1 : 9, 10 ; 3 : 9 ; 13 : 19 ; Jer. 23 : 14 ; Ezek. 16 : 46-56 ; Zeph. 2 : 9 ; Matt. 10 : 15 ; Rom. 9 : 29 ; 2 Pet. 2 : 6, etc.). No trace of it or of the other cities of the plain has been discovered, so complete was their destruction. Just opposite the site of Zoar, on the south-west coast of the Dead Sea, is a range of low hills, forming a mass of mineral salt called Jebel Usdum, "the hill of Sodom." It has been concluded from this and from other considerations that the cities of the plain stood at the southern end of the Dead Sea. Others, however, with much greater probability, contend that they stood at the northern end of the sea.

Sod'oma (Rom. 9 : 29 ; R.V., "Sodom"), the Greek form for Sodom.

Sod'omites, those who imitated the licentious wickedness of Sodom (Deut. 23 : 17 ; 1 Kings 14 : 24 ; Rom. 1 : 26, 27). Asa destroyed them "out of the land" (1 Kings 15 : 12), as did also his son Jehoshaphat (22 : 46).

Solemn meeting (Isa. 1 : 13), the convocation on the eighth day of the Feast of Tabernacles (Lev. 23 : 36 ; Num. 29 : 35). It is the name given also to the convocation held on the seventh day of the Passover (Deut. 16 : 8). So great was the degeneracy of the times that men came forth from these most religious of assemblies prepared to sin with less scruple than before (comp. Isa. 58 : 4).

Sol'omon—*peaceful*—(Heb. *Shelômôh*), David's second son by Bathsheba—*i.e.*, the first after their legal marriage (2 Sam. 12). He was probably born about B.C. 1035 (1 Chr. 22 : 5 ; 29 : 1). He succeeded his

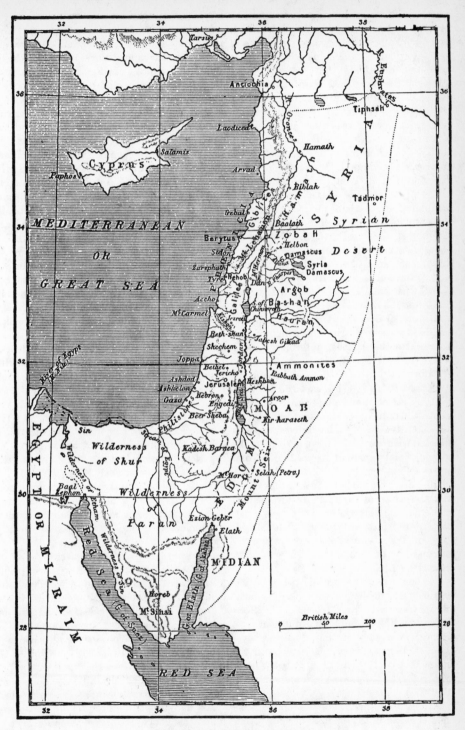

THE DOMINIONS OF SOLOMON.

father on the throne in early manhood, probably about sixteen or eighteen years of age. Nathan, to whom his education was intrusted, called him Jedidiah—*i.e.*, "beloved of the Lord" (2 Sam. 12:24, 25). He was the first king of Israel "born in the purple." His father chose him as his successor, passing over the claims of his elder sons: "Assuredly Solomon my son shall reign after me." His history is recorded in 1 Kings 1–11 and 2 Chr. 1–9. His elevation to the throne took place before his father's death, and was hastened on mainly by Nathan and Bathsheba, in consequence of the rebellion of Adonijah (1 Kings 1:5–40). During his long reign of forty years the Hebrew monarchy gained its highest splendour. This period has well been called the "Augustan age" of the Jewish annals. The first half of his reign was, however, by far the brighter and more prosperous; the latter half was clouded by the idolatries into which he fell, mainly from his heathen intermarriages (1 Kings 11:1–8; 14:21, 31).

Before his death David gave parting instructions to his son (1 Kings 2; 1 Chr. 22, 28, 29). As soon as he had settled himself in his kingdom, and arranged the affairs of his extensive empire, he entered into an alliance with Egypt by the marriage of the daughter of Pharaoh (1 Kings 3), of whom, however, nothing further is recorded. He surrounded himself with all the luxuries and the external grandeur of an Eastern monarch, and his government prospered. He entered into an alliance with Hiram, king of Tyre, who in many ways greatly assisted him in his numerous undertakings. (See HIRAM.)

For some years before his death David was engaged in the active work of collecting materials (1 Chr. 29:6–9; 2 Chr. 2:3–7) for building a temple in Jerusalem as a permanent abode for the ark of the covenant. He was not permitted to build the house of God (1 Chr. 22:8); that honour was reserved to his son Solomon. (See TEMPLE.)

After the completion of the temple Solomon engaged in the erection of many other buildings of importance in Jerusalem and in other parts of his kingdom. For the long space of thirteen years he was engaged in the erection of a royal palace on Ophel (1 Kings 7:1–12). It was 100 cubits long, 50 broad, and 30 high. Its lofty roof was supported by forty-five cedar pillars, so that the hall was like a forest of cedar wood, and hence probably it received the name of "The House of the Forest of Lebanon." In front of this "house" was another building, which was called the Porch of Pillars, and in front of this again was the "Hall of Judgment," or Throneroom (1 Kings 7:7; 10:18–20; 2 Chr. 9:17–19), "the King's Gate," where he administered justice and gave audience to his people. This palace was a building of great magnificence and beauty. A portion of it was set apart as the residence of the queen consort, the daughter of Pharaoh. From the palace there was a private staircase of red and scented sandal wood which led up to the temple.

Solomon also constructed great works for the purpose of securing a plentiful supply of water for the city (Eccl. 2:4–6). He then built Millo (LXX., "Acra") for the defence of the city, completing a line of ramparts around it (1 Kings 9:15, 24; 11:27). He erected also many other fortifications for the defence of his kingdom at various points where it was exposed to the assault of enemies (1 Kings 9:15–19; 2 Chr. 8:2–6). Among his great undertakings must also be mentioned the building of Tadmor (*q.v.*) in the wilderness as a commercial depôt, as well as a military outpost.

During his reign Palestine enjoyed great commercial prosperity. Extensive traffic was carried on by land with Tyre and Egypt and Arabia, and by sea with Spain and India and the coasts of Africa, by which Solomon accumulated vast stores of wealth and of the produce of all nations (1 Kings 9:26–28; 10:11, 12; 2 Chr. 8:17, 18; 9:21). This was the "golden age" of Israel. The royal magnificence and splendour of Solomon's court were unrivalled. He had seven hundred wives and three hundred concubines, an evidence at once of his pride, his wealth, and his sensuality.

The maintenance of his household involved immense expenditure. The provision required for one day was "thirty measures of fine flour, and threescore measures of meal, ten fat oxen, and twenty oxen taken out of the pastures, and an hundred sheep, beside harts, and roebucks, and fallow-deer, and fatted fowl" (1 Kings 4 : 22, 23).

Solomon's reign was not only a period of great material prosperity, but was equally remarkable for its intellectual activity. He was the leader of his people also in this uprising amongst them of new intellectual life. "He spake three thousand proverbs : and his songs were a thousand and five. And he spake of trees, from the cedar tree that is in Lebanon even unto the hyssop that springeth out of the wall : he spake also of beasts, and of fowl, and of creeping things, and of fishes" (1 Kings 4 : 32, 33).

His fame was spread abroad through all lands, and men came from far and near "to hear the wisdom of Solomon." Among others thus attracted to Jerusalem was "the queen of the south" (Matt. 12 : 42), the queen of Sheba, a country in Arabia Felix. "Deep, indeed, must have been her yearning, and great his fame, which induced a secluded Arabian queen to break through the immemorial custom of her dreamy land, and to put forth the energy required for braving the burdens and perils of so long a journey across a wilderness. Yet this she undertook, and carried it out with safety." (1 Kings 10 : 1–13; 2 Chr. 9 : 1–12.) She was filled with amazement by all she saw and heard : "there was no more spirit in her." After an interchange of presents she returned to her native land.

But that golden age of Jewish history passed away. The bright day of Solomon's glory ended in clouds and darkness. His decline and fall from his high estate is a sad record. Chief among the causes of his decline were his polygamy and his great wealth. "As he grew older he spent more of his time among his favourites. The idle king living among these idle women —for 1,000 women, with all their idle and mischievous attendants, filled the palaces and pleasure-houses which he had built

(1 Kings 11 : 3)—learned first to tolerate and then to imitate their heathenish ways. He did not, indeed, cease to believe in the God of Israel with his mind. He did not cease to offer the usual sacrifices in the temple at the great feasts. But his heart was not right with God; his worship became merely formal; his soul, left empty by the dying out of true religious fervour, sought to be filled with any religious excitement which offered itself. Now for the first time a worship was publicly set up amongst the people of the Lord which was not simply irregular or forbidden, like that of Gideon (Judg. 8 : 27), or the Danites (Judg. 18 : 30, 31), but was downright idolatrous." (1 Kings 11 : 7 ; 2 Kings 23 : 13.)

This brought upon him the divine displeasure. His enemies prevailed against him (1 Kings 11 : 14–22, 23–25, 26–40), and one judgment after another fell upon the land. And now the end of all came, and he died, after a reign of forty years, and was buried in the city of David, and "with him was buried the short-lived glory and unity of Israel." "He leaves behind him but one weak and worthless son, to dismember his kingdom and disgrace his name."

"The kingdom of Solomon," says Rawlinson, "is one of the most striking facts in the Biblical history. A petty nation, which for hundreds of years has with difficulty maintained a separate existence in the midst of warlike tribes, each of which has in turn exercised dominion over it and oppressed it, is suddenly raised by the genius of a soldier-monarch to glory and greatness. An empire is established which extends from the Euphrates to the borders of Egypt, a distance of 450 miles ; and this empire, rapidly constructed, enters almost immediately on a period of peace which lasts for half a century. Wealth, grandeur, architectural magnificence, artistic excellence, commercial enterprise, a position of dignity among the great nations of the earth, are enjoyed during this space, at the end of which there is a sudden collapse. The ruling nation is split in twain—the subject-races fall off, the pre-eminence lately gained being wholly lost—the scene of struggle, strife, oppression, recovery, inglorious submission, and desperate effort, re-commences."—*Historical Illustrations.*

Sol'omon, Song of, called also, after the Vulgate, the "Canticles." It is the "song of songs" (1:1), as being the finest and most precious of its kind; the noblest song, "das Hohelied," as Luther calls it. The Solomonic authorship of this book has been called in question, but evidences, both internal and external, fairly establish the traditional view that it is the product of Solomon's pen.

It is an allegorical poem setting forth the mutual love of Christ and the Church, under the emblem of the bridegroom and the bride. (Compare Matt. 9:15; John 3:29; Eph. 5:23, 27, 29; Rev. 19:7-9; 21:2, 9; 22:17. Compare also Ps. 45; Isa. 54:4-6; 62:4, 5; Jer. 2:2; 3:1, 20; Ezek. 16; Hos. 2:16, 19, 20.)

Sol'omon's Porch (John 10:23; Acts 3:11; 5:12), a colonnade, or cloister probably, on the eastern side of the temple. It is not mentioned in connection with the first temple, but Josephus mentions a porch, so called, in Herod's temple (*q.v.*).

Son of God. The plural, "sons of God," is used (Gen. 6:2, 4) to denote the pious descendants of Seth. In Job 1:6; 38:7 this name is applied to the angels. Hosea uses the phrase (1:10) to designate the gracious relation in which men stand to God.

In the New Testament this phrase frequently denotes the relation into which we are brought to God by adoption (Rom. 8:14, 19; 2 Cor. 6:18; Gal. 4:5, 6; Phil. 2:15; 1 John 3:1, 2). It occurs thirty-seven times in the New Testament as the distinctive title of our Saviour. He does not bear this title in consequence of his miraculous birth, nor of his incarnation, his resurrection, and exaltation to the Father's right hand. This is a title of nature and not of office. The sonship of Christ denotes his equality with the Father. To call Christ the Son of God is to assert his true and proper divinity. The second Person of the Trinity, because of his eternal relation to the first Person, is the Son of God. He is the Son of God as to his

divine nature, while as to his human nature he is the Son of David (Rom. 1:3, 4. Comp. Gal. 4:4; John 1:1-14; 5:18-25; 10:30-38, which prove that Christ was the Son of God before his incarnation, and that his claim to this title is a claim of equality with God).

When used with reference to creatures, whether men or angels, this word is always in the plural. In the singular it is always used of the second Person of the Trinity, with the single exception of Luke 3:38, where it is used of Adam.

Son of man. (1.) Denotes mankind generally, with special reference to their weakness and frailty (Job 25:6; Ps. 8:4; 144:3; 146:3; Isa. 51:12, etc.).

(2.) It is a title frequently given to the prophet Ezekiel, probably to remind him of his human weakness.

(3.) In the New Testament it is used forty-three times as a distinctive title of the Saviour. In the Old Testament it is used only in Ps. 80:17 and Dan. 7:13 with this application. It denotes the true humanity of our Lord. He had a true body (Heb. 2:14; Luke 24:39) and a rational soul. He was perfect man.

Songs, of Moses (Ex. 15; Num. 21:17; Deut. 32; Rev. 15:3), Deborah (Judg. 5), Hannah (1 Sam. 2), David (2 Sam. 22, and Psalms), Mary (Luke 1:46-55), Zacharias (Luke 1:68-79), the angels (Luke 2:13), Simeon (Luke 2:29), the redeemed (Rev. 5:9; 19), Solomon (see SOLOMON, SONGS OF).

Sooth'sayer, one who pretends to prognosticate future events. Baalam is so called (Josh. 13:22; Heb. *kôsem*, a "diviner," as rendered 1 Sam. 6:2; rendered "prudent," Isa. 3:2). In Isa. 2:6 and Micah 5:12 (Heb. *yonenîm — i.e.,* "diviners of the clouds") the word is used of the Chaldean diviners who studied the clouds. In Dan. 2:27; 5:7 the word is the rendering of the Chaldee *gazrin—i.e.,* "deciders" or "determiners"—here applied to Chaldean astrologers, "who, by casting nativities from the place of the stars at one's birth, and by various arts of computing and divining, foretold the fortunes and destinies of individuals."—Gesenius, *Lex. Heb.* (See SORCERER.)

Sop, a morsel of bread (John 13 : 26 ; comp. Ruth 2 : 14). Our Lord took a piece of unleavened bread, and dipping it into the broth of bitter herbs at the Paschal meal, gave it to Judas. (Comp. Ruth 2 : 14.)

So'pater—*the father who saves*—probably the same as Sosipater, a kinsman of Paul (Rom. 16 : 21), a Christian of the city of Berea who accompanied Paul into Asia (Acts 20 : 4-6).

Sor'cerer, from the Latin *sortiarius,* one who casts lots, or one who tells the lot of others. (See DIVINATION.)

In Dan. 2 : 2 it is the rendering of the Hebrew *mekhashphîm*—*i.e.,* mutterers, men who professed to have power with evil spirits. The practice of sorcery exposed to severest punishment (Mal. 3 : 5 ; Rev. 21 : 8 ; 22 : 15).

So'rek—*choice vine*—the name of a valley, *i.e.,* a torrent-bed, now the *Wâdy Sŭrâr,* "valley of the fertile spot," which drains the western Judean hills, and flowing by Makkedah and Jabneel, falls into the sea some eight miles south of Joppa. This was the home of Delilah, whom Samson loved (Judg. 16 : 4).

Sosi'pater. (See SOPATER.)

Sos'thenes—*safe in strength*—the chief ruler of the synagogue at Corinth, who was seized and beaten by the mob in the presence of Gallio, the Roman governor, when he refused to proceed against Paul at the instigation of the Jews (Acts 18 : 12-17). The motives of this assault against Sosthenes are not recorded, nor is it mentioned whether it was made by Greeks or Romans. Some identify him, but without sufficient grounds, with one whom Paul calls "Sosthenes our brother," a convert to the faith (1 Cor. 1 : 1).

South—Heb. *Negeb*—that arid district to the south of Palestine through which lay the caravan route from Central Palestine to Egypt (Gen. 12 : 9 ; 13 : 1, 3 ; 46 : 1-6). "The Negeb comprised a considerable but irregularly-shaped tract of country, its main portion stretching from the mountains and lowlands of Judah in the north to the mountains of Azazemeh in the south, and from the Dead Sea and southern Ghor on the east to the Mediterranean on the

west." In Ezek. 20 : 46 (21 : 1 in Heb.) three different Hebrew words are all rendered "south." (1) "Set thy face toward the south" (*Teman,* the region on the right—1 Sam. 33 : 24) ; (2) "Drop thy word toward the south" (*Negeb,* the region of dryness—Josh. 15 : 4) ; (3) "Prophesy against the forest of the south field" (*Darôm,* the region of brightness—Deut. 33 : 23). In Job 37 : 9 the word "south" is literally "chamber," used here in the sense of treasury (comp. 38 : 22 ; Ps. 135 : 7). This verse is rendered in the Revised Version "out of the chamber," etc.

Sov'ereignty of God, his absolute right to do all things according to his own good pleasure (Dan. 4 : 25, 35 ; Rom. 9 : 15-23 ; 1 Tim. 6 : 15 ; Rev. 4 : 11).

Spain. Paul expresses his intention (Rom. 15 : 24, 28) to visit Spain. There is, however, no evidence that he ever carried it into effect, although some think that he probably did so between his first and second imprisonment. (See TARSHISH.)

Spar'row. Mentioned among the offerings made by the very poor. Two sparrows were sold for a farthing (Matt. 10 : 29), and five for two farthings (Luke 12 : 6). The Hebrew word thus rendered is *tsippôr,* which properly denotes the whole family of small birds which feed on grain (Lev. 14 : 4 ; Ps. 84 : 3 ; 102 : 7). The Greek word of the New Testament is *strouthion* (Matt. 10 : 29-31), which is thus correctly rendered.

Spi'cery—Heb. *nechôth,* identified with the Arabic *naka'at,* the gum tragacanth, obtained from the *astralagus,* of which there are about twenty species found in Palestine. The tragacanth of commerce is obtained from the *A. tragacantha.* "The gum exudes plentifully under the heat of the sun on the leaves, thorns, and extremity of the twigs."

Spi'ces, aromatic substances, of which several are named in Ex. 30. They were used in the sacred anointing oil (Ex. 25 : 6 ; 35 : 8 ; 1 Chr. 9 : 29), and in embalming the dead (2 Chr. 16 : 14 ; Luke 23 : 56 ; 24 : 1 ; John 19 : 39, 40). Spices were stored by Hezekiah in his treasure-house (2 Kings 20 : 13 ; Isa. 39 : 2).

Spi'der. The trust of the hypocrite is

compared to the spider's web or house (Job 8:14). It is said of the wicked by Isaiah that they "weave the spider's web" (59:5)—*i.e.*, their works and designs are, like the spider's web, vain and useless. The Hebrew word here used is *'akkâbîsh*, "a swift weaver."

In Prov. 30:28 a different Hebrew word (*semâmîth*) is used. It is rendered in the Vulgate by *stellio*, and in the Revised Version by "lizard." It may, however, represent the spider, of which there are, it is said, about seven hundred species in Palestine.

Spies. When the Israelites reached Kadesh for the first time, and were encamped there, Moses selected twelve spies from among the chiefs of the divisions of the tribes, and sent them forth to spy the land of Canaan (Num. 13), and to bring back to him a report of its actual condition. They at once proceeded on their important errand, and went through the land as far north as the district round Lake Merom. After about six weeks' absence they returned. Their report was very discouraging, and the people were greatly alarmed, and in a rebellious spirit proposed to elect a new leader and return to Egypt. Only two of the spies, Caleb and Joshua, showed themselves on this occasion stout-hearted and faithful. All their appeals and remonstrances were in vain. Moses announced that as a punishment for their rebellion they must now wander in the wilderness till a new generation should arise which would go up and possess the land. The spies had been forty days absent on their expedition, and for each day the Israelites were to be wanderers for a year in the desert. (See ESHCOL.)

Two spies were sent by Joshua "secretly" —*i.e.*, unknown to the people (Josh. 2:1)— "to view the land and Jericho" after the death of Moses, and just before the tribes under his leadership were about to cross the Jordan. They learned from Rahab (*q.v.*), in whose house they found a hiding-place, that terror had fallen on all the inhabitants of the land because of the great things they had heard that Jehovah had done for them (Ex. 15:14–16; comp. 23:27; Deut. 2:25; 11:25). As the result of their mission they reported: "Truly Jehovah hath delivered into our hands all the land; for even all the inhabitants of the country do faint because of us."

Spike'nard (Heb. *nêrd*), a much-valued perfume (Cant. 1:12; 4:13, 14). It was "very precious"—*i.e.*, very costly (Mark 14:3; John 12:3, 5). It is the root of an Indian plant, the *Nardostachys jatamansi*, of the family of *Valerianæ*, growing on the Himalaya mountains. It is distinguished by its having many hairy spikes shooting out from one root. It is called by the Arabs *sunbul Hindi*, "the Indian spike." In the New Testament this word is the rendering of the Greek *nardos pistikē*. The margin of the Revised Version in these passages has "pistic nard," pistic being perhaps a local name. Some take it to mean *genuine*, and others *liquid*. The most probable opinion is that the word *pistikē* designates the nard as genuine or faithfully prepared.

Spir'it (Heb. *ruaḥ;* Gr. *pneuma*), properly wind or breath. In 2 Thess. 2:8 it means "breath," and in Eccl. 8:8 the vital principle in man. It also denotes the rational, immortal soul by which man is distinguished (Acts 7:59; 1 Cor. 5:5; 6:20; 7:34), and the soul in its separate state (Heb. 12:23), and hence also an apparition (Job 4:15; Luke 24:37, 39), an angel (Heb. 1:14), and a demon (Luke 4:36; 10:20). This word is used also metaphorically as denoting a tendency (Zech. 12:10; Luke 13:11).

In Rom. 1:4, 1 Tim. 3:16, 2 Cor. 3:17, 1 Pet. 3:18, it designates the divine nature.

Spirit, Holy. See HOLY GHOST.

Sponge occurs only in the narrative of the crucifixion (Matt. 27:48; Mark 15:36; John 19:29). It is ranked as a zoophyte. It is found attached to rocks at the bottom of the sea.

Spouse (Cant. 4:8–12; Hos. 4:13, 14) may denote either husband or wife, but in the Scriptures it denotes only the latter.

Spring (Heb. *'ain*, "the bright open source—the *eye* of the landscape"). To be carefully distinguished from "well" (*q.v.*).

"Springs" mentioned in Josh. 10:40 (Heb. *'ashdoth*) should rather be "declivities" or "slopes" (R.V.)—*i.e.*, the undulating ground lying between the lowlands (the shephêlah) and the central range of hills.

Sta'chys—*spike; an ear of corn*—a convert at Rome whom Paul salutes (Rom. 16:9).

Stac'te (Heb. *nâtâph*), one of the components of the perfume which was offered on the golden altar (Ex. 30:34; R.V. marg., "opobalsamum"). The Hebrew word is from a root meaning "to distil," and it has been by some interpreted as distilled myrrh. Others regard it as the gum of the storax tree, or rather shrub, the *Styrax officinale.* "The Syrians value this gum highly, and use it medicinally as an emulcent in pectoral complaints, and also in perfumery."

Star, Morning, a name figuratively given to Christ (Rev. 22:16; comp. 2 Pet. 1:19). When Christ promises that he will give the "morning star" to his faithful ones, he "promises that he will give to them himself, that he will impart to them his own glory and a share in his own royal dominion; for the star is evermore the symbol of royalty (Matt. 2:2), being therefore linked with the sceptre (Num. 24:17). All the glory of the world shall end in being the glory of the Church."—Trench's *Comm.*

Star'gazers (Isa. 47:13), those who pretend to tell what will occur by looking upon the stars. The Chaldean astrologers "divined by the rising and setting, the motions, aspects, colour, degree of light, etc., of the stars."

Stars. The eleven stars (Gen. 37:9); the seven (Amos 5:8); wandering (Jude 13); seen in the east at the birth of Christ, probably some luminous meteors miraculously formed for this specific purpose (Matt. 2:2-10); stars worshipped (Deut. 4:19; 2 Kings 17:16; 21:3; Jer. 19:13); spoken of symbolically (Num. 24:17; Rev. 1:16, 20; 12:1). (See ASTROLOGERS.)

Sta'ter, Greek word rendered "piece of money" (Matt. 17:27, A.V.; and "shekel" in R.V.). It was equal to two didrachmas

("tribute money," 17:24), or four drachmas, and to about 2s. 6d. of our money. (See SHEKEL.)

Steel. The "bow of steel" in (A.V.) 2 Sam. 22:35; Job 20:24; Ps. 18:34 is in the Revised Version "bow of brass" (Heb. *kĕshĕth-nĕḥûshâh*). In Jer. 15:12 the same word is used, and is also rendered in the Revised Version "brass." But more correctly it is copper (*q.v.*), as brass in the ordinary sense of the word (an alloy of copper and zinc) was not known to the ancients.

Steph'anas—*crown*—a member of the church at Corinth, whose family were among those the apostle had baptized (1 Cor. 1:16; 16:15, 17). He has been supposed by some to have been the "jailer of Philippi" (comp. Acts 16:33). The First Epistle to the Corinthians was written from Philippi some six years after the jailer's conversion, and he was with the apostle there at that time.

Ste'phen, one of the seven deacons, who became a preacher of the gospel. He was the first Christian martyr. His personal character and history are recorded in Acts 6. "He fell asleep" with a prayer for his persecutors on his lips (7:60). Devout men carried him to his grave (8:2).

It was at the feet of the young Pharisee, Saul of Tarsus, that those who stoned him laid their clothes (comp. Deut. 17:5-7) before they began their cruel work. The scene which Saul then witnessed and the words he heard appear to have made a deep and lasting impression on his mind (Acts 22:19, 20).

The speech of Stephen before the Jewish ruler is the first apology for the universalism of the gospel as a message to the Gentiles as well as the Jews. It is the longest speech contained in the Acts, a place of prominence being given to it as a defence.

Sto'ics, a sect of Greek philosophers at Athens, so called from the Greek word *stoa* —*i.e.*, a "porch" or "portico," where they were wont to assemble (Acts 17:18). They have been called "the Pharisees of Greek paganism." The founder of the Stoics was Zeno, who flourished about B.C. 300. He taught his disciples that a man's happiness consisted in bringing himself into harmony with the course of the universe. They were trained to bear evils with indifference, and so to be independent of externals. Materialism, pantheism, fatalism, and pride were the leading features of this philosophy.

Stom'acher (Isa. 3 : 24), an article of female attire, probably some sort of girdle around the breast.

Stone. Stones were commonly used for buildings, also as memorials of important events (Gen. 28 : 18; Josh. 24 : 26, 27; 1 Sam. 7 : 12, etc.). They were gathered out of cultivated fields (Isa. 5 : 2; comp. 2 Kings 3 : 19). This word is also used figuratively of believers (1 Pet. 2 : 4, 5), and of the Messiah (Ps. 118 : 22; Isa. 28 : 16; Matt. 21 : 42; Acts 4 : 11, etc.). In Dan. 2 : 45 it refers also to the Messiah. He is there described as "cut out of the rock" (*q.v.*).

A "heart of stone" denotes great insensibility (1 Sam. 25 : 37).

Stones were set up to commemorate remarkable events, as by Jacob at Bethel (Gen. 28 : 18), at Padan-aram (35 : 4), and on the occasion of parting with Laban (31 : 45-47); by Joshua at the place on the banks of the Jordan where the people first "lodged" after crossing the river (Josh. 21 : 8), and also in "the midst of Jordan," where he erected another set of twelve stones (4 : 1-9); and by Samuel at "Ebenezer" (1 Sam. 7 : 12).

Stones, Precious. Frequently referred to (1 Kings 10 : 2; 2 Chr. 3 : 6; 9 : 10; Rev. 18 : 16; 21 : 19). There are about twenty different names of such stones in the Bible. They are figuratively introduced to denote value, beauty, durability (Cant. 5 : 14; Isa. 54 : 11, 12; Lam. 4 : 7).

Stork. Heb. *ḥăsîdâh*, meaning "kindness," indicating thus the character of the bird, which is noted for its affection for its young. It is in the list of birds forbidden to be eaten by the Levitical law (Lev. 11 : 19; Deut. 14 : 18). It is like the crane, but larger in size. Two species are found in Palestine—the white, which are dispersed in pairs over the whole country; and the black, which live in marshy places and in great flocks. They migrate to Palestine

periodically (about the 22nd of March). Jeremiah alludes to this (Jer. 8 : 7). At the appointed time they return with unerring sagacity to their old haunts, and reoccupy their old nests. "There is a well-authenticated account of the devotion of a stork which, at the burning of the town of Delft, after repeated and unsuccessful attempts to carry off her young, chose rather to remain and perish with them than leave them to their fate. Well might the Romans call it the *pia avis !*."

In Job 39 : 13 (A.V.), instead of the expression "or wings and feathers unto the ostrich" (marg., "the feathers of the stork and ostrich"), the Revised Version has "are her pinions and feathers kindly" (marg., instead of "kindly," reads "like the stork's"). The object of this somewhat obscure verse seems to be to point out a contrast between the stork, as distinguished for her affection for her young, and the ostrich, as distinguished for her indifference.

Zechariah (5 : 9) alludes to the beauty and power of the stork's wings.

Strain at. Simply a misprint for "strain out" (Matt. 23 : 24).

Stran'ger. This word generally denotes a person from a foreign land residing in Palestine. Such persons enjoyed many privileges in common with the Jews, but still were separate from them. The relation of the Jews to strangers was regulated by special laws (Deut. 23 : 3; 24 : 14-21; 25 : 5; 26 : 10-13).

A special signification is also sometimes attached to this word. In Gen. 23 : 4 it denotes one resident in a foreign land; Ex. 23 : 19, one who is not a Jew; Num. 3 : 10, one who is not of the family of Aaron; Ps. 69 : 8, an alien or an unknown person.

The Jews were allowed to purchase strangers as slaves (Lev. 25 : 44, 45), and to take usury from them (Deut. 23 : 20).

Straw. Used in brick-making (Ex. 5 : 7-18). Used figuratively in Job 41 : 27; Isa. 11 : 7; 25 : 10; 65 : 25.

Steal'ing. See THEFT.

Ston'ing, a form of punishment (Lev. 20 : 2; 24 : 14; Deut. 13 : 10; 17 : 5; 22 : 21) prescribed for certain offences. Of Achan

(Josh. 7 : 25), Naboth (1 Kings 21), Stephen (Acts 7 : 59), Paul (Acts 14 : 19; 2 Cor. 11 : 25).

Stream of Egypt (Isa. 27 : 12), the *Wâdy el-'Arîsh*, called also "the river of Egypt" (Num. 34 : 5; Josh. 15 : 4), and "the brook of Egypt" (2 Kings 24 : 7). It is the natural boundary of Egypt. Occasionally in winter, when heavy rains have fallen among the mountains inland, it becomes a turbulent rushing torrent. The *present* boundary between Egypt and Palestine is about midway between el-'Arîsh and Gaza.

Street. The street called "Straight" at Damascus (Acts 9 : 11) is "a long broad street, running from east to west, about a mile in length, and forming the principal thoroughfare in the city." In Oriental towns streets are usually narrow and irregular and filthy (Ps. 18 : 42; Isa. 10 : 6). "It is remarkable," says Porter, "that all the important cities of Palestine and Syria — Samaria, Cæsarea, Gerasa, Bozrah, Damascus, Palmyra—had their 'straight streets' running through the centre of the city, and lined with stately rows of columns. The most perfect now remaining are those of Palmyra and Gerasa, where long ranges of the columns still stand."—*Through Samaria, etc.*

Stripes as a punishment were not to exceed forty (Deut. 25 : 1-3), and hence arose the custom of limiting them to thirty-nine (2 Cor. 11 : 24). Paul claimed the privilege of a Roman citizen in regard to the infliction of stripes (Acts 16 : 37, 38; 22 : 25-29). Our Lord was beaten with stripes (Matt. 27 : 26).

Subscrip'tions. The subscriptions to Paul's epistles are no part of the original. In their present form they are ascribed to Euthalius, a bishop of the fifth century. Some of them are obviously incorrect.

Sub'urbs, the immediate vicinity of a city or town (Num. 35 : 3, 7; Ezek. 45 : 2). In 2 Kings 23 : 11 the Hebrew word there used (*parvârim*) occurs nowhere else. The Revised Version renders it "precincts." The singular form of this Hebrew word (*parvar*) is supposed by some to be the same as Parbar (*q.v.*), which occurs twice in 1 Chr. 26 : 18.

Suc'coth—*booths.* (1.) The first encampment of the Israelites after leaving Rameses (Ex. 12 : 37); the civil name of Pithom (*q.v.*).

(2.) A city on the east of Jordan, identified with *Tell Dar'ala*, a high mound, a mass of *débris*, in the plain north of Jabbok and about one mile from it (Josh. 13 : 27). Here Jacob (Gen. 32 : 17, 30; 33 : 18), on his return from Padan-aram after his interview with Esau, built a house for himself and made booths for his cattle.

The princes of this city churlishly refused to afford help to Gideon and his 300 men when "faint yet pursuing" they followed one of the bands of the fugitive Midianites after the great victory at Gilboa. After overtaking and routing this band at Karkor, Gideon on his return visited the rulers of the city with severe punishment. "He took the elders of the city, and thorns of the wilderness and briers, and with them he taught the men of Succoth" (Judg. 8 : 13-17). At this place were erected the foundries for casting the metal-work for the temple (1 Kings 7 : 46).

Suc'coth-be'noth—*tents of daughters*—supposed to be the name of a Babylonian deity, the goddess Zir-banit, the wife of Merodach, worshipped by the colonists in Samaria (2 Kings 17 : 30).

Sukki'ims—*dwellers in tents*—(Vulg. and LXX., "troglodites;" *i.e.*, cave-dwellers in the hills along the Red Sea). Shishak's army, with which he marched against Jerusalem, was composed partly of this tribe (2 Chr. 12 : 3).

Sun (Heb. *shĕmĕsh*), first mentioned along with the moon as the two great luminaries of heaven (Gen. 1 : 14-18). By their motions and influence they were intended to mark and divide times and seasons. The worship of the sun was one of the oldest forms of false religion (Job 31 : 26, 27), and was common among the Egyptians and Chaldeans and other pagan nations. The Jews were warned against this form of idolatry (Deut. 14 : 19; 17 : 3; comp. 2 Kings 23 : 11; Jer. 19 : 13).

Suph (Deut. 1 : 1, R.V.; marg., "some ancient versions have the Red Sea," as in the A.V.). Some identify it with Suphah (Num. 21 : 14, marg., A.V.) as probably the name of a place. Others identify it with *es - Sufâh* = Maaleh-acrabbim (Josh. 15:3), and others again with Zuph (1 Sam. 9:5). It is most probable, however, that, in accordance with the ancient versions, this word is to be regarded as simply an abbreviation of *Yam-suph—i.e.*, the "Red Sea."

Su'phah (Num. 21:14, marg.; also R.V.), a place at the south-eastern corner of the Dead Sea, the *Ghôr es-Safieh.* This name is found in an ode quoted from the "Book of the Wars of the Lord," probably a collection of odes commemorating the triumphs of God's people (comp. 21:14, 17, 18, 27–30).

Sup'per, the principal meal of the day among the Jews. It was partaken of in the early part of the evening (Mark 6:21; John 12:2; 1 Cor. 11:21). (See LORD'S SUPPER.)

Sure'ty, one who becomes responsible for another. Christ is the surety of the better covenant (Heb. 7:22). In him we have the assurance that all its provisions will be fully and faithfully carried out. Solomon warns against incautiously becoming security for another (Prov. 6:1–5; 11:15; 17:18; 20:16).

Susan'chites, the inhabitants of Shushan, who joined the other adversaries of the Jews in the attempt to prevent the rebuilding of the temple (Ezra 4:9).

Susan'na—*lily*—with other pious women, ministered to Jesus (Luke 8:3).

Su'si, the father of Gaddi, who was one of the twelve spies (Num. 13:11).

Swal'low. (1.) Heb. *sîs* (Isa. 38:14; Jer. 8:7), the Arabic for the swift, which "is a regular migrant, returning in myriads every spring, and so suddenly that while one day not a swift can be seen in the country, on the next they have overspread the whole land, and fill the air with their shrill cry." The swift (*cypselus*) is ordinarily classed with the swallow, which it resembles in its flight, habits, and migration.

(2.) Heb. *derôr—i.e.*, "the bird of freedom" (Ps. 84:3; Prov. 26:2), properly rendered swallow, distinguished for its swiftness of flight, its love of freedom, and the impossibility of retaining it in cap-

tivity. In Isa. 38:14 and Jer. 8:7 the word thus rendered (*'agûr*) properly means "crane" (as in the R.V.).

Swan, mentioned in the list of unclean birds (Lev. 11:18; Deut. 14:16), is sometimes met with in the Jordan and the Sea of Galilee.

Swel'ling of Jordan (Jer. 12:5), literally the "pride" of Jordan (as in R.V.)—*i.e.*, the luxuriant thickets of tamarisks, poplars, reeds, etc., which were the lair of lions and other beasts of prey. The reference is not to the overflowing of the river banks. (Comp. 49:19; 50:44; Zech. 11:3).

Swine (Heb. *hazîr*), regarded as the most unclean and the most abhorred of all animals (Lev. 11:7; Isa. 65:4; 66:3, 17; Luke 15:15, 16). A herd of swine were drowned in the Sea of Galilee (Luke 8:32, 33). Spoken of figuratively in Matt. 7:6 (see Prov. 11:22). It is frequently mentioned as a wild animal, and is evidently the wild boar (Arab. *khanzîr*), which is common among the marshes of the Jordan valley (Ps. 80:13).

Sword of the Hebrew was pointed, sometimes two-edged, was worn in a sheath, and suspended from the girdle (Ex. 32:27; 1 Sam. 31:4; 1 Chr. 21:27; Ps. 149:6: Prov. 5:4; Ezek. 16:40; 21:3–5).

It is a symbol of divine chastisement (Deut. 32:25; Ps. 7:12; 78:62), and of a slanderous tongue (Ps. 57:4; 64:3; Prov. 12:18). The word of God is likened also to a sword (Heb. 4:12; Eph. 6:17; Rev. 1:16). Gideon's watchword was, "The sword of the Lord" (Judg. 7:20).

Syc'amine tree, mentioned only in Luke 17:6. It is rendered by Luther "mulberry tree"(*q.v.*), which is most probably the correct rendering. It is found of two species—the black mulberry (*Morus nigra*) and the white mulberry (*Mourea*), which are common in Palestine. The silkworm feeds on their leaves. The rearing of them is one of the chief industries of the peasantry of Lebanon and of other parts of the land. It is of the order of the fig-tree.

Some contend, however, that this name denotes the sycamore-fig of Luke 19:4.

Syc'amore, more properly sycomore (Heb. *shikmôth* and *shikmim*, Gr. *syco-*

mōros), a tree which in its general character resembles the fig-tree, while its leaves resemble those of the mulberry; hence it is called the fig-mulberry (*Ficus sycomorus*). At Jericho, Zacchæus climbed a sycamore-tree to see Jesus as he passed by (Luke 19 : 4). This tree was easily destroyed by frost (Ps. 78 : 47), and therefore it is found mostly in the "vale" (1 Kings 10 : 27; 2 Chr. 1 : 15: in both passages the R.V. has properly "lowland")—*i.e.*, the "low country," the shephêlah, where the climate is mild. Amos (7 : 14) refers to its fruit, which is of an inferior character; so also probably Jeremiah (24 : 2). It is to be distinguished from our sycamore (the *Acer pseudo-platanus*), which is a species of maple often called a plane-tree.

Sy'char—*liar* or *drunkard* (see Isa. 28 : 1, 7)—has been from the time of the Crusaders usually identified with Sychem or Shechem (John 4 : 5). It has now, however, as the result of recent explorations, been identified with '*Askar*, a small Samaritan town on the southern base of Ebal, about a mile to the north of Jacob's well.

Sy'chem. See SHECHEM.

Sye'ne—*opening* (Ezek. 29 : 10; 30 : 6)—a town of Egypt, on the borders of Ethiopia, now called *Assouan*, on the right bank of the Nile, notable for its quarries of beautiful red granite called "syenite." It was the frontier town of Egypt in the south, as Migdol was in the north-east.

Syn'agogue (Gr. *sunagōgē*—*i.e.*, "an assembly"), found only once in the Authorized Version of Ps. 74 : 8, where the margin of Revised Version has "places of assembly," which is probably correct; for while the origin of synagogues is unknown, it may well be supposed that buildings or tents for the accommodation of worshippers may have existed in the land from an early time, and thus the system of synagogues would be gradually developed.

Some, however, are of opinion that it was specially during the Babylonian captivity that the system of synagogue worship, if not actually introduced, was at least reorganized on a systematic plan (Ezek. 8 : 1; 14 : 1). The exiles gathered together for the reading of the law and the pro-

phets as they had opportunity, and after their return synagogues were established all over the land (Ezra 8 : 15; Neh. 8 : 2). In after years, when the Jews were dispersed abroad, wherever they went they erected synagogues and kept up the stated services of worship (Acts 9 : 20; 13 : 5; 17 : 1; 17 : 17; 18 : 4). The form and internal arrangements of the synagogue would greatly depend on the wealth of the Jews who erected it, and on the place where it was built. "Yet there are certain traditional peculiarities which have doubtless united together by a common resemblance the Jewish synagogues of all ages and countries. The arrangements for the women's place in a separate gallery or behind a partition of lattice-work; the desk in the centre, where the reader, like Ezra in ancient days, from his 'pulpit of wood,' may 'open the book in the sight of all the people and read in the book of the law of God distinctly, and give the sense, and cause them to understand the reading' (Neh. 8 : 4, 8); the carefully closed ark on the side of the building nearest to Jerusalem, for the preservation of the rolls or manuscripts of the law; the seats all round the building, whence 'the eyes of all them that are in the synagogue' may 'be fastened' on him who speaks (Luke 4 : 20); the 'chief seats' (Matt. 23 : 6) which were appropriated to the 'ruler' or 'rulers' of the synagogue, according as its organization may have been more or less complete;"—these were features common to all the synagogues.

Where perfected into a system, the services of the synagogue, which were at the same hours as those of the temple, consisted—(1) of prayer, which formed a kind of liturgy—there were in all eighteen prayers; (2) the reading of the Scriptures in certain definite portions; and (3) the exposition of the portions read. (See Luke 4 : 15, 22; Acts 13 : 14.)

The synagogue was also sometimes used as a court of judicature, in which the rulers presided (Matt. 10 : 17; Mark 5 : 22; Luke 12 : 11; 21 : 12; Acts 13 : 15; 22 : 19); also as public schools.

The establishment of synagogues wherever the Jews were found in sufficient numbers helped greatly to keep alive Israel's hope of the coming of the Messiah, and to prepare the way for the spread of the gospel in other lands. The worship of the Christian Church was afterwards modelled after that of the synagogue.

Christ and his disciples frequently taught in the synagogues (Matt. 13 : 54; Mark 6 : 2; John 18 : 20; Acts 13 : 5, 15, 44; 14 : 1; 17 : 2–4, 10, 17; 18 : 4, 26; 19 : 8).

To be "put out of the synagogue," a phrase used by John (9 : 22; 12 : 42; 16 : 2), means to be excommunicated.

Syn′tyche—*fortunate; affable*—a female member of the church at Philippi, whom Paul beseeches to be of one mind with Euodias (Phil. 4 : 2, 3).

Syr′acuse, a city on the south-east coast of Sicily, where Paul landed and remained three days when on his way to Rome (Acts 28 : 12). It was distinguished for its magnitude and splendour. It is now a small town of some 13,000 inhabitants.

Syr′ia (Heb. *Aram*), the name in the Old Testament given to the whole country which lay to the north-east of Phœnicia, extending to beyond the Euphrates and the Tigris. Mesopotamia is called (Gen. 24 : 10; Deut. 23 : 4) *Aram-naharaim* (= Syria of the two rivers), also Padan-aram (Gen. 25 : 20). Other portions of Syria were also known by separate names, as *Aram-maahah* (1 Chr. 19 : 6), *Aram-beth-rehob* (2 Sam. 10 : 6), *Aram-zobah* (2 Sam. 10 : 6, 8). All these separate little kingdoms afterwards became subject to Damascus. In the time of the Romans, Syria included also a part of Palestine and Asia Minor.

"From the historic annals now accessible to us, the history of Syria may be divided into three periods :—The first, the period when the power of the Pharaohs was dominant over the fertile fields or plains of Syria and the merchant cities of Tyre and Sidon, and when such mighty conquerors as Thothmes III. and Rameses II. could claim dominion and levy tribute from the nations from the banks of the Euphrates to the borders of the Libyan desert. Second, this was followed by a short period of independence, when the Jewish nation in the south was growing in power, until it reached its early zenith in the golden days of Solomon; and when Tyre and Sidon were rich cities, sending their traders far and wide, over land and sea, as missionaries of civilization, while in the north the confederate tribes of the Hittites held back the armies of the kings of Assyria. The third, and to us most interesting, period is that during which the kings of Assyria were dominant over the plains of Syria; when Tyre, Sidon, Ashdod, and Jerusalem bowed beneath the conquering armies of Shalmaneser, Sargon, and Sennacherib; and when at last Memphis and Thebes yielded to the power of the rulers of Nineveh and Babylon, and the kings of Assyria completed with terrible fulness the bruising of the reed of Egypt so clearly foretold by the Hebrew prophets."—Boscawen.

Syr′iac (2 Kings 18 : 26; Ezra 4 : 7; Dan. 2 : 4), more correctly rendered "Aramaic," including both the Syriac and the Chaldee languages. In the New Testament there are several Syriac words, such as "Eloï, Eloi, lama sabachthani?" (Mark 15 : 34; Matt. 27 : 46 gives the Heb. form, "Eli, Eli"), "Raca" (Matt. 5 : 22), "Ephphatha" (Mark 7 : 34), "Maran-atha" (1 Cor. 16 : 22).

A Syriac version of the Old Testament, containing all the canonical books, along with some apocryphal books (called the *Peshitto*—*i.e.*, simple translation, and not a paraphrase), was made early in the second century, and is therefore the first Christian translation of the Old Testament. It was made directly from the original, and not from the LXX. Version. The New Testament was also translated from Greek into Syriac about the same time. It is noticeable that this version does not contain the Second and Third Epistles of John, 2 Peter, Jude, and the Apocalypse. These were, however, translated subsequently and placed in the version. (See VERSION.)

Sy′rophenician, "a Greek, a Syrophenician by nation" (Mark 7 : 26)—*i.e.*, a Gentile born in the Phœnician part of Syria. (See PHENICIA.)

When our Lord retired into the borderland of Tyre and Sidon (Matt. 15 : 21), a

Syro-phœnician woman came to him, and earnestly besought him, in behalf of her daughter, who was grievously afflicted with a demon. Her faith in him was severely tested by his silence (Matt. 15 : 23), refusal (24), and seeming reproach that it was not meet to cast the children's bread to dogs (26). But it stood the test, and her petition was graciously granted, because of the greatness of her faith (28).

T

Ta'anach—*a sandy place*—an ancient royal city of the Canaanites, on the southwestern border of the plain of Esdraelon, 4 miles south of Megiddo. Its king was conquered by Joshua (12 : 21). It was assigned to the Levites of the family of Kohath (17 : 11–18 ; 21 : 25). It is mentioned in the song of Deborah (Judg. 5 : 19). It is identified with the small modern village of *Ta'annûk*.

Ta'anath-shi'loh—*approach to Shiloh*—a place on the border of Ephraim (Josh. 16 : 6), probably the modern *T'ana*, a ruin 7 miles south-east of Shechem, on the ridge east of the Mukhnah plain.

Tab'baoth—*impressions ; rings*—"the children of," returned from the Captivity (Ezra 2 : 43).

Tab'bath—*famous*—a town in the tribe of Ephraim (Judg. 7 : 22), to the south of Bethshean, near the Jordan.

Ta'beal—*goodness of God*—the father of one whom the kings of Syria and Samaria in vain attempted to place on the throne of Ahaz (Isa. 7 : 6–14).

Ta'beel, a Persian governor of Samaria, who joined others in the attempt to prevent the rebuilding of Jerusalem (Ezra 4 : 7).

Tab'erah—*burning*—a place in the wilderness of Paran, where the "fire of the Lord" consumed the murmuring Israelites (Num. 11 : 3 ; Deut. 9 : 22). It was also called Kibroth-hattaavah (*q.v.*).

Ta'bering, playing on a small drum or tabret. In Nahum 2 : 7, where alone it occurs, it means beating on the breast, as players beat on the tabret.

Tab'ernacle. (1.) A house or dwelling-place (Job 5 : 24 ; 18 : 6, etc.).

(2.) A portable shrine (comp. Acts 19 : 24) containing the image of Moloch (Amos 5 : 26 ; marg. and R.V., "Siccuth").

(3.) The human body (2 Cor. 5 : 1, 4) ; a tent, as opposed to a permanent dwelling.

(4.) The sacred tent (Heb. *mishkân*, "the dwelling-place"); the movable tent-temple which Moses erected for the service of God, according to the "pattern" which God himself showed to him on the mount (Ex. 25 : 9 ; Heb. 8 : 5). It is called "the tabernacle of the congregation," rather "of meeting"—*i.e.*, where God promised to meet with Israel (Ex. 29 : 42); the "tabernacle of the testimony" (Ex. 38 : 21 ; Num. 1 : 50), which does not, however, designate the whole structure, but only the enclosure which contained the "ark of the testimony" (Ex. 25 : 16, 22 ; Num. 9 : 15); the "tabernacle of witness" (Num. 17 : 8); the "house of the Lord" (Deut. 23 : 18); the "temple of the Lord" (Josh. 6 : 24); a "sanctuary" (Ex. 25 : 8).

A particular account of the materials which the people provided for the erection and of the building itself is recorded in Ex. 25-40. The execution of the plan mysteriously given to Moses was intrusted to Bezaleel and Aholiab, who were specially endowed with wisdom and artistic skill—probably gained in Egypt—for this purpose (Ex. 35 : 30–35). The people provided materials for the tabernacle so abundantly that Moses was under the necessity of restraining them (36 : 6). These stores, from which they so liberally contributed for this purpose, must have consisted in a great part of the gifts which the Egyptians so readily bestowed on them on the eve of the Exodus (12 : 35, 36).

The tabernacle was a rectangular enclosure, in length about 45 feet (*i.e.*, reckoning a cubit at 18 inches) and in breadth and height about 15. Its two sides and its western end were made of boards of acacia wood, placed on end, resting in sockets of brass, the eastern end being left open (Ex. 26:22). This framework was covered with four coverings—the first of linen, in which figures of the symbolic cherubim were wrought with needlework in blue and purple and scarlet threads, and probably also with threads of gold (Ex. 26:1-6;

THE TABERNACLE IN THE WILDERNESS.

A. The Tabernacle Covered.
B. Brazen Laver.
C. Altar of Burnt-Offering.
D. Court of the Tabernacle.

30:8-13). Above this was a second covering of twelve curtains of black goats'-hair cloth, reaching down on the outside almost to the ground (Ex. 26:7-11). The third covering was of rams' skins dyed red, and the fourth was of badgers' skins (Heb. *tahash*—i.e., the dugong, a species of seal), Ex. 25:5; 26:14; 35:7, 23; 36:19; 39:34.

Internally it was divided by a veil into two chambers, the exterior of which was called the holy place, also "the sanctuary" (Heb. 9:2) and the "first tabernacle" (6); and the interior, the holy of holies, "the holy place," "the holiest," the "second tabernacle" (Ex. 28:29; Heb. 9:3, 7). The veil separating these two chambers was a double curtain of the finest workmanship, which was never passed except by the high priest once a year, on the great Day of Atonement. The holy place was separated from the outer court which enclosed the tabernacle by a curtain, which hung over the six pillars which stood at the east end of the tabernacle, and by which it was entered.

The order as well as the typical character of the services of the tabernacle are recorded in Heb. 9; 10:19-22.

The holy of holies, a cube of 10 cubits, contained the "ark of the testimony"—i.e., the oblong chest containing the two tables of stone, the pot of manna, and Aaron's rod that budded.

The holy place was the western and larger chamber of the tabernacle. Here were placed the table for the shewbread, the golden candlestick, and the golden altar of incense.

Round about the tabernacle was a *court*, enclosed by curtains hung upon sixty pillars (Ex. 27:9-18). This court was 150 feet long and 75 feet broad. Within it were placed the altar of burnt offering, which measured 7½ feet in length and breadth and 4½ feet high, with horns at the four corners, and the laver of brass (Ex. 30:18), which stood between the altar and the tabernacle.

The whole tabernacle was completed in seven months. On the first day of the first month of the second year after the Exodus, it was formally set up, and the cloud of the divine presence descended on it (Ex. 30:23-38; 40:9-11).

It cost 29 talents 730 shekels of gold, 100 talents 1,775 shekels of silver, 70 talents 2,400 shekels of brass (Ex. 38:24-31).

The tabernacle was so constructed that it could easily be taken down and conveyed from place to place during the wanderings in the wilderness. The first encampment of the Israelites after crossing the Jordan was at Gilgal, and there the tabernacle remained for seven years (Josh. 4:19). It was afterwards removed to Shiloh (Josh. 18:1), where it remained during the time of the Judges, till the days of Eli, when the ark, having been carried out into the camp when the Israelites were at war with the Philistines, was taken by the enemy (1 Sam. 4), and was never afterwards restored to its

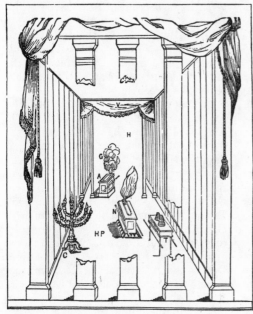

THE TABERNACLE UNVEILED.

H. The Holy of Holies, containing the Ark (A) of the Covenant with the Shechinah (G).

V. The Veil separating the Holy of Holies from the Holy Place.

H P. The Holy Place, containing the Golden Candlestick (C); the Table of Shewbread (T); and the Altar of Incense (N).

place in the tabernacle. The old tabernacle erected by Moses in the wilderness was transferred to Nob (1 Sam. 21:1), and after the destruction of that city by Saul (22:9; 1 Chr. 16:39, 40), to Gibeon. It is mentioned for the last time in 1 Chr. 21:29. A new tabernacle was erected by David at Jerusalem (2 Sam. 6:17; 1 Chr. 16:1), and the ark was brought up from Perez-uzzah and deposited in it (1 Chr. 9:19; 2 Chr. 1:4).

The word thus rendered ('ôhel) in Ex. 33:7 denotes simply a tent, probably Moses' own tent, for the tabernacle was not yet erected.

Tab'ernacles, Feast of, the third of the great annual festivals of the Jews (Lev. 23:33–43). It is also called the "feast of ingathering" (Ex. 23:16; Deut. 16:13). It was celebrated immediately after the harvest, in the month Tisri, and the celebration lasted for eight days (Lev. 33:34). During that period the people left their homes and lived in booths formed of the branches of trees. The sacrifices offered at this time are mentioned in Num. 29:13–38. It was at the time of this feast that Solomon's temple was dedicated (1 Kings 8:2). Mention is made of it after the return from the Captivity. This feast was designed (1) to be a memorial of the wilderness wanderings, when the people dwelt in booths (Lev. 23:43), and (2) to be a harvest thanksgiving (Neh. 8:9–18). The Jews, at a later time, introduced two appendages to the original festival—*viz.*, (1) that of drawing water from the Pool of Siloam, and pouring it upon the altar (John 7:2, 37), as a memorial of the water from the rock in Horeb; and (2) of lighting the lamps at night, a memorial of the pillar of fire by night during their wanderings.

"The feast of Tabernacles, the harvest festival of the Jewish Church, was the most popular and important festival after the Captivity. At Jerusalem it was a gala day. It was to the autumn pilgrims, who arrived on the 14th (of the month Tisri, the feast beginning on the 15th) day, like entrance into a silvan city. Roofs and court-yards, streets and squares, roads and gardens, were green with boughs of citron and myrtle, palm and willow. The booths recalled the pilgrimage through the wilderness. The ingathering of fruits prophesied of the spiritual harvest."—Valling's *Jesus Christ*, p. 133.

Tab'itha (in Greek called **Dorcas**)—*gazelle*—a disciple at Joppa. She was distinguished for her alms-deeds and good works. Peter, who was sent for from Lydda on the occasion of her death, prayed over the dead body, and said, "Tabitha, arise." And she opened her eyes and sat up; and Peter "gave her his hand, and raised her up; and calling the saints and widows, he presented her alive" (Acts 9 : 36–43).

Ta′bles (Mark 7 : 4) means banqueting-couches or benches, on which the Jews reclined when at meals. This custom, along with the use of raised tables like ours, was introduced among the Jews after the Captivity. Before this they had, properly speaking, no table. That which served the purpose was a skin or piece of leather spread out on the carpeted floor. Sometimes a stool was placed in the middle of this skin. (See ABRAHAM'S BOSOM; BANQUET; MEALS.)

Ta′bor—*a height.* (1.) Now *Jebel et-Tur*, a cone-like prominent mountain, 11 miles west of the Sea of Galilee. It is about 1,843 feet high. The view from the summit of it is said to be singularly extensive and grand. This is alluded to in Ps. 89 : 12; Jer. 46 : 18. It was here that Barak encamped before the battle with Sisera (*q.v.*)—Judg. 4 : 6–14. There is an old tradition, which, however, is unfounded, that it was the scene of the transfiguration of our Lord. (See HERMON.) "The prominence and isolation of Tabor, standing, as it does, on the border-land between the northern and southern tribes, between the mountains and the central plain, made it a place of note in all ages, and evidently led the psalmist to associate it with Hermon—the one emblematic of the south, the other of the north." There are some who still hold that this was the scene of the transfiguration (*q.v.*).

(2.) A town of Zebulun (1 Chr. 6 : 77).

(3.) The "plain of Tabor" (1 Sam. 10 : 3) should be, as in the Revised Version, "the oak of Tabor." This was probably the Allon-bachuth of Gen. 35 : 8.

Tab′let, probably a string of beads worn round the neck (Ex. 35 : 22; Num. 31 : 50). In Isa. 3 : 20 the Hebrew word means a perfume-box, as it is rendered in the Revised Version.

Tab′ret (Heb. *tôph*), a timbrel (*q.v.*) or tambourine, generally played by women

(Gen. 31 : 27; 1 Sam. 10 : 5; 18 : 6). In Job 17 : 6 the word (Heb. *tôpheth*) "tabret" should be, as in the Revised Version, "an abhorring" (marg., "one in whose face they spit;" lit., "a spitting in the face").

Tab′rimon—*good is Rimmon*—the father of Benhadad, king of Syria (1 Kings 15 : 18).

Tach′es, hooks or clasps by which the tabernacle curtains were connected (Ex. 26 : 6, 11, 33; 35 : 11).

Tach′monite = Hach′monite, a name given to Jashobeam (2 Sam. 23 : 8; comp. 1 Chr. 11 : 11).

Tack′ling (Isa. 33 : 23), the ropes attached to the mast of a ship. In Acts 27 : 19 this word means generally the furniture of the ship or the "gear" (27 : 17), all that could be removed from the ship.

Tad′mor—*palm*—a city built by Solomon "in the wilderness" (2 Chr. 8 : 4). In 1 Kings 9 : 18, where the word occurs in the Authorized Version, the Hebrew text and the Revised Version read "Tamar," which is properly a city on the southern border of Palestine and toward the wilderness (comp. Ezek. 47 : 19; 48 : 28). In 2 Chr. 8 : 14 Tadmor is mentioned in connection with Hamath-zobah. It is called Palmyra by the Greeks and Romans. It stood in the great Syrian wilderness—176 miles from Damascus and 130 from the Mediterranean—and was the centre of a vast commercial traffic with Western Asia. It was also an important military station. (See SOLOMON.) "Remains of ancient temples and palaces, surrounded by splendid colonnades of white marble, many of which are yet standing, and thousands of prostrate pillars, scattered over a large extent of space, attest the ancient magnificence of this city of palms, surpassing that of the renowned cities of Greece and Rome."

Tahap′anes = Tah′panhes = Tehaph′-nehes (called "Daphne" by the Greeks, now *Tell Defenneh*), an ancient Egyptian city, on the Tanitic branch of the Nile, about 16 miles from Pelusium. The Jews from Jerusalem fled to this place after the death of Gedaliah (*q.v.*), and settled there for a time (Jer. 2 : 16; 43 : 7; 44 : 1; 46 : 14). A platform of brick-work, which there is every

RUINS OF TADMOR.

reason to believe was the pavement at the entry of Pharaoh's palace, has been discovered at this place. "Here," says the discoverer, Mr. Petrie, "the ceremony described by Jeremiah [43 : 8-10; "brick-kiln"—*i.e.*, pavement of brick] took place before the chiefs of the fugitives assembled on the platform, and here Nebuchadnezzar spread his royal pavilion."

Tah'penes, the wife of Pharaoh, who gave her sister in marriage to Hadad the Edomite (1 Kings 11 : 19, 20).

Tah'tim-hod'shi—*the land of the newly inhabited*—(2 Sam. 24 : 6). It is conjectured that, instead of this word, the reading should be, "the Hittites of Kadesh," the Hittite capital, on the Orontes. It was apparently some region east of the Jordan and north of Gilead.

Tale. (1.) Heb. *tokhĕn*, "a task," as weighed and measured out = tally—*i.e.*, the number told off; the full number (Ex. 5 :

18; see 1 Sam. 18 : 27; 1 Chr. 9 : 28). In Ezek. 45 : 11 rendered "measure."

(2.) Heb. *hĕgĕh*, "a thought;" "meditation" (Ps. 90 : 9); meaning properly "as a whisper of sadness," which is soon over, or "as a thought." The LXX. and Vulgate render it "spider;" the Authorized Version and Revised Version, "as a tale" that is told. In Job 37 : 2 this word is rendered "sound;" Revised Version margin, "muttering;" and in Ezek. 2 : 10, "mourning."

Talent of silver contained 3,000 shekels (Ex. 38 : 25, 26), and was equal to 94⅞ lbs. avoirdupois. The Greek talent, however, as in the LXX., was only 82¼ lbs. It was in the form of a circular mass, as the Hebrew name *kikkâr* denotes. A talent of gold was double the weight of a talent of silver (2 Sam. 12 : 30). Parable of the talents (Matt. 18 : 24; 25 : 15).

Tali'tha cu'mi (Mark 5 : 41), a Syriac or Aramaic expression, meaning, "Little maid, arise." Peter, who was present when the miracle was wrought, recalled the actual words used by our Lord, and told them to Mark.

Tal'mai—*abounding in furrows.* (1.) One of the Anakim of Hebron, who were slain by the men of Judah under Caleb (Num. 13:22; Josh. 15:14; Judg. 1:10).

(2.) A king of Geshur, to whom Absalom fled after he had put Amnon to death (2 Sam. 3:3; 13:37). His daughter, Ma-achah, was one of David's wives, and the mother of Absalom (1 Chr. 3:2).

Tal'mon—*oppressed.* (1.) A Levite porter (1 Chr. 9:17; Neh. 11:19).

(2.) One whose descendants returned with Zerubbabel to Jerusalem (Ezra 2:41; Neh. 7:45); probably the same as (1).

Ta'mar—*palm.* (1.) A place mentioned by Ezekiel (47:19; 48:28), on the south-eastern border of Palestine. Some suppose this was "Tadmor" (*q.v.*).

(2.) The daughter-in-law of Judah, to whose eldest son, Er, she was married (Gen. 38:7). After her husband's death, she was married to Onan, his brother (19), and on his death, Judah promised to her that his third son, Shelah, would become her husband. This promise was not fulfilled, and hence Tamar's revenge and Judah's great guilt (38:12–30).

(3.) A daughter of David (2 Sam. 13:1–32; 1 Chr. 3:9), whom Amnon shamefully outraged and afterwards "hated exceedingly," thereby illustrating the law of human nature noticed even by the heathen, "Proprium humani ingenii est odisse quem læseris"—*i.c.*, "It is the property of human nature to hate one whom you have injured."

(4.) A daughter of Absalom (2 Sam. 14:27).

Tam'arisk. Heb. *'eshel* (Gen. 21:33; 1 Sam. 22:6; 31:13, in the R.V.; but in A.V., "grove," "tree"); Arab. *asal.* Seven species of this tree are found in Palestine. It is a "very graceful tree, with long feathery branches and tufts closely clad with the minutest of leaves, and surmounted in spring with spikes of beautiful pink blossoms, which seem to envelop the whole tree in one gauzy sheet of colour" (Tristram's *Nat. Hist.*).

Tam'muz, a corruption of Dumuzi, the Accadian sun-god (the Adonis of the Greeks), the husband of the goddess Ishtar. In the Chaldean calendar there was a month set apart in honour of this god—the month of June to July, the beginning of the summer solstice. At this festival, which lasted six days, the worshippers, with loud lamentations, bewailed the funeral of the god—they sat "weeping for Tammuz" (Ezek. 8:14).

The name, also borrowed from Chaldea, of one of the months of the Hebrew calendar.

Tanhu'meth—*consolation*—a Netophathite; one of the captains who supported Gedaliah (2 Kings 25:23; Jer. 40:8).

Tan'is (Ezek. 30:14, marg.). See ZOAN.

Tap'puah—*apple-region.* (1.) A town in the valley or lowland of Judah; formerly a royal city of the Canaanites (Josh. 12:17; 15:34). It is now called *Tuffûh*, about 12 miles west of Jerusalem.

(2.) A town on the border of Ephraim (Josh. 16:8). The "land" of Tappuah fell to Manasseh, but the "city" to Ephraim (17:8).

(3.) **En-tappuah**—*the well of the apple* —probably one of the springs near *Yassuf* (Josh. 17:7).

Ta'rah—*stopping; station*—an encampment of the Hebrews in the wilderness (Num. 33:27, 28).

Tares, the bearded darnel, mentioned only in Matt. 13:25–30. It is the *Lolium temulentum,* a species of rye-grass, the seeds of which are a strong soporific poison. It bears the closest resemblance to wheat till the ear appears, and only then the difference is discovered. It grows plentifully in Syria and Palestine.

Tar'get (1 Sam. 17:7, A.V., after the LXX. and Vulg.), a kind of small shield. The margin has "gorget," a piece of armour for the throat. The Revised Version more correctly renders the Hebrew word (*kidon*) by "javelin." The same Hebrew word is used in Josh. 8:18 (A.V., "spear;" R.V., "javelin"); Job 39:23 (A.V., "shield;" R.V., "javelin"); 41:29 (A.V., "spear;" R.V., "javelin").

Tar'shish, a Sanscrit or Aryan word, meaning "the sea coast." (1.) One of the "sons" of Javan (Gen. 10:4; 1 Chr. 1:7).

(2.) The name of a place which first comes into notice in the days of Solomon. The question as to the locality of Tarshish has given rise to not a little discussion. Some think there was a Tarshish in the East, on the Indian coast, seeing that "ships of Tarshish" sailed from Ezion-geber, on the Red Sea (1 Kings 9:26; 22:48; 2 Chr. 9:21). Some, again, argue that Carthage was the place so named. There can be little doubt, however, that this is the name of a Phœnician port in Spain, between the two mouths of the Guadalquivir (the name given to the river by the Arabs, and meaning "the great wâdy" or water-course). It was founded by a Carthaginian colony, and was the farthest western harbour of Tyrian sailors. It was to this port Jonah's ship was about to sail from Joppa. It has well been styled "the Peru of Tyrian adventure;" it abounded in gold and silver mines.

It appears that this name also is used without reference to any locality. "Ships of Tarshish" is an expression sometimes denoting simply ships intended for a long voyage (Isa. 23:1, 14), ships of a large size (sea-going ships), whatever might be the port to which they sailed. Solomon's ships were so styled (1 Kings 10:22; 22:49).

Tar'sus, the chief city of Cilicia. It was distinguished for its wealth and for its schools of learning, in which it rivalled, nay, excelled even Athens and Alexandria, and hence was spoken of as "no mean city." It was the native place of the Apostle Paul (Acts 21:39). It stood on the banks of the river Cydnus, about 12 miles north of the Mediterranean. It is said to have been founded by Sardanapalus, king of Assyria. It is now a filthy, ruinous Turkish town, called *Tersous.* (See PAUL.)

Tar'tak—*prince of darkness*—one of the gods of the Arvites, who colonized part of Samaria after the deportation of Israel by Shalmaneser (2 Kings 17:21).

Tar'tan, an Assyrian word, meaning "the commander-in-chief." (1.) One of Sennacherib's messengers to Hezekiah (2 Kings 18:17).

(2.) One of Sargon's generals (Isa. 20:1).

Tat'nai—*gift*—a Persian governor (Heb. *peḥâh*—*i.e.,* "satrap;" modern "pasha") "on this side the river"—*i.e.,* of the whole tract on the west of the Euphrates. This Hebrew title *peḥâh* is given to governors of provinces generally. It is given to Nehemiah (5:14) and to Zerubbabel (Hag. 1:1). It is sometimes translated "captain" (1 Kings 20:24; Dan. 3:2, 3), sometimes also "deputy" (Esther 8:9; 9:3). With others, Tatnai opposed the rebuilding of the temple (Ezra 5:6); but at the command of Darius, he assisted the Jews (6:1-13).

Tav'erns, The three, a place on the great "Appian Way," about 11 miles from Rome, designed for the reception of travellers, as the name indicates. Here Paul, on his way to Rome, was met by a band of Roman Christians (Acts 28:15). The "*Tres Tabernæ* was the first *mansio* or *mutatio*—that i, halting-place for relays—from Rome, or the last on the way to the city. At this point three roads run into the Via Appia—that from Tusculum, that from Alba Longa, and that from Antium; so necessarily here would be a halting-place, which took its name from the three shops there—the general store, the blacksmith's, and the refreshment-house.....Tres Tabernæ is translated as Three Taverns, but it more correctly means three shops" (Forbes's *Footsteps of St. Paul,* p. 22).

Taxes, first mentioned in the command (Ex. 30:11-16) that every Jew from twenty years and upward should pay an annual tax of "half a shekel for an offering to the Lord." This enactment was faithfully observed for many generations (2 Chr. 24:6; Matt. 17:24).

Afterwards, when the people had kings to reign over them, they began, as Samuel had warned them (1 Sam. 8:10-18), to pay taxes for civil purposes (1 Kings 4:7; 9:13; 12:4). Such taxes, in increased amount, were afterwards paid to the foreign princes that ruled over them.

In the New Testament the payment of taxes, imposed by lawful rulers, is enjoined as a duty (Rom. 13:1-7; 1 Pet. 2:13, 14). Mention is made of the tax (*telos*) on merchandise and travellers (Matt. 17:25); the annual tax (*phoros*) on property (Luke 20 : 22; 23 : 2); the poll-tax (*kēnsos*, "tribute," Matt. 17 : 25; 22 : 17; Mark 12 : 14); and the temple-tax ("tribute money" = two drachmas = half shekel, Matt. 17 : 24-27; comp. Ex. 30 : 13). (See TRIBUTE.)

Tax′ing (Luke 2 : 2; R.V., "enrolment"), "when Cyrenius was governor of Syria," is simply a census of the people, or an enrolment of them with a view to their taxation. The decree for the enrolment was the occasion of Joseph and Mary's going up to Bethlehem. It has been argued by some that Cyrenius (*q.v.*) was governor of Cilicia and Syria both at the time of our Lord's birth and some years afterwards. This decree for the taxing referred to the whole Roman world, and not to Judea alone. (See CENSUS.)

Te′beth (Esther 2 : 16), a word probably of Persian origin, denoting the cold time of the year; used by the later Jews as denoting the tenth month of the year. Assyrian *tebituv*, "rain."

Teil tree (an old name for the lime-tree, the *tilia*), Isa. 6 : 13, the terebinth, or turpentine-tree, the *Pistacia terebinthus* of botanists. The Hebrew word here used (*êlâh*) is rendered oak (*q.v.*) in Gen. 35 : 4; Judg. 6 : 11, 19; Isa. 1 : 29, etc. In Isa. 61 : 3 it is rendered in the plural "trees;" Hos. 4 : 13, "elm" (R.V., "terebinth"). In 1 Sam. 17 : 2, 19 it is taken as a proper name, "Elah" (R.V. marg., "terebinth").

"The terebinth of Mamre, or its lineal successor, remained from the days of Abraham till the fourth century of the Christian era, and on its site Constantine erected a Christian church, the ruins of which still remain."

This tree "is seldom seen in clumps or groves, never in forests, but stands isolated and weird-like in some bare ravine or on a hill-side where nothing else towers above the low brushwood" (Tristram).

Te′kel—*weighed* (Dan. 5 : 27).

Teko′a, Teko′ah—*pitching of tents; fastening down*—a town of Judah, about 12 miles south of Jerusalem, and visible from the city. From this place Joab procured a "wise woman," who pretended to be in great affliction, and skilfully made

her case known to David. Her address to the king was in the form of an apologue, similar to that of Nathan (2 Sam. 12 : 1-6). The object of Joab was, by the intervention of this woman, to induce David to bring back Absalom to Jerusalem (2 Sam. 14 : 2, 4, 9).

This was also the birth-place of the prophet Amos (1 : 1).

It is now the village of *Teku′a*, on the top of a hill among ruins, 5 miles south of Bethlehem, and close to Beth-haccerem ("Herod's mountain").

Tel-a′bib—*hill of corn*—a place on the river Chebar, the residence of Ezekiel (Ezek. 3 : 15). The site is unknown.

Tela′im—*young lambs*—a place at which Saul gathered his army to fight against Amalek (1 Sam. 15 : 4); probably the same as Telem (2).

Telas′sar or **Thelasar** (Isa. 37 : 12; 2 Kings 19 : 12), a province in the south-east of Assyria, probably in Babylonia. Some have identified it with *Tel Afer*, a place in Mesopotamia, some 30 miles from Sinjar.

Te′lem—*oppression*. (1.) A porter of the temple in the time of Ezra (10 : 24).

(2.) A town in the southern border of Judah (Josh. 15 : 24); probably the same as Telaim.

Tel-hare′sha—*hill of the wood*—a place in Babylon from which some captive Jews returned to Jerusalem (Ezra 2 : 59; Neh. 7 : 61).

Tel-me′lah—*hill of salt*—a place in Babylon from which the Jews returned (*id.*).

Te′ma—*south; desert*—one of the sons of Ishmael, and father of a tribe so called (Gen. 25 : 15; 1 Chr. 1 : 30; Job 6 : 19; Isa. 21 : 14; Jer. 25 : 23) which settled at a place to which he gave his name, some 250 miles south-east of Edom, on the route between Damascus and Mecca, in the northern part of the Arabian peninsula, toward the Syrian desert; the modern *Teyma*'.

Te′man—*id.* (1.) A grandson of Esau, one of the "dukes of Edom" (Gen. 36 : 11, 15, 42).

(2.) A place in Southern Idumea, the land of "the sons of the east," frequently mentioned in the Old Testament. It was noted for the wisdom of its inhabitants (Amos 1:12; Obad. 8; Jer. 49:7; Ezek. 25:13). It was divided from the hills of Paran by the low plain of Arabah (Hab. 3:3).

Te′manite—*a man of Teman*—the designation of Eliphaz, one of Job's three friends (Job 2:11; 22:1).

Teme′ni, one of the sons of Ashur, the father of Tekoa (1 Chr. 4:6).

Tem′ple, first used of the tabernacle, which is called "the temple of the Lord" (1 Sam. 1:9). In the New Testament the word is used figuratively of Christ's human body (John 2:19, 21). Believers are called "the temple of God" (1 Cor. 3:16, 17). The Church is designated "an holy temple in the Lord" (Eph. 2:21). Heaven is also called a temple (Rev. 7:5). We read also of the heathen "temple of the great goddess Diana" (Acts 19:27).

This word is generally used in Scripture of the sacred house erected on the summit of Mount Moriah for the worship of God. It is called "the temple" (1 Kings 6:17); "the temple [R.V., 'house'] of the Lord" (2 Kings 11:10); "thy holy temple" (Ps. 70:1); "the house of the Lord" (2 Chr. 23:5, 12); "the house of the God of Jacob" (Isa. 2:3); "the house of my glory" (60:7); an "house of prayer" (56:7; Matt. 21:13); "an house of sacrifice" (2 Chr. 7:12); "the house of their sanctuary" (2 Chr. 36:17); "the mountain of the Lord's house" (Isa. 2:2); "our holy and our beautiful house" (64:11); "the holy mount" (27:13); "the palace for the Lord God" (1 Chr. 29:1); "the tabernacle of witness" (2 Chr. 24:6); "Zion" (Ps. 74:2; 84:7). Christ calls it "my Father's house" (John 2:16).

Tem′ple, Solomon's. Before his death David had "with much labour" provided materials in great abundance for the building of the temple on the summit of Mount Moriah (1 Chr. 22:14; 29:4; 2 Chr. 3:1), on the east of the city, on the spot where Abraham had offered up Isaac (Gen. 22:1–12). In the beginning of his reign Solomon set about giving effect to the desire that had been so earnestly cherished by his father, and prepared additional materials for the building. From subterranean quarries at Jerusalem he obtained huge blocks of stone for the foundations and walls of the temple. These stones were prepared for their places in the building under the eye of Tyrian master-builders. He also entered into a compact with Hiram II., king of Tyre, for the supply of whatever else was needed for the work, particularly timber from the forests of Lebanon, which was brought in great rafts by the sea to Joppa, whence it was dragged to Jerusalem (1 Kings 5). As the hill on which the temple was to be built did not afford sufficient level space, a huge wall of solid masonry of great height, in some places more than 200 feet high, was raised across the south of the hill, and a similar wall on the eastern side, and in the spaces between were erected many arches and pillars, thus raising up the general surface to the required level. Solomon also provided for a sufficient water supply for the temple by hewing in the rocky hill vast cisterns, into which water was conveyed by channels from the "pools" near Bethlehem. One of these cisterns, the "great sea," was capable of containing three millions of gallons. The overflow was led off by a conduit to the Kidron.

In all these preparatory undertakings a space of about three years was occupied; and now the process of the erection of the great building began, under the direction of skilled Phœnician builders and workmen, in the fourth year of Solomon's reign, 480 years after the Exodus (1 Kings 6; 2 Chr. 3). Many thousands of labourers and skilled artisans were employed in the work. Stones prepared in the quarries underneath the city (1 Kings 5:17, 18) of huge dimension (see QUARRIES) were gradually placed on the massive walls, and closely fitted together without any mortar between, till the whole structure was completed. No sound of hammer or axe or any tool of iron was heard as the structure arose (6:7). "Like some tall palm the noiseless fabric sprang." The building was 60 cubits long, 20 cubits wide, and 30 cubits high. The engineers of the Palestine Exploration Fund, in their explorations around the temple area, discovered what is believed to have been the "chief corner stone" of the temple, "the most interesting stone in the world." It lies at the bottom of the south-eastern angle, and is 3 feet 8 inches high by 14 feet long. It rests on the solid rock at a depth of 79 feet 3 inches below the present surface. (See PINNACLE.) In examining the walls the engineers were "struck with admiration at the vastness of the blocks and the general excellence of the workmanship."

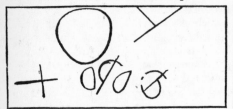

Stone with Phœnician marks found at Jerusalem.

At length, in the autumn of the eleventh year of his reign, seven and a half years after it had been begun, the temple was completed in all its architectural magnificence and beauty. For thirteen years there it stood, on the summit of Moriah, silent and unused. The reasons for this strange delay in its consecration are unknown. At the close of these thirteen years preparations for the dedication of the temple were made on a scale of the greatest magnificence. The ark was solemnly brought from the tent in which David had deposited it to the place prepared for it in the temple, and the glory-cloud, the symbol of the divine presence, filled the house. Then Solomon ascended a platform which had been erected for him, in the sight of all the people, and lifting up his hands to heaven poured out his heart to God in prayer (1 Kings 8; 2 Chr. 6, 7). The feast of dedication, which lasted seven days, followed by the feast of tabernacles, marked a new era in the history of Israel. On the eighth day of the feast of tabernacles, Solomon dismissed the vast assemblage of the people, who returned to their homes filled with joy and gladness. "Had Solomon done no other service beyond the building of the temple, he would still have influenced the religious life of his people down to the latest days. It was to them a perpetual reminder and visible symbol of God's presence and protection, a strong bulwark of all the sacred traditions of the law, a witness to duty, an impulse to historic study, an inspiration of sacred song."

The temple consisted of—(1.) The *oracle* or most holy place (1 Kings 6 : 19; 8 : 6), called also the "inner house" (6 : 27), and the "holiest of all" (Heb. 9 : 3). It was 20 cubits in length, breadth, and height. It was floored and wainscotted with cedar (1 Kings 6 : 16), and its walls and floor were overlaid with gold (6 : 20, 21, 30). There was a two-leaved door between it and the holy place overlaid with gold (2 Chr. 4 : 22); also a veil of blue purple and crimson and fine linen (2 Chr. 3 : 14; comp. Ex. 26 : 33). It had no windows (1 Kings 8 : 12). It was indeed the dwelling-place of God. (2.) The *holy place* (*q.v.*)—1 Kings 8 : 8-10—called also the "greater house" (2 Chr. 3 : 5) and the "temple" (1 Kings 6 : 17). (3.) The *porch* or entrance before the temple on the east (1 Kings 6 : 3; 2 Chr. 3 : 4; 29 : 7). In the porch stood the two pillars Jachin and Boaz (1 Kings 7 : 21; 2 Kings 11 : 14; 23 : 3). (4.) The *chambers*, which were built about the temple on the southern, western, and northern sides (1 Kings 6 : 5-10). These formed a part of the building.

Round about the building were—(1.) *The court of the priests* (2 Chr. 4 : 9), called the "inner court" (1 Kings 6 : 36). It contained the altar of burnt-offering (2 Chr. 15 : 8), the brazen sea (4 : 2-5, 10), and ten lavers (1 Kings 7 : 38, 39). (2.) *The great court*, which surrounded the whole temple (2 Chr. 4 : 9). Here the people assembled to worship God (Jer. 19 : 14; 26 : 2).

This temple erected by Solomon was many times pillaged during the course of its history — (1) 1 Kings 14 : 25, 26; (2) 2 Kings 14 : 14; (3) 2 Kings 16 : 8, 17, 18; (4) 2 Kings 18 : 15, 16. At last it was pillaged and destroyed by Nebuchadnezzar (2 Kings 24 : 13; 2 Chr. 36 : 7). He burned the temple, and carried all its treasures with him to Babylon (2 Kings 25 : 9-17; 2 Chr. 36 : 19; Isa. 64 : 11). These sacred vessels were at length, at the close of the

Captivity, restored to the Jews by Cyrus (Ezra 1 : 7–11).

Temple, the Second. After the return from captivity, under Zerubbabel (*q.v.*) and the high priest Jeshua, arrangements were almost immediately made to reorganize the long-desolated kingdom. The body of pilgrims, forming a band of 42,360, including children, having completed the long and dreary journey of some four months, from the banks of the Euphrates to Jerusalem, were animated in all their proceedings by a strong religious impulse, and therefore one of their first cares was to restore their ancient worship by rebuilding the temple. On the invitation of Zerubbabel, the governor, who showed them a remarkable example of liberality by contributing personally 1,000 golden darics (probably about £6,000), besides other gifts, the people with great enthusiasm poured their gifts into the sacred treasury (Ezra 2). First they erected and dedicated the altar of Jehovah on the exact spot where it had formerly stood, and they then cleared away the charred heaps of *débris* which occupied the site of the old temple; and in the second month of the second year (B.C. 535), amid great public excitement and rejoicing (Ps. 106 ; 107 ; 118), the foundations of the second temple were laid. A wide interest was felt in this great movement, although it was regarded with mingled feelings by the spectators (Hag. 2 : 3; Zech. 4 : 10). The Samaritans made proposals for a co-operation in the work. Zerubbabel and Jeshua and the elders, however, declined all such co-operation : Judah must build the temple without help. Immediately evil reports were spread regarding the Jews. The Samaritans sought to "frustrate their purpose" (Ezra 4 : 5), and sent messengers to Ecbatana and Susa, with the result that the work was suspended. Seven years after this Cyrus died ingloriously, having killed himself in Syria when on his way back from Egypt to the east, and was succeeded by his son Cambyses (B.C. 529–522), on whose death the "false Smerdis," an impostor, occupied the throne for some seven or eight months, and then Darius

Hystaspes became king (B.C. 522). In the second year of this monarch the work of rebuilding the temple was resumed and carried forward to its completion (Ezra 5 : 6–17 ; 6 : 1–15), under the stimulus of the earnest counsels and admonitions of the prophets Haggai and Zechariah. It was ready for consecration in the spring of B.C. 516, twenty years after the return from captivity.

This second temple had not the ark, the Urim and Thummim, the holy oil, the sacred fire, the tables of stone, the pot of manna, and Aaron's rod. As in the tabernacle, there was in it only one golden lamp for the holy place, one table of shewbread, and the incense altar, with golden censers, and many of the vessels of gold that had belonged to Solomon's temple that had been carried to Babylon but restored by Cyrus (Ezra 1 : 7–11).

This second temple also differed from the first in that, while in the latter there were numerous "trees planted in the courts of the Lord," there were none in the former. The second temple also had for the first time a space, being a part of the outer court, provided for proselytes who were worshippers of Jehovah, although not subject to the laws of Judaism.

The temple, when completed, was consecrated amid great rejoicings on the part of all the people (Ezra 6 : 16), although there were not wanting outward evidences that the Jews were no longer an independent people, but were subject to a foreign power.

Hag. 2 : 9 is rightly rendered in the Revised Version, "The latter glory of this house shall be greater than the former," instead of, "The glory of this latter house," etc., in the Authorized Version. The temple, during the different periods of its existence, is regarded as but one house, the one only house of God (comp. 2 : 3). The glory here predicted is spiritual glory and not material splendour. "Christ himself, present bodily in the temple on Mount Zion during his life on earth, present spiritually in the Church now, present in the holy city, the heavenly Jerusalem, of which he is the temple, calling forth spiritual worship and devotion......is the glory here predicted " (Perowne).

Temple, Herod's. The temple erected by the exiles on their return from Babylon had stood for about five hundred years, when Herod the Great became king of Judea. The building had suffered considerably from natural decay as well as from the assaults of hostile armies, and Herod, desirous of gaining the favour of the Jews, proposed to rebuild it. This offer was accepted, and the work was begun (B.C. 18), and carried out at great labour and expense, and on a scale of surpassing splendour. The main part of the building was completed in ten years, but the erection of the outer courts and the embellishment of the whole were carried on during the entire period of our Lord's life on earth (John 2 : 16, 19-21), and the temple was completed only A.D. 65. But it was not long permitted to exist. Within forty years after our Lord's crucifixion, his prediction of its overthrow was accomplished (Luke 19 : 41-44). The Roman legions took the city of Jerusalem by storm, and notwithstanding the strenuous efforts Titus made to preserve the temple, his soldiers set fire to it in several places, and it was utterly destroyed (A.D. 70), and was never rebuilt.

Several remains of Herod's stately temple have by recent explorations been brought to light. It had two courts—one intended for the Israelites only, and the other, a large outer court, called "the court of the Gentiles," intended for the use of strangers of all nations. These two courts were separated by a low wall, as Josephus states, of some 4½ feet high, with thirteen openings. Along the top of this dividing wall were placed at regular intervals pillars, bearing in Greek an inscription to the effect that no stranger was, on the pain of death, to pass from the court of the Gentiles into that of the Jews. At the entrance to a graveyard at the northwestern angle of the Haram wall, a stone was discovered by M. Ganneau in 1871, built into the wall, bearing the following inscription in Greek capitals : "No stranger is to enter within the partition wall and enclosure around the sanctuary. Whoever

is caught will be responsible to himself for his death, which will ensue."

There can be no doubt that the stone thus discovered was one of those originally placed on the boundary wall which separated the Jews from the Gentiles, of which Josephus speaks.

It is of importance to notice that the word rendered "sanctuary" in the inscription was used in a specific sense of the inner court, the court of the Israelites, and is the word rendered "temple" in John 2 : 15 and Acts 21 : 28, 29. When Paul speaks of the middle wall of partition (Eph. 2 : 14), he probably makes allusion to this dividing wall. Within this partition wall stood the temple proper, consisting of—(1) the court of the women, 8 feet higher than the outer court; (2) 10 feet higher than this court was the court of Israel; (3) the court of the priests, again 3 feet higher; and lastly (4) the temple floor, 8 feet above that; thus in all 29 feet above the level of the outer court.

The summit of Mount Moriah, on which the temple stood, is now occupied by the *Haram esh-Sherif*—*i.e.*, "the sacred enclosure." This enclosure is about 1,500 feet from north to south, with a breadth of about 1,000 feet, covering in all a space of about 35 acres. About the centre of the enclosure is a raised platform, 16 feet above the surrounding space, and paved with large stone slabs, on which stands the Mohammedan mosque called *Kubbet es-Sahkra* —*i.e.*, the "Dome of the Rock," or the Mosque of Omar. This mosque covers the site of Solomon's temple. In the centre of the dome there is a bare projecting rock, the highest part of Moriah, measuring 60 feet by 40, standing 6 feet above the floor of the mosque, called the *sahkra*—*i.e.*, "rock." Over this rock the altar of burnt-offerings stood. It was the threshing-floor of Araunah the Jebusite. The exact position on this "sacred enclosure" which the temple occupied has not been yet definitely ascertained. Some affirm that Herod's temple covered the site of Solomon's temple and palace, and in addition enclosed a square of 300 feet at the southwestern angle. The temple courts thus are

DOME OF THE ROCK (KUBBET ES-SAHKRA).

supposed to have occupied the southern portion of the "enclosure," forming in all a square of more than 900 feet. It is argued by others that Herod's temple occupied a square of 600 feet at the southwest of the "enclosure."

Tempta'tion. (1.) Trial; a being put to the test. Thus God "tempted [Gen. 22: 1; R.V., 'did prove'] Abraham;" and afflictions are said to tempt—*i.e.*, to try—men (James 1:2, 12; comp. Deut. 8:2), putting their faith and patience to the test. (2.) Ordinarily, however, the word means solicitation to that which is evil, and hence Satan is called "the tempter" (Matt. 4: 3). Our Lord was in this way tempted in the wilderness. That temptation was not internal, but by a real, active, subtle being. It was not self-sought. It was submitted to as an act of obedience on his part. "Christ was led, driven. An unseen personal force bore him a certain violence is implied in the words" (Matt. 4:1–11).

The scene of the temptation of our Lord is generally supposed to have been the mountain of Quarantania (*q.v.*), "a high and precipitous wall of rock, 1,200 or 1,500 feet above the plain west of Jordan, near Jericho."

Temptation is common to all (Dan. 12: 10; Zech. 13:9; Ps. 66:10; Luke 22:31, 40; Heb. 11:17; James 1:12; 1 Pet. 1:7; 4:12). We read of the temptation of Joseph (Gen. 39), of David (2 Sam. 24; 1 Chr. 21), of Hezekiah (2 Chr. 32:31), of Daniel (Dan. 6), etc. So long as we are in this world we are exposed to temptations, and need ever to be on our watch against them.

Tent. (1.) Heb. '*ohĕl* (Gen. 9:21, 27). This word is used also of a dwelling or habitation (1 Kings 8:66; Isa. 16:5; Jer. 4:20), and of the temple (Ezek. 41:1). When used of the tabernacle, as in 1 Kings 1:39, it denotes the covering of goat's hair which was placed over the *mishcân*.

(2.) Heb. *mishcân* (Cant. 1:8), used also of a dwelling (Job 18:21; Ps. 87:2), the grave (Isa. 22:16; comp. 14:18), the temple (Ps. 46:4; 84:2; 132:5), and of the tabernacle (Ex. 25:9; 26:1; 40:9; Num. 1:50, 53; 10:11). When distinguished

from '*ohĕl*, it denotes the twelve interior curtains which lay upon the framework of the tabernacle (*q.v.*).

(3.) Heb. *kŭbbâh* (Num. 25:8), a dome-like tent devoted to the impure worship of Baal-peor.

(4.) Heb. *ṣuccâh* (2 Sam. 11:11), a tent or booth made of green boughs or branches (see Gen. 33:17; Lev. 23:34, 42; Ps. 18: 11; Jonah 4:5; Isa. 4:6; Neh. 8:15–17, where the word is variously rendered).

Jubal was "the father of such as dwell in tents" (Gen. 4:20). The patriarchs were "dwellers in tents" (Gen. 9:21, 27; 12:8; 13:12; 26:17); and during their wilderness wanderings all Israel dwelt in tents (Ex. 16:16; Deut. 33:18; Josh. 7: 24). Tents have always occupied a prominent place in Eastern life (1 Sam. 17: 54; 2 Kings 7:7; Ps. 120:5; Cant. 1:5). Paul the apostle's occupation was that of a tent-maker (Acts 18:3); *i.e.*, perhaps a maker of tent cloth.

Tenth deal—*i.e.*, the tenth part of an ephah (as in the R.V.), equal to an omer or six pints. The recovered leper, to complete his purification, was required to bring a trespass, a sin, and a burnt offering, and to present a meal offering, a tenth deal or an omer of flour for each, with oil to make it into bread or cakes (Lev. 14:10, 21; comp. Ex. 16:36; 29:40).

Te'rah—*the wanderer; loiterer*—for some unknown reason emigrated with his family from his native mountains in the north to the plains of Mesopotamia. He had three sons—Haran, Nahor, and Abraham—and one daughter, Sarah. He settled in "Ur of the Chaldees," where his son Haran died, leaving behind him his son Lot. Nahor settled at Haran, a place on the way to Ur. Terah afterwards migrated with Abraham (probably his youngest son) and Lot (his grandson), together with their families, from Ur, intending to go with them to Canaan; but he tarried at Haran, where he spent the remainder of his days, and died at the age of two hundred and five years (Gen. 11:24–32; Josh. 24:2). What a wonderful part the descendants of this Chaldean shepherd have played in the history of the world!

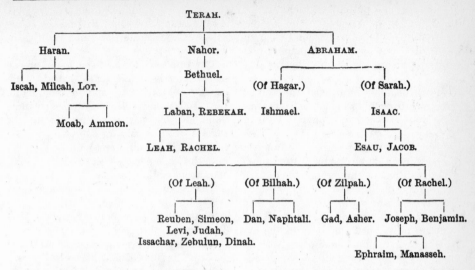

Ter'aphim—*givers of prosperity*—idols in human shape, large or small, analogous to the images of ancestors which were revered by the Romans. In order to deceive the guards sent by Saul to seize David, Michal his wife prepared one of the household teraphim, putting on it the goat's-hair cap worn by sleepers and invalids, and laid it in a bed, covering it with a mantle. She pointed it out to the soldiers, and alleged that David was confined to his bed by a sudden illness (1 Sam. 19: 13–16). Thus she gained time for David's escape. It

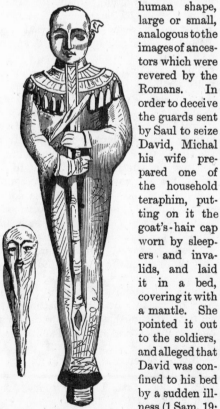

TERAPHIM.

seems strange to read of teraphim, images of ancestors, preserved for superstitious purposes, being in the house of David. Probably they had been stealthily brought by Michal from her father's house. "Perhaps," says Bishop Wordsworth, "Saul, forsaken by God and possessed by the evil spirit, had resorted to teraphim (as he afterwards resorted to witchcraft); and God overruled evil for good, and made his very teraphim (by the hand of his own daughter) to be an instrument for David's escape."—Deane's *David*, p. 32. Josiah attempted to suppress this form of idolatry (2 Kings 23:24). The ephod and teraphim are mentioned together in Hos. 3:4. It has been supposed by some (Cheyne's *Hosea*) that the "ephod" here mentioned, and also in Judg. 8:24–27, was not the part of the sacerdotal dress so called (Ex. 28:6–14), but an image of Jehovah overlaid with gold or silver (comp. Judg. 17, 18; 1 Sam. 21:9; 23:6, 9; 30:7, 8), and is thus associated with the teraphim.

Ter'ebinth (R.V. marg. of Deut. 11:30, etc.), the *Pistacia terebinthus* of botanists; a tree very common in the south and east of Palestine. (See OAK.)

Te'resh—*severe*—a eunuch or chamberlain in the palace of Ahasuerus, who conspired with another to murder him. The plot was detected by Mordecai, and the conspirators were put to death (Esther 2: 21; 6:2).

Ter'tius—*the third*—a Roman Christian whom Paul employed as his amanuensis in writing his epistle to the Romans (16: 22).

Tertul'lus, a modification of "Tertius;" a Roman advocate, whom the Jews employed to state their case against Paul in the presence of Felix (Acts 24:1-9). The charges he adduced against the apostle were—"First, that he created disturbances among the Romans throughout the empire —an offence against the Roman government (*crimen majestatis*). Secondly, that he was a ringleader of the sect of the Nazarenes; disturbed the Jews in the exercise of their religion, guaranteed by the state; introduced new gods—a thing prohibited by the Romans. And thirdly, that he attempted to profane the temple—a crime which the Jews were permitted to punish."

Tes'tament occurs twelve times in the New Testament (Heb. 9:15, etc.) as the rendering of the Gr. *diathēkē*, which is twenty times rendered "covenant" in the Authorized Version, and always so in the Revised Version. The Vulgate translates incorrectly by *testamentum*, whence the names "Old" and "New Testament," by which we now designate the two sections into which the Bible is divided. (See BIBLE.)

Tes'timony. (1.) Witness or evidence (2 Thess. 1:10).

(2.) The Scriptures, as the revelation of God's will (2 Kings 11:12; Ps. 19:7; 119: 88; Isa. 8:16, 20).

(3.) The altar raised by the Gadites and Reubenites (Josh. 22:10).

Tes'timony, Tabernacle of, the tabernacle, the great glory of which was that it contained "the testimony"—*i.e.*, the "two tables" (Ex. 38:21). The ark in which these tables were deposited was called the "ark of the testimony" (40:3), and also simply the "testimony" (27:21; 30:6).

Te'trarch, strictly the ruler over the fourth part of a province; but the word denotes a ruler of a province generally (Matt. 14:1; Luke 3:1, 19; 9:7; Acts

13:1). Herod and Phasael, the sons of Antipater, were the first tetrarchs in Palestine. Herod the tetrarch had the title of king (Matt. 14:9).

Thaddæ'us—*breast*—the name of one of the apostles (Mark 3:18), called "Lebbæus" in Matt. 10:3, and in Luke 6:15, 16, "Judas the brother of James;" while John (14:22), probably referring to the same person, speaks of "Judas, not Iscariot." These different names all designate the same person—*viz.*, Jude or Judas, the author of the epistle.

Tha'hash—*a badger*—a son of Nahor, Abraham's brother (Gen. 22:24).

Thar'shish (1 Kings 10:22; 22:48). See TARSHISH.

The'atre, only mentioned in Acts 19: 29, 31. The ruins of this theatre at Ephesus still exist, and they show that it was a magnificent structure, capable of accommodating some 56,700 persons. It was the largest structure of the kind that ever existed. Theatres, as places of amusement, were unknown to the Jews.

The'bez—*brightness*—a place some 11 miles north-east of Shechem, on the road to Scythopolis, the modern *Tâbâs*. Abimelech led his army against this place, because of its participation in the conspiracy of the men of Shechem; but as he drew near to the strong tower to which its inhabitants had fled for safety, and was about to set fire to it, a woman cast a fragment of millstone at him, and "all to brake his skull" —*i.e.*, "altogether brake," etc. His armourbearer thereupon "thrust him through, and he died" (Judg. 9:50-55).

Theft. Punished by restitution, the proportions of which are noted in 2 Sam. 12:6. If the thief could not pay the fine, he was to be sold to a Hebrew master till he could pay (Ex. 22:1-4). A night-thief might be smitten till he died, and there would be no blood-guiltiness for him (22:2). A manstealer was to be put to death (21:16). All theft is forbidden (Ex. 20:15; 21:16; Lev. 19:11; Deut. 5:19; 24:7; Ps. 50:18; Zech. 5:3; Matt. 19:18; Rom. 13:9; Eph. 4:28; 1 Pet. 4:15).

Theoc'racy, a word first used by Josephus to denote that the Jews were under the direct government of God himself. The nation was in all things subject to the will of their invisible King. All the people were the servants of Jehovah, who ruled over their public and private affairs, communicating to them his will through the medium of the prophets. They were the subjects of a heavenly, not of an earthly, king. They were Jehovah's own subjects, ruled directly by him (comp. 1 Sam. 8: 6-9).

Theoph'ilus—*lover of God*—a Christian, probably a Roman, to whom Luke dedicated both his Gospel (Luke 1:3) and the Acts of the Apostles (1:1). Nothing beyond this is known of him. From the fact that Luke applies to him the title "most excellent"—the same title Paul uses in addressing Felix (Acts 23:26; 24:3) and Festus (26:25)—it has been concluded that Theophilus was a person of rank, perhaps a Roman officer.

Thessalo'nians, Epistles to the. The *first* epistle to the Thessalonians was the first of all Paul's epistles. It was in all probability written from Corinth, where he abode a "long time" (Acts 18:11, 18), early in the period of his residence there, about the end of A.D. 52.

The *occasion* of its being written was the return of Timotheus from Macedonia, bearing tidings from Thessalonica regarding the state of the church there (Acts 18:1-5; 1 Thess. 3:6). While, on the whole, the report of Timothy was encouraging, it also showed that divers errors and misunderstandings regarding the tenor of Paul's teaching had crept in amongst them. He addresses them in this letter with the view of correcting these errors, and especially for the purpose of exhorting them to purity of life, reminding them that their sanctification was the great end desired by God regarding them.

The subscription erroneously states that this epistle was written from Athens.

The *second* epistle to the Thessalonians was probably also written from Corinth, and not many months after the first.

The *occasion* of the writing of this epistle was the arrival of tidings that the tenor of the first epistle had been misunderstood,

especially with reference to the second advent of Christ. The Thessalonians had embraced the idea that Paul had taught that "the day of Christ was at hand"—that Christ's coming was just about to happen. This error is corrected (2:1-12), and the apostle prophetically announces what first must take place. "The apostasy" was first to arise. Various explanations of this expression have been given, but that which is most satisfactory refers it to the Church of Rome.

Thessaloni'ca, a large and populous city on the Thermaic bay. It was the capital of one of the four Roman districts of Macedonia, and was ruled by a prætor. It was named after Thessalonica, the wife of Cassander, who built the city. She was so called by her father, Philip, because he first heard of her birth on the day of his gaining a victory over the Thessalians. On his second missionary journey, Paul preached in the synagogue here—the chief synagogue of the Jews in that part of Macedonia—and laid the foundations of a church (Acts 17: 1-4; 1 Thess. 1:9). The violence of the Jews drove him from the city, when he fled to Berea (Acts 17:5-10). The "rulers of the city" before whom the Jews "drew Jason," with whom Paul and Silas lodged, are in the original called *politarchai*, an unusual word, which was found, however, inscribed on an arch in Thessalonica. This discovery confirms the accuracy of the historian. Paul visited the church here on a subsequent occasion (20:1-3). This city long retained its importance. It is the most important town of European Turkey, under the name of *Saloniki*, with a mixed population of about 85,000.

Theu'das—*thanksgiving*—referred to by Gamaliel in his speech before the council at Jerusalem (Acts 5:36). He headed an insurrection against the Roman authority. Beyond this nothing is known of him.

Thick clay (Hab. 2:6) is correctly rendered in the Revised Version "pledges." The Chaldean power is here represented as a rapacious usurer, accumulating the wealth that belonged to others.

Thieves, The two (Luke 23:32, 39-43), robbers, rather brigands, probably followers of Barabbas. Our Lord's cross was placed between those of the "malefactors," to add to the ignominy of his position. According to tradition, Demas or Dismas was the name of the penitent thief hanging on the right, and Gestas of the impenitent on the left.

Thistle. (1.) Heb. *hoah* (2 Kings 14 : 9 ; Job 31 : 40). In Job 41 : 2 the Hebrew word is rendered "thorn," but in the Revised Version "hook." It is also rendered "thorn" in 2 Chr. 33 : 11 ; Prov. 26 : 9 ; Cant. 2 : 2 ; "brambles" in Isa. 34 : 13. It is supposed to be a variety of the wild plum-tree, but by some it is regarded as the common thistle, of which there are many varieties in Palestine.

(2.) Heb. *dardar*, meaning "a plant growing luxuriantly" (Gen. 3 : 18 ; Hos. 10 : 8) ; Gr. *tribŏlos*, "a triple point" (Matt. 7 : 16 ; Heb. 6 : 8, "brier," R.V. "thistle"). This was probably the star-thistle, called by botanists *Centaurea calcitropa*, or "caltrops," a weed common in corn-fields. (See THORNS.)

Thom'as—*twin*—one of the twelve (Matt. 10 : 3 ; Mark 3 : 18, etc.). He was also called Didymus (John 11 : 16 ; 14 : 5), which is the Greek equivalent of the Hebrew name. All we know regarding him is recorded in the fourth Gospel (John 11 : 15, 16 ; 14 : 4, 5 ; 20 : 24, 25, 26–29). From the circumstance that in the lists of the apostles he is always mentioned along with Matthew, who was the son of Alphæus (Mark 3 : 18), and that these two are always followed by James, who was also the son of Alphæus, it has been supposed that these three—Matthew, Thomas, and James — were brothers.

Thorn. (1.) Heb. *hedek* (Prov. 15 : 19), rendered "brier" in Micah 7 : 4. Some thorny plant, of the *Solanum* family, suitable for hedges. This is probably the so-called "apple of Sodom," which grows very abundantly in the Jordan valley. "It is a shrubby plant, from 3 to 5 feet high, with very branching stems, thickly clad with spines, like those of the English brier, with leaves very large and woolly on the under side, and thorny on the midriff."

(2.) Heb. *kŏtz* (Gen. 3 : 18 ; Hos. 10 : 8),

rendered *akantha* by the LXX. In the New Testament this word *akantha* is also rendered "thorns" (Matt. 7 : 16 ; 13 : 7 ; Heb. 6 : 8). The word seems to denote any thorny or prickly plant (Jer. 12 : 13). It has been identified with the *Ononis spinosa* by some.

(3.) Heb. *na'atzûtz* (Isa. 7 : 19 ; 55 : 13). This word has been interpreted as denoting the *Zizyphus spina Christi*, or the jujube-tree. It is supposed by some that the crown of thorns placed in wanton cruelty by the Roman soldiers on our Saviour's brow before his crucifixion was plaited of branches of this tree. It overruns a great part of the Jordan valley. It is sometimes called the lotus-tree. "The thorns are long and sharp and recurved, and often create a festering wound." It often grows to a great size. (See CROWN OF THORNS.)

(4.) Heb. *'âṭâd* (Ps. 58 : 9) is rendered in the LXX. and Vulgate by *Rhamnus*, or *Lycium Europæum*, a thorny shrub, which is common all over Palestine. From its resemblance to the box it is frequently called the box-thorn.

Thorn in the flesh (2 Cor. 12 : 7–10). Many interpretations have been given of this passage. (1.) Roman Catholic writers think that it denotes suggestions to impiety.

(2.) Luther, Calvin, and other Reformers interpret the expression as denoting temptation to unbelief.

(3.) Others suppose the expression refers to "a pain in the ear or head," epileptic fits, or, in general, to some severe physical infirmity, which was a hindrance to the apostle in his work (comp. 1 Cor. 2 : 3 ; 2 Cor. 10 : 10 ; 11 : 30 ; Gal. 4 : 13, 14 ; 6 : 17). With a great amount of probability, it has been alleged that his malady was defect of sight, consequent on the dazzling light which shone around him at his conversion —acute ophthalmia. This would account for the statements in Gal. 4 : 14 ; 2 Cor. 10 : 10 ; also Acts 23 : 5, and for his generally making use of the help of an amanuensis (comp. Rom. 16 : 22, etc.).

(4.) Another view which has been maintained is that this "thorn" consisted in an infirmity of temper, to which he occasionally gave way, and which interfered with his success (comp. Acts 15 : 39 ; 23 : 2-5). If we consider the fact, "which the experience of God's saints in all ages has conclusively established, of the difficulty of subduing an infirmity of temper, as well as the pain, remorse, and humiliation such an infirmity is wont to cause to those who groan under it, we may be inclined to believe that not the least probable hypothesis concerning the 'thorn' or 'stake' in the flesh is that the loving heart of the apostle bewailed as his sorest trial the misfortune that, by impatience in word, he had often wounded those for whom he would willingly have given his life" (Lias's *Second Cor.*, *Introd.*).

Thou'sands (Micah 5 : 2), another name for "families" or "clans" (see Num. 1 : 16 ; 10 : 4 ; Josh. 22 : 14, 21). Several "thousands" or "families" made up a "tribe."

Threshing. See AGRICULTURE.

Thresh'old. (1.) Heb. *miphtân*, probably a projecting beam at a higher point than the threshold proper (1 Sam. 5 : 4, 5 ; Ezek. 9 : 3 ; 10 : 4, 18 ; 46 : 2 ; 47 : 1); also rendered "door" and "door-post."

(2.) *'Asuppîm*, pl. (Neh. 12 : 25), rendered correctly "storehouses" in the Revised Version. In 1 Chr. 26 : 15, 17 the Authorized Version retains the word as a proper name, while in the Revised Version it is translated "storehouses."

Throne (Heb. *kiṣṣ'ê*), a royal chair or seat of dignity (Deut. 17 : 18 ; 2 Sam. 7 : 13 ; Ps. 45 : 6); an elevated seat with a canopy and hangings, which cover it. It denotes the seat of the high priest in 1 Sam. 1 : 9 ; 4 : 13, and of a provincial governor in Neh. 3 : 7 and Ps. 122 : 5. The throne of Solomon is described at length in 1 Kings 10 : 18-20.

Thum'mim—*perfection* (LXX., "truth ;" Vulg., "veritas")—Ex. 28 : 30 ; Deut. 33 : 8 ; Judg. 1 : 1 ; 20 : 18 ; 1 Sam. 14 : 3, 18 ; 23 : 9 ; 2 Sam. 21 : 1. What the "Urim and Thummim" were cannot be determined with any certainty. All we certainly know is that they were a certain divinely-given means by which God imparted, through the high priest, direction and counsel to Israel when these were needed. The method by which this was done can be only a matter of mere

conjecture. They were apparently material objects, quite distinct from the breastplate, but something added to it after all the stones had been set in it—something in addition to the breastplate and its jewels. They may have been, as some suppose, two small images, like the teraphim (comp. Judg. 17 : 5 ; 18 : 14, 17, 20 ; Hos. 3 : 4), which were kept in the bag of the breastplate, by which, in some unknown way, the high priest could give forth his divinely-imparted decision when consulted. They were probably lost at the destruction of the temple by Nebuchadnezzar. They were never seen after the return from captivity.

Thun'der, often referred to in Scripture (Job 40 : 9 ; Ps. 77 : 18 ; 104 : 7). James and John were called by our Lord "sons of thunder" (Mark 3 : 17). In Job 39 : 19, instead of "thunder," as in the Authorized Version, the Revised Version translates (*ra'amah*) by "quivering main" (marg., "shaking"). Thunder accompanied the giving of the law at Sinai (Ex. 19 : 16). It was regarded as the voice of God (Job 37 : 2 ; Ps. 18 : 13 ; 81 : 7 ; comp. John 12 : 29). In answer to Samuel's prayer (1 Sam. 12 : 17, 18), God sent thunder, and "all the people greatly feared," for at such a season (the wheat-harvest) thunder and rain were almost unknown in Palestine.

Thyati'ra, a city of Asia Minor, on the borders of Lydia and Mysia. Its modern name is *Ak-hissar*—i.e., "white castle." Here was one of the seven churches (Rev. 1 : 11 ; 2 : 18-26). Lydia, the seller of purple, or rather of cloth dyed with this colour, was from this city (Acts 16 : 14). It was and still is famous for its dyeing. Among the ruins, inscriptions have been found relating to the guild of dyers in that city in ancient times.

Thy'ine wood, mentioned only in Rev. 18 : 12 among the articles which would cease to be purchased when Babylon fell. It was called *citrus*, citron wood, by the Romans. It was the *Callitris quadrivalvis* of botanists, of the cone-bearing order of trees, and of the cypress tribe of this order. The name of this wood is derived from the Greek word *thuein*, "to sacrifice," and it was so called because it was burnt in sacrifices, on account of its fragrance. The wood of this tree was reckoned very valuable, and was used for making articles of furniture by the Greeks and Romans. Like the cedars of Lebanon, it is disappearing from the forests of Palestine.

Tibe′rias, a city, the modern *Tŭbaríeh,* on the western shore of the Sea of Tiberias. It is said to have been founded by Herod Antipas (A.D. 16), on the site of the ruins of an older city called Rakkath, and to have been thus named by him after the Emperor Tiberius. It is mentioned only three times in the history of our Lord (John 6:1, 23; 21:1).

In 1837 about one-half of the inhabitants perished by an earthquake. The population of the city is now about six thousand, nearly the one-half being Jews. "We do not read that our Lord ever entered this city. The reason of this is probably to be found in the fact that it was practically a heathen city, though standing upon Jewish soil. Herod, its founder, had brought together the arts of Greece, the idolatry of Rome, and the gross lewdness of Asia. There were in it a theatre for the performance of comedies, a forum, a stadium, a palace roofed with gold in imitation of those in Italy, statues of the Roman gods, and busts of the deified emperors. He who was not sent but to the lost sheep of the house of Israel might well hold himself aloof from such scenes as these" (Manning's *Those Holy Fields*).

After the fall of Jerusalem (A.D. 70), Tiberias became one of the chief residences of the Jews in Palestine. It was for more than three hundred years their metropolis. From about A.D. 150 the Sanhedrin settled here, and established rabbinical schools, which rose to great celebrity. Here the Jerusalem (or Palestinian) Talmud was compiled about the beginning of the fifth century. To this same rabbinical school also we are indebted for the *Masora,* a "body of traditions which transmitted the readings of the Hebrew text of the Old Testament, and preserved, by means of the vowel-system, the pronunciation of the Hebrew." In its original form, and in all manuscripts, the Hebrew is written without vowels; hence,

when it ceased to be a spoken language, the importance of knowing what vowels to insert between the consonants. This is supplied by the Masora, and hence these vowels are called the "Masoretic vowel-points."

Tiberias, Sea of, called also the Sea of Galilee (*q.v.*) and of Gennesaret. In the Old Testament it is called the Sea of Chinnereth or Chinneroth. John (21:1) is the only evangelist who so designates this lake. His doing so incidentally confirms the opinion that he wrote after the other evangelists, and at a period subsequent to the taking of Jerusalem (A.D. 70). Tiberias had by this time become an important city, having been spared by the Romans, and made the capital of the province when Jerusalem was destroyed. It thus naturally gave its name to the lake.

Tibe′rius Cæsar—*i.e.,* as known in Roman history, Tiberius Claudius Nero—only mentioned in Luke 3:1. He was the stepson of Augustus, whom he succeeded on the throne, A.D. 14. He was noted for his vicious and infamous life. In the fifteenth year of his reign John the Baptist entered on his public ministry, and under him also our Lord taught and suffered. He died A.D. 37. He is frequently referred to simply as "Cæsar" (Matt. 22:17, 21; Mark 12:14, 16, 17; Luke 20:22, 24, 25; 23:2; John 19:12, 13).

Tib′ni—*building of Jehovah*—the son of Ginath, a man of some position, whom a considerable number of the people chose as monarch. For the period of four years he contended for the throne with Omri (1 Kings 16:15-23), who at length gained the mastery, and became sole monarch of Israel. Tibni was put to death.

Ti′dal (in the LXX. called "Thorgal"), styled the "king of nations" (Gen. 14:1-10). The probability is that the word rendered nations (*goyyim*) denotes the country called Gutium, east of Tigris and north of Elam.

Tig′lath-Pile′ser I. (not mentioned in Scripture) was the most famous of the monarchs of the first Assyrian empire (about B.C. 1110). After his death, for two hundred years the empire fell into decay. The history of David and Solomon falls

TIGLATH-PILESER.

within this period. He was succeeded by his son, Shalmaneser II.

Tig'lath-Pile'ser III., the Assyrian throne-name of Pul (*q.v.*). He appears in the Assyrian records as gaining, in the fifth year of his reign (about B.C. 741), a victory over Azariah (= Uzziah in 2 Chr. 26 : 1), king of Judah, whose achievements are described in 2 Chr. 26 : 6-15. He is first mentioned in Scripture, however, as gaining a victory over Pekah, king of Israel, and Rezin of Damascus, who were confederates. He put Rezin to death, and punished Pekah by taking a considerable portion of his kingdom, and carrying off (B.C. 734) a vast number of its inhabitants into captivity (2 Kings 15 : 29; 16 : 5-9; 1 Chr. 5 : 6, 26)—the Reubenites, the Gadites, and half the tribe of Manasseh—whom he settled in Gozan. In the Assyrian annals it is further related that, before he returned from Syria, he held a court at Damascus, and received submission and tribute from the neighbouring kings, among whom were Pekah of Samaria and "Yahu-khazi [*i.e.*, Ahaz], king of Judah" (comp. 2 Kings 16 : 10-16).

He was the founder of what is called "the second Assyrian empire," an empire meant to embrace the whole world, the centre of which should be Nineveh. He died B.C. 728, and was succeeded by a general of his army,

TAMBOURINE.

Ululâ, who assumed the name Shalmaneser IV.

Timæ'us —*defiled*—the father of blind Bartimæus (Mark 10 : 46).

Tim'brel (Heb. *tôph*), a small drum or tambourine; a tabret (*q.v.*). The antiquity of this musical instrument appears from the scriptural allusions to it (Gen. 31 : 27; Ex. 15 : 20; Judg. 11 : 34, etc.) (See MUSIC.)

Tim'nah—*a portion.* (1.) A town of Judah (Josh. 15 : 10). The Philistines took possession of it in the days of Ahaz (2 Chr. 28 : 18). It was about 20 miles west of Jerusalem. It has been identified with Timnatha of Dan (Josh. 19 : 43), and also with Timnath (Judg. 14 : 1, 5).

(2.) A city in the mountains of Judah (Josh. 15 : 57)= *Tibna* near *Jeba'*.

(3.) A "duke" or sheik of Edom (Gen. 36 : 40).

Tim'nath—Gen. 38 : 12, 14. (1.) Heb. *Timnathah*, which is appropriately rendered in the Revised Version, "To Timnah," a town in Judah.

(2.) The town where Samson sojourned, probably identical with "Timnah" (1) (Judg. 14 : 1-18).

Tim'nath-he'res—*portion of the sun*—where Joshua was buried (Judg. 2 : 9). It was "in the mount of Ephraim, in the north side of the hill Gaash," 10 miles south-west of Shechem. The same as the following.

Tim'nath-se'rah—*remaining portion*—the city of Joshua in the hill country of Ephraim, the same as Timnath-heres (Josh. 19 : 50; 24 : 30). "Of all sites I have seen," says Lieutenant Conder, "none is so striking as that of Joshua's home, surrounded as it is with deep valleys and wild rugged hills." Opposite the town is a hill, on the northern side of which there are many excavated sepulchres. Among these is the supposed tomb of Joshua, which is said to be "the most striking monument in the country." It is a "square chamber with five excavations in three of its sides. the central one forming a passage leading into a second chamber beyond. A great number of lamp-niches cover the walls of the porch—upwards of two hundred—arranged in vertical rows. A single cavity with a niche for a lamp has been thought to be the resting-place of the warrior-chief of Israel." The modern *Kefr Hâris*, 10 miles south-west of Shechem.

Tim'nite, *a man of Timnah.* Samson's father-in-law is so styled (Judg. 15 : 6).

Ti'mon—*honouring*—one of the seven deacons at Jerusalem (Acts 6 : 5). Nothing further is known of him.

Timo'theus, the Greek form of the

name of Timothy (Acts 16:1, etc.; the R.V. always "Timothy").

Tim'othy—*honouring God*—a young disciple who was Paul's companion in many of his journeyings. His mother, Eunice, and his grandmother, Lois, are mentioned as eminent for their piety (2 Tim. 1:5). We know nothing of his father but that he was a Greek (Acts 16:1). He is first brought into notice at the time of Paul's second visit to Lystra (16:2), where he probably resided, and where it seems he was converted during Paul's first visit to that place (1 Tim. 1:2; 2 Tim. 3:11). The apostle having formed a high opinion of his "own son in the faith," arranged that he should become his companion (Acts 16:3), and took and circumcised him, so that he might conciliate the Jews. He was designated to the office of an evangelist (1 Tim. 4:14), and went with Paul in his journey through Phrygia, Galatia, and Mysia; also to Troas and Philippi and Berea (Acts 17:14). Thence he followed Paul to Athens, and was sent by him with Silas on a mission to Thessalonica (17:15; 1 Thess. 3:2). We next find him at Corinth (1 Thess. 1:1; 2 Thess. 1:1) with Paul. He passes now out of sight for a few years, and is again noticed as with the apostle at Ephesus (Acts 19:22), whence he is sent on a mission into Macedonia. He accompanied Paul afterwards into Asia (20:4), where he was with him for some time. When the apostle was a prisoner at Rome, Timothy joined him (Phil. 1:1), where it appears he also suffered imprisonment (Heb. 13:23). During the apostle's second imprisonment he wrote to Timothy, asking him to rejoin him as soon as possible, and to bring with him certain things which he had left at Troas—his cloak and parchments (2 Tim. 4:13).

According to tradition, after the apostle's death he settled in Ephesus as his sphere of labour, and there found a martyr's grave.

Timothy, First Epistle to. Paul in this epistle speaks of himself as having left Ephesus for Macedonia (1:3), and hence not Laodicea, as mentioned in the subscrip-

tion; but probably Philippi, or some other city in that region, was the *place* where this epistle was written. During the interval between his first and second imprisonments he probably visited the scenes of his former labours in Greece and Asia, and then found his way into Macedonia, whence he wrote this letter to Timothy, whom he had left behind in Ephesus.

It was probably written about A.D. 66 or 67.

The epistle consists mainly—(1) of counsels to Timothy regarding the worship and organization of the Church, and the responsibilities resting on its several members; and (2) of exhortation to faithfulness in maintaining the truth amid surrounding errors.

Timothy, Second Epistle to, was probably written a year or so after the first, and from Rome, where Paul was for a second time a prisoner, and was sent to Timothy by the hands of Tychicus. In it he entreats Timothy to come to him before winter, and to bring Mark with him (comp. Phil. 2:22). He was anticipating that "the time of his departure was at hand" (2 Tim. 4:6), and he exhorts his "son Timothy" to all diligence and steadfastness, and to patience under persecution (1:6-15), and to a faithful discharge of all the duties of his office (4:1-5), with all the solemnity of one who was about to appear before the Judge of quick and dead.

Tin—Heb. *bĕdîl* (Num. 31:22; Ezek. 22:18, 20), a metal well known in ancient times. It is the general opinion that the Phœnicians of Tyre and Sidon obtained their supplies of tin from the British Isles. In Ezek. 27:12 it is said to have been brought from Tarshish, which was probably a commercial emporium supplied with commodities from other places. In Isa. 1:25 the word so rendered is generally understood of *lead*, the alloy with which the silver had become mixed (ver. 22). The fire of the Babylonish Captivity would be the means of purging out the idolatrous alloy that had corrupted the people.

Tink'ling ornaments (Isa. 3:18), anklets of silver or gold, etc., such as are still used by women in Syria and the East.

Tiph'sah—*passing over; ford*—one of the boundaries of Solomon's dominions (1 Kings 4:24), probably "Thapsacus, a great and wealthy town on the western bank of the Euphrates," about 100 miles north-east of Tadmor. All the land traffic between the east and the west passed through it. Menahem undertook an expedition against this city, and "smote Tiphsah and all that were therein" (2 Kings 15:16). This expedition implied a march of some 300 miles from Tirzah if by way of Tadmor, and about 400 if by way of Aleppo; and its success showed the strength of the Israelite kingdom, for it was practically a defiance to Assyria. Conder, however, identifies this place with *Khŭrbet Tafsah*, some 6 miles west of Shechem.

Ti'ras, the youngest of the sons of Japheth (Gen. 10:2; 1 Chr. 1:5).

Tires. "To tire" the head is to adorn it (2 Kings 9:30). As a noun the word is derived from "tiara," and is the rendering of the Heb. *p'ēr*, a "turban" or an ornament for the head (Ezek. 24:17; R.V., "headtire;" 24:23). In Isa. 3:18 the word *sahărônîm* is rendered "round tires like the moon," and in Judg. 8:21, 26 "ornaments," but in both cases "crescents" in the Revised Version.

Tir'hakah, the last king of Egypt of the Ethiopian (the fifteenth) dynasty. He was the brother-in-law of So (*q.v.*). He probably ascended the throne about B.C. 692, having been previously king of Ethiopia (2 Kings 19:9; Isa. 37:9), which with Egypt now formed one nation. He was a great warrior, and but little is known of him. The Assyrian armies under Esarhaddon, and again under Assur-bani-pal, invaded Egypt and defeated Tirhakah, who afterwards retired into Ethiopia, where he died, after reigning twenty-six years.

Tir'shatha, a word probably of Persian origin, meaning "severity," denoting a high civil dignity. The Persian governor of Judea is so called (Ezra 2:63; Neh. 7:65, 70). Nehemiah is called by this name in Neh. 8:9; 10:1, and the "governor" (*peḥah*) in 5:18. Probably, therefore, tirshatha = pehah = the modern *pasha*.

Tir'za—*pleasantness*. (1.) An old royal city of the Canaanites, which was destroyed by Joshua (Josh. 12:24). Jeroboam chose it for his residence, and he removed to it from Shechem, which at first he made the capital of his kingdom. It remained the chief residence of the kings of Israel till Omri took Samaria (1 Kings 14:17; 15:21; 16:6, 8, etc.). Here Zimri perished amid the flames of the palace to which in his despair he had set fire (1 Kings 16:18), and here Menahem smote Shallum (15:14, 16). Solomon refers to its beauty (Cant. 6:4). It has been identified with the modern mud hamlet *Teïasîr*, 11 miles north of Shechem. Others, however, would identify it with *Tellûza*, a village about 6 miles east of Samaria.

(2.) The youngest of Zelophehad's five daughters (Num. 26:33; Josh. 17:3).

Tish'bite. Elijah the prophet was thus named (1 Kings 17:1; 21:17, 28, etc.). In 1 Kings 17:1 the word rendered "inhabitants" is in the original the same as that rendered "Tishbite," hence that verse may be read as in the LXX., "Elijah the Tishbite of Tishbi in Gilead." Some interpret this word as meaning "stranger," and read the verse, "Elijah the stranger from among the strangers in Gilead." This designation is probably given to the prophet as denoting that his birthplace was Tishbi, a place in Upper Galilee (mentioned in the apocryphal book of Tobit), from which for some reason he migrated into Gilead. Josephus, the Jewish historian (*Ant.* 8:13, 2), however, supposes that Tishbi was some place in the land of Gilead. It has been identified by some with *el-Ishtib*, a place some 22 miles due south of the Sea of Galilee, among the mountains of Gilead.

Tis'ri, the first month of the civil year, and the seventh of the ecclesiastical year. See ETHANIM (1 Kings 8:2). Called in the Assyrian inscriptions *Tasaritu*—i.e., "beginning."

Tithe, a *tenth* of the produce of the earth consecrated and set apart for special purposes. The dedication of a tenth to God was recognized as a duty before the time of Moses. Abraham paid tithes to Melchizedek (Gen. 14:20; Heb. 7:6); and

Jacob vowed unto the Lord and said, "Of all that thou shalt give me I will surely give the tenth unto thee."

The first Mosaic law on this subject is recorded in Lev. 27 : 30–32. Subsequent legislation regulated the destination of the tithes (Num. 18 : 21–24, 26–28 ; Deut. 12 : 5, 6, 11, 17; 14 : 22, 23). The paying of the tithes was an important part of the Jewish religious worship. In the days of Hezekiah one of the first results of the reformation of religion was the eagerness with which the people brought in their tithes (2 Chr. 31 : 5, 6). The neglect of this duty was sternly rebuked by the prophets (Amos 4 : 4 ; Mal. 3 : 8–10). It cannot be affirmed that the Old Testament law of tithes is binding on the Christian Church, nevertheless the principle of this law remains, and is incorporated in the gospel (1 Cor. 9 : 13, 14); and if, as is the case, the motive that ought to prompt to liberality in the cause of religion and of the service of God be greater now than in Old Testament times, then Christians ought to go beyond the ancient Hebrew in consecrating both themselves and their substance to God.

Every Jew was required by the Levitical law to pay three tithes of his property —(1) one tithe for the Levites ; (2) one for the use of the temple and the great feasts; and (3) one for the poor of the land.

Tit′tle—*a point*—(Matt. 5 : 18 ; Luke 16 : 17), the minute point or stroke added to some letters of the Hebrew alphabet to distinguish them from others which they resemble ; hence, the very least point.

Ti′tus—*honourable*—was with Paul and Barnabas at Antioch, and accompanied them to the council at Jerusalem (Gal. 2 : 1–3; Acts 15 : 2), although his name nowhere occurs in the Acts of the Apostles. He appears to have been a Gentile, and to have been chiefly engaged in ministering to Gentiles ; for Paul sternly refused to have him circumcised, inasmuch as in his case the cause of gospel liberty was at stake. We find him, at a later period, with Paul and Timothy at Ephesus, whence he was sent by Paul to Corinth for the purpose of getting the contributions of the church there in behalf of the poor saints at Jerusalem sent forward (2 Cor. 8 : 6 ; 12 : 18). He rejoined the apostle when he was in Macedonia, and cheered him with the tidings he brought from Corinth (7 : 6–15). After this his name is not mentioned till after Paul's first imprisonment, when we find him engaged in the organization of the church in Crete, where the apostle had left him for this purpose (Titus 1 : 5). The last notice of him is in 2 Tim. 4 : 10, where we find him with Paul at Rome during his second imprisonment. From Rome he was sent into Dalmatia, no doubt on some important missionary errand. We have no record of his death. He is not mentioned in the Acts.

Titus, Epistle to, was probably written about the same time as the first epistle to Timothy, with which it has many affinities. "Both letters were addressed to persons left by the writer to preside in their respective churches during his absence. Both letters are principally occupied in describing the qualifications to be sought for in those whom they should appoint to offices in the church; and the ingredients of this description are in both letters nearly the same. Timothy and Titus are likewise cautioned against the same prevailing corruptions, and in particular against the same misdirection of their cares and studies. This affinity obtains not only in the subject of the letters, which from the similarity of situation in the persons to whom they were addressed might be expected to be somewhat alike, but extends in a great variety of instances to the phrases and expressions. The writer accosts his two friends with the same salutation, and passes on to the business of his letter by the same transition (comp. 1 Tim. 1 : 2, 3 with Titus 1 : 1, 5; 1 Tim. 1 : 4 with Titus 1 : 13, 14; 3 : 9; 1 Tim. 4 : 12 with Titus 2 : 7, 15)." — Paley's *Horæ Paulinæ.*

The *date* of its composition may be concluded from the circumstance that it was written after Paul's visit to Crete (Titus 1 : 5). That visit could not be the one referred to in Acts 27 : 7, when Paul was on his voyage to Rome as a prisoner, and where he continued a prisoner for two years. We may warrantably suppose that after his release Paul sailed from Rome into Asia and took Crete by the way, and that there he left Titus "to set in order the things that were wanting." Thence he went to Ephesus, where he left Timothy, and from Ephesus to Macedonia, where he wrote First Timothy, and thence to Nicopolis in Epirus, from which *place* he wrote to Titus, about A.D. 66 or 67.

In the subscription to the epistle it is said to have been written from "Nicopolis of Macedonia," but no such place is known. The subscriptions to the epistles are of no authority, as they are not authentic.

Tob, The land of, a district on the east of Jordan, about 13 miles south-east of the Sea of Galilee, to which Jephthah fled from his brethren (Judg. 11:3, 5). It was on the northern boundary of Perea, between Syria and the land of Ammon (2 Sam. 10:6, 8). Its modern name is *Taiyibeh.*

Tob-adoni'jah—*good is Jehovah, my Lord*—a Levite sent out by Jehoshaphat to instruct the people of Judah in the law (2 Chr. 17:8).

Tobi'ah—*pleasing to Jehovah*—the "servant," the "Ammonite," who joined with those who opposed the rebuilding of Jerusalem after the Exile (Neh. 2:10). He was a man of great influence, which he exerted in opposition to the Jews, and "sent letters" to Nehemiah "to put him in fear" (Neh. 6:17–19). "Eliashib the priest" prepared for him during Nehemiah's absence "a chamber in the courts of the house of God," which on his return grieved Nehemiah sore, and therefore he "cast forth all the household stuff of Tobiah out of the chamber" (13:7, 8).

Tobi'jah—*id.*—a Levite sent out through Judah by Jehoshaphat to teach the people (2 Chr. 17:8).

To'chen—*measured*—a town of Simeon (1 Chr. 4:32).

Togar'mah. (1.) A son of Gomer, and grandson of Japheth (Gen. 10:3).

(2.) A nation which traded in horses and mules at the fairs of Tyre (Ezek. 27:14; 38:6); probably an Armenian or a Scythian race; descendants of (1).

To'hu, one of Samuel's ancestors (1 Sam. 1:1).

To'i, a king of Hamath, who sent "Joram his son unto King David to salute him," when he "heard that David had smitten all the host of Hadadezer" (2 Sam. 8:9, 10). Called Tou (1 Chr. 18:9, 10).

To'la—*a scarlet worm.* (1.) Eldest son of Issachar (Gen. 46:13).

(2.) A judge of the tribe of Issachar who "judged" Israel twenty-three years (Judg. 10:1, 2), when he died, and was buried in Shamir. He was succeeded by Jair.

To'lad—*productive*—a town of Simeon, in the south of Judah (1 Chr. 4:29).

To'laites, descendants of Tola (Num. 26:23; 1 Chr. 7:1, 2).

Toll, one of the branches of the king of Persia's revenues (Ezra 4:13; 7:24), probably a tax levied from those who used the bridges and fords and highways.

Tombs of the Hebrews were generally excavated in the solid rock, or were natural caves. Mention is made of such tombs in Judg. 8:32; 2 Sam. 2:32; 2 Kings 9:28; 23:30. They were sometimes made in gardens (2 Kings 21:26; 23:16; Matt. 28:60). They are found in great numbers in and around Jerusalem and all over the land. They were sometimes whitewashed (Matt. 23:27, 29). The body of Jesus was laid in Joseph's new rock-hewn tomb, in a garden near to Calvary. All evidence is in favour of the opinion that this tomb was somewhere near the Damascus gate, and outside the city, and cannot be identified with the so-called "holy sepulchre." The mouth of such rocky tombs was usually closed by a large stone (Heb. *gôlal*), which could only be removed by the united efforts of several men (Matt. 28:2; comp. John 11:39). (See SEPULCHRE.)

Tongues, Confu'sion of, at Babel, the cause of the early separation of mankind and their division into nations. The descendants of Noah built a tower to prevent their dispersion; but God "confounded their language" (Gen. 11:1–8), and they were scattered over the whole earth. Till this time "the whole earth was of one language and of one speech." (See SHINAR.)

Tongues, Gift of, granted on the day of Pentecost (Acts 2:4), in fulfilment of a promise Christ had made to his disciples (Mark 16:17). What this gift actually was has been a subject of much discussion. Some have argued that it was merely an outward sign of the presence of the Holy Spirit among the disciples, typifying his manifold gifts, and showing that salvation was to be extended to all nations. But the words of Luke (Acts 2:9) clearly show that the various peoples in Jerusalem at the time of Pentecost did really hear themselves addressed in their own special language with which they were naturally acquainted (comp. Joel 2:28, 29).

Among the gifts of the Spirit the apostle enumerates in 1 Cor. 12:10-14:30, "divers kinds of tongues" and the "interpretation of tongues." This "gift" was a different manifestation of the Spirit from that on Pentecost, although it resembled it in many particulars. Tongues were to be "a sign to them that believe not."

Tooth, one of the particulars regarding which retaliatory punishment was to be inflicted (Ex. 21:24; Lev. 24:20; Deut. 19:21). "Gnashing of teeth" = rage, despair (Matt. 8:12; Acts 7:54); "cleanness of teeth" = famine (Amos 4:6); "children's teeth set on edge" = children suffering for the sins of their fathers (Ezek. 18:2).

To'paz—Heb. *piṭdâh* (Ezek. 28:13; Rev. 21:20)—a golden yellow or "green" stone brought from Cush or Ethiopia (Job 28:19). It was the second stone in the first row in the breastplate of the high priest, and had the name of Simeon inscribed on it (Ex. 28:17). It is probably the chrysolite of the moderns.

To'phel—*lime*—a place in the wilderness of Sinai (Deut. 1:1), now identified with *Tâfyleh* or *Tâfileh*, on the west side of the Edomitish mountains.

To'phet = **Topheth**—from Heb. *tôph*, "a drum," because the cries of children here sacrificed by the priests of Moloch were drowned by the noise of such an instrument; or from *taph* or *toph*, meaning "to burn," and hence a *place of burning*—the name of a particular part in the valley of Hinnom. "Fire being the most destructive of all elements, is chosen by the sacred writers to symbolize the agency by which God punishes or destroys the wicked. We are not to assume from prophetical figures that material fire is the precise agent to be used. It was not the agency employed in the destruction of Sennacherib, mentioned in Isa. 30:33......
Tophet properly begins where the Vale of Hinnom bends round to the east, having the cliffs of Zion on the north, and the Hill of Evil Counsel on the south. It terminates at *Beer 'Ayub*, where it joins the Valley of Jehoshaphat. The cliffs on the southern side especially abound in ancient tombs. Here the dead carcasses of beasts and every offal and abomination were cast, and left to be either devoured by that worm that never died or consumed by that fire that was never quenched." Thus Tophet came to represent the place of punishment. (See HINNOM.)

Torch'es. On the night of his betrayal, when our Lord was in the garden of Gethsemane, Judas, "having received a band of men and officers from the chief priests and Pharisees, cometh thither with lanterns and torches and weapons" (John 18:1-3). Although it was the time of full moon, yet in the valley of the Kidron "there fell great, deep shadows from the declivity of the mountain and projecting rocks; there were there caverns and grottoes, into which a fugitive might retreat; finally, there were probably a garden-house and tower, into whose gloom it might be necessary for a searcher to throw light around."—Lange's *Commentary*. (Nahum 2:3, "torches," Revised Version, "steel," probably should be "scythes" for war-chariots.)

Tor'ment—Gr. *basanos* (Matt. 4:24)—the "touch-stone" of justice; hence inquisition by torture, and then any disease which racks and tortures the limbs.

Tor'toise (Heb. *tsâbh*). Ranked among the unclean animals (Lev. 11:29). Land tortoises are common in Syria. The LXX. renders the word by "land crocodile." The word, however, more probably denotes a lizard, called by the modern Arabs *dhabb*.

Tow (Judg. 16 : 9). See FLAX.

Tow'ers, of Babel (Gen. 11 : 4), Edar (Gen. 35 : 21), Penuel (Judg. 8 : 9, 17), Shechem (9 : 46), David (Cant. 4 : 4), Lebanon (7 : 4), Syene (Ezek. 29 : 10), Hananeel (Zech. 14 : 10), Siloam (Luke 13 : 4). There were several towers in Jerusalem (2 Chr. 26 : 9 ; Ps. 48 : 12). They were erected for various purposes, as watch-towers in vineyards (Isa. 5 : 2 ; Matt. 21 : 33) and towers for defence.

Tow'er of the furnaces (Neh. 3 : 11 ; 12 : 38), a tower at the north-western angle of the second wall of Jerusalem. It was probably so named from its contiguity to the "bakers' street" (Jer. 37 : 21).

Trachoni'tis—*a rugged region*—corresponds to the Heb. *Argob* (*q.v.*), the Greek name of a region on the east of Jordan (Luke 3 : 1) ; one of the five Roman provinces into which that district was divided. It was in the tetrarchy of Philip, and is now called the *Lejah.*

Tradi'tion, any kind of teaching, written or spoken, handed down from generation to generation. In Mark 7 : 3, 9, 13, Col. 2 : 8, this word refers to the arbitrary interpretations of the Jews. In 2 Thess. 2 : 15 ; 3 : 6, it is used in a good sense. Peter (1 Pet. 1 : 18) uses this word with reference to the degenerate Judaism of the "strangers scattered" whom he addresses (comp. Acts 15 : 10 ; Matt. 15 : 2-6 ; Gal. 1 : 14).

Trance (Gr. *ekstăsis*, from which the word "ecstasy" is derived) denotes the state of one who is "out of himself." Such were the trances of Peter and Paul—Acts 10 : 11 ; 11 : 5 ; 22 : 17—ecstasies, "a preternatural, absorbed state of mind preparing for the reception of the vision"—comp. 2 Cor. 12 : 1-4). In Mark 5 : 42 and Luke 5 : 26 the Greek word is rendered "astonishment," "amazement" (comp. Mark 16 : 8 ; Acts 3 : 10).

Transfigura'tion, the, of our Lord on a "high mountain apart," is described by each of the three evangelists (Matt. 17 : 1-8 ; Mark 9 : 2-8 ; Luke 9 : 28-36). The fullest account is given by Luke, who, no doubt, was informed by Peter, who was present on the occasion. What these evangelists record was an absolute historical reality,

and not a mere vision. The concurrence between them in all the circumstances of the incident is exact. John seems to allude to it also (John 1 : 14). Forty years after the event Peter distinctly makes mention of it (2 Pet. 1 : 16-18). In describing the sanctification of believers, Paul also seems to allude to this majestic and glorious appearance of our Lord on the "holy mount" (Rom. 12 : 2 ; 2 Cor. 3 : 18).

The place of the transfiguration was probably Mount Hermon (*q.v.*), and not Mount Tabor, as is commonly supposed.

Treas'ure cities, store cities which the Israelites built for the Egyptians (Ex. 1 : 11). (See PITHOM.) Towns in which the treasures of the kings of Judah were kept were so designated (1 Chr. 27 : 25).

Treas'ure houses, the houses or magazines built for the safe keeping of treasure and valuable articles of any kind (Ezra 5 : 17 ; 7 : 20 ; Neh. 10 : 38 ; Dan. 1 : 2).

Treas'ury (Matt. 27 : 6 ; Mark 12 : 41 ; John 8 : 20). It does not appear that there was a separate building so called. The name was given to the thirteen brazen chests, called "trumpets," from the form of the opening into which the offerings of the temple worshippers were put. These stood in the outer "court of the women." "Nine chests were for the appointed money-tribute and for the sacrifice-tribute—*i.e.*, money-gifts instead of the sacrifices ; four chests for freewill-offerings for wood, incense, temple decoration, and burnt-offerings" (Lightfoot's *Hor. Heb.*).

Tree of the knowledge of good and evil, stood in the midst of the garden of Eden, beside the tree of life (Gen. 2, 3). Adam and Eve were forbidden to take of the fruit which grew upon it. But they disobeyed the divine injunction, and so sin and death by sin entered our world and became the heritage of Adam's posterity. (See ADAM.)

Tree of life, stood also in the midst of the garden of Eden (Gen. 2 : 9 ; 3 : 22). Some writers have advanced the opinion that this tree had some secret virtue, which was fitted to preserve life. Probably the lesson conveyed was that life was to be sought by man, not in himself or in his own power, but from without, from Him who is emphatically the Life (John 1:4; 14:6). Wisdom is compared to the tree of life (Prov. 3:18). The "tree of life" spoken of in the Book of Revelation (Rev. 2:7; 22:2, 14) is an emblem of the joys of the celestial paradise.

Tres'pass offering (Heb. *'âshâm*, "debt"), the law concerning, given in Lev. 5:14–6:7; also in Num. 5:5–8. The idea of sin as a "debt" pervades this legislation. The *'âshâm*, which was always a ram, was offered in cases where sins were more private. (See OFFERING.)

Tribe, a collection of families descending from one ancestor. The "twelve tribes" of the Hebrews were the twelve collections of families which sprang from the sons of Jacob. In Matt. 24:30 the word has a wider significance. The tribes of Israel are referred to as types of the spiritual family of God (Rev. 7). (See KINGDOM OF ISRAEL; OF JUDAH.)

Tribula'tion, trouble or affliction of any kind (Deut. 4:30; Matt. 13:21; 2 Cor. 7:4). In Rom. 2:9 "tribulation and anguish" are the penal sufferings that shall overtake the wicked. In Matt. 24:21, 29, the word denotes the calamities that were to attend the destruction of Jerusalem.

Trib'ute, a tax imposed by a king on his subjects (2 Sam. 20:24; 1 Kings 4:6; Rom. 13:6).

In Matt. 17:24–27 the word denotes the temple rate (the "didrachma," the "half-shekel," as rendered by the R.V.) which was required to be paid for the support of the temple by every Jew above twenty years of age (Ex. 30:12; 2 Kings 12:4; 2 Chr. 24:6, 9). It was not a civil but a religious tax.

In Matt. 22:17, Mark 12:14, Luke 20:22, the word may be interpreted as denoting the capitation tax which the Romans imposed on the Jewish people. It may, however, be legitimately regarded as denoting any tax whatever imposed by a foreign power on the people of Israel. The "tribute money" shown to our Lord (Matt. 22:19) was the *denarius*, bearing Cæsar's superscription. It was the tax paid by every Jew to the Romans. (See PENNY.)

Trin'ity, a word not found in Scripture, but used to express the doctrine of the unity of God as subsisting in three distinct Persons. This word is derived from the Gr. *trias*, first used by Theophilus (A.D. 168–183), or from the Lat. *trinitas*, first used by Tertullian (A.D. 220), to express this doctrine.

The propositions involved in the doctrine are these:—1. That God is one, and that there is but one God (Deut. 6:4; 1 Kings 8:60; Isa. 44:6; Mark 12:29, 32; John 10:30). 2. That the Father is a distinct divine Person (*hypostasis, subsistentia, persona, suppositum intellectuale*) — distinct from the Son and the Holy Spirit. 3. That Jesus Christ was truly God, and yet was a Person distinct from the Father and the Holy Spirit. 4. That the Holy Spirit is also a distinct divine Person.

Tro'as, a city on the coast of Mysia, in the north-west of Asia Minor, named after ancient Troy, which was at some little distance from it (about 4 miles) to the north. Here Paul, on his second missionary journey, saw the vision of a "man of Macedonia," who appeared to him, saying, "Come over, and help us" (Acts 16:8–11). He visited this place also on other occasions, and on one of these visits he left his cloak and some books there (2 Cor. 2:12; 2 Tim. 4:13). The ruins of Troas extend over many miles, the site being now mostly covered with a forest of oak trees. The modern name of the ruins is *Eski Stamboul* —*i.e.*, Old Constantinople.

Trogyl'lium, a town on the western coast of Asia Minor, where Paul "tarried" when on his way from Assos to Miletus, on his third missionary journey (Acts 20:5).

Troph'imus—*a foster-child*—an Ephesian who accompanied Paul during a part of his third missionary journey (Acts 20:4; 21:29). He was with Paul in Jerusalem, and the Jews, supposing that the apostle had brought him with him into the temple, raised a tumult which resulted in Paul's imprisonment. (See TEMPLE, HEROD'S.) In writing to Timothy, the apostle says, "Trophimus have I left at Miletum sick" (2 Tim. 4:20). This must refer to some event not noticed in the Acts.

Trum'pets were of a great variety of forms, and were made of divers materials. Some were made of silver (Num. 10 : 2), and were used only by the priests in announcing the approach of festivals and in giving signals of war. Some were also made of rams' horns (Josh. 6 : 8). They were blown at special festivals, and to herald the arrival of special seasons (Lev. 23 : 24; 25 : 9; 1 Chr. 15 : 24; 2 Chr. 29 : 27; Ps. 81 : 3; 98 : 6).

"Trumpets" are among the symbols used in the Book of Revelation (Rev. 1 : 10; 8 : 2). (See HORN.)

Trumpets, Feast of, was celebrated at the beginning of the month Tisri, the first month of the civil year. It received its name from the circumstance that the trumpets usually blown at the commencement of each month were on that occasion blown with unusual solemnity (Lev. 23 : 23–25; Num. 10 : 10; 29 : 1–6). It was one of the seven days of holy convocation. The special design of this feast, which is described in these verses, is not known.

Truth. Used in various senses in Scripture. In Prov. 12 : 17, 19, it denotes that which is opposed to falsehood. In Isa. 59 : 14, 15, Jer. 7 : 28, it means fidelity or truthfulness. The doctrine of Christ is called "the truth of the gospel" (Gal. 2 : 5), "the truth" (2 Tim. 3 : 7; 4 : 4). Our Lord says of himself, "I am the way, and the truth" (John 14 : 6).

Tryphe'na and **Trypho'sa,** two female Christians, active workers, whom Paul salutes in his epistle to the Romans (16 : 12).

Tu'bal. (1.) The fifth son of Japheth (Gen. 10 : 2).

(2.) A nation, probably descended from the son of Japheth. It is mentioned by Isaiah (66 : 19), along with Javan, and by Ezekiel (27 : 13), along with Meshech, among the traders with Tyre, also among the confederates of Gog (Ezek. 38 : 2, 3; 39 : 1), and with Meshech among the nations which were to be destroyed (32 : 26). This nation was probably the Tiberini of the Greek historian Herodotus, a people of the Asiatic highland west of the Upper Euphrates, the southern range of the Caucasus, on the east of the Black Sea.

Tu'bal-cain, the son of Lamech and Zillah, "an instructor of every artificer in brass and iron" (Gen. 4 : 22; R.V., "the forger of every cutting instrument of brass and iron").

Tur'tle, Turtle-dove. Its peculiar peaceful and gentle habit is often referred to in Scripture. A pair was offered in sacrifice by Mary at her purification (Luke 2 : 24). The pigeon and the turtle-dove were the only birds permitted to be offered in sacrifice (Lev. 1 : 14; 5 : 7; 14 : 22; 15 : 14, 29, etc.). The Latin name of this bird, *turtur*, is derived from its note, and is a repetition of the Hebrew name *tôr*. Three species are found in Palestine—(1) the turtle-dove (*Turtur auritus*), (2) the collared turtle (*T. risorius*), and (3) the palm turtle (*T. Senegalensis*). But it is to the first of these species which the various passages of Scripture refer. It is a migratory bird (Jer. 8 : 7; Cant. 2 : 11, 12). "Search the glades and valleys, even by sultry Jordan, at the end of March, and not a turtle-dove is to be seen. Return in the second week of April, and clouds of doves are feeding on the clovers of the plain. They stock every tree and thicket......They overspread the whole face of the land." "Immediately on its arrival it pours forth from every garden, grove, and wooded hill its melancholy yet soothing ditty unceasingly from early dawn till sunset. It is from its plaintive and continuous note, doubtless, that David, pouring forth his heart's sorrow to God, compares himself to a turtle-dove" (Ps. 74 : 19).

Tych'icus — *chance* — an Asiatic Christian, a "faithful minister in the Lord" (Eph. 6 : 21, 22), who, with Trophimus, accompanied Paul on a part of his journey from Macedonia to Jerusalem (Acts 20 : 4). He is alluded to also in Col. 4 : 7, Titus 3 : 12, and 2 Tim. 4 : 12 as having been with Paul at Rome, whence he sent him to Ephesus, probably for the purpose of building up and encouraging the church there.

Type occurs only once in Scripture (1 Cor. 10 : 11, A.V. marg.). The Greek word *tupos* is rendered "print" (John 20 : 25), "figure" (Acts 7 : 43; Rom. 5 : 14), "fashion" (Acts 7 : 44), "manner" (Acts 23 : 25), "form" (Rom. 6 : 17), "example" or "ensample" (1 Cor. 10:6, 11; Phil. 3:17; 1 Thess. 1:7; 2 Thess. 3:9; 1 Tim. 4:12). It properly means a "model" or "pattern" or "mould" into which clay or wax was pressed, so that it might take the figure or exact shape of the mould. The word type is generally used to denote a resemblance between something present and something future, which is called the "antitype."

Tyran'nus—*prince*—a Greek rhetorician, in whose "school" at Ephesus Paul disputed daily for the space of two years with those who came to him (Acts 19:9). Some have supposed that he was a Jew, and that his "school" was a private synagogue.

Tyre—*a rock*—now *es-Sûr;* an ancient Phœnician city, about 23 miles, in a direct line, north of Acre, and 20 south of Sidon. It was a vast commercial emporium, maintaining commercial relations with almost all lands—"the crowning city, whose merchants are princes, and whose traffickers are the honourable of the earth." Sidon was the oldest Phœnician city, but Tyre had a longer and more illustrious history. The commerce of the whole world was gathered into the warehouses of Tyre. "Tyrian merchants were the first who ventured to navigate the Mediterranean waters; and they founded their colonies on the coasts and neighbouring islands of the Ægean Sea, in Greece, on the northern coast of Africa, at Carthage and other places, in Sicily and Corsica, in Spain at Tartessus, and even beyond the pillars of Hercules at Gadeira (Cadiz). The Phœnicians exerted an important influence upon the early development of Greece by acting as a channel of civilization and art, and the nations of Europe are indebted to them for their knowledge of that greatest of all inventions—the alphabet" (Driver's *Isaiah*). In the time of David a friendly alliance was entered into between the Hebrews and the Tyrians, who were long ruled over by their native kings (2 Sam. 5:11; 1 Kings 5:1; 2 Chr. 2:3).

Tyre consisted of two distinct parts—a rocky fortress on the mainland, called "Old Tyre," and the city, built on a small rocky island about half-a-mile distant from the shore. It was a place of great strength. It was besieged by Shalmaneser, who was assisted by the Phœnicians of the mainland for five years, and by Nebuchadnezzar (B.C. 586–573) for thirteen years, apparently without success. It afterwards fell under the power of Alexander the Great, after a siege of seven months, but continued to maintain much of its commercial importance till the Christian era. It is referred to in Matt. 11:21 and Acts 12:20. In A.D. 1291 it was taken by the Saracens, and has remained a desolate ruin ever since.

"The purple dye of Tyre had a worldwide celebrity on account of the durability of its beautiful tints, and its manufacture proved a source of abundant wealth to the inhabitants of that city."

Both Tyre and Sidon "were crowded with glass-shops, dyeing and weaving establishments; and among their cunning workmen not the least important class were those who were celebrated for the engraving of precious stones." (2 Chr. 2:7, 14.)

The wickedness and idolatry of this city are frequently denounced by the prophets, and its final destruction predicted (Isa. 23:1; Jer. 25:22; Ezek. 26:2–4; 27:2; 28:2; Amos 1:9, 10; Zech. 9:2–4). After passing through many vicissitudes, it is now only "a cluster of miserable huts, inhabited by about 3,500 impoverished Metawelies and Arab Christians, destitute alike of education, of arts, and of enterprise, carrying on with Egypt a small trade in tobacco from the neighbouring hills, and in lava millstones from the Hauran." The harbour is almost wholly filled up with the wreck of the ancient city, which also covers the ground for a distance of about 2 miles beyond the present town. The soil is almost a "mass of ruins" of building stones, shafts of pillars, and fragments of marble for many feet below the surface.

Here a church was founded soon after the death of Stephen, and Paul, on his return from his third missionary journey, spent a week in intercourse with the disciples there (Acts 21:4). Here the scene at Miletus was repeated on his leaving them. They all, with their wives and children, accompanied him to the sea-shore. The sea-voyage of the apostle terminated at Ptolemais, about 38 miles from Tyre. Thence he proceeded on foot to Cæsarea (Acts 21 : 5–8).

Tyropœ′on Valley (*i.e.*, " Valley of the Cheesemongers "), the name given by Josephus the historian to the valley or rugged ravine which in ancient times separated Mount Moriah from Mount Zion. This valley, now filled up with a vast accumulation of rubbish, and almost a plain, was spanned by bridges, the most noted of which was Zion Bridge, which was probably the ordinary means of communication between the royal palace on Zion and the temple. A fragment of the arch (*q.v.*) of this bridge (called "Robinson's Arch"), where it projects from the sanctuary wall, was discovered by Robinson in 1839. This arch was destroyed by the Romans when Jerusalem was taken.

The western wall of the temple area rose up from the bottom of this valley to the height of 84 feet, where it was on a level with the area, and above this, and as a continuance of it, the wall of Solomon's cloister rose to the height of about 50 feet, " so that this section of the wall would originally present to view a stupendous mass of masonry, scarcely to be surpassed by any mural masonry in the world."

U

U′cal, the name of a person to whom Agur's words are addressed (Prov. 30 : 1).

U′lai, the *Eulæus* of the Greeks; a river of Susiana. It was probably the eastern branch of the Choasper (*Kerkhan*), which divided into two branches some 20 miles above the city of Susa. Hence Daniel (8 : 2, 16) speaks of standing " between the banks of Ulai "—*i.e.*, between the two streams of the divided river.

Um′mah — *vicinity* — a town of Asher (Josh. 19 : 30).

Unc′tion (1 John 2 : 20, 27; R. V., "anointing"). Kings, prophets, and priests were anointed, in token of receiving divine grace. All believers are, in a secondary sense, what Christ was in a primary sense, " the Lord's anointed."

U′nicorn, described as an animal of great ferocity and strength (Num. 23 : 22; 24 : 8; Isa. 34 : 7), and untamable (Job 39 : 9). It was in reality a two-horned animal; but the exact reference of the word so rendered (*reêm*) is doubtful. Some have supposed it to be the buffalo; others, the white antelope, called by the Arabs *ri'm*. Most probably, however, the word denotes the *Bos primigenius* (" primitive ox "), which is now extinct all over the world. This was the *auerochs* of the Germans, and the *urus* described by Cæsar (*Gal. Bel.*, vi. 28) as inhabiting the Hercynian forest. The word thus rendered has been found in an Assyrian inscription written over the wild ox or bison, which some also suppose to be the animal intended (comp. Deut. 33 : 17; Ps. 22 : 21; 29 : 6; 92 : 10).

Un′ni—*afflicted.* (1.) A Levite whom David appointed to take part in bringing the ark up to Jerusalem from the house of Obed-edom by playing the psaltery on that occasion (1 Chr. 15 : 18, 19).

(2.) A Levite who returned with Zerubbabel from the Captivity (Neh. 12 : 9).

Uphar′sin—*and they divide*—one of the words written by the mysterious hand on the wall of Belshazzar's palace (Dan. 5 : 25). It is a pure Chaldean word. "Peres" is only a simple form of the same word.

U′phaz, probably another name for Ophir (Jer. 10 : 9). Some, however, regard it as the name of an Indian colony in Yemen, southern Arabia; others as a place on or near the river Hyphasis (now the *Ghana*), the south-eastern limit of the Punjaub.

Ur—*light,* or *the moon city*—a city " of the Chaldees," the birthplace of Haran (Gen. 11 : 28, 31), the largest city of Shinar or northern Chaldea, and the principal commercial centre of the country as well as the centre of political power. It stood

MODERN TYRE.

near the mouth of the Euphrates, on its western bank, and is represented by the mounds (of bricks cemented by bitumen) of *el-Mugheir—i.e.*, " the bitumined," or " the town of bitumen," now 150 miles from the sea and some 6 miles from the Euphrates, a little above the point where it receives the *Shat el-Hie*, an affluent from the Tigris. It was formerly a maritime city, as the waters of the Persian Gulf reached thus far inland. Ur was the port of Babylonia, whence trade was carried on

with the dwellers on the gulf, and with the distant countries of India, Ethiopia, and Egypt. It was abandoned about B.C. 500, but long continued, like Erech, to be a great sacred cemetery city, as is evident from the number of tombs found there. (See ABRAHAM.)

The oldest king of Ur known to us is Ur-Ba'u (servant of the goddess Ba'u), as Hommel reads the name, or Ur-Gur, as others read it. He lived some twenty-eight hundred years B.C., and took part in

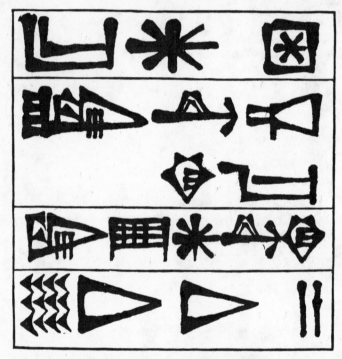

CUNEIFORM INSCRIPTION ON BRICKS FOUND AT UR.

building the famous temple of the moon-god Sin in Ur itself. The illustration here given represents his cuneiform inscription, written in the Sumerian language, and stamped upon every brick of the temple in Ur. It reads: "Ur-Ba'u, king of Ur, who built the temple of the moon-god."

"Ur was consecrated to the worship of Sin, the Babylonian moon-god. It shared this honour, however, with another city, and this city was Haran, or Harran. Harran was in Mesopotamia, and took its

name from the highroad which led through it from the east to the west. The name is Babylonian, and bears witness to its having been founded by a Babylonian king. The same witness is still more decisively borne by the worship paid in it to the Babylonian moon-god and by its ancient temple of Sin. Indeed, the temple of the moon-god at Harran was perhaps even more famous in the Assyrian and Babylonian world than the temple of the moon god at Ur.

"Between Ur and Harran there must, consequently, have been a close connection in early times, the record of which has not yet been recovered. It may be that Harran owed its foundation to a king of Ur; at any rate the two cities were bound together by the worship of the same deity—the closest and most enduring bond of union that existed in the ancient world. That Terah should have migrated from Ur to Harran, therefore, ceases to be extraordinary. If he left Ur at all, it was the most natural place to which to go. It was like passing from one court of a temple into another.

"Such a remarkable coincidence between the Biblical narrative and the evidence of archæological research cannot be the result of chance. The narrative must be historical; no writer of late date, even if he were a Babylonian, could have invented a story so exactly in accordance with what we now know to have been the truth. For a story of the kind to have been the invention of Palestinian tradition is equally impossible. To the unprejudiced mind there is no escape from the conclusion that the history of the migration of Terah from Ur to Harran is founded on fact" (*Sayce*).

Uri'ah—*the Lord is my light.* (1.) A Hittite, the husband of Bathsheba, whom David first seduced, and then after Uriah's death married. He was one of the band of David's "mighty men." The sad story of the cruel wrongs inflicted upon him by David and of his mournful death are simply told in the sacred record (2 Sam. 11:2-12:26). (See BATHSHEBA; DAVID.)

(2.) A priest of the house of Ahaz (Isa. 8:2).

(3.) The father of Meremoth, mentioned in Ezra 8:33.

U'riel—*God is my light.* (1.) A Levite of the family of Kohath (1 Chr. 6:24).

(2.) The chief of the Kohathites at the time when the ark was brought up to Jerusalem (1 Chr. 15:5, 11).

(3.) The father of Michaiah, one of Rehoboam's wives, and mother of Abijah (2 Chr. 13:2).

Uri'jah—*the Lord is my light.* (1.) A high priest in the time of Ahaz (2 Kings 16:10-16), at whose bidding he constructed an idolatrous altar like one the king had seen at Damascus, to be set up instead of the brazen altar.

(2.) One of the priests who stood at the right hand of Ezra's pulpit when he read and expounded the law (Neh. 8:4).

(3.) A prophet of Kirjath-jearim in the reign of Jehoiakim, king of Judah (Jer. 26:20-23). He fled into Egypt from the cruelty of the king, but having been brought back he was beheaded and his body "cast into the graves of the common people."

U'rim—*lights* (Vulg. "doctrina;" LXX. "revelation"). See THUMMIM.

U'sury, the sum paid for the use of money, hence interest; not, as in the modern sense, exorbitant interest. The Jews were forbidden to exact usury (Lev. 25:36, 37), only, however, in their dealings with each other (Deut. 23:19, 20). The violation of this law was viewed as a great crime (Ps. 15:5; Prov. 28:8; Jer. 15:10). After the Return, and later, this law was much neglected (Neh. 5:7, 10).

Uz—*fertile land.* (1.) The son of Aram, and grandson of Shem (Gen. 10:23; 1 Chr. 1:17).

(2.) One of the Horite "dukes" in the land of Edom (Gen. 36:28).

(3.) The eldest son of Nahor, Abraham's brother (Gen. 22:21, R.V.).

Uz, The land of, where Job lived (1:1; Jer. 25:20; Lam. 4:21), probably somewhere to the east or south-east of Palestine and north of Edom. It is mentioned in Scripture only in these three passages.

U'zal—*a wanderer*—a descendant of Joktan (Gen. 10:27; 1 Chr. 1:21), the founder apparently of one of the Arab tribes; the name also probably of the province they occupied and of their chief city.

Uz'za—*strength*—a garden in which Manasseh and Amon were buried (2 Kings 21:18, 26). It was probably near the king's palace in Jerusalem, or may have formed part of the palace grounds. Manasseh may probably have acquired it from some one of this name.

Uz'zah—*strength*—a son of Abinadab, in whose house the men of Kirjath-jearim placed the ark when it was brought back from the land of the Philistines (1 Sam. 7 : 1). He with his brother Ahio drove the cart on which the ark was placed when David sought to bring it up to Jerusalem. When the oxen stumbled, Uzzah, in direct violation of the divine law (Num. 4 : 15), put forth his hand to steady the ark, and was immediately smitten unto death. The place where this occurred was henceforth called Perez-uzzah (1 Chr. 13 : 11). David on this feared to proceed further, and placed the ark in the house of Obed-edom the Gittite (2 Sam. 6 : 2-11; 1 Chr. 13 : 6-13).

Uz'zen-she'rah, a town probably near Beth-horon. It derived its name from the daughter of Ephraim (1 Chr. 7 : 24).

Uz'zi—*the Lord is my strength.* (1.) The son of Bukki, and a descendant of Aaron (1 Chr. 6 : 5, 51 ; Ezra 7 : 4).

(2.) A grandson of Issachar (1 Chr. 7 : 2, 3).

(3.) A son of Bela, and grandson of Benjamin (1 Chr. 7 : 7).

(4.) A Benjamite, a chief in the tribe (1 Chr. 9 : 8).

(5.) A son of Bani. He had the oversight of the Levites after the return from captivity (Neh. 11 : 22).

(6.) The head of the house of Jedaiah, one of "the chief of the priests" (Neh. 12 : 19).

(7.) A priest who assisted in the dedication of the walls of Jerusalem (Neh. 12 : 42).

Uzzi'ah, a contracted form of **Azari'ah** —*the Lord is my strength.* (1.) One of Amaziah's sons, whom the people made king of Judah in his father's stead (2 Kings 14 : 21 ; 2 Chr. 26 : 1). His long reign of about fifty - two years was "the most prosperous excepting that of Jehoshaphat since the time of Solomon." He was a vigorous and able ruler, and "his name spread far abroad, even to the entering in of Egypt" (2 Chr. 26 : 8, 14). In the earlier part of his reign, under the influence of Zechariah, he was faithful to Jehovah, and "did that which was right in the sight of the Lord" (2 Kings 15 : 3 ; 2 Chr. 26 : 4, 5); but toward the close of his long life "his heart was lifted up to his destruction," and he wantonly invaded the priest's office (2 Chr. 26 : 16), and entering the sanctuary proceeded to offer incense on the golden altar. Azariah the high priest saw the tendency of such a daring act on the part of the king, and with a band of eighty priests he withstood him (2 Chr. 26 : 17), saying, "It appertaineth not to thee, Uzziah, to burn incense." Uzziah was suddenly struck with leprosy while in the act of offering incense (26 : 19-21), and he was driven from the temple and compelled to reside in "a several house" to the day of his death (2 Kings 15 : 5, 27 ; 2 Chr. 26 : 3). He was buried in a separate grave "in the field of the burial which belonged to the kings" (2 Kings 15 : 7 ; 2 Chr. 26 : 23). "That lonely grave in the royal necropolis would eloquently testify to coming generations that all earthly monarchy must bow before the inviolable order of the divine will, and that no interference could be tolerated with that unfolding of the purposes of God, which, in the fulness of time, would reveal the Christ, the true High Priest and King for evermore" (Dr. Green's *Kingdom of Israel, etc.*).

(2.) The father of Jehonathan, one of David's overseers (1 Chr. 27 : 25).

Uz'ziel—*strength of God.* (1.) One of the sons of Kohath, and uncle of Aaron (Ex. 6 : 18; Lev. 10 : 4).

(2.) A Simeonite captain (1 Chr. 4 : 39-43).

(3.) A son of Bela, and grandson of Benjamin (1 Chr. 7 : 7).

(4.) One of the sons of Heman (1 Chr. 25 : 4) ; called also Azareel (18).

(5.) A son of Jeduthan (2 Chr. 29 : 14).

(6.) The son of Harhaiah (Neh. 3 : 8).

FACSIMILE FROM CODEX VATICANUS (*reduced one-fourth of original*).
2 Thessalonians iii. 10–18, and Hebrews i.-ii. 1, 2.

ΠΟΛΥΜΕΡѠΣΚΑΙΠΟΛΥ
ΤΡΟΠΩΣΠΑΛΑΙΟΘΣΛΑ
ΛΗСΑСΤΟΙСΠΑΤΡΑСΙΝ
ΕΝΤΟΙСΠΡΟΦΗΤΑΙС·
ΕΠΕСΧΑΤΟΥΤѠΝΗΜΕ
ΡѠΝΤΟΥΤѠΝΕΛΑΛΗ
СΕΝΗΜΙΝΕΝΥΙѠϿΝΕ

Πολυμερῶς καὶ πολυ
τρόπως πάλαι ὁ Θ̄ς [θεὸς] λα
λήσας τοῖς πατράσιν
ἐν τοῖς προφήταις
ἐπ᾽ ἐσχάτου τῶν ἡμε
ρῶν τούτων ἐλάλη
σεν ἡμῖν ἐν υἱῷ, ὃν ἔ

FACSIMILE FROM CODEX VATICANUS (*exact size of original*).—Hebrews i. 1.

V

Vag'abond, from Lat. *vagabundus,* "a wanderer," "a fugitive;" not used opprobriously (Gen. 4:12, R.V., "wanderer;" Ps. 109:10; Acts 19:13, R.V., "strolling").

Vajez'atha—*purity; worthy of honour* —one of Heman's sons, whom the Jews slew in the palace of Shushan (Esther 9:9).

Val'ley. (1.) Heb. *bik'ah,* a "cleft" of the mountains (Deut. 8:7; 11:11; Ps. 104:8; Isa. 41:18); also a low plain bounded by mountains, as the plain of Lebanon at the foot of Hermon around the sources of the Jordan (Josh. 11:17; 12:7), and the valley of Megiddo (2 Chr. 35:22).

(2.) *'Eměk,* "deep;" "a long, low plain" (Job 39:10, 21; Ps. 65:13; Cant. 2:1), such as the plain of Esdraelon; the "valley of giants" (Josh. 15:8), usually translated "valley of Rephaim" (2 Sam. 5:18); of Elah (1 Sam. 17:2), of Berachah (2 Chr. 20:26); the king's "dale" (Gen. 14:17); of Jehoshaphat (Joel 3:2, 12), of Achor (Josh. 7:24; Isa. 65:10), Succoth (Ps. 60:6), Ajalon (Josh. 10:12), Jezreel (Hos. 1:5).

(3.) *Gê,* "a bursting," a "flowing together," a narrow glen or ravine, such as the valley of the children of Hinnom (2 Kings 23:10); of Eshcol (Deut. 1:24); of Sorek (Judg. 16:4), etc.

The "valley of vision" (Isa. 22:1) is usually regarded as denoting Jerusalem, which "may be so called," says Barnes (*Com. on Isa.*), "either (1) because there were several valleys *within* the city and adjacent to it, as the vale between Mount Zion and Moriah, the vale between Mount Moriah and Mount Ophel, between these and Mount Bezetha, and the valley of Jehoshaphat, the valley of the brook Kidron, etc., without the walls of the city; or (2) more probably it was called the *valley* in reference to its being *compassed with hills* rising to a considerable elevation above the city" (Ps. 125:2; comp. also Jer. 21:13, where Jerusalem is called a "valley").

(4.) Heb. *nahal,* a wâdy or water-course (Gen. 26:19; Cant. 6:11).

Vash'ti—*beautiful*—the queen of Ahasuerus, who was deposed from her royal dignity because she refused to obey the king when he desired her to appear in the banqueting hall of Shushan the palace (Esther 1:10–12). (See ESTHER.)

Vatica'nus, Codex, is said to be the oldest extant vellum manuscript. It and the *Codex Sinaiticus* are the two oldest uncial manuscripts. They were probably written in the fourth century. The Vaticanus was placed in the Vatican Library at Rome by Pope Nicolas V. in 1448, its previous history being unknown. It originally consisted in all probability of a complete copy of the Septuagint and of the New Testament. It is now imperfect, and consists of 759 thin, delicate leaves, of which the New Testament fills 142. Like the Sinaiticus, it is of the greatest value to Biblical scholars in aiding in the formation of a correct text of the New Testament. It is referred to by critics as *Codex B.*

Veil, vail. (1.) Heb. *mitpahath* (Ruth 3:15; marg., "sheet" or "apron;" R.V., "mantle"). In Isa. 3:22 this word is plural, rendered "wimples;" R.V., "shawls" —*i.e.,* wraps.

(2.) *Maṣṣêkâh* (Isa. 25:7; in Isa. 28:20 rendered "covering"). The word denotes something spread out and covering or concealing something else (comp. 2 Cor. 3:13–15).

(3.) *Maṣvěh* (Ex. 34:33, 35), the veil on the face of Moses. This verse should be read, "And *when* Moses had done speaking with them, he put a veil on his face," as in the Revised Version. When Moses spoke to them he was without the veil; only when he ceased speaking he put on the veil (comp. 2 Cor. 3:13, etc.).

(4.) *Pârôheth* (Ex. 26:31–35), the veil of the tabernacle and the temple, which hung between the holy place and the most holy (2 Chr. 3:14). In the temple a partition wall separated these two places. In it were two folding-doors, which are supposed to have been always open, the en-

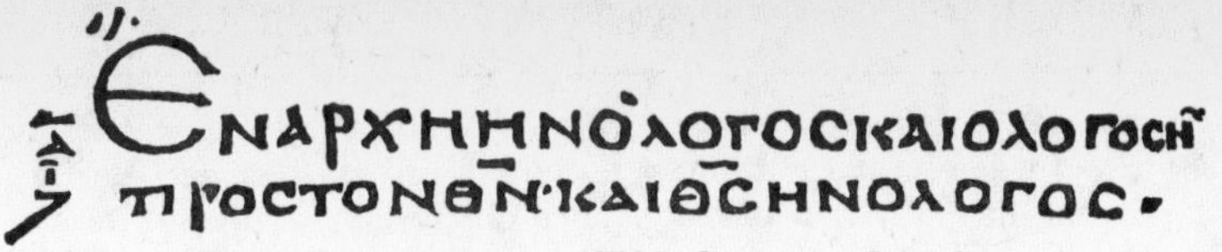

ΕΝΑΡΧΗΗΝΟΛΟΓΟCΚΑΙΟΛΟΓΟϹΗ̄
ΠΡΟCΤΟΝΘΝ̄·ΚΑΙΘϹΗΝΟΛΟΓΟϹ·

Codex ALEXANDRINUS: Fifth Century.—John i. 1.

Εν αρχη ην ο λογος και ο λογος η̄ | προς τον ϑ[εο]ν· και ϑ[εο]ς ην ο λογος.

Η ΑΓΑΠΗ
ΟΥΔΕΠΟΤΕΕΚΠΙΠΤΕΙ

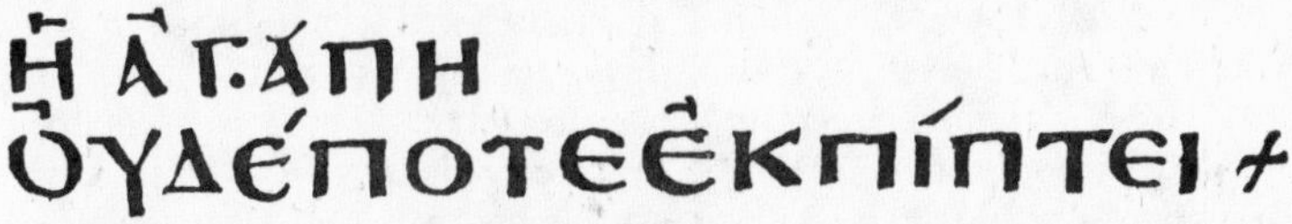

Codex CLAROMONTANUS: Sixth Century; Greek Text.—1 Cor. xiii. 8.

ἡ ἀγάπη | οὐδέποτε ἐκπίπτει

ΤΗΝΕΚΚΛΗϹΙΛΝ
ΤΟΥΙϹῩ

Codex LAUDIANUS: Sixth Century; Greek Text.—Acts xx. 28.

την εκκλησιαν | του κ[υριο]υ

ΤΟΥΛΟΓΟΥΟΥ

Codex PURPUREUS: Sixth Century.—John xv. 20.

του λογου ου

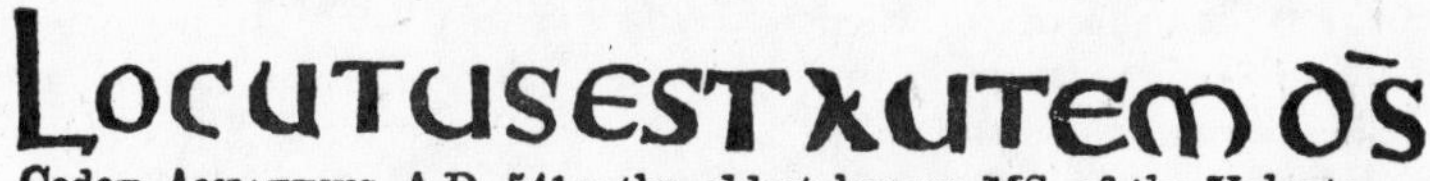

Locutusestxutem d̄s

Codex AMIATINUS, A.D. 541: the oldest known MS. of the Vulgate.—
Acts vii. 6. Locutus est autem d[eu]s

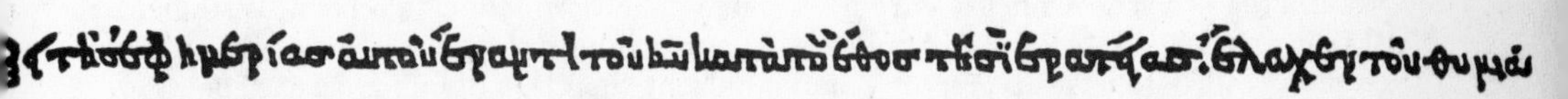

Codex COLBERTINUS: Eleventh Century; the "Queen of the Cursives."—Luke i. 8, 9.

ξει τῆσ ἐφημερίασ αὐτοῦ ἔναντι τοῦ κ[υρίο]υ κατὰ τὸ ἔϑοσ τῆσ ἱερατείασ. ἔλαχεν τοῦ ϑυμιᾶ

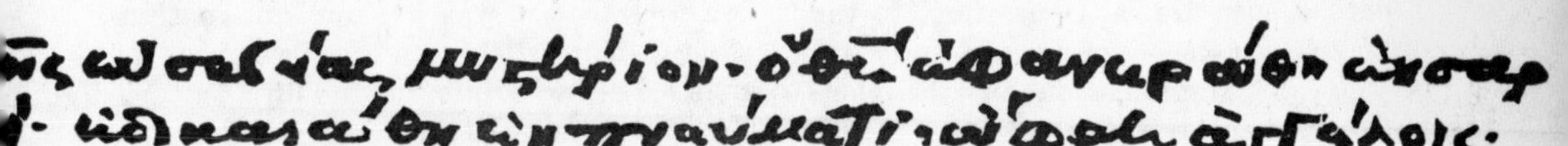

Codex LEICESTRENSIS: Fourteenth Century.—1 Tim. iii. 16.

ῆς εὐσεβε(?)ίας μυστήριον· ὁ ϑ[εὸ]ς ἐφανερώϑη ἐν σαρ | κί· ἐδικαιώϑη ἐν πνεύματι· ὤφϑη ἀγγέλοις·

SPECIMENS OF VARIOUS VERSIONS. *(See also Articles "Sinaiticus" and "Vaticanus.")*

trance being concealed by the veil which the high priest lifted when he entered into the sanctuary on the day of Atonement. This veil was rent when Christ died on the cross (Matt. 27 : 51; Mark 15 : 38; Luke 23 : 45).

(5.) *Tzâ'iph* (Gen. 24 : 65). Rebekah "took a vail and covered herself." (See also 38 : 14, 19.) Hebrew women generally appeared in public without veils (12 : 14; 24 : 16; 29 : 10; 1 Sam. 1 : 12).

(6.) *Radhîdh* (Cant. 5 : 7, R. V. "mantle;" Isa. 3 : 23). The word probably denotes some kind of cloak or wrapper.

(7.) *Mâsâk*, the veil which hung before the entrance to the holy place (Ex. 26 : 36, 37).

Ver'sion, a translation of the holy Scriptures. This word is not found in the Bible, nevertheless, as frequent references are made in this work to various ancient as well as modern versions, it is fitting that some brief account should be given of the most important of these. These versions are important helps to the right interpretation of the Word. (See SAMARITAN PENTATEUCH.)

1. The *Targums.* After the return from the Captivity, the Jews, no longer familiar with the old Hebrew, required that their Scriptures should be translated for them into the Chaldaic or Aramaic language and interpreted. These translations and paraphrases were at first oral, but they were afterwards reduced to writing, and thus targums — *i.e.,* "versions" or "translations"—have come down to us. The chief of these are—(1.) The Onkelos Targum— *i.e.,* the targum of Akelas = Aquila, a targum so called to give it greater popularity by comparing it with the Greek translation of Aquila mentioned below. This targum originated about the second century after Christ. (2.) The targum of Jonathan ben Uzziel comes next to that of Onkelos in respect of age and value. It is more a paraphrase on the Prophets, however, than a translation. Both of these targums issued from the Jewish school which then flourished at Babylon.

2. The *Greek Versions.* (1.) The oldest of these is the *Septuagint,* usually quoted as the LXX. The origin of this the most important of all the versions is involved in much obscurity. It derives its name from the popular notion that seventy-two translators were employed on it by the direction of Ptolemy Philadelphus, king of Egypt, and that it was accomplished in seventy-two days, for the use of the Jews residing in that country. There is no historical warrant for this notion. It is, however, an established fact that this version was made at Alexandria; that it was begun about 280 B.C., and finished about 200 or 150 B.C.; that it was the work of a number of translators who differed greatly both in their knowledge of Hebrew and of Greek; and that from the earliest times it has borne the name of "The Septuagint"— *i.e.,* The Seventy.

"This version, with all its defects, must be of the greatest interest—(*a*) as preserving evidence for the text far more ancient than the oldest Hebrew manuscripts; (*b*) as the means by which the Greek language was wedded to Hebrew thought; (*c*) as the source of the great majority of quotations from the Old Testament by writers of the New Testament.

(2.) The New Testament manuscripts fall into two divisions—Uncials, written in Greek capitals, with no distinction at all between the different words, and very little even between the different lines; and Cursives, in small Greek letters, and with divisions of words and lines. The change between the two kinds of Greek writing took place about the tenth century. Only five manuscripts of the New Testament approaching to completeness are more ancient than this dividing date. The *first,* numbered A, is the Alexandrian manuscript. Though brought to this country by Cyril Lucar, patriarch of Constantinople, as a present to Charles I., it is believed that it was written, not in that capital, but in Alexandria; whence its title. It is now dated in the fifth century A.D. The *second,* known as B, is the Vatican manuscript. (See VATICANUS.) The *third,* C, or the Ephraem manuscript, was so called because it was written over the writings of Ephraem, a Syrian theo-

logical author, a practice very common in the days when writing materials were scarce and dear. It is believed that it belongs to the fifth century, and perhaps a slightly earlier period of it than the manuscript A. The *fourth*, D, or the manuscript of Beza, was so called because it belonged to the reformer Beza, who found it in the monastery of St. Irenæus at Lyons in 1562 A.D. It is imperfect, and is dated in the sixth century. The *fifth* (called Aleph) is the Sinaitic manuscript. (See SINAITICUS.)

3. The *Syriac Versions*. (See SYRIAC.)

4. The *Latin Versions*. A Latin version of the Scriptures, called the "Old Latin," which originated in North Africa, was in common use in the time of Tertullian (A.D. 150). Of this there appear to have been various copies or recensions made. That made in Italy, and called the *Itala*, was reckoned the most accurate. This translation of the Old Testament seems to have been made not from the original Hebrew but from the LXX.

This version became greatly corrupted by repeated transcription, and to remedy the evil Jerome (A.D. 329–420) was requested by Damasus, the bishop of Rome, to undertake a complete revision of it. It met with opposition at first, but was at length, in the seventh century, recognized as the "Vulgate" version. It appeared in a printed form about A.D. 1455, the first book that ever issued from the press. The Council of Trent (1546) declared it "authentic." It subsequently underwent various revisions, but that which was executed (1592) under the sanction of Pope Clement VIII. was adopted as the basis of all subsequent editions. It is regarded as the sacred original in the Roman Catholic Church. All modern European versions have been more or less influenced by the Vulgate. This version reads *ipsa* instead of *ipse* in Gen. 3:15, "*She* shall bruise thy head."

5. There are several other ancient versions which are of importance for Biblical critics, but which we need not mention particularly, such as the *Ethiopic*, in the fourth century, from the LXX.; two *Egyptian* versions, about the fourth century—the Memphitic, circulated in Lower Egypt, and the Thebaic, designed for Upper Egypt, both from the Greek; the *Gothic*, written in the German language, but with the Greek alphabet, by Ulphilas (died A.D. 388), of which only fragments of the Old Testament remain; the *Armenian*, about A.D. 400; and the *Slavonic*, in the ninth century, for ancient Moravia. Other ancient versions, as the Arabic, the Persian, and the Anglo-Saxon, may be mentioned.

6. The history of the *English* versions begins properly with Wyckliffe. Portions, however, of the Scriptures were rendered into Saxon (as the Gospel according to John, by Bede, A.D. 735), and also into English (by Orme, called the "Ormulum," a portion of the Gospels and of the Acts in the form of a metrical paraphrase, toward the close of the seventh century), long before Wyckliffe; but it is to him that the honour belongs of having first rendered the whole Bible into English (A.D. 1380). This version was made from the Vulgate, and renders Gen. 3:15 after that Version, "*She* shall trede thy head."

This was followed by Tyndale's translation (1525-1531); Miles Coverdale's (1535-1553); Thomas Matthew's (1537)—really, however, the work of John Rogers, the first martyr under the reign of Queen Mary. This was properly the first Authorized Version, Henry VIII. having ordered a copy of it to be got for every church. This took place in less than a year after Tyndale was martyred for the crime of translating the Scriptures. In 1539 Richard Taverner published a revised edition of Matthew's Bible. The Great Bible, so called from its great size, called also Cranmer's Bible, was published in 1539 and 1568. In the strict sense, the "Great Bible" is "the only authorized version; for the Bishops' Bible and the present Bible [the A.V.] never had the formal sanction of royal authority." Next in order was the Geneva version (1557-1560); the Bishops' Bible (1568); the Rheims and Douai versions, under Roman Catholic auspices (1582, 1609); the Authorized Version (1611); and the Revised Version of

And he sayde: Lorde, I beleue, and worshipped hym. Jesus sayde: I am come vnto iudgemente into this worlde: that they whiche se not, myght se, and they whiche se, myghte be made blynde. And some of the Phariseis whiche were with hym, hearde these wordes, and sayd vnto hym: are we blind also? Jesus sayde vnto them: if ye were blynde ye shoulde haue no synne. But now ye saye, we se, therfore your synne remayneth.

Iohn xb. d.

☞The Notes.

a. Vve must vnderstande that there be .ij. kindes of sinners. They that acknowledge their sinnes, and repente vnfaynedlye, are hearde and forgeuen of God. Math.ix.xi. Ezech.xviy. But they that do of an insidelitye continue in their sinnefull abbominable lyuinge, and dispayre of the mercy of God, shall neuer be hearde .i.Io.v.

The x.Chapter.

❧ *Christe is the true shepherde, and the dore of the shepe. Some saye: Christe hath the deuell, and is madde. Some saye: he speaketh not the wordes of one that hath the deuell, because he telleth the trueth, the Iewes take vp stones to caste at hym, call his preachynge blasphemy, and go aboute to take him.*

✚ The Gospell on the Tewesdaye after Whitsondaye.

Erely, verely I saye vnto you: he that entreth not in by the dore into the shepefolde, but clymmeth vp some other waye, the same is a theefe and a robber. But he that goeth in by the dore, is the shepeherde of the shepe: to him the porter the New Testament in 1880 and of the Old Testament in 1884.

Vil'lages (Judg. 5 : 7, 11). The Hebrew word thus rendered (*perâzon*) means habitations in the open country, unwalled villages (Deut. 3 : 5; 1 Sam. 6 : 18). Others, however, following the LXX. and the Vulgate versions, render the word "rulers."

Vine, one of the most important products of Palestine. The first mention of it is in the history of Noah (Gen. 9 : 20). It is afterwards frequently noticed both in the Old and New Testaments, and in the ruins of terraced vineyards there are evidences that it was extensively cultivated by the Jews. It was cultivated in Palestine before the Israelites took possession of it. The men sent out by Moses brought with them from the Valley of Eshcol a cluster of grapes so large that "they bare it between two upon a staff" (Num. 13 : 23). The vineyards of En-gedi (Cant. 1 : 14), Heshbon, Sibmah, Jazer, Elealeh (Isa. 16 : 8–10; Jer. 48 : 32, 34), and Helbon (Ezek. 27 : 18), as well as of Eshcol, were celebrated.

The Church is compared to a vine (Ps. 80 : 8), and Christ says of himself, "I am the vine" (John 15 : 1). In one of his parables also (Matt. 21 : 33) our Lord compares his Church to a vineyard which "a certain householder planted, and hedged round about," etc.).

Hos. 10 : 1 is rendered in the Revised Version, "Israel is a luxuriant vine, which putteth forth his fruit," instead of "Israel is an empty vine, he bringeth forth fruit unto himself," of the Authorized Version.

Vine of Sodom, referred to only in Deut. 32 : 32. Among the many conjectures as to this tree, the most probable is that it is the *'ösher* of the Arabs, which abounds in the region of the Dead Sea. Its fruit are the so-called "apples of Sodom," which, though beautiful to the eye, are exceedingly bitter to the taste. (See EN-GEDI.) The people of Israel are referred to here by Moses as being utterly corrupt, bringing forth only bitter fruit.

Vin'egar—Heb. *hõmetz*, Gr. *oxos*, Fr. *vin aigre; i.e.,* "sour wine." The Hebrew

word is rendered vinegar in Ps. 69 : 21, a prophecy fulfilled in the history of the crucifixion (Matt. 27 : 34). This was the common sour wine (*posca*) daily made use of by the Roman soldiers. They gave it to Christ, not in derision, but from compassion, to assuage his thirst. Prov. 10 : 26 shows that there was also a stronger vinegar, which was not fit for drinking. The comparison, "vinegar upon nitre," probably means "vinegar upon soda" (as in the marg. of the R.V.), which then effervesces.

Vi'ol—Heb. *nebel* (Isa. 5 : 12, R.V., "lute;" 14 : 11)—a musical instrument, usually rendered "psaltery" (*q.v.*).

Vi'per. In Job 20 : 16, Isa. 30 : 6; 59 : 5, the Heb. word *eph'eh* is thus rendered. The Hebrew word, however, probably denotes a species of poisonous serpents known by the Arabic name of *'el ephah.* Tristram has identified it with the sand viper, a species of small size common in sandy regions, and frequently found under stones by the shores of the Dead Sea. It is rapid in its movements, and highly poisonous. In the New Testament *echidne* is used (Matt. 3 : 7; 12 : 34; 23 : 33) for any poisonous snake. The viper mentioned in Acts 28 : 3 was probably the *vipera aspis,* or the Mediterranean viper. (See ADDER.)

Vir'gin. In a prophecy concerning our Lord, Isaiah (7 : 14) says, "A virgin [R.V. marg., 'the virgin'] shall conceive, and bear a son" (comp. Luke 1 : 31-35).

The people of the land of Zidon are thus referred to by Isaiah (23 : 12), "O thou oppressed virgin, daughter of Zidon ;" and of the people of Israel, Jeremiah (18 : 13) says, "The virgin of Israel hath done a very horrible thing."

Vi'sion (Luke 1 : 22), a vivid apparition, not a dream (comp. Luke 24 : 23; Acts 26 : 19; 2 Cor. 12 : 1).

Vows, voluntary promises which, when once made, were to be kept if the thing vowed was right. They were made under a great variety of circumstances (Gen. 28 : 18–22; Lev. 7 : 16; Num. 30 : 2-13; Deut. 23 : 18; Judg. 11 : 30, 39; 1 Sam. 1 : 11; Jonah 1 : 16; Acts 18 : 18; 21 : 23).

Vul'ture. (1.) Heb. *dâ'ah* (Lev. 11 : 14). In the parallel passage (Deut. 14 : 13) the

Hebrew word used is *râ'ah*, rendered "glede;" LXX., "gups;" Vulg., "milvus." A species of ravenous bird, distinguished for its rapid flight. "When used without the epithet 'red,' the name is commonly confined to the black kite. The habits of the bird bear out the allusion in Isa. 34:15, for it is, excepting during the winter three months, so numerous everywhere in Palestine as to be almost gregarious." (See EAGLE.)

(2.) In Job 28:7 the Heb. *'ayyâh* is thus rendered. The word denotes a clamorous and a keen-sighted bird of prey. In Lev. 11:14 and Deut. 14:13 it is rendered "kite" (*q.v.*).

W

Wa'fers, thin cakes (Ex. 16:31; 29:2, 23; Lev. 2:4; 7:12; 8:26; Num. 6:15, 19) used in various offerings.

Wa'ges. Rate of (mentioned only in Matt. 20:2); to be punctually paid (Lev. 19:13; Deut. 24:14, 15); judgments threatened against the withholding of (Jer. 22:13; Mal. 3:5; comp. James 5:4); paid in money (Matt. 20:1-14); to Jacob in kind (Gen. 29:15, 20; 30:28; 31:7, 8, 41).

Wag'gon—Heb. *'âghâlâh;* so rendered in Gen. 45:19, 21, 27; 46:5; Num. 7:3, 7, 8, but elsewhere rendered "cart" (1 Sam. 6:7, etc.). This vehicle was used for peaceful purposes. In Ezek. 23:24, however, it is the rendering of a different Hebrew word, and denotes a war-chariot.

Wail'ing-place, Jews', a section of the western wall of the temple area, where the Jews assemble every Friday afternoon to bewail their desolate condition (Ps. 79:1, 4, 5). The stones in this part of the wall are of great size, and were placed, as is generally believed, in the position in which they are now found in the time of Solomon. "The congregation at the wailing-place is one of the most solemn gatherings left to the Jewish Church, and as the writer gazed at the motley concourse he experienced a feeling of sorrow that the remnants of the chosen race should be heartlessly thrust outside the sacred enclosure of their fathers' holy temple by men of an alien race and an alien creed. Many of the elders, seated on the ground, with their backs against the wall, on the west side of the area, and with their faces turned toward the eternal house, read out of their well-thumbed Hebrew books passages from the prophetic writings, such as Isa. 64:9-12" (King's *Recent Discoveries, etc.*). The wailing-place of the Jews, viewed in its past spiritual and historic relations, is indeed "the saddest nook in this vale of tears." (See LAMENTATIONS, BOOK OF.)

Wall. Cities were surrounded by walls, as distinguished from "unwalled villages" (Ezek. 38:11; Lev. 25:29-34). They were made thick and strong (Num. 13:28; Deut. 3:5). Among the Jews walls were built of stone, some of those in the temple being of great size (1 Kings 6:7; 7:9-12; 20:30; Mark 13:1, 2). The term is used metaphorically of security and safety (Isa. 26:1; 60:18; Rev. 21:12-20). (See FENCE.)

Wan'dering of the Israelites in the wilderness in consequence of their rebellious fears to enter the Promised Land (Num. 14:26-35). They wandered for forty years before they were permitted to cross the Jordan (Josh. 4:19; 5:6).

The record of these wanderings is given in Num. 33:1-49. Many of the stations at which they camped cannot now be identified.

Questions of an intricate nature have been discussed regarding the "Wanderings," but it is enough for us to take the sacred narrative as it stands, and rest assured that "He led them forth by a right way" (Ps. 107:1-7, 33-35). (See WILDERNESS.)

War. The Israelites had to take possession of the Promised Land by conquest. They had to engage in a long and bloody war before the Canaanitish tribes were finally subdued. Except in the case of Jericho and Ai, the war did not become aggressive till after the death of Joshua. Till then the attack was always first made by the Canaanites. Now the measure of the iniquity of the Canaanites was full, and Israel was employed by God to sweep them away from off the face of the earth. In entering on this new stage of the war, the tribe of Judah, according to divine direction, took the lead.

In the days of Saul and David the people of Israel engaged in many wars with the nations around, and after the division of the kingdom into two they often warred with each other. They had to defend themselves also against the inroads of the Egyptians, the Assyrians, and the Babylonians.

JEWS' WAILING-PLACE.

The whole history of Israel from first to last presents but few periods of peace.

The Christian life is represented as a warfare, and the Christian graces are also represented under the figure of pieces of armour (Eph. 6:11-17; 1 Thess. 5:8; 2 Tim. 2:3, 4). The final blessedness of believers is attained as the fruit of victory (Rev. 3:21).

Wars of the Lord, The Book of the (Num. 21:14, 15), some unknown book so called (comp. Gen. 14:14-16; Ex. 17:8-16; Num. 14:40-45; 21:1-3, 21-25, 33-35; 31. The wars here recorded might be thus designated).

Ward, a prison (Gen. 40:3, 4); a watch-station (Isa. 21:8); a guard (Neh. 13:30).

Wash'ing (Mark 7:1-9). The Jews, like other Orientals, used their fingers when taking food, and therefore washed their hands before doing so, for the sake of cleanliness. Here the reference is to the ablutions prescribed by tradition, according to which "the disciples ought to have gone down to the side of the lake, washed their hands thoroughly, 'rubbing the fist of one hand in the hollow of the other, then placed the ten finger-tips together, holding the hands up, so that any surplus water might flow down to the elbow, and thence to the ground.'" To neglect to do this had come to be regarded as a great sin—a sin equal to the breach of any of the ten command-

WASHING THE HANDS.

ments. Moses had commanded washings oft, but always for some definite cause; but the Jews multiplied the legal observance till they formed a large body of precepts. To such precepts about ceremonial washing Mark here refers. (See ABLUTION.)

Watches, the periods into which the time between sunset and sunrise was divided. They are so called because watchmen relieved each other at each of these periods. There are frequent references in Scripture to the duties of watchmen who were appointed to give notice of the approach of an enemy (2 Sam. 18:24-27; 2 Kings 9:17-20; Isa. 21:5-9). They were sometimes placed for this purpose on watch-towers (2 Kings 17:9; 18:8). Ministers or teachers are also spoken of under this title (Jer. 6:17; Ezek. 33:2-9; Heb. 13:17).

The watches of the night were originally three in number—(1) "the beginning of the watches" (Lam. 2:19); (2) "the middle watch" (Judg. 7:19); and (3) "the morning watch" (Ex. 14:24; 1 Sam. 11:11), which extended from two o'clock to sunrise. But in the New Testament we read of four watches, a division probably introduced by the Romans (Matt. 14:25; Mark 6:48; Luke 12:38). (See DAY.)

Watch'ings (2 Cor. 6:5), lit. "sleeplessnesses," the result of "manual labour, teaching, travelling, meditating, praying, cares, and the like" (Meyer's *Com.*).

Wa'ter of jeal'ousy, a phrase employed (not, however, in Scripture) to denote the water used in the solemn ordeal prescribed by the law of Moses (Num. 5:11-31) in cases of "jealousy."

Water of purifica'tion, used in cases of ceremonial cleansings at the consecration of the Levites (Num. 8:7). It signified, figuratively, that purifying of the heart which must characterize the servants of God.

Water of separa'tion, used along with the ashes of a red heifer for the ceremonial cleansing of persons defiled by contact with a dead body (Num. 19).

Waterspouts (Ps. 42:7; marg. R.V., "cataracts"). If we regard this psalm as descriptive of David's feelings when banished from Jerusalem by the revolt of Absalom, this word may denote "waterfalls," inasmuch as Mahanaim, where he abode, was near the Jabbok, and the region abounded with rapids and falls.

Wave offerings, parts of peace-offerings were so called, because they were waved by the priests (Ex. 29:24, 26, 27; Lev. 7:20-34; 8:27; 9:21; 10:14, 15, etc.), in token of a solemn special presentation to God. They then became the property of the priests. The first-fruits—a sheaf of barley—offered at the feast of Pentecost (Lev. 23:17-20), and wheat-bread—the first-fruits of the second harvest—offered at the Passover (10-14), were wave-offerings.

Wax. Made by melting the combs of bees. Mentioned (Ps. 22:14; 68:2; 97:5; Micah 1:4) in illustration.

Wean. Among the Hebrews children (whom it was customary for the mothers to nurse—Ex. 2:7–9; 1 Sam. 1:23; Cant. 8:1) were not generally weaned till they were three or four years old.

Wea'sel (Heb. *hôledh*), enumerated among unclean animals (Lev. 11:29). Some think that this Hebrew word rather denotes the mole (*Spalax typhlus*) common in Palestine. There is no sufficient reason, however, to depart from the usual translation. The weasel tribe are common also in Palestine.

Weav'ing, weavers. Weaving was an art practised in very early times (Ex. 35:35). The Egyptians were specially skilled in it (Isa. 19:9; Ezek. 27:7), and some have regarded them as its inventors.

In the wilderness, the Hebrews practised it (Ex. 26:1, 7; 28:4, 39; Lev. 13:47). It is referred to in subsequent times as specially the women's work (2 Kings 23:7; Prov. 31:13, 24).

No mention of the loom is found in Scripture, but we read of the "shuttle" (Job 7:6), "the pin" of the beam (Judg. 16:14), "the web" (13,14), and "the beam" (1 Sam. 17:7; 2 Sam. 21:19). The rendering, "with pining sickness," in Isa. 38:12 (A.V.) should be, as in the Revised Version, "from the loom," or, as in the margin, "from the thrum." We read also of the "warp" and "woof" (Lev. 13:48, 49, 51–53, 58, 59), but the Revised Version margin has, instead of "warp," "woollen or knitted stuff."

Week. From the beginning, time was divided into weeks, each consisting of six days of working and one of rest (Gen. 2:2, 3; 7:10; 8:10, 12; 29:28). The references to this division of days becomes afterwards more frequent (Ex. 34:22; Lev. 12:5; Num. 28:26; Deut. 16:16; 2 Chr. 8:13; Jer. 5:24; Dan. 9:24–27; 10:2, 3). It has been found to exist among almost all nations.

Weeks, Feast of. See PENTECOST.

Weights. Reduced to English troy-weight, the Hebrew weights were:—

(1.) The *gerah* (Lev. 27:25; Num. 3:47), a Hebrew word, meaning a *grain* or *kernel*, and hence a small weight. It was the twentieth part of a shekel, and equal to 12 grains.

(2.) *Bekah* (Ex. 38:26), meaning "a half" —*i.e.*, "half a shekel," equal to 5 pennyweight.

(3.) *Shekel*, "a weight," only in the Old Testament, and frequently in its original form (Gen. 23:15, 16; Ex. 21:32; 30:13, 15; 38:24–29, etc.). It was equal to 10 pennyweight.

(4.) *Ma'neh*, "a part" or "portion" (Ezek. 45:12), equal to 60 shekels—*i.e.*, to 2 lbs. 6 oz.

(5.) *Talent of silver* (2 Kings 5:22), equal to 3,000 shekels—*i.e.*, 125 lbs.

(6.) *Talent of gold* (Ex. 25:39), double the preceding—*i.e.*, 250 lbs.

Well (Heb. *beer*), to be distinguished from a fountain (Heb. *'ain*). A "beer" was a deep shaft, bored far under the rocky surface by the art of man, which contained water which percolated through the strata in its sides. Such wells were those of Jacob and Beersheba, etc. (see Gen. 21:19, 25, 30, 31; 24:11; 26:15, 18–25, 32, etc.). In the Pentateuch this word *beer*, so rendered, occurs twenty-five times.

West'ward—*sea-ward*—*i.e.*, toward the Mediterranean (Deut. 3:27).

Whale. The Hebrew word *tan* (plural, *tannin*) is so rendered in Job 7:12 (A.V.; but R.V., "sea-monsters"). It is rendered by "dragons" in Deut. 32:33; Ps. 91:13; Jer. 51:34; Ps. 74:13 (marg., "whales;" and marg. of R.V., "sea-monsters"); Isa. 27:1; and "serpent" in Ex. 7:9 (R.V. marg., "any large reptile," and so in ver. 10, 12). The words of Job (7:12), uttered in bitter irony, where he asks, "Am I a sea or a whale?" simply mean, "Have I a wild, untamable nature, like the waves of the sea, which must be confined and held within bounds, that they cannot pass?" "The serpent of the sea—which was but the wild, stormy sea itself—wound itself around the land, and threatened to swallow it up......Job inquires if he must be watched and plagued like this monster, lest he throw the world into disorder" (Davidson's *Job*).

The whale tribe are included under the

general Hebrew name *tannin* (Gen. 1:21; Lam. 4:3). "Even the sea-monsters [*tanninim*] draw out the breast." The whale brings forth its young alive, and suckles them.

It is to be noticed of the story of Jonah's being "three days and three nights in the whale's belly," as recorded in Matt. 12:40, that here the Gr. *kētos* means properly any kind of sea-monster of the shark or the whale tribe, and that in the book of Jonah (1:17) it is only said that "a great fish" was prepared to swallow Jonah. This fish may have been, therefore, some great shark. The white shark is known to frequent the Mediterranean Sea, and is sometimes found 30 feet in length.

Wheat, one of the earliest cultivated grains. It bore the Hebrew name *ḥiṭṭâh*, and was extensively cultivated in Palestine. There are various species of wheat. That which Pharaoh saw in his dream was the *Triticum compositum*, which bears several ears upon one stalk (Gen. 41:5). The "fat of the kidneys of wheat" (Deut. 32:14), and the "finest of the wheat" (Ps. 81:16; 147:14), denote the best of the kind. It was exported from Palestine in great quantities (1 Kings 5:11; Ezek. 27:17; Acts 12:20).

Parched grains of wheat were used for food in Palestine (Ruth 2:14; 1 Sam. 17:17; 2 Sam. 17:28). The disciples, under the sanction of the Mosaic law (Deut. 23:25), plucked ears of corn, and rubbing them in their hands, ate the grain unroasted (Matt. 12:1; Mark 2:23; Luke 6:1). Before any of the wheat-harvest, however, could be eaten, the first-fruits had to be presented before the Lord (Lev. 23:14).

Wheel (Heb. *galgal;* rendered "wheel" in Ps. 83:13, and "a rolling thing" in Isa. 17:13; R.V. in both, "whirling dust"). This word has been supposed to mean the wild artichoke, which assumes the form of a globe, and in autumn breaks away from its roots, and is rolled about by the wind in some places in great numbers.

White, a symbol of purity (2 Chr. 5:12; Ps. 51:7; Isa. 1:18; Rev. 3:18; 7:14). Our Lord, at his transfiguration, appeared in raiment "white as the light" (Matt. 17:2, etc.).

Wid'ows to be treated with kindness (Ex. 22:22; Deut. 14:29; 16:11, 14; 24:17, 19-21; 26:12; 27:19, etc.). In the New Testament the same tender regard for them is inculcated (Acts 6:1-6; 1 Tim. 5:3-16) and exhibited.

Wife. The ordinance of marriage was sanctioned in Paradise (Gen. 2:24; Matt. 19:4-6). Monogamy was the original law under which man lived, but polygamy early commenced (Gen. 4:19), and continued to prevail all down through Jewish history. The law of Moses regulated but did not prohibit polygamy. A man might have a plurality of wives, but a wife could have only one husband.

A wife's legal rights (Ex. 21:10) and her duties (Prov. 31:10-31; 1 Tim. 5:14) are specified. She could be divorced in special cases (Deut. 22:13-21), but could not divorce her husband. Divorce was restricted by our Lord to the single case of adultery (Matt. 19:3-9). The duties of husbands and wives in their relations to each other are distinctly set forth in the New Testament (1 Cor. 7:2-5; Eph. 5:22-33; Col. 3:18, 19; 1 Pet. 3:1-7).

Wil'derness. (1.) Heb. *midhbar*, denoting not a barren desert but a district or region suitable for pasturing sheep and cattle (Ps. 65:12; Isa. 42:11; Jer. 23:10; Joel 1:19; 2:22); an uncultivated place. This word is used of the wilderness of Beersheba (Gen. 21:14), on the southern border of Palestine; the wilderness of the Red Sea (Ex. 13:18); of Shur (15:22), a portion of the Sinaitic peninsula; of Sin (17:1), Sinai (Lev. 7:38), Moab (Deut. 2:8), Judah (Judg. 1:16), Ziph, Maon, En-gedi (1 Sam. 23:14, 24; 24:1), Jeruel and Tekoa (2 Chr. 20:16, 20), Kadesh (Ps. 29:8).

"The wilderness of the sea" (Isa. 21:1). Principal Douglas, referring to this expression, says: "A mysterious name, which must be meant to describe Babylon (see especially ver. 9), perhaps because it became the place of discipline to God's people, as the wilderness of the Red Sea had been (comp. Ezek. 20:35). Otherwise it is in contrast with the symbolic title in Isa. 22:1. Jerusalem is the "valley of vision," rich in spiritual husbandry; whereas Babylon, the rival centre of influence, is spiritually barren and as restless as the sea (comp. 57 : 20)."— *A Short Analysis of the O.T.*

(2.) *Jĕshîmŏn*, a desert waste (Deut. 32 : 10; Ps. 68 : 7).

(3.) *'Arábáh*, the name given to the valley from the Dead Sea to the eastern branch of the Red Sea. In Deut. 1 : 1; 2 : 8, it is rendered "plain" (R.V., "Arabah").

(4.) *Tziyyáh*, a "dry place" (Ps. 78 : 17; 105 : 41).

(5.) *Tôhú*, a "desolate" place—a place "waste" or "unoccupied" (Deut. 32 : 10; Job 12 : 24; comp. Gen. 1 : 2, "without form").

The wilderness region in the Sinaitic peninsula through which for forty years the Hebrews wandered is generally styled "the wilderness of the wanderings." This entire region is in the form of a triangle, having its base toward the north and its apex toward the south. Its extent from north to south is about 250 miles, and at its widest point it is about 150 miles broad. Throughout this vast region of some 1,500 square miles there is not a single river. The northern part of this triangular peninsula is properly the "wilderness of the wanderings" (*et-Tîh*). The western portion of it is called the "wilderness of Shur" (Ex. 15 : 22), and the eastern the "wilderness of Paran."

The "wilderness of Judæa" (Matt. 3 : 1) is a wild, barren region, lying between the Dead Sea and the Hebron Mountains. It is the "Jeshimon" mentioned in 1 Sam. 23 : 19.

Wil'lows. (1.) Heb. *'arábim* (Lev. 23 : 40; Job 40 : 22; Isa. 15 : 7; 44 : 3, 4; Ps. 137 : 1, 2). This was supposed to be the weeping willow, called by Linnæus *Salix Babylonica*, from the reference in Ps. 137. This tree is frequently found "on the coast, overhanging wells and pools. There is a conspicuous tree of this species over a pond in the plain of Acre, and others on the Phœnician plain." There are several species of the *salix* in Palestine, but it is not indigenous to Babylonia, nor was it culti-

vated there. Some are of opinion that the tree intended is the tamarisk or poplar.

(2.) Heb. *tzaphtzaphah* (Ezek. 17 : 5), called by the Arabs the *safsaf*, the general name for the willow. This may be the *Salix Ægyptica* of naturalists.

Tristram thinks that by the "willow by the water-courses," the *Nerium oleander*, the rose-bay oleander, is meant. He says, "It fringes the Upper Jordan, dipping its wavy crown of red into the spray in the rapids under Hermon, and is nurtured by the oozy marshes in the Lower Jordan nearly as far as to Jericho......On the Arnon, on the Jabbok, and the Yarmuk it forms a continuous fringe. In many of

ROSE-BAY OLEANDER.

the streams of Moab it forms a complete screen, which the sun's rays can never penetrate to evaporate the precious moisture. The wild boar lies safely ensconced under its impervious cover."

Wim'ple—Isa. 3 : 22—(R.V.,"shawls"), a wrap or veil. The same Hebrew word is rendered "vail" (R.V., "mantle") in Ruth 3 : 15.

Win'dow, properly only an opening in a house for the admission of light and air, covered with lattice-work, which might be opened or closed (2 Kings 1 : 2; Acts 20 : 9). The spies in Jericho and Paul at Damascus were let down from the windows of houses abutting on the town wall

(Josh. 2:15; 2 Cor. 11:33). The clouds are metaphorically called the "windows of heaven" (Gen. 7:11; Mal. 3:10). The word thus rendered in Isa. 54:12 ought rather to be rendered "battlements" (LXX., "bulwarks;" R.V., "pinnacles"), or as Gesenius renders it, "notched battlements—*i.c.*, suns or rays of the sun" = having a radiated appearance like the sun.

Winds, blowing from the four quarters of heaven (Jer. 49:36; Ezek. 37:9; Dan. 8:8; Zech. 2:6). The east wind was parching (Ezek. 17:10; 19:12), and is sometimes mentioned as simply denoting a strong wind (Job 27:21; Isa. 27:8). This wind prevails in Palestine from February to June, as the west wind (Luke 12:54) does from November to February. The south was a hot wind (Job 37:17; Luke 12:55). It swept over the Arabian peninsula. The rush of invaders is figuratively spoken of as a whirlwind (Isa. 21:1); a commotion among the nations of the world as a striving of the four winds (Dan. 7:2). The winds are subject to the divine power (Ps. 18:10; 135:7).

Wine. The common Hebrew word for wine is *yayin*, from a root meaning "to boil up," "to be in a ferment." Others derive it from a root meaning "to tread out," and hence the juice of the grape trodden out. The Greek word for wine is *oinos*, and the Latin *vinum*. But besides this common Hebrew word, there are several others which are thus rendered.

(1.) '*Ashîshâh* (2 Sam. 6:19; 1 Chr. 16:3; Cant. 2:5; Hos. 3:1), which, however, rather denotes a solid cake of pressed grapes, or, as in the Revised Version, a cake of raisins.

(2.) '*Asîs*, "sweet wine," or "new wine," the product of the same year (Cant. 8:2; Isa. 49:26; Joel 1:5; 3:18; Amos 9:13), from a root meaning "to tread," hence juice trodden out or pressed out, thus referring to the method by which the juice is obtained. The power of intoxication is ascribed to it.

(3.) *Hômetz.* See VINEGAR.

(4.) *Hĕmĕr*, Deut. 32:14 (rendered "blood of the grape"), Isa. 27:2 ("red wine"), Ezra 6:9; 7:22; Dan. 5:1, 2, 4. This word conveys the idea of "foaming," as in the process of fermentation, or when poured out. It is derived from the root *hâmar*, meaning "to boil up," and also "to be red," from the idea of boiling or becoming inflamed.

(5.) '*Enâbh*, a grape (Deut. 32:14). The last clause of this verse should be rendered as in the Revised Version, "and of the blood of the grape ['enabh] thou drankest wine [hemer]." In Hos. 3:1 the phrase in Authorized Version, "flagons of wine," is in the Revised Version correctly "cakes of raisins." (Comp. Gen. 49:11; Num. 6:3; Deut. 23:24, etc., where this Hebrew word is rendered in the plural "grapes.")

(6.) *Mĕsĕkh*, properly a mixture of wine and water with spices that increase its stimulating properties (Isa. 5:22). Ps. 75:8, "The wine [yayin] is red; it is full of mixture [mesekh];" Prov. 23:30, "mixed wine;" Isa. 65:11, "drink offering" (R.V., "mingled wine").

(7.) *Tîrôsh*, properly "must," translated "wine" (Deut. 28:51); "new wine" (Prov. 3:10); "sweet wine" (Micah 6:15; R.V., "vintage"). This Hebrew word has been traced to a root meaning "to take possession of," and hence it is supposed that *tîrôsh* is so designated because in intoxicating it takes possession of the brain. Among the blessings promised to Esau (Gen. 27:28) mention is made of "plenty of corn and tîrôsh." Palestine is called "a land of corn and tîrôsh" (Deut. 33:28; comp. Isa. 36:17). See also Deut. 28:51; 2 Chr. 32:28; Joel 2:19; Hos. 7:5, ("whoredom and wine [yayin] and new wine [tîrôsh])."

(8.) *Sôbhĕ* (root meaning "to drink to excess," "to suck up," "absorb"), found only in Isa. 1:22, Hos. 4:18 ("their drink;" Gesen. and marg. of R.V., "their carouse"), and Nah. 1:10 ("drunken as drunkards;" lit., "soaked according to their drink;" R.V., "drenched, as it were, in their drink"—*i.e.*, according to their sôbhĕ).

(9.) *Shêkâr*, "strong drink," any intoxicating liquor; from a root meaning "to drink deeply," "to be drunken"—a generic term applied to all fermented liquors, however obtained. Num. 28 : 7, "strong wine" (R.V., "strong drink"). It is sometimes distinguished from wine—*c.g.*, Lev. 10 : 9, "Do not drink wine [*yayin*] nor strong drink [*shêkâr*];" Num. 6 : 3; Judg. 13 : 4, 7; Isa. 28 : 7 (in all these places rendered "strong drink"). Translated "strong drink" also in Isa. 5 : 11; 24 : 9; 29 : 9; 56 : 12; Prov. 20 : 1; 31 : 6; Micah 2 : 11.

(10.) *Yekebh* (Deut. 16 : 13, but in R.V. correctly "wine-press"), a vat into which the new wine flowed from the press. Joel 2 : 24, "their vats;" 3 : 13, "the fats;" Prov. 3 : 10, "Thy presses shall burst out with new wine [*tîrôsh*];" Hag. 2 : 16; Jer. 48 : 33, "wine-presses;" 2 Kings 6 : 27; Job. 24 : 11.

(11.) *Shemârim* (only in plural), "lees" or "dregs" of wine. In Isa. 25 : 6 it is rendered "wine on the lees"—*i.e.*, wine that has been kept on the lees, and therefore *old wine.*

(12.) *Mêsěk*, "a mixture," mixed or spiced wine, not diluted with water, but mixed with drugs and spices to increase its strength, or, as some think, mingled with the lees by being shaken (Ps. 75 : 8; Prov. 23 : 30).

In Acts 2 : 13 the word *gleukos*, rendered "new wine," denotes properly "sweet wine." It must have been intoxicating.

In addition to wine the Hebrews also made use of what they called *debash*, which was obtained by boiling down must to one-half or one-third of its original bulk. In Gen. 43 : 11 this word is rendered "honey." It was a kind of syrup, and is called by the Arabs at the present day *dibs*. This word occurs in the phrase "a land flowing with milk and honey" (*děbash*)—Ex. 3 : 8, 17; 13 : 5; 33 : 3; Lev. 20 : 24; Num. 13 : 27. (See HONEY.)

Our Lord miraculously supplied wine at the marriage feast in Cana of Galilee (John 2 : 1–11). The Rechabites were forbidden the use of wine (Jer. 35). The Nazarites also were to abstain from its use during the period of their vow (Num. 6 : 1–4); and those who were dedicated as Nazarites rrom their birth were perpetually to abstain from it (Judg. 13 : 4, 5; Luke 1 : 15; 7 : 33). The priests, too, were for-

bidden the use of wine and strong drink when engaged in their sacred functions (Lev. 10 : 1, 9–11). "Wine is little used now in the East, from the fact that Mohammedans are not allowed to taste it, and very few of other creeds touch it. When it is drunk, water is generally mixed with it, and this was the custom in the days of Christ also. The people indeed are everywhere very sober in hot climates; a drunken person, in fact, is never seen" (Geikie's *Life of Christ*). The sin of drunkenness, however, must have been not uncommon in the olden times, for it is mentioned either metaphorically or literally more than seventy times in the Bible.

A drink-offering of wine was presented with the daily sacrifice (Ex. 29 : 40, 41), and also with the offering of the first-fruits (Lev. 23 : 13), and with various other sacrifices (Num. 15 : 5, 7, 10).

Wine was used at the celebration of the Passover. And when the Lord's Supper was instituted, the wine and the unleavened bread then on the paschal table were by our Lord set apart as memorials of his body and blood.

Several emphatic warnings are given in the New Testament against excess in the use of wine (Luke 21 : 34; Rom. 13 : 13; Eph. 5 : 18; 1 Tim. 3 : 8; Titus 1 : 7).

Wine'fat (Mark 12 : 1). The original word (*hypolēnion*) so rendered occurs only here in the New Testament. It properly denotes the trough or lake (*lacus*), as it was called by the Romans, into which the juice of the grapes ran from the trough above it. It is here used, however, of the whole apparatus. In the parallel passage in Matt. 21 : 33 the Greek word *lēnos* is used. This properly denotes the upper one of the two vats. (See WINE-PRESS.)

Wine-press. Consisted of two vats or receptacles—(1) a trough (Heb. *gath*, Gr. *lēnos*) into which the grapes were thrown and where they were trodden upon and bruised (Isa. 16 : 10; Lam. 1 : 15; Joel 3 : 13); and (2) a trough or vat (Heb. *yekebh*, Gr. *hypolēnion*) into which the juice ran from the trough above—the *gath* (Neh. 13 : 15; Job 24 : 11; Isa. 63 : 2, 3; Hag. 2 : 16; Joel 2 : 24). Wine-presses are found in almost every part of Palestine. They are "the only sure relics we have of the old days of Israel before the Captivity. Between Hebron and Beersheba they are found on all the hill slopes; they abound in southern Judea; they are no less common in the many valleys of Carmel; and they are numerous in Galilee." The "treading of the wine-press" is emblematic of divine judgment (Isa. 63:2; Lam. 1:15; Rev. 14:19, 20).

WINE-PRESS.

Win'now. Corn was winnowed—(1.) By being thrown up by a shovel against the wind. As a rule this was done in the evening or during the night, when the west wind from the sea was blowing, which was a moderate breeze and fitted for the purpose. The north wind was too strong, and the east wind came in gusts. (2.) By the use of a fan or van, by which the chaff was blown away (Ruth 3:2; Isa. 30:24; Jer. 4:11, 12; Matt. 3:12).

Wise, wisdom, a moral rather than an intellectual quality. To be "foolish" is to be godless (Ps. 14:1; comp. Judg. 19:23; 2 Sam. 13:13). True wisdom is a gift from God to those who ask it (Job 28:12–28; Prov. 3:13-18; Rom. 1:22; 16:27; 1 Cor. 1:17-21; 2:6-8; James 1:5). "Wisdom" in Prov. 1:20; 8:1; 9:1-5 may be regarded not as a mere personification of the attribute of wisdom, but as a

divine person, "Christ the power of God and the wisdom of God" (1 Cor. 1:24).

In Matt. 11:19 it is the personified principle of wisdom that is meant.

Wise men mentioned in Dan. 2:12 included three classes—(1) astrologers, (2) Chaldeans, and (3) soothsayers. The word in the original (ḥakamîm) probably means "medicine men." In Chaldea medicine was only a branch of magic. The "wise men" of Matt. 2:7, who came from the East to Jerusalem, were magi from Persia or Arabia.

Witch. Occurs only in Ex. 22:18, as the rendering of mĕkhashshêpheh, the feminine form of the word, meaning "enchantress" (R. V., "sorceress"), and in Deut. 18:10, as the rendering of mĕkhashshephêth, the masculine form of the word, meaning "enchanter."

Witch'craft (1 Sam. 15:23; 2 Kings 9:22; 2 Chr. 33:6; Micah 5:12; Nahum 3:4; Gal. 5:20). In the popular sense of the word no mention is made either of witches or of witchcraft in Scripture.

The "witch of En-dor" (1 Sam. 28) was a necromancer—i.e., one who feigned to hold converse with the dead. The damsel with "a spirit of divination" (Acts 16:16) was possessed by an evil spirit, or, as the words are literally rendered, "having a spirit, a pithon." The reference is to the heathen god Apollo, who was regarded as the god of prophecy.

Wit'ness. More than one witness was required in criminal cases (Deut. 17:6; 19:15). They were the first to execute the sentence on the condemned (Deut. 13:9; 17:7; 1 Kings 21:13; Matt. 27:1; Acts 7:57, 58). False witnesses were liable to punishment (Deut. 19:16-21). It was also an offence to refuse to bear witness (Lev. 5:1).

Wit'ness of the Spirit (Rom. 8:16), the consciousness of the gracious operation of the Spirit on the mind—"a certitude of the Spirit's presence and work continually asserted within us"—manifested "in his comforting us, his stirring us up to prayer, his reproof of our sins, his drawing us to works of love, to bear testimony before the world," etc.

Wiz'ard, a pretender to supernatural knowledge and power—"a knowing one," as the original Hebrew word signifies.

Such an one was forbidden on pain of death to practise his deceptions (Lev. 19: 31; 20:6, 27; 1 Sam. 28:3; Isa. 8:19; 19:3).

Wolf—Heb. *zĕĕb*—frequently referred to in Scripture as an emblem of treachery and cruelty. Jacob's prophecy, "Benjamin shall ravin as a wolf" (Gen. 49:27), represents the warlike character of that tribe (see Judg. 19-21). Isaiah represents the peace of Messiah's kingdom by the words, "The wolf also shall dwell with the lamb" (Isa. 11:6). The habits of the wolf are described in Jer. 5:6; Hab. 1:8; Zeph. 3:3; Ezek. 22:27; Matt. 7:15; 10:16; Acts 20:29. Wolves are still sometimes found in Palestine, and are the dread of shepherds, as of old.

Wo'man was "taken out of man" (Gen. 2:23), and therefore the man has the pre-eminence. "The head of the woman is the man;" but yet honour is to be shown to the wife, "as unto the weaker vessel" (1 Cor. 11:3, 8, 9; 1 Pet. 3:7). Several women are mentioned in Scripture as having been endowed with prophetic gifts, as Miriam (Ex. 15:20), Deborah (Judg. 4: 4, 5), Huldah (2 Kings 22:14), Noadiah (Neh. 6:14), Anna (Luke 2:36, 37), and the daughters of Philip the evangelist (Acts 21:8, 9). Women are forbidden to teach publicly (1 Cor. 14:34, 35; 1 Tim. 2:11, 12). Among the Hebrews it devolved upon women to prepare the meals for the household (Gen. 18:6; 2 Sam. 13:8), to attend to the work of spinning (Ex. 35: 26; Prov. 31:19), and making clothes (1 Sam. 2:19; Prov. 31:21), to bring water from the well (Gen. 24:15; 1 Sam. 9:11), and to care for the flocks (Gen. 29:6; Ex. 2:16).

The word "woman," as used in Matt. 15:28, John 2:4 and 20:13, 15, implies tenderness and courtesy and not disrespect. Only where revelation is known has woman her due place of honour assigned to her.

Wood. See FOREST.

Wood-offering (Neh. 10:34; 13:31). It would seem that in the time of Nehe-miah arrangements were made, probably on account of the comparative scarcity of wood, by which certain districts were required, as chosen by lot, to furnish wood to keep the altar fire perpetually burning (Lev. 6:13).

Wool, one of the first materials used for making woven cloth (Lev. 13:47, 48, 52, 59; 19:19). The first-fruit of wool was to be offered to the priests (Deut. 18:4). The law prohibiting the wearing of a garment "of divers sorts, as of woollen and linen together" (Deut. 22:11) may, like some other laws of a similar character, have been intended to express symbolically the separateness and simplicity of God's covenant people. The wool of Damascus, famous for its whiteness, was of great repute in the Tyrian market (Ezek. 27:18).

Word, The (Gr. *Logos*), one of the titles of our Lord, found only in the writings of John (John 1:1-14; 1 John 1:1; Rev. 19: 13). As such, Christ is the revealer of God. His office is to make God known. "No man hath seen God at any time; the only begotten Son, which is in the bosom of the Father, he hath declared him" (John 1: 18). This title designates the divine nature of Christ. As the Word, he "was in the beginning" and "became flesh." "The Word was with God" and "was God," and was the Creator of all things (comp. Ps. 33: 6; 107:20; 119:89; 147:18; Isa. 40:8).

Word of God (Heb. 4:12, etc.). The Bible so called because the writers of its several books were God's organs in communicating his will to men. It is his "word," because he speaks to us in its sacred pages. Whatever the inspired writers here declare to be true and binding upon us, God declares to be true and binding. This word is infallible, because written under the guidance of the Holy Spirit, and therefore free from all error of fact or doctrine or precept. (See INSPIRA-TION; BIBLE.) All saving knowledge is obtained from the word of God. In the case of adults it is an indispensable means of salvation, and is efficacious thereunto by the gracious influence of the Holy Spirit (John 17:17; Acts 26:17, 18; 2 Tim. 3: 15, 16; 1 Pet. 1:23).

Works, Good. The old objection against the doctrine of salvation by grace, that it does away with the necessity of good works, and lowers the sense of their importance (Rom. 6), although it has been answered a thousand times, is still alleged by many. They say if men are not saved by works, then works are not necessary. If the most moral of men are saved in the same way as the very chief of sinners, then good works are of no moment. And more than this, if the grace of God is most clearly displayed in the salvation of the vilest of men, then the worse men are the better.

The objection has no validity. The gospel of salvation by grace shows that good works are necessary. It is true, unchangeably true, that without holiness no man shall see the Lord. "Neither adulterers, nor thieves, nor covetous, nor drunkards" shall inherit the kingdom of God.

Works are "good" only when—(1) they spring from the principle of love to God. The moral character of an act is determined by the moral principle that prompts it. Faith and love in the heart are the essential elements of all true obedience. Hence good works only spring from a believing heart—can only be wrought by one reconciled to God (Eph. 2:10; James 2:18:22). (2.) Good works have the glory of God as their object; and (3) they have the revealed will of God as their only rule (Deut. 12:32; Rev. 22:18, 19).

Good works are an expression of gratitude in the believer's heart (John 14:15, 23; Gal. 5:6). They are the fruits of the Spirit (Titus 2:10–12), and thus spring from grace, which they illustrate and strengthen in the heart.

Good works of the most sincere believers are all imperfect, yet like their persons they are accepted through the mediation of Jesus Christ (Col. 3:17), and so are rewarded; they have no merit intrinsically, but are rewarded wholly of grace.

Works, Covenant of, entered into by God with Adam as the representative of the human race (comp. Gen. 9:11, 12; 17:1–21), so styled because perfect obedience was its condition, thus distinguishing it from the covenant of grace. (See COVENANT OF WORKS.)

Worm. (1.) Heb. *şâş* (Isa. 51:8), denotes the caterpillar of the clothes-moth.

(2.) The manna bred worms (*tolaʿîm*), but on the Sabbath there was not any worm (*rimmâh*) therein (Ex. 16:20, 24). Here these words refer to caterpillars or larvæ, which feed on corrupting matter.

These two Hebrew words appear to be interchangeable (Job 25:6; Isa. 14:11). *Tolaʿîm* in some places denotes the caterpillar (Deut. 28:39; Jonah 4:7), and *rimmâh*, the larvæ, as bred from putridity (Job 17:14; 21:26; 24:20). In Micah 7:17, where it is said, "They shall move out of their holes like worms," perhaps serpents or "creeping things," or as in the Revised Version, "crawling things," are meant.

The word is used figuratively in Job 25:6; Ps. 22:6; Isa. 41:14; Mark 9:44, 46, 48; Isa. 66:24.

Worm'wood—Heb. *laʿanâh*—the *Artemisia absinthium* of botanists. It is noted for its intense bitterness (Deut. 29:18; Prov. 5:4; Jer. 9:15; Amos 5:7). It is a type of bitterness—affliction, remorse, punitive suffering. In Amos 6:12 this Hebrew word is rendered "hemlock" (R.V., "wormwood"). In the symbolical language of the Apocalypse (Rev. 8:10, 11) a star is represented as falling on the waters of the earth, causing the third part of the water to turn wormwood.

The name by which the Greeks designated it, *absinthion*, means "undrinkable." The *absinthe* of France is distilled from a species of this plant. The "southernwood" or "old man," cultivated in cottage gardens on account of its fragrance, is another species of it.

Wor'ship, homage rendered to God, which it is sinful (idolatry) to render to any created being (Ex. 34:14; Isa. 2:8). Such worship was refused by Peter (Acts 10:25, 26) and by an angel (Rev. 22:8, 9).

Wor'shipper (Gr. *neocoros* = temple-sweeper = sacristan; R.V. "temple-keeper" [Acts 19:35] of the great goddess Diana). This name *neocoros* appears on most of the extant Ephesian coins.

Wrestle (Eph. 6:12). See GAMES.

Writ'ing. The art of writing must have been known in the time of the early Pharaohs. Moses is commanded "to write for a memorial in a book" (Ex. 17:14) a record of the attack of Amalek. Frequent mention is afterwards made of writing (28:11, 21, 29, 36; 31:18; 32:15, 16; 34:1, 28; 39:6, 14, 30). The origin of this art is unknown, but there is reason to conclude that in the age of Moses it was well known. The inspired books of Moses are the most ancient extant writings, although there are written monuments as old as about B.C. 2000. The words expressive of "writing," "book," and "ink," are common to all the branches or dialects of the Semitic language, and hence it has been concluded that this art must have been known to the earliest Semites before they separated into their various tribes, and nations, and families.

"The Old Testament and the discoveries of Oriental archæology alike tell us that the age of the Exodus was throughout the world of Western Asia an age of literature and books, of readers and writers, and that the cities of Palestine were stored with the contemporaneous records of past events inscribed on imperishable clay. They further tell us that the kinsfolk and neighbours of the Israelites were already acquainted with alphabetic writing, that the wanderers in the desert and the tribes of Edom were in contact with the cultured scribes and traders of Ma'in [Southern Arabia], and that the 'house of bondage' from which Israel had escaped was a land where the art of writing was blazoned not only on the temples of the gods, but also on the dwellings of the rich and powerful." —*Sayce.* (See DEBIR; PHŒNICIA.)

The "Book of the Dead" was a collection of prayers and formulæ, by the use of which the souls of the dead were supposed to attain to rest and peace in the next world. It was composed at various periods from the earliest time to the Persian conquest. It affords an interesting glimpse into the religious life and system of belief among the ancient Egyptians. We learn from it that they believed in the existence of one Supreme Being, the immortality of the soul, judgment after death, and the resurrection of the body. It shows, too, a high state of literary activity in Egypt in the time of Moses. It refers to extensive libraries then existing. That of Ramessium, in Thebes, *e.g.*, built by Rameses II., contained 20,000 books.

When the Hebrews entered Canaan it is evident that the art of writing was known to the original inhabitants, as appears, *e.g.*, from the name of the city Debir having been at first Kirjath-sepher—*i.e.*, the "city of the book," or the "book town" (Josh. 10:38; 15:15; Judg. 1:11).

The first mention of letter-writing is in the time of David (2 Sam. 11:14, 15). Letters are afterwards frequently spoken of (1 Kings 21:8, 9, 11; 2 Kings 10:1, 2, 6, 7; 19:14; 2 Chr. 21:12–15; 30:1, 6–9, etc.).

Y

Yarn. Found only in 1 Kings 10:28, 2 Chr. 1:16. The Heb. word *mikveh*, *i.e.*, "a stringing together," so rendered, rather signifies a host, or company, or a *string* of horses. The Authorized Version has: "And Solomon had horses brought out of Egypt, and linen yarn: the king's merchants received the linen yarn at a price;" but the Revised Version correctly renders: "And the horses which Solomon had were brought out of Egypt; and the king's merchants received them in droves, each drove at a price."

Year—Heb. *shânâh*—meaning "repetition" or "revolution" (Gen. 1:14; 5:3). Among the ancient Egyptians the year consisted of twelve months of thirty days each, with five days added to make it a complete revolution of the earth round the sun. The Jews reckoned the year in two ways—(1) according to a sacred calendar, in which the year began about the time of the vernal equinox, with the month Abib; and (2) according to a civil calendar, in which the year began about the time of the autumnal equinox, with the month Nisan. The month Tisri is now the beginning of the Jewish year.

Yesh'ebi, the Hebrew word rendered "inhabitants" in Josh. 17:7, but probably rather the name of the village *Yeshepheh*, probably *Yassûf*, 8 miles south of Shechem.

Yoke. (1.) Fitted on the neck of oxen for the purpose of binding to them the traces by which they might draw the plough, etc. (Num. 19:2; Deut. 21:3). It was a curved piece of wood called *'ôl*.

(2.) In Jer. 27:2; 28:10, 12 the word in the Authorized Version rendered "yoke" is *môtâh*, which properly means a "staff," or as in the Revised Version, "bar."

These words in the Hebrew are both used figuratively of severe bondage, or affliction, or subjection (Lev. 26:13; 1 Kings 12:4; Isa. 47:6; Lam. 1:14; 3:27). In the New Testament the word "yoke" is also used to denote servitude (Matt. 11:29, 30; Acts 15:10; Gal. 5:1).

(3.) In 1 Sam. 11:7, 1 Kings 19:21, Job 1:3 the word thus translated is *tzĕmĕd*, which signifies a pair, two oxen yoked or coupled together, and hence in 1 Sam. 14:14 it represents as much land as a yoke of oxen could plough in a day, like the Latin *jugum*. In Isa. 5:10 this word in the plural is translated "acres."

Yoke-fellow (Phil. 4:3), one of the apostle's fellow-labourers. Some have conjectured that Epaphroditus is meant. Wyckliffe renders the phrase "the german felowe"—*i.e.*, "thee, germane [= genuine] comrade."

Z

Za'anaim—*wanderings; the unloading of tents*—so called probably from the fact of nomads in tents encamping amid the cities and villages of that region, a place in the north-west of Lake Merom, near Kedesh, in Naphtali. Here Sisera was slain by Jael, "the wife of Heber the Kenite," who had pitched his tent in the "plain [R.V., 'as far as the oak'] of Zaanaim" (Judg. 4:11).

It has been, however, suggested by some that, following the LXX. and the Talmud, the letter *b*, which in Hebrew means "in,' should be taken as a part of the word following, and the phrase would then be "unto the oak of Bitzanaim," a place which has been identified with the ruins of *Bessûm*, about half-way between Tiberias and Mount Tabor.

Za'anan—*place of flocks*—mentioned only in Micah 1:11. It may be identified with Zenan, in the plain country of Judah (Josh. 15:37).

Zaanan'nim = Zaanaim (Josh. 19:33).

Za'avan—*terror*—one of the "dukes of Edom" (Gen. 36:27); called also Zavan (1 Chr. 1:42).

Za'bad—*gift*. (1.) One of David's valiant men (1 Chr. 11:41), the descendant of Ahlai, of the "children of Sheshan" (2:31).

(2.) A descendant of Tahath (7:21).

(3.) The son of Shemath. He conspired against Joash, king of Judah, and slew him (2 Chr. 24:25, 26). He is called also Jozachar (2 Kings 12:21).

(4.) Ezra 10:27.

(5.) Ezra 10:33.

(6.) Ezra 10:43.

Zab'bai—*wanderer; pure*. (1.) Ezra 10:28.

(2.) The father of Baruch, who "earnestly repaired" part of the wall of Jerusalem (Neh. 3:20; marg., "Zaccai").

Zab'bud—*gift*—Ezra 8:14.

Zab'di—*gift of Jehovah*. (1.) An ancestor of Achan (Josh. 7:1, 17, 18). He is probably the "Zimri" of 1 Chr. 2:6.

(2.) A Benjamite (1 Chr. 8:19).

(3.) Called "the Shephmite," one of David's officers, who had charge of his vineyards (1 Chr. 27:27).

(4.) A Levite, one of the sons of Asaph (Neh. 11:17); probably the same as Zichri (1 Chr. 9:15), and Zaccur (Neh. 12:35).

Zab'diel—*gift of God*. (1.) The father of Jashobeam, who was one of David's officers (1 Chr. 27:2).

(2.) An overseer of the priests after the Captivity (Neh. 11:14).

Za'bud—*gift*—the son of Nathan, who was "king's friend" in the court of Solomon (1 Kings 4:5).

Zab'ulon (Matt. 4:13, 15; Rev. 7:8). See ZEBULUN.

Zac'cai—*pure*—one whose "sons" returned with Zerubbabel to Jerusalem (Ezra 2:9; Neh. 7:14). (See ZABBAI.)

Zacchæ'us—*pure*—a superintendent of customs; a chief tax-gatherer (*publicanus*) at Jericho (Luke 19:1-10). "The collection of customs at Jericho, which at this time produced and exported a considerable quantity of balsam, was undoubtedly an important post, and would account for Zacchæus being a rich man." Being short of stature, he hastened on before the multitude who were thronging about Christ as he passed through Jericho on his way to Jerusalem, and climbed up a sycamore tree that he might be able to see him. When our Lord reached the spot he looked up to the publican among the branches, and addressing him by name, told him to make haste and come down, as he intended that day to abide at his house. This led to the remarkable interview recorded by the evangelist, and to the striking parable of the ten pounds (Luke 19:12-27). From that day forth Zacchæus doubtless became a disciple of Christ, but of his subsequent history we have no record.

Zac'cur—*mindful*. (1.) Father of Shammua, who was one of the spies sent out by Moses (Num. 13:4).

(2.) A Merarite Levite (1 Chr. 24:27).

(3.) A son of Asaph, and chief of one of the courses of singers as arranged by David (1 Chr. 25:2, 10).

(4.) Son of Imri (Neh. 3:2).

(5.) A Levite (Neh. 10:12).

(6.) The son of Mattaniah (Neh. 13:13).

Zachari'ah—*remembered by the Lord*. (1.) Son of Jeroboam II., king of Israel.

On the death of his father there was an interregnum of ten years, at the end of which he succeeded to the throne, which he occupied only six months, having been put to death by Shallum, who usurped the throne. "He did that which was evil in the sight of the Lord, as his fathers had done" (2 Kings 14:29; 15:8-12). In him the dynasty of Jehu came to an end.

(2.) The father of Abi, who was the mother of Hezekiah (2 Kings 18:2).

Zachari'as. (1.) A priest of the course of Abia, the eighth of the twenty-four courses into which the priests had been originally divided by David (1 Chr. 23:1-19). Only four of these courses or "families" of the priests returned from the Exile (Ezra 2:36-39); but they were then re-distributed under the old designations. The priests served at the temple twice each year, and only for a week each time. Zacharias's time had come for this service. During this period his home would be one of the chambers set apart for the priests on the sides of the temple ground. The offering of incense was one of the most solemn parts of the daily worship of the temple, and lots were drawn each day to determine who should have this great honour—an honour which no priest could enjoy more than once during his lifetime.

While Zacharias ministered at the golden altar of incense in the holy place, it was announced to him by the angel Gabriel that his wife Elisabeth, who was also of a priestly family, now stricken in years, would give birth to a son who was to be called John, and that he would be the forerunner of the long-expected Messiah (Luke 1:12-17). As a punishment for his refusing to believe this message, he was struck dumb and "not able to speak till the day that these things should be performed" (20). Nine months passed away, and Elisabeth's child was born, and when in answer to their inquiry Zacharias wrote on a "writing tablet," "His name is John," his mouth was opened, and he praised God (60-79). The child (John the Baptist), thus "born out of due time," "waxed strong in spirit" (1:80).

(2.) The "son of Barachias," mentioned as having been slain between the temple and the altar (Matt. 23:35; Luke 11:51). "Barachias" here may be another name for Jehoiada, as some think. (See ZECHARIAH.)

Za'cher—*memorial*—a son of Jehiel (1 Chr. 8:31; 9:35); called Zechariah (9:37).

Za'dok—*righteous*. (1.) A son of Ahitub, of the line of Eleazer (2 Sam. 8:17; 1 Chr. 24:3), high priest in the time of David (2 Sam. 20:25) and Solomon (1 Kings 4:4). He is first mentioned as coming to take part with David at Hebron (1 Chr. 12:27, 28). He was probably on this account made ruler over the Aaronites (27:17). Zadok and Abiathar acted as high priests on several important occasions (1 Chr. 15:11; 2 Sam. 15:24-29, 35, 36); but when Adonijah endeavoured to secure the throne, Abiathar went with him, and therefore Solomon "thrust him out from being high priest," and Zadok, remaining faithful to David, became high priest alone (1 Kings 2:27, 35; 1 Chr. 29:22). In him the line of Phinehas resumed the dignity, and held it till the fall of Jerusalem. He was succeeded in his sacred office by his son Azariah (1 Kings 4:2; comp. 1 Chr. 6:3-14).

(2.) The father of Jerusha, who was wife of King Uzziah, and mother of King Jotham (2 Kings 15:33; 2 Chr. 27:1).

(3.) "The scribe" set over the treasuries of the temple by Nehemiah along with a priest and a Levite (Neh. 13:13).

(4.) The sons of Baana, one of those who assisted in rebuilding the wall of Jerusalem (Neh. 3:4, 29).

Za'ir—*little*—a place probably east of the Dead Sea, where Joram discomfited the host of Edom who had revolted from him (2 Kings 8:21).

Zal'mon—*shady*. (1.) One of David's warriors, called the Ahohite (2 Sam. 23:28); called also Ilai (1 Chr. 11:29).

(2.) A wood near Shechem, from which Abimelech and his party brought boughs and "put them to the hold" of Shechem, "and set the hold on fire" (Judg. 9:48). Probably the southern peak of Gerizim, now called *Jebel Sulman*. (See SALMON.)

Zalmo'nah—*shady*—one of the stations of the Israelites in the wilderness (Num. 33:41, 42).

Zalmun'na, one of the two kings of Midian whom the "Lord delivered" into the hands of Gideon. He was slain afterwards with Zebah (Judg. 8:5-21). (See ZEBAH.)

Zamzum'mims, a race of giants; "a people great, and many, and tall, as the Anakims" (Deut. 2:20, 21). They were overcome by the Ammonites, "who called them Zamzummims." They belonged to the Rephaim, and inhabited the country afterwards occupied by the Ammonites. It has been conjectured that they might be Ham-zuzims—*i.e.*, Zuzims dwelling in Ham, a place apparently to the south of Ashteroth (Gen. 14:5), the ancient Rabbath-ammon.

Zano'ah—*marsh*. (1.) A town in the low country or *shephêlah* of Judah, near Zorah (Josh. 15:34). It was re-occupied after the return from the Captivity (Neh. 11:30). *Zanû'ah* in Wâdy Ismail, 10 miles west of Jerusalem, occupies probably the same site.

(2.) A town in the hill country of Judah, some 10 miles to the south-west of Hebron (Josh. 15:56).

Zaph'nath-paane'ah, the name which Pharaoh gave to Joseph when he raised him to the rank of prime minister or grand vizier of the kingdom (Gen. 41:45). This is a pure Egyptian word, and has been variously explained. Some think it means "creator," or "preserver of life." Brugsch interprets it as "governor of the district of the place of life"—*i.e.*, of Goshen, the chief city of which was Pithom, "the place of life." Others explain it as meaning "a revealer of secrets," or "the man to whom secrets are revealed."

Zar'ephath — *smelting-shop*, "a workshop for the refining and smelting of metals"—a small Phoenician town, now *Sûrafend*, about a mile from the coast, almost midway on the road between Tyre and Sidon. Here Elijah sojourned with a poor widow during the "great famine," when the "heaven was shut up three years and six months" (Luke 4:26; 2 Kings 7:1-4). It is called Sarepta in the New Testament (Luke 4:26).

Zar'etan. When the Hebrews crossed the Jordan, as soon as the feet of the priests were dipped in the water, the flow of the stream was arrested. The point of arrest was the "city of Adam beside Zaretan," probably near Succoth, at the mouth of the Jabbok, some 30 miles up the river from where the people were encamped. There the water "stood and rose upon an heap." Thus the whole space of 30 miles of the river-bed was dry, that the tribes might pass over (Josh. 3:16, 17; comp. Ps. 104:3).

Za'reth-sha'har—*the splendour of the dawn*—a city "in the mount of the valley" (Josh. 13:19). It is identified with the ruins of *Zâra*, near the mouth of the Wâdy Zerka Main, on the eastern shore of the Dead Sea, some 3 miles south of the Callirrhoe. Of this town but little remains. "A few broken basaltic columns and pieces of wall about 200 yards back from the shore, and a ruined fort rather nearer the sea, about the middle of the coast line of the plain, are all that are left" (Tristram's *Land of Moab*).

Zar'than, a place near Succoth, in the plain of the Jordan, "in the clay ground," near which Hiram cast the brazen utensils for the temple (1 Kings 7:46); probably the same as Zartan. It is also called Zeredathah (2 Chr. 4:17). (See ZEREDA.)

Zat'thu—*a sprout*—Neh. 10:14.

Zat'tu—*id.*—one whose descendants returned from the Captivity with Zerubbabel (Ezra 2:8; Neh. 7:13); probably the same as Zatthu.

Za'za—*plenty*—a descendant of Judah (1 Chr. 2:33).

Zeal, an earnest temper; may be enlightened (Num. 25:11–13; 2 Cor. 7:11; 9:2), or ignorant and misdirected (Rom. 10:2; Phil. 3:6). As a Christian grace, it must be grounded on right principles and directed to right ends (Gal. 4:18). It is sometimes ascribed to God (2 Kings 19:31; Isa. 9:7; 37:32; Ezek. 5:13).

Zeal'ots, a sect of Jews which originated with Judas the Gaulonite (Acts 5:37). They refused to pay tribute to the Romans, on the ground that this was a violation of the principle that God was the only king of Israel. They rebelled against the Romans, but were soon scattered, and became a lawless band of mere brigands. They were afterwards called *Sicarii,* from their use of the *sica*—i.e., the Roman dagger.

Zebadi'ah—*gift of Jehovah*. (1.) A son of Asahel, Joab's brother (1 Chr. 27:7).

(2.) A Levite who took part as one of the teachers in the system of national education instituted by Jehoshaphat (2 Chr. 17:7, 8).

(3.) The son of Ishmael, "the ruler of the house of Judah in all the king's matters" (2 Chr. 19:8–11).

(4.) A son of Beraiah (1 Chr. 8:15).

(5.) A Korhite porter of the Lord's house (1 Chr. 26:2). Three or four others of this name are also mentioned.

Ze'bah—*man-killer,* or *sacrifice*—one of the two kings who led the vast host of the Midianites who invaded the land of Israel, and over whom Gideon gained a great and decisive victory (Judg. 8). Zebah and Zalmunna had succeeded in escaping across the Jordan with a remnant of the Midianite host, but were overtaken at Karkor, probably in the Hauran, and routed by Gideon. The kings were taken alive and brought back across the Jordan; and confessing that they had personally taken part in the slaughter of Gideon's brothers, they were put to death (comp. 1 Sam. 12:11; Isa. 10:26; Ps. 83:11).

Zeba'im (Ezra 2:57; Neh. 7:59). "Pochereth of Zebaim" should be read as in the Revised Version, "Pochereth-hazzabaim" ("snaring the antelopes"), probably the name of some hunter.

Zeb'edee, a Galilean fisherman, the husband of Salome (*q.v.*), and the father of James and John, two of our Lord's disciples (Matt. 4:21; 27:56; Mark 15:40). He seems to have been a man of some position in Capernaum, for he had two boats (Luke 5:4) and "hired servants" (Mark 1:20) of his own. No mention is made of him after the call of his two sons by Jesus.

Zebo'im—*gazelles* or *roes*. (1.) One of the "five cities of the plain" of Sodom, generally coupled with Admah (Gen. 10:19; 14:2; Deut. 29:23; Hos. 11:8). It had a king of its own (Shemeber), and was therefore a place of some importance. It was destroyed along with the other cities of the plain.

(2.) A valley or rugged glen somewhere near Gibeah in Benjamin (1 Sam. 13:18). It was probably the ravine now bearing the name *Wâdy Shakh-ed-Dub'a*, or "ravine of the hyena," north of Jericho.

(3.) A place mentioned only in Neh. 11:34, inhabited by the Benjamites after the Captivity.

Zebu′dah—*given*—the wife of Josiah and mother of Jehoiakim (2 Kings 23:36).

Ze′bul—*habitation*—the governor of Shechem under Abimelech (Judg. 9:28, 30, 36). He informed his master of the intention of the people of Shechem to transfer their allegiance to the Hivite tribe of Hamor. This led to Abimelech's destroying the city, when he put its entire population to the sword, and sowed the ruins with salt (Judg. 9:28-45).

Zeb′ulonite, the designation of Elon, the judge who belonged to the tribe of Zebulun (Judg. 12:11, 12).

Zeb′ulun—*dwelling*—the sixth and youngest son of Jacob and Leah (Gen. 30:20). Little is known of his personal history. He had three sons (46:14).

Zeb′ulun, Tribe of, numbered at Sinai (Num. 1:31) and before entering Canaan (26:27). It was one of the tribes which did not drive out the Canaanites, but only made them tributary (Judg. 1:30). It took little interest in public affairs. It responded, however, readily to the summons of Gideon (6:35), and afterwards assisted in enthroning David at Hebron (1 Chr. 12:33, 40). Along with the other northern tribes, Zebulun was carried away into the land of Assyria by Tiglath-pileser (2 Kings 15:29).

In Deborah's song the words, "Out of Zebulun they that handle the pen of the writer" (Judg. 5:14) has been rendered in the R.V., "They that handle the marshal's staff." This is a questionable rendering. "The word *sôpher* ('scribe' or 'writer') defines the word *shebhĕt* ('rod' or 'pen') with which it is conjoined. The 'rod of the scribe' on the Assyrian monuments was the stylus of wood or metal, with the help of which the clay tablet was engraved, or the papyrus inscribed with characters. The scribe who wielded it was the associate and assistant of the 'lawgivers.'" (Sayce).

Zeb′ulun, Lot of, in Galilee, to the north of Issachar and south of Asher and Naphtali (Josh. 19:10-16), and between the Sea of Galilee and the Mediterranean. According to ancient prophecy this part of Galilee enjoyed a large share of our Lord's public ministry (Isa. 9:1, 2; Matt. 4:12-16).

Zechari′ah—*Jehovah is renowned* or *remembered*. (1.) A prophet of Judah—the eleventh of the twelve minor prophets. Like Ezekiel, he was of priestly extraction. He describes himself (1:1) as "the son of Berechiah." In Ezra 5:1 and 6:14 he is called "the son of Iddo," who was properly his grandfather. His prophetical career began in the second year of Darius (B.C. 520), about sixteen years after the return of the first company from exile. He was contemporary with Haggai (Ezra 5:1).

His *book* consists of two distinct parts— (1) chapters 1 to 8, inclusive, and (2) 9 to the end. It begins with a preface (1:1-6), which recalls the nation's past history, for the purpose of presenting a solemn warning to the present generation. Then follows a series of eight visions (1:7-6:8), succeeding one another in one night, which may be regarded as a symbolical history of Israel, intended to furnish consolation to the returned exiles and stir up hope in their minds. The symbolical action, the crowning of Joshua (6:9-15), describes how the kingdoms of the world become the kingdom of God's Christ.

Chapters 7 and 8, delivered two years later, are an answer to the question whether the days of mourning for the destruction of the city should be any longer kept, and an encouraging address to the people, assuring them of God's presence and blessing.

The second part of the book (ch. 9-14) bears no date. It is probable that a considerable interval separates it from the first part. It consists of two burdens.

The *first burden* (ch. 9-11) gives an outline of the course of God's providential dealings with his people down to the time of the Advent.

The *second burden* (ch. 12–14) points out the glories that await Israel in "the latter day"—the final conflict and triumph of God's kingdom.

(2.) The son or grandson of Jehoiada, the high priest in the times of Ahaziah and Joash. After the death of Jehoiada he boldly condemned both the king and the people for their rebellion against God (2 Chr. 24:20), which so stirred up their resentment against him that at the king's commandment they stoned him with stones, and he died "in the court of the house of the Lord" (24:21). Christ alludes to this deed of murder in Matt. 23:35, Luke 11:51. (See ZACHARIAS [2].)

(3.) A prophet, who had "understanding in the seeing of God," in the time of Uzziah, who was much indebted to him for his wise counsel (2 Chr. 26:5).

Besides these, there is a large number of persons mentioned in Scripture bearing this name of whom nothing is known.

(4.) One of the chiefs of the tribe of Reuben (1 Chr. 5:7).

(5.) One of the porters of the tabernacle (1 Chr. 9:21).

(6.) 1 Chr. 9:37.

(7.) Two Levites who assisted at the bringing up of the ark from the house of Obed-edom (1 Chr. 15:20–24).

(8.) A Kohathite Levite (1 Chr. 24:25).

(9.) A Merarite Levite (1 Chr. 26:11).

(10.) The father of Iddo (1 Chr. 27:21).

(11.) One who assisted in teaching the law to the people in the time of Jehoshaphat (2 Chr. 17:7).

(12.) A Levite of the sons of Asaph (2 Chr. 20:14).

(13.) One of Jehoshaphat's sons (2 Chr. 21:2).

(14.) The father of Abijah, who was the mother of Hezekiah (2 Chr. 29:1).

(15.) One of the sons of Asaph (2 Chr. 29:13).

(16.) One of the "rulers of the house of God" (2 Chr. 35:8).

(17.) A chief of the people in the time of Ezra, who consulted him about the return from captivity (Ezra 8:16); probably the same as mentioned in Neh. 8:4.

(18.) Neh. 11:12.

(19.) Neh. 12:16.

(20.) Neh. 12:35, 41.

(21.) Isa. 8:2.

Ze'dad—*side; sloping place*—a town in the north of Palestine, near Hamath (Num. 34:8; Ezek. 47:15). It has been identified with the ruins of *Sŭdŭd*, between Emesa (*Hums*) and Baalbec, but that is uncertain.

Zedeki'ah — *righteousness of Jehovah.* (1.) The last king of Judah. He was the third son of Josiah, and his mother's name was Hamutal, the daughter of Jeremiah of Libnah, and hence he was the brother of Jehoahaz (2 Kings 23:31; 24:17, 18). His original name was Mattaniah; but when Nebuchadnezzar placed him on the throne as the successor to Jehoiachin he changed his name to Zedekiah. The prophet Jeremiah was his counsellor, yet "he did evil in the sight of the Lord" (2 Kings 24:19, 20; Jer. 52:2, 3). He ascended the throne at the age of twenty-one years. The kingdom was at that time tributary to Nebuchadnezzar; but, despite the strong remonstrances of Jeremiah and others, as well as the example of Jehoiachin, he threw off the yoke of Babylon, and entered into an alliance with Hophra, king of Egypt. This brought up Nebuchadnezzar, "with all his host" (2 King 25:1), against Jerusalem. During this siege, which lasted about eighteen months, "every worst woe befell the devoted city, which drank the cup of God's fury to the dregs" (2 Kings 25:3; Lam. 4:4, 5, 10). The city was plundered and laid in ruins. Zedekiah and his followers, attempting to escape, were made captive and taken to Riblah. There, after seeing his own children put to death, his own eyes were put out, and, being loaded with chains, he was carried captive (B.C. 588) to Babylon (2 Kings 25:1–7; 2 Chr. 36:12; Jer. 32:4, 5; 34:2, 3; 39:1–7; 52:4–11; Ezek. 12:12), where he remained a prisoner—how long is unknown—to the day of his death.

After the fall of Jerusalem, Nebuzaraddan was sent to carry out its complete destruction. The city was razed to the ground. Only a small number of vine-dressers and husbandmen were permitted to remain in the land (Jer. 52:16). Gedaliah, with a Chaldean guard stationed at Mizpah, ruled over Judah (2 Kings 25:22, 23; Jer. 40:1, 2, 5, 6).

(2.) The son of Chenaanah, a false prophet in the days of Ahab (1 Kings 22:11, 24; 2 Chr. 18:10, 23).

(3.) The son of Hananiah, a prince of Judah in the days of Jehoiakim (Jer. 36:12).

Ze'eb—*the wolf*—one of the two leaders of the great Midianite host which invaded Israel and was utterly routed by Gideon. The division of that host, which attempted to escape across the Jordan, under Oreb and Zeeb, was overtaken by the Ephraimites, who, in a great battle, completely vanquished them, their leaders being taken and slain (Judg. 7:25; Ps. 83:11; Isa. 10:26).

Ze'lah—*slope; side*—a town in Benjamin, where Saul and his son Jonathan were buried (2 Sam. 21:14). It was probably Saul's birthplace.

Ze'lek — *cleft* — an Ammonite; one of David's valiant men (2 Sam. 23:37).

Zelo'phehad—*first-born*—of the tribe of Manasseh, and of the family of Gilead; died in the wilderness. Having left no sons, his daughters, concerned lest their father's name should be "done away from among his family," made an appeal to Moses, who, by divine direction, appointed it as "a statute of judgment" in Israel that daughters should inherit their father's portion when no sons were left (Num. 27:1-11). But that the possession of Zelophehad might not pass away in the year of jubilee from the tribe to which he belonged, it was ordained by Moses that his daughters should not marry any one out of their father's tribe; and this afterwards became a general law (Num. 36).

Zelo'tes (Luke 6:15). See SIMON; ZEALOTS.

Zemara'im. (1.) A town of Benjamin (Josh. 18:22); now the ruin, rather two ruins, *es-Sŭmrâh*, 4 miles north of Jericho.

(2.) A mount in the highlands of Ephraim, to the north of Jerusalem (2 Chr. 13:4-20). Here the armies of Abijah and Jeroboam engaged in a bloody battle, which issued in the total defeat of the king of Israel, who never "recovered strength again," and soon after died.

Zem'arite, the designation of one of the Phœnician tribes (Gen. 10:18) who inhabited the town of Sumra, at the western base of the Lebanon range.

Zem'ira — *vine-dresser* — a Benjamite; one of the sons of Becher (1 Chr. 7:8).

Ze'nas, a disciple called "the lawyer," whom Paul wished Titus to bring with him (Titus 3:13). Nothing more is known of him.

Zephani'ah—*Jehovah has concealed*, or *Jehovah of darkness*. (1.) The son of Cushi, and great-grandson of Hezekiah, and the ninth in the order of the minor prophets. He prophesied in the days of Josiah, king of Judah (B.C. 641-610), and was contemporary with Jeremiah, with whom he has much in common.

The book of his prophecies consists of:—

(*a*) An introduction (1:1-6), announcing the judgment of the world, and the judgment upon Israel, because of their transgressions.

(*b*) The description of the judgment (1:7-18).

(*c*) An exhortation to seek God while there is still time (2:1-3).

(*d*) The announcement of judgment on the heathen (2:4-15).

(*e*) The hopeless misery of Jerusalem (3:1-7).

(*f*) The promise of salvation (3:8-20).

His description of the great day of judgment in 1:14, 15 suggested to Thomas a Celano (A.D. 1250) the subject of the famous Latin hymn *Dies Iræ*.

(2.) The son of Maaseiah, the "second priest" in the reign of Zedekiah, often mentioned in Jeremiah as having been sent from the king to inquire (Jer. 21:1) regarding the coming woes which he had denounced, and to entreat the prophet's intercession that the judgment threatened might be averted (Jer. 29:25, 26, 29; 37:3; 38:1, 4; 52:24). He, along with some other captive Jews, was put to death by the king of Babylon "in Riblah in the land of Hamath" (2 Kings 25:21).

(3.) A Kohathite ancestor of the prophet Samuel (1 Chr. 6:36).

(4.) The father of Josiah, the priest who dwelt in Jerusalem when Darius issued the decree that the temple should be rebuilt (Zech. 6 : 10).

Ze′phath—*beacon; watch-tower*—a Canaanite town; called also Hormah (*q.v.*)—Judg. 1 : 17. It has been identified with the pass of *es-Sufah*, but with greater probability with *S′beita*.

Zeph′athah, a valley in the west of Judah, near Mareshah; the scene of Asa's conflict with Zerah the Ethiopian (2 Chr. 14:9–13). Identified with the *Wâdy Safieh*.

Ze′rah—*sunrise*. (1.) An "Ethiopian," probably Osorkon II., the successor of Shishak on the throne of Egypt. With an enormous army, the largest we read of in Scripture, he invaded the kingdom of Judah in the days of Asa (2 Chr. 14 : 9–15). He reached Zephathah, and there encountered the army of Asa. This is the only instance "in all the annals of Judah of a victorious encounter in the field with a first-class heathen power in full force." The Egyptian host was utterly routed, and the Hebrews gathered "exceeding much spoil." Three hundred years elapsed before another Egyptian army—that of Necho (B.C. 609)—came up against Jerusalem.

(2.) A son of Tamar (Gen. 38 : 30); called also Zara (Matt. 1 : 3).

(3.) A Gershonite Levite (1 Chr. 6 : 21,41).

Ze′red = Zared — *luxuriance; willow bush*—a brook or valley communicating with the Dead Sea near its southern extremity (Num. 21:12; Deut. 2:14). It is called the "brook of the willows" (Isa. 15:7) and the "river of the wilderness" (Amos 6:14). It has been identified with the *Wâdy el-Aksy.*

Zer′eda—*the fortress*—a city on the north of Mount Ephraim; the birthplace of Jeroboam (1 Kings 11:26). It is probably the same as Zaretan (Josh. 3:16), Zererath (Judg. 7:22), Zartanah (1 Kings 4:12), or the following.

Zered′athah, a place in the plain of Jordan; the same as Zarthan (2 Chr. 4:17; 1 Kings 7:46). Here Solomon erected the foundries in which Hiram made the great castings of bronze for the temple.

Zer′erath (Judg. 7:22), perhaps identical with Zereda or Zeredathah. Some identify it with *Zahrah*, a place about 3 miles west of Beth-shean.

Ze′resh—*star of Venus*—the wife of Haman, whom she instigated to prepare a gallows for Mordecai (Esther 5:10).

Zeru′ah—*stricken*—mother of Jeroboam, the first king of the ten tribes (1 Kings 11:26).

Zerub′babel—*the seed of Babylon*—the son of Salathiel or Shealtiel (Hag. 1:1; Zorobabel, Matt. 1:12); called also the son of Pedaiah (1 Chr. 3:17-19)—*i.e.*, according to a frequent usage of the word "son;" the grandson or the nephew of Salathiel. He is also known by the Persian name of Sheshbazzar (Ezra 1:8, 11). In the first year of Cyrus, king of Persia, he led the first band of Jews, numbering 42,360 (Ezra 2:64), exclusive of a large number of servants, who returned from captivity at the close of the seventy years. In the second year after the Return, he erected an altar and laid the foundation of the temple on the ruins of that which had been destroyed by Nebuchadnezzar (3:8-13; ch. 4-6). All through the work he occupied a prominent place, inasmuch as he was a descendant of the royal line of David.

Zerui′ah—*stricken of the Lord*—David's sister, and the mother of Abishai, Joab, and Asahel (1 Chr. 2:16), who were the three leading heroes of David's army, and being his nephews, they were admitted to the closest companionship with him.

Ze′tham—*olive planter*—a Levite (1 Chr. 23:8).

Ze′than, a Benjamite (1 Chr. 7:10).

Zi′a—*fear*—a Gadite (1 Chr. 5:13).

Zi′ba—*post; statue*—"a servant in the house of Saul" (2 Sam. 9:2), who informed David that Mephibosheth, a son of Jonathan, was alive. He afterwards dealt treacherously toward Mephibosheth, whom he slanderously misrepresented to David.

Zib′eon—*robber;* or *dyed*. (1.) A Hivite (Gen. 36:2).

(2.) A Horite, and son of Seïr (Gen. 36:20).

Zib′ia—*gazelle*—a Benjamite (1 Chr. 8:9).

Zib′iah, the mother of King Joash (2 Kings 12:1; 2 Chr. 24:1).

Zich′ri—*remembered; illustrious*. (1.) A Benjamite chief (1 Chr. 8:19).

(2.) Another of the same tribe (1 Chr. 8:23).

SIDON.

Zid'dim—*sides*—a town of Naphtali (Josh. 19 : 35), has been identified with *Kefr-Hattîn*, the "village of the Hittites," about 5 miles west of Tiberias.

Zidki'jah—*the Lord is righteous*—one who sealed the covenant with Nehemiah (Neh. 10 : 1).

Zi'don—*a fishery*—a town on the Mediterranean coast, about 25 miles north of Tyre. It received its name from the "first-born" of Canaan, the grandson of Noah (Gen. 10 : 15, 19). It was the first home of the Phœnicians on the coast of Palestine, and from its extensive commercial relations became a "great" city (Josh. 11 : 8 ; 19 : 28). It was the mother city of Tyre. It lay within the lot of the tribe of Asher, but was never subdued (Judg. 1 : 31). The Zidonians long oppressed Israel (Judg. 10 : 12). From the time of David its glory began to wane, and Tyre, its "virgin daughter" (Isa. 23 : 12), rose to its place of pre-eminence. Solomon entered into a matrimonial alliance with the Zi-, donians, and thus their form of idolatrous worship found a place in the land of Israel (1 Kings 11 : 1, 33). This city was famous for its manufactures and arts, as well as for its commerce (1 Kings 5 : 6 ; 1 Chr. 22 : 4 ; Ezek. 27 : 8). It is frequently referred to by the prophets (Isa. 23 : 2, 4, 12 ; Jer. 25 : 22 ; 27 : 3 ; 47 : 4 ; Ezek. 27 : 8 ; 28 : 21, 22 ; 32 : 30 ; Joel 3 : 4). Our Lord visited the "coasts" of Tyre and Zidon = Sidon (*q.v.*)—Matt. 15 : 21 ; Mark 7 : 24 ; Luke 4 : 26 ; and from this region many came forth to hear him preaching (Mark 3 : 8 ; Luke 6 : 17). From Sidon, at which the ship put in after leaving Cæsarea, Paul finally sailed for Rome (Acts 27 : 3, 4).

This city is now a ruin, called *Saida*. Among its remains many ancient tombs have been found. In 1855, the sarcophagus of Eshmanezer was discovered. From a Phœnician inscription on its lid, it appears that he was a "king of the Sidonians," probably in the eleventh century B.C., and that his mother was a priestess of Ashtoreth, "the goddess of the Sidonians." In this inscription Baal is mentioned as the chief god of the Sidonians.

Zif—*brightness ; splendour ; i.e.,* "the flower month"—mentioned only in 1 Kings 6 : 1, 37, as the "second month." It was called *Iyar* by the later Jews. (See MONTH.)

Zi'ha—*drought.* (1.) The name of a family of Nethinim (Ezra 2 : 43 ; Neh. 7 : 46).

(2.) A ruler among the Nethinim (Neh. 11 : 21).

Zik'lag, a town in the Negeb, or south country of Judah (Josh. 15 : 31), in the possession of the Philistines when David fled to Gath from Ziph with all his followers. Achish, the king, assigned him Ziklag as his place of residence. There he dwelt for over a year and four months. From this time it pertained to the kings of Judah (1 Sam. 27 : 6, 7). During his absence with his army to join the Philistine expedition against the Israelites (29 : 11), it was destroyed by the Amalekites (30 : 1, 2), whom David, however, pursued and utterly routed, returning all the captives (1 Sam. 30 : 26-31). Two days after his return from this expedition, David received tidings of the disastrous battle of Gilboa and of the death of Saul (2 Sam. 1 : 1-12). He now left Ziklag and returned to Hebron, along with his two wives, Ahinoam and Abigail, and his band of 600 men. It has been identified with '*Aslûj*, a heap of ruins south of Beersheba. Conder, however, identifies it with *Khirbet Zuheilîkah*, ruins found on three hills half a mile apart, some seventeen miles north-west of Beersheba, on the confines of Philistia, Judah, and Amalek.

Zil'lah—*shadow*—one of the wives of Lamech, of the line of Cain, and mother of Tubal-cain (Gen. 4 : 19, 22).

Zil'pah — *drooping* — Leah's handmaid, and the mother of Gad and Asher (Gen. 30 : 9-13).

Zil'thai—*shadow (i.e.,* protection) *of Jehovah.* (1.) A Benjamite (1 Chr. 8 : 20).

(2.) One of the captains of the tribe of Manasseh who joined David at Ziklag (1 Chr. 12 : 20).

Zim'mah—*mischief.* (1.) A Gershonite Levite (1 Chr. 6 : 20).

(2.) Another Gershonite Levite (1 Chr. 6 : 42).

(3.) The father of Joah (2 Chr. 29 : 12).

Zim'ran—*vine-dressers; celebrated*—one of the sons of Abraham by Keturah (Gen. 25:2).

Zim'ri—*praise-worthy.* (1.) A son of Salu, slain by Phinehas, the son of Eleazar, because of his wickedness in bringing a Midianitish woman into his tent (Num. 25:6-15).

(2.) Murdered Elah at Tirzah, and succeeded him on the throne of Israel (1 Kings 16:8-10). He reigned only seven days, for Omri, whom the army elected as king, laid siege to Tirzah, whereupon Zimri set fire to the palace and perished amid its ruins (11-20). Omri succeeded to the throne only after four years of fierce war with Tibni, another claimant to the throne.

Zin—*a low palm-tree*—the south-eastern corner of the desert et-Tîh, the wilderness of Paran, between the Gulf of Akabah and the head of the Wâdy Guraîyeh (Num. 13:21). To be distinguished from the wilderness of Sin (*q.v.*).

Zi'na—*ornament*—one of the sons of Shimei (1 Chr. 23:10).

Zi'on—*sunny; height*—one of the eminences on which Jerusalem was built. It was surrounded on all sides, except the north, by deep valleys, that of the Tyropœon (*q.v.*) separating it from Moriah (*q.v.*), which it surpasses in height by 105 feet. It was the south-eastern hill of Jerusalem.

When David took it from the Jebusites (Josh. 15:63; 2 Sam. 5:7) he built on it a citadel and a palace, and it became "the city of David" (1 Kings 8:1; 2 Kings 19:21, 31; 1 Chr. 11:5). In the later books of the Old Testament this name was sometimes used (Ps. 87:2; 149:2; Isa. 33:14; Joel 2:1) to denote Jerusalem in general, and sometimes God's chosen Israel (Ps. 51:18; 87:5).

In the New Testament (see SION) it is used sometimes to denote the Church of God (Heb. 12:22), and sometimes the heavenly city (Rev. 14:1).

Zi'or—*littleness*—a city in the mountains of Judah (Josh. 15:54); the modern *Si'aîr*, 4½ miles north-north-east of Hebron.

Ziph—*flowing.* (1.) A son of Jehaleleel (1 Chr. 4:16).

(2.) A city in the south of Judah (Josh. 15:24), probably at the pass of *Sufâh.*

(3.) A city in the mountains of Judah (Josh. 15:55), identified with the uninhabited ruins of *Tell ez-Zif*, about 5 miles south-east of Hebron. Here David hid himself during his wanderings (1 Sam. 23:19; Ps. 54, title).

Zi'phah, a descendant of Judah (1 Chr. 4:16).

Ziph'ron—*sweet odour*—a city on the northern border of Palestine (Num. 34:9), south-east of Hamath.

Zip'por—*a little bird*—the father of Balak, king of Moab (Num. 22:2, 4).

Zippo'rah—*a female bird.* Reuel's daughter, who became the wife of Moses (Ex. 2:21). In consequence of the event recorded in Ex. 4:24-26, she and her two sons, Gershom and Eliezer, when so far on the way with Moses toward Egypt, were sent back by him to her own kinsfolk, the Midianites, with whom they sojourned till Moses afterwards joined them (18:2-6).

Zith'ri—*the Lord protects*—a Levite, son of Uzziel (Ex. 6:22).

Ziz—*projecting; a flower*—a cleft or pass, probably that near En-gedi, which leads up from the Dead Sea (2 Chr. 20:16) in the direction of Tekoa; now *Tell Hasdsah.*

Zi'za—*splendour; abundance.* (1.) A Simeonite prince (1 Chr. 4:37-43).

(2.) A son of Rehoboam (2 Chr. 11:20).

Zi'zah, a Gershonite Levite (1 Chr. 23:11).

Zo'an (Old Egypt. *Sänt* = "stronghold," the modern *Sân*). A city on the Tanitic branch of the Nile, called by the Greeks Tanis. It was built seven years after Hebron in Palestine (Num. 13:22). This great and important city was the capital of the Hyksôs, or Shepherd kings, who ruled Egypt for more than 500 years. It was the frontier town of Goshen. Here Pharaoh was holding his court at the time of his various interviews with Moses and Aaron. "No trace of Zoan exists; Tanis was built over it, and city after city has been built over the ruins of that" (Harper, *Bible and Modern Discovery*). Extensive mounds of ruins, the wreck of the ancient city, now mark its site (Isa. 19:11, 13; 30:4; Ezek. 30:14). "The whole constitutes one of the grandest and oldest ruins in the world."

This city was also called "the Field of Zoan" (Ps. 78 : 12, 43) and "the Town of Rameses" (q.v.), because the oppressor rebuilt and embellished it, probably by the forced labour of the Hebrews, and made it his northern capital.

Zo'ar—*small*—a town on the east or south-east of the Dead Sea, to which Lot and his daughters fled from Sodom (Gen. 19 : 22, 23). It was originally called Bela (14 : 2, 8). It is referred to by the prophets Isaiah (15 : 5) and Jeremiah (48 : 34). Its ruins are still seen at the opening of the ravine of Kerak, the Kir-Moab referred to in 2 Kings 3, the modern *Tell esh-Shaghûr*.

Zo'bah = **Aram-Zobah** (Ps. 60, title), a Syrian province or kingdom to the south of Cœle-Syria, and extending from the eastern slopes of Lebanon north and east toward the Euphrates. Saul and David had war with the kings of Zobah (1 Sam. 14 : 47; 2 Sam. 8 : 3; 10 : 6).

Zo'har—*brightness*. (1.) The father of Ephron the Hittite (Gen. 23 : 8).

(2.) One of the sons of Simeon (Gen. 46 : 10; Ex. 6 : 15).

Zo'heleth—*the serpent-stone*—a rocky plateau near the centre of the village of Siloam, and near the fountain of En-rogel, to which the women of the village resort for water (1 Kings 1 : 5–9). Here Adonijah (q.v.) feasted all the royal princes except Solomon and the men who took part with him in his effort to succeed to the throne. While they were assembled here Solomon was proclaimed king, through the intervention of Nathan. On hearing this, Adonijah fled and took refuge in the sanctuary (1 Kings 1 : 49-53). He was afterwards pardoned.

Zoheleth projects into or slightly overhangs the Kidron valley. It is now called *ez-Zehwell* or *Zahweileh*.

Zo'heth—*snatching* (?)—one of the sons of Ishi (1 Chr. 4 : 20).

Zo'phah—*spreading out*—a son of Helem (1 Chr. 7 : 35), a chief of Asher.

Zo'phar—*chirping*—one of Job's friends

who came to condole with him in his distress (Job 2 : 11. The LXX. render here "king of the Mineans" = Ma'in, Maonites, Judg. 10 : 12, in Southern Arabia. He is called a Naamathite, or an inhabitant of some unknown place called Naamah.

Zo'phim, Field of—*field of watchers*—a place in Moab on the range of Pisgah (Num. 23 : 14). To this place Balak brought Balaam, that he might from thence curse the children of Israel. Balaam could only speak the word of the Lord, and that was blessing. It is the modern *Tal'at-es-Safa*. (See PISGAH.)

Zo'rah—*place of wasps*—a town in the low country of Judah, afterwards given to Dan (Josh. 19 : 41; Judg. 18 : 2), probably the same as Zoreah (Josh. 15 : 33). This was Samson's birthplace (Judg. 13 : 2, 25), and near it he found a grave (16 : 31). It was situated on the crest of a hill overlooking the valley of Sorek, and was fortified by Rehoboam (2 Chr. 11 : 10). It has been identified with *Sur'ah*, in the Wâdy Sŭrâr, 8 miles west of Jerusalem.

Zorob'abel (Matt. 1 : 12; Luke 3 : 27). See ZERUBBABEL.

Zuph—*honeycomb*—a Kohathite Levite, ancestor of Elkanah and Samuel (1 Sam. 1 : 1); called also Zophai (1 Chr. 6 : 26).

Zuph, Land of (1 Sam. 9 : 5, 6), a district in which lay Samuel's city, Ramah. It was probably so named after Elkanah's son, Zuph (1 Chr. 6 : 26, marg.).

Zur—*rock*. (1.) One of the five Midianite kings whom the Israelites defeated and put to death (Num. 31 : 8).

(2.) A Benjamite (1 Chr. 8 : 30).

Zu'riel—*rock of God*—chief of the family of the Merarites (Num. 3 : 35) at the time of the Exodus.

Zu'rishad'dai—*rock of the Almighty*—the father of Shelumiel, who was chief of the tribe of Simeon when Israel was encamped at Sinai (Num. 1 : 6; 2 : 12).

Zu'zims—*restless; sprouting*—were smitten "in Ham" by Chedorlaomer and his allies (Gen. 14 : 5). Some have identified this tribe with the Zamzummims (q.v.).

APPENDIX.

CONTENTS.

I.—CHRONOLOGICAL TABLES.

1. *The Old Testament to the Death of Solomon.*

(According to Ussher. See "Chronology.")

B.C.
4004 .. The creation.
3874 .. Birth of Seth.
3382 .. Birth of Enoch, the seventh from Adam.
3317 .. Birth of Methuselah.
3130 .. Birth of Lamech.
3074 .. Death of Adam, aged 930 years.
3017 .. Translation of Enoch in the three hundred
    and sixty-fifth year of his age.
2948 .. Birth of Noah.
2348 .. Death of Methuselah, aged 969 years.
2348 .. The deluge.
2233 .. Dispersion of mankind; confusion of
    tongues at Babel.
2126 .. Birth of Terah, Abram's father.
1998 .. Death of Noah, aged 950 years, 350 years
    after the flood.
1996 .. Birth of Abram. He was 75 years old when
    his father Terah died.
1922 .. Terah, with his family, leaves Ur of the
    Chaldees, and dwells in Haran.

B.C.
1921 .. Abram enters the land of Canaan.
1913 .. Abram rescues Lot, who had been taken
    prisoner by Chedorlaomer (Gen. 14: 4-20).
1910 .. Birth of Ishmael.
1897 .. Destruction of Sodom and Gomorrah.
1896 .. Isaac born, Abraham being 100 years old.
1859 .. Sarah died at Hebron, in the one hundred
    and twenty-seventh year of her age.
1821 .. Abraham died, aged 175 years, 100 years
    after his entrance into the land of Ca-
    naan.
1773 .. Ishmael died, aged 137 years.
1760 .. Jacob fled into Mesopotamia to escape his
    brother's rage.
1739 .. Jacob returns to Canaan from Mesopotamia.
1729 .. Joseph is sold to the Midianites.
1716 .. Isaac died, aged 180 years.
1715 .. Joseph made governor over the whole of
    Egypt.
1708 .. The seven years of famine begin.

B.C.

1706..Jacob, with his family, goes down into Egypt.

1689..Death of Jacob.

1635..Joseph dies, aged 110 years.

1571..Birth of Moses.

1531..Moses flees into the land of Midian.

1491..Moses returns to Egypt at the command of God.

1491..Exodus.

1451..Death of Miriam, Moses' sister.

1451..In the fifth month of this year Aaron dies on Mount Hor, aged 123 years.

1451..In the twelfth month of this year Moses dies on Mount Nebo, aged 120 years.

1451..Entrance of the tribes into Canaan.

1444..The first Sabbatical year. From hence the year of jubilee is to be reckoned.

1444..The tabernacle set up in Shiloh, where it remained 328 years.

1427..Joshua dies, aged 110 years. Then follows a period of anarchy and confusion. The people sink into idolatry, and are brought under subjection to Cushan, king of Mesopotamia, for 8 years.

B.C.

1400..Othniel, the first of the judges, delivers Israel. Israel continued to be governed by judges for about 450 years, to the time of Samuel.

1091..Saul anointed king by Samuel.

1085..David, the son of Jesse, born.

1065..David anointed king (1 Sam. 16:13).

1055..Death of Saul at Gilboa.

1055..David goes to Hebron, and is there anointed king by the men of Judah, and there he reigns 7½ years.

1048..The captains and elders of all the tribes coming to Hebron anoint David as king over all Israel. Jerusalem now becomes the seat of his kingdom. Here he reigned 33 years.

1023..Rebellion of Absalom.

1015..Solomon anointed king by the command of his father David.

1012..Solomon begins to build the temple, which was finished in 7½ years.

1004..The temple dedicated at the Feast of Tabernacles.

976..Death of Solomon, after reigning 40 years. The kingdom is now divided.

2. *The Kingdoms of Judah and Israel to the Close of the Old Testament.*

Relation of the Two Kingdoms to each other.	Kingdom of Judah.	B.C.	Kingdom of Israel.	Contemporaneous Persons and Events in Heathen Countries.
I. Mutual hostility from B.C. 976 to B.C. 918.	Rehoboam. Son of Solomon and Naamah. Reigned 17 years.	976	Jeroboam. Son of Nebat. Reigned 22 years. *Prophet:* Ahijah.	
	Land invaded and Jerusalem plundered by Shishak, and Rehoboam made tributary (1 Kings 14:25, 26). *Prophets:* Shemaiah and Iddo.	973		Shishak, king of Egypt.
	Abijah or **Abijam.** Son of Rehoboam and Maachah. Reigned 3 years (1 Kings 15:1, 2).	959		
	Asa (1 Kings 15:9). Son of Abijah. Cushite invasion. War with Zĕrah the Ethiopian (2 Chr. 14:9). Alliance with Ben-hadad I. (1 Kings 15:18). Reigned 41 years. *Prophets:* Oded, Azariah, Hanani, and Jehu.	956 955	**Nadab** (1 Kings 15:25). Son of Jeroboam. Murdered by Baasha, after a brief reign.	**Osorkon II.** (= probably Zĕrah), king of Egypt, the invader of Judah (2 Chr. 14:9).

Relation of the Two Kingdoms to each other.	Kingdom of Judah	B.C.	Kingdom of Israel.	Contemporaneous Persons and Events in Heathen Countries.
		953	**Baasha** (1 Kings 15:28). Son of Ahijah of Issachar. He exterminated the entire house of Jeroboam (1 Kings 11:29–39; 15:29). Reigned 24 years. *Prophet:* Jehu.	Ben-hadad I., king of Syria.
		944		The poet Hesiod in Greece.
		931	**Elah** (1 Kings 16:8). Son of Baasha. Was assassinated, after reigning 2 years, by Zimri, one of his captains, who "destroyed all the house of Baasha" (1 Kings 16:11).	
		929	**Zimri.** Reigned only 7 days (1 Kings 16:10).	
		929	**Omri.** Civil war with Tibni for 4 years (1 Kings 16:21).	
		925	**Omri.** Reigned alone 6 years (1 Kings 16:23).	
		924	**Samaria made the capital** (1 Kings 16:24). Invaded by the Syrians (1 Kings 20:34).	
II. Alliance between the kingdoms, and common hostility to Syria, from B.C. 918 to B.C. 883.		918	**Ahab** (1 Kings 16:29, 31). Son of Omri. He changed the state religion, and so "made a prodigious step downwards" by introducing the impure and debasing worship of the Phœnician gods. Reigned 22 years. *Prophets:* Elijah and Micaiah.	Ethbaal, king of Tyre and Sidon. Ben-hadad II., king of Damascus.
	Jehoshaphat (1 Kings 22:41). Son of Asa and Azubah. Joined "affinity with Ahab" (2 Chr. 18:1) Associated with him his son Jehoram, when 16 years of age, the two reigning conjointly for 8 years. *Prophets:* Eliezer and Jahaziel.	915		
		900		Homer flourished.

Relation of the Two Kingdoms to each other.	Kingdom of Judah.	B.C.	Kingdom of Israel.	Contemporaneous Persons and Events in Heathen Countries.
		900	Battle at Ramoth-gilead, in which Ahab was slain (1 Kings 22:37).	
		898	Ahaziah (1 Kings 22:51, 52). Son of Ahab. Reigned 2 years. *Prophet:* Elisha.	Lycurgus in Sparta.
		897	Jehoram or Joram. Son of Ahab (2 Kings 3:2). The last king of the house of Omri. War against Mesha (2 Kings 3:4-27). Was put to death by Jehu (2 Kings 9:1-23; comp. 1 Kings 21:21), after reigning 12 years.	
	Jehoram (2 Kings 8:16; 2 Chr. 21:11-13). Son of Jehoshaphat. His reign was one of the darkest and most unfortunate in Judean history (2 Chr. 21:12-20). Reigned as sole ruler 8 years.	892		
	Ahaziah. Youngest son of Jehoram and Athalia (2 Kings 8:25; 2 Chr. 22:1-3). Was put to death by Jehu (2 Kings 9:24; comp. 2 Chr. 22:9), after reigning 1 year.	884		Hazael of Syria.
III. Renewal of mutual hostilities, and gradual decline of both kingdoms (B.C. 883 to B.C. 588).	Athaliah (2 Kings 11:3). Daughter of Ahab and Jezebel. Usurped the throne, and reigned 6 years. The last survivor of the house of Omri. Was put to death by Jehoiada.	883	Jehu (2 Kings 10:36). Son of Nimshi. With him began the most powerful and the longest lived of all the Israelite dynasties. Reigned 28 years. *Prophet:* Jonah.	
	Joash or Jehoash (2 Kings 11:4; 12:1). Son of Ahaziah and Zibia. Was slain on his sick-bed in the castle of Millo. Reigned 40 years. *Prophet:* Joel.	877		Pygmalion, king of Tyre.
		869		Carthage founded by Dido, the Phœnician queen, 143 years after the building of the temple.

Relation of the Two Kingdoms to each other.	Kingdom of Judah.	B.C.	Kingdom of Israel.	Contemporaneous Persons and Events in Heathen Countries.
		855	Jehoahaz (2 Kings 13 : 1). Eldest son of Jehu. Ravages of the Syrians. Reigned 17 years.	
Syrians invade Judah.		840		
		839	Jehoash or Joash (2 Kings 13 : 10). Defeats the Syrians thrice. Conquers Judah. Reigned 16 years.	
	Amaziah (2 Kings 14 : 1). Son of Joash and Jehoaddan. Conquers Edom. Defeat at Beth-shemesh (2 Kings 14 : 13). Reigned 29 years.	838	Death of Elisha (2 Kings 13 : 14).	Ben-hadad III., king of Syria.
		823	Jeroboam II. (2 Kings 14 : 23). Son of Joash. The greatest of all the kings of Samaria. Reigned 41 years.	
		820		Empire of the Medes founded by Arbaces.
		814		Kingdom of Macedon founded by Caranus.
	Uzziah or Azariah (2 Kings 15 : 1, 2). Son of Amaziah and Jecholiah. Reigned 52 years. Prophet: Amos.	809		
		784	Interregnum. A period of anarchy of 11 years and some months. Prophet: Hosea.	
		776		The Grecian era. Computation by Olympiads, periods of 4 years, begins.
		771	Zachariah (2 Kings 15 : 8). Son of Jeroboam II. Slain by Shallum. Reigned 6 months.	
		770	Shallum (2 Kings 15 : 13). Reigned 1 month.	Pul, king of Assyria.
		770	Menahem (2 Kings 15 : 17). Israel invaded by Pul. Menahem becomes a vassal of Assyria (2 Kings 15 : 19).	

Relation of the Two Kingdoms to each other.	Kingdom of Judah.	B.C.	Kingdom of Israel.	Contemporaneous Persons and Events in Heathen Countries.
		761	Pekahiah. Son of Menahem (2 Kings 15:23–26). Reigned 2 years.	
	Jotham (2 Kings 15:32, 33). Son of Uzziah and Jerusha. Reigned 16 years. *Prophets:* Micah and Isaiah.	759 758	Pekah (2 Kings 15:27, 28). Forms an alliance with Rezin. War with Judah. The kingdom attacked by Tiglath-pileser. Reigned 20 years.	
		752		Foundation of Rome.
		747		Nabonassar, king of Babylon. Rezin, king of Syria.
	Ahaz (2 Kings 16:1). Son of Jotham. The party in Jerusalem in favour of an alliance with Assyria predominates (2 Kings 16:7). Reigned 16 years. *Prophets:* Isaiah and Oded.	742		Tiglath-pileser, king of Assyria.
		740 734	Interregnum of 9 years.	Syracuse founded.
		730	Hoshea (2 Kings 17:1). Son of Elah. Enters into an alliance with So, king of Egypt. The last and best king of Israel. Reigned 9 years.	So, king of Egypt.
		727		Shalmaneser IV. succeeds Tiglath-pileser, and besieges Samaria, making Hoshea tributary.
	Hezekiah (2 Kings 18:1). Son of Ahaz and Abijah. The party in favour of an alliance with Egypt predominates till the defeat of Tirhakah at Eltekeh. From this time the views of Isaiah, who opposed all alliances with foreign powers, prevailed during the rest of Hezekiah's reign.	726		
	First invasion of Judah by Sennacherib. Hezekiah submits. Renewed invasion. Destruction of Sennacherib's army.	721 714	Fall of Samaria, Israel in exile in Assyria, and the land peopled by colonists from Assyria. Destruction of the commonwealth of Israel, after a separate existence of 253 years (2 Kings 18:10).	Sargon seizes the throne of Assyria, and takes Samaria, the siege of which was begun by Shalmaneser. Merodach-baladan conquers Babylon.
	Hezekiah's illness. Reigned 29 years. *Prophet:* Isaiah.	712		

Kingdom of Judah.	B.C.	Contemporaneous Persons and Events in Heathen Countries.
	705	Sargon murdered, and succeeded by his son Sennacherib.
Manasseh (2 Kings 21:1). Son of Hezekiah. Great national apostasy. Carried captive to Babylon (2 Chr. 33:11). His repentance and restoration. Reigned 55 years. *Prophets:* Micah, Isaiah, and probably Nahum.	697	
	681	Sennacherib murdered, and succeeded by his son Esarhaddon (2 Kings 19:37).
	668–626	Assurbanipal, king of Assyria.
	666–612	Psammetichus I., king of Egypt, was succeeded by his son Necho II.
Amon (2 Kings 21:19). Was murdered after a reign of 2 years. *Prophet:* Nahum.	642	
Josiah (2 Kings 22:1). National revival of religion.	640 629 625	Fall of Nineveh. Nabopolassar, father of Nebuchadnezzar, independent in Babylon.
Finding of the book of the law. Slain at Megiddo. Reigned 31 years. *Prophets:* Jeremiah, Zephaniah, Habakkuk, and Huldah.	621	
	612–596	Necho II., king of Egypt.
Jehoahaz or Shallum (1 Chr. 3:15). Josiah's third son. "Did evil in the sight of the Lord." Reigned 3 months, when he was deposed by Necho, who took him to Egypt (2 Kings 23:33).	609	Necho II., on his way to assail the Babylonians at Carchemish, encountered and defeated the army of Josiah near Megiddo (*q.v.*). Josiah was fatally wounded (2 Chr. 35:24), and Palestine became tributary to Egypt.
Jehoiakim or Eliakim. Josiah's second son. Made king by Necho (2 Kings 23:36). Judah becomes tributary to Nebuchadnezzar (2 Kings 24:1). *Commencement of the 70 years' captivity.*	609 606	Nebuchadnezzar overcame the powerful army of the Egyptians, under Necho II., at Carchemish (Jer. 46:8–21), on the Middle Euphrates. Syria and Palestine now became tributary to Babylon (2 Kings 24:1). Daniel and other noble and royal youths are taken captive to Babylon.
Jehoiakim, despite the warnings of Jeremiah, rebelled against Nebuchadnezzar, who marched at the head of a large army into Syria and besieged Jerusalem. Jehoiakim was put to death, and Jehoiakin was placed on the throne by Nebuchadnezzar.	602	
Jehoiakin (Jeconiah or Coniah). Being suspicious of Jehoiakin's loyalty, Nebuchadnezzar led an army against Jerusalem and plundered it, carrying away many captives (2 Kings 24:10–16), among whom were the king and all his household. He placed Mattaniah on the vacant throne, giving him the name of Zedekiah. *Second conquest of Jerusalem.* Reigned 3 months.	599	

Kingdom of Judah.	B.C.	Contemporaneous Persons and Events in Heathen Countries.
Mattaniah (Zedekiah). He rebelled against Nebuchadnezzar, his suzerain, and formed an alliance with Hophra, king of Egypt (2 Kings 24 : 20; Jer. 44 : 30; Ezek. 17 : 15). Nebuchadnezzar came "with all his host" against Jerusalem (2 Kings 25 : 1). Egypt proved again for the Jews a "bruised reed" (2 Kings 18 : 21), and failed to help them. Jerusalem was besieged for a year and a half, and was visited with dire distress, famine, and pestilence. The defences of the city gave way, and the Babylonian army entered it. The doomed city drank the cup of God's fury to the dregs. The king and all his followers were taken captive, and brought to Riblah. There his son was put to death in his presence, and his own eyes were then put out, and he became a captive in Babylon to the day of his death (Jer. 52 : 11). *The second captivity.* Reigned 11 years. *Prophet:* Ezekiel.	599	
	596–591 594 591–572	Psammetichus II., king of Egypt. Solon at Athens. Hophra, king of Egypt.
Gedaliah. Appointed governor by Nebuchadnezzar (2 Kings 25 : 22). Was killed by Ishmael. Jerusalem destroyed. Many of the people carried captive to Babylon. *The third captivity.* The rest fled to Egypt (2 Kings 25 : 26). Judah lies desolate (2 Chr. 36 : 21; Zech. 7 : 14).	588	
Palestine.		
	562	Nebuchadnezzar dies, after a reign of 43 years, and is succeeded by his son Evil-merodach.
	558	Media and Persia united into one kingdom under Cyrus.
	559	Neriglissar (probably = Nergal-sharezer), Nebuchadnezzar's son-in-law, succeeds Evil-merodach.
	555	Nabonadius, the last king of Babylon. Belshazzar, his son, latterly associated with him as king. Belshazzar commanded at Babylon while his father Nabonadius took the field against Cyrus.
	538	During the siege of Babylon by Cyrus, Belshazzar made a great feast, and that night the city was taken, and Belshazzar was slain, the empire passing to the Medes and Persians. Then Darius the Mede "took the kingdom," Cyrus making him governor of the Medo-Persian empire, with the title of King. Daniel cast into the den of lions.

Palestine.	B.C.	Contemporaneous Persons and Events in Heathen Countries.
Palestine becomes a province of the Persian empire. Return of the *first* caravan "of the children of the province"—*i.e.*, of Judea—under Zerubbabel, whom Cyrus made tirshatha or governor of Judea. Only about 50,000 Jews returned on this occasion.	536	Cyrus's first year, on the death of Darius. Issues his edict in favour of the Jewish captives (Ezra 1 : 1–4 ; 6 : 3–5 ; comp. Isa. 44 : 28).
Rebuilding of the temple begun.	535	
Daniel sees the vision recorded in ch. 10–12. The Samaritans oppose the building of the temple.	534	
	529	Tarquinius Superbus at Rome. Ahasuerus (Cambyses, Cyrus's son) succeeds Cyrus as king of Persia (Ezra 4 : 6).
Building of the temple suspended.	521	
Zerubbabel and Jeshua renew the building in the second year of Darius, roused thereto by the prophets Haggai and Zechariah.	520	
Darius discovers and re-enacts Cyrus's decree.	519	
	516	Babylon was destroyed by Darius Hystaspes.
The temple completed and dedicated in the sixth year of Darius.	515	
	490	Battle of Marathon.
	486	Xerxes I. (Ahasuerus of Esther).
	483	In the third year of his reign, he holds a great assembly previous to his invasion of Greece, and divorces Queen Vashti. Probably not till after his return from the disastrous invasion did he marry Hadassa (Esther).
	480	Battles of Thermopylæ and Salamis.
The Jews are under Persian governors. Many abuses appear among them.	479	Battle of Platea. Sea-fight of Mycale.
	478	Esther made queen.
	466	Xerxes slain by two of his courtiers; succeeded by his son Artaxerxes (Longimanus)
Ezra obtains a commission from Artaxerxes (Longimanus), and leads a *second* company of exiles back to Jerusalem (Ezra 7 : 8).	457	
Nehemiah, cupbearer of Artaxerxes, appointed governor of Jerusalem. Is opposed by Sanballat and Tobiah.	446	
Nehemiah returns to Persia.	433	
Nehemiah revisits Jerusalem, and reforms many abuses.	432	
	431	Peloponnesian War begins.
	423	Socrates, Xenophon, and Thucydides at Athens.
Death of Nehemiah.	413	
Ezra and the Great Synagogue, including the prophets Haggai, Zechariah, and Malachi, probably gathered together the several books which form the Old Testament canon.	397 354	Demosthenes.
Temple built on Gerizim by the Samaritans.	332	Alexander the Great takes the city of Tyre.

3. *Chronology according to the Assyrian Inscriptions.*

The following dates, as given by Sayce from the Assyrian Inscriptions, may be compared with those in Ussher's Chronology :—

B.C.

858–823..Shalmaneser II., king of Assyria, succeeded his father Assur-natsir-pal. His long reign was one continuous history of campaigns against his neighbours, his chief object of attack being the growing power of Damascus.

853..Ahab, son of Omri, as ally of Damascus against Shalmaneser (1 Kings 20 : 34). In the time of Ahab the Assyrians first became acquainted with the kingdom of Israel. Samaria was ever afterwards called by them Beth-Omri "the house of Omri."

851..Death of Ahab.

850..Shalmaneser's campaign against the Syrian king Hadadezer (=Ben-hadad II.).

845..Shalmaneser's second campaign against Hadadezer.

843..Hadadezer murdered by Hazael, king of Syria (2 Kings 13 : 22).

841..Jehu pays tribute to Assyria.

840..Shalmaneser's campaign against Hazael proved disastrous to the Syrians.

843..Shalmaneser again sent his troops against "Hazael of the country of Damascus," and captured four of his cities, after which he made no further incursions into the west.

823..Samas-Rimmon II. succeeded his father Shalmaneser II. on the Assyrian throne.

810–781..Rimmon-nirari, grandson of Shalmaneser, ascended the throne.

804..Damascus taken by the Assyrians and reduced to a condition of vassalage.

781..Shalmaneser III. ascends the throne of Assyria.

773..Assyrian campaign against Damascus.

771..Assur-dân III. becomes king of Assyria.

756 .Jotham made regent with his father Uzziah.

753..Assur-nirari king of Assyria.

745..The first Assyrian empire came to an end "partly from internal decay, partly through the attacks of its Armenian neighbours. The last representative (Assur-nirari) of the old dynasty died or was slain in the same year. Pulu (Pul), a military captain of obscure origin, seized the vacant throne." He founded the second Assyrian empire, taking the name of Tiglath-pileser (III.), after the name of one of the most famous monarchs of the older dynasty some four centuries before.

743–40..Tiglath-pileser II. wars against Hamath. Submission of Uzziah.

742..Uzziah sends help to Hamath.

741..Death of Jotham and accession of Ahaz.

738..Azariah (= Uzziah) defeated by Tiglath-pileser, who exacts tribute from Menahem of Samaria and Rezon of Damascus.

734..Damascus besieged by the Assyrians. The tribes beyond Jordan are carried away captive. Jehoahaz of Judah becomes a vassal of Tiglath-pileser.

732..Damascus taken and Rezon slain.

729..Pekah put to death. Hoshea ascends the throne.

728..Ululâ of Tinu, a usurper, takes the name of Shalmaneser (IV.) (2 Kings 17 : 3), and ascends the Assyrian throne.

723..Samaria besieged by Shalmaneser V. The siege lasted three years.

722..On the death of Shalmaneser one of his captains, a soldier of fortune, seized the vacant throne, and took the name of Sargon.

721..Merodach - baladan of Chaldea conquers Babylon.

712–11..Embassy sent by Merodach-baladan to Hezekiah with the view of exciting trouble in the west, so as to divide the forces of Sargon, who was now threatening an invasion of Babylonia. The illness of Hezekiah was only the pretext for this embassy.

711..Capture of Jerusalem and Ashdod by Sargon.

705..Sennacherib, Sargon's son, king of Assyria.

701..Sennacherib's disastrous campaign against Judah.

697..Death of Hezekiah, and accession of his son Manasseh. The name of "Manasseh king of Judah" twice occurs on the Assyrian monuments.

691..Babylon razed to the ground by Sennacherib.

681..Sennacherib murdered, and was succeeded by his son Esarhaddon, who rebuilt Babylon, and sought to win over the Babylonians by residing in it during half the year.

676..Manasseh appears among the Assyrian tributaries.

668..Esarhaddon dies, and is succeeded by his son Assur-bani-pal (Sardanapalos).

665..Destruction of Thebes (="No Amon"=Nî of the Inscriptions) by the Assyrians. This city was "swept like a deluge" because Egypt, under Urduman, son of Tirhakah, had revolted from Assyria (Nah. 3 : 8, 10).

609..Josiah of Judah, in the name of his suzerain, "the king of Assyria," opposed the march of Pharaoh. He was slain in battle (2 Kings 23 : 29).

606(?)..Fall of Nineveh, Esarhaddon II. (Sarakos) being the last king. "The bloody city" became a heap of ruins. "The Assyrian empire vanished from the earth, and its very existence soon became little more than a name. The Oriental ground over which it had tyrannized became the fighting-ground of three rival powers—the Babylonians, the Egyptians, and the so-called Medes" (*Sayce*).

4. Between the Testaments.

From the death of Nehemiah to the fall of the Medo-Persian empire before the Macedonian little is known of the Jews. The high priests were practically the rulers of the people. They were assisted by a council of one hundred and twenty members, called the Great Synagogue. The royal house of David sank into oblivion, prophecy was suspended, and the Jews gradually became more and more exclusive and austere, both religiously and socially.

(1.) The Hellenistic Domination.

	B.C.
Alexander the Great defeated Darius (Codomannus) and founded the Macedonian empire — the Greek empire in Asia	331–167
Death of Alexander the Great at Babylon	323
Alexander's four generals (the *diadochi*) divide his empire between them. Palestine becomes a part of Syria	323
Judea is annexed to Egypt when the Græco-Egyptian kingdom is founded, and the Jews come under the dominion of the Ptolemies. The Jews are scattered over the heathen world	301–221
The Old Testament began to be translated into Greek by learned Jews in Alexandria for the use of the African Jews. The translation was probably completed during the next century. It is called the *Septuagint* (*q.v.*) Version	291
Antiochus III., the Great, overruns Palestine	219
Ptolemy IV. of Egypt recovers Palestine	217
The Jews submit to Antiochus the Great	205
Antiochus the Great defeats the Egyptians, and Palestine becomes a part of the Græco-Syrian kingdom	197
Antiochus IV. (Epiphanes) usurps the Græco-Syrian throne	175
Antiochus cruelly persecutes the Jews, ordering all his subjects on pain of death to adopt the Græco-Syrian religion and customs	170–167

(2.) The Period of the Maccabees and the Ashmonœan Kings.

	B.C.
A band of patriotic Jews, headed by Matthias the Ashmonæan, rebel against the tyranny of Antiochus	166
Antiochus dies at Tabæ in Persia, being stricken with a loathsome disease (comp. Acts 12: 23), which he recognizes as a	

	B.C.
judgment sent upon him for his treatment of the Jews	164
After a period of varying success, the Maccabean commonwealth, introducing the era of Jewish independence, is established	143
The Ashmonæan kings rule over Judea	106–65
Pompey annexes Syria to Rome, and Judea becomes from this time a Roman dependency	63
Julius Cæsar appoints Antipater, son of Antipas, an Idumæan chief, first procurator of Judea, Samaria, and Galilee, and henceforward the Herodian family supplants the Ashmonæan	47
Antipater makes his son Herod joint (with his brother Phasaël) tetrarch of Judea and Galilee	41

(3.) The Herodian Kingdom.

	B.C.
Herod the Great takes Jerusalem, and becomes the founder of the Herodian kingdom. End of the Ashmonæan line	37
Battle of Actium	31
Egypt becomes a Roman province, and is the chief seat of the Jewish Dispersion	30
Herod rebuilds Samaria, and attempts to introduce among the Jews Greek and Roman customs	27
Augustus emperor of Rome	B.C. 27–A.D. 14
Herod founds the Græco-Roman city and port of Cæsarea	B.C. 22
Erects a temple to Augustus at Paneas	20
Begins the rebuilding of the temple	18
Building of Cæsarea finished. It is dedicated to Augustus	10
Birth of John the Baptist	5
Birth of our Lord, as now generally received. Death of Herod the Great at Jericho. Archelaus becomes king in his stead	4

5. *The New Testament History.*

Palestine.	B.C.	Rome.
Nativity of Christ. See above.	4	Cyrenius (Quirinus) prefect (*legatus*) of
Antipater murdered by his father.	2	Syria—the first time (Luke 2:2).
	A.D.	
Nativity of Christ, according to Tertullian and Eusebius.	1	
Judea becomes a Roman province, and is annexed to the province of Syria.	6	
Jesus at the age of twelve visits the temple.	8	Cyrenius again *legatus* of Syria. Completes the "taxing" (Acts 5:37).
	14	Tiberius succeeds Augustus.
Caiaphas made high priest.	17	
Pontius Pilate fifth procurator.	26	
John the Baptist imprisoned and beheaded by Herod Antipas.	30	
Crucifixion of our Lord. The Pentecostal effusion.	33	
Martyrdom of Stephen. Conversion of Saul of Tarsus.	36	
Herod Agrippa I. succeeded his uncle Herod Philip II. in the tetrarchy of Trachonitis and Ituræa.	37	Death of Tiberius. Accession of Caligula.
Saul's first visit to Jerusalem (Gal. 1:18). Herod Antipas, tetrarch of Galilee and Peræa, deposed and banished. Was succeeded by Herod Agrippa.	40	
Herod Agrippa I. gained Judea and Samaria. Conversion of Cornelius.	41	Death of Caligula. Accession of Claudius.
The first Gentile church at Antioch.	43	
Herod Agrippa I., king of Judea and Samaria, beheaded James (Zebedee's son) —Acts 12:2, 23. Herod Agrippa dies at Cæsarea (Acts 12:1, 6, 11, 19, 23).	44	
Paul's first missionary journey (about 3 years)—Acts 13–14. "Saul, who is also called Paul" (Acts 13:9).	47	
Council at Jerusalem (Acts 15:1–35). The epistle of the council to the Gentile Christians in Syria and Cilicia is probably the oldest written document of the Christian Church.	50	
Felix procurator. Paul's second missionary journey (more than 3 years)—Acts 15:36–18:23.	51	
Wrote from Corinth the epistles to the *Thessalonians* (1 Thess. 1:7, 8; Acts 18:5).	52	Decree of Claudius banishing the Jews from Rome.
	54–68	Nero emperor, successor of Claudius.
Paul's third missionary journey (about 4 years)—Acts 18:23–21:14.	54	
During his stay at Ephesus (Acts 19) wrote epistle to the *Galatians* (Acts 20:2; Gal. 6:11), and probably *First Corinthians* (1 Cor. 16:8).	57 or 58	
Wrote from Macedonia *Second Corinthians* (2 Cor. 1:23; 7:5).	57	
Wrote from Corinth epistle to *Romans* at close of his stay there (Acts 20:3; 1 Cor.16:6).	58	

Palestine.	A.D.	Rome.
Paul visits Jerusalem. Is brought before Felix, and imprisoned for two years at Cæsarea (Acts 21 : 17–26).	58	
Paul before the procurator Porcius Festus. Is sent a prisoner to Rome.	60	
Arrives at Rome in spring of	61	
Paul writes from Rome his epistles to the *Ephesians, Colossians, Philemon,* and the *Philippians,* and probably *Hebrews.*	61–63	
Paul probably released.	63	
Paul's movements after his release are uncertain. Some think that at Corinth he wrote the *First Epistle to Timothy* and the *Epistle to Titus.*	64	Great fire at Rome. First general persecution of the Christians.
Arrested at Ephesus, and sent prisoner to Rome.	65	
Wrote *Second Epistle to Timothy* from Rome. Was martyred (?).	66	
Others think that Paul wrote *First Epistle to Timothy* from Macedonia, and the *Epistle to Titus* from Ephesus, and that he spent the winter of this year at Nicopolis, where he was taken prisoner and sent to Rome, whence he wrote the	67	
Second Epistle to Timothy. Suffered martyrdom (?).	68	Nero killed by his secretary, Epaphroditus, "in the thirtieth year of his age and in the fourteenth of his reign."
	69	Vespasian emperor.
Destruction of Jerusalem by Titus, the Roman general.	70	
John probably writes his Gospel and Epistles.	80–90	
	91	Titus emperor.
John writes the book of Revelation.	95	Domitian emperor.
	96	Second general persecution of Christians.
	97	Nerva emperor.
Death of John.	98	Trajan emperor.

II.—MIRACLES RECORDED IN THE OLD TESTAMENT.

1. The flood .... Gen. 7, 8.
2. Destruction of Sodom and Gomorrah .... 19:24.
3. Lot's wife turned into a "pillar of salt" .... 19:26.
4. Birth of Isaac at Gerar .... 21:1.
5. The burning bush not consumed .... Ex. 3:3.
6. Aaron's rod changed into a serpent .... 7:10–12.
7. The ten plagues of Egypt— (1) waters become blood, (2) frogs, (3) lice, (4) flies, (5) murrain, (6) boils, (7) thunder and hail, (8) locusts, (9) darkness, (10) death of the first-born .... 7:20–12:30.
8. The Red Sea divided; Israel passes through .... 14:21–31.

9. The waters of Marah sweetened .... Ex. 15:23–25.
10. Manna sent daily, except on Sabbath .... 16:14–35.
11. Water from the rock at Rephidim .... 17:5–7.
12. Nadab and Abihu consumed for offering "strange fire" Lev. 10:1, 2.
13. Some of the people consumed by fire at Taberah .... Num. 11:1–3.
14. The earth opens and swallows up Korah and his company; fire and plague follow at Kadesh .... 16:32.
15. Aaron's rod budding at Kadesh .... 17:8.
16. Water from the rock, smitten twice by Moses, Desert of Zin .... 20:7–11.

17. The brazen serpent in the Desert of Zin............. Num. 21 : 8, 9.
18. Balaam's ass speaks....... 22 : 21–35.
19. The Jordan divided, so that Israel passed over dryshod Josh. 3 : 14–17.
20. The walls of Jericho fall down .... 6 : 6–20.
21. The sun and moon stayed. Hailstorm.............. 10 : 12–14.
22. The strength of Samson .... Judg. 14–16.
23. Water from a hollow place "that is in Lehi"........ 15 : 19.
24. Dagon falls twice before the ark. Emerods on the Philistines.............. 1 Sam. 5 : 1–12.
25. Men of Beth-shemesh smitten for looking into the ark................... 6 : 19.
26. Thunderstorm causes a panic among the Philistines at Eben-ezer.............. 7 : 10–12.
27. Thunder and rain in harvest at Gilgal............. 12 : 18.
28. Sound in the mulberry trees at Rephaim............. 2 Sam. 5 : 23–25.
29. Uzzah smitten for touching the ark at Perez-uzzah... 6 : 6, 7.
30. Jeroboam's hand withered. His new altar destroyed at Bethel.............. 1 Kings 13 : 4–6.
31. Widow of Zarephath's meal and oil increased....... 17 : 14–16.
32. Widow's son raised from the dead .... 17 : 17–24.
33. Drought, fire, and rain at Elijah's prayer, and Elijah fed by ravens........... 17, 18.
34. Ahaziah's captains consumed by fire near Samaria...... 2 Kings 1 : 10–12.
35. Jordan divided by Elijah and Elisha near Jericho...... 2 : 7, 8, 14.
36. Elijah carried up into heaven 2 : 11.

37. Waters of Jericho healed by Elisha's casting salt into them.................... 2 Kings 2 : 21, 22.
38. Bears out of the wood destroy forty-two "young men"..................... 2 : 24.
39. Water provided for Jehoshaphat and the allied army 3 : 16–20.
40. The widow's oil multiplied . 4 : 2–7.
41. The Shunammite's son given, and raised from the dead at Shunem.............. 4 : 32–37.
42. The deadly pottage cured with meal at Gilgal...... 4 : 38–41.
43. An hundred men fed with twenty loaves at Gilgal... 4 : 42–44.
44. Naaman cured of leprosy. Gehazi afflicted with it... 5 : 10–27.
45. The iron axe-head made to swim, river Jordan...... 6 : 5–7.
46. Ben-hadad's plans discovered. Hazael's thoughts, etc..................... 6 : 12.
47. The Syrian army smitten with blindness at Dothan. 6 : 18.
48. The Syrian army cured of blindness at Samaria..... 6 : 20.
49. Elisha's bones revive the dead..................... 13 : 21.
50. Sennacherib's army destroyed, Jerusalem....... 19 : 35.
51. Shadow of sun goes back ten degrees on the sun-dial of Ahaz, Jerusalem......... 20 : 9–11.
52. Uzziah struck with leprosy, Jerusalem.............. 2 Chr. 26 : 16–21.
53. Shadrach, Meshach, and Abed-nego delivered from the fiery furnace, Babylon Dan. 3 : 10–27.
54. Daniel saved in the lions' den 6 : 16–23.
55. Jonah in the whale's belly. Safely landed........... Jonah 2 : 1–10.

III.—MIRACLES RECORDED IN THE GOSPELS.

1. *Peculiar to Matthew.*

(1.) Cure of two blind men.......... 9 : 27–31. | (2.) Piece of money in the fish's mouth 17 : 24–27.

2. *Peculiar to Mark.*

(1.) The deaf and dumb man........ 7 : 31–37. | (2.) The blind man of Bethsaida .... 8 : 22–26.

3. *Peculiar to Luke.*

(1.) Jesus passes unseen through the crowd...................... 4 : 28–30.
(2.) The miraculous draught of fishes 5 : 4–11.
(3.) The raising of the widow's son at Nain .... 7 : 11–18.
(4.) The woman with the spirit of infirmity......................... 13 : 11–17.
(5.) The man with the dropsy........ 14 : 1–6.
(6.) The ten lepers .... 17 : 11–19.
(7.) The healing of Malchus......... 22 : 50, 51.

4. *Peculiar to John.*

(1.) Water made wine........ ...... 2 : 1–11.
(2.) Cure of nobleman's son, Capernaum 4 : 46–54.
(3.) Impotent man at Bethsaida cured 5 : 1–9.
(4.) Man born blind cured.......... 9 : 1–7.
(5.) Lazarus raised from the dead.... 11 : 38–44.
(6.) Draught of fishes................ 21 : 1–14.

5. *Common to Matthew and Mark.*
    (1.) Syrophœnician woman's daughter cured .... Matt. 15 : 28. | Mark 7 : 24.
    (2.) Four thousand fed .... 15 : 32. | 8 : 1.
    (3.) Fig-tree blasted .... 21 : 18. | 11 : 12.

6. *Common to Matthew and Luke.*
    (1.) Centurion's servant healed .... Matt. 8 : 5. | Luke 7 : 1.
    (2.) Blind and dumb demoniac cured .... 12 : 22. | 11 : 14.

7. *Common to Mark and Luke.*
    Demoniac cured in synagogue at Capernaum................. Mark 1 : 23. | Luke 4 : 33.

8. *Common to Matthew, Mark, and Luke.*
    (1.) Peter's wife's mother cured .... Matt. 8 : 14. | Mark 1 : 30. | Luke 4 : 38.
    (2.) The tempest stilled........................... 8 : 23. | 4 : 37. | 8 : 22.
    (3.) Demoniacs of Gadara cured.................. 8 : 28. | 5 : 1. | 8 : 26.
    (4.) Leper healed .... 8 : 2. | 1 : 40. | 5 : 12.
    (5.) Jairus's daughter raised...................... 9 : 23. | 5 : 23. | 8 : 41.
    (6.) Woman's issue of blood cured............... 9 : 20. | 5 : 25. | 8 : 43.
    (7.) Man sick of the palsy cured.................. 9 : 2. | 2 : 3. | 5 : 18.
    (8.) Man's withered hand cured................... 12 : 10. | 3 : 1. | 6 : 6.
    (9.) A lunatic child cured .... 17 : 14. | 9 : 14. | 9 : 37.
    (10.) Two blind men cured .... 20 : 29. | 10 : 46. | 18 : 35.

9. *Common to Matthew, Mark, and John.*
    Jesus walks on the sea........................ Matt. 14 : 25. | Mark 6 : 48. | John 6 : 15.

10. *Common to all the evangelists.*
    Jesus feeds 5,000 "in a desert place" Matt. 14 : 15. | Mark 6 : 30. | Luke 9 : 10. | John 6 : 1-14.

In addition to the above miracles wrought by Christ there are four miraculous events connected with his life :—

1. The conception by the Holy Ghost Luke 1 : 35. | 3. The resurrection............. John 21 : 1-14.
2. The transfiguration............. Matt. 17 : 1-8. | 4. The ascension............... Luke 2 : 42-51.

IV.—PARABLES RECORDED IN THE OLD TESTAMENT.

Spoken by	Concerning	Spoken at	Recorded
Balaam...........	The Moabites and Israelites...........	Mount Pisgah...	Num. 23 : 24.
Jotham............	Trees making a king..................	Mount Gerizim..	Judg 9 : 7-15.
Samson..........	Sweetness coming forth from the strong.	Timnath	Judg. 14 : 14.
Nathan..........	The poor man's ewe lamb.............	Jerusalem......	2 Sam. 12 : 1-4.
Woman of Tekoah..Two brothers striving.................		Jerusalem......	14 : 1.
One of the sons of the prophets ... } The escaped prisoner.................		Near Samaria...	1 Kings 20 : 35-49.
Jehoash, king of Israel......... } The thistle and the cedar.............		Jerusalem......	2 Kings 14 : 9.
Isaiah............	The vineyard yielding wild grapes.....	Jerusalem......	Isa. 5 : 1-6.
Ezekiel	Lion's whelps	Babylon	Ezek. 19 : 2-9.
	The great eagles and the vine.........	Babylon........	17 : 3-10.
	The boiling pot......................	Babylon........	24 : 3-5.

V.—PARABLES RECORDED IN THE GOSPELS.

1. *Peculiar to Matthew.*

(1.) The tares...................... 13 : 24-30. | (7.) The two sons.................. 21 : 28-32.
(2.) The hid treasure............... 13 : 44. | (8.) Marriage of the king's son...... 22 : 1-14.
(3.) The pearl of great price......... 13 : 45, 46. | (9.) The ten virgins .... 25 : 1-13.
(4.) The drag net.................. 13 : 47-50. | (10.) The talents .... 25 : 14-30.
(5.) The unmerciful servant. .... 18 : 23-35. | (11.) Sheep and goats.............. 25 : 31-46.
(6.) The labourers in the vineyard.... 20 : 1-16.

2. *Peculiar to Mark.*

(1.) The seed growing secretly. . . . . . . 4 : 26–29. | (2.) Watchfulness. . . . . 13 : 34, 35.

3. *Peculiar to Luke.*

(1.) The two debtors . . . . 7 : 41–43.
(2.) The good Samaritan. . . . . 10 : 25–37.
(3.) The importunate friend at midnight . . . . 11 : 5–8.
(4.) The rich fool. . . . . 12 : 16–21.
(5.) The servants watching . . . . 12 : 35–40.
(6.) The steward . . . . 12 : 42–48.
(7.) Barren fig-tree. . . . . 13 : 6–9.
(8.) The great supper . . . . 14 : 16–24.
(9.) Building a tower, and a king going to war . . . . 14 : 28–33.

(10.) The lost piece of silver. . . . . 15 : 8–10.
(11.) The prodigal son. . . . . 15 : 11–32.
(12.) The unjust steward . . . . 16 : 1–13.
(13.) The rich man and Lazarus. . . . . . 16 : 19–31.
(14.) The master and servant . . . . 17 : 7–10.
(15.) The unjust judge and the importunate widow. . . . . 18 : 1–8.
(16.) The Pharisee and publican. . . . . . 18 : 10–14.
(17.) The pounds. 19 : 12–27.

4. There are *no parables*, as a special form of allegory, found in *John*. The word rendered "parable" in John 10 : 6 is not the word so rendered in the Synoptics. The word which John uses (*paroimia*) is better translated "allegory." It occurs elsewhere only in John 16 : 25, 29 and 2 Pet. 2 : 22, where it is rendered "proverb."

5. *Common to Matthew and Luke.*

		Luke
(1.) The house on the rock and on the sand. . . . . Matt. 7 : 24–27.		Luke 6 : 46–49.
(2.) Leaven. . . . . 13 : 33, 34.		13 : 18–21.
(3.) The lost sheep . . . . 18 : 12–14.		15 : 1–10.

6. *Common to Matthew, Mark, and Luke.*

	Matt.	Mark	Luke
(1.) Candle under a bushel.	Matt. 5 : 15.	Mark 4 : 21.	Luke 8 : 16.
(2.) New cloth and an old garment.	9 : 16.	2 : 21.	5 : 36.
(3.) New wine in old bottles	9 : 17.	2 : 22.	5 : 37, 38.
(4.) The sower.	13 : 1–23.	4 : 1–9.	8 : 4–15.
(5.) The mustard seed	13 : 31, 32.	4 : 30, 34.	13 : 18–20.
(6.) The vineyard	21 : 33–46.	12 : 1–12.	20 : 9–19.
(7.) The fig-tree	24 : 32–35.	13 : 28–31.	21 : 29–33

VI.—WEIGHTS, MEASURES, AND MONEY.

1. *Hebrew Measures of Weight.*

	EQUIVALENTS IN TROY WEIGHT.			
	lbs.	*oz.*	*dwt.*	*grs.*
Gerah.	0	0	0	12
Bekah = 10 gerahs.	0	0	5	0
Shekel = 2 bekahs.	0	0	10	0
Maneh (silver = 60 shekels).	2	6	0	0
Talent.	125	0	0	0

2. *Measures of Length.*

	ENGLISH EQUIVALENTS.	
	ft.	*in.*
Digit (Jer. 52 : 21).	0	0.912
Palm = 4 digits (Ex. 25 : 25).	0	3.648
Span = 3 palms (Ex. 28 : 16).	0	10.944
Cubit = 2 spans (Gen. 6 : 15).	1	9.888
Pace (2 Sam. 6 : 13).	3	0
Fathom (Acts 27 : 28).	6	0.8
Reed (Ezek. 40 : 3–5 ; 42 : 16) = 6 cubits.	10	11.328
Furlong or stadium = 600 Greek feet (53¼ feet less than an English furlong)	606	9

Mile (Roman) = 1,000 Roman paces = 1,618 English yards.

Day's journey (Num. 11 : 31 ; Luke 2 : 44), ordinarily about 25 to 30 miles, but when the Jews travelled in company, about 10 miles.

3. *Measures of Capacity for Liquids.*

EQUIVALENTS IN ENGLISH WINE MEASURE.

	galls.	pints.
A caph	0	0.625
A log (Lev. 14 : 10, etc.)	0	0.833
A cab (mentioned only 2 Kings 6 : 25)	0	3.33
A hin (Ex. 29 : 40 ; 30 : 24 ; Num. 15 : 4, 7, 9)	1	2
A sĕăh ("measure," 2 Kings 7 : 1, 16), called also (Heb.) *shalish*— *i.e.*, "a third," as being the third part of an ephah (Isa. 40 : 12 ; Ps. 80 : 5)	2	4
A bath, the largest liquid measure (1 Kings 7 : 26, 38 ; 2 Chr. 2 : 10 ; Ezra 7 : 22 ; Isa. 5 : 10). Same as an ephah (Ex. 16 : 36 ; Lev. 5 : 11 ; 6 : 10 ; Num. 5 : 15, etc.)	7	4.5
A kor, "which is an homer" (Isa. 5 : 10 ; Ezek. 45 : 14) = 10 ephahs	75	5
Firkin (John 2 : 6)	9	0

4. *Dry Measure.*

EQUIVALENTS IN ENGLISH CORN MEASURE.

	pecks.	galls.	pints.
Cab (2 Kings 6 : 25 = *choenix*, "measure" ; Rev. 6 : 6)	0	0	2.833
Omer (Ex. 16 : 36) = tenth deal = $\frac{1}{10}$ of an ephah (Ex. 29 : 40 ; Lev. 23 : 13)	0	0	5.1
Seah (plural, "measures," Gen. 18 : 6 ; 1 Sam. 25 : 18 ; Matt. 13 : 33)	1	0	1
Ephah = 3 seahs (Ezek. 45 : 11)	3	0	3
Letek = 5 ephas ("half-homer," Hos. 3 : 2)	16	0	0
Homer, called also kor = 2 leteks (Num. 11 : 32 ; Hos. 3 : 2)	32	0	0

5. *Jewish Money.*

ENGLISH EQUIVALENTS.

	£	s.	d.
Gerah = $\frac{1}{20}$ part of a shekel (Ex. 30 : 13)	0	0	1.3687
Bekah = $\frac{1}{2}$ shekel (Ex. 38 : 26)	0	1	1.6875
Shekel (silver at 5s. per oz., Ex. 30 : 13 ; Isa. 7 : 23 ; Matt. 17 : 27)	0	2	3.375
Shekel of gold	1	16	6
Maneh ("pound," 1 Kings 10 : 17) = 50 shekels	5	14	0.75
Talent of silver = 60 manehs	342	3	9
Talent of gold	5475	0	0

6. *Roman Money.*

ENGLISH EQUIVALENTS.

	£	s.	d.
Mite (*lepton*)—Mark 12 : 42—the smallest copper coin = about .46875 of an English farthing.			
Farthing (*quadrans* ; Gr. *kodrantes*)—Matt. 5 : 26 ; Mark 12 : 42 = 2 mites = the fourth of an *as.*			
Farthing (*assarion*)—Matt. 10 : 29 ; Luke 12 : 6 = the Roman *as*	0	0	0¾
Penny (denarius = drachma)—Matt. 22 : 19	0	0	7½
Pound (*mina*)—Luke 19 : 13, 16, 18, etc. = 100 drachmæ	3	2	6

THE END